A SHAKESPEAREAN GENEALOGY

This chart reflects Shakespeare's history plays and is thus not historically accurate. Many descendants of Henry II and Edward III are omitted. On occasion, Shakespeare combined or simply invented historical figures. These deviations from fact are explained in the notes.

In the chart, the names of Kings and Queens are printed in capitals, and the dates of their reigns are printed in bold. The names of characters appearing in the plays are underlined.

Henry
d. 1183

Edward, Prince of
Wales 1330–1376

RICHARD II
1367–1400
(1377–99)

William of
Hatfield

Lionel, Duke of
Clarence 1338–1368

Philippa
m. Edmund
Mortimer, Earl
of March

RICHARD I
1157–1199
(1189–99)

Philip Faulconbridge*
(Richard Plantagenet)

John of Gaunt,
Duke of Lancaster
1340–1399
m. Blanche of
Lancaster
m. Constance of
Castile
m. Katherine
Swynford

HENRY IV
1367–1413
(1399–1413)

Thomas Beaufort,
Duke of Exeter
1377–1427

Henry Beaufort,
Bishop of Winchester
1375–1447

John Beaufort,
Earl of Somerset
1372–1409

Joan Beaufort
m. Ralph Neville,
Earl of
Westmoreland

HENRY II
1133–1189
(1154–89)
m. Eleanor
of Aquitaine
d. 1204

Geoffrey, d. 1186
m. Constance
of Brittany

Arthur
1187–1203

JOHN 1167–1216
(1199–1216)

HENRY III
1207–1272
(1216–72)

EDWARD I
1239–1307
(1272–1307)

EDWARD II
1284–1327
(1307–27)

Edmund of Langley,
Duke of York
1341–1402

Edward, Duke of
Aumerle d. 1415

Richard, Earl
of Cambridge
d. 1415 m. Anne
Mortimer (above)

EDWARD III
1312–1377
(1327–77)
m. Philippa of
Hainault

Thomas of
Woodstock, Duke of
Gloucester 1355–1397

Anne

Eleanor
m. Alfonso VIII,
King of Castile

Blanche, d. 1252
m. Louis VIII
of France

William of
Windsor

*Philip Faulconbridge, the bastard son of Richard I, had no historical existence. Such a character appears in the play *The Life and Death of King John* and is referred to in passing in Holinshed's *Chronicles*.

† In the character of Edmund Mortimer, Shakespeare combines two historical figures. The Edmund Mortimer who married Catrin, daughter of Owain Glyndŵr, was the grandson of Lionel, Duke of Clarence, and the younger brother of Roger, Earl of March. He died in 1409. Shakespeare combines him with his nephew, the Edmund Mortimer recognized by Richard II as his heir (d. 1424). This second Edmund was the brother of Anne Mortimer and the uncle of Richard Plantagenet.

‡ The character of the Duke of Somerset combines Henry Beaufort with his younger brother Edmund (d. 1471), who succeeded him as Duke.

Elizabeth Mortimer ("Kate") m. Henry Percy ("Hotspur") 1364–1403 — Henry, Earl of Northumberland 1394–1455

EDWARD IV 1442–1483 (1461–83) m. Elizabeth Woodville d. 1492 — EDWARD V 1470–1483 (1483)

Richard, Duke of York 1472–1483

Elizabeth of York 1465–1503 m. HENRY VII (below)

Edmund, Earl of Rutland 1443–1460

Edmund Mortimer†

George, Duke of Clarence 1449–1478 m. Isabel Neville (below)

Anne Mortimer m. Richard, Earl of Cambridge (below) — Richard Plantagenet, Duke of York 1411–1460 m. Cicely Neville (below) — RICHARD III 1452–1485 (1483–85) m. Anne Neville (below) — Edward, Prince of Wales

HENRY V 1387–1422 (1413–22) m. Catherine 1401–1437 — HENRY VI 1421–1471 (1422–61) m. Margaret of Anjou d. 1482 — Edward, Prince of Wales 1453–1471 m. Anne Neville (below) — Arthur m. Catherine of Aragon (below)

Thomas, Duke of Clarence d. 1421

John of Lancaster, Duke of Bedford 1389–1435

Margaret m. James IV of Scotland — James V of Scotland

Mary, Queen of Scots

JAMES I 1566–1625 (1603–25)

Humphrey, Duke of Gloucester 1391–1447 m. Eleanor Cobham d. 1454

John Beaufort, Duke of Somerset 1403–1444 — Margaret Beaufort m. Edmund Tudor, Earl of Richmond — HENRY VII 1457–1509 (1485–1509) m. Elizabeth of York (above) — HENRY VIII 1491–1547 (1509–47) m. Catherine of Aragon

MARY I 1516–1558 (1553–58) m. Philip of Spain

Edmund Beaufort, Duke of Somerset 1406–1455 — Henry Beaufort, Duke of Somerset 1436–1464‡

m. Anne Boleyn

ELIZABETH I 1533–1603 (1558–1603)

Isabel Neville d. 1476 m. George, Duke of Clarence (above)

m. Jane Seymour

EDWARD VI 1537–1553 (1547–53)

Richard Neville, Earl of Salisbury 1400–1460 — Richard Neville, Earl of Warwick 1428–1471 — John Neville, Marquess of Montague d. 1471

Anne Neville d. 1485 m. Edward, Prince of Wales (above)

m. Anne of Cleves

m. Katherine Howard

m. Katherine Parr

Cicely Neville m. Richard Plantagenet, Duke of York (above)

m. RICHARD III (above)

Mary m. Charles Brandon — Frances

Jane Grey 1537–1554

Humphrey, Duke of Buckingham 1402–1460 — Humphrey Stafford d. 1455 — Henry, Duke of Buckingham 1454?–1483 — Edward, Duke of Buckingham 1478–1521

1377–1625

RICHARD II, 1377–99 RICHARD was the eldest son of EDWARD THE BLACK PRINCE, himself the eldest son of KING EDWARD III, who ruled England from 1327 to 1377. When the BLACK PRINCE died in battle in France in 1376, RICHARD became the legitimate heir to the throne. He ruled from EDWARD's death in 1377 until he was deposed in 1399 by HENRY BOLINGBROKE, the eldest son of JOHN OF GAUNT, DUKE OF LANCASTER. Because he was the fourth son of EDWARD III, GAUNT and his Lancastrian descendants had weaker hereditary claims to the throne than did RICHARD. When deposed, RICHARD had no children to succeed him, but he recognized EDMUND MORTIMER, FIFTH EARL OF MARCH, as his heir presumptive. This MORTIMER was descended from LIONEL, DUKE OF CLARENCE, the third son of EDWARD III, and therefore also had stronger hereditary claims to the throne than did BOLINGBROKE. SHAKESPEARE combined this MORTIMER with his uncle EDMUND MORTIMER, who married OWAIN GLYNDŴR'S DAUGHTER.

HENRY IV, 1399–1413 HENRY BOLINGBROKE, eldest son of JOHN OF GAUNT, seized the throne from RICHARD II in 1399. When HENRY died in 1413, he was succeeded by his eldest son, PRINCE HAL, who became HENRY V.

HENRY V, 1413–22 HENRY V became king in 1413 and reigned until his death in 1422. He was succeeded by his son, HENRY VI.

HENRY VI, 1422–61 HENRY VI was less than one year old when he succeeded his father, HENRY V. In the young king's minority, his uncle HUMPHREY, DUKE OF GLOUCESTER, was named Lord Protector, and the kingdom was ruled by an aristocratic council. HENRY VI assumed personal authority in 1437. He was deposed in 1461 by his third cousin, who was crowned EDWARD IV. HENRY was murdered in 1471.

EDWARD IV, 1461–83 EDWARD, the eldest son of RICHARD, DUKE OF YORK, seized the throne from HENRY VI in 1461. His Yorkist claim to the throne derived from his grandmother, ANNE MORTIMER, who was descended from LIONEL, third son of EDWARD III, and was sister to that EDMUND MORTIMER recognized by RICHARD II as his heir presumptive; EDWARD IV's grandfather, RICHARD, EARL OF CAMBRIDGE, was the son of EDMUND OF LANGLEY, fifth son of EDWARD III. EDWARD IV reigned until his death in 1483. His heir was his eldest son (EDWARD), but the throne was usurped by his brother RICHARD, DUKE OF GLOUCESTER.

RICHARD III, 1483–85 RICHARD III was the youngeer brother of EDWARD IV. After the death of EDWARD IV in 1483, RICHARD prevented the coronation of EDWARD V with a claim of illegitimacy and succeeded to the throne himself. EDWARD and his younger brother, RICHARD, DUKE OF YORK, were murdered in the Tower of London. RICHARD III was killed at the Battle of Bosworth Field in 1485, and the kingdom fell to the victor, HENRY TUDOR, EARL OF RICHMOND.

HENRY VII, 1485–1509 HENRY TUDOR seized the throne from RICHARD III in 1485. He was descended from JOHN OF GAUNT by JOHN's third marriage, with CATHERINE SWYNFORD. He married ELIZABETH, daughter of EDWARD IV, uniting the houses of Lancaster and York. He died in 1509 and was succeeded by his son, HENRY VIII.

HENRY VIII, 1509–47 HENRY was the second son of HENRY VII. His older brother, ARTHUR, died in 1502. HENRY VIII's first wife was CATHERINE OF ARAGON, who bore his daughter MARY. His second wife, ANNE BOLEYN, was the mother of ELIZABETH. His third wife, JANE SEYMOUR, bore him a son, who succeeded to the throne as EDWARD VI after HENRY VIII died in 1547.

EDWARD VI, 1547–53 EDWARD VI was nine years old when he became king. From 1547 to 1549, the realm was governed by a Lord Protector, the DUKE OF SOMERSET; power then passed to JOHN DUDLEY, DUKE OF NORTHUMBERLAND. When EDWARD VI died in 1553, NORTHUMBERLAND attempted unsuccessfully to prevent the succession of MARY TUDOR by installing as queen his daughter-in-law, LADY JANE GREY, a great-granddaughter of HENRY VII.

MARY I, 1553–58 MARY, daughter of HENRY VIII and his first wife, CATHERINE OF ARAGON, came to the throne in 1553. She married KING PHILIP OF SPAIN but died childless. She was succeeded by her half sister, ELIZABETH.

ELIZABETH I, 1558–1603 ELIZABETH, the daughter of HENRY VIII and his second wife, ANNE BOLEYN, became queen after the death of her half sister, MARY, in 1558. She ruled until her death in 1603. She was succeeded by her cousin JAMES.

JAMES I, 1603–1625 JAMES VI OF SCOTLAND became JAMES I OF ENGLAND in 1603. His claim to the throne of England derived from his great-grandmother, MARGARET TUDOR, a daughter of HENRY VII who married JAMES IV OF SCOTLAND. JAMES ruled England and Scotland until his death in 1625; he was succeeded by his son, CHARLES I.

THE NORTON SHAKESPEARE

THIRD EDITION

Comedies

TEXTUAL EDITORS

THE NORTON SHAKESPEARE

THIRD EDITION

Comedies

Stephen Greenblatt, *General Editor*
HARVARD UNIVERSITY

Walter Cohen
UNIVERSITY OF MICHIGAN

Suzanne Gossett, *General Textual Editor*
LOYOLA UNIVERSITY CHICAGO (EMERITA)

Jean E. Howard
COLUMBIA UNIVERSITY

Katharine Eisaman Maus
UNIVERSITY OF VIRGINIA

Gordon McMullan, *General Textual Editor*
KING'S COLLEGE LONDON

W · W · NORTON & COMPANY · NEW YORK · LONDON

W. W. Norton & Company has been independent since its founding in 1923, when William Warder Norton and Mary D. Herter Norton first published lectures delivered at the People's Institute, the adult education division of New York City's Cooper Union. The firm soon expanded its program beyond the Institute, publishing books by celebrated academics from America and abroad. By mid-century, the two major pillars of Norton's publishing program—trade books and college texts—were firmly established. In the 1950s, the Norton family transferred control of the company to its employees, and today—with a staff of 400 and a comparable number of trade, college, and professional titles published each year—W. W. Norton & Company stands as the largest and oldest publishing house owned wholly by its employees.

Editor: Julia Reidhead
Managing Editor, College: Marian Johnson
Associate Editor: Emily Stuart
Manuscript Editors: Harry Haskell, Alice Vigliani
Media Editor: Carly Fraser Doria
Media Project Editor: Kristin Sheerin
Production Manager: Eric Pier-Hocking
Digital Production: Mateus Texeira, Colleen Caffrey
Marketing Manager, Literature: Kim Bowers
Photo Editor: Trish Marx
Composition: Westchester Book Company
Manufacturing: RR Donnelley

The Library of Congress has catalogued the full edition as follows:
Shakespeare, William, 1564–1616.
The Norton Shakespeare / Stephen Greenblatt, General Editor, Harvard University; Walter Cohen, University of Michigan; Suzanne Gossett, General Textual Editor, Loyola University Chicago (Emerita); Jean E. Howard, Columbia University; Katharine Eisaman Maus, University of Virginia; Gordon McMullan, General Textual Editor, King's College London.—Third edition.
pages cm
Includes bibliographical references and index.
ISBN 978-0-393-93499-1 (hardcover)
I. Greenblatt, Stephen, 1943– editor. II. Cohen, Walter, 1949– editor. III. Gossett, Suzanne, editor. IV. Howard, Jean E. (Jean Elizabeth), 1948– editor. V. Maus, Katharine Eisaman, 1955– editor. VI. McMullan, Gordon, 1962– editor. VII. Title.
PR2754.G74 2015
822.3'3—dc23

2015018869

This edition: ISBN 978-0-393-93861-6

W. W. Norton & Company, Inc., 500 Fifth Avenue, New York, NY 10110-0017
wwnorton.com

W. W. Norton & Company Ltd., Castle House, 75/76 Wells Street, London W1T 3QT

Contents

Additional works, media, contextual materials, and bibliographies are
available in the Digital Edition

COMEDIES

Appendices

Illustrations

Preface

This Third Edition of *The Norton Shakespeare* is both a continuation and a new beginning. Readers who have already found the format of the printed book and its editorial apparatus to their liking will get what they are looking for. The emphasis continues to be on the pleasure of reading, with a particular attention to undergraduates who may be encountering Shakespeare for the first time. "If then you do not like him," wrote Shakespeare's first editors almost four hundred years ago, "surely you are in some manifest danger not to understand him." We have from the start made every effort, through the glosses, notes, introductions, and other materials, to facilitate understanding and hence to enhance liking. We are careful not to overburden Shakespeare's words with explication or to crowd the page with distracting commentary. The clear, uncluttered, single-column format is designed to encourage absorption. But we try to offer enough help to allow the beauty and the luminous intelligence of these stupendous works to shine.

We have in this edition carefully revised each of our introductions (including the long General Introduction) and reviewed every one of our notes and glosses, altering and adding where appropriate. Our goal has been to hold onto what our readers have told us works well, but also to update the introductions, bibliographies, filmographies, and other materials to reflect current scholarship, shifting emphases, and newly released films. An entirely new feature of this edition is an illuminating Performance Note, by Brett Gamboa (Dartmouth College), that accompanies each of the plays. These notes describe the particular and recurrent theatrical challenges with which actors and directors have grappled in mounting any given work. The strategies devised over the centuries in response to these challenges are a fascinating point of entry into critical issues of interpretation. The notes are also an invaluable guide to what audiences should look for when they attend a new production.

From its inception, *The Norton Shakespeare* has paid exceptionally close attention to the accuracy as well as the accessibility of the texts and, in particular, to the challenge posed by those plays that exist in multiple substantive versions. For the Third Edition, all of Shakespeare's plays and poems have been newly edited, from scratch, by an international team of leading textual scholars. This hugely ambitious and complex undertaking has been based on the principle of single-text editing— that is, where more than one early authoritative text of a given play has survived, rather than merging them into one (as has been traditionally done), we have edited each text in its own right. We thereby offer the reader texts as close as possible to the original versions as read by Shakespeare's contemporaries. A lively and accessible new General Textual Introduction fully articulates this principle, explores the nature of the documents that have come down to us from Shakespeare's own time, and explains in detail the editorial practices on which this new text of the complete works is meticulously based.

Approximately half of Shakespeare's plays appeared both in small-format versions (quartos), printed in the playwright's own lifetime, and in the large-format First Folio (1623), published seven years after his death. As early as the eighteenth century, careful readers began to notice that there were differences, sometimes minor and sometimes quite significant, between these printings of the same plays. Starting with the landmark Shakespeare editions of Alexander Pope (1723) and Lewis Theobald (1733), editors initiated the practice of blending the different versions together, picking and choosing as their taste dictated or as they imagined that Shakespeare would have done, had he himself produced a definitive text. Hence, for example, the two distinct texts of *King Lear* were routinely fashioned into a single text, with editors combining lines that appear only in one or the other early version and choosing among hundreds of variant readings.

From its inception, *The Norton Shakespeare* rejected this editorial method (known as "conflation"). We have continued in the current print edition our hallmark practice of offering, on facing pages, the 1608 Quarto text of *King Lear* and the substantial revision of the play as printed in the First Folio (1623). While each version may be read independently—we have provided glosses and footnotes for each—the significant points of difference between the two are immediately apparent and available for comparison. It is thus possible to watch in extraordinarily sharp focus changes in the early modern text of one of Shakespeare's greatest plays. We recognize at the same time that a combined text, in one form or another, has long served as the *King Lear* upon which innumerable performances of the play have been based and on which a huge body of literary criticism has been written. Hence in addition to providing the Quarto and Folio texts, we wanted to offer readers a version of this great tragedy that combines the two without entirely erasing their differences. The solution that we provide in these pages is what in the first two editions of *The Norton Shakespeare* we used in the comparable case of *Hamlet*. We print the Folio text of *King Lear*, but we have moved the lines that are solely in the Quarto into the body of the play. In doing so, however, we did not want simply to produce a conflated version. We have therefore indented the Q-only passages, printed them in a slightly different typeface, and numbered them in such a way as to make clear their provenance. We call this a "scars-and-stitches" solution, since, though still eminently readable and enjoyable, it clearly marks the points of insertion and difference.

The Norton Shakespeare, then, includes three separate texts of *King Lear*. The reader can compare them, analyze the role of editors in constructing the texts we now call Shakespeare's, explore in detail the kinds of decisions that playwrights, editors, and printers make and remake, witness firsthand the historical transformation of what might at first glance seem fixed and unchanging. We offer extraordinary access to this supremely brilliant, difficult, compelling play.

Hamlet, the other great tragedy at the very center of Shakespeare's achievement, similarly exists in multiple versions: the 1604 Second Quarto (Q2), the longest of the early editions; the 1623 Folio text (F), which lacks some 200 lines found in Q2 but includes more than 70 lines not found there; and, casting a fascinating light on the more familiar version of the tragedy, the drastically different First Quarto (Q1, the so-called Bad Quarto). As in the case of *Lear*, editors for centuries have routinely conflated the Q2 and F *Hamlets*.

The realities of bookbinding—not to mention our recognition of the limited time in the typical undergraduate syllabus—preclude our offering in the print edition four *Hamlets* (Q1, Q2, F, and combined) to parallel the three *Lears*. What we have provided in these pages instead is a new incarnation of the solution we came up with in the first two editions of *The Norton Shakespeare*. While basing our *Hamlet* on the Q2 text, we have moved the Folio passages, among which are some of the tragedy's most famous lines, into the body of the play. But, as with the "scars-and-stitches" *Lear*, we have made it possible for readers who are interested to see what has been added.

The growing interest in the possibility of teaching the First Quarto of *Hamlet* has also led us to add that strange text, in fully glossed and annotated form, alongside the more familiar version of Shakespeare's most famous tragedy. Readers can wonder at a *Hamlet* in which the hero muses "To be, or not to be—ay, there's the point," and they can see how drastically one theater troupe in Shakespeare's own time probably cut the play for performance.

These and other changes all serve to keep *The Norton Shakespeare* fresh and current. But this Third Edition, as I have already suggested, is much more than a careful revision and updating. It is a thoroughgoing rethinking both of the entire Shakespeare corpus and of the whole way in which Shakespeare is experienced by contemporary readers. For the purposes of this preface, a single feature of the newly edited text should be emphasized: it was created not only for the print edition, but also for a new and exciting Digital Edition. From its inception the print edition featured both the Quarto and the Folio texts of *King Lear,* and we have now added the First Quarto of *Hamlet.* Our Digital Edition makes available fully glossed and annotated Quarto and Folio versions of the plays—fifteen in all—for which more than one early authoritative text exists, thereby offering the reader access to these plays as they were first experienced by Shakespeare's contemporaries. This means not only the two versions of *Lear,* which can be viewed in side-by-side scrolling format for comparison as well as individually, and not only the three versions of *Hamlet.* It also means multiple versions, with fascinating variants, of such beloved, centrally important plays as *Romeo and Juliet, Othello, Richard II, Richard III, Henry V, Love's Labor's Lost,* and *A Midsummer Night's Dream.* There are Quarto and Folio versions as well of 2 and 3 *Henry VI, Titus Andronicus, 2 Henry IV, The Merry Wives of Windsor,* and *Troilus and Cressida.* The Digital Edition also offers an appendix of selected scenes from a number of multiple-version plays, presented side-by-side so that they can easily be compared for teaching purposes. For anyone interested in Shakespeare's practices of composition and revision and in the fascinating process through which his plays, passing through the printing house, have managed to reach us, the digital *Norton Shakespeare* is an unprecedented resource.

Links to the widely respected *Norton Facsimile of the First Folio of Shakespeare,* edited by Charlton Hinman, and to quarto facsimile pages make it possible for readers to see for themselves the original materials with which the editors have been working to create this new text of the complete works.

In the digital *Norton Shakespeare* we also include for the first time an edition of the full text of *Sir Thomas More,* a multi-authored play, unpublished in the period, whose manuscript includes a section in Shakespeare's own hand, the only surviving one of its kind. We also include an edition of *Edward III,* another play of which Shakespeare appears to have been part-author. Both texts are interesting as examples of the collaborative nature of much Elizabethan and Jacobean theater, a collaboration reflected as well in the late plays *Pericles, Henry VIII, The Two Noble Kinsmen,* the lost *Cardenio,* and—more debatably—such works as *1 Henry VI, Titus Andronicus,* and *Timon of Athens.*

This extraordinary wealth of texts, all complete with introductions, notes, and glosses, has been made possible by the vastness of the digital space. That space has allowed us to supplement the useful aids in the print edition—including maps, genealogies, a glossary, a short bibliography, a timeline, and a selection of key documents—with further resources. For the Digital Edition, the volume editors have created expanded bibliographies for the study of Shakespeare's works, and Misha Teramura (Harvard University), who edited and glossed the documents in the print text, has assembled and edited a larger archive of Tudor and Stuart documents relevant to Shakespeare and his theater world.

The remarkable expansion of texts is only the beginning. The resources of the Digital Edition have made possible innovations that were, until very recently, only a teacher's idle daydreams. Shakespeare scholars have long understood that the decisions editors make—for example, choosing one variant over another, or adding stage directions, or making consistent the multiple speech prefixes often used for a single character—can affect the meaning of the plays. But on the printed page it has been difficult to call attention to the significance of these decisions without interrupting the flow of the reading experience, while the long lists of textual variants printed at the ends of plays are so much raw data, rarely consulted or understood by anyone but experts. Now, by clicking a marginal icon, readers can summon illuminating Textual Comments for each play, written by the textual editor, that focus on textual-editing decision points influencing interpretation. It is possible for all interested readers now to understand textual cruxes and to see—and, for that matter, to call into question—key editorial choices.

Similarly, a crucially important dimension of Shakespeare's texts, as everyone grasps, is that they were originally intended for performance. Hence the brief discussion in the General Introduction of the theatrical scene Shakespeare encountered and helped to transform is now greatly enriched in "The Theater of Shakespeare's Time," a lively and original essay by Holger Schott Syme (University of Toronto). Syme conjures up a fiercely competitive world of multiple theater companies and rival venues, all scrambling for plays that will survive the attention of the government censor and lure crowds of spectators to part with their pennies.

Performance is obviously not only a matter of historical interest. It remains, for most of us and certainly for our students, central to the full experience of the plays. But, without overfreighting the page, it has been difficult to highlight this dimension in the printed book. Descriptions of famous performances, from Garrick to the present, rarely capture the significance of key interpretive choices by actors or directors. Now clicking on marginal icons keyed to particular moments in the texts allows one to read incisive and insightful Performance Comments that supplement the Performance Note preceding each play. These comments, by Brett Gamboa, highlight passages that are particularly famous challenges in performance and explore how a director or actor's interpretive choices affect meaning. Taken individually, the Performance Comments call attention to specific decisions that must be made in the realization of a play; taken together, they constitute a brilliant exploration of the performative dimensions of Shakespeare's art.

The performative dimension is enhanced by two further features of the Digital Edition. First, there are recordings of all of the songs—66 of them—in the plays, from the award-winning *Shakespeare's Songbook* audio companion by Ross Duffin. It is now possible for readers to take in fully the pervasive presence of music in Shakespeare's plays, something that the printed stage direction *"Music"* cannot hope to do. Second, there are over eight hours of spoken-word audio of key passages and scenes and those that pose particular challenges to readers. These have been specially recorded for the Digital Edition by the highly regarded company, Actors from the London Stage. With a simple click it is now possible for readers to hear the words on the page come alive in the voices of gifted actors.

The digital *Norton Shakespeare* brings together in one place an unparalleled array of resources for understanding and enjoying Shakespeare. These resources are not the primitive accumulation of materials, of dubious utility or reliability, which often makes the web an untrustworthy guide. Rather, each of the texts and other material has received the same careful scholarly and pedagogical attention that has made the print edition a success. But we are aware that different readers will have different interests and needs, often varying from time to time. The reading experience of the Digital Edition, including the visibility of icons, line numbers, glosses, and notes, can be easily customized, so that with a click readers can either "quiet" the page or access Norton's abundant reading help. The Digital Edition platform provides customizable highlighting, annotating, and comment-sharing tools that facilitate active reading.

The publisher also provides instructors with a wealth of free resources beyond the Digital Edition. An Instructor Resource Disc created for the new edition features the more than eight hours of spoken-word audio recorded by Actors from the London Stage, 150 songs, and over 100 images from the book in both JPEG and PowerPoint for easy classroom presentation. The images are available for download on the publisher's instructor resource page, wwnorton.com/instructors. In addition, the Norton Shakespeare YouTube channel brings together a carefully curated and regularly updated collection of the best of the web's Shakespeare video resources, allowing instructors to easily show clips from stage and film in class.

The extraordinary labor of love that has led to this new and revised edition of *The Norton Shakespeare* has involved a large number of collaborators. The volume editors owe a substantial debt of thanks to the readers of the earlier editions. Our readers have formed a large, engaged community, and their endorsements, observations, and suggestions for revision and expansion have proved invaluable. We have also profited from the highly detailed reviews of each individual feature of the edition commissioned by the publisher and performed with exemplary seriousness by many of our most esteemed professional colleagues.

At the very center of the Third Edition is the newly edited text of the Complete Works, an enormous, exhaustive, and exhausting enterprise. We wish to acknowledge with deepest gratitude the extraordinary labors of our gifted team of textual editors, listed on the title-page spread, led with an exemplary blend of discipline, patience, intellectual seriousness, and scholarly rigor by Gordon McMullan and Suzanne Gossett.

The *Norton Shakespeare* editors have had the valuable—indeed, indispensable—support of our publisher and a host of undergraduate and graduate research assistants, colleagues, friends, and family, whose names we gratefully note in the Acknowledgments that follow. All of these companions have helped us find in this long collective enterprise what the "Dedicatorie Epistle" to the First Folio promises to its readers: delight. We make the same promise to the readers of our edition and invite them to continue the great Shakespearean collaboration.

STEPHEN GREENBLATT
CAMBRIDGE, MASSACHUSETTS

Volume Editors' Acknowledgments

The creation of this edition has drawn heavily on the resources, experience, and skill of its remarkable publisher, W. W. Norton. Norton's record of success in academic publishing has sometimes made it seem like a giant, akin to the multinational corporations that dominate the publishing world, but it is in fact the only major publishing house that is employee-owned. Our principal guide has been our brilliant editor Julia Reidhead, whose calm intelligence, common sense, and steady focus have been essential in enabling us to reach our goal. With this Third Edition, we were blessed once again with the indispensable judgment and project-editorial expertise of Marian Johnson, managing editor, college department, as well as scrupulous manuscript editing by Alice Vigliani and Harry Haskell. Carly Fraser Doria, literature media editor, skillfully guided us through the new waters of the Digital Edition, following Cliff Landesman's innovative lead. Assistant editor Emily Stuart managed with remarkable skill and graciousness the complexities of manuscript preparation and review. Kim Yi, managing editor, digital media, and Kristin Sheerin, digital project editor, oversaw the monumental checking and proofing of files. In addition, we are deeply grateful to Cara Folkman, media assistant editor; JoAnn Simony and Elizabeth Audley, digital file coordinators; Eric Pier-Hocking, production manager; and Debra Morton Hoyt, corporate art director, who, along with designer Timothy Hsu, created our Ortelius-inspired cover design. Thanks also to Mary Jo Mecca for design and construction of the jester hat. For invaluable help in creating the Digital Edition, we would like to thank Jane Chu and Colleen Caffrey, digital designers, and Mateus Teixiera and Kristian Sanford, digital production.

The editors have, in addition, had the valuable—indeed, indispensable—support of a host of undergraduate and graduate research assistants, colleagues, friends, and family. Even a partial listing of those to whom we owe our heartfelt thanks is very long, but we are all fortunate enough to live in congenial and supportive environments, and the edition has been part of our lives for a long time. We owe special thanks for sustained dedication and learning to our colleagues, friends, and principal assistants:

Stephen Greenblatt wishes to thank his talented research assistants at Harvard, including Maria Devlin, Seth Herbst, Rhema Hokama, David Nee, Elizabeth Weckhurst, Benjamin Woodring, Catherine Woodring, and, above all, Misha Teramura. In addition, he is grateful for valuable assistance from Rebecca Cook and Aubrey Everett, along with advice and counsel from many friends, colleagues, and students. Thanks also go to C. Edward McGee (University of Waterloo), Barbara D. Palmer (late of the University of Mary Washington), Sylvia Thomas (the Yorkshire Archaeological Society), and John M. Wasson (late of Washington State University). He acknowledges a special and enduring debt to Ramie Targoff (Brandeis University).

Walter Cohen wishes to thank Marjorie Levinson (University of Michigan).

Jean Howard would like to acknowledge the help of each of her excellent research assistants at Columbia University: Bryan Lowrance, John Kuhn, Alexander Paulsson Lash, Chris McKeen, and especially Emily Shortslef, whose scholarly contributions have been indispensable and impeccable and whose good cheer is astonishingly unflagging.

We gratefully acknowledge the reviewers who provided thoughtful critiques for particular plays or of the project as a whole: Bernadette Andrea (University of Texas at San Antonio), John M. Archer (New York University), Oliver Arnold (University of California–Berkeley), Amanda Bailey (University of Connecticut), JoAnn D. Barbour

(Texas Woman's University), Catherine Belsey (Swansea University), Barbara Bono (University at Buffalo), Michael D. Bristol (McGill University), Karen Britland (University of Wisconsin–Madison), James C. Bulman (Allegheny College), William C. Carroll (Boston University), Kent Cartwright (University of Maryland, College Park), Joseph Cerami (Texas A&M University), Julie Crawford (Columbia University), Jonathan Crewe (Dartmouth College), Stephen Deng (Michigan State University), Christy Desmet (University of Georgia), Donald R. Dickson (Texas A&M University), Mario DiGangi (Graduate Center of the City University of New York), Tobias Doering (University of Munich), Frances Dolan (University of California–Davis), John Drakakis (University of Stirling), Heather Dubrow (Fordham University), Holly Dugan (George Washington University), Amy E. Earhart (Texas A&M University), Katherine E. Eggert (University of Colorado–Boulder), Lars D. Engle (University of Tulsa), Christopher John Fitter (Rutgers University), Mary Floyd-Wilson (University of North Carolina–Chapel Hill), Susan Caroline Frye (University of Wyoming), Brett Gamboa (Dartmouth College), Evelyn Gajowski (University of Nevada, Las Vegas), Hugh Hartridge Grady, Jr. (Arcadia University), Kenneth Gross (University of Rochester), Elizabeth Hanson (Queen's University), Jonathan Gil Harris (George Washington University), Michael Hattaway (New York University), Diana Henderson (Massachusetts Institute of Technology), Terence Allan Hoagwood (Texas A&M University), Lucia Kristina Hodgson (Texas A&M University), Peter Holbrook (The University of Queensland), Peter Holland (University of Notre Dame), John W. Huntington (University of Illinois at Chicago), Lorna Hutson (University of St. Andrews), Coppélia Kahn (Brown University), Jeffrey Knapp (University of California–Berkeley), Yu Jin Ko (Wellesley College), Paul A. Kottman (The New School), Bryon Lew (Trent University), Genevieve Love (Colorado College), Julia R. Lupton (University of California–Irvine), Ellen MacKay (Indiana University), Cristina Malcolmson (Bates College), Lawrence G. Manley (Yale University), Steven Mentz (St. John's University), Erin Minear (College of William and Mary), Arash Moradi (Shiraz University), Ian Moulton (Arizona State University), Steven Mullaney (University of Michigan), Cyrus Mulready (State University of New York–New Paltz), Karen Newman (Brown University), Mary A. O'Farrell (Texas A&M University), Laurie E. Osborne (Colby College), Simon Palfrey (Oxford University), Garry Partridge (Texas A&M University), Thomas Pendleton (Iona College), Peter G. Platt (Barnard College), Christopher Pye (Williams College), Phyllis R. Rackin (University of Pennsylvania), Sally Robinson (Texas A&M University), Mary Beth Rose (University of Illinois at Chicago), Suparna Roychoudhury (Mount Holyoke College), Elizabeth D. Samet (United States Military Academy at West Point), Melissa E. Sanchez (University of Pennsylvania), Michael Schoenfeldt (University of Michigan), Laurie J. Shannon (Northwestern University), Jyotsna Singh (Michigan State University), Elizabeth Spiller (Florida State University), Tiffany Stern (Oxford University), Richard Strier (University of Chicago), Ayanna Thompson (George Washington University), Douglas Trevor (University of Michigan), Henry S. Turner (Rutgers University), Brian Walsh (Yale University), Tiffany Jo Werth (Simon Fraser University), Adam Zucker (University of Massachusetts).

General Textual Editors' Acknowledgments

First and foremost, we are grateful to Stephen Greenblatt for inviting us to imagine, and then to create, a wholly new text of Shakespeare for the Third Edition of *The Norton Shakespeare*; to the volume editors—Jean Howard, Katharine Maus, and Walter Cohen—for working closely with us and for supporting the single text–editing principle we adopted; and to Julia Reidhead, the edition's publisher, for her gracious engagement and direction at every stage. And of course we are hugely grateful to the remarkable team of editors with whom we have worked, all of whom, without exception, accepted the invitation with alacrity, edited superbly, completed their work in timely fashion, and tolerated the necessary processes stemming from the need to ensure that each individual play functions both in its own right and as part of the edition as a whole. We want to thank and acknowledge them all. We also wish to thank Lacey Conley, who provided invaluable research assistance at crucial moments in the creation of the text. None of this would have been possible without the indefatigable work of the team at Norton. Marian Johnson, managing editor, college, provided invaluable wisdom and care for the newly edited text. Cliff Landesman's enthusiasm for the project and his willingness to explore—and help us understand—the digital possibilities were invaluable. Carly Fraser Doria and Emily Stuart responded with remarkable generosity, patience, and professionalism to our requests and anxieties. And we are particularly grateful to Norton's copy editors, Alice Vigliani and Harry Haskell, for their wonderfully precise work on the texts of the plays.

Editors tend to fight like cats in a sack over the choices they make when editing Shakespeare—they did this in the eighteenth century, and they try their best to keep up the tradition today—yet they also know that they are in fact highly mutually dependent, and it matters a great deal to us to note that we have had a second set of collaborators in the creation of this new text, none of whom has had actual direct involvement in *The Norton Shakespeare*, Third Edition—due in some cases to working on equivalent editions for other presses—but without whose textual and critical work we could not have acquired the knowledge we needed to create this edition. These include David Bevington, Peter Blayney, A. R. Braunmuller, R. A. Foakes, John Jowett, David Scott Kastan, Laurie Maguire, Sonia Massai, Eric Rasmussen, Tiffany Stern, Gary Taylor, Stanley Wells, and Martin Wiggins. And we would like in particular to acknowledge our considerable debt to Richard Proudfoot, who mentored us both in the fine art of editing and whose knowledge of the Shakespearean text and generosity with that knowledge are unsurpassed. We should acknowledge too certain key resources without which our editorial work would have been, practically speaking, impossible: these include the British Library's remarkable Shakespeare in Quarto website and the online text and facsimiles provided by the Internet Shakespeare Edition (a remarkable enterprise led by the generous and endlessly energetic Michael Best).

Finally, we should also note that any edition of Shakespeare is merely one in a very long line, and all modern Shakespearean editors are indebted to the extraordinary work of the earliest toilers in the field—from Shakespeare's friends Heminges and Condell assembling the First Folio and thus providing the crucial basis for all subsequent work on the Shakespeare canon, to the anonymous editors of the Second, Third, and Fourth Folios, to the crucial work of Rowe, Capell, Pope, Johnson, Theobald, and their successors in the eighteenth, nineteenth, and twentieth centuries. How they did any of it without word-processing software and the resources of the Internet we cannot for the life of us figure out.

Gordon McMullan and Suzanne Gossett

General Introduction

STEPHEN GREENBLATT

"He was not of an age, but for all time!"

There are writers whose greatness is recognized only long after they have vanished from the earth. There are writers championed by a coterie of devoted followers who tend the flame of admiration against the cold world's indifference. There are writers beloved in their native land but despised abroad, and others neglected at home yet celebrated on distant shores. Shakespeare is none of these. His genius was recognized almost immediately. The famous words with which we have begun were written by his friend and rival Ben Jonson. They have been echoed innumerable times, across the centuries, across national and linguistic boundaries, across the demarcation lines of race and class, religion and ideology. Shakespeare belongs not simply to a particular culture—English culture of the late sixteenth and early seventeenth centuries—but to world culture, the dense network of constraints and entitlements, dreams and practices that help to make us fully human. Indeed, so absolute is Shakespeare's achievement that he has himself come to seem like great creating nature. His works embody the imagination's power to transcend time-bound beliefs and assumptions, particular historical circumstances, and specific artistic conventions. If we should ever be asked as a species to bring forward one artist who has most fully expressed the human condition, we could with confidence elect Shakespeare to speak for us. As it is, when we do ask ourselves the most fundamental questions about life—about love and hatred, ambition, desire, and fear, the demand for justice and the longing for a second chance—we repeatedly turn to Shakespeare for the words we wish to hear.

The near-worship Shakespeare inspires is one of the salient facts about his art. But we must at the same time acknowledge that this art is the product of peculiar historical circumstances and specific conventions, four centuries distant from our own. The acknowledgment is important because Shakespeare the working dramatist did not typically lay claim to the transcendent, visionary truths attributed to him by his most fervent admirers; his characters more modestly say, in the words of the magician Prospero, that their project was "to please" (*The Tempest*, Epilogue, line 13). The starting point, and perhaps the ending point as well, in any encounter with Shakespeare is simply to enjoy him, to savor his imaginative richness, to take pleasure in his infinite delight in language.

"If then you do not like him," Shakespeare's first editors wrote in 1623, "surely you are in some manifest danger not to understand him." Over the years, accommodations have been devised to make liking Shakespeare easier for everyone. When aspects of his language began to seem difficult, texts were published with notes and glosses. When the historical events he depicted receded into obscurity, explanatory introductions were written. When the stage sank to melodrama and light opera, Shakespeare made his appearance in suitably revised dress. When the populace had a craving for hippodrama, plays performed entirely on horseback, *Hamlet* was dutifully rewritten and mounted. When audiences went mad for realism, live frogs croaked in productions of *A Midsummer Night's Dream*. When the stage was stripped

1

bare and given over to stark exhibitions of sadistic cruelty, Shakespeare was our contemporary. And when the theater ceded some of its cultural centrality to radio, film,
and television, Shakespeare moved effortlessly to Hollywood and the sound stages of
the BBC.

This virtually universal appeal is one of the most astonishing features of the
Shakespeare phenomenon: plays that were performed before glittering courts thrive
in junior high school auditoriums; enemies set on destroying one another laugh at
the same jokes and weep at the same catastrophes; some of the richest and most complex English verse ever written migrates with spectacular success into German and
Italian, Hindi, Swahili, and Japanese. Is there a single, stable, continuous object that
underlies all of these migrations and metamorphoses? Certainly not. The global dif-
fusion and long life of Shakespeare's works depend on their extraordinary malleability, their protean capacity to elude definition and escape secure possession. His art is
the supreme manifestation of the mobility of culture. At the same time, this art is
not without identifiable shared features: across centuries and continents, family
resemblances link many of the wildly diverse manifestations of plays such as *Romeo
and Juliet*, *Hamlet*, and *Twelfth Night*. Moreover, if there is no clear limit or end point,
there is a reasonably clear beginning, the England of the late sixteenth and early
seventeenth centuries, when the plays and poems collected in *The Norton Shakespeare* made their first appearance.

An art virtually without end or limit but with an identifiable, localized, historical
origin: Shakespeare's achievement defies the facile opposition between transcendent
and time-bound. It is not necessary to choose between an account of Shakespeare as
the scion of a particular culture and an account of him as a universal genius who
created works that continually renew themselves across national and generational
boundaries. On the contrary: crucial clues to understanding his art's remarkable
power to soar beyond the time and place of its origin lie in the very soil from which
that art sprang.

Shakespeare's World

Life and Death

Life expectancy at birth in early modern England was exceedingly low by our standards: under thirty years, compared with over seventy today. Infant mortality rates
were extraordinarily high, and it is estimated that in the poorer parishes of London
only about half the children survived to the age of fifteen, while the children of aristocrats fared only a little better. In such circumstances, some parents must have
developed a certain detachment—one of Shakespeare's contemporaries writes of losing "some three or four children"—but there are many expressions of intense grief, so
that we cannot assume that the frequency of death hardened people to loss or made it
routine.

Still, the spectacle of death, along with that other great threshold experience, birth,
must have been far more familiar to Shakespeare and his contemporaries than to
ourselves. There was no equivalent in early modern England to our hospitals, and most
births and deaths occurred at home. Physical means for the alleviation of pain and
suffering were extremely limited—alcohol might dull the terror, but it was hardly an
effective anesthetic—and medical treatment was generally both expensive and worthless, more likely to intensify suffering than to lead to a cure. This was a world without
a concept of antiseptics, with little actual understanding of disease, with few effective
ways of treating earaches or venereal disease, let alone the more terrible instances of
what Shakespeare calls "the thousand natural shocks that flesh is heir to."

The worst of these shocks was the bubonic plague, which repeatedly ravaged
England, and particularly English towns, until the third quarter of the seventeenth

Bill recording plague deaths in London, 1609.

century. The plague was terrifyingly sudden in its onset, rapid in its spread, and almost invariably lethal. Physicians were helpless in the face of the epidemic, though they prescribed amulets, preservatives, and sweet-smelling substances (on the theory that the plague was carried by noxious vapors). In the plague-ridden year of 1564, the year of Shakespeare's birth, some 254 people died in his native Stratford-upon-Avon, out of a total population of 800. The year before, some 20,000 Londoners are thought to have died; in 1593, almost 15,000; in 1603, 36,000, or over a sixth of the city's inhabitants. The social effects of these horrible visitations were severe: looting, violence, and despair, along with an intensification of the age's perennial poverty, unemployment, and food shortages. The London plague regulations of 1583, reissued with modifications in later epidemics, ordered that the infected and their households should be locked in their homes for a month; that the streets should be kept clean; that vagrants should be expelled; and that funerals and plays (as occasions in which large numbers of people gathered and infection could be spread) should be restricted or banned entirely. Comparable restrictions were not placed on gatherings for religious observance, since it was hoped that God would heed the desperate prayers of his suffering people.

The plague, then, had a direct and immediate impact on Shakespeare's own profession. City officials kept records of the weekly number of plague deaths; when these surpassed a certain number, the theaters were peremptorily closed. The basic idea was not only to prevent contagion but also to avoid making an angry God still angrier with the spectacle of idleness. While restricting public assemblies may in fact have slowed the epidemic, other public policies in times of plague, such as killing the cats and dogs, may have made matters worse (since the disease was spread not by these animals but by the fleas that bred on the black rats that infested the poorer neighborhoods). Moreover, the playing companies, driven out of London by the closing of the theaters, may have carried plague to the provincial towns.

Even in good times, when the plague was dormant and the weather favorable for farming, the food supply in England was precarious. A few successive bad harvests, such as occurred in the mid-1590s, could cause serious hardship, even starvation. Not surprisingly, the poor bore the brunt of the burden: inflation, low wages, and rent increases left large numbers of people with very little cushion against disaster. Further, at its best, the diet of most people seems to have been seriously deficient. The lower classes then, as throughout most of history, subsisted on one or two foodstuffs, usually low in protein. The upper classes disdained green vegetables and milk and gorged themselves on meat. Illnesses that we now trace to vitamin deficiencies were rampant. Some but not much relief from pain was provided by the beer that Elizabethans, including children, drank almost incessantly. (Home brewing aside, enough beer was sold in England for every man, woman, and child to have consumed forty gallons a year.)

Wealth

Despite rampant disease, the population of England in Shakespeare's lifetime grew steadily, from approximately 3,060,000 in 1564 to 4,060,000 in 1600 and 4,510,000 in 1616. Though the death rate was more than twice what it is in England today, the birthrate was almost three times the current figure. London's population in particular soared, from 60,000 in 1520 to 120,000 in 1550, 200,000 in 1600, and 375,000 a half-century later, making it the largest and fastest-growing city not only in England but in all of Europe. Every year in the first half of the seventeenth century, about 10,000 people migrated to London from other parts of England—wages in London tended to be around 50 percent higher than in the rest of the country—and it is estimated that one in eight English people lived in London at some point in their lives. The economic viability of Shakespeare's profession was closely linked to this extraordinary demographic boom: between 1567 and 1642, theater historians have estimated, the London playhouses were paid anywhere between 50 and 75 million visits.

As these visits to the theater indicate, in the capital city and elsewhere a substantial number of English men and women, despite hardships that were never very distant, had money to spend. After the disorder and dynastic wars of the fifteenth century, England in the sixteenth and early seventeenth centuries was for the most part a nation at peace, and with peace came a measure of enterprise and prosperity: the landowning classes busied themselves building great houses, planting orchards and hop gardens, draining marshlands, bringing untilled acreage under cultivation. The artisans and laborers who actually accomplished these tasks, though they were generally paid very little, often managed to accumulate something, as did the small freeholding farmers, the yeomen, who are repeatedly celebrated in the period as the backbone of English national independence and well-being. William Harrison's *Description of Britain* (1577) lovingly itemizes the yeoman's precious possessions: "fair garnish of pewter on his cupboard, with so much more odd vessel going about the house, three or four featherbeds, so many coverlets and carpets of tapestry, a silver salt [cellar], a bowl for wine (if not a whole nest) and a dozen of spoons." There are comparable accounts of the hard-earned acquisitions of the city dwellers—masters and apprentices in small workshops, shipbuilders, wool merchants, cloth makers, chandlers, tradesmen, shopkeepers, along with lawyers, apothecaries, schoolteachers, scriveners, and the like—whose pennies from time to time enriched the coffers of the players.

The chief source of England's wealth in the sixteenth century was its textile industry, an industry that depended on a steady supply of wool. The market for English textiles was not only domestic. In 1565, woolen cloth alone made up more than three-fourths of England's exports. (The remainder consisted mostly of other textiles and raw wool, with some trade in lead, tin, grain, and skins.) The Company of Merchant Adventurers carried cloth not only to nearby countries like France, Holland, and Germany but also to distant ports on the Baltic and Mediterranean, establishing links with Russia and Morocco (each took about 2 percent of London's cloth in 1597–98). English lead and tin, as well as fabrics, were sold in Tuscany and Turkey, and merchants found a market for Newcastle coal on the island of Malta. In the latter half of the century, London, which handled more than 85 percent of all exports, regularly shipped abroad more than 100,000 woolen cloths a year, at a value of at least £750,000. This figure does not include the increasingly important and profitable trade in so-called New Draperies, including textiles that went by such exotic names as bombazines, callamancoes, damazellas, damizes, mockadoes, and virgenatoes. When the Earl of Kent in *King Lear* insults Oswald as a "filthy, worsted-stocking knave" (2.2.14–15) or when the aristocratic Biron in *Love's Labor's Lost* declares that he will give up "taffeta phrases, silken terms precise, / Three-piled hyperboles" and woo henceforth "in russet 'yeas,' and honest kersey 'noes'" (5.2.407–08, 414), Shakespeare is assuming that a substantial portion of his audience will be alert to the social significance of fabric.

There is amusing confirmation of this alertness from an unexpected source: the report of a visit made to the Fortune playhouse in London in 1614 by a foreigner, Father Orazio Busino, the chaplain of the Venetian embassy. Father Busino neglected to mention the name of the play he saw, but like many foreigners, he was powerfully struck by the presence of gorgeously dressed women in the audience. In Venice, there was a special gallery for courtesans, but socially respectable women would not have been permitted to attend plays, as they could in England. In London, not only could middle- and upper-class women go to the theater, but they could also wear masks and mingle freely with male spectators and women of ill repute. The bemused cleric was uncertain about the ambiguous social situation in which he found himself:

> These theaters are frequented by a number of respectable and handsome ladies, who come freely and seat themselves among the men without the slightest hesitation. On the evening in question his Excellency and the Secretary were pleased to play me a trick by placing me amongst a bevy of young women. Scarcely was I seated ere a very elegant dame, but in a mask, came and placed herself beside me. . . . She asked me for my address both in French and English; and, on my turning a deaf ear, she determined to honor me by showing me some fine diamonds on her fingers, repeatedly taking off not fewer than three gloves, which were worn one over the other. . . . This lady's bodice was of yellow satin richly embroidered, her petticoat of gold tissue with stripes, her robe of red velvet with a raised pile, lined with yellow muslin with broad stripes of pure gold. She wore an apron of point lace of various patterns: her head-tire was highly perfumed, and the collar of white satin beneath the delicately-wrought ruff struck me as extremely pretty.

Father Busino may have turned a deaf ear on this "elegant dame" but not a blind eye: his description of her dress is worthy of a fashion designer and conveys something of the virtual clothes cult that prevailed in England in the late sixteenth and early seventeenth centuries, a cult whose major shrine, outside the royal court, was the theater.

Imports, Patents, and Monopolies

England produced some luxury goods, but the clothing on the backs of the most fashionable theatergoers was likely to have come from abroad. By the late sixteenth century, the English were importing substantial quantities of silks, satins, velvets, embroidery, gold and silver lace, and other costly items to satisfy the extravagant tastes of the elite and of those who aspired to dress like the elite. The government tried to put a check on the sartorial ambitions of the upwardly mobile by passing sumptuary laws—that is, laws restricting to the ranks of the aristocracy the right to wear certain of the most precious fabrics. But the very existence of these laws, in practice almost impossible to enforce, only reveals the scope and significance of the perceived problem.

Sumptuary laws were in part a conservative attempt to protect the existing social order from upstarts. Social mobility was not widely viewed as a positive virtue, and moralists repeatedly urged people to stay in their place. Conspicuous consumption that was tolerated, even admired, in the aristocratic elite was denounced as sinful and monstrous in less exalted social circles. English authorities were also deeply concerned throughout the period about the effects of a taste for luxury goods on the balance of trade. One of the principal English imports was wine: the "sherris" whose virtues Falstaff extols in *2 Henry IV* came from Xeres in Spain; the malmsey in which poor Clarence is drowned in *Richard III* was probably made in Greece or in the Canary Islands (from whence came Sir Toby Belch's "cup of canary" in *Twelfth Night*); and the "flagon of rhenish" that Yorick in *Hamlet* had once poured on the Gravedigger's head came from the Rhine region of Germany. Other imports included canvas, linen, fish, olive oil, sugar, molasses, dates, oranges and lemons, figs, raisins, almonds, capers, indigo, ostrich feathers, and that increasingly popular drug tobacco.

Joint stock companies were established to import goods for the burgeoning English market. The Merchant Venturers of the City of Bristol (established in 1552) handled great shipments of Spanish sack, the light, dry wine that largely displaced the vintages of Bordeaux and Burgundy when trade with France was disrupted by war. The Muscovy Company (established in 1555) traded English cloth and manufactured goods for Russian furs, oil, and beeswax. The Venice Company and the Turkey Company—uniting in 1593 to form the wealthy Levant Company—brought silk and spices home from Aleppo and carpets from Constantinople. The East India Company (founded in 1600), with its agent at Bantam in Java, brought pepper, cloves, nutmeg, and other spices from East Asia, along with indigo, cotton textiles, sugar, and saltpeter from India. English privateers "imported" American products, especially sugar, fish, and hides, in huge quantities, along with more precious cargoes. In 1592, a privateering expedition principally funded by Sir Walter Ralegh captured a huge Portuguese carrack (sailing ship), the *Madre de Dios*, in the Azores and brought it back to Dartmouth. The ship, the largest that had ever entered any English port, held 536 tons of pepper, cloves, cinnamon, cochineal, mace, civet, musk, ambergris, and nutmeg, as well as jewels, gold, ebony, carpets, and silks. Before order could be established, the English seamen began to pillage this immensely rich prize, and witnesses said they could smell the spices on all the streets around the harbor. Such piratical expeditions were rarely officially sanctioned by the state, but the Queen had in fact privately invested £1,800, for which she received about £80,000.

In the years of war with Spain, 1586–1604, the goods captured by the privateers annually amounted to 10–15 percent of the total value of England's imports. But organized theft alone could not solve England's balance-of-trade problems. Statesmen were particularly worried that the nation's natural wealth was slipping away in exchange for unnecessary things. In his *Discourse of the Commonweal* (1549), the prominent humanist Sir Thomas Smith exclaims against the importation of such trifles as mirrors, paper, laces, gloves, pins, inkhorns, tennis balls, puppets, and playing cards. And more than a century later, the same fear that England was trading its riches for trifles and wasting away in idleness was expressed by the Bristol merchant John Cary. The solution, Cary argues in "An Essay on the State of England in Relation to Its Trade" (1695), is to expand productive domestic employment. "People are or may be the Wealth of a Nation," he writes, "yet it must be where you find Employment for them, else they are a Burden to it, as the Idle Drone is maintained by the Industry of the laborious Bee, so are all those who live by their Dependence on others, as Players, Ale-House Keepers, Common Fiddlers, and such like, but more particularly Beggars, who never set themselves to work."

Stage players, all too typically associated here with vagabonds and other idle drones, could have replied in their defense that they not only labored in their vocation

Forging a magnet, 1600. The metal on the anvil is aligned North/South (Septentrio/Auster). From *De Magnete* by William Gilbert.

but also exported their skills abroad: English actors routinely performed on the Continent. But their labor was not regarded as a productive contribution to the national wealth, and plays were in truth no solution to the trade imbalances that worried authorities.

The government attempted to stem the flow of gold overseas by establishing a patent system initially designed to encourage skilled foreigners to settle in England by granting them exclusive rights to produce particular wares by a patented method. Patents were granted for such things as the making of hard white soap (1561), ovens and furnaces (1563), window glass (1567), sailcloths (1574), drinking glasses (1574), sulfur, brimstone, and oil (1577), armor and horse harness (1587), starch (1588), white writing paper made from rags (1589), aqua vitae and vinegar (1594), playing cards (1598), and mathematical instruments (1598).

By the early seventeenth century, English men and women were working in a variety of new industries like soap making, pin making, knife making, and the brewing of alegar and beeregar (ale- and beer-based vinegar). But although the ostensible purpose of the government's economic policy was to increase the wealth of England, encourage technical innovation, and provide employment for the poor, the effect of patents was often the enrichment of a few and the hounding of poor competitors by wealthy monopolists, a group that soon extended well beyond foreign-born entrepreneurs to the favorites of the monarch who vied for the huge profits to be made. "If I had a monopoly out" on folly, the Fool in *King Lear* protests, glancing at the "lords and great men" around him, "they would have part in't." The passage appears only in the Quarto version of the play (*History of King Lear* 4.140–41); it may have been cut for political reasons from the Folio. For the issue of monopolies provoked bitter criticism and parliamentary debate for decades. In 1601, Elizabeth was prevailed upon to revoke a number of the most hated monopolies, including aqua vitae and vinegar, bottles, brushes, fish livers, the coarse sailcloth known as poldavis and mildernix, pots, salt, and starch. The whole system was revoked during the reign of James I by an act of Parliament.

Haves and Have-Nots

When in the 1560s Elizabeth's ambassador to France, Sir Thomas Smith, wrote a description of England, he saw the commonwealth as divided into four sorts of people: "gentlemen, citizens, yeomen artificers, and laborers." At the forefront of the class of gentlemen was the monarch, followed by a very small group of nobles—dukes, marquesses, earls, viscounts, and barons—who either inherited their exalted titles, as the eldest male heirs of their families, or were granted them by the monarch. Under Elizabeth, this aristocratic peerage numbered between 50 and 60 individuals; James's promotions increased the number to nearer 130. Strictly speaking, Smith notes, the younger sons of the nobility were only entitled to be called "esquires," but in common speech they were also called "lords."

Below this tiny cadre of aristocrats in the social hierarchy of gentry were the knights, a title of honor conferred by the monarch, and below them were the "simple gentlemen." Who was a gentleman? According to Smith, "whoever studieth the laws of the realm, who studieth in the universities, who professeth liberal sciences, and to be short, who can live idly and without manual labor, and will bear the port, charge and countenance of a gentleman, he shall be called master . . . and shall be taken for a gentleman." To "live idly and without manual labor": where in Spain, for example, the crucial mark of a gentleman was "blood," in England it was "idleness," in the sense of sufficient income to afford an education and to maintain a social position without having to work with one's hands.

For Smith, the class of gentlemen was far and away the most important in the kingdom. Below were two groups that had at least some social standing and claim to authority: the citizens, or burgesses, those who held positions of importance and responsibility in their cities, and yeomen, farmers with land and a measure of economic independence. At the bottom of the social order was what Smith calls "the fourth sort of men which do not rule." The great mass of ordinary people have, Smith writes, "no voice nor authority in our commonwealth, and no account is made of them but only to be ruled." Still, even they can bear some responsibility, he notes, since they serve on juries and are named to such positions as churchwarden and constable.

In everyday practice, as modern social historians have observed, the English tended to divide the population not into four distinct classes but into two: a very small empowered group—the "richer" or "wiser" or "better" sort—and all the rest who were without much social standing or power, the "poorer" or "ruder" or "meaner" sort. References to the "middle sort of people" remain relatively rare until after Shakespeare's lifetime; these people are absorbed into the rulers or the ruled, depending on speaker and context.

The source of wealth for most of the ruling class, and the essential measure of social status, was land ownership, and changes to the social structure in the sixteenth and seventeenth centuries were largely driven by the land market. The property that passed into private hands as the Tudors and early Stuarts sold off confiscated monastic estates and then their own crown lands for ready cash amounted to nearly a quarter of all the land in England. At the same time, the buying and selling of private estates was on the rise throughout the period. Land was bought up not only by established landowners seeking to enlarge their estates but also by successful merchants, manufacturers, and urban professionals; even if the taint of vulgar money-making lingered around such figures, their heirs would be taken for true gentlemen. The rate of turnover in land ownership was great; in many counties, well over half the gentle families in 1640 had appeared since the end of the fifteenth century. The class that Smith called "simple gentlemen" was expanding rapidly: in the fifteenth century, they had held no more than a quarter of the land in the country, but by the later seventeenth, they controlled almost half. Over the same period, the land held by the great aristocratic magnates held steady at 15–20 percent of the total.

Riot and Disorder

London was a violent place in the first half of Shakespeare's career. There were thirty-five riots in the city in the years 1581–1602, twelve of them in the volatile month of June 1595. These included protests against the deeply unpopular Lord Mayor Sir John Spencer, attempts to release prisoners, anti-alien riots, and incidents of "popular market regulation." There is an unforgettable depiction of a popular uprising in *Coriolanus,* along with many other glimpses in Shakespeare's works, including Jack Cade's grotesque rebellion in *2 Henry VI,* the plebeian violence in *Julius Caesar,* and Laertes' "riotous head" in *Hamlet.*

The London rioters were mostly drawn from the large mass of poor and discontented apprentices who typically chose as their scapegoats foreigners, prostitutes, and gentlemen's servingmen. Theaters were very often the site of the social confrontations that sparked disorder. For two days running in June 1584, disputes between apprentices and gentlemen triggered riots outside the Curtain Theater involving up to a thousand participants. On one occasion, a gentleman was said to have exclaimed that "the apprentice was but a rascal, and some there were little better than rogues that took upon them the name of gentlemen, and said the prentices were but the scum of the world." These occasions culminated in attacks by the apprentices on London's law schools, the Inns of Court.

The most notorious and predictable incidents of disorder came on Shrove Tuesday (the Tuesday before the beginning of Lent), a traditional day of misrule when apprentices ran riot. Shrove Tuesday disturbances involved attacks by mobs of young men on the brothels of the South Bank, in the vicinity of the Globe and other public theaters. The city authorities took precautions to keep these disturbances from getting completely out of control, but evidently did not regard them as serious threats to public order.

Of much greater concern throughout the Tudor and early Stuart years were the frequent incidents of rural rioting. Though in *The Winter's Tale* Shakespeare provides a richly comic portrayal of a rural sheepshearing festival, the increasingly intensive production of wool had its grim side. When a character in Thomas More's *Utopia* (1516) complains that "the sheep are eating the people," he is referring to the practice of enclosure: throughout the sixteenth and early seventeenth centuries, many acres of croplands once farmed in common by rural communities were fenced in by wealthy landowners and turned into pasturage. The ensuing misery, displacement, and food shortages led to repeated protests, some of them violent and bloody, along with a series of government proclamations, but the process of enclosure was not reversed. The protests were at their height during Shakespeare's career: in the years 1590–1610, the frequency of anti-enclosure rioting doubled from what it had been earlier in Elizabeth's reign.

Although they often became violent, anti-enclosure riots were usually directed not against individuals but against property. Villagers—sometimes several hundred, often fewer than a dozen—gathered to tear down newly planted hedges. The event often took place in a carnival atmosphere, with songs and drinking, that did not prevent the participants from acting with a good deal of political canniness and forethought. Especially in the Jacobean period, it was common for participants to establish a fund for legal defense before commencing their assault on the hedges. Women were frequently involved, and on a number of occasions wives alone participated in the destruction of the enclosure, since there was a widespread, though erroneous, belief that married women acting without the knowledge of their husbands were immune from prosecution. In fact, the powerful Court of Star Chamber consistently ruled that both the wives and their husbands should be punished.

Although Stratford was never the scene of serious rioting, enclosure controversies turned violent more than once in Shakespeare's lifetime. In January 1601, Shakespeare's friend Richard Quiney and others leveled the hedges of Sir Edward Greville, lord of Stratford manor. Quiney was elected bailiff of Stratford in September of that year but did not live to enjoy the office for long. He died from a blow to the head struck by one of Greville's men in a tavern brawl. Greville, responsible for the administration of justice, neglected to punish the murderer.

There was further violence in January 1615, when William Combe's men threw to the ground two local aldermen who were filling in a ditch by which Combe was enclosing common fields near Stratford. The task of filling in the offending ditch was completed the next day by the women and children of Stratford. Combe's enclosure scheme was eventually stopped in the courts. Though he owned land whose value would have been affected by this controversy, Shakespeare took no active role in it, since he had previously come to a private settlement with the enclosers insuring him against personal loss.

Most incidents of rural rioting were small, localized affairs, and with good reason: when confined to the village community, riot was a misdemeanor; when it spread outward to include multiple communities, it became treason, punishable by death. The greatest of

The Peddler. From Jost Amman, *The Book of Trades* (1568).

the anti-enclosure riots, those in which hundreds of individuals from a large area participated, commonly took place on the eve of full-scale regional rebellions. The largest of these disturbances, Kett's Rebellion, involved some 16,000 peasants, artisans, and townspeople who rose up in 1549 under the leadership of a Norfolk tanner and landowner, Robert Kett, to protest economic exploitation. The agrarian revolts in Shakespeare's lifetime were on a much smaller scale. In the abortive Oxfordshire Rebellion of 1596, a carpenter named Bartholomew Steer attempted to organize a rising against the hated enclosures. The optimistic Steer allegedly promised his followers that "it was but a month's work to overrun England" and informed them "that the commons long since in Spain did rise and kill all gentlemen . . . and since that time have lived merrily there." Steer expected several hundred men to join him on Enslow Hill on November 21, 1596, for the start of the rising; no more than twenty showed up. They were captured, imprisoned, and tortured. Several were executed, but Steer apparently cheated the hangman by dying in prison.

Rebellions, most often triggered by hunger and oppression, continued into the reign of James I. The Midland Revolt of 1607, which may be reflected in *Coriolanus*, consisted of a string of agrarian risings in the counties of Northamptonshire, Warwickshire, and Leicestershire, involving assemblies of up to five thousand rebels in various places. The best known of their leaders was John Reynolds, called "Captain Powch" because of the pouch he wore, whose magical contents were supposed to defend the rebels from harm. (According to the chronicler Edmund Howes, when Reynolds was captured and the pouch opened, it contained "only a piece of green cheese.") The rebels, who were called by themselves and others both "Levelers" and "Diggers," insisted that they had no quarrel with the King but only sought an end to injurious enclosures. But Robert Wilkinson, who preached a sermon against the leaders at their trial, credited them with the intention to "level all states as they leveled banks and ditches." Most of the rebels got off relatively lightly, but, along with other ringleaders, Captain Powch was executed.

The Legal Status of Women

English women were not under the full range of crushing constraints that afflicted women in some countries in Europe. Foreign visitors were struck by their relative freedom, as shown, for example, by the fact that respectable women could venture unchaperoned into the streets and attend the theater. Yet while England was ruled for over forty years by a powerful woman, the great majority of women in the kingdom had very restricted social, economic, and legal standing. To be sure, a tiny number of influential aristocratic women, such as the formidable Countess of Shrewsbury, Bess of Hardwick, wielded considerable power. But, these rare exceptions aside, women were denied any rightful claim to institutional authority or personal autonomy. When Sir Thomas Smith thinks of how he should describe his country's social order, he declares that "we do reject women, as those whom nature hath made to keep home and to nourish their family and children, and not to meddle with matters abroad, nor to bear office in a city or commonwealth." Then, with a kind of glance over his shoulder, he makes an exception of those few for whom "the blood is respected, not the age nor the sex": for example, the Queen.

Single women, whether widowed or unmarried, could, if they were of full age, inherit and administer land, make a will, sign a contract, possess property, sue and be sued, without a male guardian or proxy. But married women had no such rights under English common law, the system of law based on court decisions rather than on codified written laws. Early modern writings about women and the family constantly return to a political model of domination and submission, in which the husband and father justly rules over wife and children as the monarch rules over the state. The husband's dominance in the family was the justification for the common-law rule that prohibited married women from possessing property, administering land, signing contracts, or bringing lawsuits in their own names: married women were described as legally "covered" by their husbands. Yet this conception of a woman's role conveniently ignores the fact that a *majority* of the adult women at any time in Shakespeare's England were not married. They were either widows or spinsters (a term that was not yet pejorative), and thus for the most part managed their own affairs. Even within marriage, women typically had more control over certain spheres than moralizing writers on the family cared to admit. For example, village wives oversaw the production of eggs, cheese, and beer, and sold these goods in the market. As seamstresses, pawnbrokers, second-hand clothing dealers, peddlers and the like—activities not controlled by the all-male craft guilds—women managed to acquire some economic power of their own, and, of course, they participated as well in the unregulated, black-market economy of the age and in the underworld of thievery and prostitution.

Women were not in practice as bereft of property as, according to English common law, they should have been. Demographic studies indicate that the inheritance system called primogeniture, the orderly transmission of property from father to eldest male heir, was more often an unfulfilled wish than a reality. Some 40 percent of marriages failed to produce a son, and in such circumstances fathers often left their land to their daughters, rather than to brothers, nephews, or male cousins. In many families, the father died before his male heir was old enough to inherit property, leaving the land, at least temporarily, in the hands of the mother. And while they were less likely than their brothers to inherit land ("real property"), daughters normally inherited a substantial share of their parents' personal property (cash and movables).

In fact, the legal restrictions upon women, though severe in Shakespeare's time, actually worsened in subsequent decades. English common law was significantly less egalitarian in its approach to wives and daughters than were alternative legal codes (manorial, civil, and ecclesiastical) still in place in the late sixteenth century. The eventual triumph of common law stripped women of many traditional rights, slowly driving them out of economically productive trades and businesses.

Limited though it was, the economic freedom of Elizabethan and Jacobean women far exceeded their political and social freedom—the opportunity to receive a grammar school or university education, to hold office in church or state, to have a voice in public debates, or even simply to speak their mind fully and openly in ordinary conversation. Women who asserted their views too vigorously risked being perceived as shrewish and labeled "scolds." Both urban and rural communities had a horror of scolds. In the Elizabethan period, such women came to be regarded as a threat to public order, to be dealt with by the local authorities. The preferred methods of correction included public humiliation—of the sort Katherina endures in *The Taming of the Shrew*—and such physical abuse as slapping, bridling with a bit or muzzle, and half-drowning by means of a contraption called the "cucking stool" (or "ducking stool"). This latter punishment originated in the Middle Ages, but its use spread in the sixteenth century, when it became almost exclusively a punishment for women. From 1560 onward, cucking stools were built or renovated in many English provincial towns; between 1560 and 1600, the contraptions were installed by rivers or ponds in Norwich, Bridport, Shrewsbury, Kingston-upon-Thames, Marlborough, Devizes, Clitheroe, Thornbury, and Great Yarmouth.

Such punishment was usually intensified by a procession through the town to the sound of "rough music," the banging together of pots and pans. The same cruel festivity accompanied the "carting" or "riding" of those accused of being whores. In some parts of the country, villagers also took the law into their own hands, publicly shaming women who married men much younger than themselves or who beat or otherwise domineered over their husbands. One characteristic form of these charivaris, or rituals of shaming, was known in the West Country as the Skimmington Ride. Villagers would rouse the offending couple from bed with rough music and stage a raucous pageant in which a man, holding a distaff, would ride backward on a donkey, while his "wife" (another man dressed as a woman) struck him with a ladle. In these cases, the collective ridicule and indignation were evidently directed at least as much at the henpecked husband as at his transgressive wife.

Women and Print

Books published for a female audience surged in popularity in the late sixteenth century, reflecting an increase in female literacy. (It is striking how many of Shakespeare's women are shown reading.) This increase is probably linked to a Protestant longing for direct access to the Scriptures, and the new books marketed specifically for women included devotional manuals and works of religious instruction. But there were also practical guides to such subjects as female education (for example, Giovanni Bruto's *Necessary, Fit, and Convenient Education of a Young Gentlewoman*, 1598), midwifery (James Guillemeau's *Child-birth; or, the Happy Delivery of Women*, 1612), needlework (Federico di Vinciolo's *New and Singular Patterns and Works of Linen*, 1591), cooking (Thomas Dawson's *The Good Housewife's Jewel*, 1587), gardening (Pierre Erondelle's *The French Garden*, 1605), and married life (Patrick Hanney's *A Happy Husband; or, Directions for a Maid to Choose Her Mate*, 1619). As the authors' names suggest, many of these works were translations, and almost all were written by men.

Starting in the 1570s, writers and their publishers increasingly addressed works of recreational literature (romance, fiction, and poetry) partially or even exclusively to women. Some books, such as Robert Greene's *Mamillia, a Mirror or Looking-Glass for the Ladies of England* (1583), directly specified in the title their desired audience. Others, such as Sir Philip Sidney's influential and popular romance *Arcadia* (1590–93), solicited female readership in their dedicatory epistles. The ranks of Sidney's followers eventually included his own niece, Mary Wroth, whose romance *Urania* was published in 1621.

In the literature of Shakespeare's time, women readers were not only wooed but also frequently railed at, in a continuation of a popular polemical genre that had long inspired heated charges and countercharges. Both sides in the polemic generally agreed that it was the duty of women to be chaste, dutiful, and modest in demeanor; the argument was whether women fulfilled or fell short of this proper role. Ironically, then, a modern reader is more likely to find inspiring accounts of courageous women not in the books written in defense of female virtue but in attacks on those who refused to be silent and obedient.

The most famous English skirmish in this controversy took place in a rash of pamphlets at the end of Shakespeare's life. Joseph Swetnam's crude *Arraignment of Lewd, Idle, Froward, and Unconstant Women* (1615) provoked three fierce responses attributed to women: Rachel Speght's *A Muzzle for Melastomus*, Esther Sowernam's *Esther Hath Hang'd Haman*, and Constantia Munda's *Worming of a Mad Dog*, all in 1617. There was also an anonymous play, *Swetnam the Woman-Hater Arraigned by Women* (first performed around 1618), in which Swetnam, depicted as a braggart and a lecher, is put on trial by women and made to recant his misogynistic lies.

Prior to the Swetnam controversy, only one English woman, writing under the pseudonym "Jane Anger," had published a defense of women (*Jane Anger Her Protection for Women*, 1589). Learned women writers in the sixteenth century tended not to become involved in public debate but rather to undertake a project to which it was difficult for even obdurately chauvinistic males to object: the translation of devotional literature into English. Thomas More's daughter Margaret More Roper translated Erasmus (*A Devout Treatise upon the Pater Noster*, 1524); Francis Bacon's mother, Anne Cooke Bacon, translated Bishop John Jewel (*An Apology or Answer in Defence of the Church of England*, 1564); Anne Locke Prowse, a friend of John Knox, translated the *Sermons of John Calvin* in 1560; and Mary Sidney, the Countess of Pembroke, completed the metrical version of the Psalms that her brother Sir Philip

Sidney had begun. Elizabeth Tudor (the future queen) herself translated, at the age of eleven, Marguerite de Navarre's *Le Miroir de l'âme pécheresse* (*The Glass of the Sinful Soul,* 1544). The translation was dedicated to her stepmother, Katherine Parr, herself the author of a frequently reprinted book of prayers.

There was in the sixteenth and early seventeenth centuries a social stigma attached to print. Far from celebrating publication, authors, and particularly female authors, often apologized for exposing themselves to the public gaze. Nonetheless, a number of women ventured in print beyond pious translations. Some, including Elizabeth Tyrwhitt, Anne Dowriche, Isabella Whitney, Mary Sidney, and Aemilia Lanyer, composed and published their own poems. Aemilia Lanyer's *Salve Deus Rex Judaeorum,* published in 1611, is a poem in praise of virtuous women, from Eve and the Virgin Mary to her noble patron, the Countess of Cumberland. "A Description of Cookeham," appended to the poem, is one of the first English country house poems, a celebration in verse of an aristocrat's rural estate.

The first Tudor woman to translate a play was the learned Jane Lumley, who composed an English version of Euripides' *Iphigenia at Aulis* (ca. 1550). The first known original play in English by a woman was by Elizabeth Cary, Viscountess Falkland, whose *Tragedy of Mariam, the Fair Queen of Jewry* was published in 1613. This remarkable play, which was not intended to be performed, includes speeches in defense of women's equality, though the most powerful of these is spoken by the villainous Salome, who schemes to divorce her husband and marry her lover. Cary, who bore

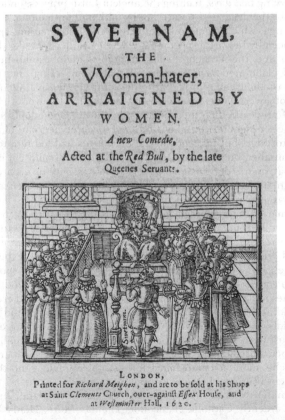

Title page of *Swetnam the Woman-Hater, Arraigned by Women* (1620), a play written in response to Joseph Swetnam's *The Arraignment of Lewd, Idle, Forward, and Unconstant Women* (1615); the woodcut depicts the trial of Swetnam in act 4.

eleven children, herself had a deeply troubled marriage, which effectively came to an end in 1625 when, defying her husband's staunchly Protestant family, she openly converted to Catholicism. Her biography was written by one of her four daughters, all of whom became nuns.

Henry VIII and the English Reformation

There had long been serious ideological and institutional tensions in the religious life of England, but officially, at least, England in the early sixteenth century had a single religion, Catholicism, whose acknowledged head was the pope in Rome. In 1517, drawing upon long-standing currents of dissent, Martin Luther, an Augustinian monk and professor of theology at the University of Wittenberg, challenged the authority of the pope and attacked several key doctrines of the Catholic Church. According to Luther, the Church, with its elaborate hierarchical structure centered in Rome, its rich monasteries and convents, and its enormous political influence, had become hopelessly corrupt, a conspiracy of venal priests who manipulated popular superstitions to enrich themselves and amass worldly power. Luther began by vehemently attacking the sale of indulgences—certificates promising the remission of punishments to be suffered in the afterlife by souls sent to purgatory to expiate their sins. These indulgences were a fraud, he argued; purgatory itself had no foundation in the Bible, which in his view was the only legitimate source of religious truth. Christians would be saved not by scrupulously following the ritual practices fostered by the Catholic Church—observing fast days, reciting the ancient Latin prayers, endowing chantries to say prayers for the dead, and so on—but by faith and faith alone.

This challenge, which came to be known as the Reformation, spread and gathered force, especially in northern Europe, where major leaders like the Swiss pastor Ulrich Zwingli and the French theologian John Calvin established institutional structures and elaborated various and sometimes conflicting doctrinal principles. Calvin, whose thought came to be particularly influential in England, emphasized the obligation of governments to implement God's will in the world. He advanced too the doctrine of predestination, by which, as he put it, "God adopts some to hope of life and sentences others to eternal death." God's "secret election" of the saved made Calvin uncomfortable, but his study of the Scriptures had led him to conclude that "only a small number, out of an incalculable multitude, should obtain salvation." It might seem that such a conclusion would lead to passivity or even despair, but for Calvin predestination was a mystery bound up with faith, confidence, and an active engagement in the fashioning of a Christian community.

The Reformation had a direct and powerful impact on those territories, especially in northern Europe, where it gained control. Monasteries, many of them fabulously wealthy, were sacked, their possessions and extensive landholdings seized by princes or sold off to the highest bidder; the monks and nuns, expelled from their cloisters, were encouraged to break their vows of chastity and find spouses, as Luther and his wife, a former nun, had done. In the great cathedrals and in hundreds of smaller churches and chapels, the elaborate altarpieces, bejeweled crucifixes, crystal reliquaries holding the bones of saints, and venerated statues and paintings were attacked as "idols" and often defaced or destroyed. Protestant congregations continued, for the most part, to celebrate the most sacred Christian ritual, the Eucharist, or Lord's Supper, but they did so in a profoundly different spirit from that of the Catholic Church—more as commemoration than as miracle—and they now prayed not in the ancient liturgical Latin but in the vernacular.

The Reformation was at first vigorously resisted in England. Indeed, with the support of his ardently Catholic chancellor, Thomas More, Henry VIII personally wrote (or at least lent his name to) a vehement, often scatological attack on Luther's character and views, an attack for which the pope granted him the honorific title "Defender of the Faith." Protestant writings, including translations of the Scriptures into English, were seized by officials of the church and state and burned. Protestants who made their views known were persecuted, driven to flee the country, or arrested, put on trial, and burned at the stake. But the situation changed drastically and decisively when in 1527 Henry decided to seek an annulment from his first wife, Catherine of Aragon, in order to marry Anne Boleyn.

Catherine had given birth to six children, but since only a daughter, Mary, survived infancy, Henry did not have the son he craved. Then as now, the Catholic Church did not ordinarily grant divorce, but Henry's lawyers argued on technical grounds that the marriage was invalid (and therefore, by extension, that Mary was illegitimate and hence unable to inherit the throne). Matters of this kind were far less doctrinal than diplomatic: Catherine, the daughter of Ferdinand of Aragon and Isabella of Castile, had powerful allies in Rome, and the pope ruled against Henry's petition. A series of momentous events followed, as England lurched away from the Church of Rome. In 1531, Henry charged the entire clergy of England with having usurped royal authority in the administration of canon law (the ecclesiastical law that governed faith, discipline, and morals, including such matters as divorce). Under extreme pressure, including the threat of mass confiscations and imprisonment, the Convocation of the Clergy begged for pardon, made a donation to the royal coffers of over £100,000, and admitted that the King was "supreme head of the English Church and clergy" (modified by the rider "as far as the law of Christ allows"). On May 15 of the next year, the convocation submitted to the demand that the King be the final arbiter of canon law; on the next day, Thomas More resigned his post.

In 1533, Henry's marriage to Catherine was officially declared null and void, and on June 1 Anne Boleyn was crowned queen (a coronation Shakespeare depicts in his late play *Henry VIII*). The King was promptly excommunicated by Pope Clement VII. In the following year, the parliamentary Act of Succession confirmed the effects of the annulment and required an oath from all adult male subjects confirming the new dynastic settlement. Thomas More and John Fisher, the Bishop of Rochester, were among the small number who refused. The Act of Supremacy, passed later in the year, formally declared the King to be "Supreme Head of the Church in England" and again required an oath to this effect. In 1535 and 1536, further acts made it treasonous to refuse the oath of royal supremacy or, as More had tried to do, to remain silent. The first victims were three Carthusian monks who rejected the oath—"How could the King, a layman," said one of them, "be Head of the Church of

The Pope as Antichrist riding the Beast of the Apocalypse. From *Fiery Trial of God's Saints* (1611; author unknown).

England?"—and in May 1535, they were duly hanged, drawn, and quartered. A few weeks later, Fisher and More were convicted and beheaded. Between 1536 and 1539, the monasteries were suppressed and their vast wealth seized by the crown.

Royal defiance of the authority of Rome was a key element in the Reformation but did not by itself constitute the establishment of Protestantism in England. On the contrary, in the same year that Fisher and More were martyred for their adherence to Roman Catholicism, twenty-five Protestants, members of a sect known as Anabaptists, were burned for heresy on a single day. Through most of his reign, Henry remained an equal-opportunity persecutor, ruthless to Catholics loyal to Rome but also hostile to some of those who espoused Reformation ideas, though many of these ideas gradually established themselves on English soil.

Even when Henry was eager to do so, it proved impossible to eradicate Protestantism, as it would later prove impossible for his successors to eradicate Catholicism. In large part this tenacity arose from the passionate, often suicidal heroism of men and women who felt that their souls' salvation depended on the precise character of their Christianity. It arose too from a mid-fifteenth-century technological innovation that made it almost impossible to suppress unwelcome ideas: the printing press. Early Protestants quickly grasped that with a few clandestine presses they could defy the Catholic authorities and flood the country with their texts. "How many printing presses there be in the world," wrote the Protestant polemicist John Foxe, "so many blockhouses there be against the high castle" of the pope in Rome, "so that either the pope must abolish knowledge and printing or printing at length will root him out." By the century's end, it was the Catholics who were using the clandestine press to propagate their beliefs in the face of Protestant persecution.

The greatest insurrection of the Tudor age was not over food, taxation, or land but over religion. On Sunday, October 1, 1536, stirred up by their vicar, the traditionalist parishioners of Louth in Lincolnshire, in the north of England, rose up in defiance of the ecclesiastical delegation sent to enforce royal supremacy. The rapidly spreading rebellion, which became known as the Pilgrimage of Grace, was led by the lawyer Robert Aske. The city of Lincoln fell to the rebels on October 6, and though it was soon retaken by royal forces, the rebels seized cities and fortifications throughout Yorkshire, Durham, Northumberland, Cumberland, Westmoreland, and northern Lancashire. Carlisle, Newcastle, and a few castles were all that were left to the King in the north. The Pilgrims soon numbered 40,000, led by some of the region's most prominent noblemen. The Duke of Norfolk, representing the crown, was forced to negotiate a truce, with a promise to support the rebels' demands that the King restore the monasteries, shore up the regional economy, suppress heresy, and dismiss his evil advisers. The Pilgrims kept the peace for the rest of 1536, on the naive assumption that their demands would be met. But Henry moved suddenly early in 1537 to impose order and capture the ringleaders; 130 people, including lords, knights, heads of religious houses, and, of course, Robert Aske, were executed.

In 1549, two years after the death of Henry VIII, the west and north of England were the sites of further unsuccessful risings for the restoration of Catholicism. The Western Rising is striking for its blend of Catholic universalism and intense regionalism among people who did not yet regard themselves as English. One of the rebels' articles, protesting against the imposition of the English Bible and religious service, declares, "We the Cornish men (whereof certain of us understand no English) utterly refuse this new English." The rebels besieged but failed to take the city of Exeter. As with almost all Tudor rebellions, the number of those executed in the aftermath of the failed rising was far greater than those killed in actual hostilities.

The Children of Henry VIII: Edward, Mary, and Elizabeth

Upon Henry's death in 1547, his ten-year-old son, Edward VI, came to the throne, with his maternal uncle Edward Seymour named as Duke of Somerset and Lord

Protector (regent while the King was still a minor). Both Edward and his uncle were staunch Protestants, and reformers hastened to transform the English church accordingly. During Edward's reign, Archbishop Thomas Cranmer formulated the forty-two articles of religion that became the core of Anglican orthodoxy and wrote the first Book of Common Prayer, which was officially adopted in 1549 as the basis of English worship services.

Somerset fell from power in 1549 and was replaced as Lord Protector by John Dudley, later Duke of Northumberland. When Edward fell seriously ill, probably of tuberculosis, Northumberland persuaded him to sign a will depriving his half-sisters Mary (the daughter of Catherine of Aragon) and Elizabeth (the daughter of Anne Boleyn) of their claim to royal succession. The Lord Protector was scheming to have his daughter-in-law, the Protestant Lady Jane Grey, a great-granddaughter of Henry VII, ascend to the throne. But when Edward died in 1553, Mary marshaled support, quickly secured the crown from Lady Jane (who had been titular queen for nine days), and had Lady Jane executed, along with her husband and Northumberland.

Queen Mary immediately took steps to return her kingdom to Roman Catholicism. Though she was unable to get Parliament to agree to return church lands seized under Henry VIII, she restored the Catholic Mass, once again affirmed the authority of the pope, and put down a rebellion that sought to depose her. Seconded by her ardently Catholic husband, Philip II, King of Spain, she initiated a series of religious persecutions that earned her (from her enemies) the name "Bloody Mary." Hundreds of Protestants took refuge abroad in cities such as Calvin's Geneva; almost three hundred less fortunate Protestants were condemned as heretics and burned at the stake.

Mary died childless in 1558, and her younger half-sister Elizabeth became queen. Elizabeth's succession had been by no means assured. For if Protestants regarded the marriage of Henry VIII to Catherine as invalid and hence deemed Mary illegitimate, so Catholics regarded his marriage to Anne Boleyn as invalid and deemed Elizabeth illegitimate. Henry VIII himself seemed to support both views, since only

The Family of Henry VIII: An Allegory of the Tudor Succession, by Lucas de Heere (ca. 1572). Henry, in the middle, is flanked by Mary to his right, and Edward and Elizabeth to his left.

three years after divorcing Catherine, he beheaded Anne Boleyn on charges of treason and adultery and urged Parliament to invalidate the marriage. Moreover, though
during her sister's reign Elizabeth outwardly complied with the official Catholic
religious observance, Mary and her advisers were deeply suspicious, and the young
princess's life was in grave danger. Poised and circumspect, Elizabeth warily evaded
the traps that were set for her. As she ascended the throne, her actions were scrutinized for some indication of the country's future course. During her coronation procession, when a girl in an allegorical pageant presented her with a Bible in English
translation—banned under Mary's reign—Elizabeth kissed the book, held it up rev-
erently, and laid it to her breast; when the abbot and monks of Westminster Abbey
came to greet her in broad daylight with candles (a symbol of Catholic devotion) in
their hands, she briskly dismissed them with the telling words "Away with those
torches! We can see well enough." England had returned to the Reformation.

Many English men and women, of all classes, remained inwardly loyal to the old
Catholic faith; Shakespeare's father and mother may well have been among these.
But English authorities under Elizabeth moved steadily, if cautiously, toward ensuring at least an outward conformity to the official Protestant settlement. Recusants,
those who refused to attend regular Sunday services in their parish churches, were
fined heavily. Anyone who wished to receive a university degree, to be ordained as a
priest in the Church of England, or to be named as an officer of the state had to swear
an oath to the royal supremacy. Commissioners were sent throughout the land to
confirm that religious services were following the officially approved liturgy and to
investigate any reported backsliding into Catholic practice or, alternatively, any
attempts to introduce more radical reforms than the Queen and her bishops had chosen to embrace. For many of the Protestant exiles who streamed back to England
were eager not only to undo the damage Mary had done but to carry the Reformation
much further. They sought to dismantle the church hierarchy, to purge the calendar
of folk customs deemed pagan and the church service of ritual practices deemed
superstitious, to dress the clergy in simple garb, and, at the extreme edge, to smash
"idolatrous" statues, crucifixes, and altarpieces. Pressing for a stricter code of life
and a simplified system of worship, the religious radicals came to be called Puritans.
Throughout her long reign, however, Elizabeth herself remained cautiously conservative and determined to hold in check what she regarded as the religious zealotry of
Catholics, on the one side, and Puritans, on the other.

Shakespeare's plays tap into the ongoing confessional tensions: "sometimes," Maria
in *Twelfth Night* says of the sober, festivity-hating steward Malvolio, "he is a kind of
puritan" (2.3.129). But the plays tend to avoid the risks of direct engagement: "The devil
a puritan that he is, or anything constantly," Maria adds a moment later, "but a time-
pleaser" (2.3.135–36). *The Winter's Tale* features a statue that comes to life—exactly
the kind of magical image that Protestant polemicists excoriated as Catholic superstition and idolatry—but the play is set in the pre-Christian world of the Delphic Oracle.
And as if this careful distancing might not be enough, the play's ruler goes out of his
way to pronounce the wonder legitimate: "If this be magic, let it be an art / Lawful as
eating" (5.3.110–11).

In the space of a single lifetime, England had gone officially from Roman Catholicism, to Catholicism under the supreme headship of the English king, to a guarded
Protestantism, to a more radical Protestantism, to a renewed and aggressive Roman
Catholicism, and finally to Protestantism again. Each of these shifts was accompanied by danger, persecution, and death. It was enough to make some people wary. Or
skeptical. Or extremely agile.

The English Bible

Luther had undertaken a fundamental critique of the Catholic Church's sacramental
system, a critique founded on the twin principles of salvation by faith alone (*sola fide*)

and the absolute primacy of the Bible (*sola scriptura*). *Sola fide* contrasted faith with "works," by which was meant primarily the whole elaborate system of rituals sanctified, conducted, or directed by the priests. Protestants proposed to modify or reinterpret many of these rituals or, as with the rituals associated with purgatory, to abolish them altogether. *Sola scriptura* required direct lay access to the Bible, which meant in practice the widespread availability of vernacular translations. The Roman Catholic Church had not always and everywhere opposed such translations, but it generally preferred that the populace encounter the Scriptures through the interpretations of the priests, trained to read the Latin translation known as the Vulgate. In times of great conflict, this preference for clerical mediation hardened into outright prohibition of vernacular translation and into persecution and book burning.

Zealous Protestants set out, in the teeth of fierce opposition, to put the Bible into the hands of the laity. A remarkable translation of the New Testament, by an English Lutheran named William Tyndale, was printed on the Continent and smuggled into England in 1525; Tyndale's translation of the Pentateuch, the first five books of the Hebrew Bible, followed in 1530. Many copies of these translations were seized and burned, as was the translator himself, but the printing press made it extremely difficult for authorities to eradicate books for which there was a passionate demand. The English Bible was a force that could not be suppressed, and it became, in its various forms, the single most important book of the sixteenth century.

Tyndale's translation was completed by an associate, Miles Coverdale, whose rendering of the Psalms proved to be particularly influential. Their joint labor was the basis for the Great Bible (1539), the first authorized version of the Bible in English, a copy of which was ordered to be placed in every church in the kingdom. With the accession of Edward VI, many editions of the Bible followed, but the process was sharply reversed when Mary came to the throne in 1553. Along with people condemned as heretics, English Bibles were burned in great bonfires.

Marian persecution was indirectly responsible for what would become the most popular as well as most scholarly English Bible, the translation known as the Geneva Bible (1560), prepared, with extensive, learned, and often fiercely polemical marginal notes, by English exiles in Calvin's Geneva and widely diffused in England after Elizabeth came to the throne. In addition, Elizabethan church authorities ordered a careful revision of the Great Bible, and this version, known as the Bishops' Bible (1568), was the one read in the churches. The success of the Geneva Bible in particular prompted those Elizabethan Catholics who now in turn found themselves in exile to bring out a vernacular translation of their own in order to counter the Protestant readings and glosses. This Catholic translation, the so-called Rheims Bible (1582), may have been known to Shakespeare, but he seems to have been far better acquainted with the Geneva Bible, and he would also have repeatedly heard the Bishops' Bible read aloud. Scholars have identified over three hundred references to the Bible in Shakespeare's work; in one version or another, the Scriptures had a powerful impact on his imagination.

A Female Monarch in a Male World

In the last year of Mary's reign, 1558, the Scottish Calvinist minister John Knox thundered against what he called "the monstrous regiment of women." When the Protestant Elizabeth came to the throne the following year, Knox and his religious brethren were less inclined to denounce female rulers, but in England as elsewhere in Europe there remained a widespread conviction that women were unsuited to wield power over men. Many men seem to have regarded the capacity for rational thought as exclusively male; women, they assumed, were led only by their passions. While gentlemen mastered the arts of rhetoric and warfare, gentlewomen were expected to display the virtues of silence and good housekeeping. Among upper-class males, the will to dominate others was acceptable and indeed admired; the same will in women was condemned as a grotesque and dangerous aberration.

The Armada portrait: note Elizabeth's hand on the globe.

Apologists for the Queen countered these prejudices by appealing to historical precedent and legal theory. History offered inspiring examples of just female rulers, notably Deborah, the biblical prophetess who judged Israel. In the legal sphere, crown lawyers advanced the theory of "the king's two bodies." As England's crowned head, Elizabeth's person was mystically divided between her mortal "body natural" and the immortal "body politic." While the queen's natural body was inevitably subject to the failings of human flesh, the body politic was timeless and perfect. In political terms, therefore, Elizabeth's sex was a matter of no consequence, a thing indifferent.

Elizabeth, who had received a fine humanist education and an extended, dangerous lesson in the art of survival, made it immediately clear that she intended to rule in more than name only. She assembled a group of trustworthy advisers, foremost among them William Cecil (later named Lord Burghley), but she insisted on making many of the crucial decisions herself. Like many Renaissance monarchs, Elizabeth was drawn to the idea of royal absolutism, the theory that ultimate power was properly concentrated in her person and indeed that God had appointed her to be his deputy in the kingdom. Opposition to her rule, in this view, was not only a political act but also a kind of impiety, a blasphemous grudging against the will of God. Apologists for absolutism contended that God commands obedience even to manifestly wicked rulers whom he has sent to punish the sinfulness of humankind. Such arguments were routinely made in speeches and political tracts and from the pulpits of churches, where they were incorporated into the Book of Homilies, which clergymen were required to read out to their congregations.

In reality, Elizabeth's power was not absolute. The government had a network of spies, informers, and agents provocateurs, but it lacked a standing army, a national police force, an efficient system of communication, and an extensive bureaucracy. Above all, the Queen had limited financial resources and needed to turn periodically to an independent and often recalcitrant Parliament, which by long tradition had the sole right to levy taxes and to grant subsidies. Members of the House of Commons were elected from their boroughs, not appointed by the monarch, and though the Queen had considerable influence over their decisions, she could by no means dictate policy. Under these constraints, Elizabeth ruled through a combination of adroit political maneuvering and imperious command, all the while enhancing her authority in the eyes of both court and country by means of an extraordinary cult of love.

"We all loved her," Elizabeth's godson Sir John Harington wrote, with just a touch of irony, a few years after the Queen's death, "for she said she loved us." Ambassadors, courtiers, and parliamentarians all submitted to Elizabeth's cult of love, in which the Queen's gender was transformed from a potential liability into a significant asset. Those who approached her generally did so on their knees and were expected to address her with extravagant compliments fashioned from the period's most passionate love poetry; she in turn spoke, when it suited her to do so, in the language of love poetry. The court moved in an atmosphere of romance, with music, dancing, plays, and the elaborate, fancy-dress entertainments called masques. The Queen adorned herself in gorgeous clothes and rich jewels. When she went on one of her summer "progresses," ceremonial journeys through her land, she looked like an exotic, sacred image in a religious cult of love, and her noble hosts virtually bankrupted themselves to lavish upon her the costliest pleasures. England's leading artists, such as the poet Edmund Spenser and the painter Nicholas Hilliard, enlisted themselves in the celebration of Elizabeth's mystery, likening her to the goddesses of classical mythology: Diana, Astraea, Phoebe, Flora. Her cult drew its power from cultural discourses that ranged from the secular (her courtiers could pine for her as a chaste, unattainable maiden) to the sacred (the veneration that under Catholicism had been due to the Virgin Mary could now be directed toward England's semidivine queen).

There was a sober, even grim aspect to these poetical fantasies: Elizabeth was brilliant at playing one dangerous faction off against another, now turning her gracious smiles on one favorite, now honoring his hated rival, now suddenly looking elsewhere and raising an obscure upstart to royal favor. And when she was disobeyed or when she felt that her prerogatives had been challenged, she was capable of an anger that, as Harington put it, "left no doubtings whose daughter she was." Thus when Sir Walter Ralegh, one of the Queen's glittering favorites, married without her knowledge or consent, he found himself promptly imprisoned in the Tower of London. And when the Protestant polemicist John Stubbs ventured to publish a pamphlet stridently denouncing the Queen's proposed marriage to the French Catholic Duke of Alençon, Stubbs and his publisher were arrested and had their right hands chopped off. (After receiving the blow, the now prudent Stubbs lifted his hat with his remaining hand and cried, "God save the Queen!")

The Queen's marriage negotiations were a particularly fraught issue. When she came to the throne at twenty-five years old, speculation about a suitable match, already widespread, intensified and remained for decades at a fever pitch, for the stakes were high. If Elizabeth died childless, the Tudor line would come to an end. The nearest heir was her cousin Mary, Queen of Scots, a Catholic whose claim was supported by France and by the papacy and whose penchant for sexual and political intrigue confirmed the worst fears of English Protestants. The obvious way to avert the nightmare was for Elizabeth to marry and produce an heir, and the pressure upon her to do so was intense.

More than the royal succession hinged on the question of the Queen's marriage; Elizabeth's perceived eligibility was a vital factor in the complex machinations of international diplomacy. A dynastic marriage between the Queen of England and a foreign ruler would forge an alliance powerful enough to alter the balance of power in Europe. The English court hosted a steady stream of ambassadors from kings and princes eager to win the hand of the royal maiden, and Elizabeth, who prided herself on speaking fluent French and Italian (and on reading Latin and Greek), played her romantic part with exemplary skill, sighing and spinning the negotiations out for months and even years. Most probably, she never meant to marry any of her numerous foreign (and domestic) suitors. Such a decisive act would have meant the end of her independence, as well as the end of the marriage game by which she played one power off against another. One day she would seem to be on the verge of accepting a proposal; the next, she would vow never to forsake her virginity. "She is a princess," the French ambassador remarked, "who can act any part she pleases."

The Kingdom in Danger

Beset by Catholic and Protestant extremists, Elizabeth contrived to forge a moderate compromise that enabled her realm to avert the massacres and civil wars that poisoned France and other countries on the Continent. But menace was never far off, and there were constant fears of conspiracy, rebellion, and assassination. Many of the fears swirled around Mary, Queen of Scots, who had been driven from her own kingdom in 1568 by a powerful faction of rebellious nobles and had taken refuge in England. Her presence, under a kind of house arrest, was a source of intense anxiety and helped generate continual rumors of plots. Some of these plots were real enough, others imaginary, still others traps set in motion by the secret agents of the government's intelligence service under the direction of Sir Francis Walsingham. The situation worsened greatly after Spanish imperial armies invaded the Netherlands in order to stamp out Protestant rebels (1567), after the St. Bartholomew's Day Massacre of Protestants (Huguenots) in France (1572), and after the assassination there of Europe's other major Protestant leader, William of Orange (1584).

The Queen's life seemed to be in even greater danger after the proclamation of Pope Gregory XIII in 1580 that the assassination of the great heretic Elizabeth (who had been excommunicated a decade before) would not constitute a mortal sin. The immediate effect of the proclamation was to make existence more difficult for English Catholics, most of whom were loyal to the Queen but who fell under grave suspicion. Suspicion was intensified by the clandestine presence of English Jesuits, trained at seminaries abroad and smuggled back into England to serve the Roman Catholic cause. When Elizabeth's spymaster Walsingham unearthed an assassination plot in the correspondence between the Queen of Scots and the Catholic Anthony Babington, the wretched Mary's fate was sealed. After vacillating, a very reluctant Elizabeth signed the death warrant in February 1587, and her cousin was beheaded.

The long-anticipated military confrontation with Catholic Spain was now unavoidable. Elizabeth learned that Philip II, her former brother-in-law and onetime suitor, was preparing to send an enormous fleet against her island realm. It was to sail to the Netherlands, where a Spanish army would be waiting to embark and invade England. Barring its way was England's small fleet of well-armed and highly maneuverable fighting vessels, backed up by ships from the merchant navy. The Invincible Armada reached English waters in July 1588, only to be routed in one of the most famous and decisive naval battles in European history. Then, in what many viewed as an act of God on behalf of Protestant England, the Spanish fleet was dispersed and all but destroyed by violent storms.

As England braced itself to withstand the invasion that never came, Elizabeth appeared in person to review a detachment of soldiers assembled at Tilbury. Dressed in a white gown and a silver breastplate, she declared that though some among her councillors had urged her not to appear before a large crowd of armed men, she would never fail to trust the loyalty of her faithful and loving subjects. Nor did she fear the Spanish armies. "I know I have the body of a weak and feeble woman," Elizabeth declared, "but I have the heart and stomach of a king, and of England too." In this celebrated speech, Elizabeth displayed many of her most memorable qualities: her self-consciously histrionic command of grand public occasion, her subtle blending of magniloquent rhetoric and the language of love, her strategic appropriation of traditionally masculine qualities, and her great personal courage. "We princes," she once remarked, "are set on stages in the sight and view of all the world."

The English and Otherness

Shakespeare's London had a large population of resident aliens, mainly artisans and merchants and their families, from Portugal, Italy, Spain, Germany, and above all France and the Netherlands. Many of these people were Protestant refugees, and they were accorded some legal and economic protection by the government. But they were not always welcomed by the local populace. Throughout the sixteenth century, London was the site of repeated demonstrations and, on occasion, bloody riots against the communities of foreign artisans, who were accused of taking jobs away from Englishmen. There was widespread hostility as well toward the Welsh, the Scots, and especially the Irish, whom the English had for centuries been struggling unsuccessfully to subdue. The kings of England claimed to be rulers of Ireland, but in reality they effectively controlled only a small area known as the Pale, extending north from Dublin. The great majority of the Irish people remained stubbornly Catholic and, despite endlessly reiterated English repression, burning of villages, destruction of crops, and massacres, incorrigibly independent.

Shakespeare's *Henry V* (1598–99) seems to invite the audience to celebrate the conjoined heroism of English, Welsh, Scots, and Irish soldiers all fighting together as a "band of brothers" against the French. But such a way of imagining the national community must be set against the tensions and conflicting interests that often set these brothers at each other's throats. As Shakespeare's King Henry realizes, a feared or hated foreign enemy helps at least to mask these tensions, and indeed, in the face of the Spanish Armada, even the bitter gulf between Catholic and Protestant Englishmen seemed to narrow significantly. But the patriotic alliance was only temporary.

Another way of partially masking the sharp differences in language, belief, and custom among the peoples of the British Isles was to group these people together in contrast to the Jews. Medieval England's Jewish population, the recurrent object of persecution, extortion, and massacre, had been officially expelled by King Edward I in 1290. Therefore few if any of Shakespeare's contemporaries would have encountered on English soil Jews who openly practiced their religion. Elizabethan England probably did, however, harbor a small number of so-called Marranos, Spanish or Portuguese Jews who had officially converted to Christianity but secretly continued to observe Jewish practices. One of those suspected to be Marranos was Elizabeth's own physician, Roderigo Lopez, who was tried in 1594 for an alleged plot to poison the Queen. Convicted and condemned to the hideous execution reserved for traitors, Lopez went to his death, in the words of the Elizabethan historian

A Jewish man depicted poisoning a well. From Pierre Boaistuau, *Certain Secret Wonders of Nature* (1569).

William Camden, "affirming that he loved the Queen as well as he loved Jesus Christ; which coming from a man of the Jewish profession moved no small laughter in the standers-by." It is difficult to gauge the meaning here of the phrase "the Jewish profession," used to describe a man who never as far as we know professed Judaism, just as it is difficult to gauge the meaning of the crowd's cruel laughter.

Elizabethans appear to have been fascinated by Jews and Judaism but quite uncertain whether the terms referred to a people, a foreign nation, a set of strange practices, a living faith, a defunct religion, a villainous conspiracy, or a messianic inheritance. Protestant reformers brooded deeply on the Hebraic origins of Christianity; government officials ordered the arrest of those "suspected to be Jews"; villagers paid pennies to itinerant fortune-tellers who claimed to be descended from Abraham or masters of cabalistic mysteries; and London playgoers, perhaps including some who laughed at Lopez on the scaffold, enjoyed the spectacle of the downfall of the wicked Barabas in Christopher Marlowe's *Jew of Malta* (ca. 1589) and the forced conversion of Shylock in Shakespeare's *Merchant of Venice* (1596–97). Jews were not officially permitted to resettle in England until the middle of the seventeenth century, and even then their legal status was ambiguous.

Shakespeare's England also had a small African population whose skin color was the subject of pseudo-scientific speculation and theological debate. Some Elizabethans believed that Africans' blackness resulted from the climate of the regions in which they lived, where, as one traveler put it, they were "so scorched and vexed with the heat of the sun, that in many places they curse it when it riseth." Others held that blackness was a curse inherited from their forefather Chus, the son of Ham, who had, according to Genesis, wickedly exposed the nakedness of the drunken Noah. George Best, a proponent of this theory of inherited skin color, reported that "I myself have seen an Ethiopian as black as coal brought into England, who taking a fair English woman to wife, begat a son in all respects as black as the father was, although England were his native country, and an English woman his mother: whereby it seemeth this blackness proceedeth rather of some natural infection of that man."

Man with head beneath his shoulders. From a Spanish edition of Mandeville's *Travels*. See *Othello* 1.3.144–45: "and men whose heads / Grew beneath their shoulders." Such men were frequently reported by medieval travelers to the East.

As the word "infection" suggests, Elizabethans frequently regarded blackness as a physical defect, though the blacks who lived in England and Scotland throughout the sixteenth century were also treated as exotic curiosities. At his marriage to Anne of Denmark, James I entertained his bride and her family by commanding four naked black youths to dance before him in the snow. (The youths died of exposure shortly afterward.) In 1594, in the festivities celebrating the baptism of James's son, a "Black-Moor" entered pulling an elaborately decorated chariot that was, in the original plan, supposed to be drawn in by a lion. There was a black trumpeter in the courts of Henry VII and Henry VIII, while Elizabeth had at least two black servants, one an entertainer and the other a page. Africans became increasingly popular as servants in aristocratic and gentle households in the last decades of the sixteenth century.

Some of these Africans were almost certainly slaves, though the legal status of slavery in England was ambiguous. In Cartwright's Case (1569), the court ruled "that England was too Pure an Air for Slaves to breathe in," but there is evidence that black slaves were owned in Elizabethan and Jacobean England. Moreover, by the mid-sixteenth century, the English had become involved in the profitable trade that carried African slaves to the New World. In 1562, John Hawkins embarked on his first slaving voyage, transporting some three hundred blacks from the Guinea coast to Hispaniola, where they were sold for £10,000. Elizabeth is reported to have said of this venture that it was "detestable, and would call down the Vengeance of Heaven upon the Undertakers." Nevertheless, she invested in Hawkins's subsequent voyages and loaned him ships.

English men and women of the sixteenth century experienced an unprecedented increase in knowledge of the world beyond their island, for a number of reasons. Religious persecution compelled both Catholics and Protestants to live abroad; wealthy gentlemen (and, in at least a few cases, ladies) traveled in France and Italy to view the famous cultural monuments; merchants published accounts of distant lands such as Turkey, Morocco, and Russia; and military and trading ventures took English ships to still more distant shores. In 1496, a Venetian tradesman living in Bristol, John Cabot, was granted a license by Henry VII to sail on a voyage of exploration; with his son Sebastian, he discovered Newfoundland and Nova Scotia. Remarkable feats of seamanship and reconnaissance soon followed: on his ship the *Golden Hind,* Sir Francis Drake circumnavigated the globe in 1579 and laid claim to California on behalf of the Queen; a few years later, a ship commanded by Thomas Cavendish also completed a circumnavigation. Sir Martin Frobisher explored bleak Baffin Island in search of a Northwest Passage to the Orient; Sir John Davis explored the west coast of Greenland and discovered the Falkland Islands off the coast of Argentina; Sir Walter Ralegh ventured up the Orinoco Delta, in what is now Venezuela, in search of the mythical land of El Dorado. Accounts of these and other exploits were collected by a clergyman and promoter of empire, Richard Hakluyt, and published as *The Principal Navigations* (1589; expanded edition 1599).

"To seek new worlds for gold, for praise, for glory," as Ralegh characterized such enterprises, was not for the faint of heart: Drake, Cavendish, Frobisher, and Hawkins all died at sea, as did huge numbers of those who sailed under their command. Elizabethans sensible enough to stay at home could do more than read written accounts of their fellow countrymen's far-reaching voyages. Expeditions brought back native plants (including, most famously, tobacco), animals, cultural artifacts, and, on occasion, samples of the native peoples themselves, most often seized against their will. There were exhibitions in London of a kidnapped Eskimo with his kayak and of Native Virginians with their canoes. Most of these miserable captives, violently uprooted and vulnerable to European diseases, quickly perished, but even in death they were evidently valuable property: when the English will not give one small coin "to relieve a lame beggar," one of the characters in *The Tempest* wryly remarks, "they will lay out ten to see a dead Indian" (2.2.30–31).

Perhaps most nations learn to define what they are by defining what they are not. This negative self-definition is, in any case, what Elizabethans seemed constantly to be doing, in travel books, sermons, political speeches, civic pageants, public exhibitions, and theatrical spectacles of otherness. The extraordinary variety of these exercises (which include public executions and urban riots, as well as more benign forms of curiosity) suggests that the boundaries of national identity were by no means clear and unequivocal. Even peoples whom English writers routinely, viciously stigmatize

An Indian dance. From Thomas Hariot, *A Brief and True Report of the New Found Land of Virginia* (1590).

as irreducibly alien—Italians, Indians, Turks, and Jews—have a surprising instability in the Elizabethan imagination and may appear for brief, intense moments as power-ful models to be admired and emulated before they resume their place as emblems of despised otherness.

James I and the Union of the Crowns

Though under great pressure to do so, the aging Elizabeth steadfastly refused to name her successor. It became increasingly apparent, however, that it would be James Stu-art, the son of Mary, Queen of Scots, and by the time Elizabeth's health began to fail, several of her principal advisers, including her chief minister, Robert Cecil, had been for several years in secret correspondence with him in Edinburgh. Crowned King James VI of Scotland in 1567 when he was but one year old, Mary's son had been raised as a Protestant by his powerful guardians, and in 1589 he married a Protestant princess, Anne of Denmark. When Elizabeth died on March 24, 1603, English offi-cials reported that on her deathbed the Queen had named James to succeed her.

Upon his accession, James—now styled James VI of Scotland and James I of England—made plain his intention to unite his two kingdoms. As he told Parliament in 1604, "What God hath conjoined then, let no man separate. I am the husband, and all of the whole isle is my lawful wife; I am the head and it is my body; I am the

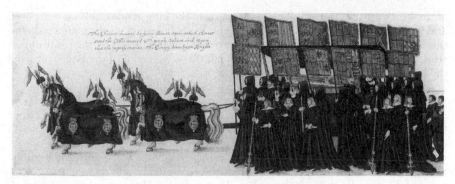

Funeral procession of Queen Elizabeth. From a watercolor sketch by an unknown artist (1603).

shepherd and it is my flock." But the flock was less perfectly united than James optimistically envisioned: English and Scottish were sharply distinct identities, as were Welsh and Cornish and other peoples who were incorporated, with varying degrees of willingness, into the realm.

Fearing that to change the name of the kingdom would invalidate all laws and institutions established under the name of England, a fear that was partly real and partly a cover for anti-Scots prejudice, Parliament balked at James's desire to be called "King of Great Britain" and resisted the unionist legislation that would have made Great Britain a legal reality. Though the English initially rejoiced at the peaceful transition from Elizabeth to her successor, there was a rising tide of resentment against James's advancement of Scots friends and his creation of new knighthoods. Lower down the social ladder, English and Scots occasionally clashed violently on the streets: in July 1603, James issued a proclamation against Scottish "insolencies," and in April 1604, he ordered the arrest of "swaggerers" waylaying Scots in London. The ensuing years did not bring the amity and docile obedience for which James hoped, and, though the navy now flew the Union Jack, combining the Scottish cross of St. Andrew and the English cross of St. George, the unification of the kingdoms remained throughout his reign an unfulfilled ambition.

Unfulfilled as well were James's lifelong dreams of ruling as an absolute monarch. Crown lawyers throughout Europe had long argued that a king, by virtue of his power to make law, must necessarily be above law. But in England sovereignty was identified not with the king alone or with the people alone but with the "King in Parliament." Against his absolutist ambitions, James faced the crucial power to raise taxes that was vested not in the monarch but in the elected members of the Parliament. He faced as well a theory of republicanism that traced its roots back to ancient Rome and that prided itself on its steadfast and, if necessary, violent resistance to tyranny. Shakespeare's fascination with monarchy is apparent throughout his work, but in his Roman plays in particular, as well as in his long poem *The Rape of Lucrece*, he manifests an intense imaginative interest in the idea of a republic.

The Jacobean Court

With James as with Elizabeth, the royal court was the center of diplomacy, ambition, intrigue, and an intense jockeying for social position. As always in monarchies, proximity to the king's person was a central mark of favor, so that access to the royal bedchamber was one of the highest aims of the powerful, scheming lords who followed James from his sprawling London palace at Whitehall to the hunting lodges and country estates to which he loved to retreat. A coveted office, in the Jacobean as in the Tudor court, was the Groom of the Stool, the person who supervised the disposal of the king's wastes. The officeholder was close to the king at one of his most exposed and vulnerable moments and enjoyed the further privilege of sleeping on a pallet at the foot of the royal bed and assisting the monarch in putting on the royal undershirt. Another, slightly less privileged official, the Gentleman of the Robes, dressed the king in his doublet and outer garments.

The royal lifestyle was increasingly expensive. Unlike Elizabeth, James had to maintain separate households for his queen and for the heir apparent, Prince Henry. (Upon Henry's death at the age of eighteen in 1612, his younger brother, Prince Charles, became heir, eventually succeeding his father in 1625.) James was also extremely generous to his friends, amassing his own huge debts in the course of paying off theirs. As early as 1605, he told his principal adviser that "it is a horror to me to think of the height of my place, the greatness of my debts, and the smallness of my means." This smallness notwithstanding, James continued to lavish gifts upon handsome favorites such as the Earl of Somerset, Robert Carr, and the Duke of Buckingham, George Villiers.

The attachment James formed for these favorites was highly romantic. "God so love me," the King wrote to Buckingham, "as I desire only to live in the world for your sake, and that I had rather live banished in any part of the earth with you than live a sorrowful widow's life without you." Such sentiments, not surprisingly, gave rise to widespread rumors of homosexual activities at court. The rumors are certainly plausible, though the surviving evidence of same-sex relationships, at court or elsewhere, is extremely difficult to interpret. A statute of 1533 made "the detestable and abominable vice of buggery committed with mankind or beast" a felony punishable by death. (English law

declined to recognize or criminalize lesbian acts.) The effect of the draconian laws against sodomy seems to have been to reduce actual prosecutions to the barest minimum: for the next hundred years, there are no known cases of trials resulting in a death sentence for homosexual activity alone. If the legal record is therefore unreliable as an index of the extent of homosexual relations, the literary record (including, most famously, the majority of Shakespeare's sonnets) is equally opaque. Any poetic avowal of male-male love may simply be a formal expression of affection based on classical models, or, alternatively, it may be an expression of passionate physical and spiritual love. The interpretive difficulty is compounded by the absence in the period of any clear reference to a homosexual "identity," though there are many references to same-sex acts and feelings. What is clear is that male friendships at the court of James and elsewhere were suffused with eroticism, at once exciting and threatening, that subsequent periods policed more anxiously.

James I. Attributed to John De Critz the Elder (ca. 1606).

In addition to the extravagant expenditures on his favorites, James

Two Young Men. By Crispin van den Broeck.

was also the patron of ever more elaborate feasts and masques. Shakespeare's work provides a small glimpse of these in *The Tempest,* with its exotic banquet and its "majestic vision" of mythological goddesses and dancing nymphs and reapers. The actual Jacobean court masques, designed by the great architect, painter, and engineer Inigo Jones, were spectacular, fantastic, technically ingenious, and staggeringly costly celebrations of regal magnificence. With their exquisite costumes and their elegant blend of music, dancing, and poetry, the masques, generally performed by the noble lords and ladies of the court, were deliberately ephemeral exercises in conspicuous expenditure and consumption: by tradition, at the end of the performance, the private audience would rush forward and tear to pieces the gorgeous scenery. And though masques were enormously sophisticated entertainments, often on rather esoteric allegorical themes, they could on occasion collapse into grotesque excess. In a letter of 1606, Sir John Harington describes a masque in honor of the visiting Danish king in which the participants, no doubt toasting their royal majesties, had had too much to drink. A lady playing the part of the Queen of Sheba attempted to present precious gifts, "but, forgetting the steps arising to the canopy, overset her caskets into his Danish Majesty's lap. . . . His Majesty then got up and would dance with the Queen of Sheba; but he fell down and humbled himself before her, and was carried to an inner chamber and laid on a bed." Meanwhile, Harington writes, the masque continued with a pageant of Faith, Hope, and Charity, but Charity could barely keep her balance, while Hope and Faith "were both sick and spewing in the lower hall." This was, we can hope, not a typical occasion.

While the English seem initially to have welcomed James's free-spending ways as a change from the parsimoniousness of Queen Elizabeth, they were dismayed by its consequences. Elizabeth had died owing £400,000. In 1608, the royal debt had risen to £1,400,000 and was increasing by £140,000 a year. The money to pay off this debt, or at least to keep it under control, was raised by various means. These included customs farming (leasing the right to collect customs duties to private individuals); the highly unpopular impositions (duties on the import of nonnecessities, such as spices, silks, and currants); the sale of crown lands; the sale of baronetcies; and appeals to an increasingly grudging and recalcitrant Parliament. In 1614, Parliament demanded an end to impositions before it would relieve the King and was angrily dissolved without completing its business.

James's Religious Policy and the Persecution of Witches

Before his accession to the English throne, the King had made known his view of Puritans, the general name for a variety of Protestant sects that were agitating for a radical reform of the church, the overthrow of its conservative hierarchy of bishops, and the rejection of a large number of traditional rituals and practices. In a book he wrote, *Basilikon Doron* (1599), James denounced "brainsick and heady preachers" who were prepared "to let King, people, law and all be trod underfoot." Yet he was not entirely unwilling to consider religious reforms. In religion, as in foreign policy, he was above all concerned to maintain peace.

On his way south to claim the throne of England in 1603, James was presented with the Millenary Petition (signed by one thousand ministers), which urged him as "our physician" to heal the disease of lingering "popish" ceremonies. He responded by calling a conference on the ceremonies of the Church of England, which duly took place at Hampton Court Palace in January 1604. The delegates who spoke for reform were moderates, and there was little in the outcome to satisfy Puritans. Nevertheless, while the Church of England continued to cling to such remnants of the Catholic past as wedding rings, square caps, bishops, and Christmas, the conference did produce some reform in the area of ecclesiastical discipline. It also authorized a new English translation of the Bible, known as the King James Bible, which was printed in 1611, too late to have been extensively used by Shakespeare. Along with Shakespeare's works, the King James Bible has probably had the profoundest influence on the subsequent history of English literature.

Having arranged this compromise, James saw his main task as ensuring conformity. He promulgated the 1604 Canons (the first definitive code of canon law since the Reformation), which required all ministers to subscribe to three articles. The first affirmed royal supremacy; the second confirmed that there was nothing in the Book of Common Prayer "contrary to the Word of God" and required ministers to use only the authorized services; the third asserted that the central tenets of the Church of England

The "swimming" of a suspected witch.

were "agreeable to the Word of God." There were strong objections to the second and third articles from those of Puritan leanings inside and outside the House of Commons. In the end, many ministers refused to conform or subscribe to the articles, but only about ninety of them, or 1 percent of the clergy, were deprived of their livings. In its theology and composition, the Church of England was little changed from what it had been under Elizabeth. In hindsight, what is most striking are the ominous signs of growing religious divisions that would by the 1640s burst forth in civil war and the execution of James's son Charles.

James seems to have taken seriously the official claims to the sacredness of kingship, and he certainly took seriously his own theories of religion and politics, which he had printed for the edification of his people. He was convinced that Satan, perpetually warring against God and His representatives on earth, was continually plotting against him. James thought moreover that he possessed special insight into Satan's wicked agents, the witches, and in 1597, while King of Scotland, he published his *Demonology*, a learned exposition of their malign threat to his godly rule. Hundreds of witches, he believed, were involved in a 1589 conspiracy to kill him by raising storms at sea when he was sailing home from Denmark with his new bride.

In the 1590s, Scotland embarked on a virulent witch craze of the kind that had since the fifteenth century repeatedly afflicted France, Switzerland, and Germany, where many thousands of women (and a much smaller number of men) were caught in a nightmarish web of wild accusations. Tortured into making lurid confessions of infant cannibalism, night flying, and sexual intercourse with the devil at huge, orgiastic "witches' Sabbaths," the victims had little chance to defend themselves and were routinely burned at the stake.

In England too there were witchcraft prosecutions, though on a much smaller scale and with significant differences in the nature of the accusations and the judicial procedures. Witch trials began in England in the 1540s; statutes against witchcraft were enacted in 1542, 1563, and 1604. English law did not allow judicial torture, stipulated lesser punishments in cases of "white magic," and mandated jury trials. Juries acquitted more than half of the defendants in witchcraft trials; in Essex, where the judicial records are particularly extensive, some 24 percent of those accused were executed, while the remainder of those convicted were pilloried and imprisoned or sentenced and reprieved. The accused were generally charged with *maleficium*, an evil deed—usually harming neighbors, causing destructive storms, or killing farm animals—but not with worshipping Satan.

After 1603, when James came to the English throne, he somewhat moderated his enthusiasm for the judicial murder of witches, for the most part defenseless, poor women resented by their neighbors. Though he did nothing to mitigate the ferocity of the ongoing witch hunts in his native Scotland, he did not try to institute Scottish-style persecutions and trials in his new realm. This relative waning of persecutorial eagerness principally reflects the differences between England and Scotland, but it may also bespeak some small, nascent skepticism on James's part about the quality of evidence brought against the accused and about the reliability of the "confessions" extracted from them. It is sobering to reflect that plays like Shakespeare's *Macbeth* (1606), Thomas Middleton's *Witch* (before 1616), and Thomas Dekker, John Ford, and William Rowley's *Witch of Edmonton* (1621) seem to be less the allies of skepticism than the exploiters of fear.

The Playing Field

Cosmic Spectacles

The first permanent, freestanding public theaters in England date only from Shakespeare's own lifetime: a London playhouse, the Red Lion, is mentioned in 1567, and

James Burbage's playhouse, The Theatre, was built in 1576. (The innovative use of these new stages, crucial to a full understanding of Shakespeare's achievement, is discussed in a separate essay in this volume, by the theater historian Holger Schott Syme.) But it is quite misleading to identify English drama exclusively with these specially constructed playhouses, for in fact there was a rich and vital theatrical tradition in England stretching back for centuries. Many towns in late medieval England were the sites of annual festivals that mounted elaborate cycles of plays depicting the great biblical stories, from the creation of the world to Christ's Passion and its miraculous aftermath. Most of these plays have been lost, but the surviving cycles, such as those from York, are magnificent and complex works of art. They are sometimes called "mystery plays," either because they were performed by the guilds of various crafts (known as "mysteries") or, more likely, because they represented the mysteries of the faith. The cycles were most often performed on the annual feast day instituted in the early fourteenth century in honor of the Corpus Christi, the sacrament of the Lord's Supper, which is perhaps the greatest of these religious mysteries.

The Feast of Corpus Christi, celebrated on the Thursday following Trinity Sunday, helped give the play cycles their extraordinary cultural resonance, but it also contributed to their downfall. For along with the specifically liturgical plays traditionally performed by religious confraternities and the "saints' plays," which depicted miraculous events in the lives of individual holy men and women, the mystery cycles were closely identified with the Catholic Church. Protestant authorities in the sixteenth century, eager to eradicate all remnants of popular Catholic piety, moved to suppress the annual procession of the Host, with its gorgeous banners, pageant carts, and cycle of visionary plays. In 1548, the Feast of Corpus Christi was abolished. Towns that continued to perform the mysteries were under increasing pressure to abandon them. It is sometimes said that the cycles were already dying out from neglect, but recent research has shown that many towns and their guilds were extremely reluctant to give them up. Desperate offers to strip away any traces of Catholic doctrine and to submit the play scripts to the authorities for their approval met with unbending opposition from the government. In 1576, the courts gave York permission to perform its cycle but only if

> in the said play no pageant be used or set forth wherein the Majesty of God the Father, God the Son, or God the Holy Ghost or the administration of either the Sacraments of baptism or of the Lord's Supper be counterfeited or represented, or anything played which tend to the maintenance of superstition and idolatry or which be contrary to the laws of God . . . or of the realm.

Such "permission" was tantamount to an outright ban. The local officials in the city of Norwich, proud of their St. George and the Dragon play, asked if they could at least parade the dragon costume through the streets, but even this modest request was refused. It is likely that as a young man Shakespeare had seen some of these plays: when Hamlet says of a noisy, strutting theatrical performance that it "out-Herods Herod," he is alluding to the famously bombastic role of Herod of Jewry in the mystery plays. But by the century's end, the cycles were no longer performed by live actors in great civic celebrations. They survived, if at all, in the debased form of puppet shows.

Early English theater was by no means restricted to these civic and religious festivals. Payments to professional and amateur performers appear in early records of towns and aristocratic households, though the Latin terms—*ministralli, histriones, mimi, lusores*, and so forth—are not used with great consistency and make it difficult to distinguish among minstrels, jugglers, stage players, and other entertainers. Performers acted in town halls and the halls of guilds and aristocratic mansions, on scaffolds erected in town squares and marketplaces, on pageant wagons in the streets, and in inn yards. By the fifteenth century, and probably earlier, there were organized companies of players traveling under noble patronage. Such companies earned a living providing amusement, while enhancing the prestige of the patron.

Panorama of London, showing two theaters, both round and both flying flags: a flying
flag indicated that a performance was in progress. The Globe is in the foreground, and
the Hope, or Beargarden, is to the left.

A description of a provincial performance in the late sixteenth century, written by
one R. Willis, provides a glimpse of what seems to have been the usual procedure:

> In the City of Gloucester the manner is (as I think it is in other like corporations)
> that when the Players of Interludes come to town, they first attend the Mayor
> to inform him what nobleman's servant they are, and so to get license for their
> public playing; and if the Mayor like the Actors, or would show respect to their
> Lord and Master, he appoints them to play their first play before himself and
> the Aldermen and common Council of the City and that is called the Mayor's
> play, where everyone that will come in without money, the Mayor giving the play-
> ers a reward as he thinks fit to show respect unto them.

In addition to their take from this "first play," the players would almost certainly have
supplemented their income by performing in halls and inn yards, where they could
on some occasions charge an admission fee. It was no doubt a precarious existence.

The "Interludes" mentioned in Willis's description of the Gloucester performances
are likely plays that were, in effect, staged dialogues on religious, moral, and political
themes. Such works could, like the mysteries, be associated with Catholicism, but they
were also used in the sixteenth century to convey polemical Protestant messages, and
they reached outside the religious sphere to address secular concerns as well. Henry
Medwall's *Fulgens and Lucrece* (ca. 1490–1501), for example, pits a wealthy but dissolute nobleman against a virtuous public servant of humble origins, while John Heywood's *Play of the Weather* (ca. 1525–33) stages a debate among social rivals, including
a gentleman, a merchant, a forest ranger, and two millers. The structure of such plays
reflects the training in argumentation that students received in Tudor schools and, in
particular, the sustained practice in examining all sides of a difficult question. Some of
Shakespeare's amazing ability to look at critical issues from multiple perspectives may
be traced back to this practice and the dramatic interludes it helped to inspire.

Another major form of theater that flourished in England in the fifteenth century
and continued on into the sixteenth was the morality play. Like the mysteries, moralities addressed questions of the ultimate fate of the soul. They did so, however, not by
rehearsing scriptural stories but by dramatizing allegories of spiritual struggle. Typically, a person named Human or Mankind or Youth is faced with a choice between a
pious life in the company of such associates as Mercy, Discretion, and Good Deeds
and a dissolute life among riotous companions like Lust or Mischief. Plays like *Mankind* (ca. 1465–70) and *Everyman* (ca. 1495) show how powerful these unpromising-
sounding dramas could be, in part because of the extraordinary comic vitality of the

evil character, or the Vice, and in part because of the poignancy and terror of an individual's encounter with death. Shakespeare clearly grasped this power. The hunchbacked Duke of Gloucester in *Richard III* gleefully likens himself to "the formal Vice, Iniquity." And when Othello wavers between Desdemona and Iago (himself a Vice figure), his anguished dilemma echoes the fateful choice repeatedly faced by the troubled, vulnerable protagonists of the moralities.

If such plays sound a bit like sermons, it is because they were. Clerics and actors shared some of the same rhetorical skills. It would be misleading to regard church-going and playgoing as comparable entertainments, but in attacking the stage, ministers often seemed to regard the professional players as dangerous rivals. "To leave a Sermon to go to a Play," warned the preacher John Stoughton, "is to forsake the Church of God; to betake oneself to the Synagogue of Satan, to fall from Heaven to Hell." The players themselves were generally too discreet to rise to the challenge; it would have been foolhardy to present the theater as the church's direct competitor. Yet in its moral intensity and its command of impassioned language, the stage frequently emulates and outdoes the pulpit.

Music and Dance

Playacting took its place alongside other forms of public expression and entertainment as well. Perhaps the most important, from the perspective of the theater, were music and dance, since these were directly and repeatedly incorporated into plays. Many plays, comedies and tragedies alike, include occasions that call upon the characters to dance: hence Beatrice and Benedict join the other masked guests at the dance in *Much Ado About Nothing;* in *Twelfth Night,* the befuddled Sir Andrew, at the instigation of the drunken Sir Toby Belch, displays his skill, such as it is, in capering; Romeo and Juliet first see each other at the Capulet ball; the witches dance in a ring around the hideous caldron and perform an "antic round" to cheer Macbeth's spirits; and, in one of Shakespeare's strangest and most wonderful scenes, the drunken Antony in *Antony and Cleopatra* joins hands with Caesar, Enobarbus, Pompey, and others to dance "the Egyptian Bacchanals."

Moreover, virtually all plays in the period, including Shakespeare's, apparently ended with a dance. Brushing off the theatrical gore and changing their expressions from woe to pleasure, the actors in plays like *Romeo and Juliet* and *Julius Caesar* would presumably have received the audience's applause and then bid for a second round of applause by performing a stately pavane or a lively jig. The vogue may have begun to wane in the early seventeenth century, but only to give way to other post-play enter-tainments, such as the improvisation game known as "themes" where someone in the audience would shout out a theme or question (for example, "Why barks that dog?") and the actor would come up with an extempore response. (The clown Robert Armin, who played the Fool in *King Lear*, was apparently an expert at this game.) Jigs, with their comical leaping dance steps often accompanied by scurrilous ballads, remained popular enough to draw not only large crowds but also official disapproval. A court order of 1612 complained about the "cut-purses and other lewd and ill-disposed persons" who flocked to the theater at the end of every play to be entertained by "lewd jigs, songs, and dances." The players were warned to suppress these disreputable entertainments on pain of imprisonment.

The displays of dancing onstage clearly reflected a widespread popular interest in dancing outside the walls of the playhouse as well. Renaissance intellectuals conjured up visions of the universe as a great cosmic dance, poets figured relations between men and women in terms of popular dance steps, stern moralists denounced dancing as an incitement to filthy lewdness, and, perhaps as significant, men of all classes evidently spent a great deal of time worrying about how shapely their legs looked in tights and how gracefully they could leap. Shakespeare assumes that his audience will be quite familiar with a variety of dances. "For, hear me, Hero," Beatrice tells her friend, "wooing, wedding, and repenting is as a Scotch jig, a measure, and a cinquepace" (*Much Ado About Nothing* 2.1.61–62). Her speech dwells on the comparison a bit, teasing out its implications, but it still does not make much sense if you do not already know something about the dances and perhaps occasionally venture to perform them yourself.

Closely linked to dancing and even more central to the stage was music, both instrumental and vocal. In the early sixteenth century, the Reformation had been disastrous for sacred music: many church organs were destroyed, choir schools were closed, the glorious polyphonic liturgies sung in the monasteries were suppressed. But by the latter part of the century, new perspectives were reinvigorating English music. Latin Masses were reset in English, and tunes were written for newly translated, metrical psalms. More important for the theater, styles of secular music were developed that emphasized music's link to humanist eloquence, its ability to heighten and to rival rhetorically powerful texts.

This link is particularly evident in vocal music, at which Elizabethan composers excelled. Renowned composers William Byrd, Thomas Morley, John Dowland, and others wrote a rich profusion of madrigals (part songs for two to eight voices unaccompanied) and ayres (songs for solo voice, generally accompanied by the lute). These works, along with hymns, popular ballads, rounds, catches, and other forms of song, enjoyed immense popularity, not only in the royal court, where musical skill was regarded as an important accomplishment, and in aristocratic households, where professional musicians were employed as entertainers, but also in less exalted social circles. In his *Plain and Easy Introduction to Practical Music* (1597), Morley tells a

Frans Hals, *The Clown with the Lute* (1625).

story of social humiliation at a failure to perform that suggests that a well-educated Elizabethan was expected to be able to sing at sight. Even if this is an exaggeration in the interest of book sales, there is evidence of impressively widespread musical literacy, reflected in a splendid array of music for the lute, viol, recorder, harp, and virginal, as well as the marvelous vocal music.

Whether it is the aristocratic Orsino luxuriating in the dying fall of an exquisite melody or bully Bottom craving "the tongs and the bones," Shakespeare's characters frequently call for music. They also repeatedly give voice to the age's conviction that there was a deep relation between musical harmony and the harmonies of the well-ordered individual and state. "The man that hath no music in himself," warns Lorenzo in *The Merchant of Venice*, "nor is not moved with concord of sweet sounds, / Is fit for treasons, stratagems, and spoils" (5.1.83–85). This conviction in turn reflects a still deeper link between musical harmony and the divinely created harmony of the cosmos. When Ulysses in *Troilus and Cressida* wishes to convey the image of universal chaos, he speaks of the untuning of a string (1.3.108–09).

The playing companies must have regularly employed trained musicians, and many actors (like the actor who in playing Pandarus in *Troilus and Cressida* is supposed to accompany himself on the lute) must have possessed musical skill. When Shakespeare's company began to use an indoor theater, the Blackfriars, as a second venue, it became famous for its orchestra, and, among other composers, the King's Musician, Robert Johnson, seems to have written songs for the actors to sing. Unfortunately, we possess the original settings for very few of Shakespeare's songs, possibly because many of them may have been set to popular tunes of the time that everyone knew and no one bothered to write down.

Alternative Entertainments

Plays, music, and dancing were by no means the only shows in town. There were jousts, tournaments, royal entries, religious processions, pageants in honor of newly installed civic officials or ambassadors arriving from abroad; wedding masques, court masques, and costumed entertainments known as "disguisings" or "mummings"; juggling acts, fortune-tellers, exhibitions of swordsmanship, mountebanks, folk healers, storytellers, magic shows; bearbaiting, bullbaiting, cockfighting, and other blood sports; folk festivals such as Maying, the Feast of Fools, Carnival, and Whitsun Ales. For several years, Elizabethan Londoners were delighted by a trained animal—Banks's Horse—that performed elaborate dance steps and could, it was thought, do arithmetic and answer questions. And there was always the grim but compelling spectacle of public shaming, mutilation, and execution.

Most English towns had stocks and whipping posts. Drunks, fraudulent merchants, adulterers, and quarrelers could be placed in carts or mounted backward on asses and paraded through the streets for crowds to jeer and throw refuse at. Women accused of being scolds, as we have already remarked, could be publicly muzzled by an iron device called a "brank" or tied to a cucking stool and dunked in the river. Convicted criminals could have their ears cut off, their noses slit, their foreheads branded. Public beheadings (generally reserved for the elite) and hangings were common. Those convicted of treason were sentenced to be "hanged by the neck, and being alive cut down, and your privy members to be cut off, and your bowels to be taken out of your belly and there burned, you being alive."

Shakespeare occasionally takes note of these alternative entertainments: at the end of *Macbeth*, for example, with his enemies closing in on him, the doomed tyrant declares, "They have tied me to a stake. I cannot fly, / But bearlike I must fight the course" (5.7.1–2). The audience is reminded then that it is witnessing the human equivalent of a popular spectacle—a bear chained to a stake and attacked by fierce dogs—that they could have paid to watch at an arena near the Globe. And when, a few moments later, Macduff enters carrying Macbeth's head, the audience is seeing the theatrical equiva-

An Elizabethan hanging.

lent of the execution of criminals and traitors that they could have also watched in the flesh, as it were, nearby. In a different key, the audiences who paid to see *A Midsummer Night's Dream* or *The Winter's Tale* got to enjoy the comic spectacle of a Maying and a Whitsun Pastoral, while the spectators of *The Tempest* could gawk at what the Folio list of characters calls a "savage and deformed slave" and to enjoy an aristocratic magician's wedding masque in honor of his daughter.

The Enemies of the Stage

In 1624, a touring company of players arrived in Norwich and requested permission to perform. Permission was denied, but the municipal authorities, "in regard of the honorable respect which this City beareth to the right honorable the Lord Chamberlain," gave the players twenty shillings to get out of town. Throughout the sixteenth and early seventeenth centuries, there are many similar records of civic officials prohibiting performances and then, to appease a powerful patron, paying the actors to take their skills elsewhere. As early as the 1570s, there is evidence that the London authorities, while mindful of the players' influential protectors, were energetically trying to drive the theater out of the city.

Why should what we now regard as one of the undisputed glories of the age have aroused so much hostility? One answer, curiously enough, is traffic: plays drew large audiences—the public theaters could accommodate thousands—and residents objected to the crowds, the noise, and the crush of carriages. Other, more serious concerns were public health and crime. It was thought that numerous diseases, including the dreaded bubonic plague, were spread by noxious odors, and the packed playhouses were obvious breeding grounds for infection. (Patrons often tried to protect themselves by sniffing nosegays or stuffing cloves into their nostrils.) The large crowds drew pickpockets, cutpurses, and other scoundrels. On more than one occasion, if Shakespeare's fellow actor Will Kemp may be believed, pickpockets, caught in the act during a performance, were tied to a post onstage "for all people to wonder at." The theater was, moreover, a well-known haunt of prostitutes and, it was alleged, a place where innocent

Syphilis victim in tub. Frontispiece to the play *Cornelianum Dolium* (1638), possibly written by Thomas Randolph. The tub inscription translates as "I sit on the throne of love, I suffer in the tub"; and the banner as "Farewell, O sexual pleasures and lusts."

maids were seduced and respectable matrons corrupted. It was darkly rumored that "chambers and secret places" adjoined the theater galleries, and in any case, taverns, disreputable inns, and whorehouses were close at hand.

There were other charges as well. Plays in the public, outdoor amphitheaters were performed in the afternoon and therefore drew people, especially the young, away from their work. They were schools of idleness, luring apprentices from their trades, law students from their studies, housewives from their kitchens, and potentially pious souls from the sober meditations to which they might otherwise devote themselves. Wasting their time and money on disreputable shows, citizens exposed themselves to sexual provocation and outright political sedition. Even when the content of plays was morally exemplary—and, of course, few plays were so gratifyingly highminded—the theater itself, in the eyes of most mayors and aldermen, was inherently disorderly.

The attack on the stage by civic officials was echoed and intensified by many of the age's moralists and religious leaders, especially those associated with Puritanism. While English Protestants earlier in the sixteenth century had attempted to counter the Catholic mystery cycles and saints' plays by mounting their own doctrinally correct dramas, by the century's end a fairly widespread consensus, even among those mildly sympathetic toward the theater, held that the stage and the pulpit were in tension with one another. After 1591, a ban on Sunday performances was strictly enforced, and in 1606, Parliament passed an act imposing a hefty fine of £10 on any person who shall "in any stage-play, interlude, show, May-game, or pageant, jestingly or profanely speak or use the holy name of God, or of Christ Jesus, or of the Holy Ghost, or of the Trinity (which are not to be spoken but with fear and reverence)." If changes in the printed texts are a reliable indication, the players seem to have complied at least to some degree with the ruling. The Folio (1623) text of *Richard III*, for example, omits the Quarto's (1597) four uses of "zounds" (for "God's wounds"), along with a mention of "Christ's dear blood shed for our grievous sins"; "God's my judge" in *The Merchant of Venice* becomes "well I know"; "By Jesu" in *Henry V* becomes a very proper "I say"; and in all the plays, "God" is from time to time metamorphosed to "Jove."

But for some of the theater's more extreme critics, these modest expurgations were tiny bandages on a gaping wound. In his huge book *Histriomastix* (1633), William Prynne regurgitates a half-century of frenzied attacks on the "sinful, heathenish, lewd, ungodly Spectacles." In the eyes of Prynne and his fellow antitheatricalists, stage plays were part of a demonic tangle of obscene practices proliferating like a cancer in the body of society. It is "manifest to all men's judgments," he writes, that effeminate mixed dancing, dicing, stage-plays, lascivious pictures, wanton fashions, face-painting, health-drinking, long hair, love-locks, periwigs, women's curling, powdering and cutting of their hair, bonfires, New-year's gifts, May-games, amorous pastorals, lascivious effeminate music, excessive laughter, luxurious disorderly Christmas-keeping, mummeries . . . [are] wicked, unchristian pastimes.

Given the anxious emphasis on effeminacy, it is not surprising that denunciations of this kind obsessively focused on the use of boy actors to play the female parts. The enemies of the stage charged that theatrical transvestism excited illicit sexual desires, both heterosexual and homosexual.

Since cross-dressing violated a biblical prohibition (Deuteronomy 22:5), religious antitheatricalists attacked it as wicked regardless of its erotic charge; indeed, they often seemed to consider any act of impersonation as inherently wicked. In their view, the theater itself was Satan's domain. Thus a Cambridge scholar, John Greene, reports the sad fate of "a Christian woman" who went to the theater to see a play: "She entered in well and sound, but she returned and came forth possessed of the devil. Whereupon certain godly brethren demanded Satan how he durst be so bold, as to enter into her a Christian. Whereto he answered, that *he found her in his own house,* and therefore took possession of her as his own" (italics in original). When the "godly brethren" came to power in the mid-seventeenth century, with the overthrow of Charles I, they saw to it that the playhouses, shut down in 1642 at the onset of the Civil War, remained closed. Public theater did not resume until the restoration of the monarchy in 1660.

Faced with enemies among civic officials and religious leaders, Elizabethan and Jacobean playing companies relied on the protection of their powerful patrons. As the liveried servants of aristocrats or of the monarch, the players could refute the charge that they were mere vagabonds, and they claimed, as a convenient legal fiction, that their public performances were necessary rehearsals in anticipation of those occasions when they would be called upon to entertain their noble masters. But harassment by the mayor and aldermen of the City of London—an area roughly one mile square, defined by the old Roman walls—continued unabated, and the players were forced to build their theaters outside the immediate jurisdiction of these authorities, either in the suburbs or in the areas known as the "liberties." A liberty was a piece of land within the City of London itself that was not directly subject to the authority of the Lord Mayor. The most significant liberty from the point of view of the theater was the area near St. Paul's Cathedral called "the Blackfriars," where, until the dissolution of the monasteries in 1538, there had been a Dominican priory. It was here that in 1608 Shakespeare's company, then called the King's Men, took over an indoor playhouse in which they performed during the winter months, reserving the open-air Globe in the suburb of Southwark for the warmer months.

Censorship and Regulation

In addition to those authorities who campaigned to shut down the theater, there were others whose task was to oversee, regulate, and censor it. Given the outright hostility of the former, the latter may have seemed to the London players equivocal allies rather than enemies. After all, plays that passed the censor were at least licensed to be performed and hence conceded to have some limited legitimacy. In April 1559, at the very start of her reign, Queen Elizabeth drafted a proposal that for the first time envisaged a system for the prior review and regulation of plays throughout her kingdom:

The Queen's Majesty doth straightly forbid all manner interludes to be played either openly or privately, except the same be notified beforehand, and licensed within any city or town corporate, by the mayor or other chief officers of the same, and within any shire, by such as shall be lieutenants for the Queen's Majesty in the same shire, or by two of the Justices of Peace inhabiting within that part of the shire where any shall be played. . . . And for instruction to every of the said officers, her Majesty doth likewise charge every of them, as they will answer: that they permit none to be played wherein either matters of religion or of the governance of the estate of the commonweal shall be handled or treated upon, but by men of authority, learning and wisdom, nor to be handled before any audience, but of grave and discreet persons.

This proposal, which may not have been formally enacted, makes an important distinction between those who are entitled to address sensitive issues of religion and politics—authors "of authority, learning and wisdom" addressing audiences "of grave and discreet persons"—and those who are forbidden to do so.

The London public theater, with its playwrights who were the sons of glovers, shoemakers, and bricklayers and its audiences in which the privileged classes mingled with rowdy apprentices, masked women, and servants, was clearly not a place to which the government wished to grant freedom of expression. In 1581, the Master of the Revels, an official in the Lord Chamberlain's department whose role had hitherto been to provide entertainment at court, was given an expanded commission. Sir Edmund Tilney, the functionary who held the office, was authorized

to warn, command, and appoint in all places within this our Realm of England, as well within franchises and liberties as without, all and every player or players with their playmakers, either belonging to any nobleman or otherwise . . . to appear before him with all such plays, tragedies, comedies, or shows as they shall in readiness or mean to set forth, and them to recite before our said Servant or his sufficient deputy, whom we ordain, appoint, and authorize by these presents of all such shows, plays, players, and playmakers, together with their playing places, to order and reform, authorize and put down, as shall be thought meet or unmeet unto himself or his said deputy in that behalf.

What emerged from this commission was in effect a national system of regulation and censorship. One of its consequences was to restrict virtually all licensed theater to the handful of authorized London-based playing companies. These companies would have to submit their plays for official scrutiny, but in return they received implicit, and on occasion explicit, protection against the continued fierce opposition of the local authorities. Plays reviewed and allowed by the Master of the Revels had been deemed fit to be performed before the monarch; how could mere aldermen legitimately claim that such plays should be banned as seditious?

The key question, of course, is how carefully the Master of the Revels scrutinized the plays brought before him either to hear or, more often from the 1590s onward, to peruse. What was Tilney, who served in the office until his death in 1610, or his successor, Sir George Buc, who served from 1610 to 1621, looking for? What did they insist be cut before they would release what was known as the "allowed copy," the only version licensed for performance? Unfortunately, the office books of the Master of the Revels in Shakespeare's time have been lost; what survives is a handful of scripts on which Tilney, Buc, and their assistants jotted their instructions. These suggest that the readings were rather painstaking, with careful attention paid to possible religious, political, and diplomatic repercussions. References, direct or strongly implied, to any living Christian prince or any important English nobleman, gentleman, or government official were particularly sensitive and likely to be struck. Renaissance political life was highly personalized; people in power were exceptionally alert to insult and zealously patrolled the boundaries of their prestige and reputation.

Moreover, the censors knew that audiences and readers were quite adept at applying theatrical representations distanced in time and space to their own world. At a time of riots against resident foreigners, Tilney read *Sir Thomas More,* a play in which Shakespeare probably had a hand, and instructed the players to cut scenes that, though set in

1517, might have had an uncomfortable contemporary resonance. "Leave out the insurrection wholly," Tilney's note reads, "and the cause thereof and begin with Sir Thomas More at the Mayor's sessions, with a report afterwards of his good service done being sheriff of London upon a mutiny against the Lombards only by a short report and not otherwise at your own perils. E. Tilney." Of course, as Tilney knew perfectly well, most plays succeed precisely by mirroring, if only obliquely, their own times, but this particular reflection evidently seemed to him too dangerous or provocative.

The topical significance of a play depends in large measure on the particular moment in which it is performed, and on certain features of the performance—for example, a striking resemblance between one of the characters and a well-known public figure—that the script itself will not necessarily disclose to us at this great distance, or even disclosed to the censor at the time. Hence the Master of the Revels noted angrily of one play performed in 1632 that "there were diverse personated so naturally, both of lords and others of the court, that I took it ill." Hence too a play that was deemed allowable when it was first written and performed could return, like a nightmare, to disturb a different place and time. The most famous instance of such a return involves Shakespeare, for on the day before the Earl of Essex's attempted coup against Queen Elizabeth in 1601, someone paid the Lord Chamberlain's Men (Shakespeare's company at the time) forty shillings to revive their old play about the deposition and murder of Richard II. "I am Richard II," the Queen declared. "Know ye not that?" However distressed she was by this performance, the Queen significantly did not take out her wrath on the players: neither the playwright nor his company was punished, nor was the Master of the Revels criticized for allowing the play in the first place. It was Essex and several of his key supporters, including the man who commissioned the performance, who lost their heads.

Evidence suggests that the Master of the Revels often regarded himself not as the strict censor of the theater but as its friendly guardian, charged with averting catastrophes. He was a bureaucrat concerned less with subversive ideas per se than with potential trouble. That is, there is no record of a dramatist being called to account for his heterodox beliefs; rather, plays were censored if they risked offending influential people, including important foreign allies, or if they threatened to cause public disorder by exacerbating religious or other controversies. The distinction is not a stable one, but it helps to explain the intellectual boldness, power, and freedom of a censored theater in a society in which the perceived enemies of the state were treated mercilessly. Shakespeare could have Lear articulate a searing indictment of social injustice—

> Robes and furred gowns hide all. Plate sins with gold,
> And the strong lance of justice hurtless breaks.
> Arm it in rags, a pigmy's straw does pierce it.
>
> (4.5.159–61)

—and evidently neither the Master of the Revels nor the courtiers in their robes and furred gowns protested. But when the Spanish ambassador complained about Thomas Middleton's anti-Spanish allegory *A Game at Chess,* performed at the Globe in 1624, the whole theater was shut down, the players were arrested, and the King professed to be furious at his official for licensing the play in the first place and allowing it to be performed for nine consecutive days.

In addition to the system for the licensing of plays for performance, there was a system for the licensing of plays for publication. At the start of Shakespeare's career, such press licensing was the responsibility of the Court of High Commission, headed by the Archbishop of Canterbury and the Bishop of London. Their deputies, a panel of junior clerics, were supposed to review the manuscripts, granting licenses to those worthy of publication and rejecting any they deemed "heretical, seditious, or unseemly for Christian ears." Without a license, the Stationers' Company, the guild of the book trade, was not supposed to register a manuscript for publication. In practice, as various complaints and attempts to close loopholes attest, some playbooks were printed without a license. In 1607, the system was significantly revised when Sir George Buc began to license plays for the press. When Buc succeeded to the post of Master of the Revels in 1610, the powers to license plays for the stage and the page were vested in one man.

Theatrical Innovations

The theater continued to flourish under this system of regulation after Shakespeare's death in 1616; by the 1630s, as many as five playhouses were operating daily in London. When the theater reemerged in 1660 after the eighteen-year hiatus imposed by Puritan rule, it quickly resumed its cultural importance, but not without a number of significant changes. Major innovations in staging resulted principally from continental influences on the English artists who accompanied the court of Charles II into exile in France, where they supplied it with masques and other theatrical entertainments.

The institutional conditions and business practices of the two companies chartered by Charles after the Restoration in 1660 also differed from those of Shakespeare's theater. In place of the more collective practice of Shakespeare's company, the Restoration theaters were controlled by celebrated actor-managers who not only assigned themselves starring roles, in both comedy and tragedy, but also assumed sole responsibility for many business decisions, including the setting of their colleagues' salaries. At the same time, the power of the actor-manager, great as it was, was limited by the new importance of outside capital. No longer was the theater, with all of its properties from script to costumes, owned by the "sharers," that is, by those actors who held shares in the joint stock company. Instead, entrepreneurs would raise capital for increasingly fantastic sets and stage machinery that could cost as much as £3,000, an astronomical sum, for a single production. This investment in turn not only influenced the kinds of new plays written for the theater but helped to transform old plays that were revived, including Shakespeare's.

In his diary entry for August 24, 1661, Samuel Pepys notes that he has been "to the Opera, and there saw Hamlet, Prince of Denmark, done with scenes very well, but above all, Betterton did the prince's part beyond imagination." This is Thomas Betterton's first review, as it were, and it is typical of the enthusiasm he would inspire throughout his fifty-year career on the London stage. Pepys's brief and scattered remarks on the plays he voraciously attended in the 1660s are precious because they are among the few records from the period of concrete and immediate responses to theatrical performances. Modern readers might miss the significance of Pepys's phrase "done with scenes": this production of Hamlet was only the third play to use the movable sets first introduced to England by its producer, William Davenant. The central historical fact that makes the productions of this period so exciting is that public theater had been banned altogether for eighteen years until the Restoration of Charles II.

A brief discussion of theatrical developments in the Restoration period will enable us at least to glance longingly at a vast subject that lies outside the scope of this introduction: the rich performance history that extends from Shakespeare's time to our own, involving tens of thousands of productions and adaptations for theater, opera, dance, Broadway musicals, and of course films. The scale of this history is vast in space as well as time: already in the late sixteenth and early seventeenth centuries, troupes of English actors performed as far afield as Poland and Bohemia.

While producing masques at the court of Charles I, the poet William Davenant had become an expert on stage scenery, and when the theaters reopened, he set to work on converting an indoor tennis court into a new kind of theater. He designed a broad open platform like that of the Elizabethan stage, but at the back of this platform he added or expanded a space, framed by a proscenium arch, in which scenes could be displayed. These elaborately painted scenes could be moved on and off, using grooves on the floor. The perspectival effect for a spectator of one central painted panel with two "wings" on either side was that of three sides of a room. This effect anticipated that of the familiar "picture frame" stage, developed fully in the nineteenth century, and began a subtle shift in theater away from the elaborate verbal descriptions that are so central to Shakespeare and toward the evocative visual poetry of the set designer's art.

Another convention of Shakespeare's stage, the use of boy actors for female roles, gave way to the more complete illusion of women playing women's parts. The King issued a decree in 1662 forcefully permitting, if not requiring, the use of actresses. The royal decree is couched in the language of social and moral reform: the introduction of actresses will require the "reformation" of scurrilous and profane passages in plays, and this in turn will help forestall some of the objections that shut the theaters down in 1642. In reality, male theater audiences, composed of a narrower range of courtiers and aristocrats than in Shakespeare's time, met this intended reform with the assumption that the new actresses were fair game sexually; most actresses (with the partial exception of those who married male members of their troupes) were regarded as, or actually became, whores. But despite the social stigma, and the fact that their salaries were predictably lower than those of their male counterparts, the stage saw some formidable female stars by the 1680s.

The first recorded appearance of an actress was that of a Desdemona in December 1660. Betterton's Ophelia in 1661 was Mary Saunderson (ca. 1637–1712), who became Mrs. Betterton a year later. The most famous Ophelia of the period was Susanna Mountfort, who appeared in that role for the first time at the age of fifteen in 1705. The performance by Mountfort that became legendary occurred in 1720, after a disappointment in love, or so it was said, had driven her mad. Hearing that *Hamlet* was being performed, Mountfort escaped from her keepers and reached the theater, where she concealed herself until the scene in which Ophelia enters in her state of insanity. At this point, Mountfort rushed onto the stage and, in the words of a contemporary, "was in truth Ophelia herself, to the amazement of the performers and the astonishment of the audience."

David Garrick and George Anne Bellamy in a celebrated production of *Romeo and Juliet* at Drury Lane, London. Engraving after a painting by Benjamin Wilson (1753).

That the character Ophelia became increasingly and decisively identified with the mad scene owes something to this occurrence, but it is also a consequence of the text used for Restoration performances of *Hamlet*. Having received the performance rights to a good number of Shakespeare's plays, Davenant altered them for the stage in the 1660s, and many of these acting versions remained in use for generations. In the case of *Hamlet*, neither Davenant nor his successors did what they so often did with other plays by Shakespeare, that is, alter the plot radically and interpolate other material. But many of the lines were cut or "improved." The cuts included most of Ophelia's sane speeches, such as her spirited retort to Laertes' moralizing; what remained made her part almost entirely an emblem of "female love melancholy."

Thomas Betterton (1635–1710), the prototype of the actor-manager, who would be the dominant figure in Shakespeare interpretation and in the English theater generally through the nineteenth century, made Hamlet his premier role. A contemporary who saw his last performance in the part (at the age of seventy-four, a rather old Prince of Denmark) wrote that to *read* Shakespeare's play was to encounter "dry, incoherent, & broken sentences," but that to see Betterton was to "prove" that the play was written "correctly." Spectators especially admired his reaction to the Ghost's appearance in the Queen's bedchamber: "his Countenance . . . thro' the violent and sudden Emotions of Amazement and Horror, turn[ed] instantly on the Sight of his fathers Spirit, as pale as his Neckcloath, when every Article of his Body seem's affected with a Tremor inexpressible." A piece of stage business in this scene, Betterton's upsetting his chair on the Ghost's entrance, became so thoroughly identified with the part that later productions were censured if the actor left it out. This business could very well have been handed down from Richard Burbage, the star of Shakespeare's original production, for Davenant, who had coached Betterton in the role, had known the performances of Joseph Taylor, who had succeeded Burbage in it. It is strangely gratifying to notice that Hamlets on stage and screen still occasionally upset their chairs.

Shakespeare's Life and Art

Playwrights, even hugely successful playwrights, were not ordinarily the objects of popular curiosity in early modern England. Many plays in this period were issued without the name of the author—there was no equivalent to our copyright system, and publishers were not required to specify on their title pages who wrote the texts they printed. Only occasionally were there significant exceptions, motivated by the pursuit of profit. Though by 1597 seven of Shakespeare's plays had been printed, the title pages did not identify him as the author. Beginning in 1598 Shakespeare's name, spelled in various ways, began to appear, and indeed several plays almost certainly not written by him were printed with his name. His name—Shakespeare, Shake-speare, Shakspeare, Shaxberd, Shakespere, and the like—had evidently begun to sell plays. During his lifetime more published plays were attributed to Shakespeare than to any other contemporary dramatist.

But this marketplace interest did not extend to the details of his life. It is both revealing and frustrating that the First Folio editors, John Heminges and Henry Condell—who knew Shakespeare well—were virtually silent about their friend's personal history. Though they included the author's picture, they did not bother to include his birth and death dates, his marital status, the names of his surviving children, his intellectual and social affiliations, his endearing or annoying quirks of character, let alone anything more psychologically revealing, such as the "table talk" carefully recorded by followers of Martin Luther. Shakespeare may have been a very private man, but, as he was dead when the edition was produced, it is unlikely to have been his own wishes that dictated the omissions. The editors evidently assumed that the potential buyers of the book—and this was an expensive commercial venture—would not be particularly interested in what we would now regard as essential biographical details.

Such presumed indifference is, in all likelihood, chiefly a reflection of Shakespeare's modest origins. He flew below the radar of ordinary Elizabethan and Jacobean social curiosity. In the wake of the death of the poet Sir Philip Sidney, Fulke Greville wrote a fascinating biography of his friend, but Sidney was a dashing aristocrat, linked by birth and marriage to the great families of the realm, and he died tragically of a wound he received on the battlefield. Writers of a less exalted station did not excite the same interest, unless, like Ben Jonson, they cultivated an extravagant public persona, or, like another of Shakespeare's contemporaries, Christopher Marlowe, they ran afoul of the authorities and got themselves murdered. The fact that there are no police reports, Privy Council orders, indictments, or postmortem inquests about Shakespeare, as there are about Marlowe, tells us something significant about Shakespeare's life—he possessed a gift for staying out of trouble—but it is not the kind of detail on which biographers thrive.

Yet Elizabethan England was a record-keeping society, and centuries of archival labor have turned up a substantial number of traces of its greatest playwright and his family. By themselves the traces would have relatively little interest, but in the light of Shakespeare's plays and poems, they have come to seem like precious relics and manage to achieve a considerable resonance.

Shakespeare's Family

William Shakespeare's grandfather, Richard, farmed land by the village of Snitterfield, near the small, pleasant market town of Stratford-upon-Avon, about ninety-six miles northwest of London. The playwright's father, John, moved in the mid-sixteenth century to Stratford, where he became a successful glover, landowner, moneylender, and dealer in wool and other agricultural goods. In or about 1557, he married Mary Arden, the daughter of a prosperous and well-connected farmer from the same area, Robert Arden of Wilmcote.

John Shakespeare was evidently highly esteemed by his fellow townspeople, for he held a series of important posts in local government. In 1556, he was appointed ale taster, an office reserved for "able persons and discreet," in 1558 was sworn in as a constable, and in 1561 was elected as one of the town's fourteen burgesses. As burgess, John served as one of the two chamberlains, responsible for administering borough property and revenues. In 1567, he was elected bailiff, Stratford's highest elective office and the equivalent of mayor. Though John Shakespeare signed all official documents with a cross or other sign, it is likely, though not certain, that he knew how to read and write. Mary, who also signed documents only with her mark, is less likely to have been literate.

According to the parish registers, which recorded baptisms and burials, the Shakespeares had eight children, four daughters and four sons, beginning with a daughter, Joan, born in 1558. A second daughter, Margaret, was born in December 1562 and died a few months later. William Shakespeare ("Gulielmus, filius Johannes Shakespeare"), their first son, was baptized on April 26, 1564. Since there was usually a few days' lapse between birth and baptism, it is conventional to celebrate Shakespeare's birthday on April 23, which happens to coincide with the Feast of St. George, England's patron saint, and with the day of Shakespeare's death fifty-two years later.

William Shakespeare had three younger brothers, Gilbert, Richard, and Edmund, and two younger sisters, Joan and Anne. (It was often the custom to recycle a name, so the first-born Joan must have died before the birth in 1569 of another daughter christened Joan, the only one of the girls to survive childhood.) Gilbert, who died in his forty-fifth year in 1612, is described in legal records as a Stratford haberdasher; Edmund followed William to London and became a professional actor, though evidently of no

Southeast Prospect of Stratford-upon-Avon, 1746. From *Gentleman's Magazine* (December 1792).

particular repute. He was only twenty-eight when he died in 1607 and was given an expensive funeral, perhaps paid for by his successful older brother.

At the high point of his public career, John Shakespeare, the father of this substantial family, applied to the Herald's College for a coat of arms, which would have marked his (and his family's) elevation from the ranks of substantial middle-class citizenry to that of the gentry. But the application went nowhere, for soon after he initiated what would have been a costly petitioning process, John apparently fell on hard times. The decline must have begun when William was still living at home, a boy of twelve or thirteen. From 1576 onward, John Shakespeare stopped attending council meetings. He became caught up in costly lawsuits, started mortgaging his land, and incurred substantial debts. In 1586, he was finally replaced on the council; in 1592, he was one of nine Stratford men listed as absenting themselves from church out of fear of being arrested for debt.

The reason for the reversal in John Shakespeare's fortunes is unknown. Some have speculated that it may have stemmed from adherence to Catholicism, since those who remained loyal to the old faith were subject to increasingly vigorous and costly discrimination. But if John Shakespeare was a Catholic, as seems possible, it would not necessarily explain his decline, since other Catholics (and Puritans) in Elizabethan Stratford and elsewhere managed to hold on to their offices. In any case, his fall from prosperity and local power, whatever its cause, was not absolute. In 1601, the last year of his life, his name was included among those qualified to speak on behalf of Stratford's rights. And he was by that time entitled to bear a coat of arms, for in 1596, some twenty years after the application to the Herald's office had been initiated, it was successfully renewed. There is no record of who paid for the bureaucratic procedures that made the grant possible, but it is likely to have been John's oldest son, William, by that time a highly successful London playwright. By elevating his father, he would have made himself a gentleman as well.

Education

Stratford was a small provincial town, but it had long been the site of an excellent free school, originally established by the church in the thirteenth century. The main purpose of such schools in the Middle Ages had been to train prospective clerics; since many aristocrats could neither read nor write, literacy by itself conferred no special distinction and was not routinely viewed as desirable. But the situation began to change markedly in the sixteenth century. Protestantism placed a far greater emphasis upon lay literacy: for the sake of salvation, it was crucially important to be intimately acquainted with the Holy Book, and printing made that book readily available. Schools became less strictly bound up with training for the church and more linked to the general acquisition of "literature," in the sense both of literacy and of cultural knowledge. In keeping with this new emphasis on reading and with humanist educational reform, the school was reorganized during the reign of Edward VI (1547–53). School records from the period have not survived, but it is almost certain that William Shakespeare attended the King's New School, as it was renamed in Edward's honor.

Scholars have painstakingly reconstructed the curriculum of schools of this kind and have even turned up the names and rather impressive credentials of the schoolmasters who taught at the King's New School when Shakespeare was of school age. (The principal teacher at that time was Thomas Jenkins, an Oxford graduate, who received £20 a year and a rent-free house.) A child's education in Elizabethan England began at age four or five with two years at what was called the "petty school," attached to the main grammar school. The little scholars carried a "hornbook," a sheet of paper or parchment framed in wood and covered, for protection, with a transparent layer of horn. On the paper was written the alphabet and the Lord's Prayer, which were reproduced as well in the slightly more advanced *ABC with the Catechism,* a combination primer and rudimentary religious guide.

After students demonstrated some ability to read, education for most girls came to a halt, but boys could go on, at about age seven, to the grammar school. Shakespeare's images of the experience are not particularly cheerful. In his famous account of the Seven Ages of Man, Jaques in *As You Like It* describes

> the whining schoolboy with his satchel
> And shining morning face, creeping like snail
> Unwillingly to school.

> (2.7.145–47)

The schoolboy would have crept quite early: the day began at 6:00 A.M. in summer and 7:00 A.M. in winter and continued until 5:00 P.M., with very few breaks or holidays.

At the core of the curriculum was the study of Latin, the mastery of which was in effect a prolonged male puberty rite involving much discipline and pain as well as pleasure. A late sixteenth-century Dutchman (whose name fittingly was Batty)

The Cholmondeley Ladies (ca. 1600–1610). Artist unknown. This striking image brings to mind Shakespeare's fascination with twinship, both identical (notably in *The Comedy of Errors*) and fraternal (in *Twelfth Night*).

proposed that God had created the human buttocks so that they could be severely beaten without risking permanent injury. Such thoughts dominated the pedagogy of the age, so that even an able young scholar, as we might imagine Shakespeare to have been, could scarcely have escaped recurrent flogging.

Shakespeare evidently reaped some rewards for the miseries he probably endured: his works are laced with echoes of many of the great Latin texts taught in grammar schools. One of his earliest comedies, *The Comedy of Errors,* is a brilliant variation on a theme by the Roman playwright Plautus, whom Elizabethan schoolchildren often performed as well as read; and one of his earliest tragedies, *Titus Andronicus,* is heavily indebted to Seneca. These are among the most visible of the classical influences that are often more subtly and pervasively interfused in Shakespeare's works. He seems to have had a particular fondness for *Aesop's Fables,* Apuleius's *Golden Ass,* and above all Ovid's *Metamorphoses.* His learned contemporary Ben Jonson remarked that Shakespeare had "small Latin and less Greek," but from this distance what is striking is not the limits of Shakespeare's learning but rather the unpretentious ease, intelligence, and gusto with which he draws upon what he must have first encountered as laborious study.

Traces of a Life

In November 1582, William Shakespeare, at the age of eighteen, married twenty-six-year-old Anne Hathaway, who came from the village of Shottery near Stratford. Their first daughter, Susanna, was baptized six months later. This circumstance, along with the fact that Anne was eight years Will's senior, has given rise to a mountain of speculation, all the more lurid precisely because there is no further evidence. Shakespeare depicts in several plays situations in which marriage is precipitated by a pregnancy, but he also registers, in *Measure for Measure* (1.2.133ff), the Elizabethan belief that a "true contract" of marriage could be legitimately made and then consummated simply by the mutual vows of the couple in the presence of witnesses.

On February 2, 1585, the twins Hamnet and Judith Shakespeare were baptized in Stratford. Hamnet died at the age of eleven, when his father was already living for much of the year in London as a successful playwright. These are Shakespeare's only known children, though in the mid-seventeenth century the playwright and impresario William Davenant hinted that he was Shakespeare's bastard son. Since people did not ordinarily advertise their illegitimacy, the claim, though impossible to verify, at least suggests the unusual strength of Shakespeare's posthumous reputation.

William Shakespeare's father, John, died in 1601; his mother died seven years later. They would have had the satisfaction of witnessing their eldest son's prosperity, and not only from a distance, for in 1597 William purchased New Place, the second-largest house in Stratford. In 1607, the playwright's daughter Susanna married a successful and well-known physician, John Hall. The next year, the Halls had a daughter, Elizabeth, Shakespeare's first grandchild. In 1616, the year of Shakespeare's death, his daughter Judith married a vintner, Thomas Quiney, with whom she had three children. Shakespeare's widow, Anne, died in 1623, at the age of sixty-seven. His first-born, Susanna, died at the age of sixty-six in 1649, the year that King Charles I was beheaded by the parliamentary army. Judith lived through Cromwell's Protectorate and on to the Restoration of the monarchy; she died in February 1662, at the age of seventy-seven. By the end of the century, the line of Shakespeare's direct heirs was extinct.

Patient digging in the archives has turned up other traces of Shakespeare's life as a family man and a man of means: assessments, small fines, real estate deeds, minor actions in court to collect debts. In addition to his fine Stratford house and a large garden and cottage facing it, Shakespeare bought substantial parcels of land in the vicinity. When in *The Tempest* the wedding celebration conjures up a vision of "barns and garners never empty," Shakespeare could have been glancing at what the legal documents record as his own "tithes of corn, grain, blade, and hay" in the fields near

Stratford. At some point after 1610, Shakespeare seems to have begun to shift his attention from the London stage to his Stratford properties, though the term "retirement" implies a more decisive and definitive break than appears to have been the case. By 1613, when the Globe Theater burned down during a performance of Shakespeare and Fletcher's *Henry VIII,* Shakespeare was probably residing for the most part in Stratford, but he retained his financial interest in the rebuilt playhouse and probably continued to have some links to his theatrical colleagues. Still, by this point, his career as a playwright was substantially over. Legal documents from his last years show him concerned to protect his real estate interests in Stratford.

A half-century after Shakespeare's death, a Stratford vicar and physician, John Ward, noted in his diary that Shakespeare and his fellow poets Michael Drayton and Ben Jonson "had a merry meeting, and it seems drank too hard, for Shakespeare died of a fever there contracted." It is not inconceivable that Shakespeare's last illness was somehow linked, if only coincidentally, to the festivities on the occasion of the wedding in February 1616 of his daughter Judith (who was still alive when Ward made his diary entry). In any case, on March 25, 1616, Shakespeare revised his will, and on April 23 he died. Two days later, he was buried in the chancel of Holy Trinity Church beneath a stone bearing an epitaph he is said to have devised:

> Good friend for Jesus' sake forbear,
> To dig the dust enclosed here:
> Blest be the man that spares these stones,
> And curst be he that moves my bones.

The verses are hardly among Shakespeare's finest, but they seem to have been effective: though bones were routinely dug up to make room for others—a fate imagined with unforgettable intensity in the graveyard scene in *Hamlet*—his own remains were undisturbed. Like other vestiges of sixteenth- and early seventeenth-century Stratford, Shakespeare's grave has for centuries now been the object of a tourist industry that borders on a religious cult.

Shakespeare's will has been examined with an intensity befitting this cult; every provision and formulaic phrase, no matter how minor or conventional, has borne a heavy weight of interpretation, none more so than the sole bequest to his wife, Anne, of "my second-best bed." Scholars have pointed out that Anne would in any case have been provided for by custom and that the terms are not necessarily a deliberate slight, but the absence of the customary words "my loving wife" or "my well-beloved wife" is difficult to ignore.

Portrait of the Playwright as Young Provincial

The great problem with the surviving traces of Shakespeare's life is not that they are few but that they are unspectacular. Christopher Marlowe was a double or triple agent, accused of brawling, sodomy, and atheism. Ben Jonson, who somehow clambered up from bricklayer's apprentice to classical scholar, served in the army in Flanders, killed a fellow actor in a duel, converted to Catholicism in prison in 1598, and returned to the Church of England in 1610. Provincial real estate investments and the second-best bed cannot compete with such adventurous lives. Indeed, the relative ordinariness of Shakespeare's social background and life has contributed to a persistent current of speculation that the glover's son from Stratford-upon-Avon was not in fact the author of the plays attributed to him.

The anti-Stratfordians, as those who deny Shakespeare's authorship are sometimes called, almost always propose as the real author someone who came from a higher social class and received a more prestigious education. Francis Bacon, the Earl of Oxford, the Earl of Southampton, even Queen Elizabeth, have been advanced, among many others, as glamorous candidates for the role of clandestine playwright. Several famous people, including Mark Twain and Sigmund Freud, have espoused these theories, though very few scholars have joined them. Since Shakespeare was quite well known in his own time as the author of the plays that bear his name, there would need to have been an extraordinary conspiracy to conceal the identity of the real master who (the theory goes) disdained to appear in the vulgarity of print or on the public stage. Like many conspiracy theories, the extreme implausibility of this one seems only to increase the fervent conviction of its advocates.

To the charge that a middle-class author from a small town could not have imagined the lives of kings and nobles, one can respond by citing the exceptional qualities that Ben Jonson praised in Shakespeare: "excellent *Phantsie*; brave notions, and gentle expressions." Even in ordinary mortals, the human imagination is a strange faculty; in Shakespeare, it seems to have been uncannily powerful, working its mysterious, transforming effects on everything it touched. His imagination was intensely engaged by what he found in books. He seems throughout his life to have been an intense, voracious reader, and it is fascinating to witness his creative encounters with Raphael Holinshed's *Chronicles of England, Scotland, and Ireland*, Plutarch's *Lives of the Noble Grecians and Romans*, Ovid's *Metamorphoses*, Montaigne's *Essays*, and the Bible, to name only some of his favorite books. But books were clearly not the only objects of Shakespeare's attention; like most artists, he drew upon the whole range of his life experiences.

To those accustomed to instant telecommunication, photography, film, and digital media, that range might seem narrowly circumscribed, but in fact something like the opposite was the case. Though we inhabit a vast virtual world, our experiential world is deliberately reduced, carefully screened, and tightly delimited. Most of us are born, sicken, and die in special institutions set apart from everyday life. We have invented means to quiet toothaches, heal wounds, and put us to sleep through painful surgeries. Those we condemn as criminals are penned up and punished behind high, windowless walls. We scarcely ever see our political representatives in person, and when we vote, we enter small, private booths. We take our entertainments most often in the dark or in the privacy of our homes, and those homes are generally walled off from the homes of others. Our meat bears little or no visible relation to the animal from which it comes; the slaughtering and butchering is discretely done out of sight. Our wastes disappear down drains; our rubbish is collected and disposed of; we live and move about in a well-lit, heavily policed, massively controlled environment.

None of this was the case in Shakespeare's world. Virtually anyone who grew up in the late sixteenth century would have had occasion to hear the sharp cries of childbirth and the groans of dying. There were a small number of hospitals and lazar houses (for lepers), but for the most part the sick, the maimed, and the mad mingled with everyone else in the crowded, muddy streets. The sufferings attendant on ordinary life were inescapable, and very few palliatives were available. (There were limits to the oblivion that the strongest ale could bring.) Malefactors, as we have seen, were most often punished in public, often hideously. There was nothing remotely equivalent to our taste for privacy. Servants were ubiquitous, and it was a rare person who had the privilege or perhaps the inclination to escape into solitude. Guests at an inn would often find themselves sharing a room or even a bed with a complete stranger. Smells and tastes—in a world without flush toilets and refrigeration—were intense, and so too were colors, for Elizabethans of any means favored vividly dyed and elaborately worked clothing. There were no streetlights, and the days faded into nights that were pitch dark and often dangerous.

Nothing here is particular to Shakespeare's biography; these were the conditions in this period of everyone's life. And what would astonish or appall us, if we were suddenly carried back into the past, would simply have been taken for granted as the way things are by most of those born into that world. But Shakespeare seems precisely not to have taken anything for granted: he seems to have carefully noted everything, from the carter who urinates in the chimney and complains of his fleabites (*1 Henry IV* 2.1.19–20) to the mad beggar who sticks sprigs of rosemary into his numbed arms (*King Lear* 2.2.177–79) to the merchant who keeps his money locked up in a desk that is covered with a Turkish tapestry (*Comedy of Errors* 4.1.103–04).

Shakespeare may have begun this practice of noting quite early in his life. When he was a very young boy—not quite four years old—his father was chosen by the Stratford council as the town bailiff. The bailiff of an Elizabethan town was a significant position; he served the borough as a justice of the peace and performed a variety of other functions, including coroner and clerk of the market. He dealt routinely with an unusually wide spectrum of local society, for on the one hand he distributed alms and on the other he negotiated with the lord of the manor. More to the point, for our purposes, the office was attended with considerable ceremony. The bailiff and his deputy were entitled to appear in public in furred gowns, attended by sergeants bearing maces before them. On Rogation Days (three days of prayer for the harvest, before Ascension Day), they would solemnly pace out the parish boundaries, and they would similarly walk in processions on market and fair days. On Sundays, the sergeants would accompany the bailiff to church, where he would sit with his wife in a front pew, and he would have a comparable seat of honor at sermons in the Guild Chapel. On special occasions, there would also be plays in the Guildhall, at which the bailiff would be seated in the front row.

On a precocious child (or even, for that matter, on an ordinary child), this ceremony must have had a significant impact. It would have conveyed irresistibly the power of clothes (the ceremonial gown of office) and of symbols (the mace) to transform identity as if by magic. It would have invested the official in question—Shakespeare's own father—with immense power, distinction, and importance, awakening what we may call a lifelong dream of high station. And perhaps, pulling slightly against this dream, it would have provoked an odd feeling that the father's clothes do not fit, a perception that the office is not the same as the man, and an intimate, firsthand knowledge that when the robes are put off, their wearer is inevitably glimpsed in a far different, less exalted light.

The honoring of the bailiff was only one of the political rituals that Shakespeare could easily have witnessed as a young man growing up in the provinces. As we have seen, Queen Elizabeth was fond of going on what were known as "progresses," triumphant ceremonial journeys around her kingdom. In 1574—when Shakespeare was ten years old—one of these progresses took her to Warwick, near Stratford-upon-Avon. The crowds that gathered to watch were participating in an elaborate celebration of charismatic power: the courtiers in their gorgeous clothes, the nervous local officials bedecked in velvets and silks, and at the center, carried in a special litter like a bejeweled icon, the virgin queen. The Queen cultivated this charisma, taking over in effect some of the iconography associated with the worship of the Virgin Mary, but she was also paradoxically fond of calling attention to the fact that she was after all quite human. For example, on this occasion at Warwick, after the trembling Recorder, presumably a local civil official of high standing, had made his official welcoming speech, Elizabeth offered her hand to him to be kissed: "Come hither, little Recorder," she said. "It was told me that you would be afraid to look upon me or to speak boldly; but you were not so afraid of me as I was of you; and I now thank you for putting me in mind of my duty." Of course, the charm of this royal "confession" of nervousness depends on its manifest implausibility: it is, in effect, a theatrical performance of humility by someone with immense confidence in her own histrionic power.

A royal progress was not the only form of spectacular political activity that Shakespeare might well have seen in the 1570s; it is still more likely that he would have witnessed parliamentary elections, particularly since his father was qualified to vote. In 1571, 1572, 1575, and 1578, there were shire elections conducted in Warwick, elections that would certainly have attracted well over a thousand voters. These were often memorable events: large crowds came together; there was usually heavy drinking and carnivalesque festivity; and at the same time, there was enacted, in a very different register from that of the monarchy, a ritual of empowerment. The people, those entitled to vote by virtue of meeting the property and residence requirements, chose their own representatives by giving their votes—their voices—to candidates for office. Here, legislative sovereignty was conferred not by God but by the consent of the community, a consent marked by shouts and applause.

Recent cultural historians have been so fascinated by the evident links between the spectacles of the absolutist monarchy and the theater that they have largely ignored the significance of this alternative public arena, one that generated intense excitement throughout the country. A child who was a spectator at a parliamentary election in the 1570s might well have found the occasion enormously compelling. It is striking, in any case, how often the adult Shakespeare returns to scenes of mass consent, and striking too how much the theater depends on assembling crowds and soliciting popular acclamation.

The most frequent occasions for the gathering together of crowds were neither elections nor theatrical performances, but rather the religious services that all Elizabethans were expected to attend at least once a week. (Recurrent absences were noted and investigated.) Protestant spokesmen routinely condemned the Catholic Mass as a form of perverse theatrical performance: a "play of sacred miracles," a "wonderful pageant," a "devil Theater." The Catholic Mass, as it had been celebrated for centuries, was outlawed, and with it a range of other Catholic rites. On occasion those rites were still practiced in secret, at considerable danger, and it is possible that Shakespeare could have been among those present. He was certainly present at the services of the English Church, whose ceremonies led by berobed priests, guided by the resonant prose of the Book of Common Prayer, and held in settings whose magnificence continues to astonish us, had their own intense histrionic power.

The young Shakespeare, whether true believer or skeptic or something in between ("So have I heard, and do in part believe it," says Hamlet's friend Horatio [1.1.164]), might have carried away from such ceremonies several impressions: an intimation of immense, cosmic forces that may impinge upon human life; a heightened understanding of the power of language to form and exalt the spirit; an awareness of intense, even murderous competition and rivalry among competing rituals; and perhaps a sense of the longing to believe that may be awakened and shaped in large crowds.

I have placed Shakespeare himself in each of these scenes—which together sketch the root conditions of the Elizabethan theater—because some people have found it difficult to conceive how this one man, with his provincial origins and his restricted range of experience, could have so rapidly and completely mastered the central imaginative themes of his times. Moreover, it is sometimes difficult to grasp how seeming abstractions such as market society, monarchical state, and theological doctrine were actually experienced directly by distinct individuals. Shakespeare's plays were social and collective events, but they also bore the stamp of a particular artist, one endowed with a remarkable capacity to craft lifelike illusions, a daring willingness to articulate an original vision, and a loving command, at once precise and generous, of language. These plays are stitched together from shared cultural experiences, inherited dramatic devices, and the pungent vernacular of the day, but we should not lose sight of the extent to which they articulate an intensely personal vision, a bold shaping of the available materials. Four centuries of feverish biographical speculation, much of it foolish, bear witness to a basic intuition: the richness of these plays, their inexhaustible openness, is the consequence not only of the auspicious collective conditions of the culture but also of someone's exceptional skill, inventiveness, and courage at taking those conditions and making of them something rich and strange.

The Theater of the Nation

What precisely were the collective conditions disclosed by the spectacles that Shakespeare would likely have witnessed? First, the growth of Stratford-upon-Avon, the bustling market town of which John Shakespeare was bailiff, is a small version of a momentous sixteenth-century development that made Shakespeare's career possible: the making of an urban "public." That development obviously depended on adequate numbers; the period experienced a rapid and still unexplained growth in population. With it came an expansion and elaboration of market relations: markets became less periodic, more continuous, and more abstract—centered, that is, not on the familiar materiality of goods but on the liquidity of capital and goods. In practical terms, this meant that it was possible to conceive of the theater not only as festive entertainment for special events—Lord Mayor's pageants, visiting princes, seasonal festivals, and the like—but as a permanent, year-round business venture. The venture relied on revenues from admission—it was an innovation of this period to have money advanced in the expectation of pleasure rather than offered to servants afterward as a reward—and counted on habitual playgoing, with a concomitant demand for new plays from competing theater companies: "But that's all one, our play is done," sings the Clown at the end of *Twelfth Night* and adds a glance toward the next afternoon's proceeds: "And we'll strive to please you every day" (5.1.393–94).

Second, the royal progress is an instance of what the anthropologist Clifford Geertz has called the Theater State, a state that manifests its power and meaning in exemplary public performances. Professional companies of players, like the one Shakespeare belonged to, understood well that they existed in relation to this Theater State and would, if they were fortunate, be called upon to serve it. Unlike Ben Jonson, Shakespeare did not, as far as we know, write royal entertainments on commission, but his plays were frequently performed before Queen Elizabeth and then before King James and Queen Anne, along with their courtiers and privileged guests. There are many fascinating glimpses of these performances, including a letter from Walter Cope to Robert Cecil, early in James's reign. "Burbage is come," Cope writes, referring to the leading actor of Shakespeare's company, "and says there is no new play that the Queen hath not seen, but they have revived an old one, called *Love's Labor's Lost,* which for wit and mirth he says will please her exceedingly. And this is appointed to be played tomorrow night at my Lord of Southampton's." Not only would such theatrical performances have given great pleasure—evidently, the Queen had already exhausted the company's new offerings—but they conferred prestige upon those who commanded them and those in whose honor they were mounted.

Monarchical power in the period was deeply allied to spectacular manifestations of the ruler's glory and disciplinary authority. The symbology of power depended on regal magnificence, reward, punishment, and pardon, all of which were heavily theatricalized. Indeed, the conspicuous public display does not simply serve the interests of power; on many occasions in the period, power seemed to exist in order to make pageantry possible, as if the nation's identity were only fully realized in theatrical performance. It would be easy to exaggerate this perception: the subjects of Queen Elizabeth and King James were acutely aware of the distinction between shadow and substance. But they were fascinated by the political magic through which shadows could be taken for substantial realities, and the ruling elite was largely complicit in the formation and celebration of a charismatic absolutism. At the same time, the claims of the monarch who professes herself or himself to be not the representative of the nation but its embodiment were set against the counterclaims of the House of Commons. And this institution too, as we have glimpsed, had its own theatrical rituals, centered on the crowd whose shouts of approval, in heavily stage-managed elections, chose the individuals who would stand for the polity and participate in deliberations held in a hall whose resemblance to a theater did not escape contemporary notice.

Third, in outlawing the Catholic Mass and banning the medieval mystery plays, along with pilgrimages and other rituals associated with holy shrines and sacred images, English Protestant authorities hoped to hold a monopoly on religious observances. But they inevitably left some people, perhaps substantial numbers of them, mourning what they had lost. Playing companies could satisfy at least some of the popular longings and appropriate aspects of the social energy no longer allowed a theological outlet. That is, official attacks on certain Catholic practices made it more possible for the public theater to appropriate and exploit their allure. Hence, for example, the plays that celebrated the solemn miracle of the Catholic Mass were banned, along with the most elaborate church vestments, but in *The Winter's Tale* Dion can speak in awe of what he witnessed at Apollo's temple:

> I shall report,
> For most it caught me, the celestial habits—
> Methinks I so should term them—and the reverence
> Of the grave wearers. Oh, the sacrifice!
> How ceremonious, solemn, and unearthly
> It was i'th' off'ring!
>
> (3.1.3–8)

And at the play's end, the statue of the innocent mother breathes, comes to life, and embraces her child.

The theater in Shakespeare's time, then, is intimately bound up with all three crucial cultural formations: market society, the Theater State, and the church. But it is important to note that the institution is not *identified* with any of them. The theater may be a market phenomenon, but it is repeatedly and bitterly attacked as the enemy of diligent, sober, productive economic activity. Civic authorities generally regarded the theater as a pestilential nuisance, a parasite on the body of the commonwealth, a temptation to students, apprentices, housewives, even respectable merchants to leave their serious business and lapse into idleness and waste. That waste, it might be argued, could be partially recuperated if it went for the glorification of a guild or the entertainment of an important dignitary, but the only group regularly profiting from the theater were the players and their disreputable associates.

For his part, Shakespeare made a handsome profit from the commodification of theatrical entertainment, but he seems never to have written "city comedy"—plays set in London and more or less explicitly concerned with market relations—and his characters express deep reservations about the power of money and commerce: "That smooth-faced gentleman, tickling commodity," Philip the Bastard observes in *King John,* "wins of all, / Of kings, of beggars, old men, young men, maids" (2.1.569–73). We could argue that the smooth-faced gentleman is none other than Shakespeare himself, for his drama famously mingles kings and clowns, princesses and panderers. But the mingling is set against a romantic current of social conservatism: in *Twelfth Night,* the aristocratic heiress Olivia falls in love with someone who appears far beneath her in wealth and social station, but it is revealed that he (and his sister Viola) are of noble blood; in *The Winter's Tale,* Leontes' daughter Perdita is raised as a shepherdess, but her noble nature shines through her humble upbringing, and she marries the Prince of Bohemia; the strange island maiden with whom Ferdinand, son of the King of Naples, falls madly in love in *The Tempest* turns out to be the daughter of the rightful Duke of Milan. Shakespeare pushes against this conservative logic in *All's Well That Ends Well,* but the noble young Bertram violently resists the unequal match thrust upon him by the King, and the play's mood is notoriously uneasy.

Similarly, Shakespeare's theater may have been patronized and protected by the monarchy—after 1603, his company received a royal patent and was known as the King's Men—but the two institutions were by no means identical in their interests or their ethos. To be sure, *Richard III* and *Macbeth* incorporate aspects of royal propaganda, but given the realities of censorship, Shakespeare's plays, and the period's drama as a whole, are surprisingly independent and complex in their political vision. There is, in any case, a certain inherent tension between kings and player kings: Elizabeth and James may both have likened themselves to actors onstage, but they were loath to admit their dependence on the applause and money, freely given or freely withheld, of the audience. The charismatic monarch insists that the sacredness of authority resides in the body of the ruler, not in a costume that may be worn and then discarded by an actor. Kings are not *representations* of power—or do not admit that they are—but claim to be the thing itself. The government institution that was actually based on the idea of representation, Parliament, had theatrical elements, as we have seen, but it significantly excluded any audience from its deliberations. And Shakespeare's oblique portraits of parliamentary representatives, the ancient Roman tribunes Sicinius Velutus and Junius Brutus in *Coriolanus,* are anything but flattering.

Finally, the theater drew significant energy from the liturgy and rituals of the late medieval church, but as Shakespeare's contemporaries widely remarked, the playhouse and the church were scarcely natural allies. Not only did the theater represent a potential competitor to worship services, and not only did ministers rail against prostitution and other vices associated with playgoing, but theatrical representation itself, even when ostensibly pious, seemed to many to empty out whatever it presented, turning substance into mere show. The theater could and did use the period's deep currents of religious feeling, but it had to do so carefully and with an awareness of conflicting interests.

Shakespeare Comes to London

How did Shakespeare decide to turn his prodigious talents to the stage? When did he make his way to London? How did he get his start? Concerning these and similar questions we have a mountain of speculation but no secure answers. There is not a single surviving record of Shakespeare's existence from 1585, when his twins were baptized in Stratford church, until 1592, when a rival London playwright made an envious remark about him. In the late seventeenth century, the delightfully eccentric collector of gossip John Aubrey was informed that prior to moving to London the young Shakespeare had been a schoolteacher in the country. Aubrey also recorded a story that Shakespeare had been a rather unusual apprentice butcher: "When he killed a calf, he would do it in a high style, and make a speech."

These and other legends, including one that has Shakespeare whipped for poaching game, fill the void until the unmistakable reference in Robert Greene's *Groatsworth of Wit Bought with a Million of Repentance* (1592). An inspired hack writer with a university education, a penchant for self-dramatization, a taste for wild living, and a strong streak of resentment, Greene, in his early thirties, was dying in poverty when he penned his last farewell, piously urging his fellow dramatists Christopher Marlowe, Thomas Nashe, and George Peele to abandon the wicked stage before they were brought low, as he had been, by a new arrival: "For there is an upstart crow, beautified with our feathers, that with his 'Tiger's heart wrapped in player's hide' supposes he is as well able to bombast out a blank verse as the best of you, and, being an absolute *Johannes Factotum,* is in his own conceit the only Shake-scene in a country." If "Shake-scene" is not enough to identify the object of his attack, Greene parodies a line from Shakespeare's early play *3 Henry VI:* "O tiger's heart wrapped in a woman's hide" (1.4.137). Greene is accusing Shakespeare of being an upstart, a plagiarist, an egomaniacal jack-of-all-trades—and, above all perhaps, a popular success.

By 1592, then, Shakespeare had already arrived on the highly competitive London theatrical scene. He was successful enough to be attacked by Greene and, a few months later, defended by Henry Chettle, another hack writer who had seen Greene's manuscript through the press (or, some scholars speculate, had written the attack himself and passed it off as the dying Greene's). Chettle expresses his regret that he did not suppress Greene's diatribe and spare Shakespeare "because myself have seen his demeanor no less civil than he excellent in the quality he professes." Besides, Chettle adds, "divers of worship have reported his uprightness of dealing, which argues his honesty and his facetious [polished] grace in writing that approves his art." "Divers of worship": not only was Shakespeare established as an accomplished writer and actor, but he evidently had aroused the attention and the approbation of several socially prominent people. In Elizabethan England, aristocratic patronage, with the money, protection, and prestige it alone could provide, was probably a professional writer's most important asset.

This patronage, or at least Shakespeare's quest for it, is most visible in the dedications in 1593 and 1594 of his narrative poems *Venus and Adonis* and *The Rape of Lucrece* to the young nobleman Henry Wriothesley, Earl of Southampton. It may be glimpsed as well, perhaps, in the sonnets, with their extraordinary adoration of the fair youth, though the identity of that youth has never been determined. What return Shakespeare got for his exquisite offerings is likewise unknown. We do know that among wits and gallants, the narrative poems won Shakespeare a fine reputation as an immensely stylish and accomplished poet. An amateur play performed at Cambridge University at the end of the sixteenth century, *The Return from Parnassus*, makes fun of this vogue, as a foolish character effusively declares, "I'll worship sweet Mr. Shakespeare, and to honor him will lay his *Venus and Adonis* under my pillow." Many readers at the time may have done so: the poem went through sixteen editions before 1640, more than any other work by Shakespeare.

Patronage was crucially important not only for individual artists but also for the actors, playwrights, and investors who pooled their resources to form professional theater companies. The public playhouses had enemies, especially among civic and religious authorities, who wished greatly to curb performances or to ban them altogether. An Act of Parliament of 1572 included players among those classified as vagabonds, threatening them therefore with the horrible punishments meted out to those regarded as economic parasites. The players' escape route was to be nominally enrolled as apprentices in guilds, as if they were learning to be goldsmiths or grocers rather than actors. Alternatively, as we have noted, they could be officially listed as the servants of high-ranking noblemen.

When Shakespeare came to London, presumably in the late 1580s, there were more than a half-dozen of these companies operating under the patronage of various aristocrats. We do not know for which of these companies, several of which had toured in Stratford, he originally worked, nor whether he began, as legend has it, by holding gentlemen's horses outside the theater or by serving as a prompter's assistant and then graduated to acting and playwriting. Shakespeare is listed among the actors in Ben Jonson's *Every Man in His Humor* (performed in 1598) and *Sejanus* (performed in 1603), but we do not know for certain what roles he played, nor are there records of any of his other performances. Tradition has it that he played Adam in *As You Like It* and the Ghost in *Hamlet,* but he was clearly not one of the leading actors of the day.

Shakespeare may initially have been associated with the company of Ferdinando Stanley, Lord Strange; that company included actors with whom Shakespeare was later linked. Or he may have belonged to the Earl of Pembroke's Men, since there is evidence that they performed *The Taming of a Shrew* and a version of *3 Henry VI.* At any event, by 1594, Shakespeare was a member of the Chamberlain's Men, for his name, along with those of Will Kemp and Richard Burbage, appears on a record of those "servants to the Lord Chamberlain" paid for performance at the royal palace at Greenwich on December 26 and 28. Shakespeare stayed with this company, which during the reign of King James received royal patronage and became the King's Men, for the rest of his career.

Many playwrights in Shakespeare's time worked freelance, moving from company to company as opportunities arose, collaborating on projects, adding scenes to old plays, scrambling from one enterprise to another. But certain playwrights, among them the most successful, wrote for a single company, often agreeing contractually to give that company exclusive rights to their theatrical works. Shakespeare seems to have followed such a pattern. For the Chamberlain's Men, later the King's Men, he wrote an average of two plays per year. His company initially performed in The Theatre, a playhouse built in 1576 by an entrepreneurial actor and trained craftsman, James Burbage, the father of the actor Richard, who was to perform many of Shakespeare's greatest roles. When in 1597 their lease on this playhouse expired, the Chamberlain's Men passed through a difficult time, but they formed a joint stock company, raising sufficient capital to lease a site and put up a splendid new playhouse in the suburb of Southwark, on the south bank of the Thames. This playhouse, the Globe, opened in 1599. Shakespeare is listed in the legal agreement as one of the principal investors, and when the company began to use Blackfriars as their indoor playhouse around 1610, he was a major shareholder in that theater as well. The Chamberlain's Men dominated the theater scene, and the shares were quite valuable. Then as now, the theater was an extremely risky enterprise—most of those who wrote plays and performed in them made pathetically little money—but Shakespeare was a notable exception. The fine house in Stratford and the coat of arms he succeeded in acquiring were among the fruits of his multiple mastery, as actor, playwright, and investor of the London stage.

Edward Alleyn. Artist unknown. Alleyn was the great tragic actor of the Admiral's Men (the principal rival to Shakespeare's company). He was famous especially for playing the major characters of Christopher Marlowe.

The Shakespearean Trajectory

Though Shakespeare's England was in many ways a record-keeping society, no reliable record survives that details the performances, year by year, in the London theaters. Every play had to be licensed by the Master of the Revels, but the records kept by the relevant government officials from 1579 to 1621 have not survived. A major theatrical entrepreneur, Philip Henslowe, kept a careful account of his expenditures, including what he paid for the scripts he commissioned, but unfortunately Henslowe's main business was with the Rose and the Fortune theaters and not with the playhouses at which Shakespeare's company performed. A comparable ledger must have been kept by the shareholders of the Chamberlain's Men, but it has not survived. Shakespeare himself apparently did not undertake to preserve all his writings for posterity, let alone to clarify the chronology of his works or to specify which plays he wrote alone and which with collaborators.

The principal source for Shakespeare's works is the 1623 Folio volume of *Mr. William Shakespeares Comedies, Histories, & Tragedies.* The world owes this work,

IF YOV KNOW NOT ME,
You know no body.
OR,
The troubles of Queene ELIZABETH.

LONDON.
Printed by *B. A.* and *T. F.* for *Nathanaell Butter.* 1 6 3 2.

Title page of *If You Know Not Me, You Know Nobody; or, the Troubles of Queen Elizabeth* (1632).

lovingly edited after his death by two of the playwright's friends, an incalculable debt: without it, nearly half of Shakespeare's plays, including many of his greatest masterpieces, would have been lost forever. The edition does not, however, include any of Shakespeare's nondramatic poems, and it omits four plays in which Shakespeare is now thought to have had a significant hand, *Edward III, Pericles, Cardenio,* and *The Two Noble Kinsmen,* along with his probable contribution to the multiauthored *Sir Thomas More.* (A number of other plays were attributed to Shakespeare, both before and after his death, but scholars have not generally accepted any of these into the established canon.) Moreover, the Folio edition does not print the plays in chronological order, nor does it attempt to establish a chronology. We do not know how much time would normally have elapsed between the writing of a play and its first performance, nor, with a few exceptions, do we know with any certainty the month or even the year of the first performance of any of Shakespeare's plays. The quarto editions of those plays that were published during Shakespeare's lifetime obviously establish a date by which we know a given play had been written, but they give us little more than an end point, because there was likely to be a substantial though indeterminate gap between the first performance of a play and its publication.

With enormous patience and ingenuity, however, scholars have gradually assembled a considerable archive of evidence, both external and internal, for dating the composition of the plays. Besides actual publication, the external evidence includes explicit reference to a play, a record of its performance, or (as in the case of Greene's attack on the "upstart crow") the quoting of a line, though all of these can be maddeningly ambiguous. The most important single piece of external evidence appears in 1598 in *Palladis Tamia,* a long book of jumbled reflections by the churchman Francis Meres that includes a survey of the contemporary literary scene. Meres finds that "the sweet, witty soul of Ovid lives in mellifluous and honey-tongued Shakespeare, witness his *Venus and Adonis,* his *Lucrece,* his sugared Sonnets among his private friends, etc." Meres goes on to list Shakespeare's accomplishments as a playwright as well:

> As Plautus and Seneca are accounted the best for Comedy and Tragedy among the Latins: so Shakespeare among the English is the most excellent in both kinds for the stage; for Comedy, witness his *Gentlemen of Verona,* his *Errors,* his *Love labors lost,* his *Love labors won,* his *Midsummers night dream,* & his *Merchant of Venice:* for Tragedy his *Richard the 2, Richard the 3, Henry the 4, King John, Titus Andronicus* and his *Romeo and Juliet.*

Meres thus provides a date by which twelve of Shakespeare's plays had definitely appeared (including one, *Love's Labor's Won,* that appears either to have been lost or to be known to us by a different title). Unfortunately, Meres provides no clues about the order of appearance of these plays, and there are no other comparable lists.

Faced with the limitations of the external evidence, scholars have turned to a bewildering array of internal evidence, ranging from datable sources and topical allusions on the one hand to evolving stylistic features (ratio of verse to prose, percentage of rhyme to blank verse, colloquialisms, use of extended similes, and the like) on the other. Thus, for example, a cluster of plays with a high percentage of rhymed verse may follow closely upon Shakespeare's writing of the rhymed poems *Venus and Adonis* and *The Rape of Lucrece* and therefore be datable to 1594–95. Similarly, vocabulary overlap probably indicates proximity in composition, so if four or five plays share relatively "rare" vocabulary, it is likely that they were written in roughly the same period. Again, there seems to be a pattern in Shakespeare's use of colloquialisms, with a steady increase from *As You Like It* (1599–1600) to *Coriolanus* (1608), followed in the late romances by a retreat from the colloquial.

Ongoing computer analysis should provide further guidance in the future, though the precise order of the plays, still very much in dispute, is never likely to be settled to universal satisfaction. Still, certain broad patterns are now widely accepted. These patterns can be readily grasped in *The Norton Shakespeare,* which presents the plays according to our best estimate of their chronological order.

Shakespeare began his career, probably in the early 1590s, by writing both comedies and history plays. The attack by Greene suggests that he made his mark with the series of theatrically vital, occasionally brilliant, and often crude plays based on the foreign and domestic broils that erupted during the unhappy reign of the Lancastrian Henry VI. Modern readers and audiences are more likely to find the first sustained evidence of unusual power in *Richard III* (ca. 1592), a play that combines a richly imagined central character, a dazzling command of histrionic rhetoric, and an overarching moral vision of English history.

At virtually the same time that he was setting his stamp on the genre of the history play, Shakespeare was writing his first—or first surviving—comedies. Here, there are even fewer signs than in the histories of an apprenticeship. *The Comedy of Errors,* one of his early works in this genre, already displays a rare command of the resources of comedy: mistaken identity, madcap confusion, and the threat of disaster, giving way in the end to reconciliation, recovery, and love. Shakespeare's other comedies from the first half of the 1590s, *The Two Gentlemen of Verona, The Taming of the Shrew,* and *Love's Labor's Lost,* are no less remarkable for their sophisticated variations on familiar comic themes, their inexhaustible rhetorical inventiveness, and their poignant intimation, in the midst of festive celebration, of loss.

Successful as are these early histories and comedies, and indicative of an extraordinary theatrical talent, Shakespeare's achievement in the later 1590s would still have been all but impossible to foresee. Starting with *A Midsummer Night's Dream* (1595–96), Shakespeare wrote an unprecedented series of romantic comedies—*The Merchant of Venice, Much Ado About Nothing, The Merry Wives of Windsor, As You Like It,* and *Twelfth Night* (1600–1601)—whose poetic richness and emotional complexity remain unmatched. In the same period, he wrote a sequence of profoundly searching and ambitious history plays—*Richard II, 1* and *2 Henry IV,* and *Henry V*—which together explore the death throes of feudal England and the birth of the modern nation-state ruled by a charismatic monarch. Both the comedies and histories of this period are marked by their capaciousness, their ability to absorb characters who press up against the outermost boundaries of the genre: the comedy *The Merchant of Venice* somehow contains the figure, at once nightmarish and poignant, of Shylock, while the *Henry IV* plays, with their somber vision of crisis in the family and the state, bring to the stage one of England's greatest comic characters, Falstaff.

If in the mid- to late 1590s Shakespeare reached the summit of his art in two major genres, he also manifested a lively interest in a third. As early as 1592–93, he wrote the crudely violent tragedy *Titus Andronicus,* the first of several plays on themes from Roman history, and a few years later, in *Richard II*, he created in the protagonist a figure who achieves by the play's close the stature of a tragic hero. In the same year that Shakespeare wrote the wonderfully farcical "Pyramus and Thisbe" scene in *A Midsummer Night's Dream*, he probably also wrote the deeply tragic realization of the same story in *Romeo and Juliet*. But once again, the lyric anguish of *Romeo and Juliet* and the tormented self-revelation of *Richard II*, extraordinary as they are, could not have led anyone to predict the next phase of Shakespeare's career, the great tragic dramas that poured forth in the early years of the seventeenth century: *Hamlet, Othello, King Lear, Macbeth, Antony and Cleopatra,* and *Coriolanus.* These plays, written between 1600 and 1608, seem to mark a major shift in sensibility, an existential and metaphysical darkening that many readers think must have drawn upon a deep personal anguish, perhaps caused by the decline and death of Shakespeare's father, John, in 1601.

Whatever the truth of these speculations—and we have no direct, personal testimony either to support or to undermine them—there appears to have occurred in the same period a shift as well in Shakespeare's comic sensibility. The comedies written between 1601 and 1607, *Troilus and Cressida, Measure for Measure,* and *All's Well That Ends Well,* are sufficiently different from the earlier comedies—more biting in tone, more uneasy with comic conventions, more ruthlessly questioning of the values of the characters and the resolutions of the plots—that they led many twentieth-century scholars to classify them as "problem plays" or "dark comedies." This category has recently begun to fall out of favor, since Shakespeare criticism is perfectly happy to demonstrate that *all* of the plays are "problem plays." But there is another group of plays, among the last Shakespeare wrote, that continue to constitute a distinct category. *Pericles, Cymbeline, The Winter's Tale,* and *The Tempest*—written between 1607 and 1611, when the playwright had developed a remarkably fluid, dreamlike sense of plot and a poetic style that could veer, apparently effortlessly, from the tortured to the ineffably sweet—have been known since the late nineteenth century as the "romances." These plays share an interest in the moral and emotional life less of the adolescents who dominate the earlier comedies than of their parents. The romances are deeply concerned with patterns of loss and recovery, suffering and redemption, despair and renewal. They have seemed to many critics to constitute a deliberate conclusion to a career that began in histories and comedies and passed through the dark and tormented tragedies.

One effect of the practice of printing Shakespeare's plays in a reconstructed chronological order, as this edition does, is to produce a kind of authorial plot, a progress from youthful exuberance and a heroic grappling with history, through psychological anguish and radical doubt, to a mature serenity built upon an understanding of loss. The ordering of Shakespeare's "complete works" in this way reconstitutes the figure of the author as the beloved hero of his own, lived romance. There are numerous reasons to treat this romance with considerable skepticism: the precise order of the plays remains in dispute, the obsessions of the earliest plays crisscross with those of the last, the drama is a collaborative art form, and the relation between authorial consciousness and theatrical representation is murky. Yet a longing to identify Shakespeare's personal trajectory, to chart his psychic and spiritual as well as professional progress, is all but irresistible.

The Fetishism of Dress

Whatever the personal resonance of Shakespeare's own life, his art is deeply enmeshed in the collective hopes, fears, and fantasies of his time. For example, throughout his plays, Shakespeare draws heavily upon his culture's investment in costume, symbols of authority, visible signs of status—the fetishism of dress he must have witnessed from early childhood. Disguise in his drama is often assumed to be incredibly effective: when Henry V borrows a cloak, when Portia dresses in a jurist's robes, when Viola puts on a young man's suit, it is as if each has become unrecognizable, as if identity resided in clothing. At the end of *Twelfth Night*, even though Viola's true identity has been disclosed, Orsino continues to call her Cesario; he will do so, he says, until she resumes her maid's garments, for only then will she be transformed into a woman:

> Cesario, come—
> For so you shall be while you are a man—
> But when in other habits you are seen,
> Orsino's mistress and his fancy's queen.
> (5.1.371–74)

The pinnacle of this fetishism of costume is the royal crown, for whose identity-conferring power men are willing to die, but the principle is everywhere, from the filthy blanket that transforms Edgar into Poor Tom to the coxcomb that is the badge of the licensed fool. Antonio, wishing to express his utter contempt, spits on Shylock's "Jewish gaberdine," as if the clothing were the essence of the man; Kent, pouring insults on the loathsome Oswald, calls him a "filthy worsted-stocking knave"; and innocent Imogen, learning that her husband has ordered her murder, thinks of herself as an expensive cast-off dress, destined to be ripped at the seams:

> Poor I am stale, a garment out of fashion,
> And for I am richer than to hang by th' walls,
> I must be ripped: to pieces with me.
> (*Cymbeline* 3.4.50–52)

What can be said, thought, felt in this culture seems deeply dependent on the clothes one wears—clothes that one is, in effect, *permitted* or *compelled* to wear, since there is little freedom in dress. Shakespearean drama occasionally represents something like such freedom: after all, Viola in *Twelfth Night* chooses to put off her "maiden weeds," as does Rosalind, who declares, "We'll have a swashing and a martial outside" (*As You Like It* 1.3.116). But these choices are characteristically made under the pressure of desperate circumstances, here shipwreck and exile. Part of the charm of Shakespeare's heroines is their ability to transform distress into an opportunity for self-fashioning, but the plays often suggest that there is less autonomy than meets the eye. What looks like an escape from cultural determinism may be only a deeper form of constraint. We may take, as an allegorical emblem of this constraint, the transformation of the beggar Christopher Sly in the playful Induction to *The Taming of the Shrew* into a nobleman. The transformation seems to suggest that you are free to make of yourself whatever you choose to be—the play begins with the drunken Sly claiming the dignity of his pedigree ("Look in the Chronicles" [Induction 1.3–4])—but in fact he is only the subject of the mischievous lord's experiment, designed to demonstrate the interwovenness of clothing and identity. "What think you," the lord asks his huntsman,

> if he were conveyed to bed,
> Wrapped in sweet clothes, rings put upon his fingers,
> A most delicious banquet by his bed,
> And brave attendants near him when he wakes—
> Would not the beggar then forget himself?

To which the huntsman replies, in words that underscore the powerlessness of the drunken beggar, "Believe me, lord, I think he cannot choose" (Induction 1.33–38).

Petruccio's taming of Katherina is similarly constructed around an imposition of identity, an imposition closely bound up with the right to wear certain articles of clothing. When the haberdasher arrives with a fashionable lady's hat, Petruccio refuses it over his wife's vehement objections: "This doth fit the time, / And gentlewomen wear such caps as these." "When you are gentle," Petruccio replies, "you shall have one, too, /

And not till then" (4.3.70–73). At the play's close, Petruccio demonstrates his authority by commanding his tamed wife to throw down her cap: "Off with that bauble; throw it underfoot" (5.2.122). Here as elsewhere in Shakespeare, acts of robing and disrobing are intensely charged, a charge that culminates in the trappings of monarchy. When Richard II, in a scene that was probably censored during the reign of Elizabeth from the stage as well as the printed text, is divested of his crown and scepter, he experiences the loss as the eradication of his name, the symbolic melting away of his identity:

> Alack the heavy day,
> That I have worn so many winters out
> And know not now what name to call myself.
> Oh, that I were a mockery king of snow,
> Standing before the sun of Bolingbroke
> To melt myself away in water-drops.
> (4.1.250–55)

When Lear tears off his regal "lendings" in order to reduce himself to the nakedness of the Bedlam beggar, he is expressing not only his radical loss of social identity but the breakdown of his psychic order as well, expressing therefore his reduction to the condition of the "poor bare forked animal" that is the primal form of undifferentiated existence. And when Cleopatra determines to kill herself in order to escape public humiliation in Rome, she magnificently affirms her essential being by arraying herself as she had once done to encounter Antony:

> Show me, my women, like a queen. Go, fetch
> My best attires. I am again for Cydnus
> To meet Mark Antony.
> (5.2.226–28)

Such scenes are a remarkable intensification of the everyday symbolic practice of Renaissance English culture, its characteristically deep and knowing commitment to illusion: "I know perfectly well that the woman in her crown and jewels and gorgeous gown is an aging, irascible, and fallible mortal—she herself virtually admits as much—yet I profess that she is the virgin queen, timelessly beautiful, wise, and just." Shakespeare understood how close this willed illusion was to the spirit of the theater, to the actors' ability to work on what the chorus in *Henry V* calls the "imaginary forces" of the audience. But there is throughout Shakespeare's works a counterintuition that, while it does not exactly overturn this illusion, renders it poignant, vulnerable, fraught. The "masculine usurp'd attire" that is donned by Viola, Rosalind, Portia, Jessica, and other Shakespeare heroines alters what they can say and do, reveals important aspects of their character, and changes their destiny, but it is, all the same, not theirs and not all of who they are. They have, the plays insist, natures that are neither transformed nor altogether concealed by their dress: "Pray God defend me," exclaims the frightened Viola. "A little thing would make me tell them how much I lack of a man" (*Twelfth Night* 3.4.271–72).

The Paradoxes of Identity

The gap between costume and identity is not simply a matter of what women supposedly lack; virtually all of Shakespeare's major characters, men and women, convey the sense of both a *self-division* and an *inward expansion*. The belief in a complex inward realm beyond costumes and status is a striking inversion of the clothes cult: we know perfectly well that the characters have no inner lives apart from what we see on the stage, and yet we believe that they continue to exist when we do not see them, that they exist apart from their represented words and actions, that they have hidden dimensions. How is this conviction aroused and sustained? In part, it is the effect of what the characters themselves say: "My grief lies all within," Richard II tells Bolingbroke,

> And these external manner of laments
> Are merely shadows to the unseen grief
> That swells with silence in the tortured soul.
> (4.1.288–91)

Similarly, Hamlet, dismissing the significance of his outward garments, declares, "I have that within which passes show— / These but the trappings and the suits of woe" (1.2.85–86). And the distinction between inward and outward is reinforced throughout this play and elsewhere by an unprecedented use of the aside and the soliloquy.

The soliloquy is a continual reminder in Shakespeare that the inner life is by no means transparent to one's surrounding world. Prince Hal seems open and easy with his mates in Eastcheap, but he has a hidden reservoir of disgust:

> I know you all, and will a while uphold
> The unyoked humor of your idleness.
> Yet herein will I imitate the sun,
> Who doth permit the base contagious clouds
> To smother up his beauty from the world,
> That, when he please again to be himself,
> Being wanted he may be more wondered at
> By breaking through the foul and ugly mists
> Of vapors that did seem to strangle him.
> (I Henry IV 1.2.170–78)

"When he please again to be himself": the line implies that identity is a matter of free choice—you decide how much of yourself you wish to disclose—but Shakespeare employs other devices that suggest more elusive and intractable layers of inwardness. There is a peculiar, recurrent lack of fit between costume and character, in fools as in princes, that is not simply a matter of disguise and disclosure. If Hal's true identity is partially "smothered" in the tavern, it is not completely revealed either in his soldier's armor or in his royal robes, nor do his asides reach the bedrock of unimpeachable self-understanding.

Identity in Shakespeare repeatedly slips away from the characters themselves, as it does from Richard II after the deposition scene and from Lear after he has given away his land and from Macbeth after he has gained the crown. The slippage does not mean that they retreat into silence; rather, they embark on an experimental, difficult fashioning of themselves and the world, most often through role-playing. "I cannot do it," says the deposed and imprisoned Richard II. "Yet I'll hammer't out" (5.5.5). This could serve as the motto for many Shakespearean characters: Viola becomes Cesario, Rosalind calls herself Ganymede, Kent becomes Caius, Edgar presents himself as Poor Tom, Hamlet plays the madman that he has partly become, Hal pretends that he is his father and a highwayman and Hotspur and even himself. Even in comedy, these ventures into alternate identities are rarely matters of choice; in tragedy, they are always undertaken under pressure and compulsion. And often enough it is not a matter of role-playing at all, but of a drastic transformation whose extreme emblem is the harrowing madness of Lear and of Leontes.

There is a moment in *Richard II* in which the deposed king asks for a mirror and then, after musing on his reflection, throws it to the ground. The shattering of the glass serves to remind us not only of the fragility of identity in Shakespeare but of its characteristic appearance in fragmentary mirror images. The plays continually generate alternative reflections, identities that intersect with, underscore, echo, or otherwise set off that of the principal character. Hence, Desdemona and Iago are not only important figures in Othello's world—they also seem to embody partially realized aspects of himself; Falstaff and Hotspur play a comparable role in relation to Prince Hal, Fortinbras and Horatio in relation to Hamlet, Gloucester and the Fool in relation to Lear, and so forth. In many of these plays, the complementary and contrasting characters figure in subplots, subtly interwoven with the play's main plot and illuminating its concerns. The note so conspicuously sounded by Fortinbras at the close of *Hamlet*—what the hero might have been, "had he been put on"—is heard repeatedly in Shakespeare and contributes to the overwhelming intensity, poignancy, and complexity of the characters. This is a world in which outward appearance is everything and nothing, in which individuation is at once sharply etched and continually blurred, in which the victims of fate are haunted by the ghosts of the possible, in which everything is simultaneously as it must be and as it need not have been.

Are these alternatives signs of a struggle between contradictory and irreconcilable perspectives in Shakespeare? In certain plays—notably, *Measure for Measure*, *All's Well That Ends Well*, *Coriolanus*, and *Troilus and Cressida*—the tension seems both high and entirely unresolved. But Shakespearean contradictions are more often reminiscent of the capacious spirit of Montaigne, who refused any systematic order that would betray his sense of reality. Thus, individual characters are immensely important in Shakespeare—he is justly celebrated for his unmatched skill in the invention of particular dramatic identities, marked with distinct speech patterns, manifested in social status, and confirmed by costume and gesture—but the principle of individuation is not the rock on which his theatrical art is founded. After the masks are stripped away, the pretenses exposed, the claims of the ego shattered, there is a mysterious remainder; as the shamed but irrepressible Paroles declares in *All's Well That Ends Well*, "Simply the thing I am / Shall make me live" (4.3.316–17). Again and again the audience is made to sense a deeper energy, a source of power that at once discharges itself in individual characters and seems to sweep right through them.

The Poet of Nature

In *The Birth of Tragedy*, Nietzsche called a comparable source of energy that he found in Greek tragedy "Dionysos." But the god's name, conjuring up Bacchic frenzy, does not seem appropriate to Shakespeare. In the late seventeenth and eighteenth centuries, it was more plausibly called Nature: "The world must be peopled," says the delightful Benedict in *Much Ado About Nothing* (2.3.213), and there are frequent invocations elsewhere of the happy, generative power that brings couples together—

> Jack shall have Jill,
> Naught shall go ill,
> The man shall have his mare again, and all shall be well.
> (*A Midsummer Night's Dream* 3.2.461–63)

—and the melancholy, destructive power that brings all living things to the grave: "Golden lads and girls all must, / As chimney-sweepers, come to dust" (*Cymbeline* 4.2.261–62).

But the celebration of Shakespeare as a poet of nature—often coupled with an inane celebration of his supposedly "natural" (that is, untutored) genius—has its distinct limitations. For Shakespearean art brilliantly interrogates the "natural," refusing to take for granted precisely what the celebrants think is most secure. His comedies are endlessly inventive in showing that love is not simply natural: the playful hint of bestiality in the line quoted above, "the man shall have his mare again" (from a play in which the Queen of the Fairies falls in love with an ass-headed laborer), lightly unsettles the boundaries between the natural and the perverse. These boundaries are called into question throughout Shakespeare's work, from the cross-dressing and erotic crosscurrents that deliciously complicate the lives of the characters in *Twelfth Night* and *As You Like It* to the terrifying violence that wells up from the heart of the family in *King Lear* or from the sweet intimacy of sexual desire in *Othello*. Even the boundary between life and death is not secure, as the ghosts in *Julius Caesar, Hamlet,* and *Macbeth* attest, while the principle of natural death (given its most eloquent articulation by old Hamlet's murderer, Claudius!) is repeatedly tainted and disrupted.

Disrupted too is the idea of order that constantly makes its claim, most insistently in the history plays. Scholars have observed the presence in Shakespeare's works of the so-called Tudor myth—the ideological justification of the ruling dynasty as a restoration of national order after a cycle of tragic violence. The violence, Tudor apologists claimed, was divine punishment unleashed after the deposition of the anointed king, Richard II, for God will not tolerate violations of the sanctified order. Traces of this propaganda certainly exist in the histories—Shakespeare may, for all we know, have personally subscribed to its premises—but a closer scrutiny of his plays has disclosed so many ironic reservations and qualifications and subversions as to call into question any straightforward adherence to a political line. The plays manifest a profound fascination with the monarchy and with the ambitions of the aristocracy, but the fascination is never simply endorsement. There is always at least the hint of a slippage between the great figures, whether admirable or monstrous, who stand at the pinnacle of authority and the vast, miscellaneous mass of soldiers, scriveners, ostlers, poets, whores, gardeners, thieves, weavers, shepherds, country gentlemen, sturdy beggars, and the like who make up the commonwealth. And the idea of order, though eloquently articulated (most memorably by Ulysses in *Troilus and Cressida*), is always shadowed by a relentless spirit of irony.

The Play of Language

If neither the individual nor nature nor order will serve, can we find a single comprehensive name for the underlying force in Shakespeare's work? Certainly not. The work is too protean and capacious. But much of the energy that surges through this astonishing body of plays and poems is closely linked to the power of language. Shakespeare was the supreme product of a rhetorical culture, a culture steeped in the arts of persuasion and verbal expressiveness. In 1512, the great Dutch humanist Erasmus published a work called *De copia* that taught its readers how to cultivate "copiousness," verbal richness, in discourse. (Erasmus obligingly provides, as a sample, a list of 144 different ways of saying "Thank you for your letter.") Recommended modes of variation include putting the subject of an argument into fictional form, as well as the use of synonym, substitution, paraphrase, metaphor, metonymy, synecdoche, hyperbole, diminution, and a host of other figures of speech. To change emotional tone, he suggests trying *ironia, interrogatio, admiratio, dubitatio, abominatio*—the possibilities seem infinite.

In Renaissance England, certain syntactic forms or patterns of words known as "figures" (also called "schemes") were shaped and repeated in order to confer beauty or heighten expressive power. Figures were usually known by their Greek and Latin names, though in an Elizabethan rhetorical manual, *The Art of English Poesy,* George Puttenham made a valiant if short-lived attempt to give them English equivalents, such as "*Hyperbole,* or the Overreacher," "*Ironia,* or the Dry Mock," and "*Ploce,* or the Doubler." Those who received a grammar school education throughout Europe at almost any point between the Roman Empire and the eighteenth century probably knew by heart the names of up to one hundred such figures, just as they knew by heart their multiplication tables. According to one scholar's count, Shakespeare knew and made use of about two hundred.

As certain grotesquely inflated Renaissance texts attest, lessons from *De copia* and similar rhetorical guides could encourage mere prolixity and verbal self-display. But though he shared his culture's delight in rhetorical complexity, Shakespeare always understood how to swoop from baroque sophistication to breathtaking simplicity. Moreover, he grasped early in his career how to use figures of speech, tone, and rhythm not only to provide emphasis and elegant variety but also to articulate the inner lives of his characters. Take, for example, these lines from *Othello*, where, as scholars have noted, Shakespeare deftly combines four common rhetorical figures— *anaphora, parison, isocolon,* and *epistrophe*—to depict with painful vividness Othello's psychological torment:

> By the world,
> I think my wife be honest, and think she is not;
> I think that thou art just, and think thou art not.
> I'll have some proof.
>
> (3.3.380–83)

Anaphora is simply the repetition of a word at the beginning of a sequence of sentences or clauses ("I/I"). *Parison* is the correspondence of word to word within adjacent sentences or clauses, either by direct repetition ("think/think") or by the matching of noun with noun, verb with verb ("wife/thou"; "be/art"). *Isocolon* gives exactly the same length to corresponding clauses ("and think she is not/and think thou art not"), and *epistrophe* is the mirror image of *anaphora,* in that it is the repetition of a word at the end of a sequence of sentences or clauses ("not/not"). Do we need to know the Greek names for these figures in order to grasp the effectiveness of Othello's lines? Of course not. But Shakespeare and his contemporaries, convinced that rhetoric provided the most natural and powerful means by which feelings could be conveyed to readers and listeners, were trained in an analytical language that helped at once to promote and to account for this effectiveness. In his 1593 edition of *The Garden of Eloquence,* Henry Peacham remarks that *epistrophe* "serveth to leave a word of importance in the end of a sentence, that it may the longer hold the sound in the mind of the hearer," and in *Directions for Speech and Style* (ca. 1599), John Hoskins notes that *anaphora* "beats upon one thing to cause the quicker feeling in the audience."

Shakespeare also shared with his contemporaries a keen understanding of the ways that rhetorical devices could be used not only to express powerful feelings but to hide them: after all, the artist who created Othello also created Iago, Richard III, and Lady Macbeth. He could deftly skewer the rhetorical affectations of Polonius in *Hamlet* or the pedant Holofernes in *Love's Labor's Lost.* He could deploy stylistic variations to mark the boundaries not of different individuals but of different social realms; in *A Midsummer Night's Dream,* for example, the blank verse of Duke Theseus is played off against the rhymed couplets of the well-born young lovers, and both in turn contrast with the prose spoken by the artisans. At the same time that he thus marks boundaries between both individuals and groups, Shakespeare shows a remarkable ability to establish unifying patterns of imagery that knit together the diverse strands of his plot and suggest subtle links among characters who may be scarcely aware of how much they share with one another.

One of the hidden links in Shakespeare's own works is the frequent use he makes of a somewhat unusual rhetorical figure called *hendiadys.* An example from the Roman poet Virgil is the phrase *pateris libamus et auro,* "we drink from cups and gold" (*Georgics* 2.192). Rather than serving as an adjective or a dependent noun, as in "golden cups" or "cups of gold," the word "gold" serves as a substantive joined to another substantive, "cups," by a conjunction, "and." Shakespeare uses the figure over three hundred times in all, and since it does not appear in ancient or medieval lists of tropes and schemes and is treated only briefly by English rhetoricians, he may have come upon it directly in Virgil. *Hendiadys* literally means "one through two," though Shakespeare's versions often make us quickly, perhaps only subliminally, aware of the complexity of what ordinarily passes for straightforward perceptions. When Othello, in his suicide speech, invokes the memory of "a malignant and a turbaned Turk," the figure of speech at once associates enmity with cultural difference and keeps them slightly apart. And when Macbeth speaks of his "strange and self-abuse," the *hendiadys* seems briefly to hold both "strange" and "self" up for scrutiny. It would be foolish to make too much of any single feature in Shakespeare's varied and diverse creative achievement, and yet this curious rhetorical scheme has something of the quality of a fingerprint.

But all of his immense rhetorical gifts, though rich, beautiful, and supremely useful, do not adequately convey Shakespeare's relation to language, which is less strictly functional than a total immersion in the arts of persuasion may imply. An Erasmian admiration for copiousness cannot fully explain Shakespeare's astonishing vocabulary of some 25,000 words. (His closest rival among the great English poets of the period was John Milton, with about 12,000 words, and most major writers, let alone ordinary people, have much smaller vocabularies.) This immense word hoard, it is worth noting, was not the result of scanning a dictionary; in the late sixteenth century, there were no large-scale English dictionaries of the kind to which we are now accustomed. Shakespeare seems to have absorbed new words from virtually every discursive realm he ever encountered, and he experimented boldly and tirelessly with them. These experiments were facilitated by a flexibility in grammar, orthography, and diction that the more orderly, regularized English of the later seventeenth and eighteenth centuries suppressed.

Owing in part to the number of dialects in London, pronunciation was variable, and there were many opportunities for phonetic association between words: the words "bear," "barn," "bier," "bourn" "born," and "barne" could all sound like one another. Homonyms were given greater scope by the fact that the same word could be spelled so many different ways—Christopher Marlowe's name appears in the records as Marlowe, Marloe, Marlen, Marlyne, Merlin, Marley, Marlye, Morley, and Morle—and by the fact that a word's grammatical function could easily shift, from noun to verb, verb to adjective, and so forth. Since grammar and punctuation did not insist on relations of coordination and subordination, loose, nonsyntactic sentences were common, and etymologies were used to forge surprising or playful relations between distant words.

It would seem inherently risky for a popular playwright to employ a vocabulary so far in excess of what most mortals could possibly possess, but Shakespeare evidently counted on his audience's linguistic curiosity and adventurousness, just as he counted on its general and broad-based rhetorical competence. He was also usually careful to provide a context that in effect explained or translated his more arcane terms. For example, when Macbeth reflects with horror on his murderous hands, he shudderingly imagines that even the sea could not wash away the blood; on the contrary, his bloodstained hand, he says, "will rather / The multitudinous seas incarnadine." The meaning of the unfamiliar word "incarnadine" is explained by the next line: "Making the green one red" (2.2.64–66).

What is most striking is not the abstruseness or novelty of Shakespeare's language but its extraordinary vitality, a quality that the playwright seemed to pursue with a kind of passionate recklessness. Perhaps Samuel Johnson was looking in the right direction when he complained that the "quibble," or pun, was "the fatal Cleopatra for which [Shakespeare] lost the world, and was content to lose it." For the power that continually discharges itself throughout the plays, at once constituting and unsettling everything it touches, is the polymorphous power of language, language that seems both costume and that which lies beneath the costume, personal identity and that which challenges the merely personal, nature and that which enables us to name nature and thereby distance ourselves from it.

Shakespeare's language has an overpowering exuberance and generosity that often resembles the experience of love. Consider, for example, Oberon's description in A Midsummer Night's Dream of the moment when he saw Cupid shoot his arrow at the fair vestal: "Thou rememberest," he asks Puck,

> Since once I sat upon a promontory
> And heard a mermaid on a dolphin's back
> Uttering such dulcet and harmonious breath
> That the rude sea grew civil at her song

> And certain stars shot madly from their spheres
> To hear the sea-maid's music?
>
> (2.1.148–54)

Here, Oberon's composition of place, lightly alluding to a classical emblem, is infused with a fantastically lush verbal brilliance. This brilliance, the result of masterful alliterative and rhythmical technique, seems gratuitous; that is, it does not advance the plot, but rather exhibits a capacity for display and self-delight that extends from the fairies to the playwright who has created them. The rich music of Oberon's words imitates the "dulcet and harmonious breath" he is intent on recalling, breath that has, in his account, an oddly contradictory effect: it is at once a principle of order, so that the rude sea is becalmed like a lower-class mob made civil by a skilled orator, and a principle of disorder, so that celestial bodies in their fixed spheres are thrown into mad confusion. And this contradictory effect, so intimately bound up with an inexplicable, supererogatory, and intensely erotic verbal magic, is a key to *A Midsummer Night's Dream*, with its exquisite blend of confusion and discipline, lunacy and hierarchical ceremony.

The fairies in this comedy seem to embody a pervasive sense found throughout Shakespeare's work that there is something uncanny about language, something that is not quite human, at least in the conventional and circumscribed sense of the human that dominates waking experience. In the comedies, this intuition is alarming but ultimately benign: Oberon and his followers trip through the great house at the play's close, blessing the bride-beds and warding off the nightmares that lurk in marriage and parenthood. But there is in Shakespeare an alternative, darker vision of the uncanniness of language, a vision also embodied in creatures that test the limits of the human—not the fairies of *A Midsummer Night's Dream* but the weird sisters of *Macbeth*. When in the tragedy's opening scene the witches chant, "Fair is foul, and foul is fair," they unsettle through the simplest and most radical act of linguistic equation (x is y) the fundamental distinctions through which a moral order is established. And when Macbeth appears onstage a few minutes later, his first words unconsciously echo what we have just heard from the witches' mouths: "So foul and fair a day I have not seen" (1.3.39). What is the meaning of this linguistic "unconscious"? On the face of things, Macbeth presumably means only that the day of fair victory is also a day of foul weather, but the fact that he echoes the witches (something that we hear but that he cannot know) intimates an occult link between them, even before their direct encounter. It is difficult, perhaps impossible, to specify exactly what this link signifies—generations of emboldened critics have tried without notable success—but we can at least affirm that its secret lair is in the play's language, like a half-buried pun whose full articulation will entail the murder of Duncan, the ravaging of his kingdom, and Macbeth's own destruction.

Macbeth is haunted by half-buried puns, equivocations, and ambiguous grammatical constructions known as amphibologies. They manifest themselves most obviously in the words of the witches, from the opening exchanges to the fraudulent assurances that deceive Macbeth at the close, but they are also present in his most intimate and private reflections, as in his tortured broodings about his proposed act of treason:

> If it were done when 'tis done, then 'twere well
> It were done quickly. If th'assassination
> Could trammel up the consequence and catch
> With his surcease success—that but this blow
> Might be the be-all and the end-all!—here,
> But here, upon this bank and shoal of time,
> We'd jump the life to come.
>
> (1.7.1–7)

The dream is to reach a secure and decisive end, to catch as in a net (hence "trammel up") all of the slippery, unforeseen, and uncontrollable consequences of regicide, to hobble time as one might hobble a horse (another sense of "trammel up"), to stop the flow ("success") of events, to be, as Macbeth later puts it, "settled." But Macbeth's words themselves slip away from the closure he seeks; they slide into one another, trip over themselves, twist and double back and swerve into precisely the sickening uncertainties their speaker most wishes to avoid. And if we sense a barely discernible note of comedy in Macbeth's tortured language, a discordant playing with the senses of the word "done" and the hint of a childish tongue twister in the phrase "catch / With his surcease success," we are in touch with a dark pleasure to which Shakespeare was all his life addicted.

Look again at the couplet from *Cymbeline:* "Golden lads and girls all must, / As chimney-sweepers, come to dust." The playwright who insinuated a pun into the solemn dirge is the same playwright whose tragic heroine in *Antony and Cleopatra,* pulling the bleeding body of her dying lover into the pyramid, says, "Our strength is all gone into heaviness" (4.15.34). He is the playwright whose Juliet, finding herself alone on the stage, says, "My dismal scene I needs must act alone" (*Romeo and Juliet* 4.3.19), and the playwright who can follow the long, wrenching periodic sentence that Othello speaks, just before he stabs himself, with the remark "O bloody period!" (5.2.349). The point is not merely the presence of puns in the midst of tragedy (as there are stabs of pain in the midst of Shakespearean comedy); it is rather the streak of wildness that they so deliberately disclose, the sublimely indecorous linguistic energy of which Shakespeare was at once the towering master and the most obedient, worshipful servant.

From Page to Stage: Shakespeare at Work

Shakespeare's extraordinary imaginative and linguistic power left its mark, like a personal signature, on everything he wrote. But his plays became the property of the theatrical company in which he was a shareholder. The company could choose to sell its plays to printers who might hope to profit if the public was eager to read as well as to watch a popular hit. But relatively few plays excited that level of public interest. Moreover, playing companies did not always think it was in their interest to have their scripts circulating in print, at least while the plays were actively in repertory: players evidently feared competition from rival companies and thought that reading might dampen playgoing. Plays were on occasion printed quickly, in order to take advantage of their popularity, but they were most often sold to the printers when the theaters were temporarily closed by plague, or when the company was in need of capital (four of Shakespeare's plays were published in 1600, presumably to raise money to pay the debts incurred in building the new Globe), or when a play had grown too old to revive profitably. There is no conclusive evidence that Shakespeare disagreed with this professional caution. There was clearly a market for his plays in print as well as onstage, and he himself may have taken pride in what he wrote as suitable for reading as well as viewing. But unlike Jonson, who took the radical step of rewriting his own plays for publication in the 1616 folio of his *Works,* Shakespeare evidently never undertook to constitute his plays as a canon. If in the sonnets he imagines his verse achieving a symbolic immortality, this dream apparently did not extend to his plays, at least through the medium of print.

Moreover, there is no evidence that Shakespeare had an interest in asserting authorial rights over his scripts, or that he or any other working English playwright had a public "standing," legal or otherwise, from which to do so. (Jonson was ridiculed for his presumption.) There is no indication whatever that he could, for example, veto changes in his scripts or block interpolated scenes or withdraw a play from production if a particular interpretation, addition, or revision did not please him. To be sure, in his advice to the players, Hamlet urges that those who play the clowns "speak no more than is set down for them," but—apart from the question of whether the prince speaks for the playwright—the play-within-the-play in *Hamlet* is precisely an instance of a script altered to suit a particular occasion. It seems likely that Shakespeare would have routinely accepted the possibility of such alterations. Moreover, he would of necessity have routinely accepted the possibility, and in certain cases the virtual inevitability, of cuts in order to stage his plays in the two to two and one-half hours that was the normal performing time. There is an imaginative generosity in many of Shakespeare's scripts, as if he were deliberately offering his fellow actors more than they could use on any one occasion and hence giving them abundant materials with which to reconceive and revivify each play again and again, as they or their audiences liked it. The Elizabethan theater, like most theater in our own time, was a collaborative enterprise, and the collaboration almost certainly extended to decisions about selection, trimming, shifts of emphasis, and minor or major revision.

Writing for the theater for Shakespeare was never simply a matter of sitting alone at his desk and putting words on paper; it was a social process as well as individual act. We do not know the extent to which this process frustrated him; in Sonnet 66 he writes of "art made tongue-tied by authority." Shakespeare may have been forced on occasion to cut lines and even whole scenes to which he was attached; shifting political circumstances may have occasioned rewriting, possibly against his will; or his fellow players may have insisted that they could not successfully perform what he had written, compelling him to make changes he did not welcome. But compromise and collaboration are part of what it means to be in the theater, and Shakespeare was, supremely, a man of the theater.

As a man of the theater, Shakespeare understood that whatever he set down on paper was not the end of the story. It would inevitably be shaped by the words he spoke to his fellow actors and by their own ideas concerning emphasis, stage business, tone, pacing, possible cuts, and so forth. It could be modified too by the intervention of the government censor or by intimations that some powerful figure might take offense at something in the script. To the extent that the agreed-upon alterations were ever written down, they were recorded in the promptbook used for a particular performance, and that promptbook could in turn be modified for a subsequent performance in a different setting.

For many years, it was thought that Shakespeare himself did little or no revising. Some recent editors have argued persuasively that there are many signs of authorial revision, even wholesale rewriting. But there is no sign that Shakespeare sought through such revision to bring each of his plays to its "perfect," "final" form. On the contrary, many of the revisions seem to indicate that the scripts remained open texts that the playwright and his company expected to add to, cut, and rewrite as the occasion demanded.

Ralph Waldo Emerson once compared Shakespeare and his contemporary Francis Bacon in terms of the relative "finish" of their work. All of Bacon's work, wrote Emerson, "lies along the ground, a vast unfinished city." Each of Shakespeare's dramas, by contrast, "is perfect, hath an immortal integrity. To make Bacon's work complete, he must live to the end of the world." Recent scholarship suggests that Shakespeare was more like Bacon than Emerson thought. Neither the Folio nor the quarto texts of Shakespeare's plays bear the seal of final authorial intention, the mark of decisive closure that has served, at least ideally, as the guarantee of textual authenticity. We want to believe, as we read the text, "This is the play as Shakespeare himself wanted it read," but there is no license for such a reassuring sentiment. To be "not of an age, but for all time" means in Shakespeare's case not that the plays have achieved a static perfection, but that they are creatively, inexhaustibly unfinished.

The Status of the Artist

That we have been so eager to link certain admired scripts to a single known playwright is closely related to changes in the status of artists in the Renaissance, changes that led to a heightened interest in the hand of the individual creator. Like medieval painting, medieval drama gives us few clues as to the particular individuals who fashioned the objects we admire. We know something about the places in which these objects were made, the circumstances that enabled their creation, the spaces in which they were placed, but relatively little about the particular artists themselves. It is easy to imagine a wealthy patron or a civic authority in the late Middle Ages commissioning a play on a particular subject (appropriate, for example, to a seasonal ritual, a religious observance, or a political festivity) and specifying the date, place, and length of the performance, the number of actors, even the costumes to be used, but it is more difficult to imagine him specifying a particular playwright and still less insisting that the entire play be written by this dramatist alone. Only with the Renaissance do we find a growing insistence on the name of the maker, the signature that heightens the value and even the meaning of the work by implying that it is the emanation of a single, distinct shaping consciousness.

In the case of Renaissance painting, we know that this signature does not necessarily mean that every stroke was made by the master. Some of the work, possibly the greater part of it, may have been done by assistants, with only the faces and a few finishing touches from the hand of the illustrious artist to whom the work is confidently attributed. As the skill of individual masters became more explicitly valued, contracts began to specify how much was to come from the brush of the principal painter. Consider, for example, the Italian painter Luca Signorelli's contract of 1499 for frescoes in Orvieto Cathedral:

> The said master Luca is bound and promises to paint [1] all the figures to be done on the said vault, and [2] especially the faces and all the parts of the figures from the middle of each figure upwards, and [3] that no painting should be done on it without Luca himself being present. . . . And it is agreed [4] that all the mixing of colors should be done by the said master Luca himself.

Such a contract at once reflects a serious cash interest in the characteristic achievement of a particular artist and a conviction that this achievement is compatible with the presence of other hands, provided those hands are subordinate, in the finished work. For paintings on a smaller scale, it was more possible to commission an exclusive performance. Thus the contract for a small altarpiece by Signorelli's great teacher, Piero della Francesca, specifies that "no painter may put his hand to the brush other than Piero himself."

There is no record of any comparable concern for exclusivity in the English theater. Unfortunately, the contracts that Shakespeare and his fellow dramatists almost certainly signed have not, with one significant exception, survived. But plays written for the professional theater are by their nature an even more explicitly collective art form than paintings; they depend for their full realization on the collaboration of others, and that collaboration may well extend to the fashioning of the script. It seems that some authors may simply have been responsible for providing plots that others then dramatized; still others were hired to "mend" old plays or to supply prologues, epilogues, or songs. A particular playwright's name came to be attached to a certain identifiable style—a characteristic set of plot devices, a marked rhetorical range, a tonality of character—but this name may refer in effect more to a certain product associated with a particular playing company than to the individual artist who may or may not have written most of the script. The one contract whose details do survive, that entered into by Richard Brome and the actors and owners of the Salisbury Court Theater in 1635, does not stipulate that Brome's plays must be written by him alone or even that he must be responsible for a certain specifiable proportion of each script. Rather, it specifies that the playwright "should not nor would write any play or any part of a play to any other players or playhouse, but apply all his study and endeavors therein for the benefit of the said company of the said playhouse." The Salisbury Court players want rights to everything Brome writes for the stage; the issue is not that the plays associated with his name be exclusively *his* but rather that he be exclusively *theirs*.

Recent textual scholarship, then, has been moving steadily away from a conception of Shakespeare's plays as direct, unmediated emanations from the mind of the author and toward a conception of them as working scripts, composed and continually reshaped as part of a collaborative commercial enterprise in competition with other, similar enterprises. One consequence has been the progressive weakening of the idea of the solitary, inspired genius, in the sense fashioned by Romanticism and figured splendidly in the statue of Shakespeare in the public gardens in Germany's Weimar, the city of Goethe and Schiller: the poet, with his sensitive, expressive face and high domed forehead sitting alone and brooding, a skull at his feet, a long-stemmed rose in his crotch. In place of this projection of German Romanticism, we have now a playwright and sometime actor who is also (to his considerable financial advantage) a major shareholder in the company—the Chamberlain's Men, later the King's Men—to which he loyally supplies for most of his career an average of two plays per year.

As a shareholder Shakespeare had to concern himself with such matters as economic cycles, lists of plague deaths, the cost of costumes, government censorship, city ordinances, the hiring and firing of personnel, and innumerable other factors that affected his enterprise. Practical considerations did not merely affect the context of his writing for the stage; they also shaped the form of what he wrote. His plays were not monuments, fixed in every detail and immobilized forever. They were like living beings, destined to change as a condition for their very survival.

One of the very first biographical mentions of Shakespeare, in the Reverend Thomas Fuller's *History of the Worthies of England* (1662), seems to have grasped this principle of mobility. Fuller reports—or imagines—the "wit-combats" that Shakespeare and Jonson had at the Mermaid Tavern:

> which two I behold like a Spanish great galleon and an English man of war; Master Jonson (like the former) was built far higher in learning, solid but slow in his performances. Shakespeare, with the English man of war, lesser in bulk, but lighter in sailing, could turn with all tides, tack about, and take advantage of all winds by the quickness of his wit and invention.

The encounters Fuller describes may be apocryphal, but to "turn with all tides, tack about, and take advantage of all winds" is a canny description of the highly mobile texts that Shakespeare fashioned and bequeathed to posterity.

Conjuring Shakespeare

The Elizabethan and Jacobean public had an interest in reading plays as well as seeing them. There was a lively market in such texts, often rushed into print to catch public excitement, and there is even evidence that at certain performances it was possible for audiences at the playhouse to purchase a copy of the very play they were watching.

Shakespeare's attitude to this market is unclear. Unlike Ben Jonson, he never personally edited and oversaw the publication of his plays, either individually or as a collection, but he may, for all we know, have imagined some day doing so. Perhaps death simply overtook him before he reached that goal. Certainly the Folio editors, though they were themselves fellow actors, thought of his plays as literary works. In 1623, seven years after the playwright's death, Heminges and Condell believed they could sell copies of their expensive collection of Shakespeare's plays—"What euer you do," they urge their readers, "buy"—by insisting that their texts were "as he conceiued them."

"As he conceived them": potential readers in the early seventeenth century then were already interested in access to Shakespeare's "conceits"—his "wit," his imagination, and his creative power—and were willing to assign a high value to the products of his particular, identifiable skill, one distinguishable from that of his company and of his rival playwrights. After all, Jonson's dedicatory poem in the Folio praises Shakespeare not as the playwright of the incomparable King's Men but as the equal of Aeschylus, Sophocles, and Euripides. And if we now see Shakespeare's dramaturgy in the context of his contemporaries and of a collective artistic practice, readers continue to have little difficulty recognizing that most of the plays attached to his name tower over those of his rivals.

The First Folio included an engraving purporting to show what Shakespeare looked like, but in the little poem that accompanied this image Jonson urged the reader to "look / Not on his Picture, but his Book." The words on the page then should conjure up the author himself; they should ideally give the reader unmediated access to the astonishing forge of imaginative power that was the mind of the dramatist. Such is the vision—at its core closely related to the preservation of the divinely inspired text in the great scriptural religions—that has driven many of the great editors who have for centuries produced successive editions of Shakespeare's works. The vision was not yet fully formed in the First Folio, for Heminges and Condell still felt obliged to apologize to their noble patrons for dedicating to them a collection of mere "trifles." But by the eighteenth century, there were no longer any ritual apologies for Shakespeare; instead, there was growing recognition of the supreme artistic importance of his works.

At the same time, from the eighteenth century onward, there was growing recognition of the uncertain, conflicting, and in some cases corrupt state of the surviving texts. Every conceivable step, it was thought, must be undertaken to correct mistakes, strip away corruptions, and return the texts to their pure and unsullied form. Noticing that there were multiple texts of fully half of the plays and noticing too that these texts often contain significant variants, editors routinely conflated the distinct versions into a single text in an attempt to reconstruct the ideal, definitive, complete, and perfect copy that they imagined Shakespeare must have aspired to and eventually reached for each of his plays. In doing so they succeeded in producing something that Shakespeare himself never wrote.

Heminges and Condell, who knew the author and had access to at least some of his manuscripts, lamented the fact that Shakespeare did not live "to have set forth and overseen his own writings." But even had he done so—or, alternatively, even if a cache of his manuscripts were discovered in a Warwickshire attic tomorrow—all of the editorial problems would not be solved, though the textual landscape would change, nor would all of the levels of mediation be swept away. The written word has strange powers: it seems to hold onto something of the very life of the person who has written it, but it also seems to pry that life loose from the writer, exposing it to vagaries of history and chance quite independent of those to which the writer was personally subject. Moreover, with the passing of centuries, the language itself and the whole frame of reference within which language and symbols are understood have decisively changed. The most learned modern scholar still lives at a huge experiential remove from Shakespeare's world and, even holding a precious copy of the First Folio in hand, cannot escape having to read across a vast chasm of time what is, after all, an edited text. The rest of us cannot so much as indulge in the fantasy of direct access: our eyes inevitably wander to the glosses and the explanatory notes.

Abandoning the dream of direct access to Shakespeare's final and definitive intentions is not a cause for despair, nor should it lead us to throw our hands up and declare that one text is as good as another. What it does is to encourage us to be actively interested in the editorial principles that underlie the particular edition that we are using. It is said that the great artist Brueghel once told an inquisitive connoisseur who had come to his studio, "Keep your nose out of my paintings; the smell of the paint will poison you." In the case of Shakespeare, it is increasingly important to bring one's nose close to the page, as it were, and sniff the ink. More precisely, it is important to understand the rationale for the choices that the editors have made.

The rationale behind *The Norton Shakespeare* is described at length in the Textual Introduction to this volume. What should be stressed here is the fact that

Shakespeare was the master of the unfinished, the perpetually open. The notion of finding a perfectly fixed text of one of his plays, the copy that he directly handed over to the printer as his "final" version, goes against everything we know about his personal practice and about Elizabethan and Jacobean theater. Shakespeare wrote his plays to be performed by professional players in a range of different settings, at different times, and before different publics. The project required considerable flexibility. As a working playwright, he seems to have thought about the creation of "parts" or roles, often with specific actors in mind though always with the understanding that the personnel might change. Taken all together, of course, the parts made up a whole, but both the individual pieces and the larger structure they formed were and have remained open. The editors of *The Norton Shakespeare* have tried to record and preserve this openness.

Speaking only for myself, I will confess a further ambition: I would like to meet Shakespeare in person. I think that throughout his career Shakespeare produced in effect detachable parts of himself, parts that derived from his personhood (his social relationships, his acquired knowledge, his temperament, his memories, his inner life, and so forth) but that moved independently in the world. He created out of himself hundreds of secondary agents, his characters, some of whom seem even to float free of the particular narrative structures in which they perform their given roles and to take on an agency we ordinarily reserve for biological persons. As an artist he literally gave his life to these agents, transferring his personal energies to them.

I do not mean that Shakespeare's characters are all self-portraits in the sense of referring back to his individual existence (though some of them almost certainly do). I mean rather that Shakespeare's life is, in an unusually intense and vivid way, in his works. And therefore when I open the printed book or scroll through the Digital Edition, I feel his eerie presence and want to call out, with the words Ben Jonson wrote in his dedicatory poem to the First Folio, "My Shakespeare, rise!"

General Textual Introduction

GORDON McMULLAN AND SUZANNE GOSSETT

Most people read an edition of Shakespeare's plays and poems because they want to read the plays and poems, not because they wish to dwell on the material origins of the texts they are reading—where the texts came from, how the manuscripts looked, who printed them, for whom they were printed, how the publishing practices of the English Renaissance made them what they are. Yet attention to the text itself is, we believe, an integral part of understanding the meaning of Shakespeare's works, considerably enhancing the pleasure of the reading experience. Seeing Shakespeare in the theater, reading Shakespeare on the page: both can offer extraordinary, multiply layered experiences of entertainment and intellectual uplift, a sense of unparalleled access to the past, and often simply a great deal of fun. We have edited the text of Shakespeare with these pleasures, and the reader's choices, in mind, and we wish to share with you a sense of the further levels of engagement that close attention to the origins of the text itself can bring.

For us, first and foremost, the *textual* is inseparable from the *critical*. That is, the "themes" we locate in Shakespeare, the sense of the place of the plays and poems in Shakespeare's world and in our own, the ways in which these remarkable writings require us to reflect on being human, on being gendered, on living in community, on having an ethnicity and a class status, all have their foundation in the words we read— and if we don't know whether the words we are reading are the "right" ones, or if we don't have the tools to reflect on the challenges presented by the very idea of "right" words, then we may miss out on key aspects of the Shakespearean experience. The fantasies of the "anti-Stratfordians" (people who claim Shakespeare's works were written by one or another equally implausible candidate) serve to remind us of the obsession of our age with Shakespearean *authenticity,* with the urge to ensure that the Shakespeare we see performed, or that we read or study, is the *real* Shakespeare, the *authentic* Shakespeare. The primary question we address in our textual introduction is central to this debate—"How authentic is the text I am reading?"—and in order to do this we need to reflect on two things: on the nature of the Shakespearean text and on the complex idea of "authenticity." Once we have done that, we can begin to explain some of the decisions we made in editing the texts that together form *The Norton Shakespeare.*

The "Authentic" Shakespeare

For centuries, playgoers and readers had two questions answered for them in advance: which plays and poems to read as "Shakespeare's" (the reader logically assumed that if a play or poem was in the "complete works," then it was Shakespeare's, and if not, not), and, beyond that, which *text* of a given Shakespeare play or poem to read. This second question might seem odd. Surely there is only one *Hamlet* and that is the *Hamlet* Shakespeare wrote? Yet not only does more than one authoritative text of certain plays (above all, as it happens, of *Hamlet*) exist, some of which are very different from each other, but the word "authoritative" raises a third question—notably, "On what grounds do we decide that a printed text is close to what Shakespeare actually wrote?" Moreover, the first of these questions is itself not straightforward. The boundaries of the Shakespeare canon—those texts accepted as being written in whole or in part by Shakespeare—have always been porous. Neither *Pericles* nor *The Two Noble Kinsmen,* for instance, was included in the First Folio, yet both have long been attributed to Shakespeare (in each case, as it happens, to Shakespeare working jointly with another playwright, as pretty much all his fellow Elizabethan and Jacobean playwrights did), and both are now invariably included in "Complete Works" editions. Some plays have been considered part of the Shakespeare canon for far less time. *Edward III,* for instance, now appears in editions as a "Shakespeare and others" play, where a couple of decades ago it did not. Times change, evidence surfaces, and methods of attributing authorship develop. As a result, other plays continue to hover at the edges of the canon. At the time of writing, the newest contender for inclusion is a celebrated play by Thomas Kyd called *The Spanish Tragedy,* for which, it is suggested, Shakespeare supplied extra scenes, capitalizing on the play's success. *The Spanish Tragedy* does not appear in the present edition of *The Norton Shakespeare,* but if in due course we are sufficiently convinced by the arguments for its inclusion, then in it will come. What the French thinker Jacques Derrida called "the logic of the supplement" operates here: each time you add something to a volume called "Complete" you make it *more* complete, but the fact that you needed to add something to complete a volume already claiming to be "complete" has the effect of undermining the very possibility of completeness. For editors of Shakespeare, this is unavoidable—and to be celebrated, not resented.

It is not only the *external* borders of the Shakespeare canon that are fluid; the *internal* borders too—the choice of words within a given play or poem—have never, to the surprise of many readers, been firmly fixed. Shakespeare lovers are aware, perhaps, that Hamlet's flesh is too "solid," "sullied," or "sallied," depending on which version of the play one reads; they may also have wondered which of two "others"—"the base Judean" or "the base Indian"—is the one to which Othello really means to compare himself just before his suicide; but they may not realize that these celebrated instances of Shakespearean textual choice are part of a much broader canvas of instabilities, uncertainties, and options. This means that not only the choice of play, but the choice of *text* of that play, affects the reader's experience of Shakespeare.

The key question arising here is that of the "right" reading, the "authentic" reading, a status usually taken to require a direct relationship to the author. The mental adjustment needed is to accept that, quite often, there may be either *no* "right" reading or *more than one*. We cannot ever know exactly what Shakespeare wrote because (with one limited, debated exception) we do not have the holograph manuscript (a manuscript in his own handwriting) of any of his plays or poems. Shakespeare's own manuscripts of the plays in the First Folio or in the various quartos that predate the Folio have not survived, and so editors are unable to do the one thing they would most like to be able to do, which is to compare what Shakespeare actually wrote with what was printed. The apparent exception is the lines in the surviving manuscript of *Sir Thomas More* that are largely accepted as being in Shakespeare's hand—but, maddeningly, this is the one play in the Shakespeare canon as currently constituted that never found its way into print in the late sixteenth or early seventeenth century. So, even in the case of the one brief section of extant manuscript generally thought to be in Shakespeare's hand, we cannot make a direct comparison between what was written and what was printed.

It was long believed that Shakespeare never revised his texts (a myth prompted by the prefatory material to the First Folio) and therefore that there must have been one, and only one, lost master original from which all subsequent texts derive. But further complicating the notion of the "authentic Shakespeare" is the existence of short, variant quarto texts of several plays. Because certain of these are noticeably inferior to the Folio (or, sometimes, to a fuller quarto) text of the same play, they were traditionally referred to as "bad quartos." In recent years, scholars have sought to replace the unhelpful connotations of "bad" with neutral descriptive terms such as "short quartos," but the point of origin of these texts remains unclear. Are they "authentic"? One long-standing argument has it that they are "reported" texts, the product of "pirate" printers who sat a handful of actors down and persuaded them to recall not only their own lines but the entire play—this, it is claimed, explains the discrepancy in quality between the lines of certain characters in these quartos (e.g., Mercutio in the First Quarto of *Romeo and Juliet*, whose lines are nearly identical to those in the much fuller Second Quarto) and those of others. These quartos vary considerably, from the brief, highly problematic quarto of *The Merry Wives of Windsor* to the much more independent and interpretively convincing First Quarto of *Hamlet*. It has sometimes been proposed that these quartos may represent Shakespeare's early drafts. A further possibility, championed recently as a development of increasing editorial openness to the possibility that Shakespeare did occasionally revise his own work, is that the short quartos represent "theatrical" versions of the plays, whereas the lengthy Folio texts represent more overtly "literary" versions designed with readers in mind. It may be that we will never fully understand how these quartos came to be so different from the fuller, ostensibly more authoritative versions in the First Folio and elsewhere, but it seems essential to present them in all their intriguing difference. Our editorial principles and the technology we adopt in this edition allow us to include fully edited versions of all these quartos, so that the reader may understand the complexity of deciding what constitutes "authentic" Shakespeare.

The Text in the Print House

One reason it is hard to know what Shakespeare actually wrote is that all early modern printed texts include interpretations, adjustments, and misreadings of the manuscripts on which they are based (which may have been the author's own or a neater scribal copy), as well as mechanical errors made by the compositors in the process of setting the type for printing. Moreover, workers in the Renaissance print house did not simply transfer the words passively from writer to reader; they actively intervened in what they printed. There was no fixed way to spell words in Shakespeare's day—Shakespeare himself spelled his own name differently at different times when signing documents—and compositors made the most of this irregularity to even out or "justify" the line they were setting (for example, by adding or removing a final "e" on an individual word). Similarly, there was no sense that the printer's duty was to print exactly what he found in the manuscript with which he was working. On the contrary, since early modern play manuscripts typically included little or no punctuation, it was the job of the compositor setting the type to add punctuation so as to enable and enhance the reader's experience. One of the most misleading of Shakespearean myths, one prevalent among actors even today, is the claim that the punctuation in the First Folio expresses "Shakespeare's instructions to actors": those theater professionals who have carefully timed their pauses and breaths according to the arrangement of commas and semicolons in the First Folio may be sad to learn that they are almost certainly basing their practice on the habits of Compositor A or Compositor J (since we almost never know the names of the workers in the print houses, compositors are usually referred to by letter).

To understand how the printing process affected the texts we read, it helps to know how the two principal formats in which Shakespeare's plays were printed—folio and quarto—were put together. A folio is made up of standard-sized sheets of paper printed with two pages on each side, then folded in half and assembled with several other such folded sheets inserted inside each other to form a "gathering" or "quire"; these gatherings are then stitched together to form the book. A quarto is made of the same standard-sized sheets of paper but is printed with four pages on each side and then folded twice (so that it is a quarter the size of the original sheet and half the size of a folio); each set of four leaves is either stitched together with other sets or inserted into a number of others to form a gathering as with a folio; the gatherings are then sewn through the central fold to form a book (which is why, very occasionally, you might come across a book where some of the pages need cutting apart if the print is to be read; the folding of the sheet to form eight pages will always require two edges to be cut after binding). Try folding a sheet of paper and you will see how this works. If you write the page numbers from one to eight on the folded sheet and then unfold it again, you will see that pages 1, 4, 5, and 8 (the "outer forme") are on one side and 2, 3, 6, and 7 (the "inner forme") are on the other, and that only some pages on each side are printed consecutively. (Scholars in fact tend to specify locations in early printed texts not by page numbers, which are notoriously unreliable in books from Shakespeare's day, but by what are called "signatures," which express the physical construction of the book—that is, the number of leaves collected together as a gathering and the number of gatherings that make up the book. Thus B2, or B2r, signifies the front side—recto—of the second sheet in gathering B, while C3v means the reverse side— verso—of the third sheet in gathering C.) A compositor setting either an inner or an outer form was thus not setting the type in the order of the plot, and you can imagine the loss of understanding this might produce at moments of complication in the text, even in an experienced professional. And then of course there is the Elizabethan equivalent of the coffee break to consider: one compositor would at times take over from another and carry on setting the type, and you can see where this has happened because the new compositor has different habits—his own preferences for abbreviating speech prefixes, say—and in a context where there are two characters with similar names he might misunderstand the speech prefix for the one and set it as the other, thus attributing a speech to the wrong speaker—all of which makes it that much harder to determine the nature of the manuscript from which the compositors were working.

If you look at the illustration on the next page, you can see a visual summary of the print workers' tasks. In the right foreground a boy is examining a forme (the frame into which the type is locked for printing) that has been set with type; he seems to be doing a last check against the manuscript while waiting for the forme to be placed in the press. To the far left, a pair of compositors is setting type from typecases, with the manuscript copy from which they are working stuck to the wall in front of them; behind them, a worker is replacing used type into a typecase arranged alphabetically and vertically ("upper-case" letters, i.e., capitals, at the top, "lower-case" below); to his right, a bespectacled proofreader checks an as-yet-uncorrected sheet against copy; in the background, a figure who is just possibly a woman (there is evidence that women worked in, and sometimes even, as printers' widows, owned, print houses) is using absorbent, wool-stuffed leather balls to apply ink to the forme before it is placed on the bed of the press; and, finally, the pressman pulls the bar across to lower the central weight of the press onto the conjunction of inked type and blank paper and thus imprint the sheet.

The first sheet pulled would be handed to the proofreader for checking, and he would mark errors for correction; when he finished, the press would be stopped, the (now very inky) type adjusted to make the corrections, and the process would then continue. The pressman would, however, keep printing sheets during the twenty minutes it might take the proofreader to work through the proof, and those uncorrected sheets (a hundred or so) would be stacked together indiscriminately with the corrected ones in the overall print run (which was 1,200 or so copies in the case of the First Folio), not separated or discarded. The result is that early printed books are a blend of uncorrected and corrected sheets, and no individual copy of a book such

Unknown engraver, after Stradanus (Jan van der Straet), *Invention of Book Printing,*
from *Nova reperta* (New inventions and discoveries of modern times; ca. 1599–1603).

as the Folio is likely to be exactly the same as any other, given the random distribution of uncorrected sheets. If you look closely at the list of textual variants to this
edition, you will see that editors sometimes note when they have selected a corrected
reading from a copy of the base text other than the primary one from which they are
working.

One printing-house factor likely to affect the text was the need for print workers
to "cast off," that is, to work out how many lines of a given manuscript would fit on a
printed page, and to make pencil annotations in the manuscript to mark where page
breaks would fall in print. Occasionally mistakes would be made, and you can see in
the printed text where either a compositor has realized that he still has a lot of words
to set but little space to play with, and so keeps everything tight, or where he is, by
contrast, running out of words yet still has a fair amount of page to fill, and so
deploys white space, printers' ornaments, and the like. For examples of these composition strategies, see pages 80 and 81.

of Romeo and Iuliet.

On Thurſday next be married to the Countie.
  Iu. : Tell me not Frier that thou hearſt of it,
Vnleſſe thou tell me how we may preuent it.
Giue me ſome ſudden counſell : els behold
Twixt my extreames and me, this bloodie Knife
Shall play the Vmpeere, arbitrating that
Which the Commiſsion of thy yeares and arte
Could to no iſſue of true honour bring.
Speake not, be briefe : for I deſire to die,
If what thou ſpeakſt, ſpeake not of remedie.
  Fr : Stay *Iuliet*, I doo ſpie a kinde of hope,
VVhich craues as deſperate an execution,
As that is deſperate we would preuent.
If rather than to marrie Countie *Paris*
Thou haſt the ſtrength or will to ſlay thy ſelfe,
Tis not vnlike that thou wilt vndertake
A thing like death to chyde away this ſhame,
That coapſt with death it ſelfe to flye from blame.
And if thou dooſt, Ile giue thee remedie.
  Iul : Oh bid me leape (rather than marrie *Paris*)
From off the battlements of yonder tower :
Or chaine me to ſome ſteepie mountaines top,
VVhere roaring Beares and ſauage Lions are :
Or ſhut me nightly in a Charnell-houſe,
VVith reekie ſhankes, and yeolow chaples ſculls :
Or lay me in tombe with one new dead :
Things that to heare them namde haue made me tremble ;
And I will doo it without feare or doubt,
To keep my ſelfe a faithfull vnſtaind VVife
To my deere Lord, my deereſt *Romeo*.
  Fr : Hold *Iuliet*, hie thee home, get thee to bed,
Let not thy Nurſe lye with thee in thy Chamber :
And when thou art alone, take thou this Violl,
And this diſtilled Liquor drinke thou off :
VVhen preſently through all thy veynes ſhall run
A dull and heauie ſlumber, which ſhall ſeaze

             H 3   Each

Q1 *Romeo and Juliet*, H3r. An example of a "tight" page where the casting-off seems to have been efficient.

The excellent Tragedie

Each vitall spirit: for no Pulse shall keepe
His naturall progresse, but surcease to beate:
No signe of breath shall testifie thou liust,
And in this borrowed likenes of shrunke death,
Thou shalt remaine full two and fortie houres,
And when thou art laid in thy Kindreds Vault,
Ile send in hast to *Mantua* to thy Lord,
And he shall come and take thee from thy graue.

  Iul: Frier I goe, be sure thou send for my deare *Romeo*.
            Exeunt.

   Enter olde Capolet, his Wife, Nurse, and
       Seruingman.

  Capo: Where are you sirra?
  Ser: Heere forsooth.
  Capo: Goe, prouide me twentie cunning Cookes.
  Ser: I warrant you Sir, let me alone for that, Ile knowe
them by licking their fingers.
  Capo: How canst thou know them so?
  Ser: Ah Sir, tis an ill Cooke cannot licke his owne fin-
gers.
  Capo: Well get you gone.

      Exit Seruingman.

But wheres this Head-strong?
  Moth: Shees gone (my Lord) to Frier *Laurence* Cell
To be confest.
  Capo: Ah, he may hap to doo some good of her,
A headstrong selfewild harlotrie it is.

              Enter

Q1 *Romeo and Juliet*, H3v. An example of a "loose" page—note the white space and use of the ornament.

These moments of professional adjustment necessarily affect the texts we have inherited, and a close look at the early printed page may explain why lines that seem metrically regular have been set as prose, say, or as fragmented verse lines. Here from the First Quarto of *King Lear* is an example of verse lines that have been squeezed into prose in order to save space:

> *The Historie of King Lear.*
>
> like a riotous Inne;epicurisme,and lust make more like a tauerne
> or brothell, then a great pallace; the shame it selfe doth speake
> for instant remedie; be thou desired by her, that else will take the
> thing shee begs, a little to disquantitie your traine, and the re-
> mainder that shall still depend, to bee such men as may besort
> your age, that know themselues and you.
>
> *Lear.* Darkenes,and Deuils!saddle my horses, call my traine
> together; degenerate bastard, ile not trouble thee; yet haue I left
> a daughter.
>
> *Gon.* You strike my people;and your disordred rabble,make
> seruants of their betters,   *Enter Duke.*
>
> *Lear.* We that too late repent. O sir,are you come?is it your
> will that wee prepare any horses?ingratitude!thou marble har-
> ted fiend, more hideous when thou shewest thee in a child,then
> the Sea-monster; detested kite, thou list my traine, and men of
> choise and rarest parts, that all particulars of dutie knowe, and
> in the most exact regard, support the worships of their name?O
> most small fault, how vgly did'st thou in *Cordelia* shewe, that
> like an engine wrencht my frame of nature from the fixt place;
> drew from my heart all loue,and added to the gall,O *Lear!Lear!*
> beat at this gate that let thy folly in, and thy deere iudgement
> out; goe,goe, my people.
>
> *Duke.* My Lord,I am giltles,as I am ignorant.
>
> *Lear.* It may be so my Lord: harke *Nature*,heare deere God-
> desse; suspend thy purpose, if thou did'st intend to make this
> creature fruitful,into her wombe conuey sterility; drie vp in hir
> the organs of increase,and from her derogate body neuer spring
> a babe to honour her; if shee must teeme, create her childe of
> spleene, that it may liue and bee a thourt disseaturd torment to
> her; let it stampe wrinckles in her brow of youth; with accent
> teares , fret channels in her cheeks;turne all her mothers paines
> and benefits to laughter and contempt, that shee may feele,that
> she may feele, how sharper then a serpents tooth it is, to haue a
> thanklesse child; goe, goe,my people.
>
> *Duke.* Now Gods that we adore, whereof comes this!
>
> *Gon.* Neuer afflict your selfe to know the cause; but let his
> disposition haue that scope that dotage giues it.
>
> *Lear.* What,fiftie of my followers at a clap,within a fortnight?
>
>   D 2   *Duke.*

Q1 *King Lear*, D2r

And here from the First Quarto of *Henry V* is an example of prose that has been set as rough verse (notice how the first word of each line of Fluellen's speeches is capitalized) in order to stretch it out to fill the available space:

of Henry the fift.

So hath he sworne the like to me.

K. How think you *Flewellen*,is it lawfull he keep his oath?

Fl. And it please your maiesty,tis lawful he keep his vow.
If he be periur'd once,he is as arrant a beggerly knaue,
As treads vpon too blacke shues.

Kin. His enemy may be a gentleman of worth.

Flew. And if he be as good a gentleman as Lucifer
And Belzebub,and the diuel himselfe,
Tis meete he keepe his vowe.

Kin. Well sirrha keep your word.
Vnder what Captain seruest thou?

Soul. Vnder Captaine *Gower.*

Flew. Captaine *Gower* is a good Captaine
And hath good littrature in the warres.

Kin. Go call him hither.

Soul. I will my Lord.

Exit souldier.

Kin. Captain *Flewellen*,when *Alonson* and I was
Downe together,*I* tooke this gloue off from his helmet,
Here *Flewellen*, weare it. *If* any do challenge it,
He is a friend of *Alonsons,*
And an enemy to mee.

Fle. Your maiestie doth me as great a fauour
As can be desired in the harts of his subiects,
I would see that man now that should chalenge this gloue:
And it please God of his grace,*I* would but see him,
That is all.

Kin. *Flewellen* knowst thou Captaine *Gower?*

Fle. Captaine *Gower* is my friend.
And if it like your maiestie,*I* know him very well.

Kin. Go call him hither.

Flew. *I* will and it shall please your maiestie.

Kin. Follow *Flewellen* closely at the heeles,
The gloue he weares, it was the souldiers:

F 2

It

Q1 Henry V, F2r

Understanding these print-house procedures clarifies how at each stage of the printing process error and variety may be introduced: at the stage of "casting off," at the stage of setting the type from manuscript (especially if the writer had difficult handwriting), at the stages of proofreading and press correction, and in the assembly of corrected and uncorrected sheets into the book itself. Clearly, we need to be wary of assuming that the material features of the early texts unconditionally transmit "authorial intention."

What Kind of Edition Is This?

Editions always exist for readers. There is no more fundamental question for an editor than "For whom am I editing?" because the answer determines very substantially the nature of the edition produced. No edition can be designed for every imaginable reader; on the contrary, specific kinds of editing are done with specific sets of readers in mind. "Diplomatic" editions, for instance, are designed for scholars: they reproduce all the features of the original text without correction or alteration, but for most readers they would make for an unappealing reading experience. An "old-spelling" edition is another possibility: it is edited (that is, an editor has emended the text where error is apparent and included other aids to reading, such as stage directions), but it remains in the spelling (and, perhaps, the punctuation) of Shakespeare's day and is thus again likely to be difficult going for most contemporary readers. Modern-spelling editions are designed to make early modern texts as accessible as possible: the editor makes necessary corrections to the text, adds stage directions where they are needed to clarify the action, makes consistent certain variable features of the original, and modernizes the spelling and punctuation of those texts (while keeping a close eye on moments when the modernizing of spelling or punctuation might change the actual meaning). It is this latter course—the modern-spelling edition designed to offer maximum accessibility for contemporary readers—that *The Norton Shakespeare* adopts, but with certain developments and enhancements and with a specific set of principles for editorial choice.

We—the team of editors who together created this edition—have edited the works of Shakespeare—that is, the existing early texts—from scratch on the basis of a set of principles known as "single-text editing." The first two editions of *The Norton Shakespeare* were based on the text created in 1986 for Oxford University Press—a groundbreaking edition that transformed the modern editing of Shakespeare—but editorial practice has changed since that time, and Norton has created a new text for the present moment. This text is new both in its physical construction and in its theoretical underpinnings.

First, this, the Third Edition of *The Norton Shakespeare*, is "born digital." That is, we have taken the opportunity offered by the interactive ebook format to offer readers and classroom teachers an unprecedented set of options that will allow them to engage with, not just be passive recipients of, the words before them. The Digital Edition allows readers to open textual and performance comments by clicking on icons in the margin next to the line they are reading; to toggle from the text to a facsimile of the original printed folio or quarto; to hear all the songs scattered through the plays; and to listen to eight hours of selected scenes read by professional actors. In addition, readers can view the Quarto and Folio versions of *King Lear* side by side, scrolling as they choose; side-by-side viewing is also available for selected scenes from six plays and for two versions of a sonnet. Readers using the print and electronic editions in combination will be able to move between thumbing through the printed book and navigating the ebook not only for added portability but also in order to find additional versions of fifteen plays plus many enhancements, not least a selection of Textual Comments designed to underline the interconnections of textual decisions and the meaning of the plays.

Second, this edition adopts a new approach to the Shakespearean text, one made possible in part by the opportunities offered by the digital platform. Our underlying editorial principle has been, at its simplest, to edit the *text*, not the *work*. Let us explain what we mean by this with reference in particular to the plays (though there are similar issues with the sonnets). Shakespeare's plays exist in imperfect ways— none of them ideal, none of them perfectly representing what Shakespeare wrote or what his first audiences heard. Editors have always recognized that these surviving printed texts vary in their origins, though all must bear in some way "traces" of the original literary works that Shakespeare wrote out with quill and paper. Lying behind the surviving texts are, variously, authorial drafts, "fair" or scribal copies, theatrical promptbooks, and occasionally unfinished materials—often a mixture of more than one of these. One older editorial tradition sought to address the imperfections present in the texts as a result of this variable provenance by reconstructing, to a greater or lesser extent, an imagined original, creating an edition that—drawing on their professional knowledge of the writing habits of Shakespeare and his contemporaries, of Elizabethan handwriting, and of the printing process—the editors believed to be nearer to what Shakespeare and his audiences would have known or wanted than the actual surviving text with its flaws and imperfections. Of course editors need to correct many of those flaws and imperfections: to give readers a comprehensible reading experience, you must address errors and other distractions. But we believe it is not necessary or even desirable to try to reconstruct a "perfect" work that may never have existed in this form. Consequently, we have made the decision not to do what editors have normally done for centuries, which is to emend at will by merging the differing elements of distinct early texts of a given play, but rather to provide carefully considered editions of each of the early authoritative texts of works for which more than one such text survives. Similarly, in dealing with plays for which only one text survives, we have stayed as close as possible to that text when sense can be made of it, not adopting a traditional emendation if it appears to us to be the product of editorial preference rather than necessary for sense. In other words, we have chosen to edit the *texts* we actually have, not the *play* or the *poem* we do not, to accept uncertainty, and to exercise a certain skepticism toward earlier claims that sometimes made the editor seem a substitute for Shakespeare.

As we have noted, this edition was "born digital"—that is, we set out to invert the prior hierarchy of page and screen by creating an edition that would reach its fullest potential in digital form. Both the print and the digital editions are, in different ways, "complete works." The print volume includes all the poems, some of which exist in various manuscripts and others in print; there is usually only one form of each of these, though we include the entire *Passionate Pilgrim*, which was falsely ascribed to Shakespeare alone but does include some of his poems in variant forms. It—the print volume—includes all the plays too, providing one text for each play (except for *Hamlet*, for which we offer two editions, the First Quarto and a text merging the Second Quarto with materials from the Folio, and *King Lear*, for which we offer editions of the Quarto and the Folio, plus a merged text including all materials in both: for an account of the inclusion of these merged editions, or "conflations," in an edition based on single-text editing principles, see page 87, below. In deciding which of several texts to include in the bound volume we have used a pragmatic and flexible measure. Rather than (as has been done in the past) claiming to be able to determine and present the text that was Shakespeare's "original" version—or his "final" version, or the one that the company probably performed—we have in the case of plays that exist in significantly different texts printed the text that is most complete and apparently most finished. This often means the text in the First Folio, where about half the plays appear for the first time in the only text we have. But when—as, for example, in the case of *Romeo and Juliet* or of *1 Henry IV*—the Folio text is itself derived from a good quarto, we choose that earlier quarto as the base text from which our print edition is created.

We encourage readers to work with both versions, digital and print, to gain the most possible from *The Norton Shakespeare*. Editing Shakespeare digitally enables us to offer readers the opportunity to read, compare, and contrast the two (or, in the case of *Hamlet*, three) early texts of each of the plays for which multiple texts exist. Whether the plays exist in one substantive text or several, we have taken the same approach to the editing—modernizing spelling and punctuation on principles that are consistent across the edition, providing additional stage directions where they are required to clarify the action, and trusting the original text wherever possible, emending only where absolutely necessary and not "reconstructing" material in addition to that provided by the surviving texts.

The primary impact of these choices is, naturally, on those plays for which more than one early substantive text exists. For instance, we provide (in the Digital Edition) edited texts of Quarto *Othello* and Folio *Othello*—two different texts representing, we believe, two subtly different plays. Even when two separate early texts are nearly identical, the differences can be fascinating. Thus, in *Othello*, the female protagonist, Desdemona, infuriates her father by marrying an older man who is both black and a convert from Islam. Her father, who initially voices a series of racist reasons for assuming that Othello had brainwashed his daughter into eloping with him, sees her as shy and almost worryingly asexual (she has shown no interest in the eligible men he has introduced her to), but Othello's narrative of the process by which he wooed her suggests that she is more actively aware of her sexuality than her father believes: "My story being done, / She gave me for my pains a world of sighs. / [. . .] She thanked me / And bade me, if I had a friend that loved her, / I should but teach him how to tell my story, / And that would woo her" (Q 1.3.145–46, 150–53).

> She gaue me for my paines a world of fighes;
> She fwore Ifaith twas ftrange,twas paffing ftrange ;
> Twas pittifull,twas wondrous pittifull;

Q1 *Othello*, C3v

So the Quarto. The slightly later Folio version of the play alters one key word: "My story being done, / She gave me for my pains a world of kisses" (F 1.3.158–59).

> She gaue me for my paines a world of kiffes:
> She fwore in faith 'twas ftrange : 'twas paffing ftrange,
> 'Twas pittifull: 'twas wondrous pittifull.

F *Othello*, ss5v

Thus there are two equally coherent versions of the same line, different in one small but significant way. By providing editions of both texts, we avoid the necessity of preferring the one reading over the other (male editors have typically preferred "sighs," just as the editorial tradition seems generally to assume, in the phrasing of inserted stage directions, that men kiss women, not that women and men kiss each other), and we open up for our readers a degree of choice—to read the Quarto with its sighing Desdemona or the Folio with its more ardent, kissing Desdemona—and their decision about which version to read will impact the way they see the tragedy unfolding and thus their interpretation of the play. In this way, the study of the material features of the text and of the meaning of the play are inseparable.

This tiny difference between Quarto *Othello* and Folio *Othello* may represent revised authorial intention or some incidental external influence; we cannot know for certain. But there is a category of difference between Quarto and Folio that reminds us that when we read Shakespeare's plays we are dealing with the substantially collaborative process that is theatrical production—and thus with texts that have in various ways gone through the performance process. The severe reduction in Emilia's and Desdemona's parts in act 4 of Quarto *Othello*—the cutting, for instance, of the "Willow Song" that Desdemona sings before she goes to bed for the last time or of Emilia's wry lines about husbands—may be due not to authorial choice, a decision on Shakespeare's part to reduce the prominence of the women at this late stage of the play, but to theatrical necessity, that is, the presumed absence from the King's Men at one point of boy actors with sufficient singing ability or stamina. Often we can only guess at the reasons for such changes, but the point is that they are very often material and environmental, not intentional in the sense of being deliberate changes made for artistic reasons by the author. Yet they cannot be dismissed simply as "inauthentic," not only because we do not know Shakespeare's role at such moments but also because all staged plays are necessarily constructed through collaborative engagement between text and actor. Furthermore, for readers and playgoers across subsequent centuries, these renegotiated texts, offering evidence of multiple inputs for a range of practical reasons, were the "real" Shakespeare. Knowing about the practical processes of playwriting, performance, and printing enables the reader to gain a fuller understanding of the nature of the Shakespearean text as an expression of the highly socialized process of dramatic creativity.

We have noted in passing that, across the centuries, the borders of the Shakespeare canon have been fluid. For a century and a half, the *King Lear* that audiences saw in the theater was not Shakespeare's *King Lear* as we know it, but an adaptation of the play created by Irish poet and playwright Nahum Tate in the late seventeenth century that radically cut and altered the original, even providing a happy ending that suited the theatrical expectations of the day but looks to us bewilderingly inappropriate. Once the popularity of the Tate version had faded, the *King Lear* that audiences began to see reverted to "Shakespeare's *King Lear*"—or, rather, to a particular version of that play, one that editors (and directors) assembled from the two markedly different early texts, Quarto and Folio, by including as many of the different lines as possible from each and merging or "conflating" them into a play a few hundred lines longer than either of the early texts. The paradox is obvious—in the process of trying to present the reader with a "Shakespearean" text, editors produced a text different from either of the ones for which Shakespeare was responsible—yet for readers from the mid-nineteenth to the late twentieth centuries, this elongated version of *King Lear* was the one they read and grew to know and love as "Shakespeare's" play.

This history underpins the decision of *The Norton Shakespeare* to include, alongside editions of the early texts of *Hamlet* and *King Lear*, a further, "scars and stitches" conflated edition of each—that is, an edition of each play that, by way of indentation and a distinctive yet quiet difference in font, makes the process of conflation visible without intruding excessively on the pleasure of the reading experience. We provide these multiple options because they will enable readers to see how these texts changed, developed, and were remade across time. In the case of *King Lear*, it is very possible that Shakespeare was involved in reworking his tragedy a couple of years after he had first written it and it had gone into regular production, and readers can reflect on that dynamic process by comparing the two early versions; equally, they can choose to read the "scars and stitches" edition, which both replicates the experience of nineteenth- and twentieth-century readers who came to know the play through traditional conflated editions and makes visible the process through which that conflation was achieved. Thus in the Digital Edition we offer three versions of *King Lear*—and four of *Hamlet*—so as to enable readers to witness the dynamic and contingent processes that go into the bringing-into-the-present of Shakespeare's plays.

"Single-Text Editing" and the Treatment of Error

The Norton Shakespeare seeks to minimize intervention by the editor, but there are nonetheless occasions when the editor must assist the reader in making sense of the text and where it is not immediately obvious how to do so. In order to explain our decision making at such moments, we will offer some examples. Readers will see that for all texts in this edition, both print and digital, we offer in the Digital Edition a set of Textual Variants, compressed notes in which editors mark each moment where the edited version is in some way different from the "base text," that is, from the original quarto or folio text from which the edition is formed, specifying where the preferred word or other feature originates—from another early text, or from the editorial tradition, or from our own choice. No edition of a Shakespeare play can simply present the exact words of its base text, because no early text is free from error or complication. How many times, after all, reading a modern printed book, have you spotted errors, omissions, or typos? Even with the vast technological transformations since Shakespeare's death, the printing process remains flawed; so you would expect that any text printed in (or somewhat after) Shakespeare's day—created on a manually operated press using fiddly metal type set by hand in wooden frames, in often cramped conditions, using toxic ink, and always under pressure to speed up the process to keep the business afloat—would include a fair number of such errors. As we have noted, the print-house workers were actively involved in the creation of the Shakespearean text, an involvement that is by no means limited to error—but human error is inevitable and pervasive.

Consequently, editors working on the basis of single-text editing must always balance their commitment to the text against the possibility of error. Our basic premise is that the editor should not attempt to alter or "improve"—by following a different text, the editorial tradition, or her own informed invention—any reading that can make sense, even if that meaning seems a little strained. While such difficulties may arise from print-house errors, they may instead be signs of the semantic or syntactical differences between our current version of the English language and that of the late sixteenth and early seventeenth centuries. Single-text editing compels editors—and their readers—to make an effort to understand the given text, rather than to slide into something apparently more familiar. This is known as the principle of the "harder reading" (in Latin, *lectio difficilior*), and it expresses our urge not to risk obliterating the powerful specificity and difference of Shakespeare's works, even as it remains the editor's task to address error when it is undoubtedly present.

The multiplicity of early authoritative texts sometimes confronts the editor adhering to single-text-editing principles with difficult decisions. For example, at one point in the Folio text of *Troilus and Cressida,* Thersites is abusing Patroclus: "Let thy bloud be thy direction till thy death," he sneers, "then, if she that laies thee out sayes thou art a fair coarse [i.e., corpse], I'll be sworne and sworne upon't, she never shrowded any but Lazars." The earlier Quarto reads the central section as follows: "if she that layes thee out sayes thou art not a fair course," and it seems clear that the Folio corrects the Quarto reading, since the "not" makes nonsense of the meaning ("You'll be so ugly by the time you die that if the person laying out your corpse says you're beautiful then the only possible conclusion would be that the dead bodies she usually buries must all be lepers"). The editor therefore emends by removing the "not" from her Quarto edition on the grounds that while single-text editing normally requires her to maintain differences between cognate texts—that is, between texts of the same play that have reached us through different processes of transmission—she must not do this at the expense of sense.

By contrast, the two texts of *King Lear* provide a fine instance of the presence or absence of a word—again, as it happens, "not"—offering equal sense in two cognate texts. At the very end of the long first scene in the Folio, Lear's daughters Goneril and Regan talk together about their aging father's increasingly erratic behavior, and

Goneril notes that "the obseruation we haue made of it hath beene little"—an expression of regret for not taking notice of these mood swings before they led to the current crisis:

> *Gon.* You fee how full of changes his age is, the ob-
> feruation we haue made of it hath beene little; he alwaies
> lou'd our Sifter moft, and with what poore iudgement he
> hath now caft her off, appeares too groffely.

F *King Lear*, qq3r

In the Quarto, however, Goneril notes that "the obseruation we haue made of it hath *not* bin little" (our italics)—that is, that the sisters have in fact been aware of the problem for quite a while:

> *Gon.* You fee how full of changes his age is the obferuation we
> haue made of it hath not bin little; hee alwaies loued our fifter
> moft, and with what poore iudgement hee hath now caft her
> off, appeares too groffe.

Q1 *King Lear*, C1r

It is this earlier version that is invariably chosen by conflating editors and is thus the reading that those who already know *King Lear* will recognize. Yet it is not the only meaningful option. Both readings make sense, even if one is less familiar, and the advantage of single-text editing is that the editor is not forced to choose one option and thus to dilute the possibilities for meaning on both page and stage.

We briefly mentioned earlier one of the best-known cruxes in *Othello,* the moment at which the protagonist, just prior to his suicide, compares himself to a racial other who also failed to recognize the extraordinary value of what he had until he lost it. In the Quarto, the lines read "one whose hand, / Like the base *Indian*, threw a pearle away, / Richer then all his Tribe"; this has, marginally, been the version preferred by editors across time:

> Perplext in the extreame ; of one whofe hand,
> Like the bafe *Indian*, threw a pearle away,
> Richer then all his Tribe : of one whofe fubdued eyes,

Q1 *Othello*, N2r

In the Folio, the lines read "one, whose hand / (Like the base Iudean) threw a Pearle away / Richer then all his Tribe"—the "Judean" here probably being associated with Christ's betrayer, Judas Iscariot, and thus, for Shakespeare's audiences, with Jews in general:

> Perplexed in the extreame : Of one, whofe hand
> (Like the bafe Iudean) threw a Pearle away
> Richer then all his Tribe : Of one, whofe fubdu'd Eyes,

F *Othello*, vv5v

Note two elements here. First, the punctuation differs; neither version can be said to be either *better* or *more authorial* than the other in this regard (the parentheses in the Folio, for instance, are probably the preference of the King's company scribe, Ralph Crane, who transcribed several plays for inclusion in the Folio). Second, the difference between "*Indian*" and "Iudean" could be attributed to two kinds of easy error: a misreading of a scratchy secretary-hand "i" for "e" (or vice versa)—

Sample minuscules in secretary hand from Ronald B. McKerrow, *An Introduction to Bibliography for Literary Students*, Oxford 1927.

—and an accidental inversion of the individual type "n" for "u" (or vice versa) by the compositor. The vice versas underline the impossibility of deciding which is "correct," and the presence in *The Norton Shakespeare* of editions of both early texts removes the need for the imposition of editorial preference.

Single-text editing thus seeks to minimize editorial intervention while remaining aware of the needs of the reader and offering clarification (e.g., in the form of expanded or inserted stage directions, which we mark with square brackets) of action, speaker, or other elements of the original that may delay the reader's progress through the play. For these pragmatic reasons, we have chosen to maintain certain traditional overarching elements that could be considered to run counter to the theory of single-text editing. An instance is our division of almost all play texts into acts and scenes, an editorial practice that dates back to the eighteenth century. Such neat divisions are by no means always present in the base texts—either in the Folio, which is not always consistent or precise in its divisions (*Love's Labor's Lost,* for instance, has two different acts marked "*Actus Quartus*"; Folio *Hamlet* stops marking act divisions after act 2), or in the various quartos, many of which either mark scene divisions only or offer no divisions or numbers at all. Act divisions only became fully formalized with the development of indoor playhouses, where the necessity of trimming the candles every half-hour or so required breaks in the action; they thus apply far less to Elizabethan plays than to Jacobean. Our working premise for this edition, however, is that many of our readers will wish to locate scholarly discussions of these plays by critics who, almost without exception, cite speeches by act and scene number; thus, we offer act and scene numbers for all main texts and reserve scene divisions only for a handful of quartos that do not fall into the usual divisions.

The single-text editor's task is not necessarily more straightforward when she is dealing with plays with only one early authoritative text. One of the key questions anyone editing on single-text-editing principles has to ask is when to emend and when to leave alone. An instance comes in *All's Well That Ends Well*, which opens (in our modernized version) with this stage direction:

> *Enter young* BERTRAM, *Count of Roussillon, his mother* [*the Dowager* COUNTESS], *and* HELEN, *Lord* LAFEU, *all in black.*

The "*and*" seems to be in an odd place here; that is, you might expect it to be positioned between "HELEN" and "*Lord*," completing the list. Yet it comes instead between "*Mother*" and "HELEN." Is this simply a mistake by the compositor? It could easily be. Often, editors simply move the "*and*" to what seems to be the logical place between "HELEN" and "*Lord*." But what if there is a different logic to its positioning? It might be that Shakespeare is using the conjunction to separate two pairs: to connect Bertram and his mother on the one hand, and Helen and Lafeu on the other. Equally, the "*and*" might serve to connect the Countess and Helen, a connection that proves particularly resilient in the action to follow. Rather than limit the possibilities, we leave the stage direction as it is in the Folio, simply modernizing and standardizing the names and clarifying (with "dowager") that the Countess is the widow of Bertram's father. A theater director might wish to think about the staging options this stage direction offers.

All of these editorial challenges inevitably require the creation of something hybrid, something impure, despite the earnest intentions of the regularizing editor. Editing is always negotiation, and it is always compromise. This does not mean it is slapdash or arbitrary; on the contrary, it must be exceptionally precise, requiring a level of patience and concentration that is not everyone's forte. The paradox for editors is that the outcome of good work—words or lines or stage directions that took a great deal of experience, research, and agonizing to establish—will be simply, and rightly, invisible to the reader. In this, the editor's lot is not so very different—structurally, if not creatively—from that of the collaborating playwright. Effective collaboration is about effacing the joins between the work of different contributors—we presume that Shakespeare and Fletcher, composing *Henry VIII* and *The Two Noble Kinsmen* together, would not have wanted audience members to register when the writing of a given scene switched from the one to the other—and the quiet collaboration across time that is the work of the editor ought by definition to be hidden, at least in the case of editions created for the general reader and the advanced student who do not want or need the intrusion of the mediator.

Shakespeare and the Multiplication of Meaning

Most people, reading a Shakespeare poem or play, have in mind the question "What did Shakespeare mean here?" as they reflect on the words, especially if the words are not easy to make sense of. Despite the profound ways in which the Romantic construction of authorship as a process of untrammeled, transcendent individual inspiration has been questioned and deconstructed over the last half-century, the general understanding of the processes of writing, as of all forms of creativity, remains firmly bound up with ideas of intention, of textual "ownership," of the creative artist as "author"— that is, as the sole source of "authority" in respect of the form and meaning of a given text. We have tried in this introduction to suggest that the meanings of Shakespeare's plays and poems have a wider range of starting points, emerge from a more complex, varied, and fascinating creative base, than simply what the poet himself "meant"—in other words, that Shakespearean "authenticity" is a multivalent concept, one that includes at its core what the author meant but also a range of other, contiguous collaborations, negotiations, and origins for meaning. The Shakespearean text is fluid and multiple, and the nature of the engagement of both editor and reader with that text should, we believe, follow suit. We have much to gain by being open to the increased possibilities this transformed understanding can bring. The very words themselves are, in so many ways, unfixed in their meanings; the ways through which they came into the public domain in Shakespeare's own day—in manuscript, on the stage, in the various print formats available to those seeking to profit from publication—are also multiple; and the ways in which the plays and poems have been presented and re-presented in subsequent centuries make "multiple" seem a gross understatement. Shakespeare seems to have re-thought and re-imagined his own writings; his colleagues in the King's Men negotiated and adapted his work to suit conditions; publishers printed it in a range of ways, official and unofficial, working with Shakespeare himself on the poems if not on the plays (we have no evidence that Shakespeare—unlike his friend and rival Ben Jonson—oversaw the printing of his plays, whereas he clearly did pay attention to the publication of his poems), and his former colleagues gathered most, though not all, of the plays into a single, rather grandiose Folio in 1623, initiating the long tradition of editing the works to make them available for the "great variety of readers." *The Norton Shakespeare* offers its readers a set of options for reading and understanding Shakespeare that makes the most both of the digital technologies and of the editorial practices of the present, giving the reader choices—of text, of taxonomy, of glossarial support—and in the process providing the means for a new generation actively to discover, engage with, learn from, and—above all—be thrilled and moved by these astonishing works in all their fabulous multiplicity.

The Theater of Shakespeare's Time

HOLGER SCHOTT SYME

Early modern London was a theatrical city like no other, as the travel writer Fynes Moryson proudly proclaimed: "as there be, in my opinion, more plays in London than in all parts of the world I have seen, so do these players or comedians excel all others in the world." Moryson wrote just after Shakespeare's death, around 1619, but the world of playacting he described had thrived in and around England's capital long before Shakespeare arrived there. The decades between 1567, when the first theater built in England since the Romans opened its doors, and 1642, when playacting was prohibited by Parliament, saw an unprecedented and still unparalleled flourishing of theatrical artistry. Moryson's account emphasizes not just the quality of London's actors, but also the sheer quantity of plays on offer: as far as he was concerned, there was more theater in the city than anywhere else in the world. The historical record bears out his impression. English acting companies, driven by a constant hunger for new work, kept dozens of dramatists busy writing a staggering number of plays—more than 2,500 works, of which just over 500 survive. Theaters sprang up all around London in the 1570s. Throughout Shakespeare's career, there were never fewer than four acting venues in operation; some years, up to nine theaters were competing for audiences. Different spaces and different companies catered to different tastes and income brackets: the tiny indoor location of the Boys of St. Paul's, an acting company of youths, could accommodate fewer than 100 of the wealthy courtiers and law students who were their typical spectators; the Swan Theater, on the other hand, the largest of the open-air venues that were the most common type of theater in Shakespeare's London, had room for over 3,000 people from all social backgrounds. The theater was rich and varied, an engine of artistic experiment and a place where traditions flourished; it was an art form both elite and popular; it provided entertainment for kings and queens even as their governments worried that it was difficult to control, attracting large and boisterous crowds and posing a threat to public health during plague outbreaks.

In London, theater was everywhere. But *what* was it? Who performed it, where, under what circumstances, using what methods and techniques, and for whom?

History

Before we can approach these questions, a few words about historical evidence are in order. Theater is a transitory art, not designed to leave behind lasting records or traces; it is, as Shakespeare never tired of noting, a kind of dream. In Shakespeare's time, it was a pursuit about which the government cared only intermittently, and was therefore rarely the subject of official recordkeeping. Much of what we know about playhouses and acting companies derives from squabbles over money and the lawsuits that followed. What information survives is just enough to make theater historians realize how much has been lost. For instance, with few exceptions, we do not know who performed which roles. We cannot name a single character Shakespeare played. Even for the most famous actors of the age, we can list at most a handful of parts. Nor do we

93

know how popular most of Shakespeare's plays were. His history plays, more than his tragedies or comedies, sold well as books—but did they do as well on stage? We would like to think so, but without attendance records, we cannot know for sure. *Much Ado About Nothing* was never reprinted on its own after its initial publication in 1600. Does that mean it was a theatrical flop too? Probably not—else why print it at all? But we cannot be certain.

One extant document contains a tremendous amount of information: Philip Henslowe's business record, known as his *Diary*. Henslowe was a financier who owned three theaters and served as a financial manager of sorts for the acting companies that rented his venues. The *Diary* includes performance records from 1592 through 1597, mostly for the Lord Admiral's Men. It allows us to get a sense of this company's business practices, its repertory of plays, its inventory of props and costumes, and its dealings with playwrights and artisans. And the *Diary* makes us realize just how many plays have disappeared: it mentions about 280 titles, of which at most 31 survive.

This may all sound rather depressing, as if the story of Shakespeare's theater were ultimately irretrievable. But it is not. We can interpret archaeological discoveries; extrapolate from extant records such as Henslowe's or the accounts of court officials; trace contemporary responses to the theater in letters, diaries, satires, and polemics; and study plays and their stage directions to understand what features playwrights expected in playhouses and how they intended to use them. We can make the most of what survives to construct a tentative and careful, but not baseless, narrative of what this world may have been like.

Playhouses

Theater in Shakespeare's London was predominantly an outdoor activity. Most playhouses were open-air spaces much larger than the few indoor venues. The building simply called The Theatre, in the suburb of Shoreditch, north of the City of London, created a model in 1576 that many playhouses would follow for the next forty years. It was a fourteen-sided polygonal structure, nearly round, with an external diameter of about seventy-two feet; audiences stood in the open yard or sat in one of three galleries. There was probably a permanent stage, which thrust out into the yard, with the galleries behind it serving as a balcony over the performance area and, where they were walled off, providing a backstage area (the "tiring house" in early modern terminology). The Theatre may not have had a roof over its stage. The Rose Theater in Southwark, across the Thames from the City of London, was built without such a roof in 1587; one was added during renovations in 1592. The shape of the stage also changed over time: archaeological excavations have shown that the Rose's original stage was relatively shallow, not extending far into the yard. In 1592, the space was redesigned to allow the stage to thrust out farther, creating a deeper playing area surrounded by standing spectators on three sides. This model would be followed in later playhouses, but whereas the Rose's stage (and probably those of other early theaters as well) tapered toward the front, later ones were rectangular and thus quite large. Judging from the erosion around the stage area in the excavated Rose, audiences responded with enthusiasm to the new configuration, pressing as close to the action as possible.

This first generation of playhouses also included The Theatre's close neighbor in Shoreditch, the Curtain, built in 1577 and named not after a stage curtain, which these theaters did not have, but after its location, the "Curtain Estate." The Theatre, the Curtain, and the Rose resembled one another in size and shape and had room for 2,000–2,500 spectators. The next generation of theaters did not depart from the earlier model in shape, but anticipated larger crowds. The Swan (1595), the Globe (1599), and the last outdoor theater erected in London, the Hope (1613), had a capacity of about 3,000. They were impressive buildings not just because of their size but

This view of London's northern suburbs shows the Curtain playhouse (the three-story polygonal structure with the flag on the left). It aptly illustrates the almost rural location of these early theaters: the Curtain stands adjacent to farmhouses and windmills.

also because they were beautifully decorated, as foreign visitors reported. Johannes de Witt, a Dutchman, described the Swan in 1596 as an "amphitheater of obvious beauty," admiring its wooden columns painted to look like marble.

Although some of the later playhouses modified the formula set by The Theatre, all the open-air venues shared a common spatial and social logic. They all separated their audience into those standing in the yard (the "groundlings" or "understanders"), who paid a penny to enter the theater, and those who sat in one of the galleries, paying two pennies for the lower level or three for the upper levels, where the benches had cushions. The most exclusive seats, at sixpence, were in the "lords' rooms," probably located in the sections of the galleries closest to the stage, and possibly in the balcony over the stage. Fashionable gallants and wealthy show-offs could also sit on the stage itself, paying an additional sixpence for a stool. Neither the "lords' rooms" nor the stools onstage gave the best view of the play, but they provided unparalleled opportunities to put fancy clothes on display: these were seats for being seen. Stage-sitting was often satirized as a vain and foolish habit, and the groundlings evidently objected to the rich fops blocking their view. As Shakespeare's contemporary Thomas Dekker describes the scene at one of the outdoor theaters, the "scarecrows in the yard hoot at you, hiss at you, spit at you, yea, throw dirt even in your teeth: 'tis most Gentlemanlike patience to endure all this, and to laugh at the silly animals."

The theaters, though hierarchically structured, were unusually inclusive: audience members from all social spheres could gain admission and enjoy the same spectacles. Social hierarchies became dangerously porous in this shared space, as Dekker's stage-sitters experienced firsthand: the commoners in the yard could hurl abuse and even dirt at the gentle and noble audience members onstage. Lords had to suffer close proximity with their social inferiors. However, the playhouses' inclusiveness had limits, too: the poor and royalty were unlikely to enter a theater. Neither Queen Elizabeth I nor King James I ever did.

Purpose-built theaters were not the only places where plays were performed. From the mid-1570s on, four inns also regularly hosted acting companies: the Bell, the Bull, the Cross Keys, and the Bell Savage. Only one of them, the Bell, seems to have had an indoor hall for play performances; the others had yards in which a stage could be erected. These yards had open galleries to give guests access to rooms on the upper floors, so that the overall structure of the auditorium was similar to the theaters: an open yard surrounded by galleries, at least some of which would have had benches. Unlike the theaters, however, which stood in the suburbs surrounding London, the inns were within or just outside the city walls. This location made them favored acting sites in the winter, when the roads were unpredictable and the days

A Victorian photograph of the Elizabethan galleried yard of the White Hart Inn in Southwark, similar to the layout of the inns used for performing plays.

were short, making it difficult for audience members to return to the City before the gates were shut at nightfall. But the inns irked London authorities. No venues other than churches allowed for the assembly of as many people as inn yards did, and play performances could attract particularly unruly crowds. For the authorities, these places created a threat of public disorder right in the heart of the City, and for over two decades, Lord Mayors and aldermen made intermittent attempts to shut down acting at the inns. It seems they succeeded by 1596, since references to regular performances in those venues cease after that year.

No adult acting company regularly performed in an indoor space in London between 1576 and 1610. There were a number of such venues, though, notably a very small theater near St. Paul's Cathedral, with room for only a select few, and a somewhat larger space inside the former Blackfriars friary. Both were active in the 1570s and 1580s, when two children's companies used them—acting troupes made up of choirboys from the royal chapels and St. Paul's Cathedral. By the time Shakespeare arrived in London, however, the old Blackfriars had closed, and neither space was used during the 1590s. But the boys' companies started performing again around the turn of the century, acting exclusively indoors.

This reemergence lies behind the conversation between Rosencrantz and Hamlet about the "eyrie of children" that produce plays mocking "the common stages." Although the boys' companies could not seriously jeopardize the adult troupes' economic success, their reappearance around 1600 apparently made their grown-up competitors look unfashionable among the trendiest patrons. Exclusivity was the hallmark of these companies and their indoor theaters, which were referred to as "private" playhouses; unlike the "common" theaters, these venues kept the wider world out both architecturally and socially. Entrance fees were much higher, probably starting at sixpence (the price of the costliest seats in the open-air theaters) and going up to over two shillings.

The boys also performed less frequently than the adult companies. They made the most of their elite status, thriving on satirical plays and a willingness to court controversy that sometimes landed them in hot water with persons of influence. Their financial situation was as unstable as their favor with the authorities. When King James, in March 1608, shut down the children's company that was using a recently constructed theater inside the former Blackfriars monastery, he unwittingly made theater history. Soon thereafter, the decades-old division between outdoor adult and indoor boys' companies came to an end. In 1610, near the end of Shakespeare's career, the King's Men adopted the Blackfriars as a second venue. Even after that, however, most audiences would still have experienced plays in the outdoor playhouses that remained the most popular, accessible, and visible acting venues in and around London.

Companies and Repertories

What was an acting company in Shakespeare's time? Formally, a group of players serving a noble patron. A law of 1572 had forced performers to find official sponsors to avoid legal prosecution as "vagrants" and "masterless men." That is why the troupe with which Shakespeare was associated for most of his documented career was first known as the Lord Chamberlain's Servants, and after 1603 as the King's Servants: these actors were officially servants of the Lord Chamberlain (the member of the Privy Council in charge of the royal household), and later of King James I. (Modern scholars generally refer to these companies as the Lord Chamberlain's Men and the King's Men.) All companies resident in London for at least part of the year were associated with high-ranking noblemen. After 1603, most of these troupes came under royal patronage, formally serving the King, the Queen, or a member of their family.

In all likelihood, the connection between patrons and companies was fairly loose, although the players technically formed part of their patrons' households. Take the example of James's son-in-law, the Count Palatine: his troupe, the Palsgrave's Men, operated under that name from 1613 to 1632, although their supposed patron only lived in England for a few months from 1612 to 1613. Links may have been closer where companies were sponsored by nobles of lower rank, as was common throughout the kingdom. Dozens of these groups appear in contemporary records. They toured the towns, cities, and stately homes surrounding their lords' seats, returning at Christmas to entertain families and guests. Whether they visited London is unclear, as is the question of what plays they performed; but some of them were so active on the road that they probably traveled to the country's biggest city as well.

What most defined a company were its leading members: the actors who would typically take on all major roles and who jointly owned the troupe's stock of costumes, props, and, crucially, play scripts. There were between six and a dozen of these "sharers." They not only formed the heart of any acting company, but also had an immediate financial interest in its success, as they divided the weekly profits among themselves. But there was more to a troupe of actors than its sharers. When the King's Men received their royal patent, or license, in 1603, the document not only identified the nine sharers (Shakespeare among them) as "servants" of James I, but also recognized that those servants required further "associates" to stage plays. These hired actors could in some cases be as closely associated with a company as the sharers. John Sinncklo, for example, was a member of the Chamberlain's Men for most of their existence and is mentioned by name in the stage directions to three of Shakespeare's plays. He was apparently an extraordinarily thin man and is often linked with very skinny characters—in *1 Henry IV* he played the Beadle whom Doll Tearsheet calls a "thin man in a censer." Sinncklo was a fixture of Chamberlain's Men productions for playwrights and audiences alike, and an integral part of their identity. Yet despite this status,

Sincklo continued to be an employee rather than an owner of the company for the rest of his recorded life.

The theatrical power of one other set of actors likewise outstripped their institutional power within the company: the male youths who played all female roles. These "boys"—in reality, adolescents who would not have started acting before they were twelve or thirteen and sometimes continued into their early twenties—were associated with the companies as sharers' apprentices. In effect, therefore, none of the actors who played Shakespeare's great female roles, from Tamora to Lady Macbeth to Hermione, were officially members of an acting troupe; rather, they belonged to a sharer's household. Each boy was contracted to serve his master for at least seven years, in return for instruction, room, and board. But officially, they would not have been in training as actors, since there was no guild for actors (and thus no official training available). Instead, they formally became apprentices in the trade governed by the guild to which their master belonged. For example, John Heminges, one of the leading sharers in Shakespeare's troupe, was a member of the Company of Grocers, the guild that oversaw that trade. Over thirty years, he had about ten apprentices. Since Heminges did not actually work as a grocer, these youths were probably boy actors, being trained as stage performers. If they completed their term, though, they could pay a fee and become "freemen" of the Company of Grocers and citizens of London— positions that came with many legal advantages and privileges. Although many boy actors did not become leading men, the social status they gained by formally completing an apprenticeship left them free to make their way in life after their careers as players had ended.

Although increasingly integrated into London's social life over the course of Shakespeare's career, most acting companies also spent part of the year touring market towns and stately homes. Acting was frowned upon if not strictly forbidden in London during Lent, the forty days or so before Easter, and companies had to go elsewhere to secure an income then; there was also a long-standing custom of traveling during the summer, when days were longer and roads more reliable (see the map of touring routes in the map appendix, below). Many companies only knew this itinerant existence, and it was their work that the young Shakespeare may have seen in Stratford. But around the time he began working as a theater professional some companies had started to regard London as their home. By the 1590s, that group included Lord Strange's Men, the Admiral's Men, and the Earl of Pembroke's Men. They established long-term relationships with the owners of playhouses where they performed more or less permanently. The Admiral's Men became associated with the Rose and later the Fortune, both theaters belonging to Philip Henslowe. The Chamberlain's Men, founded in 1594, started at The Theatre, owned by James Burbage (whose son Richard would soon emerge as the troupe's young star). Pembroke's Men may have been the resident company at the Swan once that playhouse opened in 1595. A further troupe probably occupied the Curtain. By 1599 yet another company, the Earl of Derby's Men, took up residence at the Boar's Head. In fact, so many acting troupes

Money was collected in small, round earthenware containers that had to be smashed after a performance. Many fragments of these were found during the excavation of the Rose playhouse.

performed in London that there were never fewer than four venues in operation during Shakespeare's career, and in some years the city sustained nine theaters.

The proprietors of most of those playhouses rented their buildings to the actors for a share of the revenues: half the takings from the galleries belonged to the landlord, while the sharers in the company retained all income from the yard and the other half of the takings from the galleries. Troupes and theater owners thus divided profits as well as risk: if a play flopped, the landlord also lost income, just as he gained from popular offerings. Some owners, Henslowe in particular, acted as the company's financial manager, keeping stock of belongings and conducting transactions on the actors' behalf.

Despite the great variety of playhouses and acting companies, or perhaps because of it, some venues developed specific profiles. This happened surprisingly early in the history of London theater. Writing in 1579, the antitheatrical polemicist Stephen Gosson excluded some plays from his general criticism, praising two "shown at the Bull"; two others "usually brought into the Theater"; and especially "the two prose books played at the Bell Savage, where you shall find never a word without wit, never a line without pith, never a letter placed in vain." Within a few years of opening, then, two of the inns and The Theatre were already known for specific plays one could expect to see there—whereas the four venues Gosson does not mention may have staged precisely the kinds of plays of which he disapproved.

All the same, few playhouses or acting companies were famous exclusively for a handful of titles or a particular kind of drama. The repertories of most troupes, including the Chamberlain's Men and King's Men, were inclusive in their approach to themes and genres and combined old favorites with new and potentially challenging material. The King's Men's 1603 patent describes them as performing not only "comedies, tragedies, histories"—the kinds of plays we might expect from Shakespeare's company—but also "interludes, morals, pastorals." Shakespeare's works do not represent all these categories, and they likely do not represent the full range of shows his troupe staged. If Henslowe's *Diary* is a reliable model, companies commissioned ten to twenty plays each year, and new plays dominated their repertory. If a play failed to draw crowds, it disappeared quickly. If it had staying power, it would remain in circulation for a while, but few became recognized classics destined to be revived every couple of years. In general, it seems that audiences enjoyed periodically reencountering older scripts, but had a more voracious appetite for fresh material—although old stories might frequently return in novel versions. Companies would produce their own take on plays from competing repertories: the Admiral's Men paid Ben Jonson in 1602 for a script about Richard III, for instance; and the Chamberlain's Men bought Jonson's *Every Man in His Humor* in 1598, probably hoping to capitalize on a 1597 hit at the Rose, George Chapman's *Comedy of Humors*. Even a single troupe's repertory might feature multiple plays drawn from the same stories or materials. The King's Men owned another *Richard II* play, which they staged at the Globe in April 1611—within weeks of performances of *Macbeth*, *Cymbeline*, and *The Winter's Tale*. Of those three Shakespearean offerings, the latter two were then still quite new; but *Macbeth* would have been a revival, an indication that it was a success when first performed.

The repertory system required daily turnover. Staging the same play for days at a time, let alone for weeks, was practically unheard of. The nine consecutive performances of Thomas Middleton's *A Game at Chess* at the Globe in 1624 were described as extraordinary at the time—nowadays, of course, a run of nine nights would be notable for its brevity. We can get a glimpse of what a typical selection of shows would have looked like in Shakespeare's company from Henslowe's *Diary*, which contains the only surviving sample of the Chamberlain's Men's repertory (staged in collaboration with the Admiral's Men in June 1594):

MON 3 June	*Hesther and Ahasuerus*
TUE 4 June	*The Jew of Malta*
WED 5 June	*Titus Andronicus*

THU 6 June	*Cutlack*
SAT 8 June	*Belin Dun*
SUN 9 June	*Hamlet*
MON 10 June	*Hesther and Ahasuerus*
TUE 11 June	*The Taming of a Shrew*
WED 12 June	*Titus Andronicus*
THU 13 June	*The Jew of Malta*

The two companies performed seven different plays in ten days. Of those, two were tragedies based on fictional plots (*The Jew of Malta* and *Titus Andronicus*), two were tragedies set in the distant northern European past (*Cutlack* and *Hamlet*—the latter not Shakespeare's version), one was a biblical drama (*Hesther and Ahasuerus*), one was a history or tragedy drawn from the English chronicles (*Belin Dun*, about a high-wayman hanged by King Henry I), and one was a comedy (*The Taming of a Shrew*—again, not Shakespeare's). One play was brand-new (*Belin Dun*); one recent (*Titus Andronicus*, first performed in January 1594); two quite old (*The Jew of Malta* and *The Taming of a Shrew* were probably written before 1590); and we know nothing about the others.

The two companies' combined offerings constitute a representative mixture of old and new; of different geographical settings and historical periods; of tragic, heroic, moral, and comedic entertainments. Variety was a predictable feature of any company's stock of plays. Predictability, however, was not. For theatergoers keen to see a performance of *Titus* after its successful June 5 outing, finding out when the play was going to be mounted next was neither easy nor straightforward (we now know that their next chance would have come on June 12). They may have relied on word of mouth, as the actors commonly announced the next day's play at the end of a show; they might have encountered the players marching through the City in the morning hours, advertising that day's performance; or they may have read the news on one of the playbills posted daily all over the City to inform audiences what was being staged where. But would-be spectators had to keep their eyes peeled: while repertories responded to popular demand, they did not follow an easily foreseeable schedule. Since *Titus* did well, it would certainly be back onstage soon. But exactly when was uncertain.

Why Shakespeare's Company Was Different

The playhouse in which the Chamberlain's Men and the King's Men performed after 1599, the Globe, was a unique building project. In 1597 James Burbage's lease for the land on which The Theatre stood ran out, and a year later the Chamberlain's Men were forced to vacate the premises and move to the neighboring Curtain. The building itself, however, still belonged to Burbage, and after his death in 1597, to his sons Cuthbert and Richard, the latter Shakespeare's fellow sharer. The Burbages therefore took the extraordinary step of having a carpenter dismantle the structure and use the salvaged timber to build a new playhouse. This would be erected on a plot of land on the other side of London, south of the river and across the street from Henslowe's Rose Theater. This new theater, the Globe, would be significantly bigger than its predecessor. As archaeological digs have revealed, it was probably a sixteen-sided polygon with a diameter of about eighty-five feet, nearly fourteen feet more than The Theatre's. It was operational by September 1599, when the Swiss traveler Thomas Platter saw a performance of *Julius Caesar* at what he called "the straw-thatched house"—almost certainly the Globe, which had a thatched roof over the galleries and stage.

Opening a new playhouse right next to the small and aging Rose might look like an aggressive gesture on the Burbages' part, bringing the Chamberlain's Men into direct competition with the Admiral's Men. In such a turf-war narrative, Burbage and company look like history's winners: Henslowe and his son-in-law Edward Alleyn almost immediately started building a new playhouse elsewhere. The Admiral's Men abandoned the Rose in 1600 and moved into their new home, the Fortune, in Clerkenwell, northwest of the City and far away from the Globe. But there is no reason to think that a desire to ramp up competition motivated the Burbages' decision. For one thing, this kind of thinking would have been out of step with the general atmosphere of mutual respect among London's acting companies. For another, the very speed with which Henslowe and Alleyn acted supports a different story. In fact, the Burbages may have chosen the Southwark location because they knew that Henslowe had started to look for a suitable site for a new playhouse and that the Admiral's Men would soon leave their old home.

What made the Globe a remarkable project was neither its builders' allegedly aggressive approach to the theatrical marketplace nor its size or design, which were no more impressive than the Swan's. The Globe was unique for the way it was financed: it belonged not to a separate landlord, but to members of the acting company itself.

How did this come about? It may be that when the Burbages decided to move their playhouse in 1598, they did not have sufficient funds for that enterprise. In 1596, their father had spent the very large sum of £600 to transform a medieval hall inside the former Blackfriars monastery into a theater. The purpose of this investment is uncertain: the doomed lease negotiations for The Theatre had not yet begun, so James Burbage might have been trying to expand his activities as a theater owner rather than replace his old playhouse. He had only been his son's company's landlord for a little over a year when he bought the Blackfriars, and may very well have had another company in mind for the new space. Whatever the case, the new venue was the largest indoor performance space in London, and probably the first hall theater designed for an adult company. But the undertaking failed. Almost instantly, a group of wealthy inhabitants of the Blackfriars precinct successfully protested against the plan. The composition of that group is enlightening: it contained Lord Hunsdon, the patron of Shakespeare's company; and Hunsdon's recently deceased father had tried to buy part of the same property Burbage was after the year before. If the new playhouse was meant for the Chamberlain's Men, it is certainly strange that both these patrons of the company attempted to prevent its construction.

In any event, the property was not a viable alternative when Richard Burbage and his fellows lost The Theatre. Whether for financial reasons or because neither Cuthbert nor Richard Burbage wanted to play the role of theater owner and landlord, the brothers devised a solution that would for the first time put a venue mostly in actors' hands. Half the enterprise belonged to the Burbages (since they contributed the timber from The Theatre), but the remaining 50 percent was divided equally among five of the seven or eight remaining sharers in the Chamberlain's Men: John Heminges, William Kemp, Augustine Phillips, Thomas Pope, and William Shakespeare. At Christmas 1598, this consortium signed the lease for the plot of land in Southwark. They subsequently covered the construction costs of £700, exactly what The Theatre had cost to build in 1576.

Having a playhouse owned by the majority of the sharers in an acting company was a unique business model. These sharers now were responsible for the upkeep of the building, but they also, as landlords, received a portion of the entire revenue from every show (the Globe used the same rental agreement as the Rose, splitting performance income between landlords and actors). Beyond economics, the agreement created an unparalleled strong bond between these actors and their venue. It practically ensured that the Globe became their default home, and that its joint owners would remain members of the same acting company. The Globe was made for the Chamberlain's Men—but the Chamberlain's Men, in a sense, were also made by the Globe.

What happened to the Blackfriars property in the meantime? It stood empty for three years; and then, in 1600, it became an active theater after all. That year, Richard Burbage, clearly unwilling to adopt his father's or Henslowe's business model, leased

This section of Wenceslaus Hollar's 1647 "Long View" of London, drawn from South-wark, shows the Globe in its rebuilt state. The Globe is the round building in the middle, misidentified as a "Beere bayting" arena. The round building to its right, mislabeled "The Globe," is in fact the Hope playhouse, which by the 1620s was used exclusively as a bearbaiting venue.

the Blackfriars venue outright to the manager of a boys' acting company—for a flat annual fee of £40, and for twenty-one years. No revenue sharing, no managerial services: Burbage washed his hands of his father's failed endeavor. (The boys' company did not face the same opposition as the 1596 venture, perhaps because it performed as rarely as once a week, or because it represented a more up-market kind of playing.)

Eventually, the Blackfriars would become the King's Men's second venue: they probably started performing plays there sometime in 1610, at the very end of Shakespeare's career. But neither the company nor the Burbages were in any rush to move indoors. In 1604, the boys' company's manager tried to return the building to them and cut the twenty-one-year lease short, but the Burbages were uninterested. Only after the King forced out the children's troupe in 1608 did they agree to terminate the lease. The brothers owned the property and certainly had no financial incentive to search for investors. And yet the Burbages immediately turned the Blackfriars into another shared venture, splitting costs and revenues equally among themselves, one outsider, and four King's Men's sharers, including Shakespeare. The idea here was evidently not to maximize personal gain, but to enhance the company's profile—and its leaders' fortunes.

Within a decade, the Blackfriars turned into *the* place for new, fashionable plays. But during Shakespeare's lifetime, it never outshone the older outdoor space. For the first years of the new theater's existence, references to King's Men plays mention only the Globe; prominent audience members, including foreign princes, still visited the open-air venue; and in 1613, the company emphatically reaffirmed its commitment to its traditional playhouse. That year, the building's cost-effective thatched roof caught

A different section of Hollar's panorama shows the Blackfriars precinct across the river from the Globe and Hope theaters. Just to the left of center, next to the spire of St. Bride's Church, the long roof with two tall chimneys marks the probable location of the Blackfriars theater.

fire during the first performance of Shakespeare and Fletcher's *Henry VIII*. The Globe burned down, leaving the King's Men with only an indoor theater at their disposal. However, instead of redefining themselves as the Blackfriars company, they extended their lease on the Southwark plot, invested the enormous sum of £1,400, and rebuilt their playhouse—with decorations that made it, in the words of an eyewitness, "the fairest that ever was in England." This time, the galleries and stage had tiled roofs.

If the Chamberlain's/King's Men were unique in forming such a strong interconnection between actors and theaters, they also benefited from the unusual privilege of having an in-house playwright. No other company in the 1590s seems to have had a sharer who could also provide, on average, two plays a year. In addition, Shakespeare apparently performed other tasks for his company that would normally have been farmed out to hired dramatists, which included writing new scenes for old plays. The sheets in the *Sir Thomas More* manuscript that are probably in Shakespeare's handwriting are one example: there, he provided a long scene for a collaboratively authored text that needed major patching to be stageable. There is also evidence that additions to Thomas Kyd's *Spanish Tragedy* first printed in 1602 are by Shakespeare; if so, he wrote them for a Chamberlain's Men revival of this early classic (originally staged around 1587). The role of Hieronimo in the play was one of Richard Burbage's star turns, so we know the script found its way into the company's repertory at some point in the late 1590s or early 1600s.

Although the Chamberlain's Men were unusually fortunate to have Shakespeare as a sharer, we should not overestimate his place in their repertory. He was no Thomas Dekker, the dramatist who between 1597 and 1603 wrote or coauthored 41 new plays for a range of companies. Nor was Shakespeare as productive as Thomas Heywood, who claimed to have authored or cowritten more than 220 plays in a career spanning forty years. Given a need for at least ten fresh scripts a year, Shakespeare's contributions to his company's repertory were valuable, even indispensable—but they could never make up more than a fraction of the new material commissioned every year. Even if demand for new plays slowed in the 1620s, after the King's Men had accumulated a stock of reliably popular offerings, those of Shakespeare's works that had proved their lasting appeal would always be part of a much larger set of scripts. And the company treated Shakespeare's plays much like other authors' works, hiring playwrights to spruce up the old texts and make them newly exciting for audiences; in Shakespeare's case, it was Thomas Middleton who revised *Measure for Measure*, *Macbeth*, and possibly others.

At Court

Thinking of theater as a commercial enterprise taking place in venues accessible to all who paid the price of admission means leaving out one important aspect of early modern theater: private performances for aristocratic audiences. Companies were occasionally paid to stage their plays inside the London houses of noble clients, but such interactions with the highest social ranks were intermittent and unpredictable. The court, on the other hand, annually required actors to provide entertainments during lengthy revels between Christmas and Twelfth Night, and usually at Shrovetide (the three days before Ash Wednesday). Under Elizabeth I, there was only one court, her own, and theatrical activities were limited to those two holiday periods. With the ascension of James I, however, the number of royal courts multiplied—besides the King's own, Queen Anne, Prince Henry, and later Prince Charles also maintained courts with their own occasions for entertainment—and playing was no longer limited to holidays. The records show that the royally sponsored adult companies could be summoned to one of the palaces at any time. Officially, the courts' desire for theater justified the actors' need to play all year round in public venues, despite the City authorities' concerns: companies constantly had to rehearse and try out plays in front of live audiences so they could be ready to perform whenever a royal patron needed them.

The person in charge of organizing royal entertainments was the Master of the Revels, an officer who worked for the Lord Chamberlain. Under Elizabeth, the office was held by Sir Edmund Tilney. His job was not an easy one: he was responsible for choosing the appropriate companies and plays from the multitude available in London. In his early years, Tilney's approach seemed scattershot, with up to seven different troupes playing at court per season. The sheer complexity of keeping that many companies organized may have led to the foundation of an elite troupe under Elizabeth's own patronage, the Queen's Men, who dominated court entertainments for a few years after 1583. In 1594, the Master of the Revels apparently undertook a second effort to streamline holiday performances, this time relying not on a single troupe, but on a pair—and his superior, the Lord Chamberlain, adopted one of those companies as his own. For five years thereafter, Tilney could draw on two consistently excellent groups of actors, the Chamberlain's Men and the Admiral's Men.

As in 1583, though, this approach gave the Queen's revels a rather different complexion from the popular theaters. The Queen's Men were the leading company for about ten years after their creation, but other troupes eventually reappeared in the court season. Similarly, Shakespeare's company and their colleagues at the Rose were prominent but far from alone in London, and their competitors also turned up on Tilney's payroll again before long. Derby's Men, Worcester's Men, Hertford's Men, and the boys' companies all performed at court within a few years of the establishment of the Lord Chamberlain's troupe in 1594. Tilney's tenure as Master of the Revels was marked by repeated, ultimately futile efforts to limit actors' access to courtly employment—efforts seemingly designed to shut out the unrestrained variety of the public theatrical marketplace.

Under James I, the Lord Chamberlain's office finally acknowledged the size and diversity of London's theater world. Abandoning the model of a separate set of privileged companies with access to the court, the crown instead brought all major London companies gradually under royal patronage. By 1615, five adult troupes were being officially sponsored by members of James's family. Only those companies were asked to perform at court, but they were probably also the only acting outfits remaining in London: there were not enough playhouses to accommodate more than five permanent adult companies.

Even if the diversity of companies performing at court came to reflect the situation in the public playhouses over the course of Shakespeare's career, the repertory the actors drew on for their courtly performances remained distinct in surprising ways. We might expect that kings and queens, princes, ambassadors, and wealthy courtiers would have made for the most discerning and demanding audience imaginable, but the records tell a different story. Often, the plays staged at court were already several years old; by the 1610s, Revels playlists begin to feel like compilations of the classics that had their place in every company's repertory but could not normally compete with the appeal of new material. The court's, or the Master of the Revels', taste was broadly on the conservative side.

Though the records list almost no specific play titles from Elizabeth's reign, those surviving from James's time suggest that the King and his inner circle liked their Shakespeare well aged. In 1604, there were *A Midsummer Night's Dream*, nine years old; *The Merry Wives of Windsor*, seven years old; and *The Comedy of Errors*, over ten years old. The next year, we have recorded performances of *Henry V*, six or seven years after its first staging; and of *The Merchant of Venice*, at least seven years old, but performed twice within three days in James's presence in February 1605. These were the typical Shakespearean offerings. Exceptions occurred, including the still-new *Tempest* and *Winter's Tale* in November 1611, but for the most part, the Master of the Revels assembled an unadventurous repertory in which certain favorites often reappear. *Twelfth Night*, *The Winter's Tale*, *Othello*, and *1 Henry IV* show up every few years, as do some of Ben Jonson's plays (*Volpone* and *The Alchemist* in particular) and titles whose continued popularity at court now seems puzzling (such as the anonymous *Greene's Tu Quoque* and *The Merry Devil of Edmonton*). A company that performed for the royal households as often as did the King's Men must have adjusted to their courtly audience's expectations to some degree, and may therefore have been less quick to follow the latest artistic fashions than a company less in demand at court. But even so, Shakespeare and his fellows probably saw acting for their royal patrons as quite a different challenge from playing for London audiences. And in spite of the unquestionable importance of their connection to the royal household, the fact that they performed publicly far more frequently and depended on the income from those performances probably meant that their day-to-day activities were less influenced by the preferences of the court than we might imagine.

The Regulation of Playing and Its Failures

Organizing court entertainments was the most important aspect of the Master of the Revels' job, but he had another major responsibility: the licensing of new plays. Every script had to be submitted to him for approval, and only manuscripts bearing his license and signature were allowed to be performed. In their censorship activities, Tilney and his successors concentrated mainly on three concerns: no actual persons could be slandered or attacked; plays had to steer clear of incendiary topics and language; and, after a law banning profanity onstage had been passed in 1606, actors were no longer allowed to utter oaths using the name of God in any form. In the main, though, the Master of the Revels was not the acting companies' antagonist. For instance, Tilney did not simply reject *Sir Thomas More*, although he found the play objectionable on a number of counts; instead, he suggested changes that would enable him to give the players his license.

That relatively benign mode of control could quickly shift into an aggressive register when the players crossed a line. Companies that staged plays without first having them licensed, if discovered, were severely reprimanded. Stricter actions followed whenever a performance offended a person of high rank and influence. Playhouses were sometimes shut down as a consequence, and actors and playwrights found themselves in prison while under investigation. When these perceived transgressions happened (and they happened infrequently), the state was typically unable to explain what had gone wrong, especially if the play had been licensed. Playwrights would routinely offer the likeliest theory: the actors had ad-libbed, adding content the Master of the Revels had not seen and the author(s) had not written. There was certainly a kernel of truth to those defenses. Live performance is invariably different from the script on which it is based. But although that insight was not unknown to Shakespeare's contemporaries, it never seemed to affect the official system of licensing, which continued to operate unchanged throughout the early modern period.

Beyond the licensing requirements, there are few signs that the state took any sustained interest in regulating the theatrical marketplace, in London or elsewhere in the country. Nor were such efforts especially effective when they did occur. One of the most significant interventions took place in July 1597, apparently in response to a now-lost play, *The Isle of Dogs*, performed by Pembroke's Men at the Swan. This performance caused a massive scandal, landed some actors and the playwright Ben Jonson in jail under investigation for sedition, shut down all the theaters, and ruined Pembroke's Men financially. We do not know what made the play so offensive, but it must have been a serious trespass. The Privy Council's reaction to what it regarded as the players' "lewd and mutinous behaviour" was unprecedentedly severe; an order went out to stop all performances and have all playhouses demolished within three months. As telling as this order, though, is what happened next: almost nothing. The company was broken up, but no theaters were destroyed. Henslowe's *Diary* shows no signs that he was concerned about loss of income, and before long a new London-based company established itself in a new theater, the Boar's Head. For the next few years, the Privy Council attempted to control the number of troupes and playhouses in London, but every one of its annual letters to the local authorities expresses frustration about the inefficient implementation of the previous set of orders. No letters on the subject written after 1602 survive.

The Privy Council's general indifference to tightly regulating the theaters and its relatively hands-off attitude, even in the brief period when it adopted restrictive policies, did not align well with the wishes of the Lord Mayor and aldermen of the City, for whom the theaters posed a perennial challenge to public order. However, even the City authorities were not consistent in their opposition: they habitually relied on actors and playwrights for the annual civic entertainments, especially the Lord Mayor's pageants. Some aldermen befriended players, and actors participated in parish-level government (Shakespeare's colleagues Henry Condell and John Heminges were church wardens; Edward Alleyn and Philip Henslowe served as members of the vestry, or parish council, of St. Saviour's Church in Southwark). And although opposition to regular performances at the inns in the City was fairly consistent over twenty years, this policy may not have been the reason that all the large playhouses were built in the suburbs. Rather, high property prices and the scarcity of plots of land large enough for an amphitheater-style structure inside the densely packed City probably forced theater-builders to look beyond the city walls. Having large gathering places close to their gates but beyond their control vexed London authorities, but their anger may have been fueled by more than a simple desire to prohibit playacting: the theaters made a lot of money, and none of that income could be taxed by the City—despite the fact that the vast majority of playgoers would have been Londoners. The Mayor and his aldermen thus had many reasons for feeling aggrieved. Not only did they have to suffer the threat of riots and public disturbances sparked at the theaters, but they could not even collect fees and taxes in return.

The one cause that brought the interests of City and Privy Council together was also the single biggest economic threat to the acting companies, and the most frequent reason for playhouse closures: the plague. While the transmission of diseases was not well understood in early modern England, the authorities knew that crowds spread illness. Hence the government would order the theaters to shut whenever plague deaths reached a certain level (these figures had to be recorded and reported parish by parish every week). Sometimes, such closures were a precaution and did not last long. But on a number of occasions during Shakespeare's career, the theaters were closed for many months, with disastrous consequences for the London-based companies. A plague outbreak in 1593 halted performances for almost the entire year, forced all companies to tour, and caused a major reorganization of the theatrical landscape—out of which the Chamberlain's Men emerged as a new troupe formed from the fragments of its disbanded predecessors. At least as devastating was the horrific eruption of plague that shut down all playing in London from March 1603 to September 1604, and the less severe but longer episode that kept the theaters closed from August 1608 to the end of 1610. The first decade of James's reign was an especially chaotic and challenging time for the London companies, as there were lengthy plague closures even in the years when the playhouses were periodically open. If the world of London theater changed fundamentally after Shakespeare's retirement in 1613, the great watershed may not have been the introduction of multiple royal patrons or of new indoor performance venues, but instead the comparative stability offered by an extended period without plague outbreaks. In any case, it seems clear that the greatest threat to an acting company's fortunes was not the Privy Council, the censor, or local authorities, but a mysterious, unpredictable, and lethal disease.

Casting

We have already glimpsed some of the details of how an early modern acting company was put together: at its core were the sharers, the actors who jointly owned the troupe's assets; then there were a number of male youths, usually apprenticed to the sharers, who played women and children; and then there was a group of hired men, who had no financial stake in the group's success, as they were paid a set salary, although some (such as John Sincklo) stayed loyally with the same troupe. Beyond those actors, most London companies employed someone who functioned like a modern stage manager, the book-holder. That person was responsible for maintaining play scripts and organizing the backstage action during performances; he likely also acted as a prompter. Finally, there were employees who collected admission fees, cleaned the theater, and probably doubled as stagehands. Some of these workers were women, a female presence in an otherwise entirely male business.

Senior actors developed a degree of professional specialization. The most obvious experts were the clowns or fools, often among the most prominent members of any company. Richard Tarlton was the first of the great and famous Elizabethan clowns, and he was the Queen's Men's undisputed star until his death in 1588. Will Kemp, a sharer in the Chamberlain's Men as well as, for a short while, in the Globe, took over Tarlton's crown as the funniest man on English stages. After Kemp left the company in 1599, Robert Armin inherited his role as clown. The styles of these comedic performers differed, with Tarlton famed as an improviser and singer, Kemp known for his athleticism, and Armin for his subtler verbal wit, but they all had one thing in common: their responsibilities included the comic entertainments performed after plays

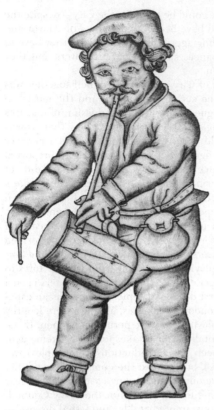

This portrait of Richard Tarlton, drawn by John Scottowe in or around 1588, shows Tarlton dressed as a jester, playing the tabor (a kind of drum) and pipe.

were done. Hence, they regularly appeared before audiences as themselves or as recognizable stage personae. They were certainly among the most readily identifiable faces of the company.

Unlike other roles, the clowns' parts in plays were often not fully scripted, and allowed for improvisation—the excessive use of which Hamlet criticizes when he tells the players to "let those that play your clowns speak no more than is set down for them." It is thus no coincidence that even as playwriting became a profession separate from acting, famous clowns still continued to be known as dramatists as well: Tarlton, Kemp, and Armin all wrote, as did John Shank, John Singer, and William Rowley. The line between the play and its performance, between the playwright's text and what the actors said and did, was particularly blurred in these performers' roles—and we should not assume that authors (or anyone else) found this especially troubling. It would be an error to read Hamlet's views as Shakespeare's, let alone the audience's: by all accounts, including Hamlet's, theatergoers enjoyed the clowns' ad-libbing and did not mind if such riffing delayed the progress of the play. We should, however, take seriously Hamlet's use of the plural "clowns." The company's specialist clown would never have been the only actor with comedic skills. *Hamlet* itself requires at least two clowns, the two gravediggers, even if Armin took on three of the plays' foolish roles and acted Polonius, Osric, and the first gravedigger (a casting choice the structure of the play allows). *Twelfth Night*, similarly, calls for a designated clown, but also needs another comically gifted actor as Sir Andrew Aguecheek. Shakespeare's company included a number of such performers. Thomas Pope, one of its founding sharers, had a reputation as a comedian, as did Richard Cowley, a hired man with the Chamberlain's Men who became a sharer in the King's Men.

If not all comic parts always went to the same performer, the same is true of dramatic leads. Two great tragic actors dominate all narratives of Shakespeare's stage: Edward Alleyn, the Admiral's Men's star, and Richard Burbage, the Chamberlain's and King's Men's leading player. Both rose to prominence in the 1590s. Alleyn, Burbage's senior by three years, gained fame first. However, although he led the longer life (Burbage died in 1619, Alleyn in 1626), his career as an actor lasted nowhere near as long as his colleague's: sometime before 1606, Alleyn retired from the stage to devote his attention to even more profitable ventures, whereas Burbage continued acting until his death. But even these two titans of the stage would not have taken the lead in every play: that is not how ensembles work. Alleyn certainly performed the title characters in Christopher Marlowe's *Tamburlaine* and *Doctor Faustus* and Barabas in *The Jew of Malta*, though he may not have originated those roles; beyond these, we know of five other parts in which he acted, four of them from lost plays. Burbage's list is not much longer. An elegy written shortly after his death laments that with him died characters that no other actor could bring to life as powerfully: "No more young Hamlet, old Hieronimo, / Kind Lear, the grievèd Moor." He was closely associated, then, with three of Shakespeare's plays and Kyd's *Spanish Tragedy*; notably, those works were at least ten years old when he died.

We might expect that Burbage, at the height of his fame, played all the largest parts, but the elegy suggests otherwise: Othello is a smaller role than Iago. What is more, when the Chamberlain's Men were established in 1594, Burbage was only twenty-five, the youngest sharer, and had not yet risen to the level of prominence he would later attain; and the company included other well-known actors: George Bryan, John Heminges, Augustine Phillips, and William Sly. Initially, Burbage's name would not have been the most recognizable among these, and even when his reputation ultimately eclipsed the others', he would—and could—not have been the only choice for leads. Think of Shakespeare's plays from the mid-1590s: Burbage probably played Romeo, but what about *Richard II*? Would Burbage have been a better fit for the king or for the usurper Bolingbroke? In *The Merchant of Venice*, Shylock is the star turn nowadays, but Bassanio may have been the likelier role for Burbage, with older actors, like Bryan or Phillips, taking the roles of the other two male leads, Antonio and Shylock—or Thomas Pope, if Shylock was considered a comic part. Or take, as a final example, *Titus Andronicus*. Titus is the largest role, but Burbage may well have been a better fit for Aaron, a younger and more agile character.

A contemporary portrait of Richard Burbage. Burbage sometimes worked as a visual artist, and some scholars believe this painting to be a self-portrait.

Matching actors' ages to those of their characters, though, is a complicated business, and a casting consideration that was treated differently in Shakespeare's time from now. Burbage played Lear when he was no older than thirty-seven; and he was famous in the role of Hieronimo—an elderly father figure—by 1601, when he was just thirty-two. The same actor, then, might have acted the aged King Lear, "old Hieronimo," and "young Hamlet" within the span of a few days. And yet, despite this apparent disregard for verisimilitude, it was the supposedly lifelike quality of his acting that made Burbage famous. A writer in the 1660s reported on his ability to "wholly transfor[m] himself into his part, putting off himself with his clothes, as he never assumed himself again until the play was done." Part of Burbage's power was that he could seemingly become another person, even if that meant aging by decades. If the effect was a kind of make-believe, however, the means were an orator's, not those of modern psychological realism. What contemporary witnesses praise is Burbage's facility with speech, with finding the right vocal affect and the right quality of voice to express his character. As important was his aptitude at suiting his physical movement to the role, finding what were called the right "actions." That term probably referred to an elaborate arsenal of gestures and body positions that was systematic enough that audiences could read and make sense of actors' movements: putting a hand on the heart, holding one's face in one's hands, making a fist, and so on. Even if Burbage seemed able to go beyond conventions and give his actions an unusually personal or individual quality, though, it is clear that what seemed lifelike in Shakespeare's theater had little to do with a modern understanding of stage realism.

Burbage's specific talent may have been self-transformation; Alleyn, on the other hand, was known and remembered for his extraordinary stage presence. But both actors used a similar technical arsenal. Alleyn, like Burbage, was praised for his "excellent action"—as Thomas Nashe wrote in 1592, not even the greatest Roman actors "could ever perform more in action than famous Ned Alleyn." If Burbage disappeared into his roles, Alleyn was celebrated for the awe-inspiring quality he himself lent the characters he played. We do not know what his acting would have looked like onstage, but its outsized effect was not universally popular. Hamlet's criticism of players that "so strutted and bellowed" that "they imitated humanity so abominably" may refer to actors of Alleyn's ilk, perhaps an implicit statement that the Chamberlain's Men favored a different approach to performance. After Alleyn's death, in the reign of Charles I, the larger-than-life style associated with him was frowned upon by some writers and by spectators at some theaters. But there is no evidence that Burbage's brand of acting displaced Alleyn's within Shakespeare's lifetime. More probably, the two actors' particular aptitudes represented the pinnacles of two different but not incompatible acting techniques that in other players' work appeared in mixed forms. Both of these men were exceptional figures, after all. The Admiral's Men were not a company of many Alleyns, nor were the Chamberlain's Men a troupe of Burbages. What most performers and audiences probably understood "acting" (or "playing") to mean is captured vividly in these lines from *Richard III*:

> Come, cousin, canst thou quake, and change thy color,
> Murder thy breath in middle of a word,
> And then begin again, and stop again,
> As if thou wert distraught and mad with terror?
>
> (3.5.1–4)

What Richard is asking Buckingham here is whether he can act—and Buckingham replies that he can indeed "counterfeit the deep tragedian," in part because he can use the appropriate actions (looks, trembling, starts, smiles). Both characters describe a kind of performance that is highly codified, quite predictable, and not exactly lifelike; but both share the confidence that a talented actor can turn hackneyed gestures and tics into a convincing impression of reality.

If actors were capable of creating something like reality out of obvious fictions, and if those fictions could stretch to having an actor in his thirties play an old king one day and a young prince the next, then it cannot have been difficult for performers and audiences to come to terms with the widespread practice of doubling. All but the actors cast in the largest roles routinely played multiple characters, often leaving the stage as one person only to return shortly thereafter, wearing a new hat or a different cloak, as an entirely different character. Doubling meant that most early modern plays, although they may feature thirty or more characters, could be staged by around fourteen actors. In *The Merchant of Venice*, for example, the same player could take the parts of Old Gobbo, Tubal, the Jailer, and the Duke; or Morocco, Arragon, and the Duke—in either case, characters ranging widely in age and social status.

Like doubling, the casting of male youths in all female parts was a firmly established theatrical convention, though one that had less to do with pragmatic considerations than with a strong moral rationale. The idea of women putting their bodies on public display, even if fully clothed, was widely regarded as immoral and likened to prostitution. All-male casts were so deeply ingrained in English theatergoers' expectations that seeing actual women play female roles startled those who traveled abroad, where female actors were common. Some expressed their surprise that women could in fact act; others compared the Continental female performers critically to English boy players, whom they considered preferable not on moral but on artistic grounds. The women, these witnesses argued, played their characters too close to life, not artfully enough. A degree of artifice was as desirable in the boy actors' performances as in those delivered by the men. But as with the adult players, that artfulness did not diminish the potential impact of the show, as a famous account of a 1610 staging of *Othello* in Oxford attests. There, the scholar Henry Jackson recalls how Desdemona's death affected him: "although she always acted her whole part supremely well, yet when she was killed she was even more moving, for when she fell back upon the bed she implored the pity of the spectators by her very face." The boy player disappears behind the female pronouns, as if the artifice of the performance had become invisible. At the same time, Jackson registers that the body onstage, female or not, is not quite like a real corpse either; it responds to, and demands a response from, "the spectators." Yet, despite his recognition that the actor, or the character, is manipulating the audience's emotions, Jackson still responds emotionally and is in fact moved. The convention of using male youths for

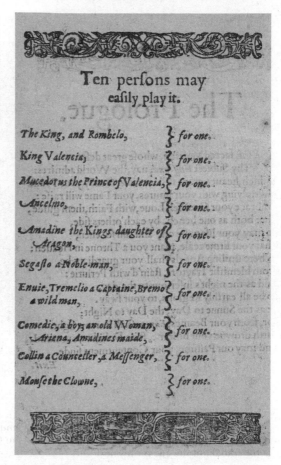

A chart from the second edition of the very popular anonymous play *Mucedorus* (1606), showing which actors can play more than one part.

female parts, then, was of a piece with the broader understanding of acting in Shakespeare's time as an art that deployed heightened artifice in order to create an affectively powerful semblance of real life.

Staging and Its Meanings

The staging of a new play in Shakespeare's time did not begin in a rehearsal room or in a theater, but in an actor's home. One of the first tasks of the company book-holder in readying a new script for performance was the preparation of the players' individual parts: each actor received only his own lines, along with the cues to which he was to respond and a handful of stage directions. Initially, then, most actors did not know who else was onstage with them, how many lines those other characters had, how much time passed between the scenes in which they appeared, or even who would give them their cues—nor what those characters said before the two or three words that made up the cue. Since companies performed together almost every day and actors often lived close to each other, informal discussions must have taken place to clarify relationships between characters, but any performer's primary duty would have been to learn

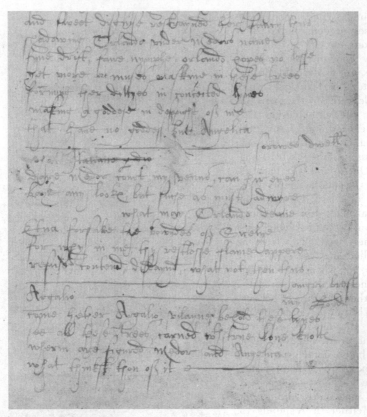

A section of Edward Alleyn's part for the role of Orlando in Robert Greene's *Orlando Furioso*. The long lines across the page mark breaks in Orlando's speech; at their end, the actor could find the cue for his next line.

his part in relative isolation, finding appropriate actions and intonations for his lines and memorizing cues. For leads, this was a formidable responsibility. Parts were written on strips of paper that were glued together to form a roll—which is why the terms "role" and "part" are synonymous. The scrolls for leads could reach remarkable length and heft. The one extant early modern part, Alleyn's copy of Orlando in Robert Greene's *Orlando Furioso*, is six inches wide and an impressive thirteen feet long, but its 530 lines probably did not overly tax an actor who had mastered more than 1,100 lines in *The Jew of Malta* and nearly 900 lines in the second part of *Tamburlaine*.

By Shakespeare's time, the solitary actor preparing his role could have predicted how the play would be staged with some certainty. The setup illustrated in the 1596 drawing of the Swan Theater is broadly representative of what a performer could expect in any venue: a rectangular, flat, largely empty stage; no sets in the modern sense, and few large furniture items; two pillars, probably set back from the edges of the stage by a few feet; at least two stage doors, and possibly a third in the center; and a balcony where scenes described as taking place "aloft" or "above" would be staged, though sections of it may also have offered additional audience seating, and part of it may have been used as a "music room." Even if there was no central stage door, there would have been an area between the two entrances that lay concealed behind an arras or a curtain that could be drawn to reveal pre-set tableaux, such as Hermione's statue in *The Winter's Tale*, Ferdinand and Miranda's chess game in *The Tempest*, or the caskets in *The Merchant of Venice*. There was also a trapdoor giving access to the space underneath the stage (sometimes called hell)—the place from which the ghost of Hamlet's father calls out to his son and his friends. In some theaters,

The interior of the Swan Theater, a sixteenth-century copy of a drawing by the Dutch traveler Johannes de Witt.

there was a pulley system that allowed objects, such as the figure of Jupiter in *Cymbeline*, to be lowered to the stage from the roof above it. That roof was often called the heavens, so that the stage as a whole represented a Christian microcosm, with hell, earth, and heaven enclosed in a round—*Hamlet*'s "distracted globe" or *Henry V*'s "wooden O."

This fairly stable, symbolically rich staging setup lent itself to an emblematic

The modern Globe on London's South Bank. This 1997 reconstruction is significantly larger than the original, but it captures the general idea of what an early modern theater may have looked like.

approach to performance. Figures appearing in the balcony are not always more powerful than those on the stage itself, but their position above could be dramatically exploited that way. When Tamora appears "aloft" alongside Saturninus in *Titus Andronicus*, for example, the staging suggests her elevation from prisoner of war to empress—a shift that officially does not take place until twenty lines later. The appearance of a prisoner and a foreigner in the location symbolically associated with supreme national power, however, also instantly signals how much of a topsy-turvy world Saturninus's Rome is about to become. This kind of visual logic of power returns in many plays that deal with the subjects of governance or rule: the descent of Richard II from the balcony to the stage when he surrenders to Bolingbroke is a particularly rich example. However, the emblematic use of the stage (where "above" means "powerful") could always be layered onto other modes of representation. In *Richard II*, the balcony also stands for an actual space "above," the battlements of Flint Castle; as the stage direction has it, Richard and his allies "enter on the walls." The stage to which he descends likewise is not simply "below" but also the "base court," the castle's lower court where Bolingbroke is waiting. From the perspective of the actor working with his part, the scene and its stage directions would have carried these various representational meanings—the text informed him both of Richard's movement from sun-like power to debasement before his enemy, and of the fact that the scene is taking place in two different locations in a castle. But the directions also had additional pragmatic value, as "on the walls" told the actor that he would have to enter on the balcony.

Stage directions such as these are explicit. Far more common are "internal" stage directions: textual references to actions characters perform. Often, these are straightforward: for instance, Bolingbroke's "there I throw my gage" in *Richard II*. But they can also be quite opaque. In *Hamlet*, when Polonius says, "Take this from this if this be otherwise," the line only tells the actor to perform some kind of gesture—he needs to indicate what "this" should be taken from what other "this" if Polonius is wrong. The most common interpretation is "my head from my shoulders" (indicated with appropriate gestures), but he may also be talking about his staff of office and his hand, or

A performance at the modern Globe.

his chain of office and his neck, or something else. The line requires actions to complete it, but it does not prescribe those actions.

Explicit and implicit stage directions allowed for a very short rehearsal period: they made it possible for the actor to conceive much of his performance alone. The text may not always tell him what to do, but it will often tell him when he needs to do *something*. However, there are also many cases where Shakespeare's plays seem to presuppose a good deal of back and forth between actors. For example, when Hamlet tells his mother to "leave wringing of your hands" in 3.4, the youth playing Gertrude would have needed to know to perform that action before Hamlet tells him to stop it—but there may have been no indication of this in his part. So while the part system allowed players to prepare for much, and while the established shape and features of playhouses by the 1590s made it possible for actors to anticipate many staging decisions before ever rehearsing a play, Shakespeare's texts also contain many instances where a successful performance depends on the players going beyond their individual parts.

Even if rehearsal periods were short, it is hard to imagine that the elaborate dumbshows, masques, and battle scenes featured in some plays were not carefully prepared. But rehearsal in the modern sense did not exist, mainly because the modern idea of character work did not exist. Renaissance actors did not spend long hours developing ideas about their characters' biographies, inner lives, or hidden feelings. Acting was primarily a physical and oratorical art and, in its conventionality, quite predetermined. What made any individual performance surprising and unpredictable were the specific effects achieved by bringing together a particular text with a conventionalized physical and vocal arsenal. But rehearsal also did not have to address many of the technological challenges that only came into being in the modern theater. In an outdoor venue without artificial lighting, actors do not need to hit their "marks"; an expansive stage lit only by sunlight allows for greater freedom of movement than one illuminated by an elaborate lighting design. Lastly, staging was determined in part by the architecture of the playhouses. Certain spots on stage worked especially well for certain set pieces. Soliloquies, for instance, were at their most powerful not when delivered front and center, but instead from a position farther away from the audience, off-center, and underneath the stage roof, which provided the greatest sense of acoustic intimacy. Therefore, an actor preparing a speech could predict with some certainty where onstage he would deliver it.

Of course there is more to staging a play than speaking lines and finding positions. Nowadays, sets are of paramount importance. In Shakespeare's time, they were all but nonexistent, except for some big-impact items: the Rose Theater owned a hell-mouth, probably covering the trapdoor, for devils to enter and exit in plays such as Marlowe's *Doctor Faustus*. Tombs, caves, and cages also appear in Henslowe's inventory, as do magical trees and severed heads. One other cost factor of modern productions, however, loomed similarly large in Shakespeare's time: costumes. Dresses in particular could be more expensive to commission than new plays, and companies maintained a rich stock of costumes; in 1598, the Admiral's Men owned at least eighty complete men's outfits. Most of these were generic items, but some were character-specific: "Harry the Fifth's velvet gown," "Longshanks' suit," or "Merlin's gown and cape."

What the actors wore was the most noteworthy visual aspect of staging. On a basic level, costumes identified characters. If the actor playing Tubal in *The Merchant of Venice* also played the jailor and the Duke, his three characters would have been distinguished initially and immediately by different garments. But costumes did more than facilitate identification. Dress signified social rank. It instantly allowed audiences to place characters, without having heard them speak or knowing anything else about them. More important, dress could set the scene: a nightgown signaled where and when an action took place; a forester's outfit told the audience to imagine a woodland setting; an innkeeper's costume moved the scene to a tavern. And dress denoted historical periods—as can be seen in Henry Peacham's famous illustration of *Titus Andronicus*. In this 1590s drawing, Titus's garments—Roman armor and a toga accessorized with a laurel wreath—immediately inform the viewer that this is a classical figure, and that the play is set in ancient Rome.

Yet Peacham's picture also shows that costume functioned in multiple registers on Shakespeare's stage. Titus wears Roman dress, and the short tunics of the three figures on the right also suggest quasiclassical costumes. But Tamora, on her knees in a flowing, embroidered gown and wearing a nonclassical crown, signifies less an ancient figure (Goth or Roman) than royalty. Her garments, unlike those of the characters beside her, are designed to situate her not in history, but in a particular social sphere. The outfits of the two leftmost characters follow a different logic yet again: they are Elizabethan soldiers, with breeches, halberds, and contemporary helmets. Their costume has no historical function; its sole purpose is to identify them as having a particular occupation. Dress, then, could signify in multiple, mutually contradictory ways at the same time on Shakespeare's stage. What Peacham's image

Henry Peacham's illustration of a scene from *Titus Andronicus* (ca. 1595).

suggests visually is that *Titus Andronicus*, while set in Rome, is also concerned with general questions of monarchic power and soldierly virtue. All three of those aspects of the play could be communicated through costume. If the picture portrays a kind of theater capable of sustaining anachronistic and logical contradictions in the pursuit of its thematic goals, it is representative of the broader, and pervasive, anachronism of Shakespearean drama, in which church bells ring and books rather than scrolls are read in *Julius Caesar's* Rome, while the title character wears that most Elizabethan of male garments, a doublet. No matter how far back in historical time these plays were set, they also always took place in the present moment.

Audience members seem to have consumed a wide range of foods at the theater. Archaeologists found oyster shells, remnants of crab, and a large quantity of nutshells and fruit seeds at the Rose Theater site.

Impressive and expensive as the actors' costumes could be, their visual impact would necessarily have been lessened by the daylight playing conditions: performers were not isolated in space and light as they can be in modern theaters, but always competed for attention with the audience itself, with the equally splendid figures in the lords' rooms and on stage stools, and with whatever distracting things spectators chose to do while the play was in progress: play cards, smoke tobacco, solicit prostitutes (or johns). Aurally, too, Shakespeare's stage was not as insulated as a modern theater. Spectators were rowdier and more audibly present than audiences now. But the sounds of the city would also have infiltrated the open-air space: church bells, the noise of bears and hounds from the nearby bearbaiting arenas, the cries of street vendors, and perhaps even the sound of performances at neighboring playhouses might all have been heard. Going to a play in early modern London was never exclusively about the action and words onstage; it was always also about the theater itself, its temporary inhabitants, and the places where the theaters stood. Visually and aurally, the stage was in competition with the world, but it also found ways of integrating that world into its fictions.

Although the early modern theatrical experience was shaped by a host of immediate sensory perceptions, it equally depended on the audience's ability to refashion those impressions in their minds—even as plays insisted on drawing attention to the material reality of the stage. The Prologue to *Henry V* illustrates this condition perfectly. On the one hand, it mocks the apparent inadequacy of the theater, an "unworthy scaffold," a "cockpit" laughably ill suited to representing the "vasty fields of France"; it mercilessly reminds the audience where they are. At the same time, the Prologue also encourages the listeners to ignore all these carefully catalogued shortcomings and allow the play to work "on your imaginary forces," pleading with them to "piece out our imperfections with your thoughts." The Prologue seems to indulge in a risky game: it explains in detail why the theater should fail even as it dares the audience to make it work. But this risk lay at the heart of Shakespeare's theatrical art. We can detect it in the use of boy actors as much as in contradictory costuming choices and willful anachronisms. It found its most daring expression in the frequent use of narrative, seemingly the least theatrical form of writing. Antonio's tearful farewell to Bassanio in *The Merchant of Venice*; the deaths of the Dukes of Suffolk and York in *Henry V*; the reunion of Perdita and Leontes in *The Winter's Tale*; most remarkably, the death of as charismatic a character as Falstaff, in *Henry V*: again and again, Shakespeare chose to have events such as these reported by other characters rather than staging them before his spectators' eyes. In these scenes, the words and their demands on the audience's imagination do not just compete with what is visible, as they always did in the early modern playhouse. These narrations do more than that: they celebrate and rely on the power of words to take audiences out of the theater altogether, to transport them, without any visual aid whatsoever, to places and encounters that even the characters in the play itself only imagine.

And yet, despite placing such trust in language's capacity to transform reality, both the scenes and their author depended on their actors' ability to make audiences believe those words. If language's appeal to the imagination was meant to pull theatergoers out of their immediate sensory experience and into an engagement with a world of fiction, that goal could be achieved only by virtue of the very bodies, costumes, and props whose specific presence audiences were encouraged to transform into representations of an alternative reality. If a play worked, it enabled its viewers almost to forget the theaters whose splendor impressed so many visitors; allowed them to imagine for a moment that the words they heard did not come from a scroll of paper, that they had not been preapproved and licensed by a government official, purchased by a profit-hungry company, and written by a commercial playwright. Ultimately, then, in spite of the theater's undeniably powerful architectural, social, cultural, and visual presence in the lives of Shakespeare's contemporaries, its success in creating alternative, fictional worlds depended on an audience capable of understanding that all this splendor was not an end in itself. That is the marvelous paradox of Shakespeare's theater: it invested a great deal of goods, money, and physical labor in an effort to persuade people not to ignore those material realities altogether, but to use them as a means of accessing greater, still more wondrous, and wholly imaginary worlds beyond.

COMEDIES

Shakespearean Comedy

by

KATHARINE EISAMAN MAUS

> BEGGAR   Is not a comonty a Christmas gambol,
> or a tumbling trick?
> PAGE   No . . . it is a kind of history.
> *(The Taming of the Shrew*, Induction 2)

When, after Shakespeare's death, his colleagues in his theater company, the King's Men, collected and printed his works in the First Folio, they organized them into three groups: comedies, tragedies, and histories. Since the late nineteenth century, several plays written late in Shakespeare's career—*Pericles, The Winter's Tale, Cymbeline*, and *The Tempest*—have been relegated (as they are in *The Norton Shakespeare*) to a separate group, the romances. With the romances subtracted, Shakespeare's comic output comes to twelve plays, plus *Troilus and Cressida* and the coauthored *Two Noble Kinsmen*, which are sometimes classified as comedies and sometimes as tragedies.

Writing about 350 B.C.E., the Greek philosopher Aristotle speculated that comedy had originated in the *phallaka*, ribald songs that accompanied a fertility rite in which young men paraded a large model of an erect penis through a village to celebrate a bountiful grape harvest. The procession of youths who sang these songs was called a *komos*, from which the word "comedy" is perhaps derived. At this historical remove it is impossible to recover exactly how "phallic songs" might have been detached from their original performance circumstances and developed into staged drama. Yet many modern critics as well as Aristotle have remarked upon comedy's association with ancient myths of seasonal rebirth and renewal, and with festivities in which sexuality and fertility are celebrated, inhibitions loosened, bodily pleasures indulged, bounds of decorum overturned.

Shakespeare's England was familiar neither with grape harvests nor with the *phallaka*, and causal connections between its traditions of merrymaking and the development of a comic tradition are even harder to draw here than in the Greek case. Still, in many of his comedies Shakespeare suggests an affinity between the plays and the festivities of his own agrarian culture. May Day, on May 1, and Midsummer Night, at the summer solstice, celebrated the effects of the burgeoning spring and fertile summer for plants, animals, and people. The period between Christmas Eve and Epiphany, or Twelfth Night, was a time of revelry sometimes presided over by a "lord of misrule" who issued topsy-turvy edicts and encouraged playful role-playing and overindulgence in food and drink. Several of Shakespeare's comedies—*A Midsummer Night's Dream, Twelfth Night*, and *The Merry Wives of Windsor*—make overt references to such holidays or incorporate some of their rituals into the action. The dialogue between Spring and Winter in *Love's Labor's Lost*, and many of the songs in *As You Like It* and *Twelfth Night*, evoke the seasonal round that all these festivals commemorate and honor. Some Protestant reformers repudiated these "holidays of indulgence" because of their pagan or Catholic origin, and because of their scandalous mixture of sacred and profane; perhaps the contemporary controversy over these traditional celebrations sharpened Shakespeare's interest in them.

An Ancient Greek cup showing a phallic procession.

Medieval and Renaissance England was home to a rich indigenous tradition of clowning that flourished during holiday seasons but was not necessarily tied to special occasions. Many medieval morality plays—dramas in which a religious or moral dilemma is allegorically represented—feature boisterously anarchic "Vices," or devil characters, who comment irreverently on the action while sowing playful mayhem onstage. Wealthy men sometimes employed professional fools in their household, whose function was to amuse their employers with ridiculous banter. Although a number of written parts for Vice characters have survived, neither the Vice nor the professional fool necessarily tied his performance to a script. He was like a modern jazz performer, improvising ingeniously, rather than like a classical musician who aims to render a beautiful interpretation of a fully notated score. In *Twelfth Night*, the heroine Viola remarks upon the agile intelligence the professional clown's spur-of-the-moment preposterousness requires:

> He must observe their mood on whom he jests,
> The quality of persons, and the time,
> And, like the haggard [hunting hawk], check at every feather
> That comes before his eye. This is a practice
> As full of labor as a wise man's art.
>
> (3.1.55–59)

Laborious, and perilous too. The fool was permitted some liberty of speech, because his humor was often obscene, satirical, or disrespectful. Still, his uninhibited, irreverent commentary risked offending those more powerful than himself. In Shakespeare's plays every professional fool is threatened at some point with a whipping for having presumptuously overstepped his bounds. "The more pity that fools may not speak wisely what wise men do foolishly," remarks one of these fools, the clown Touchstone, in *As You Like It* (1.2.76–77).

Once the public theaters became established in London in the 1570s, the stage became a place where professional clowns could entertain larger and more diverse audiences: Will Kemp, a member of Shakespeare's theater company in the 1590s, was famous for his witty jests and pranks both onstage and off. Hamlet's advice to the acting company that visits him in Elsinore suggests both the scene-stealing appeal of improvisatory clowning and its potential to deform a carefully crafted play with random interpolations:

> And let those that play your clowns speak no more than is set down for them;
> for there be of them that will themselves laugh to set some quantity of barren

spectators to laugh too, though in the meantime some necessary question of the play be then to be considered. That's villainous and shows a most pitiful ambition in the fool that uses it.

(3.2.34–40)

Yet scripted comedies retain some of the clown's typical focus upon what the fool Feste, in *Twelfth Night*, calls "present mirth"—an emphasis on enjoyment in the here-and-now regardless of context or consequences.

In scripted drama, the word "comedy" can refer to anything from a short entertaining scene or improvisation to a whole play. Renaissance playwrights did not necessarily maintain strict demarcations between genres—they were prone to "mingling kings and clowns," as Shakespeare's contemporary Philip Sidney noted disapprovingly in *The Defense of Poetry*. Shakespeare's tragedies and history plays often contain comic episodes or subplots. In fact Falstaff, arguably Shakespeare's greatest comic character, makes his most memorable appearances in the history plays *1* and *2 Henry IV*; in *Macbeth*, a drunken porter staggers onstage to make obscene jokes immediately after Macbeth, offstage, has murdered Duncan; in *King Lear,* the Fool provides moments of extremely dark humor that blur the distinction between the tragic and the comically absurd.

Yet by Shakespeare's time comedy, considered as a distinctive kind of play, was more than merely a series of jokes and funny sketches, or a collection of festive customs. As the Page informs the Beggar in *The Taming of the Shrew*, a comedy "is a kind of history": that is, it has a plot. Plays "with happy endings," which we would classify as comedies, were much the most popular kind of dramatic entertainment on the English stage, far outnumbering tragedies. The most widely influential patterns for these plays were derived from the classical Roman dramatists Plautus and Terence, who were read in Latin, and sometimes performed or declaimed, in grammar schools of the kind Shakespeare attended as a boy in Stratford. Plautus and Terence had, in turn, appropriated plots and characters from Greek predecessors, most of whose works have since been lost. Their kind of drama is often called New Comedy to distinguish it from Old Comedy, an earlier Greek form that had satirized well-known living people and commented on current events.

Although individual New Comedies naturally vary, they generally feature stock characters and follow a predictable pattern. A youth is in love with an apparently unsuitable maiden—often a slave girl. Various stock characters help or hinder his love: the "heavy father" or uncle who prohibits the union and sometimes lusts after the maiden

Will Kemp, the clown in Shakespeare's company during the 1590s. From the title page of *Kemp's Nine Day's Wonder . . .* (1603).

himself; the ingenious slave who plots on the youth's behalf while remarking self-delightedly upon his own tricky skill; the stupid slave who misconstrues the speech and action of other characters; the braggart soldier home from war who exaggerates his exploits in battle but turns out to be a ridiculous coward. Sometimes the true identities of various characters are unclear, either because they have suffered some mishap that has obscured their family history, or because they are in disguise. As the play proceeds, one or both of the lovers find themselves in peril—"the course of true love never did run smooth," as Shakespeare's Lysander remarks in *A Midsummer Night's Dream* (1.1.134)—yet in the end nobody dies. Ultimately confusions are sorted out and family members reunited and reconciled; often the maiden turns out to be freeborn and therefore marriage material. The couple may then be ushered to wedded bliss.

New Comedy registers the surprising triumph of the apparently weak over the apparently powerful: of youth over age, of love over property, of wit over authority, of pleasure-seekers over prudent calculators. At the same time, the end of the play channels the characters' unruly energies into a form that seems ultimately to reinforce rather than challenge the status quo. The tricky slave may hoodwink his masters, but he does not flee his household or agitate for the abolition of servitude. The lovers, though they flout their parents' authority, enter into marriage and prepare to become parents themselves in their turn. New Comedy implies that rebelliousness marks a phase of life; it is not a precursor to revolutionary social change. Human beings follow a predictable cycle just as the seasons do, with one life stage succeeding another in due course, and the younger generation replacing the old.

Plautus's and Terence's plays were a treasure-trove for later writers. The plots were easy to recycle, because they were generalized rather than tied to particular people and current events, as Old Comedy had been. New Comedy represents human eccentricities as perennial; absurd behavior apparently takes much the same form in ancient Greece or Rome, in Italy in the 1400s, and in England in the 1590s. Moreover, New Comedy was well adapted to societies in which, like Shakespeare's England, censorship and slander laws prohibited the lampooning of powerful individuals and most public discussion of contemporary political affairs. The romance novella, adapting and recombining New Comic plot devices, flourished all over Renaissance Europe; Shakespeare knew versions from Italy, Spain, and France, as well as romances written in the late sixteenth century by such English writers as Thomas Lodge, Robert Greene, and Barnabe Riche. When, following age-old precedent, Shakespeare appropriates his plots from others, he sometimes adapts plot formulas directly from the classical originals, and sometimes relies upon one of their mediated forms. In *The Comedy of Errors* he goes straight to a classical source, Plautus's *Menaechmi*, but he follows more recent renditions of New Comic devices for the plots of *The Two Gentlemen of Verona, The Merry Wives of Windsor, As You Like It, Twelfth Night, Much Ado About Nothing, Measure for Measure,* and *All's Well That Ends Well.*

The "marriage plot" of New Comedy is absolutely fundamental to Shakespeare's comic drama: most of his comedies involve multiple courtships and weddings. Sometimes, indeed, Shakespeare alters the expected formula, as in *Love's Labor's Lost,* in which the women defer the weddings for at least a year, or in *Measure for Measure,* in which most of the concluding marriages are apparently loveless ones. Yet in these cases, the familiarity of the pattern means that characters as well as audiences register these changes as troubling departures from the norm. "Our wooing doth not end like an old play," complains Biron in *Love's Labor's Lost,* "Jack hath not Jill" (5.2.860–61). Many of Shakespeare's comedies also feature situations drawn from New Comic tradition: characters in disguise, separated family members reunited at the end of the play, smart-mouthed servant characters turning the tables on their masters, and (in *The Merry Wives of Windsor* and *All's Well That Ends Well*) cowardly braggart soldiers.

Aristotle and the Latin poet Horace had maintained that comedy typically dealt with people of low or ordinary social status, whereas tragedy dealt with kings and nobles. Indeed, classical New Comedies typically feature urban characters of the middling sort. Yet the Renaissance romances derived from them move up the social scale, so that the main characters are often kings and dukes, princesses and countesses. While Shakespeare's plays have plenty of lower-status characters in supporting roles, the marriage plots tend to retain this upscale orientation. In *Love's Labor's Lost*, a king and his nobles square off against a princess and her ladies; in *As You Like It*, the daughters of two dukes fall in love with noblemen brothers; *The Two Gentlemen of Verona*, *Twelfth Night*, *A*

A woodcut from a 1493 edition of Terence, showing a performance of *The Eunuch*.

Midsummer Night's Dream, Measure for Measure, and *All's Well That Ends Well* all involve characters of high degree in the marriage plot. The Countess Olivia, in *Twelfth Night*, suggests how indelible the markers of status were imagined to be. Olivia falls in love with a woman, Viola, disguised as a man, who is employed as a servant. When Olivia asks after her beloved's parentage, Viola replies that it is "above my fortunes . . . I am a gentleman" (1.5.260–61). After Viola departs, Olivia soliloquizes:

> "I am a gentleman." I'll be sworn thou art.
> Thy tongue, thy face, thy limbs, actions, and spirit
> Do give thee five-fold blazon.
>
> (1.5.273–75)

Although unaware of Viola's true sex, Olivia has no trouble at all accurately assessing Viola's class origins, which her behavior seems to set forth for all to view, as a gentleman's coat of arms, or "blazon," reveals his identity and family background. Even less exalted heroes and heroines, such as Katherina and Petruccio in *The Taming of the Shrew*, or the Antipholus twins in *The Comedy of Errors*, or the Page and Ford families in *The Merry Wives of Windsor*, live above the social line, critical in Shakespeare's time, that separated the landowning, professional, servant-employing classes from the vast majority who earned their living through manual toil.

Nonetheless, the emphasis in comedy tends to be on traits human beings share, not on those that elevate one person over another. Shakespeare's comedies tend not to focus upon the fate of a magnificent titular hero, as the tragedies do, but to feature a large collection of protagonists. Often the different characters participate in several interlocking plots, a technique that originated in classical theater and was much elaborated in the Middle Ages and Renaissance. *The Two Gentlemen of Verona* follows the initially diverging but eventually reconnecting adventures of Valentine and his faithless friend Proteus. *The Taming of the Shrew* deals not only with Katherina and Petruccio, but with Bianca and Lucentio, and Hortensio and the Widow; and this entire action is prefaced by a framing story about a practical joke on a drunken tinker. *Much Ado About Nothing* pairs the courtship of Claudio and Hero with the courtship of Beatrice and Benedict. *The Merry Wives of Windsor* combines Falstaff's attempt to seduce two middle-aged wives with a competition among several other men for the nubile daughter of one of the wives. *A Midsummer Night's Dream* attends to the wedding of Duke Theseus and Hippolyta, to the marital quarrels of Oberon and Titania, to the mishaps of four Athenian lovers lost in the woods, and to the attempts of a group of artisans to rehearse a play for the Duke's wedding.

The multiplot action encourages the audience to take a wide view, to make comparisons among various characters who are doing more or less the same thing—for instance, falling in love—in different ways. No single story, no single individual has a monopoly on the stage, nor, implicitly, a monopoly on the truth. Often the collisions among the various plotlines are surprising and funny: *The Comedy of Errors*, indeed, is a tissue of such unlikely interpenetrations, as bewildered characters find themselves hijacked again and again into the wrong story. Not until the entire cast is assembled at the end of the play can the multiple farcical misunderstandings be sorted out. In most of Shakespeare's comedies the multiplot structure helps to foreground the importance of "hap," or fortune, in the outcome of the plot, as apparently independent causal sequences intersect and react upon one another. In *A Midsummer Night's Dream*, the chance encounter of the fairies Oberon and Robin with the Athenian lovers in the woods proves unexpectedly fateful for the lovers. In *As You Like It*, an inexplicable twist of fate brings Orlando, roaming far from home, to the same forest to which his beloved Rosalind has fled, and then later brings Orlando's older brother to the same forest, where Orlando can happen upon him just in the nick of time to save him from being eaten by a lioness. In *Twelfth Night*, the lovesick Olivia, seeking to marry a man who is, unbeknownst to her, actually a woman in disguise, accidentally stumbles instead upon her beloved's identical twin brother, a shipwreck survivor who has just arrived in town that morning. For the audience, the pleasure of such plots depends upon an interplay between the completely predictable "happy ending" and the unforeseen, wildly fortuitous means by which the characters arrive there.

In the crowded comic world, the aggressively self-actualizing individual who tries to carve out his own destiny tends to make himself ridiculous. By contrast, those who surrender themselves to circumstances often benefit from the workings of accident or providence. *Twelfth Night* rewards Viola, the lucky survivor of a shipwreck who waits for time to untangle her dilemmas, but humiliates the unctuous steward Malvolio, who strives assiduously to better his social standing. Moreover, in a world in which rules of probability seem not to hold, laughably foolish characters often prove weirdly discerning: Bottom in *A Midsummer Night's Dream*, Launce in *The Two Gentlemen of Verona*, Dogberry in *Much Ado About Nothing*, Pompey in *Measure for Measure*. Another important source of insight is the professional fool with his honed expertise as an improviser of absurdity: *As You Like It*'s Touchstone, *Twelfth Night*'s Feste, or *All's Well*'s Lavatch. These characters' crackpot misprisions and sly puns, bringing unrelated words and meanings into unanticipated conjunctions, are the verbal equivalents of the multilayered plot structure, in which apparently incompatible elements collide in productive chance encounters.

In an influential analysis, the critic Northrop Frye claimed that the comic world typically includes many characters and plots because comedy, as a genre, concerns itself with the renewal of an entire community, a renewal for which the concluding marriages are a kind of metaphor. As a practical matter, in order to perpetuate themselves, societies need their adult, fertile members to procreate, for, as Benedict comments in *Much Ado About Nothing*, "the world must be peopled" (2.3.213). The marriage of two people thus serves a social purpose beyond their individual gratification, as Shakespeare frequently reminds us by including some reference at the end of the play to the newlyweds' prospective children. Interestingly, the two genres with which Shakespeare was deeply concerned as a young dramatist for a large swathe of the mid- to late-1590s—chronicle history and comedy—both concern themselves with the construction of a community, but consider the problem from different, even complementary angles. While the history play is concerned with matters of state, the fate of nations, and a struggle for political power, comedy is concerned with domestic life and the relations among family members and neighbors. Thus features that seem marginal or supplemental in the history plays become central in the comedies, and vice versa. In the history plays wars typically determine the outcome of events, so valor in battle is highly prized; in *1* and *2 Henry IV*, Prince Harry must renounce his association with the fat, pleasure-loving, admittedly cowardly Falstaff and embrace his own heroic destiny. In comedy, however, war is pushed to the margins. In *As You Like It*, the bad duke musters an army to defeat the good duke, but, offstage, happens to meet a holy man who converts him to a hermit's life, so the threat of force simply evaporates. Moreover, bravery in battle is no longer a proxy for merit in other areas of life. As *Much Ado About Nothing* opens, a group of men are returning from a military campaign: the soldier most remarked upon, who "hath borne himself beyond the promise of his age, doing in the figure of a lamb the feats of a lion" (1.1.11–13), is Claudio, whose ferocious misogyny eventually brings the play close to tragedy. In *All's Well*

Falstaff and Mistress Quickly. Detail from the frontispiece to *The Wits; or, Sport upon Sport* (1662), a collection of short dramatic pieces, one of which featured Falstaff and his exploits.

That Ends Well, Bertram likewise wins high honors on the battlefield, but treats both his wife and his would-be lover shamefully.

One effect of this refocusing of perspective is that women, most of whom were excluded from politics but central to domestic life in Elizabethan England, become likewise central to Shakespearean comedy. Whereas the young women in classical New Comedies tend to be fairly pallid—in some plays the "love interest" does not even appear onstage—Shakespeare's comic women are highly realized and distinctive. He has a special partiality for vocal, opinionated heroines, who are dramatically much more compelling than the demure females held up for admiration by most Renaissance conduct books. In one of Shakespeare's first plays, *The Taming of the Shrew*, Katherina, the "shrew" or overbearing woman of the title, puts up furious resistance to her marriage to the eccentric Petruccio, before finally testifying to her "taming" in a long public speech of flamboyantly abject submission that makes her once again the center of attention. In later plays, a clever woman—a softened, better-socialized version of the shrew—typically stage-manages some of the crucial action of the play. Beatrice, in *Much Ado About Nothing*, interrupts her raillery with Benedict to facilitate the rehabilitation of her cousin, who has been falsely accused of unchastity. In *As You Like It*, the talkative, quirky Rosalind presides over much of the action in male disguise, finally ushering in the marriage god Hymen to officiate at the weddings with which the play concludes. In *Twelfth Night*, the "fair shrew" Maria devises an elaborate practical joke on the killjoy Malvolio. In *The Merchant of Venice*, Portia disguises herself as a young male lawyer and saves the life of her new husband's best friend in a stunning courtroom reversal. In *All's Well That Ends Well*, Helen is even more enterprising, first curing the King of a deadly malady, and then following her caddish husband from France to Italy and arranging to get pregnant by him without his knowledge.

Despite their high-spiritedness, their frankness about their desires, their volubility, and, in some cases, their willingness to don transvestite disguise—all traits associated with promiscuity in Renaissance treatises about women—the premarital virginity of Shakespeare's comic heroines is a nonnegotiable requirement, both for the men that love them and, apparently, for Shakespeare himself. The social value of

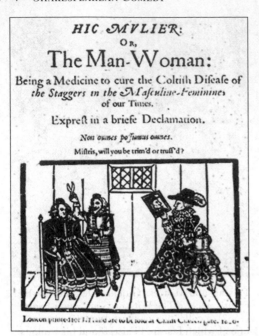

HIC MVLIER:
OR,
The Man-Woman:

Being a Medicine to cure the Coltish Difeafe of
the Staggers in the Mafculine-Feminines
of our Times.

Expreſt in a briefe Declamation.

Non omnes poſſumus omnes.

Miſtris, will you be trim'd or truſs'd?

London printed for I.T. and are to be fold at Chrift Churce gate. 1620

Title page of *Hic Mulier: or, The Man-Woman*
(1620), a pamphlet denouncing the "unnatural"
practice of women wearing men's clothing and
adopting masculine styles (the women in this
image are at a men's barber). *Hic Mulier* was
answered by *Haec Vir: or, The Womanish-Man*
(also 1620).

chastity is suggested in *Measure for Measure* 5.1.178–84, when the Duke and others enumerate the categories of respectable women: they may be "maids"—that is, virgins— "wives," or "widows." The only other category is "punk," or prostitute. Not surprisingly, then, Portia in *The Merchant of Venice* declares that if a husband does not claim her by passing the casket test devised by her father, she will live "chaste as Diana," the goddess of virginity; taking a lover outside of marriage does not seem to occur to her as an option. In *A Midsummer Night's Dream*, when the eloping lovers Hermia and Lysander find themselves lost in the wood by night, Hermia insists that they sleep at some distance from one another: "such separation as may well be said / Becomes a virtuous bachelor and a maid" (2.2.58–59). As a "virtuous bachelor," Lysander respects her scruples, but when the fairy Robin Goodfellow comes upon the sleeping couple, he misconstrues the situation: "Pretty soul, she durst not lie / Near this lack-love, this kill-courtesy" (2.2.76–77). Fairies, the play suggests, live by different rules of sexual conduct than mortals do. In other plays the standards for servant women and for minor characters are considerably more relaxed than they are for the genteel heroines. In *Much Ado About Nothing*, when Hero is imagined to have talked out of the window at night with a man, her fiancé and father agree that she has so shamed herself that she might as well die. Yet her maid Margaret, for whom Hero was mistaken, apparently escapes without rebuke when the confusion becomes known. Similarly, Jacquenetta, the milkmaid in *Love's Labor's Lost*, turns out to be pregnant by one of her two suitors at the end of the play; her evident consent to premarital intimacy contrasts with the behavior of the princess and her ladies-in-waiting, who engage their lovers in elegant mockery but at the same time carefully preserve their "maiden honor, yet as pure / As the unsullied lily" (5.2.352–53).

The wit of Shakespeare's heroines, then, is not simply anarchic or subversive: it coexists with implicit constraints upon their conduct. In Renaissance England, women's political and legal rights were severely restricted, yet Shakespeare's women, although often more intelligent and resourceful than the men with whom they are paired, only rarely chafe openly against their subordination or argue for a reconfiguration of gender roles. There are two rather different reasons for their acquiescence. One is that the comedies generally represent the restrictions upon women's freedom as easy to evade. In *The Merry Wives of Windsor*, Mistress Ford and Mistress Page, the merry wives of the title, will be ruined socially if their husbands discover that they are entertaining a man who is paying court to them. Twice one of the husbands bursts in with a posse of neighbors to investigate their supposed adulterous scheming. Yet instead of being intimidated by this show of male authority, or inveighing against the double standard for sexual behavior, the wives deliberately place themselves in risky situations, taking enormous pleasure in their narrow escapes and easily making fools of both the jealous husband and the would-be lover. In other comedies, faced with some restriction or impediment, women simply pass themselves off as men. In *As You Like It*, for instance, Celia and Rosalind know that two women traveling alone will be vulnerable to robbery and rape, so Rosalind disguises herself as a male "youth," and they arrive at their destination safely. In *The Merchant of Venice*, Portia likewise disguises herself as a young man in order to gain access to the male preserve of the courtroom. In both cases, male disguise allows the heroine to combine her superior intelligence with the social privileges accorded to men.

Yet if the constraints of gender seem simple for a clever woman to renegotiate, they also, in many plays, do not seem especially onerous to those who must live within them. Shakespeare's heroines are not chaste because chastity needs to be imposed forcibly upon them, but because they accept their culture's notion of admirable conduct and take pride in their physical "purity." Moreover, many of Shakespeare's comic heroines associate erotic feeling with a happy acceptance of inferiority to the beloved man. In *A Midsummer Night's Dream*, Helena, desperate for Demetrius's affection, is especially abject:

> I am your spaniel, and, Demetrius,
> The more you beat me I will fawn on you.
> Use me but as your spaniel: spurn me, strike me,
> Neglect me, lose me—only give me leave,
> Unworthy as I am, to follow you.
>
> (2.1.203–07)

Other women in Shakespeare's comedies possess more self-respect, but even Portia in *The Merchant of Venice*, who (disguised as a youthful lawyer) will shortly take masterful charge of a Venetian courtroom, considers herself, in comparison to her intended husband Bassanio, "an unlessoned girl, unschooled, unpracticed":

> Happiest of all is that her gentle spirit
> Commits itself to yours to be directed
> As from her lord, her governor, her king.
>
> (3.2.159–65)

A married woman in Shakespeare's time could not own property in her own name: her estate was normally, upon marriage, at her husband's disposal. Portia alludes to this rule, called *couverture*, as her speech continues:

> But now I was the lord
> Of this fair mansion, master of my servants,
> Queen o'er myself; and even now, but now,
> This house, these servants, and this same myself
> Are yours, my lord's.
>
> (3.2.167–71)

Portia is both cleverer and much wealthier than her intended, but instead of seeing the obligation to defer to her new husband as a degradation of her status, Portia embraces it, as if a willingness to relinquish her authority were an intrinsic part of her experience of love.

Shakespeare's comic heroines, then, triumph not in spite of but because of the restrictions placed upon them: in other words, they find constraint enabling. This paradox has generated a certain amount of disagreement among Shakespeare's critics. Some see him as a proto-feminist because of the way his heroines challenge gender norms by donning transvestite disguises, devising "bed tricks," or distinguishing themselves in the male professions of law or medicine. Other critics emphasize the conservatism of the heroine's goal: marriage to a husband whom she accepts as her "lord." In fact, the heroine's preeminence in comedy seems of a piece with the almost magical conferral of power upon the ordinarily powerless that is an intrinsic aspect of the comic pattern. Often her successes seem inexplicable by ordinary means: in *As You Like It*, Rosalind describes herself as a magician's disciple, and in *All's Well That Ends Well*, "though miracles are past"—that is, the remarkable events described in the Bible no longer occur—Helen's cure of the King is called "the rarest argument of wonder that hath shot out in our latter times" (2.3.1, 6–7).

In classical New Comedy, as I have already mentioned, an older authority figure, usually a father, refused to permit the marriage of the young lovers and thus created an obstacle that the action of the play had to overcome. Shakespeare sometimes uses this convention: in *A Midsummer Night's Dream*, Hermia flees Athens with her lover Lysander because her father Egeus, backed by law, is trying to force her to marry Demetrius. In *The Merchant of Venice*, the Jewish Jessica must elope with Lorenzo, a Christian her father would never countenance. In *The Merry Wives of Windsor*, Ann and Fenton outwit both her parents, who have other matches for her in mind. Yet often in Shakespearean comedy, the young lovers woo without the interference, or even with the positive assistance, of parents and other older authority figures. In *The Two Gentlemen of Verona*, *Love's Labor's Lost*, and *Twelfth Night*, parents are elsewhere, or dead. In *As You Like It*, Rosalind's father does not recognize her, because she is in disguise, and he has nothing to do with her marriage plans. In *The Merchant of Venice*, Bassanio's father is apparently deceased, and while Portia's late father has devised an apparently arbitrary test for her suitors, it ends up selecting the man with whom she is already in love. In *Much Ado About Nothing*, Claudio asks his commanding officer, as his father-surrogate, to help him arrange a marriage with Hero, whose father is likewise accommodating; in the same play, friends and relatives intervene to "undertake one of Hercules' labors, which is to bring Signor Benedict and the lady Beatrice into a mountain of affection, th'one with th'other" (2.1.321–23). In *All's Well That Ends Well*, the older generation is more enthusiastic about the union of the poor physician's daughter Helen and the aristocrat Bertram than are the young people themselves, generously dismissing the class difference between husband and wife and ignoring property considerations as well.

By minimizing, in many plays, the importance of parental prohibition, Shakespeare focuses attention instead on the way the young lovers create their own roadblocks to marriage. In their jubilant multiple weddings, the comedies generally celebrate the delights of heterosexual love, and Shakespeare seems to take as axiomatic that this celebration pleases the audience as well. Such titles as *Twelfth Night, or What You Will* and *As You Like It* suggest that Shakespeare sees his comedies as pleasurably gratifying his audience's wishful fantasies. The epilogues of several comedies invite the audience to share in the concluding festivities. In *A Midsummer Night's Dream*, after the lovers troop off to bed—to beget healthy children, we are told—Robin Goodfellow asks the audience to "give me your hands": he both requests applause for the actors' performance and suggests that the world of the play and the world of the audience are continuous, and that the spectators of the play are part of the happy community of the comic conclusion. In *As You Like It*, even more explicitly, Rosalind's Epilogue makes the connection between the comedy's onstage flirtations and a heightened sexual atmosphere among the play's spectators: "I charge you, O women, for the love you bear to men, to like as much of this play as please you. And I charge you, O men, for the love you bear to women—as I perceive by your simpering, none of you hates them—that between you and the women, the play may please" (lines 200–204).

Yet Shakespeare tempers this affirmative view of heterosexual attraction and gratification with some attention to inherently contradictory or recalcitrant aspects of sexuality. In fact, over the course of his career as a comic dramatist he seems to grow more pessimistic, so that in his last two comedies, *Measure for Measure* and *All's Well That Ends Well*, love's difficulties and disappointments come close to overwhelming its rewards. As we have seen, sexual congress between men and women is a social necessity—a community cannot survive unless its members procreate.

Nonetheless, sexual passion figures, in Shakespearean comedy as in most Renaissance love poetry, as profoundly resistant to social control: a highly subjective, even solipsistic or isolating experience.

> The lunatic, the lover, and the poet
> Are of imagination all compact.
> (*A Midsummer Night's Dream* 5.1.7–8)

Again and again Shakespeare stresses that, in love, there is no accounting for taste: beauty lies in the eye of the beholder, and socially mandated standards of beauty mean little to individual beholders. In *Love's Labor's Lost*, Biron's male friends tease him unmercifully for loving a "black" or dark-complexioned woman, because the ideal female beauty in Shakespeare's day was fair-haired and white-skinned, but Biron staunchly defends his preference. In *Much Ado About Nothing*, when Claudio enthuses about Hero, "the sweetest lady that ever I looked on," Benedict replies that "I can see yet without spectacles, and I see no such matter" (1.1.53–56). In *A Midsummer Night's Dream*, Helena, unrequitedly in love with Demetrius, compares herself to Hermia, the woman Demetrius does love:

> Through Athens I am thought as fair as she.
> But what of that? Demetrius thinks not so.
> ·
> Love looks not with the eyes but with the mind,
> And therefore is winged Cupid painted blind.
> (1.1.227–35)

Yet at the same time as the lover's experience seems unshared by others, it also seems to come from outside the self, an alien invader. "What's this, what's this?" asks the shocked Angelo in *Measure for Measure*, surprised by his sudden, overpowering desire for Isabella (2.3.165). Both Biron, in *Love's Labor's Lost*, and Benedict, in *Much Ado About Nothing*, ridicule the follies of lovers until, unexpectedly, they fall in love themselves: "What, I love, I sue, I seek a wife?" Biron asks himself incredulously (3.1.174). In *A Midsummer Night's Dream*, the fairies interfere with attachments between the human lovers by treating their eyes with juice squeezed from a flower obtained by supernatural means from the other side of the globe. Yet ordinary sexual passion, generated from "within" the lover, apparently operates exactly the same way as the exotic flower juice operating from "without." In fact Demetrius, one of the lovers, must remain permanently under the influence of the fairies' flower-juice in order for the final pairing off to proceed.

How can this mysterious, giddy impulse be subjected to discipline? In particular, how can it be harnessed to what the Queen in *Love's Labor's Lost* calls the "world-without-end bargain" of marriage (5.2.777), a bond that could not, in Shakespeare's time, be dissolved by divorce? "Tell me how long you would have her after you have possessed her," the disguised Rosalind commands her lover Orlando, who answers, "Forever and a day." "Say 'a day' without the 'ever,'" Rosalind advises him (*As You Like It* 4.1.124–27). Shakespeare's plays are full of jokes about the brief half-life of erotic attraction, a desire that seems immense but that will disappear as soon as its sexual goal is achieved. In *Much Ado About Nothing*, Balthasar sings:

> Sigh no more, ladies, sigh no more.
> Men were deceivers ever,
> One foot in sea, and one on shore,
> To one thing constant never.
> ·
> The fraud of men was ever so,
> Since summer first was leafy.
> (2.3.57–68)

Elsewhere, women's fickle affections are said to betray men, their infidelities imposing the shame of the "cuckold's horn" upon their husbands. In *Much Ado About Nothing*, Benedict worries that if he marries, he will inevitably "hang my bugle in an invisible baldric," or horn-belt (1.1.205–06); in *As You Like It*, the Duke's men, coming home from hunting the deer, sing a song that ends in a jolly insult to the listener and his presumed lineage:

> Take thou no scorn to wear the horn.
> It was a crest e'er thou wast born.
> Thy father's father wore it,
> And thy father bore it.
>   (4.2.14–17)

It is not surprising, then, that Shakespeare's comedies should be much concerned with the problem of constancy, and with the making and breaking of vows, since a vow is essentially an assurance about the future. As the weaker parties to the love-transaction, women are especially likely to insist upon the importance of the vow, since they have more to lose if it is breached. In *The Merchant of Venice*, as we have seen, Portia subjects herself and her estate to her new husband Bassanio, but she does so conditionally:

> This house, these servants, and this same myself
> Are yours, my lord's. I give them with this ring,
> Which when you part from, lose, or give away,
> Let it presage the ruin of your love.
>   (3.2.170–73)

In the event, Bassanio does give away the ring. In *The Two Gentlemen of Verona* and *A Midsummer Night's Dream*, some of the men, despite their professed ardor, likewise do not remain faithful to the women they have courted; and in *Love's Labor's Lost*, the women warily impose a year's waiting period on the men in an attempt to test their dependability. If love is often instantly kindled, it must be perpetuated by promises, and the dependability of those promises rests upon the trustworthiness of the persons who make them.

Shakespeare's comedies thus hold in suspension two apparently disparate views of love: one highly idealized and idealizing, the other subjecting the idealism to critique and mockery. Shakespeare was certainly not the first to take a double view of "lovers' follies": they had long generated much of the humor in New Comic plot situations. In many classical and Renaissance New Comedies, the enthusiastic young lover is laughably wholehearted and naïve, the subject of his friends' sardonic commentary. Shakespeare often complicates this simple paradigm. Many of his most appealing characters deal with the complexities of sexual love neither by repudiating love nor by abandoning their capacity for critical detachment. Rather, they fall in love but simultaneously remain entirely cognizant of their own absurdity; in other words, they combine the roles of lover and love's critic. Biron in *Love's Labor's Lost* and Benedict in *Much Ado About Nothing* both play this double game, and in *As You Like It* Rosalind, in her disguise as "Ganymede," regales her lover Orlando with what she represents as sage advice. "Men have died from time to time, and worms have eaten them, but not for love," she assures him briskly (4.1.93–94). And later: "men are April when they woo, December when they wed; maids are May when they are maids, but the sky changes when they are wives" (4.1.127–30). Yet after Orlando departs, Rosalind exclaims to her cousin Celia: "O coz, coz, my pretty little coz, that thou didst know how many fathom deep I am in love" (4.1.175–76). Viola, in *Twelfth Night*, performs the same trick of detachment with less humor and more pathos, recounting her own story of apparently unrequited love to her beloved, Duke Orsino, as a story about her sister:

King Solomon *in flagrante delicto*. From the *The Deceit of Women* (1558?).

ORSINO   And what's her history?
VIOLA A blank, my lord. She never told her love
    But let concealment, like a worm i'the bud,
    Feed on her damask cheek. She pined in thought,
    And, with a green and yellow melancholy,
    She sat like Patience on a monument,
    Smiling at grief.

                                          (2.4.106–12)

Whether this oblique utterance counts as "telling" her love is, of course, an open question, as uncertain, or "blank," as Viola perceives her own future to be. The self-aware lover, alert to the excesses of passionate sexual attachment but at the same time fully immersed in them, is a natural ally of the clown, with his professional expertise in ironic participation. Thus in *As You Like It*, Touchstone throws in his lot with Rosalind and Celia, and Viola comments appreciatively upon Feste's skill in *Twelfth Night*.

If one problem for lovers is a temporal one—how to make a fleeting, if powerful, impulse the basis of a permanent relationship—another is how to reconcile the heterosexual, potentially procreative liaison with other kinds of relationship. While, compared to other comic dramatists, Shakespeare tends to play down intergenerational strife, he again and again shows the emotional demands of heterosexual pairing in conflict with powerful same-sex loyalties. In the early *Two Gentlemen of Verona*, best friends Valentine and Proteus fall in love with the same woman: Proteus betrays his friend in an attempt to get Silvia for himself, and then Valentine (without consulting Silvia) cedes her to Proteus:

    And that my love may appear plain and free,
    All that was mine in Silvia I give thee.

                                          (5.4.83–84)

The "love" to which Valentine refers here is not his love for his betrothed but his devotion to his male companion, which apparently trumps all other obligations. Another turn of the plot is required to return Silvia to Valentine and to pair Proteus with his original girlfriend, Julia. Shakespeare will not return to the depiction of so bald a rivalry between friends until the late, collaborative play *The Two Noble Kinsmen*, but in many other comedies a man's new love affair with a woman competes with his prior attachment to another man. In *Twelfth Night*, Sebastian owes his life to Antonio, a noble pirate who feels for him "desire, / More sharp than filèd steel" (3.3.4–5). Following Sebastian to Illyria, where there is a price on his head, Antonio risks his life only to see Sebastian snatched away by the marriage-minded Olivia. In *The Merchant of Venice*, Bassanio must choose between his loyalty to Portia, whom he has just married, and his obligation to his friend Antonio—and initially chooses Antonio. In *A Midsummer Night's Dream*, it is the women—the fairy queen Titania and her Indian votress, and the mortal women Hermia and Helena—whose intimacies are ruptured by heterosexual passion. As the men quarrel over them and Hermia and Helena quarrel between themselves, Helena exclaims:

> —oh, is all quite forgot,
> All schooldays' friendship, childhood innocence?
> We, Hermia, like two artificial gods
> Have with our needles created both one flower,
> Both on one sampler, sitting on one cushion,
> Both warbling of one song, both in one key,
> As if our hands, our sides, voices, and minds
> Had been incorporate. So we grew together
> Like to a double cherry, seeming parted,
> But yet an union in partition.
>
> (3.2.201–10)

Here, as in the other plays, Shakespeare leaves unspecified whether the emotional closeness between two persons of the same sex is ever physically consummated. But like marriage, female friendship as Helena describes it mysteriously makes one out of two: the word "incorporate," for instance, derives from a Latin word meaning "made into a single body." The implication is that whether or not such relationships are ever homosexually expressed, their intensity rivals that of heterosexual love.

Nonetheless, the potentially procreative marriages with which the comedy ends cannot occur if the characters sort permanently with persons of their own sex. Often therefore, as here, idyllic moments of same-sex love are imagined retrospectively, as something already lost. At other times, same-sex attachment must be renounced. Thus in *Much Ado About Nothing*, Beatrice requires her lover Benedict to challenge his friend Claudio to a duel for having slandered her cousin Hero. Benedict initially recoils, but then relents to her demand, a sign that his primary allegiance has shifted from his comrades-in-arms to the woman whom he will marry at the end of the play. In *The Merchant of Venice*, Portia forgives her husband Bassanio for having given away his wedding ring only after Bassanio's close friend Antonio pledges, essentially, that he will no longer claim priority in Bassanio's affections. In *A Midsummer Night's Dream*, the fairy queen Titania at first retains her Indian votress's child out of a sense of loyalty to the dead votress, but ends up tamely relinquishing the child to her husband Oberon. Still, because Shakespeare portrays same-sex friendship as so rewarding and significant, some sense of loss as well as gain lingers over the happiness of the comic conclusion. Moreover, some characters cannot or refuse to be included in the marital finale. Thus, in *Twelfth Night*, as so many of the main characters form heterosexual couples, the valiant Antonio is left isolated, an isolation the directors of some productions have emphasized by having him exit separately at the end of the play. In *As You Like It*, the "melancholy" Jacques simply declines to participate in the wedding revelry: "So—to your pleasures! / I am for other than for dancing measures" (5.4.183–84). Such characters make vivid the fact that not everybody is "the marrying kind," and that the inclusiveness of the comic conclusion has its limits.

Also left out of the comic conclusion, or only shakily reintegrated, are characters who might be considered scapegoats. The word "scapegoat" originates in an ancient ceremony in which a community ritually cleansed itself by delegating the responsibility for all its sins to a single person or animal—a goat in ancient Israel, a slave or foreigner in ancient Greece—who was then punished and expelled. In modern parlance, a scapegoat is someone unfairly blamed as an individual for faults or crimes that are actually committed by a group. In many of his plays Shakespeare manifests keen interest in the psychological mechanism by which people project their faults onto others, and the way uniting against a despised "outsider" can help a community cohere more tightly. Thus in *The Merchant of Venice*, the Christians revile the Jew Shylock, whose bald pursuit of self-interest and refusal to mix financial arrangements with friendship lay bare unwelcome truths about their own handling of money. Likewise the prim Malvolio, in *Twelfth Night*, is treated as a madman for having dared to imagine for himself the social advancement through marriage which the glamorous twins Sebastian and Viola actually achieve. The residents of Windsor humiliate Falstaff, in *The Merry Wives of Windsor*, for thinking that he can trade sex for money, even while Ann's parents plan to marry her off to one of her wealthy suitors rather than to the man she loves. Don John, the scheming bastard in *Much Ado About Nothing*, embodies the possibility of extramarital sexual activity, the prospect of which triggers so much of the suspicion and pain in the play. In all these cases the scapegoat is indeed guilty, sometimes murderously so. Yet the community's investment in punishing him seems excessive, in a way that exposes its hypocrisy or blindness to its own motives.

In a few of the comedies, the scapegoat character remains completely beyond the pale at the end of the play: in *Much Ado About Nothing*, the Duke cheerfully anticipates devising "brave tortures" for his bastard brother Don John the day after the weddings. More often, there is some attempt at reconciliation, an effort to encircle the offender and keep him within the community after all. In *The Merry Wives of Windsor*, Falstaff is tormented but then invited to a feast, and in *All's Well That Ends Well*, the pretentious, unscrupulous Parolles is first exposed as a liar and a coward, and then given a small pension. The attempt at reconciliation may seem profoundly hurtful, as when Shylock is given his life with the proviso that he convert to Christianity, a form of "mercy" that seems merely to substitute psychological for physical violence. Or the conciliatory gesture may be rejected: in *Twelfth Night*, despite Olivia's attempts to make peace, Malvolio storms off with a vow to "be revenged on the whole pack of you."

Yet despite these darker notes forgiveness remains critically important in Shakespearean comedy. And since, as we have seen, the obstacles to happy love are so often self-imposed, not only the scapegoat characters are in need of it. A good deal of pain in the plays is the result of immature or unworthy young men behaving badly: Proteus in *The Two Gentlemen of Verona*, Demetrius in *A Midsummer Night's Dream*, Oliver in *As You Like It*, Bassanio in *The Merchant of Venice*, Claudio in *Much Ado About Nothing*, Angelo in *Measure for Measure*, Bertram in *All's Well That Ends Well*. All these characters, with greater or lesser motive and with more or less serious consequences, violate the bonds of relationship and must be forgiven at the end of the play. At times, indeed, they seem to get off too lightly: their efforts at repentance unconvincing, the pardons they are extended unmerited, and the women with whom they are matched too good for them.

In Shakespeare's hands, however, comedy is not merely a genre that celebrates youth and fertility, but one that mandates the charitable inclusion of nearly everyone. And typically that imagined community includes not only the characters onstage but the audience of the play as well. The actor playing Robin Goodfellow, in the closing lines of the Epilogue to *A Midsummer Night's Dream*, bids us to "give me your hands, if we be friends"—both a hint for applause and an invitation into the play's magical, fortunate world. The comedies offer to their audiences, as we like it, the heartwarming possibility of getting more than we deserve.

SELECTED BIBLIOGRAPHY

Bamber, Linda. *Comic Women, Tragic Men: Gender and Genre in Shakespeare*. Stanford, CA: Stanford UP, 1982. Looks at Shakespearean comedy as the special domain of women, imagined as the Other by a male dramatist.

Barber, C. L. *Shakespeare's Festive Comedy*. Princeton, NJ: Princeton UP, 1959. Discusses Shakespeare's comedy in terms of Elizabethan holiday rituals.

Briggs, Julia. "Shakespeare's Bed-Tricks." *Essays in Criticism* 44 (1994): 293–314. Provides an overview of Shakespeare's use of the "bed trick" (sexual substitution) in many of his comedies.

Carroll, William. *The Metamophoses of Shakespearean Comedy*. Princeton, NJ: Princeton UP, 1985. Examines the themes of change and fluidity in the comedies.

Danson, Lawrence. *Shakespeare's Dramatic Genres*. Oxford: Oxford UP, 2000. Offers a brief, student-oriented overview that includes a chapter on the comedies.

Dutton, Richard, and Jean Howard, eds. *A Companion to Shakespeare's Works*. Vol. 3: *The Comedies*. Malden, MA: Blackwell, 2005. Includes twelve essays on topics such as cross-dressing, rhetoric, homoeroticism, and geography, as well as essays on individual plays.

Frye, Northrop. "The Argument of Comedy." *The Anatomy of Criticism*. Princeton, NJ: Princeton UP, 1957. Presents a very influential general account of comic plot.

Leggatt, Alexander, ed. *The Cambridge Companion to Shakespearean Comedy*. Cambridge: Cambridge UP, 2003. Includes thirteen essays on the literary and social background and on recurrent themes such as "confusion" and "sexual disguise."

Salingar, Leo. *Shakespeare and the Traditions of Comedy*. Cambridge: Cambridge UP, 1974. Looks at Shakespeare's debt to medieval and classical comedy and romance.

Wheeler, Richard. *Shakespeare's Development and the Problem Comedies: Turn and Counter-Turn*. Berkeley: U of California P, 1981. Presents psychoanalytically tinged discussion of Shakespeare's late comedies.

The Two Gentlemen of Verona

Readers and playgoers have often found both startling and disconcerting the events that conclude *The Two Gentlemen of Verona*. Proteus, a young man thwarted in his love for Silvia, who loves Proteus's friend Valentine, says that since wooing her with words has not worked, he will follow the soldier's path and "love you gainst the nature of love—force ye" (5.4.58). At that moment, Valentine steps out of hiding and stops the attempted rape by denouncing Proteus as a treacherous friend. Overcome with remorse for the betrayal of Valentine, though not explicitly for his attempted sexual violence, Proteus begs forgiveness. Generously, Valentine says he is content. He then announces that he will give Silvia to Proteus as a sign of the renewal of the friendship between the two men. A near rape and the offer of a woman as an object of exchange between men—is this the stuff of comedy?

Apparently a number of directors, actors, and critics have thought not. In the mid-eighteenth century, it became common to cut Valentine's offer to give Silvia to his friend, a stage tradition that largely held until William Charles Macready, the famous actor and producer of Shakespeare's plays, reintroduced the lines in 1841. As late as 1952, however, Denis Carey's production at the Bristol Old Vic again deleted Valentine's offer. Some critics have been so certain Shakespeare could not have written the scene as it stands that they argued that it was altered in the playhouse. How do we explain why Shakespeare concluded his comedy with events that to many people have seemed so distasteful and so disconcerting?

One answer might be that Shakespeare was simply a young dramatist not fully in control of his craft. *The Two Gentlemen of Verona* is, after all, one of his earliest plays, perhaps the earliest. It bears marks of its early date of composition. It has, for example, the smallest cast of any of the plays. Many scenes contain only two or three speakers, as if Shakespeare had not yet mastered the skill of orchestrating a full complement of stage voices and bodies. It is marked as well by a number of plot inconsistencies and confusing details. Valentine and Proteus leave Verona to go to the Emperor's court, for example, but end up attaching themselves to the Duke of Milan—an important nobleman, certainly, but not the Emperor. Likewise, the geographical placement of some scenes is vague. The characters speak of Verona, Milan, Mantua, and Padua, but the names often are used interchangeably and seem collectively to be Shakespeare's shorthand for "Italy" rather than distinct places.

In other ways, however, the play is both an accomplished theatrical piece and a genuine precursor of many aspects of Shakespeare's later comic techniques and structures. The play features lovers whose fickle or thwarted passions lead them into all sorts of difficulties: treachery to friends, banishment, disguise. These difficulties get sorted out only after most of the drama's significant players decamp to a forest outside Milan. There, in a green world complete with a band of outlaws, the fickle Proteus reverts to his original love for Julia, Silvia's disapproving father forgoes his objections to Valentine, friendship is renewed between the two young men, the outlaws are pardoned and unworthy lovers dismissed. The utopian possibilities for social renewal in a world beyond the walls and customs of the city are celebrated in this play as they will later be in *A Midsummer Night's Dream*, *As You Like It*, and other Shakespearean romantic comedies of the 1590s. *Two Gentlemen* also contains the first of Shakespeare's cross-dressed heroines, the faithful Julia, who follows her fickle lover from Verona to Milan and then, as his page, accompanies him into the woods in his pursuit of Silvia. Male disguise allows Julia a freedom of action and movement not normally granted to early modern women, but, as was often to be the case in later Shakespearean comedies, this freedom has as its ultimate goal the heroine's embrace of marriage.

The excellence of much of the play, then, suggests that the difficulties many have experienced with the ending stem not from Shakespeare's relative inexperience as a dramatist, but rather from the subject matter of the play itself—that is, from Shakespeare's ambitious attempt to probe the relationship between two kinds of bonds: friendship between men and love between a man and a woman. In the Renaissance, each of these was a privileged relationship, but their relative worth was a matter for debate and disagreement. In staging his exploration of the claims of love and friendship, Shakespeare drew on two different sources. The first was a Spanish prose romance published in 1542, Jorge de Montemayor's *Diana Enamorada*. Translated into French in 1578 and into English in the 1580s, it was published in English in 1598. Shakespeare, then, could have read the story in French or in the unpublished English version. He could also have learned of it from an anonymous play performed at court in 1585, *The History of Felix and Philomena*, now lost.

The Montemayor romance focuses on a man's unfaithfulness in love. Don Felix leaves Felismena for Celia; Felismena pursues him in the guise of a page; Celia falls in love with the page and conveniently dies when the page rejects her. Shakespeare retains much of this material in the Proteus–Silvia–Julia triangle but adds the Valentine plot, probably drawn from the story of two friends, Titus and Gisippus, told by Boccaccio and then recounted in book 2, chapter 12, of Thomas Elyot's *Book of the Governor* (1531). In this story, Titus falls in love with the woman Gisippus is to marry, and Gisippus gives the woman to his friend. Later, Gisippus takes upon himself the blame for a murder Titus is wrongly accused of committing.

Male friendship ("Steadfast is the love based on inclination"). From Richard Brathwaite, *The English Gentleman*, 2nd edition (1633).

The story unabashedly advances the claims of heroic male friendship over other ties, including those of male–female love. Shakespeare's challenge in *The Two Gentlemen of Verona* is to join together aspects of these two stories. In his play, there are two pairs of lovers, not just a fickle Proteus figure moving between two women, and the close friendship between Valentine and Proteus is given a prominence equal to that of the male–female love stories.

In foregrounding the importance of male friendship, Shakespeare joined a long tradition of writers who celebrated such friendships, often comparing them favorably with the presumably more dangerous relationships men could have with women. In *The Governor*, for example, Elyot praised male friendship in terms that would be echoed in other early modern texts: "Verily it is a blessed and stable connection of sundry wills, making of two persons one in having and suffering. And therefore a friend is properly named of phi-losophers the other I. For that in them is but one mind and one possession and that which more is, a man more rejoiceth at his friend's good fortune than at his own" (book 2, chapter 11). The French essayist Michel de Montaigne, whose writings Shakespeare might have encountered in French before John Florio's English transla-tion of 1603, also praised the friendship of equals as a mingling of souls so complete that no line divides them. By contrast, Sir Francis Bacon (who also wrote an essay in praise of friendship) in his essay "Of Love" captures the fear and disdain with which passionate love between men and women was often regarded: "In life it doth much mischief, sometimes like a siren, sometimes like a fury. You may observe that amongst all the great and worthy persons (whereof the memory remaineth, either ancient or recent) there is not one that hath been transported to the mad degree of love; which shows that great spirits and great business do keep out this weak passion."

The Two Gentlemen of Verona participates both in the celebration (and critique) of male friendship and in the comic deflation of male–female love. Several times male characters speak of the strange transformations of the self that passion for a woman can induce. Proteus, choosing to stay in Verona with Julia rather than fol-low his friend to Milan for an education in courtiership, speaks of his own choice disdainfully. Of Valentine he says:

> He after honor hunts, I after love.
> He leaves his friends to dignify them more;
> I leave myself, my friends, and all, for love.
> Thou, Julia, thou hast metamorphosed me:
> Made me neglect my studies, lose my time,
> War with good counsel, set the world at naught;
> Made wit with musing weak, heart sick with thought.
> (1.1.63–69)

The play is one of Shakespeare's first explorations of what it means to be trans-formed, or "metamorphosed," by love of a woman. Perhaps he took his cue from the Roman poet Ovid's vastly popular book the *Metamorphoses*, which contained numer-ous tales of people transformed by love. In Ovid, gods sometimes assume the shapes of mortals or of animals to pursue their beloved; or women turn into trees or flowers in their flight from unwanted amorous advances. In *The Two Gentlemen of Verona*, Pro-teus's name echoes that of the sea god who could change shape at will and who was thus often associated with a fickle nature. In the above passage Proteus is the one who first mentions being metamorphosed by love, but the play rings many changes on this idea. Sometimes the transformations wrought by love seem comic to others. Speed, for example, has excellent fun laughing at the strange transformations of his master, Valentine, who, in love with Silvia, begins to act like a perfect malcontent, "metamorphosed with a mistress" (2.1.27). A malcontent, here meaning someone made melancholy by love, was a stock figure in Renaissance literature and the visual arts, sometimes rendered comic by his disordered attire or his moody alienation from his fellow men.

Sometimes, however, in this play, love is shown to have more positive conse-quences. It leads to heroic feats such as Julia's daring cross-dressed journey in pur-suit of Proteus, and to the outpouring of poetry and songs. However fickle Proteus's passion for Silvia shows him to be, it also moves him to offer her the gorgeous song "Who is Silvia? What is she / That all our swains commend her?" (4.2.37–38). In the movie *Shakespeare in Love*, in which scenes and speeches from *The Two Gentlemen of Verona* are used to indicate Shakespeare's promise as a writer of romantic comedy, this lyricism compels Viola de Lesseps, the aristocratic heroine, to fall in love with the youthful Shakespeare who wrote those verses. Within the play, Valentine, under the influence of love, is prepared to scale the walls of Silvia's tower to bear her away;

The love melancholic. Isaac Oliver, *Edward, First Lord Herbert of Cherbury* (1617).

however, not all the metamorphoses wrought by love are either comic or admirable. Love also makes men dangerous and hurtful. Under the influence of his fickle passions, Proteus abandons one woman for another, betrays Valentine's marriage plans to Silvia's father, and threatens to rape the woman he supposedly adores. Proteus speaks three soliloquies in *The Two Gentlemen of Verona* (2.4.188–210, 2.6.1–43, and 4.2.1–17), and in each he struggles with the confusion to which his mixed allegiances and desires have led him. Loving Silvia, he has betrayed Julia and betrayed Valentine, acknowledging that "I love his lady too too much, / And that's the reason I love him so little" (2.4.201–02). As moralists warned, the passion of man for woman can turn a man into a beast.

By contrast, friendship between men, though much compromised in this text, holds the promise of an ennobling intimacy. When Proteus and Valentine must part in the first scene, Proteus's language betrays the depth of his love for and dependence on his friend:

> Wilt thou be gone? Sweet Valentine, adieu.
> Think on thy Proteus when thou haply seest
> Some rare noteworthy object in thy travel.
> Wish me partaker in thy happiness
> When thou dost meet good hap; and in thy danger,
> If ever danger do environ thee,
> Commend thy grievance to my holy prayers;
> For I will be thy beadsman, Valentine.
>
> (1.1.11–18)

Here, the friend is imagined as "the other I," sharer of every joy, intimate of every thought. The delight with which Valentine later welcomes Proteus to the Duke's court and even his eventual offer of Silvia to his friend are signs of the potential depth of male bonds in the play and in early modern culture. In fact, to an early modern audience, Valentine's offer was perhaps not so shocking as it seems to contemporary audiences, but rather the unsurprising outcome of a social world that valued male friendship above most other forms of association.

But Valentine's gesture, of course, suggests the potential cost to women of these powerful male bonds. It neither serves their desires nor is made with their consent. By the way he creates the characters of Julia and Silvia, Shakespeare invites his audience to take them and their emotions seriously and makes it difficult to overlook the men's irresponsible and callous treatment of them. While Proteus is faithful neither to his male friend nor to his female beloved, the women are models of constant affection. Each, moreover, risks a good deal for her beloved. Julia courts public scandal by dressing as a boy and following Proteus to Milan; Silvia flees her father's court to follow the banished Valentine into the forest. Each, moreover, is respectful of her female rival.

Julia, in particular, is a complex figure, proud and silly in the scene in which she pretends not to want to read the letter her maid has brought her from Proteus (1.2), but impressively dignified when, disguised as a male page, she is faced with the task of being Proteus's messenger to Silvia (4.4). Asked by Silvia to describe Julia, the disguised woman says that Julia is of her color and height. She knows this, she claims, because once she wore Julia's clothes "to play the woman's part" (4.4.155) in a holiday pageant. Moreover, the part she played

> 'twas Ariadne, passioning
> For Theseus' perjury and unjust flight,
> Which I so lively acted with my tears
> That my poor mistress, movèd therewithal,
> Wept bitterly; and would I might be dead
> If I in thought felt not her very sorrow.
> (4.4.162–67)

Ariadne, of course, is an archetype of the betrayed woman. She helped her lover, Theseus, escape the man-eating Minotaur in the labyrinth on Crete, but then was abandoned by him on the island of Naxos. The abandoned Julia, so transformed by love and grief that she no longer can lay claim to her own name, finds a point of identification in Ariadne's grief and in imagining what "Julia" would have felt to see the enactment of Ariadne's story. This is a wonderfully complicated moment, a representation of a woman's grief and self-alienation and also her empathetic engagement with the story of another woman's grief. It at once reveals the cost, to women, of men's inconstancy and makes it difficult to accept that women should simply become the objects of exchange between male friends.

The nearly tragic consciousness here granted to Julia is countered in this play by the boisterous comic voices of Speed and Lance, two of Shakespeare's earliest and liveliest clowns. Their presence helps suggest that however complicated Shakespeare's exploration of the tension between love and friendship becomes, the outcome will not be fully tragic. Speed is a clever clown, excellent at puns and wordplay, devastatingly accurate in his parodic imitation of Valentine's lovesick behavior and clever enough to see, when his master cannot, that Silvia has induced Valentine to write a love letter to himself. Lance, who may have been added to the play in the later stages of composition, is a doltish clown whose command of the English language is remarkable mainly for its deficiencies. If Speed specializes in puns, the witty play on the double meaning of words, Lance specializes in malapropisms, the linguistic blunders by which one word is mistaken for another. He can, for example, when leaving home to follow his master to Milan, say that he has received his "proportion, like the prodigious son" (2.3.3), by which he means that he has received his portion, or inheritance, like the prodigal son in the

"I'll be sworn I have sat in the stocks for puddings he hath stolen" (4.4.26–27). From Geffrey Whitney, *A Choice of Emblems* (1586).

biblical story who received his inheritance and squandered it. In Lance's fractured English, nothing is communicated straightforwardly. He blunders into meaning, his linguistic mistakes turning the language of the learned and the witty on its head. In Lance's mouth, words become unfamiliar and unpredictable, always ready to yield up an obscene innuendo or to forge unlikely connections between different domains of meaning.

Lance's larger role in the play is as comically unsettling as his language. As was to be increasingly true of many of Shakespeare's low-life characters and subplots, his behavior mirrors and comments on the behavior of his "betters," but in a deflationary and unpredictable way. Lance's great love is for his dog, Crab. When he must leave for Milan, he is in an agony of grief because his dog, like a hard-hearted mistress, sheds no tears for his departure. "I think Crab my dog be the sourest-natured dog that lives. My mother weeping, my father wailing, my sister crying, our maid howling, our cat wringing her hands, and all our house in a great perplexity, yet did not this cruel-hearted cur shed one tear" (2.3.4–8). So deep is Lance's affection for his dog that when Crab, who in the end does accompany his master to Milan, disgraces himself by pissing under the Duke's table at a banquet, Lance takes the blame—and the subsequent punishment— upon himself. It is "the bit with the dog" that in *Shakespeare in Love* particularly wins the approval of Queen Elizabeth.

The highborn lovers, Proteus and Valentine, do not always show an equal devotion to their human mistresses. Lance's attachment threatens to expose both the element of absurdity lurking inside every grand passion and also the falsity of the assumption that only the wellborn are capable of self-sacrifice. In fact, Lance's affection for Crab shows just how many forms love can take, including affection that reaches across the line supposedly dividing one species from another, man from animal. Thomas Elyot, speaking of friends, claimed that their tie made "of two persons one." Lance's language about his dog expresses his feeling of just such an overwhelming and confusing intersubjective unity: "I am the dog. No, the dog is himself, and I am the dog. Oh, the dog is me, and I am myself" (2.3.19–20). Affection in this play takes many forms. However, when Lance contemplates marriage, his thoughts are less romantic than pragmatic. As Lance and Speed read a catalog of the qualities of Lance's beloved (3.1.267–350), Lance focuses on the practical: the woman's ability to fetch and carry, to sew, and to milk. And her faults, which are manifold, pale in his eyes beside her wealth. Set against the rarefied courtship rituals of his masters, Lance's pragmatism underscores the mundane aspects of the institution of marriage to which courtship will lead and beside which affection for a friend or a dog might seem more pleasurable.

Together the two clowns do much to increase the hilarity and confusion that permeate this early comedy: a play in which letters are only with great difficulty delivered to their receivers, love tokens given to one mistress are rerouted to another, and masculine affection proves remarkably fickle and unsteady. When something like order descends on this society, it does so in a locale where Lance does not go— the forest outside Milan. The initial scenes in the forest are striking in that they have the fairy-tale quality of a Robin Hood story come to life. Banished from Milan,

Valentine and Speed are beset by robbers in the forest; but these outlaws are so impressed with Valentine's bearing and his skill in languages that they make him captain of their forest band (4.1.54–66). Outside the town, living apart from women, the outlaws establish an alternative community where Valentine, despite his grief at being separated from Silvia, finds a measure of contentment. Several of Shakespeare's later comedies will depend on the contrast between the flawed life of town or court and the less fettered existence of rural spaces. *The Two Gentlemen of Verona* tries out this juxtaposition, contrasting to the betrayals and confusions of urban life and male-female courtship the straightforward male camaraderie of the forest.

The arrival of women and of Proteus, Valentine's friend-turned-rival, disrupts this harmonious male community as first Silvia appears, escorted by the timid Eglamour, and then Proteus, attended by Julia, disguised as his page. Suddenly, the potential for violence escalates as the frustrated Proteus threatens Silvia with rape, and both men lay claim to her affections. The disguised Julia can only watch. Just moments before Proteus, Silvia, and Julia arrived, Valentine had made a speech that obliquely suggests one way their encounter might end. Alone in the woods, Valentine describes how he can

> sit alone, unseen of any,
> And to the nightingale's complaining notes
> Tune my distresses and record my woes.
> (5.4.4–6)

By mentioning the nightingale, Valentine evokes a horrific tale of sexual violence. In a story made famous by Ovid in the *Metamorphoses*, the beautiful Philomela was raped by her brother-in-law, Tereus, and eventually transformed into a nightingale. The bird's song is so melancholy because it is a perpetual lament for Philomela's lost chastity.

As it turns out, no one undergoes Philomela's fate in *The Two Gentlemen of Verona*. Silvia escapes rape, just as Julia avoids Ariadne's fate when the fickle Proteus returns his affections to her. But the close of this early comedy, through its mythic allusions and flirtation with sexual violence, hints at the tragic endings that have narrowly been averted. In this regard, the play is not unlike *A Midsummer Night's Dream*, in which there is a properly comic ending with lover wedded to lover while the last act of that play includes an unintentionally comic enactment of the tragic story of Pyramus and Thisbe, lovers whose passion ended in death, not marriage. Though *Two Gentlemen* ends comically, with two marriages in prospect and male friendship restored, the violent and unexpected turnabouts in the play's concluding moments indicate the difficulty of joining a tale of heroic male friendship to a tale of romantic love between men and women. Especially for the women, the "happy" ending comes at a cost. The two marriages are arranged only after male friendship has been renewed and Valentine has offered—without consulting Silvia—to give his beloved to his friend. Though the two women get the men they have desired, Silvia never speaks again after she is offered to Proteus. Her response to all that has happened remains cloaked in silence, while Julia at the play's end is still in her male disguise (even though she has revealed her true identity). That disguise is both a reminder of the dangers she has encountered because of Proteus's fickleness and perhaps a hint that it is in the form of a boy that Julia is most pleasing to him. As we have seen, this ending since at least the eighteenth century has been controversial, perhaps because much of modern culture has come to value love between men and women over other kinds of emotional bonds. In the Renaissance, the matter was not so settled, a reminder of the different ways in which Shakespeare both is and is not our contemporary.

JEAN E. HOWARD

SELECTED BIBLIOGRAPHY

Demeter, Jason. "Pearls in Beauteous Ladies' Eyes: Shakespeare, Race, and Riots in the American Metropolis." *Journal of Narrative Theory* 41 (Fall 2011): 378–400. Analyzes how lines from *The Two Gentlemen of Verona* figured in commentary on American race relations in the 1960s and 1970s, and how Joseph Papp's 1971 musical version of the play used a multiracial cast in the context of pronounced racial tensions in New York City.

Fudge, Erica. "'The dog is himself': Humans, Animals, and Self-Control in *The Two Gentlemen of Verona*." *How to Do Things with Shakespeare: New Approaches, New Essays.* Ed. Laurie Maguire. Oxford: Blackwell, 2008. 185–209. Reading from within the emerging field of animal studies, Fudge argues that Lance's dog, Crab, pissing under a table, reveals the incivility against which humans (often unsuccessfully) define themselves.

Guy-Bray, Stephen. "Shakespeare and the Invention of the Heterosexual." *Early Modern Literary Studies* Special Issue 16 (October 2007): 12.1–28. http://purl. oclc.org/emls/si-16/brayshks.htm. Argues that in early modern culture homosociality is more important than married love and that heterosexuality, rather than being natural, has to be made up or constructed. *Two Gentlemen* shows how this works.

Hunt, Maurice. "Catholicism, Protestant Reformation, and *The Two Gentlemen of Verona*." *Shakespeare's Religious Allusiveness: Its Play and Tolerance.* Aldershot, Eng.: Ashgate, 2004. 1–17. Addresses the play's deployment of Catholic and Protestant images, metaphors, and concepts, arguing that the Catholic elements create a more memorable, lyric effect despite the play's apparent commitment to the triumph of Protestant ideas of conversion and companionate marriage.

Kiefer, Frederick. "Love Letters in *The Two Gentlemen of Verona*." *Shakespeare Studies* 18 (1986): 65–85. Explores the role of letters in the negotiation of love in *Two Gentlemen*, which contains more letters than any of Shakespeare's other comedies.

Masten, Jeffrey. "*The Two Gentlemen of Verona*." Vol. 3 of *A Companion to Shakespeare's Works: The Comedies.* Ed. Richard Dutton and Jean E. Howard. 4 vols. Oxford: Blackwell, 2003. 266–88. Argues against the idea that *Two Gentlemen* is an immature play because of its focus on male friendship rather than heterosexual love, and argues for male friendship as the abiding framework for Shakespeare's writing career.

Rivlen, Elizabeth. "Shakespeare's Apprenticeship: Performing Service in *The Comedy of Errors* and *The Two Gentlemen of Verona*." *The Aesthetics of Service in Early Modern England.* Evanston, IL: Northwestern UP, 2012. 27–51. Focuses on the ubiquity of servants in Shakespeare's early plays and their capacity not just to mirror but to alter elite identities.

Schlueter, June, ed. "*The Two Gentlemen of Verona*": *Critical Essays.* New York: Garland, 1996. Gathers eighteenth- and nineteenth-century comments on the play along with essays by twentieth-century critics and reviews of notable theater and television productions.

Shannon, Laurie. "The Early Modern Politics of Likeness." *Sovereign Amity: Figures of Friendship in Shakespearean Contexts.* Chicago: U of Chicago P, 2002. 17–53. Traces male friendship discourse from Cicero to Montaigne, showing its importance both for intimate relations between sovereign selves and also for its role in political discourse.

Slights, Camille Wells. "*The Two Gentlemen of Verona* and the Courtesy Book Tradition." *Shakespeare Studies* 16 (1983): 13–31. Argues that the play explores the fashioning of a Renaissance gentleman.

FILMS

A Spray of Plum Blossoms. 1931. Dir. Bu Wancang. China. 100 min. Set on a modern Cantonese military base, this silent film stars Ruan Lingyu, an icon of early Chinese cinema, as Julia. Highlights the intimate relationship between Julia and Silvia, with both women at times dressed in military uniforms.

The Two Gentlemen of Verona. 1983. Dir. Don Taylor. UK. 137 min. This BBC-TV version, in color, employs period music and elegant Italian settings in a performance that foregrounds the heterosexual love plot.

Shakespeare in Love. 1998. Dir. John Madden. USA. 123 min. Starring Gwyneth Paltrow and Joseph Fiennes. Includes scenes and speeches from *The Two Gentlemen of Verona* as examples of Shakespeare's early success with comedy and love lyric.

TEXTUAL INTRODUCTION

The Two Gentlemen of Verona is first mentioned in Francis Meres's list of Shakespeare's comedies and tragedies in his *Palladis Tamia* of 1598. "Shakespeare," Meres notes, "among the English is the most excellent in both kinds for the stage," adding, "for comedy, witness his Gentlemen of Verona." This, along with the play's elliptical composition and occasional lapses in dramatic coherence, has led editors and critics to agree that it is one of Shakespeare's very earliest works.

Textually speaking, the play is relatively straightforward. There is only one surviving early authoritative text—that printed in the 1623 First Folio (F)—and the issues an editor must address in presenting the play to the modern reader by and large require reflection not so much on complex cruxes as on the best ways to present certain moments in the action with the fullest clarity. That said, even the "best" of Shakespeare's play texts have been multiply mediated, and there are elements in the Folio text of *The Two Gentlemen of Verona* that make its origins less than entirely clear: editors remain divided over the nature of the underlying copy.

The play appears from certain features (e.g., a high proportion of parentheses enclosing subordinate clauses and "massed entries") to be one of several in the Folio that the interventionist King's Men scribe Ralph Crane transcribed in the early 1620s (which include *The Tempest, The Merry Wives of Windsor,* and *Measure for Measure,* plays with which *The Two Gentlemen of Verona* is grouped at the beginning of the First Folio). But what precisely was Crane transcribing? Suggestions have included a manuscript in Shakespeare's own hand (a holograph); an assemblage consisting of the "plot" (the outline of entries per scene that would have been pinned up within the tiring house) combined with the separate parts given to each actor; or a promptbook. Yet none of these alone would appear to account for all of the Folio text's inconsistencies, and the matter remains open—though editors generally think the promptbook hypothesis the least likely, presuming that many of the play's inconsistencies would necessarily have been resolved for performance and entrances indicated. In addition, the text seems to have been set by two, or perhaps three, compositors, each of whom appears to have introduced his own habits in terms of spelling, contractions, and the like (see Howard-Hill 1973).

For this edition, as for other *Norton Shakespeare* plays with massed entries, entry stage directions have been relocated as required for characters' actual entrances. At 1.3.0, for instance, F reads "*Enter Antonio and Panthino. Protheus.*" Here the initial SD becomes two distinct SDs: "*Enter* ANTONIO *and* PANTINO" (1.3.0) and, to make the action clear for the uninitiated reader, "*Enter* PROTEUS *with a letter, unaware of Antonio and Pantino's presence"* (1.3.43). (The Textual Variants note all emendations and relocations of such massed entry directions.) When Julia passes herself off as Sebastian, the page boy, and witnesses Proteus's betrayal, her cross-dressing needs to be precisely indicated from 4.2.25 on. Other clarifications include the attribution of a song to Proteus at 4.2.37 (see Digital Edition TC 9). Similarly, Turio has been replaced by a Servant at 2.4.112 (Digital Edition TC 6).

Characters' names have been modernized unless the context calls for the retention of the F spelling, e.g., at 1.3.67 (Digital Edition TC 4). Place-names in this play are at times rather loosely deployed and occasionally need rationalization: to reflect a coherent journey between Verona and Milan, for instance, the apparently erroneous mention of "Padua" (2.5.1) has been emended here to "Milan," a city for which modern English spelling has been retained except at 3.1.81 and 5.4.126, where "Milano" has been preferred for metrical reasons (Digital Edition TC 8).

Nathalie Rivère de Carles

Textual Bibliography

Howard-Hill, T. H. "The Compositors of Shakespeare's Folio Comedies." *Studies in Bibliography* 26 (1973): 62–106.
Johnson, Samuel, ed. William Shakespeare, *Works* (London, 1745).
Pope, Alexander, ed. William Shakespeare, *Works*. 6 vols. (London, 1723–25).
Theobald, Lewis, ed. William Shakespeare, *Works*. 7 vols. (London, 1733).

PERFORMANCE NOTE

Faced with realizing the simple structure and flat characterizations of *The Two Gentlemen of Verona*, many productions affect an ironic distance to the play, revealing through their actors a wry awareness of the characters' thinness and romantic excesses. With or without such irony, productions frequently take antinaturalistic approaches to the play, indulging in its lyricism, stylizing the acting, and highlighting the main characters' naive exuberance to create an atmosphere of levity and inconsequence. Such approaches potentially lessen the human stakes of the play, thereby preventing the disturbing fifth-act events from spoiling the comic resolution; or conversely, they may deepen the impact of a rape scene staged with terrifying realism, rendering the "comic" ending richer and more unsettling for the wide chasm between generic expectations and dramatic reality. Other productions develop darker aspects throughout, introducing, for instance, Proteus as a sinister Byronic figure who competes enviously with Valentine or else presenting Sylvia's (or Proteus's) father as a chillingly realistic tyrant. Such choices develop depth in characters by destabilizing their archetypal roles, along with the play's generic identity, contributing to an audience's uncertainty about its resolution.

The roles of Proteus and Julia, in fact, require considerable versatility: one is alternately tender and ruthless, the other as equivocal as constant, and both cunning, witty, impassioned, and capable of deception. Productions might also pursue complexity by suggesting that Valentine's ego and condescension at least partly explain Proteus's betrayal, or that some homoerotic attraction inspires the rivalry for one or both. Meanwhile, Silvia can be exceptionally dignified or overly entitled; the outlaws mistreated gentlemen or unsavory convicts; and Lance can tinge the play with warmth or melancholy. Other considerations in performance include managing the play's notoriously difficult ending (see Digital Edition PC 2) and deciding whether and how to resolve its many inconsistencies—e.g., Proteus sails from one landlocked city to another; the Duke of Milan seems to think he—at least in the Folio text—is in Verona (3.1.81); and the play assigns the name "Sir Eglamour" to two different men who appear to have opposite characteristics, one of whom Sylvia praises for chivalry shortly before he abandons her in the forest (5.3.6–7).

Brett Gamboa

The Two Gentlemen of Verona

THE PERSONS OF THE PLAY

DUKE of Milan, father to Silvia
SILVIA, beloved of Valentine, daughter to the Duke
PROTEUS, a gentleman of Verona
LANCE, clownish servant to Proteus
VALENTINE, a gentleman of Verona
SPEED, clownish servant to Valentine
TURIO, a foolish rival to Valentine
ANTONIO, father to Proteus
PANTINO, servant to Antonio
JULIA, beloved of Proteus
LUCETTA, waiting-woman to Julia
EGLAMOUR, agent for Silvia in her escape
HOST, where Julia lodges

Three OUTLAWS with Valentine
SERVANT to the Duke
Musicians
Ursula, maid to Silvia

1.1

[Enter] VALENTINE[1] *[and]* PROTEUS.[2]

VALENTINE   Cease to persuade, my loving Proteus.
Home-keeping youth have ever homely° wits.   *dull*
Were't not affection° chains thy tender° days   *love / young*
To the sweet glances of thy honored love,
5   I rather would entreat thy company
To see the wonders of the world abroad
Than, living dully sluggardized° at home,   *made lazy*
Wear out thy youth with shapeless° idleness.   *aimless*
But since thou lov'st, love still,° and thrive therein,   *constantly*
10 Even as I would when I to love begin.
PROTEUS   Wilt thou be gone? Sweet Valentine, adieu.
Think on thy Proteus when thou haply° seest   *by chance*
Some rare noteworthy object in thy travel.
Wish me partaker in thy happiness
15 When thou dost meet good hap;° and in thy danger,   *fortune*
If ever danger do environ° thee,   *surround*
Commend° thy grievance to my holy prayers;   *Entrust*
For I will be thy beadsman,[3] Valentine.

1.1 Location: Presumably Verona, though we learn
this only from the title.
1. St. Valentine is the patron saint of lovers; Valentine's name may thus indicate his role as faithful
lover.
2. In classical mythology, a sea god who could change
shape at will; the name suggests a fickle nature. In
1.1, Proteus is pronounced with three syllables; elsewhere in the play, often with two. In F, the names of

all the characters who appear in a given scene are
listed as it opens, even if they enter at a later point.
This edition marks entrances when characters actually appear onstage. In this scene, Speed enters at line
70, though in F his entrance is not marked and his
name is listed with that of Proteus and Valentine at
the beginning of the scene.
3. One who prays (counts the beads of a rosary) for
another's spiritual welfare.

VALENTINE And on a love-book[4] pray for my success?
20 PROTEUS Upon some book I love I'll pray for thee.
VALENTINE That's on some shallow story of deep love—
  How young Leander crossed the Hellespont.[5]
PROTEUS That's a deep story of a deeper love,
  For he was more than over-shoes[6] in love.
25 VALENTINE 'Tis true, for you are over-boots in love,
  And yet you never swam the Hellespont.
PROTEUS Over the boots? Nay, give me not the boots.°   *do not mock me*
VALENTINE No, I will not, for it boots° thee not.   *profits*
PROTEUS   What?
VALENTINE To be in love, where scorn is bought with groans,
30 Coy looks with heartsore sighs, one fading moment's mirth
  With twenty watchful,° weary, tedious nights.   *wakeful*
  If haply won, perhaps a hapless° gain;   *an unlucky*
  If lost, why then a grievous labor won;
  However,° but a folly bought with wit,   *Either way*
35 Or else a wit by folly vanquishèd.
PROTEUS So, by your circumstance,° you call me fool.   *lengthy discourse*
VALENTINE So, by your circumstance,° I fear you'll prove.   *situation*
PROTEUS 'Tis Love you cavil at.° I am not Love.   *find fault with*
VALENTINE Love is your master, for he masters you;
40 And he that is so yokèd by a fool
  Methinks should not be chronicled for wise.
PROTEUS Yet writers say, "As in the sweetest bud,
  The eating canker° dwells, so eating love   *harmful caterpillar*
  Inhabits in the finest wits of all."
45 VALENTINE And writers say, "As the most forward bud
  Is eaten by the canker ere it blow,°   *blossom*
  Even so by love the young and tender wit
  Is turned to folly, blasting° in the bud,   *withering*
  Losing his verdure° even in the prime,°   *greenness / spring*
50 And all the fair effects of future hopes."
  But wherefore waste I time to counsel thee
  That art a votary[7] to fond° desire?   *foolish*
  Once more adieu. My father at the road°   *harbor*
  Expects my coming, there to see me shipped.[8]
55 PROTEUS And thither will I bring thee, Valentine.
VALENTINE Sweet Proteus, no. Now let us take our leave.
  To Milan let me hear from thee by letters
  Of thy success° in love and what news else   *fortune (good or bad)*
  Betideth° here in absence of thy friend,   *Happens*
60 And I likewise will visit thee with mine.
PROTEUS All happiness bechance to thee in Milan.
VALENTINE As much to you at home; and so farewell.
                                              Exit.
PROTEUS He after honor hunts, I after love.

---

4. A book about love (instead of a prayer book). Valentine is teasing Proteus for making love his religion.
5. In classical mythology, Leander drowned while swimming the Hellespont (a narrow strait of water in modern Turkey separating the Gallipoli peninsula from mainland Asia) to visit his love, Hero. Shakespeare probably had read in manuscript Christopher Marlowe's poem "Hero and Leander."
6. So deep as to cover the shoes (or boots); recklessly or excessively.
7. One devoted to a particular pursuit; one bound by vows to a religious life.
8. Although Verona and Milan are inland, Shakespeare writes of Verona as if it were located, like London, on a tidal river leading to the sea.

He leaves his friends to dignify° them more;   *bring honor to*
65 I leave[9] myself, my friends, and all, for love.
Thou, Julia, thou hast metamorphosed° me: *transformed*
Made me neglect my studies, lose° my time,   *waste*
War with good counsel, set the world at naught;°   *put no value on the world*
Made wit with musing weak, heart sick with thought.°   *melancholy ideas*
[*Enter* SPEED.]
70 SPEED Sir Proteus, save you.[1] Saw you my master?
PROTEUS But now he parted hence to embark for Milan.
SPEED Twenty to one, then, he is shipped already,
And I have played the sheep[2] in losing him.
PROTEUS Indeed a sheep doth very often stray,
75 An if° the shepherd be a while away.   *An if = If*
SPEED You conclude that my master is a shepherd, then, and
I a sheep?
PROTEUS I do.
SPEED Why, then, my horns are his horns,[3] whether I wake or
80 sleep.
PROTEUS A silly answer, and fitting well a sheep.
SPEED This proves me still a sheep.
PROTEUS True, and thy master a shepherd.
SPEED Nay, that I can deny by a circumstance.°   *argument*
85 PROTEUS It shall go hard but I'll prove it by another.[4]
SPEED The shepherd seeks the sheep and not the sheep the
shepherd; but I seek my master and my master seeks not me.
Therefore I am no sheep.
PROTEUS The sheep for fodder follow the shepherd; the shep-
90 herd for food follows not the sheep. Thou for wages followest
thy master; thy master for wages follows not thee. Therefore
thou art a sheep.
SPEED Such another proof will make me cry "baa."
PROTEUS But dost thou hear? Gav'st thou my letter to Julia?
95 SPEED Ay, sir. I, a lost mutton,° gave your letter to her, a laced   *sheep*
mutton,° and she, a laced mutton, gave me, a lost mutton,   *prostitute (slang)*
nothing for my labor.
PROTEUS Here's too small a pasture for such store° of muttons.   *abundance*
SPEED If the ground be overcharged,° you were best stick[5] her.   *overburdened*
100 PROTEUS Nay, in that you are astray: 'twere best pound° you.   *empound; beat*
SPEED Nay, sir, less than a pound shall serve me for carrying
your letter.
PROTEUS You mistake. I mean the pound—a pinfold.°   *pen for stray animals*
SPEED From a pound to a pin?[6] Fold it° over and over,   *Multiply*
105 'Tis threefold too little for carrying a letter to your lover.
PROTEUS But what said she?

9. TEXTUAL COMMENT Editors since Pope have emended F's "I loue" to "I leave." Proteus's declaration that he will "leave" (neglect) everything else for love sets up a contrast between himself and Valentine, who "leaves" (departs) in order to bring honor to his friends. See Digital Edition TC 1.
1. TEXTUAL COMMENT Before 1606, when a parliamentary act prohibited actors from speaking the name of God or Christ, Speed's words of greeting here would have been "God save you." F has an apostrophe before "save," a trace of this deleted word. See Digital Edition TC 2.

2. Been foolish, with a pun on "ship." "Ship" and "sheep" were pronounced similarly.
3. As Speed's master, Valentine owns Speed's horns. Traditionally, the horns signified the cuckold and were attributed to men whose wives were unfaithful.
4. It shall fare ill with me unless I prove my claim by using another argument.
5. Stab or slaughter the extra sheep, with a pun on "stick" as meaning "have sexual intercourse with."
6. Proverbially, pins have little value (e.g., "not worth a pin"). Speed fears he is going to be paid too little for carrying the letter to Julia.

SPEED [*nodding, then saying*] Ay.°   *Yes*
PROTEUS Nod—ay? Why, that's "noddy."°   *a fool*
SPEED You mistook, sir! I say she did nod, and you ask me if
110   she did nod, and I say "Ay."
PROTEUS And that set together is "noddy."
SPEED Now you have taken the pains to set it together, take it
    for your pains.
PROTEUS No, no, you shall have it for bearing the letter.
115 SPEED Well, I perceive I must be fain° to bear with you.   *willing*
PROTEUS Why, sir, how do you bear with me?
SPEED Marry,[7] sir, the letter very orderly,° having nothing but   *dutifully*
    the word "noddy" for my pains.
PROTEUS Beshrew me° but you have a quick wit.   *Curse me (a mild oath)*
120 SPEED And yet it cannot overtake your slow purse.
PROTEUS Come, come, open the matter; in brief, what said she?
SPEED Open your purse that the money and the matter may
    be both at once delivered.
PROTEUS [*giving him money*] Well, sir, here is for your pain.
125   What said she?
SPEED Truly, sir, I think you'll hardly win her.[8]
PROTEUS Why? Couldst thou perceive so much from her?
SPEED Sir, I could perceive[9] nothing at all from her—no, not so
    much as a ducat[1] for delivering your letter. And being so hard°   *stingy; cold*
130   to me that brought your mind,° I fear she'll prove as hard to   *wishes*
    you in telling° your mind. Give her no token but stones,[2] for   *when you speak*
    she's as hard as steel.
PROTEUS What said she? Nothing?
SPEED No, not so much as "Take this for thy pains." To tes-
135   tify° your bounty, I thank you, you have testerned me;[3] in   *attest to*
    requital whereof, henceforth, carry your letters yourself!
    And so, sir, I'll commend you to my master.   [*Exit.*]
PROTEUS Go, go, be gone, to save your ship from wreck,
    Which cannot perish having thee aboard,
140   Being destined to a drier death on shore.[4]
    I must go send some better messenger.
    I fear my Julia would not deign° my lines,   *graciously accept*
    Receiving them from such a worthless post.°   *Exit.*   *messenger; blockhead*

1.2

    Enter JULIA *and* LUCETTA.
JULIA But say, Lucetta, now we are alone,
    Wouldst thou then counsel me to fall in love?
LUCETTA Ay, madam, so you stumble not unheedfully.°   *carelessly*
JULIA Of all the fair resort° of gentlemen   *company*
5   That every day with parle° encounter me,   *talk*
    In thy opinion which is worthiest love?

---

7. A mild oath suggesting surprise, from the Virgin
Mary's name.
8. You'll have a hard time winning her.
9. Punning on an obsolete meaning of "perceive" as
"receive."
1. A coin worth about three shillings and sixpence, a
generous tip.

2. Precious stones; pebbles; perhaps also testicles.
token: love-gift.
3. Given me a testern, a coin worth much less than
the ducat Speed wanted.
4. *Which . . . shore:* alluding to the proverb "He that
is born to be hanged shall never be drowned."
1.2 Location: Out of doors, maybe in Julia's garden.

LUCETTA Please you° repeat their names, I'll show my mind   *If you will*
　　According to my shallow simple skill.
JULIA What think'st thou of the fair Sir Eglamour?[1]
10 LUCETTA As of a knight well spoken, neat,° and fine;   *elegant*
　　But, were I you, he never should be mine.
JULIA What think'st thou of the rich Mercatio?
LUCETTA Well of his wealth; but of himself, so-so.
JULIA What think'st thou of the gentle Proteus?
15 LUCETTA Lord, Lord, to see what folly reigns in us.
JULIA How now? What means this passion° at his name?   *outburst of emotion*
LUCETTA Pardon, dear madam; 'tis a passing° shame   *great*
　　That I, unworthy body as I am,
　　Should censure° thus on lovely gentlemen.   *pass judgment*
20 JULIA Why not on Proteus, as of all the rest?
LUCETTA Then thus: of many good, I think him best.
JULIA Your reason?
LUCETTA I have no other but a woman's reason:
　　I think him so because I think him so.
25 JULIA And wouldst thou have me cast my love on him?
LUCETTA Ay, if you thought your love not cast away.
JULIA Why, he of all the rest hath never moved° me.   *proposed marriage to*
LUCETTA Yet he of all the rest I think best loves ye.
JULIA His little speaking shows his love but small.
30 LUCETTA Fire that's closest kept° burns most of all.   *most enclosed*
JULIA They do not love that do not show their love.
LUCETTA Oh, they love least that let men know their love.
JULIA I would I knew his mind.
LUCETTA [*handing her Proteus' letter*] Peruse this paper, madam.
35 JULIA "To Julia." Say, from whom?
LUCETTA That the contents will show.
JULIA Say, say! Who gave it thee?
LUCETTA Sir Valentine's page; and sent, I think, from Proteus.
　　He would have given it you, but I, being in the way,
40 　Did in your name receive it.[2] Pardon the fault, I pray.
JULIA Now, by my modesty, a goodly broker!°   *go-between*
　　Dare you presume to harbor wanton lines?°   *receive love letters*
　　To whisper and conspire against my youth?
　　Now trust me, 'tis an office° of great worth,   *position; duty*
45 　And you an officer fit for the place.
　　There! Take the paper! [*She gives* LUCETTA *the letter.*] See it
　　　be returned,
　　Or else return no more into my sight.
LUCETTA To plead for love deserves more fee than hate.
JULIA Will ye be gone?
LUCETTA　　　　　　　　That you may ruminate.°   *Exit.*   *meditate*
50 JULIA And yet I would I had o'erlooked° the letter.   *examined*
　　It were a shame to call her back again
　　And pray her to° a fault for which I chid her.   *ask her to commit*
　　What fool is she, that knows I am a maid
　　And would not force the letter to my view?

1. Not the same Eglamour who assists Silvia in 4.3.　　2. An inconsistency in the text. In 1.1, Speed said he
The name is found in medieval romances and by the　　delivered the letter to Julia. He may have mistaken
1590s seems to have acquired comic associations.　　Lucetta for Julia or lied to Proteus.

55 Since maids in modesty say "No" to that
    Which they would have the profferer° construe "Ay."   *giver*
    Fie, fie, how wayward is this foolish Love
    That, like a testy° babe, will scratch the nurse   *cranky*
    And presently,° all humbled, kiss the rod?[3]   *immediately after*
60 How churlishly I chid Lucetta hence,
    When willingly I would have had her here?
    How angerly I taught my brow to frown,
    When inward joy enforced my heart to smile?
    My penance is to call Lucetta back
65 And ask remission for my folly past.
    What ho! Lucetta!
            [*Enter* LUCETTA.]
LUCETTA   What would your ladyship?
JULIA   Is't near dinner-time?
LUCETTA   I would it were,
    That you might kill° your stomach° on your meat   *expend / hunger; rage*
    And not upon your maid.
            [*She drops and picks up the letter.*][4]
JULIA   What is't that you
70 Took up so gingerly?°   *cautiously*
LUCETTA   Nothing.
JULIA   Why didst thou stoop, then?
LUCETTA   To take a paper up that I let fall.
JULIA   And is that paper nothing?
75 LUCETTA   Nothing concerning me.
JULIA   Then let it lie for those that it concerns.
LUCETTA   Madam, it will not lie where it concerns,
    Unless it have a false interpreter.
JULIA   Some love of yours hath writ to you in rhyme.
80 LUCETTA   That I might sing it, madam, to a tune,
    Give me a note. Your ladyship can set[5]—
JULIA   As little by such toys° as may be possible.   *trifles*
    Best sing it to the tune of "Light o' love."[6]
LUCETTA   It is too heavy° for so light a tune.   *serious*
85 JULIA   Heavy? Belike it hath some burden,[7] then?
LUCETTA   Ay, and melodious were it, would you sing it.
JULIA   And why not you?
LUCETTA   I cannot reach so high.[8]
JULIA   Let's see your song. [*She tries to grab the letter.*][9] How
    now, minion?[1]
LUCETTA   Keep tune° there still. So you will sing it out.[2]   *in tune; in good humor*
90 And yet methinks I do not like this tune.[3]

3. Children sometimes had to kiss the stick with which they were beaten.
4. There is no indication in F of when Lucetta drops the letter that she here picks up. Some directors and editors assume that she drops it, either advisedly or inadvertently, before leaving the stage at line 49. To have her drop and immediately retrieve the letter, as here, may suggest that Lucetta is again trying to call her mistress's attention to it.
5. Set to music. Julia takes it to mean "set store by" or "give value to."
6. A popular song in Shakespeare's time.
7. Refrain; heavy load; perhaps punningly referring to the weight of a body during intercourse.
8. Sing so high a note; hope to win so high-ranking a lover.
9. TEXTUAL COMMENT The struggle between Julia and Lucetta fixes the attention of the audience on the letter, highlighting its importance in the play's erotic plotline. This edition adds stage directions to those implied in the dialogue to help readers follow the movements of this prop. See Digital Edition TC 3.
1. Hussy; with a possible pun on "minim," a musical term for a half note.
2. Finish singing it; come to the end of your anger.
3. Julia may have struck or threatened to strike Lucetta.

JULIA You do not?

LUCETTA No, madam, 'tis too sharp.°   high-pitched; bitter

JULIA You, minion, are too saucy.

LUCETTA Nay, now you are too flat°   low-pitched; blunt
95   And mar the concord° with too harsh a descant.°   harmony / melody
        There wanteth but a mean to fill your song.[4]

JULIA The mean is drowned with your unruly bass.°   low notes; bad conduct

LUCETTA Indeed, I bid the base for[5] Proteus.
        [JULIA grabs the letter.]

JULIA This babble shall not henceforth trouble me.
100   Here is a coil with protestation.°   fuss about a love vow
        [She tears the letter and drops the pieces.]
        [LUCETTA motions to pick them up.]
        Go, get you gone, and let the papers lie!
        You would be fing'ring them to anger me.

LUCETTA [aside] She makes it strange,° but she would be best   pretends not to care
        pleased
        To be so angered with another letter.   [Exit.]
105 JULIA Nay, would I were so angered with the same.
        [She picks up pieces of the letter.]
        O hateful hands to tear such loving words;
        Injurious wasps[6] to feed on such sweet honey
        And kill the bees that yield it with your stings!
        I'll kiss each several° paper for amends.   separate
110   Look, here is writ "kind Julia." Unkind Julia!
        As° in revenge of thy ingratitude   As if
        I throw thy name against the bruising stones,
        Trampling contemptuously on thy disdain.
        And here is writ "Love-wounded Proteus."
115   Poor wounded name, my bosom as a bed
        Shall lodge thee till thy wound be thoroughly healed;
        And thus I search° it with a sovereign° kiss.   probe; cleanse / healing
        But twice or thrice was "Proteus" written down.
        Be calm, good wind: blow not a word away
120   Till I have found each letter in the letter
        Except mine own name. That, some whirlwind bear
        Unto a ragged, fearful, hanging° rock   overhanging
        And throw it thence into the raging sea!
        Lo, here in one line is his name twice writ:
125   "Poor forlorn Proteus, passionate Proteus,
        To the sweet Julia"—that I'll tear away;
        And yet I will not, sith° so prettily   since
        He couples it to his complaining names.
        Thus will I fold them, one upon another:
130   Now kiss, embrace, contend, do what you will.[7]
        [Enter LUCETTA.]

LUCETTA Madam, dinner is ready and your father stays.°   waits

JULIA Well, let us go.

LUCETTA What, shall these papers lie like telltales here?

4. There lacks but a tenor part to complete your song. Her implication is that Julia lacks a man to fulfill her desires.
5. I sang the bass part for; I acted in the interests of (a phrase from the game called prisoner's base).
6. Referring to her hurtful fingers.
7. Julia uses sexually charged language when she suggests that the fragments of paper bearing her and Proteus's names might "couple," "kiss," "embrace," and "contend" (struggle against each other).

	JULIA	If you respect° them, best to take them up.	*value*
135	LUCETTA	Nay, I was taken up° for laying them down.	*scolded*
		Yet here they shall not lie for° catching cold.	*for fear of*

[*She picks up pieces of the letter.*]

	JULIA	I see you have a month's mind to° them.	*a strong desire for*
	LUCETTA	Ay, madam, you may say what sights you see;	
		I see things, too, although you judge I wink.°	*close my eyes*
140	JULIA	Come, come, will't please you go? *Exeunt.*	

1.3

Enter ANTONIO *and* PANTINO.

	ANTONIO	Tell me, Pantino, what sad° talk was that	*serious*
		Wherewith my brother held you in the cloister?°	*covered walk*
	PANTINO	'Twas of his nephew Proteus, your son.	
	ANTONIO	Why, what of him?	
	PANTINO	He wondered that your lordship	
5		Would suffer him to spend his youth at home	
		While other men, of slender° reputation,	*insignificant*
		Put forth° their sons to seek preferment° out—	*Send / advancement*
		Some to the wars to try their fortune there;	
		Some to discover islands far away;	
10		Some to the studious universities.	
		For any or for all these exercises	
		He said that Proteus your son was meet,°	*fit*
		And did request me to importune° you	*beg*
		To let him spend his time no more at home,	
15		Which would be great impeachment to his age°	*reproach in his old age*
		In having known no travel in his youth.	
	ANTONIO	Nor need'st thou much importune me to that	
		Whereon this month I have been hammering.°	*thinking hard*
		I have considered well his loss of time,	
20		And how he cannot be a perfect° man,	*complete*
		Not being tried and tutored in the world.	
		Experience is by industry achieved,	
		And perfected by the swift course of time.	
		Then tell me—whither were I best to send him?	
25	PANTINO	I think your lordship is not ignorant	
		How his companion, youthful Valentine,	
		Attends° the Emperor[1] in his royal court.	*Waits upon*
	ANTONIO	I know it well.	
	PANTINO	'Twere good, I think, your lordship sent him thither.	
30		There shall he practice° tilts and tournaments,	*take part in*
		Hear sweet discourse, converse with noblemen,	
		And be in eye of° every exercise	*witness*
		Worthy his youth and nobleness of birth.	
	ANTONIO	I like thy counsel. Well hast thou advised,	
35		And that thou mayst perceive how well I like it,	
		The execution of it shall make known.	
		Even with the speediest expedition,°	*swiftness*
		I will dispatch him to the Emperor's court.	

1.3 Location: Antonio's house in Verona.
1. One of several inconsistencies in the plot. Proteus and Valentine are later shown at the court of the Duke of Milan, not at the Emperor's court. The references to Milan continue in 2.5.1, 3.1.81, and 5.4.126, but Milan had ever only been an imperial court in the fourth century C.E. Shakespeare is either inflating the political significance of the Duke of Milan's court or making a mistake.

PANTINO   Tomorrow, may it please you, Don Alfonso
40   With other gentlemen of good esteem
      Are journeying to salute the Emperor
      And to commend their service to his will.
ANTONIO   Good company—with them shall Proteus go.
        [*Enter* PROTEUS *with a letter, unaware of Antonio*
            and Pantino's presence.]
      And in good time!° Now will we break with him.[2]   *at the right moment*
45 PROTEUS   Sweet love, sweet lines, sweet life!
      Here is her hand, the agent of her heart.
      Here is her oath for love, her honor's pawn.°   *pledge*
      Oh, that our fathers would applaud our loves
      To seal our happiness with their consents.
50   O heavenly Julia!
    ANTONIO   How now? What letter are you reading there?
    PROTEUS   May't please your lordship, 'tis a word or two
      Of commendations° sent from Valentine,   *greetings*
      Delivered by a friend that came from him.
55 ANTONIO   Lend me the letter. Let me see what news.
    PROTEUS   There is no news, my lord, but that he writes
      How happily he lives, how well beloved
      And daily gracèd° by the Emperor,   *honored*
      Wishing me with him, partner of his fortune.
60 ANTONIO   And how stand you affected° to his wish?   *disposed*
    PROTEUS   As one relying on your lordship's will,
      And not depending on his friendly wish.
    ANTONIO   My will is something sorted with° his wish.   *in agreement with*
      Muse° not that I thus suddenly proceed,   *Wonder*
65   For what I will, I will, and there an end.
      I am resolved that thou shalt spend some time
      With Valentinus[3] in the Emperor's court.
      What maintenance° he from his friends° receives,   *money / family*
      Like exhibition° thou shalt have from me.   *The same allowance*
70   Tomorrow be in readiness to go.
      Excuse it not,[4] for I am peremptory.°   *resolved*
    PROTEUS   My lord, I cannot be so soon provided.°   *equipped*
      Please you deliberate a day or two.
    ANTONIO   Look what° thou want'st shall be sent after thee.   *Whatever*
75   No more of stay: tomorrow thou must go!
      Come on, Pantino, you shall be employed
      To hasten on his expedition. [*Exeunt* ANTONIO *and* PANTINO.]
    PROTEUS   Thus have I shunned the fire for fear of burning
      And drenched me in the sea where I am drowned.
80   I feared to show my father Julia's letter,
      Lest he should take exceptions° to my love,   *object*
      And with the vantage of mine own excuse[5]
      Hath he excepted most° against my love.   *raised most obstacles*
      Oh, how this spring of love resembleth
85   The uncertain glory of an April day,

2. Reveal the plan to him.
3. TEXTUAL COMMENT This is the only instance of
the spelling "Valentinus" in F. This use of Latin,
which was the primary diplomatic language in the
sixteenth century, may suggest that Antonio envisions a political purpose to Proteus's journey. See

Digital Edition TC 4.
4. Do not offer reasons why you should be excused
from this.
5. And by taking advantage of my lie (that the letter
came from Valentine).

Which now shows all the beauty of the sun,
And by and by a cloud takes all away!
       [*Enter* PANTINO.]
PANTINO   Sir Proteus, your father calls for you.
He is in haste; therefore I pray you go.
90   PROTEUS   Why, this it is: my heart accords thereto,
And yet a thousand times it answers "No."[6]   *Exeunt.*

2.1

Enter VALENTINE *and* SPEED. [VALENTINE *drops*
     a glove.]
SPEED   Sir, your glove.
VALENTINE   Not mine. My gloves are on.
SPEED   Why, then, this may be yours, for this is but one.[1]
VALENTINE   Ha? Let me see—ay, give it me, it's mine.
     Sweet ornament that decks° a thing divine.   *decorates*
5   Ah, Silvia, Silvia!
SPEED [*calling*]   Madam Silvia! Madam Silvia!
VALENTINE   How now, sirrah?[2]
SPEED   She is not within hearing, sir.
VALENTINE   Why, sir, who bade you call her?
10   SPEED   Your worship, sir, or else I mistook.
VALENTINE   Well, you'll still be° too forward.   *persist in being*
SPEED   And yet I was last chidden° for being too slow.   *chided (scolded)*
VALENTINE   Go to,[3] sir. Tell me, do you know Madam Silvia?
SPEED   She that your worship loves?
15   VALENTINE   Why, how know you that I am in love?
SPEED   Marry, by these special marks: first, you have learned,
     like Sir Proteus, to wreathe° your arms, like a malcontent;[4]   *fold*
     to relish° a love-song, like a robin-redbreast; to walk alone,   *sing*
     like one that had the pestilence;° to sigh, like a schoolboy   *plague*
20   that had lost his ABC;° to weep, like a young wench that had   *primer; spelling book*
     buried her grandam; to fast, like one that takes° diet; to   *keeps to a*
     watch,° like one that fears robbing; to speak puling,° like a   *lie awake / whiningly*
     beggar at Hallowmas.[5] You were wont,° when you laughed,   *formerly accustomed*
     to crow like a cock; when you walked, to walk like one of the
25   lions; when you fasted, it was presently° after dinner; when   *immediately*
     you looked sadly, it was for want of money. And now you are
     metamorphosed with a mistress, that when I look on you I
     can hardly think you my master.
VALENTINE   Are all these things perceived in me?
30   SPEED   They are all perceived without ye.°   *in your appearance*
VALENTINE   Without me?[6] They cannot.
SPEED   Without you? Nay, that's certain, for without° you were   *unless*
     so simple, none else would.° But you are so without these fol- *(perceive them)*
     lies[7] that these follies are within you and shine through you

---

6. *my . . . "No"*: suggesting that Proteus is divided
between desire to go and desire to stay. *accords thereto:*
agrees to it.
2.1 Location: Milan.
1. A pun—"one" could be pronounced like "on."
2. Fellow; a form of address to social inferiors.
3. Expression of impatience.

4. A person made melancholy and discontented by
love. Such people were often depicted with folded arms.
5. All Saints' Day, November 1, when it was customary to give charity to beggars.
6. Valentine has taken Speed to mean, "They are all
perceived when you are absent."
7. But you are so outwardly marked by these follies.

35 like the water in an urinal,° that not an eye that sees you but   *glass jar for urine*
    is a physician to comment on your malady.
    VALENTINE But tell me, dost thou know my lady Silvia?
    SPEED She that you gaze on so as she sits at supper?
    VALENTINE Hast thou observed that? Even she, I mean.
40 SPEED Why, sir, I know[8] her not.
    VALENTINE Dost thou know her by my gazing on her, and yet
    know'st her not?
    SPEED Is she not hard-favored,° sir?   *ugly*
    VALENTINE Not so fair, boy, as well-favored.°   *gracious; esteemed*
45 SPEED Sir, I know that well enough.
    VALENTINE What dost thou know?
    SPEED That she is not so fair as—of you—well favored.°   *looked on with favor*
    VALENTINE I mean that her beauty is exquisite but her favor°   *graciousness*
    infinite.
50 SPEED That's because the one is painted° and the other out of   *(with cosmetics)*
    all count.[9]
    VALENTINE How painted? And how out of count?
    SPEED Marry, sir, so painted to make her fair that no man
    counts of° her beauty.   *takes account of; values*
55 VALENTINE How esteem'st thou me? I account of her beauty.
    SPEED You never saw her since she was deformed.[1]
    VALENTINE How long hath she been deformed?
    SPEED Ever since you loved her.
    VALENTINE I have loved her ever since I saw her, and still I
60 see her beautiful.
    SPEED If you love her, you cannot see her.
    VALENTINE Why?
    SPEED Because Love is blind. Oh, that you had mine eyes, or
    your own eyes had the lights° they were wont to have when   *power to see clearly*
65 you chid at Sir Proteus for going ungartered![2]
    VALENTINE What should I see then?
    SPEED Your own present folly and her passing° deformity. For   *excessive*
    he, being in love, could not see to garter his hose, and you,
    being in love, cannot see to put on your hose.
70 VALENTINE Belike, boy, then you are in love, for last morning
    you could not see to wipe my shoes.
    SPEED True, sir! I was in love with my bed. I thank you, you
    swinged° me for my love, which makes me the bolder to   *beat*
    chide you for yours.
75 VALENTINE In conclusion, I stand affected to° her.   *in love with*
    SPEED I would you were set[3] so your affection would cease.
    VALENTINE Last night she enjoined° me to write some lines   *instructed*
    to one she loves.
    SPEED And have you?
80 VALENTINE I have.
    SPEED Are they not lamely writ?
    VALENTINE No, boy, but as well as I can do them.
         [*Enter* SILVIA.]
    Peace, here she comes.

8. Punning on "know" as meaning "to be sexually
familiar with."
9. *out of all count:* innumerable.
1. Altered (Speed implies that Valentine's love for
Silvia distorts his view of her).

2. Garters kept stockings from falling down. Going
"ungartered" was a traditional sign of love melancholy.
3. Seated; satisfied. Speed has interpreted "stand"
as carrying its bawdy connotation of "having an
erection."

SPEED [*aside*] Oh, excellent motion!° Oh, exceeding puppet!°   *puppet show / (Silvia)*
85   Now will he interpret⁴ to her!
VALENTINE Madam and mistress, a thousand good-morrows.
SPEED [*aside*] Oh, give° ye good e'en!° Here's a million of   *God give / evening*
     manners.
SILVIA Sir Valentine and servant,⁵ to you two thousand.
90   SPEED [*aside*] He should give her interest, and she gives it
     him.⁶
VALENTINE As you enjoined me, I have writ your letter
     Unto the secret nameless friend of yours,
     Which I was much unwilling to proceed in
95   But for my duty to your ladyship.
          [*He gives her the letter.*]
SILVIA I thank you, gentle servant. 'Tis very clerkly° done.   *like a scholar*
VALENTINE Now trust me, madam, it came hardly off,°   *was not done easily*
     For being ignorant to whom it goes
     I writ at random, very doubtfully.
100 SILVIA Perchance you think too much of so much pains?
VALENTINE No, madam. So it stead° you, I will write,   *help*
     Please you command a thousand times as much.
     And yet—
SILVIA A pretty period.° Well, I guess the sequel,°   *pause / what is next*
105 And yet I will not name it. And yet I care not.
     And yet take this again. [*She offers him the letter.*] And yet I
          thank you,
     Meaning henceforth to trouble you no more.
SPEED [*aside*] And yet you will. And yet another "yet."
VALENTINE What means your ladyship? Do you not like it?
110 SILVIA Yes, yes. The lines are very quaintly° writ,   *skillfully*
     But, since unwillingly, take them again.
          [*She offers him the letter again.*]
     Nay, take them.
VALENTINE   Madam, they are for you.
SILVIA Ay, ay. You writ them, sir, at my request,
     But I will none of them. They are for you.
115 I would have had them writ more movingly.
VALENTINE Please you, I'll write your ladyship another.
SILVIA And when it's writ, for my sake read it over,
     And if it please you, so. If not, why, so.
VALENTINE If it please me, madam? What then?
120 SILVIA Why if it please you, take it for your labor.
     And so, good morrow, servant.   *Exit.*
SPEED [*aside*] Oh, jest unseen, inscrutable, invisible
     As a nose on a man's face or a weathercock on a steeple!
     My master sues° to her, and she hath taught her suitor,   *appeals*
125 He being her pupil, to become her tutor.
     Oh, excellent device!° Was there ever heard a better?   *trick*
     That my master, being scribe, to himself should write the
          letter?
VALENTINE How now, sir? What are you reasoning with
     yourself?

4. Provide commentary (as if in a puppet show).   6. He should surpass her in compliments, but she
5. In courtly love literature, a man devoted to a lady   surpasses him.
is called her servant.

SPEED   Nay, I was rhyming. 'Tis you that have the reason.
130 VALENTINE   To do what?
SPEED   To be a spokesman from Madam Silvia.
VALENTINE   To whom?
SPEED   To yourself. Why, she woos you by a figure.°   device; indirect means
VALENTINE   What figure?
135 SPEED   By a letter, I should say.
VALENTINE   Why, she hath not writ to me.
SPEED   What need she, when she hath made you write to
    yourself? Why, do you not perceive the jest?
VALENTINE   No, believe me.
140 SPEED   No believing you indeed, sir. But did you perceive her
    earnest?[7]
VALENTINE   She gave me none, except an angry word.
SPEED   Why, she hath given you a letter.
VALENTINE   That's the letter I writ to her friend.
145 SPEED   And that letter hath she delivered, and there an end.
VALENTINE   I would it were no worse.
SPEED   I'll warrant you, 'tis as well.
    For often have you writ to her, and she, in modesty,
    Or else for want of idle time, could not again reply;
150   Or fearing else some messenger that might her mind
        discover,
    Herself hath taught her love himself to write unto her lover!
    All this I speak in print,° for in print I found it.[8]   very precisely
    Why muse you, sir? 'Tis dinner-time.
VALENTINE   I have dined.°   (on love)
155 SPEED   Ay, but hearken, sir. Though the chameleon[9] Love can
    feed on the air, I am one that am nourished by my victuals
    and would fain° have meat. Oh, be not like your mistress: be   be eager to
    moved, be moved![1]   Exeunt.

2.2

Enter PROTEUS *and* JULIA.

PROTEUS   Have patience, gentle Julia.
JULIA   I must, where is no remedy.
PROTEUS   When possibly I can, I will return.
JULIA   If you turn not,° you will return the sooner.   are not unfaithful
5   [*She gives him a ring.*][1] Keep this remembrance for thy
    Julia's sake.
PROTEUS   Why, then, we'll make exchange. Here, take you this.
        [*He gives her a ring.*]
JULIA   And seal the bargain with a holy kiss.
        [*They kiss.*]
PROTEUS   Here is my hand for my true constancy.
    And when that hour o'erslips° me in the day   passes by
10   Wherein I sigh not, Julia, for thy sake,
    The next ensuing hour some foul mischance

7. To be serious. Valentine takes "perceive" to mean "receive," and takes "earnest" to mean "pledge" or "money given to seal a bargain."
8. Speed's reference to a printed speech probably shouldn't be taken literally. More likely, he is making fun of Valentine's inability to understand Silvia's trick by stressing his own care with language.
9. A small lizard that can exist for long periods without food and was thought to feed on air.
1. Be kind; be induced (to eat).
2.2 Location: Probably Julia's house or garden.
1. The action in this scene resembles a betrothal ceremony, and thus in the Elizabethan period a legally binding agreement to marry.

Torment me for my love's forgetfulness.
My father stays° my coming. Answer not.   *awaits*
The tide is now. [JULIA *weeps*.] Nay, not thy tide of tears.
15   That tide will stay° me longer than I should.   *delay*
Julia, farewell.   [*Exit* JULIA.]
           What, gone without a word?
Ay, so true love should do. It cannot speak,
For truth hath better deeds than words to grace° it.   *adorn*
           [*Enter* PANTINO.]

PANTINO   Sir Proteus, you are stayed for.

PROTEUS   Go. I come, I come.
20   Alas, this parting strikes poor lovers dumb.   *Exeunt.*

2.3

Enter LANCE[1] [*with his dog Crab*[2]].

LANCE   Nay, 'twill be this hour ere I have done weeping; all
the kind° of the Lances have this very fault. I have received   *family; kin*
my proportion,° like the prodigious[3] son, and am going with   *portion*
Sir Proteus to the Imperial's° court. I think Crab my dog be   *(for "Emperor's")*
5   the sourest-natured dog that lives.[4] My mother weeping, my
father wailing, my sister crying, our maid howling, our cat
wringing her hands, and all our house in a great perplexity,
yet did not this cruel-hearted cur shed one tear. He is a
stone, a very pebble-stone, and has no more pity in him than
10   a dog. A Jew would have wept to have seen our parting![5]
Why, my grandam, having no eyes,° look you, wept herself   *being blind*
blind at my parting. Nay, I'll show you the manner of it.[6]
This shoe is my father. No, this left shoe is my father. No,
no, this left shoe is my mother. Nay, that cannot be so nei-
15   ther. Yes, it is so, it is so: it hath the worser sole.[7] This shoe
with the hole[8] in it is my mother, and this my father. A vengeance on't: there 'tis.[9] Now, sir, this staff is my sister, for,
look you, she is as white as a lily and as small° as a wand.°   *slender / small stick*
This hat is Nan, our maid. I am the dog. No, the dog is him-
20   self, and I am the dog. Oh, the dog is me, and I am myself.
Ay, so, so. Now come I to my father: "Father, your blessing."
Now should not the shoe speak a word for weeping? Now
should I kiss my father—well, he weeps on. Now come I to
my mother: oh, that she could speak now, like a wood
25   woman![1] Well, I kiss her. Why, there 'tis: here's my mother's
breath[2] up and down.° Now come I to my sister: mark the   *exactly*
moan she makes.[3] Now the dog all this while sheds not a

2.3 Location: A street in Verona.
1. A shortened form of "Lancelot."
2. "Crab" may mean "crab apple" or a "crabbed, ill-tempered person."
3. Lance frequently confuses one word with another. His reference here is to the biblical parable of the prodigal son, who wastes his inheritance but is welcomed home again (Luke 15:11–32).
4. PERFORMANCE COMMENT Crab is quite often played by a real dog, adding an exciting potential for randomness and even sabotage. See Digital Edition PC 1.
5. Alluding to proverbs claiming that Jews and dogs lack pity.
6. Here Lance takes off his shoes to demonstrate the points in his following speech.

7. Punning on "soul" and alluding to medieval debates about whether women had souls.
8. Punning on "hole" as "female genitalia."
9. Presumably Lance is now satisfied with his positioning of the shoes.
1. TEXTUAL COMMENT F has "would-woman," a term that editors have long emended. This edition emends to "wood," meaning "mad" or "enraged, furious," which reflects Lance's description of his mother's grief at his departure. See Digital Edition TC 5.
2. Comparing the smelly shoe to his mother's breath.
3. Perhaps Lance makes his staff "moan" by swishing it in the air.

tear nor speaks a word; but see how I lay the dust with my
tears.
    [*Enter* PANTINO.]

30 PANTINO Lance, away, away! Aboard! Thy master is shipped,
and thou art to post° after with oars.° What's the matter?   *hurry / in a rowboat*
Why weep'st thou, man? Away, ass, you'll lose° the tide if   *miss*
you tarry any longer.

LANCE It is no matter if the tied[4] were lost, for it is the unkind-
35 est tied that ever any man tied.

PANTINO What's the unkindest tide?

LANCE Why, he that's tied here, Crab, my dog.

PANTINO Tut, man! I mean thou'lt lose the flood,° and in los-   *miss the tide*
ing the flood, lose thy voyage, and in losing thy voyage, lose
40 thy master, and in losing thy master, lose thy service, and in
losing thy service— [LANCE *silences him*.] Why dost thou
stop my mouth?

LANCE For fear thou shouldst lose thy tongue.

PANTINO Where should I lose my tongue?

45 LANCE In thy tale.

PANTINO In thy tail!°   *rear end*

LANCE Lose the tide, and the voyage, and the master, and the
service, and the tied. Why, man, if the river were dry, I am
able to fill it with my tears; if the wind were down, I could
50 drive the boat with my sighs.

PANTINO Come, come away, man. I was sent to call° thee.   *summon*

LANCE Sir, call me what thou dar'st!

PANTINO Wilt thou go?

LANCE Well, I will go.   *Exeunt.*

2.4

Enter VALENTINE, SILVIA, TURIO, *and* SPEED.

SILVIA Servant!

VALENTINE Mistress?

SPEED Master, Sir Turio frowns on you.

VALENTINE Ay, boy, it's for love.

5 SPEED Not of you.

VALENTINE Of my mistress, then.

SPEED 'Twere good you knocked° him.   [*Exit.*]   *struck*

SILVIA Servant, you are sad.

VALENTINE Indeed, madam, I seem so.

10 TURIO Seem you that you are not?

VALENTINE Haply° I do.   *Perhaps*

TURIO So do counterfeits.

VALENTINE So do you.

TURIO What seem I that I am not?

15 VALENTINE Wise.

TURIO What instance° of the contrary?   *evidence*

VALENTINE Your folly.

TURIO And how quote° you my folly?   *detect; observe*

VALENTINE I quote it in your jerkin.°   *short coat*

---

4. Taking "tide" for "tied," or one who is tied up, mean-   2.4 Location: The Duke's court in Milan.
ing Crab.

20 TURIO My jerkin is a doublet.°   *jacket; couple or pair*
    VALENTINE Well, then, I'll double your folly.
    TURIO How?
    SILVIA What, angry, Sir Turio? Do you change color?
    VALENTINE Give him leave, madam; he is a kind of
25   chameleon.¹
    TURIO That hath more mind to feed on your blood than live
       in your air.²
    VALENTINE You have said, sir.
    TURIO Ay, sir, and done, too, for this time.
30 VALENTINE I know it well, sir. You always end ere you begin.
    SILVIA A fine volley of words, gentlemen, and quickly shot
       off.
    VALENTINE 'Tis indeed, madam; we thank the giver.
    SILVIA Who is that, servant?
35 VALENTINE Yourself, sweet lady, for you gave° the fire. Sir   *spark*
       Turio borrows his wit from your ladyship's looks and spends
       what he borrows kindly° in your company.   *properly; naturally*
    TURIO Sir, if you spend word for word with me, I shall make
       your wit bankrupt.
40 VALENTINE I know it well, sir. You have an exchequer° of   *treasury*
       words and, I think, no other treasure to give your followers,
       for it appears by their bare liveries³ that they live by your
       bare° words.   *worthless*
           [*Enter the* DUKE *with a letter in his hand.*]
    SILVIA No more, gentlemen, no more! Here comes my father.
45 DUKE Now, daughter Silvia, you are hard beset.°   *set upon (by men)*
       —Sir Valentine, your father is in good health.
       What say you to a letter from your friends
       Of much good news?
    VALENTINE   My lord, I will be thankful
       To any happy messenger° from thence.   *bringer of happy news*
50 DUKE Know ye Don Antonio, your countryman?
    VALENTINE Ay, my good lord, I know the gentleman
       To be of worth and worthy estimation,
       And not without desert so well reputed.
    DUKE Hath he not a son?
55 VALENTINE Ay, my good lord, a son that well deserves
       The honor and regard of such a father.
    DUKE You know him well?
    VALENTINE I knew him as myself, for from our infancy
       We have conversed° and spent our hours together.   *kept company*
60   And though myself have been an idle truant,
       Omitting° the sweet benefit of time   *Neglecting*
       To clothe mine age° with angel-like perfection,   *adorn my years*
       Yet hath Sir Proteus, for that's his name,
       Made use and fair advantage of his days:
65   His years but young, but his experience old;
       His head unmellowed,° but his judgment ripe;   *without gray hair*
       And in a word, for far behind his worth

---

1. Chameleons can change color, perhaps suggesting that Turio is fickle in love.
2. Chameleons were supposed to live on air (see note to 2.1.155), but Turio would rather drink Valentine's blood.
3. By their threadbare clothing.

	Comes all the praises that I now bestow,	
	He is complete° in feature° and in mind,	*perfect / appearance*
70	With all good grace to grace a gentleman.	
	DUKE Beshrew me, sir, but if he make this good,°	*proves this to be true*
	He is as worthy for an empress' love	
	As meet° to be an emperor's counselor.	*fit*
	Well, sir, this gentleman is come to me	
75	With commendation from great potentates,°	*rulers; men of power*
	And here he means to spend his time awhile.	
	I think 'tis no unwelcome news to you.	
	VALENTINE Should I have wished a thing,° it had been he.	*anything*
	DUKE Welcome him, then, according to his worth.	
80	—Silvia, I speak to you, and you, Sir Turio;	
	For Valentine, I need not cite° him to it.	*urge*
	I will send him hither to you presently. [*Exit.*]	
	VALENTINE This is the gentleman I told your ladyship	
	Had come along with me, but that his mistress	
85	Did hold his eyes locked in her crystal looks.	
	SILVIA Belike that° now she hath enfranchised° them	*Perhaps / freed*
	Upon some other pawn for fealty.[4]	
	VALENTINE Nay, sure, I think she holds them prisoners still.	
	SILVIA Nay, then he should be blind, and being blind	
90	How could he see his way to seek out you?	
	VALENTINE Why, lady, Love hath twenty pair of eyes.	
	TURIO They say that Love hath not an eye at all.[5]	
	VALENTINE To see such lovers, Turio, as yourself.	
	Upon a homely object, Love can wink.°	*close its eyes*
	[*Enter* PROTEUS.]	
95	SILVIA Have done, have done! Here comes the gentleman.	
	VALENTINE Welcome, dear Proteus! —Mistress, I beseech	
	you	
	Confirm his welcome with some special favor.	
	SILVIA His worth is warrant for his welcome hither,	
	If this be he you oft have wished to hear from.	
100	VALENTINE Mistress, it is. Sweet lady, entertain him[6]	
	To be my fellow-servant to your ladyship.	
	SILVIA Too low a mistress for so high° a servant.	*tall; distinguished*
	PROTEUS Not so, sweet lady, but too mean° a servant	*lowly*
	To have a look of° such a worthy mistress.	*from*
105	VALENTINE Leave off discourse of disability.°	*unworthiness*
	Sweet lady, entertain him for your servant.	
	PROTEUS My duty will I boast of, nothing else.	
	SILVIA And duty never yet did want his meed.°	*lack his reward*
	Servant, you are welcome to a worthless mistress.	
110	PROTEUS I'll die on° him that says so but yourself.	*die fighting*
	SILVIA That you are welcome?	
	PROTEUS That you are worthless.	
	[*Enter* SERVANT.][7]	

---

4. *Upon . . . fealty:* Because of some other lover's pledge of faithful service.
5. Referring to the blindness of Cupid.
6. Take him into your service.
7. TEXTUAL COMMENT Even though F does not indi-

cate the entrance of a servant at this point and assigns the following line to Turio, many editors have assumed that a servant must enter here to bring the message that Silvia's father would speak with her. See Digital Edition TC 6.

SERVANT   Madam, my lord your father would speak with you.
SILVIA   I wait upon his pleasure.   [*Exit* SERVANT.]
                              —Come, Sir Turio;
        Go with me. —Once more, new servant, welcome.
115   I'll leave you to confer of° home affairs.   *talk about*
        When you have done, we look to hear from you.
PROTEUS   We'll both attend upon your ladyship.
                              [*Exeunt* SILVIA *and* TURIO.]
VALENTINE   Now tell me: how do all from whence you came?
PROTEUS   Your friends are well and have them much
        commended.°   *sent their regards*
VALENTINE   And how do yours?
120 PROTEUS   I left them all in health.
VALENTINE   How does your lady? And how thrives your love?
PROTEUS   My tales of love were wont to weary you:
        I know you joy not in a love-discourse.
VALENTINE   Ay, Proteus, but that life is altered now.
125   I have done penance for contemning° Love,   *despising*
        Whose high imperious thoughts have punished me
        With bitter fasts, with penitential groans,
        With nightly tears, and daily heartsore sighs.
        For in revenge of my contempt of love,
130   Love hath chased sleep from my enthrallèd° eyes   *enslaved*
        And made them watchers of mine own heart's sorrow.
        O gentle Proteus, Love's a mighty lord
        And hath so humbled me as° I confess   *that*
        There is no woe to° his correction,°   *equal to / punishment*
135   Nor to his service no such joy on earth.
        Now, no discourse, except it be of love!
        Now can I break my fast, dine, sup, and sleep
        Upon the very naked name of love.
PROTEUS   Enough! I read your fortune in your eye.
140   Was this the idol that you worship so?
VALENTINE   Even she; and is she not a heavenly saint?
PROTEUS   No, but she is an earthly paragon.°   *model without equal*
VALENTINE   Call her divine.
PROTEUS   I will not flatter her.
VALENTINE   Oh, flatter me; for Love delights in praises.
145 PROTEUS   When I was sick, you gave me bitter pills,
        And I must minister the like to you.
VALENTINE   Then speak the truth by° her; if not divine,   *about*
        Yet let her be a principality,°   *angel*
        Sovereign° to all the creatures on the earth.   *Superior*
PROTEUS   Except my mistress.
150 VALENTINE   Sweet, except not any,°   *make no exceptions*
        Except° thou wilt except against° my love.   *Unless / insult*
PROTEUS   Have I not reason to prefer° mine own?   *advance*
VALENTINE   And I will help thee to prefer her, too:
        She shall be dignified with this high honor,
155   To bear my lady's train, lest the base earth
        Should from her vesture° chance to steal a kiss   *garments*
        And, of so great a favor growing proud,
        Disdain to root° the summer-swelling flower   *receive the roots of*
        And make rough winter everlastingly.
160 PROTEUS   Why, Valentine, what braggartism° is this?   *excessive boasting*

VALENTINE   Pardon me, Proteus; all I can is nothing
         To her[8] whose worth makes other worthies nothing.
         She is alone.°   *unique*
PROTEUS   Then let her alone.
VALENTINE   Not for the world! Why, man, she is mine own,
165   And I as rich in having such a jewel
         As twenty seas, if all their sand were pearl,
         The water nectar, and the rocks pure gold.
         Forgive me that I do not dream on thee,°   *pay attention to you*
         Because thou seest me dote upon my love.
170   My foolish rival, that her father likes
         Only for° his possessions are so huge,   *because*
         Is gone with her along, and I must after,
         For Love, thou know'st, is full of jealousy.
PROTEUS   But she loves you?
175 VALENTINE   Ay, and we are betrothed. Nay, more, our
               marriage hour,
         With all the cunning manner of our flight,
         Determined of:° how I must climb her window,   *Decided upon*
         The ladder made of cords, and all the means
         Plotted and 'greed on for my happiness.
180   Good Proteus, go with me to my chamber
         In these affairs to aid me with thy counsel.
PROTEUS   Go on before. I shall inquire you forth.°   *seek you out*
         I must unto the road° to disembark   *harbor*
         Some necessaries that I needs must use,
185   And then I'll presently° attend you.   *at once*
VALENTINE   Will you make haste?
PROTEUS   I will.   [*Exit* VALENTINE.]
         Even as one heat another heat expels,[9]
         Or as one nail by strength drives out another,
190   So the remembrance of my former love
         Is by° a newer object quite forgotten.   *because of*
         Is it mine eye, or Valentine's praise,[1]
         Her true perfection, or my false transgression,
         That makes me, reasonless,° to reason thus?   *wrongly; without cause*
195   She is fair, and so is Julia that I love—
         That I did love, for now my love is thawed,
         Which like a waxen image 'gainst a fire
         Bears no impression of the thing it was.
         Methinks my zeal to° Valentine is cold,   *affection for*
200   And that I love him not as I was wont.
         Oh, but I love his lady too too much,
         And that's the reason I love him so little.
         How shall I dote on her with more advice°   *upon more deliberation*
         That thus without advice begin to love her?
205   'Tis but her picture° I have yet beheld,   *outer appearance*
         And that hath dazzlèd my reason's light.
         But when I look on her perfections,
         There is no reason but° I shall be blind.   *doubt that*

---

8. **all . . . her**: all I can say is nothing in comparison
with her.
9. Referring to a popular belief that the application
of heat takes away the pain of a burn.

1. Textual Comment F reads, "It is mine, or *Valen-
tines* praise?" which editors have long emended for
sense and for metrical regularity. See Digital Edition
TC 7.

If I can check my erring love, I will;
210   If not, to compass° her I'll use my skill.   *Exit.*   *win*

2.5

Enter SPEED *and* LANCE.

SPEED   Lance, by mine honesty, welcome to Milan.[1]

LANCE   Forswear° not thyself, sweet youth, for I am not wel-   *Perjure*
come. I reckon this always, that a man is never undone° till   *ruined*
he be hanged, nor never welcome to a place till some certain
5   shot° be paid, and the hostess say, "Welcome."   *tavern bill*

SPEED   Come on, you madcap. I'll to the alehouse with you
presently, where, for one shot of five pence, thou shalt have
five thousand welcomes. But, sirrah, how did thy master
part with Madam Julia?

10 LANCE   Marry, after they closed[2] in earnest, they parted very
fairly in jest.

SPEED   But shall she marry him?

LANCE   No.

SPEED   How, then? Shall he marry her?

15 LANCE   No, neither.

SPEED   What, are they broken?°   *no longer engaged*

LANCE   No. They are both as whole as a fish.[3]

SPEED   Why, then, how stands the matter with them?

LANCE   Marry, thus: when it stands well with him,[4] it stands
20   well with her.

SPEED   What an ass art thou! I understand thee not.

LANCE   What a block° art thou that thou canst not! My staff[5]   *stupid person*
understands me.

SPEED   What thou say'st?

25 LANCE   Ay, and what I do, too. Look thee, I'll but lean, and my
staff understands me.

SPEED   It stands under thee indeed.

LANCE   Why, "stand-under" and "under-stand" is all one.

SPEED   But tell me true: will't be a match?

30 LANCE   Ask my dog. If he say "Ay," it will; if he say "No," it
will; if he shake his tail and say nothing, it will.

SPEED   The conclusion is, then, that it will.

LANCE   Thou shalt never get such a secret from me but by a
parable.°   *an indirect speech*

35 SPEED   'Tis well that I get it so. But, Lance, how say'st thou[6]
that my master is become a notable lover?

LANCE   I never knew him otherwise.

SPEED   Than how?

LANCE   A notable lubber,° as thou reportest him to be.   *clumsy, stupid person*

40 SPEED   Why, thou whoreson[7] ass, thou mistak'st° me.   *misunderstand*

LANCE   Why, fool, I meant not thee; I meant thy master.[8]

2.5 Location: A street in Milan.
1. TEXTUAL COMMENT F reads "Padua," which is probably an error, since the play's other references to geography have Valentine and Proteus traveling to and from Milan. See Digital Edition TC 8.
2. Came to an agreement; embraced.
3. Lance takes "broken" to mean "in pieces" and replies with a proverb.
4. When it goes well with him; when he has an erection.

5. A stick used when walking; also a euphemism for "penis." During this dialogue Lance may play with his staff, which he says "understands" (supports; comprehends) him.
6. What can you say about the fact.
7. Literally, "son of a whore." A term of abuse frequently used in jest.
8. Punning on "mistake." Lance understood Speed to mean "you misjudge me" or "you confuse me with someone else."

SPEED   I tell thee my master is become a hot lover.

LANCE   Why, I tell thee I care not, though he burn himself in
love.[9] If thou wilt, go with me to the alehouse; if not, thou
45 art an Hebrew, a Jew, and not worth° the name of a   *worthy*
Christian.

SPEED   Why?

LANCE   Because thou hast not so much charity in thee as to
go to the ale[1] with a Christian. Wilt thou go?

50 SPEED   At thy service.   *Exeunt.*

2.6

Enter PROTEUS *alone.*

PROTEUS   To leave my Julia shall I be forsworn;°   *guilty of vow-breaking*
To love fair Silvia shall I be forsworn;
To wrong my friend I shall be much forsworn;
And e'en that power° which gave me first my oath   *(Love)*
5 Provokes me to this threefold perjury.
Love bade me swear, and Love bids me forswear;
O sweet-suggesting° Love, if thou hast sinned,   *sweetly seductive*
Teach me, thy tempted subject, to excuse it.
At first I did adore a twinkling star,
10 But now I worship a celestial sun.
Unheedful° vows may heedfully° be broken,   *Careless / advisedly*
And he wants° wit that wants resolvèd will°   *lacks / determination*
To learn° his wit t'exchange the bad for better.   *teach*
Fie, fie, unreverent tongue, to call her bad
15 Whose sovereignty so oft thou hast preferred°   *recommended*
With twenty thousand soul-confirming° oaths.   *soul-confirmed; devout*
I cannot leave° to love, and yet I do;   *cease*
But there I leave to love where I should love.
Julia I lose, and Valentine I lose;
20 If I keep them, I needs must lose myself;
If I lose them, thus find I by their loss
For Valentine, myself, for Julia, Silvia.[1]
I to myself am dearer than a friend,
For love is still° most precious in itself,   *always*
25 And Silvia—witness heaven that made her fair—
Shows Julia but° a swarthy Ethiop.[2]   *to be merely*
I will forget that Julia is alive,
Rememb'ring that my love to her is dead;
And Valentine I'll hold an enemy,
30 Aiming at Silvia as a sweeter friend.
I cannot now prove constant to myself
Without some treachery used to Valentine.
This night he meaneth with a corded° ladder   *rope*
To climb celestial Silvia's chamber window,
35 Myself in counsel, his competitor.[3]
Now presently I'll give her father notice
Of their disguising and pretended° flight,   *intended*

9. *burn himself in love:* be too passionate; suffer the
burning sensations of venereal disease.
1. Referring to a church-ale, a charitable festival at
which ale was sold in aid of the church or to relieve
the poor.
2.6 Location: The Duke's court in Milan.

1. Proteus claims that to hold on to his selfhood and
his love (Silvia), he must give up Julia and Valentine.
2. Ethiopian, or black African. The comparison rests
on a European idealization of female fairness or
whiteness.
3. Myself in on the secret as his partner.

Who, all enraged, will banish Valentine—
For Turio he intends shall wed his daughter.
40   But, Valentine being gone, I'll quickly cross°   *thwart*
By some sly trick blunt Turio's dull proceeding.
Love, lend me wings to make my purpose swift,
As thou hast lent me wit to plot this drift.°   *Exit.*   *scheme*

2.7

Enter JULIA *and* LUCETTA.

JULIA   Counsel, Lucetta; gentle girl, assist me,
And e'en in kind love I do conjure° thee,   *entreat*
Who art the table° wherein all my thoughts   *notebook; tablet*
Are visibly charactered° and engraved,   *written*
5   To lesson° me and tell me some good mean°   *teach / way*
How with my honor I may undertake
A journey to my loving Proteus.
LUCETTA   Alas, the way is wearisome and long.
JULIA   A true-devoted pilgrim is not weary
10   To measure° kingdoms with his feeble steps;   *make his way through*
Much less shall she that hath Love's wings to fly,
And when the flight is made to one so dear,
Of such divine perfection, as Sir Proteus.
LUCETTA   Better forbear till Proteus make return.
15   JULIA   Oh, know'st thou not his looks are my soul's food?
Pity the dearth° that I have pinèd in   *famine*
By longing for that food so long a time.
Didst thou but know the inly° touch of love,   *inward*
Thou wouldst as soon go kindle fire with snow
20   As seek to quench the fire of love with words.
LUCETTA   I do not seek to quench your love's hot fire,
But qualify° the fire's extreme rage,   *lessen*
Lest it should burn above the bounds of reason.
JULIA   The more thou damm'st it up, the more it burns!
25   The current that with gentle murmur glides,
Thou know'st, being stopped, impatiently doth rage.
But when his fair course is not hinderèd,
He makes sweet music with th'enameled° stones,   *shiny*
Giving a gentle kiss to every sedge°   *plant*
30   He overtaketh in his pilgrimage;
And so by many winding nooks he strays
With willing sport to the wild ocean.
Then let me go and hinder not my course.
I'll be as patient as a gentle stream,
35   And make a pastime of each weary step
Till the last step have brought me to my love,
And there I'll rest as after much turmoil
A blessèd soul doth in Elysium.[1]
LUCETTA   But in what habit° will you go along?   *clothing*
40   JULIA   Not like a woman, for I would prevent°   *forestall*
The loose encounters of lascivious men.
Gentle Lucetta, fit° me with such weeds°   *equip / clothing*
As may beseem some well-reputed page.

2.7 Location: Julia's house.   1. In Greek mythology, the final abode, after
death, of blessèd souls.

LUCETTA   Why, then, your ladyship must cut your hair.
45   JULIA   No, girl, I'll knit° it up in silken strings   *bind*
          With twenty odd-conceited° true-love knots.²   *strangely devised*
          To be fantastic° may become a youth   *fanciful*
          Of greater time° than I shall show° to be.   *age / appear*
    LUCETTA   What fashion, madam, shall I make your breeches?
50   JULIA   That fits as well as "Tell me, good my lord,
          What compass° will you wear your farthingale?"³   *fullness*
          Why, ev'n what fashion thou best likes, Lucetta.
    LUCETTA   You must needs have them with a codpiece,⁴ madam.
    JULIA   Out, out,° Lucetta! That will be ill favored.°   *Not so / unbecoming*
55   LUCETTA   A round hose,⁵ madam, now's not worth a pin
          Unless you have a codpiece to stick pins on.
    JULIA   Lucetta, as thou lov'st me, let me have
          What thou think'st meet and is most mannerly.°   *seemly; modest*
          But tell me, wench, how will the world repute me
60   For undertaking so unstaid° a journey?   *reckless*
          I fear me it will make me scandalized.°   *disgraced*
    LUCETTA   If you think so, then stay at home and go not.
    JULIA   Nay, that I will not.
    LUCETTA   Then never dream on infamy, but go!
65   If Proteus like your journey when you come,
          No matter who's displeased when you are gone:
          I fear me he will scarce be pleased withal.°   *with it*
    JULIA   That is the least, Lucetta, of my fear.
          A thousand oaths, an ocean of his tears,
70   And instances of infinite° of love   *an infinity*
          Warrant me° welcome to my Proteus.   *Assure me I will be*
    LUCETTA   All these are servants to deceitful men.
    JULIA   Base men that use them to so base effect!
          But truer stars did govern Proteus' birth:⁶
75   His words are bonds, his oaths are oracles,
          His love sincere, his thoughts immaculate,
          His tears pure messengers sent from his heart,
          His heart as far from fraud as heaven from earth.
    LUCETTA   Pray heaven he prove so when you come to him.
80   JULIA   Now, as thou lov'st me, do him not that wrong
          To bear a hard opinion of his truth.
          Only deserve my love by loving him,
          And presently° go with me to my chamber   *at once*
          To take a note of what I stand in need of
85   To furnish me upon my longing° journey.   *love-prompted*
          All that is mine I leave at thy dispose,°   *in your care*
          My goods, my lands, my reputation;
          Only in lieu thereof dispatch me hence.°   *help me hurry away*
          Come, answer not, but to it presently;
90   I am impatient of my tarriance.°   *Exeunt.*   *delay*

---

2. Ornamental ribbons supposed to symbolize love.
3. Hooped petticoat.
4. A pouch attached to the front of men's breeches, covering the genital area. In the Elizabethan period, codpieces could be elaborately decorated, as with
pins (line 56).
5. Breeches fitting the legs and thighs tightly and puffed out at the hips.
6. The stars' position at one's birth supposedly determined one's character.

3.1

Enter DUKE, TURIO, [*and*] PROTEUS.

DUKE Sir Turio, give us leave,° I pray, awhile;   *leave us alone*
  We have some secrets to confer about.   [*Exit* TURIO.]
  Now tell me, Proteus, what's your will with me?
PROTEUS My gracious lord, that which I would discover°   *reveal*
5 The law of friendship bids me to conceal.
  But when I call to mind your gracious favors
  Done to me, undeserving as I am,
  My duty pricks° me on to utter that   *urges*
  Which else no worldly good should draw from me.
10 Know, worthy prince, Sir Valentine my friend
  This night intends to steal away your daughter.
  Myself am one made privy to the plot.
  I know you have determined to bestow her
  On Turio, whom your gentle daughter hates,
15 And should she thus be stol'n away from you,
  It would be much vexation to your age.
  Thus for my duty's sake I rather chose
  To cross° my friend in his intended drift°   *thwart / plan*
  Than by concealing it heap on your head
20 A pack of sorrows, which would press you down,
  Being unprevented,° to your timeless° grave.   *unstopped / early*
DUKE Proteus, I thank thee for thine honest care,
  Which to requite° command me¹ while I live.   *repay*
  This love of theirs myself have often seen,
25 Haply° when they have judged me fast asleep,   *Perchance*
  And oftentimes have purposed to forbid
  Sir Valentine her company and my court.
  But fearing lest my jealous aim might err
  And so unworthily disgrace the man—
30 A rashness that I ever yet have shunned—
  I gave him gentle looks, thereby to find
  That which thyself hast now disclosed to me.
  And that thou mayst perceive my fear of this,
  Knowing that tender youth is soon suggested,°   *tempted*
35 I nightly lodge her in an upper tower,
  The key whereof myself have ever kept;
  And thence she cannot be conveyed away.
PROTEUS Know, noble lord, they have devised a mean°   *plan*
  How he her chamber window will ascend
40 And with a corded ladder fetch her down,
  For which the youthful lover now is gone,
  And this way comes he with it presently,
  Where, if it please you, you may intercept him.
  But, good my lord, do it so cunningly
45 That my discovery° be not aimèd° at;   *disclosure / guessed*
  For love of you, not hate unto my friend,
  Hath made me publisher of this pretense.²
DUKE Upon mine honor, he shall never know
  That I had any light° from thee of this.   *information*
    [*Enter* VALENTINE.]

3.1 Location: The Duke's court in Milan.   2. Has caused me to make this plan public.
1. Ask anything of me.

50 PROTEUS   Adieu, my lord. Sir Valentine is coming.

[*Exit* PROTEUS.]

DUKE   Sir Valentine, whither away so fast?³

VALENTINE   Please it° your grace, there is a messenger   *If it please*
   That stays° to bear my letters to my friends,   *waits*
   And I am going to deliver them.

55 DUKE   Be they of much import?

VALENTINE   The tenor° of them doth but signify   *general sense*
   My health and happy being at your court.

DUKE   Nay, then, no matter. Stay with me awhile.
   I am to break with thee of° some affairs   *disclose to you*
60   That touch me near, wherein thou must be secret.
   'Tis not unknown to thee that I have sought
   To match my friend Sir Turio to my daughter.

VALENTINE   I know it well, my lord, and sure the match
   Were° rich and honorable. Besides, the gentleman   *Would be*
65   Is full of virtue, bounty, worth, and qualities
   Beseeming° such a wife as your fair daughter.   *Suited to*
   Cannot your grace win her to fancy him?

DUKE   No, trust me: she is peevish, sullen, froward,°   *perverse*
   Proud, disobedient, stubborn, lacking duty,
70   Neither regarding° that she is my child   *taking into account*
   Nor fearing me as if I were her father.⁴
   And, may I say to thee, this pride of hers
   Upon advice° hath drawn my love from her,   *After consideration*
   And where° I thought the remnant° of mine age   *whereas / remainder*
75   Should have been cherished by her childlike duty,
   I now am full resolved to take a wife
   And turn her out to who will take her in.
   Then let her beauty be her wedding dower,
   For me and my possessions she esteems not.

80 VALENTINE   What would your grace have me to do in this?

DUKE   There is a lady in Milano⁵ here
   Whom I affect,° but she is nice° and coy,   *love / hard to please*
   And naught esteems° my agèd eloquence.   *does not value*
   Now therefore would I have thee to my tutor—
85   For long agone° I have forgot° to court;   *ago / forgotten how*
   Besides, the fashion of the time is changed—
   How and which way I may bestow° myself   *conduct*
   To be regarded in her sun-bright eye.

VALENTINE   Win her with gifts if she respect° not words.   *heed*
90   Dumb jewels often in their silent kind°   *nature*
   More than quick words do move a woman's mind.

DUKE   But she did scorn a present that I sent her.

VALENTINE   A woman sometimes scorns what best contents her.
   Send her another: never give her o'er,
95   For scorn at first makes after-love the more.
   If she do frown, 'tis not in hate of you,
   But rather to beget more love in you.
   If she do chide, 'tis not to have you gone,

---

3. Valentine may be crossing the stage without noticing the Duke or starting to retreat on seeing him.
4. Nor respecting me as a father should be respected.
5. F reads "in Verona," another sign of inconsistency
in regard to the play's setting. In this line "Verona" is
replaced by "Milano" rather than "Milan" for greater
metrical regularity.

	Forwhy° the fools° are mad if left alone.	*Because / (women)*
100	Take no repulse, whatever she doth say:	
	For° "Get you gone" she doth not mean "Away!"	*By*
	Flatter and praise, commend, extol their graces;	
	Though ne'er so black,° say they have angels' faces.	*dark-complexioned*
	That man that hath a tongue, I say, is no man	
105	If with his tongue he cannot win a woman.	
	DUKE But she I mean is promised by her friends	
	Unto a youthful gentleman of worth,	
	And kept severely from resort of men,	
	That no man hath access by day to her.	
110	VALENTINE Why, then, I would resort to her by night.	
	DUKE Ay, but the doors be locked and keys kept safe,	
	That no man hath recourse to her by night.	
	VALENTINE What lets but one may enter° at her window?	*hinders one from entering*
	DUKE Her chamber is aloft, far from the ground,	
115	And built so shelving° that one cannot climb it	*projecting so far out*
	Without apparant hazard of his life.	
	VALENTINE Why, then, a ladder quaintly° made of cords	*skillfully*
	To cast up, with a pair of anchoring hooks,	
	Would serve to scale another Hero's⁶ tower,	
120	So° bold Leander would adventure it.	*Provided*
	DUKE Now, as thou art a gentleman of blood,°	*well-born; passionate*
	Advise me where I may have such a ladder.	
	VALENTINE When would you use it? Pray, sir, tell me that.	
	DUKE This very night. For Love is like a child	
125	That longs for everything that he can come by.	
	VALENTINE By seven o'clock I'll get you such a ladder.	
	DUKE But hark thee! I will go to her alone.	
	How shall I best convey the ladder thither?	
	VALENTINE It will be light, my lord, that you may bear it	
130	Under a cloak that is of any length.	
	DUKE A cloak as long as thine will serve the turn?	
	VALENTINE Ay, my good lord.	
	DUKE Then let me see thy cloak;	
	I'll get me one of such another length.	
	VALENTINE Why, any cloak will serve the turn, my lord.	
135	DUKE How shall I fashion me to wear° a cloak?	*get used to wearing*
	I pray thee, let me feel thy cloak upon me.	
	[*He snatches the cloak and finds a rope ladder and a letter hidden within.*]	
	What letter is this same? What's here? "To Silvia"?	
	And here an engine° fit for my proceeding!	*instrument (the ladder)*
	I'll be so bold to break the seal for once.	
140	[*Reads.*] "My thoughts do harbor° with my Silvia nightly,	*dwell*
	And slaves they are to me that send them flying.	
	Oh, could their master come and go as lightly,	
	Himself would lodge where senseless° they are lying.	*without feeling*
	My herald° thoughts in thy pure bosom rest them	*message-bearing*
145	While I, their king, that thither them importune,°	*command*
	Do curse the grace° that with such grace° hath blest them,	*good fortune / favor*

6. See note to 1.1.22. Hero, Leander's beloved, lived in a tower.

	Because myself do want° my servant's fortune.	*lack*
	I curse myself, for° they are sent by me,	*because*
	That they should harbor where their lord should be."	
150	What's here? "Silvia, this night I will enfranchise thee."	
	'Tis so! And here's the ladder for the purpose.	
	Why, Phaëton,[7] for° thou art Merops' son,	*since*
	Wilt thou aspire to guide the heavenly car,	
	And with thy daring folly burn the world?	
155	Wilt thou reach° stars because they shine on thee?	*grasp at*
	Go, base intruder, overweening° slave,	*presumptuous*
	Bestow thy fawning smiles on equal mates,°	*mates of your own rank*
	And think my patience, more than thy desert,	
	Is privilege for° thy departure hence.	*Allows*
160	Thank me for this more than for all the favors	
	Which, all too much, I have bestowed on thee.	
	But if thou linger in my territories	
	Longer than swiftest expedition°	*speed*
	Will give thee time to leave our royal court,	
165	By heaven, my wrath shall far exceed the love	
	I ever bore my daughter or thyself!	
	Be gone. I will not hear thy vain excuse,	
	But, as thou lov'st thy life, make speed from hence. *[Exit.]*	

VALENTINE   And why not death, rather than living torment?

170	To die is to be banished from myself,	
	And Silvia is myself. Banished from her	
	Is self from self: a deadly banishment.	
	What light is light if Silvia be not seen?	
	What joy is joy if Silvia be not by?	
175	Unless it be to think that she is by	
	And feed upon the shadow° of perfection.	*image; memory*
	Except I be by Silvia in the night,	
	There is no music in the nightingale.	
	Unless I look on Silvia in the day,	
180	There is no day for me to look upon.	
	She is my essence, and I leave° to be	*cease*
	If I be not by her fair influence[8]	
	Fostered, illumined, cherished, kept alive.	
	I fly not death to fly his deadly doom:[9]	
185	Tarry I here, I but attend on° death,	*wait for*
	But fly I hence, I fly away from life.	

[*Enter* PROTEUS *and* LANCE.]

PROTEUS   Run, boy, run, run, and seek him out.

LANCE   So-ho! So-ho![1]

PROTEUS   What seest thou?

190   LANCE   Him we go to find. There's not a hair on 's head but 'tis
a Valentine.[2]

---

7. Famous in Greek mythology for his reckless ambition, Phaëton set the world on fire when he tried to drive the chariot of his father, Helios, the sun god. Phaëton's mother, Clymene, was married to Merops, not Helios, making Phaëton illegitimate. The rest of the line, naming Merops as Phaëton's father, may question Phaëton's status as the son of Helios (and so his ability to drive the sun god's chariot) or may be an ironic means of calling attention to his illegitimacy.

8. Alluding to the popular belief that the stars exert power, or "influence," over individuals.
9. I cannot escape death by fleeing the Duke's death sentence.
1. A cry in hare hunting and hawking.
2. Punning on "hare" and on Valentine's name. Every part, down to the "hair," of the creature he sees suggests a "valentine," or stereotypical lover.

PROTEUS Valentine?

VALENTINE No.

PROTEUS Who, then? His spirit?

195 VALENTINE Neither.

PROTEUS What, then?

VALENTINE Nothing.

LANCE Can nothing speak? Master, shall I strike?

PROTEUS Who wouldst thou strike?

200 LANCE Nothing.

PROTEUS Villain, forbear.

LANCE Why, sir, I'll strike nothing. I pray you—

PROTEUS Sirrah, I say forbear. —Friend Valentine, a word.

VALENTINE My ears are stopped and cannot hear good news,

205 So much of bad already hath possessed them.

PROTEUS Then in dumb silence will I bury mine,°   (*my news*)

 For they are harsh, untunable,° and bad.   *out of tune*

VALENTINE Is Silvia dead?

PROTEUS   No, Valentine!

VALENTINE No Valentine indeed for sacred Silvia.

 Hath she forsworn me?

210 PROTEUS   No, Valentine.

VALENTINE No Valentine, if Silvia have forsworn me.

 What is your news?

LANCE Sir, there is a proclamation that you are vanished.°   (*for "banished"*)

PROTEUS That thou art banishèd—oh, that's the news—

215 From hence, from Silvia, and from me thy friend.

VALENTINE Oh, I have fed upon this woe already,

 And now excess of it will make me surfeit.°   *sicken*

 Doth Silvia know that I am banishèd?

PROTEUS Ay, ay, and she hath offered to the doom,°   *sentence*

220 Which unreversed stands in effectual force,[3]

 A sea of melting pearl, which some call tears.

 Those at her father's churlish feet she tendered;°   *offered*

 With them, upon her knees, her humble self,

 Wringing her hands, whose whiteness so became them

225 As if but now they waxèd° pale for woe.   *turned*

 But neither bended knees, pure hands held up,

 Sad sighs, deep groans, nor silver-shedding tears[4]

 Could penetrate her uncompassionate sire,

 But Valentine, if he be ta'en, must die.

230 Besides, her intercession chafed him so,

 When she for thy repeal° was suppliant,   *recall from exile*

 That to close° prison he commanded her,   *tightly enclosed*

 With many bitter threats of biding° there.   *staying permanently*

VALENTINE No more, unless the next word that thou speak'st

235 Have some malignant power upon my life.

 If so, I pray thee breathe it in mine ear,

 As ending anthem° of my endless dolor.°   *final hymn / grief*

PROTEUS Cease to lament for that° thou canst not help   *what*

 And study° help for that which thou lament'st.   *devise*

240 Time is the nurse and breeder of all good.

 Here, if thou stay, thou canst not see thy love;

---

3. Which, unless reversed, will be enforced.   4. Tears that flow like silver streams.

Besides, thy staying will abridge thy life.
Hope is a lover's staff; walk hence with that
And manage it° against despairing thoughts.　　　　　*use it as a weapon*
245 Thy letters may be here, though thou art hence,
Which, being writ to me, shall be delivered
Even in the milk-white bosom of thy love.
The time now serves not to expostulate.°　　　　　*complain; argue*
Come, I'll convey thee through the city gate,
250 And ere I part with thee confer at large°　　　　　*discuss at length*
Of all that may concern thy love affairs.
As thou lov'st Silvia, though not for thyself,
Regard thy danger and along with me.

VALENTINE　I pray thee, Lance, an if° thou seest my boy,　　　　　*an if = if*
255 Bid him make haste and meet me at the North Gate.

PROTEUS　Go, sirrah, find him out. —Come, Valentine.

VALENTINE　O my dear Silvia! Hapless Valentine!

[*Exeunt* PROTEUS *and* VALENTINE.]

LANCE　I am but a fool, look you, and yet I have the wit to
think my master is a kind of a knave. But that's all one,° if he　　　　　*all right*
260 be but one knave.[5] He lives not now that knows me to be in
love; yet I am in love, but a team of horse shall not pluck that
from me, nor who 'tis I love; and yet 'tis a woman, but what
woman I will not tell myself; and yet 'tis a milkmaid; yet 'tis
not a maid,° for she hath had gossips;[6] yet 'tis a maid, for she　　　　　*virgin*
265 is her master's maid and serves for wages. She hath more
qualities° than a water-spaniel,[7] which is much in a bare°　　　　　*abilities / mere*
Christian. Here is the catalog of her condition. [*He produces
a paper.*] "*Imprimis*:[8] she can fetch and carry." —Why, a
horse can do no more. Nay, a horse cannot fetch, but only
270 carry. Therefore is she better than a jade.° "*Item*: she can　　　　　*inferior horse*
milk." Look you, a sweet virtue in a maid with clean hands.

[*Enter* SPEED.]

SPEED　How now, Signor Lance? What news with your
mastership?

LANCE　With my master's ship? Why, it is at sea.

275 SPEED　Well, your old vice still: mistake the word.[9] What
news, then, in your paper?

LANCE　The black'st news that ever thou heard'st.

SPEED　Why, man? How black?

LANCE　Why, as black as ink.

280 SPEED　Let me read them.

LANCE　Fie on thee, jolt-head;° thou canst not read.　　　　　*blockhead*

SPEED　Thou liest. I can.

LANCE　I will try thee. Tell me this: who begot thee?

SPEED　Marry, the son of my grandfather.

285 LANCE　O illiterate loiterer! It was the son of thy grandmother.
This proves that thou canst not read.

SPEED　Come, fool, come. Try me in thy paper.

5. If he is only moderately a rascal; only a knave in one area (love).
6. Women who attended at childbirth; people who served as sponsors at the baptism of a newborn child.
7. A dog used for hunting waterfowl.
8. The paper employs the language of official docu- ments. "*Imprimis*," Latin for "in the first place," was used to begin inventories. "*Item*" (line 270), meaning "also," was used to introduce subsequent articles in a list.
9. *your . . . word*: your customary fault of making blunders with language.

LANCE [*giving* SPEED *the paper*]   There—and Saint Nicholas[1]
    be thy speed.°   *protection*

290 SPEED   "*Imprimis*: she can milk."
    LANCE   Ay, that she can.
    SPEED   "*Item*: she brews good ale."
    LANCE   And thereof comes the proverb: "Blessing of your
    heart, you brew good ale."

295 SPEED   "*Item*: she can sew."
    LANCE   That's as much as to say: "Can she so?"
    SPEED   "*Item*: she can knit."
    LANCE   What need a man care for a stock° with a wench   *dowry*
    when she can knit him a stock?°   *stocking*

300 SPEED   "*Item*: she can wash and scour."
    LANCE   A special virtue, for then she need not be washed and
    scoured.[2]
    SPEED   "*Item*: she can spin."
    LANCE   Then may I set the world on wheels,° when she can   *take life easy*

305 spin for her living.
    SPEED   "*Item*: she hath many nameless° virtues."   *inexpressible*
    LANCE   That's as much as to say "bastard virtues," that indeed
    know not their fathers and therefore have no names.
    SPEED   Here follow her vices.

310 LANCE   Close at the heels of her virtues.
    SPEED   "*Item*: she is not to be fasting in respect of° her breath." *on account of*
    LANCE   Well, that fault may be mended with a breakfast.
    Read on.
    SPEED   "*Item*: she hath a sweet mouth."[3]

315 LANCE   That makes amends for her sour breath.
    SPEED   "*Item*: she doth talk in her sleep."
    LANCE   It's no matter for that so she sleep not in her talk.
    SPEED   "*Item*: she is slow in words."
    LANCE   O villain, that set this down among her vices! To be

320 slow in words is a woman's only virtue. I pray thee, out
    with't, and place it for her chief virtue!
    SPEED   "*Item*: she is proud."°   *haughty; lascivious*
    LANCE   Out with that, too! It was Eve's legacy,[4] and cannot be
    ta'en from her.

325 SPEED   "*Item*: she hath no teeth."
    LANCE   I care not for that neither, because I love crusts.
    SPEED   "*Item*: she is curst."°   *shrewish*
    LANCE   Well, the best is, she hath no teeth to bite.
    SPEED   "*Item*: she will often praise° her liquor."   *appraise (by tasting)*

330 LANCE   If her liquor be good, she shall; if she will not, I will,
    for good things should be praised.
    SPEED   "*Item*: she is too liberal."°   *bold; wanton*
    LANCE   Of her tongue she cannot, for that's writ down she is
    slow of; of her purse she shall not, for that I'll keep shut.

---

1. The patron saint of schoolchildren and scholars.
2. *washed and scoured*: slang for "knocked down and beaten."
3. A sweet tooth; a wanton nature.
4. In the Garden of Eden, Satan, in the form of a serpent, tempted Eve, wife of the first man, Adam, to eat fruit from the tree of knowledge of good and evil, which God had forbidden humans to taste. Eve was thus guilty of the sin of pride for disobeying God and putting her will before his command. See Genesis 2:15–3:24.

335 Now, of another thing⁵ she may, and that cannot I help.
     Well, proceed.
     SPEED "*Item*: she hath more hair than wit, and more faults
     than hairs, and more wealth than faults."
     LANCE Stop there! I'll have her. She was mine and not mine
340 twice or thrice in that last article. Rehearse° that once more.   *Repeat*
     SPEED "*Item*: she hath more hair than wit—"
     LANCE "More hair than wit." It may be. I'll prove it. The
     cover of the salt hides the salt,° and therefore it is more°   *saltcellar / greater*
     than the salt; the hair that covers the wit is more than the
345 wit, for the greater hides the less. What's next?
     SPEED "And more faults than hairs."
     LANCE That's monstrous! Oh, that that were out!
     SPEED "And more wealth than faults."
     LANCE Why, that word makes the faults gracious.° Well, I'll   *pleasing*
350 have her, and if it be a match—as nothing is impossible—
     SPEED What then?
     LANCE Why, then will I tell thee that thy master stays° for   *waits*
     thee at the North Gate.
     SPEED For me?
355 LANCE For thee? Ay, who art thou? He hath stayed for a bet-
     ter man than thee.
     SPEED And must I go to him?
     LANCE Thou must run to him, for thou hast stayed so long
     that going° will scarce serve the turn.   *walking*
360 SPEED Why didst not tell me sooner? Pox of⁶ your love letters!
                                                               [*Exit.*]
     LANCE Now will he be swinged° for reading my letter. An   *beaten*
     unmannerly slave, that will thrust himself into secrets. I'll
     after, to rejoice in the boy's correction.   *Exit.*

3.2

     Enter DUKE *and* TURIO.
     DUKE Sir Turio, fear not but that she will love you
     Now Valentine is banished from her sight.
     TURIO Since his exile she hath despised me most,
     Forsworn my company, and railed at me,
5   That° I am desperate° of obtaining her.   *So that / hopeless*
     DUKE This weak impress° of love is as a figure   *impression*
     Trenchèd° in ice, which with an hour's heat   *Cut*
     Dissolves to water and doth lose his form.
     A little time will melt her frozen thoughts,
10   And worthless Valentine shall be forgot.
              [*Enter* PROTEUS.]
     How now, Sir Proteus? Is your countryman,
     According to our proclamation, gone?
     PROTEUS Gone, my good lord.
     DUKE My daughter takes his going grievously?
15   PROTEUS A little time, my lord, will kill that grief.
     DUKE So I believe, but Turio thinks not so.

---

5. "Purse" (line 334) and "another thing" were colloquial terms for "female genitalia."

6. May disease take (a curse).
3.2 Location: Scene continues.

Proteus, the good conceit° I hold of thee—   *opinion*
For thou hast shown some sign of good desert—
Makes me the better° to confer with thee.   *the more willing*

20 PROTEUS Longer than I prove loyal to your grace
Let me not live to look upon your grace.

DUKE Thou know'st how willingly I would effect
The match between Sir Turio and my daughter?

PROTEUS I do, my lord.

25 DUKE And also, I think, thou art not ignorant
How she opposes her° against my will?   *herself*

PROTEUS She did, my lord, when Valentine was here.

DUKE Ay, and perversely she persevers so!
What might we do to make the girl forget

30 The love of Valentine, and love Sir Turio?

PROTEUS The best way is to slander Valentine
With falsehood, cowardice, and poor descent:
Three things that women highly hold in hate.

DUKE Ay, but she'll think that it is spoke in hate.

35 PROTEUS Ay, if his enemy deliver° it.   *report*
Therefore it must with circumstance° be spoken   *supporting detail*
By one whom she esteemeth as his friend.

DUKE Then you must undertake to slander him.

PROTEUS And that, my lord, I shall be loath to do.

40 'Tis an ill office for a gentleman,
Especially against his very° friend.   *true*

DUKE Where your good word cannot advantage° him,   *profit*
Your slander never can endamage° him;   *harm*
Therefore the office is indifferent,°   *neutral*

45 Being entreated to it by your friend.[1]

PROTEUS You have prevailed, my lord. If I can do it
By aught° that I can speak in his dispraise,   *anything*
She shall not long continue love to him.
But say this weed° her love from Valentine: *uproot*

50 It follows not that she will love Sir Turio.

TURIO Therefore, as you unwind her love from him,
Lest it should ravel and be good to none,
You must provide to bottom it on me;[2]
Which must be done by praising me as much

55 As you in worth dispraise Sir Valentine.

DUKE And, Proteus, we dare trust you in this kind
Because we know, on Valentine's report,
You are already Love's firm votary,°   *disciple*
And cannot soon revolt and change your mind.

60 Upon this warrant shall you have access
Where you with Silvia may confer at large—
For she is lumpish,° heavy, melancholy,   *low-spirited*
And for your friend's sake will be glad of you—
Where you may temper° her, by your persuasion,   *mold*

65 To hate young Valentine and love my friend.

PROTEUS As much as I can do, I will effect.
But you, Sir Turio, are not sharp enough:
You must lay lime[3] to tangle° her desires   *capture*

---

1. Being asked to do it by a friend like me.   3. Birdlime, a sticky substance used to trap birds.
2. To wind it like a skein of thread upon me.

By wailful sonnets whose composèd° rhymes   *well-crafted*
70 Should be full fraught° with serviceable vows.[4]   *laden*
  DUKE   Ay, much is the force of heaven-bred poesy.
  PROTEUS   Say that upon the altar of her beauty
    You sacrifice your tears, your sighs, your heart;
    Write till your ink be dry, and with your tears
75 Moist it again, and frame some feeling line
    That may discover° such integrity.°   *reveal / sincerity*
    For Orpheus'[5] lute was strung with poets' sinews,°   *nerves*
    Whose golden touch could soften steel and stones,
    Make tigers tame and huge leviathans°   *whales*
80 Forsake unsounded deeps to dance on sands.
    After your dire-lamenting elegies,°   *love poems*
    Visit by night your lady's chamber window
    With some sweet consort;° to their instruments   *band of musicians*
    Tune° a deploring dump.° The night's dead silence   *Sing / sad melody*
85 Will well become such sweet-complaining grievance.
    This, or else nothing, will inherit° her.   *win*
  DUKE   This discipline° shows thou hast been in love.   *instruction*
  TURIO   And thy advice this night I'll put in practice.
    Therefore, sweet Proteus, my direction-giver,
90 Let us into the city presently
    To sort° some gentlemen well skilled in music.   *select*
    I have a sonnet that will serve the turn
    To give the onset° to thy good advice.   *start*
  DUKE   About it, gentlemen.
95 PROTEUS   We'll wait upon your grace till after supper,
    And afterward determine our proceedings.
  DUKE   Even now about it. I will pardon you.°   *Exeunt.* *excuse you from service*

4.1

Enter certain OUTLAWS.
  FIRST OUTLAW   Fellows, stand fast: I see a passenger.°   *traveler*
  SECOND OUTLAW   If there be ten, shrink not, but down with 'em.
      [*Enter* VALENTINE *and* SPEED.]
  THIRD OUTLAW   Stand,° sir, and throw us that° you have about ye. *Halt / that which*
    If not, we'll make you sit and rifle° you.   *search*
5 SPEED [*to* VALENTINE]   Sir, we are undone! These are the
    villains
    That all the travelers do fear so much.
  VALENTINE [*to the* OUTLAWS]   My friends—
  FIRST OUTLAW   That's not so, sir! We are your enemies—
  SECOND OUTLAW   Peace! We'll hear him.
10 THIRD OUTLAW   Ay, by my beard will we; for he is a proper° man. *handsome*
  VALENTINE   Then know that I have little wealth to lose.
    A man I am crossed with adversity.
    My riches are these poor habiliments°   *clothes*
    Of which, if you should here disfurnish° me,   *deprive*
15 You take the sum and substance that I have.
  SECOND OUTLAW   Whither travel you?

---

4. Promises to be of service.   entrancing music.
5. A figure in Greek mythology famous for his   **4.1** Location: A forest between Mantua and Milan.

VALENTINE To Verona.

FIRST OUTLAW Whence came you?

VALENTINE From Milan.

20 THIRD OUTLAW Have you long sojourned there?

VALENTINE Some sixteen months,[1] and longer might have
    stayed

    If crooked° fortune had not thwarted me.   evil

FIRST OUTLAW What, were you banished thence?

VALENTINE   I was.

SECOND OUTLAW   For what offense?

VALENTINE For that which now torments me to rehearse:°   tell

25 I killed a man,[2] whose death I much repent,

    But yet I slew him manfully in fight,

    Without false vantage or base treachery.°   unfair advantage

SECOND OUTLAW Why, ne'er repent it, if it were done so.

    But were you banished for so small a fault?

30 VALENTINE I was, and held me glad of such a doom.°   sentence

FIRST OUTLAW Have you the tongues?°   skill in languages

VALENTINE My youthful travel therein made me happy,°   fortunate; skilled

    Or else I often had been miserable.

THIRD OUTLAW By the bare scalp of Robin Hood's fat friar,°   (Friar Tuck)

35 This fellow were a king for our wild faction.°   band

FIRST OUTLAW We'll have him! Sirs, a word.

              [OUTLAWS talk apart.]

SPEED [to VALENTINE] Master, be one of them! It's an honor-
    able kind of thievery.

VALENTINE Peace, villain.

40 FIRST OUTLAW [to VALENTINE] Tell us this: have you anything
    to take to?[3]

VALENTINE Nothing but my fortune.°   luck

THIRD OUTLAW Know, then, that some of us are gentlemen,

    Such as the fury of ungoverned youth

45 Thrust from the company of awful° men.   respectable

    Myself was from Verona banishèd

    For practicing° to steal away a lady,   plotting

    An heir, and near allied unto the Duke.

SECOND OUTLAW And I from Mantua, for a gentleman

50 Who, in my mood,° I stabbed unto the heart.   anger

FIRST OUTLAW And I for suchlike petty crimes as these.

    But to the purpose, for we cite our faults

    That they may hold excused our lawless lives;

    And partly seeing you are beautified

55 With goodly shape, and by your own report

    A linguist and a man of such perfection

    As we do in our quality° much want—   profession

SECOND OUTLAW Indeed, because you are a banished man,

    Therefore, above the rest,[4] we parley° to you: talk

60 Are you content to be our general,

---

1. A claim not consonant with the play's overall time
scheme. Either this is a textual inconsistency or Valentine is lying.
2. Why Valentine lies here is much debated. He may

be protecting Silvia's reputation or trying to impress
the outlaws.
3. Any way to support yourself.
4. For that above all other reasons.

        To make a virtue of necessity
        And live as we do in this wilderness?
    THIRD OUTLAW   What say'st thou? Wilt thou be of our
        consort?°   *company*
        Say "Ay," and be the captain of us all.
65   We'll do thee homage and be ruled by thee,
        Love thee as our commander and our king.
    FIRST OUTLAW   But if thou scorn our courtesy, thou diest.
    SECOND OUTLAW   Thou shalt not live to brag what we have
        offered.
    VALENTINE   I take your offer and will live with you,
70   Provided that you do no outrages
        On silly° women or poor passengers.°   *defenseless / travelers*
    THIRD OUTLAW   No, we detest such vile base practices.
        Come, go with us, we'll bring thee to our crew°   *band of men*
        And show thee all the treasure we have got,
75   Which, with ourselves, all rest at thy dispose.°   *Exeunt.*   *disposal*

4.2

    Enter PROTEUS.
    PROTEUS   Already have I been false to Valentine,
        And now I must be as unjust to Turio.
        Under the color° of commending him   *pretext*
        I have access my own love to prefer.°   *advance*
5   But Silvia is too fair, too true, too holy
        To be corrupted with my worthless gifts.
        When I protest true loyalty to her,
        She twits° me with my falsehood to my friend.   *reproaches*
        When to her beauty I commend my vows,
10   She bids me think how I have been forsworn
        In breaking faith with Julia, whom I loved.
        And notwithstanding all her sudden quips,°   *sharp rebukes*
        The least whereof would quell a lover's hope,
        Yet, spaniel-like, the more she spurns my love,
15   The more it grows and fawneth on her still.
        [Enter TURIO *with Musicians.]*
        But here comes Turio. Now must we to her window
        And give some evening music to her ear.
    TURIO   How now, Sir Proteus? Are you crept before us?
    PROTEUS   Ay, gentle Turio, for you know that love
20   Will creep° in service where it cannot go.°   *crawl / walk*
    TURIO   Ay, but I hope, sir, that you love not here.
    PROTEUS   Sir, but I do, or else I would be hence.
    TURIO   Who? Silvia?
    PROTEUS   Ay, Silvia—for your sake.
    TURIO   I thank you for your own.° *[to Musicians]* Now,   *own sake*
        gentlemen,
25   Let's tune, and to it lustily awhile.
        [Enter JULIA, *in page-boy's clothes, as Sebastian, and*
        the HOST. *They talk apart.]*
    HOST   Now, my young guest, methinks you're alicholly;° I pray   *melancholy*
    you, why is it?

4.2 Location: Outside the Duke's palace under Silvia's window by moonlight.

JULIA   Marry, mine host, because I cannot be merry.

HOST   Come, we'll have you merry. I'll bring you where you
30   shall hear music and see the gentleman that you asked for.

JULIA   But shall I hear him speak?

HOST   Ay, that you shall.

JULIA   That will be music.

HOST   Hark, hark.[1]

35 JULIA   Is he among these?

HOST   Ay. But peace, let's hear 'em.

[Music.]

PROTEUS [*sings*][2]   Who is Silvia? What is she
        That all our swains° commend her?   *lovers*
        Holy, fair, and wise is she.
40   The heaven such grace did lend her
        That she might admirèd be.

        Is she kind as she is fair?
        For beauty lives with kindness.
        Love° doth to her eyes repair°   *(Cupid) / pay a visit*
45   To help° him of his blindness,   *cure*
        And, being helped, inhabits there.

        Then to Silvia let us sing
        That Silvia is excelling.
        She excels each mortal thing
50   Upon the dull earth dwelling.
        To her let us garlands bring.

HOST   How now? Are you sadder than you were before? How
    do you, man? The music likes° you not?   *pleases*

JULIA   You mistake; the musician likes me not.

55 HOST   Why, my pretty youth?

JULIA   He plays false,[3] father.

HOST   How, out of tune on the strings?

JULIA   Not so, but yet so false that he grieves my very heartstrings.

HOST   You have a quick° ear.   *perceptive*

60 JULIA   Ay, I would I were deaf; it makes me have a slow° heart.   *heavy*

HOST   I perceive you delight not in music.

JULIA   Not a whit when it jars so.°   *is so discordant*

HOST   Hark, what fine change° is in the music.   *modulation*

JULIA   Ay, that "change" is the spite.

65 HOST   You would have them always play but one thing?

JULIA   I would always have one play but one thing. But, Host,
    doth this Sir Proteus that we talk on often resort unto this
    gentlewoman?

HOST   I tell you what Lance, his man, told me: he loved her
70   out of all nick.°   *excessively*

JULIA   Where is Lance?

HOST   Gone to seek his dog, which tomorrow, by his master's
    command, he must carry for a present to his lady.

JULIA   Peace, stand aside. The company parts.

---

1. Probably music plays.
2. TEXTUAL COMMENT This song is not ascribed to
anyone in F, but Julia's later comments in lines 54–

58 suggest that it is Proteus who sings while playing
a stringed instrument. See Digital Edition TC 9.
3. Is unfaithful; plays out of tune.

75 PROTEUS　Sir Turio, fear not you. I will so plead
　　That you shall say my cunning drift° excels.　　　　　　　　　*scheme*
TURIO　Where meet we?
PROTEUS　　　　　　　　At Saint Gregory's[4] well.
TURIO　　　　　　　　　　　　　　Farewell.
　　　　　　　[*Exeunt* TURIO *and Musicians.*]
　　　　　[*Enter* SILVIA *above.*°]　　　　　　　　　(at her window)
PROTEUS　Madam, good even to your ladyship.
SILVIA　I thank you for your music, gentlemen.
80　　Who is that that spake?
PROTEUS　One, lady, if you knew his pure heart's truth,
　　You would quickly learn to know him by his voice.
SILVIA　Sir Proteus, as I take it.
PROTEUS　Sir Proteus, gentle lady, and your servant.
SILVIA　What's your will?
85 PROTEUS　　　　　　　That I may compass yours.[5]
SILVIA　You have your wish. My will is even this,
　　That presently you hie° you home to bed.　　　　　　　　　*speed*
　　Thou subtle, perjured, false, disloyal man,
　　Think'st thou I am so shallow, so conceitless,°　　　　　　*witless*
90　　To be seducèd by thy flattery
　　That hast deceived so many with thy vows?
　　Return, return, and make thy love amends.
　　For me—by this pale queen of night[6] I swear—
　　I am so far from granting thy request
95　　That I despise thee for thy wrongful suit,
　　And by and by intend to chide myself
　　Even for this time I spend in talking to thee.
PROTEUS　I grant, sweet love, that I did love a lady,
　　But she is dead.
JULIA [*aside*]　　　　'Twere false, if° I should speak it;　　*even if*
100　　For I am sure she is not burièd.
SILVIA　Say that she be; yet Valentine, thy friend,
　　Survives, to whom, thyself art witness,
　　I am betrothed. And art thou not ashamed
　　To wrong him with thy importunacy?°　　　　　　*improper requests*
105 PROTEUS　I likewise hear that Valentine is dead.
SILVIA　And so suppose am I, for in his grave,
　　Assure thyself, my love is burièd.
PROTEUS　Sweet lady, let me rake it from the earth.
SILVIA　Go to thy lady's grave and call hers thence,
110　　Or, at the least, in hers sepulcher° thine.　　　　　　　　*bury*
JULIA [*aside*]　He heard not that.
PROTEUS　Madam, if your heart be so obdurate,°　　　　　　*hardened*
　　Vouchsafe° me yet your picture for my love,　　　　　　　*grant*
　　The picture that is hanging in your chamber.
115　　To that I'll speak, to that I'll sigh and weep;
　　For since the substance of your perfect self

---

4. Patron saint of musicians and singers.
5. *compass:* win. Punning on "will." That I may win
your good will; that I may conquer your sexual desire.

6. The moon, imagined as Diana, goddess of
chastity.

Is else devoted,[7] I am but a shadow,°   *mere nothing*
And to your shadow° will I make true love.   *image*

JULIA [*aside*]   If 'twere a substance, you would sure deceive it
120   And make it but a shadow, as I am.

SILVIA   I am very loath to be your idol, sir.
But since your falsehood shall become you well°   *make you fit*
To worship shadow and adore false shapes,
Send to me in the morning, and I'll send it.°   *(the picture)*
And so, good rest.   [*Exit.*]

125 PROTEUS   As wretches have o'ernight
That wait for execution in the morn.   [*Exit.*]

JULIA   Host, will you go?

HOST   By my halidom,° I was fast asleep.   *holy relic (an oath)*

JULIA   Pray you, where lies° Sir Proteus?   *lodges*

130 HOST   Marry, at my house. Trust me, I think 'tis almost day.

JULIA   Not so; but it hath been the longest night
That e'er I watched, and the most heaviest.°   [*Exeunt.*]   *saddest*

4.3

Enter EGLAMOUR.

EGLAMOUR   This is the hour that Madam Silvia
Entreated me to call and know her mind:
There's some great matter she'd employ me in.
Madam, madam!
         [*Enter* SILVIA *above.*]

SILVIA   Who calls?

EGLAMOUR   Your servant and your friend;
5   One that attends your ladyship's command.

SILVIA   Sir Eglamour, a thousand times good morrow!

EGLAMOUR   As many, worthy lady, to yourself.
According to your ladyship's impose,°   *command*
I am thus early come to know what service
10   It is your pleasure to command me in.

SILVIA   O Eglamour, thou art a gentleman—
Think not I flatter, for I swear I do not—
Valiant, wise, remorseful,° well accomplished.   *compassionate*
Thou art not ignorant what dear goodwill
15   I bear unto the banished Valentine,
Nor how my father would enforce me marry
Vain Turio, whom my very soul abhors.
Thyself hast loved, and I have heard thee say
No grief did ever come so near thy heart
20   As when thy lady and thy true love died,
Upon whose grave thou vowed'st pure chastity.
Sir Eglamour, I would° to Valentine—   *would go*
To Mantua, where I hear he makes abode;
And for° the ways are dangerous to pass   *because*
25   I do desire thy worthy company,
Upon whose faith and honor I repose.°   *rely*
Urge not[1] my father's anger, Eglamour,

---

7. Is devoted to someone else.   1. Do not offer as an excuse.
4.3 Location: The same place, the next morning.

But think upon my grief, a lady's grief,
And on the justice of my flying hence
30   To keep me from a most unholy match,
Which heaven and fortune still° rewards with plagues.   *always*
I do desire thee, even from a heart
As full of sorrows as the sea of sands,
To bear me company and go with me;
35   If not, to hide what I have said to thee,
That I may venture to depart alone.
EGLAMOUR   Madam, I pity much your grievances,
Which, since I know they virtuously are placed,
I give consent to go along with you,
40   Recking° as little what betideth° me   *Caring / happens to*
As much I wish all good befortune° you.   *befall*
When will you go?
SILVIA   This evening coming.
EGLAMOUR   Where shall I meet you?
SILVIA   At Friar Patrick's cell,
Where I intend holy confession.
45   EGLAMOUR   I will not fail your ladyship.
Good morrow, gentle lady.
SILVIA   Good morrow, kind Sir Eglamour.   *Exeunt.*

4.4

Enter LANCE [*with his dog Crab*].
LANCE   When a man's servant shall play the cur° with him,   *act like a stupid dog*
look you, it goes hard. One that I brought up of° a puppy,   *from*
one that I saved from drowning when three or four of his
blind brothers and sisters went to it.° I have taught him even   *met their death*
5   as one would say precisely, "Thus I would teach a dog." I was
sent to deliver him as a present to Mistress Silvia from my
master, and I came no sooner into the dining chamber but
he steps me to¹ her trencher° and steals her capon's leg. Oh,   *wooden plate*
'tis a foul thing when a cur cannot keep° himself in all com-   *behave*
10   panies! I would have, as one should say, one that takes upon
him to be a dog indeed, to be, as it were, a dog at° all things.   *adept at*
If I had not had more wit than he, to take a fault upon me
that he did, I think verily he had been hanged for't; sure as I
live, he had suffered for't. You shall judge. He thrusts me
15   himself into the company of three or four gentleman-like
dogs under the Duke's table. He had not been there—bless
the mark²—a pissing while³ but all the chamber smelt him.
"Out with the dog," says one; "What cur is that?" says
another; "Whip him out," says the third; "Hang him up,"
20   says the Duke. I, having been acquainted with the smell
before, knew it was Crab and goes me to the fellow that
whips the dogs: "Friend," quoth I, "you mean to whip the
dog?" "Ay, marry do I," quoth he. "You do him the more
wrong," quoth I, "'twas I did the thing you wot° of." He   *know*
25   makes me no more ado, but whips me out of the chamber.

4.4 Location: The same place, somewhat later.
1. *he steps me to:* he (the dog) steps forward to
Lance's embarrassment or to his detriment. Here and
in line 14, "thrusts me," Lance is describing the dog's

actions and their negative effect on himself.
2. An apology for offensive language.
3. Slang for "a very short time." Lance here employs
it literally.

How many masters would do this for his servant? Nay, I'll be
sworn I have sat in the stocks[4] for puddings[5] he hath stolen,
otherwise he had been executed! I have stood on the pillory[6]
for geese he hath killed, otherwise he had suffered for't! [*to*
30 *Crab*] Thou think'st not of this now. Nay, I remember the
trick you served me when I took my leave of Madam Silvia.
Did not I bid thee still mark° me, and do as I do? When didst   *watch*
thou see me heave up my leg and make water against a gentle-
woman's farthingale?° Didst thou ever see me do such a   *hooped petticoat*
35 trick?
                    [*Enter* PROTEUS *and* JULIA *as Sebastian.*]
PROTEUS [*to* JULIA]   Sebastian[7] is thy name? I like thee well
And will employ thee in some service° presently.   *work; sexual business*
JULIA   In what you please; I'll do what I can.
PROTEUS   I hope thou wilt. [*to* LANCE] How now, you whore-
    son peasant,
40 Where have you been these two days loitering?
LANCE   Marry, sir, I carried Mistress Silvia the dog you
    bade me.
PROTEUS   And what says she to my little jewel?
LANCE   Marry, she says your dog was a cur, and tells you cur-
45 rish thanks is good enough for such a present.
PROTEUS   But she received my dog?
LANCE   No, indeed, did she not. Here have I brought him
    back again.
PROTEUS   What, didst thou offer her this from me?
50 LANCE   Ay, sir. The other squirrel[8] was stolen from me by the
hangman's° boys in the marketplace, and then I offered her   *fit for the hangman*
mine own, who is a dog as big as ten of yours, and therefore
the gift the greater.
PROTEUS   Go, get thee hence and find my dog again,
55 Or ne'er return again into my sight.
Away, I say! Stayest thou to vex me here?
A slave that still an end° turns me to shame.   *always*
                    [*Exit* LANCE *with Crab.*]
—Sebastian, I have entertained thee
Partly that I have need of such a youth
60 That can with some discretion do my business—
For 'tis no trusting to yon foolish lout—
But chiefly for thy face and thy behavior,
Which, if my augury° deceive me not,   *fortune-telling skills*
Witness good bringing-up, fortune, and truth.
65 Therefore know thou for this I entertain thee.
Go presently, and take this ring with thee:
Deliver it to Madam Silvia.
She loved me well delivered° it to me.   *who gave*
JULIA   It seems you loved not her, to leave° her token.[9]   *part with*
She is dead, belike?°   *perchance*

4. An instrument of punishment in which the offender
sat with feet clamped between two wooden planks
into which ankle holes had been cut.
5. Dishes made of animal intestines or stomachs
stuffed with meat and spices.
6. An instrument of punishment similar to the stocks.
One stood with head and hands clamped between

wooden planks.
7. A name sometimes associated with male homoeroticism and the arrow-pierced body of St. Sebastian.
8. A disparaging reference to the small dog Proteus
intended to give Silvia.
9. TEXTUAL COMMENT For a discussion of "love" and
"leave" in this line, see Digital Edition TC 1.

70 PROTEUS   Not so; I think she lives.

JULIA Alas!

PROTEUS Why dost thou cry "Alas"?

JULIA I cannot choose but pity her.

PROTEUS Wherefore shouldst thou pity her?

75 JULIA Because methinks that she loved you as well
As you do love your lady Silvia.
She dreams on him that has forgot her love;
You dote on her that cares not for your love.
'Tis pity love should be so contrary,
80 And thinking on it makes me cry "Alas."

PROTEUS Well, give her that ring, and therewithal°   along with it
This letter. [He points.] That's her chamber. Tell my lady
I claim the promise for her heavenly picture.
Your message done, hie home unto my chamber,
85 Where thou shalt find me sad and solitary.   [Exit.]

JULIA How many women would do such a message?
Alas, poor Proteus, thou hast entertained
A fox to be the shepherd of thy lambs!
Alas, poor fool,¹ why do I pity him
90 That with his very heart despiseth me?
Because he loves her, he despiseth me;
Because I love him, I must pity him.
This ring I gave him when he parted from me
To bind him to remember my goodwill.
95 And now am I, unhappy messenger,
To plead for that which I would not obtain,
To carry that which I would have refused,
To praise his faith which I would have dispraised.
I am my master's true confirmèd love,
100 But cannot be true servant to my master
Unless I prove false traitor to myself.
Yet will I woo for him, but yet so coldly
As, heaven it knows, I would not have him speed.°   succeed
       [Enter SILVIA, attended by her maid Ursula.]
Gentlewoman, good day! I pray you, be my mean°   agent; means
105 To bring me where to speak with Madam Silvia.

SILVIA What would you with her, if that I be she?

JULIA If you be she, I do entreat your patience
To hear me speak the message I am sent on.

SILVIA From whom?

110 JULIA From my master, Sir Proteus, madam.

SILVIA Oh, he sends you for a picture?

JULIA Ay, madam.

SILVIA Ursula, bring my picture there.
       [Ursula passes her the picture.]
Go, give your master this. Tell him from me
115 One Julia, that his changing thoughts forget,
Would better fit his chamber than this shadow.°   portrait

JULIA [handing SILVIA a letter]² Madam, please you peruse
this letter.

---

1. Julia is referring to herself.
2. Possibly the first letter is from Proteus to Julia.
Whether Julia offers it to Silvia by mistake or deliber-

ately (as she later seems deliberately to mistake two
rings) is open to question.

Pardon me, madam, I have unadvised°   *inadvertently*
Delivered you a paper that I should not—
[*She takes the letter back and gives* SILVIA *another.*]
120   This is the letter to your ladyship.
SILVIA [*pointing at the first letter*]   I pray thee, let me look on
    that again.
JULIA   It may not be. Good madam, pardon me.
SILVIA   There, hold. I will not look upon your master's lines:
  I know they are stuffed with protestations
125   And full of new-found° oaths which he will break   *newly made*
  As easily as I do tear his paper.
    [*She tears the second letter.*]
JULIA   Madam, he sends your ladyship this ring.
SILVIA   The more shame for him that he sends it me,
  For I have heard him say a thousand times
130   His Julia gave it him at his departure.
  Though his false finger have profaned the ring,
  Mine shall not do his Julia so much wrong.
JULIA   She thanks you.
SILVIA   What say'st thou?
135 JULIA   I thank you, madam, that you tender° her.   *show concern for*
  Poor gentlewoman, my master wrongs her much.
SILVIA   Dost thou know her?
JULIA   Almost as well as I do know myself.
  To think upon her woes I do protest
140   That I have wept a hundred several times.
SILVIA   Belike she thinks that Proteus hath forsook her?
JULIA   I think she doth, and that's her cause of sorrow.
SILVIA   Is she not passing° fair?   *exceedingly*
JULIA   She hath been fairer, madam, than she is.
145   When she did think my master loved her well,
  She, in my judgment, was as fair as you.
  But since she did neglect her looking glass
  And threw her sun-expelling mask[3] away,
  The air hath starved° the roses in her cheeks   *withered*
150   And pinched the lily tincture° of her face,   *white color*
  That now she is become as black as I.
SILVIA   How tall was she?
JULIA   About my stature: for at Pentecost,[4]
  When all our pageants of delight° were played,   *pleasing performances*
155   Our youth got me to play the woman's part,[5]
  And I was trimmed° in Madam Julia's gown,   *dressed*
  Which served me as fit, by all men's judgments,
  As if the garment had been made for me.
  Therefore I know she is about my height,
160   And at that time I made her weep a-good,°   *in earnest*
  For I did play a lamentable° part.   *pitiable*
  Madam, 'twas Ariadne, passioning
  For Theseus' perjury and unjust flight,[6]

3. A mask to block the sun worn by upper-class Englishwomen to preserve their light complexions.
4. Religious days seven weeks after Easter, when plays and theatrical pageants were staged in many English towns.
5. Act the female role, as boys conventionally did in the Elizabethan theater.
6. In Greek mythology, Ariadne hanged herself after she was abandoned by her lover, Theseus. *passioning*: sorrowing.

Which I so lively° acted with my tears   *convincingly*
165 That my poor mistress, movèd therewithal,
Wept bitterly; and would I might be dead
If I in thought felt not her very sorrow.
SILVIA   She is beholden to thee, gentle youth.
Alas, poor lady, desolate and left!
170 I weep myself to think upon thy words.
Here, youth: there is my purse. I give thee this
For thy sweet mistress' sake, because thou lov'st her.
Farewell.
JULIA   And she shall thank you for't if e'er you know her—
                       [*Exit* SILVIA *with Ursula.*]
175 A virtuous gentlewoman, mild and beautiful!
I hope my master's suit will be but cold,°   *unsuccessful*
Since she respects my mistress' love so much.
Alas, how love can trifle with itself!
Here is her picture. Let me see. I think
180 If I had such a tire,° this face of mine   *headdress*
Were full as lovely as is this of hers;
And yet the painter flattered her a little,
Unless I flatter with myself too much.
Her hair is auburn, mine is perfect yellow:
185 If that be all the difference in his love,
I'll get me such a colored periwig.°   *wig*
Her eyes are gray as glass, and so are mine;
Ay, but her forehead's low, and mine's as high.[7]
What should it be that he respects° in her   *esteems*
190 But I can make respective° in myself,   *worthy of esteem*
If this fond Love were not a blinded god?
        [*She picks up the portrait.*]
Come, shadow, come, and take this shadow up,[8]
For 'tis thy rival. O thou senseless form,
Thou shalt be worshipped, kissed, loved, and adored!
195 And, were there sense° in his idolatry,   *reason*
My substance should be statue in thy stead.[9]
I'll use thee kindly for thy mistress' sake
That used me so; or else, by Jove I vow,
I should have scratched out your unseeing eyes
200 To make my master out of love with thee!   *Exit.*

5.1

Enter EGLAMOUR.
EGLAMOUR   The sun begins to gild the western sky,
And now it is about the very hour
That Silvia at Friar Patrick's cell should meet me.
She will not fail, for lovers break not hours,°   *appointments*
5 Unless it be to come before their time,
So much they spur their expedition.°   *hasten their progress*
        [*Enter* SILVIA.]
See where she comes. Lady, a happy evening!

---

7. Mine's as high as hers is low. High foreheads were considered a sign of beauty.
8. Probably addressing herself as a "shadow," or mere nothing, Julia means "pick up Silvia's portrait" or "take up the challenge posed by this woman."
9. My person ("substance") should be an idol ("statue") to Proteus rather than Silvia's picture.
5.1 Location: An abbey in Milan.

SILVIA Amen, amen! Go on, good Eglamour,
　　Out at the postern° by the abbey wall;　　　　　　　　　　　　*back door or side door*
10　　I fear I am attended° by some spies.　　　　　　　　　　　　　　　　*followed*
EGLAMOUR Fear not; the forest is not three leagues off;
　　If we recover° that, we are sure° enough.　　　　*Exeunt.*　　　　　*reach / safe*

5.2
Enter TURIO, PROTEUS, *and* JULIA [*as Sebastian*].
TURIO Sir Proteus, what says Silvia to my suit?
PROTEUS O sir, I find her milder than she was,
　　And yet she takes exceptions at° your person.　　　　　　　　　　　*objects to*
TURIO What? That my leg is too long?
5　PROTEUS No, that it is too little.
TURIO I'll wear a boot to make it somewhat rounder.
JULIA [*aside*] But love will not be spurred to what it loathes.[1]
TURIO What says she to my face?
PROTEUS She says it is a fair one.
10　TURIO Nay, then the wanton lies! My face is black.
PROTEUS But pearls are fair; and the old saying is,
　　"Black men are pearls in beauteous ladies' eyes."
JULIA [*aside*] 'Tis true, such pearls[2] as put out ladies' eyes,
　　For I had rather wink° than look on them.　　　　　　　　　　　*shut my eyes*
15　TURIO How likes she my discourse?
PROTEUS Ill when you talk of war.
TURIO But well when I discourse of love and peace?
JULIA [*aside*] But better indeed when you hold your peace.
TURIO What says she to my valor?
20　PROTEUS O sir, she makes no doubt of that.
JULIA [*aside*] She needs not when she knows it cowardice.
TURIO What says she to my birth?
PROTEUS That you are well derived.°　　　　　　　　　　　　　　　*descended*
JULIA [*aside*] True: from a gentleman to a fool.
25　TURIO Considers she my possessions?
PROTEUS Oh, ay, and pities them.
TURIO Wherefore?
JULIA [*aside*] That such an ass should owe° them.　　　　　　　　　*own*
PROTEUS That they are out by lease.°　　　　　　　　　　　　　　*rented out*
　　[*Enter the* DUKE.]
30　JULIA Here comes the Duke.
DUKE How now, Sir Proteus? How now, Turio?
　　Which of you saw Eglamour of late?
TURIO Not I.
PROTEUS　　　　　Nor I.
DUKE　　　　　　　　　Saw you my daughter?
PROTEUS　　　　　　　　　　　　　Neither.
DUKE Why, then, she's fled unto that peasant° Valentine,　　　　　*rascal*
35　　And Eglamour is in her company.
　　'Tis true, for Friar Laurence[3] met them both

5.2 Location: The Duke's court in Milan.
1. F assigns this line to Proteus and lines 13 and 14 to Turio, but it makes more sense to assign them to the disguised Julia, whose covert comments on the words of Proteus and Turio provide the scene with much of its humor.

2. Punning on the medical meaning of "pearl" as a thin film or cataract growing over the eye.
3. Possibly a slip for "Friar Patrick," mentioned in the preceding scene and at line 41 below, although there may be more than one friar in the forest.

As he, in penance, wandered through the forest.
Him he knew well, and guessed that it was she,
But, being masked, he was not sure of it.
40 Besides, she did intend confession
At Patrick's cell this even, and there she was not.
These likelihoods confirm her flight from hence.
Therefore, I pray you, stand not to discourse,
But mount you presently and meet with me
45 Upon the rising of the mountain foot
That leads toward Mantua, whither they are fled.
Dispatch,° sweet gentlemen, and follow me. [*Exit.*] *Hurry*
TURIO Why, this it is to be a peevish° girl *silly; perverse*
That flies her fortune when it follows her.
50 I'll after, more to be revenged on Eglamour
Than for the love of reckless Silvia. [*Exit.*]
PROTEUS And I will follow, more for Silvia's love
Than hate of Eglamour that goes with her. [*Exit.*]
JULIA And I will follow, more to cross that love
55 Than hate for Silvia, that is gone for love. [*Exit.*]

5.3

[Enter] OUTLAWS *[and]* SILVIA *[as their captive].*
FIRST OUTLAW Come, come, be patient. We must bring you to
 our captain.
SILVIA A thousand more mischances than this one
 Have learned° me how to brook° this patiently. *taught / endure*
5 SECOND OUTLAW Come, bring her away.
FIRST OUTLAW Where is the gentleman that was with her?° *(Eglamour)*
THIRD OUTLAW Being nimble-footed, he hath outrun us,
 But Moses and Valerius[1] follow him.
 Go thou with her to the west end of the wood;
10 There is our captain. We'll follow him that's fled.
 The thicket is beset;° he cannot scape. *surrounded*
   [Exeunt SECOND *and* THIRD OUTLAWS.]
FIRST OUTLAW Come, I must bring you to our captain's cave.
 Fear not; he bears an honorable mind
 And will not use a woman lawlessly.
15 SILVIA O Valentine, this I endure for thee! *Exeunt.*

5.4

Enter VALENTINE.
VALENTINE How use° doth breed a habit in a man! *custom*
 This shadowy desert,° unfrequented woods, *uninhabited spot*
 I better brook° than flourishing peopled towns. *endure*
 Here can I sit alone, unseen of any,
5 And to the nightingale's complaining notes[1]
 Tune my distresses and record my woes.
 O thou° that dost inhabit in my breast, *(addressing Silvia)*
 Leave not the mansion[2] so long tenantless
 Lest, growing ruinous, the building fall

5.3 Location: At the frontiers of the Mantua forest.
1. Presumably, Moses and Valerius are fellow members of the outlaw band.
5.4 Location: Another part of the forest.

1. In classical mythology, Philomela was turned into a nightingale after Tereus raped her; her song is a lament.
2. Referring to his body as Silvia's home.

10   And leave no memory of what it was!
     Repair me with thy presence, Silvia!
     Thou gentle nymph, cherish thy forlorn swain.
          [*Shouts within.*]
     What hallooing? And what stir is this today?
     These are my mates, that make their wills their law,
15   Have° some unhappy passenger° in chase.   *Who have / traveler*
     They love me well, yet I have much to do
     To keep them from uncivil outrages.
     Withdraw thee, Valentine.
          [VALENTINE *hides. Enter* PROTEUS, SILVIA, *and* JULIA
          as Sebastian.]
                Who's this comes here?
    PROTEUS   Madam, this service I have done for you—
20   Though you respect not aught your servant doth—
     To hazard life and rescue you from him
     That would have forced your honor° and your love.   *violated your chastity*
     Vouchsafe me for my meed° but one fair look!   *reward*
     A smaller boon° than this I cannot beg,   *request*
25   And less than this I am sure you cannot give.
    VALENTINE [*aside*]   How like a dream is this I see and hear!
     Love, lend me patience to forbear awhile.
    SILVIA   Oh, miserable, unhappy that I am!
    PROTEUS   Unhappy were you, madam, ere I came;
30   But by my coming I have made you happy.
    SILVIA   By thy approach° thou mak'st me most unhappy.   *amorous advances*
    JULIA [*aside*]   And me, when he approacheth to your presence.
    SILVIA   Had I been seizèd by a hungry lion
     I would have been a breakfast to the beast
35   Rather than have false Proteus rescue me.
     O heaven, be judge how I love Valentine,
     Whose life's as tender° to me as my soul.   *precious*
     And full as much, for more there cannot be,
     I do detest false perjured Proteus.
40   Therefore be gone; solicit me no more.
    PROTEUS   What dangerous action, stood it next to death,
     Would I not undergo for one calm° look!   *gentle*
     Oh, 'tis the curse in love, and still approved,°   *always confirmed*
     When women cannot love where they're beloved.
45   SILVIA   When Proteus cannot love where he's beloved!
     Read over Julia's heart, thy first best love,
     For whose dear sake thou didst then rend thy faith
     Into a thousand oaths, and all those oaths
     Descended into perjury° to love me!   *Were forsworn*
50   Thou hast no faith left now unless thou'dst two,[3]
     And that's far worse than none. Better have none
     Than plural faith, which is too much by one,
     Thou counterfeit° to thy true friend.   *deceiver; false friend*
    PROTEUS   In love
     Who respects friend?
    SILVIA   All men but Proteus.

---

3. You have no faithfulness left now unless you were to have two lovers (Julia and Silvia).

55 PROTEUS Nay, if the gentle spirit of moving words
        Can no way change you to a milder form,
        I'll woo you like a soldier, at arm's end,°   *at swordpoint*
        And love you 'gainst the nature of love—force ye.
            [*He seizes her.*]
    SILVIA O heaven!
60 PROTEUS I'll force thee yield to my desire.
    VALENTINE [*stepping forward*] Ruffian! Let go that rude
        uncivil touch,
        Thou friend of an ill fashion!
    PROTEUS   Valentine!
    VALENTINE Thou common° friend—that's without faith or   *superficial*
        love,
        For such is a friend now. Treacherous man,
65   Thou hast beguiled my hopes! Naught but mine eye
        Could have persuaded me. Now I dare not say
        I have one friend alive; thou wouldst disprove me.
        Who should be trusted when one's right hand
        Is perjured to the bosom?° Proteus,   *false to the heart*
70   I am sorry I must never trust thee more,
        But count the world a stranger for thy sake![4]
        The private wound is deepest. O time most accursed,
        'Mongst all foes that a friend should be the worst!
    PROTEUS My shame and guilt confounds me.
75   Forgive me, Valentine. If hearty sorrow
        Be a sufficient ransom for offense,
        I tender't° here. I do as truly suffer   *offer it*
        As e'er I did commit.
    VALENTINE   Then I am paid,
        And once again I do receive thee° honest.   *accept you as*
80   Who by repentance is not satisfied
        Is nor of heaven nor earth, for these are pleased;
        By penitence th'Eternal's wrath's appeased.
        And that my love may appear plain and free,
        All that was mine in Silvia[5] I give thee.[6]
    JULIA O me unhappy!
            [*She faints.*]
    PROTEUS   Look to the boy.
85 VALENTINE   Why, boy!
        Why, wag!° How now? What's the matter? Look up. Speak.   *sweet boy*
    JULIA O good sir, my master charged me to deliver a ring to
        Madam Silvia, which out of my neglect was never done.
    PROTEUS Where is that ring, boy?
    JULIA   Here 'tis. This is it.
            [*She gives* PROTEUS *a ring.*]
90 PROTEUS How? Let me see.
        Why, this is the ring I gave to Julia!
    JULIA Oh, cry you mercy, sir; I have mistook!
            [*She produces another ring.*] This is the ring you sent to Silvia.

4. But cut myself off from the world (in disillusionment) because of your treachery.
5. All my claims to Silvia; all that was mine, in the
person of Silvia; all the love I gave to Silvia.

6. PERFORMANCE COMMENT Each production's
approach to Valentine's offer can help condemn or
redeem him while either neutralizing or intensifying the
sequence's disturbing aspects. See Digital Edition PC 2.

PROTEUS   But how cam'st thou by this ring? At my depart
95   I gave this unto Julia.
JULIA   And Julia herself did give it me—
      [*She reveals herself.*] And Julia herself hath brought it
      hither.
PROTEUS   How? Julia?
JULIA   Behold her that gave aim to° all thy oaths   *was the object of*
100   And entertained 'em deeply in her heart.
      How oft hast thou with perjury cleft the root!°   *bottom of her heart*
      O Proteus, let this habit° make thee blush!   *disguise*
      Be thou ashamed that I have took upon me
      Such an immodest raiment, if shame live
105   In a disguise of love.[7]
      It is the lesser blot, modesty finds,
      Women to change their shapes° than men their minds.   *appearances; clothes*
PROTEUS   Than men their minds? 'Tis true. O heaven, were
      man
      But constant, he were perfect! That one error
110   Fills him with faults, makes him run through all th'sins;
      Inconstancy falls off ere it begins.[8]
      What is in Silvia's face but I may spy
      More fresh in Julia's, with a constant° eye?   *faithful*
VALENTINE   Come, come, a hand from either.
115   Let me be blest to make this happy close.°   *ending; union*
      'Twere pity two such friends should be long foes.
            [JULIA *and* PROTEUS *join hands.*]
PROTEUS   Bear witness, heaven, I have my wish forever.
JULIA   And I mine.
           [*Enter* OUTLAWS *with the* DUKE *and* TURIO *as their*
           captives.]
OUTLAWS   A prize, a prize, a prize!
VALENTINE   Forbear, forbear, I say! It is my lord the Duke.
           [OUTLAWS *release their captives.*]
120   [*to the* DUKE] Your grace is welcome to a man disgraced:
      Banished Valentine.
DUKE   Sir Valentine?
TURIO   Yonder is Silvia, and Silvia's mine.
VALENTINE   Turio, give back,° or else embrace thy death!   *stand back*
      Come not within the measure° of my wrath.   *reach*
125   Do not name Silvia thine; if once again,
      Milano° shall not hold thee. Here she stands: *Milan*
      Take but possession of her with a touch—
      I dare thee but to breathe upon my love.
TURIO   Sir Valentine, I care not for her, I.
130   I hold him but a fool that will endanger
      His body for a girl that loves him not.
      I claim her not, and therefore she is thine.
DUKE   The more degenerate and base art thou
      To make such means° for her as thou hast done   *efforts*

---

7. *if . . . love*: if a disguise one wears for the sake of
love can be considered shameful; if one who pretends
to feel love is capable of feeling shame.

8. The inconstant man begins to deceive, or "fall
off," even before he swears constancy.

135 And leave her on such slight conditions.°   *trivial reasons*
 —Now, by the honor of my ancestry,
 I do applaud thy spirit, Valentine,
 And think thee worthy of an empress' love.
 Know, then, I here forget all former griefs,°   *grievances*
140 Cancel all grudge, repeal° thee home again,   *recall*
 Plead a new state in thy unrivaled merit,⁹
 To which I thus subscribe:° Sir Valentine,   *bear witness*
 Thou art a gentleman, and well derived;
 Take thou thy Silvia, for thou hast deserved her.
145 VALENTINE I thank your grace; the gift hath made me happy.
 I now beseech you, for your daughter's sake,
 To grant one boon° that I shall ask of you.   *favor*
 DUKE I grant it for thine own, whate'er it be.
 VALENTINE These banished men that I have kept withal° *lived with*
150 Are men endued with worthy qualities.
 Forgive them what they have committed here,
 And let them be recalled from their exile.
 They are reformèd, civil, full of good,
 And fit for great employment, worthy lord.
155 DUKE Thou hast prevailed; I pardon them and thee.
 Dispose of them as thou know'st their deserts.
 —Come, let us go. We will include all jars°   *end all discord*
 With triumphs,° mirth, and rare solemnity.° *pageants / festivity*
 VALENTINE And, as we walk along, I dare be bold
160 With our discourse to make your grace to smile.
 What think you of this page, my lord?
 DUKE I think the boy hath grace in him; he blushes.
 VALENTINE I warrant you, my lord, more grace than boy.¹
 DUKE What mean you by that saying?
165 VALENTINE Please you, I'll tell you as we pass along,
 That you will wonder° what hath fortunèd.° *marvel at / happened*
 Come, Proteus, 'tis your penance but to hear
 The story of your loves discoverèd.°   *revealed*
 That done, our day of marriage shall be yours,
170 One feast, one house, one mutual happiness. *Exeunt.*

---

9. Argue (that there is) a new situation created by 1. He has more feminine charm ("grace") than male
your unparalleled merit. gender (that is, "he" is really a girl).

The Taming of the Shrew

One of Shakespeare's first comedies—probably written in 1592 or earlier—*The Taming of the Shrew* is also one of his most controversial, focusing as it does on the battle between the sexes and on the process by which a strong-willed woman is made to submit to the control of her husband. When the play is read, and especially when it is experienced in performance, it is, however, much more interesting and complex than its title might suggest. An early example of Shakespeare's extraordinary theatrical craftsmanship, it consists of two interwoven plots and a frame tale. This complex structure allows for contrasts and parallels in the development of the play's main themes, complicating how the audience thinks about the drama's examination of the relationship between the sexes and the possibility that people can change their social identities as a result of either choice or coercion. Not surprisingly, *The Taming of the Shrew* has elicited wildly varying reactions from generations of readers, audiences, actors, and directors, easily speaking to present-day debates about gender equality and the persistence of attitudes and practices that make such equality often seem a chimera.

In the frame story, a poor tinker, Christopher Sly, who in the speech prefixes in the First Folio is simply called "Beggar," is made to believe that he is a nobleman with servants, a wife, fine food, and even erotic artwork at his command. This hoax, shown in the play's first two scenes (called "Inductions"), is engineered by a real lord who has found Sly drunk and asleep outside a tavern. The Lord's trick leads to many jokes at Sly's expense. While the tinker likes playing the part of a nobleman, he doesn't do it very well. His language, especially, betrays him. For example, Sly doesn't know how to address a lady, anxiously inquiring of his servants what to call his elegant spouse and settling on the absurd title "Madam wife" (Induction 2.108). The comedy of this scene is compounded by the fact that Sly's "wife" is really the Lord's page, Bartholomew, dressed up to impersonate a woman. Sly thus mistakes the sex of the person he would take to bed. He is also ignorant of the tastes and customs of the nobility, asking for cheap ale when he should call for sack, the sweet wine favored by gentlemen.

While these blunders make Sly an object of humor, he is also the figure for whose viewing pleasure the main play's two central plots unroll. As a temporary lord, Sly has a troupe of actors to entertain him. At least until he falls asleep, Sly watches them enact a comedy about courtship and marriage in which the primary plot involves a strong-willed woman, Katherina Minola, who is "tamed" by a fortune-seeking suitor named Petruccio. In the other plot, Katherina's seemingly demure sister, Bianca, is pursued by three adoring suitors and eventually elopes with one of them without her father's knowledge or consent. All three actions are united by themes of disguise and transformation. Snatched from the mud and given the clothes and the privileges of a lord, Sly is temporarily translated from one social class and identity to another, even though his behavior and the snickers of his "attendants" repeatedly remind the audience that he is not *really* a nobleman. In their pursuit of Bianca, several of her suitors also don disguises. One, Hortensio, poses as a teacher of music and mathematics; another, Lucentio, pretends to be Cambio, a language instructor; meanwhile, Lucentio's servant Tranio assumes his master's identity and in that disguise poses as yet another of Bianca's many admirers. Love makes men willing to transform themselves, although in this plot these changes are reversible. When the disguised gentlemen tire of acting as scholars-for-hire, they simply reclaim their houses, fortunes, and social positions and demote their servants.

In the main plot, more subtle questions of disguise arise. Petruccio, to teach Katherina that she must obey him, acts the part of "shrew tamer," a role in which he appears at his own wedding in outlandish and ragged clothes and, during a sojourn at his country house, turns the world on its head by denying Katherina sleep, food, and any exercise of her own will. But if his servant Grumio is to be believed, this may not simply be a one-time disguise. Hearing of his master's plan to wed the rich and shrewish Katherina, Grumio says:

> O' my word, an she knew him as well as I do, she would think scolding would do little good upon him. She may perhaps call him half a score knaves or so. Why, that's nothing; an he begin once, he'll rail in his rope tricks. I'll tell you what, sir, an she stand him but a little, he will throw a figure in her face and so disfigure her with it that she shall have no more eyes to see withal than a cat. You know him not, sir.   (1.2.106–13)

Grumio's words raise doubts about Petruccio's "real" nature. Is he temporarily adopting the role of a shrew tamer and verbal bully, or is that his customary mode of being or a role that he has previously adopted in dealing with servants and other social inferiors? And as Petruccio attempts to transform Katherina from shrew to obedient spouse, new questions arise. Is he forcing her to deform her nature or helping her experiment with a role that might bring out untapped aspects of her personality or lead to greater control of her social environment? Is there, in fact, anything like a "real self," or is personhood a succession of social roles adopted because of coercion, social expectations, material circumstances, or the drive for social mastery?

The multiple instances of disguise and transformation in the three plots raise questions about how malleable people's identities really are and how much they are determined or constrained by social circumstance. The play invites us to see, for example, that lords and gentlemen can play with their social roles more successfully and with less risk than can tinkers. Sly's transformation is thrust upon him; but his lack of wealth and education makes it impossible for him to "pass" as nobility without the complicity of the lord who found him asleep outside the tavern. His transformation is precarious, a mere dream from which he will have to awaken, no matter how much he might want to continue as a lord. By contrast, Lucentio has more cultural capital and more ability to play with his identity. His role as a Latin master is nothing *but* a temporary stratagem, a part that his education enables him to play to perfection but that his social rank permits him to cast aside when he has won his bride.

Similarly, the social fact of gender sets different limits on possible presentations and transformations of self. Petruccio's outrageous behavior—striking his servants and starving his wife—makes him admired by other men. Hortensio, for example, one of Bianca's suitors who eventually marries a wealthy widow, decides to model himself after Petruccio and to take lessons from him on how to tame a wife. But what is deemed to be Katherina's outrageous behavior—striking a sister and defying a father and would-be husband—elicits only scorn and condemnation. Like class, gender limits one's permissible or possible range of action and the transformations of self one can effect. Unless she is willing to endure severe privation and penalties, Katherina can only undergo one kind of transformation—toward greater docility and subservience to her husband. In such circumstances, it is difficult to determine—as many critics wish to do—whether Katherina finds her "real" self through her encounters with Petruccio. Like many characters in the play, she can only improvise a self in relation to the social constraints and possibilities available to her, and the constraints operating upon a tinker or a woman are very different from those affecting a university-educated gentleman or a lord.

The social hierarchies that shape the possibilities for personal transformations are, in the Sly frame tale, given a peculiarly English inflection. The Sly episodes refer repeatedly to the Warwickshire countryside that was Shakespeare's own birthplace. Sly mentions Greet, an actual village near Stratford, and Barton Heath (probably Barton-on-the-Heath, another village close to Stratford), and the men enumerated as his tavern companions—Stephen Sly, John Naps, Peter Turf, and Henry Pimpernel—for the most part have homely English names. Moreover, the contrast between Sly and the lord who carries him to his house evokes the gap in sixteenth-century rural England between poor laborers, barely making a living at a succession of marginal jobs, and wealthy landowners. As arable and common land was fenced in or enclosed to increase the opportunities for grazing sheep, many landowners made huge profits, wool being one of England's most important exports. But enclosures, a number of which occurred in the Stratford region, also caused hardship for small tenant farmers forced off the enclosed land and, in some cases, driven into vagrancy.

Sly's appellation as "Beggar" suggests a fixed social identity. A poor man with a checkered employment history, he describes himself as "old Sly's son of Barton Heath, by birth a peddler, by education a cardmaker, by transmutation a bear-herd, and now by present profession a tinker" (Induction 2.17–19). A cardmaker makes the metal combs used to prepare wool for spinning; thus, Sly has had some tangential involvement with the wool industry, although he seems primarily to have led an itinerant life mending pots, selling cheap goods from a peddler's pack, and running up whatever tab he could at the local tavern. The Induction reveals the enormous gap in wealth and education separating this man from the leisured aristocrats who pick him up on the way home from hunting and use him for their evening's sport. The trick they play upon him is a fantastic one, but the details of the lord's privilege and Sly's drunken poverty are evoked with vivid realism. For such a man as Sly, what hope is there of becoming a lord?

By contrast, Bianca and her suitors exist in an Italian setting at many removes from Sly's English-countryside milieu. The events in this story line are drawn directly from George Gascoigne's *Supposes* (1566), itself an adaption of a work by Ariosto, *I Suppositi*, which employs the disguised identities, clever servants, and gullible fathers found in classical comedy. Wealth is also a crucial factor in this plot, for despite his speeches about the necessity for suitors to gain his daughters' love, Baptista is willing to give them to their wealthiest wooers. The suitors' money comes mostly

Woodcut of a "jovial" tinker, a person who mends pots, as Christopher Sly was said to do. From the Magdalene College Pepys Ballad Collection (1616).

from trade. Bianca's suitors testify to the number of ships they have at sea and to the luxury goods and property they have acquired through their ventures. In this world of prosperous urban merchants, Baptista can indulge his daughters with some training in the arts and languages, but he still expects to control their marriage choices. Katherina he delivers to the frankly fortune-hunting Petruccio, but his supposedly compliant daughter, Bianca—whose name, meaning "white," implies her virtue and purity—slips from his grasp. She not only elopes, but in the play's final banquet scene she refuses to come when her new husband summons her, suggesting that her earlier docility may have been a calculated pose. If her sister is gradually tamed, Bianca ultimately reveals her own considerable capacity for willfulness, her education and social position having given her the wherewithal to manipulate the courtship process to her own advantage.

It is against this backdrop that the particular features of the main plot become apparent. The relationship between Katherina and Petruccio has long been regarded as the play's most riveting story line. In fact, in the eighteenth century the famous actor David Garrick produced a shortened version of the play simply called *Catharine and Petruchio*, which cut the Bianca plot and held the stage for nearly one hundred years. The interest in Katherina and Petruccio is understandable, for Shakespeare created for them a story of taming at once enjoyable and deeply troubling. Though set in Italy, this plot line feels English, connected in subterranean ways to the world of Christopher Sly. For one thing, Petruccio is not just a creature of the city; he has a farmhouse that serves as this play's "green world," or place of transformations. Moreover, Petruccio is distinguished in many ways from the other Italian suitors. He has, for example, a sullen and quarrelsome servant, Grumio, in every respect the antithesis of the clever attendants, Tranio and Biondello, who help Lucentio win Bianca and, in fact, seem to do most of their master's thinking and plotting for him. This may be a kind of affectionate joke made at the expense of English domestic servants, who, despite their crude ways, at least aren't shown as mastering their masters. Moreover, while Hortensio, Gremio, and Lucentio woo Bianca with song and poetry, Petruccio woos Katherina by contradicting her every word and taming her, like a hawk, by making her go hungry and sleepless. The language of blood sport permeates both the Induction and the Petruccio scenes. The lord who picks up Sly has just returned from hunting and speaks knowledgeably about the abilities of each of his hounds; Petruccio repeatedly compares the taming of a wife to the transformation of a wild hawk into a docile hunting falcon, aligning wife taming with other manly English sports.

Finally, of course, the source for the Petruccio-Katherina plot is not an Italian comedy, as in the Bianca-Lucentio plot, but a folk story about taming a difficult wife. Variants of this type of story circulated throughout northern Europe in Shakespeare's day, including the vicious English ballad entitled "A Merry Jest of a Shrewd and Curst Wife Lapped in Morel's Skin for Her Good Behavior." In this ballad, a strong-willed wife is beaten bloody by her husband and then wrapped inside the salted skin of a dead horse named Morel. This mode of taming is more physically brutal than that employed by Petruccio, but both the play and the ballad assume that a husband can use extreme means to curb the will of a froward wife. Despite his Italian name, then, Petruccio is in many ways an Englishman; and the play implicitly suggests that unlike his Italian counterpart, the true Englishman defines his manhood through the firm and, if necessary, cruel mastery of wife and servant. By contrast, the less assertive Lucentio takes direction from his servant, supplicates his betrothed on bended knee, and ends up with a wife he cannot master.

Shakespeare's subtle Englishing of Katherina and Petruccio may have heightened the original audience's interest in and even identification with them, but the men and women in that audience may not have been equally drawn to what they witnessed. In the wake of the modern women's movement, certainly, the very idea of "taming" a woman and curbing her tongue has seemed offensive to many readers and viewers.

Cucking stool used to discipline scolds, shrews, and witches.

In *The Taming of the Shrew,* language is a vehicle for domination. Sly cannot effectively play a lord because he has not mastered the language of the elite. Katherina can be eloquent, but because of her gender her verbal independence is read by her father and suitors as a sign of shrewishness. In part, Petruccio tames Katherina's tart tongue by aggressive use of his own. A clear sign that he has succeeded occurs in 4.6, when, at her husband's behest, Katherina calls the sun the moon and an old man a budding virgin. Her words at this point no longer express her own perceptions but her husband's blatantly willful reading of reality. In the play's last scene, she makes a lengthy speech about a wife's duty to obey her husband that conforms to the patriarchal ideology of the day and her husband's wishes but is disturbingly far from her earlier expression of women's right to independent speech and thought.

Some directors have found this curbing of the female tongue and will so intolerable that they have made production choices that downplay the extent of Katherina's submission to Petruccio or that mitigate the linguistic coercion and physical cruelty that are part of his taming methods. For example, in many productions Katherina delivers her last speech about wifely duty while signaling, by winks and gestures, that she does not really believe it, or the director omits the lines in which Katherina offers to put her hand beneath her husband's foot as a token of submission. Such choices signal a desire to "save" Shakespeare from accusations that his play celebrates a crude form of male dominance.

Even in Shakespeare's own day, not everyone, including not all men, would have found Petruccio's behavior laudable. In 1611 John Fletcher, a young playwright in Shakespeare's company, the King's Men, wrote *The Woman's Prize, or the Tamer Tamed,* which answered Shakespeare's play by having Petruccio tamed by his second wife, Maria. The existence of this play suggests that some people took pleasure in seeing an aggressive husband brought to heel. In fact, the proper relationship between husband and wife was a matter of widespread discussion and debate in the early modern period, with many people suggesting limits to men's dominance within marriage. Some Protestant preachers enjoined husbands to use no violence against their wives and to treat them as spiritual equals and domestic helpmeets. They lauded marriage not merely as an economic arrangement but as a union demanding mutual affection and respect

Husband dominator. From a German
playing card by Peter Flötner (1520).

from both parties. In practice, many
women exercised considerable authority
in their households: managing servants,
helping to arrange their children's marriages, and overseeing many local market negotiations. At the same time, few
women disputed that in the last analysis
husbands were masters of their wives
and that the household was "a little commonwealth," a realm in which the husband's supremacy over wife and children
mirrored the supremacy of the monarch
over his subjects. Disorder in the domestic realm was treated as a serious matter,
intimating the possibility of a breakdown
of order and hierarchy in the culture at
large.

Strong-willed women were particularly
apt to be labeled as disorderly in early
modern towns and villages, even if their
"crimes" involved nothing more than talk-
ativeness. A shrew, in fact, was commonly
defined as a woman with a wagging tongue
who, partly because of her garrulousness,
was not properly submissive to her husband. The ideal wife, by contrast, was
imagined in the prescriptive literature as
chaste, silent, and obedient. The talk-
ativeness that could mark a woman as a shrew could also be interpreted as a sign of
her sexual promiscuity, on the theory that one kind of looseness leads to another.
Women deemed unruly were subject to various kinds of punishment. These could
include being "cucked"—ducked into water on a "cucking stool"—or being fitted with
a scold's bridle, a torturous harness that fitted around a woman's head with a metal bit
that went into her mouth and prevented her from speaking and sometimes caused
her to gag and her mouth to bleed or her teeth to be knocked loose. The husbands of
disorderly and aggressive women could also be punished for failure to control their
wives. Charivaris, or "rough ridings," were shaming rituals in which neighbors came to
the house of a disorderly woman and made her or her husband ride backward through
the town on a horse while bystanders shouted and played cacophonous music. This
signaled that the world had been turned upside down and rendered inharmonious by
her disorderliness and his inability to control his wife.

In *The Taming of the Shrew,* no man is submitted to a "rough riding" even though
at the end of the play both Lucentio and Hortensio seem to have lost control of
their wives. Instead, all the attention focuses on the taming of Katherina and on
the strategies employed by Petruccio to make her compliant with his will. On the
eighteenth- and nineteenth-century stage, Petruccio often carried a whip, symbol
of his power to control his wife and servants with physical force. Whether or not he
literally carries a whip, Petruccio employs coercion—verbal, psychological, and
physical—to control his wife, subjecting her to public humiliation and private deprivation in order to teach her proper submissiveness to the authority of her husband.
In so doing, he reinforces the hierarchical principle upon which the entire Elizabethan social order was premised, warning not only unruly men but also servants and
beggars that, except in jest, they cannot usurp the places of their masters. But is
this account of *The Taming of the Shrew* adequate? Is the play as fiercely repressive

as some critics assume? It is precisely on this point that readers, critics, and actors differ.

Some critics, for example, emphasize how Shakespeare mitigates the violence of many versions of the folktale on which the main plot is modeled. Katherina is not, for example, beaten and wrapped in a salted horsehide, nor does Petruccio force her to sleep with him before their return to Padua. In his farmhouse, he keeps her awake by disordering the bed and talking at her, but only after their return to the relative safety and familiarity of her father's house does he speak of his intention to "bed" her. In short, sexual conquest does not seem to be part of his taming practices. Perhaps more important, many actors, audiences, and critics have seen in Katherina and Petruccio's relationship an attractive mutuality and vitality they find difficult to reconcile with the idea that the play is simply a lesson in how to subordinate a woman. For example, when Petruccio first woos Katherina in 2.1, the two of them engage in a verbal sparring match that is dazzling in its complexity and speed. Puns and insults fly back and forth, with Katherina giving as good as she gets. The following exchange is typical:

> PETRUCCIO   Come, come, you wasp, i'faith you are too angry.
> KATHERINA   If I be waspish, best beware my sting.
> PETRUCCIO   My remedy is then to pluck it out.
> KATHERINA   Ay, if the fool could find it where it lies.
> PETRUCCIO   Who knows not where a wasp does wear his sting?
>   In his tail.
> KATHERINA   In his tongue.
> PETRUCCIO   Whose tongue?
> KATHERINA   Yours, if you talk of tales, and so farewell.
> PETRUCCIO   What, with my tongue in your tail?
>   Nay, come again, good Kate, I am a gentleman—
> KATHERINA   That I'll try.
>   *She strikes him.*
> PETRUCCIO   I swear I'll cuff you if you strike again.
>   (2.1.209–19)

This is a beautifully orchestrated encounter, with Katherina and Petruccio trading rapid-fire, one-line insults and deftly topping one another's puns. Their exchange has erotic intensity. These two are taking one another's measure, listening intently, struggling for advantage. Petruccio is not above talking dirty, and Katherina is not above making physical contact, albeit with a blow and not a caress. This is light-years away from the vapid wooing of Lucentio and Bianca, hiding behind the screen of school Latin.

On the stage, something vital and alive goes on between Katherina and Petruccio, and they have often been compared with Shakespeare's other witty couples, such as Benedict and Beatrice in *Much Ado About Nothing*, iconoclasts who seem more real and finally better and more equally matched than the more conventional couples with whom they are contrasted. Many critics, in fact, have argued that the real love story of the play belongs to Katherina and Petruccio, and that his taming of her is merely a way of showing her the advantages of outwardly conforming to society's expectations so that she can have the husband, the home, and the social approval she surely must crave. Many critics argue that it is Katherina's spirit that attracts Petruccio and that her spirit is never broken, just redirected, as in the final scene when Katherina takes out her aggressions not against her husband but against the other wives, whom she lectures on their marriage duties. In fact, some critics have argued that in watching Petruccio discipline and abuse his servants and the tailor who makes a dress for Katherina, Katherina learns how to direct her aggression against social inferiors, or against other women, rather than against her husband—an outcome that would grant her some social power at the expense of making her, like Petruccio, a bully.

The debate about how to interpret *The Taming of the Shrew* will surely continue. In performance, directors and actors sometimes emphasize the drama's playful and farcical elements, sometimes its dark, violent, and repressive potential. For example, how should one stage the final lines of Katherina's lecture to Bianca and the widow about the marital duties of a good wife? In these lines Katherina offers to put her hand beneath her husband's foot, a reference to an ancient and out-of-date marriage custom. But does she, and how does Petruccio respond? One could stage this moment as Petruccio's final triumph over a beaten spouse: she kneels; he puts his foot on her extended hand; he smiles out at the audience and she remains expressionless, dazed and broken before being abruptly dragged to her feet and commanded to kiss her victorious husband, a kiss that feels likes a violation. Or at the other extreme, when Katherina kneels with hand extended, Petruccio could kneel also and take her hand in his, eyes fixed on hers, oblivious to the onlookers both onstage and in the audience. Completely enveloped in one another's gaze, the tableau could suggest they have moved beyond the exaggerated postures of shrew and shrew tamer into something that feels like mutual love. In this case, the words "Come on and kiss me, Kate" might be uttered as an entreaty, and not a command, to which Katherina willingly responds. Neither interpretive choice is "right," but the contrast suggests the diametrically different ways in which key moments in this text can be realized in performance.

Critics and readers remain similarly divided as to what they see in this tale of woman tamed. Most agree, however, that *The Taming of the Shrew* deals with issues that deserve the thoughtful and sometimes heated critical debate the play has engendered. For example, while Katherina's taming does not involve the kinds of physical brutality in the "Merry Jest" ballad, it is nonetheless true that in Petruccio's farmhouse Katherina is deprived of sleep, food, and the protection of family and female companionship—techniques akin to modern methods of torture and brainwashing. As Katherina says, she is "starved for meat, giddy for lack of sleep, / With oaths kept waking and with brawling fed" (4.3.9–10). This is horrifying, even if the horror is mitigated by the laughter-inducing techniques of knockabout farce. Grumio makes the audience laugh as he tantalizes Katherina with one kind of food and then another, while ultimately withholding them all, but this does not erase the fact that Katherina is hungry and that her hunger is used to starve her into complying with Petruccio's wishes. There is similar cruelty lurking behind the trick played on Sly in the Induction. The beggar is tantalized with the prospect of riches he can never retain. *The Taming of the Shrew* makes a joke out of the enormous gap between the poverty of a tinker and the privilege of a lord, comedy from the physical and psychic trials that lie in wait for a strong-willed woman.

It is perhaps appropriate to conclude by focusing again on the role of Sly. As he watches the play the actors perform for him, he at first makes comments on the action, but these stop after the first act, and he presumably falls asleep onstage. In another contemporary play, however, called *The Taming of a Shrew*, Sly makes interjections throughout, including a brief speech in which he vows to go home and tame his own wife, having learned from Petruccio how it is done. Scholars disagree about the relationship of *The Taming of the Shrew* and *The Taming of a Shrew*: they dispute which came first and whether Shakespeare had a hand in both (for a fuller discussion, see the Textual Introduction). Among the many differences between the two texts, however, is Sly's continuing stage prominence right to the end of *The Taming of a Shrew* and his final assertion that

> I'll to my
> Wife presently and tame her too,
> An if she anger me.

No one knows for certain if Shakespeare wrote these lines or why they don't appear in *The Taming of the Shrew*. Like almost everything else connected to this play, they are subject to various interpretations. Perhaps because they are put in Sly's mouth they are discredited, taken as another example of the reductiveness of his responses to the pastimes of the cultural elite—in this case, to the play staged in the Lord's house by the traveling players. Maybe *only* a tinker would take this as the "message" of the play. However, perhaps Sly's response to what he has just watched indicates why this vital and attractive play seems to many readers to traffic in dangerous matters and to be easily used to justify the crudest kinds of male tyranny. It is a little disconcerting that *even* a downtrodden tinker can find comfort in the thought that while he is neither a lord nor a gentleman, he shares with them the same right to tame his wife "an if she anger me." Impoverished and ridiculed, Sly nonetheless feels entitled by virtue of his gender to dominate his spouse, perhaps thereby compensating for his powerlessness in other areas. In short, there is always something lower than a beggar—a beggar's wife. The play published in the First Folio does not contain Sly's speech, but in our day *The Taming of the Shrew* nonetheless remains, along with *The Merchant of Venice*, one of Shakespeare's most controversial plays: a spur to thought and to debate, a reminder of the serious matters that often lie at the heart of Shakespeare's "festive" comedies.

JEAN E. HOWARD

SELECTED BIBLIOGRAPHY

Aspinall, Dana E., ed. *The Taming of the Shrew: Critical Essays*. New York: Routledge, 2002. A broad selection of twentieth-century critical essays about the play, plus reviews of notable film, television, and stage versions.

Bailey, Amanda. "Livery and Its Discontents in *The Taming of the Shrew*." *Flaunting: Style and the Subversive Male Body in Renaissance England*. Toronto: U of Toronto P, 2007. 51–76. Examines how the excesses of male fashion could destabilize the early modern social order, including the disorder produced by servants who dress above their stations.

Boose, Lynda. "Scolding Brides and Bridling Scolds: Taming the Woman's Unruly Member." *Shakespeare Quarterly* 42 (1991): 179–213. Draws on the research of nineteenth-century scholars to recover the early modern punishments, including iron gags and cucking stools, used against women accused of being shrews or scolds.

Dolan, Frances E. "Household Chastisements: Gender, Authority and 'Domestic Violence.'" *Renaissance Culture and the Everyday*. Ed. Patricia Fumerton and Simon Hunt. Philadelphia: U of Pennsylvania P, 1999. 204–25. Scrutinizes forms of nearly invisible early modern domestic violence in which superiors discipline social subordinates, and argues that in *The Taming of the Shrew* Katherina is schooled by Petruccio to learn more socially acceptable targets for her anger, including the besting of servants.

Evett, David. "'Surprising Confrontations': Discourses of Service in *The Taming of the Shrew*." *Discourses of Service in Shakespeare's England*. New York: Palgrave Macmillan, 2005. 35–54. Explores the many different representations of servants and service in *The Taming of the Shrew,* and argues that the play posits "willing service" as the best alternative to coercion or rebellion within the master-servant relationship.

Haring-Smith, Tori. *From Farce to Metadrama: A Stage History of "The Taming of the Shrew," 1594–1983*. Westport, CT: Greenwood, 1985. A comprehensive stage history of the play and of some major adaptations from the late 1590s to the early 1980s.

Henderson, Diana E. "The Return of the Shrew: New Media, Old Stories, and Shakespearean Comedy." *Collaborations with the Past: Reshaping Shakespeare across Time and Media*. Ithaca, NY: Cornell UP, 2006. 155–201. Presents an excellent analysis of twentieth-century film versions of *The Taming of the Shrew* from the

Mary Pickford/Douglas Fairbanks Jr. version of 1929 to *10 Things I Hate About You* in 1999.

Marcus, Leah. "The Shakespearean Editor as Shrew-Tamer." *English Literary Renaissance* 22 (1992): 177–200. Examines and queries the historical process by which *The Taming of a Shrew* came to be regarded not as a source for Shakespeare's *The Taming of the Shrew*, but as a debased derivative of it.

Newman, Karen. "Renaissance Family Politics and Shakespeare's *Taming of the Shrew*." *Fashioning Femininity and English Renaissance Drama*. Chicago: U of Chicago P, 1991. 33–50. Argues that Katherina's linguistic freedom constitutes her main threat to male authority and that that freedom is never completely curtailed.

Smith, Amy L. "Performing Marriage with a Difference: Wooing, Wedding, and Bedding in *The Taming of the Shrew*." *Comparative Drama* 36 (2002): 289–320. Uses Judith Butler's theories of performativity to argue that within Katherina and Petruccio's self-conscious performance of courtship and marriage lies the potential for a critical reworking of gender norms, rather than outright submission to or resistance of them.

FILMS

The Taming of the Shrew. 1929. Dir. Samuel Taylor. USA. 63 min. One of the first "talkies," this black-and-white film, starring Douglas Fairbanks as Petruccio and Mary Pickford as Katherina, ends with Pickford's famous "wink" at the conclusion of her speech of submission.

Kiss Me Kate. 1953. Dir. George Sidney. USA. 109 min. Film version of the Cole Porter musical starring Howard Keel and Kathryn Grayson in which a group of actors is shown performing Shakespeare's play, the events of which mirror their own circumstances. Songs include "Brush Up Your Shakespeare" and "Where Is the Life That Late I Led?"

The Taming of the Shrew. 1967. Dir. Franco Zeffirelli. USA. 122 min. Broad-comedy performance starring the real-life couple of Elizabeth Taylor and Richard Burton as Katherina and Petruccio.

The Taming of the Shrew. 1980. Dir. Jonathan Miller. UK. 127 min. Intelligent BBC/Time-Life version starring John Cleese as Petruccio and Sarah Badel as Katherina with sets modeled on Vermeer interiors.

10 Things I Hate About You. 1999. Dir. Gil Junger. USA. 97 min. Loose adaptation of Shakespeare's plot in which Julia Stiles plays a headstrong character, Kat Stratford, who comes to an accommodation with bad boy Heath Ledger as Patrick Verona.

TEXTUAL INTRODUCTION

The Taming of the Shrew was published for the first time in the 1623 First Folio, and it is that text that forms the basis for this edition. However, another play that seems to be closely related also circulated during the period: *The Taming of a Shrew. A Shrew* was first published as a quarto in 1594 and was reprinted in 1596 and 1607. The play shares many features with *The Shrew* beyond the similarity of their titles, including the plot of a woman who is "tamed" by her husband and a subplot of her sister and her various suitors. *A Shrew* is, however, dissimilar enough—the location and character names differ, the shrew has two sisters, the frame story is completed, the play is significantly shorter—that *A Shrew* and *The Shrew* cannot be understood as different names for one play. But there is no consensus about the relationship between these two plays. Various theories have been proposed to account for the similarities and differences between the two. Some scholars have suggested that *A Shrew* is an anonymous play that served as a source for Shakespeare's *The Shrew*. Others argue that *A*

Shrew derives from *The Shrew*, either as an imperfect copy of Shakespeare's play or as a memorial reconstruction of it. It has also been proposed that both *The Shrew* and *A Shrew* are imperfect derivatives of an even earlier *Shrew* play. While the Oxford editors believed that *The Shrew* was a source for *A Shrew*, the most recent editor (2010) for the Arden Shakespeare argues that *A Shrew* likely came before *The Shrew*.

Dating *The Shrew* is complicated first of all by its uncertain relationship to *A Shrew*. *A Shrew* was entered into the Stationers' Register on May 2, 1594 (the year it was first published), and its title page describes the play as having been performed by Pembroke's Men; if that is the case, the play must have been written before 1593, when that company went bankrupt. Consequently, if *The Shrew* predates *A Shrew*, it must have been written by 1592. Yet linguistic analysis shows similarities between *The Shrew* and *The Comedy of Errors* and *Love's Labor's Lost*, both written around 1594–95. Francis Meres's 1598 *Palladis Tamia: Wit's Treasury* mentions neither *A Shrew* nor *The Shrew* among Shakespeare's comedies—perhaps an omission, or perhaps evidence that *The Shrew* had not yet been written and that *A Shrew* is not Shakespeare's play.

Internal evidence for dating is not much more helpful. *The Shrew* includes the use of "*Sincklo*" as the speech prefix for one of the players in the Induction. Scholars agree that Sincklo is John Sincler, a hired man who was active as a player during the 1590s and early 1600s. More perplexing is the connection between Sincler and a character named "Soto," since the only Soto in an extant play is found in John Fletcher's *Women Pleased*, written sometime around 1619–23, well after Shakespeare's death. But these lines could have been inserted later. Finally, it has been argued that *A Shrew*'s gender politics are consistent with official Elizabethan gender views, while *The Shrew*'s are more akin to Jacobean visions of a companionate marriage. In summary, as with the relationship between *A Shrew* and *The Shrew*, there has been no consensus on the date of *The Shrew*, but it seems most likely to have been written in the early part of the decade, probably in 1591–92.

Questions about the play's date of composition and its relationship to *A Shrew*, however, have little bearing on editing *The Shrew*. The two are separate plays, and the decisions made in editing *The Shrew* are based on its text in the Folio and not on *A Shrew*'s text. A few notable issues arise in editing *The Shrew*, particularly concerning the play's irregular act divisions. The Folio starts the play with "*Actus primus. Scoena Prima.*" It was Alexander Pope who first labeled the two opening scenes as part of the Induction, a move that all subsequent editors have followed. There are also irregularities in subsequent act divisions. The Folio marks no act 2 and no scene divisions; the act and scenes inserted have been fairly consistent across the editorial tradition, and they are detailed here in the Textual Variants.

The character of Hortensio is more complicated to handle: he is not part of the "bidding" for Bianca in 2.1, despite being one of her wooers, and partway through the play Tranio seems to take over what has been Hortensio's role as Petruccio's old friend. These changes suggest that there might have been a revision to his character, but it is not possible to recover the earlier version of the play if there was one. There are also a number of clearly incorrect speech prefixes for his character, as indicated in the Textual Variants.

The stage directions in the Folio are often more detailed than is typical for early modern plays, describing actions, demeanor, and order of entry in some cases: for example, at the equivalent of 2.1.38, the Folio reads, "*Enter Gremio, Lucentio, in the habit of a meane man, Petruchio with Tranio, his boy bearing a Lute and Bookes.*" As is usual in early modern play texts, there are missing entrances and exits, and other directions appear incomplete: the Haberdasher, for instance, is given an entrance but is never provided with an exit. The placement and wording of stage directions can affect the way readers and audiences respond to the play; for some examples, see the Textual Comments.

SARAH WERNER

PERFORMANCE NOTE

To moderate anticipated moral opposition to a comedy that hinges on female subjection, directors of *The Taming of the Shrew* often endeavor not to engage audiences emotionally, but in fact to distance them from the action. In this they may follow Shakespeare, who stresses the plot's artificiality via framing scenes wherein characters deceive a drunkard, even regarding his own identity, then mount a performance full of role playing and disguise. Directors can complement the play's ostentatious theatricality by keeping Sly onstage throughout the *Taming* play, or conspicuously doubling him and others in the main plot, for example, with Sly and the Hostess renewing their feud as Petruccio and Katherina. Productions also routinely employ *commedia*-inflected or blatantly cartoonish characterizations and settings (such as the "wild west") to explain the play's violence and antifeminism as routine elements of farce. On the other hand, some directors unapologetically showcase the play's brutality, cutting the Induction scenes and trimming the Bianca subplot so that the violence leveled at Katherina appears more disturbing for the comparative simplicity of its representation.

In the further interests of rendering the taming plot more palatable, some productions shift the play's genre toward romantic comedy, softening objections to Katherina's gradual submission by presenting her interactions with Petruccio as mutually complicit banter or foreplay. Some productions depict Baptista as Katherina's main oppressor and offer Petruccio as a handsome alternative and a means of escape. Others make a feminist heroine of Katherina, implying that her incongruous behavior in the finale is a deliberate ploy to win Petruccio's bet, suggestive even of the power she holds in their present or future relationship. Still others, conversely, make her a tragic figure, brainwashed and/or beaten into submission. Petruccio, meanwhile, can be a cunning sadist or a dull brute, a dashing hero or a zany (clown), depending on whether the production casts Katherina more as victim or virago. The portrayal of Bianca inevitably influences Katherina's reception, since her sweetness can be sincere or yet another of the play's disguises—often revealed by productions' having her flout her sister behind their father's back, thus partly excusing the shrewishness for which Katherina is notorious.

Brett Gamboa

The Taming of the Shrew

[THE PERSONS OF THE PLAY]

In the Induction:
Christopher Sly, a BEGGAR
HOSTESS
LORD
Bartholomew, PAGE to the Lord
HUNTSMEN attending the Lord
SERVANTS attending the Lord
PLAYERS

In the play-within-a-play:
BAPTISTA Minola, a gentleman of Padua
KATHERINA, elder daughter to Baptista
BIANCA, younger daughter to Baptista

PETRUCCIO, a gentleman of Verona, suitor to Katherina
GRUMIO ⎫
CURTIS ⎪
NATHANIEL ⎬ servants to Petruccio
PHILIP ⎪
JOSEPH ⎪
PETER ⎭
GREMIO, a rich old man of Padua, suitor to Bianca
HORTENSIO, suitor to Bianca, later disguised as Licio
LUCENTIO, a gentleman of Pisa, suitor to Bianca, later disguised as Cambio
TRANIO ⎫ servants to Lucentio
BIONDELLO ⎭

VINCENTIO, father to Lucentio
PEDANT, later disguised as Vincentio

WIDOW
TAILOR
HABERDASHER
OFFICER
SERVANTS
Attendants]

Induction 1
Enter [a] BEGGAR *[called] Christopher Sly and [a]* HOSTESS.[1]
BEGGAR   I'll feeze° you, in faith.   *fix; beat*
HOSTESS   A pair of stocks,[2] you rogue.

Induction 1 Location: In front of a country tavern.
1. TEXTUAL COMMENT To emphasize his societal role, the Folio (F) consistently uses "Beggar" for the character that editors usually refer to as "Sly." This edition follows F's use of roles rather than proper names to refer to the Induction's characters. See

Digital Edition TC 1.
2. A threat to have him put in the stocks (an instrument of public punishment consisting of two wooden planks with semicircles carved into them; the criminal sat with his or her feet clamped between the planks).

BEGGAR You're a baggage;° the Slys are no rogues. Look in *whore*
the chronicles;[3] we came in with Richard Conqueror.[4]
5 Therefore *paucas palabras*:[5] let the world slide.° Sessa![6] *go by*
HOSTESS You will not pay for the glasses you have burst?° *broken*
BEGGAR No, not a denier.[7] Go by, Saint Jeronimy![8] Go to thy
cold bed, and warm thee.
HOSTESS I know my remedy: I must go fetch the headborough.° *constable*
10 BEGGAR Third, or fourth, or fifth borough, I'll answer him by
law. I'll not budge an inch, boy.[9] Let him come, and kindly.° *and welcome! (ironic)*
Falls asleep.

[*Exit* HOSTESS.][1]
Wind horns.° Enter a LORD *from hunting, with his train* *Horns sound*
[*of* HUNTSMEN *and* SERVANTS].
LORD Huntsman, I charge thee, tender well° my hounds. *care well for*
Breathe Meriman[2]—the poor cur is embossed°— *exhausted*
And couple Clowder with the deep-mouthed brach.[3]
15 Saw'st thou not, boy, how Silver made it good
At the hedge corner, in the coldest fault?[4]
I would not lose the dog for twenty pound.
FIRST HUNTSMAN Why, Belman is as good as he, my lord.
He cried upon it at the merest loss,[5]
20 And twice today picked out the dullest scent.
Trust me, I take him for the better dog.
LORD Thou art a fool. If Echo were as fleet,° *fast*
I would esteem him worth a dozen such.
But sup° them well and look unto them all. *feed*
25 Tomorrow I intend to hunt again.
FIRST HUNTSMAN I will, my lord.
LORD [*seeing* BEGGAR] What's here? One dead or drunk? See,
doth he breathe?
SECOND HUNTSMAN He breathes, my lord. Were he not warmed
with ale,
This were a bed but cold to sleep so soundly.
30 LORD Oh, monstrous beast! How like a swine he lies.
Grim death, how foul and loathsome is thine image.[6]
Sirs, I will practice on° this drunken man. *play a trick on*
What think you if he were conveyed to bed,
Wrapped in sweet° clothes, rings put upon his fingers, *scented*
35 A most delicious banquet by his bed,
And brave° attendants near him when he wakes— *finely dressed*
Would not the beggar then forget himself?
FIRST HUNTSMAN Believe me, lord, I think he cannot choose.° *do otherwise*
SECOND HUNTSMAN It would seem strange unto him when he
waked.

---

3. Histories, especially histories of England such as Raphael Holinshed's *Chronicles of England, Scotland, and Ireland* (2nd ed., 1587).
4. A blunder for "William the Conqueror," who took the English throne in 1066.
5. Misquoting *pocas palabras*, Spanish for "few words," a phrase from Thomas Kyd's *Spanish Tragedy* (ca. 1587).
6. Probably equivalent to "Be quiet."
7. *denier:* French coin of little value.
8. Misquoting a popular line—"Hieronimo, beware! go by, go by!"—from Kyd's *Spanish Tragedy* and confusing Hieronimo, Kyd's hero, with Saint Jerome.
9. Term of abuse applicable to either sex.

1. TEXTUAL COMMENT The Folio does not provide a stage direction for the Hostess's exit, which must occur before the Lord arrives. This edition has her remain onstage while the Beggar taunts her as "boy" and refuses to pay, thus heightening their antagonism. See Digital Edition TC 2.
2. Give Meriman time to recover his breath.
3. And put Clowder on a leash with the female hound ("brach") who bays deeply.
4. When the scent was faintest.
5. When the scent had been completely lost.
6. Your likeness (invoking the common comparison between sleep and death).

40 LORD Even as a flatt'ring° dream or worthless fancy.   *pleasing*
   Then take him up and manage well the jest.
   Carry him gently to my fairest chamber,
   And hang it round with all my wanton pictures.°   *erotic artworks*
   Balm° his foul head in warm distillèd waters,   *Anoint*
45 And burn sweet wood to make the lodging sweet.[7]
   Procure me music ready when he wakes
   To make a dulcet° and a heavenly sound.   *melodious*
   And, if he chance to speak, be ready straight°   *at once*
   And with a low, submissive reverence°   *deep bow*
50 Say, "What is it your honor will command?"
   Let one attend him with a silver basin
   Full of rosewater and bestrewed with flowers;
   Another bear the ewer,° the third a diaper,°   *water jug / towel*
   And say, "Will't please your lordship cool your hands?"
55 Someone be ready with a costly suit,
   And ask him what apparel he will wear;
   Another tell him of his hounds and horse
   And that his lady mourns at his disease.
   Persuade him that he hath been lunatic
60 And, when he says he is,° say that he dreams,   *is indeed mad*
   For he is nothing but a mighty lord.
   This do, and do it kindly,° gentle sirs: *naturally; fittingly*
   It will be pastime passing° excellent   *exceedingly*
   If it be husbanded with modesty.°   *prudently managed*
65 FIRST HUNTSMAN My lord, I warrant you we will play our part
   As° he shall think by our true diligence   *So*
   He is no less than what we say he is.
   LORD Take him up gently and to bed with him,
   And each one to his office° when he wakes.   *assigned role*
                  [*The* BEGGAR *is carried out.*]
              Sound trumpets.
70 Sirrah,[8] go see what trumpet 'tis that sounds.
                              [*Exit a* SERVANT.]
   Belike° some noble gentleman that means,   *Perhaps*
   Traveling some journey, to repose° him here.   *rest*
              Enter [SERVANT].
   How now? Who is it?
   SERVANT   An't° please your honor, players   *If it*
   That offer service to your lordship.
              Enter PLAYERS.
75 LORD Bid them come near.
   —Now, fellows, you are welcome.
   PLAYERS   We thank your honor.
   LORD Do you intend to stay with me tonight?
   FIRST PLAYER So please your lordship to accept our duty.° *services; respect*
   LORD With all my heart. This fellow I remember
80 Since once he played a farmer's eldest son.
   —'Twas where you wooed the gentlewoman so well.
   I have forgot your name, but sure that part
   Was aptly fitted° and naturally performed.   *well suited (to you)*

---

7. Aromatic woods like juniper were often burned to   8. A form of address to social inferiors.
make a room smell fragrant.

SECOND PLAYER   I think 'twas Soto[9] that your honor means.

85   LORD   'Tis very true. Thou didst it excellent.
—Well, you are come to me in happy time,°   *at the right time*
The rather for° I have some sport in hand   *Especially since*
Wherein your cunning° can assist me much.   *skill*
There is a lord will hear you play tonight.
90   But I am doubtful of your modesties,°   *self-control*
Lest over-eying of° his odd behavior—   *noticing; staring at*
For yet his honor never heard a play—
You break into some merry passion°   *fit of laughter*
And so offend him. For I tell you, sirs,
95   If you should smile, he grows impatient.

FIRST PLAYER   Fear not, my lord, we can contain ourselves,
Were he the veriest antic° in the world.   *most eccentric fellow*

LORD [*to a* SERVANT]   Go, sirrah, take them to the buttery,[1]
And give them friendly welcome, every one.
100   Let them want° nothing that my house affords.   *lack*

Exit one [SERVANT] *with the players.*

[*to another* SERVANT] Sirrah, go you to Bartholomew, my page,
And see him dressed in all suits° like a lady.   *in every detail*
That done, conduct him to the drunkard's chamber
And call him "Madam," do him obeisance.°   *pay him respects*
105   Tell him° from me, as he will win my love,   *(Bartholomew, the page)*
He bear himself with honorable° action   *becoming*
Such as he hath observed in noble ladies
Unto their lords by them accomplishèd.°   *performed*
Such duty to the drunkard let him do
110   With soft low tongue° and lowly courtesy,   *voice*
And say, "What is't your honor will command
Wherein your lady and your humble wife
May show her duty and make known her love?"
And then with kind embracements, tempting kisses,
115   And with declining head into his bosom,[2]
Bid him shed tears, as being overjoyed
To see her noble lord restored to health,
Who for this seven years hath esteemed him°   *thought himself to be*
No better than a poor and loathsome beggar.
120   And if the boy have not a woman's gift
To rain a shower of commanded° tears,   *produced on demand*
An onion will do well for such a shift,°   *purpose*
Which in a napkin being close conveyed°   *secretly carried*
Shall in despite[3] enforce a watery eye.
125   See this dispatched with all the haste thou canst;
Anon° I'll give thee more instructions.   *Soon*

Exit a [SERVANT].

I know the boy will well usurp° the grace,   *assume*
Voice, gait, and action of a gentlewoman.
I long to hear him call the drunkard "husband,"

---

9. Possibly a reference to a character of this name in
John Fletcher's *Women Pleased*. Since that play was
first acted around 1620, the reference must either be
a late addition to Shakespeare's text or else refer to a

character in an earlier play, now lost.
1. Pantry, often used to store liquor as well as food.
2. And with his head bowing down onto his chest.
3. In spite of an inability to cry.

130 And how my men will stay° themselves from laughter   *restrain*
When they do homage to this simple peasant.
I'll in to counsel them. Haply° my presence   *Perhaps*
May well abate the over-merry spleen[4]
Which otherwise would grow into extremes.   [*Exeunt.*]

Induction 2

Enter aloft[1] the drunkard [BEGGAR] *with* [SERVANTS]—
some with apparel, basin and ewer, and other
appurtenances—and LORD.

BEGGAR   For God's sake, a pot of small ale!°   *weak, cheap ale*
FIRST SERVANT   Will't please your lordship drink a cup of
sack?°   *costly imported wine*
SECOND SERVANT   Will't please your honor taste of these
conserves?°   *candied fruits*
THIRD SERVANT   What raiment° will your honor wear today?   *clothing*
5 BEGGAR   I am Christophero Sly. Call not me "honor" nor
"lordship." I ne'er drank sack in my life—and if you give me
any conserves, give me conserves of beef.° Ne'er ask me what   *salted beef*
raiment I'll wear, for I have no more doublets° than backs,   *jackets*
no more stockings than legs, nor no more shoes than feet—
10 nay, sometime more feet than shoes, or such shoes as my
toes look through the over-leather.
LORD   Heaven cease this idle humor[2] in your honor.
Oh, that a mighty man of such descent,
Of such possessions and so high esteem,
15 Should be infusèd with so foul a spirit.
BEGGAR   What, would you make me mad? Am not I Christopher Sly, old Sly's son of Barton Heath,[3] by birth a peddler,
by education a cardmaker,[4] by transmutation a bear-herd,°   *keeper of a tame bear*
and now by present profession a tinker?° Ask Marian Hackett,   *pot mender*
20 the fat alewife[5] of Wincot, if she know me not. If she say I
am not fourteen pence on the score[6] for sheer° ale, score   *for nothing but*
me up for the lying'st knave in Christendom. What, I am not
bestraught.° Here's—   *crazy*
THIRD SERVANT   Oh, this it is that makes your lady mourn.
25 SECOND SERVANT   Oh, this is it that makes your servants
droop.
LORD   Hence comes it that your kindred shuns your house,
As beaten hence by your strange lunacy.
O noble lord, bethink thee of thy birth.
Call home thy ancient° thoughts from banishment   *former*
30 And banish hence these abject lowly dreams.
Look how thy servants do attend on thee,

4. May lessen the impulse to laugh. Emotional out-
bursts, including laughter, were thought to originate
in the spleen.
Induction 2 Location: A bedroom in the Lord's house.
1. Upon the gallery above the stage. Whether this
long and complex scene was in fact performed "aloft"
is open to question. At a later point (1.1.244–49),
F has the Beggar commenting from above on the play
presented by the traveling actors who arrive in Induction 1. If Induction 2 is played on the main stage, the
Beggar must at some point ascend to the gallery, or
he must observe the entire play from the side of the
main stage.

2. Heaven put an end to this foolish fantasy. According to Renaissance medical theory, humors, or bodily
fluids, determined one's disposition.
3. Possibly Barton-on-the-Heath, a village not far from
Stratford-upon-Avon.
4. Maker of metal combs used to prepare wool for
spinning.
5. Female proprietor of a tavern. Wincot is a small
village near Stratford; individuals named Hacket
were living there in 1591.
6. In debt. Accounts were originally kept by notch-
ing, or "scoring," a stick, later by making marks on a
wall or a door.

Each in his office ready at thy beck.°   *command*
Wilt thou have music? (*Music.*) Hark, Apollo[7] plays,
And twenty cagèd nightingales do sing.
35   Or wilt thou sleep? We'll have thee to a couch
Softer and sweeter than the lustful bed
On purpose trimmed up for Semiramis.[8]
Say thou wilt walk: we will bestrew the ground.
Or wilt thou ride? Thy horses shall be trapped,°   *fitted with adornments*
40   Their harness studded all with gold and pearl.
Dost thou love hawking? Thou hast hawks will soar
Above the morning lark. Or wilt thou hunt?
Thy hounds shall make the welkin° answer them   *sky*
And fetch shrill echoes from the hollow earth.
45 FIRST SERVANT   Say thou wilt course,° thy greyhounds are   *hunt hares*
     as swift
As breathèd° stags—ay, fleeter than the roe.[9]   *well-exercised*
SECOND SERVANT   Dost thou love pictures?[1] We will fetch thee
     straight
Adonis[2] painted by a running brook
And Cytherea all in sedges° hid,   *water rushes*
50   Which seem to move and wanton° with her breath,   *play amorously*
Even as the waving sedges play wi'th' wind.
LORD   We'll show thee Io[3] as she was a maid,
And how she was beguilèd and surprised,
As lively° painted as the deed was done.   *realistically*
55 THIRD SERVANT   Or Daphne[4] roaming through a thorny wood,
Scratching her legs that one shall swear she bleeds,
And at that sight shall sad Apollo weep,
So workmanly° the blood and tears are drawn.   *skillfully*
LORD   Thou art a lord and nothing but a lord.
60   Thou hast a lady far more beautiful
Than any woman in this waning age.[5]
FIRST SERVANT   And till the tears that she hath shed for thee,
Like envious° floods o'errun her lovely face,   *spiteful*
She was the fairest creature in the world—
65   And yet° she is inferior to none.   *still*
BEGGAR   Am I a lord? And have I such a lady?
Or do I dream? Or have I dreamed till now?
I do not sleep. I see, I hear, I speak.
I smell sweet savors° and I feel soft things.   *odors*
70   Upon my life, I am a lord indeed,
And not a tinker, nor Christopher Sly.
Well, bring our lady hither to our sight—
And once again, a pot o'th' smallest° ale!   *weakest*

7. Greek god of music, who played the lyre.
8. Legendary Queen of Assyria, known for her great beauty and many sexual adventures.
9. Small deer proverbial for its swiftness.
1. Probably the "wanton pictures" referred to earlier (Induction 1.43). As described in the following lines, they are conventional erotic scenes, mostly derived from Ovid's *Metamorphoses*.
2. In classical mythology, a beautiful boy whom Aphrodite (Cytherea) loved. This scene shows Aphro-

dite spying on Adonis while he bathes in the brook.
3. Raped by Zeus, who concealed himself in a cloud or thick mist, she was then turned into a cow by Hera, Geek goddess of marriage.
4. A nymph who was turned into a laurel tree as she fled from Apollo.
5. Alluding to the popular belief that the world had steadily degenerated from the perfection of paradise or the classical Golden Age.

SECOND SERVANT Will't please your mightiness to wash your
    hands?
75 Oh, how we joy to see your wit restored!
    Oh, that once more you knew but what you are!
    These fifteen years you have been in a dream
    Or, when you waked, so waked as if you slept.
BEGGAR These fifteen years? By my fay,° a goodly nap.   *faith*
80 But did I never speak of° all that time?   *during*
FIRST SERVANT Oh, yes, my lord, but very idle words.
    For though you lay here in this goodly chamber,
    Yet would you say ye were beaten out of door
    And rail upon the hostess of the house°   *tavern*
85 And say you would present° her at the leet°   *accuse / local court*
    Because she brought stone jugs and no sealed quarts.[6]
    Sometimes you would call out for Cicely Hackett.
BEGGAR Ay, the woman's maid of the house.
THIRD SERVANT Why, sir, you know no house nor no such maid,
90 Nor no such men as you have reckoned up,
    As Stephen Sly and old John Naps of Greet[7]
    And Peter Turf and Henry Pimpernel
    And twenty more such names and men as these,
    Which never were nor no man ever saw.
95 BEGGAR Now Lord be thankèd for my good amends.°   *recovery*
ALL Amen.
BEGGAR   I thank thee; thou shalt not lose by it.
    Enter [Bartholomew the PAGE,[8] *disguised as a] lady,*
    with Attendants.
PAGE How fares my noble lord?
BEGGAR Marry,[9] I fare° well, for here is cheer° enough.   *get on; feed / food*
    Where is my wife?
100 PAGE Here, noble lord. What is thy will with her?
BEGGAR Are you my wife and will not call me "husband"?
    My men should call me "lord"; I am your goodman.[1]
PAGE My husband and my lord, my lord and husband:
    I am your wife in all obedience.
105 BEGGAR I know it well. —What must I call her?
LORD "Madam."
BEGGAR   "Alice Madam" or "Joan Madam"?[2]
LORD "Madam" and nothing else: so lords call ladies.
BEGGAR Madam wife, they say that I have dreamed
    And slept above some fifteen year or more.
110 PAGE Ay, and the time seems thirty unto me,
    Being all this time abandoned° from your bed.   *banned*
BEGGAR 'Tis much. Servants, leave me and her alone.
        [Exeunt LORD *and* SERVANTS.*]*[3]

---

6. She served from unmarked stone jugs rather than from the officially measured and stamped ("sealed") quarts.

7. Greet is a small village not far from Stratford. The names may be those of Stratford citizens.

8. TEXTUAL COMMENT Editors have often referred to the page as Bartholomew, the name by which the Lord addresses him, but as it does with the Beggar, this edition uses *"Page"* to emphasize the character's societal role rather than his individuality. See Digital Edition TC 3.

9. Mild oath, derived from the Virgin Mary's name.

1. Husband: a term normally not used by lords.

2. Misusing the usual title for a noblewoman. "Alice" and "Joan" are names rarely associated with the upper classes in Elizabethan texts.

3. TEXTUAL COMMENT The Folio has no stage direction here that would indicate how the Induction scenes are distinguished from the Petruccio and Katherina play or whether the Lord exits with his men, but those attending on the Beggar probably obey his command and leave the stage along with the Lord here. See Digital Edition TC 4.

Madam, undress you and come now to bed.
PAGE   Thrice noble lord, let me entreat of you
115 To pardon me yet for a night or two,
Or if not so, until the sun be set.
For your physicians have expressly charged,
In peril to incur[4] your former malady,
That I should yet absent me from your bed.
120 I hope this reason stands for my excuse.
BEGGAR   Ay, it stands[5] so that I may hardly tarry° so long. But   *delay*
I would be loath to fall into my dreams again. I will there-
fore tarry in despite of the flesh and the blood.
      Enter a MESSENGER.
MESSENGER   Your honor's players, hearing your amendment,
125 Are come to play a pleasant comedy.
For so your doctors hold it very meet,°   *suitable*
Seeing too much sadness hath congealed your blood
And melancholy is the nurse of frenzy,[6]
Therefore they thought it good you hear a play
130 And frame your mind to mirth and merriment,
Which bars° a thousand harms and lengthens life.   *prevents*
BEGGAR   Marry, I will let them play it. Is not a comonty° a   *(for "comedy")*
Christmas gambol° or a tumbling trick?   *frolic; game*
PAGE   No, my good lord, it is more pleasing stuff.
135 BEGGAR   What, household stuff?°   *furnishings; events*
PAGE   It is a kind of history.°   *story*
BEGGAR   Well, we'll see't.   [*Exit* MESSENGER.]
Come, madam wife, sit by my side,
And let the world slip. We shall ne'er be younger.[7]
      [BEGGAR *and* PAGE *sit and watch the play.*]

1.1

      Flourish.° *Enter* LUCENTIO *and his man* TRANIO.   *Fanfare of trumpets*
LUCENTIO   Tranio, since for° the great desire I had   *because of*
To see fair Padua, nursery of arts,[1]
I am arrived for° fruitful Lombardy,   *before*
The pleasant garden of great Italy,
5 And by my father's love and leave am armed
With his good will and thy good company—
My trusty servant well approved° in all—   *reliable*
Here let us breathe° and haply institute   *pause; rest*
A course of learning and ingenious° studies.   *liberal; intellectual*
10 Pisa, renownèd for grave citizens,
Gave me my being and my father first,°   *before me*
A merchant of great traffic° through the world,   *business*
Vincentio, come of the Bentivolii.[2]
Vincentio's son, brought up in Florence,
15 It shall become° to serve° all hopes conceived,[3]   *befit / fulfill*

4. *In peril to incur:* Because of the risk of bringing on.
5. Punning on "stand" as meaning "to have an erection."
6. According to Renaissance humoral theory, excessive sadness could cause thickening of the blood and thus delirium, or "frenzy." *nurse:* nourisher.
7. PERFORMANCE COMMENT As the Induction scenes are among the very few that Shakespeare set in Elizabethan England, some modern directors have chosen to establish that historical context, while others seek

to update it by presenting Sly as a contemporary of the audience's. See Digital Edition PC 1.
1.1 Location: A street in Padua.
1. A center for learning ("arts"). Padua's famous university attracted some English students in Shakespeare's time and was renowned for the study of law and medicine.
2. Descended from the Bentivolii (perhaps a reference to the famous Bentivoglio family of Bologna).
3. That is, by relatives and friends.

To deck° his fortune with his virtuous deeds.   *adorn*
And therefore, Tranio, for the time I study
Virtue, and that part of philosophy
Will I apply° that treats of happiness   *pursue; study*
20 By virtue specially to be achieved.
Tell me thy mind, for I have Pisa left
And am to Padua come as he that leaves
A shallow plash° to plunge him in the deep,   *pool*
And with satiety seeks to quench his thirst.
25 TRANIO *Mi pardonato,*° gentle master mine,   *Pardon me*
I am in all affected° as yourself;   *inclined*
Glad that you thus continue your resolve
To suck the sweets of sweet philosophy.
Only, good master, while we do admire
30 This virtue and this moral discipline,
Let's be no stoics nor no stocks,[4] I pray,
Or so devote to Aristotle's checks[5]
As Ovid be an outcast quite abjured.[6]
Balk logic° with acquaintance that you have,   *Bandy words*
35 And practice rhetoric in your common talk.
Music and poesy use to quicken° you.   *revive; animate*
The mathematics and the metaphysics,
Fall to them as you find your stomach° serves you.   *appetite*
No profit grows where is no pleasure ta'en:
40 In brief, sir, study what you most affect.°   *like*
LUCENTIO Gramercies,° Tranio, well dost thou advise.   *Thank you*
If, Biondello, thou wert come ashore,[7]
We could at once put us in readiness
And take a lodging fit to entertain
45 Such friends as time in Padua shall beget.
But stay a while, what company is this?
TRANIO Master, some show to welcome us to town.
        Enter BAPTISTA *with his two daughters,* KATHERINA
        and BIANCA; GREMIO, *a pantaloon,*[8] [*and*] HORTENSIO,
        [*suitor*] *to Bianca.* LUCENTIO [*and*] TRANIO *stand by.*
BAPTISTA Gentlemen, importune° me no farther,   *pester*
For how I firmly am resolved you know:
50 That is, not to bestow° my youngest daughter   *give in marriage*
Before I have a husband for the elder.
If either of you both love Katherina,
Because I know you well and love you well,
Leave shall you have to court her at your pleasure.
55 GREMIO To cart her[9] rather. She's too rough for me.
There, there, Hortensio, will you° any wife?   *do you want*
KATHERINA[1] [*to* BAPTISTA] I pray you, sir, is it your will

---

4. Wooden posts devoid of feeling. Punning on "stoics," the Greek philosophers who advocated both indifference to pleasure or pain and patient endurance.
5. Restraints. Aristotle defined virtue as a mean, the
avoiding of excess (or deficiency).
6. *As . . . abjured:* That Ovid be renounced. Ovid was
a Roman poet whose erotic writings were popular in
the Renaissance. His *Ars Amatoria* (*The Art of Love*)
is mentioned by Lucentio at 4.2.8.
7. Padua, an inland city, did not have a port. Shakespeare's knowledge of Italian geography seems to
have been shaky.

8. Foolish old man: a stock character from the Italian
commedia dell'arte whose usual role was to hinder
young lovers.
9. To carry her through the street in, or tied to, a cart.
This was a common punishment for disorderly women.
1. TEXTUAL COMMENT Although F uses "*Kate*" or "*Kat*"
as the speech prefix and "*Katerina*" or "*Katherina*" in
the stage directions for this character, this edition consistently uses "*Katherina*" (pronounced with a "t" rather
than a "th" sound). Petruccio's shortening of her name
to "Kate" is one of the ways by which he attempts to
assert his authority over her. See Digital Edition TC 5.

To make a stale of me[2] amongst these mates?°   *fellows; husbands*
HORTENSIO   "Mates," maid? How mean you that? No mates
    for you,
60   Unless you were of gentler, milder mold.°   *nature*
KATHERINA   I'faith, sir, you shall never need to fear;
    Iwis it is not halfway to her heart.[3]
    But if it were, doubt not, her care should be
    To comb your noddle° with a three-legged stool   *hit your head*
65   And paint° your face and use you like a fool.   *(with blood)*
HORTENSIO   From all such devils, good Lord deliver us.
GREMIO   And me too, good Lord.
TRANIO   Hush, master, here's some good pastime toward;°   *in view*
    That wench is stark mad or wonderful froward.°   *incredibly willful*
70 LUCENTIO   But in the other's silence do I see
    Maid's mild behavior and sobriety.
    Peace, Tranio.
TRANIO   Well said, master; mum and gaze your fill.
BAPTISTA   Gentlemen, that I may soon make good
75   What I have said —Bianca, get you in,
    And let it not displease thee, good Bianca,
    For I will love thee ne'er the less, my girl.
KATHERINA   A pretty peat.° It is best put finger in the eye,[4] an°   *pet; spoiled child / if*
    she knew why.
80 BIANCA   Sister, content you° in my discontent.   *satisfy yourself*
    [*to* BAPTISTA] Sir, to your pleasure° humbly I subscribe:°   *will / submit*
    My books and instruments shall be my company,
    On them to look and practice by myself.
LUCENTIO   Hark, Tranio, thou mayst hear Minerva[5] speak.
85 HORTENSIO   Signor Baptista, will you be so strange?°   *unnatural; cruel*
    Sorry am I that our good will effects°   *causes*
    Bianca's grief.
GREMIO   Why, will you mew° her up,   *confine (like a falcon)*
    Signor Baptista, for° this fiend of hell,   *because of*
    And make her bear the penance° of her tongue?   *punishment*
90 BAPTISTA   Gentlemen, content ye; I am resolved.
    Go in, Bianca.   [*Exit* BIANCA.]
    And for I know she taketh most delight
    In music, instruments, and poetry,
    Schoolmasters will I keep within my house,
95   Fit to instruct her youth. If you, Hortensio,
    Or Signor Gremio, you, know any such,
    Prefer° them hither; for to cunning° men   *Recommend / skillful*
    I will be very kind and liberal
    To mine own children in good bringing up.
100   And so farewell. Katherina, you may stay,
    For I have more to commune with Bianca.   *Exit.*
KATHERINA   Why, and I trust I may go too, may I not? What,
    shall I be appointed hours, as though, belike, I knew not
    what to take and what to leave? Ha.   *Exit.*

---

2. To make me a laughingstock or a prostitute or a
decoy (for Bianca).
3. Certainly, marriage does not even half interest
her. (Katherina speaks of herself in the third person

here.)
4. *put finger in the eye*: to weep.
5. Roman goddess of wisdom.

105 GREMIO You may go to the devil's dam!⁶ Your gifts are so
good here's none will hold° you. Their love⁷ is not so great,   *tolerate*
Hortensio, but we may blow our nails° together and fast it   *wait patiently*
fairly out.⁸ Our cake's dough on both sides.⁹ Farewell. Yet
for the love I bear my sweet Bianca, if I can by any means
110 light on a fit man to teach her that wherein she delights, I
will wish° him to her father.   *recommend*
HORTENSIO So will I, Signor Gremio. But a word, I pray.
Though the nature of our quarrel yet never brooked parle,¹
know now upon advice° it toucheth° us both—that we may   *reflection / concerns*
115 yet again have access to our fair mistress and be happy rivals
in Bianca's love—to labor and effect one thing specially.
GREMIO What's that, I pray?
HORTENSIO Marry, sir, to get a husband for her sister.
GREMIO A husband? A devil!
120 HORTENSIO I say a husband.
GREMIO I say a devil. Think'st thou, Hortensio, though her
father be very rich, any man is so very° a fool to be married   *completely*
to hell?
HORTENSIO Tush, Gremio. Though it pass° your patience and   *exceeds*
125 mine to endure her loud alarums,° why, man, there be good   *calls to arms; scoldings*
fellows in the world, an° a man could light on them, would   *if*
take her with all faults, and money enough.
GREMIO I cannot tell, but I had as lief° take her dowry with   *would as willingly*
this condition: to be whipped at the high cross² every
130 morning.
HORTENSIO Faith, as you say, there's small choice in rotten
apples. But come, since this bar in law° makes us friends, it   *legal obstacle*
shall be so far forth friendly maintained³ till by helping Baptista's eldest daughter to a husband, we set his youngest free
135 for a husband, and then have to't° afresh. Sweet Bianca!   *begin the fight*
Happy man be his dole;⁴ he that runs fastest, gets the ring.⁵
How say you, Signor Gremio?
GREMIO I am agreed, and would I had given him the best
horse in Padua to begin his wooing that would thoroughly
140 woo her, wed her, and bed her, and rid the house of her.
Come on.
Exeunt GREMIO *and* HORTENSIO. TRANIO *and*
LUCENTIO *remain.*
TRANIO I pray, sir, tell me, is it possible
That love should of a sudden take such hold?
LUCENTIO O Tranio, till I found it to be true,
145 I never thought it possible or likely.
But see, while idly I stood looking on,
I found the effect of love-in-idleness⁶
And now in plainness do confess to thee,
That art to me as secret° and as dear   *intimate*

6. The devil's mother, imagined as the stereotypical
shrew and said to be worse than the devil himself.
7. Love of them (that is, of women).
8. And abstain as best we can.
9. Proverbial expression of failure.
1. *brooked parle*: permitted discussion.
2. Cross set on a pedestal in the town center, the
normal site for punishment in an English village.
3. *it . . . maintained*: we'll pursue the matter as friends.

4. May the winner's fate be that of a happy man.
5. A proverb alluding to the ring that riders in a
jousting match try to catch on their lances. Also punning on "ring" as referring to both "wedding ring"
and female genitalia.
6. Punning on a flower known as "love-in-idleness,"
whose juice was thought to induce love. (See *A Midsummer Night's Dream* 2.1.166–68.)

150   As Anna[7] to the Queen of Carthage was:
      Tranio, I burn, I pine, I perish, Tranio,
      If I achieve not this young modest girl.
      Counsel me, Tranio, for I know thou canst;
      Assist me, Tranio, for I know thou wilt.

155   TRANIO   Master, it is no time to chide you now;
      Affection is not rated° from the heart.   *driven out by scolding*
      If love have touched you, naught remains but so,
      Redime te captum quam queas minimo.[8]

  LUCENTIO   Gramercies,° lad! Go forward, this contents;   *Thanks*
160   The rest will comfort, for thy counsel's sound.

  TRANIO   Master, you looked so longly° on the maid   *persistently*
      Perhaps you marked not what's the pith° of all.   *main point*

  LUCENTIO   Oh, yes, I saw sweet beauty in her face,
      Such as the daughter of Agenor[9] had
165   That made great Jove to humble him to her hand
      When with his knees he kissed the Cretan strand.

  TRANIO   Saw you no more? Marked you not how her sister
      Began to scold and raise up such a storm
      That mortal ears might hardly endure the din?

170   LUCENTIO   Tranio, I saw her coral lips to move
      And with her breath she did perfume the air;
      Sacred and sweet was all I saw in her.

  TRANIO   Nay, then 'tis time to stir him from his trance.
      —I pray, awake, sir! If you love the maid,
175   Bend thoughts and wits to achieve her. Thus it stands:
      Her elder sister is so curst° and shrewd°   *quarrelsome / shrewish*
      That till the father rid his hands of her,
      Master, your love must live a maid at home,
      And therefore has he closely mewed her up
180   Because° she will not be annoyed with° suitors.   *So that / troubled with*

  LUCENTIO   Ah, Tranio, what a cruel father's he.
      But art thou not advised,° he took some care   *aware*
      To get her cunning schoolmasters to instruct her?

  TRANIO   Ay, marry am I, sir, and now 'tis plotted.

  LUCENTIO   I have it, Tranio.

185   TRANIO   Master, for° my hand,   *by*
      Both our inventions° meet and jump° in one.   *schemes / agree*

  LUCENTIO   Tell me thine first.

  TRANIO   You will be schoolmaster
      And undertake the teaching of the maid:
      That's your device.°   *plan*

  LUCENTIO   It is. May it be done?
190   TRANIO   Not possible: for who shall bear your part
      And be in Padua here Vincentio's son,
      Keep house and ply his book,° welcome his friends,   *study*
      Visit his countrymen and banquet them?

  LUCENTIO   Basta,° content thee, for I have it full.°   *Enough / fully planned*

---

7. Sister to Dido, Queen of Carthage. In both Virgil's *Aeneid* and Christopher Marlowe's *Dido, Queen of Carthage* (1594), Dido tells Anna of her secret love for Aeneas.
8. Latin: Ransom yourself from captivity at the low- est possible price. A phrase from Terence, quoted as it appears in William Lily's *A Short Introduction of Grammar*, a standard Elizabethan school text.
9. Europa. Jove transformed himself into a bull and carried her across the sea to Crete to rape her.

195   We have not yet been seen in any house,
Nor can we be distinguished by our faces
For man or master. Then it follows thus:
Thou shalt be master, Tranio, in my stead,
Keep house and port° and servants, as I should;   *social position*
200   I will some other be, some Florentine,
Some Neapolitan, or meaner° man of Pisa.   *poorer*
'Tis hatched and shall be so. Tranio, at once
Uncase° thee: take my colored hat and cloak.[1]   *Undress*
    [TRANIO *and* LUCENTIO *exchange clothes.*][2]
When Biondello comes, he waits on thee,
205   But I will charm° him first to keep his tongue.   *persuade; use magic on*
TRANIO   So had you need.
    In brief, sir, since it your pleasure is
And I am tied to be obedient—
For so your father charged me at our parting:
210   "Be serviceable° to my son," quoth he,   *diligent in service*
Although I think 'twas in another sense—
I am content to be Lucentio,
Because so well I love Lucentio.
LUCENTIO   Tranio, be so, because Lucentio loves,
215   And let me be a slave t'achieve that maid
Whose sudden sight hath thralled° my wounded[3] eye.   *enslaved*
    Enter BIONDELLO.
Here comes the rogue. Sirrah, where have you been?
BIONDELLO   Where have I been? Nay, how now, where are
you? Master, has my fellow Tranio stolen your clothes, or
220   you stolen his, or both? Pray, what's the news?
LUCENTIO   Sirrah, come hither; 'tis no time to jest,
And therefore frame your manners to the time.
Your fellow Tranio here, to save my life,
Puts my apparel and my countenance on,
225   And I for my escape have put on his:
For in a quarrel since I came ashore
I killed a man and fear I was descried.°   *observed*
Wait you on him, I charge you, as becomes,°   *is fitting*
While I make way from hence to save my life.
You understand me?
230 BIONDELLO   Ay, sir; ne'er a whit.°   *not at all*
LUCENTIO   And not a jot of "Tranio" in your mouth;
Tranio is changed into Lucentio.
BIONDELLO   The better for him; would I were so, too.
TRANIO   So could I, faith, boy, to have the next wish after,
235   That Lucentio indeed had Baptista's youngest daughter.
But, sirrah, not for my sake, but your master's, I advise
You use your manners discreetly in all kind of companies.
When I am alone, why, then I am Tranio,
But in all places else, your master Lucentio.

---

1. The outfit of an Elizabethan gentleman. Servants usually wore uniforms, like the "blue coats" of Petruccio's servants (4.1.76–77).
2. F does not indicate at what point in this exchange Lucentio and Tranio trade clothes; perhaps they begin during Lucentio's previous speech. This exchange of clothes, emphasizing the ease with which social identity is shifted, is an important visual enactment of one of the play's main preoccupations.
3. Wounded by Cupid's arrow.

240 LUCENTIO Tranio, let's go.
One thing more rests° that thyself execute:°   *remains / must do*
To make one among these wooers. If thou ask me why,
Sufficeth my reasons are both good and weighty.   *Exeunt.*
The Presenters[4] above speak.

SERVANT My lord, you nod; you do not mind° the play.   *pay attention to*
245 BEGGAR Yes, by Saint Anne,[5] do I, a good matter surely. Comes
there any more of it?

PAGE My lord, 'tis but begun.

BEGGAR 'Tis a very excellent piece of work, madam lady. Would
'twere done.
They sit and mark.°   *observe*

1.2

Enter PETRUCCIO *and his man* GRUMIO.

PETRUCCIO Verona, for a while I take my leave
To see my friends in Padua, but of all
My best belovèd and approvèd friend,
Hortensio. And I trow° this is his house.   *believe*
5 Here, sirrah Grumio, knock, I say.

GRUMIO Knock, sir? Whom should I knock? Is there any man
has rebused[1] your worship?

PETRUCCIO Villain, I say, knock me here[2] soundly.

GRUMIO Knock you here, sir? Why, sir, what am I, sir, that I
10 should knock you here, sir?

PETRUCCIO Villain, I say, knock me at this gate,
And rap me well or I'll knock your knave's pate.°   *head*

GRUMIO My master is grown quarrelsome. I should knock
you first,
And then I know after who comes by the worst.[3]

15 PETRUCCIO Will it not be?
Faith, sirrah, an° you'll not knock, I'll ring it.[4]   *if*
I'll try how you can *sol-fa*° and sing it.   *sing a scale*
He wrings him by the ears.

GRUMIO Help, masters, help! My master is mad.

PETRUCCIO Now knock when I bid you, sirrah villain.
Enter HORTENSIO.

20 HORTENSIO How now, what's the matter? My old friend
Grumio and my good friend Petruccio? How do you all at
Verona?

PETRUCCIO Signor Hortensio, come you to part the fray?
Con tutto il cuore ben trovato,[5] may I say.

25 HORTENSIO *Alla nostra casa ben venuto,*
Molto honorato signor mio Petruccio.[6]
Rise, Grumio, rise, we will compound° this quarrel.   *settle*

GRUMIO Nay, 'tis no matter, sir, what he 'lleges° in Latin. If   *alleges*
this be not a lawful cause for me to leave his service— Look

---

4. Figures who introduce and comment on the
action of a play for the audience.
5. A common oath. Saint Anne was the mother of
the Virgin Mary and the patron saint of married
women.
1.2 Location: In front of Hortensio's house in Padua.
1. Grumio regularly blunders and puns. Here he
means "abused" or "rebuked," or perhaps both.
2. Knock here for me: a conventional usage that Gru-

mio misunderstands or pretends to understand as
"strike me." *Villain:* low-born man (often a contemptuous term of address).
3. *I should . . . worst:* You want me to give the first
blow, but then I know I'd have the worst of it.
4. I'll ring the bell; with a pun on "wring."
5. With all my heart, welcome (Italian).
6. Welcome to our house, my most honored Signor
Petruccio.

30   you, sir: he bid me knock him and rap him soundly, sir.
       Well, was it fit for a servant to use his master so, being per-
       haps, for aught I see, two-and-thirty, a pip out?[7]
       Whom would to God I had well knocked at first,
       Then had not Grumio come by the worst.

35   PETRUCCIO   A senseless villain. Good Hortensio,
       I bade the rascal knock upon your gate
       And could not get him for my heart to do it.

    GRUMIO   Knock at the gate? O heavens, spoke you not these
       words plain? "Sirrah, knock me here, rap me here, knock me
40   well, and knock me soundly"? And come you now with
       knocking at the gate?

    PETRUCCIO   Sirrah, be gone, or talk not, I advise you.

    HORTENSIO   Petruccio, patience; I am Grumio's pledge.°   *guarantor*
       Why this' a heavy chance[8] twixt him and you,
45   Your ancient,° trusty, pleasant servant Grumio.   *long-standing*
       And tell me now, sweet friend, what happy gale
       Blows you to Padua here from old Verona?

    PETRUCCIO   Such wind as scatters young men through the
       world
       To seek their fortunes farther than at home,
50   Where small experience grows. But in a few,°   *in short*
       Signor Hortensio, thus it stands with me:
       Antonio, my father, is deceased,
       And I have thrust myself into this maze,[9]
       Haply to wive and thrive as best I may.
55   Crowns° in my purse I have, and goods at home,   *Five-shilling coins*
       And so am come abroad to see the world.

    HORTENSIO   Petruccio, shall I then come roundly° to thee   *speak plainly*
       And wish thee to a shrewd, ill-favored wife?
       Thou'dst thank me but a little for my counsel;
60   And yet I'll promise thee she shall be rich
       And very rich. But thou'rt too much my friend,
       And I'll not wish thee to her.

    PETRUCCIO   Signor Hortensio, twixt such friends as we,
       Few words suffice; and therefore if thou know
65   One rich enough to be Petruccio's wife—
       As wealth is burden° of my wooing dance—   *refrain; chief theme*
       Be she as foul° as was Florentius' love,[1]   *ugly*
       As old as Sibyl,[2] and as curst and shrewd
       As Socrates' Xanthippe,[3] or a worse,
70   She moves° me not, or not° removes, at least,°   *annoys / nor / at all*
       Affection's edge° in me, were she as rough   *intensity*
       As are the swelling Adriatic seas.
       I come to wive it wealthily in Padua;
       If wealthily, then happily in Padua.

7. Drunk; a bit crazy. Probably alluding to the card game one-and-thirty, in which the aim is to accumulate exactly thirty-one points. To collect thirty-two means the player has overshot or been excessive. A "pip" is a spot on a card; hence, "a pip out" means "off by one."
8. *Why . . . chance:* This is a sad occurrence.
9. This uncertain world; this unpredictable business of "wiving and thriving."
1. Florent, the knight in John Gower's *Confessio*

Amantis, who had to marry the ugly old woman who had saved his life by answering a riddle he had been commanded to solve. On their wedding night, as a reward for his compliance, she became young and beautiful. A version of this story also appears in Chaucer's *Wife of Bath's Tale.*
2. The Cumaean Sibyl, a prophetess in classical mythology, had immortality without eternal youth.
3. The philosopher's notoriously shrewish wife.

75 GRUMIO [*to* HORTENSIO]   Nay, look you, sir, he tells you flatly
what his mind is. Why, give him gold enough and marry him
to a puppet or an aglet-baby,[4] or an old trot° with ne'er a   *hag*
tooth in her head, though she have as many diseases as two
and fifty horses. Why, nothing comes amiss, so money comes
80 withal.°   *with it*
HORTENSIO   Petruccio, since we are stepped thus far in,
I will continue that° I broached in jest.   *what*
I can, Petruccio, help thee to a wife
With wealth enough, and young and beauteous,
85 Brought up as best becomes a gentlewoman.
Her only fault, and that is faults enough,
Is that she is intolerable curst°   *shrewish*
And shrewd and froward,° so beyond all measure   *willful*
That were my state° far worser than it is,   *fortune*
90 I would not wed her for a mine of gold.
PETRUCCIO   Hortensio, peace; thou know'st not gold's effect.
Tell me her father's name and 'tis enough,
For I will board[5] her, though she chide as loud
As thunder when the clouds in autumn crack.
95 HORTENSIO   Her father is Baptista Minola,
An affable° and courteous gentleman;   *pleasant*
Her name is Katherina Minola,
Renowned in Padua for her scolding tongue.
PETRUCCIO   I know her father, though I know not her,
100 And he knew my deceasèd father well.
I will not sleep, Hortensio, till I see her,
And therefore let me be thus bold with you
To give you over° at this first encounter—   *leave you*
Unless you will accompany me thither.
105 GRUMIO [*to* HORTENSIO]   I pray you, sir, let him go while the
humor° lasts. O'my word, an she knew him as well as I do,   *mood*
she would think scolding would do little good upon him.
She may perhaps call him half a score knaves or so. Why,
that's nothing; an he begin once, he'll rail in his rope tricks.[6]
110 I'll tell you what, sir, an she stand° him but a little, he will   *withstand; arouse*
throw a figure[7] in her face and so disfigure her with it that
she shall have no more eyes to see withal than a cat. You
know him not, sir.
HORTENSIO   Tarry, Petruccio, I must go with thee,
115 For in Baptista's keep° my treasure is.   *custody; stronghold*
He hath the jewel of my life in hold,
His youngest daughter, beautiful Bianca,
And her withholds from me and other more,°   *others besides*
Suitors to her and rivals in my love,
120 Supposing it a thing impossible,
For those defects I have before rehearsed,
That ever Katherina will be wooed.
Therefore this order hath Baptista ta'en:

---

4. Small figure used as a tag or an ornament on
dresses, laces, and other goods.
5. Woo aggressively; go aboard, as in a sea battle;
have sexual intercourse with.
6. An obscure phrase: "rope tricks" may refer to rhetorical or sexual feats. Grumio's point seems to be
that when Petruccio "rails," he will be more aggressive than Katherina.
7. A figure of speech.

That none shall have access unto Bianca
125 Till Katherine the Curst have got a husband.
GRUMIO   "Katherine the Curst,"
A title for a maid of all titles the worst.
HORTENSIO   Now shall my friend Petruccio do me grace°   *a favor*
And offer me disguised in sober robes
130 To old Baptista as a schoolmaster
Well seen° in music to instruct Bianca,   *skilled*
That so I may by this device at least
Have leave and leisure to make love to her
And unsuspected court her by herself.

Enter GREMIO [*with a paper*]⁸ *and* LUCENTIO *disguised*
[*as Cambio, a schoolmaster*].

135 GRUMIO   Here's no knavery!⁹ See, to beguile the old folks,
how the young folks lay their heads together. —Master,
master, look about you. Who goes there, ha?
HORTENSIO   Peace, Grumio, it is the rival of my love.
Petruccio, stand by a while.
140 GRUMIO   A proper stripling° and an amorous.   *handsome youth (ironic)*
[HORTENSIO, PETRUCCIO, *and* GRUMIO *stand aside*.]
GREMIO   Oh, very well, I have perused the note.°   *listing of books*
Hark you, sir, I'll have them° very fairly bound—   *(the books)*
All books of love, see that at any hand°—   *in any case*
And see you read no other lectures to her;
145 You understand me. Over and beside
Signor Baptista's liberality
I'll mend° it with a largesse.° Take your paper, too,   *increase / gift*
And let me have them very well perfumed,
For she is sweeter than perfume itself
150 To whom they go to. What will you read to her?
LUCENTIO   Whate'er I read to her, I'll plead for you
As for my patron, stand you so assured,
As firmly as yourself were still in place;°   *always present*
Yea, and perhaps with more successful words
155 Than you, unless you were a scholar, sir.
GREMIO   Oh, this learning, what a thing it is!
GRUMIO   Oh, this woodcock,¹ what an ass it is!
PETRUCCIO [*to* GRUMIO]   Peace, sirrah.
HORTENSIO   Grumio, mum. —God save you, Signor Gremio.
160 GREMIO   And you are well met, Signor Hortensio.
Trow° you whither I am going? To Baptista Minola.   *Know*
I promised to enquire carefully
About a schoolmaster for the fair Bianca,
And by good fortune I have lighted well
165 On this young man, for learning and behavior
Fit for her turn,° well-read in poetry   *use*
And other books, good ones, I warrant ye.
HORTENSIO   'Tis well. And I have met a gentleman
Hath promised me to help one to another,

8. Presumably Lucentio's list of books for Bianca's
studies.
9. Spoken sarcastically; perhaps referring to the
plotting of Petruccio and Hortensio rather than to

that of Gremio and Lucentio, whom Grumio may not
yet have seen.
1. Wild bird easily caught and so thought to be
stupid.

170 A fine musician to instruct our mistress;
So shall I no whit be behind in duty
To fair Bianca, so beloved of me.
GREMIO Beloved of me, and that my deeds shall prove.
GRUMIO And that his bags° shall prove.   *money bags*
175 HORTENSIO Gremio, 'tis now no time to vent° our love.   *express*
Listen to me and if you speak me fair,°   *courteously*
I'll tell you news indifferent° good for either.   *equally*
Here is a gentleman, whom by chance I met,
Upon agreement from us to his liking°   *If we accept his terms*
180 Will undertake to woo curst Katherine,
Yea, and to marry her, if her dowry please.
GREMIO So said, so done, is well.
Hortensio, have you told him all her faults?
PETRUCCIO I know she is an irksome brawling scold.
185 If that be all, masters, I hear no harm.
GREMIO No, say'st me so, friend? What countryman?
PETRUCCIO Born in Verona, old Antonio's son.
My father dead, my fortune lives for me,°   *is mine*
And I do hope good days and long to see.
190 GREMIO O sir, such a life with such a wife were strange.°   *unknown; rare*
But if you have a stomach, to't o'God's name;
You shall have me assisting you in all.
But will you woo this wildcat?
PETRUCCIO   Will I live?
GRUMIO Will he woo her? Ay, or I'll hang her.
195 PETRUCCIO Why came I hither but to that intent?
Think you a little din can daunt mine ears?
Have I not in my time heard lions roar?
Have I not heard the sea, puffed up with winds,
Rage like an angry boar chafed with sweat?
200 Have I not heard great ordnance° in the field,   *cannon*
And heaven's artillery thunder in the skies?
Have I not in a pitched battle heard
Loud larums,° neighing steeds, and trumpets clang?   *calls to arms*
And do you tell me of a woman's tongue
205 That gives not half so great a blow° to hear   *loud noise*
As will a chestnut in a farmer's fire?
Tush, tush, fear° boys with bugs.°   *frighten / bogeymen*
GRUMIO   For he fears none.
GREMIO Hortensio, hark:
This gentleman is happily° arrived,   *fortunately*
210 My mind presumes, for his own good and yours.
HORTENSIO I promised we would be contributors
And bear his charge° of wooing whatsoe'er.   *expense*
GREMIO And so we will, provided that he win her.
GRUMIO I would I were as sure of a good dinner.
Enter TRANIO, *brave*°[, *as Lucentio*], *and* BIONDELLO.   *richly dressed*
215 TRANIO Gentlemen, God save you. If I may be bold,
Tell me, I beseech you, which is the readiest way
To the house of Signor Baptista Minola?
BIONDELLO He that has the two fair daughters: is't he you
mean?
220 TRANIO Even he, Biondello.
GREMIO Hark you, sir, you mean not her to—

TRANIO   Perhaps him and her, sir; what have you to do?[2]
PETRUCCIO   Not her that chides, sir, at any hand, I pray.
TRANIO   I love no chiders, sir. Biondello, let's away.
LUCENTIO [aside]   Well begun, Tranio.
225 HORTENSIO   Sir, a word ere you go:
         Are you a suitor to the maid you talk of, yea or no?
TRANIO   An if I be, sir, is it any offense?
GREMIO   No, if without more words you will get you hence.
TRANIO   Why, sir, I pray, are not the streets as free
         For me as for you?
230 GREMIO   But so is not she.
TRANIO   For what reason, I beseech you.
GREMIO   For this reason, if you'll know:
         That she's the choice° love of Signor Gremio.   chosen; excellent
HORTENSIO   That she's the chosen of Signor Hortensio.
235 TRANIO   Softly, my masters. If you be gentlemen
         Do me this right:° hear me with patience.   justice
         Baptista is a noble gentleman
         To whom my father is not all unknown,
         And were his daughter fairer than she is,
240   She may more suitors have, and me for one.
         Fair Leda's daughter[3] had a thousand wooers;
         Then well one more may fair Bianca have.
         And so she shall: Lucentio shall make one,
         Though Paris came[4] in hope to speed° alone.   succeed
245 GREMIO   What, this gentleman will out-talk us all.
LUCENTIO   Sir, give him head; I know he'll prove a jade.°   worn-out horse
PETRUCCIO   Hortensio, to what end are all these words?
HORTENSIO   Sir, let me be so bold as ask you:
         Did you yet ever see Baptista's daughter?
250 TRANIO   No, sir, but hear I do that he hath two:
         The one as famous for a scolding tongue
         As is the other for beauteous modesty.
PETRUCCIO   Sir, sir, the first's for me, let her go by.
GREMIO   Yea, leave that labor to great Hercules,
255   And let it be more than Alcides' twelve.[5]
PETRUCCIO   Sir, understand you this of me, in sooth:°   truth
         The youngest daughter, whom you hearken° for,   lie in wait; yearn
         Her father keeps from all access of suitors
         And will not promise her to any man
260   Until the elder sister first be wed.
         The younger then is free and not before.
TRANIO   If it be so, sir, that you are the man
         Must stead° us all, and me amongst the rest,   help
         An if you break the ice, and do this feat—
265   Achieve° the elder, set the younger free   Win
         For our access—whose hap shall be° to have her   he who is lucky enough
         Will not so graceless be, to be ingrate.°   ungrateful
HORTENSIO   Sir, you say well, and well you do conceive.°   understand
         And since you do profess to be a suitor,

2. What business is it of yours?
3. Helen of Troy. In Marlowe's *Doctor Faustus,* her face is said to have "launched a thousand ships."
4. Even if Paris (who stole Helen of Troy from her husband) were to come.

5. Hercules, the hero of classical mythology who successfully performed twelve seemingly impossible tasks ("labors"), was also called Alcides (descendant of Alcaeus).

270 You must as we do, gratify° this gentleman,   *reward*
To whom we all rest generally beholden.
TRANIO   Sir, I shall not be slack. In sign whereof,
Please ye we may contrive° this afternoon   *pass, spend (time)*
And quaff carouses° to our mistress' health,   *toasts*
275 And do as adversaries do in law:
Strive mightily, but eat and drink as friends.
GRUMIO, BIONDELLO   Oh, excellent motion!° Fellows, let's be   *proposal*
gone.
HORTENSIO   The motion's good indeed, and be it so.
Petruccio, I shall be your *ben venuto*.°   *Exeunt.*   *welcome (your host)*

2.1

Enter KATHERINA *and* BIANCA [*with her hands tied*].
BIANCA   Good sister, wrong me not, nor wrong yourself
To make a bondmaid° and a slave of me—   *female servant*
That I disdain. But for these other goods,°   *possessions*
Unbind my hands. I'll pull them off myself,
5 Yea, all my raiment to my petticoat,
Or what you will command me will I do,
So well I know my duty to my elders.
KATHERINA   Of all thy suitors here I charge° tell   *command you*
Whom thou lov'st best. See thou dissemble° not.   *deceive*
10 BIANCA   Believe me, sister, of all the men alive,
I never yet beheld that special face
Which I could fancy more than any other.
KATHERINA   Minion,° thou liest. Is't not Hortensio?   *Hussy*
BIANCA   If you affect° him, sister, here I swear   *love*
15 I'll plead for you myself, but you shall have him.
KATHERINA   Oh, then belike you fancy riches more:
You will have Gremio to keep you fair.
BIANCA   Is it for him you do envy me so?
Nay, then, you jest, and now I well perceive
20 You have but jested with me all this while.
I prithee, sister Kate, untie my hands.
[KATHERINA] *strikes her.*
KATHERINA   If that be jest, then all the rest was so.
Enter BAPTISTA.
BAPTISTA   Why, how now, dame, whence grows this insolence?
Bianca, stand aside; poor girl, she weeps.
25 Go ply thy needle, meddle not with her.
[*to* KATHERINA] For shame, thou hilding° of a devilish spirit,   *worthless creature*
Why dost thou wrong her, that did ne'er wrong thee?
When did she cross thee with a bitter word?
KATHERINA   Her silence flouts° me, and I'll be revenged.   *mocks*
[*She*] *flies after* BIANCA.
30 BAPTISTA   What, in my sight? —Bianca, get thee in.
Exit [BIANCA].
KATHERINA   What, will you not suffer me?° Nay, now I see   *let me have my way*
She is your treasure: she must have a husband,
I must dance barefoot on her wedding day[1]
And, for your love to her, lead apes in hell.[2]

2.1 Location: Baptista's house in Padua.
1. Proverbially expected of older unmarried sisters.
2. *lead apes in hell:* the proverbial destiny of unmarried women.

35 Talk not to me. I will go sit and weep
Till I can find occasion of revenge.   [*Exit* KATHERINA.]
BAPTISTA Was ever gentleman thus grieved as I?
But who comes here?
   Enter GREMIO; LUCENTIO [*disguised as Cambio*] *in the*
   habit of a mean man;° PETRUCCIO *with* [HORTENSIO   *man of low social rank*
   disguised as Licio; and] TRANIO [*disguised as Lucentio*]
   with his boy [BIONDELLO] *bearing a lute and books.*
GREMIO Good morrow, neighbor Baptista.
40 BAPTISTA Good morrow, neighbor Gremio. —God save you,
gentlemen.
PETRUCCIO And you, good sir. Pray, have you not a daughter
Called Katherina, fair and virtuous?
BAPTISTA I have a daughter, sir, called Katherina.
45 GREMIO [*to* PETRUCCIO] You are too blunt; go to it orderly.°   *properly*
PETRUCCIO You wrong me, Signor Gremio; give me leave.
—I am a gentleman of Verona, sir,
That, hearing of her beauty and her wit,
Her affability and bashful modesty,
50 Her wondrous qualities and mild behavior,
Am bold to show myself a forward° guest   *eager*
Within your house to make mine eye the witness
Of that report, which I so oft have heard.
And for an entrance to my entertainment[3]
55 I do present you with a man of mine,
Cunning in music and the mathematics,
To instruct her fully in those sciences,
Whereof I know she is not ignorant.
Accept of him, or else you do me wrong.
60 His name is Licio, born in Mantua.
BAPTISTA You're welcome, sir, and he for your good sake.
But for my daughter Katherine, this I know:
She is not for your turn,° the more my grief.   *She will not suit you*
PETRUCCIO I see you do not mean to part with her,
65 Or else you like not of my company.
BAPTISTA Mistake me not, I speak but as I find.°   *as the facts stand*
Whence are you, sir? What may I call your name?
PETRUCCIO Petruccio is my name, Antonio's son,
A man well known throughout all Italy.
70 BAPTISTA I know him well;[4] you are welcome for his sake.
GREMIO Saving° your tale, Petruccio, I pray let us that are   *With all respect to*
poor petitioners speak too. *Baccare*,° you are marvelous *Stand back (mock Latin)*
forward.
PETRUCCIO Oh, pardon me, Signor Gremio; I would fain be
75 doing.[5]
GREMIO I doubt it not, sir. But you will curse your wooing
neighbors. [*to* BAPTISTA] This is a gift[6] very grateful,° I am   *pleasing*
sure of it. To express the like kindness, myself, that have
been more kindly beholden to you than any, freely give unto
80 you this young scholar, that hath been long studying at
Rheims,[7] as cunning in Greek, Latin, and other languages

---

3. And as an entrance fee for my reception ("entertainment") as a suitor.
4. Baptista probably means he knows him by
reputation.

5. I am eager to get on with it (with a pun on "doing"
as meaning "have sexual intercourse").
6. That is, Petruccio's gift of Hortensio/Licio.
7. French city famous for its university.

as the other in music and mathematics. His name is Cambio;[8] pray accept his service.

BAPTISTA   A thousand thanks, Signor Gremio. Welcome, good
85   Cambio. [to TRANIO] But, gentle sir, methinks you walk like
a stranger. May I be so bold to know the cause of your
coming?

TRANIO   Pardon me, sir, the boldness is mine own,
That, being a stranger in this city here,
90   Do make myself a suitor to your daughter,
Unto Bianca, fair and virtuous.
Nor is your firm resolve unknown to me,
In the preferment of the eldest sister.
This liberty is all that I request:
95   That upon knowledge of my parentage,
I may have welcome 'mongst the rest that woo
And free access and favor as the rest.
And toward the education of your daughters,
I here bestow a simple instrument
100   And this small packet of Greek and Latin books.
If you accept them, then their worth is great.

BAPTISTA   Lucentio is your name;[9] of whence, I pray?

TRANIO   Of Pisa, sir, son to Vincentio.

BAPTISTA   A mighty man of Pisa; by report
105   I know him well. You are very welcome, sir.
[to HORTENSIO] Take you the lute [to LUCENTIO] and you the
set of books;
You shall go see your pupils presently.°   *immediately*
Holla, within!

        Enter a SERVANT.

            Sirrah, lead these gentlemen
To my daughters, and tell them both
110   These are their tutors; bid them use them well.

        [*Exit* SERVANT *with* HORTENSIO *and* LUCENTIO.]
We will go walk a little in the orchard°   *garden*
And then to dinner. You are passing° welcome,   *extremely*
And so I pray you all to think yourselves.

PETRUCCIO   Signor Baptista, my business asketh haste,
115   And every day I cannot come to woo.
You knew my father well and in him me,
Left solely heir to all his lands and goods,
Which I have bettered rather than decreased.
Then tell me, if I get your daughter's love,
120   What dowry shall I have with her to wife?

BAPTISTA   After my death, the one half of my lands,
And in possession° twenty thousand crowns.   *upon the marriage*

PETRUCCIO   And for that dowry I'll assure her of
Her widowhood,[1] be it that she survive me,
125   In all my lands and leases whatsoever.
Let specialties° be therefore drawn between us,   *explicit contracts*
That covenants may be kept on either hand.

BAPTISTA   Ay, when the special thing is well obtained—
That is her love, for that is all in all.

---

8. Italian for "exchange."   the name in one of the schoolbooks.
9. How Baptista knows this is unclear. He may read   1. Widow's share of the estate.

130 PETRUCCIO   Why, that is nothing. For I tell you, father,
　　　I am as peremptory° as she proud minded,　　　　　　　　　　*stubborn*
　　　And where two raging fires meet together
　　　They do consume the thing that feeds their fury.
　　　Though little fire grows great with little wind,
135　　Yet extreme gusts will blow out fire and all.²
　　　So I to her and so she yields to me,
　　　For I am rough and woo not like a babe.
　　BAPTISTA   Well mayst thou woo, and happy be thy speed;°　　　*fortune*
　　　But be thou armed for some unhappy words.
140 PETRUCCIO   Ay, to the proof,³ as mountains are for winds,
　　　That shakes not though they blow perpetually.
　　　　　Enter HORTENSIO [*disguised as Licio*] *with his*
　　　　　head broke.
　　BAPTISTA   How now, my friend, why dost thou look so pale?
　　HORTENSIO   For fear, I promise you, if I look pale.
　　BAPTISTA   What, will my daughter prove a good musician?
145 HORTENSIO   I think she'll sooner prove a soldier.
　　　Iron may hold with° her, but never lutes.　　　　　　　　　　*withstand*
　　BAPTISTA   Why, then, thou canst not break° her to the lute?　　*train*
　　HORTENSIO   Why, no, for she hath broke the lute to me.
　　　I did but tell her she mistook her frets⁴
150　And bowed° her hand to teach her fingering,　　　　　　　　　*bent*
　　　When, with a most impatient devilish spirit,
　　　"Frets,⁵ call you these?" quoth she. "I'll fume° with them."　*be in a rage*
　　　And with that word she struck me on the head,
　　　And through the instrument my pate made way,
155　And there I stood amazèd for a while,
　　　As on a pillory,⁶ looking through the lute,
　　　While she did call me rascal, fiddler,
　　　And twangling Jack,° with twenty such vile terms,　　　　　　*knave*
　　　As° had she studied to misuse me so.　　　　　　　　　　　　*As if*
160 PETRUCCIO   Now by the world, it is a lusty° wench.　　　　　　*lively*
　　　I love her ten times more than e'er I did.
　　　Oh, how I long to have some chat with her.
　　BAPTISTA [*to* HORTENSIO]   Well, go with me and be not so
　　　　discomfited.
　　　Proceed in practice° with my younger daughter;　　*Continue your lessons*
165　She's apt to learn and thankful for good turns.
　　　Signor Petruccio, will you go with us,
　　　Or shall I send my daughter Kate to you?
　　PETRUCCIO   I pray you do.　　　*Exeunt all but* PETRUCCIO.
　　　　　　　　　　　I'll attend° her here　　　　　　　　　　　*await*
　　　And woo her with some spirit when she comes.
170　Say that she rail, why, then I'll tell her plain
　　　She sings as sweetly as a nightingale.
　　　Say that she frown, I'll say she looks as clear
　　　As morning roses newly washed with dew.
　　　Say she be mute and will not speak a word,

2. Implying that those who have opposed Katherina
so far have been too weak ("little wind") and that he
will subdue her with his "extreme gusts."
3. In impenetrable armor. Proof armor was tested for
its strength.
4. Placed her fingers upon the wrong bars ("frets")
on the lute's fingerboard.
5. Katherina plays on "frets" as also meaning "annoy-
ances" or "vexations."
6. An instrument of public punishment in which the
offender's head and hands were fastened in wooden
clamps.

175	Then I'll commend her volubility	
	And say she uttereth piercing° eloquence.	*moving*
	If she do bid me pack,° I'll give her thanks,	*go away*
	As though she bid me stay by her a week.	
	If she deny to wed, I'll crave° the day	*beg to know*
180	When I shall ask the banns[7] and when be married.	
	But here she comes, and now, Petruccio, speak.	

     Enter KATHERINA.

	Good morrow, Kate, for that's your name, I hear.	
	KATHERINA Well have you heard, but something° hard of	*somewhat*
	hearing:	
	They call me Katherine that do talk of me.	
185	PETRUCCIO You lie, in faith, for you are called plain Kate,	
	And bonny° Kate, and sometimes Kate the curst.	*comely*
	But Kate, the prettiest Kate in Christendom,	
	Kate of Kate Hall,[8] my super dainty Kate—	
	For dainties are all cates[9]—and therefore, Kate,	
190	Take this of me, Kate of my consolation:	
	Hearing thy mildness praised in every town,	
	Thy virtues spoke of and thy beauty sounded,[1]	
	Yet not so deeply as to thee belongs,	
	Myself am moved to woo thee for my wife.	
195	KATHERINA Moved, in good time.° Let him that moved you	*indeed*
	hither	
	Remove you hence. I knew you at the first	
	You were a movable.[2]	
	PETRUCCIO Why, what's a movable?	
	KATHERINA A joint-stool.[3]	
	PETRUCCIO Thou hast hit it: come, sit on me.	
	KATHERINA Asses are made to bear[4] and so are you.	
200	PETRUCCIO Women are made to bear and so are you.	
	KATHERINA No such jade° as you, if me you mean.	*worn-out horse*
	PETRUCCIO Alas, good Kate, I will not burden[5] thee,	
	For knowing° thee to be but young and light.[6]	*Because I know*
	KATHERINA Too light° for such a swain° as you to catch,	*quick / bumpkin*
205	And yet as heavy as my weight should be.[7]	
	PETRUCCIO "Should be"? Should—buzz.[8]	
	KATHERINA Well ta'en, and like a buzzard.[9]	
	PETRUCCIO O slow-winged turtle,° shall a buzzard take thee?	*turtledove*
	KATHERINA Ay, for a turtle, as he takes a buzzard.[1]	
	PETRUCCIO Come, come, you wasp, i'faith you are too angry.	
210	KATHERINA If I be waspish, best beware my sting.	

---

7. Have the banns read. Banns were required announcements in church of a forthcoming wedding.
8. Either an obscure allusion or an ironic reference to Katherina's home as a place that is famous because she lives there.
9. For delicacies ("dainties") are called "cates."
1. Proclaimed; tested for depth.
2. Piece of furniture; changeable person.
3. Wooden stool made by a joiner.
4. Carry loads; bear children; bear the weight of a lover.
5. Lie on you in sexual intercourse; make you pregnant; make accusations against you; accompany you with a musical refrain, or "burden."
6. Not heavy; wanton; lacking a musical accompa-

niment.
7. She is claiming social prominence ("weight") and refusing the implication that she is wanton ("light") or like a coin that has been clipped so that it is lighter than it should be.
8. Punning on "be" and "bee," Petruccio suggests Katherina should make a buzzing sound.
9. A hawk that cannot be trained to "take," or capture, prey; a fool.
1. Obscure line probably meaning that if a fool ("buzzard") mistakes me for a faithful love ("turtledove"), he'll be making as big a mistake as the turtledove makes when it captures a buzzing insect (another meaning of "buzzard").

	PETRUCCIO	My remedy is then to pluck it out.	
	KATHERINA	Ay, if the fool could find it where it lies.	
	PETRUCCIO	Who knows not where a wasp does wear his sting?	
		In his tail.	
	KATHERINA	In his tongue.	
	PETRUCCIO	Whose tongue?	
215	KATHERINA	Yours, if you talk of tales,° and so farewell.	*gossip; genitals*
	PETRUCCIO	What, with my tongue in your tail?	
		Nay, come again, good Kate, I am a gentleman—	
	KATHERINA	That I'll try.°	*test*

She strikes him.

	PETRUCCIO	I swear I'll cuff you if you strike again.	
220	KATHERINA	So may you lose your arms.[2]	
		If you strike me, you are no gentleman,	
		And if no gentleman, why, then, no arms.	
	PETRUCCIO	A herald,° Kate? Oh, put me in thy books.[3]	*An authority on heraldry*
	KATHERINA	What is your crest,[4] a coxcomb?[5]	
225	PETRUCCIO	A combless cock,[6] so Kate will be my hen.	
	KATHERINA	No cock of mine; you crow too like a craven.°	*cock that won't fight*
	PETRUCCIO	Nay, come, Kate, come. You must not look so sour.	
	KATHERINA	It is my fashion when I see a crab.°	*crab apple; sour person*
	PETRUCCIO	Why, here's no crab, and therefore look not sour.	
230	KATHERINA	There is, there is.	
	PETRUCCIO	Then show it me.	
	KATHERINA	Had I a glass,° I would.	*mirror*
	PETRUCCIO	What, you mean my face?	
	KATHERINA	Well aimed° of such a young one.	*A good guess*
235	PETRUCCIO	Now, by Saint George,° I am too young for you.	*England's patron saint*
	KATHERINA	Yet you are withered.	
	PETRUCCIO	'Tis with cares.	
	KATHERINA	I care not.	
	PETRUCCIO	Nay, hear you, Kate. In sooth you scape° not so.	*escape*
	KATHERINA	I chafe° you if I tarry. Let me go.	*annoy; inflame*
	PETRUCCIO	No, not a whit; I find you passing gentle.	
240		'Twas told me you were rough and coy° and sullen,	*disdainful*
		And now I find report a very liar,	
		For thou art pleasant, gamesome,° passing° courteous,	*playful / very*
		But slow in speech, yet sweet as springtime flowers.	
		Thou canst not frown, thou canst not look askance,°	*scornfully*
245		Nor bite the lip, as angry wenches will,	
		Nor hast thou pleasure to be cross in talk;	
		But thou with mildness entertain'st thy wooers	
		With gentle conference,° soft and affable.	*conversation*
		Why does the world report that Kate doth limp?	
250		Oh, sland'rous world! Kate, like the hazel twig,	
		Is straight and slender and as brown in hue	
		As hazelnuts, and sweeter than the kernels.	
		Oh, let me see thee walk: thou dost not halt.°	*limp*
	KATHERINA	Go, fool, and whom thou keep'st command.[7]	

2. Lose your claim to a coat of arms (sign of noble status); loosen your grip on me.
3. Heralds kept books listing gentlemen and their coats of arms.
4. Image on a coat of arms; a fleshy ridge or comb on a rooster's head.
5. Court fool's cap (resembling a cock's comb or crest).
6. A cock with its comb cut down (and thought, therefore, to be gentle), with a pun on "cock" as "penis."
7. And command your servants (not me).

255 PETRUCCIO   Did ever Dian[8] so become a grove
    As Kate this chamber with her princely gait?
    Oh, be thou Dian, and let her be Kate,
    And then let Kate be chaste and Dian sportful.°   *playful; amorous*
    KATHERINA   Where did you study all this goodly speech?
260 PETRUCCIO   It is *extempore*, from my mother wit.°   *native intelligence*
    KATHERINA   A witty mother, witless else° her son.   *otherwise*
    PETRUCCIO   Am I not wise?
    KATHERINA   Yes, keep you warm.[9]
    PETRUCCIO   Marry, so I mean, sweet Katherine, in thy bed.
265 And therefore setting all this chat aside,
    Thus in plain terms: your father hath consented
    That you shall be my wife, your dowry 'greed on,
    And will you, nill you,° I will marry you.   *if you will or not*
    Now, Kate, I am a husband for your turn,°   *needs*
270 For by this light, whereby I see thy beauty—
    Thy beauty that doth make me like thee well—
    Thou must be married to no man but me,

        Enter BAPTISTA, GREMIO, [*and*] TRANIO [*disguised*
        as Lucentio].

    For I am he am born to tame you, Kate,
    And bring you from a wild Kate° to a Kate   *(punning on "wildcat")*
275 Conformable° as other household Kates.   *Submissive*
    Here comes your father. Never make denial;
    I must and will have Katherine to my wife.
    BAPTISTA   Now, Signor Petruccio, how speed you with my
    daughter?
280 PETRUCCIO   How but well, sir, how but well?
    It were impossible I should speed amiss.
    BAPTISTA   Why, how now, daughter Katherine, in your dumps?°   *dejected*
    KATHERINA   Call you me daughter? Now I promise you
    You have showed a tender fatherly regard,
285 To wish me wed to one half-lunatic,
    A madcap ruffian and a swearing Jack,
    That thinks with oaths to face the matter out.°   *get his way brazenly*
    PETRUCCIO   Father, 'tis thus: yourself and all the world
    That talked of her have talked amiss of her.
290 If she be curst, it is for policy,°   *part of a scheme*
    For she's not froward,° but modest as the dove.   *willful*
    She is not hot, but temperate as the morn.
    For patience she will prove a second Grissel,[1]
    And Roman Lucrece[2] for her chastity.
295 And to conclude, we have 'greed so well together
    That upon Sunday is the wedding day.
    KATHERINA   I'll see thee hanged on Sunday first.
    GREMIO   Hark, Petruccio, she says she'll see thee hanged first.
    TRANIO   Is this your speeding?° Nay, then, goodnight our part.[3]   *progress*
300 PETRUCCIO   Be patient, gentlemen. I choose her for myself.

---

8. Goddess of the hunt and of chastity.
9. Alluding to the proverbial phrase "enough wit to keep oneself warm," implying that the person has few brains.
1. Griselda, proverbial for "wifely patience." Chau-

cer's *Clerk's Tale* offers one version of her story.
2. In Roman legend, a married woman who killed herself after being raped by Tarquin. Shakespeare's *Rape of Lucrece* recounts the story.
3. Good-bye to our chances (of gaining Bianca).

If she and I be pleased, what's that to you?
'Tis bargained twixt us twain, being alone,
That she shall still be curst in company.
I tell you, 'tis incredible to believe
305 How much she loves me. Oh, the kindest Kate!
She hung about my neck, and kiss on kiss
She vied° so fast, protesting oath on oath,   went me one better
That in a twink° she won me to her love.   instant
Oh, you are novices. 'Tis a world° to see   worth a world
310 How tame, when men and women are alone,
A meacock° wretch can make the curstest shrew.   timid
—Give me thy hand, Kate. I will unto Venice
To buy apparel 'gainst° the wedding day.   in preparation for
—Provide the feast, father, and bid the guests;
315 I will be sure my Katherine shall be fine.°   richly dressed
BAPTISTA   I know not what to say, but give me your hands.
God send you joy, Petruccio, 'tis a match.
GREMIO and TRANIO   Amen, say we; we will be witnesses.
PETRUCCIO   Father and wife and gentlemen, adieu.
320 I will to Venice; Sunday comes apace.
We will have rings and things and fine array,
And kiss me, Kate. "We will be married o'Sunday."
                    Exeunt PETRUCCIO and KATHERINA.
GREMIO   Was ever match clapped up° so suddenly?   settled
BAPTISTA   Faith, gentlemen, now I play a merchant's part
325 And venture madly on a desperate mart.°   risky bargain
TRANIO   'Twas a commodity lay fretting by you;[4]
'Twill bring you gain or perish on the seas.
BAPTISTA   The gain I seek is quiet in the match.
GREMIO   No doubt but he hath got a quiet catch.
330 But now, Baptista, to your younger daughter.
Now is the day we long have looked for;
I am your neighbor and was suitor first.
TRANIO   And I am one that love Bianca more
Than words can witness or your thoughts can guess.
335 GREMIO   Youngling, thou canst not love so dear° as I.   deeply; expensively
TRANIO   Graybeard, thy love doth freeze.
GREMIO   But thine doth fry.
Skipper,° stand back; 'tis age that nourisheth.   Irresponsible youth
TRANIO   But youth in ladies' eyes that flourisheth.
BAPTISTA   Content you, gentlemen, I will compound° this   settle
    strife.
340 'Tis deeds must win the prize, and he of both°   whichever of you
That can assure my daughter greatest dower
Shall have my Bianca's love.
Say, Signor Gremio, what can you assure her?
GREMIO   First, as you know, my house within the city
345 Is richly furnished with plate and gold,
Basins and ewers to lave° her dainty hands,   wash
My hangings all of Tyrian[5] tapestry.

4. It (that is, Katherina) was a piece of merchandise
deteriorating in value or a sexually available woman
fretting with irritation while in your possession.

5. Crimson or purple. (The Mediterranean city of
Tyre was famous for dye of this color.)

In ivory coffers I have stuffed my crowns;°   *coins*
In cypress chests my arras counterpoints,°   *tapestry bedcovers*
350   Costly apparel, tents,° and canopies,   *bed curtains*
      Fine linen, Turkey cushions bossed° with pearl,   *embossed*
      Valance° of Venice gold in needlework,   *Fringe on bed drapery*
      Pewter and brass, and all things that belongs
      To house or housekeeping. Then at my farm
355   I have a hundred milch kine° to the pail,   *dairy cows*
      Sixscore fat oxen standing in my stalls,
      And all things answerable to° this portion.   *on the same scale as*
      Myself am struck° in years, I must confess,   *advanced*
      And if I die tomorrow this is hers,
360   If whilst I live she will be only mine.
     TRANIO   That only came well in. Sir, list to me:
      I am my father's heir and only son.
      If I may have your daughter to my wife,
      I'll leave her houses three or four as good
365   Within rich Pisa walls as any one
      Old Signor Gremio has in Padua,
      Besides two thousand ducats by the year
      Of fruitful land,[6] all which shall be her jointure.°   *marriage settlement*
      —What, have I pinched° you, Signor Gremio?   *distressed*
370   GREMIO [*aside*]   Two thousand ducats by the year of land?
      My land amounts not to so much in all.
      —That she shall have, besides an argosy°   *a merchant ship*
      That now is lying in Marseilles' road.°   *harbor*
      —What, have I choked you with an argosy?
375   TRANIO   Gremio, 'tis known my father hath no less
      Than three great argosies, besides two galliasses°   *large cargo ships*
      And twelve tight° galleys: these I will assure her   *watertight*
      And twice as much, whate'er thou offer'st next.
     GREMIO   Nay, I have offered all; I have no more,
380   And she can have no more than all I have.
      [*to* BAPTISTA] If you like me, she shall have me and mine.
     TRANIO   Why, then the maid is mine from all the world
      By your firm promise: Gremio is outvied.°   *outbid*
     BAPTISTA   I must confess your offer is the best,
385   And let° your father make her the assurance,   *provided*
      She is your own. Else, you must pardon me,
      If you should die before him, where's her dower?
     TRANIO   That's but a cavil:° he is old, I young.   *frivolous objection*
     GREMIO   And may not young men die as well as old?
390   BAPTISTA   Well, gentlemen, I am thus resolved:
      On Sunday next you know
      My daughter Katherine is to be married.
      [*to* TRANIO] Now on the Sunday following shall Bianca
      Be bride to you, if you make this assurance;
395   If not, to Signor Gremio.
      And so I take my leave and thank you both.   *Exit.*
     GREMIO   Adieu, good neighbor. —Now I fear thee not.
      Sirrah, young gamester, your father were a fool

---

6. *Besides . . . land:* As well as fertile land that brings in an income of 2,000 ducats (Venetian gold coins) each year.

To give thee all and in his waning age
400 Set foot under thy table.[7] Tut, a toy!°   *nonsense*
An old Italian fox is not so kind, my boy.   *Exit.*
TRANIO   A vengeance on your crafty withered hide!
Yet I have faced it with a card of ten.[8]
'Tis in my head to do my master good:
405 I see no reason° but supposed Lucentio   *possible action*
Must get° a father called supposed Vincentio.   *beget; obtain*
And that's a wonder: fathers commonly
Do get their children, but in this case of wooing,
A child shall get a sire, if I fail not of my cunning.   *Exit.*

3.1

Enter LUCENTIO [*disguised as Cambio*], HORTENSIO
[*disguised as Licio*], *and* BIANCA.

LUCENTIO   Fiddler, forbear.° You grow too forward, sir.   *desist*
Have you so soon forgot the entertainment
Her sister Katherine welcomed you withal?°   *with*
HORTENSIO   But, wrangling pedant, this is
5 The patroness of heavenly harmony.
Then give me leave to have prerogative,°   *precedence*
And when in music we have spent an hour,
Your lecture° shall have leisure for as much.   *lesson*
LUCENTIO   Preposterous[1] ass, that never read so far
10 To know the cause why music was ordained!°   *ordered; appointed*
Was it not to refresh the mind of man
After his studies or his usual pain?°   *labor*
Then give me leave to read philosophy
And while I pause, serve in° your harmony.   *serve up (contemptuous)*
15 HORTENSIO   Sirrah, I will not bear these braves° of thine.   *insults*
BIANCA   Why, gentlemen, you do me double wrong
To strive for that which resteth in my choice.
I am no breeching[2] scholar in the schools:
I'll not be tied to hours nor 'pointed times,
20 But learn my lessons as I please myself.
And to cut off all strife: here sit we down,
[*to* HORTENSIO] Take you your instrument, play you the
whiles;°   *in the meantime*
His lecture will be done ere you have tuned.
HORTENSIO   You'll leave his lecture when I am in tune?[3]
25 LUCENTIO   That will be never; tune your instrument.
BIANCA   Where left we last?
LUCENTIO   Here, madam:
[*He reads.*]   "*Hic ibat Simois, hic est Sigeia tellus,*
Hic steterat Priami regia celsa senis."[4]
30 BIANCA   Construe them.°   *Translate the lines*

---

7. Become your dependent.
8. I have bluffed and won with a card of little value
(a ten spot).
3.1 Location: Baptista's house in Padua.
1. Literally, putting last what should come first;
reversing the natural order of things.
2. Youthful (in breeches); liable to be whipped
(breeched).

3. When my lute is in the proper pitch. Lucentio
responds with a pun on "in tune" as meaning "in harmony" with Bianca.
4. Latin lines from Penelope's letter to her husband,
Ulysses, in Ovid's *Heroides*: "Here flowed the Simois;
here is the Sigeian land; here stood old Priam's lofty
palace."

LUCENTIO *Hic ibat*, as I told you before; *Simois*, I am Lucentio; *hic est*, son unto Vincentio of Pisa; *Sigeia tellus*, disguised thus to get your love; *hic steterat*, and that Lucentio
that comes a-wooing; *Priami*, is my man Tranio; *regia*, bear-
35   ing my port;° *celsa senis*, that we might beguile the old   *taking my social place*
pantaloon.°   *foolish old man*

HORTENSIO Madam, my instrument's in tune.

BIANCA Let's hear. Oh, fie, the treble jars.°   *is discordant*

LUCENTIO Spit in the hole,[5] man, and tune again.

40   BIANCA [*to* LUCENTIO] Now let me see if I can construe it. *Hic
ibat Simois*, I know you not; *hic est Sigeia tellus*, I trust you
not; *hic staterat Priami*, take heed he hear us not; *regia*, presume not; *celsa senis*, despair not.

HORTENSIO Madam, 'tis now in tune.

LUCENTIO   All but the base.

45   HORTENSIO The base is right; 'tis the base knave that jars.
[*aside*] How fiery and forward our pedant is.
Now for my life, the knave doth court my love.
Pedascule,° I'll watch you better yet.   *Little pedant*

BIANCA [*to* LUCENTIO] In time I may believe, yet I mistrust.

50   LUCENTIO Mistrust it not, for sure Aeacides[6]
Was Ajax, called so from his grandfather.

BIANCA I must believe my master, else I promise you
I should be arguing still upon that doubt.
But let it rest. —Now, Licio, to you:
55   Good master, take it not unkindly, pray,
That I have been thus pleasant with you both.

HORTENSIO [*to* LUCENTIO] You may go walk and give me leave°   *allow me leisure*
a while.
My lessons make no music in three parts.°   *for three voices*

LUCENTIO Are you so formal,° sir? Well, I must wait.   *precise*
60   [*aside*] And watch withal, for, but° I be deceived,   *unless*
Our fine musician groweth amorous.

HORTENSIO Madam, before you touch the instrument,
To learn the order of my fingering,
I must begin with rudiments of art,
65   To teach you gamut[7] in a briefer sort,°   *quicker way*
More pleasant, pithy, and effectual
Than hath been taught by any of my trade;
And there it is in writing, fairly drawn.

BIANCA Why, I am past my gamut long ago.

70   HORTENSIO Yet read the gamut of Hortensio.

BIANCA [*reading*] "Gamut I am, the ground° of all accord: *lowest note; basis*
  A *re*, to plead Hortensio's passion;
  B *mi*, Bianca, take him for thy lord;
  C *fa*, *ut*, that loves with all affection;
75   D *sol*, *re*, one clef, two notes[8] have I;
  E *la*, *mi*, show pity or I die."

---

5. Moisten the lute's peg hole (to aid tuning). Lucentio speaks contemptuously and may not be giving
serious advice.
6. Aeacides, or Ajax, was named after his grandfather Aeacus. Lucentio pretends to continue the

lesson.
7. A musical scale, named after its lowest note,
"gamma-ut."
8. Referring perhaps to his one love and two identities.

Call you this gamut? Tut, I like it not.
Old fashions please me best; I am not so nice°   *capricious*
To change true rules for old inventions.
    Enter a MESSENGER.
80 MESSENGER Mistress, your father prays you leave your books
And help to dress your sister's chamber up.
You know tomorrow is the wedding day.
BIANCA Farewell, sweet masters both, I must be gone.
                    [*Exeunt* BIANCA *and* MESSENGER.]
LUCENTIO Faith, mistress, then I have no cause to stay.
                             [*Exit.*]
85 HORTENSIO But I have cause to pry into this pedant:
Methinks he looks as though he were in love.
Yet if thy thoughts, Bianca, be so humble°   *low*
To cast thy wandering eyes on every stale,°   *bait; lure*
Seize thee that list.⁹ If once I find thee ranging,°   *unfaithful*
90 Hortensio will be quit with thee by changing.¹   *Exit.*

3.2

    Enter BAPTISTA, GREMIO, TRANIO [*disguised as*
    Lucentio], [LUCENTIO *disguised as Cambio*],¹
      KATHERINA, BIANCA, *and others, Attendants.*
BAPTISTA Signor Lucentio, this is the 'pointed day
That Katherine and Petruccio should be married,
And yet we hear not of our son-in-law.
What will be said, what mockery will it be,
5 To want° the bridegroom when the priest attends   *lack*
To speak the ceremonial rites of marriage?
What says Lucentio to this shame of ours?
KATHERINA No shame but mine. I must forsooth° be forced   *truly*
To give my hand opposed against my heart
10 Unto a mad-brain rudesby° full of spleen,²   *unmannerly fellow*
Who wooed in haste and means to wed at leisure.
I told you, I, he was a frantic° fool,   *mad*
Hiding his bitter jests in blunt behavior,
And to be noted for a merry man,
15 He'll woo a thousand, 'point the day of marriage,
Make friends, invite, and proclaim the banns,
Yet never means to wed where he hath wooed.
Now must the world point at poor Katherine
And say, "Lo, there is mad Petruccio's wife,
20 If it would please him come and marry her."
TRANIO Patience, good Katherine, and Baptista, too.
Upon my life Petruccio means but well,
Whatever fortune stays° him from his word.   *incident keeps*
Though he be blunt, I know him passing wise;
25 Though he be merry, yet withal he's honest.³

9. Let anyone who wants you take you.
1. Will get even with you or get rid of you by finding another love.
3.2 Location: In front of Baptista's house.
1. Although Lucentio speaks no lines in the events leading up to and including Petruccio's arrival for his wedding, this edition, like many others, includes him, disguised as Cambio, among the characters who enter at this point.
2. Caprice; impulsiveness. Contemporary medical theorists claimed that high and low spirits originated in the spleen.
3. Some critics find Tranio's familiarity with Petruccio improbable. Possibly these lines were originally meant to be spoken by Hortensio.

KATHERINA   Would Katherine had never seen him, though.
                    Exit weeping [with BIANCA *following].*[4]
BAPTISTA   Go, girl, I cannot blame thee now to weep,
For such an injury would vex a very saint,
Much more a shrew of impatient humor.
                    Enter BIONDELLO.

30 BIONDELLO   Master, master, news! Old news and such news
as you never heard of!
BAPTISTA   Is it new and old too? How may that be?
BIONDELLO   Why, is it not news to hear of Petruccio's coming?
BAPTISTA   Is he come?
35 BIONDELLO   Why, no, sir.
BAPTISTA   What, then?
BIONDELLO   He is coming.
BAPTISTA   When will he be here?
BIONDELLO   When he stands where I am and sees you there.
40 TRANIO   But say, what to thine old news?
BIONDELLO   Why, Petruccio is coming in a new hat and an old
jerkin;° a pair of old breeches thrice turned;[5] a pair of boots   *jacket*
that have been candlecases,[6] one buckled, another laced; an
old rusty sword ta'en out of the town armory, with a broken
45 hilt and chapelesse,[7] with two broken points;[8] his horse
hipped,° with an old mothy saddle and stirrups of no kin-   *lame in the hips*
dred,° besides possessed with the glanders[9] and like to mose   *unmatched*
in the chine;[1] troubled with the lampass,[2] infected with the
fashions,° full of windgalls,[3] sped with spavins,[4] rayed with   *farcins (small tumors)*
50 the yellows,° past cure of the fives,[5] stark spoiled with the   *disfigured by jaundice*
staggers,[6] begnawn with the bots,[7] weighed in the back° and   *swaybacked*
shoulder-shotten,[8] near-legged before[9] and with a half-
cheeked[1] bit and a headstall[2] of sheep's leather which, being
restrained° to keep him from stumbling, hath been often   *tightened*
55 burst and now repaired with knots, one girth° six times   *saddle strap*
pieced,° and a woman's crupper of velour[3] which hath two   *mended*
letters for her name fairly set down in studs and here and
there pieced with packthread.°   *twine*
BAPTISTA   Who comes with him?
60 BIONDELLO   O sir, his lackey, for all the world caparisoned°   *outfitted*
like the horse, with a linen stock° on one leg and a kersey   *stocking*
boot-hose[4] on the other, gartered with a red and blue list,°   *strip of cloth*

---

4. TEXTUAL COMMENT The Folio does not provide an
exit for Bianca in this scene before her re-entry at line
177. This edition has her leave with Katherina to
emphasize the way the marriage transaction is a competition between men. See Digital Edition TC 6.
5. Turned inside out three times (to make them last
longer).
6. In other words, discarded and used to store old
candle ends.
7. Without the metal tip that protects the sword's
point.
8. With two laces that don't hold up his hose; with
two points (instead of one) on his broken sword.
9. The first in a catalog of horse diseases, most of
which are described in Gervase Markham's *Discourse
of Horsemanship* (1593). The glanders caused swellings and nasal discharge.
1. Obscure phrase, probably meaning the horse was

apt to suffer discharge from the nostrils, indicating
the last stage of glanders.
2. A disease characterized by swellings in the mouth.
3. Soft tumors usually appearing on the fetlock, so
called because they were thought to contain air.
4. Rendered useless by swelling of the leg joints.
5. Swelling of glands below the ears.
6. A disease causing loss of balance.
7. Eaten by intestinal worms.
8. With sprained shoulders.
9. With knock-kneed forelegs.
1. *half-cheeked*: improperly attached.
2. The part of the bridle that fits around the horse's
head. Sheepskin would be inferior to the animal
skins normally used.
3. *crupper*: strap that passes under a horse's tail to
keep the saddle straight; *velour*: velvet.
4. A coarse wool stocking.

an old hat, and the humor of forty fancies pricked in't for a
feather[5]—a monster, a very monster in apparel, and not like
65   a Christian footboy or a gentleman's lackey.
    TRANIO   'Tis some odd humor pricks° him to this fashion,   *incites, urges*
    Yet oftentimes he goes but mean appareled.
    BAPTISTA   I am glad he's come, howsoe'er he comes.
    BIONDELLO   Why, sir, he comes not.
70   BAPTISTA   Didst thou not say he comes?
    BIONDELLO   Who, that Petruccio came?
    BAPTISTA   Ay, that Petruccio came.
    BIONDELLO   No, sir, I say his horse comes with him on his back.
    BAPTISTA   Why, that's all one.
75   BIONDELLO   Nay by Saint Jamy,
          I hold you a penny,
          A horse and a man
          Is more than one,
          And yet not many.
        Enter PETRUCCIO *and* GRUMIO.
80   PETRUCCIO   Come, where be these gallants? Who's at home?
    BAPTISTA   You are welcome, sir.
    PETRUCCIO   And yet I come not well.
    BAPTISTA   And yet you halt° not.   *limp*
    TRANIO   Not so well appareled as I wish you were.
85   PETRUCCIO   Were it better I should rush in thus?
    But where is Kate? Where is my lovely bride?
    How does my father? Gentles,[6] methinks you frown,
    And wherefore gaze this goodly company
    As if they saw some wondrous monument,
90   Some comet or unusual prodigy?°   *extraordinary thing*
    BAPTISTA   Why, sir, you know this is your wedding day.
    First were we sad, fearing you would not come,
    Now sadder that you come so unprovided.°   *unprepared*
    Fie, doff this habit,° shame to your estate,°   *outfit / social place*
95   An eyesore to our solemn festival.
    TRANIO   And tell us what occasion of import
    Hath all so long detained you from your wife
    And sent you hither so unlike yourself?
    PETRUCCIO   Tedious it were to tell and harsh to hear.
100   Sufficeth I am come to keep my word,
    Though in some part enforcèd to digress,°   *deviate from my plan*
    Which at more leisure I will so excuse
    As you shall well be satisfied with all.
    But where is Kate? I stay too long from her;
105   The morning wears, 'tis time we were at church.
    TRANIO   See not your bride in these unreverent° robes.   *disrespectful*
    Go to my chamber, put on clothes of mine.
    PETRUCCIO   Not I, believe me; thus I'll visit her.
    BAPTISTA   But thus, I trust, you will not marry her.
110   PETRUCCIO   Good sooth,° even thus. Therefore ha' done with   *Yes indeed*
    words:

---

5. Possibly an absurdly fanciful decoration attached
to the hat instead of a feather.

6. The polite term of address to men and women of
the gentry.

To me she's married, not unto my clothes.
Could I repair what she will wear° in me   *wear out (in sex)*
As I can change these poor accoutrements,
'Twere well for Kate and better for myself.
115   But what a fool am I to chat with you,
When I should bid good morrow to my bride
And seal the title with a lovely° kiss!   *loving*

                        Exit [with GRUMIO].

TRANIO   He hath some meaning in his mad attire.
We will persuade him, be it possible,
120   To put on better ere he go to church.
BAPTISTA   I'll after him and see the event° of this.   *outcome*

                Exit [with GREMIO, BIONDELLO, and Attendants].

TRANIO [to LUCENTIO]   But, sir, to love concerneth us to add[7]
Her father's liking, which to bring to pass,
As before imparted to your worship,
125   I am to get a man—whate'er he be,
It skills° not much, we'll fit him to our turn—   *matters*
And he shall be Vincentio of Pisa
And make assurance here in Padua
Of greater sums than I have promisèd.
130   So shall you quietly enjoy your hope°   *what you hope for*
And marry sweet Bianca with consent.
LUCENTIO   Were it not that my fellow schoolmaster
Doth watch Bianca's steps so narrowly,
'Twere good, methinks, to steal our marriage,°   *elope*
135   Which once performed, let all the world say no,
I'll keep mine own, despite of all the world.
TRANIO   That by degrees we mean to look into,
And watch our vantage° in this business.   *opportunity*
We'll overreach the graybeard Gremio,
140   The narrow-prying° father Minola,   *overly suspicious*
The quaint° musician, amorous Licio,   *skillful; crafty*
All for my master's sake, Lucentio.

                        Enter GREMIO.

Signor Gremio, came you from the church?
GREMIO   As willingly as e'er I came from school.
145   TRANIO   And is the bride and bridegroom coming home?
GREMIO   A bridegroom, say you? 'Tis a groom° indeed—   *crude, lower-class man*
A grumbling groom, and that the girl shall find.
TRANIO   Curster° than she? Why, 'tis impossible.   *More cantankerous*
GREMIO   Why, he's a devil, a devil, a very fiend.
150   TRANIO   Why, she's a devil, a devil, the devil's dam.°   *mother*
GREMIO   Tut, she's a lamb, a dove, a fool to him.[8]
I'll tell you, Sir Lucentio, when the priest
Should ask if Katherine should be his wife,
"Ay, by gog's wounds,"[9] quoth he and swore so loud
155   That all amazed the priest let fall the book,
And, as he stooped again to take it up,
This mad-brained bridegroom took° him such a cuff   *gave*
That down fell priest and book, and book and priest.
"Now take them up," quoth he, "if any list."°   *choose*

---

7. To the love between Bianca and Lucentio it is
necessary for us to add.

8. A good-natured innocent compared with him.
9. By God's (Christ's) wounds (a common oath).

160 TRANIO What said the wench when he rose again?
GREMIO Trembled and shook: for why,° he° stamped and swore,   *because / (Petruccio)*
As if the vicar meant to cozen¹ him.
But after many ceremonies done,
He calls for wine—"a health," quoth he, as if
165 He had been aboard° carousing to his mates   *(a ship)*
After a storm—quaffed off the muscatel²
And threw the sops all in the sexton's face,
Having no other reason
But that his beard grew thin and hungerly°   *sparsely; as if hungry*
170 And seemed to ask him° sops as he was drinking.   *ask him for*
This done, he took the bride about the neck
And kissed her lips with such a clamorous smack
That at the parting all the church did echo.
And I, seeing this, came thence for very shame,
175 And after me I know the rout° is coming.   *crowd*
Such a mad marriage never was before.
    Music plays.
Hark, hark, I hear the minstrels play.
    Enter PETRUCCIO, KATHERINA, BIANCA, HORTENSIO
    [*as* Licio], BAPTISTA[, *and* GRUMIO].
PETRUCCIO Gentlemen and friends, I thank you for your pains.
I know you think to dine with me today
180 And have prepared great store of wedding cheer,°   *food and drink*
But so it is my haste doth call me hence,
And therefore here I mean to take my leave.
BAPTISTA Is't possible you will away tonight?
PETRUCCIO I must away today before night come.
185 Make° it no wonder: if you knew my business,   *Consider*
You would entreat me rather go than stay.
And, honest° company, I thank you all   *worthy*
That have beheld me give away myself
To this most patient, sweet, and virtuous wife.
190 Dine with my father, drink a health to me,
For I must hence, and farewell to you all.
TRANIO Let us entreat you stay till after dinner.
PETRUCCIO It may not be.
GREMIO   Let me entreat you.
PETRUCCIO It cannot be.
KATHERINA   Let me entreat you.
PETRUCCIO I am content.
195 KATHERINA   Are you content to stay?
PETRUCCIO I am content you shall entreat me stay;
But yet not stay, entreat me how you can.
KATHERINA Now, if you love me, stay.
PETRUCCIO   Grumio, my horse.
GRUMIO Ay, sir, they be ready, the oats have eaten the horses.³
200 KATHERINA Nay, then,
Do what thou canst, I will not go today,
No, nor tomorrow, not till I please myself.

1. Cheat (by not performing a legally binding ceremony).
2. Wine with small cakes, or "sops," soaked in it, traditionally drunk by the newly married couple and their guests.
3. Either Grumio gets it the wrong way around, or he is joking about the great quantity of oats the horses have eaten.

The door is open, sir, there lies your way.
You may be jogging whiles your boots are green.[4]

205 For me, I'll not be gone till I please myself.
'Tis like you'll prove a jolly° surly groom,   *an arrogant*
That take it on you at the first so roundly.[5]

PETRUCCIO   O Kate, content thee; prithee, be not angry.

KATHERINA   I will be angry; what hast thou to do?[6]

210 —Father, be quiet; he shall stay° my leisure.   *await*

GREMIO   Ay, marry, sir, now it begins to work.

KATHERINA   Gentlemen, forward to the bridal dinner.
I see a woman may be made a fool
If she had not a spirit to resist.

215 PETRUCCIO   They shall go forward, Kate, at thy command.
—Obey the bride, you that attend on her.
Go to the feast, revel and domineer,°   *feast sumptuously*
Carouse full measure to her maidenhead,
Be mad and merry or go hang yourselves.

220 But for my bonny Kate, she must with me.
Nay, look not big,° nor stamp, nor stare, nor fret.   *defiant*
I will be master of what is mine own.
She is my goods, my chattels; she is my house,
My household stuff, my field, my barn,

225 My horse, my ox, my ass, my anything,
And here she stands, touch her whoever dare.[7]
I'll bring mine action on° the proudest he   *attack; sue (in court)*
That stops my way in Padua. —Grumio,
Draw forth thy weapon; we are beset with thieves,

230 Rescue thy mistress if thou be a man.
—Fear not, sweet wench, they shall not touch thee, Kate;
I'll buckler° thee against a million.   *shield*

    Exeunt PETRUCCIO, KATHERINA[, *and* GRUMIO].

BAPTISTA   Nay, let them go, a couple of quiet ones.

GREMIO   Went they not quickly, I should die with laughing.

235 TRANIO   Of all mad matches never was the like.

LUCENTIO   Mistress, what's your opinion of your sister?

BIANCA   That being mad herself, she's madly mated.

GREMIO   I warrant him, Petruccio is Kated.[8]

BAPTISTA   Neighbors and friends, though bride and
    bridegroom wants°   *are missing*

240 For to supply° the places at the table,   *to fill*
You know there wants no junkets° at the feast.   *sweetmeats*
Lucentio, you shall supply the bridegroom's place,
And let Bianca take her sister's room.

TRANIO   Shall sweet Bianca practice how to bride it?

245 BAPTISTA   She shall, Lucentio. Come, gentlemen, let's go.

       Exeunt.

---

4. You can be off now while your boots are new ("green"). Proverbial expression for getting an early start or getting rid of an unwelcome guest.
5. That takes charge at the outset so outspokenly.
6. What business is it of yours?
7. Petruccio warns others to leave Katherina alone.

In cataloging the ways she is one of his possessions, he alludes to the Tenth Commandment, which forbids coveting a neighbor's wife or property.
8. Mated with a "Kate"; afflicted with Katherina (imagined as a disease).

4.1

Enter GRUMIO.

GRUMIO Fie, fie on all tired jades,° on all mad masters, and   *worn-out horses*
all foul° ways. Was ever man so beaten? Was ever man so   *muddy*
rayed?° Was ever man so weary? I am sent before to make a   *dirtied*
fire, and they are coming after to warm them. Now were not
5 I a little pot and soon hot,[1] my very lips might freeze to my
teeth, my tongue to the roof of my mouth, my heart in my
belly, ere I should come by a fire to thaw me; but I with blowing the fire shall warm myself, for considering the weather,
a taller[2] man than I will take cold. Holla, ho, Curtis!

Enter CURTIS.

10 CURTIS Who is that calls so coldly?
GRUMIO A piece of ice. If thou doubt it, thou mayst slide from
my shoulder to my heel with no greater a run but my head
and my neck. A fire, good Curtis.
CURTIS Is my master and his wife coming, Grumio?
15 GRUMIO Oh, ay, Curtis, ay, and therefore fire, fire, cast on no
water.[3]
CURTIS Is she so hot a shrew as she's reported?
GRUMIO She was, good Curtis, before this frost; but thou
know'st winter tames man, woman, and beast, for it hath
20 tamed my old master and my new mistress and myself, fellow Curtis.
CURTIS Away, you three-inch° fool, I am no beast.   *short*
GRUMIO Am I but three inches? Why, thy horn[4] is a foot, and
so long am I at the least. But wilt thou make a fire, or shall I
25 complain on thee to our mistress, whose hand—she being
now at hand—thou shalt soon feel, to thy cold comfort, for
being slow in thy hot office?°   *fire-making duties*
CURTIS I prithee, good Grumio, tell me, how goes the world?
GRUMIO A cold world, Curtis, in every office but thine, and
30 therefore, fire. Do thy duty and have thy duty,° for my mas-   *take your reward*
ter and mistress are almost frozen to death.
CURTIS There's fire ready, and therefore, good Grumio, the
news.
GRUMIO Why, "Jack boy, ho boy"[5] and as much news as wilt
35 thou.
CURTIS Come, you are so full of coney-catching.[6]
GRUMIO Why, therefore fire, for I have caught extreme cold.
Where's the cook? Is supper ready, the house trimmed,
rushes strewed,[7] cobwebs swept, the servingmen in their
40 new fustian,° their white stockings, and every officer° his   *coarse cloth / servant*
wedding garment on? Be the Jacks fair within, the Jills fair
without,[8] the carpets° laid, and everything in order?   *table coverings*
CURTIS All ready, and therefore, I pray thee, news.

4.1 Location: Petruccio's country house.
1. Proverbial for a small person who quickly becomes angry.
2. Punning on "taller" as meaning "sturdier."
3. Alluding to the popular song "Scotland's Burning," in which the words "Fire, fire" are followed by "Cast on water, cast on water."
4. The proverbial sign of a cuckold; an erect penis. Grumio implies that he is "long" enough to cuckold Curtis.
5. A line from another popular song.
6. Trickery, with a play on the "catches," or songs, of which Grumio is fond. A coney is a rabbit.
7. Scattered on the floor.
8. Jacks and Jills were manservants and maidservants; also leather drinking vessels and metal drinking vessels.

GRUMIO   First, know my horse is tired, my master and mis-
45   tress fallen out.
CURTIS   How?
GRUMIO   Out of their saddles into the dirt, and thereby hangs
    a tale.
CURTIS   Let's ha't, good Grumio.
50   GRUMIO   Lend thine ear.
CURTIS   Here.
GRUMIO [*cuffing him*]   There.
CURTIS   This 'tis to feel a tale, not to hear a tale.
GRUMIO   And therefore 'tis called a sensible tale,[9] and this
55   cuff was but to knock at your ear and beseech listening.
    Now I begin: *Inprimis*,° we came down a foul° hill, my mas-   *First / muddy*
    ter riding behind my mistress.
CURTIS   Both of° one horse?   *on*
GRUMIO   What's that to thee?
60   CURTIS   Why, a horse.
GRUMIO   Tell thou the tale: but hadst thou not crossed° me,   *interrupted*
    thou shouldst have heard how her horse fell, and she under
    her horse. Thou shouldst have heard in how mirey a place,
    how she was bemoiled,° how he left her with the horse upon   *covered with mud*
65   her, how he beat me because her horse stumbled, how she
    waded through the dirt to pluck him off me, how he swore,
    how she prayed that never prayed before, how I cried, how
    the horses ran away, how her bridle was burst, how I lost my
    crupper, with many things of worthy memory which now
70   shall die in oblivion, and thou return unexperienced° to thy   *ignorant; unknowing*
    grave.
CURTIS   By this reckoning he is more shrew than she.
GRUMIO   Ay, and that thou and the proudest of you all shall
    find when he comes home. But what° talk I of this? Call   *why*
75   forth Nathaniel, Joseph, Nicholas, Philip, Walter, Sugarsop,
    and the rest. Let their heads be slickly combed, their blue
    coats[1] brushed, and their garters of an indifferent° knit; let   *ordinary; a matching*
    them curtsy with their left legs and not presume to touch a
    hair of my master's horsetail till they kiss their hands.[2] Are
80   they all ready?
CURTIS   They are.
GRUMIO   Call them forth.
CURTIS [*calling*]   Do you hear, ho? You must meet my master
    to countenance[3] my mistress.
85   GRUMIO   Why, she hath a face of her own.
CURTIS   Who knows not that?
GRUMIO   Thou, it seems, that calls for company to countenance
    her.
CURTIS   I call them forth to credit[4] her.
    Enter four or five [SERVANTS].
90   GRUMIO   Why, she comes to borrow nothing of them.
NATHANIEL   Welcome home, Grumio.
PHILIP   How now, Grumio.

---

9. Reasonable; capable of being felt.
1. The usual servant uniform.
2. A greeting signifying inordinate submissiveness.
3. Greet, pay respects to; with a pun in the next line

on "countenance" as meaning "face."
4. Honor, with pun in next line on "credit" as meaning "offer financial assistance."

JOSEPH What, Grumio.

NICHOLAS Fellow Grumio.

95 NATHANIEL How now, old lad.

GRUMIO Welcome, you; how now, you; what, you; fellow, you.
And thus much for greeting. Now, my spruce° companions,   *smartly dressed*
is all ready and all things neat?

NATHANIEL All things are ready. How near is our master?

100 GRUMIO E'en at hand, alighted by this, and therefore be not—
Cock's° passion, silence; I hear my master.   *God's (a common oath)*

Enter PETRUCCIO *and* KATHERINA.[5]

PETRUCCIO Where be these knaves? What, no man at door
To hold my stirrup nor to take my horse?
Where is Nathaniel, Gregory, Philip?

105 ALL SERVANTS Here, here, sir; here, sir.

PETRUCCIO "Here, sir; here, sir; here, sir; here, sir."
You logger-headed° and unpolished grooms!   *stupid*
What, no attendance? No regard? No duty?
Where is the foolish knave I sent before?

110 GRUMIO Here, sir, as foolish as I was before.

PETRUCCIO You peasant swain,° you whoreson,° malt-horse   *farm laborer / bastard*
drudge,[6]
Did I not bid thee meet me in the park[7]
And bring along these rascal knaves with thee?

GRUMIO Nathaniel's coat, sir, was not fully made,

115 And Gabriel's pumps° were all unpinked° i'th' heel;   *shoes / not ornamented*
There was no link[8] to color Peter's hat,
And Walter's dagger was not come from sheathing.°   *having a sheath fixed*
There were none fine but Adam, Rafe, and Gregory;
The rest were ragged, old, and beggarly.

120 Yet as they are, here are they come to meet you.

PETRUCCIO Go rascals, go, and fetch my supper in.

Exeunt SERVANTS.

[*Sings.*] "Where is the life that late I led?
Where are those—"[9]
Sit down, Kate, and welcome. Soud, soud, soud, soud.[1]

Enter SERVANTS *with supper.*

125 Why, when, I say? —Nay, good, sweet Kate, be merry.
—Off with my boots, you rogues; you villains, when?
[*Sings.*] "It was the Friar of orders gray,
As he forth walkèd on his way."[2]
Out, you rogue, you pluck my foot awry!

130 Take that, and mend the plucking of the other.
—Be merry, Kate. —Some water here, what, ho!

Enter one with water.

Where's my spaniel Troilus? Sirrah, get you hence
And bid my cousin Ferdinand come hither.
—One, Kate, that you must kiss and be acquainted with.

---

5. TEXTUAL COMMENT The interactions between Petruccio and his servants that begin here could be staged in a number of different ways. For instance, the servants may or may not be in on Petruccio's plan to scare Katherina. See Digital Edition TC 7.
6. Stupid, menial worker. The slow, heavy malt horse was used to grind malt by turning a treadmill.
7. A piece of ground comprising woodland and pasture

attached to a country house and used for recreation.
8. Torch, the smoke of which was used to blacken shoes.
9. Probably a fragment of a ballad, now lost, lamenting a newlywed's loss of freedom.
1. An expression of impatience.
2. Another fragment of a lost song, perhaps one of the many songs about a friar's seduction of a nun.

135   —Where are my slippers? Shall I have some water?
       —Come, Kate, and wash, and welcome heartily.
       —You whoreson villain, will you let it fall?
       KATHERINA Patience, I pray you, 'twas a fault unwilling.
       PETRUCCIO A whoreson, beetle-headed,° flap-eared knave!   *thick-headed*
140   —Come, Kate, sit down, I know you have a stomach.°   *an appetite; temper*
       Will you give thanks, sweet Kate, or else shall I?
       —What's this, mutton?
       FIRST SERVANT   Ay.
       PETRUCCIO   Who brought it?
       PETER   I.
       PETRUCCIO 'Tis burnt, and so is all the meat.
       What dogs are these? Where is the rascal cook?
145   How durst you villains bring it from the dresser°   *cook; sideboard*
       And serve it thus to me that love it not?
       There, take it to you, trenchers,° cups, and all,   *plates*
       You heedless jolt-heads° and unmannered slaves.   *careless blockheads*
       What, do you grumble? I'll be with you straight.
                          [*Exeunt* SERVANTS.]
150   KATHERINA I pray you, husband, be not so disquiet;
       The meat was well, if you were so contented.
       PETRUCCIO I tell thee, Kate, 'twas burnt and dried away,
       And I expressly am forbid to touch it,
       For it engenders choler,³ planteth anger,
155   And better 'twere that both of us did fast,
       Since of ourselves,° ourselves are choleric,   *by our natures*
       Than feed it with such over-roasted flesh.
       Be patient, tomorrow't shall be mended,
       And for this night we'll fast for company.°   *together*
160   Come, I will bring thee to thy bridal chamber.
                          Exeunt [PETRUCCIO *and* KATHERINA;
                                        GRUMIO *remains*].
           Enter SERVANTS *severally.*
       NATHANIEL Peter, didst ever see the like?
       PETER He kills her in her own humor.⁴
           Enter CURTIS, *a servant.*
       GRUMIO Where is he?
       CURTIS In her chamber, making a sermon of continency° to   *on self-control*
165   her, and rails and swears and rates° that she, poor soul,   *scolds*
       knows not which way to stand, to look, to speak, and sits as
       one new risen from a dream. Away, away, for he is coming
       hither.
                          [*Exeunt* SERVANTS *and* GRUMIO.]
           Enter PETRUCCIO.
       PETRUCCIO Thus have I politicly° begun my reign,   *cunningly*
170   And 'tis my hope to end successfully.
       My falcon⁵ now is sharp° and passing° empty,   *hungry / extremely*
       And till she stoop⁶ she must not be full gorged,°   *fully fed*
       For then she never looks upon her lure.°   *falconer's bait*
       Another way I have to man my haggard,°   *tame my female hawk*

---

3. It causes anger. An excess of the choleric humor   5. In what follows, Petruccio likens his methods of
was believed to provoke anger.   disciplining Katherina to the training of a wild hawk.
4. He subdues her choleric humor by outdoing her in   6. Fly to the bait; submit to my authority.
bad temper.

175 To make her come and know her keeper's call,
That is, to watch her° as we watch these kites°   *keep her awake / hawks*
That bait and beat⁷ and will not be obedient.
She ate no meat today, nor none shall eat;
Last night she slept not, nor tonight she shall not.
180 As with the meat, some undeservèd fault
I'll find about the making of the bed,
And here I'll fling the pillow, there the bolster,⁸
This way the coverlet, another way the sheets.
Ay, and amid this hurly I intend°   *will pretend*
185 That all is done in reverend care of her.
And in conclusion, she shall watch° all night,   *stay awake*
And if she chance to nod, I'll rail and brawl
And with the clamor keep her still awake.
This is a way to kill a wife with kindness,
190 And thus I'll curb her mad and headstrong humor.
He that knows better how to tame a shrew,
Now let him speak; 'tis charity to show.°   *Exit.*   *(his methods)*

4.2

Enter TRANIO [*disguised as Lucentio*] *and* HORTENSIO
[*disguised as Licio*].
TRANIO   Is't possible, friend Licio, that Mistress Bianca
Doth fancy any other but Lucentio?
I tell you, sir, she bears me fair in hand.°   *leads me on*
HORTENSIO   Sir, to satisfy you in what I have said,
5   Stand by and mark the manner of his teaching.
[*They stand aside.*]
Enter BIANCA [*and* LUCENTIO *disguised as Cambio*].
LUCENTIO   Now, mistress, profit you in what you read?
BIANCA   What, master, read you? First resolve° me that.   *answer*
LUCENTIO   I read that I profess,° *The Art to Love.*¹   *what I practice*
BIANCA   And may you prove, sir, master of your art.
10   LUCENTIO   While you, sweet dear, prove mistress of my heart.
[*They stand aside.*]
HORTENSIO   Quick proceeders,² marry! Now tell me, I pray,
You that durst swear that your mistress Bianca
Loved none in the world so well as Lucentio—
TRANIO   O despiteful° love, unconstant womankind!   *cruel*
15   I tell thee, Licio, this is wonderful.°   *astonishing*
HORTENSIO   Mistake no more: I am not Licio,
Nor a musician, as I seem to be,
But one that scorn to live in this disguise
For such a one° as leaves a gentleman   *(Bianca)*
20   And makes a god of such a cullion.°   *base fellow*
Know, sir, that I am called Hortensio.
TRANIO   Signor Hortensio, I have often heard
Of your entire° affection to Bianca,   *sincere*

---

7. That flutter and flap their wings (instead of settling on the falconer's fist).
8. *bolster:* a long, firm pillow used to support the
sleeper's head.
4.2 Location: Padua, in front of Baptista's house.
1. Ovid's *Ars Amatoria,* in which the poet calls him-

self the "Professor of Love" and treats erotic love as a
skill or an art.
2. Taking up the allusion to a university degree
implicit in Bianca's "master of your art," Hortensio
puns on "proceeding" from a bachelor's to a master's
degree.

And since mine eyes are witness of her lightness°   *sexual infidelity*
25 I will with you, if you be so contented,
Forswear Bianca and her love forever.
HORTENSIO See how they kiss and court! Signor Lucentio,
Here is my hand, and here I firmly vow
Never to woo her more, but do forswear her
30 As one unworthy all the former favors
That I have fondly° flattered them withal.   *foolishly*
TRANIO [*shaking hands*] And here I take the like unfeignèd
oath,
Never to marry with her, though she would entreat.
Fie on her, see how beastly° she doth court him.   *lewdly*
35 HORTENSIO Would all the world but he had quite forsworn.³
For me, that I may surely keep mine oath,
I will be married to a wealthy widow,
Ere three days pass, which hath as long loved me
As I have loved this proud disdainful haggard.°   *intractable woman; hawk*
40 And so farewell, Signor Lucentio.
Kindness in women, not their beauteous looks,
Shall win my love; and so I take my leave
In resolution, as I swore before.   [*Exit.*]
TRANIO Mistress Bianca, bless you with such grace
45 As 'longeth° to a lover's blessèd case.°   *belongs / state*
Nay, I have ta'en you napping, gentle love,
And have forsworn you with Hortensio.
BIANCA Tranio, you jest—but have you both forsworn me?
TRANIO Mistress, we have.
LUCENTIO   Then we are rid of Licio.
50 TRANIO I'faith he'll have a lusty° widow now   *lively; lustful*
That shall be wooed and wedded in a day.
BIANCA God give him joy.
TRANIO Ay, and he'll tame her.
BIANCA He says so, Tranio?
55 TRANIO Faith, he is gone unto the taming school.
BIANCA The taming school? What, is there such a place?
TRANIO Ay, mistress, and Petruccio is the master
That teacheth tricks eleven-and-twenty long⁴
To tame a shrew and charm her chattering tongue.⁵
Enter BIONDELLO.
60 BIONDELLO O master, master, I have watched so long
That I am dog-weary, but at last I spied
An ancient angel⁶ coming down the hill
Will serve the turn.
TRANIO   What is he, Biondello?
BIONDELLO Master, a marcantant⁷ or a pedant,°   *schoolmaster*
65 I know not what, but formal in apparel,
In gait and countenance surely like a father.

3. I wish that everyone but Cambio had given her over (so that she will be left an old maid as she deserves; Hortensio apparently assumes that Bianca would never marry a poor musician).
4. Who teaches tricks that are exactly appropriate or of just the right number. An allusion to the card game one-and-thirty, in which the object is to accumulate exactly thirty-one points. See note to 1.2.32.

5. Tranio's apparent knowledge of Hortensio's plans is puzzling and may be an indication that some text has been lost.
6. Worthy old man. Punning on "angel" as meaning both "valuable gold coin" and "divine messenger." The coin had a picture of the archangel Michael on it.
7. Biondello's version of *mercatante*, an older Italian word for "merchant."

LUCENTIO   And what of him, Tranio?
TRANIO   If he be credulous and trust my tale,
I'll make him glad to seem° Vincentio   *pretend to be*
70   And give assurance to Baptista Minola
As if he were the right Vincentio.
Take in your love and then let me alone.
                    [*Exeunt* LUCENTIO *and* BIANCA.]
        Enter a PEDANT.[8]
PEDANT   God save you, sir.
TRANIO   And you, sir. You are welcome.
Travel you far on, or are you at the farthest?
75   PEDANT   Sir, at the farthest for a week or two,
But then up farther, and as far as Rome,
And so to Tripoli,[9] if God lend me life.
TRANIO   What countryman, I pray?
PEDANT   Of Mantua.
TRANIO   Of Mantua, sir? Marry, God forbid!
80   And come to Padua careless of your life?
PEDANT   My life, sir? How, I pray? For that goes hard.[1]
TRANIO   'Tis death for anyone in Mantua
To come to Padua. Know you not the cause?
Your ships are stayed° at Venice, and the Duke,   *detained*
85   For private quarrel twixt your Duke and him,
Hath published and proclaimed it openly.
'Tis marvel, but that you are but newly come,
You might have heard it else proclaimed about.[2]
PEDANT   Alas, sir, it is worse for me than so,°   *my plight is even worse*
90   For I have bills for money by exchange[3]
From Florence and must here deliver them.
TRANIO   Well, sir, to do you courtesy
This will I do, and this I will advise you.
First tell me, have you ever been at Pisa?
95   PEDANT   Ay, sir, in Pisa have I often been,
Pisa renowned for grave citizens.
TRANIO   Among them know you one Vincentio?
PEDANT   I know him not, but I have heard of him:
A merchant of incomparable wealth.
100   TRANIO   He is my father, sir, and sooth to say,
In count'nance somewhat doth resemble you.
BIONDELLO   As much as an apple doth an oyster, and all one.°   *but no matter*
TRANIO   To save your life in this extremity,
This favor will I do you for his sake—
105   And think it not the worst of all your fortunes
That you are like to Sir Vincentio.
His name and credit° shall you undertake,°   *social status / assume*
And in my house you shall be friendly lodged.
Look that you take upon you° as you should—   *act your part*

8. TEXTUAL COMMENT Although F is consistent in labeling this character as a Pedant (a stock comic type), because he is said at line 90 to have "bills for money," some editors have designated him a "merchant" like the corresponding character in George Gascoigne's comedy *Supposes* (1566). See Digital Edition TC 8.

9. The north African trading center or the city in Syria.
1. *goes hard:* is difficult to deal with.
2. *but that . . . about:* if you hadn't just arrived, you would have heard it announced everywhere.
3. Promissory notes that the bearer could exchange for cash.

110   You understand me, sir? So shall you stay
      Till you have done your business in the city.
      If this be court'sy, sir, accept of it.
    PEDANT   O sir, I do and will repute° you ever   *consider*
      The patron of my life and liberty.
115   TRANIO   Then go with me to make the matter good.
      This, by the way, I let you understand:
      My father is here looked for every day
      To pass assurance° of a dowry in marriage   *convey legal guarantee*
      Twixt me and one Baptista's daughter here;
120   In all these circumstances I'll instruct you.
      Go with me to clothe you as becomes you.   *Exeunt.*

4.3

    Enter KATHERINA *and* GRUMIO.
    GRUMIO   No, no, forsooth, I dare not for my life.
    KATHERINA   The more my wrong, the more his spite appears.[1]
      What, did he marry me to famish me?
      Beggars that come unto my father's door
5   Upon entreaty have a present° alms;   *immediate*
      If not, elsewhere they meet with charity.
      But I, who never knew how to entreat,
      Nor never needed that I should entreat,
      Am starved for meat, giddy for lack of sleep,
10   With oaths kept waking and with brawling fed,
      And that which spites° me more than all these wants,   *vexes*
      He does it under name of perfect love,
      As who should say,° if I should sleep or eat   *As if to say*
      'Twere deadly sickness or else present° death.   *instant*
15   I prithee, go and get me some repast;
      I care not what, so it be wholesome food.
    GRUMIO   What say you to a neat's foot?°   *ox foot or calf's foot*
    KATHERINA   'Tis passing good; I prithee, let me have it.
    GRUMIO   I fear it is too choleric° a meat.   *conducive to anger*
20   How say you to a fat tripe finely broiled?
    KATHERINA   I like it well; good Grumio, fetch it me.
    GRUMIO   I cannot tell, I fear 'tis choleric.
      What say you to a piece of beef and mustard?
    KATHERINA   A dish that I do love to feed upon.
25   GRUMIO   Ay, but the mustard is too hot a little.
    KATHERINA   Why, then the beef and let the mustard rest.
    GRUMIO   Nay, then I will not. You shall have the mustard
      Or else you get no beef of Grumio.
    KATHERINA   Then both or one or anything thou wilt.
30   GRUMIO   Why, then the mustard without the beef.
    KATHERINA   Go, get thee gone, thou false deluding slave,
        [*She*] *beats him.*
      That feed'st me with the very name° of meat.   *only the name*
      Sorrow on thee and all the pack of you
      That triumph thus upon my misery.
35   Go, get thee gone, I say.
        Enter PETRUCCIO *and* HORTENSIO *with meat.*

4.3 Location: Petruccio's country house.
1. The more injustice I suffer, the more he seems to want me to suffer.

PETRUCCIO How fares my Kate? What, sweeting,° all amort?°   *sweetheart / dejected*
HORTENSIO Mistress, what cheer?
KATHERINA   Faith, as cold as can be.
PETRUCCIO Pluck up thy spirits, look cheerfully upon me.
  Here, love, thou seest how diligent I am
40 To dress° thy meat myself and bring it thee.   *prepare*
  I am sure, sweet Kate, this kindness merits thanks.
  What, not a word? Nay, then, thou lov'st it not,
  And all my pains is sorted to no proof.°   *are to no purpose*
  —Here, take away this dish.
45 KATHERINA I pray you, let it stand.
PETRUCCIO The poorest service is repaid with thanks,
  And so shall mine before you touch the meat.
KATHERINA I thank you, sir.
HORTENSIO Signor Petruccio, fie, you are to blame.
50 —Come, Mistress Kate, I'll bear you company.
PETRUCCIO [*aside*] Eat it up all, Hortensio, if thou lovest me.
  —Much good do it unto thy gentle heart.
  Kate, eat apace. And now, my honey love,
  Will we return unto thy father's house
55 And revel it as bravely as the best,
  With silken coats and caps, and golden rings,
  With ruffs and cuffs and farthingales² and things,
  With scarves and fans and double change of brav'ry,°   *finery*
  With amber bracelets, beads, and all this knav'ry.°   *tricks of dress*
60 What, hast thou dined? The tailor stays thy leisure
  To deck thy body with his ruffling° treasure.   *ornate (with ruffles)*
     Enter TAILOR.
  Come, tailor, let us see these ornaments;
  Lay forth the gown.
     Enter HABERDASHER.
         What news with you, sir?
HABERDASHER Here is the cap your worship did bespeak.
65 PETRUCCIO Why, this was molded on a porringer°—   *porridge bowl*
  A velvet dish.³ Fie, fie, 'tis lewd and filthy.
  Why, 'tis a cockle° or a walnut shell,   *mollusk shell*
  A knack,° a toy, a trick,° a baby's cap.   *knickknack / trifle*
  Away with it! Come, let me have a bigger.
70 KATHERINA I'll have no bigger; this doth fit the time,°   *suit current fashion*
  And gentlewomen wear such caps as these.
PETRUCCIO When you are gentle, you shall have one too,
  And not till then.
HORTENSIO   That will not be in haste.
KATHERINA Why, sir, I trust I may have leave to speak,
75 And speak I will. I am no child, no babe.
  Your betters have endured me say my mind,
  And if you cannot, best you stop your ears.
  My tongue will tell the anger of my heart,
  Or else my heart, concealing it, will break,
80 And rather than it shall, I will be free,

2. *ruffs*: fashionable high collars made of starched linen or lace. *cuffs*: bands, often made of lace, sewn onto sleeves for ornament. *farthingales*: hooped petticoats.
3. It's merely a dish made of velvet. Velvet caps were often associated with prostitutes.

Even to the uttermost as I please in words.

PETRUCCIO   Why, thou say'st true; it is paltry cap,
A custard-coffin,[4] a bauble, a silken pie.
I love thee well in that thou lik'st it not.

85 KATHERINA   Love me or love me not, I like the cap,
And it I will have, or I will have none.

PETRUCCIO   Thy gown? Why, ay: come, tailor, let us see't.
O mercy, God, what masquing stuff[5] is here?
What's this? A sleeve? 'Tis like a demi-cannon.°   *large cannon*
90 What, up and down, carved like an apple tart?[6]
Here's snip and nip and cut and slish and slash,
Like to a cithern in a barber's shop.
Why, what a devil's name, tailor, call'st thou this?

HORTENSIO   I see she's like° to have neither cap nor gown.   *likely*

95 TAILOR   You bid me make it orderly and well,
According to the fashion and the time.

PETRUCCIO   Marry, and did,° but if you be remembered,   *Indeed I did*
I did not bid you mar it to the time.
Go, hop me[7] over every kennel° home,   *gutter*
100 For you shall hop without my custom,° sir.   *patronage; business*
I'll none of it. Hence, make your best of it.

KATHERINA   I never saw a better fashioned gown,
More quaint,° more pleasing, nor more commendable.   *elegant*
Belike° you mean to make a puppet of me.   *It seems*

105 PETRUCCIO   Why true, he means to make a puppet of thee.

TAILOR   She says your worship means to make a puppet of her.

PETRUCCIO   Oh, monstrous arrogance! Thou liest, thou thread,
thou thimble,
Thou yard, three-quarters, half-yard, quarter, nail,[8]
Thou flea, thou nit,° thou winter cricket, thou!   *egg of a louse*
110 Braved° in mine own house with° a skein of thread?   *Defied; adorned / by*
Away, thou rag, thou quantity,° thou remnant,   *fragment*
Or I shall so bemete° thee with thy yard°   *measure; beat / ruler*
As thou shalt think on prating[9] whilst thou liv'st.
I tell thee, I, that thou hast marred her gown.

115 TAILOR   Your worship is deceived. The gown is made
Just as my master had direction;
Grumio gave order how it should be done.

GRUMIO   I gave him no order; I gave him the stuff.°   *material*

TAILOR   But how did you desire it should be made?

120 GRUMIO   Marry, sir, with needle and thread.

TAILOR   But did you not request to have it cut?

GRUMIO   Thou hast faced° many things.   *trimmed; defied*

TAILOR   I have.

GRUMIO   Face not me. Thou hast braved° many men; brave°   *dressed finely / defy*
125 not me. I will neither be faced nor braved. I say unto thee, I

---

4. Pastry crust around a custard or an open pie (perhaps with a pun on "costard," slang for "head").
5. Extravagant clothing suitable for theatrical
masques.
6. With slits like the top of an apple pie. The gown's
sleeves may have been designed so as to reveal fabric
of another color underneath.

7. You can go hopping.
8. Measure of cloth, a sixteenth of a yard; Petruccio
is literally belittling the tailor. "Yard" is slang for
"penis."
9. You will think twice before you talk idly, with a
pun on "prat" as slang for "beat on the buttocks."

bid thy master cut out the gown, but I did not bid him cut it
to pieces. Ergo,° thou liest.   *Therefore*
TAILOR   Why, here is the note of the fashion to testify.
PETRUCCIO   Read it.
130   GRUMIO   The note lies in 's throat if he° say I said so.   *it*
TAILOR [*reading*]   "Inprimis,° a loose-bodied gown."[1]   *First*
GRUMIO   Master, if ever I said "loose-bodied gown," sew me in
        the skirts of it, and beat me to death with a bottom° of   *spool*
        brown thread. I said "a gown."
135   PETRUCCIO   Proceed.
TAILOR   "With a small compassed° cape."   *flared*
GRUMIO   I confess the cape.
TAILOR   "With a trunk° sleeve."   *wide*
GRUMIO   I confess two sleeves.
140   TAILOR   "The sleeves curiously° cut."   *carefully; elaborately*
PETRUCCIO   Ay, there's the villainy.
GRUMIO   Error i'th' bill,° sir, error i'th' bill! I commanded the   *order (for the dress)*
        sleeves should be cut out and sewed up again, and that I'll
        prove upon thee, though thy little finger be armed in a
145   thimble.
TAILOR   This is true that I say; an° I had thee in place where,°   *if / in a suitable place*
        thou shouldst know it.
GRUMIO   I am for thee straight. Take thou the bill,[2] give me
        thy mete-yard,° and spare not me.   *yardstick*
150   HORTENSIO   God-a-mercy, Grumio, then he shall have no
        odds.°   *advantage*
PETRUCCIO   Well, sir, in brief, the gown is not for me.
GRUMIO   You are i'th' right, sir, 'tis for my mistress.
PETRUCCIO [*to* TAILOR]   Go take it up unto° thy master's use.[3]   *take it away for*
155   GRUMIO   Villain, not for thy life. Take up my mistress' gown
        for thy master's use?
PETRUCCIO   Why, sir, what's your conceit° in that?   *meaning*
GRUMIO   O sir, the conceit is deeper than you think for. "Take
        up my mistress' gown to his master's use." Oh, fie, fie, fie.
160   PETRUCCIO [*aside to* HORTENSIO]   Hortensio, say thou wilt see
        the tailor paid.
        —Go take it hence, be gone, and say no more.
HORTENSIO   Tailor, I'll pay thee for thy gown tomorrow,
        Take no unkindness of his hasty words.
        Away, I say. Commend me to thy master.
                        Exeunt TAILOR [*and* HABERDASHER].
165   PETRUCCIO   Well, come, my Kate, we will unto your father's
        Even in these honest mean habiliments.
        Our purses shall be proud, our garments poor,
        For 'tis the mind that makes the body rich.
        And as the sun breaks through the darkest clouds,
170   So honor 'peareth° in the meanest habit.   *can be seen*
        What, is the jay more precious than the lark
        Because his feathers are more beautiful?
        Or is the adder better than the eel,

---

1. A loose-fitting dress. In the next line, Grumio
takes this to mean a dress suitable for a wanton, or
loose, woman.

2. Grumio puns on "bill" as also meaning a "weapon"
or "halberd," a staff with a blade attached.

3. *use:* sexual purposes.

Because his painted skin contents the eye?
175 Oh, no, good Kate; neither art thou the worse
For this poor furniture° and mean array.   *clothing; attire*
If thou account'st it shame, lay it on me,°   *blame me*
And therefore frolic: we will hence forthwith
To feast and sport us° at thy father's house.   *amuse ourselves*
180 [*to* GRUMIO] Go, call my men, and let us straight to him,
And bring our horses unto Long-lane end.
There will we mount and thither walk on foot.
Let's see, I think 'tis now some seven o'clock,
And well we may come there by dinner time.°   *about noon*
185 KATHERINA   I dare assure you, sir, 'tis almost two,
And 'twill be supper time° ere you come there.   *about 6 p.m.*
PETRUCCIO   It shall be seven ere I go to horse.
Look what I speak, or do, or think to do,
You are still crossing° it. —Sirs, let't alone.   *contradicting*
190 I will not go today, and ere I do,
It shall be what o'clock I say it is.
HORTENSIO   Why, so this gallant will command the sun.
                             [*Exeunt.*]

4.4

Enter TRANIO [*disguised as Lucentio*] *and the* PEDANT
dressed like Vincentio, booted and bareheaded.[1]
TRANIO   Sir, this is the house. Please it you that I call?
PEDANT   Ay, what else? And but[2] I be deceived,
Signor Baptista may remember me
Near twenty years ago in Genoa—
5 TRANIO   Where we were lodgers at the Pegasus.[3]
'Tis well, and hold your own° in any case   *keep to your role*
With such austerity as 'longeth° to a father.   *belongs*
    Enter BIONDELLO.
PEDANT   I warrant you. But, sir, here comes your boy;
'Twere good he were schooled.
10 TRANIO   Fear you not him. —Sirrah Biondello,
Now do your duty thoroughly, I advise you.
Imagine 'twere the right Vincentio.
BIONDELLO   Tut, fear not me.
TRANIO   But hast thou done thy errand to Baptista?
15 BIONDELLO   I told him that your father was at Venice
And that you looked for him this day in Padua.
TRANIO   Thou'rt a tall° fellow; hold thee° that to drink.   *worthy / take*
Here comes Baptista. Set your countenance, sir.
    Enter BAPTISTA *and* LUCENTIO [*disguised as Cambio*].
TRANIO   Signor Baptista, you are happily met.
20 [*to* PEDANT] Sir, this is the gentleman I told you of.
I pray you, stand good father to me now;
Give me Bianca for my patrimony.

4.4 Location: Padua, in front of Baptista's house.
1. In F, the Pedant is mistakenly given a second entry at line 18, where he is described as "booted and bare-headed," indicating that he is dressed for travel but has taken off his hat, perhaps in deference to Baptista, whom he is about to meet. The present stage direction conflates F's two stage directions regarding the Pedant's entrance.
2. Unless (the Pedant is rehearsing his speech to Baptista).
3. Common name for an inn (marked by a sign of the flying horse of classical mythology).

PEDANT   Soft,° son. —Sir, by your leave, having come to   *Just a moment*
 Padua
 To gather in some debts, my son Lucentio
25 Made me acquainted with a weighty cause
 Of love between your daughter and himself.
 And for the good report I hear of you,
 And for the love he beareth to your daughter
 And she to him, to stay him° not too long   *keep him waiting*
30 I am content, in a good father's care,[4]
 To have him matched. And if you please to like
 No worse than I, upon some agreement
 Me shall you find ready and willing
 With one consent to have her so bestowed;
35 For curious° I cannot be with you,   *overly particular*
 Signor Baptista, of whom I hear so well.
BAPTISTA   Sir, pardon me in what I have to say;
 Your plainness and your shortness please me well.
 Right true it is your son Lucentio here
40 Doth love my daughter, and she loveth him,
 Or both dissemble deeply their affections.
 And therefore if you say no more than this,
 That like a father you will deal with him
 And pass° my daughter a sufficient dower,   *grant*
45 The match is made and all is done:
 Your son shall have my daughter with consent.
TRANIO   I thank you, sir. Where, then, do you know best
 We be affied° and such assurance ta'en   *betrothed*
 As shall with either part's agreement stand?[5]
50 BAPTISTA   Not in my house, Lucentio, for you know
 Pitchers have ears,[6] and I have many servants.
 Besides, old Gremio is harkening still,°   *always listening*
 And haply° we might be interrupted.   *perhaps*
TRANIO   Then at my lodging, an it like you.°   *if it please you*
55 There doth my father lie,° and there this night   *lodge*
 We'll pass° the business privately and well.   *settle*
 Send for your daughter by your servant here;
 My boy shall fetch the scrivener° presently.   *scribe; notary*
 The worst is this: that at so slender warning
60 You are like to have a thin and slender pittance.°   *scanty meal*
BAPTISTA   It likes me well. —Cambio, hie° you home,   *hurry*
 And bid Bianca make her ready straight.
 And if you will, tell what hath happened:
 Lucentio's father is arrived in Padua,
65 And how she's like to be Lucentio's wife.   [*Exit* LUCENTIO.][7]
BIONDELLO   I pray the gods she may with all my heart.

---

4. Content with the care that should be shown by a good father.
5. As shall confirm the agreements of both parties.
6. Proverbial for "Someone may be eavesdropping." The handles of a pitcher are its "ears."
7. F does not mark an exit for Lucentio/Cambio here, but it makes sense that he would follow Baptista's order. If Lucentio exits here and Biondello at line 66 as in F, or at line 67 as in this text, then their re-entry a few lines later can mark a new scene. Some editors assume that Biondello and perhaps Lucentio never leave the stage since Biondello says (at 4.5.5–6) that he has been left behind by Tranio to explain things to Lucentio. In that case, no scene break would be introduced after Baptista exits.

TRANIO   Dally not with the gods, but get thee gone.
                                    Exit [BIONDELLO].[8]
    Signor Baptista, shall I lead the way?
    Welcome: one mess° is like to be your cheer.°   *dish / entertainment*
70 Come, sir, we will better it in Pisa.
BAPTISTA   I follow you.   *Exeunt.*

4.5

Enter LUCENTIO [*disguised as Cambio*] *and* BIONDELLO.
BIONDELLO   Cambio.
LUCENTIO   What say'st thou, Biondello?
BIONDELLO   You saw my master wink and laugh upon you?
LUCENTIO   Biondello, what of that?
5   BIONDELLO   Faith, nothing, but he's left me here behind to
    expound the meaning or moral of his signs and tokens.
LUCENTIO   I pray thee, moralize° them.   *interpret*
BIONDELLO   Then thus: Baptista is safe, talking with the
    deceiving father of a deceitful son.
10 LUCENTIO   And what of him?
BIONDELLO   His daughter is to be brought by you to the supper.
LUCENTIO   And then?
BIONDELLO   The old priest at Saint Luke's church is at your
    command at all hours.
15 LUCENTIO   And what of all this?
BIONDELLO   I cannot tell, except they are busied about a
    counterfeit assurance.° Take you assurance[1] of her, *cum*   *betrothal agreement*
    privilegio ad imprimendum solum;[2] to th' church take the
    priest, clerk, and some sufficient honest witnesses.
20 If this be not that you look for, I have no more to say,
    But bid Bianca farewell forever and a day.
LUCENTIO   Hear'st thou, Biondello?
BIONDELLO   I cannot tarry. I knew a wench married in an
    afternoon as she went to the garden for parsley to stuff a
25 rabbit, and so may you, sir. And so adieu, sir, my master
    hath appointed me to go to Saint Luke's to bid the priest be
    ready to come against° you come with your appendix.[3]   *by the time*
                                    Exit.
LUCENTIO   I may and will, if she be so contented.
    She will be pleased, then wherefore should I doubt?
30 Hap what hap may, I'll roundly go about her.[4]
    It shall go hard° if Cambio go without her.   *Exit.*[5]   *be unfortunate*

8. F here has a mysterious stage direction: "*Enter Peter.*" Some editors have argued that this is the name of an actor inadvertently introduced into the stage directions. Others assume it is the name of one of Lucentio's servants, who enters to tell the disguised Tranio and Baptista that their meal is ready; this possibility is not entirely satisfactory, especially since Baptista and Tranio still have to *proceed* to Lucentio's house for their meal. Perhaps something has been lost or garbled in this portion of the scene.
4.5 Location: Scene continues.

1. Make yourself sure.
2. With the exclusive right to print (a Latin phrase used by printers on the title pages of their books). Biondello urges Lucentio to confirm his "exclusive right" to Bianca and may be punning on "print" as meaning "to father a child."
3. Appendage (the bride).
4. Come what may, I'll pursue her eagerly.
5. At the corresponding point in *A Shrew*, Sly, still onstage, comments on the action.

4.6

Enter PETRUCCIO, KATHERINA, [*and*] HORTENSIO.[1]

PETRUCCIO   Come on, i'God's name, once more toward our
    father's.
    Good lord, how bright and goodly shines the moon.
KATHERINA   The moon? The sun. It is not moonlight now.
PETRUCCIO   I say it is the moon that shines so bright.
5 KATHERINA   I know it is the sun that shines so bright.
PETRUCCIO   Now by my mother's son, and that's myself,
    It shall be moon, or star, or what I list,°   *please*
    Or e'er° I journey to your father's house.   *Before*
    —Go on, and fetch our horses back again.
10   Evermore crossed° and crossed, nothing but crossed.   *contradicted*
HORTENSIO [*to* KATHERINA]   Say as he says, or we shall never go.
KATHERINA   Forward, I pray, since we have come so far,
    And be it moon, or sun, or what you please.
    And if you please to call it a rush candle,[2]
15   Henceforth I vow it shall be so for me.
PETRUCCIO   I say it is the moon.
KATHERINA   I know it is the moon.
PETRUCCIO   Nay, then, you lie: it is the blessèd sun.
KATHERINA   Then God be blessed, it is the blessèd sun;
20   But sun it is not when you say it is not,
    And the moon changes even as your mind.[3]
    What you will have it named, even that it is,
    And so it shall be so for Katherine.
HORTENSIO   Petruccio, go thy ways;° the field is won.   *do as you wish*
25 PETRUCCIO   Well, forward, forward, thus the bowl should run
    And not unluckily against the bias.[4]
    But soft, company is coming here.

        Enter VINCENTIO.

    Good morrow, gentle mistress, where away?
    —Tell me, sweet Kate, and tell me truly, too,
30   Hast thou beheld a fresher gentlewoman?
    Such war of white and red within her cheeks!
    What stars do spangle heaven with such beauty
    As those two eyes become that heavenly face?
    —Fair lovely maid, once more good day to thee.
35   —Sweet Kate, embrace her for her beauty's sake.
HORTENSIO   'A° will make the man mad to make the woman of   *He*
    him.°   *call him a woman*
KATHERINA   Young budding virgin, fair, and fresh, and sweet,
    Whither away, or whither is thy abode?
40   Happy the parents of so fair a child;
    Happier the man whom° favorable stars   *to whom*
    Allots thee for his lovely bedfellow.

4.6 Location: A road somewhere between Petruccio's house and Padua.
1. TEXTUAL COMMENT Only Petruccio, Katherina,
and Hortensio are named in this entrance, but stage
tradition often includes Grumio in the scene, as
someone needs to perform the duties of a servant.
See Digital Edition TC 9.
2. Candle made from rush dripped in grease, thus giving poor light.
3. Implying that Petruccio is mad as well as fickle.
Lunatics and women were imagined to be governed
by the moon.
4. A metaphor from the game of bowls in which the
ball, or bowl, was weighted so that it ran along a "bias,"
or curving path.

PETRUCCIO   Why, how now, Kate, I hope thou art not mad;
This is a man, old, wrinkled, faded, withered,
45   And not a maiden, as thou say'st he is.
KATHERINA   Pardon, old father, my mistaking eyes,
That have been so bedazzled with the sun
That everything I look on seemeth green.°   *youthful*
Now I perceive thou art a reverend father.
50   Pardon, I pray thee, for my mad mistaking.
PETRUCCIO   Do, good old grandsire, and withal° make known   *in addition*
Which way thou travelest; if along with us,
We shall be joyful of thy company.
VINCENTIO   Fair sir, and you, my merry mistress,
55   That with your strange encounter° much amazed me,   *greeting*
My name is called Vincentio, my dwelling Pisa,
And bound I am to Padua, there to visit
A son of mine, which long I have not seen.
PETRUCCIO   What is his name?
VINCENTIO   Lucentio, gentle sir.
60   PETRUCCIO   Happily met, the happier for thy son.
And now by law, as well as reverend age,
I may entitle thee my loving father:
The sister to my wife, this gentlewoman,
Thy son by this hath married.[5] Wonder not,
65   Nor be not grieved; she is of good esteem,
Her dowry wealthy, and of worthy birth,
Beside, so qualified° as may beseem   *with such qualities*
The spouse of any noble gentleman.
Let me embrace with old Vincentio,
70   And wander we to see thy honest son,
Who will of thy arrival be full joyous.
VINCENTIO   But is this true, or is it else your pleasure
Like pleasant travelers to break a jest°   *crack a joke*
Upon the company you overtake?
75   HORTENSIO   I do assure thee, father, so it is.
PETRUCCIO   Come, go along and see the truth hereof,
For our first merriment hath made thee jealous.°   *suspicious*
          Exeunt [PETRUCCIO, KATHERINA, *and* VINCENTIO].
HORTENSIO   Well, Petruccio, this has put me in heart;
Have to my widow, and if she be froward,°   *difficult*
80   Then hast thou taught Hortensio to be untoward.°   *Exit.*   *unmannerly*

5.1

Enter [GREMIO *first, followed separately by*]
BIONDELLO, LUCENTIO [*as himself*], *and* BIANCA.
BIONDELLO [*to* LUCENTIO]   Softly and swiftly, sir, for the priest
is ready.
LUCENTIO   I fly, Biondello; but they may chance to need thee at
home, therefore leave us.   *Exeunt* [LUCENTIO *and* BIANCA].

---

5. By now has married. It is unclear how Petruccio
and Hortensio know this, especially since Hortensio
has heard "Lucentio" (Tranio) forswear Bianca (in
4.2). The inconsistency may suggest textual alteration in the role of Hortensio.
5.1 Location: Padua, in front of Lucentio's house.

5 BIONDELLO Nay, faith, I'll see the church o'your back,[1] and
then come back to my mistress as soon as I can.   [*Exit.*][2]

GREMIO I marvel Cambio comes not all this while.

    Enter PETRUCCIO, KATHERINA, VINCENTIO, GRUMIO
    with Attendants.

PETRUCCIO Sir, here's the door; this is Lucentio's house.
My father's bears° more toward the marketplace;   *lies*
10 Thither must I, and here I leave you, sir.

VINCENTIO You shall not choose but drink before you go.
I think I shall command your welcome here,
And by all likelihood some cheer is toward.°   *food is being prepared*
    [*He*] *knocks.*

GREMIO They're busy within; you were best knock louder.

    PEDANT [*disguised as Vincentio, above,*] *looks out of
    the window.*

15 PEDANT What's he that knocks as he would beat down the
gate?

VINCENTIO Is Signor Lucentio within, sir?

PEDANT He's within, sir, but not to be spoken withal.

VINCENTIO What if a man bring him a hundred pound or two
20 to make merry withal?

PEDANT Keep your hundred pounds to yourself; he shall need
none so long as I live.

PETRUCCIO [*to* VINCENTIO] Nay, I told you your son was well
beloved in Padua. —Do you hear, sir? To leave frivolous circumstances,° I pray you tell Signor Lucentio that his father   *matters*
is come from Pisa and is here at the door to speak with him.

PEDANT Thou liest: his father is come from Padua and here
looking out at the window.

VINCENTIO Art thou his father?

30 PEDANT Ay, sir, so his mother says, if I may believe her.

PETRUCCIO Why, how now, gentleman? Why, this is flat knavery, to take upon you another man's name.

PEDANT Lay hands on the villain! I believe 'a° means to   *he*
cozen° somebody in this city under my countenance.°   *cheat / name; person*
    Enter BIONDELLO.

35 BIONDELLO I have seen them in the church together, God
send 'em good shipping.° But who is here? Mine old master   *fair sailing*
Vincentio! Now we are undone and brought to nothing.

VINCENTIO Come hither, crackhemp.[3]

BIONDELLO I hope I may choose, sir.

40 VINCENTIO Come hither, you rogue. What, have you forgot me?

BIONDELLO Forgot you? No, sir, I could not forget you, for I
never saw you before in all my life.

VINCENTIO What, you notorious villain, didst thou never see
thy master's father, Vincentio?

45 BIONDELLO What, my old worshipful old master? Yes, marry,
sir, see where he looks out of the window.

---

1. At your back. Probably, I'll see the church as you
leave it after the wedding.
2. In F, Lucentio and Bianca exit first (after line 4)
and Biondello presumably follows after line 6, though
no exit is explicitly marked for him. Gremio, onstage

before this trio, apparently does not see them stealing away to the church.
3. Rogue (deserving to stretch the hangman's hemp
rope).

VINCENTIO   Is't so indeed?
    He beats BIONDELLO.
BIONDELLO   Help, help, help! Here's a madman will murder me!
                                           [Exit.]
PEDANT   Help, son! Help, Signor Baptista!   *[Exit above.]*
50 PETRUCCIO   Prithee, Kate, let's stand aside and see the end of
    this controversy.
        Enter PEDANT *[below] with* SERVANTS, BAPTISTA,
        TRANIO *[disguised as Lucentio].*
TRANIO *[to* VINCENTIO*]*   Sir, what are you that offer° to beat   *presume*
    my servant?
VINCENTIO   What am I, sir? Nay, what are you, sir? O immor-
55   tal gods! O fine villain! A silken doublet, a velvet hose, a
    scarlet cloak, and a copatain° hat! Oh, I am undone, I am   *high-crowned*
    undone. While I play the good husband at home, my son and
    my servant spend all at the university.
TRANIO   How now, what's the matter?
60 BAPTISTA   What, is the man lunatic?
TRANIO   Sir, you seem a sober ancient gentleman by your
    habit, but your words show you a madman. Why, sir, what
    'cerns° it you if I wear pearl and gold? I thank my good   *concerns*
    father, I am able to maintain it.
65 VINCENTIO   Thy father? O villain, he is a sailmaker in
    Bergamo.[4]
BAPTISTA   You mistake, sir; you mistake, sir. Pray, what do
    you think is his name?
VINCENTIO   His name? As if I knew not his name: I have
70   brought him up ever since he was three years old, and his
    name is Tranio.
PEDANT   Away, away, mad ass. His name is Lucentio, and he is
    mine only son and heir to the lands of me, Signor Vincentio.
VINCENTIO   Lucentio? Oh, he hath murdered his master! Lay
75   hold on him, I charge you in the Duke's name. O my son, my
    son! Tell me, thou villain, where is my son Lucentio?
TRANIO   Call forth an officer.
        [Enter an Officer.]
    Carry this mad knave to the jail. Father Baptista, I charge
    you see that he be forthcoming.°   *available when needed*
80 VINCENTIO   Carry me to the jail?
GREMIO   Stay, officer, he shall not go to prison.
BAPTISTA   Talk not, Signor Gremio: I say he shall go to prison.
GREMIO   Take heed, Signor Baptista, lest you be coney-
    catched° in this business. I dare swear this is the right   *duped*
85   Vincentio.
PEDANT   Swear if thou dar'st.
GREMIO   Nay, I dare not swear it.
TRANIO   Then thou wert best say that I am not Lucentio.
GREMIO   Yes, I know thee to be Signor Lucentio.
90 BAPTISTA   Away with the dotard, to the jail with him.
        Enter BIONDELLO, LUCENTIO, *and* BIANCA.

---

4. An Italian town associated with Harlequin, the witty, resourceful servant of the Italian *commedia dell'arte.*

VINCENTIO   Thus strangers may be haled° and abused. Oh,   *dragged about*
    monstrous villain!

BIONDELLO   Oh, we are spoiled, and yonder he is! Deny him,
    forswear him, or else we are all undone.

Exeunt BIONDELLO, TRANIO, *and* PEDANT *as fast as
                                        may be.*

95   LUCENTIO   Pardon, sweet father.

        [*He*] *kneels.*

VINCENTIO   Lives my sweet son?

BIANCA   Pardon, dear father.

BAPTISTA   How hast thou offended? Where is Lucentio?

LUCENTIO   Here's Lucentio, right son to the right Vincentio,

100   That have by marriage made thy daughter mine
        While counterfeit supposes⁵ bleared thine eyne.°   *deceived your eyes*

GREMIO   Here's packing° with a witness,⁶ to deceive us all.   *plotting*

VINCENTIO   Where is that damned villain Tranio,
        That faced and braved° me in this matter so?   *defied*

105   BAPTISTA   Why, tell me, is not this my Cambio?

BIANCA   Cambio is changed into Lucentio.

LUCENTIO   Love wrought these miracles. Bianca's love
        Made me exchange my state° with Tranio,   *social position*
        While he did bear my countenance in the town;

110   And happily I have arrived at the last
        Unto the wishèd haven of my bliss.
        What Tranio did, myself enforced him to;
        Then pardon him, sweet father, for my sake.

VINCENTIO   I'll slit the villain's nose that would have sent me

115   to the jail.

BAPTISTA   But do you hear, sir? Have you married my daughter
        without asking my good will?

VINCENTIO   Fear not, Baptista, we will content you, go to. But
        I will in to be revenged for this villainy.   *Exit.*

120   BAPTISTA   And I to sound the depth° of this knavery.   *Exit.*   *discover the extent*

LUCENTIO   Look not pale, Bianca, thy father will not frown.

        Exeunt [LUCENTIO *and* BIANCA].

GREMIO   My cake is dough,⁷ but I'll in among the rest,
        Out of hope of all° but my share of the feast.   [*Exit.*]   *With hope of nothing*

KATHERINA   Husband, let's follow to see the end of this ado.

125   PETRUCCIO   First kiss me, Kate, and we will.

KATHERINA   What, in the midst of the street?

PETRUCCIO   What, art thou ashamed of me?

KATHERINA   No, sir, God forbid, but ashamed to kiss.

PETRUCCIO   Why, then, let's home again. —Come, sirrah, let's

130   away.

KATHERINA   Nay, I will give thee a kiss. Now, pray thee, love,
        stay.

PETRUCCIO   Is not this well? Come, my sweet Kate.
        Better once than never, for never too late.⁸

                                        Exeunt.

---

5. False ideas. Possibly an allusion to Gascoigne's
Supposes (1566), which was Shakespeare's main
source for the Bianca and Lucentio plot.
6. With clear evidence; without any doubt.

7. Proverbial expression for a failed project.
8. Two proverbs combined: "Better late than never"
and "It is never too late to mend."

5.2

Enter BAPTISTA, VINCENTIO, GREMIO, *the* PEDANT,
LUCENTIO, BIANCA, [PETRUCCIO, KATHERINA,
HORTENSIO, *and the*] WIDOW, [*followed by*]
BIONDELLO, GRUMIO, *and* TRANIO *with the* [SERVANTS]
bringing in a banquet.[1]

LUCENTIO At last, though long,° our jarring notes agree,		*after a long time*
And time it is when raging war is done		
To smile at scapes° and perils overblown.		*escapes*
My fair Bianca, bid my father welcome,		
5 While I with selfsame° kindness welcome thine.		*identical*

Brother Petruccio, sister Katherina,
And thou, Hortensio, with thy loving widow,
Feast with the best, and welcome to my house.
My banquet is to close our stomachs up
10   After our great good cheer.° Pray you, sit down,   *feast; happiness*
For now we sit to chat as well as eat.

PETRUCCIO   Nothing but sit and sit, and eat and eat.
BAPTISTA   Padua affords this kindness, son Petruccio.
PETRUCCIO   Padua affords nothing but what is kind.
15   HORTENSIO   For both our sakes I would that word were true.
PETRUCCIO   Now, for my life, Hortensio fears[2] his widow.
WIDOW   Then never trust me if I be afeard.°   *afraid*
PETRUCCIO   You are very sensible, and yet you miss my sense:
   I mean Hortensio is afeard of you.
20   WIDOW   He that is giddy thinks the world turns round.[3]
PETRUCCIO   Roundly° replied.   *Boldly*
KATHERINA   Mistress, how mean you that?
WIDOW   Thus I conceive by him.[4]
PETRUCCIO   Conceives° by me! How likes Hortensio that?   *Becomes pregnant*
HORTENSIO   My widow says thus she conceives her tale.[5]
25   PETRUCCIO   Very well mended. Kiss him for that, good widow.
KATHERINA   "He that is giddy thinks the world turns round."
   I pray you tell me what you meant by that.
WIDOW   Your husband, being troubled with a shrew,
   Measures my husband's sorrow by his woe:
30   And now you know my meaning.
KATHERINA   A very mean meaning.
WIDOW   Right, I mean you.
KATHERINA   And I am mean indeed, respecting you.[6]
PETRUCCIO   To her, Kate!
HORTENSIO   To her, Widow!
35   PETRUCCIO   A hundred marks,[7] my Kate does put her down.°   *defeat her*
HORTENSIO   That's my office.[8]
PETRUCCIO   Spoke like an officer.[9] Ha' to thee,° lad.   *Here's to you*
   [*He*] *drinks to* HORTENSIO.

5.2 Location: Lucentio's house in Padua.
1. Light meal of fruit, sweetmeats, and wine following the main meal.
2. Is afraid of. The widow takes it to mean "frightens."
3. That is, people judge everything by their own experience, implying that Petruccio is afraid of his wife.
4. Thus I understand him.
5. Thus she understands or intends her remark, with a pun on "tail" as meaning "genitalia."

6. I am moderate (like the mathematical "mean") compared with you; I demean myself in dealing with you.
7. A substantial wager, since 1 mark was equivalent to 13 shillings and 4 pence, or two-thirds of a pound. An unskilled laborer might earn 6 to 8 pounds in a year.
8. That's my job, with a pun on "put her down" as meaning "force or lay her down in sexual intercourse."
9. Like one who knows his duty.

BAPTISTA   How likes Gremio these quick-witted folks?

GREMIO   Believe me, sir, they butt together[1] well.

40 BIANCA   Head and butt? An hasty-witted body
Would say your head and butt were head and horn.[2]

VINCENTIO   Ay, mistress bride, hath that awakened you?

BIANCA   Ay, but not frighted me; therefore I'll sleep again.

PETRUCCIO   Nay, that you shall not, since you have begun:

45 Have at° you for a better jest or two.   *I shall come at*

BIANCA   Am I your bird? I mean to shift my bush,[3]
And then pursue me as you draw your bow.
You are welcome all.

          Exeunt BIANCA[, KATHERINA, *and* WIDOW].

PETRUCCIO   She hath prevented° me. Here, Signor Tranio,   *stopped; anticipated*

50 This bird you aimed at, though you hit her not—
Therefore a health to all that shot and missed.

TRANIO   O sir, Lucentio slipped° me like his greyhound,   *unleashed*
Which runs himself and catches for his master.

PETRUCCIO   A good swift° simile, but something currish.°   *witty / base; doglike*

55 TRANIO   'Tis well, sir, that you hunted for yourself:
'Tis thought your deer does hold you at a bay.[4]

BAPTISTA   Oh, oh, Petruccio, Tranio hits you now.

LUCENTIO   I thank thee for that gird,° good Tranio.   *taunt*

HORTENSIO   Confess, confess: hath he not hit you here?

60 PETRUCCIO   'A° has a little galled° me, I confess.   *He / wounded*
And as the jest did glance away from me,
'Tis ten to one it maimed you two outright.

BAPTISTA   Now in good sadness,° son Petruccio,   *in all seriousness*
I think thou hast the veriest shrew of all.

65 PETRUCCIO   Well, I say no, and therefore, sir, assurance:
Let's each one send unto° his wife,   *summon*
And he whose wife is most obedient
To come at first when he doth send for her
Shall win the wager which we will propose.

HORTENSIO   Content;° what's the wager?   *Agreed*

70 LUCENTIO   Twenty crowns.°   *coins worth five shillings*

PETRUCCIO   Twenty crowns?
I'll venture so much of° my hawk or hound,   *on*
But twenty times so much upon my wife.

LUCENTIO   A hundred, then.

HORTENSIO   Content.

PETRUCCIO   A match.° 'Tis done.   *Agreed*

HORTENSIO   Who shall begin?

75 LUCENTIO   That will I.
Go, Biondello, bid your mistress come to me.

BIONDELLO   I go.   *Exit.*

BAPTISTA   Son, I'll be your half Bianca comes.[5]

LUCENTIO   I'll have no halves; I'll bear it all myself.

      Enter BIONDELLO.

How now, what news?

---

1. They thrust their heads or horns together, with a pun on "butt" as meaning "buttocks."
2. Would say your butting head was a cuckold's horned head.
3. Alluding to the Elizabethan sport of shooting sitting birds with a bow and arrow. There may also be a bawdy pun on "bush" as meaning "pubic area" and

the target of Petruccio's (phallic) arrow.
4. Your deer turns on you and holds you at a distance. Punning on "deer" and "dear."
5. I'll put up half the stake (and therefore collect half of any winnings) in wagering that Bianca will come first.

80   BIONDELLO   Sir, my mistress sends you word
     That she is busy and she cannot come.
     PETRUCCIO   How? "She's busy and she cannot come."
     Is that an answer?
     GREMIO   Ay, and a kind one, too.
     Pray God, sir, your wife send you not a worse.
85   PETRUCCIO   I hope better.
     HORTENSIO   Sirrah Biondello, go and entreat my wife to come
     to me forthwith.
                                          Exit BIONDELLO.
     PETRUCCIO   Oh, ho, "entreat" her. Nay, then she must needs
     come.
     HORTENSIO   I am afraid, sir, do what you can,
     Yours will not be entreated.
                      Enter BIONDELLO.
90   Now, where's my wife?
     BIONDELLO   She says you have some goodly jest in hand.
     She will not come; she bids you come to her.
     PETRUCCIO   Worse and worse. "She will not come." Oh, vile,
     Intolerable, not to be endured!
95   Sirrah Grumio, go to your mistress,
     Say I command her come to me.   *Exit* [GRUMIO].
     HORTENSIO   I know her answer.
     PETRUCCIO   What?
     HORTENSIO   She will not.
     PETRUCCIO   The fouler fortune mine, and there an end.[6]
                      Enter KATHERINA.
     BAPTISTA   Now, by my halidom,° here comes Katherina.   *by all I hold sacred*
100 KATHERINA   What is your will, sir, that you send for me?
     PETRUCCIO   Where is your sister and Hortensio's wife?
     KATHERINA   They sit conferring by the parlor fire.
     PETRUCCIO   Go fetch them hither. If they deny° to come,   *refuse*
     Swinge me them soundly forth[7] unto their husbands.
105 Away, I say, and bring them hither straight.
                                          [*Exit* KATHERINA.]
     LUCENTIO   Here is a wonder, if you talk of a wonder.
     HORTENSIO   And so it is. I wonder what it bodes.
     PETRUCCIO   Marry, peace it bodes, and love, and quiet life,
     An awful° rule and right supremacy   *awe-inspiring*
110 And, to be short, what not° that's sweet and happy.   *everything*
     BAPTISTA   Now fair befall thee, good Petruccio.
     The wager thou hast won, and I will add
     Unto their losses twenty thousand crowns,
     Another dowry to another daughter,
115 For she is changed as she had never been.[8]
     PETRUCCIO   Nay, I will win my wager better yet
     And show more sign of her obedience,
     Her new-built virtue and obedience.
                 Enter KATHERINA, BIANCA, *and* WIDOW.
     See where she comes and brings your froward° wives   *willful*

---

6. Worse luck for me (if you're right), and that's that.   8. As if she had never existed before; as if she had
7. Beat them soundly for me, and bring them out.   never been what she was before (a shrew).

120   As prisoners to her womanly persuasion.
        Katherine, that cap of yours becomes you not.
        Off with that bauble; throw it underfoot.
    WIDOW   Lord, let me never have a cause to sigh
        Till I be brought to such a silly pass.
125   BIANCA   Fie, what a foolish duty call you this?
    LUCENTIO   I would your duty were as foolish too.
        The wisdom of your duty, fair Bianca,
        Hath cost me five hundred crowns since supper time.
    BIANCA   The more fool you for laying° on my duty.   *gambling*
130   PETRUCCIO   Katherine, I charge thee tell these headstrong
        women
        What duty they do owe their lords and husbands.
    WIDOW   Come, come, you're mocking; we will have no telling.
    PETRUCCIO   Come on, I say, and first begin with her.
    WIDOW   She shall not.
135   PETRUCCIO   I say she shall, and first begin with her.
    KATHERINA   Fie, fie, unknit that threatening unkind brow,
        And dart not scornful glances from those eyes
        To wound thy lord, thy king, thy governor.
        It blots° thy beauty as frosts do bite the meads,°   *disfigures / meadows*
140   Confounds thy fame° as whirlwinds shake fair buds   *Ruins your reputation*
        And in no sense is meet° or amiable.   *fitting*
        A woman moved° is like a fountain troubled,   *angry*
        Muddy, ill-seeming,° thick, bereft of beauty,   *ugly*
        And while it is so none so dry or thirsty
145   Will deign to sip or touch one drop of it.
        Thy husband is thy lord, thy life, thy keeper,
        Thy head, thy sovereign, one that cares for thee,
        And for thy maintenance commits his body
        To painful labor both by sea and land,
150   To watch the night in storms, the day in cold,
        Whilst thou liest warm at home, secure and safe,
        And craves no other tribute at thy hands
        But love, fair looks, and true obedience—
        Too little payment for so great a debt.
155   Such duty as the subject owes the prince,
        Even such a woman oweth to her husband.
        And when she is froward, peevish,° sullen, sour,   *obstinate*
        And not obedient to his honest will,
        What is she but a foul contending rebel
160   And graceless traitor to her loving lord?
        I am ashamed that women are so simple°   *foolish*
        To offer war where they should kneel for peace,
        Or seek for rule, supremacy, and sway
        When they are bound to serve, love, and obey.
165   Why are our bodies soft and weak and smooth,
        Unapt to° toil and trouble in the world,   *Unfitted for*
        But that our soft conditions° and our hearts   *dispositions*
        Should well agree with our external parts?
        Come, come, you froward and unable worms.°   *weak creatures*
170   My mind hath been as big° as one of yours,   *proud*
        My heart° as great, my reason haply more   *spirit*
        To bandy word for word and frown for frown.
        But now I see our lances are but straws,

Our strength as weak,° our weakness past compare,   (as straws)
175   That seeming to be most which we indeed least are.
Then vail your stomachs, for it is no boot,[9]
And place your hands below your husband's foot—
In token of which duty, if he please,
My hand is ready, may it do him ease.°[1]   give him comfort
180   PETRUCCIO   Why, there's a wench. Come on and kiss me, Kate.
LUCENTIO   Well, go thy ways, old lad, for thou shalt ha't.[2]
VINCENTIO   'Tis a good hearing° when children are toward.[3]   thing to hear
LUCENTIO   But a harsh hearing when women are froward.
PETRUCCIO   Come, Kate, we'll to bed.
185   —We three are married, but you two are sped.°   defeated
'Twas I won the wager, though you hit the white,[4]
And being a winner,° God give you good night.   since I am a winner
                              Exit PETRUCCIO.[5]
HORTENSIO   Now go thy ways, thou hast tamed a curst shrew.
LUCENTIO   'Tis a wonder, by your leave, she will be tamed so.
                              [Exeunt.][6]

9. Then lower your pride, for it is of no profit.
1. PERFORMANCE COMMENT Though Katherina's final speech may suggest she has been tamed, many actors have delivered it in ways that undercut or ironize its meaning. See Digital Edition PC 2.
2. You shall have the prize.
3. Obedient (as opposed to "froward," line 119).
4. Hit the target (with a pun on "Bianca," which means "white" in Italian).

5. TEXTUAL COMMENT The sense of the play's resolution will be affected by editorial and performance choices about how Petruccio and Katherina exit the stage. F lists an exit only for Petruccio here, although many editors have Katherina leave the stage with him. See Digital Edition TC 10.
6. In A Shrew, the Christopher Sly story concludes the play.

The Comedy of Errors

In his essay "On Cripples," Shakespeare's great contemporary Michel de Montaigne alludes to a strange case of impersonation in a small rural community in southwestern France. There, a cunning imposter succeeded in assuming the identity of Martin Guerre, a man who had disappeared some years earlier. The imposter lived in the community for three years, sleeping with Guerre's wife and farming his land, until the real Martin Guerre unexpectedly returned. Convicted of fraud, the imposter confessed and was hanged.

Montaigne was dismayed by the execution, for he felt that the evidence was too murky, the imposture too convincing, and human identity too elusive a possession to justify capital punishment. The court, he writes, should have emulated the ancient Greek tribunal that, confronted by a similarly baffling case, ordered the parties to come back in a hundred years. Montaigne was not only advising judicial caution; he was urging his readers to take everyday life less automatically, to acknowledge the inevitability of ignorance and error, and to respond to their own existence with wonder. "I have seen no more evident monstrosity and miracle in the world than myself," he writes in the same essay in which he talks about Martin Guerre. "We become habituated to anything strange by use and time; but the more I frequent myself and know myself, the more my deformity astonishes me, and the less I understand myself."

Montaigne's reflections on Martin Guerre have no direct bearing on *The Comedy of Errors*, but they alert us to the play's wholesale unsettling of the familiar. The comfortable assumptions that condition a normal life—I know who I am; these things belong to me and not to someone else; these are the people I love, command, work for, do business with, or avoid—are undermined by the tangled interactions of two sets of identical twins. Antipholus of Syracuse and Antipholus of Ephesus, along with their servants, Dromio of Syracuse and Dromio of Ephesus, have been raised apart from one another in separate cities and are unaware that their paths are now unexpectedly crossing. Through a breathless succession of zany doublings and confusions, Shakespeare's comedy discloses the hidden strangeness of ordinary existence. An invitation to dinner, a simple transaction with a goldsmith, the operation of commercial and civil laws, the relationship between master and servant, the bond between husband and wife (or mistress or sister-in-law)—all become unhinged, as if by sorcery. "There's not a man I meet but doth salute me," says Antipholus of Syracuse, "As if I were their well-acquainted friend, / And everyone doth call me by my name" (4.3.1–3). These are the familiar practices of everyday life, but to this stranger who is, unbeknownst to him, being mistaken for his identical (and identically named) twin, they confirm the unsavory reputation of Ephesus as a place of "nimble jugglers," "Dark-working sorcerers," "Soul-killing witches," and "Disguisèd cheaters" (1.2.98–101).

The audience knows, of course, that Antipholus's uncanny experiences have been caused neither by witchcraft nor by deliberate identity theft. The wonder that seems to suffuse everything is the result of nothing more magical or malicious than twinship and a shared name; hence, we could say, such wonder is spurious or misplaced, the result of misunderstandings. "This is the fairy land" (2.2.190), exclaims one of the Dromios, mystified by the succession of inexplicable events, and his similarly disoriented master invokes the notorious wiles of far-off Lapland. But in *The Comedy of Errors*, there is in reality only daylight and the familiar city street of Roman comedy, a street reassuringly adapted to the commercial world of Shakespeare's

An Italian merchant pictured on a Florentine playing card.

London. Disorientation and danger lurk, to be sure, in this conventional urban landscape—Antipholus of Syracuse suspects he is the victim of sorcery, Antipholus of Ephesus is treated as a madman, Adriana fears the loss of her husband's love, Luciana is convinced that her brother-in-law is trying to seduce her, the servants are constantly beaten for faults they have not in fact committed, and poor Egeon is condemned to die at day's end. Yet though the pressure of time weighs heavily on virtually all of the characters, enmeshed as they are in humiliating, menacing, and apparently insoluble difficulties, the confusions that bedevil their lives are all neatly resolved by the appointed hour of 5:00 P.M.

This comic resolution, however, does not quite make weirdness or wonder altogether evaporate from the play. Montaigne urged his readers to abandon their confident belief in the ordered rationality of life and to find the marvelous in the everyday. Identical twins are fairly commonplace and the fact that two people can bear the same name even more so, but Shakespeare's play calls attention to all that is potentially disorienting in such familiar circumstances. The end of *The Comedy of Errors* seems to restore order and reason—to make the ordinary world ordinary again—but the closing gestures lightly unsettle this restoration. The Abbess, who turns out to be Egeon's long-lost wife and the mother of the twin Antipholuses, finds a strange image, at once touching and grotesque, to describe her experiences: she declares that she has been pregnant for thirty-three years and has only now given birth. Though officially everything has been sorted out, in fact everything is just beginning. A family that has had virtually no shared experience has been suddenly reconstituted and will need to rework all the relationships among its members. The Antipholus brothers, physically indistinguishable, have almost nothing else in common. Adriana is formally reconciled with her estranged husband but has no assurance that things will improve. And the twin Dromios, unable to determine which of them is the elder and should therefore go first through the door, decide that they will draw lots for seniority; meanwhile, they will dispense with hierarchy and go through the door hand in hand.

More telling, perhaps, the questions raised by the strange case of Martin Guerre linger unresolved at the end of Shakespeare's comedy: What is the self? What are the guarantees of identity? Who possesses a name, and by what right? How is individuality secured? How can one person represent another? The drama is the perfect medium for an exploration of these questions, for the form of the drama itself invites reflection on the extent to which it is possible for one person to assume the identity of another.

From this perspective, *The Comedy of Errors* is not, as it is sometimes said to be, a simple and even simpleminded farce, the crude work of a novice playwright, but a remarkably subtle and acute deployment of the very conditions of the theater to engage with problems that haunted Shakespeare throughout his career.

While it is a mistake to view it as mere apprentice work, *The Comedy of Errors* is nonetheless one of the earliest of Shakespeare's plays (and it is also, perhaps not coincidentally, the shortest). Its exact date of composition and first performance are unknown; there was a performance at Gray's Inn, one of London's law schools, on December 28, 1594, but the play's thematic and stylistic resemblances to Shakespeare's other early comedies, *The Two Gentlemen of Verona, Love's Labor's Lost*, and *The Taming of the Shrew*, have led many scholars to conclude that he wrote it some years earlier. It was not printed until 1623, as part of the First Folio.

The anonymous recorder of the Gray's Inn performance—apparently something of a debacle because of the pushing and shoving of unexpectedly large crowds—noted the play's resemblance to an ancient comedy, the *Menaechmi*, written by the Roman playwright Plautus. Shakespeare probably read this much-admired play in Latin, since an English translation, by William Warner, was not printed until 1595. The *Menaechmi* is a brilliant, energetic farce, fast-paced, funny, and, as farces often are, cold at heart. A prologue carefully explains the premise: a Syracusan merchant took one of his twin sons, seven years old, on a business trip abroad. During a festival, he accidentally became separated from the son. The boy was found by a childless trader, who took him off to Epidamnum; the father, crazed with grief, died a few days later. When news of the catastrophe reached Syracuse, the remaining son was given the name of his missing brother.

The action of Plautus's play is set some years later, when Menaechmus of Syracuse, searching for his twin, finds himself in Epidamnum. Greeted warmly by perfect strangers, Menaechmus realizes that some mistake is being made, but he is not filled with dread. "I can lose nothing," he cheerfully tells his slave, as he accepts food, gifts, and sexual favors from a woman who, evidently confusing him with someone else, imagines that she is his mistress. What most strikes him is that it is all free of charge. His twin, a prosperous citizen who is normally comfortable in an entourage that includes wife, household slaves, mistress, and an obnoxious hanger-on nicknamed the Sponge, is frustrated by the fact that everyone seems to have gone mad, and in fact, he becomes enraged when he himself is treated as a madman. The dizzying confusions steadily mount until the brothers find themselves face-to-face and, with delicious slowness, figure out that they are the long-separated identical twins. The brothers plan to return together to Syracuse, and the play ends with the announcement of the forthcoming auction of Menaechmus's property: "slaves, household effects, house, land, etcetera—and a wife, should there be any purchaser."

Though he took over much of Plautus's farce, Shakespeare made highly revealing changes and additions. For a start, he shifted the setting from Epidamnum to Ephesus, a city associated with sorcery, exorcism, mystery cults, and early Christianity. As if to multiply the comic confusion generated by one set of identical twins, he added a second set—the servants, who, for reasons that are not really explained, bear like their masters a single name. (The device of the identical slaves is borrowed from another play by Plautus, the *Amphitruo*.) Shakespeare also chose to double the plot by framing the main action with the anguished figure of the Syracusan merchant Egeon, caught up in his city's murderous commercial struggle with rival city Ephesus. The melancholy personal history that Egeon relates is adapted not from the ancient comedy but from a medieval romance, the tale of Apollonius of Tyre as told by the fourteenth-century poet John Gower in his *Confessio Amantis* (a tale to which Shakespeare again turned many years later for the plot of *Pericles*). Egeon's fate quickly recedes from the audience's attention, but the threat to his life provides a somber context for the play's hilarity, and his return to the stage at the close, on the way to the place of execution, suddenly raises the stakes of the resolution. The closing scene

Traso

Parmeno

Gnato

A scene in the street/the street as scene.
Woodcut from a German edition of Terence's
Eunuchus (1486).

highlights the romance elements that Shakespeare introduced into his frenetic scheme of mistaken identity: the reuniting of parents and children who had been tragically separated, the miraculous recovery of a beloved spouse long presumed dead, and a sense of wonder that does not entirely evaporate with the solving of the puzzle. Plautus's Epidamnum is a city full of rogues, parasites, and courtesans, a place where you can lose your cloak, your chain, and your money; Shakespeare's Ephesus is a place where you can lose—or regain—your identity, your marriage, and your life.

Egeon's story in *The Comedy of Errors* has a shape that merits attention: he is condemned to death through the operation of an inflexible law that even the sympathetic Duke cannot mitigate, and then, through a wondrous turn of events, his life is spared, and he recovers the loved ones he thought he had lost forever. Even though the play is set in pagan antiquity, in this shape we may sense the psychic and moral rhythm of Christianity: the mortal penalty of the harsh law is wiped out, altogether unexpectedly and gratuitously, by a miraculous, loving dispensation. The farcical core of the play is at a considerable remove from this portentous rhythm, but Christianity's influence is not restricted to the frame. Since Shakespeare and his age were relatively indifferent to anachronism, Antipholus of Syracuse can say to his servant, "Now, as I am a Christian, answer me" (1.2.77), and the servant can cross himself and call for his rosary beads (2.2.189). The fear of demonic possession takes a specifically Christian form when Satan himself is exorcised by Doctor Pinch. And although pagan antiquity had shrines such as the Temple of Diana at Ephesus (where the tale of Apollonius of Tyre reaches its climax), the priory and its abbess seem to belong in a Christian community, a community invoked by the very name of Ephesus, where St. Paul preached and to which he wrote an influential epistle.

A central concern of the Epistle to the Ephesians is marriage, where, in the words of Genesis, "two shall be one flesh." Paul spells out what is required: "Wives, submit yourselves unto your own husbands, as unto the Lord. . . . Husbands, love your wives, even as Christ also loved the church." These strikingly asymmetrical admonitions make themselves felt throughout *The Comedy of Errors*. Where Plautus's Menaechmus cheerfully cheats on his wife, Shakespeare's married twin seems to have some traces of moral restraint. Antipholus turns to the courtesan only when his wife, Adriana, seems to lock him out of his own house—and even then, protesting to his friends that his wife's suspicions are unfounded, he seems mainly interested in dinner and pleasant conversation. Where the nameless wife in Plautus is above all outraged that her husband has stolen from her a gown and a bracelet to bestow as presents on his mistress, Shakespeare's Adriana is obsessed with the possibility that her husband no

"I'll to the mart" (3.2.187). London's Royal Exchange, founded by Sir Thomas Gresham, 1565. Etching by Wenceslaus Hollar (1644).

longer loves her. It is this tormenting fear of marital estrangement that has driven her to a querulousness that only confirms her overwhelming craving for perfect union:

> Ah, do not tear away thyself from me;
> For know, my love, as easy mayst thou fall
> A drop of water in the breaking gulf
> And take unmingled thence that drop again
> Without addition or diminishing,
> As take from me thyself, and not me too.
> (2.2.125–30)

The oneness that is envisioned here, the poignant longing for wholeness, and the fear of pollution and self-loss have no place in the emotional register of the *Menaechmi.* Where Plautus's farce ends with a joke about offering the wife for sale, *The Comedy of Errors* ends with the characters, reconciled and reunited, entering the abbey for a feast.

Near the close of Shakespeare's play, the Abbess seems to reflect the spirit of St. Paul's admonition to wives when she observes that by robbing her husband of the "sweet recreation" that he should find at home, Adriana's "jealous fits" have driven him mad (5.1.76, 85). This criticism echoes both Antipholus's own complaint that his wife is "shrewish" (3.1.2) and the distinctly Pauline opinions voiced by Adriana's sister, Luciana. Luciana—a character for whom there is no precedent in Plautus—argues that males of every species are "masters to their females, and their lords" (2.1.24) and therefore that Adriana should patiently submit to her husband. Such views, similar to those expressed by the "reformed" Katherina in *The Taming of the Shrew,* are given considerable prominence in *The Comedy of Errors,* and yet they are neither unchallenged nor unequivocally endorsed. Adriana observes wryly that her sister is single and hence that her views on marriage are untested by experience. And the Abbess's moralizing diagnosis—that Antipholus would not have mistreated Adriana or gone mad if she had reined in her tongue—turns out to be merely another of the mistaken conjectures that all of the characters incessantly advance in their attempts to account for the day's weird events.

There is a kind of laughter that functions as social regulation: comedy, writes Sir Philip Sidney in his *Defense of Poesy* (ca. 1583), "is an imitation of the common errors of our life," which the dramatist represents "in the most ridiculous and scornful sort that may be, so as it is impossible that any beholder can be content to be such a one." By such means shrewish wives, philandering husbands, and negligent servants are disciplined and put back in their proper places. But in *The Comedy of Errors*, though the errors are ridiculous enough, they are hardly common, and the audience's laughter seems something other than scornful or regulative. None of the explanatory accounts—not even the moral values and providential rhythm of Christianity with which Shakespeare has infused his pagan plot—seems entirely adequate as a response to the chain of mad mistakings. The characters are subject not to a divine plan or to the social order but to fortune. And if this fortune turns out to have the happy air of providence—epitomized by the reuniting of the divided and dispersed family—there seems to be no particularly uplifting lesson to be learned.

Shakespeare's play is cannily alert to the arbitrariness of human relations. An innocent merchant is condemned to death: no one thinks he is a malefactor, but he will be executed for being in the wrong place at the wrong time. One set of twins is destined through poverty to be the servants, casually beaten and abused, of the other set. The servants, called "knaves" and "villains," are in no way less intelligent or able than their masters; their fate is the consequence of the accident of birth. A man, "master of his liberty" (2.1.7), gads about the city, bestowing gifts on a courtesan. His neglected wife, fuming at home, must "practice to obey" (2.1.29). The wife protests the double standard—"Why should their liberty than ours be more?" (2.1.10)—and in doing so gives voice to a question that haunts virtually the entire social nexus of the play. At stake are not only the weird, unintended consequences of the day's zany misrecognitions; rather, those misrecognitions cast a sharp, satirical light on the gender and class distinctions that make up the structure of everyday life. "I have served him from the hour of my nativity to this instant," Dromio of Ephesus bitterly remarks, "and have nothing at his hands for my service but blows" (4.4.30–32).

Yet if *The Comedy of Errors* casts doubt on the supposed naturalness and justice of the ways things are, it does not imagine the possibility of a radical transformation. In the midst of the farcical confusions, characters repeatedly long for greater justice, equality, and emotional fulfillment, but Shakespeare does not encourage us to believe that such an existence can be realized. There may be a happy resolution, but there is no escape from the pervasive, fundamentally inequitable social order and from the mercantile world based on credit, trade, exchange, bonds, and debt.

Several of Shakespeare's best-loved comedies are structured around alternative worlds: the familiar, daylit realm of the court or city is set against the magical realm of the woods and the enchanted night. But in *The Comedy of Errors*, there is only the single urban setting, a setting that would have reminded contemporary audiences of the bustling city that stretched out beyond the walls of the playhouse. In the sixteenth century, London had become the center of a commercial culture that Shakespeare deftly sketches with quick strokes. We learn that Antipholus keeps a purse of ducats locked "in the desk / That's covered o'er with Turkish tapestry" (4.1.103–04), that the courtesan considers a ring worth forty ducats "too much to lose" (4.3.92), and that the goldsmith plans to discharge his overdue debt to a merchant with the money that Antipholus has promised to pay him for the gold chain. That gold chain functions as a convenient symbol of the interlinked network of obligations and exchanges in which the twins—who seem as like one another as two coins of equal value—are caught and which their uncontrolled interchangeability temporarily disrupts.

A closer look reveals that Antipholus of Ephesus and Antipholus of Syracuse are not in fact interchangeable. The former is confident, well connected, and somewhat irascible; the latter is anxious, insecure, and driven by restless longing:

> I to the world am like a drop of water
> That in the ocean seeks another drop,
> Who, falling there to find his fellow forth,
> Unseen, inquisitive, confounds himself.
>   (1.2.35–38)

This poignant sense of self-loss, which anticipates the alienation and existential anxiety of the tragedies, is intensified by the mad confusions that follow: the events of *The Comedy of Errors* may be deliciously amusing to the audience, but to the characters they are mystifying and even nightmarish. Antonin Artaud, a modern writer who championed what he called the "Theater of Cruelty," praises the Marx Brothers' movies in terms that seem at least as relevant to Shakespeare's comedy: "In order to understand the powerful, total, definitive, absolute originality . . . of films like *Animal Crackers*," Artaud writes, "you would have to add to humor the notion of something disquieting and tragic, a fatality (neither happy nor unhappy, difficult to formulate) which would hover over it like the cast of an appalling malady upon an exquisitely beautiful profile." And yet it is not the nightmare that triumphs but laughter— laughter at what another sixteenth-century writer, George Gascoigne, called "supposes." Gascoigne defined a suppose as "a mistaking or imagination of one thing for another," and it is with a frantic succession of these supposes, all equally wide of the mark, that the baffled characters of *The Comedy of Errors* occupy themselves.

The "imagination of one thing for another" could serve as a definition of the theater. The spectators of Shakespeare's comedy have paid for the pleasure of watching identity slip away from the characters' grasp, as if in the home or the marketplace who you are is no more secure than it is onstage. They have paid, too, for the pleasure of watching identity serendipitously return, as if Shakespeare's theater had the magic power to restore the human family, however broken and scattered, and to restore stability to the battered self. If neither the loss nor the recovery is altogether plausible, the delicious intertwining of the two seems designed to provoke what Montaigne urged upon his readers: a skeptical wonder.

STEPHEN GREENBLATT

SELECTED BIBLIOGRAPHY

Christensen, Ann C. "'Because their business still lies out a' door': Resisting the Separation of the Spheres in Shakespeare's *The Comedy of Errors*." *Literature and History* 5 (1996): 19–37. Examines how *The Comedy of Errors* charts the growing divide both between public and private and between the commercial and domestic spheres.

Finkelstein, Richard. "*The Comedy of Errors* and the Theology of Things." *Studies in English Literature, 1500–1900* 52 (2012): 325–44. Argues that by exploring the connection between spiritual and commercial capital, *The Comedy of Errors* places increased emphasis on the possibility of redemption not through religious means but through the marketplace.

Frye, Northrop. "The Argument of Comedy." *English Institute Essays*. New York: AMS Press, 1948. 58–73. Argues that Shakespeare's comic form is a synthesis of Aristophanes' Old Comedy and the New Comedy of Plautus and Terence.

Hunt, Maurice. "Slavery, English Servitude and *The Comedy of Errors*." *English Literary Renaissance* 27 (1997): 31–56. Looks at how the rough treatment of the Dromio twins and their ambiguous status—somewhere between servants and slaves— reflect similar features of Elizabethan servitude.

Miola, Robert S., ed. *"The Comedy of Errors": Critical Essays.* New York: Routledge, 2001. See esp. Laurie Maguire, "The Girls from Ephesus," 355–91. A collection of essays on *The Comedy of Errors* spanning a range of topics, including stage history, performance studies, genre conventions, and gender studies. In her essay, Maguire argues that Shakespeare's comedy explores contrasting models for female conduct, one independent and the other submissive.

Parker, Patricia. "The Bible and the Marketplace: *The Comedy of Errors.*" *Shakespeare from the Margins: Language, Culture, Context.* Chicago: U of Chicago P, 1996. 56–82. Asserts that while displaying a wealth of biblical allusions, Shakespeare's comedy attempts at the same time to undermine the Bible as a cultural authority.

Perry, Curtis. "Commerce, Community, and Nostalgia in *The Comedy of Errors.*" *Money and the Age of Shakespeare: Essays in New Economic Criticism.* Ed. Linda Woodbridge. New York: Palgrave Macmillan, 2003. 39–51. Looks at how the longing for family in *The Comedy of Errors* reveals the alienating forces of the market economy.

Sohrawardy, Ameer. "Twin Obligations in Soloman Plaatje's *Diphosho-phosho.*" *Native Shakespeares: Indigenous Appropriations on a Global Stage.* Ed. Craig Dionne and Parmita Kapadia. Burlington, VT: Ashgate, 2008. 187–200. Argues that South African writer Solomon Plaatje's controversial translation of *The Comedy of Errors* into Setswana constitutes an intertextual challenge to Shakespeare's play.

van Elk, Martine. "'This sympathized one day's error': Genre, Representation, and Subjectivity in *The Comedy of Errors.*" *Shakespeare Quarterly* 60 (2009): 47–72. Dissects how the play's foundations in both romance and farce reveal not only a clash of genres but also competing modes of self-representation.

Witmore, Michael. "The Avoidance of Ends in *The Comedy of Errors.*" *Culture of Accidents: Unexpected Knowledges in Early Modern England.* Stanford, CA: Stanford UP, 2001. 62–81. Asserts that rather than constituting a series of haphazard accidents, *The Comedy of Errors* is a self-conscious exploration of the problems inherent in representing accidents within the context of larger narratives.

FILM

The Comedy of Errors. 1983. Dir. James Cellan Jones. UK. 109 min. A BBC-TV production, with Roger Daltrey (lead singer of The Who) as the Dromios.

TEXTUAL INTRODUCTION

The base text for *The Comedy of Errors* is the First Folio of 1623, the earliest and only authoritative text of the play. With some notable exceptions, the Folio text is a good one, and most textual scholars agree that some form of the author's own manuscript was used as the copy text. Certain features of the text support this conclusion, including a particularly high degree of variation and uncertainty in speech prefixes and unnecessary or unnecessarily specific information in the stage directions.

Three different characters—Egeon, the First Merchant, and the Second Merchant—are identified with the same speech prefix, "*Mer.*" We learn from the stage direction opening the second act that Adriana is "*wife to Antipholis Sereptus,*" a description that is not used in the dialogue but that does derive from Shakespeare's source, Plautus's *Menaechmi.* The corresponding twin, Antipholus of Syracuse, is identified as "*Antipholis Erotes*" in the stage direction at 1.2.0, presumably resulting in the speech prefix "*E. Ant.*" (for Antipholus of Syracuse) in act 2. Confusingly, the same prefix is later used for Antipholus of Ephesus in act 5. A reference to Pinch's vocation as "*a Schoole-master*" in the stage direction marking his entrance at 4.4.38 provides information that is dramatically irrelevant. Another example of inconsistency is the identification of Adriana's kitchen maid as "*Luce*" throughout 3.1 and "*Nell*" in the dialogue at 3.2.110. Though the later reference is clearly to the character from 3.1, "*Luce*" cannot be a compositor's error, as the name appears consistently in the stage directions, speech prefixes, and dialogue of 3.1. Another example of such confusion occurs in 3.2, where Luciana is identified as "*Iuliana*" in the opening stage direction and "*Iulia*" in the first speech prefix.

References to locations in the stage directions, "*from the Bay*" (4.1.84) and "*from the Courtizans*" (4.1.13), may suggest an authorial desire to guide the theatrical staging, though they are not consistently included. It is also possible that location directions could have been added to the playing company manuscript while preparing the play for production. In the *Norton Shakespeare* text, references to characters in stage directions and speech prefixes have been regularized, though elsewhere the goal has been to stay as close as possible to the Folio text, retaining inconsistencies such as the name Luce/Nell for the same character.

The Folio's act divisions have been retained, and scene divisions have been added following the editorial tradition.

JAMES A. KNAPP

PERFORMANCE NOTE

The Comedy of Errors requires theater companies to present two pairs of twins that are mistaken for one another by the Ephesians, yet easily distinguished by the audience. Most pursue an illusion of likeness by casting actors of similar height and complexion and dressing them to match, though there exists a strong countertradition of doubling the roles, using one actor for the Antipholuses and another for the Dromios. The latter choice asks actors to differentiate the twins by slight changes in costume, voice, or personality (e.g., playing an urbane against a more rustic brother), and it also requires body doubles, curtain tricks, or textual revision so that the twins can meet each other in the final scene. Other productions cast "twins" starkly different in appearance, testing the audience's credulity and even the value of credibility in the theater. Given the play's farcical atmosphere and interest in exchanges—for example, of marks, blows, rope's ends, and rings—matching (for instance) a slim white Dromio to a portly black one, as Hudson Valley Shakespeare's 2002 production did, can prove an emphatic thematic complement to the action.

In light of its strong farcical elements, *The Comedy of Errors* tends to inspire highly stylized productions, often influenced by clowning and other traditional comic forms. The population of Ephesus—full of "courtesans," "witches," and "sorcerers"—is naturally conducive to *commedia*-inflected productions, which can help explain and excuse the play's wanton violence. Productions can also present the violence more naturalistically, complicating the genre and underscoring the play's presentation of master–servant relationships. In the same vein, productions face crucial choices in portraying Adriana, who even in highly farcical productions can stand out as the lone realistic figure in a sea of types. Presenting Adriana as a sensible, emotionally accessible woman can distinguish her as a sympathetic center, complicating the comic resolution with aspects of romance, while playing her as an archetypically jealous wife can help assure that the audience's focus remains with the Antipholi as they move through an unqualified farce.

BRETT GAMBOA

The Comedy of Errors

[THE PERSONS OF THE PLAY

Solinus, DUKE of Ephesus
EGEON, a merchant of Syracuse, father of the Antipholus twins
ANTIPHOLUS OF EPHESUS } twin brothers, sons of Egeon
ANTIPHOLUS OF SYRACUSE
DROMIO OF EPHESUS } twin brothers, bondmen of the Antipholuses
DROMIO OF SYRACUSE
ADRIANA, wife of Antipholus of Ephesus
LUCIANA, her sister
LUCE, Adriana's kitchen maid, also known as Nell
BALTHASAR, a merchant
ANGELO, a goldsmith
Doctor PINCH, a schoolmaster
FIRST MERCHANT, friend to Antipholus of Ephesus
SECOND MERCHANT, to whom Angelo owes a debt
Emilia, an ABBESS at Ephesus
COURTESAN
JAILER
MESSENGER
OFFICERS
Headsman, Attendants]

1.1

Enter [Solinus,] the DUKE of Ephesus, with [EGEON] the
Merchant of Syracuse, JAILER, and other Attendants.

EGEON¹ Proceed, Solinus, to procure my fall,
And by the doom° of death end woes and all.   *sentence*
DUKE Merchant of Syracusa,² plead no more.
I am not partial° to infringe our laws.   *inclined*
5 The enmity and discord which of late
Sprung from the rancorous outrage of your Duke
To merchants, our well-dealing³ countrymen,
Who, wanting° guilders⁴ to redeem° their lives,   *lacking / ransom*
Have sealed° his rigorous statutes with their bloods,   *ratified*
10 Excludes all pity from our threat'ning looks.
For since the mortal° and intestine jars°   *deadly / internal strife*
Twixt thy seditious countrymen and us,

1.1 Location: The play is set in Ephesus (modern Turkish *Efes*), a wealthy and important ancient Greek city-state in Asia Minor. Much of the action takes place, as in this opening scene, in a public space, a street or "mart" (i.e., marketplace). There are also three distinct houses, signified, as in the stage setting of ancient Roman comedy, by three doors, each possibly bearing a different sign. The house of Antipholus of Ephesus, identified as the Phoenix, is flanked by that of the courtesan, identified as the Porcupine. The priory in the last act may have borne anachronistically the sign of the cross.
1. TEXTUAL COMMENT The first speech prefix given to

this character in the Folio (F) is "*Marchant*," and it is not until the end of the scene that we learn his proper name: Egeon. Never identified in the Folio speech prefixes as Egeon, he is also called "*Mer.,*" "*Merch.,*" "*Mar. Fat.,*" "*Fa.,*" "*Fath.,*" and "*Father.*" See Digital Edition TC 1.
2. Syracusa or Syracuse (modern Italian *Siracusa*, on the southeast coast of Sicily) was a powerful ancient city-state founded by Greek settlers.
3. Honest-trading; more generally, civil or well-behaved; fair in their business transactions.
4. Money, not specifically referring to Dutch or German coins.

	It hath in solemn synods° been decreed,	*assemblies*
	Both by the Syracusians and ourselves,	
15	To admit no traffic to⁵ our adverse° towns.	*hostile*
	Nay more, if any born at Ephesus	
	Be seen at any Syracusian marts° and fairs;	*markets*
	Again, if any Syracusian born	
	Come to the bay of Ephesus, he dies,	
20	His goods confiscate to the Duke's dispose,°	*disposal*
	Unless a thousand marks⁶ be levièd°	*raised*
	To quit° the penalty and to ransom him.	*pay*
	Thy substance,° valued at the highest rate,	*goods*
	Cannot amount unto a hundred marks;	
25	Therefore by law thou art condemned to die.	

EGEON Yet this my comfort: when your words are done,
My woes end likewise with the evening sun.

DUKE Well, Syracusian, say in brief the cause
Why thou departed'st from thy native home,
30   And for what cause thou cam'st to Ephesus.

EGEON A heavier task could not have been imposed,
Than I° to speak my griefs unspeakable. *Than for me*
Yet that the world may witness that my end
Was wrought by nature,⁷ not by vile offense,
35   I'll utter what my sorrow gives me leave.
In Syracusa was I born, and wed
Unto a woman happy but for me,⁸
And by me,° had not our hap° been bad. *by me made happy / luck*
With her I lived in joy; our wealth increased
40   By prosperous voyages I often made
To Epidamnum,⁹ till my factor's° death, *agent's*
And the great care of goods at random° left, *untended*
Drew me from kind embracements of my spouse,
From whom my absence was not six months old
45   Before her self—almost at fainting under
The pleasing punishment that women bear°— *pregnancy*
Had made provision for her following me,
And soon and safe arrivèd where I was.
There had she not been long, but she became
50   A joyful mother of two goodly sons;
And, which was strange, the one so like the other
As° could not be distinguished but by names. *That they*
That very hour, and in the selfsame inn,
A mean woman° was delivered *woman of low birth*
55   Of such a burden male, twins both alike.
Those, for° their parents were exceeding poor, *because*
I bought and brought up to attend my sons.
My wife, not meanly° proud of two such boys, *in no small degree*
Made daily motions° for our home return. *requests*
60   Unwilling, I agreed. Alas, too soon
We came aboard.
A league from Epidamnum had we sailed
Before the always wind-obeying deep

---

5. To allow no trade between.
6. A mark was two-thirds of a pound in English money, although there was no coin of this amount.
7. Was brought about by natural feeling: a father's love.

8. Fortunate except in her association with me.
9. Plautus's setting for the *Menaechmi*, now Durrës in Albania; Shakespeare's play, however, seems to treat it as if it were in Greece.

Gave any tragic instance° of our harm.   *sign*
65   But longer did we not retain much hope,
For what obscurèd light the heavens did grant
Did but convey unto our fearful minds
A doubtful warrant° of immediate death,   *A fearsome confirmation*
Which though my self would gladly have embraced,
70   Yet the incessant weepings of my wife—
Weeping before° for what she saw must come—   *in advance*
And piteous plainings° of the pretty babes   *cries*
That mourned for fashion, ignorant what to fear,[1]
Forced me to seek delays° for them and me.   *reprieves*
75   And this it was—for other means was none—
The sailors sought for safety by our boat,°   *lifeboat*
And left the ship then sinking ripe[2] to us.
My wife, more careful° for the latter-born,°   *anxious / younger*
Had fastened him unto a small spare mast,
80   Such as seafaring men provide for storms.
To him one of the other twins was bound,
Whilst I had been like heedful of° the other.   *equally attentive to*
The children thus disposed,° my wife and I,   *placed*
Fixing our eyes on whom our care was fixed,
85   Fastened ourselves at either end the mast,
And floating straight,° obedient to the stream,   *immediately*
Was carried towards Corinth, as we thought.
At length the sun, gazing upon the earth,
Dispersed those vapors° that offended° us,   *clouds / harmed*
90   And by the benefit of his wishèd light
The seas waxed calm, and we discoverèd
Two ships from far, making amain° to us: *speeding*
Of Corinth that, of Epidaurus[3] this.
But ere they came—oh, let me say no more!
95   Gather the sequel by that went before.[4]
DUKE   Nay, forward, old man. Do not break off so,
For we may pity, though not pardon thee.
EGEON   Oh, had the gods done so, I had not now
Worthily° termed them merciless to us.   *Justly*
100   For ere the ships could meet by° twice five leagues   *come within*
We were encountered by a mighty rock,
Which being violently borne upon,
Our helpful ship° was splitted in the midst;   *(the mast)*
So that in this unjust divorce of us,
105   Fortune had left to both of us alike°   *equally*
What° to delight in, what to sorrow for.   *Something*
Her° part, poor soul, seeming as burdenèd   *(My wife's)*
With lesser weight,[5] but not with lesser woe,
Was carried with more speed before the wind,
110   And in our sight they three were taken up
By fishermen of Corinth, as we thought.
At length another ship had seized on us,°   *hauled us up*
And knowing whom it was their hap° to save,   *luck*

1. That imitated the adults' lamentation without
understanding it.
2. At the point of sinking; softened and ready to drop.
3. Either modern Dubrovnik, on the Adriatic and
north of Durrës (Epidamnum), or the Greek city actually called Epidaurus, near Corinth.
4. Deduce what followed from that which I have
already recounted.
5. Lighter than her husband and the other child.

Gave healthful welcome to their shipwrecked guests,
115 And would have reft° the fishers of their prey,⁶   *deprived*
Had not their bark° been very slow of sail;   *vessel*
And therefore homeward did they bend their course.
Thus have you heard me severed from my bliss,
That by misfortunes was my life prolonged
120 To tell sad stories of my own mishaps.
DUKE   And for the sake of them thou sorrowest for,
Do me the favor to dilate at° full   *relate in*
What have befall'n of them and thee till now.
EGEON   My youngest boy,⁷ and yet my eldest care,
125 At eighteen years became inquisitive
After his brother, and importuned me
That his attendant—so his case was like,⁸
Reft of his brother but retained his name⁹—
Might bear him company in the quest of him;
130 Whom whilst I labored of a love to see,¹
I hazarded the loss of whom I loved.
Five summers have I spent in farthest Greece,
Roaming clean through the bounds of Asia,
And coasting° homeward came to Ephesus,   *sailing*
135 Hopeless to find,° yet loath to leave unsought   *find them*
Or° that or any place that harbors men.   *Either*
But here must end the story of my life,
And happy were I in my timely death
Could all my travels² warrant° me they live.   *assure*
140 DUKE   Hapless° Egeon, whom the fates have marked   *Unlucky*
To bear the extremity of dire mishap!
Now, trust me, were it not against our laws,
Against my crown, my oath, my dignity—
Which princes, would they, may not disannul³—
145 My soul should sue as advocate for thee.
But though thou art adjudgèd° to the death,   *sentenced*
And passèd sentence may not be recalled
But° to our honor's great disparagement,°   *Except / disgrace*
Yet will I favor thee in what I can.⁴
150 Therefore, merchant, I'll limit° thee this day   *allot*
To seek thy health° by beneficial help.   *deliverance*
Try all the friends thou hast in Ephesus;
Beg thou, or borrow, to make up the sum,
And live. If no, then thou art doomed to die.
155 —Jailer, take him to thy custody.
JAILER   I will, my lord.
EGEON   Hopeless and helpless doth Egeon wend,°   *go*
But to procrastinate° his lifeless end.   *Exeunt.*   *postpone*

---

6. Those whom they have fished out of the sea.
7. An inconsistency of detail (see line 78).
8. *so . . . like:* in this way his situation was similar.
9. Bore the name of the brother from whom he was separated.

1. *Whom . . . see:* Since I longed to see my lost son.
2. Journeys; "travails," efforts.
3. *would . . . disannul:* even if they wished to, cannot cancel or overrule.
4. Yet I will bend the law's strictness as much as I can.

1.2

Enter ANTIPHOLUS [OF SYRACUSE], [FIRST] MERCHANT,
and DROMIO [OF SYRACUSE].

FIRST MERCHANT   Therefore give out° you are of Epidamnum,   *say*
  Lest that your goods too soon be confiscate.
  This very day a Syracusian merchant
  Is apprehended for arrival here,
5 And, not being able to buy out° his life,   *ransom*
  According to the statute of the town
  Dies ere the weary sun set in the west.
  There is your money that I had to keep.°   *in my keeping*
ANTIPHOLUS OF SYRACUSE [*to* DROMIO OF SYRACUSE]   Go bear
  it to the Centaur,[1] where we host,°   *lodge*
10 And stay there, Dromio, till I come to thee.
  Within this hour it will be dinnertime.[2]
  Till that,° I'll view the manners of the town,   *then*
  Peruse° the traders, gaze upon the buildings,   *Observe*
  And then return and sleep within mine inn;
15 For with long travel I am stiff and weary.
  Get thee away.
DROMIO OF SYRACUSE   Many a man would take you at your
  word,
  And go indeed, having so good a mean.[3]   *Exit.*
ANTIPHOLUS OF SYRACUSE   A trusty villain,[4] sir, that very oft,
20 When I am dull° with care and melancholy,   *gloomy*
  Lightens my humor[5] with his merry jests.
  What,° will you walk with me about the town   *Now then*
  And then go to my inn and dine with me?
FIRST MERCHANT   I am invited, sir, to certain merchants,
25 Of whom I hope to make much benefit.
  I crave your pardon; soon° at five o'clock,   *promptly*
  Please° you, I'll meet with you upon the mart,   *If it please*
  And afterward consort° you till bedtime.   *accompany*
  My present business calls me from you now.
30 ANTIPHOLUS OF SYRACUSE   Farewell till then. I will go lose
  myself
  And wander up and down to view the city.
FIRST MERCHANT   Sir, I commend you to your own content.°   *pleasures; peace*
                                                            Exit.
ANTIPHOLUS OF SYRACUSE   He that commends me to mine
  own content
  Commends me to the thing I cannot get.
35 I to the world am like a drop of water
  That in the ocean seeks another drop,
  Who, falling there to find his fellow forth,[6]
  Unseen, inquisitive, confounds° himself.   *mingles; destroys*
  So I, to find a mother and a brother,
40 In quest of them, unhappy, lose myself.
    Enter DROMIO OF EPHESUS.

1.2 Location: A street in Ephesus.
1. The name of an inn; taverns, inns, and shops were
frequently identified by a pictorial sign.
2. Noon, time for the midday meal.
3. Opportunity, but punning on "means" ("wealth").
4. Servant or slave ("villein"); also, rogue or scoun-

drel (often used affectionately).
5. Mood, determined by the humors, bodily fluids
that formed the basis of Elizabethan medical
psychology.
6. To locate a matching drop.

Here comes the almanac of my true date.[7]
—What now? How chance° thou art returned so soon? *What happened that*
DROMIO OF EPHESUS   Returned so soon? Rather approached
    too late.
The capon burns, the pig falls from the spit,
45   The clock hath strucken twelve upon the bell;
My mistress made it one[8] upon my cheek.
She is so hot° because the meat is cold; *angry*
The meat is cold because you come not home;
You come not home because you have no stomach;° *appetite*
50   You have no stomach, having broke your fast.° *eaten*
But we that know what 'tis to fast and pray
Are penitent[9] for your default° today. *fault*
ANTIPHOLUS OF SYRACUSE   Stop in your wind,° sir. Tell me *Shut your mouth*
    this, I pray:
Where have you left the money that I gave you?
55   DROMIO OF EPHESUS   Oh, sixpence that I had o'Wednesday
    last,
To pay the saddler for my mistress' crupper?[1]
The saddler had it, sir, I kept it not.
ANTIPHOLUS OF SYRACUSE   I am not in a sportive humor now.
Tell me, and dally not, where is the money?
60   We being strangers here, how dar'st thou trust
So great a charge from° thine own custody? *responsibility out of*
DROMIO OF EPHESUS   I pray you, jest, sir, as° you sit at dinner. *when*
I from my mistress come to you in post.° *haste*
If I return I shall be post[2] indeed,
65   For she will scour° your fault upon my pate.° *score; flog / head*
Methinks your maw,° like mine, should be your clock *stomach*
And strike[3] you home without a messenger.
ANTIPHOLUS OF SYRACUSE   Come, Dromio, come, these jests
    are out of season;
Reserve them till a merrier hour than this.
70   Where is the gold I gave in charge to thee?
DROMIO OF EPHESUS   To me, sir? Why, you gave no gold to me.
ANTIPHOLUS OF SYRACUSE   Come on, sir knave,[4] have done
    your foolishness,
And tell me how thou hast disposed° thy charge. *dealt with*
DROMIO OF EPHESUS   My charge was but to fetch you from
    the mart
75   Home to your house, the Phoenix,[5] sir, to dinner;
My mistress and her sister stays° for you. *wait*
ANTIPHOLUS OF SYRACUSE   Now, as I am a Christian,[6] answer me
In what safe place you have bestowed my money,
Or I shall break that merry sconce° of yours *head*
80   That stands° on tricks when I am undisposed.° *insists / not in the mood*

---

7. The measure of my exact age (because born on the same date).
8. *made it one*: struck one o'clock.
9. Are doing penance in the ordinary way by praying and fasting (since the meal is delayed), and also through being beaten.
1. A strap passed under a horse's tail to prevent the saddle from slipping forward.
2. Beaten, like a wooden doorpost on which tavern charges were tallied (scored).

3. Beat; ring time like a clock.
4. Ironic: "knave," like "villain," means both "servant" and "rogue."
5. Antipholus of Ephesus's house is, like the inn (line 9), identified by a sign, this one depicting the mythological bird that symbolized resurrection. Many Londoners lived above their places of business.
6. A common oath, though anachronistic in classical Greece.

Where is the thousand marks thou hadst of me?

DROMIO OF EPHESUS   I have some marks of yours upon my
    pate,
Some of my mistress' marks upon my shoulders,
But not a thousand marks between you both.
85 If I should pay your worship those again,°   *back*
Perchance you will not bear them patiently.

ANTIPHOLUS OF SYRACUSE   Thy mistress' marks? What
    mistress, slave, hast thou?

DROMIO OF EPHESUS   Your worship's wife, my mistress, at the
    Phoenix—
She that doth fast till you come home to dinner,
90 And prays that you will hie° you home to dinner.   *hasten*

ANTIPHOLUS OF SYRACUSE   What, wilt thou flout° me thus   *mock; disobey*
    unto my face,
Being forbid? There, take you that, sir knave!
    [*He strikes him.*]

DROMIO OF EPHESUS   What mean you, sir? For God sake,
    hold° your hands!   *stop*
Nay, an° you will not, sir, I'll take my heels.°   *Exit.*   *if / run away*
95 ANTIPHOLUS OF SYRACUSE   Upon my life, by some device° or   *trick*
    other
The villain is o'er-raught° of all my money.   *cheated*
They say this town is full of cozenage:°   *deception*
As° nimble jugglers[7] that deceive the eye,   *Such as*
Dark-working[8] sorcerers that change the mind,
100 Soul-killing witches that deform[9] the body,
Disguisèd cheaters, prating mountebanks,°   *fast-talking quacks*
And many suchlike liberties[1] of sin.
If it prove so, I will be gone the sooner.
I'll to the Centaur to go seek this slave.
105 I greatly fear my money is not safe.   *Exit.*

2.1

Enter ADRIANA, *wife to* ANTIPHOLUS [OF EPHESUS], *with*
    LUCIANA, *her sister.*

ADRIANA   Neither my husband nor the slave returned
That in such haste I sent to seek his master?
Sure,° Luciana, it is two o'clock.   *Surely*

LUCIANA   Perhaps some merchant hath invited him,
5 And from the mart he's somewhere gone to dinner.
Good sister, let us dine and never fret.
A man is master of his liberty.
Time is their master, and when they see time
They'll go or come. If so, be patient, sister.
10 ADRIANA   Why should their liberty than ours be more?
LUCIANA   Because their business still° lies out o'door.   *always*
ADRIANA   Look, when I serve him so, he takes it ill.[1]

---

7. Performers skilled in manipulating appearances;
the term "juggler" could mean either an actual sorcerer or a mere illusionist.
8. Operating secretly or producing darkness.
9. Injure, disfigure; change the shape of (like the
enchantress Circe of Homer's *Odyssey*, who transformed Odysseus's men into swine).

1. "Liberties" possibly refers to the district that
housed many of London's theaters (including Shakespeare's company), which were situated just outside
the City's legal jurisdictions.
2.1 Location: Before the house of Antipholus of
Ephesus.
1. Whenever I treat him so, he takes it badly.

LUCIANA   Oh, know he is the bridle of your will.[2]

ADRIANA   There's none but° asses will be bridled so.   *Only*

15 LUCIANA   Why, headstrong liberty is lashed° with woe.   *beaten; tied down*
There's nothing situate under heaven's eye
But hath his bound° in earth, in sea, in sky.   *its limits*
The beasts, the fishes, and the wingèd fowls
Are their males' subjects and at their controls.°   *under their control*
20 Man, more divine,[3] the master of all these,
Lord of the wide world and wild wat'ry seas,
Indued° with intellectual sense and souls,   *Endowed*
Of more preeminence than fish and fowls,
Are masters to their females, and their lords:[4]
25 Then let your will attend on their accords.[5]

ADRIANA   This servitude makes you to keep unwed.

LUCIANA   Not this, but troubles of the marriage bed.[6]

ADRIANA   But were you wedded, you would bear some sway.°   *wield some power*

LUCIANA   Ere I learn love, I'll practice to obey.

30 ADRIANA   How if your husband start° some other where?°   *strays; wanders / elsewhere*

LUCIANA   Till he come home again, I would forbear.°   *be patient*

ADRIANA   Patience unmoved! No marvel though she pause.[7]
They can be meek that have no other cause.°   *reason not to be*
A wretched soul, bruised with adversity,
35 We bid be quiet when we hear it cry;
But were we burdened with like° weight of pain,   *equal*
As much or more we should ourselves complain.
So thou, that hast no unkind mate to grieve thee,
With urging helpless° patience would relieve° me;   *futile / comfort*
40 But if thou live to see like right bereft,[8]
This fool-begged[9] patience in thee will be left.°   *abandoned*

LUCIANA   Well, I will marry one day, but to try.°   *test*
Here comes your man.° Now is your husband nigh.°   *servant / near*
    Enter DROMIO OF EPHESUS.

ADRIANA   Say, is your tardy master now at hand?

45 DROMIO OF EPHESUS   Nay, he's at two hands with me, and that
my two ears can witness.[1]

ADRIANA   Say, didst thou speak with him? Know'st thou his mind?

DROMIO OF EPHESUS   I? Ay, he told[2] his mind upon mine ear.
Beshrew° his hand, I scarce could understand it.   *Curse*

50 LUCIANA   Spake he so doubtfully° thou couldst not feel his   *ambiguously*
meaning?

DROMIO OF EPHESUS   Nay, he struck so plainly I could too well
feel his blows, and withal so doubtfully° that I could scarce   *dreadfully; stoutly*
understand° them.   *stand under*

55 ADRIANA   But say, I prithee,° is he coming home?   *pray thee*

---

2. He is meant to restrain your desires.
3. Nearer to God (in the great hierarchy of all beings).
4. *Man . . . lords:* Man's dominion over the creatures of earth and water derives from Genesis 1:28–29; his rule over woman is expressed in Paul's epistles, especially 1 Corinthians 11:3ff and Ephesians 5:22ff ("Wives, submit yourselves unto your husbands, as unto the Lord").
5. *attend . . . accords:* serve their wishes.
6. Compare 1 Corinthians 7:28: "And if a virgin marry, she sinneth not: nevertheless such shall have trouble in the flesh."
7. That she hesitates (to marry).
8. *like . . . bereft:* yourself similarly deprived of rights.
9. Declaredly foolish; to "beg a person for a fool" was to petition the Court of Wards for custody of a lunatic (and thus custody of all his or her possessions).
1. *he's . . . witness:* he boxed my ears with both of his hands.
2. Communicated, but playing on "struck" ("tolled").

It seems he hath great care to please his wife.[3]

DROMIO OF EPHESUS   Why, mistress, sure my master is
 horn-mad.[4]

ADRIANA   Horn-mad, thou villain?

DROMIO OF EPHESUS   I mean not cuckold mad,
 But sure he is stark mad.

60   When I desired him to come home to dinner,
 He asked me for a thousand marks in gold.
 "'Tis dinner time," quoth I. "My gold!" quoth he.
 "Your meat doth burn," quoth I. "My gold!" quoth he.
 "Will you come?" quoth I. "My gold!" quoth he;

65   "Where is the thousand marks I gave thee, villain?"
 "The pig," quoth I, "is burned." "My gold!" quoth he.
 "My mistress, sir—" quoth I. "Hang up° thy mistress!   Enough of
 I know not thy mistress. Out° on thy mistress!"   A curse

LUCIANA   Quoth who?

70 DROMIO OF EPHESUS   Quoth my master.
 "I know," quoth he, "no house, no wife, no mistress."
 So that my errand,° due unto my tongue,[5]   delivery; message
 I thank him, I bare° home upon my shoulders;   bore
 For in conclusion he did beat me there.

75 ADRIANA   Go back again, thou slave, and fetch him home.

DROMIO OF EPHESUS   Go back again and be new° beaten home?   again
 For God's sake, send some other messenger.

ADRIANA   Back, slave, or I will break thy pate across.

DROMIO OF EPHESUS   An he will bless that cross with other
 beating,[6]

80   Between you I shall have a holy[7] head.

ADRIANA   Hence, prating peasant,° fetch thy master home.   babbling fellow

DROMIO OF EPHESUS   Am I so round[8] with you, as you with me,
 That like a football you do spurn° me thus?   maltreat; kick
 You spurn me hence, and he will spurn me hither;

85   If I last in this service you must case me in leather.[9]   [Exit.]

LUCIANA   Fie, how impatience loureth° in your face!   frowns

ADRIANA   His company must do his minions grace,[1]
 Whilst I at home starve for a merry look.
 Hath homely age th'alluring beauty took

90   From my poor cheek? Then he hath wasted it.[2]
 Are my discourses dull? Barren my wit?
 If voluble and sharp° discourse be marred,   witty
 Unkindness blunts it more than marble hard.[3]
 Do their° gay vestments° his affections bait?[4]   (the minions') / clothing

---

3. Ironic: compare 1 Corinthians 7:32–33: "The unmarried careth for the things of the Lord, how he may please the Lord: But he that is married careth for the things that are of the world, how he may please his wife."
4. Uncontrolled and wild as a horned beast (a common expression, as intended by Dromio); enraged at being made a cuckold, who by popular repute grew horns (as Adriana takes it).
5. due . . . tongue: which I should have carried back in words.
6. If he will give me another beating (playing on "across," a cross made by blows on my head, and "bless," the French blesser, "to injure").

7. Blessed (because marked with the sign of the cross); also, full of holes.
8. Blunt, disrespectful (with a play on "spherical," like a football).
9. If I survive as your servant, you must cover me with leather, like a football; with a play on "last," a wooden model of a foot used in making leather shoes.
1. Must grace his paramours.
2. Caused it to waste away; squandered it.
3. More than hard marble would blunt a sharp tool.
4. Lure away (bait); lessen (abate) toward Adriana.

95   That's not my fault; he's master of my state.[5]
    What ruins are in me that can be found
    By him not ruined?[6] Then is he the ground°   *cause*
    Of my defeatures.° My decayèd fair,°   *disfigurement / beauty*
    A sunny look of his would soon repair.
100   But, too unruly deer, he breaks the pale[7]
    And feeds from° home. Poor I am but his stale.[8]   *away from*
  LUCIANA   Self-harming jealousy! Fie, beat it hence!
  ADRIANA   Unfeeling fools can with such wrongs dispense.
    I know his eye doth homage otherwhere,
105   Or else what lets° it but he would be here?   *prevents*
    Sister, you know he promised me a chain.
    Would that alone o'love he would detain,[9]
    So° he would keep fair quarter° with his bed.[1]   *If then / faith*
    I see the jewel best enamelèd
110   Will lose his beauty. Yet the gold bides° still   *remains*
    That others touch,[2] and often touching will
    Wear gold, and no man that hath a name°   *reputation*
    By falsehood and corruption doth it shame.[3]
    Since that my beauty cannot please his eye,
115   I'll weep what's left away, and weeping die.
  LUCIANA   How many fond° fools serve mad jealousy!   *infatuated*

                                  Exeunt.

2.2

Enter ANTIPHOLUS [OF SYRACUSE].

ANTIPHOLUS OF SYRACUSE   The gold I gave to Dromio is laid up
    Safe at the Centaur, and the heedful° slave   *careful*
    Is wandered forth in care to seek me out.
    By computation and mine host's report,[1]
5   I could not speak° with Dromio since at first   *could not have spoken*
    I sent him from the mart. See, here he comes.

Enter DROMIO [OF] SYRACUSE.

    How now, sir, is your merry humor altered?
    As you love strokes,° so jest with me again.   *blows*
    You know no Centaur? You received no gold?
10   Your mistress sent to have me home to dinner?
    My house was at the Phoenix?—Wast thou mad,
    That thus so madly thou didst answer me?
  DROMIO OF SYRACUSE   What answer, sir? When spake I such
    a word?
  ANTIPHOLUS OF SYRACUSE   Even now, even here, not half an
    hour since.
15   DROMIO OF SYRACUSE   I did not see you since you sent me
    hence

---

5. Estate or general condition, including clothes; also, metaphorically, kingdom.
6. *What . . . ruined:* What deterioration can be found in me that he is not responsible for?
7. He goes beyond the park boundary ("pale").
8. Lover held up to the ridicule of her rivals; prostitute.
9. *Would . . . detain:* I wish he would withhold that one manifestation of love.
1. TEXTUAL COMMENT The following five lines (109–13) as printed in the Folio appear to be corrupt and have been emended since the eighteenth century. For the passage as it originally appears, see Digital Edition TC 2.
2. *touch:* test (the fineness of gold was tested by rubbing it on a touchstone); caress, referring to her husband's infidelities.
3. *I see . . . shame:* a difficult passage, possibly owing to omitted lines. The general idea is that reputation, like gold, withstands corruption and yet may be worn away. Her husband's infidelities have not tarnished his name, but they may diminish her substance.
2.2 Location: A street in Ephesus.
1. Based on a calculation of the time elapsed and the innkeeper's account of Dromio's doings.

Home to the Centaur with the gold you gave me.

ANTIPHOLUS OF SYRACUSE   Villain, thou didst deny the gold's
    receipt,°   *receiving the gold*
And told'st me of a mistress and a dinner,
For which I hope thou felt'st² I was displeased.

20   DROMIO OF SYRACUSE   I am glad to see you in this merry vein.°   *disposition*
    What means this jest? I pray you, master, tell me?

ANTIPHOLUS OF SYRACUSE   Yea, dost thou jeer and flout me in
    the teeth?°   *to my face*
    Think'st thou I jest? Hold,° take thou that, and that!   *Stop*
        [*He*] *beats* DROMIO.

DROMIO OF SYRACUSE   Hold, sir, for God's sake! Now your
    jest is earnest.³

25   Upon what bargain⁴ do you give it me?

ANTIPHOLUS OF SYRACUSE   Because that I familiarly
    sometimes
    Do use you for my fool° and chat with you,   *jester*
    Your sauciness will jest upon my love⁵
    And make a common⁶ of my serious hours.

30   When the sun shines let foolish gnats make sport,°   *play*
    But creep in crannies when he hides his beams.
    If you will jest with me, know my aspect,⁷
    And fashion your demeanor to° my looks,   *to match*
    Or I will beat this method° in your sconce.°   *rule* / *head*

35   DROMIO OF SYRACUSE   "Sconce,"° call you it? So° you would   *Small fort* / *If*
    leave battering,⁸ I had rather have it a head. An° you use   *If*
    these blows long, I must get a sconce° for my head, and   *protective screen*
    ensconce° it too, or else I shall seek my wit° in my shoulders.   *shelter* / *brains*
    But I pray, sir, why am I beaten?

40   ANTIPHOLUS OF SYRACUSE   Dost thou not know?

DROMIO OF SYRACUSE   Nothing, sir, but that I am beaten.

ANTIPHOLUS OF SYRACUSE   Shall I tell you why?

DROMIO OF SYRACUSE   Ay, sir, and wherefore;° for, they say,   *for what reason*
    every why hath a wherefore.

45   ANTIPHOLUS OF SYRACUSE   Why first—for flouting me; and then
    wherefore—for urging° it the second time to me.   *repeating*

DROMIO OF SYRACUSE   Was there ever any man thus beaten
    out of season,°   *unjustly*
    When in the why and the wherefore is neither rhyme nor
    reason?
    Well, sir, I thank you.

50   ANTIPHOLUS OF SYRACUSE   Thank me, sir, for what?

DROMIO OF SYRACUSE   Marry,⁹ sir, for this something that you
    gave me for nothing.

ANTIPHOLUS OF SYRACUSE   I'll make you amends next: to give°   *by giving*
    you nothing for something. But say, sir, is it dinnertime?

55   DROMIO OF SYRACUSE   No, sir, I think the meat wants that° I   *lacks what*
    have.

---

2. Perceived, with an allusion to the beating.
3. Serious, with a play on "earnest" as a deposit to secure a business transaction.
4. Transaction (playing on the financial sense of "earnest"); in this context, contention or quarrel.
5. *Your . . . love:* You impertinently assume the right to joke because of my benevolence.
6. Land belonging to the whole community (Dromio

maintains an egalitarian spirit at inappropriate times).
7. Countenance, expression; in astrology, the position of a heavenly body, as the sun (lines 30–31).
8. Beating; here, with a play on "sconce," attacking with a battering ram.
9. By the Virgin Mary, a mild oath.

ANTIPHOLUS OF SYRACUSE   In good time,[1] sir, what's that?

DROMIO OF SYRACUSE   Basting.[2]

ANTIPHOLUS OF SYRACUSE   Well, sir, then 'twill be dry.

60   DROMIO OF SYRACUSE   If it be, sir, I pray you eat none of it.

ANTIPHOLUS OF SYRACUSE   Your reason?

DROMIO OF SYRACUSE   Lest it make you choleric,[3] and pur-
chase me another dry basting.°   *severe beating*

ANTIPHOLUS OF SYRACUSE   Well, sir, learn to jest in good
65   time;[4] there's a time for all things.

DROMIO OF SYRACUSE   I durst° have denied that before you   *dared*
were so choleric.

ANTIPHOLUS OF SYRACUSE   By what rule,° sir?   *principle*

DROMIO OF SYRACUSE   Marry, sir, by a rule as plain as the
70   plain bald pate of Father Time himself.[5]

ANTIPHOLUS OF SYRACUSE   Let's hear it.

DROMIO OF SYRACUSE   There's no time for a man to recover his
hair that grows bald by nature.

ANTIPHOLUS OF SYRACUSE   May he not do it by fine and
75   recovery?[6]

DROMIO OF SYRACUSE   Yes, to pay a fine° for a periwig, and   *fee*
recover the lost hair of another man.[7]

ANTIPHOLUS OF SYRACUSE   Why is Time such a niggard of
hair, being, as it is, so plentiful an excrement?°   *outward growth*

80   DROMIO OF SYRACUSE   Because it is a blessing that he bestows
on beasts, and what he hath scanted° men in hair, he hath   *given less to*
given them in wit.°   *intellect*

ANTIPHOLUS OF SYRACUSE   Why, but there's many a man hath
more hair than wit.

85   DROMIO OF SYRACUSE   Not a man of those but he hath the wit
to lose his hair.[8]

ANTIPHOLUS OF SYRACUSE   Why, thou didst conclude hairy
men plain dealers without wit.[9]

DROMIO OF SYRACUSE   The plainer dealer,[1] the sooner lost; yet
90   he loseth it in a kind of jollity.°   *sexual pleasure*

ANTIPHOLUS OF SYRACUSE   For what reason?

DROMIO OF SYRACUSE   For two, and sound° ones too.   *strong*

ANTIPHOLUS OF SYRACUSE   Nay, not sound,° I pray you.   *healthy*

DROMIO OF SYRACUSE   Sure° ones, then.   *Certain*

95   ANTIPHOLUS OF SYRACUSE   Nay, not sure° in a thing falsing.[2]   *trustworthy*

DROMIO OF SYRACUSE   Certain ones, then.

ANTIPHOLUS OF SYRACUSE   Name them.

DROMIO OF SYRACUSE   The one, to save the money that he
spends in tiring;° the other, that at dinner they should not   *hairstyling*
100   drop in his porridge.

ANTIPHOLUS OF SYRACUSE   You would all this time have proved
there is no time for all things.

---

1. Indeed! (an expression of ironical acquiescence).
2. Punning on a second meaning, "beating."
3. Angry. Choler was the hot, dry humor (see note to 1.2.21); both climate and diet were thought to affect the humors. Thus, for example, the consumption of overly dry meat was thought to be linked to a choleric disposition.
4. Opportunely; in a merry or good-humored time.
5. Time was commonly depicted as a bald old man.
6. *fine and recovery:* the legal method of transferring the ownership of property that could not normally be sold, especially to break an entail.
7. *to pay . . . man:* to buy a wig made from someone else's hair (as wigs usually were).
8. *wit . . . hair:* ironic—clever enough to catch syphilis (which may cause hair loss).
9. *conclude . . . wit:* argue that hairy men are simple, lacking in cunning and therefore being honest (plain dealers).
1. With a pun on "deal," meaning "have sex."
2. In a deceptive matter; perhaps punning on "thing" as "sexual organ."

DROMIO OF SYRACUSE   Marry, and did, sir: namely, e'en° no   *even; precisely*
time to recover hair lost by nature.
105   ANTIPHOLUS OF SYRACUSE   But your reason was not substantial,° why there is no time to recover.   *firmly based*
  DROMIO OF SYRACUSE   Thus I mend° it: Time himself is bald,   *improve*
and therefore to the world's end will have bald followers.
  ANTIPHOLUS OF SYRACUSE   I knew 'twould be a bald° conclu-   *an inane*
110   sion. But soft, who wafts° us yonder?   *beckons*
          Enter ADRIANA *and* LUCIANA.
  ADRIANA   Ay, ay, Antipholus, look strange[3] and frown;
Some other mistress hath thy sweet aspects.°   *loving looks*
I am not Adriana, nor thy wife.
The time was once when thou unurged wouldst vow
115   That never words were music to thine ear,
That never object pleasing in thine eye,
That never touch well welcome to thy hand,
That never meat sweet-savored in thy taste,
Unless I spake, or looked, or touched, or carved to° thee.   *for*
120   How comes it now, my husband, oh, how comes it,
That thou art then estrangèd from thyself?
Thy "self" I call it, being strange to me
That, undividable, incorporate,°   *united in one body*
Am better than thy dear self's better part.[4]
125   Ah, do not tear away thyself from me;
For know, my love, as easy mayst thou fall°   *let fall*
A drop of water in the breaking gulf
And take unmingled thence that drop again
Without addition or diminishing,
130   As take from me thyself and not me too.[5]
How dearly° would it touch thee to the quick,   *deeply*
Shouldst thou but° hear I were licentious,   *only*
And that this body, consecrate to thee,
By ruffian lust should be contaminate?
135   Wouldst thou not spit at me, and spurn° at me,   *strike*
And hurl the name of husband in my face,[6]
And tear the stained skin[7] of my harlot brow,
And from my false hand cut the wedding ring,
And break it with a deep-divorcing vow?
140   I know thou canst, and therefore see° thou do it!   *make sure*
I am possessed with° an adulterate blot;[8]   *in possession of*
My blood is mingled with the crime of lust:
For if we two be one, and thou play false,
I do digest the poison of thy flesh,
145   Being strumpeted° by thy contagion.   *made a whore*
Keep then fair league[9] and truce with thy true bed,
I live dis-stained, thou undishonorèd.[1]

---

3. Look distant, but suggesting "without recognition," as if a foreigner—which he is.
4. Either his better qualities or his soul (which is better than his body). Adriana's plea depends on the doctrine of marriage as "one flesh" articulated in Genesis
2:23–24 and echoed in Paul's mystical view of the
church as wedded to God. Compare Ephesians
5:28–33.
5. *not me too:* not take me away from myself as
well.
6. And bitterly confront me with my degraded mar-

riage vow.
7. Mark of impure character, as if she had been
legally branded as a harlot.
8. The stain, or disgrace, of adultery.
9. *Keep . . . league:* If you keep faithful alliance.
1. TEXTUAL COMMENT The Folio's "distain'd," often
changed by editors to "unstained," is here emended
to the archaic word "dis-stained," referring to the
removal of color during the dying process. See Digital Edition TC 3.

ANTIPHOLUS OF SYRACUSE   Plead you to me, fair dame? I know
 you not.
 In Ephesus I am but two hours old,
150 As strange unto your town as to your talk,
 Who, every word by all my wit being scanned,°   *analyzed*
 Wants° wit in all, one word to understand.   *Lacks*
LUCIANA   Fie, brother,° how the world is changed with you! *brother-in-law*
 When were you wont to use° my sister thus?   *treat*
155 She sent for you by Dromio home to dinner.
ANTIPHOLUS OF SYRACUSE   By Dromio?
DROMIO OF SYRACUSE   By me?
ADRIANA   By thee; and this thou didst return° from him: *bring back*
 That he did buffet thee and, in his blows,
160 Denied my house for° his, me for his wife.   *to be*
ANTIPHOLUS OF SYRACUSE   Did you converse, sir, with this
 gentlewoman?
 What is the course and drift of your compact?[2]
DROMIO OF SYRACUSE   I, sir? I never saw her till this time.
ANTIPHOLUS OF SYRACUSE   Villain, thou liest; for even her
 very° words   *exact*
165 Didst thou deliver to me on the mart.
DROMIO OF SYRACUSE   I never spake with her in all my life.
ANTIPHOLUS OF SYRACUSE   How can she thus then call us by
 our names?—
 Unless it be by inspiration.°   *divine revelation*
ADRIANA   How ill agrees it with° your gravity° *does it suit / dignity*
170 To counterfeit° thus grossly° with your slave, *dissemble / blatantly*
 Abetting him to thwart me in my mood!
 Be it my wrong you are from me exempt,[3]
 But wrong not that wrong with a more contempt.[4]
 Come, I will fasten on this sleeve of thine:
175 Thou art an elm, my husband; I, a vine,[5]
 Whose weakness married to thy stronger state°   *condition*
 Makes me with thy strength to communicate.°   *share*
 If aught possess thee from me,[6] it is dross,°   *worthless*
 Usurping ivy, brier, or idle moss,
180 Who, all° for want of pruning, with intrusion,° *entirely / invasively*
 Infect thy sap and live on thy confusion.[7]
ANTIPHOLUS OF SYRACUSE *[aside]*   To me she speaks; she moves° *uses*
 me for her theme.°   *topic*
 What, was I married to her in my dream?
 Or sleep I now and think I hear all this?
185 What error drives our eyes and ears amiss?
 Until I know this sure uncertainty,
 I'll entertain° the offered fallacy.°   *accept / delusion*
LUCIANA   Dromio, go bid the servants spread° for dinner. *lay the table*
DROMIO OF SYRACUSE *[aside]*   Oh, for my beads!° I cross me[8] *rosary beads*
 for° a sinner.   *as*
190 This is the fairy land. Oh, spite of spites!

---

2. What is the purpose and meaning of your conspiracy?
3. *Be . . . exempt:* Grant that it is my fault that you are alienated from me.
4. But do not add to that injury with mockery.
5. This image occurs both in Ovid's *Metamorphoses*

14.665–66 and in Psalm 128:3, included in the Elizabethan homily on marriage.
6. If anything takes possession of you away from (or apart from) me.
7. *live . . . confusion:* take life from your destruction.
8. Make the sign of the cross (to ward off evil).

We talk with goblins, owls,[9] and sprites.°   *spirits*
If we obey them not, this will ensue:
They'll suck our breath or pinch us black and blue.[1]

LUCIANA Why prat'st° thou to thyself and answer'st not?   *babble*
195 Dromio, thou drone,° thou snail, thou slug, thou sot!°   *idler / blockhead*

DROMIO OF SYRACUSE I am transformèd, master, am I not?

ANTIPHOLUS OF SYRACUSE I think thou art in mind, and so
     am I.

DROMIO OF SYRACUSE Nay, master, both in mind and in my
     shape.

ANTIPHOLUS OF SYRACUSE Thou hast thine own form.

DROMIO OF SYRACUSE   No, I am an ape.[2]

200 LUCIANA If thou art changed to aught,° 'tis to an ass.   *anything*

DROMIO OF SYRACUSE 'Tis true: she rides° me, and I long for   *tyrannizes*
     grass.[3]
     'Tis so, I am an ass; else it could never be,
     But I should know her as well as she knows me.

ADRIANA Come, come, no longer will I be a fool
205 To put the finger in the eye and weep
     Whilst man and master laughs my woes to scorn.[4]
     Come, sir, to dinner. —Dromio, keep the gate.
     —Husband, I'll dine above with you today,
     And shrive you of[5] a thousand idle pranks.
210 —Sirrah,[6] if any ask you for your master,
     Say he dines forth,° and let no creature enter.   *out*
     Come, sister. —Dromio, play the porter well.

ANTIPHOLUS OF SYRACUSE Am I in earth, in heaven, or in hell?
     Sleeping or waking? Mad or well advised?°   *sane*
215 Known unto these, and to myself disguised?
     I'll say as they say, and persever so,
     And in this mist at all adventures° go.   *whatever occurs*

DROMIO OF SYRACUSE Master, shall I be porter at the gate?

ADRIANA Ay, and let none enter, lest I break your pate.°   *head*
220 LUCIANA Come, come, Antipholus, we dine too late.

                                        [*Exeunt.*]

                         3.1

          Enter ANTIPHOLUS OF EPHESUS, *his man* DROMIO
          [OF EPHESUS], ANGELO *the goldsmith, and* BALTHASAR
          the merchant.

ANTIPHOLUS OF EPHESUS Good Signor Angelo, you must
     excuse us all.
     My wife is shrewish° when I keep not hours.°   *ill tempered / am late*
     Say that I lingered with you at your shop
     To see the making of her carcanet,°   *jeweled necklace*
5   And that tomorrow you will bring it home.
     But here's a villain that would face me down[1]—
     He met me on the mart, and that I beat him,
     And charged him with[2] a thousand marks in gold,

---

9. A possible reference to witchcraft.
1. Traditional recreations for fairies.
2. An imitation (of myself); a fool.
3. Freedom, as when a horse is put out to pasture.
4. *laughs . . . scorn:* make a mockery of my pain.
5. And act as your confessor to hear and pardon.

6. Standard term for addressing inferiors.
3.1 Location: Before the house of Antipholus of Ephesus.
1. That would insist despite my denial that.
2. And accused him of possessing.

And that I did deny my wife and house!
10 —Thou drunkard, thou, what didst thou mean by this?
DROMIO OF EPHESUS   Say what you will, sir, but I know what
I know.
That you beat me at the mart I have your hand³ to show.
If the skin were parchment, and the blows you gave were ink,
Your own handwriting would tell you what I think.
ANTIPHOLUS OF EPHESUS   I think thou art an ass.
15 DROMIO OF EPHESUS   Marry, so it doth appear
By the wrongs I suffer and the blows I bear.
I should kick, being kicked, and being at that pass,°   *in that predicament*
You would keep from my heels and beware of an ass.
ANTIPHOLUS OF EPHESUS   You're sad,° Signor Balthasar. Pray   *serious*
God our cheer°   *fare*
20 May answer° my good will and your good welcome here.   *equal*
BALTHASAR   I hold your dainties cheap, sir, and your wel-
come dear.⁴
ANTIPHOLUS OF EPHESUS   O Signor Balthasar, either at flesh
or fish,
A table full of welcome makes scarce° one dainty dish.   *scarcely makes*
BALTHASAR   Good meat, sir, is common; that every churl°   *peasant*
affords.
25 ANTIPHOLUS OF EPHESUS   And welcome more common, for
that's nothing but words.
BALTHASAR   Small cheer° and great welcome makes a merry   *Little food*
feast.
ANTIPHOLUS OF EPHESUS   Ay, to a niggardly host and more
sparing° guest.   *temperate*
But though my cates° be mean,° take them in good part.   *provisions / poor*
Better cheer may you have, but not with better heart.
30 But soft,⁵ my door is locked. [*to* DROMIO OF EPHESUS] Go, bid
them let us in.
DROMIO OF EPHESUS [*calling*]   Maud, Bridget, Marian, Cicely,
Gillian, Ginn!
[*Enter* DROMIO OF SYRACUSE *within.*]
DROMIO OF SYRACUSE [*within*]   Mome, Malt-horse, Capon,
Coxcomb, Idiot, Patch!⁶
Either get thee from the door, or sit down at the hatch.⁷
Dost thou conjure for° wenches, that thou call'st for such   *summon by spells*
store°   *plenty*
35 When one is one too many? Go, get thee from the door.
DROMIO OF EPHESUS   What patch is made our porter? My
master stays° in the street.   *waits*
DROMIO OF SYRACUSE [*within*]   Let him walk from whence he
came, lest he catch cold on 's° feet.   *on his*
ANTIPHOLUS OF EPHESUS   Who talks within there? Ho, open
the door!
DROMIO OF SYRACUSE [*within*]   Right, sir, I'll tell you when,
an° you'll tell me wherefore.   *if*
40 ANTIPHOLUS OF EPHESUS   Wherefore? For my dinner: I have
not dined today.

3. The mark of Antipholus's hand.
4. I value your welcome more highly than the delicacies of your table.
5. An exclamation of surprise.

6. Dolt, plodding oaf, eunuch, fool, idiot, clown.
7. Literally, sit down at the gate or half door, but
playing on the proverbial phrase "set a hatch (gate)
before the door" of the tongue: keep silent.

DROMIO OF SYRACUSE [*within*]   Nor today here you must not.
    Come again when you may.
ANTIPHOLUS OF EPHESUS   What art thou that keep'st me out
    from the house I owe?°   *own*
DROMIO OF SYRACUSE [*within*]   The porter for this time,° sir,   *for now*
    and my name is Dromio.
DROMIO OF EPHESUS   O villain, thou hast stol'n both mine
    office° and my name: *function*
45 The one ne'er got me credit, the other mickle blame.[8]
    If thou hadst been Dromio today in my place,
    Thou wouldst have changed thy face[9] for a name or thy
        name for an ass.
        Enter LUCE [*within*].[1]
LUCE [*within*]   What a coil° is there, Dromio? Who are those   *disturbance*
    at the gate?
DROMIO OF EPHESUS   Let my master in, Luce.
LUCE [*within*]   Faith, no, he comes too late,
    And so tell your master.
50 DROMIO OF EPHESUS   O Lord, I must laugh,
    Have at you[2] with a proverb: "Shall I set in my staff?"[3]
LUCE [*within*]   Have at you with another, that's —"When?
    Can you tell?"[4]
DROMIO OF SYRACUSE [*within*]   If thy name be called Luce,
    Luce, thou hast answered him well.
ANTIPHOLUS OF EPHESUS   Do you hear, you minion?° You'll   *subordinate*
    let us in, I trow?[5]
LUCE [*within*]   I thought to have asked you.
55 DROMIO OF SYRACUSE [*within*]   And you said no.°   *(already)*
DROMIO OF EPHESUS   So come help.
        [DROMIO OF EPHESUS *and* ANTIPHOLUS OF EPHESUS
        knock at the door.]
                            Well struck! There was blow for blow.[6]
ANTIPHOLUS OF EPHESUS   Thou baggage,° let me in.   *good-for-nothing*
LUCE [*within*]   Can you tell for whose sake?
DROMIO OF EPHESUS   Master, knock the door hard.
LUCE [*within*]   Let him knock till it ache.
ANTIPHOLUS OF EPHESUS   You'll cry for this, minion, if I beat
    the door down.
60 LUCE [*within*]   What needs all that, and a pair of stocks in
    the town?[7]
        Enter ADRIANA [*within*].
ADRIANA [*within*]   Who is that at the door that keeps° all this   *keeps up*
    noise?
DROMIO OF SYRACUSE [*within*]   By my troth, your town is
    troubled with unruly boys.

8. My reputation ("name") has never brought me
credit, but in the course of my duties I have received
much reproof ("mickle blame").
9. I.e., tried to change your identity (?). F's reading is
obscure, and most editors emend the line: for example,
"Thou wouldst have changed thy face for an aim" (i.e.,
you would have exchanged your face for a target).
1. TEXTUAL COMMENT The Folio refers to Adriana's
kitchen maid as both "Luce" and "Nell," signaling
perhaps a change in Shakespeare's mind while writing the play. We have chosen to retain both names.
See Digital Edition TC 4.
2. A challenge or warning in a fight (as with a quar-

ter staff): Now I attack you.
3. "Shall I take up residence?" (proverbial).
4. Proverbial response of defiance.
5. TEXTUAL COMMENT In order to preserve the rhyme
scheme, the Folio's "hope" has been emended to
"trow" ("believe"). See Digital Edition TC 5.
6. Blows to the door in response to verbal blows from
within.
7. Why should I worry when there is a legal punishment for such behavior? *stocks:* instrument of punishment in which a person was seated with his or her
legs locked in a wooden frame.

ANTIPHOLUS OF EPHESUS   Are you there, wife? You might
    have come before.

ADRIANA [*within*]   Your wife, sir knave? Go, get you from the
    door.

65 DROMIO OF EPHESUS   If you went in pain, master, this knave
    would go sore.[8]

ANGELO   Here is neither cheer, sir, nor welcome; we would
    fain° have either.   *gladly*

BALTHASAR   In° debating which was best, we shall part° with   *After / depart*
    neither.

DROMIO OF EPHESUS   They stand at the door, master; bid
    them welcome hither.

ANTIPHOLUS OF EPHESUS   There is something in the wind°   *afoot*
    that we cannot get in.

70 DROMIO OF EPHESUS   You would say so, master, if your
    garments were thin.°   (*taking "wind" literally*)
    Your cake[9] here is warm within; you stand here in the cold.
    It would make a man mad as a buck[1] to be so bought and sold.°   *betrayed*

ANTIPHOLUS OF EPHESUS   Go fetch me something. I'll break
    ope° the gate.   *open*

DROMIO OF SYRACUSE [*within*]   Break° any breaking here, and   *Do*
    I'll break your knave's pate.

75 DROMIO OF EPHESUS   A man may break° a word with you, sir,   *speak*
    and words are but wind;
    Ay, and break it in your face, so he break it° not behind.   *break wind*

DROMIO OF SYRACUSE [*within*]   It seems thou want'st break-
    ing.[2] Out upon thee, hind!°   *slave; fellow*

DROMIO OF EPHESUS   Here's too much "out upon thee"! I pray
    thee, let me in.

DROMIO OF SYRACUSE [*within*]   Ay, when fowls have no
    feathers and fish have no fin.

80 ANTIPHOLUS OF EPHESUS   Well, I'll break in! —Go borrow me
    a crow.°   *crowbar*

DROMIO OF EPHESUS   A crow without feather? Master, mean
    you so?
    For a fish without a fin, there's a fowl without a feather.
    [*to* DROMIO OF SYRACUSE] If a crow help us in, sirrah, we'll
    pluck a crow° together.   *settle accounts*

ANTIPHOLUS OF EPHESUS   Go, get thee gone; fetch me an iron
    crow.

85 BALTHASAR   Have patience, sir. Oh, let it not be so.
    Herein you war against your reputation,
    And draw within the compass of suspect°   *scope of suspicion*
    Th'unviolated honor of your wife.
    Once this:° your long experience of her wisdom,   *In brief*
90   Her sober virtue, years,° and modesty,   *maturity*
    Plead on her part some cause° to you unknown;   *explanation; excuse*
    And doubt not, sir, but she will well excuse°   *explain*
    Why at this time the doors are made° against you.   *barred*
    Be ruled by me: depart in patience,
95   And let us to the Tiger[3] all to dinner,

---

8. If you, the master, get punished as a knave, so will
I, the actual servant ("knave").
9. Referring either to Adriana or to the meal.
1. Angry, with an allusion to cuckoldry (see 2.1.57

and note).
2. Need a beating; need to be "broken in," or tamed
like a horse.
3. The name of an inn; see 1.2.9.

And about evening come yourself alone
To know the reason of this strange restraint.°   *exclusion*
If by strong hand you offer° to break in   *attempt*
Now in the stirring passage° of the day,   *traffic*
100 A vulgar° comment will be made of it,   *public; lewd*
And that supposèd° by the common rout°   *assumed / mob*
Against your yet ungallèd estimation,[4]
That may with foul intrusion enter in
And dwell upon your grave when you are dead.
105 For slander lives upon succession,°   *perpetuates itself*
Forever housèd where it gets possession.
ANTIPHOLUS OF EPHESUS   You have prevailed. I will depart in
    quiet,
And in despite of mirth° mean to be merry.   *ridicule*
I know a wench of excellent discourse,
110 Pretty and witty; wild, and yet, too, gentle.
There will we dine. This woman that I mean
My wife—but I protest without desert°—   *my deserving*
Hath oftentimes upbraided me withal.°   *scolded me about*
To her will we to dinner. [*to* ANGELO] Get you home
115 And fetch the chain. By this° I know 'tis made.   *this time*
Bring it, I pray you, to the Porcupine,
For there's the house.° That chain will I bestow—   *That is where she lives*
Be it for nothing but to spite my wife—
Upon mine hostess there. Good sir, make haste:
120 Since mine own doors refuse to entertain° me,   *welcome*
I'll knock elsewhere to see if they'll disdain me.
ANGELO   I'll meet you at that place some hour hence.
ANTIPHOLUS OF EPHESUS   Do so. This jest shall cost me some
    expense.   *Exeunt.*

3.2

Enter [LUCIANA] *with* ANTIPHOLUS OF SYRACUSE.

LUCIANA   And may it be that you have quite forgot
A husband's office?° Shall, Antipholus,   *duty*
Even in the spring of love, thy love-springs° rot?   *young shoots of love*
Shall love in building grow so ruinous?[1]
5 If you did wed my sister for her wealth,
Then for her wealth's sake use° her with more kindness;   *treat*
Or if you like elsewhere, do it by stealth:
Muffle° your false love with some show of blindness.[2]   *Hide*
Let not my sister read it in your eye.
10 Be not thy tongue thy own shame's orator.
Look sweet, speak fair, become disloyalty;[3]
Apparel vice like virtue's harbinger.°   *herald*
Bear a fair presence,° though your heart be tainted: *Present a pleasant front*
Teach sin the carriage° of a holy saint.   *bearing*
15 Be secret false: what° need she be acquainted?   *why*
What simple thief brags of his own attaint?°   *crime*
'Tis double wrong to truant with° your bed   *be unfaithful to*

---

4. *yet . . . estimation:* as yet uninjured reputation.
3.2 Location: Scene continues.
1. Shall love become a ruin at the time of its building?
2. Seem to blindfold yourself so that your glances do

not reveal your faithlessness.
3. *become disloyalty:* put an attractive face on your
unfaithfulness.

And let her read it in thy looks at board.°   *table*
Shame hath a bastard fame, well managèd;°   *if properly handled*
20 Ill deeds is° doubled with an evil word.   *are*
Alas, poor women, make us but believe,
Being compact of credit,⁴ that you love us.
Though others have the arm, show us the sleeve.⁵
We in your motion turn,⁶ and you may move° us.   *control; touch*
25 Then, gentle brother, get you in again.
Comfort my sister, cheer her, call her wife.
'Tis holy sport to be a little vain°   *false*
When the sweet breath of flattery conquers strife.
ANTIPHOLUS OF SYRACUSE   Sweet mistress, what your name is
    else I know not,
30 Nor by what wonder you do hit of° mine.   *on*
Less in your knowledge and your grace you show not
Than our earth's wonder,⁷ more than earth° divine.   *mortal flesh*
Teach me, dear creature, how to think and speak.
Lay open to my earthy gross conceit,⁸
35 Smothered in errors, feeble, shallow, weak,
The folded° meaning of your words' deceit.   *hidden*
Against my soul's pure truth why labor you
To make it wander in an unknown field?
Are you a god? Would you create me new?°   *anew*
40 Transform me then, and to your power I'll yield.
But if that I am I, then well I know
Your weeping sister is no wife of mine,
Nor to her bed no homage° do I owe.   *duty*
Far more, far more, to you do I decline.°   *incline; submit*
45 Oh, train° me not, sweet mermaid,⁹ with thy note   *entice*
To drown me in thy sister's flood of tears.
Sing, siren, for thyself, and I will dote.
Spread o'er the silver waves thy golden hairs,
And as a bed I'll take thee, and there lie,
50 And in that glorious supposition° think: *(that the hair is a bed)*
He gains by death that° hath such means to die.¹   *who*
Let love, being light,² be drowned if she sink.
LUCIANA   What, are you mad, that you do reason so?
ANTIPHOLUS OF SYRACUSE   Not mad, but mated³—how, I do
    not know.
55 LUCIANA   It is a fault that springeth from your eye.°   *from looking lustfully*
ANTIPHOLUS OF SYRACUSE   For gazing on your beams,° fair   *eyes*
    sun, being by.
LUCIANA   Gaze where you should, and that will clear your sight.
ANTIPHOLUS OF SYRACUSE   As good to wink,° sweet love, as   *shut one's eyes*
    look on° night.   *at*

---

4. Being made of credulity; gullible.
5. Although others have the reality of your love, present us the appearance.
6. We are subject to your influence (as heavenly bodies were believed to follow the rotations of concentric celestial spheres).
7. *Less . . . wonder:* You seem as wise and as gracious as the wonder of the world (probably an allusion to Queen Elizabeth, before whom the play might have been performed).

8. *earthy gross conceit:* clumsy mortal understanding.
9. Siren; in Greek legend, mermaids' singing lured sailors to their death (see line 47).
1. Perhaps with a pun on "to die" as the Elizabethan expression for "to have an orgasm."
2. The line has two implications: only false love could sink, because true love is too light and buoyant; and love deserves drowning because it is giddy and wanton.
3. Amazed, confounded; in love; married.

LUCIANA   Why call you me love? Call my sister so.

ANTIPHOLUS OF SYRACUSE   Thy sister's sister.

LUCIANA   That's my sister.

60 ANTIPHOLUS OF SYRACUSE   No,
    It is thyself, mine own self's better part,
    Mine eye's clear eye, my dear heart's dearer heart,
    My food, my fortune, and my sweet hope's aim,
    My sole earth's heaven, and my heaven's claim.[4]

65 LUCIANA   All this my sister is, or else should be.

ANTIPHOLUS OF SYRACUSE   Call thyself sister, sweet, for I am
        thee.°   thine
    Thee will I love, and with thee lead my life.
    Thou hast no husband yet, nor I no wife.
    Give me thy hand.

LUCIANA   Oh, soft, sir, hold you still;
70   I'll fetch my sister to get her good will.   Exit.

                Enter DROMIO [OF SYRACUSE].

ANTIPHOLUS OF SYRACUSE   Why, how now, Dromio, where
        runn'st thou so fast?

DROMIO OF SYRACUSE   Do you know me, sir? Am I Dromio?
        Am I your man? Am I myself?

75 ANTIPHOLUS OF SYRACUSE   Thou art Dromio, thou art my
        man, thou art thyself.

DROMIO OF SYRACUSE   I am an ass, I am a woman's man, and
        besides° myself.   in addition

ANTIPHOLUS OF SYRACUSE   What woman's man? And how
80   besides thyself?

DROMIO OF SYRACUSE   Marry, sir, besides myself, I am due to
        a woman: one that claims me, one that haunts me, one that
        will have me.

ANTIPHOLUS OF SYRACUSE   What claim lays she to thee?

85 DROMIO OF SYRACUSE   Marry, sir, such claim as you would lay
        to your horse, and she would have me as a beast—not that I,
        being a beast, she would have me, but that she, being a very
        beastly creature, lays claim to me.

ANTIPHOLUS OF SYRACUSE   What is she?

90 DROMIO OF SYRACUSE   A very reverend° body; ay, such a one as   worthy
        a man may not speak of without he say, "sir reverence."[5] I
        have but lean luck in the match, and yet is she a wondrous
        fat marriage.

ANTIPHOLUS OF SYRACUSE   How dost thou mean, a fat
95   marriage?

DROMIO OF SYRACUSE   Marry, sir, she's the kitchen wench,°   servant
        and all grease; and I know not what use to put her to, but to
        make a lamp of her and run from her by her own light. I
        warrant° her rags and the tallow in them will burn a Poland   guarantee
100   winter.[6] If she lives till doomsday, she'll burn a week longer
        than the whole world.[7]

ANTIPHOLOUS OF SYRACUSE   What complexion is she of?

---

4. My only heaven on earth and only claim on heaven.
5. "Saving your reverence," an apology for a potentially offensive remark.

6. The length of a winter in Poland—a long time.
7. Than the rest of the world (the popular Christian
belief being that the earth would end in fire).

DROMIO OF SYRACUSE Swart° like my shoe, but her face noth-   *Dark*
ing like so clean kept. For why?° She sweats a man may go   *How so?*
105 over shoes[8] in the grime of it.
ANTIPHOLUS OF SYRACUSE That's a fault that water will mend.
DROMIO OF SYRACUSE No, sir, 'tis in grain.° Noah's flood   *ingrained*
could not do it.
ANTIPOHOLUS OF SYRACUSE What's her name?
110 DROMIO OF SYRACUSE Nell, sir. But her name and three
quarters—that's an ell° and three quarters—will not mea-   *more than a yard*
sure her from hip to hip.
ANTIPHOLUS OF SYRACUSE Then she bears some breadth?
DROMIO OF SYRACUSE No longer from head to foot than from
115 hip to hip. She is spherical, like a globe. I could find out°   *discover*
countries in her.
ANTIPHOLUS OF SYRACUSE In what part of her body stands
Ireland?
DROMIO OF SYRACUSE Marry, sir, in her buttocks. I found it
120 out by the bogs.°   *peat marsh; sponginess*
ANTIPHOLUS OF SYRACUSE Where Scotland?
DROMIO OF SYRACUSE I found it by the barrenness, hard in
the palm of the hand.[9]
ANTIPHOLUS OF SYRACUSE Where France?
125 DROMIO OF SYRACUSE In her forehead, armed and reverted,[1]
making war against her hair.[2]
ANTIPHOLUS OF SYRACUSE Where England?
DROMIO OF SYRACUSE I looked for the chalky cliffs,[3] but I could
find no whiteness in them. But I guess it stood in her chin,
130 by° the salt rheum° that ran between France and it.   *judging by / mucus*
ANTIPHOLUS OF SYRACUSE Where Spain?
DROMIO OF SYRACUSE Faith, I saw it not, but I felt it hot in her
breath.[4]
ANTIPHOLUS OF SYRACUSE Where America, the Indies?
135 DROMIO OF SYRACUSE O sir, upon her nose, all o'er embellished with rubies, carbuncles, sapphires,[5] declining their rich
aspect[6] to the hot breath of Spain, who sent whole armadas
of carracks to be ballast[7] at her nose.
ANTIPHOLUS OF SYRACUSE Where stood Belgium, the
140 Netherlands?
DROMIO OF SYRACUSE O, sir, I did not look so low.[8] To conclude, this drudge or diviner° laid claim to me, called me   *witch*
Dromio, swore I was assured° to her, told me what privy°   *betrothed / private; secret*
marks I had about me—as the mark of my shoulder, the
145 mole in my neck, the great wart on my left arm—that I,
amazed, ran from her as a witch.

---

8. She sweats so much that a man may be up to his ankles.
9. Hard with calluses and dry (a moist hand prover-bially indicated fertility; hence a dry hand could connote barrenness).
1. In rebellion (perhaps referring to syphilitic sores).
2. TEXTUAL COMMENT In the Folio's "heire," there is a pun on "hair" and "heir" that is no longer possible in standard English orthography. See Digital Edition TC 6.

3. Teeth; an allusion to the white chalk cliffs of Dover.
4. As if she had been eating pungent food.
5. Glistening skin blemishes (as well as precious stones).
6. Casting their gaze down; paying tribute to.
7. *armadas . . . ballast:* fleets of galleons to be loaded.
8. The Netherlands and Belgium were also known as the Low Countries; the words offer a sexual double-entendre.

And I think, if my breast had not been made of faith and my
    heart of steel,[9]
She had transformed me to a curtal° dog and made me turn   *tailless*
    i'th' wheel.°   *turn a roasting spit*
ANTIPHOLUS OF SYRACUSE   Go, hie thee presently.° Post° to   *now / Hasten*
    the road,°   *harbor*
150   An if° the wind blow any way from shore,°   *An if=If / out to sea*
    I will not harbor in this town tonight.
    If any bark put forth, come to the mart,
    Where I will walk till thou return to me.
    If everyone knows us, and we know none,
155   'Tis time, I think, to trudge,° pack, and be gone.   *depart*
DROMIO OF SYRACUSE   As from a bear a man would run for life,
    So fly I from her that would be my wife.   *Exit.*
ANTIPHOLUS OF SYRACUSE   There's none but witches do
    inhabit here,
    And therefore 'tis high time that I were hence.
160   She that doth call me husband, even my° soul   *my very*
    Doth for a wife abhor. But her fair sister,
    Possessed with such a gentle sovereign° grace,   *excellent*
    Of such enchanting presence and discourse,
    Hath almost made me traitor to myself.
165   But lest myself be guilty to° self-wrong,   *of*
    I'll stop mine ears against the mermaid's song.
        Enter ANGELO *with the chain.*
ANGELO   Master Antipholus.
ANTIPHOLUS OF SYRACUSE   Ay, that's my name.
ANGELO   I know it well, sir. Lo, here's the chain
170   I thought to have ta'en° you at the Porcupine.   *overtaken*
    The chain unfinished made me stay° thus long.   *delay*
ANTIPHOLUS OF SYRACUSE   What is your will that I shall do
    with this?
ANGELO   What please° yourself, sir. I have made it for you.   *pleases*
ANTIPHOLUS OF SYRACUSE   Made it for me, sir? I bespoke° it not.   *ordered*
175   ANGELO   Not once, nor twice, but twenty times you have.
    Go home with it, and please your wife withal,°   *with it*
    And soon at suppertime I'll visit you,
    And then receive my money for the chain.
ANTIPHOLUS OF SYRACUSE   I pray you, sir, receive the money
    now,
180   For fear you ne'er see chain nor money more.
ANGELO   You are a merry man, sir; fare you well.   *Exit.*
ANTIPHOLUS OF SYRACUSE   What I should think of this, I
    cannot tell.
    But this I think: there's no man is so vain°   *foolish*
    That would refuse so fair an offered chain.
185   I see a man here needs not live by shifts,°   *his own efforts*
    When in the streets he meets such golden gifts.
    I'll to the mart, and there for Dromio stay.
    If any ship put out, then straight° away.   *Exit.*   *immediately*

---

9. Compare Ephesians 6:11ff: "Put on the whole armor of God, that ye may be able to stand against the assaults of the devil. . . . having on the breast plate of righteousness. . . . Above all, take the shield of faith."

4.1

Enter a [SECOND] MERCHANT, [ANGELO *the*] *goldsmith,*
and an OFFICER.

SECOND MERCHANT You know since Pentecost[1] the sum is due,
And since I have not much importuned you;
Nor now I had not,° but° that I am bound   *I would not have / except*
To Persia and want° guilders for my voyage.   *lack*
5   Therefore make present satisfaction,°   *immediate payment*
Or I'll attach° you by this officer.   *arrest*
ANGELO Even just the sum that I do owe to you
Is growing° to me by Antipholus,   *owing*
And in the instant that I met with you,
10   He had of me a chain. At five o'clock
I shall receive the money for the same.
Pleaseth you° walk with me down to his house;   *If it please you to*
I will discharge my bond, and thank you too.
Enter ANTIPHOLUS [OF] EPHESUS, [*and*] DROMIO
[OF EPHESUS] *from the Courtesan's* [*house*].
OFFICER That labor may you save; see where he comes.
15   ANTIPHOLUS OF EPHESUS [*to* DROMIO OF EPHESUS] While I go
to the goldsmith's house, go thou
And buy a rope's end;° that will I bestow°   *piece of rope / employ (as a whip)*
Among my wife and her confederates
For locking me out of my doors by day.
But soft,° I see the goldsmith. Get thee gone.   *wait*
20   Buy thou a rope, and bring it home to me.
DROMIO OF EPHESUS I buy a thousand pound a year, I buy a
rope![2]   *Exit.*
ANTIPHOLUS OF EPHESUS [*to* ANGELO] A man is well holp up°   *helped*
that trusts to you!
I promisèd your presence and the chain,
But neither chain nor goldsmith came to me.
25   Belike° you thought our love° would last too long   *Perhaps / friendship*
If it were chained together, and therefore came not.
ANGELO Saving° your merry humor, here's the note   *Without offense to*
How much your chain weighs to the utmost carat,
The fineness of the gold, and chargeful fashion,°   *costly craftsmanship*
30   Which doth amount to three odd ducats° more   *gold coins*
Than I stand debted° to this gentleman.   *indebted*
I pray you see him presently discharged,°   *paid off now*
For he is bound to sea and stays but° for it.   *waits only*
ANTIPOHOLUS OF EPHESUS I am not furnished with the
present° money.   *ready*
35   Besides, I have some business in the town.
Good signor, take the stranger to my house,
And with you take the chain, and bid my wife
Disburse the sum on the receipt thereof.
Perchance° I will be there as soon as you.   *Perhaps*
40   ANGELO Then you will bring the chain to her yourself?
ANTIPHOLUS OF EPHESUS No, bear it with you, lest I come not
time° enough.   *soon*

4.1 Location: A street in Ephesus.
1. Christian festival observed on the seventh Sunday after Easter, in commemoration of the descent of the Holy Ghost on the disciples on the day of the Jewish harvest holiday of Shavuoth.
2. Perhaps in exasperated contrast with Antipholus of Syracuse's earlier demand for a thousand marks (1.2.81).

ANGELO   Well, sir, I will. Have you the chain about you?

ANTIPHOLUS OF EPHESUS   An if I have not, sir, I hope you have,
   Or else you may return without your money.

45   ANGELO   Nay, come, I pray you, sir, give me the chain.
   Both wind and tide stays° for this gentleman,   *wait*
   And I, to blame, have held him here too long.

ANTIPHOLUS OF EPHESUS   Good lord! You use this dalliance°   *trifling delay*
   to excuse
   Your breach of promise to° the Porcupine.   *to go to*

50   I should have chid you for not bringing it,
   But like a shrew° you first begin to brawl.   *sour person*

SECOND MERCHANT [*to* ANGELO]   The hour steals on. I pray
   you, sir, dispatch.°   *hurry*

ANGELO   You hear how he importunes me. The chain!

ANTIPHOLUS OF EPHESUS   Why, give it to my wife and fetch
   your money.

55   ANGELO   Come, come, you know I gave it you even° now.   *just*
   Either send the chain, or send me by some token.³

ANTIPHOLUS OF EPHESUS   Fie, now you run this humor out of
   breath.°   *exhaust this joke*
   Come, where's the chain? I pray you, let me see it.

SECOND MERCHANT   My business cannot brook° this dalliance.   *tolerate*

60   Good sir, say whe'er° you'll answer° me or no.   *whether / repay*
   If not, I'll leave him to the officer.

ANTIPHOLUS OF EPHESUS   I answer you? What should I answer
   you?

ANGELO   The money that you owe me for the chain.

ANTIPHOLUS OF EPHESUS   I owe you none till I receive the
   chain.

65   ANGELO   You know I gave it you half an hour since.

ANTIPHOLUS OF EPHESUS   You gave me none. You wrong me
   much to say so.

ANGELO   You wrong me more, sir, in denying it.
   Consider how it stands upon° my credit.⁴   *affects*

SECOND MERCHANT   Well, officer, arrest him at my suit.

70   OFFICER [*to* ANGELO]   I do, and charge you in the Duke's name
   to obey me.

ANGELO [*to* ANTIPHOLUS OF EPHESUS]   This touches° me in   *injures*
   reputation.
   Either consent to pay this sum for me,
   Or I attach° you by this officer.   *arrest*

ANTIPHOLUS OF EPHESUS   Consent to pay thee that° I never   *for what*
   had?

75   Arrest me, foolish fellow, if thou dar'st.

ANGELO   Here is thy fee:⁵ arrest him, officer.
   I would not spare my brother in this case,
   If he should scorn me so apparently.°   *openly*

OFFICER [*to* ANTIPHOLUS OF EPHESUS]   I do arrest you, sir. You
   hear the suit.

80   ANTIPHOLUS OF EPHESUS   I do obey thee, till I give thee bail.
   [*to* ANGELO] But sirrah, you shall buy this sport as dear⁶

---

3. With some sign of yours (so that Adriana will   5. Public officers were entitled to private payment.
know to pay me).   6. You shall pay as dearly for this amusement.
4. Financial standing; more generally, reputation.

As all the metal in your shop will answer.°   *amount to*
ANGELO   Sir, sir, I shall have law° in Ephesus—   *my legal rights*
    To your notorious shame, I doubt it not.

        Enter DROMIO [OF] SYRACUSE *from the bay.*

85 DROMIO OF SYRACUSE   Master, there's a bark of Epidamnum
    That stays but till her owner comes aboard,
    And then, sir, she bears away. Our freightage,° sir,   *luggage; goods*
    I have conveyed aboard, and I have bought
    The oil, the balsamum,[7] and aqua vitae.°   *alcohol*
90   The ship is in her trim,° the merry wind   *ready to sail*
    Blows fair from land; they stay for naught° at all   *nothing*
    But for their owner, master, and yourself.
  ANTIPHOLUS OF EPHESUS   How now? A madman? Why, thou
     peevish° sheep,[8]   *bleating*
    What ship of Epidamnum stays for me?
95 DROMIO OF SYRACUSE   A ship you sent me to, to hire waftage.°   *buy our passage*
  ANTIPHOLUS OF EPHESUS   Thou drunken slave! I sent thee for
    a rope,
    And told thee to what purpose and what end.
  DROMIO OF SYRACUSE   You sent me for a rope's end° as soon!   *a beating*
    You sent me to the bay, sir, for a bark.
100 ANTIPHOLUS OF EPHESUS   I will debate this matter at more leisure
    And teach your ears to list° me with more heed.   *listen to*
    To Adriana, villain, hie thee straight.°   *go immediately*
    Give her this key, and tell her in the desk
    That's covered o'er with Turkish tapestry
105   There is a purse of ducats. Let her send it.
    Tell her I am arrested in the street,
    And that shall bail me.° Hie thee, slave, be gone!   *pay my bail*
    —On, officer, to prison, till it come.

        Exeunt [all but DROMIO OF SYRACUSE].

  DROMIO OF SYRACUSE   To Adriana. That is where we dined,
110 Where Dowsabel[9] did claim me for her husband.
    She is too big, I hope, for me to compass.[1]
    Thither I must, although against my will;
    For servants must their masters' minds° fulfill.   *Exit.*   *wishes*

4.2

      Enter ADRIANA *and* LUCIANA.

  ADRIANA   Ah, Luciana, did he tempt thee so?
    Mightst thou perceive austerely in his eye[1]
    That he did plead in earnest, yea or no?
    Looked he or° red or pale, or sad or merrily?   *either*
5   What observation mad'st thou in this case
    Of his heart's meteors tilting[2] in his face?
  LUCIANA   First he denied you had in him no° right.   *any*
  ADRIANA   He meant he did me none, the more my spite.°   *grief*
  LUCIANA   Then swore he that he was a stranger here.

---

7. A healing resin.
8. Idiot, punning on "ship" in the next line (the words were similarly pronounced).
9. English form of "Dulcibella," a generic name for a sweetheart.
1. Encompass; a pun on the cartographic description

of Nell's body (see 3.2.110–41).
4.2 Location: Before the house of Antipholus of Ephesus.
1. By the seriousness of his expression.
2. Conflicting emotions, as if heavenly bodies were engaged in combat ("tilting").

10	ADRIANA	And true he swore, though yet forsworn[3] he were.
	LUCIANA	Then pleaded I for you.
	ADRIANA	And what said he?
	LUCIANA	That love I begged for you, he begged of me.
	ADRIANA	With what persuasion did he tempt thy love?
	LUCIANA	With words that in an honest suit° might move.	courtship
15		First he did praise my beauty, then my speech.
	ADRIANA	Didst speak him fair?°	encourage him
	LUCIANA	Have patience, I beseech.
	ADRIANA	I cannot, nor I will not hold me still.°	silent
		My tongue, though not my heart, shall have his° will.	its
		He is deformèd, crooked, old, and sere,°	withered
20		Ill-faced, worse-bodied, shapeless° everywhere,	ill shaped
		Vicious, ungentle, foolish, blunt, unkind,
		Stigmatical in making,[4] worse in mind.
	LUCIANA	Who would be jealous, then, of such a one?
		No evil lost is wailed when it is gone.
25	ADRIANA	Ah, but I think him better than I say,
		And yet would herein others' eyes were worse.[5]
		Far from her nest the lapwing[6] cries away;
		My heart prays for him, though my tongue do curse.

Enter DROMIO [OF] SYRACUSE.

	DROMIO OF SYRACUSE	Here go—the desk, the purse! Sweet
		now, make haste![7]
	LUCIANA	How hast thou lost thy breath?
30	DROMIO OF SYRACUSE	By running fast.
	ADRIANA	Where is thy master, Dromio? Is he well?
	DROMIO OF SYRACUSE	No, he's in Tartar limbo,[8] worse than hell.
		A devil in an everlasting[9] garment hath him,
		One whose hard heart is buttoned up with steel;
35		A fiend, a fairy,[1] pitiless and rough;
		A wolf, nay worse, a fellow all in buff;[2]
		A back friend,[3] a shoulder-clapper,° one that	arresting officer
		countermands°	prohibits
		The passages of alleys, creeks, and narrow lands;[4]
		A hound that runs counter[5] and yet draws dryfoot well;[6]
40		One that before the judgment[7] carries poor souls to hell.
	ADRIANA	Why, man, what is the matter?
	DROMIO OF SYRACUSE	I do not know the matter,° he is	dispute
		'rested ° on the case.[8]	arrested

3. *true . . . forsworn:* he is behaving like a stranger to me, but he is lying and is being false to his marriage vows if he claims to be one.
4. Deformed in his physical makeup.
5. And nevertheless wish others' eyes to be deceived (and so think him ugly).
6. A bird (the peewit) that diverts attention away from her nest to protect her young; Adriana wishes to turn other women's attention away from Antipholus's attractions.
7. Dromio is possibly speaking to himself as he rushes in.
8. Hellish prison. "Tartar" is short for "Tartarus," the classical hell, but it also suggests the Tartars, a central Asian people reputed by Elizabethans to be particularly savage. "Limbo" was common slang for "prison."
9. Term for the durable material used in the Elizabethan period for the uniform of prison officers; eter-

nal, like hell's punishments.
1. Malevolent fairy, like the goblins in 2.2.191–93.
2. Stout leather used in uniforms.
3. False friend; also referring to the officer's hand on the culprit's back during an arrest.
4. The traffic through alleys, small passageways, and narrow pathways. *lands:* launds; glades or clearings, pathways through woods.
5. Runs in the opposite direction to the prey; also perhaps alluding to the Counter, as several debtors' prisons in London were known.
6. *draws . . . well:* tracks game by the scent of its foot.
7. *before the judgment:* in a court of law, with an allusion to the Day of Judgment.
8. *on the case:* in a legal action in which the injury was not specifically addressed by precedent; by means of the officer's hand on his outer clothing ("case").

ADRIANA What, is he arrested? Tell me at whose suit?

DROMIO OF SYRACUSE I know not at whose suit he is arrested well,

45 But is in a suit of buff which 'rested him, that can I tell.
Will you send him, mistress, redemption, the money in his desk?

ADRIANA Go fetch it, sister.   *Exit* LUCIANA.
                              This I wonder at,
That he unknown to me should be in debt.
Tell me, was he arrested on° a band?°   *for breaking / (i.e., bond)*

50 DROMIO OF SYRACUSE Not on a band, but on a stronger thing:
A chain, a chain! Do you not hear it ring?

ADRIANA What, the chain?

DROMIO OF SYRACUSE   No, no, the bell. 'Tis time that I were gone.
It was two ere I left him, and now the clock strikes one.[9]

ADRIANA The hours come back! That did I never hear.

55 DROMIO OF SYRACUSE Oh, yes, if any hour[1] meet a sergeant,
'a° turns back for very fear.   *he*

ADRIANA As if Time were in debt. How fondly° dost thou reason!   *foolishly*

DROMIO OF SYRACUSE Time is a very bankrupt and owes
more than he's worth to season.[2]
Nay, he's a thief too: have you not heard men say
That time comes stealing on by night and day?

60 If 'a be in debt and theft, and a sergeant in° the way,   *stands in*
Hath he not reason to turn back an hour in a day?
                    Enter LUCIANA.

ADRIANA Go, Dromio, there's the money. Bear it straight,°   *quickly*
And bring thy master home immediately.
                    [*Exit* DROMIO OF SYRACUSE.]
Come, sister, I am pressed° down with conceit:°   *depressed / imaginings*

65 Conceit, my comfort and my injury.   *Exeunt.*

4.3

Enter ANTIPHOLUS [OF] SYRACUSE.

ANTIPHOLUS OF SYRACUSE There's not a man I meet but doth
salute° me   *greet*
As if I were their well-acquainted friend,
And everyone doth call me by my name.
Some tender° money to me, some invite me,   *offer*

5 Some other give me thanks for kindnesses.
Some offer me commodities to buy.
Even now a tailor called me in his shop,
And showed me silks that he had bought for me,
And therewithal° took measure of my body.   *with that*

10 Sure, these are but imaginary wiles,°   *delusions*
And Lapland sorcerers[1] inhabit here.
                    Enter DROMIO [OF] SYRACUSE.

---

9. "On" and "one" were pronounced similarly.
1. Perhaps a pun on "ower" ("debtor") or "whore."
2. "Seisin," a legal term for "possession"; opportunity; thus, there is too little time to make good the

promises of the occasion.
4.3 Location: A street in Ephesus.
1. Lapland was known for having witches.

DROMIO OF SYRACUSE   Master, here's the gold you sent me
for. What, have you got the picture of old Adam new
appareled?[2]

15 ANTIPHOLUS OF SYRACUSE   What gold is this? What Adam dost
thou mean?

DROMIO OF SYRACUSE   Not that Adam that kept the Paradise,
but that Adam that keeps the prison; he that goes in the
calf's-skin[3] that was killed for the Prodigal;[4] he that came
behind you, sir, like an evil angel, and bid you forsake your

20 liberty.[5]

ANTIPHOLUS OF SYRACUSE   I understand thee not.

DROMIO OF SYRACUSE   No? Why, 'tis a plain case: he that went
like a bass viol[6] in a case of leather; the man, sir, that when
gentlemen are tired gives them a sob[7] and 'rests them; he,

25 sir, that takes pity on decayed° men and gives them suits of   *ruined*
durance;[8] he that sets up his rest[9] to do more exploits with
his mace° than a morris-pike.[1]   *staff of office*

ANTIPHOLUS OF SYRACUSE   What, thou mean'st an officer?

DROMIO OF SYRACUSE   Ay, sir, the sergeant of the band; he that

30 brings any man to answer it° that breaks his band;° one that   *for it / bond*
thinks a man always going to bed, and says, "God give you
good rest."°   *arrest*

ANTIPHOLUS OF SYRACUSE   Well, sir, there rest in° your foolery.   *cease*
Is there any ships puts forth tonight? May we be gone?

35 DROMIO OF SYRACUSE   Why, sir, I brought you word an hour
since that the bark *Expedition* put forth tonight, and then
were you hindered by the sergeant to tarry for the hoy[2] *Delay*.
Here are the angels[3] that you sent for to deliver you.

ANTIPHOLUS OF SYRACUSE   The fellow is distract,° and so am I,   *distracted; mad*

40 And here we wander in illusions.
Some blessèd power deliver us from hence.

        Enter a COURTESAN.

COURTESAN   Well met, well met, Master Antipholus.
I see, sir, you have found the goldsmith now.
Is that the chain you promised me today?

45 ANTIPHOLUS OF SYRACUSE   Satan, avoid![4] I charge thee, tempt
me not!

DROMIO OF SYRACUSE   Master, is this Mistress Satan?

ANTIPHOLUS OF SYRACUSE   It is the devil.

DROMIO OF SYRACUSE   Nay, she is worse: she is the devil's dam°—   *mother*
and here she comes in the habit° of a light° wench, and   *clothing / wanton*

50 thereof comes that the wenches say, "God damn me." That's

---

2. *have . . . appareled*: i.e., "is the sergeant who was
taking you into custody still with you?" Sergeants
wore leather uniforms, and Dromio's punning words
refer to the skins in which Adam was dressed after
the Fall (Genesis 3:21). There is also a possible reference to Ephesians 4:22: "put off . . . the old man,
which is corrupt . . . put on the new man, which after
God is created in righteousness."
3. The buff of the officer's garments.
4. The prodigal son of Luke 15:11–32; his father
killed a calf for a feast on his return home.
5. *bid . . . liberty*: arrested you.
6. Large stringed instrument, like a cello (continuing the jokes about the officer's leather uniform).

7. A rest (for tired horses) as well as a lament, picked
up in the following puns of "rests" and "pity."
8. *suits of durance*: lawsuits or prosecutions ending
in imprisonment; clothes made of hard-wearing
material.
9. *sets up his rest*: gambles all (punning on "arrest").
1. *morris-pike*: another word for "Moorish pike," a
lance of North African origin or design.
2. A small, slow vessel used in coastal waters. The
names of the ships are Dromio's improvisations.
3. Gold coins bearing a figure of the archangel
Michael.
4. Away! An echo of Jesus' words to Satan in Matthew 4:10: "Avoid Satan."

as much to say, "God make me a light wench." It is written,
they appear to men like angels of light.[5] Light is an effect of
fire, and fire will burn. Ergo,° light wenches will burn.[6] Come   *Therefore*
not near her.

55   COURTESAN   Your man and you are marvelous merry, sir.
Will you go with me? We'll mend° our dinner here?   *complete*
     DROMIO OF SYRACUSE   Master, if you do, expect spoon-meat,[7]
or bespeak° a long spoon.   *request*
     ANTIPHOLUS OF SYRACUSE   Why, Dromio?
60   DROMIO OF SYRACUSE   Marry, he must have a long spoon that
must eat with the devil.
     ANTIPHOLUS OF SYRACUSE [*to* COURTESAN]   Avoid, then, fiend!
     What tell'st thou me of supping?
Thou art, as you are all, a sorceress.
I conjure° thee to leave me and be gone.   *order; charge*
65   COURTESAN   Give me the ring of mine you had at dinner,
Or for my diamond the chain you promised,
And I'll be gone, sir, and not trouble you.
     DROMIO OF SYRACUSE   Some devils ask but° the parings of   *only*
one's nail, a rush,° a hair, a drop of blood, a pin, a nut, a   *straw*
70   cherry-stone; but she, more covetous, would have a chain.
Master, be wise. An if° you give it her, the devil will shake   *If*
her chain[8] and fright us with it.
     COURTESAN   I pray you, sir, my ring, or else the chain.
I hope you do not mean to cheat me so?
75   ANTIPHOLUS OF SYRACUSE   Avaunt,° thou witch! —Come,   *Go away*
     Dromio, let us go.
     DROMIO OF SYRACUSE   "Fly pride," says the peacock.[9] Mistress,
     that you know.
           Exeunt [ANTIPHOLUS OF SYRACUSE *and* DROMIO OF
                               SYRACUSE].
     COURTESAN   Now out of doubt Antipholus is mad,
Else would he never so demean° himself.   *conduct; debase*
A ring he hath of mine worth forty ducats,
80   And for the same he promised me a chain.
Both one and other he denies me now.
The reason that I gather he is mad,
Besides this present instance of his rage,
Is a mad tale he told today at dinner
85   Of his own doors being shut against his entrance.
Belike° his wife, acquainted with his fits,   *Probably*
On purpose shut the doors against his way.°   *entrance*
My way is now to hie° home to his house   *hasten*
And tell his wife that, being lunatic,
90   He rushed into my house and took perforce°   *forcibly*
My ring away. This course I fittest choose,
For forty ducats is too much to lose.   [*Exit.*]

---

5. From 2 Corinthians 11:14: "Satan himself is
transformed into an angel of light."
6. Will transmit venereal disease; will suffer in hell.
7. Soft food for babies or invalids, mentioned for the
sake of the proverb in lines 60–61.

8. Alluding to the binding of the devil in a chain in
Revelation 20:1.
9. For the conniving courtesan to complain about
cheating is, in Dromio's view, analogous to a proud
peacock decrying pride.

4.4

Enter ANTIPHOLUS [OF] EPHESUS *with* [*an* OFFICER].

ANTIPHOLUS OF EPHESUS   Fear me not, man. I will not break
away.
I'll give thee ere I leave thee so much money
To warrant thee° as I am 'rested for.   *As surety*
My wife is in a wayward mood today
5   And will not lightly° trust the messenger   *readily*
That I should be attached° in Ephesus.   *arrested*
I tell you, 'twill sound harshly in her ears.

Enter DROMIO [OF] EPHESUS *with a rope's end.*

Here comes my man. I think he brings the money.
How now, sir? Have you that I sent you for?
10   DROMIO OF EPHESUS   Here's that I warrant you will pay[1] them
all.
ANTIPHOLUS OF EPHESUS   But where's the money?
DROMIO OF EPHESUS   Why, sir, I gave the money for the rope.
ANTIPHOLUS OF EPHESUS   Five hundred ducats, villain, for a
rope?
DROMIO OF EPHESUS   I'll serve° you, sir, five hundred at the   *provide*
rate.°   *for that price*
15   ANTIPHOLUS OF EPHESUS   To what end did I bid thee hie thee
home?
DROMIO OF EPHESUS   To° a rope's end, sir, and to that end am   *For*
I returned.
ANTIPHOLUS OF EPHESUS   And to that end, sir, I will welcome
you.[2]
[*He beats* DROMIO.]
OFFICER   Good sir, be patient.
DROMIO OF EPHESUS   Nay, 'tis for me to be patient: I am in
20   adversity.[3]
OFFICER   Good now,° hold thy tongue.   *Please*
DROMIO OF EPHESUS   Nay, rather persuade him to hold° his   *hold off*
hands.
ANTIPHOLUS OF EPHESUS   Thou whoreson,[4] senseless villain!
25   DROMIO OF EPHESUS   I would I were senseless, sir, that I might
not feel your blows.
ANTIPHOLUS OF EPHESUS   Thou art sensible in° nothing but   *responsive to*
blows, and so is an ass.
DROMIO OF EPHESUS   I am an ass indeed. You may prove it by
30   my long ears.[5] I have served him from the hour of my nativity
to this instant and have nothing at his hands for my service
but blows. When I am cold, he heats me with beating; when
I am warm, he cools me with beating. I am waked with it
when I sleep, raised with it when I sit, driven out of doors
35   with it when I go from home, welcomed home with it when I
return. Nay, I bear it on my shoulders, as a beggar wont her
brat,[6] and I think when he hath lamed me, I shall beg with it[7]
from door to door.

4.4 Location: Scene continues.
1. With a beating (see 4.1.15–21).
2. I will treat you to a rope's end (a beating).
3. In painful circumstances; alluding to Psalm 94:13.
4. Literally, son of a whore; more generally, a term of
contemptuous familiarity.

5. Playing on "ears"/"years," which were pronounced
in the same way.
6. *wont her brat*: is accustomed to carrying her child.
7. I shall receive a beating (a frequent punishment
for begging).

Enter ADRIANA, LUCIANA, COURTESAN, *and a*
schoolmaster, called PINCH.

ANTIPHOLUS OF EPHESUS   Come, go along. My wife is coming
    yonder.

40 DROMIO OF EPHESUS [*to* ADRIANA]   Mistress, *respice finem,*[8]
    respect your end; or rather, to prophesy like the parrot,[9]
    "Beware the rope's end."

ANTIPHOLUS OF EPHESUS   Wilt thou still talk?
    [*He*] *beats* DROMIO.

COURTESAN [*to* ADRIANA]   How say you now? Is not your
    husband mad?

45 ADRIANA   His incivility confirms no less.
    —Good Doctor Pinch, you are a conjurer.[1]
    Establish him in his true sense[2] again,
    And I will please you° what you will demand.   *repay you with*

LUCIANA   Alas, how fiery and how sharp° he looks!   *fierce*

50 COURTESAN   Mark how he trembles in his ecstasy!°   *frenzy*

PINCH [*to* ANTIPHOLUS OF EPHESUS]   Give me your hand, and
    let me feel your pulse.

ANTIPHOLUS OF EPHESUS   There is my hand, and let it feel
    your ear.
    [*He strikes* PINCH.]

PINCH   I charge thee, Satan, housed within this man,
    To yield possession to my holy prayers,
55   And to thy state of darkness hie thee straight.
    I conjure thee by all the saints in heaven.

ANTIPHOLUS OF EPHESUS   Peace, doting wizard, peace! I am
    not mad.

ADRIANA   Oh, that thou wert not, poor distressèd soul.

ANTIPHOLUS OF EPHESUS   You minion,° you, are these your   *hussy*
    customers?
60   Did this companion° with the saffron° face   *rascal / yellow*
    Revel and feast it at my house today,
    Whilst upon me the guilty doors were shut,
    And I denied to enter in my house?

ADRIANA   O husband, God doth know you dined at home,
65   Where would you had remained until this time,
    Free from these slanders° and this open shame.   *scandals*

ANTIPHOLUS OF EPHESUS   Dined at home? [*to* DROMIO OF
    EPHESUS] Thou villain, what sayest thou?

DROMIO OF EPHESUS   Sir, sooth to say,° you did not dine at   *to speak truly*
    home.

ANTIPHOLUS OF EPHESUS   Were not my doors locked up, and I
    shut out?

70 DROMIO OF EPHESUS   Perdie,° your doors were locked, and   *By God (pardieu)*
    you shut out.

ANTIPHOLUS OF EPHESUS   And did not she herself revile me
    there?

DROMIO OF EPHESUS   Sans° fable, she herself reviled you there.   *Without*

---

8. A religious injunction to "think on your end," but
punning on *respice funem,* "think on the rope" (on
hanging).
9. Parrots were often taught to cry "rope," an exclamation or curse; the "prophecy" is that the hearer
deserves to be hanged.
1. Capable of exorcising devils; exorcism required a

"doctor"—a learned man—since it was thought that
devils needed to be addressed in Latin.
2. In his right mind. Possession and lunacy were not
necessarily medically distinct, since both involved
the displacement of reason (by passion, sickness, or
demons).

ANTIPHOLUS OF EPHESUS Did not her kitchen maid rail, taunt,
    and scorn me?
DROMIO OF EPHESUS Certes° she did. The kitchen vestal[3]   *Certainly*
    scorned you.
75 ANTIPHOLUS OF EPHESUS And did not I in rage depart from
    thence?
DROMIO OF EPHESUS In verity you did. My bones bears
    witness,
    That since have felt the vigor of his rage.
ADRIANA [*aside to* PINCH] Is't good to soothe° him in these   *humor*
    contraries?
PINCH [*aside to* ADRIANA] It is no shame.° The fellow finds   *harm*
    his vein,
80   And, yielding to him, humors well his frenzy.
ANTIPHOLUS OF EPHESUS Thou hast suborned° the goldsmith   *induced*
    to arrest me.
ADRIANA Alas, I sent you money to redeem you,
    By Dromio here, who came in haste for it.
DROMIO OF EPHESUS Money by me? Heart and good will you
    might,
85   But surely, master, not a rag° of money.   *farthing*
ANTIPHOLUS OF EPHESUS Went'st not thou to her for a purse
    of ducats?
ADRIANA He came to me, and I delivered it.
LUCIANA And I am witness with her that she did.
DROMIO OF EPHESUS God and the rope-maker bear me witness
90   That I was sent for nothing but a rope.
PINCH [*aside to* ADRIANA] Mistress, both man and master is
    possessed;
    I know it by their pale and deadly° looks.   *deathlike*
    They must be bound and laid in some dark room.[4]
ANTIPHOLUS OF EPHESUS [*to* ADRIANA] Say wherefore didst
    thou lock me forth° today,   *out*
95   [*to* DROMIO OF EPHESUS] And why dost thou deny the bag of
    gold?
ADRIANA I did not, gentle husband, lock thee forth.
DROMIO OF EPHESUS And, gentle master, I received no gold.
    But I confess, sir, that we were locked out.
ADRIANA Dissembling villain, thou speak'st false in both.
100 ANTIPHOLUS OF EPHESUS Dissembling harlot, thou art false
    in all,
    And art confederate with a damnèd pack°   *conspiracy; posse*
    To make a loathsome abject scorn of me.
    But with these nails I'll pluck out these false eyes,
    That would behold in me this shameful sport.
    Enter three or four, and offer to bind him; he strives.
105 ADRIANA Oh, bind him, bind him! Let him not come near me.
PINCH More company!° The fiend is strong within him.   *Get help*
LUCIANA Ay me, poor man, how pale and wan he looks.
ANTIPHOLUS OF EPHESUS What, will you murder me? —Thou,
    jailer, thou,

---

3. Ironic: a virgin priestess of the household goddess
Vesta's temple, responsible for keeping the fire
burning.

4. An ordinary sixteenth-century treatment for
insanity.

I am thy prisoner. Wilt thou suffer them
To make a rescue?[5]
110 OFFICER   Masters, let him go.
He is my prisoner, and you shall not have him.
PINCH Go bind this man, for he is frantic too.
          [*They bind* DROMIO OF EPHESUS.]
ADRIANA What wilt thou do, thou peevish° officer?   *stupid*
Hast thou delight to see a wretched man
115 Do outrage and displeasure° to himself?   *harm*
OFFICER He is my prisoner. If I let him go,
The debt he owes will be required of me.
ADRIANA I will discharge° thee ere I go from thee.   *repay*
Bear me forthwith unto his creditor,
120 And knowing how the debt grows,[6] I will pay it.
Good Master Doctor, see him safe conveyed
Home to my house. Oh, most unhappy day!
ANTIPHOLUS OF EPHESUS Oh, most unhappy strumpet!
DROMIO OF EPHESUS Master, I am here entered in bond for
you.
125 ANTIPHOLUS OF EPHESUS Out on thee, villain. Wherefore
      dost thou mad° me?   *goad*
DROMIO OF EPHESUS Will you be bound for nothing? Be mad,
      good master. Cry, "The devil!"[7]
LUCIANA God help poor souls, how idly do they talk.
ADRIANA Go bear him hence. Sister, go you with me.
          Exeunt [PINCH *and his assistants, carrying off*
              ANTIPHOLUS OF EPHESUS *and* DROMIO OF EPHESUS].
          OFFICER, ADRIANA, LUCIANA, *and* COURTESAN *remain.*
130 [*to* OFFICER] Say now, whose suit is he arrested at?
OFFICER One Angelo, a goldsmith. Do you know him?
ADRIANA I know the man. What is the sum he owes?
OFFICER Two hundred ducats.
ADRIANA   Say, how grows it due?
OFFICER Due for a chain your husband had of him.
135 ADRIANA He did bespeak° a chain for me, but had it not.   *order*
COURTESAN Whenas your husband, all in rage today,
Came to my house, and took away my ring—
The ring I saw upon his finger now—
Straight after did I meet him with a chain.
140 ADRIANA It may be so, but I did never see it.
Come, jailer, bring me where the goldsmith is.
I long to know the truth hereof at large.°   *in full*
          Enter ANTIPHOLUS [OF] SYRACUSE *and* DROMIO [OF]
              SYRACUSE, *with* [*their rapiers*] *drawn.*
LUCIANA God, for thy mercy, they are loose again!
ADRIANA And come with naked° swords; let's call more help   *drawn*
To have them bound again. [ADRIANA *and* LUCIANA] *run out.*
145 OFFICER   Away, they'll kill us.
          Exeunt all, as fast as may be, frighted. [ANTIPHOLUS OF
              SYRACUSE *and* DROMIO OF SYRACUSE *remain.*]

5. To release by force from legal custody.
6. *knowing . . . grows:* when I know how the debt
came about.

7. A cry of exasperation; a direct address to the devil,
which would lend support to the view that he is
possessed.

ANTIPHOLUS OF SYRACUSE   I see these witches are afraid of
    swords.
DROMIO OF SYRACUSE   She that would be your wife, now ran
    from you.
ANTIPHOLUS OF SYRACUSE   Come to the Centaur. Fetch our
    stuff from thence.
    I long that we were safe and sound aboard.

150 DROMIO OF SYRACUSE   Faith, stay here this night. They will
    surely do us no harm: you saw they speak us fair, give us gold.
    Methinks they are such a gentle nation, that but for the
    mountain of mad flesh that claims marriage of me, I could
    find in my heart to stay here still,° and turn witch.   *always*

155 ANTIPHOLUS OF SYRACUSE   I will not stay tonight for all the
    town.
    Therefore away, to get our stuff aboard.   *Exeunt.*

5.1

Enter [SECOND] MERCHANT *and* [ANGELO] *the goldsmith.*

ANGELO   I am sorry, sir, that I have hindered you,
    But I protest he had the chain of me,
    Though most dishonestly he doth deny it.
SECOND MERCHANT   How is the man esteemed here in the city?
5 ANGELO   Of very reverend reputation, sir,
    Of credit infinite, highly beloved,
    Second to none that lives here in the city.
    His word might bear my wealth at any time.[1]
SECOND MERCHANT   Speak softly. Yonder, as I think, he walks.

    Enter ANTIPHOLUS [OF SYRACUSE] *and* DROMIO
    [OF SYRACUSE] *again.*

10 ANGELO   'Tis so, and that self° chain about his neck,   *same*
    Which he forswore° most monstrously to have.   *denied on oath*
    Good sir, draw near to me, I'll speak to him.
    —Signor Antipholus, I wonder much
    That you would put me to this shame and trouble,
15   And not without some scandal to yourself,
    With circumstance° and oaths so to deny   *detailed argument*
    This chain which now you wear so openly.
    Beside the charge,° the shame, imprisonment,   *cost*
    You have done wrong to this my honest friend,
20   Who, but for staying on° our controversy,   *as a result of*
    Had hoisted sail and put to sea today.
    This chain you had of me. Can you deny it?
ANTIPHOLUS OF SYRACUSE   I think I had. I never did deny it.
SECOND MERCHANT   Yes, that you did, sir, and forswore it too.
25 ANTIPHOLUS OF SYRACUSE   Who heard me to deny it or
    forswear it?
SECOND MERCHANT   These ears of mine thou know'st did hear
    thee.
    Fie on thee, wretch! 'Tis pity that thou liv'st
    To walk where any honest men resort.
ANTIPHOLUS OF SYRACUSE   Thou art a villain to impeach° me   *accuse*
    thus.

5.1 Location: Before a priory.
1. His word alone would be enough security to borrow all I have.

30 I'll prove mine honor and mine honesty
    Against thee presently,° if thou dar'st stand.°   now / defend yourself
SECOND MERCHANT I dare, and do defy thee for a villain.
        They draw. Enter ADRIANA, LUCIANA, COURTESAN, *and
        others.*
ADRIANA Hold, hurt him not, for God sake! He is mad.
    Some get within him;² take his sword away.
35 Bind Dromio too, and bear them to my house.
DROMIO OF SYRACUSE Run, master, run! For God's sake,
    take° a house.   take cover in
    This is some priory—in, or we are spoiled.°   ruined
        Exeunt [ANTIPHOLUS OF SYRACUSE *and*
        DROMIO OF SYRACUSE] *to the priory.*
        Enter Lady ABBESS [*from the priory*].
ABBESS Be quiet, people. Wherefore throng you hither?
ADRIANA To fetch my poor distracted husband hence.
40 Let us come in that we may bind him fast
    And bear him home for his recovery.
ANGELO I knew he was not in his perfect wits.
SECOND MERCHANT I am sorry now that I did draw on him.
ABBESS How long hath this possession held the man?
45 ADRIANA This week he hath been heavy, sour, sad,
    And much different from the man he was;
    But till this afternoon his passion°   insanity
    Ne'er brake° into extremity of rage.   broke
ABBESS Hath he not lost much wealth by wreck of sea?
50 Buried some dear friend? Hath not else his eye
    Strayed° his affection in unlawful love—   Led astray
    A sin prevailing much in youthful men,
    Who give their eyes the liberty of gazing?
    Which of these sorrows is he subject to?
55 ADRIANA To none of these, except it be the last,
    Namely, some love that drew him oft from home.
ABBESS You should for that have reprehended him.
ADRIANA Why, so I did.
ABBESS   Ay, but not rough enough.
ADRIANA As roughly as my modesty would let me.
ABBESS Haply° in private.   Perhaps
60 ADRIANA   And in assemblies too.
ABBESS Ay, but not enough.
ADRIANA It was the copy of our conference.³
    In bed he slept not for my urging it;
    At board° he fed not for my urging it;   table
65 Alone, it was the subject of my theme;
    In company I often glanced° it;   alluded to
    Still° did I tell him it was vile and bad.   Continually
ABBESS And thereof came it that the man was mad.
    The venom° clamors of a jealous woman   venomous
70 Poisons more deadly than a mad dog's tooth.
    It seems his sleeps were hindered by thy railing,
    And thereof comes it that his head is light.

---

2. *get within him*: stand within his guard; Adriana is   3. *copy of our conference*: exact topic of our
requesting to have someone stand between the two   conversation.
dueling men.

Thou say'st his meat was sauced with thy upbraidings;
Unquiet meals make ill digestions.
75 Thereof the raging fire of fever bred,
And what's a fever, but a fit of madness?[4]
Thou sayest his sports were hindered by thy brawls.
Sweet recreation barred, what doth ensue
But moody and dull melancholy,
80 Kinsman to grim and comfortless despair,
And at her heels a huge infectious troop
Of pale distemperatures° and foes to life?   *illnesses; imbalances*
In food, in sport, and life-preserving rest
To be disturbed would mad or° man or beast.   *would make mad either*
85 The consequence is, then, thy jealous fits
Hath scared thy husband from the use of wits.
LUCIANA She never reprehended him but mildly
When he demeaned himself rough, rude, and wildly.
        [*to* ADRIANA] Why bear you these rebukes and answer not?
90 ADRIANA She did betray me to my own reproof.
        —Good people, enter, and lay hold on him.
ABBESS No, not a creature enters in my house.
ADRIANA Then let your servants bring my husband forth.
ABBESS Neither. He took this place for sanctuary,[5]
95 And it shall privilege him from your hands
Till I have brought him to his wits again,
Or lose my labor in assaying it.
ADRIANA I will attend my husband, be his nurse,
Diet° his sickness, for it is my office,°   *Treat / duty*
100 And will have no attorney° but myself,   *proxy*
And therefore let me have him home with me.
ABBESS Be patient, for I will not let him stir
Till I have used the approvèd° means I have,   *tested*
With wholesome syrups, drugs, and holy prayers
105 To make of him a formal° man again.   *complete; sane*
It is a branch and parcel° of mine oath,   *part*
A charitable duty of my order.
Therefore depart, and leave him here with me.
ADRIANA I will not hence and leave my husband here,
110 And ill it doth beseem your holiness
To separate the husband and the wife.[6]
ABBESS Be quiet and depart. Thou shalt not have him.
                                                        [*Exit.*]
LUCIANA [*to* ADRIANA] Complain unto the Duke of this
        indignity.
ADRIANA Come, go. I will fall prostrate at his feet,
115 And never rise until my tears and prayers
Have won his grace to come in person hither
And take perforce my husband from the Abbess.
SECOND MERCHANT By this I think the dial point's at five.
Anon° I'm sure the Duke himself in person   *Soon*
120 Comes this way to the melancholy vale,

4. Both are imbalances in the body's humors; see
note to 4.4.47.
5. Churches and other sacred buildings provided refuge from legal prosecution until the seventeenth
century.

6. Against the Abbess's defense of sanctuary, Adriana cites the competing biblical injunction against
separating individuals united in holy matrimony. See
Matthew 19 and Mark 10.

The place of death and sorry execution,
Behind the ditches of the abbey here.
ANGELO   Upon what cause?
SECOND MERCHANT   To see a reverend Syracusian merchant,
125   Who put unluckily into this bay
Against the laws and statutes of this town,
Beheaded publicly for his offense.
ANGELO   See where they come. We will behold his death.
LUCIANA   Kneel to the Duke before he pass the abbey.

Enter the DUKE *of Ephesus, and* [EGEON] *the Merchant
of Syracuse, barehead, with the Headsman,*° *and other*   *executioner*
OFFICERS.

130 DUKE   Yet once again proclaim it publicly:
If any friend will pay the sum for him,
He shall not die; so much we tender[7] him.
ADRIANA   Justice, most sacred Duke, against the Abbess!
DUKE   She is a virtuous and a reverend lady.
135   It cannot be that she hath done thee wrong.
ADRIANA   May it please your grace, Antipholus my husband,
Who I made lord of me and all I had
At your important° letters,[8] this ill day   *urgent*
A most outrageous fit of madness took him,
140   That desp'rately he hurried through the street—
With him his bondman, all as mad as he—
Doing displeasure to the citizens
By rushing in their houses, bearing thence
Rings, jewels, anything his rage° did like.   *he in his madness*
145   Once did I get him bound and sent him home,
Whilst to take order for° the wrongs I went,   *settle up*
That here and there his fury had committed.
Anon, I wot° not by what strong° escape,   *know / forcible*
He broke from those that had the guard of him,
150   And with his mad attendant and himself,
Each one with ireful passion, with drawn swords,
Met us again, and madly bent on us
Chased us away, till raising of more aid
We came again to bind them. Then they fled
155   Into this abbey, whither we pursued them,
And here the Abbess shuts the gates on us
And will not suffer us to fetch him out,
Nor send him forth, that we may bear him hence.
Therefore, most gracious Duke, with thy command,
160   Let him be brought forth and borne hence for help.
DUKE   Long since, thy husband served me in my wars,
And I to thee engaged a prince's word—
When thou didst make him master of thy bed—
To do him all the grace° and good I could.   *favor; patronage*
165   Go, some of you, knock at the abbey gate,
And bid the lady Abbess come to me.
I will determine this before I stir.

Enter a MESSENGER.

MESSENGER   O mistress, mistress, shift° and save yourself!   *do what you can*

---

7. Offer; feel tender regard for.
8. Formal instructions. Adriana may have been the Duke's ward.

My master and his man are both broke loose,
170 Beaten the maids a-row,° and bound the Doctor,   *one after another*
Whose beard they have singed off with brands° of fire,   *torches*
And ever as it blazed, they threw on him
Great pails of puddled° mire to quench the hair.   *foul*
My master preaches patience to him, and the while
175 His man with scissors nicks him like a fool,⁹
And sure—unless you send some present help—
Between them they will kill the conjurer.
ADRIANA Peace, fool, thy master and his man are here,
And that is false thou dost report to us.
180 MESSENGER Mistress, upon my life I tell you true.
I have not breathed almost since I did see it.
He cries for you, and vows, if he can take you,
To scorch your face and to disfigure you.
     Cry within.
Hark, hark, I hear him, mistress. Fly, be gone!
185 DUKE [*to* ADRIANA] Come stand by me. Fear nothing. Guard
  with halberds!°   *spears with blades*
ADRIANA Ay me, it is my husband! Witness you
That he is borne about invisible.
Even now we housed him in° the abbey here,   *chased him into*
And now he's there, past thought of human reason.
   Enter ANTIPHOLUS [OF EPHESUS] *and* DROMIO OF
   EPHESUS.
190 ANTIPHOLUS OF EPHESUS Justice, most gracious Duke, oh,
  grant me justice!
Even for the service that long since I did thee,
When I bestrid thee¹ in the wars and took
Deep scars to save thy life; even for the blood
That then I lost for thee, now grant me justice.
195 EGEON [*aside*] Unless the fear of death doth make me dote,° *grow senile*
I see my son Antipholus and Dromio.
ANTIPHOLUS OF EPHESUS Justice, sweet prince, against that
  woman there,
She whom thou gav'st to me to be my wife,
That hath abused and dishonored me,
200 Even in the strength and height of injury.
Beyond imagination is the wrong
That she this day hath shameless thrown on me.
DUKE Discover° how, and thou shalt find me just.   *Reveal*
ANTIPHOLUS OF EPHESUS This day, great Duke, she shut the
  doors upon me
205 While she with harlots° feasted in my house.   *scoundrels*
DUKE A grievous fault. Say, woman, didst thou so?
ADRIANA No, my good lord. Myself, he, and my sister
Today did dine together. So befall my soul
As this is false he burdens me withal.²
210 LUCIANA Ne'er may I look on day, nor sleep on night,
But° she tells to your highness simple truth.   *Unless*
ANGELO [*aside*] O perjured woman! They are both forsworn.

9. Cuts his hair in a foolish or fantastical fashion. 2. So . . . withal: Let the fate of my soul depend on
1. Stood over you (to defend you when you were whether what he charges me with is false.
down).

In this the madman justly chargeth them.
ANTIPHOLUS OF EPHESUS My liege, I am advisèd° what I say,   *fully aware*
215   Neither disturbed with the effect of wine,
       Nor heady-rash provoked with raging ire,
       Albeit my wrongs might make one wiser mad.
       This woman locked me out this day from dinner.
       That goldsmith there, were he not packed° with her,   *conspiring*
220   Could witness it, for he was with me then,
       Who parted with me to go fetch a chain,
       Promising to bring it to the Porcupine,
       Where Balthasar and I did dine together.
       Our dinner done, and he not coming thither,
225   I went to seek him. In the street I met him,
       And in his company that gentleman.
            [*He indicates the* SECOND MERCHANT.]
       There did this perjured goldsmith swear me down°   *contradict me in swearing*
       That I this day of him received the chain,
       Which, God he knows, I saw not. For the which,
230   He did arrest me with an officer.
       I did obey, and sent my peasant° home   *servant*
       For certain ducats; he with none returned.
       Then, fairly,° I bespoke° the officer   *courteously / asked*
       To go in person with me to my house.
235   By th' way, we met my wife, her sister, and a rabble more
       Of vile confederates. Along with them
       They brought one Pinch, a hungry, lean-faced villain;
       A mere anatomy,° a mountebank,°   *skeleton / quack*
       A threadbare juggler,° and a fortune-teller,   *illusionist*
240   A needy, hollow-eyed, sharp-looking° wretch,   *emaciated*
       A living dead man. This pernicious slave
       Forsooth took on him as° a conjurer,   *posed as*
       And gazing in mine eyes, feeling my pulse,
       And with no face, as 'twere, outfacing me,[3]
245   Cries out I was possessed. Then altogether
       They fell upon me, bound me, bore me thence,
       And in a dark and dankish vault at home
       There left me and my man, both bound together,
       Till, gnawing with my teeth my bonds in sunder,°   *apart*
250   I gained my freedom, and immediately
       Ran hither to your grace, whom I beseech
       To give me ample satisfaction
       For these deep shames and great indignities.
ANGELO My lord, in truth, thus far I witness with him:
255   That he dined not at home but was locked out.
DUKE But had he such a chain of thee, or no?
ANGELO He had, my lord, and when he ran in here
       These people saw the chain about his neck.
SECOND MERCHANT Besides, I will be sworn these ears of mine
260   Heard you confess you had the chain of him,
       After you first forswore it on the mart,
       And thereupon I drew my sword on you,
       And then you fled into this abbey here,
       From whence I think you are come by miracle.

3. And with his thin face staring me down.

265 ANTIPHOLUS OF EPHESUS I never came within these abbey
        walls,
      Nor ever didst thou draw thy sword on me.
      I never saw the chain, so help me heaven,
      And this is false you burden me withal.°   with
 DUKE Why, what an intricate impeach° is this!   complex charge
270 I think you all have drunk of Circe's cup.⁴
      If here you housed° him, here he would have been.   enclosed
      If he were mad, he would not plead so coldly.°   rationally
      [to ADRIANA] You say he dined at home; the goldsmith here
      Denies that saying. [to DROMIO OF EPHESUS] Sirrah, what say
        you?
275 DROMIO OF EPHESUS [indicating the COURTESAN] Sir, he dined
        with her, there, at the Porcupine.
 COURTESAN He did, and from my finger snatched that ring.
 ANTIPHOLUS OF EPHESUS 'Tis true, my liege, this ring I had of her.
 DUKE [to the COURTESAN] Saw'st thou him enter at the abbey
        here?
 COURTESAN As sure, my liege, as I do see your grace.
280 DUKE Why, this is strange. Go call the Abbess hither.
      I think you are all mated° or stark mad.   bewildered

                    Exit one to the ABBESS.

 EGEON Most mighty Duke, vouchsafe me speak a word.
      Haply° I see a friend will save my life   Maybe
      And pay the sum that may deliver me.
285 DUKE Speak freely, Syracusian, what thou wilt.
 EGEON [to ANTIPHOLUS OF EPHESUS] Is not your name, sir,
        called Antipholus?
      And is not that your bondman Dromio?
 DROMIO OF EPHESUS Within this hour I was his bondman,⁵ sir,
      But he, I thank him, gnawed in two my cords.
290 Now am I Dromio, and his man, unbound.
 EGEON I am sure you both of you remember me.
 DROMIO OF EPHESUS Ourselves we do remember, sir, by you:
      For lately we were bound as you are now.⁶
      You are not Pinch's patient, are you, sir?
295 EGEON Why look you strange° on me? You know me well.   unknowingly
 ANTIPHOLUS OF EPHESUS I never saw you in my life till now.
 EGEON Oh, grief hath changed me since you saw me last,
      And careful° hours with Time's deformèd° hand   sorrowful / deforming
      Have written strange defeatures° in my face.   disfigurements
300 But tell me yet, dost thou not know my voice?
 ANTIPHOLUS OF EPHESUS Neither.
 EGEON Dromio, nor thou?
 DROMIO OF EPHESUS No, trust° me, sir, nor I.   believe
 EGEON I am sure thou dost.
305 DROMIO OF EPHESUS Ay, sir, but I am sure I do not, and
        whatsoever a man denies, you are now bound to believe
        him.
 EGEON Not know my voice! O time's extremity,
      Hast thou so cracked and splitted my poor tongue

---

4. The drink by means of which the enchantress
Circe turned men into swine.
5. His indentured servant; tied up with him. (The

pun continues in line 290.)
6. By looking at you, we remember how we were
(bound).

310   In seven short years that here my only son
        Knows not my feeble key of untuned cares?[7]
        Though now this grainèd° face of mine be hid   *lined*
        In sap-consuming winter's drizzled snow,
        And all the conduits of my blood froze up,
315   Yet hath my night of life some memory;
        My wasting lamps° some fading glimmer left;   *failing eyes*
        My dull deaf ears a little use to hear.
        All these old witnesses, I cannot err,
        Tell me thou art my son Antipholus.
320   ANTIPHOLUS OF EPHESUS   I never saw my father in my life.
        EGEON   But° seven years since,° in Syracusa, boy,   *Only / ago*
        Thou know'st we parted, but perhaps, my son,
        Thou sham'st to acknowledge me in misery.
        ANTIPHOLUS OF EPHESUS   The Duke, and all that know me in
             the city,
325   Can witness with me that it is not so.
        I ne'er saw Syracusa in my life.
        DUKE   I tell thee, Syracusian, twenty years
        Have I been patron to Antipholus,
        During which time he ne'er saw Syracusa.
330   I see thy age and dangers make thee dote.
            Enter the ABBESS *with* ANTIPHOLUS [OF] SYRACUSE *and*
            DROMIO [OF] SYRACUSE.
        ABBESS   Most mighty Duke, behold a man much wronged.
            All gather to see them.
        ADRIANA   I see two husbands, or mine eyes deceive me.
        DUKE   One of these men is genius[8] to the other,
        And so, of these, which is the natural° man,   *human; mortal*
335   And which the spirit? Who deciphers them?
        DROMIO OF SYRACUSE   I, sir, am Dromio. Command him away.
        DROMIO OF EPHESUS   I, sir, am Dromio. Pray let me stay.
        ANTIPHOLUS OF SYRACUSE   Egeon, art thou not? Or else his
             ghost.
        DROMIO OF SYRACUSE   O my old master! Who hath bound
             him here?
340   ABBESS   Who ever bound him, I will loose his bonds
        And gain a husband by his liberty.
        Speak, old Egeon, if thou beest the man
        That hadst a wife once called Emilia,
        That bore thee at a burden° two fair sons.   *in one birth*
345   Oh, if thou beest the same Egeon, speak,
        And speak unto the same Emilia.
        DUKE   Why, here begins his morning story right:
        These two Antipholus', these two so like,
        And these two Dromios, one in semblance—
350   Besides her urging° of her wreck at sea—   *claim*
        These are the parents to these children,
        Which accidentally are met together.
        EGEON   If I dream not, thou art Emilia.
        If thou art she, tell me, where is that son

---

7. My weak voice born of harsh sorrows.
8. Attendant spirit. It was a classical belief that each

person had such a spirit, identical in appearance,
allotted to him or her at birth.

355 That floated with thee on the fatal° raft?   *ill-fated*
ABBESS   By men of Epidamnum, he, and I,
     And the twin Dromio, all were taken up.
     But, by and by, rude° fishermen of Corinth   *harsh; boorish*
     By force took Dromio and my son from them,
360 And me they left with those of Epidamnum.
     What then became of them, I cannot tell;
     I, to this fortune that you see me in.
DUKE   Antipholus, thou cam'st from Corinth first.°   *originally*
ANTIPHOLUS OF SYRACUSE   No, sir, not I. I came from
     Syracuse.
365 DUKE   Stay, stand apart. I know not which is which.
ANTIPHOLUS OF EPHESUS   I came from Corinth, my most
     gracious lord.
DROMIO OF EPHESUS   And I with him.
ANTIPHOLUS OF EPHESUS   Brought to this town by that most
     famous warrior,
     Duke Menaphon, your most renownèd uncle.
370 ADRIANA   Which of you two did dine with me today?
ANTIPHOLUS OF SYRACUSE   I, gentle mistress.
ADRIANA   And are not you my husband?
ANTIPHOLUS OF EPHESUS   No, I say nay to that.
ANTIPHOLUS OF SYRACUSE   And so do I. Yet did she call me so,
375 And this fair gentlewoman her sister here
     Did call me brother. [*to* LUCIANA] What I told you then,
     I hope I shall have leisure° to make good,   *opportunity*
     If this be not a dream I see and hear.
ANGELO   That is the chain, sir, which you had of me.
380 ANTIPHOLUS OF SYRACUSE   I think it be, sir. I deny it not.
ANTIPHOLUS OF EPHESUS   And you, sir, for this chain arrested
     me.
ANGELO   I think I did, sir. I deny it not.
ADRIANA   I sent you money, sir, to be your bail
     By Dromio, but I think he brought it not.
385 DROMIO OF EPHESUS   No, none by me.
ANTIPHOLUS OF SYRACUSE   This purse of ducats I received
     from you,
     And Dromio my man did bring them me.
     I see we still° did meet each other's man,   *constantly*
     And I was ta'en for him, and he for me,
390 And thereupon these errors are arose.
ANTIPHOLUS OF EPHESUS   These ducats pawn I for my father
     here.
DUKE   It shall not need. Thy father hath his life.
COURTESAN   Sir, I must have that diamond from you.
ANTIPHOLUS OF EPHESUS   There, take it, and much thanks for
     my good cheer.
395 ABBESS   Renownèd Duke, vouchsafe to take the pains
     To go with us into the abbey here,
     And hear at large discoursèd° all our fortunes.   *recounted in full*
     And all that are assembled in this place,
     That by this sympathizèd° one day's error   *shared*
400 Have suffered wrong, go, keep us company,
     And we shall make full satisfaction.
     Thirty-three years have I but gone in travail°   *labor*

Of you, my sons, and till this present hour
My heavy burden ne'er deliverèd.
405 The Duke, my husband, and my children both,
And you the calendars of their nativity,[9]
Go to a gossips' feast,[1] and go with me—
After so long grief such nativity![2]
DUKE   With all my heart, I'll gossip at° this feast.   *join in*
                 Exeunt all. The two DROMIOS *and two*
                 [ANTIPHOLUS] *Brothers remain.*
410 DROMIO OF SYRACUSE   Master, shall I fetch your stuff from
        shipboard?
ANTIPHOLUS OF EPHESUS   Dromio, what stuff of mine hast
        thou embarked?°   *placed on board*
DROMIO OF SYRACUSE   Your goods that lay at host, sir, in the
        Centaur.
ANTIPHOLUS OF SYRACUSE   He speaks to me. I am your
        master, Dromio.
        Come, go with us, we'll look to that anon.
415   Embrace thy brother there; rejoice with him.
                 Exeunt [ANTIPHOLUS OF SYRACUSE *and* ANTIPHOLUS
                 OF EPHESUS. DROMIO OF SYRACUSE *and* DROMIO OF
                                 EPHESUS *remain*].
DROMIO OF SYRACUSE   There is a fat friend at your master's
        house
        That kitchened me for you[3] today at dinner.
        She now shall be my sister, not my wife.
DROMIO OF EPHESUS   Methinks you are my glass° and not my   *mirror*
        brother:
420   I see, by you,° I am a sweet-faced youth.   *by means of you*
        Will you walk in to see their gossiping?°   *merrymaking*
DROMIO OF SYRACUSE   Not I, sir; you are my elder.[4]
DROMIO OF EPHESUS   That's a question. How shall we try° it?   *test*
DROMIO OF SYRACUSE   We'll draw cuts° for the senior. Till   *straws*
        then, lead thou first.
425 DROMIO OF EPHESUS   Nay, then, thus:
        We came into the world like brother and brother,
        And now let's go hand in hand, not one before another.
                                                 Exeunt.

9. (Addressed to the Dromios): the two servants are a record of their masters' age, having been born at the same time.
1. A feast attended by the godparents ("gossips") to celebrate the christening of a child.
2. TEXTUAL COMMENT The repetition of "nativity" and "go" in lines 406–08 has struck many editors as unpoetic and has led to many suggested emendations. See Digital Edition TC 7.
3. Who entertained me in the kitchen while mistaking me for you.
4. The elder customarily takes precedence and enters first.

Love's Labor's Lost

Love's Labor's Lost (1594–96) is an experimental play disguised as a conventional one. Its most striking feature—its language of sexualized verbal wit—goes well with its aristocratic love plot. Yet the work is complicated by an unexpected concluding twist; challenges to hierarchies of gender, class, nation, and race; a scatological and homoerotic view of bodily function; and partly buried political and religious references. Without jettisoning the spirit of romantic comedy, then, Love's Labor's Lost offers a complex view of wooing and wedding with broad social implications.

Initially, Shakespeare telegraphs what is coming next. King Ferdinand of Navarre and his three courtiers—Biron, Dumaine, and Longueville—swear to shun women for three years to pursue the studious life of an ancient Greek or Renaissance Italian philosophical academy. Yet the arrival of a diplomatic embassy led by the Princess of France and including three ladies-in-waiting—Rosaline, Katherine, and Maria—induces the men to fall in love. They are ridiculed for their about-face. In a multiple eavesdropping scene, they overhear one another confessing this change of heart and hypocritically denounce such oath breaking. In a court masque (a dramatic form in which costumed aristocrats are the performers), they disguise themselves as Russians to advance their claims, but the ladies' own disguises lead each man to woo the wrong woman. Then, roughly two hundred lines from the end, a messenger reports that the Princess's father, the King of France, has died. The world of romantic comedy—Navarre's rural retreat from the ordinary affairs of life—is invaded by death. When the men obliviously continue their wooing, the women, who all along have mistrusted their forsworn suitors (arguably with even more justification in the Quarto than in the Folio version of the play), insist on a year's separation, which returns the plot to the opening rejection of heterosexual life.

From Two Gentlemen of Verona (1591–92) to Twelfth Night (1600–1601), Shakespeare's young lovers marry off. Love's Labor's Lost's open-ended conclusion thus sets it apart from the other romantic comedies, pointing instead to the problem plays, Troilus and Cressida (1601–02), Measure for Measure (1604), and All's Well That Ends Well (1606–07). Here, as Biron remarks with the work's typical self-consciousness, "Our wooing doth not end like an old play: / Jack hath not Jill" (5.2.860–61).* Both the romantic plot and the deflating outcome are suggested by the final poetic dialogue—between Spring, associated with fertility and love, and Winter, linked to coldness and suffering. Yet Spring also brings "unpleasing" cuckoldry and Winter "a merry note" (5.2.895, 912).

Before then, the aristocrats' verbal ingenuity dominates Love's Labor's Lost. No other Shakespearean play so emphasizes its own brilliance, so centrally concerns language itself, so heavily draws on bookishness, so revels in courtly style. Love's Labor's Lost possesses the highest ratio of rhyme to blank verse among the dramatic works—rivaled only by A Midsummer Night's Dream (1594–96). Shakespeare's most heavily rhymed tragedy, Romeo and Juliet (1594–96), and history, Richard II (1595), also date from these years, sometimes thought of as Shakespeare's lyrical period. Rhyming calls attention to the medium of language itself. By contrast, when Shakespeare seeks to render speech naturalistically, to make his language a more neutral expression of thought, he resorts to blank verse or prose.

---

*All quotations are taken from the edited text of the Folio, printed here. The Digital Edition includes edited texts of both the Folio and the Quarto.

In *Love's Labor's Lost*, Shakespeare generally employs blank verse for serious moments in long speeches, while reserving rhyme for the witty repartee of love that is a microcosm of the play's larger debate structure. In the opening scene, each male courtier discusses, in blank verse, the vow of abstinence from women before capping his speech with a concluding couplet (lines 1–48, couplets at 22–23, 26–27, 31–32, 47–48). But when the men then debate the plan, they produce more studied and playful effects by switching to rhyme—usually rhymed pentameter couplets, sometimes known as heroic couplets. At times, Shakespeare shifts to quatrains rhymed *abab*. If such a passage is followed by a couplet (see, for example, 1.1.61–66), the result is the six-line stanza of Shakespeare's amatory narrative poem *Venus and Adonis* (1592–93), a work that meditates comically on gender reversal, though of a different sort from what the play offers.

If three quatrains are followed by a couplet, a sonnet is born (for instance, 1.1.80–93). There are at least eight sonnets or sonnet-like structures in the play (also 1.1.160–74; 4.2.98–111; 4.3.22–37 and 55–68; 5.2.275–90, 344–57, and 403–16). In the subplot, the braggart Armado, in love with the peasant Jaquenetta, remarks, "I am sure I shall turn sonnet" (that is, sonneteer; 1.2.164). The boom of the English love sonnet begins in 1591 with the publication of Sidney's *Astrophil and Stella*, and Shakespeare is thought to have started his own sequence around 1592–93. Three of the lords' poems to the ladies were lifted from the 1598 Quarto of the play for *The Passionate Pilgrim*, an unauthorized 1599 collection attributed to Shakespeare on the title page but actually containing poetry by various writers. Within the play, the sonnets do not promote the men's romantic goals. The ladies coolly receive their suitors' poetic protestations, and the two sonnets in dialogue belittle the men. The sonnet form turns upon itself when Biron, having embraced plain speaking, avows his love to Rosaline—"Oh, never will I . . . woo in rhyme" (5.2.403–06)—in what proves to be the opening of a sonnet.

Wooing rhetoric is also associated with male bonding. The lords begin by misogynistically excluding any woman from their company "[o]n pain of losing her tongue" (1.1.123). Once in love, they switch to a Renaissance courtier's style, derived from two influential Italian writers—the fourteenth-century lyric poet Petrarch, founder of the European sonnet craze, and the fifteenth-century Neoplatonic philosopher Ficino. In the eavesdropping scene, they express their feelings not to the ladies but inadvertently to one another, through overheard soliloquies. Biron, the King, Longueville, and Dumaine successively confess their love, whereupon Dumaine's oath breaking is denounced by Longueville, Longueville's by the King, and the King's by Biron. The scene thus enacts the rhetorical figure of chiasmus—common to many passages in the play—in which the second of two parallel structures inverts the order of the first.

Like the play's linguistic fireworks, the obtrusive patterning here underscores the artificiality of the men's behavior. Biron, who like Armado's page Mote speaks directly to the audience, is the only courtier whose initial confession is not overheard, and he alone denounces himself, albeit under compulsion. Thereafter, the courtiers imagine their wooing as collective sexual attack: "Advance your standards, and upon them, lords! / Pell-mell, down with them!" (4.3.362–63). Fittingly, the play's jaundiced view of the sexual style of men in groups results in a year of isolation that separates the courtiers not only from women—as their initial academy stipulated—but also from one another. As in *The Merchant of Venice* (1596–97), another play that punishes male lovers who break their vows, the dissolution of male bonds precedes durable heterosexual attachment. Holofernes, a character from the subplot, is the play's only professional teacher ("Pedant"), and he is often ridiculous. But education shapes the main plot as well, partly in the lords' proposed intellectual retreat but especially in the ladies' schooling of the lords, a turn of events that reverses the gendered hierarchy of Renaissance pedagogy.

The language of *Love's Labor's Lost* is also marked by sexualized punning. Here, the men are no match for the women. The following exchange occurs during the Russian masque:

KATHERINE [*as* MARIA]   What, was your visor made without a
    tongue?
LONGUEVILLE   I know the reason, lady, why you ask.
KATHERINE   Oh, for your reason! Quickly, sir, I long.
LONGUEVILLE   You have a double tongue within your mask,
    And would afford my speechless visor half.
KATHERINE   "Veal!" quoth the Dutchman. Is not veal a calf?
LONGUEVILLE   A calf, fair lady?
KATHERINE   No, a fair lord-calf.
LONGUEVILLE   Let's part the word.
KATHERINE   No, I'll not be your half.
    Take all and wean it: it may prove an ox.
LONGUEVILLE   Look how you butt yourself in these sharp mocks.
    Will you give horns, chaste lady? Do not so.
KATHERINE   Then die a calf before your horns do grow.
LONGUEVILLE   One word in private with you ere I die.
KATHERINE   Bleat softly, then: the butcher hears you cry.
                                    (5.2.243–56)

Referring to the mouthpiece keeping the mask in place, Katherine notes Longueville's silence ("without a tongue"). Longueville's second reply ("double tongue") accuses Katherine of punning, concealing her identity, being deceptive, and speaking enough for two, and then urges her to relinquish one tongue so he can speak and she will reveal her identity. Katherine's "Veal" combines Dutch for "well," German for "much," and a pun on "veil." And when the word is combined with the end of her second comment ("long"), we get "long-veal," a veiled assertion of her interlocutor's identity—Longueville. "Veal" also anticipates "calf" at the line's end—source of the passage's remaining jokes. Katherine reverses Longueville's question—his "lady" becomes her "lord"—thus branding him "a fair lord-calf," a dolt. Longueville's offer of compromise ("part the word") inspires Katherine's construal of "part" as "divide"; hence, her refusal to "be your half" (better half, or wife) and covert acknowledgment that the first half of the word ("ca") suggests her name. Longueville should raise the calf into an "ox," a castrated dolt with "horns," the symbol of cuckoldry. This argument sullies her reputation, he warns, but Katherine tells him that to avoid cuckoldry he should drop dead. Longueville asks for a tête-à-tête "ere I die" (have an orgasm), to which Katherine agrees, while warning him of his impending doom.

The ladies also best the lords by critique of male verbal excess (*sans* is French for "without"):

BIRON   My love to thee is sound, *sans* crack or flaw.
ROSALINE   *Sans* "sans," I pray you!
                        (5.2.416–17)

The men, Biron realizes, must drop their bookish language to approximate the women's norm: "Honest plain words best pierce the ears of grief" (5.2.739). Rosaline sentences him to a year of jesting among "the speechless sick and . . . groaning wretches" (5.2.837–38), where he will learn the value—or valuelessness—of wit. And the Princess usually exercises a dignified stylistic restraint that eludes the men. Yet the women's actual practice often repudiates their theory. Early on, Rosaline praises Biron's wit. The ladies then embrace the game of verbal one-upmanship and obscene punning, as the Katherine-Longueville exchange demonstrates. Thus, they violate the principle that Rosaline claims Biron has ignored:

                A jest's prosperity lies in the ear
                Of him that hears it, never in the tongue
                Of him that makes it.
                    (5.2.847–49)

The women's self-contradictory avowal of wit and sobriety alike renders them romantically desirable in a fashion alien to the stereotypes of love poetry. Their possibly cynical economic mission may depend, as Boyet, their attending lord, suggests, on the Princess's ability to win the King's love. There are repeated jibes at their appearance as well as accusations of unchastity leveled at Rosaline by Biron, Boyet, and Katherine. The sexual innuendos in Katherine and Rosaline's exchange turn on "light" (bright, frivolous, or wanton), contrasted with both "heavy" (serious, overweight, pregnant) and "dark" (black, obscure, wanton; 5.2.14–46; see also 4.3.223–73). While not erasing the ladies' moral superiority, these countertendencies justify modern productions that have treated them without idealism or sentimentality.

The subplot, in which Armado and Costard, the clown, compete for Jaquenetta's affections, provides a different critique. More a series of set pieces than a continuous story, it offers both parallels and contrasts to the main plot. The first eight scenes (in modern editions) alternate between main plot and subplot; the concluding, ninth scene unites the two sets of characters. In each plot, the characters are divided into two groups, one of which intrudes from the outside—the ladies in the main plot, Armado and his page in the subplot. Such symmetries, which reinforce the work's formalized, dancelike structure and give it an aristocratic feel, recall the comedies that John Lyly wrote in the 1580s for boy actors. But this formalism acquires special force from the subplot's rootedness in popular culture, a culture reinvoked in the concluding speeches of Spring and Winter. Costard and Jaquenetta are from the rural lower classes; Dull, the constable, who anticipates Dogberry in *Much Ado About Nothing* (1598), barely stands above them. Mote is a page; Nathaniel, Holofernes, and Armado, although of higher rank, derive from the stock characters (minister, schoolmaster, braggart) of Italian commedia dell'arte, an originally popular, improvisational theater.

The juxtaposition of the two plots exalts and deflates the aristocrats. The subplot's fractured prose and doggerel verse set off Biron's polished poetry to advantage. Holofernes is the leading practitioner of the popular characters' penchant for synonyms. An apple hangs in the "*caelo,* the sky, the welkin, the heaven, and . . . falleth . . . on . . . terra,* the soil, the land, the earth" (4.2.5–6). Armado's forte is schematic syntax: "The time when? . . . Now for the ground which. . . . Then, for the place where" (1.1.227–32). But if Armado's language is excessive, Biron's is only slightly less so. Similarly, Costard's violation of the edict against being "taken with a wench" (1.1.271–72) anticipates the failure of the aristocrats. This leveling continues when Armado's love letter to Jaquenetta is echoed by those of the lords. Armado and Biron both have their epistles delivered by Costard, whose confusion of the two exposes each writer to ridicule. The courtiers' Muscovite masque is paralleled by the popular pageant of the Nine Worthies, a scene resembling the humble theatricals of *A Midsummer Night's Dream.* Moreover, both masque and pageant anticipate the larger plot of *Love's Labor's Lost* in their failure to end as their performers wish.

Costard's verbal sparring with the King and Princess, in which he holds his own, also reduces the sense of social superiority. His pointed response to dismissal by the forsworn courtiers—"Walk aside, the true folk, and let the traitors stay" (4.3.207)—recalls his, but not their, honesty. The lords' ridicule of the Nine Worthies prompts Holofernes' telling reply: "This is not generous, not gentle, not humble" (5.2.623). Although the aristocrats learn nothing from Marcadé's announcement of the death of the Princess's father, Armado, whom Costard has just accused of getting Jaquenetta pregnant, sees the need to reform. The lords accept their one-year sentences reluctantly, whereas Armado's voluntary longer commitment echoes and reverses their opening oaths: "I am a votary: I have vowed to Jaquenetta / To hold the plough for her sweet love three years" (5.2.868–69). The oddity here is Biron. More than any other aristocratic character, he internalizes popular culture, moving from refined verse to colloquial and proverbial expression in what is one of Shakespeare's most proverb-rich plays. For instance, he is the only figure from the main plot with an extended prose speech (4.3.1–17). In Shakespeare, this sort of linguistic range is

Garden scene. From Thomas Hill, *The Gardener's Labyrinth* (1577).

often integral to a character's unique ability to negotiate life's complexities. Yet Biron proves almost as hapless as his fellow suitors.

The subplot also reflects on the main plot through scatological or homoerotic bodily imagery, which includes terms for constipation—"immured," "restrained," "bound," "purgation," "loose" (3.1.114–17)—as well as Armado's boast of intimacy with the King, who has a tendency "with his royal finger thus [to] dally with my excrement" (5.1.90). In the play of the Nine Worthies, Holofernes as Judas Maccabeus is reduced to Judas (Iscariot), betrayer of Jesus:

> BOYET Therefore, as he is an ass, let him go.
>   And so, adieu, sweet Jude. Nay, why dost thou stay?
> DUMAINE For the latter end of his name.
> BIRON For the "ass" to the "Jude"? Give it him: Jud-as, away!
>   (5.2.619–22)

Here, emphasis on "ass" activates the synonymous connotation of "end," the end of his body as well as "of his name." This material suggests that the main courtship plot is not the whole story. Aristocratic romantic language is balanced by a more excremental and homoerotic view of the body. Such passages exploit the possibilities of a transvestite theater, in which boys played the women's parts. The hints of homosexuality in the subplot answer the normative heterosexuality of the main plot. This verbal patterning expands the play's notions of the body and sexuality beyond what events themselves offer.

Such imagery also promotes religious, national, and racial xenophobia. Costard calls Armado's page "my incony [fine-quality] jew" (3.1.125), where "incony" inspires "inkle" (tape; 3.1.128), which suggests "ingle" (catamite, a boy kept by a pederast; see also 1.2.7). When Judas Maccabeus is "clipped" of his surname (5.2.593), Jewish circumcision is evoked. Holofernes' expulsion as "Jud-as" suggests the age's association of Jews with excrement and sodomy. Coming from "tawny Spain," "Dun"-colored Armado, "in all the world's new fashion planted" and hence perhaps associated with New World plantations, is also an alien figure (1.1.171, 4.3.194, 1.1.162). Yet he is less

Queen Elizabeth hunting. From George Gascoigne, *The Noble Art of Venerie or Hunting* (1575).

foreign than the Russians, much less their accompanying blackamoors, whose presence glances at racial subjugation. They could be based on a report of an earlier Tudor masque or on a contemporary amateur entertainment at one of London's law schools. The play and these two performances may draw on the period's link of Russia with dark skin. Although *Love's Labor's Lost* dramatizes a practice of scapegoating foreigners, it does not ratify this practice. Holofernes as Judas issues a pointed rebuke to the aristocrats; Armado reveals a depth of commitment unknown to them; the Russian masque backfires. Just as the play undermines convention in the central love plot, here, too, it questions—without openly attacking—cultural norms.

But the aristocrats themselves, unlike many of the popular characters, are also foreign. Behind the play lie contemporary political events that assume importance, given the plot's lack of literary sources. The comedy's King of Navarre draws on King Henri of Navarre, who established a philosophical academy and was accused of withdrawing from public life. His three courtiers are named for the historical king's aristocratic contemporaries, two of whom (the play's Biron and Dumaine) served him. The Princess may derive from Princess Marguerite de Valois, daughter of King Henri II of France. Marguerite was already Henri of Navarre's estranged wife when she led an embassy of reconciliation to him in 1578, accompanied by her ladies-in-waiting. As in *Love's Labor's Lost,* one topic of discussion was "Aquitaine—a dowry for a queen" (2.1.8).

Negotiations proceeded amid rampant adultery that undermined the vows of reconciliation and, contemporaries believed, caused renewal of France's Wars of Religion (1562–98), the bloody conflict between Protestant and Catholic aristocrats arguably noticed in the play's "civil war of wits" (2.1.225). Boyet, Marcadé, and perhaps Armado's page, Mote, also have prominent namesakes from these wars. To end the conflict and secure his claim on the French throne, Henri of Navarre converted to Catholicism in 1593, a further oath breaking that provoked criticism in Protestant England. The sympathy and judgment directed toward the play's lords, the serious treatment of their repudiated vows, the current of threatening sexuality, the emphasis on conflict, the invasion of death into the festive aristocratic world—all match this background. In short, the apparently anomalous intrusion of religious and political violence lends a surprising depth to what might otherwise be a lightweight romantic tale.

Foreignness and sexuality converge in the debate about the aristocrats' own colors. A 1984 production of the play cast a black actress as Rosaline. Although only Rosaline's hair and eyes are black, the play goes farther metaphorically. Unwillingly in love with Rosaline, Biron initially complains of her color (3.1.182–85, 4.3.2–3). But echoing Shakespeare's sonnets to the "dark lady," he later takes blackness as beauty's standard:

> KING   By heaven, thy love is black as ebony!
> . . . .
> BIRON   No face is fair that is not full so black.
> KING   Oh, paradox! Black is the badge of hell . . . .
> (4.3.241, 247–48)

If black is beautiful, even "Ethiops," who presumably share the King's distaste for their own appearance, "of their sweet complexion crack [boast]" (4.3.262). But it is not only the women whose faces suggest darkness. "Biron they call him," Rosaline remarks, "but a merrier man . . . I never spent an hour's talk withal" (2.1.66–68). The contrast is between "merrier" and "Biron," punning on a brown study, or seriousness. Before "the heavenly Rosaline," Biron imagines himself "a rude and savage man of Ind" (4.3.215–16), a claim he repeats to her: "Vouchsafe to show the sunshine of your face, / That we, like savages, may worship it" (5.2.202–03). The inclusion of the blackamoors thus accords with the play's association of its central couple with blackness.

Love's Labor's Lost went unperformed from 1642 to 1839, remaining unpopular until the mid-twentieth century. But modern enthusiasm for wordplay and demonstrations of the comedy's theatrical potential have changed things. Perhaps today its significance lies in linguistic artifice that is and is not rejected, an upper class that learns its manners from the lower, a capacious sense of bodily and sexual experience, a sympathetic evocation of blackness, a plot that takes a clear-eyed but not dismissive view of romantic love, and a company of women who ride off into the sunset without their men.

WALTER COHEN

SELECTED BIBLIOGRAPHY

Archer, John Michael. "*Love's Labour's Lost*." *A Companion to Shakespeare's Works*. Vol. 3: *The Comedies*. Ed. Richard Dutton and Jean E. Howard. Malden, MA: Blackwell, 2003. 320–37. Treats issues of race and nation in relation to language, gender, and sexuality.

Flanigan, Tom. "On Fashionable Education and the Art of Rhetoric: Reflections of a Not-Indifferent Student in *Love's Labour's Lost*." *Journal of the Wooden O Symposium* 5 (2005): 13–33. Offers a historical context for the play's treatment of education.

Hudson, Judith. "Punishing Perjury in *Love's Labour's Lost*." *Early Modern Drama and the Bible: Contexts and Readings, 1570–1625*. Ed. Adrian Streete. London: Palgrave Macmillan, 2012. 118–36. Discusses perjury in the play as both religious and secular crime.

Lewis, Cynthia. "'We Know What We Know': Reckoning in *Love's Labor's Lost*." *Studies in Philology* 105 (2008): 245–64. Examines the play's meditation on negotiations and calculations that go into formations of worth.

Londré, Felicia Hardison, ed. *"Love's Labour's Lost": Critical Essays.* New York: Routledge, 2001. Presents critical perspectives from 1598 to 2000 on theme, structure, gender, rhetoric, race, and performance history.

Maus, Katharine Eisaman. "Transfer of Title in *Love's Labour's Lost*: Language, Individualism, Gender." *Shakespeare Left and Right.* Ed. Ivo Kamps. New York: Routledge, 1991. 206–23. Explores the play's interrelated questioning of gender and linguistic norms.

Mazzio, Carla. "The Melancholy of Print: *Love's Labour's Lost*." *Historicism, Psychoanalysis, and Early Modern Culture.* Ed. Carla Mazzio and Douglas Trevor. New York: Routledge, 2000. 186–227. Analyzes the intersection of the speech(lessness) of love and early modern print culture.

Moncrief, Kathryn M. "'Teach Us, Sweet Madam': Masculinity, Femininity, and Gendered Instruction in *Love's Labor's Lost*." *Performing Pedagogy in Early Modern England: Gender, Instruction, and Performance.* Ed. Kathryn M. Moncrief and Kathryn R. McPherson. Surrey: Ashgate, 2011. 113–27. Discusses pedagogy as the inversion of traditional gendered hierarchy.

Parker, Patricia. "Preposterous Reversals: *Love's Labour's Lost*." *Modern Language Quarterly* 54 (1993): 435–82. Examines the play's obscene bodily punning as a challenge to class, gender, and sexual hierarchy.

Woods, Gillian. "Catholicism and Conversion in *Love's Labour's Lost*." *How to Do Things with Shakespeare: New Approaches, New Essays.* Ed. Laurie Maguire. Malden, MA: Blackwell, 2008. 101–30. Explores the tension between comic plot in Shakespeare and contemporary French wars of religion.

FILMS

Love's Labour's Lost. 1985. Dir. Elijah Moshinsky. UK. 120 min. Inspired by eighteenth-century European painting and music.

Love's Labour's Lost. 2000. Dir. Kenneth Branagh. UK. 93 min. Musical comedy, 1930s songs and settings, half of Shakespeare's lines retained, in the shadow of World War II, with Branagh, Alicia Silverstone, and Nathan Lane.

TEXTUAL INTRODUCTION

Despite its claim on the title page to be "Newly corrected and augmented," the 1598 Quarto of *Love's Labor's Lost* (Q) is urgently in need of editorial attention. Confusion over which character is speaking; inconsistency about which woman Biron is courting; vague stage directions; and a final line attributed to no one: all imply that the newly formed Lord Chamberlain's Men, when they first acted the play in 1594, must have relied upon a significantly different text. The kinds of errors that Q presents, such as its wide variation in names and speech prefixes, and the presence of "ghost" characters, suggest that the base text was authorial manuscript. However, evidence derived from the spelling conventions used by the printer, William White, points to the compositors working from a printed text—which would seem to endorse the title page's claim of a lost quarto, based on foul papers, reprinted by Q. For all its frustrations, the surviving Quarto remains a fascinating glimpse of Shakespeare at work, suggesting not only his process of revision but also his confidence that errors and inconsistencies would be worked out in the playhouse.

The Folio *Love's Labor's Lost* is clearly reprinted from the 1598 Quarto, yet its revisions suggest familiarity with the play in performance. It makes a concerted (if still incomplete) effort to smooth out the course of true love between Biron and Rosaline by altering speech prefixes in 2.1. It also redistributes some of the lines spoken by the Princess's "three lords," whose silent presence may have seemed indulgent, given how little scope for doubling the play affords. In F, at the beginning of

Berowne. Did not I dance with you in *Brabant* once?	*Berow.* Did not I dance with you in *Brabant* once?
Kather. Did not I dance with you in *Brabant* once?	*Rofa.* Did not I dance with you in *Brabant* once?
Ber. I know you did.	*Ber.* I know you did.
Kath. How needles was it then to aſke the queſtion?	*Rofa.* How needleſſe was it then to ask the queſtion?
Ber. You muſt not be ſo quicke.	*Ber.* You muſt not be ſo quicke.
Kath. Tis long of you that ſpur me with ſuch queſtions,	*Rofa.* 'Tis long of you y̆ ſpur me with ſuch queſtions.
Ber. Your wit's too hot, it ſpeedes too faſt, twill tire.	*Ber.* Your wit's too hot, it ſpeeds too faſt, 'twill tire.
Kath. Not till it leaue the rider in the mire.	*Rofa.* Not till it leaue the Rider in the mire.
Ber. What time a day?	*Ber.* What time a day?
Kath. The houre that ſooles ſhould aſke.	*Rofa.* The howre that ſooles ſhould aske.
Ber. Now faire befall your maſke.	*Ber.* Now faire befall your maske.
Kath. Faire fall the face it couers.	*Rofa.* Faire fall the face it couers.
Ber. And ſend you manie louers.	*Ber.* And ſend you many louers.
Kath. Amen, ſo you be none.	*Rofa.* Amen, ſo you be none.
Ber. Nay then will I be gon.	*Ber.* Nay then will I be gone.

Biron's first flirtatious exchange with Katherine in Q (2.1.114–27) (left); revised to Rosaline in F (2.1.114–27) (right).

3.1, we find a stage direction, "*Song*," which is not required until Mote sings "Concolinel" at line 3 but possibly recalls the "plot" held backstage to jog the memory of the players or musicians. The play's final lines, "The words of Mercury are harsh, / After the songs of Apollo," which were printed in a larger typeface in Q, with no speech prefix, and so look like a bibliographical comment, are spoken by Armado in F. His additional instruction (which does not appear in Q), "You that way; we this way," might be directed at the players or the audience. Finally, the text is divided into five acts, which may be editorial but could also reflect theater practice after 1607.

Unfortunately, the Folio reproduces many of the errors that make the Quarto unactable. Most egregiously, the wrongful distribution of speeches between Nathaniel and Holofernes in 4.2 remains, though the bookkeeper would have needed to correct this in order to draw up the players' parts. In 5.2, when the disguised ladies torment their suitors, "*Mar.*" has a dialogue with first Dumaine and then Longueville, when the latter should clearly encounter Katherine (lines 239–56). Furthermore, draft passages in Q, where Shakespeare has written a speech and then immediately reused the material, have been reprinted in F alongside the revised versions (4.3.290–312, 5.2.130–33). More generally, we would expect a performance manuscript to improve upon the extremely vague stage directions provided by Q, but examples in act 5 such as "*Enter Ladies*" and "*Enter the King and the rest*" remain untouched, while exit cues are missing for the King in 1.1, Dumaine in 2.1, Biron in 3.1, and Armado in 5.2.

If F's changes reflect consultation with a theatrical manuscript, this must have been severely limited—perhaps only a few pages from 2.1 and 5.2—or it may be that the annotator of Q drew upon his memory of the play in performance. This would explain one of the Folio's oddest emendations, where the line "Climb o'er the house to unlock the little gate" is rendered "That were to climb o'er the house to unlock the gate" (1.1.109). However, it is also possible that the annotator had access to a further authorial manuscript or scribal copy that was still some way from promptbook material. Ultimately, the most systematic correction of Q was done in the printing house, for the vast majority of the Folio's changes are corrections of typographical errors and attempts to standardize spelling. For example, in 1.1 "sedule" becomes "schedule," "pome" is corrected to "pompe," though the nonsense of being expressly forbidden to "fast" rather than "feast" remains (line 62). For all the infelicities that stand in 4.2, the Folio has corrected a host of small details: "indiscreet" replaces "indistreell," "scurrilitie" "squirilitie," and "forgive" "forgine," though proofreading has failed to pick up the missing "of" in "we taste and feeling," or the use of "cald" instead of "call I" (lines 25, 47). In the process of correction, F has also added a number of errors: in 1.1, "hanted" replaces Q's "haunted;" in 2.1, F prints "repaie" where Q has "repaide," and "point out" where Q has "point you." There are also omissions that look like compositorial eye-skip rather than deliberate revision—for example, nine lines introducing the verse "The fox, the ape, and the humble-bee" are missing (3.1.75–82); Holofernes' Mantuan eulogy excludes the phrase "loves thee not" (4.2.90), and 5.2 omits Armado's assertion about Hector: "When he breathed he was a man" (lines 654–55).

Without ignoring the errors added by F or the uncertain origin of its changes, some of which may have been made without Shakespeare's consent or after his death, it is undeniable that many of the corrections to Q required by modern editors have already been made in F, and that this text appears more closely to reflect the play as it was originally performed.

JANE KINGSLEY-SMITH

TEXTUAL BIBLIOGRAPHY

Kerrigan, John. "*Love's Labor's Lost* and Shakespearean Revision." *Shakespeare Quarterly* 33 (Autumn 1982): 337–39.
———. "Shakespeare at Work: The Katherine-Rosaline Tangle in *Love's Labor's Lost*." *RES* 33 (May 1982): 129–36.
Wells, Stanley. "The Copy for the Folio Text of *Love's Labour's Lost*." *RES* 33 (May 1982): 137–47.

PERFORMANCE NOTE

Love's Labor's Lost, conspicuously among Shakespeare's plays, taxes companies with the fundamental challenge of making the play intelligible. As its meager production history perhaps demonstrates, the comedy's copious servings of abstruse puns, defunct satire, and (in Biron's terms) "taffeta phrases" and "figures pedantical" threaten the accessibility of a quite straightforward plot. Onstage, though, the play's preoccupation with the written word makes way for rich theatricality. So while productions can facilitate comprehension by implying that obfuscation is a comic character trait or by cutting the script, they often engage audiences most when they emphasize the artificiality of characters and action, complementing a play that uses nearly every character as an actor or spectator in several self-consciously theatrical set pieces.

Few plays make directors think so much about style. The premise of the plot is so thin, and the secondary characters so ripe for caricature, that the whole often plays as farce: an elegant comedy of manners wherein perfectly matched lords and ladies proceed toward inevitable unions. But modern directors increasingly probe beneath the play's surfaces, satirizing the principals or building improbable sympathies for lesser characters. Some seek to frustrate generic expectations (as does the play's conclusion) by magnifying the divide between the lords' immaturity and the ladies' sophistication, or by playing the women's indifference as earnest, not affected. Thus the lords' initial vow can seem attractively naïve or foolish, and the dispute over Navarre's debt a mere pretext for romance or a source of lasting suspicion.

The choices made often reflect two overarching directorial decisions: first, whether to inflect the production with the melancholy and estrangement that characterize the comedy's eventual irresolution, or to play unadulterated comedy straight into an ending that confounds it; second, whether the mood around the couples' leave-taking is dubious or optimistic about their futures together. Along the way, productions must strike a balance between Armado's boasting and his evident loyalty and courage; Holofernes' pedantry and his potentially endearing sensitivity; Boyet's acute perception and his priggishness. Meanwhile, Costard can appear a bumpkin of accidental wit or a self-assured ally of the audience, and Jaquenetta an innocent dairymaid or a lewd social climber. Productions must also work out the mood and suddenness of Marcadé's entrance and the complex blocking required for the eavesdropping scene (4.3) and the pageant of "Nine Worthies."

BRETT GAMBOA

Love's Labor's Lost

[THE PERSONS OF THE PLAY

Ferdinand, KING of Navarre
BIRON
LONGUEVILLE } lords attending on the King
DUMAINE
Blackamoors

PRINCESS of France, later QUEEN
MARIA
KATHERINE } ladies attending on the Princess
ROSALINE
BOYET } lords attending on the Princess
Two other lords
FORESTER
MARCADÉ, a messenger from France

Don Adriano de ARMADO, a Spanish braggart
Mote, PAGE to Armado
COSTARD, a clown
JAQUENETTA, a country wench
Anthony DULL, a constable

HOLOFERNES, a schoolmaster
NATHANIEL, a curate]

1.1 (Q 1.1)
Enter Ferdinand, KING of Navarre [holding a paper],
BIRON, LONGUEVILLE, *and* DUMAINE.[1]

KING   Let Fame, that all hunt after in their lives,
  Live registered upon our brazen° tombs,   *brass; long-lasting*
  And then grace° us in the disgrace° of death   *honor / disfigurement*
  When, spite of cormorant° devouring Time,[2]   *despite ravenous*
5   Th'endeavor of this present breath° may buy   *speech; life*
  That honor which shall bate° his scythe's keen edge   *blunt*
  And make us heirs of all eternity.°   *eternally renowned*
  Therefore, brave conquerors—for so you are,
  That war against your own affections°   *passions*
10   And the huge army of the world's desires—
  Our late° edict shall strongly stand in force.   *recent*

1.1 Location: The whole play takes place in the King of Navarre's park.
1. TEXTUAL COMMENT Until Henri of Navarre's accession to the French throne in 1589, Navarre was an independent kingdom in southwestern France. For the historical background to these figures, and the spelling and pronunciation of their names, see the Introduction and especially Digital Edition TC 1 (Folio edited text).
2. Proverbial; one of the play's many proverbs, used by aristocrats and commoners alike.

Navarre shall be the wonder of the world;
Our court shall be a little academe,
Still° and contemplative in living art.³   *Peaceful*
15   You three, Biron, Dumaine, and Longueville,
Have sworn for three years' term to live with me,
My fellow-scholars, and to keep those statutes
That are recorded in this schedule° here.   *document*
Your oaths are passed,° and now subscribe° your names,   *pledged / sign*
20   That his own hand may strike his honor down
That violates the smallest branch° herein.   *clause*
If you are armed to do as sworn to do,
Subscribe to your deep oaths, and keep it too.⁴

LONGUEVILLE   I am resolved; 'tis but a three years' fast.
25   The mind shall banquet, though the body pine.
Fat paunches have lean pates,° and dainty bits°   *heads / bites*
Make rich the ribs but bankrupt quite the wits.
     [*He signs.*]

DUMAINE   My loving lord, Dumaine is mortified.°   *dead to worldliness*
The grosser manner of these world's delights
30   He throws upon the gross world's baser slaves.
To love, to wealth, to pomp, I pine and die,
With all these⁵ living in philosophy.
     [*He signs.*]

BIRON   I can but say their protestation over.°   *again*
So much, dear liege,° I have already sworn: *lord*
35   That is, to live and study here three years.
But there are other strict observances,
As not to see a woman in that term,
Which I hope well is not enrollèd° there;   *listed*
And one day in a week to touch no food,
40   And but one meal on every day beside,
The which I hope is not enrollèd there;
And then to sleep but three hours in the night,
And not be seen to wink of° all the day—   *close my eyes during*
When I was wont to think no harm all night,⁶
45   And make a dark night too of half the day—
Which I hope well is not enrollèd there.
Oh, these are barren tasks, too hard to keep:
Not to see ladies, study, fast, not sleep.

KING   Your oath is passed to pass away from these.
50   BIRON   Let me say no, my liege, an if° you please.   *an if = if*
I only swore to study with your grace,
And stay here in your court for three years' space.

LONGUEVILLE   You swore to that, Biron, and to the rest.

BIRON   By yea and nay,⁷ sir, then I swore in jest.
55   What is the end of study? Let me know.

KING   Why, that to know which else we should not know.

BIRON   Things hid and barred, you mean, from common sense?°   *ordinary perception*

---

3. The art of living (this meaning goes back to ancient Stoic thought); learning invigorated by life. *academe* (line 13): a philosophical academy like Plato's, revived during the Renaissance.
4. The first couplet to cap a blank-verse speech. For more on rhyme, see the Introduction. *armed*: equipped.
5. His three companions; the conditions prescribed

in the document; or the suggestion that philosophy is a source or substitute for the worldly attractions of line 31.
6. Proverbial. *no harm*: it harmless (to sleep).
7. Earnestly (a solemn oath based on Matthew 5:37); ambiguously.

KING Ay, that is study's godlike recompense.

BIRON Come on,[8] then. I will swear to study so,

60 To know the thing I am forbid[9] to know,
As thus: to study where I well may dine,
When I to feast expressly am forbid;
Or study where to meet some mistress fine,
When mistresses from common sense are hid;

65 Or, having sworn too hard-a-keeping° oath, *a too-demanding*
Study to break it and not break my troth.° *pledged faith*
If study's gain be thus, and this be so,
Study knows that which yet it doth not know.[1]
Swear me to this and I will ne'er say no.° *(first rhyming triplet)*

70 KING These be the stops° that hinder study quite, *obstacles*
And train° our intellects to vain delight. *allure*

BIRON Why, all delights are vain, and that most vain
Which with pain° purchased doth inherit pain;° *labor / suffering*
As,° painfully to pore upon a book *Such as*

75 To seek the light of truth, while truth the while
Doth falsely° blind the eyesight of his look.° *deceitfully / its vision*
Light seeking light doth light of light beguile;[2]
So, ere you find where light in darkness lies,
Your light grows dark by losing of your eyes.

80 Study me[3] how to please the eye indeed
By fixing it upon a fairer° eye, *woman's*
Who, dazzling so,[4] that eye shall be his heed,° *what he heeds*
And give him light that it° was blinded by. *(his eye)*
Study is like the heavens' glorious sun

85 That will not be deep searched with saucy° looks. *presumptuous; insolent*
Small° have continual plodders ever won, *Little*
Save base° authority from others' books. *Except commonplace*
These earthly godfathers of heaven's lights,° *astronomers*
That give a name to every fixèd star,

90 Have no more profit of their shining nights
Than those that walk and wot° not what they are. *know*
Too much to know is to know naught but fame,° *hearsay; reputation*
And every godfather can give a name.° *(as astronomers do)*

KING How well he's read to reason against reading!

95 DUMAINE Proceeded° well to stop all good proceeding.[5] *Argued*
LONGUEVILLE He weeds° the corn° and still lets grow the *pulls up / wheat*
weeding.° *weeds*

BIRON The spring is near when green geese are a-breeding.[6]

DUMAINE How follows that?

BIRON   Fit in his° place and time. *its*

DUMAINE In reason nothing.

BIRON   Something, then, in rhyme.[7]

---

8. Q has "Com'on," possibly punning on "common" (line 57).
9. Deliberately misinterpreting "should" (line 56) as "ought" rather than "would."
1. *If . . . know:* If study means experiencing the forbidden (line 60), study does indeed enable one to know what isn't yet known (line 56). *and:* and if.
2. The eye, from too much study (reading), is blinded (as if from looking at a bright light).
3. Study, I say: the beginning of the first sonnet (lines 80–93). This is Biron's initial claim that a man's spiritual enlightenment depends not on read-

ing books but on gazing into a beautiful woman's eyes—derived from Petrarch and Ficino. For these writers and for sonnets, see the Introduction.
4. The man (who does this) being thus bedazzled.
5. Toward a university degree.
6. When young geese are mating (as will the young lords, Biron implies). A goose is also a prostitute.
7. "In reason," it follows "nothing" (not at all); but in rhyme, "something" (somewhat)—an allusion to the proverbial phrase "neither rhyme nor reason" and perhaps to their own rhyming repartee.

100 KING   Biron is like an envious, sneaping° frost   *a malicious, biting*
     That bites the firstborn infants° of the spring.   *buds*
     BIRON   Well, say I am; why should proud° summer boast   *splendid*
     Before the birds have any cause to sing?
     Why should I joy in any abortive° birth?   *premature*
105 At Christmas I no more desire a rose
     Than wish a snow in May's newfangled shows,°   *displays of flowers*
     But like of° each thing that in season grows.   *But enjoy*
     So you to study now it is too late:
     That were to climb o'er the house to unlock the gate.[8]
110 KING   Well, sit you out.° Go home, Biron; adieu.   *don't take part*
     BIRON   No, my good lord, I have sworn to stay with you.
     And though I have for barbarism° spoke more   *on behalf of ignorance*
     Than° for that angel, Knowledge, you can say,   *Than what*
     Yet confident I'll keep what I have sworn,
115 And bide the penance of each three years' day.°   *day of the three years*
     Give me the paper. Let me read the same,
     And to the strictest decrees I'll write my name.
     KING [*handing him the paper*]   How well this yielding rescues
          thee from shame!
     BIRON [*reads*]   "Item: That no woman shall come within a mile
120 of my court."
     Hath this been proclaimed?
     LONGUEVILLE   Four days ago.
     BIRON   Let's see the penalty: "On pain of losing her tongue."
     Who devised this penalty?
     LONGUEVILLE   Marry,[9] that did I.
125 BIRON   Sweet lord, and why?
     LONGUEVILLE   To fright them hence with that dread penalty.
     BIRON   A dangerous law against gentility!°   *courtesy*
     "Item: If any man be seen to talk with a woman within the
     term of three years, he shall endure such public shame as
130 the rest of the court shall possibly devise."
     This article, my liege, yourself must break.
     For well you know, here comes in embassy
     The French King's daughter with yourself to speak—
     A maid of grace and complete majesty—
135 About surrender up of Aquitaine[1]
     To her decrepit, sick, and bedrid father.
     Therefore, this article is made in vain,
     Or vainly comes th'admired Princess hither.
     KING   What say you, lords? Why, this was quite forgot!
140 BIRON   So study evermore is overshot.°   *wide of the mark*
     While it doth study to have what it would,
     It doth forget to do the thing it should;
     And when it hath the thing it hunteth most,
     'Tis won as towns with fire:[2] so won, so lost.
145 KING   We must of force° dispense with this decree.   *necessity*
     She must lie° here, on mere° necessity.   *lodge / absolute*
     BIRON   Necessity will make us all forsworn

---

8. Set about things in a senseless, backward way—   1. A large area in southern France.
rather than climbing over the gate to unlock the house.   2. That is, destroyed in being captured.
9. Indeed (invocation of the Virgin Mary).

Three thousand times within this three years' space.
For every man with his affects° is born,   *passions*
150   Not by° might mastered, but by special grace.°   *by his own / (of God)*
If I break faith, this word° shall speak for me: *motto*
I am forsworn "on mere necessity."
So to the laws at large° I write my name,   *in general*
     [*He signs.*]
And he that breaks them in the least degree
155   Stands in attainder of° eternal shame.   *condemned to*
Suggestions° are to others as to me,   *Temptations*
But I believe, although I seem so loath,
I am the last that will last° keep his oath.   *longest; least likely*
But is there no quick° recreation granted?   *lively*
160   KING   Ay, that there is. Our court, you know, is haunted[3]
With° a refinèd traveler of° Spain,   *By / from*
A man in all the world's new fashion planted,[4]
That hath a mint of phrases in his brain;
One who° the music of his own vain tongue   *whom*
165   Doth ravish like enchanting harmony;
A man of compliments,° whom right and wrong   *fashion; attainments?*
Have chose as umpire of their mutiny.°   *discord*
This child of Fancy,° that Armado hight,°   *fantastic being / is called*
For interim° to our studies shall relate   *interlude*
170   In high-born words the worth of many a knight
From tawny° Spain, lost in the world's debate.°   *sunburned / warfare*
How you delight, my lords, I know not, I,
But I protest I love to hear him lie,
And I will use him for my minstrelsy.°   *entertainment*
175   BIRON   Armado is a most illustrious wight,°   *person*
A man of fire-new° words, fashion's own knight.   *newly coined*
LONGUEVILLE   Costard the swain[5] and he shall be our sport,
And so to study three years is but short.
     Enter [DULL,] *a constable*[,] *with* COSTARD *with*
     a letter.
DULL   Which is the Duke's° own person?   *King's*
180   BIRON   This, fellow. What wouldst?
DULL   I myself reprehend° his own person, for I am his grace's   (*blunder for "represent"*)
farborough.[6] But I would see his own person in flesh and
blood.
BIRON   This is he.
185   DULL [*to the* KING]   Señor Arm—Arm—commends° you. There's   *greets*
villainy abroad. This letter will tell you more.
COSTARD   Sir, the contempts[7] thereof are as touching me.
KING [*reads*]   A letter from the magnificent Armado![8]
BIRON   How low soever the matter, I hope in God for high words.
190   LONGUEVILLE   A high hope for a low heaven.° God grant us   *a small blessing*
patience!
BIRON   To hear, or forbear hearing?
LONGUEVILLE   To hear meekly, sir, and to laugh moderately,
or to forbear both.

---

3. *haunted*: frequented; beginning of a sonnet of fifteen lines (lines 160–74).
4. *Established*; see Introduction.
5. The costard is a large apple; also, comically, the head. *swain*: country lad.

6. Blunder for "thirdborough," a petty constable.
7. Blunder for "contents"; but also, inadvertently, "contempt."
8. Phrase used of the Spanish Armada (1588).

195 BIRON Well, sir, be it as the style shall give us cause to climb
in merriness.⁹

COSTARD The matter° is to me, sir, as concerning Jaquenetta.   *(perhaps sexual)*
The manner of it is, I was taken with the manner.°   *caught red-handed*

BIRON In what manner?

200 COSTARD In manner and form¹ following, sir—all those three. I
was seen with her in the manor house, sitting with her upon
the form,° and taken following her into the park, which put   *bench*
together is "in manner and form following." Now, sir, for the
"manner"—it is the manner of a man to speak to a woman; for

205 the "form"—in some form.

BIRON For the "following," sir?

COSTARD As it shall follow in my correction,° and God defend   *punishment*
the right!°   *(prayer before combat)*

KING Will you hear this letter with attention?

210 BIRON As we would hear an oracle.

COSTARD Such is the simplicity² of man to hearken after the
flesh.

KING [reads] "Great deputy, the welkin's vicegerent,° and sole   *heaven's deputy*
dominator of Navarre, my soul's earth's° god, and body's   *earthly*

215 fostering patron—"

COSTARD Not a word of Costard yet.

KING "So it is—"

COSTARD It may be so; but if he say it is so, he is, in telling
true, but so.°   *truly only so-so*

220 KING Peace!

COSTARD Be to me and every man that dares not fight.

KING No words!

COSTARD Of other men's secrets, I beseech you.

KING "So it is, besieged with sable-colored° melancholy, I did   *black*

225 commend the black oppressing humor° to the most wholesome   *melancholy*
physic° of thy health-giving air, and, as I am a gentleman,   *medicine*
betook myself to walk. The time when? About the sixth hour,
when beasts most graze, birds best peck, and men sit down to
that nourishment which is called supper; so much for the

230 time when. Now for the ground which—which, I mean, I
walked upon—it is ycleped° thy park. Then, for the place   *called (archaic)*
where—where, I mean, I did encounter that obscene° and   *disgusting; wanton*
most preposterous³ event that draweth from my snow-white
pen° the ebon-colored° ink, which here thou viewest, behold-   *goose quill / black*

235 est, surveyest, or seest. But to the place where: it standeth
north-north-east and by east from the west corner of thy
curious-knotted° garden. There did I see that low-   *intricately patterned*
spirited° swain, that base minnow° of thy mirth—"   *base / shrimp*

COSTARD [aside] Me?

240 KING "That unlettered,° small-knowing soul—"   *illiterate*

COSTARD [aside] Me.

KING "That shallow vassal°—"   *base wretch; vessel*

COSTARD [aside] Still me.

---

9. *style . . . merriness:* stile=fence; the humble subject of "merriness" does not ordinarily lead one "to
climb" to a high prose "style." A "style" is also a pen
and, hence, perhaps a penis that will "climb" (swell)
in "merriness" (pleasure).

1. Legal, then proverbial, phrase.
2. Simplicity (folly); perhaps a pun on "sin" as well.
3. Unnatural; in reversed position—with "obscene"
(line 232) anatomically suggesting placement of the
rear, or posterior, in front. See 5.1.77, 79, 104.

KING   "Which, as I remember, hight Costard—"

245   COSTARD   Oh, me!

KING   "Sorted° and consorted, contrary to thy established,   *Associated*
proclaimed edict and continent canon,° which with—oh,   *restraining law*
with—but with this—I passion° to say wherewith!"   *grieve*

COSTARD   With a wench.

250   KING   "With a child of our grandmother Eve, a female, or—for
thy more sweet understanding—a woman. Him I—as my ever-
esteemed duty pricks[4] me on—have sent to thee, to receive
the meed° of punishment, by thy sweet grace's officer,   *reward*
Anthony Dull: a man of good repute, carriage, bearing, and

255   estimation."

DULL   Me, an't° shall please you. I am Anthony Dull.   *if it*

KING   "For Jaquenetta—so is the weaker vessel° called which I   *woman (1 Peter 3:7)*
apprehended with the aforesaid swain—I keep her as a vessel
of thy law's fury, and shall, at the least of thy sweet notice,°   *as soon as you order*

260   bring her to trial.° Thine in all compliments of devoted and   *(legally; sexually)*
heart-burning heat of duty,

Don Adriano de Armado."

BIRON   This is not so well as I looked for, but the best that
ever I heard.

265   KING   Ay, the best for° the worst. [*to* COSTARD] But, sirrah,[5]   *best example of*
what say you to this?

COSTARD   Sir, I confess the wench.

KING   Did you hear the proclamation?

COSTARD   I do confess much of the hearing it, but little of the

270   marking of° it.   *paying attention to*

KING   It was proclaimed a year's imprisonment to be taken
with a wench.

COSTARD   I was taken with none, sir. I was taken with a damosell.

275   KING   Well, it was proclaimed "damosell."

COSTARD   This was no damosell neither, sir: she was a virgin.

KING   It is so varied° too, for it was proclaimed "virgin."   *covers that variation*

COSTARD   If it were, I deny her virginity. I was taken with a maid.

KING   This "maid" will not serve your turn, sir.

280   COSTARD   This maid will serve my turn,° sir.   *(sexually)*

KING   Sir, I will pronounce your sentence:
You shall fast a week with bran and water—

COSTARD   I had rather pray a month with mutton and
porridge.[6]

285   KING   And Don Armado shall be your keeper.
My lord Biron, see him delivered o'er,
And go we, lords, to put in practice that
Which each to other hath so strongly sworn.

[*Exeunt the* KING, LONGUEVILLE, *and* DUMAINE.]

BIRON   I'll lay° my head to any goodman's hat,   *bet*

290   These oaths and laws will prove an idle scorn.
—Sirrah, come on.

COSTARD   I suffer for the truth, sir. For true it is, I was taken
with Jaquenetta, and Jaquenetta is a true° girl, and therefore   *an honest*

4. Spurs (sexual). See also 2.1.188; 4.1.131, 137;   5. Standard term for addressing social inferiors.
4.2.11, 18, 44, 47, 51, 54.   6. Mutton soup; "mutton" is also slang for "prostitute."

welcome the sour cup of prosperity! Affliction[7] may one day
295   smile again, and until then, sit thee down,° Sorrow!   *Exeunt.*   *stay with me*

1.2 (Q 1.2)
Enter ARMADO *and Mote, his* PAGE.[1]

ARMADO   Boy, what sign is it° when a man of great spirit grows   *what does it mean*
          melancholy?
PAGE   A great sign, sir, that he will look sad.
ARMADO   Why, sadness is one and the selfsame thing,° dear imp.°   *(as melancholy) / child*
5   PAGE   No, no, O Lord, sir, no.
ARMADO   How canst thou part° sadness and melancholy, my   *distinguish between*
          tender juvenal?[2]
PAGE   By a familiar° demonstration of the working,° my tough   *plain / their operation*
          señor.[3]
10   ARMADO   Why "tough señor"? Why "tough señor"?
PAGE   Why "tender juvenal"? Why "tender juvenal"?
ARMADO   I spoke it, tender juvenal, as a congruent epitheton
          appertaining to° thy young days, which we may nominate°   *suitable term for / call*
          "tender."
15   PAGE   And I, tough señor, as an appertinent° title to your old   *appropriate*
          time, which we may name "tough."
ARMADO   Pretty and apt!
PAGE   How mean you, sir? I pretty and my saying apt, or I apt
          and my saying pretty?
20   ARMADO   Thou pretty because little.°   *(proverbial)*
PAGE   Little pretty because little. Wherefore apt?
ARMADO   And therefore apt because quick.°   *quick-witted*
PAGE   Speak you this in my praise, master?
ARMADO   In thy condign° praise.   *well-deserved*
25   PAGE   I will praise an eel with the same praise.
ARMADO   What, that an eel is ingenious?
PAGE   That an eel is quick.°   *alive*
ARMADO   I do say thou art quick in answers. Thou heat'st my
          blood.°   *You make me angry*
30   PAGE   I am answered, sir.
ARMADO   I love not to be crossed.
PAGE [*aside*]   He speaks the mere° contrary: crosses[4] love not   *absolute*
          him.
ARMADO   I have promised to study three years with the Duke.
35   PAGE   You may do it in an hour, sir.
ARMADO   Impossible!
PAGE   How many is one thrice told?°   *counted*
ARMADO   I am ill at reckoning; it fits the spirit of a tapster.°   *bartender*
PAGE   You are a gentleman and a gamester,° sir.   *gambler*
40   ARMADO   I confess both; they are both the varnish of a com-
          plete man.
PAGE   Then I am sure you know how much the gross sum of
          deuce-ace° amounts to.   *a two and a one (dice)*
ARMADO   It doth amount to one more than two.

7. Blunder for reverse order: "affliction! Prosperity."
1.2 Location: The King's park.
1. TEXTUAL COMMENT The Folio has "Moth," meaning "moth" or "mote" (speck). It is pronounced like
the latter word, and that sense may be primary. Hence,

it is spelled "Mote" in both F and Q in this edition. See
Digital Edition TC 2 (Folio edited text).
2. Youth; Juvenal, ancient Roman satirist.
3. Sir; senior.
4. Coins (often imprinted with crosses).

45	PAGE Which the base vulgar° call three?	*common people*
	ARMADO True.	
	PAGE Why, sir, is this such a piece of study?° Now, here's three	*hard work*
	studied ere you'll thrice wink, and how easy it is to put "years"	
	to the word "three" and study three years in two words the	
50	dancing horse⁵ will tell you.	
	ARMADO A most fine figure!°	*verbal turn; number*
	PAGE [*aside*] To prove you a cipher.°	*zero*
	ARMADO I will hereupon confess I am in love, and as it is base°	*ignoble*
	for a soldier to love, so am I in love with a base° wench. If draw-	*lowborn*
55	ing my sword against the humor of affection° would deliver	*inclination to love*
	me from the reprobate thought of it, I would take Desire pris-	
	oner and ransom him to any French courtier for a new-	
	devised curtsy.° I think scorn° to sigh. Methinks I should	*bowing fashion / disdain*
	outswear° Cupid. Comfort me, boy—what great men have	*renounce*
60	been in love?	
	PAGE Hercules, master.	
	ARMADO Most sweet Hercules! More authority, dear boy,	
	name more; and, sweet my child, let them be men of good	
	repute and carriage.°	*behavior*
65	PAGE Samson, master. He was a man of good carriage, great	
	carriage, for he carried the town gates on his back⁶ like a	
	porter, and he was in love.	
	ARMADO O well-knit Samson, strong-jointed Samson, I do excel	
	thee in my rapier as much as thou didst me in carrying gates.	
70	I am in love too. Who was Samson's love, my dear Mote?	
	PAGE A woman, master.	
	ARMADO Of what complexion?⁷	
	PAGE Of all the four, or the three, or the two, or one of the four.	
	ARMADO Tell me precisely of what complexion.	
75	PAGE Of the sea-water green,⁸ sir.	
	ARMADO Is that one of the four complexions?	
	PAGE As I have read, sir, and the best of them too.	
	ARMADO Green, indeed, is the color of lovers, but to have a	
	love of that color? Methinks Samson had small reason for it.	
80	He surely affected° her for her wit.°	*loved / intelligence*
	PAGE It was so, sir, for she had a green wit.⁹	
	ARMADO My love is most immaculate white and red.	
	PAGE Most maculate° thoughts, master, are masked under	*impure*
	such colors.°	*hues; pretexts*
85	ARMADO Define,° define, well-educated infant.	*Explain your meaning*
	PAGE My father's wit and my mother's tongue assist me!	
	ARMADO Sweet invocation of a child—most pretty and	
	pathetical!°	*touching*
	PAGE If she be made° of white and red,	*(also "maid")*
90	Her faults will ne'er be known,	
	For blushing cheeks by faults are bred,	
	And fears by pale white shown.	

---

5. Morocco, a performing horse trained to "count" with its hooves, was a London sensation in 1591. The Page jokingly takes the phrase "three years" as the object of "study" (line 34).
6. For the gates, see Judges 16:3. Love proved disastrous for both Hercules and Samson.
7. Temperament (Armado's meaning), as determined by the balance of bodily humors: blood, phlegm, melancholy (from black bile), choler; skin coloring (the Page's meaning).
8. Ill colored; evidence of chlorosis, an anemic condition affecting young women.
9. Immature understanding (proverbial).

Then if she fear or be to blame,
By this you shall not know,
95   For still her cheeks possess the same
Which native° she doth owe.°   *naturally / own*
A dangerous rhyme, master, against the reason of white and
red.
ARMADO   Is there not a ballad, boy, of the King and the Beggar?[1]
100   PAGE   The world was very guilty of such a ballad some three
ages since, but I think now 'tis not to be found, or if it were
it would neither serve° for the writing nor the tune.   *be acceptable*
ARMADO   I will have that subject newly writ o'er, that I may
example my digression° by some mighty precedent. Boy, I do   *justify my lapse*
105   love that country girl that I took in the park with the ratio-
nal hind,[2] Costard. She deserves well—
PAGE [*aside*]   To be whipped,° and yet a better love than my   *(as a prostitute)*
master.
ARMADO   Sing, boy. My spirit grows heavy in love.
110   PAGE [*aside*]   And that's great marvel, loving a light° wench.   *wanton*
ARMADO   I say, sing.
PAGE   Forbear till this company be passed.
Enter [COSTARD, *the*] *clown,* [DULL, *the*] *constable,*
and [JAQUENETTA, *a*] *wench.*
DULL   Sir, the Duke's pleasure is that you keep Costard safe,
and you must let him take no delight nor no penance,° but   *(for "pleasance"?)*
115   he must fast three days a week. For this damsel, I must keep
her at the park. She is allowed for the dey-woman.° Fare you   *approved as dairymaid*
well.   *Exit.*
ARMADO [*aside*]   I do betray myself with blushing. [*to* JAQUEN-
ETTA] Maid—
120   JAQUENETTA   Man.
ARMADO   I will visit thee at the lodge.
JAQUENETTA   That's hereby.[3]
ARMADO   I know where it is situate.
JAQUENETTA   Lord, how wise you are!
125   ARMADO   I will tell thee wonders.
JAQUENETTA   With that face?°   *Really?*
ARMADO   I love thee.
JAQUENETTA   So I heard you say.°   *You don't say so*
ARMADO   And so, farewell.
130   JAQUENETTA   Fair weather after you.°   *(proverbial)*
COSTARD   Come, Jaquenetta. Away!
Exeunt [DULL *and* JAQUENETTA].
ARMADO   Villain,° thou shalt fast for thy offenses ere thou be   *Peasant; rascal*
pardoned.
COSTARD   Well, sir, I hope when I do it, I shall do it on a full
135   stomach.°   *well fed; bravely*
ARMADO   Thou shalt be heavily punished.
COSTARD   I am more bound to you than your fellows,° for they   *servants*
are but lightly rewarded.
ARMADO   Take away this villain! Shut him up.
140   PAGE   Come, you transgressing slave. Away!

---

1. The ballad concerns the love of King Cophetua for   2. Peasant (or deer?) capable of reason.
the beggar maid Zenelophon. See also 4.1.65–67.   3. Nearby; neither here nor there (?).

COSTARD Let me not be pent up,° sir. I will fast, being loose.[4]   *jailed; constipated*
PAGE No, sir, that were fast and loose.° Thou shalt to prison.   *a cheating trick*
COSTARD Well, if ever I do see the merry days of desolation°   *(for "elation"?)*
that I have seen, some shall see—
145 PAGE What shall some see?
COSTARD Nay, nothing, Master Mote, but what they look upon.
It is not for prisoners to be silent in their words, and therefore
I will say nothing. I thank God I have as little patience as
another man, and therefore I can be quiet.

Exeunt [PAGE *and* COSTARD].

150 ARMADO I do affect° the very ground—which is base—where   *love*
her shoe—which is baser—guided by her foot—which is
basest—doth tread. I shall be forsworn—which is a great
argument° of falsehood—if I love. And how can that be true   *proof*
love which is falsely attempted? Love is a familiar;° Love is a   *an attendant evil spirit*
155 devil. There is no evil angel but Love. Yet Samson was so
tempted, and he had an excellent strength. Yet was Solomon
so seduced, and he had a very good wit. Cupid's butt-shaft° is   *unbarbed arrow*
too hard for Hercules' club, and therefore too much odds for a
Spaniard's rapier. The first and second cause° will not serve   *(in the dueling code)*
160 my turn. The *passado*[5] he respects not; the *duello*° he regards   *dueling code*
not. His disgrace is to be called "Boy," but his glory is to sub-
due men. Adieu, valor; rust, rapier; be still, drum: for your
manager° is in love. Yea, he loveth. Assist me, some extempo-   *wielder*
ral° god of rhyme, for I am sure I shall turn sonnet.° Devise,   *impromptu / sonneteer*
165 wit; write, pen: for I am for whole volumes in folio.°   *Exit.*   *largest book size*

2.1 (Q 2.1)

Enter the PRINCESS *of France, with three attending
ladies* [MARIA, KATHERINE, *and* ROSALINE], *and three
lords* [*including* BOYET].[1]

BOYET Now, madam, summon up your dearest spirits.°   *utmost energies*
Consider who the King your father sends,
To whom he sends, and what's his embassy:
Yourself, held precious in the world's esteem,
5 To parley with the sole inheritor°   *owner*
Of all perfections that a man may owe,
Matchless Navarre; the plea° of no less weight   *that which is claimed*
Than Aquitaine—a dowry for a queen.
Be now as prodigal of° all, dear grace,   *generous with*
10 As Nature was in making graces dear,[2]
When she did starve the general world beside°   *except (you)*
And prodigally gave them all to you.
PRINCESS Good Lord Boyet, my beauty, though but mean,°   *average*
Needs not the painted flourish° of your praise.   *embellishment*
15 Beauty is bought by judgment of the eye,
Not uttered[3] by base sale of chapmen's° tongues.   *salesmen's*
I am less proud to hear you tell° my worth   *speak of; reckon up*

4. Being free; being loose in the bowels.
5. Fencing thrust.
2.1 Location: Outside the gates of the King's court.
1. Pronounced "Boy-ett." TEXTUAL COMMENT For
this character and the "three lords," see Digital Edition TC 3 (Folio edited text).

2. *dear grace . . . graces dear:* chiasmus, an *abba* rhetorical structure common to the aristocrats' speech
and the larger movement of the play. See 4.3 and the
Introduction. The second "dear" means costly (because
rare).
3. Not spoken; not offered for sale.

<table>
<tr><td></td><td>Than you much willing to be counted wise</td><td></td></tr>
<tr><td></td><td>In spending your wit in the praise of mine.</td><td></td></tr>
<tr><td>20</td><td>But now to task the tasker:⁴ good Boyet,</td><td></td></tr>
<tr><td></td><td>You are not ignorant, all-telling Fame°</td><td>*rumor*</td></tr>
<tr><td></td><td>Doth noise abroad° Navarre hath made a vow,</td><td>*spread the rumor that*</td></tr>
<tr><td></td><td>Till painful° study shall outwear three years</td><td>*taxing*</td></tr>
<tr><td></td><td>No woman may approach his silent court.</td><td></td></tr>
<tr><td>25</td><td>Therefore, to 's° seemeth it a needful course,</td><td>*to us*</td></tr>
<tr><td></td><td>Before we enter his forbidden gates,</td><td></td></tr>
<tr><td></td><td>To know his pleasure; and in that behalf,</td><td></td></tr>
<tr><td></td><td>Bold° of your worthiness, we single you</td><td>*Confident*</td></tr>
<tr><td></td><td>As our best-moving, fair° solicitor.</td><td>*most eloquent, just*</td></tr>
<tr><td>30</td><td>Tell him the daughter of the King of France,</td><td></td></tr>
<tr><td></td><td>On serious business, craving quick dispatch,</td><td></td></tr>
<tr><td></td><td>Importunes personal conference with his grace.</td><td></td></tr>
<tr><td></td><td>Haste, signify so much, while we attend,°</td><td>*wait upon*</td></tr>
<tr><td></td><td>Like humble-visaged suitors, his high will.</td><td></td></tr>
</table>

35   BOYET   Proud of° employment, willingly I go.   *Exit.*   *Honored with*

    PRINCESS *[aside]*   All pride is willing pride,° and yours is so.   *vanity*

    —Who are the votaries,° my loving lords,   *vow takers*

    That are vow-fellows with this virtuous duke?

    LORD   Longueville is one.

    PRINCESS   Know you the man?

<table>
<tr><td>40</td><td>MARIA   I know him, madam. At a marriage feast,</td><td></td></tr>
<tr><td></td><td>   Between Lord Périgort⁵ and the beauteous heir</td><td></td></tr>
<tr><td></td><td>   Of Jacques Falconbridge, solemnized</td><td></td></tr>
<tr><td></td><td>   In Normandy, saw I this Longueville.</td><td></td></tr>
<tr><td></td><td>   A man of sovereign parts° he is esteemed:</td><td>*outstanding qualities*</td></tr>
<tr><td>45</td><td>   Well fitted in arts, glorious in arms,</td><td></td></tr>
<tr><td></td><td>   Nothing becomes him ill that he would° well.</td><td>*wishes to do*</td></tr>
<tr><td></td><td>   The only soil of° his fair virtue's gloss—</td><td>*stain on*</td></tr>
<tr><td></td><td>   If virtue's gloss will stain with any soil—</td><td></td></tr>
<tr><td></td><td>   Is a sharp wit matched with too blunt° a will,</td><td>*rough; unfeeling*</td></tr>
<tr><td>50</td><td>   Whose edge hath power to cut, whose will still° wills</td><td>*always*</td></tr>
<tr><td></td><td>   It should none spare that come within his° power.</td><td>*its*</td></tr>
</table>

    PRINCESS   Some merry, mocking lord, belike°—is't so?   *probably*

    MARIA   They say so most that most his humors know.

    PRINCESS   Such short-lived wits do wither as they grow.

55   Who are the rest?

<table>
<tr><td></td><td>KATHERINE   The young Dumaine—a well-accomplished youth,</td><td></td></tr>
<tr><td></td><td>   Of° all that virtue love, for virtue loved;</td><td>*By*</td></tr>
<tr><td></td><td>   Most power to do most harm, least knowing ill,⁶</td><td></td></tr>
<tr><td></td><td>   For he hath wit to make an ill shape good,</td><td></td></tr>
<tr><td>60</td><td>   And shape to win grace though he had no wit.⁷</td><td></td></tr>
<tr><td></td><td>   I saw him at the Duke Alençon's once,</td><td></td></tr>
<tr><td></td><td>   And much too little° of that good I saw</td><td>*short*</td></tr>
<tr><td></td><td>   Is my report to° his great worthiness.</td><td>*my report compared with*</td></tr>
</table>

---

4. Impose a task on you who have given me one; chastise the task setter.

5. Not otherwise mentioned; Périgord is in Aquitaine.

6. Potentially dangerous by virtue of his very innocence; although he theoretically could do harm, he is free of all misdeeds.

7. *For . . . wit:* He is intelligent enough to make up for a displeasing appearance, if he had one (or perhaps to make something evil seem virtuous) and good-looking enough to win favor (from people or perhaps from God), even if he lacked intelligence.

ROSALINE[8] Another of these students at that time
65 Was there with him, as I have heard a truth.
Biron[9] they call him, but a merrier man,
Within the limit of becoming° mirth, _decorous_
I never spent an hour's talk withal.° _with_
His eye begets occasion° for his wit, _finds opportunities_
70 For every object that the one doth catch
The other turns to a mirth-moving jest,
Which his fair tongue—conceit's expositor°— _thought's expounder_
Delivers in such apt and gracious words
That agèd ears play truant at° his tales _neglect work to hear_
75 And younger hearings are quite ravishèd,
So sweet and voluble° is his discourse. _fluent_
PRINCESS God bless my ladies! Are they all in love,
That every one her own hath garnishèd
With such bedecking ornaments of praise?
80 MARIA Here comes Boyet.

      Enter BOYET.

PRINCESS Now, what admittance,° lord? _reception_
BOYET Navarre had notice of your fair approach,
And he and his competitors° in oath _partners_
Were all addressed° to meet you, gentle lady, _ready_
85 Before I came. Marry,° thus much I have learnt: _Indeed_
He rather means to lodge you in the field,
Like one that comes here to besiege his court,
Than seek a dispensation for his oath
To let you enter his unpeopled° house. _servantless_

      Enter [the KING _of_] _Navarre_, LONGUEVILLE, DUMAINE,
      and BIRON.

90 Here comes Navarre.
KING Fair Princess, welcome to the court of Navarre.
PRINCESS "Fair" I give you back again, and "welcome" I have
      not yet. The roof of this court° is too high to be yours, and _sky_
      welcome to the wide fields too base to be mine.
95 KING You shall be welcome, madam, to my court.
PRINCESS I will be welcome, then. Conduct me thither.
KING Hear me, dear lady; I have sworn an oath.
PRINCESS Our Lady help my lord! He'll be forsworn.
KING Not for the world, fair madam, by my will.° _willingly (mild oath)_
100 PRINCESS Why, will° shall break it—will, and nothing else. _(sexual) desire_
KING Your ladyship is ignorant what it° is. _(the oath)_
PRINCESS Were my lord so, his ignorance were wise,
      Where now his knowledge must prove ignorance.[1]
      I hear your grace hath sworn out housekeeping.° _repudiated hospitality_
105 'Tis deadly sin to keep that oath, my lord,
      And sin to break it.
      But pardon me, I am too sudden° bold; _rashly_
      To teach a teacher ill beseemeth me.

---

8. TEXTUAL COMMENT For F's partial revision of
Q's uncertain treatment of whom Biron courts—
Katherine or Rosaline—see Digital Edition TC 4 (Folio
edited text).
9. Probable pun on "Biron/brown." "Brown" was associated with somberness or melancholy (as in a "brown

study") and is contrasted in this line with "merrier" by
means of "but."
1. Perhaps: ignorance of your sexual desire would make
you wise, but your knowledge of it will make you a fool.
Or: ignorance would be wise, but the pursuit of knowledge is not.

Vouchsafe to read the purpose of my coming,
110 And suddenly resolve° me in my suit.   *immediately answer*
        [*She hands him a letter.*]
     KING Madam, I will, if suddenly I may.
     PRINCESS You will the sooner that I were away,°   *so that I'll go*
     For you'll prove perjured if you make me stay.
        [*The* KING *reads apart.*]
     BIRON Did not I dance with you in Brabant once?
115 ROSALINE Did not I dance with you in Brabant once?
     BIRON I know you did.
     ROSALINE   How needless was it, then,
        To ask the question!
     BIRON   You must not be so quick.°   *sharp; hasty; witty*
     ROSALINE 'Tis 'long of° you that spur° me with such questions.   *due to / prod*
     BIRON Your wit's too hot. It speeds too fast; 'twill tire.
120 ROSALINE Not till it leave the rider in the mire.
     BIRON What time o'day?
     ROSALINE The hour that fools should ask.
     BIRON Now fair befall° your mask!   *good luck to*
     ROSALINE Fair fall° the face it covers.   *befall*
125 BIRON And send you many lovers.
     ROSALINE Amen, so you be none.
     BIRON Nay, then, will I be gone.
        [*The* KING *steps forward.*]
     KING Madam, your father here doth intimate
        The payment of² a hundred thousand crowns,
130   Being but th'one half of an entire sum
        Disbursèd by my father in his° wars.   *(the King of France's)*
        But say that he° or we—as neither have—   *(Navarre's father)*
        Received that sum, yet there remains unpaid
        A hundred thousand more, in surety of the which
135   One part of Aquitaine is bound to us,
        Although not valued° to the money's worth.   *equal in value*
        If, then, the King your father will restore
        But that one half which is unsatisfied,
        We will give up our right in Aquitaine,
140   And hold fair friendship with his majesty.
        But that, it seems, he little purposeth.
        For here he doth demand to have repaid
        An hundred thousand crowns, and not demands°   *rather than offering*
        On payment of a hundred thousand crowns
145   To have his title live in Aquitaine,
        Which we much rather had depart withal,°   *would surrender*
        And have the money by our father lent,
        Than Aquitaine, so gelded as it is.³
        Dear Princess, were not his requests so far
150   From reason's yielding,° your fair self should make   *what reason might concede*
        A yielding—'gainst some reason—in my breast,
        And go well satisfied to France again.
     PRINCESS You do the King my father too much wrong,

2. *intimate . . . of*: suggest he paid.
3. Navarre says that of the 200,000 crowns he's owed,
the King of France falsely claims to have paid back
half and has given him Aquitaine as collateral for
the other half, even though it isn't worth that much.

Navarre is willing to return Aquitaine and forget the
entire debt in return for 100,000 crowns, but France
wants Navarre to pay that sum and keep Aquitaine.
gelded: reduced; castrated.

And wrong the reputation of your name,
155 In so unseeming° to confess receipt   *seeming unwilling*
 Of that° which hath so faithfully been paid.   *(200,000 crowns)*
 KING I do protest I never heard of it,
 And if you prove it I'll repay it back,
 Or yield up Aquitaine.
 PRINCESS   We arrest° your word.   *seize as security*
160 Boyet, you can produce acquittances°   *receipts*
 For such a sum from special officers
 Of Charles his° father.   *(Navarre's)*
 KING   Satisfy me so.
 BOYET So please your grace, the packet is not come
 Where that and other specialties° are bound.   *legal contracts*
165 Tomorrow you shall have a sight of them.
 KING It shall suffice me; at which interview
 All liberal° reason will I yield unto.   *civilized*
 Meantime, receive such welcome at my hand
 As honor, without breach of honor, may
170 Make tender of to thy true worthiness.
 You may not come, fair Princess, in my gates,
 But here without° you shall be so received   *outside*
 As you shall deem yourself lodged in my heart,
 Though so denied further harbor in my house.
175 Your own good thoughts excuse me, and farewell.
 Tomorrow we shall visit you again.
 PRINCESS Sweet health and fair desires consort° your grace. *accompany*
 KING Thy own wish wish I thee in every place.
       Exeunt [*the* KING, LONGUEVILLE,
         DUMAINE, *and* BIRON].
 BOYET Lady, I will commend you to my own heart.
180 ROSALINE Pray you, do my commendations.
 I would be glad to see it.[4]
 BOYET I would you heard it groan.
 ROSALINE Is the fool° sick?   *poor thing*
 BOYET Sick at the heart.
185 ROSALINE Alack, let it blood.°   *bleed it (medically)*
 BOYET Would that do it good?
 ROSALINE My physic° says "Ay."   *medical knowledge*
 BOYET Will you prick 't with your eye?[5]
 ROSALINE *Non point,*° with my knife. *Not at all; it's blunt*
190 BOYET Now God save thy life!
 ROSALINE And yours from long living.
 BOYET I cannot stay thanksgiving.[6]
   [*He starts to withdraw.*]
   Enter DUMAINE.
 DUMAINE Sir, I pray you, a word. What lady is that same?
 BOYET The heir of Alençon; Katherine her name.
195 DUMAINE A gallant lady! Monsieur, fare you well. [*Exit.*]
   [*Enter* LONGUEVILLE.]
 LONGUEVILLE I beseech you, a word. What is she in the white?
   [*He indicates* MARIA.]

---

4. Know your real feelings; literally, behold your heart and, hence, see you dead.
5. "Eye" puns on "Ay" (line 187), suggesting a needle but also a vagina, impossibly serving as a penis.
6. Stay long enough to thank you (for that rude remark).

BOYET   A woman sometime, if you saw her in the light.

LONGUEVILLE   Perchance light in the light°—I desire her   *wanton if seen clearly*
  name.

BOYET   She hath but one for herself; to desire that were a
  shame.

200 LONGUEVILLE   Pray you, sir, whose daughter?

BOYET   Her mother's, I have heard.

LONGUEVILLE [*preparing to leave*]   God's blessing o'your beard!°   *(insult)*

BOYET   Good sir, be not offended.
  She is an heir of Falconbridge—

205 LONGUEVILLE   Nay, my choler° is ended.   *anger*
  She is a most sweet lady.

BOYET   Not unlike,° sir; that may be.   *Exit* LONGUEVILLE.   *unlikely*
      Enter BIRON.

BIRON   What's her name in the cap?

BOYET   Rosaline, by good hap.

210 BIRON   Is she wedded or no?

BOYET   To her will, sir, or so.°   *or something like that*

BIRON   You are welcome, sir. Adieu.

BOYET   Farewell to me, sir, and welcome to you.°   *Exit* [BIRON].   *you're welcome to go*

MARIA   That last is Biron, the merry madcap lord;
  Not a word with him but a jest—

215 BOYET   And every jest but a word.

PRINCESS   It was well done of you to take him at his word.°   *(literally; punningly)*

BOYET   I was as willing to grapple as he was to board.[7]

MARIA   Two hot sheeps,° marry.   *(pronounced like "ships")*

BOYET   And wherefore not ships?
  No sheep, sweet lamb, unless we feed on your lips.

220 MARIA   You sheep and I pasture.° Shall that finish the jest?   *pun on "pastor" (shepherd)*

BOYET   So° you grant pasture for me—   *So long as*
      [*He attempts to kiss her.*]

MARIA   Not so, gentle beast.
  My lips are no common, though several they be.[8]

BOYET   Belonging to whom?

MARIA   To my fortunes and me.

PRINCESS   Good wits will be jangling,° but, gentles,° agree!   *quarreling / gentlefolk*

225 This civil war of wits were much better used
  On Navarre and his bookmen,° for here 'tis abused.°   *scholars / misapplied*

BOYET   If my observation—which very seldom lies,
  By the heart's still rhetoric,° disclosed with eyes—   *silent eloquence*
  Deceive me not now, Navarre is infected.

230 PRINCESS   With what?

BOYET   With that which we lovers entitle "affected."°   *being in love*

PRINCESS   Your reason?

BOYET   Why, all his behaviors did make their retire°   *withdrawal*
  To the court of his eye, peeping through desire.

235 His heart, like an agate with your print impressed,[9]
  Proud with his form,° in his eye pride expressed.   *the Princess's image*
  His tongue, all impatient to speak[1] and not see,
  Did stumble with haste in his eyesight to be.

---

7. Join ships ("grapple") for hand-to-hand combat ("board"): metaphor for competitive wordplay, with sexual overtones.
8. My lips are not commonly owned grazing land, though they are pasture—they are privately owned,
enclosed land. *several:* more than one; separate; parted.
9. Engraved with your image. Agates were engraved and set in rings.
1. Impatient at being able only to speak.

All senses to that sense did make their repair,°   *resort*
240   To feel° only looking° on fairest of fair.   *experience / by looking*
     Methought all his senses were locked in his eye,
     As jewels in crystal for some prince to buy,
     Who, tend'ring° their own worth from whence they were   *displaying*
       glassed,°   *encased in crystal*
     Did point° you to buy them along as you passed.   *direct*
245   His face's own margin[2] did quote° such amazes,   *indicate*
     That all eyes saw his eyes enchanted with gazes.
     I'll give you° Aquitaine and all that is his,   *bet you get*
     An° you give him, for my sake, but one loving kiss.   *If*
     PRINCESS   Come! To our pavilion! Boyet is disposed.°   *(to be merry)*
250   BOYET   But to speak that in words which his eye hath disclosed.
                 [*Exeunt the* PRINCESS *and lords.*]
     I only have made a mouth of his eye
     By adding a tongue, which I know will not lie.
     ROSALINE[3]   Thou art an old love-monger and speakest skilfully.
     MARIA   He is Cupid's grandfather and learns news of him.
255   KATHERINE   Then was Venus° like her mother, for her father   *Cupid's mother*
       is but grim.°   *not handsome*
     BOYET   Do you hear, my mad° wenches?   *high-spirited*
     MARIA   No.
     BOYET   What, then, do you see?
     KATHERINE   Ay, our way to be gone.
     BOYET   You are too hard for me.
                          Exeunt.

3.1 (Q 3.1)

     Enter [ARMADO, *the*] braggart,[1] *and* [PAGE, *his*] *boy.*
     ARMADO   Warble, child! Make passionate° my sense of   *responsive*
       hearing.
     PAGE [*sings*]   Concolinel.[2]
     ARMADO   Sweet air!° Go, tenderness of years. Take this   *tune*
5   key, give enlargement° to the swain, bring him festinately°   *freedom / in a hurry*
       hither. I must employ him in a letter to my love.
     PAGE   Will you win your love with a French brawl?°   *dance*
     ARMADO   How meanest thou? Brawling in French?[3]
     PAGE   No, my complete master, but to jig off a tune° at the   *sing a jiglike tune*
10   tongue's end, canary° to it with the feet, humor° it with   *dance / adapt to*
       turning up your eyes, sigh a note and sing a note, sometime
       through the throat—as if you swallowed love with singing
       love—sometime through the nose—as if you snuffed up
       love by smelling love—with your hat penthouse-like° o'er the   *like an awning*
15   shop of your eyes, with your arms crossed° on your thin-   *(from love melancholy)*
       belly[4] doublet like a rabbit on a spit, or your hands in your
       pocket like a man after° the old painting; and keep not too   *in the style of*
       long in one tune, but a snip° and away. These are compli-   *snatch*

---

2. The part of a book in which comments were printed.
3. It is uncertain which of the ladies should speak these lines.
3.1 Location: The King's park.
1. The braggart soldier was a stock figure in the contemporary Italian commedia dell'arte, a theatrical form with popular roots. His theatrical ancestry can be traced back to ancient Roman comedy.

2. *Concolinel:* song title or opening. TEXTUAL COMMENT On the song and the stage direction for it, see Digital Edition TC 5 (Folio edited text).
3. "Brawling" means "quarreling," but the phrase may also refer to popular rioting against immigrant French merchants and artisans.
4. Unpadded belly or lower part; also suggesting that Armado is wasting away for love.

ments;[5] these are humors;° these betray nice° wenches that   *caprices / seduce wanton*
20   would be betrayed without these, and make them men of
note—do you note, men?—that most are affected° to these.   *given*
ARMADO   How hast thou purchased this experience?
PAGE   By my penny of observation.
ARMADO   "But oh, but oh—"
25 PAGE   "The hobbyhorse is forgot."[6]
ARMADO   Call'st thou my love "hobbyhorse"?
PAGE   No, master. The hobbyhorse is but a colt,° and your love   *young horse; wanton*
perhaps a hackney.° But have you forgot your love?   *riding horse; whore*
ARMADO   Almost I had.
30 PAGE   Negligent student! Learn her by heart.
ARMADO   By heart and in heart, boy.
PAGE   And out of heart,° master. All those three I will prove.   *disheartened*
ARMADO   What wilt thou prove?
PAGE   A man, if I live, and this "by," "in," and "without" upon
35   the instant. "By" heart you love her, because your heart cannot come by her; "in" heart you love her, because your heart
is in love with her; and "out" of heart you love her, being out
of heart that you cannot enjoy her.
ARMADO   I am all these three.
40 PAGE [*aside*]   And three times as much more, and yet nothing
at all.
ARMADO   Fetch hither the swain. He must carry me° a letter.   *for me*
PAGE [*aside*]   A message well sympathized°—a horse to be   *matched*
ambassador for an ass!
45 ARMADO   Ha, ha! What sayest thou?
PAGE   Marry, sir, you must send the ass upon the horse, for he
is very slow-gaited. But I go.
ARMADO   The way is but short. Away!
PAGE   As swift as lead, sir.
50 ARMADO   Thy meaning, pretty ingenious?
Is not lead a metal heavy, dull, and slow?
PAGE   *Minime,*° honest master; or rather, master, no.   **By no means**
ARMADO   I say lead is slow.
PAGE   You are too swift, sir, to say so.
Is that lead slow which is fired from a gun?
55 ARMADO   Sweet smoke of rhetoric!
He reputes me a cannon, and the bullet—that's he.
I shoot thee at the swain—
PAGE   Thump,° then, and I flee. [*Exit.*]   *Bang*
ARMADO   A most acute juvenal—voluble° and free of grace.   *quick-witted*
By thy favor, sweet welkin,° I must sigh in thy face.   *sky*
60 Most rude melancholy, valor gives thee place.°   *gives way to you*
       Enter PAGE *and* [COSTARD, *the*] *clown*[, *limping*].
My herald is returned.
PAGE   A wonder, master! Here's a costard broken in a shin.[7]
ARMADO   Some enigma, some riddle—come, thy l'envoy:° begin!   *explanation*

---

5. Refined behaviors.
6. A lament for the passing of the good old days; perhaps the refrain of a song. A hobbyhorse—a person costumed as a horse—was used in popular dancing; the word also meant "whore," perhaps suggested by the association between "oh" (line 24), in its suggestion of "O" and "vagina."
7. A head with a cut shin (an anatomical impossibility that provokes the Page's amusement); disappointed in love or sex (alluding to Armado's triumph over Costard); taking a loan.

COSTARD No egma, no riddle, no l'envoy, no salve in the
65 mail,[8] sir! O sir, plantain,° a plain plantain! No l'envoy, no *healing herb*
l'envoy, no salve, sir, but a plantain.
ARMADO By virtue, thou enforcest laughter; thy silly thought,
my spleen.[9] The heaving of my lungs provokes me to ridicu-
lous° smiling. O pardon me, my stars! Doth the inconsider- *mocking; absurd*
70 ate° take *salve* for l'envoy, and the word "l'envoy" for a salve? *thoughtless person*
PAGE Do the wise think them other? Is not l'envoy a *salve*?
ARMADO No, page, it is an epilogue or discourse to make plain
Some obscure precedence that hath tofore been sain.[1]
I will example° it: *give an example of*
75   The fox, the ape, and the humble-bee,° *bumblebee*
Were still at odds,[2] being but three.
There's the moral.° Now the l'envoy— *lesson*
PAGE I will add the l'envoy. Say the moral again.
ARMADO   The fox, the ape, and the humble-bee,
80   Were still at odds, being but three.
PAGE   Until the goose came out of door,
And stayed° the odds by adding four.° *stopped / a fourth*
Now will I begin your moral, and do you follow with my
l'envoy.
85   The fox, the ape, and the humble-bee,
Were still at odds, being but three.
ARMADO   Until the goose came out of door,
Staying the odds by adding four.
PAGE A good l'envoy, ending in the goose.[3] Would you desire
90 more?
COSTARD [*aside*] The boy hath sold him a bargain: a goose,° *made him a fool*
that's flat.° *certain*
[*to* ARMADO] Sir, your pennyworth° is good an° your *bargain / if*
goose be fat.
To sell a bargain well is as cunning as fast and loose.° *cheating; (of bowels)*
Let me see: a fat l'envoy? Ay, that's a fat goose.
95 ARMADO Come hither, come hither. How did this argument° *topic*
begin?
PAGE By saying that a costard was broken in a shin.
Then called you for the l'envoy.
COSTARD True, and I for a plantain—thus came your argu-
ment° in. Then the boy's fat l'envoy—the goose that you *(enema?)*
100 bought—and he ended the market.° *bargaining*
ARMADO But tell me, how was there a costard broken in a
shin?
PAGE I will tell you sensibly.° *clearly; with feeling*
COSTARD Thou hast no feeling of it, Mote. I will speak that
105 l'envoy.

---

8. Costard takes Armado to be proposing remedies
for his shin. "Egma" for "enigma" may be an error for
an "egg" solution or "enema." "L'envoy" (French
l'envoi) refers to a salve or an ointment, perhaps by
confusion with "lenify" (to soothe or purge). There is
also a pun on the Latin *salve* ("greetings"), the opposite of *"l'envoy"*'s sense of "farewell." *mail:* traveling
bag. In addition, a salve inserted in or an anal salvo
discharged from the male.

9. Amusement: the spleen was regarded as the organ
controlling laughter.
1. *Some . . . sain:* What was obscurely said before.
2. Were always quarreling; were always an odd
number.
3. Punning on the French *oie* ("goose"), the final
sound in *envoy*, "ending in the goose" also because it
is inserted in the end of the goose (prostitute, victim
of venereal disease).

I, Costard, running out, that was safely within,[4]
Fell over the threshold and broke my shin.
ARMADO   We will talk no more of this matter—
COSTARD   Till there be more matter° in the shin.   *pus; semen*
110   ARMADO   Sirrah Costard, I will enfranchise° thee.   *free*
COSTARD   Oh, marry me to one Frances?[5] I smell some l'envoy,
some goose in this!
ARMADO   By my sweet soul, I mean setting thee at liberty,
enfreedoming thy person; thou wert immured,° restrained,   *shut in*
115   captivated, bound.°   *(of bowels)*
COSTARD   True, true, and now you will be my purgation° and   *liberator; enema*
let me loose.°   *(my bowels)*
ARMADO   I give thee thy liberty, set° thee from durance,° and,   *free / imprisonment*
in lieu thereof, impose on thee nothing but this: bear this
120   significant° to the country maid Jaquenetta [*giving him a*   *token*
letter]. There is remuneration [*giving him a coin*], for the best
ward° of mine honors is rewarding my dependants. Mote,   *guard*
follow.
PAGE   Like the sequel, I. Seigneur Costard, adieu.
                                    Exeunt [ARMADO *and* PAGE].
125   COSTARD   My sweet ounce of man's flesh, my incony jew![6]
Now will I look to his remuneration. "Remuneration"? Oh,
that's the Latin word for three farthings.° Three farthings: *a coin worth 3/4 pence*
remuneration. "What's the price of this inkle?"[7] "One
penny." "No, I'll give you a remuneration." Why, it carries
130   it!° "Remuneration"? Why, it is a fairer name than "French   *carries the day*
crown."[8] I will never buy and sell out of° this word.   *without using*
              Enter BIRON.
BIRON[9]   My good knave, Costard, exceedingly well met.
COSTARD   Pray you, sir, how much carnation° ribbon may a   *flesh-colored*
man buy for a remuneration?
135   BIRON   What is a remuneration?
COSTARD   Marry, sir, halfpenny-farthing.°   *three farthings*
BIRON   Why, then, three farthings' worth of silk.
COSTARD   I thank your worship. God be wi'you.
BIRON   Stay, slave, I must employ thee.
140   As thou wilt win my favor, good my knave,
Do one thing for me that I shall entreat.
COSTARD   When would you have it done, sir?
BIRON   This afternoon.
COSTARD   Well, I will do it, sir. Fare you well.
145   BIRON   Thou knowest not what it is!
COSTARD   I shall know, sir, when I have done it.
BIRON   Why, villain, thou must know first.
COSTARD   I will come to your worship tomorrow morning.

---

4. *running out . . . within*: possible reference to bodily
emissions.
5. Punning on "enfranchise" (line 110); "Frances" was
probably a common name for a prostitute.
6. Religious reference from the mishearing of "adieu"
(line 124); playful diminutive of "jewel" or "juvenal."
incony: fine, quality.
7. Linen tape, suggested by "incony" (line 125); near

homonym of "ingle," a catamite (boy kept by a pederast), and perhaps thereby evoking the period's association of the "jew" (line 125) with sodomy.
8. A coin; syphilis (the "French disease") results in a
bald head ("crown").
9. TEXTUAL COMMENT For the problems with Biron's
speech prefixes here and elsewhere, see Digital Edition TC 6 (Folio edited text).

150 BIRON   It must be done this afternoon. Hark, slave, it is but
         this:
     The Princess comes to hunt here in the park,
     And in her train there is a gentle lady.
     When tongues speak sweetly, then they name her name,
     And Rosaline they call her. Ask for her,
155 And to her white hand see thou do commend
     This sealed-up counsel.° [*He gives him a letter.*] There's thy   message
         guerdon.° Go!   reward
         [*He gives him money.*]
   COSTARD   "Gardon"? O sweet gardon! Better than remunera-
     tion: elevenpence-farthing better.[1] Most sweet gardon! I will
     do it, sir, in print.° Gardon! Remuneration!   *Exit.*   to the letter
160 BIRON   And I, forsooth, in love? I that have been love's whip,
     A very beadle[2] to a humorous° sigh,   moody
     A critic, nay, a night-watch constable,
     A domineering pedant° o'er the boy°—   schoolmaster / Cupid
     Than whom no mortal so magnificent.
165 This wimpled,° whining, purblind,° wayward boy,   blindfolded / all-blind
     This Seigneur° Junior, giant dwarf, Dan° Cupid,   Sir; senior / Master
     Regent of love-rhymes, lord of folded arms,
     Th'anointed sovereign of sighs and groans,
     Liege of all loiterers and malcontents,
170 Dread prince of plackets, king of codpieces,[3]
     Sole imperator° and great general   Absolute ruler
     Of trotting paritors[4]—O my little heart!
     And I to be a corporal of his field,°   field officer
     And wear his colors like a tumbler's hoop!°   (adorned with ribbons)
175 What, I love, I sue, I seek a wife?
     A woman that is like a German clock:
     Still° a-repairing, ever out of frame,°   Always / order
     And never going aright, being° a watch,   though
     But being° watched that it may still go right.   Except when
180 Nay, to be perjured, which is worst of all,
     And among three to love the worst of all:
     A whitely° wanton with a velvet° brow,   pale / smooth
     With two pitch° balls stuck in her face for eyes;   tar black
     Ay, and by heaven, one that will do the deed°   sexual act
185 Though Argus[5] were her eunuch° and her guard.   harem warden
     And I to sigh for her, to watch° for her,   stay awake at night
     To pray for her? Go to!° It is a plague   Come now!
     That Cupid will impose for my neglect
     Of his almighty, dreadful, little might.
190 Well, I will love, write, sigh, pray, sue, and groan;
     Some men must love my lady, and some Joan.°   [*Exit.*]   lower-class woman

---

1. Biron has given Costard a "guerdon" of one shilling, or twelve pence, which is "elevenpence-farthing"
(eleven pence and one farthing) "better than remuneration," defined earlier by Costard as "three-
farthings" (where four farthings equal one pence;
lines 127–28).
2. Minor parish official who punished lesser offenses

(for instance, by whipping).
3. The parts of clothes covering the male sexual
organ (hence, penises, or men). *plackets:* slits in petticoats (hence, female genitalia, or women).
4. Officers who summoned sexual offenders to
ecclesiastical courts.
5. Mythical watchman with a hundred eyes.

4.1 (Q 4.1)

Enter the PRINCESS, *a* FORESTER, *her ladies* [MARIA,
KATHERINE, *and* ROSALINE], *and her lords* [*including*
BOYET].

PRINCESS   Was that the King that spurred his horse so hard,
Against the steep uprising of the hill?

BOYET   I know not, but I think it was not he.

PRINCESS   Whoe'er 'a° was, 'a showed a mounting mind.   *he*

5   Well, lords, today we shall have our dispatch.
On Saturday we will return to France.
Then Forester, my friend, where is the bush
That we must stand and play the murderer in?

FORESTER   Hereby, upon the edge of yonder coppice°—   *thicket*

10   A stand° where you may make the fairest° shoot.   *hunter's station / best*

PRINCESS   I thank my beauty, I am fair° that shoot,   *beautiful*
And thereupon thou speak'st "the fairest shoot."

FORESTER   Pardon me, madam, for I meant not so.

PRINCESS   What, what? First praise me, and then again say no?

15   Oh, short-lived pride! Not fair? Alack for woe!

FORESTER   Yes, madam, fair—

PRINCESS   Nay, never paint° me now!   *flatter*
Where fair° is not, praise cannot mend the brow.   *beauty*
Here, good my glass,° take this for telling true.   *my good mirror*
[*She gives him money.*]
Fair payment for foul words is more than due.

20   FORESTER   Nothing but fair is that which you inherit.°   *own*

PRINCESS   See, see, my beauty will be saved by merit!¹
Oh, heresy in fair, fit for these days;²
A giving hand, though foul, shall have fair praise.
But come: the bow. Now mercy° goes to kill,   *the merciful Princess*

25   And shooting well is then accounted ill.°   *unmerciful*
Thus will I save my credit in the shoot:
Not wounding, pity would not let me do't;³
If wounding, then it was to show my skill,
That more for praise than purpose meant to kill.

30   And out of question° so it is sometimes: *beyond doubt*
Glory° grows guilty of detested crimes,   *The desire for glory*
When, for fame's sake, for praise, an outward part,
We bend to that the working of the heart;
As I for praise alone now seek to spill

35   The poor deer's blood, that my heart° means no ill.   *pun on "hart" (male deer)*

BOYET   Do not curst° wives hold that self-sovereignty⁴   *shrewish*
Only for praise' sake, when they strive to be
Lords o'er their lords?

PRINCESS   Only for praise, and praise we may afford

40   To any lady that subdues a lord.

Enter [COSTARD, *the*] *clown.*

BOYET   Here comes a member of the commonwealth.°   *common people*

COSTARD   God dig-you-den° all. Pray you, which is the head lady?   *give you good evening*

4.1 Location: A hunter's station in the King's park.
1. Desert; good works (her "payment").
2. Believing in salvation by faith, Protestants considered it a common "heresy" "these days" to think, as
Catholics did, that one could be "saved by merit." *in
fair*: in regard to beauty.

3. *Thus . . . do't*: I will save my reputation as a hunter
by saying, if I miss, that pity for the deer caused me
to miss deliberately.
4. *hold that self-sovereignty*: exercise that same power
over themselves (and their husbands).

PRINCESS   Thou shalt know her, fellow, by the rest that have
45   no heads.[5]
COSTARD   Which is the greatest lady? The highest?
PRINCESS   The thickest and the tallest.
COSTARD   The thickest and the tallest? It is so; truth is truth.
     An your waist, mistress, were as slender as my wit
50   One o'these maids' girdles for your waist should be fit.
     Are not you the chief woman? You are the thickest here.
PRINCESS   What's your will, sir? What's your will?
COSTARD   I have a letter from Monsieur Biron
     To one Lady Rosaline.
55   PRINCESS   Oh, thy letter, thy letter! He's a good friend of mine.
        [*She seizes the letter.*]
     Stand aside, good bearer. —Boyet, you can carve;°   *cut meat; act affected*
     Break up° this capon.[6]   *Cut up; open*
BOYET   I am bound to serve.
        [*He reads the superscription.*]
     This letter is mistook; it importeth° none here.   *matters to*
     It is writ to Jaquenetta.
PRINCESS   We will read it, I swear.
60   Break the neck of the wax,° and everyone give ear.   *seal; (capon)*
BOYET (*reads*)   "By heaven, that thou art fair is most infalli-
     ble,° true that thou art beauteous, truth itself that thou art   *certain*
     lovely. More fairer than fair, beautiful than beauteous, truer
     than truth itself, have commiseration on thy heroical vassal.
65   The magnanimous and most illustrate° King Cophetua set°   *illustrious / set his*
     eye upon the pernicious and indubitate° beggar Zenelo-   *undoubted*
     phon,° and he it was that might rightly say, '*Veni, vidi, vici,*'[7]   *(see 1.2.99)*
     which to annothanize° in the vulgar—O base and obscure   *anatomize; annotate*
     vulgar!°—*videlicet,*° 'He came, see, and overcame.' He   *vernacular / namely*
70   came, one; see, two; overcame, three. Who came? The King.
     Why did he come? To see. Why did he see? To overcome. To
     whom came he? To the beggar. What saw he? The beggar.
     Who overcame he? The beggar. The conclusion is victory.
     On whose side? The King's. The captive is enriched. On
75   whose side? The beggar's. The catastrophe° is a nuptial. On *outcome*
     whose side? The King's? No, on both in one, or one in both.
     I am the King, for so stands the comparison; thou the beg-
     gar, for so witnesseth thy lowliness. Shall I command thy
     love? I may. Shall I enforce thy love? I could. Shall I entreat
80   thy love? I will. What shalt thou exchange for rags? Robes.
     For tittles?° Titles. For thyself? Me. Thus expecting thy   *jots; specks*
     reply, I profane my lips on thy foot, my eyes on thy picture,
     and my heart on thy every part.
        Thine in the dearest design of industry,°   *(gallantry?); diligence*
85   Don Adriano de Armado.
     Thus dost thou hear the Nemean lion[8] roar
     'Gainst thee, thou lamb, that standest as his prey.
     Submissive fall his princely feet before,
     And he from forage° will incline to play.   *raging*

5. Part of the body, literalizing metaphorical use of   7. Originally said by Julius Caesar.
"head" as "leader" (line 42); maidenhead.   8. Killed by Hercules as the first of his labors.
6. Love letter; castrated male chicken.

90   But if thou strive, poor soul, what art thou then?

      Food for his rage, repasture° for his den."   *food*

PRINCESS   What plume of feathers° is he that indited° this   *silly bird / wrote*

     letter?

    What vane?[9] What weathercock?° Did you ever hear better?   *(example of showiness)*

BOYET   I am much deceived, but I remember the style.

95 PRINCESS   Else your memory is bad, going o'er[1] it erewhile.

BOYET   This Armado is a Spaniard that keeps° here in court: *dwells*

    A phantasime,° a Monarcho,[2] and one that makes sport   *fantastic being*

    To° the Prince and his bookmates.   *For*

PRINCESS   Thou, fellow, a word.

    Who gave thee this letter?

COSTARD   I told you: my lord.

100 PRINCESS   To whom shouldst thou give it?

COSTARD   From my lord to my lady.

PRINCESS   From which lord to which lady?

COSTARD   From my lord Biron, a good master of mine,

    To a lady of France that he called Rosaline.

105 PRINCESS   Thou hast mistaken his letter. Come, lords, away!

    —Here, sweet, put up this.   [*She gives* ROSALINE *the letter.*]

                 'Twill be thine another day.°   *Your turn will come*

          Exeunt [*the* PRINCESS, *the* FORESTER, *and lords*].

BOYET   Who is the shooter? Who is the shooter?

ROSALINE   Shall I teach you to know?

BOYET   Ay, my continent° of beauty.   *container of all*

ROSALINE   Why, she that bears the bow.

    Finely put off!°   *evaded*

110 BOYET   My lady goes to kill horns, but if thou marry,

    Hang me by the neck if horns that year miscarry.[3]

    Finely put on!°   *applied*

ROSALINE   Well, then, I am the shooter.

BOYET   And who is your deer?°   *prey; dear*

ROSALINE   If we choose by the horns, yourself come not near.[4]

115   Finely put on, indeed!

MARIA   You still wrangle with her, Boyet, and she strikes at the

    brow.[5]

BOYET   But she herself is hit lower[6]—have I hit her° now?   *found her out*

ROSALINE   Shall I come upon thee with an old saying, that

    was a man when King Pépin of France was a little boy,[7] as

120   touching the hit-it?[8]

BOYET   So I may answer thee with one as old, that was a woman

    when Queen Guinevere of Britain[9] was a little wench, as

    touching the hit-it.

---

9. Weathervane, often in the form of a heraldic banner; vanity.

1. Having read; having climbed (taking "style" in line 94 as "stile," "fence").

2. Pretentious person—from the nickname of an eccentric Italian of Shakespeare's time who claimed to be a monarch of the world.

3. If you do not soon cuckold your husband; possibly, if penises fail or lead to a miscarriage. From here through line 138, there are almost continuous sexual references.

4. Probably: If you want to be safe, don't come close, because you have cuckold's horns.

5. Aims well; taunts you about your cuckold's horns.

6. In the heart; in the genitals.

7. Was already old when Charlemagne's father (d. 768) was a little boy.

8. *the hit-it:* bawdy popular round and the dance done to it.

9. Notoriously unfaithful wife of the legendary King Arthur.

ROSALINE Thou canst not hit it, hit it, hit it,
125 Thou canst not hit it, my good man.
BOYET An I cannot, cannot, cannot,
    An I cannot, another can.   *Exit* [ROSALINE].
COSTARD By my troth, most pleasant. How both did fit it!° sing well; (bawdy)
MARIA A mark° marvelous well shot, for they both did hit it. target
130 BOYET A mark? Oh, mark but that mark! "A mark," says my
    lady.
    Let the mark have a prick° in't to mete° at, if it may be. bull's-eye; penis / aim
MARIA Wide o'the bow hand.[1] I'faith, your hand is out.° out of practice
COSTARD [*aside*] Indeed, 'a° must shoot nearer, or he'll ne'er he
    hit the clout.°   bull's-eye; (bawdy)
BOYET An if my hand be out, then belike your hand is in.[2]
135 COSTARD [*aside*] Then will she get the upshoot[3] by cleaving
    the pin.°   center
MARIA Come, come, you talk greasily.° Your lips grow foul. indecently
COSTARD She's too hard for you at pricks,° sir. Challenge her archery; sex
    to bowl.
BOYET I fear too much rubbing.[4] Goodnight, my good owl.[5]
         [*Exeunt* BOYET, KATHERINE, *and* MARIA.]
COSTARD By my soul, a swain, a most simple clown!
140 Lord, lord, how the ladies and I have put him down.
    O'my troth, most sweet jests, most incony° vulgar wit, fine-quality
    When it comes so smoothly off, so obscenely,[6] as it were,
    so fit.
    Armado o'th' other side°—Oh, a most dainty° man! by contrast / elegant
    To see him walk before a lady and to bear her fan;
145 To see him kiss his hand, and how most sweetly° 'a will stylishly
    swear!
    And his page o' t'other side, that handful of wit.
    Ah heavens, it is a most pathetical nit!°   affecting little fellow
         Shout° *within.*   Loud voice; shooting
    Sola, sola!°   *Exit.*   (hunting cry)

4.2 (Q 4.2)

Enter DULL, HOLOFERNES, *the pedant*[,][1] *and*
NATHANIEL[, *the curate*].

NATHANIEL Very reverent° sport, truly, and done in the testi- respectable
    mony° of a good conscience.   with the warrant
HOLOFERNES The deer was, as you know, *sanguis*,[2] in blood,° robust
    ripe as a pomewater° who now hangeth like a jewel in the ear kind of apple
5   of *caelo*, the sky, the welkin, the heaven, and anon° falleth soon after
    like a crab° on the face of *terra*, the soil, the land, the earth. crab apple

---

1. Too far to the left side (a cry in archery).
2. If I'm out of practice (at archery, at sex), you're not.
3. Winning shot; ejaculation.
4. In the game of bowls, touching obstacles; sexual friction.
5. "Owl," a bird of night, is suggested by "Goodnight"; to "take owl" is to take offense; rhyming with "bowl," "owl" suggests "ole" (hole) in the sexual sense.
6. Inadvertently accurate; perhaps a blunder for "seemly."
4.2 Location: The King's park.
1. Holofernes—a character based on a warrior

whose decapitation by the heroine of the apocryphal Book of Judith saves Jerusalem—was a familiar tyrant in medieval religious plays; also a doctor of theology and tutor to Gargantua in Rabelais's *Gargantua and Pantagruel*. Like the braggart soldier, the pedant or schoolmaster was a stock character in commedia dell'arte (see Introduction); his prominence is due to the humanist-inspired, early Tudor educational reforms that presumably shaped Shakespeare's own formal education.
2. The Latin in this scene, some of it inaccurate, is translated only when the characters themselves fail to do so. It is often unclear whether an error is the character's or the printer's.

NATHANIEL   Truly, Master Holofernes, the epithets are sweetly
varied, like a scholar at the least; but, sir, I assure ye, it was a
buck of the first head.[3]

10 HOLOFERNES   Sir[4] Nathaniel, *haud credo*.°   *I hardly think so*

DULL   'Twas not a "auld grey doe," 'twas a pricket.[5]

HOLOFERNES   Most barbarous intimation!° Yet a kind of insinu-   *intrusion*
ation, as it were, *in via*, in way of explication, *facere*,° as it   *to make*
were, replication,° or rather *ostentare*, to show, as it were, his   *explanation*
15 inclination, after his undressed, unpolished, uneducated,
unpruned, untrained, or rather unlettered, or ratherest uncon-
firmed° fashion, to insert again° my "*haud credo*" for a deer.   *inexperienced / interpret*

DULL   I said the deer was not a "auld grey doe," 'twas a pricket.

HOLOFERNES   Twice-sod simplicity, *bis coctus*![6]
20 O thou monster, Ignorance, how deformed dost thou look!

NATHANIEL   Sir, he hath never fed of the dainties that are
bred in a book.
He hath not eat paper, as it were; he hath not drunk ink.
His intellect is not replenished; he is only an animal—only
sensible° in the duller parts.   *capable of feeling*
And such barren plants are set before us that we thankful
should be—
25 Which we of taste and feeling are—for those parts that do
fructify° in us more than he.   *bear fruit*
For as it would ill become me to be vain, indiscreet, or a
fool,
So were there a patch set on learning[7] to see him in a school.
But *omne bene*,° say I, being of an old father's° mind: *all is well / sage's*
Many can brook the weather that love not the wind.[8]

30 DULL   You two are bookmen. Can you tell, by your wit,
What was a month old at Cain's birth that's not five weeks
old as yet?

HOLOFERNES   Dictynna, goodman° Dull. Dictynna, goodman   *yeoman*
Dull.

DULL   What is "Dictima"?

35 HOLOFERNES[9]   A title to° Phoebe, to *luna*, to the moon.   *name for*

NATHANIEL   The moon was a month old when Adam was no
more,
And raught° not to five weeks when he came to fivescore.   *reached*
Th'allusion holds in the exchange.[1]

DULL   'Tis true, indeed: the collusion° holds in the exchange.   *(for "allusion")*

40 NATHANIEL   God comfort° thy capacity! I say th'allusion holds   *pity*
in the exchange.

DULL   And I say the pollution[2] holds in the exchange, for the
moon is never but a month old—and I say beside, that 'twas
a pricket that the Princess killed.

---

3. With his first head of antlers; in his fifth year.
4. Used generally of graduates, including priests
(like "Reverend").
5. Buck in its second year, with a sexual hint.
6. *Twice . . . coctus*: Twice-boiled folly, twice-cooked;
"*coctus*" also continues the sexual innuendo of "pricket"
(line 18) with the suggestion of "cock."
7. It would mean that a fool ("patch") had been put to
his studies; there would be a black mark on learning.
8. Many can endure the weather while disliking
some of its features (?); one must live with what one
cannot change (proverbial).

9. Textual Comment For the confusion of Holofernes' and Nathaniel's speech prefixes here, and the
grounds for their correction, see Digital Edition TC
7 (Folio edited text).
1. The riddle works as well with Adam as with Cain.
2. Dull's blunder for "allusion" again, but in each
case a commentary on his interlocutors. "Collusion"
can refer to a verbal trick designed to promote collusion in the sense of conspiracy; linguistic pollution
occurs when one favors difficult foreign words over
straightforward English.

45 HOLOFERNES   Sir Nathaniel, will you hear an extemporal epitaph on the death of the deer?—and, to humor the ignorant,
call I the deer the Princess killed a pricket.

NATHANIEL   *Perge,*° good Master Holofernes, *perge,*   *Proceed*
So it shall please you to abrogate scurrility.³

50 HOLOFERNES   I will something affect the letter,⁴ for it
argues° facility: *shows*
The preyful° Princess pierced and pricked a pretty pleasing   *desirous of prey*
pricket;
Some say a sore,⁵ but not a sore till now made sore with
shooting.
The dogs did yell; put "l" to sore, then "sorrel"° jumps from   *buck in its third year*
thicket.
Or° pricket, sore or else sorrel, the people fall a-hooting.   *Either*

55 If sore be sore, then "l"° to sore makes fifty sores o'sorrel.   *Roman numeral for 50*
Of one sore I an hundred make by adding but one more "l."°   *50 more; one moral*

NATHANIEL   A rare talent!°   *talon; ability*

DULL [*aside*]   If a talent be a claw, look how he claws° him   *scratches; flatters*
with a talent!

60 HOLOFERNES   This is a gift that I have simple,° simple: a fool-   *naturally*
ish, extravagant° spirit, full of forms, figures, shapes,   *wandering*
objects, ideas, apprehensions, motions,° revolutions.° These   *impulses/ reflections*
are begot in the ventricle° of memory, nourished in the   *part of the brain*
womb of *pia mater,*⁶ and delivered upon the mellowing of

65 occasion.° But the gift is good in those in whom it is acute,   *when the time is ripe*
and I am thankful for it.

NATHANIEL   Sir, I praise the Lord for you, and so may my
parishioners, for their sons are well tutored by you, and their
daughters profit very greatly under you.⁷ You are a good

70 member of the commonwealth.

HOLOFERNES   *Mehercle,*° if their sons be ingenious, they shall   *By Hercules*
want° no instruction. If their daughters be capable, I will put   *lack*
it to them.

     Enter JAQUENETTA *and* [COSTARD,] *the clown.*
But *vir sapit qui pauca loquitur*⁸—a soul feminine saluteth us.

75 JAQUENETTA   God give you good morrow, Master Person.

HOLOFERNES   Master Person? *Quasi*° Pierce-one!⁹ An if one   *As if*
should be pierced, which is the one?

COSTARD   Marry, Master Schoolmaster, he that is likest to° a   *most like*
hogshead.¹

80 HOLOFERNES   "Of piercing a hogshead"°—a good luster of   *(getting drunk?)*
conceit° in a turf of earth, fire enough for a flint, pearl   *spark of imagination*
enough for a swine.² 'Tis pretty; it is well.

JAQUENETTA   Good Master Parson, be so good as read me this
letter. It was given me by Costard, and sent me from Don

85 Armado. [*She gives* NATHANIEL *the letter.*] I beseech you,
read it.

---

3. *abrogate scurrility:* avoid indecency. Nathaniel is probably worrying about "pricket"—justifiably, given line 51, below. *"Perge"* may suggest "purging."
4. I will to some extent aspire to alliteration.
5. Deer in its fourth year.
6. Membrane surrounding the brain.
7. In conjunction with "member" (line 70), "capable" (line 72), and "put it to them" (lines 72–73), probably

bawdy.
8. "That man is wise that speaketh few things or words" (William Lily's early sixteenth-century Latin grammar, translating a common proverb).
9. Pronounced like "parson" or "person"; bawdy.
1. Large cask used for beer or wine; fool.
2. To "cast pearls before swine," a biblical phrase, was already proverbial.

HOLOFERNES "*Fauste precor, gelida quando pecus omne sub umbra Ruminat*"[3]—and so forth. Ah, good old Mantuan! I may speak of thee as the traveler doth of Venice: "*Venetia,*

90 *Venetia, Chi non ti vede, non ti pretia.*"[4] Old Mantuan, old Mantuan, who understandeth thee not, loves thee not. [*He sings.*] *Ut, re, sol, la, mi, fa.*[5] [*to* NATHANIEL] Under pardon, sir, what are the contents? Or rather, as Horace° says in   *ancient Roman poet* his—What, my soul, verses?[6]

95 NATHANIEL   Ay, sir, and very learned.

HOLOFERNES   Let me hear a staff, a stanza, a verse.[7] *Lege, domine.*°   *Read, sir*

NATHANIEL [*reads*]   "If love make me forsworn, how shall I swear to love?[8]

Ah, never faith could hold, if not to beauty vowed.

100 Though to myself forsworn, to thee I'll faithful prove;

Those thoughts to me were oaks,[9] to thee like osiers°   *willows* bowed.

Study his bias leaves° and makes his book thine eyes,   *goes off course*

Where all those pleasures live that art would comprehend.

If knowledge be the mark,° to know thee shall   *aim* suffice.

105 Well learnèd is that tongue that well can thee commend;

All ignorant that soul that sees thee without wonder,

Which is to me some praise, that I thy parts° admire.   *qualities*

Thy eye Jove's lightning bears, thy voice his dreadful thunder,

Which, not to anger bent, is music and sweet fire.

110 Celestial as thou art, O pardon, love, this wrong,

That sings heaven's praise with such an earthly tongue."

HOLOFERNES   You find not the *apostrophus*° and so miss the   *elision mark* accent. Let me supervise° the canzonet.° [*He takes the let-*   *look over / little poem* *ter.*] Here are only numbers ratified,° but for the elegancy,   *correct meters*

115 facility, and golden cadence of poesy, *caret.*° Ovidius Naso[1]   *it is lacking* was the man; and why, indeed, "Naso," but for smelling out the odoriferous flowers of fancy, the jerks of invention?° *Imi-*   *strokes of imagination* *tari*° is nothing: so doth the hound his master, the ape his   *To imitate* keeper, the tired° horse his rider. —But, *domicella*—virgin—   *attired*

120 was this directed to you?

JAQUENETTA   Ay, sir, from one Monsieur Biron, one of the strange queen's lords.[2]

---

3. The first line of a Latin poem by the Italian poet Mantuan (1448–1516), a poem well known even to schoolboys in Shakespeare's time: "Faustus, while all the cattle are chewing the cud in the cool shade, I pray you" (let us talk a little about our old love affairs).
4. Italian proverb, translated by John Florio as "Venice, who seeth thee not, praiseth thee not" (*First Fruits*, 1578).
5. Notes of the scale ("ut" is the modern "do"). If Holofernes sings them as a scale, he gets them in the wrong order; but they may represent a tune.
6. TEXTUAL COMMENT For the attribution of the mis-quotation of Latin and Italian in this speech to the printer rather than to Holofernes or Shakespeare, see Digital Edition TC 8 (Folio edited text).
7. A *staff, a stanza, a verse*: three ways of saying

"stanza."
8. The beginning of a sonnet (lines 97–111), with six stresses per line. Like the poems of Longueville (4.3.55–68) and Dumaine (4.3.96–115), it was reprinted in *The Passionate Pilgrim* (1599). See the Introduction.
9. Those resolutions that seemed to me to be as strong as oaks.
1. The full name of the ancient Roman poet Ovid was Publius Ovidius Naso; *nasus* is Latin for "nose."
2. Jaquenetta has just said (lines 84–85) that Armado wrote and Costard gave her the letter, and she can't know that Biron, who is not a "strange" (foreign) courtier attending upon the Princess, actually composed it. Probably the errors are Shakespeare's.

HOLOFERNES I will over-glance the superscript.° [*He reads.*]   address
"To the snow-white hand of the most beauteous Lady Rosa-
125   line." I will look again on the intellect° of the letter for the   meaning; contents
nomination of the party writing to the person written unto:
"Your ladyship's, in all desired employment, Biron."
NATHANIEL Master Holofernes, this Biron is one of the vota-
ries with the King, and here he hath framed a letter to a
130   sequent° of the stranger queen's, which accidentally, or by   follower
the way of progression,° hath miscarried. [*to* JAQUENETTA]   in transit
Trip and go,³ my sweet. Deliver this paper into the hand of
the King; it may concern much. Stay not thy compliment. I
forgive thy duty.⁴ Adieu.
135   JAQUENETTA Good Costard, go with me. [*to* NATHANIEL] Sir,
God save your life!
COSTARD Have with thee,° my girl.   I'll come with you
Exeunt [COSTARD *and* JAQUENETTA].
NATHANIEL Sir, you have done this in the fear of God, very
religiously, and, as a certain father° sayeth—   church father
140   HOLOFERNES Sir, tell not me of the father; I do fear colorable
colors.⁵ But to return to the verses: did they please you, Sir
Nathaniel?
NATHANIEL Marvelous well, for the pen.°   penmanship
HOLOFERNES I do dine today at the father's of a certain pupil
145   of mine where, if before repast it shall please you to gratify°   grace; please
the table with a grace, I will, on my privilege I have with the
parents of the foresaid child or pupil, undertake your *ben
venuto*,⁶ where I will prove those verses to be very unlearned,
neither savoring of poetry, wit, nor invention. I beseech your
150   society.
NATHANIEL And thank you too, for society, sayeth the text,⁷ is
the happiness of life.
HOLOFERNES And, certes,° the text most infallibly concludes   certainly
it. [*to* DULL] Sir, I do invite you too. You shall not say me nay.
155   *Pauca verba*.° Away! The gentles are at their game,⁸ and we   Few words
will to our recreation.   *Exeunt*.

4.3 (Q 4.3)

Enter BIRON *with a paper in his hand, alone.*
BIRON The King he is hunting the deer; I am coursing°   pursuing
myself. They have pitched a toil;° I am toiling in a pitch¹—   set a snare
pitch that defiles. "Defile"? A foul word. Well, sit thee down,°   stay with me
Sorrow; for so they say the fool said, and so say I, and I the
5   fool. Well proved, wit! By the Lord, this love is as mad as
Ajax. It kills sheep;² it kills me: I, a sheep. Well proved again
o'my side! I will not love. If I do, hang me. I'faith, I will not.
Oh, but her eye! By this light, but for her eye, I would not
love her; yes, for her two eyes. Well, I do nothing in the world
10   but lie, and lie in my throat.° By heaven, I do love, and it   scandalously

---

3. A common expression, the title of a popular song
and dance.
4. Do not delay in order to take leave politely. I
excuse you from making a curtsy.
5. I do mistrust plausible—but specious—arguments
(a rejection of popishness?).
6. Undertake your welcome (Italian).
7. No convincing source has been identified.

8. The gentlefolk are at their sport (hunting).
4.3. Location: Scene continues.
1. In tar; in Rosaline's eyes (?).
2. At the Greek siege of Troy, when Agamemnon
awards Achilles' armor to Odysseus, Ajax goes mad
with rage and kills a flock of sheep, believing them to
be the Greek army.

hath taught me to rhyme and to be melancholy, and here is
part of my rhyme [*indicating the paper*], and here my melancholy [*indicating his breast*]. Well, she hath one o'my sonnets
already. The clown bore it, the fool sent it, and the lady hath

15 it. Sweet clown, sweeter fool, sweetest lady! By the world, I
would not care a pin if the other three were in.°   *similarly involved*
      Enter the KING.
Here comes one with a paper. God give him grace to groan!°   *(out of love)*
      [BIRON] *stands aside.*³

KING Ay me!
BIRON [*aside*] Shot, by heaven! Proceed, sweet Cupid. Thou
20 hast thumped him with thy bird-bolt under the left pap.°   *your arrow in the heart*
      [*The* KING *unfolds a paper.*]
In faith, secrets!
KING [*reads*] "So sweet a kiss the golden sun gives not⁴
      To those fresh morning drops upon the rose,
      As thy eyebeams when their fresh rays have smote
25   The night of dew° that on my cheeks down flows.   *nightly tears*
      Nor shines the silver moon one half so bright
      Through the transparent bosom of the deep,
      As doth thy face through tears of mine give light.
      Thou shin'st in every tear that I do weep;
30   No drop but as a coach doth carry thee;
      So ridest thou, triumphing in my woe.
      Do but behold the tears that swell in me,
      And they thy glory through my grief will show.
      But do not love thyself: then thou wilt keep
35   My tears for glasses,° and still make me weep.   *mirrors*
      O Queen of queens, how far dost thou excel,
      No thought can think, nor tongue of mortal tell."
How shall she know my griefs? I'll drop the paper.
Sweet leaves° shade° folly.   *(of trees; paper) / hide*
      Enter LONGUEVILLE [*with a paper*].
                              Who is he comes here?
40 What, Longueville? And reading? Listen, ear.
      The KING *steps aside.*
BIRON [*aside*] Now, in thy° likeness, one more fool appear!   *(the King's)*
LONGUEVILLE Ay me, I am forsworn.
BIRON [*aside*] Why, he comes in like a perjure,° wearing papers.⁵ *perjurer*
KING [*aside*] In love, I hope. Sweet fellowship in shame!
45 BIRON [*aside*] One drunkard loves another of the name.°   *another drunkard*
LONGUEVILLE Am I the first that have been perjured so?
BIRON [*aside*] I could put thee in comfort: not by two that I know.
      Thou makest the triumviry,⁶ the corner cap° of society,   *three-cornered cap*
      The shape of love's Tyburn⁷ that hangs up simplicity.°   *folly*
50 LONGUEVILLE I fear these stubborn° lines lack power to move.   *rough*
      O sweet Maria, empress of my love!
      These numbers° will I tear and write in prose.   *verses*
BIRON [*aside*] Oh, rhymes are guards° on wanton Cupid's hose;   *decorative bands*

---

3. At line 74, Biron says, "here sit I in the sky." At some
point before then—perhaps here—he mounts to a
higher level.
4. The beginning of a sonnet that actually extends to
sixteen lines (lines 22–37).
5. Wearing a poem (lines 55–68). Convicted perjurers

were exposed by having to wear papers that explained
their guilt.
6. You complete the triumvirate (group of three
rulers).
7. The common place of execution in London, here
metaphorically for gallows, which were triangular.

Disfigure not his slop.°   *breeches*
LONGUEVILLE   This same shall go.[8]
         He reads the sonnet.
55   "Did not the heavenly rhetoric of thine eye,
        'Gainst whom the world cannot hold argument,
        Persuade my heart to this false perjury?
        Vows for thee broke deserve not punishment.
        A woman I forswore, but I will prove,
60   Thou being a goddess, I forswore not thee.
        My vow was earthly, thou a heavenly love;
        Thy grace° being gained cures all disgrace in me.   *favor*
        Vows are but breath, and breath a vapor is.
        Then thou, fair sun which on my earth dost shine,
65   Exhalest° this vapor-vow; in thee it is.   *Draw up*
        If broken then, it is no fault of mine.
        If by me broke, what fool is not so wise
        To lose an oath to win a paradise?"
BIRON [*aside*]   This is the liver vein[9] which makes flesh a deity.
70   A green goose° a goddess? Pure, pure idolatry!   *silly girl; whore*
        God amend us, God amend! We are much out o'th' way.°   *badly astray*
        Enter DUMAINE.
LONGUEVILLE   By whom shall I send this? —Company? Stay.
        [LONGUEVILLE *stands aside*.]
BIRON [*aside*]   All hid, all hid, an old infant play![1]
        Like a demigod here sit I in the sky,
75   And wretched fools' secrets heedfully o'er-eye.
        More sacks to the mill.° O heavens, I have my wish: *More to come!*
        Dumaine transformed! Four woodcocks° in a dish!   *fools*
DUMAINE   O most divine Kate!
BIRON [*aside*]   O most profane coxcomb!°   *fool*
80 DUMAINE   By heaven, the wonder of a mortal eye!
BIRON [*aside*]   By earth, she is not. Corporal,[2] there you lie.
DUMAINE   Her amber hairs for foul hath amber quoted.[3]
BIRON [*aside*]   An amber-colored raven was well noted.[4]
DUMAINE   As upright as the cedar!
BIRON [*aside*]   Stoop,[5] I say.
        Her shoulder is with child.°   *bulging; bowed down*
85 DUMAINE   As fair as day!
BIRON [*aside*]   Ay, as some days, but then no sun must shine.
DUMAINE   Oh, that I had my wish!
LONGUEVILLE [*aside*]   And I had mine!
KING [*aside*]   And I mine too, good Lord!
BIRON [*aside*]   Amen, so I had mine. Is not that a good word?[6]
90 DUMAINE   I would forget her, but a fever she
        Reigns in my blood, and will remembered be.
BIRON [*aside*]   A fever in your blood? Why, then, incision°   *bloodletting*

---

8. Either he has hesitated before tearing the paper or he pieces it together, as if in response to Biron's aside.
9. Style of the lover (the liver was thought of as the seat of love).
1. Hide-and-seek ("play" means "game"); perhaps also a medieval religious play in which God views the actions from above, like Biron does (line 74).
2. Officer in Cupid's army; perhaps: (she is merely) corporeal, or human. The possible application to

both Dumaine and Katherine, but in different ways, is characteristic of Biron's asides here.
3. Her amber-colored hairs have caused amber itself to be regarded as foul by comparison.
4. Dumaine is an acute observer, Biron remarks ironically, in describing Katherine's hair as amber. (Katherine more resembles the raven, a black fowl, punning on "foul," line 82.)
5. She's stooped; come down to earth.
6. Isn't that a kind wish; isn't "Amen" a "good word"?

Would let her out in saucers.[7] Sweet misprision!°   *misinterpretation*
DUMAINE　Once more I'll read the ode that I have writ.
95　BIRON [*aside*]　Once more I'll mark how love can vary° wit.   *inspire; impair*
　　　DUMAINE *reads his sonnet.*
　DUMAINE　"On a day—alack the day!—
　　　　Love, whose month is ever May,
　　　　Spied a blossom, passing° fair,   *surpassingly*
　　　　Playing in the wanton° air.   *playful*
100　　　Through the velvet leaves the wind
　　　　All unseen can° passage find,   *did*
　　　　That° the lover, sick to death,   *So that*
　　　　Wish himself the heaven's breath.
　　　　'Air,' quoth he, 'thy cheeks may blow;
105　　　Air, would I might triumph so!
　　　　But, alack, my hand is sworn
　　　　Ne'er to pluck thee from thy thorn.
　　　　Vow, alack, for youth unmeet;°   *inappropriate*
　　　　Youth so apt to pluck a sweet.
110　　　Do not call it sin in me
　　　　That I am forsworn for thee,
　　　　Thou, for whom Jove would swear
　　　　Juno but an Ethiop[8] were,
　　　　And deny himself for° Jove,   *to be*
115　　　Turning mortal for thy love.' "
　　This will I send, and something else more plain
　　That shall express my true love's fasting pain.
　　Oh, would the King, Biron, and Longueville
　　Were lovers too! Ill to example° ill   *be a precedent for*
120　Would from my forehead wipe a perjured note;[9]
　　For none offend where all alike do dote.
LONGUEVILLE [*stepping forward*]　Dumaine, thy love is far from
　　　charity,°   *Christian love*
　　That in love's grief desir'st society.°   *company*
　　You may look pale, but I should blush, I know,
125　To be o'erheard and taken napping so.
KING [*stepping forward*]　Come, sir, you blush. As his, your case
　　　is such.
　　You chide at him, offending twice as much.
　　You do not love Maria? Longueville
　　Did never sonnet for her sake compile,
130　Nor never lay his wreathèd arms athwart[1]
　　His loving bosom, to keep down his heart?
　　I have been closely° shrouded in this bush   *secretly*
　　And marked you both, and for you both did blush.
　　I heard your guilty rhymes, observed your fashion,
135　Saw sighs reek° from you, noted well your passion.   *rise*
　　"Ay me!" says one. "O Jove!" the other cries.
　　One her hairs were gold, crystal the other's eyes.
　　[*to* LONGUEVILLE] You would for paradise break faith and troth,
　　[*to* DUMAINE] And Jove for your love would infringe an oath.

---

7. Into basins used to catch the blood; by the basinful.
8. Black African (used here in racist fashion to signify ugliness).
9. Inscription (and see Biron's description of Longueville, line 43).
1. Folded arms across. (Folded arms were a sign of love melancholy.)

140   What will Biron say when that he shall hear
      Faith infringèd, which such zeal did swear?
      How will he scorn! How will he spend his wit!
      How will he triumph, leap, and laugh at it!
      For all the wealth that ever I did see,
145   I would not have him know so much by° me.   *about*
      BIRON [*stepping forward*]   Now step I forth to whip hypocrisy.
      Ah, good my liege, I pray thee, pardon me.
      Good heart, what grace hast thou thus to reprove
      These worms for loving, that art most in love?
150   Your eyes do make no coaches° in your tears;   *(ironic: see lines 29–31)*
      There is no certain princess that appears.
      You'll not be perjured; 'tis a hateful thing!
      Tush, none but minstrels like of sonneting!
      But are you not ashamed? Nay, are you not,
155   All three of you, to be thus much o'ershot?°   *wide of the mark*
      [*to* LONGUEVILLE] You found his° mote; the King your mote   *(Dumaine's)*
          did see;
      But I a beam[2] do find in each of three.
      Oh, what a scene of fool'ry have I seen—
      Of sighs, of groans, of sorrow, and of teen!°   *grief*
160   O me, with what strict patience have I sat
      To see a king transformèd to a gnat,
      To see great Hercules whipping a gig,°   *spinning a top*
      And profound Solomon tuning° a jig,   *playing*
      And Nestor[3] play at push-pin° with the boys,   *child's game*
165   And critic Timon[4] laugh at idle toys.°   *foolish fancies*
      Where lies thy grief? Oh, tell me, good Dumaine!
      And gentle Longueville, where lies thy pain?
      And where my liege's? All about the breast.
      A caudle,° ho!   *warm, healing drink*
      KING   Too bitter is thy jest.
170   Are we betrayed thus to thy overview?
      BIRON   Not you by me, but I betrayed to you.
      I that am honest, I that hold it sin
      To break the vow I am engagèd in.
      I am betrayed by keeping company
175   With men like you, men of inconstancy.
      When shall you see me write a thing in rhyme,
      Or groan for Joan, or spend a minute's time
      In pruning me?° When shall you hear that I   *preening myself*
      Will praise a hand, a foot, a face, an eye,
180   A gait, a state,° a brow, a breast, a waist,   *an attitude; bearing*
      A leg, a limb—
              Enter JAQUENETTA [*with a paper*] *and* [COSTARD, *the*]
              clown. [BIRON *catches sight of them and prepares to*
              exit.]
      KING   Soft! Whither away so fast?
      A true° man or a thief that gallops so.   *An honest*
      BIRON   I post° from love. Good lover, let me go.   *hasten*

---

2. Larger defect: "And why beholdest thou the mote
that is in thy brother's eye, but considerest [or "per-
ceivest"] not the beam that is in thine own eye?"
(Matthew 7:3–5; Luke 6:41–42).

3. Homeric hero, a type figure of wise old age; later,
portrayed in Shakespeare's *Troilus and Cressida*.
4. Cynical Greek misanthrope; later, the central
character of Shakespeare's *Timon of Athens*.

JAQUENETTA   God bless the King!

KING   What present° hast thou there?   *writing; gift*

COSTARD   Some certain treason.

185   KING   What makes treason° here?   *is treason doing*

COSTARD   Nay, it makes nothing, sir.

KING   If it mar nothing neither,
The treason and you go in peace away together.

JAQUENETTA   I beseech your grace, let this letter be read.
Our Person misdoubts° it; it was treason, he said.   *suspects*

190   KING   Biron, read it over.
            [BIRON] *reads the letter.*
Where hadst thou it?

JAQUENETTA   Of Costard.

KING   Where hadst thou it?

COSTARD   Of Dun Adramadio,⁵ Dun Adramadio.
            [BIRON *tears up the letter.*]

195   KING   How now? What is in you? Why dost thou tear it?

BIRON   A toy, my liege, a toy. Your grace needs not fear it.

LONGUEVILLE   It did move him to passion, and therefore let's
        hear it.

DUMAINE [*picking up the pieces*]   It is Biron's writing, and here
        is his name.

BIRON [*to* COSTARD]   Ah, you whoreson loggerhead!° You were   *foolish blockhead*
        born to do me shame.

200   [*to the* KING]   Guilty, my lord, guilty! I confess, I confess!

KING   What?

BIRON   That you three fools lacked me, fool, to make up
        the mess.°   *group of four at table*
He, he, and you, and you, my liege, and I,
Are pickpurses° in love, and we deserve to die.   *cheaters*
Oh, dismiss this audience, and I shall tell you more.

DUMAINE   Now the number is even.

205   BIRON   True, true, we are four.
Will these turtles° be gone?   *turtledoves; lovers*

KING   Hence, sirs, away!

COSTARD   Walk aside, the true folk, and let the traitors stay.
            [*Exeunt* COSTARD *and* JAQUENETTA.]

BIRON   Sweet lords, sweet lovers—oh, let us embrace!
As true we are as flesh and blood can be.

210   The sea will ebb and flow; heaven will show his face;
Young blood doth not obey an old decree.
We cannot cross° the cause why we are born;   *oppose*
Therefore of all hands° must we be forsworn.   *in any case*

KING   What? Did these rent° lines show some love of thine?   *torn*

215   BIRON   "Did they?" quoth you. Who sees the heavenly
        Rosaline
That, like a rude° and savage man of Ind°   *an ignorant / India*
At the first opening of the gorgeous East,
Bows not his vassal head and, stricken blind,
Kisses the base ground with obedient breast?

220   What peremptory,° eagle-sighted eye⁶   *determined*

---

5. *Dun:* error for Don meaning "gray-brown," referring to skin color and recalling "tawny Spain"
(1.1.171). *Adramadio:* error for Adriano that encom-

passes "drama," "mad," "amado" ("loved").
6. The eagle, king of birds, was thought to be the
only one able to look directly at the sun.

Dares look upon the heaven of her brow
That is not blinded by her majesty?
KING   What zeal, what fury, hath inspired thee now?
My love, her mistress, is a gracious moon;
225   She an attending star, scarce seen alight.°   *hardly visible*
BIRON   My eyes are then no eyes, nor I Biron.
Oh, but for my love, day would turn to night.
Of all complexions the culled sovereignty°   *those chosen as best*
Do meet as at a fair in her fair cheek,
230   Where several Worthies make one dignity,[7]
Where nothing wants° that want° itself doth seek.   *lacks / desire*
Lend me the flourish of all gentle tongues—
Fie, painted rhetoric! Oh, she needs it not!
To things of sale a seller's praise belongs.
235   She passes praise—then praise too short doth blot.[8]
A withered hermit, fivescore winters worn,
Might shake off fifty looking in her eye.
Beauty doth varnish age, as if new born,
And gives the crutch the cradle's infancy.
240   Oh, 'tis the sun that maketh all things shine!
KING   By heaven, thy love is black as ebony!
BIRON   Is ebony like her? Oh, word divine!
A wife of such wood were felicity.
Oh, who can give an oath? Where is a book?°   *a Bible*
245   That I may swear Beauty doth beauty lack
If that she learn not of her eye to look:[9]
No face is fair that is not full so° black.   *just as*
KING   Oh, paradox! Black is the badge of hell,
The hue of dungeons, and the school of night;[1]
250   And beauty's crest becomes the heavens well.[2]
BIRON   Devils soonest tempt, resembling spirits of light.[3]
Oh, if in black my lady's brows be decked,
It mourns that painting and usurping hair°   *makeup and false hair*
Should ravish doters with a false aspect,
255   And therefore is she born to make black fair.
Her favor° turns the fashion of the days,   *appearance*
For native blood° is counted painting now;   *natural red coloring*
And therefore red, that would avoid dispraise,
Paints itself black to imitate her brow.
260   DUMAINE   To look like her are chimney sweepers black.
LONGUEVILLE   And since her time are colliers counted bright.
KING   And Ethiops of their sweet complexion crack.°   *boast*
DUMAINE   Dark needs no candles now, for dark is light.
BIRON   Your mistresses dare never come in rain,
265   For fear their colors should be washed away.
KING   'Twere good yours did; for, sir, to tell you plain,
I'll find a fairer face not° washed today.   *that has not been*
BIRON   I'll prove her fair, or talk till doomsday here.

7. Various kinds of excellence together produce a single preeminent beauty.
8. Hence praise inevitably falls short and mars her reputation.
9. If beauty doesn't learn from Rosaline's eye how she (beauty) could look.
1. *school:* title. The phrase "school of night" has been supposed to refer to a secret society of Shakespeare's time; alternatively, it may mean that night learns to be black in black's school.
2. (And yet, you say,) the badge of your dark beauty is heavenly (said incredulously).
3. Fair beauties are not to be trusted, "for Satan himself is transformed into an angel of light" (2 Corinthians 11:14).

KING No devil will fright thee, then,° so much as she.   *(at doomsday)*
270 DUMAINE I never knew man hold vile stuff so dear.
  LONGUEVILLE [*indicating his shoe*] Look, here's thy love: my
        foot and her face see.⁴
  BIRON Oh, if the streets were pavèd with thine eyes,
    Her feet were much too dainty for such tread.
  DUMAINE Oh, vile! Then as she goes what upward° lies   *up her dress (bawdy)*
275   The street should see as she walked overhead.
  KING But what of this? Are we not all in love?
  BIRON Nothing so sure—and thereby all forsworn.
  KING Then leave this chat; and, good Biron, now prove
    Our loving lawful and our faith not torn.
280 DUMAINE Ay, marry, there: some flattery° for this evil.   *excuse*
  LONGUEVILLE Oh, some authority how to proceed,
    Some tricks, some quillets° how to cheat the devil.   *verbal tricks*
  DUMAINE Some salve for perjury.°   *oath breaking; purging*
  BIRON   'Tis more than need!°   *really essential*
    Have at you,° then, Affection's° men-at-arms!   *Here goes / Love's*
285 Consider what you first did swear unto:
    To fast, to study, and to see no woman—
    Flat treason against the kingly state of youth!
    Say, can you fast? Your stomachs are too young,
    And abstinence engenders maladies.
290 And where that you have vowed to study, lords,⁵
    In that⁶ each of you have forsworn his book,
    Can you still dream and pore and thereon look?
    For when would you, my lord, or you, or you,
    Have found the ground of study's excellence
295 Without the beauty of a woman's face?
    From women's eyes this doctrine I derive:
    They are the ground, the books, the academes
    From whence doth spring the true Promethean fire.⁷
    Why, universal plodding poisons up
300 The nimble° spirits in the arteries,   *life-giving*
    As motion and long-during° action tires   *long-lasting*
    The sinewy vigor of the traveler.
    Now, for not looking on a woman's face,
    You have in that forsworn the use of eyes,
305 And study, too, the causer of your vow.
    For where is any author in the world
    Teaches such beauty as a woman's eye?
    Learning is but an adjunct to our self,
    And where we are, our learning likewise is.
310 Then when ourselves we see in ladies' eyes,
    With ourselves—
    Do we not likewise see our learning there?
    Oh, we have made a vow to study, lords,
    And in that vow we have forsworn our books.⁸
315 For when would you, my liege, or you, or you,
    In leaden contemplation have found out

---

4. You may see her face in my (black) shoes.
5. TEXTUAL COMMENT For the presence of both a first draft and a revised version of Biron's speech in the following lines, a practice found elsewhere in the play, see Digital Edition TC 9 (Folio edited text).

And where that: And whereas.
6. Inasmuch as; in that vow.
7. Divine fire. In Greek mythology, Prometheus stole fire from heaven and gave it to humanity.
8. Our true books, women's eyes.

Such fiery numbers° as the prompting eyes   *passionate verses*
Of Beauty's tutors have enriched you with?
Other slow arts° entirely keep° the brain,   *disciplines / fill up*
320   And therefore, finding barren practicers,°   *practitioners of the "arts"*
Scarce show a harvest of their° heavy toil.   *(the practicers')*
But love, first learned in a lady's eyes,
Lives not alone immurèd° in the brain,   *only shut up*
But with the motion of all elements[9]
325   Courses° as swift as thought in every power,°   *Flows / faculty*
And gives to every power a double power,
Above° their functions and their offices.°   *Beyond / normal duties*
It adds a precious seeing to the eye:
A lover's eyes will gaze an eagle blind.[1]
330   A lover's ear will hear the lowest sound,
When the suspicious head of theft is stopped.[2]
Love's feeling is more soft and sensible°   *sensitive*
Than are the tender horns of cockled snails.°   *snails with shells*
Love's tongue proves dainty Bacchus° gross in taste.   *Greek god of wine*
335   For valor, is not love a Hercules,
Still° climbing trees in the Hesperides?[3]   *Constantly*
Subtle as Sphinx,[4] as sweet and musical
As bright Apollo's° lute, strung with his hair?   *Greek god of music*
And when love speaks, the voice of all the gods
340   Make heaven drowsy with the harmony.
Never durst poet touch a pen to write,
Until his ink were tempered with love's sighs.
Oh, then his lines would ravish savage ears
And plant in tyrants mild humility.
345   From women's eyes this doctrine I derive:
They sparkle still the right Promethean fire.
They are the books, the arts, the academes,
That show, contain, and nourish all the world,
Else none° at all in aught proves excellent.   *Without them no one*
350   Then fools you were these women to forswear,
Or keeping what is sworn you will prove fools.
For wisdom's sake—a word that all men love—
Or for love's sake—a word that loves[5] all men—
Or for men's sake—the author of these women—
355   Or women's sake—by whom we men are men—
Let us once lose our oaths to find ourselves,[6]
Or else we lose ourselves to keep our oaths.
It is religion to be thus forsworn;
For charity itself fulfills the law,[7]
360   And who can sever love from charity?
    KING   Saint Cupid, then! And, soldiers, to the field!
    BIRON   Advance your standards,° and upon them, lords!   *(with a sexual sense)*
    Pell-mell, down with them! But be first advised

---

9. Earth, air, fire, and water.
1. Can stare at the sun (here, the beloved woman) without injury longer than even an eagle can.
2. When even an alert thief (or someone listening for a thief) hears nothing.
3. Garden of golden apples that Hercules had to pick as his eleventh labor.
4. Monster in Greek mythology that killed travelers who failed to solve her riddle.

5. Meaning is uncertain: is a friend to; values; pleases; inspires with love; is lovable to.
6. "For whosoever will save his life shall lose it: and whosoever will lose his life for my sake shall find it" (Matthew 16:25).
7. "He that loveth another hath fulfilled the law" (Romans 13:8). "Love worketh no ill to his neighbor: therefore is love the fulfilling of the law" (Romans 13:10).

In conflict that you get the sun of them.[8]

365 LONGUEVILLE   Now to plain dealing—lay these glozes° by.   *verbal sophistries*
Shall we resolve to woo these girls of France?
KING   And win them, too. Therefore let us devise
Some entertainment for them in their tents.
BIRON   First, from the park let us conduct them thither.
370 Then, homeward, every man attach° the hand   *seize*
Of his fair mistress. In the afternoon
We will with some strange° pastime solace them,   *novel*
Such as the shortness of the time can shape;
For revels, dances, masques, and merry hours
375 Forerun° fair Love, strewing her way with flowers.   *Run before*
KING   Away, away! No time shall be omitted,
That will by time and may by us be fitted.°   *used well*
BIRON   *Allons, allons!*° Sowed cockle reaps no corn,[9]   *Come on, come on*
And justice always whirls in equal measure.°   *acts impartially*
380 Light° wenches may prove plagues to men forsworn;   *Frivolous*
If so, our copper buys° no better treasure.   *Exeunt.*   *base coin deserves*

5.1 (Q 5.1)
Enter [HOLOFERNES,] *the pedant,* [NATHANIEL, *the*]
curate, and DULL.

HOLOFERNES   *Satis quid sufficit.*[1]
NATHANIEL   I praise God for you, sir. Your reasons° at dinner   *discourses*
have been sharp and sententious, pleasant without scurril-
ity, witty without affectation, audacious without impudency,
5 learned without opinion,° and strange° without heresy. I did   *arrogance / original*
converse this *quondam* day° with a companion of the King's   *the other day*
who is intituled, nominated, or called Don Adriano de
Armado.
HOLOFERNES   *Novi hominem tanquam te.*[2] His humor° is   *temperament*
10 lofty, his discourse peremptory,° his tongue filed,° his eye   *overbearing / polished*
ambitious, his gait majestical, and his general behavior vain,
ridiculous, and thrasonical.[3] He is too picked,° too spruce,   *fastidious*
too affected, too odd, as it were, too peregrinate,° as I may   *exotic*
call it.
15 NATHANIEL   A most singular and choice epithet!
   [*He*] *draw*[s] *out his table-book*° [*and writes in it*].   *notebook*
HOLOFERNES   He draweth out the thread of his verbosity finer
than the staple of his argument.[4] I abhor such fanatical
phantasimes,[5] such insociable and point-device° compan-   *extremely precise*
ions, such rackers of orthography:[6] as to speak "dout" *sine*° "b,"   *without*
20 when he should say "doubt"; "det" when he should pronounce
"debt"—d, e, b, t, not d, e, t. He clepeth° a "calf," "cauf," "half,"   *calls*

---

8. Get the sun in their eyes (get the advantage); also,
probably bawdy, playing on "beget the son."
9. Wheat ("corn") was never reaped where weeds
("cockle") were sown (proverbial): in other words, we
won't get something for nothing; we must make an
effort.
5.1 Location: The King's park.
1. Should be *Satis est quod sufficit:* "Enough is
enough," but recalling the English proverb "Enough
is as good as a feast." The Latin in this scene, some of
it inaccurate, again is translated only when the characters themselves fail to do so. Here, too, it is often
unclear whether the error is the character's, the

printer's, or Shakespeare's.
2. I know the man as well as I know you.
3. Boastful, bragging. From "Thraso," the braggart
soldier in *Eunuchus,* by the Roman dramatist
Terence.
4. He's wordy. (Unintentionally ironic, coming from
Holofernes; "staple" means "fiber," "argument" means
"subject matter.")
5. Extravagant, fantastic beings.
6. Tormentors of spelling. Holofernes speaks for
those educational theorists who urged, unsuccessfully, that English words be spelled and pronounced
like their Latin roots.

"hauf," "neighbor" *vocatur*° "nebor"—"neigh" abbreviated "ne."   *is called*
This is "abhominable," which he would call "abominable." It
insinuateth me of *insanire*[7]—*ne intelligis, domine?*[8]—to make
25   frantic, lunatic.
NATHANIEL   *Laus Deo, bone intelligo.*[9]
HOLOFERNES   "*Bone*"? "*Bone*" for "*bene*"! Priscian a little
scratched;[1] 'twill serve.
      Enter [ARMADO, *the*] *braggart,* [*and* PAGE, *his*] *boy*[,
         with COSTARD].
NATHANIEL   *Videsne quis venit?*°   *Do you see who's coming?*
30   HOLOFERNES   *Video, et gaudio.*°   *I see, and rejoice.*
ARMADO   Chirrah![2]
HOLOFERNES   *Quare*° "Chirrah," not "Sirrah"?   *Why*
ARMADO   Men of peace, well encountered!
HOLOFERNES   Most military sir, salutation!
35   PAGE [*to* COSTARD]   They have been at a great feast of lan-
guages and stolen the scraps.
COSTARD [*to* PAGE]   Oh, they have lived long on the alms-
basket[3] of words. I marvel thy master hath not eaten thee for
a word, for thou art not so long by the head as "*honorific-*
40   *abilitudinitatibus.*"[4] Thou art easier swallowed than a
flap-dragon.[5]
PAGE [*to* COSTARD]   Peace! The peal° begins.   *jangling; babble*
ARMADO [*to* HOLOFERNES]   Monsieur, are you not lettered?°   *learned; literate*
PAGE   Yes, yes, he teaches boys the hornbook.° What is "a, b"   *alphabet book*
45   spelled backward with the horn on his head?°   *as a cuckold*
HOLOFERNES   "Ba," *pueritia,*° with a horn added.   *child(ishness)*
PAGE   Ba, most silly sheep with a horn. You hear his learning?
HOLOFERNES   *Quis, quis,* thou consonant?[6]
PAGE   The last of the five vowels,° if you° repeat them, or the   *"u" / ewe*
50   fifth° if I.   *you*
HOLOFERNES   I will repeat them: a, e, i—
PAGE   The sheep.[7] The other two concludes it: o, u.[8]
ARMADO   Now, by the salt° wave of the *Mediterraneum,* a sweet   *salty; witty*
touch,° a quick venue° of wit! Snip-snap, quick and home![9] It   *hit / thrust*
55   rejoiceth my intellect. True wit—
PAGE   Offered by a child to an old man, which is wit-old.[1]
HOLOFERNES   What is the figure?° What is the figure?   *figure of speech*
PAGE   Horne
HOLOFERNES   Thou disputes like an infant. Go, whip thy gig![9]   *spin your top*
60   PAGE   Lend me your horn to make one, and I will whip about
your infamy *manu cita.*[2] A gig of° a cuckold's horn!   *made of*
COSTARD   An° I had but one penny in the world, thou shouldst   *If*

---

7. Puts me in mind of madness; perhaps, drives me
mad.
8. Don't you understand, master?
9. Praise God, I understand well.
1. *Priscian a little scratched:* imperfect Latin (Priscian
was a sixth-century Latin grammarian). Holofernes is
ridiculing Nathaniel's mistake of using *bone* for *bene*.
2. Pseudo-Spanish or dialectal pronunciation of
"Sirrah"; or garbled Greek for "Hail."
3. Basket in which the leftovers of a feast were collected for the poor.
4. Dative and ablative plural of a Latin word meaning "honorableness," renowned for its length. *word:*
"mote" equals the French *mot,* which means "word."
5. A raisin floated on flaming brandy, which had to

be snapped up with the mouth and eaten in the game
of snapdragon.
6. Nonentity (because a consonant alone is sound-
less). *Quis:* Latin for "who;" also, pronounced "kiss"
and hence referring back to "ba" (lines 46–47), a
sheep's bleat but also meaning "kiss."
7. The Spanish for "sheep"—*oveja,* often spelled
oueia—seems to have been used as a device for memorizing the vowels.
8. Proves what I say (or completes the list): oh, you
(ewe).
9. And to the target.
1. Mentally feeble; "wittol," a contented cuckold.
2. With a swift hand.

have it to buy gingerbread. [*He searches his pockets.*] Hold!
There is the very remuneration I had of thy master, thou
65 halfpenny° purse of wit, thou pigeon egg of discretion. Oh,   *tiny*
an the heavens were so pleased that thou wert but my bastard! What a joyful father wouldst thou make me! Go to,
thou hast it *ad dunghill*, at the fingers' ends,° as they say.   *exactly; (scatological)*
    [*He gives him the coin.*]
HOLOFERNES Oh, I smell false Latin: "*dunghill*" for "*unguem*."°   *fingernail*
70 ARMADO Arts-man, *preambulate*.[3] We will be singled° from   *separated*
the barbarous. [*They withdraw.*] Do you not educate youth
at the charge-house° on the top of the mountain?   *endowed school*
HOLOFERNES Or *mons*, the hill.
ARMADO At your sweet pleasure, for the mountain.
75 HOLOFERNES I do, *sans*° question.   *without*
ARMADO Sir, it is the King's most sweet pleasure and affection°   *wish*
to congratulate° the Princess at her pavilion, in the *posteriors*[4]   *greet*
of this day, which the rude multitude call the afternoon.
HOLOFERNES The "*posterior*" of the day, most generous° sir, is   *noble*
80 liable,° congruent, and measurable° for the afternoon. The   *fitting / suitable*
word is well culled,[5] choice, sweet, and apt,° I do assure you,   *(synonyms)*
sir, I do assure you.
ARMADO Sir, the King is a noble gentleman and my familiar,°   *close friend*
I do assure ye, very good friend. For what is inward° between   *confidential; (sexual?)*
85 us, let it pass—I do beseech thee, remember thy courtesy; I
beseech thee, apparel thy head[6]—and among other impor-
tunate° and most serious designs, and of great import indeed,   *pressing*
too—but let that pass.[7] For I must tell thee, it will please his
grace, by the world, sometime to lean upon my poor shoulder,
90 and with his royal finger thus dally with my excrement°—   *growth of hair; feces*
with my mustachio. But, sweetheart, let that pass. By the
world, I recount no fable. Some certain special honors it
pleaseth his greatness to impart to Armado: a soldier, a man
of travel that hath seen the world. But let that pass. The very
95 all of all° is—but, sweetheart, I do implore secrecy—that   *sum of everything*
the King would have me present the Princess—sweet
chuck!°—with some delightful ostentation,° or show, or pag-   *chick / show*
eant, or antic,° or firework. Now, understanding that the   *grotesque pageant*
curate and your sweet self are good at such eruptions° and   *(scatological)*
100 sudden breaking-out° of mirth, as it were, I have acquainted   *(scatological)*
you withal° to the end to crave your assistance.   *with it*
HOLOFERNES Sir, you shall present before her the Nine Worthies.[8] —Sir Nathaniel, as concerning some entertainment
of° time, some show in the *posterior* of this day, to be ren-   *way of spending*
105 dered by our assistance the King's command, and this most
gallant, illustrate,° and learned gentleman, before the Prin-   *illustrious*
cess, I say none so fit as to present the Nine Worthies!

---

3. Scholar, walk ahead, with a play on "arse"
(behind, rather than "pre-," or ahead).
4. End (temporal and anatomical).
5. With a play on "cul," French for "backside."
6. *remember . . . head:* remember that you removed
your hat in courtesy (perhaps at line 34). I beseech
you, put it back on.
7. Suggestion of sodomy and excrement, developed
in the repeated phrase "but [butt] let that pass" (lines

85, 88, 91, 94).
8. Famous conquerors often represented in folk
plays and pageants. Usually three pagans—Hector,
Alexander, Julius Caesar; three Jews—Joshua, David,
Judas Maccabeus; and three Christians—Arthur,
Charlemagne, and Godfrey of Bouillon or Guy of
Warwick. Of these, only Alexander, Judas Maccabeus, and Hector appear in the next scene; Shakespeare adds Pompey and Hercules.

NATHANIEL   Where will you find men worthy enough to present them?

110   HOLOFERNES   Joshua, yourself;[9] myself—; and this gallant gentleman, Judas Maccabeus. This swain, because of his great limb or joint, shall pass Pompey the Great;[1] the page, Hercules—[2]

ARMADO   Pardon, sir, error! He is not quantity enough for
115   that Worthy's thumb. He is not so big as the end of his club.

HOLOFERNES   Shall I have audience?° He shall present Her-   *attention*
cules in minority.° His *Enter*° and *Exit* shall be strangling a   *childhood / entrance*
snake,[3] and I will have an Apology° for that purpose.   *explanatory speech*

PAGE   An excellent device! So if any of the audience hiss, you
120   may cry, "Well done, Hercules! Now thou crushest the snake!" That is the way to make an offense gracious, though few have the grace to do it.

ARMADO   For the rest of the Worthies?

HOLOFERNES   I will play three myself.

125   PAGE   Thrice-worthy gentleman!

ARMADO   Shall I tell you a thing?

HOLOFERNES   We attend.°   *listen*

ARMADO   We will have, if this fadge° not, an antic. I beseech   *succeed*
you, follow.

130   HOLOFERNES   *Via,*° goodman Dull. Thou hast spoken no word   *Come on*
all this while.

DULL   Nor understood none neither, sir.

HOLOFERNES   *Allons!*° We will employ thee.   *Come on!*

DULL   I'll make one° in a dance or so, or I will play on the   *join*
135   tabor° to the Worthies and let them dance the hay.°   *small drum / reel*

HOLOFERNES   Most Dull, honest Dull! To our sport. Away!

Exeunt.

5.2 (Q 5.2)

Enter ladies [the PRINCESS, MARIA, KATHERINE, *and*
ROSALINE].

PRINCESS   Sweethearts, we shall be rich ere we depart
If fairings° come thus plentifully in.   *gifts*
A lady walled about with diamonds:[1]
Look you what I have from the loving King!
[*She shows them a pendant.*]

5   ROSALINE   Madam, came nothing else along with that?

PRINCESS   Nothing but this? Yes, as much love in rhyme
As would be crammed up in a sheet of paper,
Writ on both sides the leaf, margin and all,
That he was fain to seal on Cupid's name.[2]

10   ROSALINE   That was the way to make his godhead wax,°   *grow; sealing wax*
For he hath been five thousand years° a boy.   *(age of the world)*

KATHERINE   Ay, and a shrewd unhappy gallows,[3] too.

---

9. In the event, Nathaniel plays Alexander.
1. *great . . . Great:* Costard's considerable size enables him to "pass" for Pompey the Great, suggesting "penis" through "limb" or "joint," and, through the jingle with "pump" in "Pompey," both "penis" and "pudendum."
2. TEXTUAL COMMENT For the textual uncertainty here over the casting of the Nine Worthies, see Digital Edition TC 10 (Folio edited text).

3. Hercules strangled two snakes sent by Juno to kill him in his cradle.
5.2 Location: The ladies' lodgings in the King's park.
1. This describes the gift.
2. So that he was obliged to obliterate Cupid's name with his seal.
3. Ill-natured, pernicious gallows bird, deserving to be hanged.

ROSALINE   You'll ne'er be friends with him: 'a° killed your sister.   *he*
KATHERINE   He made her melancholy, sad, and heavy,
15   And so she died. Had she been light like you,
Of such a merry, nimble, stirring spirit,
She might ha' been a grandam ere she died;
And so may you, for a light heart lives long.
ROSALINE   What's your dark° meaning, mouse, of this light°   *covert / careless*
word?
20   KATHERINE   A light° condition in a beauty dark.   *frivolous; wanton*
ROSALINE   We need more light to find your meaning out.
KATHERINE   You'll mar the light by taking it in snuff;⁴
Therefore, I'll darkly end the argument.
ROSALINE   Look what° you do, you do it still i'th' dark.°   *whatever / (bawdy)*
25   KATHERINE   So do not you, for you are a light wench.
ROSALINE   Indeed, I weigh not° you, and therefore light.   *weigh less than*
KATHERINE   You weigh me not? Oh, that's you care not for me!
ROSALINE   Great reason, for past care is still past cure.⁵
PRINCESS   Well bandied both! A set of wit well played.
30   But Rosaline, you have a favor° too.   *love token*
Who sent it, and what is it?
ROSALINE   I would you knew.
An if my face were but as fair as yours,
My favor were as great; be witness this.
   [*She shows them a brooch.*]
Nay, I have verses too, I thank Biron:
35   The numbers° true, and were the numb'ring° too   *meter / evaluation*
I were the fairest goddess on the ground.
I am compared to twenty thousand fairs°—   *beauties*
Oh, he hath drawn my picture in his letter!
PRINCESS   Anything like?
40   ROSALINE   Much in the letters,° nothing in the praise.   *black ink*
PRINCESS   Beauteous as ink°—a good conclusion.   *(that is, black)*
KATHERINE   Fair as a text° "B" in a copybook.   *formally written black*
ROSALINE   'Ware pencils,⁶ ho! Let me not die your debtor,°   *I'll pay you back*
My red dominical,⁷ my golden letter.⁸
45   Oh, that your face were not so full of Os!°   *pockmarks; pudenda*
PRINCESS   A pox of that jest! And I beshrew° all shrews.   *wish mischief upon*
But, Katherine, what was sent to you from fair Dumaine?
KATHERINE   Madame, this glove.
   [*She shows them a glove.*]
PRINCESS   Did he not send you twain?
KATHERINE   Yes, madam, and, moreover,
50   Some thousand verses of a faithful lover:
A huge translation° of hypocrisy,   *expression*
Vilely compiled, profound simplicity!°   *folly*
MARIA   This, and these pearls, to me sent Longueville.
   [*She shows them a letter and a chain of pearls.*]
The letter is too long by half a mile.
55   PRINCESS   I think no less. Dost thou not wish in heart
The chain were longer, and the letter short?

---

4. Taking it amiss; snuffing a candle.
5. Reversing the proverb's normal order: past cure is
past care.
6. Beware of introducing the subject of brushes
(used for cosmetic purposes as well as for drawing

portraits).
7. Red letter marking Sundays and feast days in an
almanac; reference to Katherine's ruddy complexion.
8. Also used to mark Sunday; reference to Katherine's fair hair.

MARIA   Ay, or I would these hands might never part.[9]
PRINCESS   We are wise girls to mock our lovers so.
ROSALINE   They are worse fools to purchase mocking so.
60   That same Biron I'll torture ere I go.
   Oh, that I knew he were but in by th' week,°   *permanently caught*
   How I would make him fawn and beg and seek,
   And wait the season and observe the times,°   *servilely attend on me*
   And spend his prodigal wits in bootless° rhymes,   *fruitless*
65   And shape his service wholly to my device,
   And make him proud to make me proud that jests.[1]
   So, pursuivant°-like, would I o'ersway his state,   *arresting officer*
   That he should be my fool and I his fate.
PRINCESS   None are so surely caught, when they are catched,
70   As wit turned fool. Folly in wisdom hatched
   Hath wisdom's warrant and the help of school
   And wit's own grace to grace a learnèd fool.
ROSALINE   The blood of youth burns not with such excess
   As gravity's° revolt to wantonness.   *a wise person's*
75   MARIA   Folly in fools bears not so strong a note°   *stigma*
   As fool'ry in the wise when wit doth dote,°   *act foolishly*
   Since all the power thereof it doth apply
   To prove, by wit, worth in simplicity.°   *folly*
   Enter BOYET.
PRINCESS   Here comes Boyet, and mirth is in his face.
80   BOYET   Oh, I am stabbed with laughter! Where's her grace?
PRINCESS   Thy news, Boyet?
BOYET   Prepare, madam, prepare!
   Arm, wenches, arm! Encounters mounted are°   *An attack is prepared*
   Against your peace. Love doth approach disguised,
   Armed in arguments—you'll be surprised!°   *taken by surprise attack*
85   Muster your wits; stand in your own defense;
   Or hide your heads like cowards and fly hence.
PRINCESS   Saint Denis to Saint Cupid![2] What are they
   That charge° their breath against us? Say, scout, say.   *level (a weapon)*
BOYET   Under the cool shade of a sycamore
90   I thought to close mine eyes some half an hour,
   When, lo, to interrupt my purposed rest,
   Toward that shade I might behold addressed°   *I could see approaching*
   The King and his companions. Warily,
   I stole into a neighbor thicket by
95   And overheard what you shall overhear:°   *hear over again*
   That, by and by, disguised they will be here!
   Their herald is a pretty knavish page,
   That well by heart hath conned his embassage.°   *learned his message*
   Action and accent° did they teach him there: *Gesture and intonation*
100   "Thus must thou speak, and thus thy body bear,"
   And ever and anon they made a doubt,°   *expressed fear*
   Presence majestical would put him out.°   *make him forget his lines*
   "For," quoth the King, "an angel shalt thou see.
   Yet fear not thou, but speak audaciously."

9. Perhaps she has twisted the chain around them;   and be glad to be ridiculed.
or, she'd never separate her hands to give one hand in   2. St. Denis (the patron saint of France) against St.
marriage to so ungenerous a man.   Cupid.
1. And be pleased to praise the one who mocks him;

105   The boy replied: "An angel is not evil.
    I should have feared her had she been a devil."
    With that, all laughed and clapped him on the shoulder,
    Making the bold wag by their praises bolder.
    One rubbed his elbow[3] thus, and fleered,° and swore   *grinned*
110   A better speech was never spoke before.
    Another with his finger and his thumb°   *(snapping his fingers)*
    Cried "*Via!*° We will do't, come what will come!"   *Come on!*
    The third he capered and cried, "All goes well!"
    The fourth turned on the toe° and down he fell.   *did a pirouette*
115   With that, they all did tumble on the ground,
    With such a zealous laughter, so profound,
    That in this spleen ridiculous° appears,   *absurd fit (of laughter)*
    To check their folly, passion's solemn tears.
    PRINCESS   But what, but what? Come they to visit us?
120   BOYET   They do, they do, and are appareled thus,[4]
    Like Muscovites or Russians, as I guess.
    Their purpose is to parley, to court, and dance,
    And every one his love-suit will advance
    Unto his several° mistress, which they'll know   *particular*
125   By favors several which they did bestow.
    PRINCESS   And will they so? The gallants shall be tasked;°   *put to the test*
    For, ladies, we will everyone be masked;
    And not a man of them shall have the grace,°   *luck*
    Despite of suit,° to see a lady's face.   *pleading; costume*
130   Hold, Rosaline! This favor thou shalt wear,
    And then the King will court thee for his dear.
    Hold, take thou this, my sweet, and give me thine.
        [*They exchange favors.*]
    So shall Biron take me for Rosaline.
    [*to* MARIA *and* KATHERINE] And change your favors too. So
        shall your loves
135   Woo contrary, deceived by these removes.°   *exchanges*
        [*They exchange favors.*]
    ROSALINE   Come on, then. Wear the favors most in sight.°   *conspicuously*
    KATHERINE   But in this changing what is your intent?
    PRINCESS   The effect of my intent is to cross theirs.
    They do it but in mocking merriment,°   *satirical mirth*
140   And mock for mock is only my intent.
    Their several counsels° they unbosom shall   *confidences*
    To loves mistook, and so be mocked withal
    Upon the next occasion that we meet,
    With visages displayed, to talk and greet.
145   ROSALINE   But shall we dance if they desire us to't?
    PRINCESS   No, to the death we will not move a foot;
    Nor to their penned speech render we no grace,
    But while 'tis spoke each turn away her face.
    BOYET   Why, that contempt will kill the speaker's heart,
150   And quite divorce his memory from his part!
    PRINCESS   Therefore I do it; and I make no doubt,
    The rest will ne'er come in if he be out.[5]

---

3. Sign of satisfaction.
4. Absence of a rhyme for "guess" and a referent for "thus" suggests that a line describing the lords' cos-tumes has been lost.
5. The rest of his prepared speech will be forgotten if he's confused ("out" of his part).

There's no such sport as sport by sport o'erthrown,
To make theirs ours and ours none but our own.
155 So shall we stay, mocking intended game,
And they, well mocked, depart away with shame.
           Sound [trumpet].
BOYET The trumpet sounds. Be masked! The maskers come!
           [The ladies put on their masks.]
           *Enter Black[a]moors with music,⁶ the boy [PAGE] with
           a speech, and the rest of the lords [LONGUEVILLE,
           DUMAINE, BIRON, and the KING] disguised.*
PAGE   "All hail, the richest beauties on the earth!"
BIRON [*aside*] Beauties no richer than rich taffeta.°   (*masks of taffeta*)
160 PAGE   "A holy parcel° of the fairest dames   *party*
           That ever turned—
           The ladies turn their backs to him.
                       their backs to mortal views."
BIRON   Their "eyes," villain, their "eyes"!
PAGE   "That ever turned their eyes to mortal views.
           Out—"
165 BOYET   True: "out,"° indeed!   (*of his part*)
PAGE   "Out of your favors, heavenly spirits,
           Vouchsafe° not to behold—"   *Be willing*
BIRON   "Once to behold," rogue!
PAGE   "Once to behold, with your sun-beamed eyes—
170 With your sun-beamed eyes—"
BOYET   They will not answer to that epithet.
           You were best call it "daughter-beamed eyes."
PAGE [*to BIRON*] They do not mark° me, and that brings me out!   *listen to*
BIRON   Is this your perfectness?° Begone, you rogue!   (*in saying your lines*)
                                         [Exit PAGE.]
           [The ladies turn to face the maskers.]
175 ROSALINE [*as the PRINCESS*]⁷ What would these strangers?°   *foreigners*
           Know their minds, Boyet.
           If they do speak our language, 'tis our will
           That some plain° man recount their purposes.   *plainspoken*
           Know what they would.
BOYET   What would you with the Princess?
180 BIRON   Nothing but peace and gentle visitation.°   *visiting*
ROSALINE   What would they, say they?
BOYET   Nothing but peace and gentle visitation.
ROSALINE   Why, that they have, and bid them so be gone.
BOYET   She says you have it, and you may be gone.
185 KING   Say to her, we have measured° many miles   *paced*
           To tread a measure° with you on this grass.   *dance*
BOYET   They say that they have measured many a mile
           To tread a measure with you on this grass.
ROSALINE   It is not so. Ask them how many inches
190 Is in one mile. If they have measured many,
           The measure, then, of one is eas'ly told.°   *counted*
BOYET   If to come hither you have measured miles,
           And many miles, the Princess bids you tell

---

6. Presumably non-speaking musicians dressed as
black Africans to provide an exotic accompaniment
(see Introduction).

7. From here to line 230, Rosaline speaks as the
Princess.

How many inches doth fill up one mile.
195 BIRON Tell her we measure them by weary steps.
BOYET She hears herself.
ROSALINE [*to* BIRON]   How many weary steps,
Of many weary miles you have o'ergone,
Are numbered in the travel of one mile?
BIRON We number nothing that we spend for you.
200 Our duty is so rich, so infinite,
That we may do it still° without account.°   *always / reckoning*
Vouchsafe to show the sunshine of your face,
That we, like savages, may worship it.
ROSALINE My face is but a moon,[8] and clouded° too.   *masked; dark*
205 KING Blessèd are clouds, to do as such clouds do!
Vouchsafe, bright moon—and these thy stars°—to shine,   *companions*
Those clouds removed, upon our watery eyne.°   *eyes*
ROSALINE O vain petitioner, beg a greater matter:
Thou now requests but moonshine in the water.°   *nothing*
210 KING Then in our measure vouchsafe but one change.[9]
Thou bidd'st me beg; this begging is not strange.°   *odd; foreign*
ROSALINE Play music, then! Nay, you must do it soon.
Not yet? No dance! Thus change I like the moon.
                    [*Music plays.*]
KING Will you not dance? How come you thus estranged?
215 ROSALINE You took the moon at full, but now she's changed.
KING Yet still she is the moon, and I the man.[1]
The music plays. Vouchsafe some motion° to it.   *movement; response*
ROSALINE Our ears vouchsafe it—
KING   But your legs should do it.
ROSALINE Since you are strangers, and come here by chance,
We'll not be nice.° Take hands.   *coy*
                    [*The ladies take the men by the hand.*]
220   We will not dance.
KING Why take you hands, then?
ROSALINE   Only to part friends.
—Curtsy, sweethearts, and so the measure ends.
                    [*The ladies curtsy and disengage their hands. The
                    music ceases.*]
KING More measure° of this measure! Be not nice.   *A larger amount*
ROSALINE We can afford no more at such a price.
225 KING Price you yourselves. What buys your company?
ROSALINE Your absence only.
KING   That can never be.
ROSALINE Then cannot we be bought; and so, adieu—
Twice to your visor, and half once to you.[2]
KING If you deny to dance, let's hold more chat.
ROSALINE In private, then.
230 KING   I am best pleased with that.
                    [*They converse apart.*]
BIRON White-handed mistress, one sweet word with thee.

---

8. Because it shines with a borrowed light.
9. Of the moon; of the figure in the dance; *measure:* dance.
1. *the man:* (in the moon). A line rhyming with

"man" seems to have dropped out.
2. Perhaps: your masked ("visor") (double) face deserves two farewells, but yourself less than one (for behaving so foolishly).

PRINCESS [*as* ROSALINE]   "Honey" and "milk" and "sugar":
  there is three.
BIRON   Nay, then, two treys,° an if you grow so nice:°   *threes (dice) / subtle*
  "Metheglin," "wort," and "malmsey"°—well run, dice!   *(three sweet drinks)*
  There's half-a-dozen sweets.
235 PRINCESS   Seventh sweet, adieu.
  Since you can cog,° I'll play no more with you.   *cheat (at dice)*
BIRON   One word in secret.
PRINCESS   Let it not be sweet.
BIRON   Thou griev'st my gall.°   *chafe my sore place*
PRINCESS   Gall?° Bitter.   *Liver bile*
BIRON   Therefore meet.°   *fitting; (let's meet?)*
  [*They converse apart.*]
DUMAINE   Will you vouchsafe with me to change a word?°   *exchange words*
MARIA [*as* KATHERINE]   Name it.
DUMAINE   Fair lady—
240 MARIA   Say you so? Fair lord!
  Take you that for° your "Fair lady."   *in exchange for*
DUMAINE   Please it you
  As much in private, and I'll bid adieu.
  [*They converse apart.*]
KATHERINE [*as* MARIA]   What, was your visor made without a
  tongue?[3]
LONGUEVILLE   I know the reason, lady, why you ask.
245 KATHERINE   Oh, for your reason! Quickly, sir, I long.
LONGUEVILLE   You have a double tongue within your mask,
  And would afford my speechless visor half.[4]
KATHERINE   "Veal!" quoth the Dutchman. Is not veal a calf?[5]
LONGUEVILLE   A calf, fair lady?
KATHERINE   No, a fair lord-calf.°   *dolt*
LONGUEVILLE   Let's part the word.°   *compromise*
250 KATHERINE   No, I'll not be your half.[6]
  Take all and wean° it: it may prove an ox.[7]   *raise*
LONGUEVILLE   Look how you butt° yourself in these sharp mocks.   *attack*
  Will you give horns,[8] chaste lady? Do not so.
KATHERINE   Then die a calf before your horns do grow.
255 LONGUEVILLE   One word in private with you ere I die.°   *have an orgasm*
KATHERINE   Bleat softly, then: the butcher hears you cry.
  [*They converse apart.*]
BOYET [*aside*]   The tongues of mocking wenches are as keen
  As is the razor's edge—invisible,
  Cutting a smaller hair than may be seen.
260 Above the sense of sense, so sensible[9]

---

3. A projection within a mask permitting it to be held in place with the mouth. Katherine is also alluding to Longueville's silence.
4. *You . . . half:* You are double-tongued (masked; punning; deceptive; speaking enough for two) and ask about my silence because you wish to give up half your speech by giving me one of the tongues (the one that keeps her mask on; this would reveal her identity).
5. *"Veal":* Well (ironic: Dutch pronunciation of "well" or German *viel*, meaning "much"; "Dutch" could mean "German"); veil (mask). Combined with Katherine's previous word, "long" (line 245), the result is "Longueville"—thus demonstrating that she

knows the identity of her disguised suitor and had anticipated his "half" (line 247) by uttering half his name. *Veau,* French for "veal," does also mean "calf" (a dunce in Renaissance English).
6. Taking "part" as "divide": half of what you are the other half of; your better half (your wife); half of "calf" ("ca," for "Katherine").
7. Dolt; castrated male.
8. Butt with horns; equip with horns; cuckold.
9. *Above . . . sense:* Above the power of the senses to apprehend (perhaps with the ironic meaning of "non-sense"); *so sensible:* so acutely felt by the hearer.

Seemeth their conference.° Their conceits° have wings   *conversation / fancies*
Fleeter than arrows, bullets, wind, thought—swifter things.
ROSALINE [*coming forward*]   Not one word more, my maids.
    Break off! Break off!
      [*The* PRINCESS, MARIA, *and* KATHERINE
        join ROSALINE.]
BIRON   By heaven, all dry-beaten with pure scoff!¹
265 KING   Farewell, mad wenches. You have simple wits!
           Exeunt [*the* KING, LONGUEVILLE, DUMAINE,
               and BIRON *with the Blackamoors*].
    [*The ladies unmask.*]
PRINCESS   Twenty adieus, my frozen Muscovites.
    Are these the breed of wits so wondered at?°   *admired*
BOYET   Tapers they are, with° your sweet breaths puffed out.°   *by / extinguished*
ROSALINE   Well-liking° wits they have—gross, gross, fat, fat!   *Plump*
270 PRINCESS   Oh, poverty in wit! Kingly-poor flout!²
    Will they not, think you, hang themselves tonight,
    Or ever but in visors show their faces?
    This pert Biron was out of count'nance° quite.   *disconcerted; masked*
ROSALINE   They were all in lamentable cases.°   *states; outfits*
275   The King was weeping-ripe for a good word.³
PRINCESS   Biron did swear himself out of all suit.⁴
MARIA   Dumaine was at my service, and his sword.
    "*Non point*,"° quoth I—my servant straight was mute.   *Not at all; it's blunt*
KATHERINE   Lord Longueville said I came o'er his heart,
    And trow you° what he called me?   *can you believe*
280 PRINCESS   "Qualm,"⁵ perhaps?
KATHERINE   Yes, in good faith.
PRINCESS   Go, sickness as thou art!
ROSALINE   Well, better wits have worn plain statute-caps.⁶
    But will you hear? The King is my love sworn.
PRINCESS   And quick Biron hath plighted faith to me.
285 KATHERINE   And Longueville was for my service born.
MARIA   Dumaine is mine as sure as bark on tree.
BOYET   Madam, and pretty mistresses, give ear:
    Immediately they will again be here
    In their own shapes,° for it can never be   *Undisguised*
290   They will digest° this harsh indignity.   *accept*
PRINCESS   Will they return?
BOYET   They will, they will, God knows;
    And leap for joy, though they are lame with blows.
    Therefore, change favors, and, when they repair,°   *return*
    Blow° like sweet roses in this summer air.   *Bloom*
295 PRINCESS   How "blow"? How "blow"? Speak to be understood!
BOYET   Fair ladies masked are roses in their bud;
    Dismasked—their damask sweet commixture⁷ shown—
    Are angels vailing° clouds, or roses blown.°   *letting fall / blooming*

---

1. Soundly beaten without bloodshed; battered by mocking words.
2. Reversed wordplay ("kingly-poor") on "well-li-king" (or like-king," line 269), possibly criticizing Rosaline's "flout" (gibe) but probably the King's (line 265).
3. The beginning of a sixteen-line dialogue sonnet. *weeping-ripe for*: near tears for lack of.
4. Avowed his passion—beyond all reason; out of character for his Russian "suit" (costume); in a mis-taken "suit" at love (to the wrong woman).
5. Heartburn: perhaps punning on "came" (line 279) and picked up in "Go" (line 281).
6. Cleverer people have been ordinary apprentices (whose headwear was regulated by statute); perhaps an allusion to fancy caps forming part of the lords' disguise.
7. Sweet red and white complexion.

PRINCESS   Avaunt, perplexity!° What shall we do   *Be off, riddler!*
300   If they return in their own shapes to woo?
ROSALINE   Good madam, if by me you'll be advised,
        Let's mock them still, as well known[8] as disguised.
        Let us complain to them what fools were here,
        Disguised like Muscovites in shapeless gear,°   *ill-cut clothes*
305   And wonder what they were, and to what end
        Their shallow shows, and prologue vilely penned,
        And their rough carriage° so ridiculous   *awkward manner*
        Should be presented at our tent to us.
BOYET   Ladies, withdraw: the gallants are at hand.
310   PRINCESS   Whip to our tents, as roes° run o'er land.   *deer*

        Exeunt [the PRINCESS, ROSALINE,
               MARIA, *and* KATHERINE].
    Enter the KING *and the rest [*LONGUEVILLE, DUMAINE,
    and BIRON, *as themselves*].

KING   Fair sir, God save you! Where's the Princess?
BOYET   Gone to her tent. Please it your majesty,
        Command me any service to her?
KING   That she vouchsafe me audience for one word.
315   BOYET   I will, and so will she, I know, my lord.   *Exit.*
BIRON   This fellow picks up wit as pigeons peas,
        And utters° it again when Jove doth please.   *speaks; sells*
        He is wit's peddler, and retails his wares
        At wakes and wassails,° meetings, markets, fairs;   *festivals and revels*
320   And we that sell by gross,° the Lord doth know,   *wholesale*
        Have not the grace to grace it with such show.
        This gallant pins the wenches on his sleeve;°   *attracts all the girls*
        Had he been Adam, he had° tempted Eve!   *would have*
        He can carve,[9] too, and lisp.° Why, this is he   *speak affectedly*
325   That kissed away his hand in courtesy.
        This is the ape of form,° Monsieur the Nice,°   *good form / fastidious*
        That when he plays at tables° chides the dice   *backgammon*
        In honorable° terms. Nay, he can sing   *polite*
        A mean most meanly,[1] and in ushering°   *as a gentleman usher*
330   Mend° him who can. The ladies call him "Sweet";   *Improve on*
        The stairs as he treads on them kiss his feet.
        This is the flower that smiles on everyone
        To show his teeth as white as whale's bone,°   *walrus ivory*
        And consciences that will not die in debt
335   Pay him the duty of "Honey-tongued Boyet."
KING   A blister on his sweet tongue, with my heart,
        That put Armado's page out of his part!

    *Enter [*BOYET *with] the ladies [*MARIA, KATHERINE,
    and ROSALINE, *and the* PRINCESS].

BIRON   See where it° comes! Behavior,° what wert thou   *(Boyet) / Fine manners*
        Till this madman° showed thee, and what art thou now?   *madcap*
340   KING   All hail, sweet madam, and fair time of day!
PRINCESS   "Fair" in "All hail"° is foul, as I conceive.   *(as in "hailstorm")*
KING   Construe my speeches better, if you may.
PRINCESS   Then wish me better—I will give you leave.

---

8. Let's mock them just as much now that they are
known for themselves.
9. He can act with social grace, flirt.

1. *he . . . meanly:* he can sing an in-between vocal
part (tenor or alto) in the appropriate way (make himself generally useful).

KING   We came to visit you, and purpose now[2]
345   To lead you to our court. Vouchsafe it, then.
PRINCESS   This field shall hold me, and so hold your vow.
Nor° God nor I delights in perjured men.   *Neither*
KING   Rebuke me not for that which you provoke:
The virtue° of your eye must break my oath.   *power*
350   PRINCESS   You nickname virtue;° "vice" you should have spoke,   *misname goodness*
For virtue's office° never breaks men's troth.   *action*
Now, by my maiden honor—yet as pure
As the unsullied lily—I protest,
A world of torments though I should endure,
355   I would not yield to be your house's guest.
So much I hate a breaking cause° to be   *cause of breaking*
Of heavenly oaths, vowed with integrity.
KING   Oh, you have lived in desolation here,
Unseen, unvisited, much to our shame.
360   PRINCESS   Not so, my lord; it is not so, I swear.
We have had pastimes here, and pleasant game.
A mess of° Russians left us but of late.   *group of four*
KING   How, madam? Russians?
PRINCESS   Ay, in truth, my lord:
Trim° gallants, full of courtship and of state.°   *Elegant / dignity*
365   ROSALINE   Madam, speak true! —It is not so, my lord.
My lady, to the manner of the days,°   *in the present fashion*
In courtesy gives undeserving praise.
We four, indeed, confronted were with four
In Russian habit. Here they stayed an hour
370   And talked apace; and in that hour, my lord,
They did not bless us with one happy° word!   *well-chosen*
I dare not call them fools, but this I think:
When they are thirsty, fools would fain have drink.°   *They are fools*
BIRON [aside]   This jest is dry° to me. —Gentle sweet,   *barren (punning)*
375   Your wits makes wise things foolish. When we greet,
With eyes' best seeing, heaven's fiery eye,
By light we lose light.[3] Your capacity
Is of that nature, that, to° your huge store,   *compared to*
Wise things seem foolish and rich things but poor.
380   ROSALINE   This proves you wise and rich, for in my eye—
BIRON   I am a fool and full of poverty.
ROSALINE   But that you take what doth to you belong,
It were a fault to snatch words from my tongue.
BIRON   Oh, I am yours, and all that I possess.
ROSALINE   All the fool mine?
385   BIRON   I cannot give you less.
ROSALINE   Which of the visors was it that you wore?
BIRON   Where? When? What visor? Why demand° you this?   *ask*
ROSALINE   There, then, that visor: that superfluous case°   *mask*
That hid the worse and showed the better face.
390   KING [aside]   We are descried!° They'll mock us now downright.   *uncovered*
DUMAINE [aside]   Let us confess and turn it to a jest.
PRINCESS   Amazed, my lord? Why looks your highness sad?

2. The beginning of another dialogue sonnet (lines   3. When we gaze intently at the sun, we go blind.
344–57).

ROSALINE Help! Hold his° brows! He'll swoon. Why look you   (Biron's)
    pale?
    Seasick, I think, coming from Muscovy!
395 BIRON Thus pour the stars down plagues for perjury.
    Can any face of brass° hold longer out?   brazen shamelessness
    Here stand I, lady. Dart thy skill at me;
    Bruise me with scorn; confound me with a flout;°   put-down
    Thrust thy sharp wit quite through my ignorance;
400 Cut me to pieces with thy keen conceit;°   intelligence
    And I will wish° thee never more to dance,   invite
    Nor never more in Russian habit wait.°   attend on you
    Oh, never will I trust to speeches penned,[4]
    Nor to the motion of a schoolboy's tongue,
405 Nor never come in visor to my friend,°   sweetheart
    Nor woo in rhyme, like a blind harper's song.
    Taffeta phrases, silken terms precise,
    Three-piled° hyperboles, spruce affectation,   Rich velvet; elaborate
    Figures° pedantical—these summer flies   (of speech)
410 Have blown me full of maggot ostentation.°   laid maggot eggs in me
    I do forswear them, and I here protest
    By this white glove—how white the hand, God knows!—
    Henceforth my wooing mind shall be expressed
    In russet° "yeas" and honest kersey° "noes."   homely / plain
415 And to begin: wench, so God help me, law!°   indeed (humble oath)
    My love to thee is sound, sans° crack or flaw.   without
ROSALINE Sans "sans," I pray you!
BIRON   Yet° I have a trick°   Still / touch
    Of the old rage.° Bear with me: I am sick.   fever
    I'll leave it by degrees. Soft, let us see:
420 Write "Lord, have mercy on us"[5] on those three.°   (his companions)
    They are infected; in their hearts it lies.
    They have the plague and caught it of your eyes.
    These lords are visited;° you are not free,   afflicted by plague
    For the lords' tokens° on you do I see.   favors; plague spots
425 PRINCESS No, they are free[6] that gave these tokens to us.
BIRON Our states are forfeit.[7] Seek not to undo us![8]
ROSALINE It is not so; for how can this be true
    That you stand forfeit, being those that sue?°   sue at law; beg; woo
BIRON Peace! For I will not have to do° with you.   deal; copulate
430 ROSALINE Nor shall not, if I do as I intend.
BIRON [to the KING, DUMAINE, and LONGUEVILLE] Speak for
    yourselves. My wit is at an end.
KING Teach us, sweet madam, for our rude transgression
    Some fair excuse.
PRINCESS   The fairest is confession.
    Were you not here, but even now, disguised?
KING Madam, I was.
435 PRINCESS   And were you well advised?°   in your right mind

---

4. The beginning of a sonnet (lines 403–16)—ironic, considering Biron's renunciation of literary effects.
5. A common inscription on the doors of plague-visited houses.
6. Generous; at liberty; free of love; free of obligation.
7. (Denying the Princess's claim in line 425 that the men are "free"): Our estates are subject to confisca-

tion; our condition as bachelors is ended; because we're in love, we've lost power over ourselves; as would-be husbands, we owe you our estates; we've acted dishonorably.
8. Don't undo our forfeiture (don't ruin us) by calling us "free" (by rejecting our love).

KING   I was, fair madam.

PRINCESS   When you then were here,
What did you whisper in your lady's ear?

KING   That more than all the world I did respect° her.   *value*

PRINCESS   When she shall challenge° this you will reject her.   *assert her claim to*

KING   Upon mine honor, no.

440   PRINCESS   Peace, peace! Forbear!
Your oath once broke, you force not° to forswear.   *find it easy*

KING   Despise me when I break this oath of mine!

PRINCESS   I will, and therefore keep it. —Rosaline,
What did the Russian whisper in your ear?

445   ROSALINE   Madam, he swore that he did hold me dear
As precious eyesight, and did value me
Above this world, adding thereto, moreover,
That he would wed me or else die my lover.

PRINCESS   God give thee joy of him! The noble lord

450   Most honorably doth uphold his word.
[*She joins their hands together.*]

KING   What mean you, madam? By my life, my troth,
I never swore this lady such an oath.

ROSALINE   By heaven, you did; and to confirm it plain,
You gave me this [*indicating a love token*], but take it, sir,
again.

455   KING   My faith, and this, the Princess I did give.
I knew her by this jewel on her sleeve.

PRINCESS   Pardon me, sir, this jewel did she wear;
And lord Biron, I thank him, is my dear.
[*to* BIRON] What, will you have me or your pearl again?

460   BIRON   Neither of either;° I remit° both twain.   *the two / surrender*
I see the trick on't.° Here was a consent,°   *of it / plot*
Knowing aforehand of our merriment,
To dash it like a Christmas comedy.
Some carry-tale, some please-man, some slight zany,

465   Some mumble-news, some trencher-knight, some Dick,[9]
That smiles his cheek in years° and knows the trick   *into wrinkles*
To make my lady laugh when she's disposed,
Told our intents before, which, once disclosed,
The ladies did change favors, and then we,

470   Following the signs, wooed but the sign of she.°   *each mistress*
Now to our perjury to add more terror,
We are again forsworn in will° and error!°   *willfully / mistakenly*
Much upon this 'tis.[1] [*He seizes* BOYET.] And might not you
Forestall° our sport, to make us thus untrue?   *Have undermined*

475   Do not you know my lady's foot by th' square,[2]
And laugh upon the apple[3] of her eye,
And stand between her back, sir, and the fire,°   *keep the heat from her*
Holding a trencher,° jesting merrily?   *serving plate*
You put our page out—

9. *carry-tale:* talebearer; *please-man:* toady; *zany:* clownish, rustic servant in commedia dell'arte; *mumble-news:* gossip; *trencher-knight:* parasite, who dines from his lord's dish ("trencher") or who has a lordly appetite; *Dick:* low fellow.
1. It happened very much like this.

2. Know how to please your mistress. *square:* a carpenter's rule (Boyet "has her measure"); possible pun on "squire" (an "apple-squire" was a pimp; see "apple," line 476 and note).
3. Pupil. Boyet can wittily catch the Princess's eye; he is on intimate terms with her.

[*At a sign from the* PRINCESS, *he releases* BOYET.]
          Go, you are allowed.°   *privileged (as a fool)*
480   Die when you will, a smock[4] shall be your shroud.
     You leer upon° me, do you? There's an eye   *look malevolently at*
     Wounds like a leaden sword.°   *harmless stage sword*
BOYET   Full merrily
     Hath this brave manège, this career, been run.
BIRON   Lo, he is tilting straight.[5] Peace! I have done.
        Enter [COSTARD, *the*] *clown.*
485   Welcome, Pure Wit. Thou part'st a fair fray.
COSTARD   O Lord, sir, they would know
     Whether the three Worthies shall come in, or no?
BIRON   What, are there but three?
COSTARD   No, sir, but it is vara° fine,   *very*
     For every one pursents° three.   *(re)presents*
BIRON   And three times thrice is nine.
490 COSTARD   Not so, sir—under° correction, sir, I hope it is not so.   *subject to*
     You cannot beg us,° sir. I can assure you, sir, we know what   *show we're fools*
       we know.
     I hope, sir, three times thrice, sir—
BIRON   Is not nine?
COSTARD   Under correction, sir, we know whereuntil° it doth   *to what*
     amount.
495 BIRON   By Jove, I always took three threes for nine.
COSTARD   O Lord, sir, it were pity you should get your living
     by reckoning,[6] sir.
BIRON   How much is it?
COSTARD   O Lord, sir, the parties themselves—the actors,
500   sir—will show whereuntil it doth amount. For mine own
     part, I am, as they say, but to perfect° one man in one poor   *present*
     man: Pompion[7] the Great, sir.
BIRON   Art thou one of the Worthies?
COSTARD   It pleased them to think me worthy of Pompey the
505   Great. For mine own part, I know not the degree° of the   *rank*
     Worthy, but I am to stand for him.
BIRON   Go! Bid them prepare.
COSTARD   We will turn it finely off,° sir. We will take some care.   *perform it*
                              Exit.
KING   Biron, they will shame us. Let them not approach.
510 BIRON   We are shame-proof, my lord; and 'tis some policy°   *clever strategy*
     To have one show worse than the King's and his company.
KING   I say they shall not come.
PRINCESS   Nay, my good lord, let me o'errule you now:
     That sport best pleases that doth least know how.
515   Where zeal strives to content, and the contents
     Dies in the zeal of that which it presents,[8]
     Their form confounded makes most form in mirth,[9]
     When great things laboring° perish in their birth.   *(to be born)*

---

4. Woman's garment (either a charge of effeminacy or equivalent to "women will be the death of you").
5. Jousting (linguistically) at once; *manège* (line 483): feat of horsemanship; *career*: short gallop at full speed.
6. It would be a shame if you had to earn your living by arithmetic.
7. Pumpkin (blunder for "Pompey").
8. *and . . . presents*: and the enthusiasm of those who present the play is fatal to the substance.
9. Artistry defeated produces the greatest comic effect.

BIRON   A right description of our sport,° my lord.   *(the Russian masque)*
    Enter [ARMADO, *the*] *braggart*[, *with a paper*].
520 ARMADO [*to the* KING]   Anointed,° I implore so much expense   *Anointed one*
    of thy royal sweet breath as will utter a brace° of words.   *pair*
    [ARMADO *and the* KING *talk apart.*]
PRINCESS   Doth this man serve God?
BIRON   Why ask you?
PRINCESS   He speaks not like a man of God's making.
525 ARMADO [*to the* KING]   That's all one, my fair, sweet, honey
    monarch; for, I protest, the schoolmaster is exceeding
    fantastical—too, too vain, too, too vain. But we will put it, as
    they say, to *fortuna de la guerre.*° [*He gives him a paper.*] I wish   *the fortune of war*
    you the peace of mind, most royal couplement.   [*Exit.*]
530 KING [*reading*]   Here is like to be a good presence of Worthies.
    He presents Hector of Troy; the swain, Pompey the Great;
    the parish curate, Alexander; Armado's page, Hercules; the
    pedant, Judas Maccabeus.
    An if these four Worthies in their first show thrive,
535   These four will change habits° and present the other five!   *costumes*
BIRON   There is five in the first show.
KING   You are deceived; 'tis not so.
BIRON   The pedant, the braggart, the hedge-priest,° the fool,   *illiterate priest*
    and the boy.
540 Abate throw at novum[1] and the whole world again
    Cannot prick out five such, take each one in 's vein.°   *characteristic manner*
KING   The ship is under sail and here she comes amain.°   *at full speed*
    Enter [COSTARD *as*] *Pompey.*
COSTARD   "I Pompey am—"
BIRON   You lie: you are not he.
COSTARD   "I Pompey am—"
BOYET   With leopard's head on knee.[2]
545 BIRON   Well said, old mocker! I must needs be friends with
    thee.
COSTARD   "I Pompey am, Pompey surnamed 'the Big'°—"   *(sexual)*
DUMAINE   "The Great."
COSTARD [*to* DUMAINE]   It is "Great," sir.
    "—Pompey surnamed 'the Great,'
550 That oft in field, with targe and shield, did make my foe to
    sweat;[3]
    And traveling along this coast, I here am come by chance,
    And lay my arms before the legs° of this sweet lass of France."   *(bawdy)*
    [*He sets down his sword and shield.*]
    [*to the* PRINCESS]   If your ladyship would say, "Thanks,
    Pompey," I had done.
555 PRINCESS   Great thanks, great Pompey.
COSTARD   'Tis not so much worth, but I hope I was perfect.° I   *I recited correctly*
    made a little fault in "Great."
BIRON   My hat to a halfpenny,° Pompey proves the best Worthy!   *I'll bet anything*
    [COSTARD *stands aside.*]
    Enter [NATHANIEL, *the*] *curate, for Alexander.*

---

1. Barring a lucky chance in the dice game of novum (in which the main throws were five and nine—like the five actors playing the Nine Worthies).
2. Embossed either on the knee piece of his armor or on his shield, which he might then be holding upside down; or Biron's "You lie" (line 543) may indicate that

Costard has fallen down.
3. The first of three lines in fourteeners (fourteen-syllable lines)—an archaic meter by the 1590s, like most of those used by the non-aristocratic characters. *targe:* shield.

NATHANIEL   "When in the world I lived, I was the world's
    commander.
560   By east, west, north, and south, I spread my conquering
    might.
    My scutcheon° plain° declares that I am Alisander."   *coat of arms / clearly*
BOYET   Your nose says no, you are not, for it stands too right.[4]
BIRON [*to* BOYET]   Your nose smells "no"[5] in this, most tender-
    smelling° knight.   *sensitive-to-smell*
PRINCESS   The conqueror is dismayed. Proceed, good Alexander.
565   NATHANIEL   "When in the world I lived, I was the world's
    commander—"
BOYET   Most true, 'tis right. You were so, Alisander.
BIRON   Pompey the Great!
COSTARD [*comes forward*]   Your servant—and Costard!
BIRON   Take away the conqueror! Take away Alisander!
570   COSTARD   O sir, you have overthrown Alisander the Con-
    queror. [*to* NATHANIEL] You will be scraped out of the painted
    cloth[6] for this. Your lion, that holds his pole-axe, sitting on a
    close stool, will be given to Ajax.[7] He will be the ninth Wor-
    thy. A conqueror and afraid to speak? Run away, for shame,
575   Alisander!   [*Exit* NATHANIEL.]
    There, an't° shall please you: a foolish mild man—an honest   *if it*
    man, look you, and soon dashed. He is a marvelous good
    neighbor, in sooth, and a very good bowler, but for Alisander?
    Alas, you see how 'tis: a little o'er-parted.° But there are Wor-   *given too hard a role*
580   thies a-coming will speak their mind in some other sort.
PRINCESS   Stand aside, good Pompey.
      [COSTARD *withdraws.*]
      Enter [HOLOFERNES, *the*] *pedant, for Judas, and*
      [PAGE,] *the boy, for Hercules.*
HOLOFERNES   "Great Hercules is presented by this imp,°   *child*
    Whose club killed Cerberus, that three-headed *canus*;[8]
    And when he was a babe, a child, a shrimp,
585   Thus did he strangle serpents in his *manus*.[9]
    Quoniam,° he seemeth in minority,°   *Since / a child*
    Ergo,° I come with this Apology."   *Therefore*
    [*to* PAGE] Keep some state° in thy exit and vanish.   *dignity*
                Exit [PAGE, *the*] *boy.*
    "Judas I am—"
590   DUMAINE   A Judas?
HOLOFERNES [*to* DUMAINE]   Not Iscariot, sir.
    "Judas I am, ycleped° 'Maccabeus'—"   *named*
DUMAINE   "Judas Maccabeus" clipped° is plain "Judas."   *shortened; circumcised*
BIRON   A kissing traitor![1] How° art thou proud, Judas?   *Why*
595   HOLOFERNES   "Judas I am—"
DUMAINE   The more shame for you, Judas!

4. Straight (alluding to Alexander's reputed crooked
neck).
5. Implying that Nathaniel smells bad; according to
the Greek biographer Plutarch, Alexander was
reputed to have "a marvelous good savor" (Thomas
North's translation).
6. Referring to the practice of representing the Worthies on wall hangings.
7. Alexander's arms, which showed a lion holding a
battle-ax (or penis) and seated (a "close-stool" is a
toilet), will be given to another warrior, Ajax (punning

on "a jakes," a toilet), a Greek hero from the Trojan
War who coveted the armor of Achilles. See 4.3.6 and
note.
8. In classical mythology, the three-headed watch-
dog ("canis") of Hades.
9. Hands; pronounced "máy-ness," hence punning on
"anus."
1. Alluding to the kiss with which Judas Iscariot
betrayed Jesus, with a pun on "clipped" (embraced,
kissed), itself punning on "ycleped" (lines 592–93).

HOLOFERNES What mean you, sir?

BOYET To make Judas hang himself.

HOLOFERNES Begin,° sir; you are my elder.   *Hang yourself first*

600 BIRON Well followed: Judas was hanged on an elder.°   *(tree)*

HOLOFERNES I will not be put out of countenance.°   *be upset*

BIRON Because thou hast no face.°   *countenance*

HOLOFERNES What is this?[2]

BOYET A cittern head.°   *guitar*

605 DUMAINE The head of a bodkin.°   *hairpin; small dagger*

BIRON A death's-face° in a ring.   *death's head*

LONGUEVILLE The face of an old Roman coin, scarce seen.°   *worn down*

BOYET The pommel° of Caesar's falchion.°   *handle / sword*

DUMAINE The carved-bone face on a flask.°   *gunpowder horn*

610 BIRON Saint George's half-cheek° in a brooch.   *profile*

DUMAINE Ay, and in a brooch of lead.°   *(indicating low rank)*

BIRON Ay, and worn in the cap of a tooth-drawer.[3] [*to*
HOLOFERNES] And now forward, for we have put thee in
countenance.°   *depicted you*

615 HOLOFERNES You have put me out of countenance.

BIRON False! We have given thee faces.

HOLOFERNES But you have outfaced° them all.   *mocked*

BIRON An thou wert a lion, we would do so.

BOYET Therefore, as he is an ass,[4] let him go.

620 And so, adieu, sweet Jude. Nay, why dost thou stay?

DUMAINE For the latter end of his name.

BIRON For the "ass" to the "Jude"? Give it him: Jud-as, away![5]

HOLOFERNES This is not generous,° not gentle,° not humble.[6]   *noble / courteous*
[*Exit.*]

BOYET [*calling after him*] A light for Monsieur Judas! It grows
dark; he may stumble.

625 PRINCESS Alas, poor Maccabeus! How hath he been baited!
Enter [ARMADO, *the*] *braggart*[, *as Hector*].

BIRON Hide thy head, Achilles![7] Here comes Hector in arms.

DUMAINE Though my mocks come home by° me, I will now   *later rebound on*
be merry.

KING Hector was but a Trojan[8] in respect of° this.   *in comparison with*

BOYET But is this Hector?

630 KING I think Hector was not so clean-timbered.°   *well built*

LONGUEVILLE His leg is too big for Hector.

DUMAINE More calf,° certain.   *part of the leg; fool*

BOYET No, he is best endued° in the small.°   *endowed / (below the calf)*

BIRON This cannot be Hector.

635 DUMAINE He's a god or a painter, for he makes faces.°   *grimaces; creates life*

ARMADO "The armipotent° Mars, of lances the almighty,   *powerful in arms*
Gave Hector a gift—"

DUMAINE A gilt nutmeg.[9]

---

2. Indicating his face. The replies refer to ornamental faces on objects.
3. Worn by a lowly dentist as a sign of his trade.
4. An ass disguises himself as a lion in one of Aesop's fables—only to have his own nature undo him. "Ass" in the sense of "backside" is punningly evoked by "end" (line 621).
5. *As*, in "Jud-as," is "the latter end of his name" (line 621), but "end" also means "ass."
6. PERFORMANCE COMMENT For more on this line, see Digital Edition PC 1.

7. Leading Greek hero in the Trojan War; Hector's chief opponent and slayer in Homer, but his inferior and a coward in *Troilus and Cressida*.
8. An ordinary guy (slang).
9. A nutmeg glazed with egg yolk, used, like "lemon" and "cloves" (lines 639, 640), to flavor drinks. A common lover's gift, the "gilt nutmeg" may also allude to Armado's makeup. "Lemon" perhaps puns on "leman" (lover, sweetheart), in which case "cloven" (line 641) would have a sexual innuendo.

BIRON   A lemon.

640   LONGUEVILLE   Stuck with cloves.

DUMAINE   No, cloven.

ARMADO   "The armipotent Mars, of lances the almighty,
　　Gave Hector a gift, the heir of Ilion;° 　　　　　　　　　　　　　*Troy*
　　A man so breathed,° that certain he would fight—yea, 　　　　　*fit*

645　　From morn till night, out of his pavilion.° 　　　　　　*jousting tent*
　　I am that flower—"

DUMAINE 　　　　　　　　That mint.

LONGUEVILLE 　　　　　　　　　　That columbine.

ARMADO   Sweet Lord Longueville, rein thy tongue!

LONGUEVILLE   I must rather give it the rein, for it runs° against 　　*jousts; races; speaks*
　　Hector.

650   DUMAINE   Ay, and Hector's a greyhound.[1]

ARMADO   The sweet war-man is dead and rotten. Sweet chucks,
　　beat not the bones of the buried! When he breathed he was a
　　man—but I will forward with my device.° [*to the* PRINCESS] 　　*performance*
　　Sweet royalty, bestow on me the sense of hearing.
　　　　　BIRON *steps forth*[, *but the* PRINCESS *ignores him*].

655   PRINCESS   Speak, brave Hector. We are much delighted.

ARMADO [*bowing*]   I do adore thy sweet grace's slipper.

BOYET   Loves her by the foot.

DUMAINE   He may not by the yard.° 　　　　　　　　　*penis (slang)*

ARMADO   "This Hector far surmounted Hannibal.[2]

660　The party is gone°— " 　　　　　　　　　　　　*Hector is dead*

COSTARD [*coming forward*]   Fellow Hector, she is gone! She
　　is two months on her way.[3]

ARMADO   What meanest thou?

COSTARD   Faith, unless you play the honest Trojan, the poor

665　wench is cast away. She's quick!° The child brags in her belly 　　*pregnant*
　　already: 'tis yours.° 　　　　　　　　　　　*(because it brags)*

ARMADO   Dost thou infamonize° me among potentates? Thou 　　*defame (a coinage)*
　　shalt die.

COSTARD   Then° shall Hector be whipped for Jaquenetta that 　　*In that case*

670　is quick by him, and hanged for Pompey that is dead by him.[4]

DUMAINE   Most rare Pompey!

BOYET   Renowned Pompey!

BIRON   Greater than great, great, great, great Pompey! Pom-
　　pey the Huge!° 　　　　　　　　　　　　　*(bawdy)*

675   DUMAINE   Hector trembles.

BIRON   Pompey is moved. More, Ates,° more, Ates! Stir them 　　*goddess of discord*
　　on! Stir them on!

DUMAINE   Hector will challenge him.

BIRON   Ay, if 'a° have no more man's blood in 's belly than will 　　*he*

680　sup° a flea. 　　　　　　　　　　　　　　　*feed*

ARMADO   By the North Pole, I do challenge thee.

COSTARD   I will not fight with a pole, like a northern° man. I'll 　　*an uncivilized (Scot)*
　　slash; I'll do it by the sword. I pray you, let me borrow my
　　arms° again. 　　　　　　　　　　　　*(from the Princess)*

---

1. Famous as a runner; "Hector" was a common
name for a greyhound.
2. Surpassed Hannibal, leader of Carthage against
Rome (with the unintentional homosexual innuendo
of "surmounted").
3. Jaquenetta is two months pregnant. Since at most

only a few days seem to have passed in the aristocratic plot, it is possible to infer that Costard is the
actual father; but this may be an example of Shakespearean double time.
4. Whom Armado has killed; whose hopes of Jaquenetta Armado has killed.

685   DUMAINE   Room for the incensed Worthies!
    COSTARD   I'll do it in my shirt.
    DUMAINE   Most resolute Pompey!
    PAGE [*to* ARMADO]   Master, let me take you a buttonhole
        lower.⁵ Do you not see? Pompey is uncasing° for the combat.   *undressing*
690   [ARMADO *backs away.*] What mean you? You will lose your
        reputation.
    ARMADO   Gentlemen and soldiers, pardon me. I will not com-
        bat in my shirt.
    DUMAINE   You may not deny it. Pompey hath made the
695   challenge.
    ARMADO   Sweet bloods,° I both may and will.   *men of fiery spirit*
    BIRON   What reason have you for't?
    ARMADO   The naked truth of it is, I have no shirt. I go wool-
        ward for penance.⁶
700   PAGE   True, and it was enjoined him in Rome° for want of linen.   *center of Catholicism*
        Since when, I'll be sworn, he wore none but a dishclout° of   *dishcloth*
        Jaquenetta's, and that he wears next his heart for a favor.
            Enter a messenger, Monsieur MARCADÉ.⁷
    MARCADÉ   God save you, madam,
    PRINCESS   Welcome, Marcadé—
        But that thou interruptest our merriment.
705   MARCADÉ   I am sorry, madam, for the news I bring
        Is heavy in my tongue. The King your father—
    PRINCESS   Dead, for° my life!   *upon*
    MARCADÉ   Even so. My tale is told.
    BIRON   Worthies, away! The scene begins to cloud.
    ARMADO   For mine own part, I breathe free breath. I have
710   seen the day of wrong through the little hole of discretion,
        and I will right myself like a soldier.⁸
            Exeunt Worthies [ARMADO, COSTARD, *and the* PAGE].
    KING   How fares your majesty?°   *(her new title)*
    QUEEN   Boyet, prepare! I will away tonight.
    KING   Madam, not so. I do beseech you: stay.
715   QUEEN   Prepare, I say! —I thank you, gracious lords,
        For all your fair endeavors, and entreat,
        Out of a new-sad soul, that you vouchsafe
        In your rich wisdom to excuse or hide°   *overlook*
        The liberal° opposition of our spirits.   *unrestrained*
720   If over-boldly we have borne ourselves
        In the converse of breath,° your gentleness°   *conversation / courtesy*
        Was guilty of it.° [*to the* KING] Farewell, worthy lord.   *Gave us license*
        A heavy heart bears not a humble tongue.
        Excuse me so, coming so short of thanks
725   For my great suit, so easily obtained.⁹
    KING   The extreme parts of time extremely forms
        All causes to the purpose of his speed,¹
        And often at his very loose° decides   *the last moment*

5. Help you to take off your doublet; take you down a
peg or two (both proverbial).
6. He has no linen between his wool outer garments
and his skin—a form of Catholic self-punishment.
7. Associated with the *danse macabre*, the dance of
death; possibly Mercury, the classical messenger of
the gods and guide of souls to the underworld; perhaps also Mar-Arcadia, a reminder that death enters

even the pastoral, Arcadian world of Navarre's park.
8. I have enough sense to acknowledge my wrongdoing and will honorably put myself in the right.
9. Even though there is no mention of the suit after
2.1, we must assume that it was settled.
1. *The extreme . . . speed:* Final moments enforce
rapid decisions.

	That which long process could not arbitrate;	
730	And though the mourning brow of progeny	
	Forbid the smiling courtesy of love	
	The holy suit° which fain it would convince,°	*marriage / give proof of*
	Yet since love's argument was first° on foot,	*already*
	Let not the cloud of sorrow jostle it	
735	From what it purposed, since to wail friends lost	
	Is not by much so wholesome-profitable	
	As to rejoice at friends but newly found.	

QUEEN I understand you not; my griefs are double.[2]

BIRON Honest plain words best pierce the ears of grief,
740 And by these badges° understand the King.   *signs; words*
    For your fair sakes have we neglected time,
    Played foul-play with our oaths. Your beauty, ladies,
    Hath much deformed us, fashioning our humors
    Even to the opposèd end of our intents;[3]
745 And what in us hath seemed ridiculous—
    As love is full of unbefitting strains,°   *impulses*
    All wanton° as a child, skipping and vain,   *careless*
    Formed by the eye, and therefore, like the eye,
    Full of straying shapes, of habits, and of forms,
750 Varying in subjects as the eye doth roll
    To every varied object in his glance—
    Which parti-coated° presence of loose° love   *foolish / unrestrained*
    Put on by us, if in your heavenly eyes
    Have misbecomed° our oaths and gravities,   *been unbecoming to*
755 Those heavenly eyes that look into these faults
    Suggested° us to make. Therefore, ladies,   *Tempted*
    Our love being yours, the error that love makes
    Is likewise yours. We to ourselves prove false
    By being once false, forever to be true
760 To those that make us both—fair ladies, you;
    And even that falsehood, in itself a sin,
    Thus purifies itself and turns to grace.

QUEEN We have received your letters full of love,
    Your favors, the ambassadors of love,
765 And in our maiden counsel rated them
    At° courtship, pleasant jest, and courtesy,   *As*
    As bombast[4] and as lining to the time;
    But more devout° than this in our respects°   *serious / consideration*
    Have we not been, and therefore met your loves
770 In their own fashion, like a merriment.

DUMAINE Our letters, madam, showed much more than jest.

LONGUEVILLE So did our looks.

ROSALINE   We did not quote° them so.   *interpret*

KING Now, at the latest minute of the hour,
    Grant us your loves.

QUEEN   A time, methinks, too short
775 To make a world-without-end° bargain in.   *an everlasting (biblical)*
    No, no, my lord, your grace is perjured much,
    Full of dear° guiltiness, and therefore this: *grievous; precious*
    If for my love—as there is no such cause[5]—

---

2. Doubled because I cannot understand you.
3. *fashioning . . . intents*: distorting our behavior into the opposite of what we intended.
4. Wool stuffing for clothes; inflated rhetoric.
5. No reason why you should feel obliged to do so.

You will do aught,° this shall you do for me: *anything*
780   Your oath I will not trust, but go with speed
        To some forlorn and naked hermitage,
        Remote from all the pleasures of the world.
        There stay until the twelve celestial signs°   *(of the zodiac)*
        Have brought about their annual reckoning.
785   If this austere insociable life
        Change not your offer, made in heat of blood—
        If frosts and fasts, hard lodging and thin weeds°   *clothes*
        Nip not the gaudy blossoms of your love,
        But that it bear this trial and last° love—   *remain*
790   Then, at the expiration of the year,
        Come challenge° me, challenge me by these deserts;   *claim*
            [*She takes his hand.*]
        And by this virgin palm, now kissing thine,
        I will be thine; and till that instant shut
        My woeful self up in a mourning-house,
795   Raining the tears of lamentation
        For the remembrance of my father's death.
        If this thou do deny, let our hands part;
        Neither entitled in the other's heart.
    KING   If this, or more than this, I would deny,
800   To flatter up° these powers of mine with rest,   *So as to pamper*
        The sudden hand of death close up mine eye.
        Hence hermit,° then! My heart is in thy breast.   *I'm off to be a hermit*
            [*They converse apart.*]
    BIRON   And what to me, my love, and what to me?
    ROSALINE   You must be purged too. Your sins are racked;
805   You are attaint° with faults and perjury.   *dishonored; infected*
        Therefore, if you my favor mean to get,
        A twelvemonth shall you spend and never rest,
        But seek the weary beds of people sick.
    DUMAINE   But what to me, my love, but what to me?
810 KATHERINE   A wife? A beard,[6] fair health, and honesty,
        With threefold love: I wish you all these three.
    DUMAINE   Oh, shall I say, "I thank you, gentle wife"?
    KATHERINE   Not so, my lord. A twelvemonth and a day
        I'll mark no words that smooth-faced wooers say.
815   Come when the King doth to my lady come.
        Then if I have much love, I'll give you some.
    DUMAINE   I'll serve thee true and faithfully till then.
    KATHERINE   Yet swear not, lest ye be forsworn again.
    LONGUEVILLE   What says Maria?
    MARIA   At the twelvemonth's end,
820   I'll change my black gown for a faithful friend.°   *lover*
    LONGUEVILLE   I'll stay° with patience, but the time is long.   *wait*
    MARIA   The liker you: few taller are so young.[7]
    BIRON   Studies my lady?° Mistress, look on me.   *Are you preoccupied*
        Behold the window of my heart, mine eye.
825   What humble suit attends° thy answer there?   *waits for*
        Impose some service on me for thy love.
    ROSALINE   Oft have I heard of you, my lord Biron,

---

6. Implying that he looks immature; perhaps also that as a hermit he'll grow a beard.

7. The more like you—although tall ("long"), you are still young.

Before I saw you, and the world's large tongue
Proclaims you for a man replete with mocks,
830 Full of comparisons° and wounding flouts,   *satirical similes*
Which you on all estates° will execute   *classes of people*
That lie within the mercy of your wit.
To weed this wormwood° from your fruitful brain,   *bitterness*
And therewithal to win me, if you please—
835 Without the which I am not to be won—
You shall this twelvemonth term, from day to day,
Visit the speechless sick and still converse°   *always associate*
With groaning wretches; and your task shall be,
With all the fierce° endeavor of your wit,   *forceful*
840 To enforce the painèd impotent° to smile.   *the sick*
  BIRON   To move wild laughter in the throat of death?
    It cannot be; it is impossible.
    Mirth cannot move a soul in agony.
  ROSALINE   Why, that's the way to choke a gibing spirit,
845   Whose influence is begot of that loose grace°   *uncritical acceptance*
    Which shallow laughing hearers give to fools.
    A jest's prosperity lies in the ear
    Of him that hears it, never in the tongue
    Of him that makes it. Then, if sickly ears,
850   Deafed with the clamors of their own dear groans,
    Will hear your idle scorns, continue then,
    And I will have you and that fault withal;°   *as well*
    But if they will not, throw away that spirit,
    And I shall find you empty of that fault,
855   Right joyful of your reformation.
  BIRON   A twelvemonth? Well, befall what will befall,
    I'll jest a twelvemonth in an hospital.
        [*The* KING *and* QUEEN *come forward.*]
  QUEEN   Ay, sweet my lord, and so I take my leave.
  KING   No, madam, we will bring° you on your way.   *escort*
860   BIRON   Our wooing doth not end like an old play:
    Jack hath not Jill. These ladies' courtesy
    Might well have made our sport a comedy.
  KING   Come, sir, it wants° a twelvemonth and a day,   *lacks*
    And then 'twill end.
  BIRON   That's too long for a play.
        Enter [ARMADO, *the*] *braggart.*
865   ARMADO   Sweet majesty, vouchsafe me—
        [*He approaches the* KING.]
  QUEEN   Was not that Hector?
  DUMAINE   The worthy knight of Troy.
  ARMADO   I will kiss thy royal finger and take leave.
    I am a votary: I have vowed to Jaquenetta
    To hold the plough° for her sweet love three years.   *To farm (bawdy)*
870   But, most esteemed greatness, will you hear the dialogue°   *debate*
    that the two learned men[8] have compiled in praise of the owl
    and the cuckoo? It should have followed in the end of our
    show.
  KING   Call them forth quickly. We will do so.

---

8. Holofernes and Nathaniel (?).

875 ARMADO Holla! Approach!

    Enter all [HOLOFERNES, NATHANIEL, COSTARD, *the*
      PAGE, DULL, *and* JAQUENETTA].

    This side is Hiems, winter; this Ver, the spring: the one main-
    tained° by the owl, t'other by the cuckoo. Ver, begin!   *supported*
                       The Song.

SPRING [*sings*]   When daisies pied and violets blue[9]
        And cuckoo-buds° of yellow hue   *(buttercups?)*
880   And lady-smocks,° all silver-white,   *cuckoo flowers*
        Do paint the meadows with delight,
        The cuckoo, then, on every tree,
        Mocks married men, for thus sings he:
        "Cuckoo!
885   Cuckoo! Cuckoo!" Oh, word of fear,[1]
        Unpleasing to a married ear.

        When shepherds pipe on oaten straws,
        And merry larks are ploughmen's clocks,
        When turtles tread,° and rooks and daws,   *turtledoves mate*
890   And maidens bleach their summer smocks,
        The cuckoo, then, on every tree,
        Mocks married men, for thus sings he:
        "Cuckoo!
        Cuckoo! Cuckoo!" Oh, word of fear,
895   Unpleasing to a married ear.

WINTER [*sings*]   When icicles hang by the wall,
        And Dick the shepherd blows his nail,[2]
        And Tom bears logs into the hall,
        And milk comes frozen home in pail,
900   When blood is nipped° and ways° be foul,   *chilled / pathways*
        Then nightly sings the staring owl:
        "Tu-whit, tu-whoo!"[3]
        A merry note,
        While greasy Joan doth keel° the pot.   *stir to cool*

905   When all aloud the wind doth blow,
        And coughing drowns the parson's saw,°   *moralizing*
        And birds sit brooding in the snow,
        And Marian's nose looks red and raw,
        When roasted crabs° hiss in the bowl,°   *crab apples / (of ale)*
910   Then nightly sings the staring owl:
        "Tu-whit, tu-whoo!"
        A merry note,
        While greasy Joan doth keel the pot.

    ARMADO   The words of Mercury are harsh
915   After the songs of Apollo.[4]
    You that way; we this way.[5]   *Exeunt.*

---

9. The dialogue is in iambic tetrameter, a song meter. *pied*: multicolored.
1. Because it sounds like "cuckold."
2. Blows on his hands to keep warm; is idle.
3. Perhaps: to it (a hunting cry, with possible sexual overtones), to woo; or: to wit, to woo (two central themes of the play).
4. Presumably the love poetry of the King and court-

iers. *words of Mercury*: probably referring to Marcadé's somber message. (See note to the stage direction following line 702.)
5. This line may distinguish the audience ("you") from the actors ("we"), the aristocratic from the humbler characters, the French ladies from the inhabitants of Navarre, or even the actor playing Spring from the one playing Winter.

A Midsummer Night's Dream

How secure is the borderline, the seventeenth-century French philosopher Blaise Pascal wondered, that divides daylight reality from the illusions of dreams? Since dreams generally have very little continuity from night to night and even from moment to moment, their effect upon us, compared to the stability of the waking world, is relatively slight. But, he observed, given their vivid intensity, all it would take would be consistency in dreaming to blur the boundaries: "If an artisan were sure to dream every night for twelve hours' duration that he was a king, I believe he would be almost as happy as a king, who should dream every night for twelve hours on end that he was an artisan." The most one can say, Pascal concluded, is that "life is a dream a little less inconstant."

Weaving its way along the borderline between reality and dream, *A Midsummer Night's Dream* eschews even so modest a conclusion. The characters, to be sure, draw many sharp distinctions—between waking and sleep, men and women, aristocrats and commoners, humans and animals, mortals and fairies. But though none of these distinctions disappears in the course of the play—on the contrary, they are constantly insisted upon—the comedy deftly and subtly calls them into question. How do you know whether you are sleeping or awake? What makes you certain that the boundaries of your identity are secure? Perhaps such questioning particularly befits a play written by an actor, part of a small all-male troupe accustomed to doubling and shifting roles rapidly across the whole spectrum of real and imagined existence.

Some scholars have speculated that the comedy's original occasion was an aristocratic wedding in an English country house, perhaps with the Queen herself in attendance, so that when, at the end of the play-within-the-play, the stage brides and grooms exit to consummate their marriage, the real newlyweds, amid the blessings and sly jokes of their guests, would also have retired to bed. But though a hall-of-mirrors event of this kind is plausible, there is no historical evidence that *A Midsummer Night's Dream* was ever performed at, let alone written expressly for, such a wedding. What we do know is that it was repeatedly performed on the London stage: the title page of the First Quarto says that it "hath been sundry times publikely acted" by the Lord Chamberlain's Men and that it was written by William Shakespeare.

The precise date that *A Midsummer Night's Dream* was written and first performed is unknown; the Elizabethan writer Francis Meres mentions it admiringly in 1598, and certain of its stylistic features have led many scholars to place it around 1594–96, the probable period of the comparably lyrical *Romeo and Juliet* and *Richard II*. Attempts to find more precise coordinates by locating an allusion to a particular royal progress in Oberon's lines about the "fair vestal thronèd by the west" (2.1.158)* or to a particular wet season in Titania's lines about the miserable weather (2.1.88ff) have been defeated by the frequency of both Queen Elizabeth's travels and English rainstorms.

Shakespeare's comedy has been beloved for more than four centuries. To be sure, there have been a few dissenters: the diarist Samuel Pepys wrote after seeing a production in 1662 that "it is the most insipid ridiculous play that ever I saw in my life," though he took note of "some good dancing and some handsome women." Most audiences have been vastly more enthusiastic. The play has inspired musical compositions,

---

*All quotations are taken from the edited text of the Quarto, printed here. The Digital Edition includes edited texts of both the Quarto and the Folio.

Cupid and his victims. From Gilles Corrozet, *Hecatomgraphie* (1540).

of which Felix Mendelssohn's Overture in E Major is the most celebrated, along with famously lavish productions. By the nineteenth century, it was routinely staged on gorgeous sets, with twinkling lights, fairies rising on midnight mushrooms, the moon shining over the Acropolis, and live rabbits hopping across carpets of flowers. But *A Midsummer Night's Dream* has proved equally at home in the simplest of settings. Generations of schoolchildren have romped through cardboard forests, while in Peter Brook's influential 1970 production for the Royal Shakespeare Company the actors performed (often on trapeze) in a three-sided, brightly lit, bare white box.

Shakespeare's visionary poetic drama appeals to an unusually broad spectrum of spectators. Though the play depicts the private pleasures of the elite, it does so with the resources of the public stage. Its humor crosses all boundaries. If it mocks working-class artisans (skilled craftsmen who are simply called "the rabble" in one Quarto stage direction), it also laughs at well-born young lovers. If it ridicules the folly of mortals, it also takes pleasure in the blunders of fairies. If it poses cunning philosophical riddles, it also delights in farce.

The language of *A Midsummer Night's Dream* reflects an unusually high incidence of the tropes familiar to those who had received advanced rhetorical and literary training, but you do not have to know the Greek names for these tropes—*anaphora, isocolon, anadiplosis,* and the like—to enjoy their effects. The Elizabethan rhetorician George Puttenham characterized the mere repetition of words—*epizeuxis*—as "a very foolish impertinency of speech," but familiarity with rhetorical handbooks is not required to know that Bottom's attempt at grand passion—

> O grim-looked night, O night with hue so black,
> O night, which ever art when day is not,
> O night, O night, alack, alack, alack . . .
>
> (5.1.168–70)

—sounds asinine. Nor do you need to have read Puttenham's subtle advice for creating musical effects in language to savor the ravishing harmonies of Oberon's words:

> once I sat upon a promontory
> And heard a mermaid on a dolphin's back
> Uttering such dulcet and harmonious breath
> That the rude sea grew civil at her song
> And certain stars shot madly from their spheres
> To hear the sea-maid's music.
>
> (2.1.149–54)

All you need to do is read the words aloud for yourself.

Let us consider, as one further example of Shakespeare's ability to make sophisticated rhetorical schemes accessible, the exchange between Lysander and Hermia in the wake of Egeus's attempt to block their betrothal:

> LYSANDER   The course of true love never did run smooth,
>   But either it was different in blood—
> HERMIA   Oh, cross! Too high to be enthralled to low.
> LYSANDER   Or else misgraffèd in respect of years—

HERMIA   Oh, spite! Too old to be engaged to young.
LYSANDER   Or else it stood upon the choice of friends—
HERMIA   Oh, hell! To choose love by another's eyes.
                                                (1.1.134–40)

The alternation of carefully calibrated single lines, or *stichomythia,* is a scheme that Shakespeare borrowed from the Roman playwright Seneca and used in different ways in many of his plays. The effect here is to convey the lovers' mutual anguish, tingeing it slightly perhaps with a gently ironic distance that evaporates in the poignant lament that follows (lines 141–49).

These rhetorical devices, along with the subtle modulations from blank verse to rhymed couplets to boisterous comic prose, are so deftly handled that their pleasures are accessible to the learned and unlearned alike. This breadth also reflects the very wide range of cultural materials that the playwright has cunningly woven together— from the classical heritage of the educated elite to popular ballads, from court culture to folklore, from refined and sophisticated entertainments to the coarser delights of burlesque.

There is no single literary source for *A Midsummer Night's Dream,* but Shakespeare is indebted for the legendary Theseus and Hippolyta to Thomas North's translation (1579) of Plutarch's *Lives of the Noble Grecians and Romans,* and still more to Chaucer's *Knight's Tale.* The play repeatedly echoes Chaucer's references to observing "the rite of May," a folk custom still current in Elizabethan England and quite possibly known to Shakespeare personally. To the dismay of Puritans, who regarded the celebration as a lascivious remnant of paganism, young men and women of all classes would go out into the woods and fields to welcome the May with singing and dancing. Shakespeare's title associates this custom with another occasion for festive release: Midsummer Eve (June 23), when the solstice was marked by holiday license and by tales of fairy spells and temporary madness.

Some Elizabethan aristocrats kept theatrical troupes as liveried servants, along with young pages who could sing and perform; and powerful magnates, both secular and religious, often had plays, masquerades, and elaborate shows staged in their houses. From this milieu Shakespeare derives a vision of what we can call the revels of power—performances designed to entertain, gratify, and reflect the values of those at the top of society. From this milieu, too, Shakespeare absorbs a sense of social hierarchy: a distinction between Duke Theseus, at once imperious and genteel, and Egeus, wealthy but distinctly lower in rank and harping on what is his by law, along with a more marked distinction between these characters and the artisans, members of the lower orders, regarded by their social superiors with condescending indulgence.

The artisans—or "rude mechanicals," as they are called—enable Shakespeare to introduce wonderful swoops into earthy prose, snatches of jigs, a comical taste for the grotesque, a glimpse of a world that usually resides beyond the horizon of courtly vision. The lovers at the pinnacle of the play's society do not know the names and trades of the "[h]ard-handed men that work in Athens here" (5.1.72) who have come to offer them entertainment, but we the audience do, and we even know something of their hopes, fears, and dreams. We know that young Francis Flute the bellows-mender has (or thinks he has) a beard coming; that Snug the joiner worries that he is a slow learner; that Bottom the weaver wants to play all the parts. As with the Pageant of the Nine Worthies in *Love's Labor's Lost,* we are invited at once to join in the mockery of the inept performers and to distance ourselves from the mockers' lame, somewhat disagreeable attempts at wisecracks. That is, the audience of *A Midsummer Night's Dream* is not simply mirrored in the play's upper classes; the real audience is given a broader perspective, a more capacious understanding, than anyone onstage.

This understanding is signaled not only in our ability to take in both the courtly and popular dimensions of the play, but also in our ability to see what escapes both aristocrats and artisans: the world of the fairies. But what are the fairies? From what social milieu do they spring? It is tempting to reply that they are denizens of the country—that is, characters drawn from the semipagan folklore of a rural England that was at least partially intact and that Shakespeare himself could easily have encountered. Reginald Scot, who wrote a brilliant attack on witchcraft persecutions (*The Discovery of Witchcraft*, 1584), suggests that Robin Goodfellow, the mischievous spirit also called a "puck," was once feared by villagers, though most recognize him now to be a figure of mere "illusion and knaverie." Yet intensive scholarly research over several generations has suggested that Shakespeare's fairies are quite unlike those his audience might have credited, half-credited, or—as Scot hoped—discredited.

The fairies of Elizabethan popular belief were often threatening and dangerous, while those of *A Midsummer Night's Dream* are generally benevolent. The former steal human infants, perhaps to sacrifice them to the devil, while the latter, even when they quarrel over the possession of a young boy, do so to bestow love and favor upon him; the former leave deformed, emaciated children in place of those they have stolen, while the latter trip nimbly through the palace blessing the bride-beds and warding off deformities. Shakespeare's fairies have some of the menacing associations of "real" fairies—Robin speaks of shrouds and gaping graves, while the quarrel between Oberon and Titania has disrupted the seasons and damaged the crops, as wicked spirits were said to do. But the fairies we see are, as Oberon says, "spirits of another sort." Though they have very little goodwill toward each other, Oberon and Titania (whose names Shakespeare took from the French romance *Huon of Bordeaux* and from Ovid, respectively) repeatedly demonstrate their goodwill toward mortals. The fairy king and queen are distressed at the unintended consequences of their quarrel, and each is involved, with romantic generosity, in the happiness of Theseus and Hippolyta. This generosity extends beyond the immediate range of their interests: in the midst of plotting to humiliate Titania, Oberon attempts to intervene on behalf of the spurned Helena, and though this intervention proves, through Robin's mistake, to lead to hopeless confusion, the fairies make amends.

Indeed, if Robin takes mischievous delight in the discord he has helped to sow among the four young lovers—"Lord, what fools these mortals be!" (3.2.115)—he is not the originator of that discord, and he is the indispensable agent for setting things right. In his role as both mischief maker and matchmaker, Robin resembles the crafty slave in comedies by the Latin playwrights Plautus and Terence, a stock character who sometimes seems to enjoy and contribute to the plot's tangles but who manages in the end to remove the obstacles that stand in the way of the young lovers.

This resemblance brings us to yet another of the cultural elements that Shakespeare cunningly interweaves in the plot of *A Midsummer Night's Dream*. From the classical literary tradition he must have first encountered in grammar school, Shakespeare derives the ancient Greek setting, the story of Pyramus and Thisbe as told in Ovid's *Metamorphoses*, the transformation of a man into an ass as told in Apuleius's *Golden Ass*, and, above all, the basic plot convention of young lovers contriving to escape the rigid will of a stern father. This literary convention, rooted in the ancient comedies of Menander, Plautus, and Terence, corresponds to certain aspects of actual life in Shakespeare's England, where lawsuits provide records of parents trying to compel children to marry against their will. But the historical problem of marital consent has a complex relation to its artistic representation. Not only does the play exaggerate the actual punitive power of the father—Egeus threatens his disobedient daughter with death (to which Theseus offers, as a grim alternative, the nunnery)—but it also exaggerates the release from this power by staging the giddy possibility of a marriage based entirely on love and desire rather than parental will.

In *A Midsummer Night's Dream*, this triumph of youth, a highly implausible dream for any Elizabethan member of the propertied classes, is brought about by yet another plot convention: the escape from the court or city to the "green world" of the forest. This theatrical structure is not characteristic of ancient Roman comedies, but

Pyramus and Thisbe. From George Wither, *A Collection of Emblems* (1635).

the festive release from the discipline and sobriety of everyday life somewhat resembles the Saturnalian rhythms found in the Greek playwright Aristophanes; still more perhaps, it reflects certain English folk customs, such as Maying. When Theseus comes upon the four exhausted lovers asleep in the woods, he thinks that "they rose up early to observe / The rite of May" (4.1.130–31).

But, of course, Theseus is wrong. The lovers were not out a-Maying. They had spent the night stumbling through the woods in a confused state of fear, anger, and desire. When it enters the charmed, moonlit space of *A Midsummer Night's Dream*, "the rite of May," along with the other rituals and representations Shakespeare stitched together in creating his play, is transformed; to use Peter Quince's term for the metamorphosed Bottom, the rites and rituals are "translated." Folk customs, the revels of power, the classical tradition as taught in schools—all are displaced from their points of origin, their enabling institutions and assumptions, and brought into a new space, the space of the Shakespearean stage.

This "translation" has, in every case, the odd effect of simultaneous elevation and enervation, celebration and parody. Just when you are ready to write something off as a joke, it becomes moving; just when you start to take something seriously, it is comically undermined. Thus, the minor Ovidian tale of Pyramus and Thisbe is greatly elaborated but also travestied; the mechanicals are at once sympathetically represented and mercilessly ridiculed; the revels of power are lovingly reproduced but also ironically distanced.

Some of the play's most wonderful moments spring from the zany conjunction of distinct and even opposed theatrical modes (a conjunction characteristically parodied in the oxymoronic title of the artisans' play, "A tedious brief scene of young Pyramus / And his love Thisbe; very tragical mirth" [5.1.56–57]). Thus, for example, exquisite love poetry and low comedy meet in the wonderful moment in which the Queen of the Fairies awakens to become enraptured at the sight of the most flatulently absurd of the mechanicals, Bottom. Bottom has been transformed with perfect appropriateness into an ass, yet it is he who is granted the play's most exquisite vision of delight and who articulates, in a comically confused burlesque of St. Paul (1 Corinthians 2:9), the deepest sense of wonder: "The eye of man hath not heard, the ear of man hath not seen, man's hand is not able to taste, his tongue to conceive, nor his heart to report what my dream was" (4.1.207–10).

It would be asinine, the play suggests, to try to expound this dream, but we can at least suggest that whatever its meaning, its existence is closely linked to the nature of the theater itself. Robin suggests as much when he proposes in his epilogue that the audience imagine that it has all along been slumbering: the play it has seen has been a collective hallucination. The play, then, is a dream about watching a play about dreams. Fittingly, the comedy devotes much of its last act to a parody of a theatrical performance, as if its most enduring concern were not the fate of the lovers but the possibility of performing plays. The entire last act of *A Midsummer Night's Dream* is unnecessary in terms of the plot: by Oberon's intervention and Theseus's fiat, the plot complications have all been resolved at the end of act 4. Knots that had seemed almost impossible to untangle—Theseus had declared in act 1 that he was powerless to overturn the ancient privilege of Athens invoked by Egeus—suddenly dissolve. The absurdly easy resolution of an apparently hopeless dilemma characterizes not only the lovers' legal but also their emotional condition, a blend of mad confusion and geometric logic that is settled, apparently permanently, with the aid of the fairies' magical love juice.

But this diagrammatic settling of affairs sits uncomfortably with all that the lovers have experienced in the woods. Both critics and directors have given different weight to this experience. Some treat the lovers as mindless comic puppets, jerked by the playwright's invisible strings, while others take more seriously the darkness that shadows their words and actions. This darkness includes emotional violence and masochism, the betrayal of friendship, the radical fickleness of desire. It extends to the play's sexual politics. Under the strain of the night's adventures, the friendship between Hermia and Helena begins to crack apart, while Lysander and Demetrius become bitter rivals. Though they are eventually reconciled, it is as if the heterosexual couplings can only be formed by painfully sundering the intimate same-sex bonds that preceded them. Shakespeare had begun to reflect on this problem as early as *The Two Gentlemen of Verona*, possibly his first play, and throughout his career he returned to it repeatedly, including in what is possibly his last play, *The Two Noble Kinsmen*. For the most part, the broken friendships are repaired, but, as with Anto-

A fairy hill. From Olaus Magnus, *Historia de Gentibus Septentrionalibus* (1558).

nio and Sebastian in *Twelfth Night* and Leontes and Polixenes in *The Winter's Tale*, there is usually a lingering sense of loss, from which even the sunnier *Midsummer Night's Dream* is not completely exempt.

In another very early play, *The Taming of the Shrew*, Shakespeare had also begun his lifelong reflection on the struggle between men and women, a struggle frequently focused on the male desire to dominate and subdue the female. In *A Midsummer Night's Dream*, tension flares in the case of the fairies into open conflict over the Indian boy, the locus of Oberon's assertion of patriarchal power and Titania's claim to independence. In the human world of the play, this tension is less immediately apparent; but in the first scene Theseus alludes to his military conquest of the Amazon queen Hippolyta, and there are other brief glimpses of cruelty, indifference, and rage. We never completely forget that the reconciliation of the quarreling fairies is brought about by the nasty demeaning of Titania or that the human lovers are sorted out by a trick.

Those who see *A Midsummer Night's Dream* as lighthearted entertainment must somehow laugh off this darkness; those who wish to emphasize the play's more troubling and discordant notes must somehow neutralize the comic register in which such notes are sounded. For example, the brutal insults hurled at Hermia by the young man who had loved her and with whom she has eloped might well seem extremely painful, but the fantastic language in which these insults are expressed—

> Get you gone, you dwarf,
> You minimus of hind'ring knot-grass made,
> You bead, you acorn.
>
> (3.2.328–30)

—distances audiences from the pain and generates laughter.

Audiences for most productions tend to oscillate between engagement and detachment. In the young lovers' choices and sufferings, we encounter a situation in which the final outcome doesn't matter greatly to us but matters greatly to them. And while we see the characters from a distance—though Hermia and Helena are distinct enough, even attentive readers occasionally find it difficult to remember which is Lysander and which Demetrius—we also experience at least glancingly *their* sense of how important the difference is, how unbearable to be matched against one's consent, how painfully difficult to make a match that corresponds to one's desires.

Desires in *A Midsummer Night's Dream* are intense, irrational, and alarmingly mobile. This mobility, the speed with which desire can be detached from one object and attached to a different object, does not diminish the exigency of the passion, for the lovers are convinced at every moment that their choices are irrefutably rational and irresistibly compelling. But there is no security in these choices, and the play is repeatedly haunted by a fear of abandonment and by the disquieting erasure of the boundary between human and animal.

The emblem, as well as the agent, of a dangerously mobile desire is the fairies' love juice. No human being in the play experiences a purely abstract, objectless desire; when you desire, you desire *someone*. But the love juice is the distilled essence of erotic mobility itself, and it is appropriately in the power of the fairies. For the fairies seem to embody the principle of what we might call polytropic desire—that is, desire that can instantaneously alight on any object, including an ass-headed man, and that can with equal instantaneousness swerve away from that object and onto another. Oberon and Titania have, we learn, long histories of amorous adventures; they are aware of each other's wayward passions; and, endowed with an extraordinary, eroticizing rhetoric, they move endlessly through the spiced, moonlit night.

If there is a link between the fairies and the erotic, there is a still more powerful link between the fairies and the imagination. Theseus makes the connection explicit when he rejects the stories that the lovers have told him: "I never may believe / These antique fables, nor these fairy toys." In a famous speech (5.1.2–22), he accounts for such fables and toys as products of the imagination. The speech reflects Theseus's misplaced confidence in his own sense of waking reality, a reality that does not include fairies. Yet paradoxically, in dismissively categorizing the lunatic, the lover, and the poet as "of imagination all compact," he manages to articulate insights that the play seems to uphold. Those in the grip of a powerful imagination may be loosed from the moorings of reason and nature, and they may inhabit a world of wish fulfillment and its converse, nightmare. But the poet whose imagination "bodies forth / The forms of things unknown" (5.1.14–15) has created *A Midsummer Night's Dream*, giving his fantasies—including the fantasy called "Theseus"—"[a] local habitation and a name." Finally, it is the imagination that enables giddy, restless, changeable mortals to attach their desires to a particular person.

For Theseus, the imagination is the agent of delusion—and there is much in the play that would seem to support this conclusion. But his account is not complete without Hippolyta's insistence that the story the four young lovers tell seems to have something that goes beyond delusion. Their minds, she observes, have been "transfigured" together, and this shared transfiguration bears witness to "something of great constancy; / But, howsoever, strange and admirable" (5.1.26–27). It is as if we were all to wake up one morning and discover we had had the same dream.

And, of course, *we* in the audience have had, as Robin's epilogue suggests, just this experience: the experience of the theater. In the theater, we confront a living representation of the complex relation between transfiguration and delusion, a relation explored with fantastic, anxious literalness in the artisans' performance of *Pyramus and Thisbe*. In reassuring the ladies that the lion is only Snug the joiner, that nothing is what it claims to be, the players simultaneously burlesque the stage and call attention to the basic elements from which any performance is made: rudimentary scenery, artisans, language, imagination, desire.

There is precious little evidence, to be sure, of either imagination or desire in the *Pyramus and Thisbe* staged at the close of *A Midsummer Night's Dream*. Their absence is part of the comical awfulness of the play-within-the-play—the reason, in effect, that it does not become the Shakespearean tragedy it so strikingly resembles, *Romeo and Juliet*. And yet, as Theseus says, "The best in this kind are but shadows, and the worst are no worse if imagination amend them." "It must be your imagination, then," Hippolyta points out, "and not theirs" (5.1.208–10). But that is true of performances far greater than that of which the artisans are capable.

In the theater, we are always aware of a gap between what we see and what is represented. In heightening our awareness of this gap, the play-within-the-play at once intensifies the illusion of reality elsewhere in the comedy (including the illusion that the actors playing their parts actually are bumbling mechanicals) and calls attention to what is required in order to bring any of the interconnected worlds of this play to life. If we are to see fairies onstage in *A Midsummer Night's Dream*, and not simply flesh-and-blood actors (probably boy actors in Shakespeare's theater), it must be our imagination that makes amends. So, too, if we are to believe in the lovers' desire and sympathize with their predicament, it must be *our* desire that animates their words.

Such, at least, is the vision of the theater suggested by the play that Bottom and company offer to the newlyweds. There is nothing really out there, their performance implies, except what the audience graciously consents to dream is there. Yet in the closing moments of the play, when the fairies emerge from the woods and venture into Theseus's mansion to bless the bride-beds, a quite different vision of theater is suggested—one in which the dreams and desires that we have are determined by forces over which we have no control, forces that only a playwright's love juice can make visible under an imaginary moon.

STEPHEN GREENBLATT

SELECTED BIBLIOGRAPHY

Barber, C. L. "May Games and Metamorphoses on a Midsummer's Night." *Shakespeare's Festive Comedy*. Princeton, NJ: Princeton UP, 2012. 135–84. Explains how *A Midsummer Night's Dream* combines folk customs, Ovidian fancy, and Elizabethan pageantry to produce a clarifying release of imagination.

Bate, Jonathan. *Shakespeare and Ovid*. New York: Oxford UP, 1993. Argues that *A Midsummer Night's Dream* indirectly dramatizes Ovid, gathering themes of myth, metamorphosis, and love into a mixed mode typical of sixteenth-century mythography.

Boehrer, Bruce. "Economies of Desire in *A Midsummer Night's Dream*." *Shakespeare Studies* 32 (2004): 99–117. Explores the competing impulses in the play to embrace and repudiate otherness in same-sex and cross-species attachments.

Briggs, K. M. *The Anatomy of Puck*. London: Routledge & Kegan Paul, 1959. Offers a survey of early modern notions about fairies, especially in English literary tradition, describing also the influence of Shakespeare's innovations.

Dash, Irene. *Women's Worlds in Shakespeare's Plays*. London: Associated UP, 1997. Looks at *A Midsummer Night's Dream* in performance, arguing that traditional staging practices have tended reductively to simplify Shakespeare's women.

Loomba, Ania. "The Great Indian Vanishing Trick—Colonialism, Property and the Family in *A Midsummer Night's Dream*." *A Feminist Companion to Shakespeare*. Ed. Dympna Callaghan. Malden, MA: Blackwell, 2000. 163–87. Argues that the Indian boy represents the shaping dialectic between non-European practices and Western domestic ideology.

Montrose, Louis. *The Purpose of Playing: Shakespeare and the Cultural Politics of the Elizabethan Theatre*. Chicago: U of Chicago P, 1996. Examines the play's relation to Elizabethan ideology through discourses of gender, physiology, social rank, and royal iconography.

Traub, Valerie. *The Renaissance of Lesbianism in Early Modern England*. Cambridge: Cambridge UP, 2002. Observes how renovated classical idioms and new scientific knowledge made female-female desire intelligible during the Renaissance.

Williams, Gary Jay. *Our Moonlight Revels: "A Midsummer Night's Dream" in the Theatre*. Iowa City: U of Iowa P, 1997. Explores the major stage, film, and opera adaptations, understood in relation to the cultures that produced them.

Young, David P. *Something of Great Constancy: The Art of "A Midsummer Night's Dream."* New Haven, CT: Yale UP, 1966. Presents an extensive, variegated study covering sources, structure, performance, and contexts.

FILMS

A Midsummer Night's Dream. 1935. Dir. William Dieterle and Max Reinhardt. USA. 133 min. Sumptuous production, with balletic fairies, a serpentine Hippolyta, an elaborate Mendelssohn score, and Mickey Rooney as Robin Goodfellow.

A Midsummer Night's Dream. 1968. Dir. Peter Hall. UK. 124 min. Noted for its miniskirted sensuality, body paint, and extremely gnarled and muddy forest. With Diana Rigg and Helen Mirren.

A Midsummer Night's Dream. 1996. Dir. Adrian Noble. UK. 105 min. Theseus and Hippolyta double as Oberon and Titania, with a frame device of a boy dreaming the play. Starring Lindsay Duncan and Alex Jennings.

A Midsummer Night's Dream. 1999. Dir. Michael Hoffman. USA. 116 min. In Victorian costume against the Tuscan backdrop, this dreamy and erotic version amplifies Bottom's role. With Kevin Kline and Michelle Pfeiffer.

The Children's Midsummer Night's Dream. 2001. Dir. Christine Edzard. UK. 115 min. Performed entirely by child actors, between eight and twelve years old.

Were the World Mine. 2008. Dir. Tom Gustafson. USA. 95 min. In this musical, a
bullied gay teenager cast as Puck (Robin) in a high school production of *A Midsummer Night's Dream* discovers the secret of love juice and uses it to turn some
of the students in his all-boys' school gay.

TEXTUAL INTRODUCTION

A Midsummer Night's Dream was entered in the Stationers' Register to Thomas
Fisher on October 8, 1600, and was published by him in the same year in quarto
format (Q1) in a text printed by Richard Bradock. The title page states that the play
has been "sundry times publickely acted, by the Right Honourable, the Lord Chamberlaine his seruants," and was "Written by William Shakespeare." The play was
reprinted in 1619 (Q2) by William Jaggard for the publisher Thomas Pavier in an edition misdated "1600." In 1623, it was included in the First Folio (F) edition of Shakespeare's *Comedies, Histories, and Tragedies*. Reprints of F were included in the subsequent
Folio editions of 1632 (F2), 1664–65 (F3), and 1685 (F4).

Q1 is believed to have been set up from Shakespeare's manuscript or a faithful
transcript thereof. It has been chosen as the primary text in the present edition on
the grounds that it provides the best witness to how Shakespeare originally conceived the play. Q2 has no independent authority but simply reprints Q1 by correcting a few printing errors while adding others. F was chiefly set up from Q2 but
contains a number of important differences that may reflect performance practice by
Shakespeare's company. The theatrical manuscript from which they are believed to
originate may date from after Shakespeare's death: an F-only stage direction asks for
"*Tawyer with a Trumpet*" (5.1.125), a reference to William Tawyer, a musician of the
King's Men according to a document of 1624, who is referred to as "Mr Heminges
man" the year after. No extant reference to Tawyer is earlier than 1623.

Although they are significant, the differences between Q1 and F *Midsummer
Night's Dream* are local and subtle rather than pervasive. The most consequential difference is that in the last act, F reassigns Philostrate's Q1 speeches to Egeus, who thus
occupies the role of Theseus's "usual manager of mirth" (5.1.35), responsible for the
wedding entertainment. As a result, the conclusion to the two texts is rather different.
In Q1's act 4, scene 1, Egeus vociferously opposes his daughter's love for Lysander.
Overruled by Theseus, who allows the lovers to get married, Egeus leaves the stage
defeated and does not reappear. In the final scene, when the lovers and the royal couple are celebrating, Hermia's father is thus conspicuously absent, excluded from the
comic ending, not unlike Malvolio in *Twelfth Night* and Shylock in *The Merchant of
Venice*. F, by contrast, has Egeus reappear in act 5, which means he is onstage at the
same time as Hermia, the daughter who did not obey him, and Lysander, the son-in-
law he did not want—which can create interesting tensions in performance.

Other significant differences include a passage early in 5.1: a lengthy speech by
Theseus in Q1 is broken up in F into eight short speeches alternatively assigned to
Lysander and Theseus (5.1.44–60). F adds numerous stage directions, signaling music
(4.1.28, 4.1.81, 5.1.384) and Lion's roaring (5.1.253), pointing out that characters lie
down (3.2.417), sleep (2.2.24, 2.2.65, 3.2.462, 4.1.100), and awake (3.2.137, 4.1.196); and
providing entrance (3.2.437, 5.1.302) and exit stage directions (2.1.244, 2.2.87, 3.1.93,
3.1.182, 3.2.101, 3.2.338, 4.1.184, 4.1.196, 4.1.212, 4.2.39, 5.1.203). At one point, F has
Robin enter earlier than Q1 does (F 3.1.46, Q 3.1.64), and on two occasions F's Bottom
exits and re-enters, whereas Q1 keeps him onstage (3.1.93–99, 5.1.150–66). F also alters
or expands some of Q1's stage directions (for example, 3.2.419). The dialogue text is
often but not always identical. Three lines are present in Q1 but absent from F (3.2.344,
4.1.190–91, 5.1.308–09), and the two texts differ in many individual words. Some of the
changes may have occurred during typesetting, including "filly" to "silly" (2.1.46),
"interchainèd" to "interchangèd" (2.2.49), and "favors" to "savors" (4.1.47), or such

minor substitutions as "off from" to "from off" (2.1.183) and "my" to "mine" (3.2.243). Yet other F changes may well be intentional—for instance, "merit" where Q1 has "friends" (1.1.139). F also omits some words present in Q1—"Ay me!" (1.1.132), "round" (2.1.175), "Helen" (3.2.173), "right" (4.2.28), and "trusty" (5.1.144)—and adds a few others, notably "here" (2.2.104), "now" (2.2.113), "passionate" (3.2.220), and "thou" (4.1.69).

Q1 and Q2 provide neither act nor scene divisions, while F divides the play into acts only. In keeping with editorial tradition and thus for the convenience of readers consulting criticism about the play, the present edition adheres to the Folio act division and inserts scene breaks when the stage is cleared and the action is discontinuous.

LUKAS ERNE

PERFORMANCE NOTE

Few plays draw attention to their artificiality like *A Midsummer Night's Dream*. In *Midsummer*, even "rude mechanicals" debate issues of theatrical representation and reception, in the course of a plot that features sudden reversals of affection, fairies visible and invisible, a man turned into an ass, and the casting, rehearsal, and performance of a play. Each production's approach to stage realism, casting, and mise-en-scène may therefore prove pivotal. Whether a production chooses to stylize the lovers' abrupt changes in affection or to mark these out as psychologically revealing, to isolate Bottom in his desire to play all the parts or to have its own actors double roles, or to cast wispy children or grown men as fairies can accentuate or hedge against the play's many advertisements of artifice.

Companies must also determine how to depict the green world and how far to complicate the play's mood and genre in their representations thereof. Benign fairy kingdoms full of flower-strewing nymphs have given way on modern stages to shadier places and menacing creatures. Is Robin Goodfellow a mischievous prankster or a predator? Should Oberon be dismayed at finding Titania matched (and mated) with an ass, or should he exult in sadistic satisfaction? Does Lysander brush Hermia aside out of adoration for Helena, or does he linger over the chance to eviscerate his former lover? Productions face a challenge in exploring the play's darker aspects, particularly the dissension and sexual aggression underlying its principal relationships, without destroying the comedy. At the return to Athens, directors must also decide whether to include Egeus in 5.1 (the Quarto text doesn't), thereby suggesting his reconciliation or continuing umbrage; whether the nobles' harsh criticism of the mechanicals' performance is superficial banter or a further means to cloud the comedy; and whether the tone of Robin's epilogue is friendly or frightening.

BRETT GAMBOA

A Midsummer Night's Dream

[THE PERSONS OF THE PLAY

THESEUS, Duke of Athens
HIPPOLYTA, Queen of the Amazons, betrothed to Theseus
EGEUS, father to Hermia
HERMIA, daughter to Egeus, in love with Lysander
LYSANDER, in love with Hermia
DEMETRIUS, in love with Hermia
HELENA, in love with Demetrius
PHILOSTRATE, Master of the Revels at the court of Theseus
Lords and Attendants on Theseus and Hippolyta

OBERON, King of the Fairies
TITANIA, Queen of the Fairies
ROBIN Goodfellow, a puck°   *an imp or a mischievous sprite*
PEASEBLOSSOM ⎫
COBWEB   ⎪
MOTH   ⎬ fairies in Titania's service
MUSTARDSEED   ⎭
Other FAIRIES

Peter QUINCE, a carpenter, Prologue in the Interlude
Nick BOTTOM, a weaver, Pyramus in the Interlude
Francis FLUTE, a bellows-mender, Thisbe in the Interlude
Tom SNOUT, a tinker, Wall in the Interlude
SNUG, a joiner, Lion in the Interlude
Robin STARVELING, a tailor, Moonshine in the Interlude]

1.1 (F 1.1)

Enter THESEUS, HIPPOLYTA, [*and* PHILOSTRATE,]
with others.

THESEUS   Now, fair Hippolyta, our nuptial hour
Draws on apace. Four happy days bring in
Another moon; but, oh, methinks, how slow
This old moon wanes! She lingers° my desires   *delays fulfillment of*
5   Like to a stepdame° or a dowager   *stepmother*
Long withering out a young man's revenue.[1]
HIPPOLYTA   Four days will quickly steep° themselves in night;   *plunge*
Four nights will quickly dream away the time;
And then the moon—like to a silver bow
10 Now bent in heaven—shall behold the night
Of our solemnities.
THESEUS   Go, Philostrate,
Stir up the Athenian youth to merriments,
Awake the pert and nimble spirit of mirth,
Turn melancholy forth to funerals;

1.1 Location: Theseus's palace in Athens.
1. *a dowager ... revenue*: a widow using up the

inheritance that will go to her husband's (young) heir
on her death.

15 The pale companion is not for our pomp.

                                            [Exit PHILOSTRATE.]

      Hippolyta, I wooed thee with my sword
      And won thy love doing thee injuries;[2]
      But I will wed thee in another key,
      With pomp, with triumph,° and with reveling.   *public festivity*

      Enter EGEUS *and his daughter* HERMIA, *and* LYSANDER
      and DEMETRIUS.

20 EGEUS Happy be Theseus, our renownèd duke!
    THESEUS Thanks, good Egeus. What's the news with thee?
    EGEUS Full of vexation come I, with complaint
      Against my child, my daughter Hermia.
      —Stand forth, Demetrius. —My noble lord,
25 This man hath my consent to marry her.
      —Stand forth, Lysander. —And, my gracious duke,
      This man hath bewitched the bosom of my child.
      —Thou, thou, Lysander, thou hast given her rhymes,
      And interchanged love tokens with my child.
30 Thou hast by moonlight at her window sung
      With feigning[3] voice verses of feigning love,
      And stolen the impression of her fantasy[4]
      With bracelets of thy hair, rings, gauds,° conceits,°   *trinkets / clever gifts*
      Knacks,° trifles, nosegays,° sweetmeats—messengers   *Knickknacks / bouquets*
35 Of strong prevailment° in unhardened youth.   *persuasiveness*
      With cunning hast thou filched my daughter's heart,
      Turned her obedience, which is due to me,
      To stubborn harshness. —And, my gracious duke,
      Be it so° she will not here before your grace   *If*
40 Consent to marry with Demetrius,
      I beg the ancient privilege of Athens:
      As she is mine, I may dispose of her,
      Which shall be either to this gentleman
      Or to her death, according to our law
45 Immediately° provided in that case.   *Expressly*
    THESEUS What say you, Hermia? Be advised, fair maid:
      To you your father should be as a god,
      One that composed° your beauties, yea, and one   *fashioned*
      To whom you are but as a form in wax
50 By him imprinted,[5] and within his power
      To leave° the figure or disfigure° it.   *maintain / destroy*
      Demetrius is a worthy gentleman.
    HERMIA So is Lysander.
    THESEUS   In himself he is,
      But in this kind,° wanting your father's voice,[6]   *respect*
55 The other must be held the worthier.
    HERMIA I would my father looked but with my eyes.
    THESEUS Rather your eyes must with his judgment look.
    HERMIA I do entreat your grace to pardon me.
      I know not by what power I am made bold,

---

2. Theseus captured Hippolyta in his military conquest of the Amazons.
3. A pun: deceitful; desiring ("faining"); soft (in music).
4. *stolen . . . fantasy:* by craftily impressing your image on her imagination, like a seal in wax, (you have) stolen her love.
5. *you are . . . imprinted:* you are merely a wax impression of his seal.
6. Lacking your father's consent or vote.

60   Nor how it may concern° my modesty   *befit*
        In such a presence here to plead my thoughts,
        But I beseech your grace that I may know
        The worst that may befall me in this case
        If I refuse to wed Demetrius.
65   THESEUS   Either to die the death° or to abjure   *be executed*
        For ever the society of men.
        Therefore, fair Hermia, question your desires,
        Know° of your youth, examine well your blood,°   *Inquire / passions*
        Whether, if you yield not to your father's choice,
70   You can endure the livery° of a nun,[7]   *habit*
        For aye° to be in shady cloister mewed,°   *ever / caged*
        To live a barren sister all your life,
        Chanting faint hymns to the cold fruitless moon.[8]
        Thrice blessèd they that master so their blood
75   To undergo such maiden pilgrimage;°   *life as a virgin*
        But earthlier happy is the rose distilled[9]
        Than that which, withering on the virgin thorn,
        Grows, lives, and dies in single blessedness.°   *in celibacy*
     HERMIA   So will I grow, so live, so die, my lord,
80   Ere I will yield my virgin patent[1] up
        Unto his lordship whose unwishèd yoke
        My soul consents not to give sovereignty.
     THESEUS   Take time to pause, and by the next new moon—
        The sealing day betwixt my love and me
85   For everlasting bond of fellowship—
        Upon that day either prepare to die
        For disobedience to your father's will,
        Or else to wed Demetrius, as he would,
        Or on Diana's altar to protest°   *vow*
90   For aye° austerity and single life.   *Forever*
     DEMETRIUS   Relent, sweet Hermia, and, Lysander, yield
        Thy crazèd title° to my certain right.   *flawed claim*
     LYSANDER   You have her father's love, Demetrius;
        Let me have Hermia's. Do you marry him.
95   EGEUS   Scornful Lysander! True, he hath my love,
        And what is mine my love shall render him;
        And she is mine, and all my right of her
        I do estate° unto Demetrius.   *settle; bestow*
     LYSANDER [*to* THESEUS]   I am, my lord, as well derived° as he,   *descended*
100   As well possessed,° my love is more than his,   *endowed with wealth*
        My fortunes every way as fairly ranked,
        If not with vantage,° as Demetrius'.   *superiority*
        And, which is more than all these boasts can be,
        I am beloved of beauteous Hermia.
105   Why should not I then prosecute° my right?   *pursue*
        Demetrius, I'll avouch it to his head,°   *face*
        Made love to° Nedar's daughter, Helena,   *Wooed*
        And won her soul, and she, sweet lady, dotes,
        Devoutly dotes, dotes in idolatry

---

7. Christian orders of nuns were established in the Middle Ages, but Elizabethans used the term as well for women devoted to a religious life in classical antiquity.
8. The emblem of Diana, goddess of chastity.

9. Preserved in a perfume (figuratively, preserved in her children). *earthlier happy*: happier on earth.
1. My right to remain a virgin.

110   Upon this spotted and inconstant² man.
      THESEUS   I must confess that I have heard so much
         And with Demetrius thought to have spoke thereof,
         But, being overfull of self-affairs,°   *my own concerns*
         My mind did lose it. —But, Demetrius, come,
115   —And come, Egeus; you shall go with me.
         I have some private schooling° for you both.   *advice*
         —For you, fair Hermia, look you arm° yourself   *prepare*
         To fit your fancies° to your father's will,   *desires*
         Or else the law of Athens yields you up,
120   Which by no means we may extenuate,°   *mitigate*
         To death or to a vow of single life.
         —Come, my Hippolyta. What cheer, my love?
         —Demetrius and Egeus, go along.
         I must employ you in some business
125   Against° our nuptial and confer with you   *In preparation for*
         Of something nearly that³ concerns yourselves.
      EGEUS   With duty and desire we follow you.
                    Exeunt [all but LYSANDER *and* HERMIA].
      LYSANDER   How now, my love, why is your cheek so pale?
         How chance the roses there do fade so fast?
130   HERMIA   Belike° for want of rain, which I could well   *Probably*
         Beteem° them from the tempest of my eyes.   *Afford; grant*
      LYSANDER   Ay me! For aught that I could ever read,
         Could ever hear by tale or history,
         The course of true love never did run smooth,
135   But either it was different in blood°—   *hereditary rank*
      HERMIA   Oh, cross!° Too high to be enthralled to low.   *vexation*
      LYSANDER   Or else misgraffèd⁴ in respect of years—
      HERMIA   Oh, spite! Too old to be engaged to young.
      LYSANDER   Or else it stood° upon the choice of friends°—   *rested / kin*
140   HERMIA   Oh, hell! To choose love by another's eyes.
      LYSANDER   Or if there were a sympathy° in choice,   *an agreement*
         War, death, or sickness did lay siege to it,
         Making it momentany° as a sound,   *momentary*
         Swift as a shadow, short as any dream,
145   Brief as the lightning in the collied° night   *coal-black*
         That in a spleen° unfolds° both heaven and earth   *swift impulse / reveals*
         And ere a man hath power to say "Behold!"
         The jaws of darkness do devour it up.
         So quick bright things come to confusion.
150   HERMIA   If then true lovers have been ever° crossed,   *always*
         It stands as an edict in destiny.
         Then let us teach our trial patience⁵
         Because it is a customary cross,
         As due to love as thoughts and dreams and sighs,
155   Wishes and tears, poor fancy's° followers.   *love's*
      LYSANDER   A good persuasion.° Therefore hear me, Hermia: *argument; principle*
         I have a widow aunt, a dowager
         Of great revenue, and she hath no child.
         From Athens is her house remote seven leagues,

---

2. *spotted and inconstant:* fickle.   4. Badly matched; improperly grafted.
3. *nearly that:* that closely.   5. Let us teach ourselves to be patient in this trial.

160 And she respects° me as her only son.   *regards*
There, gentle Hermia, may I marry thee,
And to that place the sharp Athenian law
Cannot pursue us. If thou lovest me then
Steal forth thy father's house tomorrow night,
165 And in the wood, a league without° the town,   *outside*
Where I did meet thee once with Helena
To do observance to a morn of May,°   *celebrate May Day*
There will I stay for thee.

HERMIA   My good Lysander,
I swear to thee by Cupid's strongest bow,
170 By his best arrow with the golden head,[6]
By the simplicity° of Venus' doves,[7]   *innocence*
By that which knitteth souls and prospers loves,
And by that fire which burned the Carthage Queen
When the false Trojan under sail was seen,[8]
175 By all the vows that ever men have broke,
In number more than ever women spoke,
In that same place thou hast appointed me
Tomorrow truly will I meet with thee.

LYSANDER   Keep promise, love. Look, here comes Helena.
        Enter HELENA.
180 HERMIA   God speed, fair[9] Helena! Whither away?

HELENA   Call you me fair? That "fair" again unsay.
Demetrius loves your fair; oh, happy fair!°   *fortunate beauty*
Your eyes are lodestars,° and your tongue's sweet air°   *guiding stars / melody*
More tunable° than lark to shepherd's ear   *tuneful*
185 When wheat is green, when hawthorn buds appear.
Sickness is catching; oh, were favor° so,   *looks; charms*
Your words I catch, fair Hermia, ere I go;
My ear should catch your voice, my eye your eye,
My tongue should catch your tongue's sweet melody.
190 Were the world mine, Demetrius being bated,°   *excepted*
The rest I'd give to be to you translated.
Oh, teach me how you look, and with what art
You sway the motion of Demetrius' heart.

HERMIA   I frown upon him, yet he loves me still.
195 HELENA   Oh, that your frowns would teach my smiles such
        skill!

HERMIA   I give him curses, yet he gives me love.

HELENA   Oh, that my prayers could such affection move!

HERMIA   The more I hate, the more he follows me.

HELENA   The more I love, the more he hateth me.

200 HERMIA   His folly, Helena, is no fault of mine.

HELENA   None but your beauty; would that fault were mine!

HERMIA   Take comfort: he no more shall see my face.
Lysander and myself will fly this place.
Before the time I did Lysander see

---

6. Cupid's sharp golden arrow was said to create love; his blunt lead arrow caused dislike.
7. Said to draw Venus's chariot.
8. *fire . . . seen:* Dido, Queen of Carthage, burned herself on a funeral pyre when her lover, Aeneas, sailed away.
9. The dialogue plays on the meanings "blonde," "beautiful," "beauty." Helena is presumably fair-haired and Hermia (called a "raven" at 2.2.114) a brunette.

205   Seemed Athens as a paradise to me.
        Oh, then, what graces in my love do dwell
        That he hath turned a heaven unto a hell?
    LYSANDER   Helen, to you our minds we will unfold:
        Tomorrow night, when Phoebe° doth behold   *Diana (the moon)*
210   Her silver visage in the watery glass,
        Decking with liquid pearl the bladed grass,
        A time that lovers' flights doth still° conceal,   *always*
        Through Athens' gates have we devised to steal.
    HERMIA   And in the wood where often you and I
215   Upon faint° primrose beds were wont° to lie,   *pale / accustomed*
        Emptying our bosoms of their counsel sweet,
        There my Lysander and myself shall meet,
        And thence from Athens turn away our eyes
        To seek new friends and stranger companies.°   *the company of strangers*
220   Farewell, sweet playfellow; pray thou for us,
        And good luck grant thee thy Demetrius.
        —Keep word, Lysander; we must starve our sight
        From lovers' food till morrow deep midnight.   *Exit.*
    LYSANDER   I will, my Hermia. —Helena, adieu.
225   As you on him, Demetrius dote on you.   *Exit.*
    HELENA   How happy some o'er other some[1] can be!
        Through Athens I am thought as fair as she.
        But what of that? Demetrius thinks not so.
        He will not know what all but he do know.
230   And as he errs, doting on Hermia's eyes,
        So I, admiring of his qualities.
        Things base and vile, holding no quantity,°   *shape; proportion*
        Love can transpose to form and dignity.
        Love looks not with the eyes but with the mind,[2]
235   And therefore is winged Cupid painted blind.
        Nor hath love's mind of any judgment taste,°   *any trace of judgment*
        Wings and no eyes figure° unheedy haste.   *symbolize*
        And therefore is love said to be a child
        Because in choice he is so oft beguiled.
240   As waggish° boys in game° themselves forswear,   *playful / sport; play*
        So the boy Love is perjured everywhere.
        For ere Demetrius looked on Hermia's eyne,°   *eyes*
        He hailed down oaths that he was only mine.
        And when this hail some heat from Hermia felt,
245   So he dissolved,° and showers of oaths did melt.   *broke faith; melted*
        I will go tell him of fair Hermia's flight:
        Then to the wood will he tomorrow night
        Pursue her; and for this intelligence°   *information*
        If I have thanks, it is a dear[3] expense.
250   But herein mean I to enrich my pain,
        To have his sight thither and back again.   *Exit.*

---

1. *o'er other some*: in comparison with others.
2. Love is promoted not by the evidence of the senses, but by the fancies of the mind.
3. Costly (because of the betrayal of secrecy and because it leads Demetrius to Hermia); or welcome (because the potential return is Demetrius's love regained).

1.2 (F 1.2)

Enter QUINCE *the carpenter, and* SNUG *the joiner, and*
BOTTOM *the weaver, and* FLUTE *the bellows-mender,*
and SNOUT *the tinker, and* STARVELING *the tailor.*[1]

QUINCE Is all our company here?

BOTTOM You were best to call them generally,[2] man by man,
according to the scrip.°   *script; list*

QUINCE Here is the scroll of every man's name which is
5   thought fit through all Athens to play in our interlude° before   *brief play*
the Duke and the Duchess on his wedding day at night.

BOTTOM First, good Peter Quince, say what the play treats on;
then read the names of the actors; and so grow to a point.[3]

QUINCE Marry,° our play is *The Most Lamentable Comedy*   *By the Virgin Mary*
10   *and Most Cruel Death of Pyramus and Thisbe.*[4]

BOTTOM A very good piece of work, I assure you, and a merry.
Now, good Peter Quince, call forth your actors by the scroll.
Masters, spread yourselves.

QUINCE Answer as I call you. —Nick Bottom, the weaver?

15 BOTTOM Ready. Name what part I am for, and proceed.

QUINCE You, Nick Bottom, are set down for Pyramus.

BOTTOM What is Pyramus? A lover or a tyrant?

QUINCE A lover that kills himself, most gallant, for love.

BOTTOM That will ask some tears in the true performing of
20   it. If I do it, let the audience look to their eyes. I will move
storms. I will condole° in some measure. To the rest. —Yet   *lament; arouse pity*
my chief humor° is for a tyrant. I could play Ercles[5] rarely,° *inclination / excellently*
or a part to tear a cat° in, to make all split.°   *rant / go to pieces*

The raging rocks
25   <center>And shivering shocks°</center>   *shattering blows*
Shall break the locks
Of prison gates,
And Phibbus' car[6]
Shall shine from far
30   <center>And make and mar</center>
The foolish Fates.

This was lofty. Now name the rest of the players. This is
Ercles' vein, a tyrant's vein. A lover is more condoling.

QUINCE Francis Flute, the bellows-mender?

35 FLUTE Here, Peter Quince.

QUINCE Flute, you must take Thisbe on you.

FLUTE What is Thisbe, a wandering knight?°   *knight-errant*

QUINCE It is the lady that Pyramus must love.

FLUTE Nay, faith, let not me play a woman:[7] I have a beard
40   coming.

1.2 Location: Somewhere in the city of Athens.
1. The artisans' names recall their occupations.
Quince's name is probably derived from "quoins,"
wooden wedges used by carpenters who made buildings such as houses and theaters. The name "Snug"
evokes well-finished wooden furniture made by join-
ers. A bottom was the piece of wood on which thread
was wound; Bottom's name also connotes "ass" and
"lowest point." As Flute's name suggests, domestic
bellows whistle through holes when needing repair.
Snout's name may refer either to the spouts of the
kettles he repairs or to his nose. Tailors, as Starve-

ling's name recalls, were proverbially thin.
2. Bottom's error for "individually" (he frequently
misuses words in this manner).
3. *grow to a point:* draw to a conclusion.
4. Parodying titles such as that of Thomas Preston's
*Cambyses: A Lamentable Tragedy Mixed Full of Pleas-
ant Mirth* . . . (ca. 1570).
5. Hercules (a stock ranting role in early plays).
6. The chariot of Phoebus Apollo, the sun god (the
odd spelling may represent Bottom's pronunciation).
7. On the Elizabethan stage, women's parts were
played by boys and young men.

QUINCE   That's all one.° You shall play it in a mask,[8] and you *irrelevant*
may speak as small° as you will.   *high-pitched; shrill*

BOTTOM   An° I may hide my face, let me play Thisbe too. I'll   *If*
speak in a monstrous little voice, "Thisne, Thisne!"[9] —"Ah,

45 Pyramus, my lover dear, thy Thisbe dear and lady dear."

QUINCE   No, no, you must play Pyramus; and Flute, you Thisbe.

BOTTOM   Well, proceed.

QUINCE   Robin Starveling, the tailor?

STARVELING   Here, Peter Quince.

50 QUINCE   Robin Starveling, you must play Thisbe's mother.
—Tom Snout, the tinker?

SNOUT   Here, Peter Quince.

QUINCE   You, Pyramus' father; myself, Thisbe's father; Snug the
joiner, you, the lion's part; and I hope here is a play fitted.°   *(well) cast*

55 SNUG   Have you the lion's part written? Pray you, if it be, give
it me, for I am slow of study.

QUINCE   You may do it extempore, for it is nothing but roaring.

BOTTOM   Let me play the lion too. I will roar that I will do any
man's heart good to hear me. I will roar that I will make the

60 Duke say, "Let him roar again! Let him roar again!"

QUINCE   An you should do it too terribly, you would fright the
Duchess and the ladies that they would shriek, and that
were enough to hang us all.

ALL   That would hang us, every mother's son.

65 BOTTOM   I grant you, friends, if you should fright the ladies
out of their wits, they would have no more discretion but to
hang us. But I will aggravate° my voice so that I will roar you   *(for "moderate")*
as gently as any sucking dove.[1] I will roar you an 'twere° any   *as though it were*
nightingale.

70 QUINCE   You can play no part but Pyramus; for Pyramus is a
sweet-faced man, a proper° man as one shall see in a sum-   *handsome*
mer's day, a most lovely, gentlemanlike man. Therefore you
must needs play Pyramus.

BOTTOM   Well, I will undertake it. What beard were I best to

75 play it in?

QUINCE   Why, what you will.

BOTTOM   I will discharge° it in either your straw-color beard,   *perform*
your orange-tawny[2] beard, your purple-in-grain° beard, or   *very deep red*
your French-crown-color° beard, your perfect yellow.   *gold-coin-colored*

80 QUINCE   Some of your French crowns have no hair at all,[3] and
then you will play bare-faced.° —But, masters, here are your   *beardless; undisguised*
parts,[4] and I am to entreat you, request you, and desire you
to con° them by tomorrow night, and meet me in the palace   *memorize*
wood, a mile without the town, by moonlight. There will we

85 rehearse; for if we meet in the city, we shall be dogged with
company, and our devices° known. In the meantime, I will   *plans*
draw a bill° of properties such as our play wants. I pray you,   *list*
fail me not.

---

8. Elizabethan ladies regularly wore masks to remain
anonymous and to protect their complexions.
9. Probably intended as a pet name for Thisbe; or it
may mean "in this manner" ("thissen").
1. Bottom confuses "sitting dove" and "sucking lamb."
2. Dark yellow, a recognized name for the dye. (Bot-

tom the weaver shows his professional knowledge.)
3. Referring to the baldness caused by venereal disease (called "the French disease").
4. Literally; an Elizabethan actor was generally given
only his own lines and cues.

BOTTOM We will meet, and there we may rehearse most
90 obscenely[5] and courageously. Take pains; be perfect.[6] Adieu.
QUINCE At the Duke's oak we meet.
BOTTOM Enough! Hold, or cut bowstrings.[7]   *Exeunt.*

2.1 (F 2.1)

Enter a FAIRY *at one door and* ROBIN *Goodfellow[, a
puck,][1] at another.*

ROBIN How now, spirit, whither wander you?[2]
FAIRY Over hill, over dale,
Thorough° bush, thorough briar,   *Through*
Over park, over pale,°   *enclosure; fence*
5 Thorough flood, thorough fire,
I do wander everywhere
Swifter than the moon's sphere;[3]
And I serve the Fairy Queen
To dew her orbs[4] upon the green.
10 The cowslips tall her pensioners° be;   *royal bodyguards*
In their gold coats spots you see.
Those be rubies, fairy favors,°   *gifts*
In those freckles live their savors.°   *scent*
I must go seek some dewdrops here
15 And hang a pearl in every cowslip's ear.
Farewell, thou lob° of spirits, I'll be gone.   *country bumpkin*
Our queen and all her elves come here anon.
ROBIN The King doth keep his revels here tonight.
Take heed the Queen come not within his sight,
20 For Oberon is passing fell and wrath[5]
Because that she as her attendant hath
A lovely boy stolen from an Indian king—
She never had so sweet a changeling[6]—
And jealous Oberon would have the child
25 Knight of his train, to trace° the forests wild.   *range*
But she perforce° withholds the lovèd boy,   *forcibly*
Crowns him with flowers, and makes him all her joy.
And now they never meet in grove or green,
By fountain° clear or spangled starlight sheen,°   *spring / shining starlight*
30 But they do square,° that all their elves for fear   *quarrel*
Creep into acorn cups and hide them there.
FAIRY Either I mistake your shape and making° quite,   *form*
Or else you are that shrewd° and knavish sprite   *mischievous*
Called Robin Goodfellow. Are not you he

---

5. A comic blunder, possibly for "out of sight" ("from
the scene" or "from being seen").
6. Be letter perfect in learning your parts.
7. *Hold, or cut bowstrings* (from military archery): Be
present at the rehearsal, or else quit the troupe (?).
2.1 Location: A wood near Athens.
1. TEXTUAL COMMENT A puck is an imp or a mischievous sprite; in Elizabethan folklore, Robin Goodfellow
was a puck who would do housework if well treated.
In the speech prefixes of the First Quarto (Q1) and
the Folio (F), this character is variously identified as
"Robin" and "Puck"; this edition regularizes based on
his proper name Robin Goodfellow. For more on the
issue of speech prefixes and names, see Digital Edition
TC 1 (Quarto edited text).

2. PERFORMANCE COMMENT While productions of
A Midsummer Night's Dream have traditionally
depicted the play's fairy forest as a place of beauty
and benevolence, directors in the second half of the
twentieth century began to explore the darker possibilities beneath its surface. For more, see Digital
Edition PC 1.
3. Each planet, including the moon, was thought to
be fixed in a transparent hollow globe revolving
around the earth.
4. To sprinkle her fairy rings (circles of dark grass).
5. *passing fell and wrath:* exceedingly fierce and angry.
6. Usually a child left by fairies in exchange for one
stolen, but here the stolen child.

35	That frights the maidens of the villagery,°	*villages*
	Skim milk, and sometimes labor in the quern,°	*hand mill*
	And bootless° make the breathless housewife churn,	*in vain*
	And sometime° make the drink to bear no barm,°	*at times / froth on ale*
	Mislead night-wanderers, laughing at their harm?	
40	Those that "hobgoblin" call you, and "sweet puck,"	
	You do their work, and they shall have good luck.	
	Are not you he?	
	ROBIN Thou speakest aright;	
	I am that merry wanderer of the night.	
	I jest to Oberon and make him smile	
45	When I a fat and bean-fed horse beguile,°	*trick*
	Neighing in likeness of a filly foal.	
	And sometime lurk I in a gossip's° bowl	*an old woman's*
	In very likeness of a roasted crab,[7]	
	And when she drinks, against her lips I bob,	
50	And on her withered dewlap° pour the ale.	*loose skin on neck*
	The wisest aunt° telling the saddest° tale	*old woman / most serious*
	Sometime for three-foot stool mistaketh me.	
	Then slip I from her bum, down topples she,	
	And "tailor" cries,[8] and falls into a cough;	
55	And then the whole choir° hold their hips and laugh,	*company*
	And waxen° in their mirth, and neeze,° and swear	*increase / sneeze*
	A merrier hour was never wasted there.	
	But room, fairy: here comes Oberon.	
	FAIRY And here my mistress. Would that he were gone.	

Enter [OBERON,] the King of Fairies, at one door, with his train, and [TITANIA,] the Queen, at another, with hers.[9]

60	OBERON Ill met by moonlight, proud Titania.	
	TITANIA What, jealous Oberon? —Fairy, skip hence.	
	I have forsworn his bed and company.	
	OBERON Tarry, rash wanton!° Am not I thy lord?	*impetuous creature*
	TITANIA Then I must be thy lady; but I know	
65	When thou hast stolen away from fairyland	
	And in the shape of Corin[1] sat all day	
	Playing on pipes of corn and versing love[2]	
	To amorous Phillida. Why art thou here	
	Come from the farthest step° of India	*limit*
70	But that, forsooth, the bouncing° Amazon,	*vigorous*
	Your buskined° mistress and your warrior love,	*wearing hunting boots*
	To Theseus must be wedded, and you come	
	To give their bed joy and prosperity?	
	OBERON How canst thou thus, for shame, Titania,	
75	Glance at my credit° with Hippolyta,	*Question my good name*
	Knowing I know thy love to Theseus?	
	Didst not thou lead him through the glimmering night	

7. Crab apple ("lamb's wool," a winter drink, was made with roasted apples and warm ale).
8. Possibly the old woman cries this because she ends up cross-legged on the floor, as tailors sat to do their work, or because she falls on her "tail."
9. PERFORMANCE COMMENT Many productions of the play have opted to cast actors and actresses in more than one role, such as having the same actor perform as both Theseus and Oberon. For more on doubling and its interpretive implications for the play, see Digital Edition PC 2.
1. "Corin" and "Phillida" are typical names for a shepherd and shepherdess in pastoral poetry.
2. Making or reciting love poetry. *pipes of corn:* musical instruments made of oat stalks.

From Perigenia, whom he ravishèd,
And make him with fair Aegles[3] break his faith,
80   With Ariadne, and Antiopa?[4]
TITANIA   These are the forgeries of jealousy;
And never since the middle summer's spring°   *beginning of midsummer*
Met we on hill, in dale, forest, or mead,
By pavèd fountain or by rushy[5] brook,
85   Or in° the beachèd margin° of the sea   *on / shore*
To dance our ringlets° to the whistling wind,   *circle dances*
But with thy brawls thou hast disturbed our sport.
Therefore the winds, piping to us in vain,
As in revenge have sucked up from the sea
90   Contagious fogs which, falling in the land,
Hath every pelting° river made so proud   *paltry*
That they have overborne their continents.°   *banks*
The ox hath therefore stretched his yoke in vain,
The plowman lost his sweat, and the green corn°   *grain*
95   Hath rotted ere his youth attained a beard.
The fold stands empty in the drownèd field,
And crows are fatted with the murrain° flock;   *dead of disease*
The nine-men's morris[6] is filled up with mud,
And the quaint mazes in the wanton green[7]
100   For lack of tread are undistinguishable.
The human mortals want° their winter cheer;[8]   *lack*
No night is now with hymn or carol blessed.
Therefore[9] the moon, the governess of floods,
Pale in her anger, washes° all the air,   *moistens; wets*
105   That rheumatic[1] diseases do abound.
And thorough this distemperature° we see   *bad weather; disturbance*
The seasons alter; hoary-headed frosts
Fall in the fresh lap of the crimson rose,
And on old Hiems'° chin and icy crown   *winter's*
110   An odorous chaplet° of sweet summer buds   *wreath*
Is, as in mockery, set. The spring, the summer,
The childing° autumn, angry winter, change   *fruitful*
Their wonted liveries,[2] and the mazèd° world   *bewildered*
By their increase° now knows not which is which.   *crop yield*
115   And this same progeny of evils comes
From our debate,° from our dissension;   *quarrel*
We are their parents and original.°   *origin*
OBERON   Do you amend it then; it lies in you.
Why should Titania cross her Oberon?
120   I do but beg a little changeling boy
To be my henchman.°   *page of honor*
TITANIA   Set your heart at rest.[3]

---

3. In Plutarch's *Lives*, Theseus previously had mistresses named Perigouna and Aegles. "Perigenia" may be Shakespeare's alteration.
4. Taken from Plutarch; some writers used "Antiopa" as an alternative name for the Amazonian queen whom Theseus married, although here it seems to refer to a different woman. Ariadne helped Theseus to kill the Minotaur and escape from his labyrinth on Crete; she fled with Theseus, but he deserted her on Naxos.
5. Fringed with reeds. *pavèd*: pebbled.
6. The playing area for this outdoor game (traditionally, a board game played with nine pebbles or pegs) was cut in turf.
7. Luxuriant grass. *quaint mazes*: intricate arrangements of paths (kept visible by frequent use).
8. Winter cheer would include the hymns and carols of the Yuletide. But Q1 and F read "here."
9. As in lines 88 and 93 above, referring to the consequences of their quarrel.
1. Characterized by rheum: colds, coughs, and the like.
2. Customary clothing.
3. Proverbial expression for "Abandon that idea."

The fairyland buys not the child of me.
His mother was a votress[4] of my order,
And in the spicèd Indian air by night
125 Full often hath she gossiped by my side
And sat with me on Neptune's yellow sands,
Marking the embarkèd traders° on the flood,°   *merchant ships / tide*
When we have laughed to see the sails conceive
And grow big-bellied with the wanton° wind,   *playful; amorous*
130 Which she, with pretty and with swimming[5] gait
Following°—her womb then rich with my young squire—   *Copying*
Would imitate, and sail upon the land
To fetch me trifles and return again,
As from a voyage, rich with merchandise.
135 But she, being mortal, of that boy did die,
And for her sake do I rear up her boy,
And for her sake I will not part with him.
OBERON How long within this wood intend you stay?
TITANIA Perchance till after Theseus' wedding day.
140 If you will patiently dance in our round
And see our moonlight revels, go with us.
If not, shun me, and I will spare° your haunts.   *avoid*
OBERON Give me that boy, and I will go with thee.
TITANIA Not for thy fairy kingdom. —Fairies, away!
145 We shall chide° downright if I longer stay.   *quarrel*
      Exeunt [TITANIA *and her train*].
OBERON Well, go thy way. Thou shalt not from° this grove   *go from*
Till I torment thee for this injury.
—My gentle puck, come hither. Thou rememberest
Since° once I sat upon a promontory   *When*
150 And heard a mermaid on a dolphin's back
Uttering such dulcet° and harmonious breath°   *sweet / voice; song*
That the rude° sea grew civil at her song   *rough*
And certain stars shot madly from their spheres°   *orbits*
To hear the sea-maid's music?
ROBIN   I remember.
155 OBERON That very time I saw—but thou couldst not—
Flying between the cold moon and the earth,
Cupid, all armed. A certain aim he took
At a fair vestal thronèd by the west,[6]
And loosed his love-shaft° smartly from his bow   *golden arrow*
160 As° it should pierce a hundred thousand hearts.   *As though*
But I might° see young Cupid's fiery shaft   *could*
Quenched in the chaste beams of the watery moon;
And the imperial votress passèd on
In maiden meditation, fancy-free.°   *free of love thoughts*
165 Yet marked I where the bolt° of Cupid fell.   *arrow*
It fell upon a little western flower,
Before milk-white, now purple with love's wound,
And maidens call it "love-in-idleness."[7]

---

4. A woman who has taken a vow to serve (often, religious).
5. As though gliding through the waves.
6. To the west of India; in England. *vestal:* virgin (a compliment to Queen Elizabeth, the Virgin Queen, and possibly an allusion to a specific entertainment in her honor, such as the water pageant at Elvetham in 1591).
7. Pansy. (Classical legend describes how the mulberry turned purple with Pyramus's blood and the hyacinth with Hyacinthus's, but it does not mention the pansy.)

Fetch me that flower. The herb I showed thee once:
170 The juice of it on sleeping eyelids laid
     Will make or° man or woman madly dote   *either*
     Upon the next live creature that it sees.
     Fetch me this herb, and be thou here again
     Ere the leviathan[8] can swim a league.
175 ROBIN   I'll put a girdle° round about the earth   *circle*
     In forty minutes.
     OBERON   Having once this juice,
     I'll watch Titania when she is asleep
     And drop the liquor° of it in her eyes.   *juice*
     The next thing then she waking looks upon—
180 Be it on lion, bear, or wolf, or bull,
     On meddling monkey or on busy ape—
     She shall pursue it with the soul of love.
     And ere I take this charm from off her sight—
     As I can take it with another herb—
185 I'll make her render up her page to me.
     But who comes here? I am invisible,
     And I will overhear their conference.

          Enter DEMETRIUS, HELENA *following him.*

     DEMETRIUS   I love thee not, therefore pursue me not.
     Where is Lysander and fair Hermia?
190 The one I'll stay, the other stayeth me.[9]
     Thou told'st me they were stolen unto this wood,
     And here am I, and wood° within this wood   *insane*
     Because I cannot meet my Hermia.
     Hence, get thee gone, and follow me no more.
195 HELENA   You draw me, you hard-hearted adamant,[1]
     But yet you draw not iron, for my heart
     Is true as steel.[2] Leave you° your power to draw,   *Relinquish*
     And I shall have no power to follow you.
     DEMETRIUS   Do I entice you? Do I speak you fair?[3]
200 Or rather do I not in plainest truth
     Tell you I do not nor I cannot love you?
     HELENA   And even for that do I love you the more.
     I am your spaniel, and, Demetrius,
     The more you beat me I will fawn on you.
205 Use me but as your spaniel: spurn me, strike me,
     Neglect me, lose me—only give me leave,
     Unworthy as I am, to follow you.
     What worser place can I beg in your love—
     And yet a place of high respect with me—
210 Than to be usèd as you use your dog?
     DEMETRIUS   Tempt not too much the hatred of my spirit,
     For I am sick when I do look on thee.
     HELENA   And I am sick when I look not on you.
     DEMETRIUS   You do impeach° your modesty too much   *call into question*
215 To leave the city and commit yourself

---

8. Biblical sea monster, identified with the whale.
9. The one (Lysander) I'll bring to a halt, the other (Hermia) stops me in my tracks.
1. Very hard stone supposed to have magnetic properties. *draw me:* that is, with the magnetic power of attraction.
2. Hermia contrasts the base metal iron with steel, which holds its temper.
3. Do I speak kindly to you?

Into the hands of one that loves you not,
To trust the opportunity of night
And the ill counsel of a desert° place   *deserted*
With the rich worth of your virginity.

220 HELENA   Your virtue is my privilege.° For that°   *protection / Because*
It is not night when I do see your face.
Therefore I think I am not in the night,
Nor doth this wood lack worlds of company,
For you in my respect° are all the world.   *as far as I am concerned*

225 Then how can it be said I am alone
When all the world is here to look on me?

DEMETRIUS   I'll run from thee and hide me in the brakes,°   *thickets*
And leave thee to the mercy of wild beasts.

HELENA   The wildest hath not such a heart as you.

230 Run when you will. The story shall be changed:
Apollo flies, and Daphne holds the chase;[4]
The dove pursues the griffin;[5] the mild hind°   *doe*
Makes speed to catch the tiger: bootless° speed   *useless*
When cowardice pursues and valor flies.

235 DEMETRIUS   I will not stay thy questions.[6] Let me go!
Or if thou follow me, do not believe
But I shall do thee mischief in the wood.   *[Exit.]*[7]

HELENA   Ay, in the temple, in the town, the field,
You do me mischief. Fie, Demetrius,

240 Your wrongs do set a scandal on my sex.[8]
We cannot fight for love as men may do;
We should be wooed and were not made to woo.
I'll follow thee and make a heaven of hell
To die upon the hand I love so well.   *[Exit.]*

245 OBERON   Fare thee well, nymph. Ere he do leave this grove
Thou shalt fly him, and he shall seek thy love.
      Enter [ROBIN *Goodfellow, the*] *puck.*
Hast thou the flower there? Welcome, wanderer.

ROBIN   Ay, there it is.

OBERON   I pray thee give it me.
I know a bank where the wild thyme blows,

250 Where oxlips[9] and the nodding violet grows,
Quite over-canopied with luscious woodbine,°   *honeysuckle*
With sweet musk-roses,[1] and with eglantine.°   *sweetbrier (a type of rose)*
There sleeps Titania sometime of the night,
Lulled in these flowers with dances and delight;

255 And there the snake throws° her enameled skin,   *throws off; casts away*
Weed° wide enough to wrap a fairy in.   *Garment*
And with the juice of this I'll streak° her eyes,   *anoint*
And make her full of hateful fantasies.
Take thou some of it, and seek through this grove.

260 A sweet Athenian lady is in love

---

4. A reversal of the traditional myth in which the nymph Daphne, flying from Apollo, was transformed into a laurel tree to escape him.
5. A fabulous monster with a lion's body and an eagle's head and wings.
6. I will not wait here any longer to hear you talk.
7. TEXTUAL COMMENT Neither Q1 nor F provides an exit for Demetrius in this scene; however, when exactly he leaves has important implications for the tone of Helena's speech. See Digital Edition TC 2 (Quarto edited text).
8. Your injustices to me cause me to behave in a way that disgraces my sex (by wooing him rather than being wooed).
9. Hybrid between primrose and cowslip.
1. Large rambling white roses.

With a disdainful youth. Anoint his eyes,
But do it when the next thing he espies
May be the lady. Thou shalt know the man
By the Athenian garments he hath on.
265 Effect it with some care, that he may prove
More fond° on her than she upon her love.   *doting*
And look thou meet me ere the first cock crow.[2]
ROBIN   Fear not, my lord; your servant shall do so.   *Exeunt.*

2.2 (F 2.2)

Enter TITANIA, *Queen of Fairies, with her train.*

TITANIA   Come, now a roundel° and a fairy song;   *circle dance*
Then, for the third part of a minute,[1] hence,
Some to kill cankers° in the musk-rose buds,   *caterpillars*
Some war with reremice° for their leathern wings   *bats*
5 To make my small elves coats, and some keep back
The clamorous owl that nightly hoots and wonders
At our quaint° spirits. Sing me now asleep;   *dainty*
Then to your offices, and let me rest.
  [*She lies down.*] FAIRIES *sing* [*and dance*].
FIRST FAIRY   You spotted snakes with double° tongue,   *forked*
10   Thorny hedgehogs, be not seen;
             Newts and blindworms,[2] do no wrong,
             Come not near our Fairy Queen.
CHORUS   Philomel,[3] with melody
             Sing in our sweet lullaby;
15   Lulla, lulla, lullaby, lulla, lulla, lullaby.
             Never harm,
             Nor spell, nor charm
             Come our lovely lady nigh.
             So good night, with lullaby.
20 FIRST FAIRY   Weaving spiders, come not here;
             Hence, you long-legged spinners, hence!
             Beetles black, approach not near;
             Worm nor snail, do no offense.
CHORUS   Philomel, with melody, etc.
  [TITANIA *sleeps.*]
25 SECOND FAIRY   Hence, away! Now all is well.
One aloof° stand sentinel.   *at a distance*
           [*Exeunt* FAIRIES, *leaving one sentinel.*]
       Enter OBERON. [*He squeezes the juice on Titania's eyes.*]
OBERON   What thou seest when thou dost wake,
Do it for thy true love take;
Love and languish for his sake.
30 Be it ounce° or cat or bear,   *lynx*
Pard,° or boar with bristled hair,   *Leopard*
In thy eye that shall appear
When thou wak'st, it is thy dear.
Wake when some vile thing is near.   [*Exit.*]
       Enter LYSANDER *and* HERMIA.

---

2. Some spirits were thought unable to bear daylight (compare *Hamlet* 1.1.138–56).
2.2 Location: The wood.
1. The fairies are quick enough to do their tasks in twenty seconds.

2. Newts (water lizards) and blindworms were thought to be poisonous, as were spiders (line 20).
3. Philomel, the nightingale (in classical mythology, a woman who, having been raped by her sister's husband, was transformed into a bird).

35   LYSANDER   Fair love, you faint with wandering in the wood,
       And to speak truth, I have forgot our way.
       We'll rest us, Hermia, if you think it good,
       And tarry for the comfort of the day.
     HERMIA   Be it so, Lysander. Find you out a bed,
40   For I upon this bank will rest my head.
     LYSANDER   One turf shall serve as pillow for us both;
       One heart, one bed, two bosoms, and one troth.°   *pledged faith*
     HERMIA   Nay, good Lysander: for my sake, my dear,
       Lie further off yet; do not lie so near.
45   LYSANDER   Oh, take the sense,° sweet, of my innocence!   *true meaning*
       Love takes the meaning in love's conference.[4]
       I mean that my heart unto yours is knit,
       So that but one heart we can make of it.
       Two bosoms interchainèd with an oath;
50   So, then, two bosoms and a single troth.
       Then by your side no bed-room me deny,
       For lying so, Hermia, I do not lie.[5]
     HERMIA   Lysander riddles very prettily.
       Now much beshrew[6] my manners and my pride
55   If Hermia meant to say Lysander lied.
       But, gentle friend, for love and courtesy
       Lie further off in human° modesty.   *courteous*
       Such separation as may well be said
       Becomes a virtuous bachelor and a maid,
60   So far be distant. And good night, sweet friend;
       Thy love ne'er alter till thy sweet life end.
     LYSANDER   Amen, amen, to that fair prayer say I,
       And then end life when I end loyalty.
       Here is my bed. Sleep give thee all his rest.
65   HERMIA   With half that wish the wisher's eyes be pressed.[7]
       [*They sleep separately.*]
       Enter [ROBIN *Goodfellow, the*] *puck.*
     ROBIN   Through the forest have I gone,
       But Athenian found I none
       On whose eyes I might approve°   *test*
       This flower's force in stirring love.
70   Night and silence. Who is here?
       Weeds of Athens he doth wear.
       This is he my master said
       Despisèd the Athenian maid;
       And here the maiden, sleeping sound
75   On the dank and dirty ground.
       Pretty soul, she durst not lie
       Near this lack-love, this kill-courtesy.
       Churl,° upon thy eyes I throw   *Rude fellow*
       All the power this charm doth owe.°   *own*
       [*He squeezes the juice on Lysander's eyes.*]
80   When thou wak'st, let love forbid
       Sleep his seat on thy eyelid.[8]

---

4. Love should enable lovers truly to understand each other.
5. Deceive; punning on "lie down."
6. Curse (used in a mild sense).

7. May sleep's rest be shared between us. *pressed*: closed in sleep.
8. *forbid . . . eyelid*: prevent you from sleeping.

So awake when I am gone,
For I must now to Oberon.   *Exit.*
     Enter DEMETRIUS *and* HELENA, *running.*
HELENA   Stay, though thou kill me, sweet Demetrius.
85 DEMETRIUS   I charge thee: hence, and do not haunt me thus.
HELENA   Oh, wilt thou darkling° leave me? Do not so.   *in darkness*
DEMETRIUS   Stay, on thy peril;⁹ I alone will go.   [*Exit.*]
HELENA   Oh, I am out of breath in this fond° chase.   *foolish*
    The more my prayer, the lesser is my grace.°   *reward*
90   Happy is Hermia, wheresoe'er she lies,
    For she hath blessèd and attractive° eyes.   *magnetic*
    How came her eyes so bright? Not with salt tears;
    If so, my eyes are oftener washed than hers.
    No, no; I am as ugly as a bear,
95   For beasts that meet me run away for fear.
    Therefore no marvel though Demetrius
    Do, as° a monster, fly my presence thus.   *as if I were*
    What wicked and dissembling glass of mine
    Made me compare° with Hermia's sphery eyne?°   *compete / starry eyes*
100   But who is here? Lysander, on the ground?
    Dead or asleep? I see no blood, no wound.
    Lysander, if you live, good sir, awake.
LYSANDER [*awaking*]   And run through fire I will for thy
       sweet sake.
    Transparent¹ Helena, nature shows art°   *skill; magic power*
105   That through thy bosom makes me see thy heart.
    Where is Demetrius? Oh, how fit a word
    Is that vile name to perish on my sword!
HELENA   Do not say so, Lysander; say not so.
    What though he love your Hermia? Lord, what though?
110   Yet Hermia still loves you; then be content.
LYSANDER   Content with Hermia? No, I do repent
    The tedious minutes I with her have spent.
    Not Hermia but Helena I love.
    Who will not change a raven for a dove?
115   The will of man is by his reason swayed,²
    And reason says you are the worthier maid.
    Things growing are not ripe until their season,
    So I, being young, till now ripe not to reason.
    And, touching now the point of human skill,³
120   Reason becomes the marshal⁴ to my will
    And leads me to your eyes, where I o'erlook°   *look over; read*
    Love's stories written in love's richest book.
HELENA   Wherefore was I to this keen° mockery born?   *sharp*
    When at your hands did I deserve this scorn?
125   Is't not enough, is't not enough, young man,
    That I did never—no, nor never can—
    Deserve a sweet look from Demetrius' eye,
    But you must flout my insufficiency?⁵

---

9. Stay here, or risk peril (if you follow me).
1. Radiant; capable of being seen through.
2. Renaissance psychology considered the will (that is, the passions) to be in constant conflict with, and ideally subject to, the faculty of reason.

3. Reaching (only) now the highest point of human judgment.
4. An officer who led guests to their appointed places.
5. *flout my insufficiency:* mock my shortcomings by pretending they are wonderful qualities.

Good troth,° you do me wrong—good sooth,° you do—   *Truly / indeed*
130 In such disdainful manner me to woo.
But fare you well. Perforce I must confess
I thought you lord of more true gentleness.°   *courtesy; breeding*
Oh, that a lady of one man refused
Should of° another therefore be abused!   *Exit.*   *by*
135 LYSANDER She sees not Hermia. —Hermia, sleep thou there,
And never mayst thou come Lysander near;
For as a surfeit of the sweetest things
The deepest loathing to the stomach brings,
Or as the heresies that men do leave
140 Are hated most of those they did deceive,[6]
So thou, my surfeit and my heresy,
Of all be hated, but the most of me!
And, all my powers, address° your love and might   *direct; apply*
To honor Helen and to be her knight.   *Exit.*
145 HERMIA [*awaking*] Help me, Lysander, help me! Do thy best
To pluck this crawling serpent from my breast!
Ay me, for pity! What a dream was here!
Lysander, look how I do quake with fear.
Methought a serpent ate my heart away,
150 And you sat smiling at his cruel prey.°   *act of preying*
Lysander? What, removed? Lysander! Lord!
What, out of hearing, gone? No sound, no word?
Alack, where are you? Speak an if° you hear,   *an if = if*
Speak, of° all loves! I swoon almost with fear.   *for the sake of*
155 No? Then I well perceive you are not nigh.
Either death or you I'll find immediately.
        Exit. [TITANIA *remains lying asleep.*]

3.1 (F 3.1)

Enter the clowns°[, BOTTOM, QUINCE, SNOUT,   *rustics*
   STARVELING, FLUTE, *and* SNUG].
BOTTOM Are we all met?
QUINCE Pat,° pat; and here's a marvelous convenient place for   *On the dot*
   our rehearsal. This green plot shall be our stage, this haw-
   thorn brake° our tiring-house,° and we will do it in action as   *thicket / dressing room*
5   we will do it before the Duke.
BOTTOM Peter Quince?
QUINCE What sayest thou, bully° Bottom?   *good fellow; jolly*
BOTTOM There are things in this comedy of Pyramus and
   Thisbe that will never please. First, Pyramus must draw a
10   sword to kill himself, which the ladies cannot abide. How
   answer you that?
SNOUT By'r lakin,[1] a parlous° fear.   *perilous*
STARVELING I believe we must leave the killing out, when all
   is done.[2]
15 BOTTOM Not a whit. I have a device to make all well. Write me
   a prologue, and let the prologue seem to say we will do no
   harm with our swords, and that Pyramus is not killed indeed.
   And for the more better assurance, tell them that I, Pyramus,

---

6. *as the heresies . . . deceive:* as men most hate the false opinions they once held.
3.1 Location: Remains the same, although F intro-

duces an act break.
1. By our ladykin (Virgin Mary): a mild oath.
2. When all is said and done.

20   am not Pyramus but Bottom the weaver. This will put them
      out of fear.

QUINCE   Well, we will have such a prologue, and it shall be
      written in eight and six.[3]

BOTTOM   No, make it two more: let it be written in eight and
      eight.

25 SNOUT   Will not the ladies be afeard of the lion?

STARVELING   I fear it, I promise you.

BOTTOM   Masters, you ought to consider with yourself, to bring
      in—God shield us!—a lion among ladies is a most dreadful
      thing.[4] For there is not a more fearful° wildfowl than your lion   *frightening*
30   living. And we ought to look to't.

SNOUT   Therefore another prologue must tell he is not a lion.

BOTTOM   Nay, you must name his name, and half his face
      must be seen through the lion's neck, and he himself must
      speak through, saying thus or to the same defect:° "Ladies,"   *(for "effect")*
35   or "Fair Ladies, I would wish you," or "I would request you,"
      or "I would entreat you not to fear, not to tremble. My life
      for yours.[5] If you think I come hither as a lion, it were pity
      of° my life. No, I am no such thing. I am a man as other men   *a threat to*
      are"—and there indeed let him name his name, and tell
40   them plainly he is Snug the joiner.

QUINCE   Well, it shall be so. But there is two hard things: that
      is, to bring the moonlight into a chamber—for you know
      Pyramus and Thisbe meet by moonlight.

SNOUT[6]   Doth the moon shine that night we play our play?

45 BOTTOM   A calendar, a calendar! Look in the almanac; find
      out moonshine, find out moonshine!

QUINCE   Yes, it doth shine that night.

BOTTOM   Why, then may you leave a casement of the great
      chamber window where we play open, and the moon may
50   shine in at the casement.

QUINCE   Ay, or else one must come in with a bush of thorns
      and a lantern and say he comes to disfigure,[7] or to present,°   *represent*
      the person of Moonshine. Then there is another thing: we
      must have a wall in the great chamber; for Pyramus and
55   Thisbe, says the story, did talk through the chink of a wall.

SNOUT   You can never bring in a wall. What say you, Bottom?

BOTTOM   Some man or other must present Wall; and let him
      have some plaster, or some loam, or some roughcast[8] about
      him to signify "wall"; or let him hold his fingers thus, and
60   through that cranny shall Pyramus and Thisbe whisper.

QUINCE   If that may be, then all is well. Come, sit down, every
      mother's son, and rehearse your parts. Pyramus, you begin.
      When you have spoken your speech, enter into that brake,
      and so everyone according to his cue.
            Enter ROBIN[, *invisible*].[9]

3. Alternate lines of eight and six syllables (a common ballad measure).
4. In 1594, at a feast in honor of the christening of King James's son, a tame lion that was supposed to draw a chariot was replaced by a black African man in order to avoid frightening the audience.
5. I pledge my life to defend yours.
6. Or Snug: Q1 and F abbreviate as "Sn."
7. Blunder for "figure," represent. *bush of thorns:* bundle of thornbush kindling (like the lantern, a traditional accessory of the man in the moon).
8. Mixture of lime and gravel used to plaster exterior walls.
9. TEXTUAL COMMENT Throughout the scene, the various entrances of Robin and Bottom differ between Q1 and F, with significant implications for staging possibilities. See Digital Edition TC 3 (Quarto edited text).

65 ROBIN [*aside*] What hempen homespuns[1] have we swaggering
    here
    So near the cradle of the Fairy Queen?
    What, a play toward?° I'll be an auditor—   *in preparation*
    An actor too perhaps, if I see cause.

QUINCE Speak, Pyramus. —Thisbe, stand forth.

70 BOTTOM [*as Pyramus*] "Thisbe, the flowers of odious° savors   (*for "odorous"*)
    sweet—"

QUINCE Odors—"odorous"!

BOTTOM [*as Pyramus*] "—Odors savors sweet.
    So hath thy breath, my dearest Thisbe dear.
    But hark, a voice! Stay thou but here a while,

75   And by and by I will to thee appear."   *Exit.*

QUINCE A stranger Pyramus than e'er played here.   [*Exit.*]

FLUTE Must I speak now?

QUINCE Ay, marry, must you. For you must understand he
    goes but to see a noise that he heard and is to come again.

80 FLUTE [*as Thisbe*] "Most radiant Pyramus, most lily-white
    of hue,
    Of color like the red rose on triumphant briar,
    Most brisky juvenal° and eke° most lovely Jew,[2]   *lively youth (juvenile) / also*
    As true as truest horse that yet would never tire,
    I'll meet thee, Pyramus, at Ninny's tomb—"

85 QUINCE "Ninus'[3] tomb," man! Why, you must not speak that
    yet; that you answer to Pyramus. You speak all your part at
    once, cues and all. —Pyramus, enter! Your cue is past; it is
    "never tire."

FLUTE Oh,
90   [*as Thisbe*] "As true as truest horse that yet would never tire."
        [*Enter* ROBIN, *invisible, and* BOTTOM *with the
        ass head on.*]

BOTTOM [*as Pyramus*] "If I were fair,° Thisbe, I were° only   *handsome / would be*
    thine."

QUINCE Oh, monstrous! Oh, strange! We are haunted! Pray,
    masters! Fly, masters! Help!
        [*Exeunt* QUINCE, SNOUT, STARVELING,
               FLUTE, *and* SNUG.]

ROBIN I'll follow you, I'll lead you about a round,°   *in circles*
95 Through bog, through bush, through brake, through briar.
    Sometime a horse I'll be, sometime a hound,
    A hog, a headless bear, sometime a fire,°   *will-o'-the-wisp*
    And neigh and bark and grunt and roar and burn,
    Like horse, hound, hog, bear, fire, at every turn.   *Exit.*

100 BOTTOM Why do they run away? This is a knavery of them to
    make me afeard.
        Enter SNOUT.

SNOUT O Bottom, thou art changed! What do I see on thee?

---

1. Peasants, or country bumpkins, dressed in coarse homespun fabric made from hemp.
2. Not often considered "lovely" by Elizabethan Christians; usually, a term of abuse (here, echoing the first syllable of "juvenal").
3. Mythical founder of Nineveh, whose wife, Semiramis, was believed to have founded Babylon, the setting for the story of Pyramus and Thisbe. Flute's mistake, "Ninny," means "fool."

BOTTOM   What do you see? You see an ass head of your own,[4]
do you?   [*Exit* SNOUT.]
    Enter QUINCE.

105   QUINCE   Bless thee, Bottom, bless thee! Thou art translated.°   *transformed*
                                                      Exit.

BOTTOM   I see their knavery. This is to make an ass of me, to
fright me, if they could. But I will not stir from this place,
do what they can. I will walk up and down here, and I will
sing, that they shall hear I am not afraid.

110   [*Sings.*]   The ouzel cock,° so black of hue,   *male blackbird*
            With orange-tawny bill,
            The throstle° with his note so true,   *song thrush*
            The wren with little quill°—   *feathers*

TITANIA [*awaking*]   What angel wakes me from my flowery
bed?

115   BOTTOM [*sings*]   The finch, the sparrow, and the lark,
            The plainsong[5] cuckoo gray,
            Whose note full many a man doth mark
            And dares not answer "Nay"[6]—

for indeed, who would set his wit to° so foolish a bird? Who   *pay heed to*
120   would give a bird the lie,[7] though he cry "cuckoo" never so?°   *ever so much*

TITANIA   I pray thee, gentle mortal, sing again.
Mine ear is much enamored of thy note;
So is mine eye enthrallèd to thy shape,
And thy fair virtue's force[8] perforce doth move me

125   On the first view to say, to swear, I love thee.

BOTTOM   Methinks, mistress, you should have little reason
for that. And yet, to say the truth, reason and love keep little
company together nowadays—the more the pity that some
honest neighbors will not make them friends. Nay, I can

130   gleek° upon occasion.   *make jokes*

TITANIA   Thou art as wise as thou art beautiful.

BOTTOM   Not so neither; but if I had wit enough to get out of
this wood, I have enough to serve mine own turn.°   *purpose*

TITANIA   Out of this wood do not desire to go.

135   Thou shalt remain here, whether thou wilt or no.
I am a spirit of no common rate°—   *rank*
The summer still° doth tend upon my state[9]—   *always; continually*
And I do love thee. Therefore go with me.
I'll give thee fairies to attend on thee,

140   And they shall fetch thee jewels from the deep
And sing while thou on pressèd flowers dost sleep.
And I will purge thy mortal grossness° so   *fleshly being*
That thou shalt like an airy spirit go.
Peaseblossom, Cobweb, Moth, and Mustardseed!
    Enter four FAIRIES[: PEASEBLOSSOM, COBWEB, MOTH,[1]
    and MUSTARDSEED].

PEASEBLOSSOM   Ready.

COBWEB   And I.

---

4. You see a figment of your own asinine imagination.
5. A melody sung without adornment (that is, the cuckoo's call).
6. Deny. (The cuckoo's call was associated with cuckoldry.)

7. Who would call a bird a liar?
8. The power of your good or beauteous qualities.
9. Serves me, as part of my royal retinue.
1. As it is spelled in Q1 and F, or "Mote": speck. Both words were spelled and pronounced alike.

MOTH   And I.

MUSTARDSEED   And I.

145   ALL   Where shall we go?

TITANIA   Be kind and courteous to this gentleman.
     Hop in his walks and gambol in his eyes;
     Feed him with apricots and dewberries,
     With purple grapes, green figs, and mulberries;
150   The honey bags steal from the humble-bees,°   *bumblebees*
     And for night-tapers crop their waxen thighs,
     And light them at the fiery glowworms' eyes
     To have° my love to bed and to arise;   *lead*
     And pluck the wings from painted butterflies
155   To fan the moonbeams from his sleeping eyes.
     Nod to him, elves, and do him courtesies.

PEASEBLOSSOM   Hail, mortal!

COBWEB   Hail!

MOTH   Hail!

160   MUSTARDSEED   Hail!

BOTTOM   I cry your worships mercy,[2] heartily. —I beseech
     your worship's name.

COBWEB   Cobweb.

BOTTOM   I shall desire you of more acquaintance, good Mas-
165   ter Cobweb. If I cut my finger,[3] I shall make bold with you.
     —Your name, honest gentleman?

PEASEBLOSSOM   Peaseblossom.

BOTTOM   I pray you commend me to Mistress Squash, your
     mother, and to Master Peascod,[4] your father. Good Master
170   Peaseblossom, I shall desire you of more acquaintance too.
     —Your name, I beseech you, sir?

MUSTARDSEED   Mustardseed.

BOTTOM   Good Master Mustardseed, I know your patience[5]
     well. That same cowardly, giant-like ox-beef[6] hath devoured
175   many a gentleman of your house. I promise you, your kin-
     dred hath made my eyes water ere now. I desire you of more
     acquaintance, good Master Mustardseed.

TITANIA [*to the* FAIRIES]   Come, wait upon him. Lead him to
     my bower.
     The moon methinks looks with a watery eye,
180   And when she weeps, weeps every little flower,[7]
     Lamenting some enforcèd° chastity.   *violated; involuntary*
     Tie up my lover's tongue;[8] bring him silently.   [*Exeunt.*]

3.2 (F 3.2)

Enter [OBERON,] *King of Fairies.*

OBERON   I wonder if Titania be awaked;
     Then what it was that next came in her eye,
     Which she must dote on in extremity.

        Enter ROBIN *Goodfellow.*

     Here comes my messenger. How now, mad spirit?

---

2. I beg pardon of your honors.
3. Cobwebs were used to stop bleeding.
4. Ripe pea pod (called "your father" because it suggests "codpiece"). *Squash:* Unripe pea pod.
5. What you have suffered with fortitude.
6. Because beef is often eaten with mustard, or

because oxen munch on mustard plants.
7. Dew was thought to originate on the moon.
8. Bottom is perhaps making involuntary asinine
noises.
3.2 Location: The wood.

5	What night-rule° now about this haunted grove?	*night revels; sports*
	ROBIN My mistress with a monster is in love.	
	Near to her close° and consecrated bower,	*private*
	While she was in her dull° and sleeping hour,	*drowsy*
	A crew of patches,° rude mechanicals°	*fools / rough workmen*
10	That work for bread upon Athenian stalls,°	*market stands*
	Were met together to rehearse a play	
	Intended for great Theseus' nuptial day.	
	The shallowest thick-skin of that barren sort,°	*witless lot*
	Who Pyramus presented° in their sport,	*acted*
15	Forsook his scene° and entered in a brake.	*stage*
	When I did him at this advantage take,	
	An ass's nole° I fixèd on his head.	*head*
	Anon his Thisbe must be answerèd,	
	And forth my mimic° comes. When they him spy—	*burlesque actor*
20	As wild geese that the creeping fowler° eye,	*hunter of birds*
	Or russet-pated choughs, many in sort,[1]	
	Rising and cawing at the gun's report,	
	Sever° themselves and madly sweep the sky—	*Scatter*
	So at his sight away his fellows fly,	
25	And at our stamp[2] here o'er and o'er one falls.	
	He° "Murder!" cries and help from Athens calls.	*One (workman)*
	Their sense thus weak, lost with their fears thus strong,	
	Made senseless things begin to do them wrong.	
	For briars and thorns at their apparel snatch,	
30	Some sleeves, some hats: from yielders all things catch.[3]	
	I led them on in this distracted fear	
	And left sweet Pyramus translated there,	
	When in that moment, so it came to pass,	
	Titania waked and straightway loved an ass.	
35	OBERON This falls out better than I could devise.	
	But hast thou yet latched° the Athenian's eyes	*anointed*
	With the love juice, as I did bid thee do?	
	ROBIN I took him sleeping—that is finished, too—	
	And the Athenian woman by his side,	
40	That° when he waked, of force° she must be eyed.	*So that / necessity*
	Enter DEMETRIUS *and* HERMIA.	
	OBERON Stand close. This is the same Athenian.	
	ROBIN This is the woman, but not this the man.	
	[OBERON *and* ROBIN *stand apart*.]	
	DEMETRIUS Oh, why rebuke you him that loves you so?	
	Lay breath so bitter on your bitter foe.	
45	HERMIA Now I but chide, but I should use thee worse,	
	For thou, I fear, hast given me cause to curse.	
	If thou hast slain Lysander in his sleep,	
	Being o'er shoes° in blood, plunge in the deep,	*Having waded so far*
	And kill me too.	
50	The sun was not so true unto the day	
	As he to me. Would he have stolen away	
	From sleeping Hermia? I'll believe as soon	
	This whole° earth may be bored, and that the moon	*solid*

---

1. Together, in a flock. *russet-pated choughs:* gray-headed jackdaws.
2. Editors have wondered how a fairy's presumably tiny foot could cause the human to fall.
3. Everything robs the timid.

May through the center creep and so displease
55   Her brother's noontide with the Antipodes.[4]
It cannot be but thou hast murdered him.
So should a murderer look: so dead,° so grim.   *deathly pale*
DEMETRIUS   So should the murdered look, and so should I,
Pierced through the heart with your stern cruelty.
60   Yet you, the murderer, look as bright, as clear,
As yonder Venus in her glimmering sphere.°   *orbit*
HERMIA   What's this to my Lysander? Where is he?
Ah, good Demetrius, wilt thou give him me?
DEMETRIUS   I had rather give his carcass to my hounds.
65 HERMIA   Out, dog! Out, cur! Thou driv'st me past the bounds
Of maiden's patience. Hast thou slain him, then?
Henceforth be never numbered among men.
Oh, once tell true; tell true, even for my sake:
Durst thou have looked upon him being awake,
70   And hast thou killed him sleeping? Oh, brave touch!°   *noble stroke*
Could not a worm,° an adder do so much?   *serpent*
An adder did it; for with doubler[5] tongue
Than thine, thou serpent, never adder stung.
DEMETRIUS   You spend your passion on a misprised mood.°   *in misconceived anger*
75   I am not guilty of Lysander's blood,
Nor is he dead, for aught that I can tell.
HERMIA   I pray thee, tell me then that he is well.
DEMETRIUS   And if I could, what should I get therefore?°   *for that*
HERMIA   A privilege, never to see me more;
80   And from thy hated presence part I so.
See me no more, whether he be dead or no.   *Exit.*
DEMETRIUS   There is no following her in this fierce vein.
Here therefore for a while I will remain.
So sorrow's heaviness[6] doth heavier grow
85   For debt that bankrupt sleep doth sorrow owe,[7]
Which now in some slight measure it will pay,
If for his tender here I make some stay.[8]
      [He] lies down [and sleeps].
OBERON *[to* ROBIN*]*   What hast thou done? Thou hast
    mistaken quite
And laid the love juice on some true love's sight.
90   Of thy misprision° must perforce ensue   *mistake*
Some true love turned, and not a false turned true.
ROBIN   Then fate o'errules, that, one man holding troth,°   *faith*
A million fail, confounding oath on oath.[9]
OBERON   About the wood go swifter than the wind,
95   And Helena of Athens look° thou find.   *be sure*
All fancy-sick° she is and pale of cheer°   *lovesick / face*
With sighs of love that costs the fresh blood dear.[1]
By some illusion see thou bring her here;

---

4. *that . . . Antipodes:* that the moon could creep through a hole bored through the earth's center and emerge on the other side, the Antipodes, displeasing the inhabitants by displacing the noontime sun with the darkness of night. (Apollo, the sun god, was the brother of Diana, the moon goddess.)
5. More forked (of the adder); more duplicitous (of Demetrius).

6. Sadness (punning on "heavy": drowsy).
7. *For . . . owe:* Because sorrow worsens without sleep.
8. *Which . . . stay:* I will rest here awhile, giving sleep capital ("tender") to pay off some of its debt to sorrow.
9. Among the millions of faithless men, the one true man's oath has been subverted by fate.
1. Sighs were thought to cause a loss of blood.

　　　　I'll charm his eyes against° she do appear.　　　　　　　　　*in readiness for when*
100　ROBIN　I go, I go; look how I go,
　　　　Swifter than arrow from the Tartar's bow.[2]　　　　　　　[*Exit.*]
　　OBERON [*squeezing the juice on Demetrius' eyes*]　Flower of
　　　　this purple dye,
　　　　Hit with Cupid's archery,
　　　　Sink in apple° of his eye.　　　　　　　　　　　　　　　　　*pupil*
105　　When his love he doth espy,
　　　　Let her shine as gloriously
　　　　As the Venus of the sky.
　　　　When thou wak'st, if she be by,
　　　　Beg of her for remedy.
　　　　　　　　Enter [ROBIN *Goodfellow, the*] *puck.*
110　ROBIN　Captain of our fairy band,
　　　　Helena is here at hand,
　　　　And the youth mistook by me,
　　　　Pleading for a lover's fee.°　　　　　　　　　　　　　　　*reward*
　　　　Shall we their fond° pageant see?　　　　　　　　　　　　*foolish*
115　　Lord, what fools these mortals be!
　　OBERON　Stand aside. The noise they make
　　　　Will cause Demetrius to awake.
　　ROBIN　Then will two at once woo one;
　　　　That must needs be sport alone.°　　　　　　　　　　　　*in itself*
120　And those things do best please me
　　　　That befall preposterously.°　　　　　　　　　　　　　　*ass backward*
　　　　　　[*They stand apart.*]
　　　　　　Enter LYSANDER *and* HELENA.
　　LYSANDER　Why should you think that I should woo in scorn?
　　　　Scorn and derision never come in tears.
　　　　Look when I vow, I weep, and vows so born,
125　　In their nativity all truth appears.[3]
　　　　How can these things in me seem scorn to you,
　　　　Bearing the badge of faith[4] to prove them true?
　　HELENA　You do advance° your cunning more and more.　　　*increase; display*
　　　　When truth kills truth[5]—oh, devilish-holy fray!
130　These vows are Hermia's. Will you give her o'er?
　　　　Weigh oath with oath, and you will nothing weigh.[6]
　　　　Your vows to her and me put in two scales
　　　　Will even weigh, and both as light as tales.°　　　　　　*lies; fiction*
　　LYSANDER　I had no judgment when to her I swore.
135　HELENA　Nor none, in my mind, now you give her o'er.
　　LYSANDER　Demetrius loves her, and he loves not you.
　　DEMETRIUS [*awaking*]　O Helen, goddess, nymph, perfect,
　　　　divine!
　　　　To what, my love, shall I compare thine eyne?
　　　　Crystal is muddy. Oh, how ripe in show°　　　　　　　　*appearance*
140　　Thy lips, those kissing cherries, tempting grow!
　　　　That pure congealèd white, high Taurus'[7] snow,

---

2. Tartars, a dark-skinned, supposedly savage people
in Asia Minor, were famed for their skills in archery.
3. *Look . . . appears:* The fact that I am weeping
authenticates my vow's sincerity.
4. Insignia, such as that worn on a servant's livery
(here, his tears).

5. When one vow nullifies another.
6. *you . . . weigh:* you will find that neither oath has
any substance; you, Lysander, will be found to have
no substance.
7. Range of high mountains in Asia Minor.

Fanned with the eastern wind, turns to a crow[8]
When thou hold'st up thy hand. Oh, let me kiss
This princess of pure white, this seal° of bliss!   pledge
145 HELENA Oh, spite! Oh, hell! I see you all are bent
To set against me for your merriment.
If you were civil and knew courtesy,
You would not do me thus much injury.
Can you not hate me, as I know you do,
150 But you must join in souls to mock me too?
If you were men, as men you are in show,
You would not use a gentle° lady so,   well-born; mild
To vow and swear and superpraise my parts,°   overpraise my qualities
When I am sure you hate me with your hearts.
155 You both are rivals and love Hermia,
And now both rivals to mock Helena.
A trim° exploit, a manly enterprise,   fine
To conjure tears up in a poor maid's eyes
With your derision. None of noble sort°   rank; nature
160 Would so offend a virgin and extort°   torture
A poor soul's patience, all to make you sport.
LYSANDER You are unkind, Demetrius; be not so.
For you love Hermia; this you know I know.
And here, with all good will, with all my heart,
165 In Hermia's love I yield you up my part;
And yours of Helena to me bequeath,
Whom I do love and will do till my death.
HELENA Never did mockers waste more idle breath.
DEMETRIUS Lysander, keep thy Hermia. I will none.[9]
170 If e'er I loved her, all that love is gone.
My heart to her but as guest-wise° sojourned,   as a guest
And now to Helen is it home returned,
There to remain.
LYSANDER   Helen, it is not so.
DEMETRIUS Disparage not the faith thou dost not know,
175 Lest to thy peril thou aby it dear.°   pay for it dearly
Look where thy love comes; yonder is thy dear.
            Enter HERMIA.
HERMIA Dark night, that from the eye his° function takes,   its
The ear more quick of apprehension makes,
Wherein it doth impair the seeing sense,
180 It pays the hearing double recompense.
Thou art not by mine eye, Lysander, found;
Mine ear, I thank it, brought me to thy sound.
But why unkindly didst thou leave me so?
LYSANDER Why should he stay whom love doth press to go?
185 HERMIA What love could press Lysander from my side?
LYSANDER Lysander's love, that would not let him bide:
Fair Helena, who more engilds the night
Than all yon fiery oes and eyes of light.[1]
[*to* HERMIA] Why seek'st thou me? Could not this make
    thee know

8. *turns to a crow*: appears black by contrast.
9. I will have nothing to do with her.

1. Stars (punning on the vowels and on lovers' exclamatory "oh"s and "ay"s). An "o" was a spangle.

190   The hate I bare thee made me leave thee so?
      HERMIA   You speak not as you think; it cannot be.
      HELENA   Lo, she is one of this confederacy.
      Now I perceive they have conjoined all three
      To fashion this false sport in spite of° me.   *to spite*
195   Injurious Hermia, most ungrateful maid,
      Have you conspired, have you with these contrived
      To bait[2] me with this foul derision?
      Is all the counsel° that we two have shared,   *intimacy*
      The sisters' vows, the hours that we have spent
200   When we have chid the hasty-footed time
      For parting us—oh, is all forgot,
      All schooldays' friendship, childhood innocence?
      We, Hermia, like two artificial° gods   *artfully skilled*
      Have with our needles created both one flower,
205   Both on one sampler, sitting on one cushion,
      Both warbling of one song, both in one key,
      As if our hands, our sides, voices, and minds
      Had been incorporate.° So we grew together   *of one body*
      Like to a double cherry, seeming parted,
210   But yet an union in partition,
      Two lovely berries molded on one stem;
      So with two seeming bodies but one heart,
      Two of the first,[3] like coats in heraldry,
      Due but to one and crownèd with one crest.
215   And will you rent our ancient love asunder,
      To join with men in scorning your poor friend?
      It is not friendly, 'tis not maidenly.
      Our sex as well as I may chide you for it,
      Though I alone do feel the injury.
220   HERMIA   I am amazèd at your words.
      I scorn you not; it seems that you scorn me.
      HELENA   Have you not set Lysander, as in scorn,
      To follow me and praise my eyes and face?
      And made your other love, Demetrius—
225   Who even but now° did spurn me with his foot—   *just now*
      To call me goddess, nymph, divine, and rare,
      Precious, celestial? Wherefore speaks he this
      To her he hates? And wherefore doth Lysander
      Deny your love—so rich within his soul—
230   And tender° me, forsooth, affection,   *offer*
      But by your setting on, by your consent?
      What though I be not so in grace° as you,   *favor*
      So hung upon with love, so fortunate,
      But miserable most, to love unloved?
235   This you should pity rather than despise.
      HERMIA   I understand not what you mean by this.
      HELENA   I do. Persever, counterfeit sad° looks,[4]   *serious*
      Make mouths upon° me when I turn my back,   *Make faces at*

---

2. To torment (as Elizabethans set dogs to bait a bear).
3. A technical phrase in heraldry, referring to the first quartering in a coat of arms, which may be repeated. The friends then have two bodies but a single, overarching identity.

4. TEXTUAL COMMENT Owing to the ambiguous nature of early modern spelling, Helena's response to Hermia could mean two quite different things, one of which is supported by Q1's punctuation, the other by F's. See Digital Edition TC 4 (Quarto edited text).

Wink each at other, hold the sweet jest up.°   *keep up the joke*
240   This sport well carried shall be chronicled.
If you have any pity, grace, or manners,
You would not make me such an argument.°   *a subject of merriment*
But fare ye well. 'Tis partly my own fault,
Which death or absence soon shall remedy.
245   LYSANDER   Stay, gentle Helena, hear my excuse,
My love, my life, my soul, fair Helena!
HELENA   Oh, excellent!
HERMIA [*to* LYSANDER]   Sweet, do not scorn her so.
DEMETRIUS   If she cannot entreat, I can compel.[5]
LYSANDER   Thou canst compel no more than she entreat.
250   Thy threats have no more strength than her weak prayers.
—Helen, I love thee, by my life, I do!
I swear by that which I will lose for thee
To prove him false that says I love thee not.
DEMETRIUS [*to* HELENA]   I say I love thee more than he can do.
255   LYSANDER   If thou say so, withdraw,[6] and prove it too.
DEMETRIUS   Quick, come!
HERMIA   Lysander, whereto tends all this?
LYSANDER   Away, you Ethiope![7]
     [*He tries to break away from* HERMIA.]
DEMETRIUS [*to* HERMIA]   No, no, he'll
Seem to break loose.[8] [*to* LYSANDER] Take on as° you would   *Pretend*
follow,
But yet come not. You are a tame man, go!
260   LYSANDER [*to* HERMIA]   Hang off,° thou cat, thou burr! Vile   *Let go*
thing, let loose,
Or I will shake thee from me like a serpent.
HERMIA   Why are you grown so rude? What change is this,
Sweet love?
LYSANDER   Thy love? Out, tawny Tartar, out!
Out, loathèd medicine![9] O hated potion, hence!
HERMIA   Do you not jest?
265   HELENA   Yes, sooth,° and so do you.   *truly*
LYSANDER   Demetrius, I will keep my word with thee.
DEMETRIUS   I would I had your bond, for I perceive
A weak bond[1] holds you. I'll not trust your word.
LYSANDER   What? Should I hurt her, strike her, kill her dead?
270   Although I hate her, I'll not harm her so.
HERMIA   What? Can you do me greater harm than hate?
Hate me? Wherefore? Oh, me, what news,° my love?   *what has happened*
Am not I Hermia? Are not you Lysander?
I am as fair now as I was erewhile.°   *a while ago*
275   Since night you loved me, yet since night you left me.
Why then, you left me—oh, the gods forbid—
In earnest, shall I say?
LYSANDER   Ay, by my life,
And never did desire to see thee more.

---

5. If Hermia cannot entreat you to stop, I can make you do it.
6. Come with me ("step outside").
7. Allusion to Hermia's dark hair and complexion. Elizabethans generally regarded light complexions as more beautiful than dark and often stigmatized dark-skinned peoples (such as Ethiopians or Tartars) as ugly.
8. Lysander will only pretend to break free from Hermia.
9. Any drug (including poison).
1. Hermia's weak grasp (with a pun on "bond": signed oath, the meaning in the previous line).

Therefore be out of hope, of question, of doubt;
280 Be certain, nothing truer. 'Tis no jest
That I do hate thee and love Helena.
HERMIA [*to* HELENA]   Oh, me, you juggler,° you   *trickster*
canker-blossom,²
You thief of love! What, have you come by night
And stolen my love's heart from him?
HELENA   Fine, i'faith.
285 Have you no modesty, no maiden shame,
No touch of bashfulness? What, will you tear
Impatient answers from my gentle tongue?
Fie, fie, you counterfeit, you puppet,³ you!
HERMIA   "Puppet"? Why so? —Ay, that way goes the game.
290 Now I perceive that she hath made compare
Between our statures; she hath urged her height,
And with her personage, her tall personage,
Her height, forsooth, she hath prevailed with him.
—And are you grown so high in his esteem
295 Because I am so dwarfish and so low?
How low am I, thou painted maypole?⁴ Speak!
How low am I? I am not yet so low
But that my nails can reach unto thine eyes.
HELENA   I pray you, though you mock me, gentlemen,
300 Let her not hurt me. I was never curst;°   *quarrelsome*
I have no gift at all in shrewishness.
I am a right° maid for my cowardice.   *proper*
Let her not strike me. You perhaps may think
Because she is something° lower than myself   *somewhat*
That I can match her.
305 HERMIA   "Lower"? Hark, again!
HELENA   Good Hermia, do not be so bitter with me.
I evermore did love you, Hermia,
Did ever keep your counsels, never wronged you,
Save that, in love unto Demetrius,
310 I told him of your stealth° unto this wood.   *stealing away*
He followed you; for love I followed him.
But he hath chid me hence and threatened me
To strike me, spurn me, nay, to kill me too.
And now, so° you will let me quiet go,   *if only*
315 To Athens will I bear my folly back
And follow you no further. Let me go.
You see how simple and how fond° I am.   *foolish*
HERMIA   Why, get you gone. Who is't that hinders you?
HELENA   A foolish heart that I leave here behind.
HERMIA   What, with Lysander?
320 HELENA   With Demetrius.
LYSANDER   Be not afraid; she shall not harm thee, Helena.
DEMETRIUS   No, sir, she shall not, though you take her part.
HELENA   Oh, when she is angry she is keen° and shrewd.°   *sharp / shrewish*
She was a vixen when she went to school,
325 And though she be but little, she is fierce.

---

2. A worm that devours blossoms (of love).   4. Proverbial epithet for someone tall and skinny.
3. Fraudulent imitation; but Hermia interprets "pup-   *painted:* insulting allusion to the use of cosmetics.
pet" as a reference to her height.

HERMIA "Little" again? Nothing but "low" and "little"?
    Why will you suffer her to flout me thus?
    Let me come to her.
  LYSANDER   Get you gone, you dwarf,
    You minimus of hind'ring knot-grass⁵ made,
    You bead, you acorn.

330 DEMETRIUS   You are too officious
    In her behalf that scorns your services.
    Let her alone: speak not of Helena;
    Take not her part. For if thou dost intend
    Never so little° show of love to her,   *Even the smallest*
    Thou shalt aby° it.   *pay for*

335 LYSANDER   Now she holds me not;
    Now follow, if thou dar'st, to try whose right,
    Of thine or mine, is most in Helena.
  DEMETRIUS Follow? Nay, I'll go with thee, cheek by jowl.⁶
            [*Exeunt* LYSANDER *and* DEMETRIUS.]
  HERMIA You, mistress, all this coil° is long° of you.   *turmoil / because*
    Nay, go not back.

340 HELENA   I will not trust you, I,
    Nor longer stay in your curst company.
    Your hands than mine are quicker for a fray;°   *fight*
    My legs are longer, though, to run away.   [*Exit.*]
  HERMIA I am amazed and know not what to say.   [*Exit.*]
        [OBERON *and* ROBIN *come forward.*]

345 OBERON This is thy negligence. Still° thou mistak'st   *Always*
    Or else committ'st thy knaveries willfully.
  ROBIN Believe me, king of shadows,° I mistook.   *fairy spirits*
    Did not you tell me I should know the man
    By the Athenian garments he had on?

350   And so far° blameless proves my enterprise   *to this extent*
    That I have 'nointed an Athenian's eyes;
    And so far am I glad it so did sort,°   *turn out*
    As° this their jangling° I esteem a sport.   *Since / bickering*
  OBERON Thou seest these lovers seek a place to fight.

355   Hie° therefore, Robin, overcast the night;   *Hurry*
    The starry welkin° cover thou anon   *sky*
    With drooping fog as black as Acheron,°   *(river of hell)*
    And lead these testy rivals so astray
    As° one come not within another's way.   *So that*

360   Like to Lysander sometime frame thy tongue,
    Then stir Demetrius up with bitter wrong;°   *insults*
    And sometime rail thou like Demetrius,
    And from each other look thou lead them thus
    Till o'er their brows death-counterfeiting sleep

365   With leaden legs and batty° wings doth creep.   *batlike*
    Then crush this herb into Lysander's eye,
    Whose liquor hath this virtuous° property: *potent*
    To take from thence all error with his might
    And make his eyeballs roll with wonted° sight.   *normal*

370   When they next wake, all this derision

---

5. Creeping binding weed (its sap was thought to stunt   6. Proverbial saying for "side by side."
human growth). *minimus:* diminutive thing (Latin).

Shall seem a dream and fruitless° vision,   *inconsequential*
And back to Athens shall the lovers wend°   *go*
With league° whose date° till death shall never end.   *covenant / duration*
Whiles I in this affair do thee employ,
375 I'll to my queen and beg her Indian boy;
And then I will her charmèd° eye release   *enchanted*
From monster's view, and all things shall be peace.
ROBIN My fairy lord, this must be done with haste,
For night's swift dragons⁷ cut the clouds full fast,
380 And yonder shines Aurora's harbinger,⁸
At whose approach ghosts wandering here and there
Troop home to churchyards; damnèd spirits all,
That in crossways and floods⁹ have burial,
Already to their wormy beds are gone,
385 For fear lest day should look their shames upon:
They willfully themselves exile from light
And must for aye° consort with black-browed night.   *forever*
OBERON But we are spirits of another sort.
I with the morning's love¹ have oft made sport,
390 And like a forester² the groves may tread
Even till the eastern gate, all fiery red,
Opening on Neptune° with fair blessèd beams   *(the sea)*
Turns into yellow gold his salt° green streams.   *salty*
But notwithstanding, haste, make no delay;
395 We may effect this business yet ere day.   [*Exit.*]
ROBIN Up and down, up and down,
I will lead them up and down.
I am feared in field and town.
Goblin,° lead them up and down.   *(Robin himself)*
400 Here comes one.
            Enter LYSANDER.
LYSANDER Where art thou, proud Demetrius? Speak
      thou now.
ROBIN³ Here, villain, drawn° and ready. Where art thou?   *with sword drawn*
LYSANDER I will be with thee straight.°   *immediately*
ROBIN   Follow me then
      To plainer° ground.   [*Exit* LYSANDER.]⁴   *clearer*
            Enter DEMETRIUS.
DEMETRIUS   Lysander, speak again.
405 Thou runaway, thou coward, art thou fled?
Speak! In some bush? Where dost thou hide thy head?
ROBIN Thou coward, art thou bragging to the stars,
Telling the bushes that thou look'st for wars,
And wilt not come? Come, recreant;° come, thou child.   *coward; wretch*
410 I'll whip thee with a rod. He is defiled

---

7. Imagined as drawing the chariots of the goddess of night.
8. Herald of the goddess of dawn; the morning star.
9. In which the drowned were "buried," without Christian sacrament. *crossways:* crossroads (where suicides were buried, also without Christian sacrament). Robin is differentiating here between two types of spirits: those who wandered from their churchyard graves and those who have no proper resting place.

These two types, both ghosts of former humans, are differentiated in turn from the fairy spirits by Oberon in the ensuing lines.
1. The love of Aurora, goddess of dawn (or Cephalus, a brave hunter, Aurora's lover).
2. Keeper of a royal forest or private park.
3. In what follows, Robin presumably mimics the voices of Demetrius and Lysander.
4. He might instead wander about the stage.

That draws a sword on thee.[5]

DEMETRIUS   Yea, art thou there?

ROBIN   Follow my voice; we'll try° no manhood here.   *test*

                                     Exeunt.

            [*Enter* LYSANDER.]

LYSANDER   He goes before me and still dares me on.
When I come where he calls, then he is gone.
415   The villain is much lighter-heeled than I.
I followed fast, but faster he did fly,
That° fallen am I in dark uneven way,   *With the result that*
And here will rest me.
            [*He lies down.*]
                              Come, thou gentle day.
For if but once thou show me thy gray light,
420   I'll find Demetrius and revenge this spite.
            [*He sleeps.*]
            [*Enter*] ROBIN *and* DEMETRIUS.

ROBIN   Ho, ho, ho! Coward, why com'st thou not?

DEMETRIUS   Abide° me, if thou dar'st; for well I wot°   *Wait for / know*
Thou runn'st before me, shifting every place,
And dar'st not stand nor look me in the face.
Where art thou now?

425   ROBIN   Come hither; I am here.

DEMETRIUS   Nay, then, thou mock'st me. Thou shalt buy°   *pay for*
    this dear°   *dearly*
If ever I thy face by daylight see.
Now, go thy way. Faintness constraineth me
To measure out my length on this cold bed.
            [*He lies down.*]
430   By day's approach look to be visited.
            [*He sleeps.*]
            Enter HELENA.

HELENA   O weary night, O long and tedious night,
Abate° thy hours; shine comforts from the east,   *Shorten*
That I may back to Athens by daylight
From these that my poor company detest;
435   And sleep, that sometimes shuts up sorrow's eye,
Steal me a while from mine own company.
            [*She lies down and*] *sleep*[*s*].

ROBIN   Yet but three? Come one more;
Two of both kinds makes up four.
            [*Enter* HERMIA.]
Here she comes, curst° and sad.   *angry*
440   Cupid is a knavish lad
Thus to make poor females mad.

HERMIA   Never so weary, never so in woe,
Bedabbled with the dew and torn with briars,
I can no further crawl, no further go;
445   My legs can keep no pace with my desires.
Here will I rest me till the break of day.
            [*She lies down.*]
Heavens shield Lysander, if they mean a fray.
            [*She sleeps.*]

─────────────────────

5. That is, it would be a disgrace to treat you as an honorable opponent.

ROBIN   On the ground,
　　　　Sleep sound.
450   I'll apply
　　　　To your eye,
　　　　Gentle lover, remedy.
　　　　　　　　[*He squeezes the juice on Lysander's eyes.*]
　　　　When thou wak'st,
　　　　Thou tak'st
455   True delight
　　　　In the sight
　　　　Of thy former lady's eye;
　　　　And the country proverb known,
　　　　That every man should take his own,
460   In your waking shall be shown.
　　　　Jack shall have Jill,
　　　　Naught shall go ill,
　　　　The man shall have his mare again, and all shall be well.
　　　　　　　　[*Exit. The lovers remain onstage, asleep.*]

4.1 (F 4.1)

Enter [TITANIA,] *Queen of Fairies, and* [BOTTOM, *the*]
clown [*with the ass head*], *and* FAIRIES[, PEASEBLOSSOM,
COBWEB, MOTH, *and* MUSTARDSEED], *and* [OBERON,]
the King, behind them.

TITANIA [*to* BOTTOM]   Come, sit thee down upon this flowery
　　　bed
　　　While I thy amiable° cheeks do coy,°　　　　　　　　　*lovable / caress*
　　　And stick musk-roses in thy sleek smooth head,
　　　And kiss thy fair large ears, my gentle joy.
5   BOTTOM   Where's Peaseblossom?
PEASEBLOSSOM   Ready.
BOTTOM   Scratch my head, Peaseblossom. —Where's Monsieur
　　　Cobweb?
COBWEB   Ready.
10   BOTTOM   Monsieur Cobweb, good monsieur, get you your
　　　weapons in your hand and kill me a red-hipped humble-bee
　　　on the top of a thistle; and, good monsieur, bring me the
　　　honey-bag. Do not fret yourself too much in the action,
　　　monsieur; and, good monsieur, have a care the honey-bag
15   break not. I would be loath to have you overflown with°　a　　　*submerged by*
　　　honey-bag, signor.　　　　　　　　　　　　[*Exit* COBWEB.]
　　　—Where's Monsieur Mustardseed?
MUSTARDSEED   Ready.
BOTTOM   Give me your neaf,° Monsieur Mustardseed. Pray　　　*fist*
20   you leave your courtesy,¹ good monsieur.
MUSTARDSEED   What's your will?
BOTTOM   Nothing, good monsieur, but to help Cavaliery²
　　　Cobweb to scratch. I must to the barber's, monsieur, for
　　　methinks I am marvelous hairy about the face. And I am
25   such a tender ass, if my hair do but tickle me, I must scratch.
TITANIA   What, wilt thou hear some music, my sweet love?

4.1 Location: The wood. Q1 has no act break here. F
has the four lovers sleep through the action onstage.
1. *leave your courtesy*: stop bowing, or do not stand

bareheaded.
2. Blunder for "Cavalier," perhaps influenced by the
Italian term *cavaliere*.

BOTTOM   I have a reasonable good ear in music. Let's have the
    tongs and the bones.³
TITANIA   Or say, sweet love, what thou desir'st to eat.
30 BOTTOM   Truly, a peck of provender.° I could munch your   *fodder*
    good dry oats. Methinks I have a great desire to a bottle° of   *bundle*
    hay. Good hay, sweet hay, hath no fellow.°   *equal*
TITANIA   I have a venturous fairy that shall seek
    The squirrel's hoard and fetch thee off new nuts.
35 BOTTOM   I had rather have a handful or two of dried peas.
    But, I pray you, let none of your people stir me; I have an
    exposition of° sleep come upon me.   *(for "disposition to")*
TITANIA   Sleep thou, and I will wind thee in my arms.
    —Fairies, be gone, and be always° away.   [*Exeunt* FAIRIES.]   *in every direction*
40 So° doth the woodbine⁴ the sweet honeysuckle   *Thus*
    Gently entwist; the female ivy so
    Enrings the barky fingers of the elm.
    —Oh, how I love thee, how I dote on thee!
        [*They sleep.*]
        Enter ROBIN *Goodfellow.*
OBERON [*coming forward*]   Welcome, good Robin. Seest thou
    this sweet sight?
45 Her dotage now I do begin to pity.
    For, meeting her of late behind the wood
    Seeking sweet favors° for this hateful fool,   *love tokens*
    I did upbraid her and fall out with her.
    For she his hairy temples then had rounded
50 With coronet of fresh and fragrant flowers,
    And that same dew which sometime° on the buds   *formerly*
    Was wont° to swell like round and orient⁵ pearls   *accustomed*
    Stood now within the pretty flowerets' eyes
    Like tears that did their own disgrace bewail.
55 When I had at my pleasure taunted her,
    And she in mild terms begged my patience,
    I then did ask of her her changeling child,
    Which straight she gave me, and her fairy sent
    To bear him to my bower in fairyland.
60 And now I have the boy, I will undo
    This hateful imperfection of her eyes.
    And, gentle puck, take this transformèd scalp
    From off the head of this Athenian swain,
    That he, awaking when the other° do,   *others*
65 May all to Athens back again repair
    And think no more of this night's accidents
    But as the fierce vexation of a dream.
    But first I will release the Fairy Queen.
        [*He squeezes the juice on Titania's eyes.*]
    Be as thou wast wont to be;
70 See as thou wast wont to see.
    Dian's bud o'er Cupid's flower⁶
    Hath such force and blessèd power.

---

3. Triangle and clappers (rustic musical instruments).
4. Here, "woodbine" cannot mean "honeysuckle," as it
did at 2.1.251, and thus must refer to a different plant.
5. Lustrous (the best pearls were from the Far East).

6. "Dian's bud," the herb of 2.1.184 and 3.2.366, is
perhaps *Agnus castus,* or chaste tree: said to preserve
chastity and hence the antidote to "Cupid's flower,"
or the "love-in-idleness" of 2.1.168.

Now, my Titania, wake you, my sweet queen.

TITANIA [*awaking*]   My Oberon, what visions have I seen!
75 Methought I was enamored of an ass.

OBERON   There lies your love.

TITANIA   How came these things to pass?
Oh, how mine eyes do loathe his visage now!

OBERON   Silence a while. —Robin, take off this head.
—Titania, music call, and strike more dead
80 Than common sleep of all these five[7] the sense.

TITANIA   Music, ho—music such as charmeth sleep!
             [*Music plays.*]

ROBIN [*to* BOTTOM, *removing the ass head*]   Now when thou
      wak'st with thine own fool's eyes peep.

OBERON   Sound, music! Come, my queen, take hands with me,
And rock the ground whereon these sleepers be.
             [*They dance.*]
85 Now thou and I are new in amity
And will tomorrow midnight solemnly
Dance in Duke Theseus' house triumphantly
And bless it to all fair prosperity.
There shall the pairs of faithful lovers be
90 Wedded, with Theseus, all in jollity.

ROBIN   Fairy King, attend and mark:
I do hear the morning lark.

OBERON   Then, my queen, in silence sad
Trip we after night's shade.
95 We the globe can compass° soon,   *orbit*
Swifter than the wandering moon.

TITANIA   Come, my lord, and in our flight
Tell me how it came this night
That I sleeping here was found
100 With these mortals on the ground.
             Exeunt [OBERON, TITANIA, *and* ROBIN].
      Wind horn. Enter THESEUS [*with* HIPPOLYTA, EGEUS,]
      and all his train.

THESEUS   Go, one of you, find out the forester,
For now our observation[8] is performed.
And since we have the vanguard° of the day,   *earliest part*
My love shall hear the music of my hounds.
105 Uncouple[9] in the western valley; let them go.
Dispatch, I say, and find the forester.   [*Exit an Attendant.*]
—We will, fair Queen, up to the mountain's top
And mark the musical confusion
Of hounds and echo in conjunction.
110 HIPPOLYTA   I was with Hercules and Cadmus[1] once
When in a wood of Crete they bayed° the bear   *hunted*
With hounds of Sparta.[2] Never did I hear
Such gallant chiding;° for besides the groves,   *barking*
The skies, the fountains, every region near

---

7. The lovers and Bottom.
8. "Observance to a morn of May," as at 1.1.167.
9. Release (the dogs, leashed in pairs).

1. Mythical founder of Thebes. (No source for the anecdote is known.)
2. Famous in antiquity as hunting dogs.

115   Seemed all one mutual cry. I never heard
    So musical a discord, such sweet thunder.
    THESEUS My hounds are bred out of the Spartan kind,
    So flewed,³ so sanded;° and their heads are hung   *sandy-colored*
    With ears that sweep away the morning dew;
120   Crook-kneed, and dewlapped⁴ like Thessalian bulls;
    Slow in pursuit, but matched in mouth like bells,
    Each under each.⁵ A cry more tunable⁶
    Was never holla'd to nor cheered with horn
    In Crete, in Sparta, nor in Thessaly.
125   Judge when you hear. But soft,° what nymphs are these?   *stop; look*
    EGEUS My lord, this is my daughter here asleep,
    And this Lysander, this Demetrius is,
    This Helena, old Nedar's Helena.
    I wonder of their being here together.
130   THESEUS No doubt they rose up early to observe
    The rite of May and, hearing our intent,
    Came here in grace of our solemnity.°   *ceremony*
    But speak, Egeus: is not this the day
    That Hermia should give answer of her choice?
135   EGEUS It is, my lord.
    THESEUS Go bid the huntsmen wake them with their horns.
                                     [Exit an Attendant.]
                Shout within; wind horns; [the lovers] all start up.
    Good morrow, friends. Saint Valentine⁷ is past.
    Begin these woodbirds but to couple now?
    LYSANDER Pardon, my lord.
              [The lovers kneel.]
    THESEUS   I pray you all, stand up.
              [The lovers stand.]
140   *[to* DEMETRIUS *and* LYSANDER*]* I know you two are rival
      enemies.
    How comes this gentle concord in the world,
    That hatred is so far from jealousy°   *suspicion*
    To sleep by hate and fear no enmity?
    LYSANDER My lord, I shall reply amazèdly,°   *confusedly*
145   Half sleep, half waking. But as yet, I swear,
    I cannot truly say how I came here.
    But as I think—for truly would I speak,
    And now I do bethink me, so it is—
    I came with Hermia hither. Our intent
150   Was to be gone from Athens where we might
    Without° the peril of the Athenian law—   *Outside*
    EGEUS *[to* THESEUS*]* Enough, enough, my lord; you have
      enough.
    I beg the law, the law upon his head!
    —They would have stolen away, they would, Demetrius,
155   Thereby to have defeated° you and me,   *defrauded*
    You of your wife and me of my consent,
    Of my consent that she should be your wife.

---

3. Flews were large hanging, fleshy chaps.
4. With hanging folds of skin under the neck (compare 2.1.50).
5. *matched . . . each:* harmoniously matched in the

pitch of their barking, like a set of bells.
6. A pack of hounds more well tuned.
7. Birds were said to choose their mates on Valentine's Day.

DEMETRIUS [*to* THESEUS]   My lord, fair Helen told me of their
    stealth,
    Of this their purpose hither to this wood,
160   And I in fury hither followed them,
    Fair Helena in fancy° following me.   *love*
    But, my good lord, I wot not by what power—
    But by some power it is—my love to Hermia,
    Melted as the snow, seems to me now
165   As the remembrance of an idle gaud°   *a worthless trinket*
    Which in my childhood I did dote upon;
    And all the faith, the virtue of my heart,
    The object and the pleasure of mine eye,
    Is only Helena. To her, my lord,
170   Was I betrothed ere I saw Hermia,
    But like a sickness[8] did I loathe this food;
    But, as in health come to my natural taste,
    Now I do wish it, love it, long for it,
    And will for evermore be true to it.
175 THESEUS   Fair lovers, you are fortunately met.
    Of this discourse we more will hear anon.
    —Egeus, I will overbear your will;
    For in the temple, by and by, with us
    These couples shall eternally be knit.
180   And, for° the morning now is something° worn,   *since / somewhat*
    Our purposed hunting shall be set aside.
    Away with us to Athens. Three and three,
    We'll hold a feast in great solemnity.
    —Come, Hippolyta.
            [*Exit* THESEUS *with* HIPPOLYTA, EGEUS, *and his train.*]
185 DEMETRIUS   These things seem small and undistinguishable,
    Like far-off mountains turnèd into clouds.
HERMIA   Methinks I see these things with parted eye,°   *(double vision)*
    When everything seems double.
HELENA   So methinks;
    And I have found Demetrius like a jewel,
    Mine own and not mine own.
190 DEMETRIUS   Are you sure
    That we are awake? It seems to me
    That yet we sleep, we dream. Do not you think
    The Duke was here and bid us follow him?
HERMIA   Yea, and my father.
HELENA   And Hippolyta.
195 LYSANDER   And he did bid us follow to the temple.
DEMETRIUS   Why, then, we are awake. Let's follow him,
    And by the way let's recount our dreams.
                      [*Exeunt lovers.*]
BOTTOM [*awaking*]   When my cue comes, call me, and I will
    answer. My next is "Most fair Pyramus." Heigh-ho,°   *(a call; perhaps a yawn)*
200   Quince? Flute the bellows-mender? Snout the tinker?
    Starveling? God's my life!° Stolen hence and left me asleep!   *Good Lord*
    I have had a most rare vision. I have had a dream past the
    wit of man to say what dream it was. Man is but an ass if he

---

8. Only as a person does when ill or nauseated.

go about° to expound this dream. Methought I was—there   *try*
205 is no man can tell what. Methought I was—and methought
I had—but man is but patched a fool[9] if he will offer° to say   *venture*
what methought I had. The eye of man hath not heard, the
ear of man hath not seen, man's hand is not able to taste, his
tongue to conceive, nor his heart to report[1] what my dream
210 was. I will get Peter Quince to write a ballad of this dream.
It shall be called "Bottom's Dream," because it hath no bottom;[2] and I will sing it in the latter end of a play, before the
Duke. Peradventure,° to make it the more gracious, I shall   *Perhaps*
sing it at her° death.   [*Exit.*]   *(Thisbe's?)*

4.2 (F 4.2)

Enter QUINCE, FLUTE[, SNOUT, *and* STARVELING].

QUINCE Have you sent to Bottom's house? Is he come home
yet?

STARVELING He cannot be heard of. Out of doubt° he is trans-   *Doubtless*
ported.[1]

5 FLUTE If he come not, then the play is marred. It goes not
forward, doth it?

QUINCE It is not possible. You have not a man in all Athens
able to discharge° Pyramus but he.   *perform*

FLUTE No, he hath simply the best wit° of any handicraft   *intellect*
10 man in Athens.

QUINCE Yea, and the best person° too; and he is a very par-   *looks*
amour for a sweet voice.

FLUTE You must say "paragon." A paramour is—God bless
us—a thing of naught.°   *something wicked*

Enter SNUG *the joiner.*

15 SNUG Masters, the Duke is coming from the temple, and
there is two or three lords and ladies more married. If our
sport° had gone forward, we had all been made men.[2]   *entertainment*

FLUTE Oh, sweet bully Bottom! Thus hath he lost sixpence a
day[3] during his life; he could not have 'scaped sixpence a day.
20 An° the Duke had not given him sixpence a day for playing   *If*
Pyramus, I'll be hanged. He would have deserved it. Sixpence a day in Pyramus, or nothing.

Enter BOTTOM.

BOTTOM Where are these lads? Where are these hearts?°   *mates*

QUINCE Bottom! Oh, most courageous[4] day! Oh, most happy
25 hour!

BOTTOM Masters, I am to discourse wonders; but ask me not
what; for if I tell you, I am not true Athenian. I will tell you
everything right as it fell out.

QUINCE Let us hear, sweet Bottom.

30 BOTTOM Not a word of° me. All that I will tell you is that the   *out of*
Duke hath dined. Get your apparel together, good strings°   *(to attach the beards)*

---

9. Patchwork or motley costumes were worn by jesters.
1. *The eye . . . report:* Burlesque of scripture: "The eye hath not seen, and the ear hath not heard, nei-ther have entered into the heart of man" those things that God has prepared (1 Corinthians 2:9–10 [Bish-ops' Bible]).
2. Because it is unfathomable, or has no substance

(foundation).
4.2 Location: Athens.
1. Carried away (by the fairies); transformed.
2. *we . . . men:* our fortunes would have been made.
3. As a royal pension, considerably more than the average daily wage of an Elizabethan workman.
4. Blunder for "brave," meaning "splendid."

to your beards, new ribbons to your pumps. Meet presently°   *immediately*
at the palace; every man look o'er his part. For the short and
the long is, our play is preferred.° In any case, let Thisbe have   *recommended*
35 clean linen; and let not him that plays the lion pare his nails,
for they shall hang out for the lion's claws. And, most dear
actors, eat no onions nor garlic, for we are to utter sweet
breath; and I do not doubt but to hear them say it is a sweet
comedy. No more words. Away! Go, away!   [*Exeunt.*]

5.1 (F 5.1)

Enter THESEUS, HIPPOLYTA, PHILOSTRATE[, *Lords, and
Attendants*].

HIPPOLYTA   'Tis strange, my Theseus, that° these lovers   *that which*
speak of.
THESEUS[1]   More strange than true. I never may believe
These antique[2] fables, nor these fairy toys.°   *trifles*
Lovers and madmen have such seething brains,
5   Such shaping fantasies,° that apprehend° more   *imaginations / conceive*
Than cool reason ever comprehends.
The lunatic, the lover, and the poet
Are of imagination all compact.°   *composed*
One sees more devils than vast hell can hold;
10   That is the madman. The lover, all as frantic,
Sees Helen's beauty in a brow of Egypt.[3]
The poet's eye, in a fine frenzy rolling,
Doth glance from heaven to earth, from earth to heaven.
And as imagination bodies forth
15   The forms of things unknown, the poet's pen
Turns them to shapes and gives to airy nothing
A local habitation and a name.
Such tricks hath strong imagination
That if it would but apprehend some joy,
20   It comprehends some bringer° of that joy;   *source*
Or in the night, imagining some fear,°   *object to be feared*
How easy is a bush supposed a bear!
HIPPOLYTA   But all the story of the night told over,
And all their minds transfigured so together,
25   More witnesseth than fancy's images[4]
And grows to something of great constancy;°   *consistency*
But, howsoever,° strange and admirable.°   *in any case / wondrous*

Enter [*the*] *lovers,* LYSANDER, DEMETRIUS, HERMIA,
and HELENA.

THESEUS   Here come the lovers, full of joy and mirth.
Joy, gentle friends, joy and fresh days of love
Accompany your hearts.
30 LYSANDER   More than to us
Wait in your royal walks, your board, your bed.[5]
THESEUS   Come now, what masques, what dances shall we have

5.1 Location: Athens. Theseus's palace.
1. Textual Comment Substantial portions of this
famous speech by Theseus are mislined in Q1 and F,
perhaps because Shakespeare added the lines on the
poet's imagination as an afterthought. For more
details and speculations on the original versions, see
Digital Edition TC 5 (Quarto edited text).

2. Ancient; strange, grotesque (as in "antic").
3. In a gypsy's face. *Helen:* Helen of Troy.
4. *More . . . images:* Testifies to something more than
mere figments of the imagination.
5. *More . . . bed:* May even more joy and love attend
your daily lives.

To wear away this long age of three hours
Between our after-supper and bedtime?
35 Where is our usual manager of mirth?
What revels are in hand? Is there no play
To ease the anguish of a torturing hour?
Call Philostrate.
PHILOSTRATE⁶   Here, mighty Theseus.
THESEUS Say, what abridgement⁷ have you for this evening,
40 What masque, what music? How shall we beguile
The lazy time if not with some delight?
PHILOSTRATE [*giving* THESEUS *a paper*]   There is a brief° how   *short list*
     many sports are ripe.
Make choice of which your highness will see first.
THESEUS [*reads*]⁸   "The battle with the Centaurs,⁹ to be sung
45 By an Athenian eunuch to the harp."
We'll none of that. That have I told my love
In glory of my kinsman Hercules.¹
[*Reads.*] "The riot of the tipsy Bacchanals
Tearing the Thracian singer in their rage."²
50 That is an old device,° and it was played   *show*
When I from Thebes came last a conqueror.
[*Reads.*] "The thrice-three muses mourning for the death
Of learning, late deceased in beggary."³
That is some satire, keen and critical,
55 Not sorting with° a nuptial ceremony.   *befitting*
[*Reads.*] "A tedious brief scene of young Pyramus
And his love Thisbe; very tragical mirth."
Merry and tragical? Tedious and brief?
That is hot ice and wondrous strange snow!
60 How shall we find the concord of this discord?
PHILOSTRATE   A play there is, my lord, some ten words long,
   Which is as brief as I have known a play,
   But by ten words, my lord, it is too long,
   Which makes it tedious. For in all the play
65 There is not one word apt, one player fitted.°   *appropriately cast*
   And tragical, my noble lord, it is,
   For Pyramus therein doth kill himself,
   Which, when I saw rehearsed, I must confess,
   Made mine eyes water; but more merry tears
70 The passion of loud laughter never shed.
THESEUS   What are they that do play it?
PHILOSTRATE   Hard-handed men that work in Athens here,
   Which never labored in their minds till now,

---

6. TEXTUAL COMMENT The speeches by Philostrate
throughout 5.1 in Q1 are assigned to Egeus in F; this
change significantly affects the nature of the scene and
allows for a wide variety of interpretations in performance. See Digital Edition TC 6 (Quarto edited text).
7. Pastime, something to make the evening seem
shorter.
8. TEXTUAL COMMENT In F's version of this speech,
Lysander reads out the descriptions of the entertainments on offer, while Theseus comments. For further
details on possibilities for staging this arrangement,
see Digital Edition TC 7 (Quarto edited text).
9. Probably the battle that occurred when the Cen-

taurs tried to carry off the bride of Theseus's friend
Pirithous.
1. According to Plutarch, Hercules and Theseus were
cousins.
2. The murder of the poet Orpheus by drunken
women, devotees of Dionysus.
3. Possibly a topical reference: Robert Greene, Christopher Marlowe, and Thomas Kyd, university wits
who began writing for the stage in the 1580s, all died
in desperate circumstances in 1592–94. But satiric
laments on the poverty of scholars and poets were
commonplace.

	And now have toiled° their unbreathed° memories	*taxed / unexercised*
75	With this same play against° your nuptial.	*in preparation for*

THESEUS   And we will hear it.

PHILOSTRATE   No, my noble lord,
It is not for you. I have heard it over,
And it is nothing, nothing in the world;
Unless you can find sport in their intents,

80	Extremely stretched° and conned° with cruel pain,	*strained / memorized*

To do you service.

THESEUS   I will hear that play.
For never anything can be amiss
When simpleness and duty tender it.
Go, bring them in; and take your places, ladies.

[Exit PHILOSTRATE.]

85	HIPPOLYTA I love not to see wretchedness o'ercharged,[4]	
	And duty in his service° perishing.	*its attempt to serve*

THESEUS   Why, gentle sweet, you shall see no such thing.

	HIPPOLYTA He says they can do nothing in this kind.°	*kind of thing*

THESEUS   The kinder we, to give them thanks for nothing.

90	Our sport shall be to take what they mistake.	
	And what poor duty cannot do, noble respect°	*consideration*
	Takes it in might, not merit.[5]	
	Where I have come, great clerks° have purposèd	*scholars*
	To greet me with premeditated welcomes,	
95	Where I have seen them shiver and look pale,	

Make periods in the midst of sentences,
Throttle their practiced accent[6] in their fears,
And in conclusion dumbly have broke off,
Not paying me a welcome. Trust me, sweet,

100	Out of this silence yet I picked a welcome;	
	And in the modesty of fearful° duty	*frightened*

I read as much as from the rattling tongue
Of saucy and audacious eloquence.
Love, therefore, and tongue-tied simplicity

105	In least speak most, to my capacity.°	*in my judgment*

[Enter PHILOSTRATE.]

PHILOSTRATE   So please your grace, the Prologue is
    addressed.[7]

THESEUS   Let him approach.
        Enter [QUINCE *as*] *the Prologue.*

QUINCE [*as Prologue*]   If we offend, it is with our good will.
That you should think, we come not to offend

110	But with good will. To show our simple skill,	

That is the true beginning of our end.
Consider, then, we come but in despite.

	We do not come as minding° to content you,	*intending*

Our true intent is. All for your delight

115	We are not here. That you should here repent you	

The actors are at hand; and by their show
You shall know all that you are like to know.[8]

---

4. Overburdened. *wretchedness:* incompetence or weakness; poor people.
5. *in . . . merit:* with respect to the giver's capacity, not the merit of the performance.
6. Rehearsed eloquence; usual manner of speaking.

7. The speaker of the Prologue is ready.
8. The humor of Quince's speech rests in its mispunctuation; repunctuated, it becomes a typical courteous address.

THESEUS   This fellow doth not stand upon points.[9]

LYSANDER   He hath rid his prologue like a rough° colt: he   *an unbroken*
120   knows not the stop.[1] A good moral, my lord: it is not enough
to speak, but to speak true.

HIPPOLYTA   Indeed he hath played on this prologue like a child
on a recorder: a sound, but not in government.°   *control*

THESEUS   His speech was like a tangled chain: nothing°   *not at all*
125   impaired, but all disordered.[2] Who is next?

      Enter [BOTTOM as] Pyramus, and [FLUTE as] Thisbe,
      and [SNOUT as] Wall, and [STARVELING as] Moonshine,
      and [SNUG as] Lion.

QUINCE [as Prologue]   Gentles, perchance you wonder at this
      show,
But wonder on till truth make all things plain.
This man is Pyramus, if you would know;
This beauteous lady Thisbe is, certain.
130   This man with lime and roughcast doth present
Wall, that vile wall which did these lovers sunder;
And through Wall's chink, poor souls, they are content
To whisper—at the which let no man wonder.
This man with lantern, dog, and bush of thorn
135   Presenteth Moonshine. For, if you will know,
By moonshine did these lovers think no scorn°   *(it) no disgrace*
To meet at Ninus' tomb, there, there to woo.
This grisly beast, which "Lion" hight° by name,   *is called*
The trusty Thisbe, coming first by night,
140   Did scare away, or rather did affright;
And as she fled, her mantle she did fall,°   *drop*
Which Lion vile with bloody mouth did stain.
Anon comes Pyramus, sweet youth and tall,°   *handsome*
And finds his trusty Thisbe's mantle slain;
145   Whereat with blade, with bloody, blameful blade,
He bravely broached° his boiling bloody breast;   *stabbed*
And Thisbe, tarrying in mulberry shade,
His dagger drew and died. For all the rest
Let Lion, Moonshine, Wall, and lovers twain
150   At large° discourse, while here they do remain.   *length*

      Exeunt [QUINCE as Prologue, SNUG as] Lion, [FLUTE
      as] Thisbe, and [STARVELING as] Moonshine.[3]

THESEUS   I wonder if the lion be to speak.

DEMETRIUS   No wonder, my lord; one lion may when many
asses do.

SNOUT [as Wall]   In this same interlude° it doth befall   *play*
155   That I, one Snout by name, present a wall;
And such a wall as I would have you think
That had in it a crannied hole or chink,
Through which the lovers, Pyramus and Thisbe,
Did whisper often very secretly.
160   This loam, this roughcast, and this stone doth show

---

9. Bother about niceties; heed punctuation marks.
1. How to rein the colt to a stop; punctuation mark.
2. PERFORMANCE COMMENT In performance, the tone of the Athenian nobles' criticisms of the Interlude can range from innocuous banter to cruel intimidation, thus changing the overall effect of the scene.

For more, see Digital Edition PC 3.
3. TEXTUAL COMMENT The exits and entrances for the Interlude's players differ subtly between Q1 and F, but with poignant implications. See Digital Edition TC 8 (Quarto edited text).

That I am that same wall; the truth is so.
And this the cranny is, right and sinister,[4]
Through which the fearful lovers are to whisper.
THESEUS   Would you desire lime and hair to speak better?
165   DEMETRIUS   It is the wittiest partition[5] that ever I heard dis-
course, my lord.
THESEUS   Pyramus draws near the wall: silence!
BOTTOM [as Pyramus]   O grim-looked° night, O night with   grim-looking
hue so black,
O night, which ever art when day is not,
170   O night, O night, alack, alack, alack,
I fear my Thisbe's promise is forgot.
And thou, O wall, O sweet, O lovely wall,
That stand'st between her father's ground and mine,
Thou wall, O wall, O sweet and lovely wall,
175   Show me thy chink, to blink through with mine eyne.
[SNOUT, as Wall, shows his chink.]
Thanks, courteous wall; Jove shield thee well for this.
But what see I? No Thisbe do I see.
O wicked wall, through whom I see no bliss,
Cursed be thy stones[6] for thus deceiving me!
180   THESEUS   The wall, methinks, being sensible,° should curse   capable of feeling
again.°   back
BOTTOM [to THESEUS]   No, in truth, sir, he should not. "Deceiv-
ing me" is Thisbe's cue. She is to enter now, and I am to spy
her through the wall. You shall see it will fall pat° as I told   precisely
185   you. Yonder she comes.
Enter [FLUTE as] Thisbe.
FLUTE [as Thisbe]   O wall, full often hast thou heard my
moans
For parting my fair Pyramus and me.
My cherry lips have often kissed thy stones,
Thy stones with lime and hair knit up in thee.
190   BOTTOM [as Pyramus]   I see a voice; now will I to the chink
To spy an° I can hear my Thisbe's face.   if
Thisbe?
FLUTE [as Thisbe]   My love! Thou art my love, I think.
BOTTOM [as Pyramus]   Think what thou wilt, I am thy lover's
grace,°   gracious lover
And like Limander[7] am I trusty still.
195   FLUTE [as Thisbe]   And I like Helen,[8] till the fates me kill.
BOTTOM [as Pyramus]   Not Shafalus to Procrus[9] was so true.
FLUTE [as Thisbe]   As Shafalus to Procrus, I to you.
BOTTOM [as Pyramus]   Oh, kiss me through the hole of this
vile wall.
FLUTE [as Thisbe]   I kiss the wall's hole, not your lips at all.
200   BOTTOM [as Pyramus]   Wilt thou at Ninny's tomb meet me
straightway?

4. Left; running horizontally. Or on the one side
(Pyramus's) and the other (Thisbe's).
5. Wall; formal term for part of an oration.
6. Punning, unintentionally, on "testicles."
7. Blunder for "Leander," who drowned while swimming across the Hellespont to meet his lover, Hero.

8. Helen of Troy was notoriously untrustworthy; a
blunder for "Hero."
9. Blunder for "Cephalus" and "Procris." Procris was
in fact seduced by her husband in disguise as another
man; he later accidentally killed her.

FLUTE [*as Thisbe*]   Tide° life, tide death, I come without delay.   *Betide; come*
                         [*Exeunt* BOTTOM *and* FLUTE.]

SNOUT [*as Wall*]   Thus have I, Wall, my part dischargèd so;
   And, being done, thus Wall away doth go.   [*Exit.*]

THESEUS   Now is the mural° down between the two neighbors.   *wall*

205 DEMETRIUS   No remedy, my lord, when walls are so willful to°   *as to*
   hear without warning.[1]

HIPPOLYTA   This is the silliest stuff that ever I heard.

THESEUS   The best in this kind are but shadows,[2] and the
   worst are no worse if imagination amend them.

210 HIPPOLYTA   It must be your imagination, then, and not theirs.

THESEUS   If we imagine no worse of them than they of themselves, they may pass for excellent men. Here come two
   noble beasts in, a man and a lion.
          Enter [SNUG *as*] *Lion and* [STARVELING *as*] *Moonshine*
          [*with a lantern, thornbush, and dog*].

SNUG [*as Lion*]   You ladies, you whose gentle hearts do fear

215 The smallest monstrous mouse that creeps on floor,
   May now, perchance, both quake and tremble here
   When lion rough in wildest rage doth roar.
   Then know that I as Snug the joiner am
   A lion fell,[3] nor else no lion's dam.

220 For if I should as lion come in strife
   Into this place, 'twere pity on my life.

THESEUS   A very gentle beast, and of a good conscience.

DEMETRIUS   The very best at a beast, my lord, that e'er I saw.

LYSANDER   This lion is a very fox[4] for his valor.

225 THESEUS   True; and a goose[5] for his discretion.

DEMETRIUS   Not so, my lord. For his valor cannot carry his
   discretion, and the fox carries the goose.

THESEUS   His discretion, I am sure, cannot carry his valor; for
   the goose carries not the fox. It is well. Leave it to his discre-
230 tion, and let us listen to the moon.

STARVELING [*as Moonshine*]   This lantern doth the hornèd°   *crescent*
   moon present.

DEMETRIUS   He should have worn the horns on his head.[6]

THESEUS   He is no crescent,[7] and his horns are invisible
   within the circumference.

235 STARVELING [*as Moonshine*]   This lantern doth the hornèd
   moon present;
   Myself the man i'th' moon do seem to be.

THESEUS   This is the greatest error of all the rest: the man
   should be put into the lantern; how is it else the man i'th'
   moon?

240 DEMETRIUS   He dares not come there for° the candle. For you   *for fear of*
   see it is already in snuff.[8]

HIPPOLYTA   I am aweary of this moon; would he would change!

THESEUS   It appears by his small light of discretion that he is

---

1. Informing the parents. *hear:* proverbially, "walls have ears."
2. Mere likenesses without substance. *kind:* profession (that is, actors).
3. Fierce; or skin (punning on the costume to which Snug reassuringly calls attention).

4. Symbolic of low cunning, rather than courage.
5. Symbolic of foolishness.
6. The symbol of a cuckold.
7. Waxing moon. Perhaps a joke about Starveling's thinness.
8. In need of snuffing; angry.

in the wane; but yet in courtesy, in all reason, we must stay
245   the time.
LYSANDER   Proceed, Moon.
STARVELING   All that I have to say is to tell you that the lantern is the moon, I the man i'th' moon, this thornbush my
  thornbush, and this dog my dog.
250 DEMETRIUS   Why, all these should be in the lantern, for all
  these are in the moon. But silence; here comes Thisbe.

      Enter [FLUTE as] Thisbe.

FLUTE *[as Thisbe]*   This is old Ninny's tomb. Where is my love?
SNUG *[as Lion]*   Oh!
      [Lion roars.]
      [Thisbe runs off, dropping her mantle.]
DEMETRIUS   Well roared, Lion!
255 THESEUS   Well run, Thisbe!
HIPPOLYTA   Well shone, Moon! Truly, the moon shines with a
  good grace.
      [Lion worries° Thisbe's mantle.]   *gnaws on*
THESEUS   Well moused,[9] Lion!
      Enter [BOTTOM as] Pyramus.
DEMETRIUS   And then came Pyramus.   *[Exit SNUG as Lion.]*
260 LYSANDER   And so the lion vanished.
BOTTOM *[as Pyramus]*   Sweet moon, I thank thee for thy
    sunny beams;
  I thank thee, moon, for shining now so bright.
  For by thy gracious, golden, glittering gleams
  I trust to take of truest Thisbe sight.
265   But stay, oh, spite!
  But mark, poor knight,
  What dreadful dole° is here?   *grief*
  Eyes, do you see?
  How can it be?
270   O dainty duck! O dear!
  Thy mantle good,
  What, stained with blood?
  Approach, ye Furies fell!
  O Fates,[1] come, come,
275   Cut thread and thrum,[2]
  Quail,° crush, conclude, and quell!°   *Overpower / kill*
THESEUS   This passion, and[3] the death of a dear friend, would
  go near to make a man look sad.
HIPPOLYTA   Beshrew my heart, but I pity the man.
280 BOTTOM *[as Pyramus]*   Oh, wherefore, Nature, didst thou
    lions frame,
  Since lion vile hath here deflowered[4] my dear?
  Which is—no, no, which was—the fairest dame
  That lived, that loved, that liked, that looked with cheer.
  Come, tears, confound!
285   Out, sword, and wound

---

9. The mantle is like a mouse in the mouth of a cat.
1. The three Fates in Greek mythology spun and cut
the thread of a person's life.
2. A technical term from Bottom's occupation: the
tufted end of a weaver's warp, or set of yarns placed

lengthwise in a loom when the woven fabric is cut.
3. Only if combined with. *passion:* suffering; extravagant speech.
4. Ruined (but commonly suggesting "deprived of
her virginity"); his error for "devoured."

The pap° of Pyramus,   *breast*
Ay, that left pap,
Where heart doth hop.
       [*He stabs himself.*]
Thus die I, thus, thus, thus.

290   Now am I dead;
Now am I fled.
My soul is in the sky.
Tongue, lose thy light;
Moon, take thy flight.   [*Exit* STARVELING *as Moonshine.*]

295   Now die, die, die, die, die.
       [*Pyramus dies.*]

DEMETRIUS   No die, but an ace for him; for he is but one.[5]

LYSANDER   Less than an ace, man; for he is dead, he is nothing.

THESEUS   With the help of a surgeon he might yet recover,
300   and yet prove an ass.

HIPPOLYTA   How chance Moonshine is gone before Thisbe comes back and finds her lover?

THESEUS   She will find him by starlight.
      [*Enter* FLUTE *as Thisbe.*]
Here she comes, and her passion° ends the play.   *passionate speech*

305 HIPPOLYTA   Methinks she should not use a long one for such a Pyramus; I hope she will be brief.

DEMETRIUS   A mote° will turn the balance which Pyramus,   *speck*
which[6] Thisbe, is the better: he for a man, God warrant us;
she for a woman, God bless us.

310 LYSANDER   She hath spied him already with those sweet eyes.

DEMETRIUS   And thus she means, *videlicet*:[7]

FLUTE [*as Thisbe*]   Asleep, my love?
What, dead, my dove?
O Pyramus, arise!

315   Speak, speak! Quite dumb?
Dead, dead? A tomb
Must cover thy sweet eyes.
These lily lips,
This cherry nose,

320   These yellow cowslip cheeks
Are gone, are gone.
Lovers, make moan.
His eyes were green as leeks.
O sisters three,°   *(the Fates)*

325   Come, come to me
With hands as pale as milk;
Lay them in gore,
Since you have shore°   *shorn*
With shears his thread of silk.

330   Tongue, not a word!
Come, trusty sword,
Come, blade, my breast imbrue.°   *stain with blood*
      [*She stabs herself.*]
And farewell, friends,

---

5. Pun on "die" as one of a pair of dice. *one:* the ace, or lowest throw.
6. *which . . . which:* whether . . . or.

7. As follows. *means:* moans; lodges a formal legal complaint.

Thus Thisbe ends.
335   Adieu, adieu, adieu.
        [Thisbe dies.]
THESEUS   Moonshine and Lion are left to bury the dead.
DEMETRIUS   Ay, and Wall too.
BOTTOM *[starting up]*   No, I assure you, the wall is down that
    parted their fathers. *[FLUTE rises.]* Will it please you to see
340   the epilogue or to hear a Bergomask dance[8] between two of
    our company?
THESEUS   No epilogue, I pray you; for your play needs no
    excuse. Never excuse; for when the players are all dead, there
    need none to be blamed. Marry, if he that writ it had played
345   Pyramus and hanged himself in Thisbe's garter, it would
    have been a fine tragedy; and so it is, truly, and very notably
    discharged. But come, your Bergomask; let your epilogue
    alone.   *[BOTTOM and FLUTE[9] dance; then exeunt.]*

The iron tongue of midnight hath told° twelve.   *counted; tolled*
350   Lovers, to bed; 'tis almost fairy time.
I fear we shall outsleep the coming morn
As much as we this night have overwatched.°   *stayed awake too late*
This palpable-gross° play hath well beguiled   *palpably crude*
The heavy° gait of night. Sweet friends, to bed.   *drowsy; slow*
355   A fortnight hold we this solemnity
In nightly revels and new jollity.   *Exeunt.*
      *Enter [*ROBIN *Goodfellow, the] puck[, with a broom].*
ROBIN   Now the hungry lion roars,
    And the wolf behowls the moon,
    Whilst the heavy° plowman snores,   *weary*
360   All with weary task fordone.°   *"done in"; exhausted*
    Now the wasted brands° do glow,   *burned-out logs*
    Whilst the screech-owl, screeching loud,
    Puts the wretch that lies in woe
    In remembrance of a shroud.
365   Now it is the time of night
    That the graves, all gaping wide,
    Every one lets forth his sprite[1]
    In the churchway paths to glide;
    And we fairies that do run
370   By the triple Hecate's[2] team
    From the presence of the sun,
    Following darkness like a dream,
    Now are frolic.° Not a mouse   *merry*
    Shall disturb this hallowed house.
375   I am sent with broom[3] before
    To sweep the dust behind° the door.   *from behind*
      *Enter [*OBERON *and* TITANIA,*] King and Queen of*
      Fairies, with all their train.

---

8. A dance named after Bergamo, in Italy (commonly ridiculed for its rusticity).
9. The only "two of our company" onstage at the end of the interlude. The role of Bottom may have been first performed by the actor Will Kemp, who was famous for his dancing.

1. Each grave lets forth its ghost.
2. Hecate was goddess of the moon and night, and she had three realms: heaven (as Cynthia), earth (as Diana), and hell (as Proserpine).
3. One of his traditional emblems; he helped good housekeepers and punished lazy ones.

OBERON   Through the house give glimmering light
     By the dead and drowsy fire;
     Every elf and fairy sprite
380   Hop as light as bird from briar;
     And this ditty after me
     Sing, and dance it trippingly.
TITANIA   First rehearse your song by rote,
     To each word a warbling note.
385   Hand in hand with fairy grace
     Will we sing and bless this place.
          [*The* FAIRIES *dance to a song.*][4]
OBERON   Now until the break of day
     Through this house each fairy stray.
     To the best bride-bed will we,[5]
390   Which by us shall blessèd be;
     And the issue there create°   *created; conceived*
     Ever shall be fortunate.
     So shall all the couples three
     Ever true in loving be.
395   And the blots of nature's hand
     Shall not in their issue stand;
     Never mole, harelip, nor scar,
     Nor mark prodigious,° such as are   *ominous birthmark*
     Despisèd in nativity,
400   Shall upon their children be.
     With this field-dew consecrate[6]
     Every fairy take his gait,°   *way*
     And each several° chamber bless   *separate*
     Through this palace with sweet peace;
405   And the owner of it blessed
     Ever shall in safety rest.
     Trip away, make no stay;
     Meet me all by break of day.   *Exeunt* [*all but* ROBIN].
ROBIN [*to the audience*]   If we shadows have offended,
410   Think but this, and all is mended,
     That you have but slumbered here
     While these visions did appear.
     And this weak and idle theme,
     No more yielding but° a dream,   *than*
415   Gentles, do not reprehend,
     If you pardon, we will mend.
     And as I am an honest puck,
     If we have unearnèd luck
     Now to 'scape the serpent's tongue,[7]
420   We will make amends ere long;
     Else the puck a liar call.
     So, good night unto you all.
     Give me your hands,° if we be friends,   *applause*
     And Robin shall restore amends.   [*Exit.*]

---

4. TEXTUAL COMMENT In F, the words of Oberon's speech constitute the text of the fairies' song, perhaps due to a misunderstanding in the printing house. See Digital Edition TC 9 (Quarto edited text).
5. Oberon and Titania will bless the bed of Theseus and Hippolyta.
6. Consecrated, blessed. Playfully alludes to the traditional Catholic custom of blessing the marriage bed with holy water.
7. Hissing from the audience.

The Merchant of Venice

Jew. Jew. Jew. The word echoes through *The Merchant of Venice.* The play has generated controversy for centuries. Is it anti-Semitic? Does it criticize anti-Semitism? Does it merely represent anti-Semitism without either endorsement or condemnation? Are the Christians right to call Shylock, the Jewish moneylender, a "devil," an "inexorable dog"; or is he merely the understandably resentful victim of their bigotry? Does Portia, Shylock's antagonist in the courtroom, exemplify the best in womanly virtue, or is she a manipulative virago? These questions about character suggest others that might be phrased more generally. What are the obligations of majority cultures to minorities in their midst? Do universally shared human characteristics outweigh racial and religious differences, or are such differences decisive?

Perhaps these issues seem more pressing for us than they did for Shakespeare. He hardly could have predicted Nazi genocide or other savagely efficient modern forms of "ethnic cleansing." Nor could he have foreseen the opportunities and problems faced by multiracial societies centuries after his death. Nevertheless, by Shakespeare's time, the legacy of Jew hating in western Europe was already long and bitter. Depictions of fiendish Jews were routine in medieval and Renaissance drama; the villainous protagonist of Christopher Marlowe's *Jew of Malta,* a popular success in the early 1590s, was only the latest precedent. In 1594, shortly before Shakespeare wrote *The Merchant of Venice,* an outpouring of anti-Semitic outrage was triggered by the case of Roderigo Lopez, a Portuguese Jewish convert to Christianity accused of attempting to murder Queen Elizabeth.

Of course, the existence of anti-Semitism in sixteenth-century England says little about Shakespeare's own attitudes. He could have written *The Merchant of Venice* either to capitalize on or to criticize the prejudices of his society. Interestingly, Shakespeare had probably never encountered practicing Jews, since they had been forcibly expelled from England in the Middle Ages. And England was not alone in its intolerance of religious difference. In 1492, Spain banished all non-Christians. During the sixteenth century, northern Europe saw decades of bloody conflict between Catholics and Protestants, while much of southern Europe was in the grip of the Inquisition. The impulse behind these persecutions was the conviction that a stable society required a shared belief system. A community based on consensus can indeed be impressively cohesive. Its homogeneity, however, makes it impatient of those who do not share its assumptions. Moreover, by the 1590s, when Shakespeare wrote *The Merchant of Venice,* wars of religion all over Europe were making such consensus seem increasingly elusive—something obtainable, if at all, only at appalling human cost.

Possibly Venice seemed to Shakespeare to offer an alternative social prototype. Although it had no natural resources to speak of, it was the richest city in Renaissance Europe, located where the products of Asia could most conveniently be exchanged with those of western Europe. As a town of traders, Venice was full of foreigners: Turks, Jews, Arabs, Africans, Christians of various nationalities and denominations. By sixteenth-century standards, the city was unusually tolerant of diversity. This relative toleration was intimately linked with the city's wealth: its legal guarantees of fair treatment for all were designed to keep its markets running smoothly. Antonio tells Solanio:

> The Duke cannot deny the course of law,
> For the commodity that strangers have

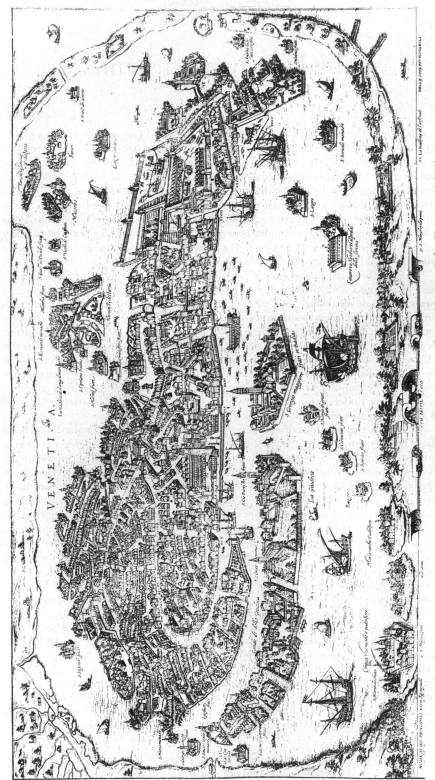

Prospect of Venice. From George Braun and Franz Hogenberg, *Civitates Orbis Terrarum* (1593).

> With us in Venice, if it be denied,
> Will much impeach the justice of the state,
> Since that the trade and profit of the city
> Consisteth of all nations.
>
> (3.3.26–31)

Shakespeare stresses, even exaggerates, this evenhanded cosmopolitanism. Historically, for instance, Venetian Jews were confined to a ghetto, gated and locked at night, but Shakespeare either did not know this fact or chose to ignore it. Venice thus provided Shakespeare with an example—perhaps the only example in sixteenth-century Europe—of a place where people with little in common culturally might coexist peacefully solely because it was materially expedient to do so. The laws of the marketplace seemed to have little to do with religion or nationality.

In *The Merchant of Venice,* the Christian gentlemen who populate the opening scenes associate friendship with generous, even reckless, expenditure. When Bassanio asks Antonio for a loan, Antonio rushes to supply him even though he does not have the money at hand. When Graziano asks a favor of Bassanio, Bassanio grants it before he even hears what it is. Later in the play, when Portia finds out that Antonio's life is forfeit because of 3,000 ducats, she instantly offers to pay twelve times that sum to redeem him. Not entirely surprisingly, Bassanio is an amiable spendthrift who does not fret too much about waste or loss:

> In my school days, when I had lost one shaft,
> I shot his fellow of the selfsame flight
> The selfsame way, with more advisèd watch,
> To find the other forth; and by adventuring both,
> I oft found both.
>
> (1.1.140–44)

"Oft" is not "always." Sometimes, presumably, Bassanio lost both arrows. His temperamental similarity to his friend Antonio, the merchant-adventurer, is an optimism about gambling at long odds.

Such prodigal panache is undeniably attractive, especially in comedy, where generic conventions typically ensure that characters beat long odds. It generates, moreover, some of the most gorgeous poetry of the play, a language of risky munificence, in which phenomenal wealth is accumulated only to be splendidly dispersed. Salerio, for instance, describes a shipwreck as a beautiful squandering of luxury goods:

> dangerous rocks
> Which, touching but my gentle vessel's side,
> Would scatter all her spices on the stream,
> Enrobe the roaring waters with my silks.
>
> (1.1.31–34)

Likewise, Portia tells Bassanio:

> for myself alone
> I would not be ambitious in my wish
> To wish myself much better, yet for you
> I would be trebled twenty times myself—
> A thousand times more fair, ten thousand times
> More rich; that only to stand high in your account
> I might in virtues, beauties, livings, friends,
> Exceed account.
>
> (3.2.150–57)

Unfortunately, it soon becomes obvious that the Christians' generosity is not extended to everybody. The magnanimous, depressive Antonio proudly acknowledges kicking and spitting on Shylock. The charming Portia ridicules her foreign suitors and rejoices in the failure of her black suitor to choose the correct casket: "Let all of his complexion choose me so" (2.7.79). These people find it hard to deal with those different from themselves: their society is based as much on the exclusion of the alien as on the inclusion of the similar. The moral ambiguity of the Christians' outlook is captured in their fondness for the loaded word *kind*, which in Renaissance English meant not only "compassionate" but "similar," or "akin." People act benevolently toward those who are of the same *kind* as themselves.

Shylock's relation to the Venetian Christians exemplifies a different social mechanism. Unable to trust to love and generosity, Shylock relies instead on contractually enforceable promises and networks of mutual material need and self-interest. Shylock's emphasis on purely economic factors means that he does not think about money the way Antonio and Bassanio do. He tends not to spend but to conserve, not to expand but to defend, not to seek risk but to minimize it. When he imagines a disaster at sea, he envisions not a spectacular swirl of silk and spices, but a sordid scenario of thievery and nibbling rats.

Although Shylock identifies strongly with his "sacred nation," his "tribe," and although he relies on fellow Jews like Tubal, the play gives little sense of Jewish community. The play represents Shylock as an isolated figure, shunned by his daughter, abandoned by his servant. His calculating, loveless existence seems to result from the way he manages his property. Or perhaps isolation has made him cautious and selfish. Shylock has little motive to be generous with the Christians who despise him, and every reason to believe that he cannot depend on others to rescue him from misfortune.

The psychological and social contrasts between the Christians and Shylock reflect both class and religious differences. The Christians' magnificent improvidence is, in Shakespeare's time, a distinctively aristocratic trait. A true gentleman refuses to be too obviously concerned with monetary expenditure, especially where friends are concerned. He also feels socially obliged to display himself properly. Bassanio spends huge sums of borrowed money equipping himself for his trip to Belmont to woo Portia, even though all he technically need do is arrive alone and select the correct casket. Coming to Portia unattended or in shabby clothes is unthinkable even though (or perhaps because) "all the wealth I had," as Bassanio freely admits, "ran in my veins" (3.2.252–53). By contrast Shylock, despite his evident wealth, is obviously no gentleman. He locks up his possessions, regrets how much his servant eats, fumes over the money he spends searching for his missing daughter.

At the same time, the opposition between the Christians and Shylock seems rooted in religious disparities. Judaism in the play is presented not in its actual complexity but as a sixteenth-century Christian like Shakespeare would have construed it, as a set of dra-

"Jews." From Jost Amman, *The Panoplia* (1568).

matically vivid contrasts with Christian norms. The law of Moses, as set down in Deuteronomy and Leviticus, specifies numerous aspects of the observant Jew's life—what to eat and wear, how to worship, how to conduct business, how to punish crimes. The Mosaic code places a high value upon justice and emphasizes the importance of adhering to the letter of the law. Shylock's Judaism reveals itself not merely in his distinctive dress and his avoidance of pork, but in his trust of literal meanings, his respect for material possessions and observable facts, his expectation that contracts will be rigorously enforced.

The typical Christian outlook is different. Christians obtain divine approval not by wearing certain garments, avoiding particular foods, or circumcising their boys, but by believing in Christ's power to save them. The central virtues in this religious system are not justice and scrupulous compliance with the law but charity and mercy, and a willingness to believe what seems incredible. In the terms Shakespeare provides in *The Merchant of Venice*, the Christian demeanor is entrepreneurial, even reckless, the spiritual equivalent of what Antonio does with his ships or Bassanio does with the money he borrows from his friend. "Give up every-

Young man in Venice. From Cesare Vecellio, *De gli habiti antichi et moderni* (1590).

thing you have and follow me," Jesus tells his would-be follower, advice echoed in the inscription on the lead casket: "Who chooseth me must give and hazard all he hath" (2.7.16). Like the word *kind,* the similarly complex word *gentle* is used repeatedly in the play to describe this distinctive set of traits: the word simultaneously refers to considerate behavior, to aristocratic family background, and to "gentile," or Christian, religious convictions.

As the play proceeds, it modifies somewhat these initially vivid contrasts between Christian and Jew by showing the sharp contrasts between what the characters claim to be and how they actually behave. For instance, Shylock pretends that he thinks of people in purely material, economic terms. Antonio may treat him badly, but when he applies for a loan, Shyock calls him "a good man." "[M]y meaning in saying he is a good man is to have you understand me that he is sufficient" (1.3.13–15): in other words, Antonio's wealth makes him a good credit risk. Within a few lines, however, Shylock informs us in an aside that he hates Antonio and wants revenge upon him. After Jessica's flight, Solanio claims that Shylock has been seen running through the streets crying, "O my ducats, O my daughter! . . . [M]y ducats, and my daughter!" (2.8.15ff). It is impossible to know how accurate this rumor might be: the equation of ducats and daughter is exactly what Christians expect of the moneygrubbing Shylock. But when Shylock finally appears onstage, he says nothing of the kind. When Tubal tells him that Jessica has exchanged a turquoise ring for a monkey, Shylock replies: "Out upon her; thou torturest me, Tubal! It was my turquoise; I had it of Leah when I was a bachelor. I would not have given it for a wilderness of monkeys" (3.1.100–102). He insists, in other words, upon the sentimental value of the turquoise ring, not upon its monetary value. His grief over his daughter's defection, and her insensitivity to his relation with her dead mother, much exceeds his financial loss. Likewise in the courtroom, Shylock is remarkable not for his businesslike prudence but for his refusal to be swayed by monetary appeals. There is something in the quality of his oppression that he refuses to convert into a payoff.

The Christians are also more complicated than they profess to be. Their faith teaches that all human beings are precious and demands that they love not only neighbors but even enemies. However, only some persons elicit a humane response, while others are disregarded or treated as nonhuman. When Salerio and Solanio ridicule Shylock, he protests: "Hath not a Jew eyes? Hath not a Jew hands, organs, dimensions, senses, affections, passions—fed with the same food, hurt with the same weapons, subject to the same diseases, healed by the same means, warmed and cooled by the same winter and summer as a Christian is?" (3.1.49–53). Shylock asserts that a common human experience of embodiment ought to override considerations of religious or racial difference. These lines are among the most memorable in the play, but the argument does not follow from the position Shylock has taken earlier. Rather, it is effective because it exposes Christian hypocrisy. Similarly, in the trial scene, Shylock points out that the Christian practice of slavery plainly treats some human beings as mere property. "You have among you many a purchased slave, / Which like your asses and your dogs and mules / You use in abject and in slavish parts / Because you bought them" (4.1.90–93). The Christians' creed mandates universal love, but they fail to behave in accord with their precepts.

These inconsistencies haunt the play's friendships and marriages. Marriage is a hybrid social relation: obviously associated with love and procreation, it is simultaneously a property relation, involving the economic alliance of individuals and families. Bassanio's courtship of Portia is doubly motivated: he loves her, and he needs her money. The language of his attraction, even at its most generous and disinterested, is full of the metaphors of commerce and exchange. And although Antonio protests against thinking of friendship purely as an economic transaction, it is not difficult to construe his self-sacrificing generosity as an attempt to buy Bassanio's love. So although the Christians attempt to differentiate spiritual values from economic ones, those values continually turn out to be intimately intertwined.

The casket test directly confronts this problem. The failures of Morocco and Aragon demonstrate that it is possible to find a plausible reason for choosing any one of the three caskets. But when Bassanio makes his choice, we see how the test works: it can be solved only by one who views its puzzles from the correct point of view. Bassanio must abstract from his particular relation with Portia to a general distinction between "ornament" and "truth":

> Look on beauty,
> And you shall see 'tis purchased by the weight,
> Which therein works a miracle in nature,
> Making them lightest that wear most of it.
> (3.2.88–91)

Surely Bassanio does not believe that because Portia is lovely, she must be unchaste. Instead, his upbringing as a Christian gentleman has acquainted him with a particular frame of mind that prefers invisible over visible things, spirit over body, metaphor over literal meaning. The same cultural background makes him willing to take chances: to "hazard all he hath" on the unprepossessing lead casket. Because every suitor gets the same chance, the casket test seems to be fair; in fact, it is rather like those "objective" intelligence tests that, in subtle or not-so-subtle ways, reward the belief systems of dominant groups while stigmatizing outsiders. In this case, the person best fitted to be Portia's husband is one who, by Christian standards, knows the limitations and right use of wealth. This knowledge enables him to value characteristics in his wife—virtue, intelligence, and beauty—that make her precious in more than monetary ways.

One of the surprises of the casket test is that it takes place at all. Portia's obedience to her dead father's apparently irrational plans for her is remarkable in comedy, for comic heroines more often, like Jessica, defy their fathers than conscientiously follow their orders. Perhaps Portia could be seen as synthesizing the best of Jewish and Christian characteristics; obeying the letter of a wise father's law, even while cultivating the spiritual virtues of love and generosity. Perhaps, then, Jewish and Christian outlooks are not *necessarily* in conflict (any more than there is a necessary conflict in being, as Portia is, both rich and beautiful). Certainly Portia's respect for the letter of the law, combined with her willingness to go beyond that letter, makes her the only character who can effectively confront Shylock in the trial scene.

When she disguises herself as a young lawyer, Portia becomes one of many Shakespearean comic heroines to assume male attire. The power that she achieves by her transvestism signals an interesting development in Shakespeare's treatment of the relations between men and women. Earlier plays often differentiate sharply between the sexes: between the male political domain and the female domestic domain in *Richard II,* between the male streetcorner and the female bedchamber in *Romeo and Juliet.* In *The Merchant of Venice* and the comedies Shakespeare wrote immediately thereafter, women seem to possess a new liberty of action. Their freedom coincides with another new development in Shakespearean comedy, the presence of a scapegoat character—someone like Shylock, who cannot be assimilated into the comic society at the end of the play. Perhaps when the most serious social threats seem to be posed by outsiders, there is more freedom for women within the "in" group: the crucial bifurcation is no longer between male and female but between "us" and "them."

Portia's legal strategy is complex, and thus the trial has several stages. At first, she both offers and recommends generosity:

> Therefore, Jew,
> Though justice be thy plea, consider this—
> That in the course of justice none of us
> Should see salvation. We do pray for mercy,
> And that same prayer doth teach us all to render
> The deeds of mercy.
>
> (4.1.195–200)

Not surprisingly, Shylock is deaf to this eloquence. Portia's argument is based on the distinctively Christian premise that salvation is an undeserved gift. She derives her authority from the Lord's Prayer: "forgive us our trespasses as we forgive those who trespass against us." But Shylock doesn't accept, or even perhaps know the existence of, a prayer that supposedly "teaches us all." Portia's plea for tolerance and compassion might seem to rest on universal premises, but in fact Portia's "we" who "pray for mercy" neatly excludes the Jew.

The judgment upon Shylock at the end of the trial has disturbed many critics and audiences. After the Christians win the case—not only saving Antonio's life but also keeping the 3,000 ducats Shylock had lent Bassanio—Portia seems to take exactly the revenge she has up to now deplored. Her legal ground is provided by a previously unmentioned law against any alien who plots the death of a Venetian citizen. The law in which Shylock trusted, because it seemed to provide a refuge from prejudice, turns out to have prejudice inscribed within it from the start. In this respect, it resembles the casket test—everybody seems to get the same chance, but in fact the test blatantly favors the insider.

Portia and the Duke apparently regard the dismissal of Shylock as merciful; his *life* is preserved, although half or all of his mere money is taken away. Portia's sentence forces Shylock to behave as a Christian citizen and father should: to worship in a Christian church, to grant money to his daughter, to recognize the difference between spiritual and economic well-being. Eschewing lethal force, the Duke demands that Shylock acquiesce in his punishment: "I am content" (4.1.392), Shylock says at last. But what else can he say? The coercive inclusion of Shylock in the Christian community seems all the more violent because it pretends to renounce coercion. If designating people outcasts is bad, compelling them to participate in a society they find intolerable may be even worse.

The Merchant of Venice thus hovers on the edge of tragedy. Shylock's ferocious negativity is poised against, and arguably elicited by, the Christians' hypocritical refusal to admit the way their spiritual lives depend on material prosperity. The presence of the scapegoated Jew lays bare the mechanisms by which Venetian society works. Shylock can be reviled and dismissed, but the possibilities that he represents do not simply vanish when he flees the courtroom. Thus the moral disquiet the play raises among directors, readers, and audiences: Christian and Jewish perspectives seem mutually invalidating, and both finally inadequate.

Shakespeare suggests the stubbornness of the problems broached by the play in the way he structures the last act. Most Shakespeare comedies return to the city or the court at the end, or at least look forward to that return; but in The Merchant of Venice, the play ends at Belmont, the nostalgically depicted, magically copious "green world." It is as if the formal demand for comic closure conflicts with Shakespeare's awareness that no neat resolution of Venice's problems is forthcoming.

Indeed, some muted version of those problems pursues the Christians even to Portia's estate. The act begins with the banter between the newlyweds Jessica and Lorenzo, who have stayed behind at Belmont in Portia's absence. It is a bit ominous that all the love stories they recall are unhappy ones. Still, the couple's affectionate teasing makes the scene a welcome change from what has immediately preceded it. Showing Jessica and Lorenzo in witty conversation minutes after the brutal expulsion of Shylock seems an attempt to confine the punitive energies of the play to the usurer alone. The scene offers an alternative vision of interaction between racial groups, one that involves love rather than hatred. Of course, this is a vision not of mutual tolerance but of assimilation: Jessica's marriage to a Christian has exempted her from Shylock's fate. In 5.1 Lorenzo describes to his wife the "music of the spheres"—a perfect heavenly harmony made inaudible by the corruption of this life. Perhaps, analogously, the Christians' failure lies not in the nature of their ideals, but in the imperfect realization of those ideals in the everyday world. The inevitable dissonance between the mundane and the ideal world does not necessarily, however, simply drain the ideal of its meaning.

The moral dilemmas posed by high but perhaps unrealizable ideals come under scrutiny yet again in the ring trick with which the play ends. In The Merchant of Venice, as in many of Shakespeare's plays, courtship and marriage coexist with, and are potentially or actually in competition with, intense same-sex friendships. In the trial scene, just before, it seems, Shylock will kill Antonio, Bassanio makes a desperate declaration:

> Antonio, I am married to a wife
> Which is as dear to me as life itself;
> But life itself, my wife, and all the world
> Are not with me esteemed above thy life.
> I would lose all—ay, sacrifice them all
> Here to this devil—to deliver you.
>   (4.1.280–85)

To which Portia, disguised as Balthazar, responds in an acid aside, "Your wife would give you little thanks for that / If she were by to hear you make the offer" (286–87). After the conclusion of the trial, Portia-as-Balthazar asks Bassanio for his wedding ring as payment for legal services. This request presents Bassanio with a harder problem than Shylock had. Bassanio can imagine breaking a written contract, but not denying the request of an ally to whom he's indebted. By giving the ring to

Balthazar, Bassanio demonstrates both that his loyalty to Antonio still outweighs his allegiance to Portia and that he has trouble governing his generous impulses. Portia's trick teaches Bassanio, and Antonio as well, that the marital relationship involves unique responsibilities and that those responsibilities impose a limit on reckless munificence. At play's end, Antonio is once again "standing surety" for Bassanio, this time to Portia rather than to Shylock, promising to help sustain rather than interfere with his friend's marriage vows.

In this moment, as happens again and again in The Merchant of Venice, oppositions between potentially tragic alternatives miraculously dissolve—between being rich and being virtuous, marrying for money and marrying for love, following paternal orders and making one's own choice, enforcing the letter of the law and enforcing its spirit, remaining faithful to one's wife and loving one's male friend. Balthazar turns out to have been Portia, Bassanio has given his ring to its original owner, and all seems to be well. But by setting the play's last act in a magical world of trust and abundance, Shakespeare stresses the artifice involved in his resolution. Even as this beautiful, troubling play comes to a close, it pointedly emphasizes the distance between the final act's charmed fictional world and the intransigent real one.

KATHARINE EISAMAN MAUS

SELECTED BIBLIOGRAPHY

Adelman, Janet. Blood Relations: Christian and Jew in "The Merchant of Venice." Chicago: U of Chicago P, 2008. Offers the most complete account of the significance of the religious conflicts in the play, focusing upon the different ways Jews and Christians understand the same biblical stories.

Bailey, Amanda. "Shylock and the Slaves: Owing and Owning in The Merchant of Venice." Shakespeare Quarterly 62 (2011): 1–24. Considers the "pound of flesh" bargain in the context of actual procedures for punishing delinquent debtors in early modern England.

Barber, C. L. "The Merchants and the Jew of Venice: Wealth's Communion and an Intruder." Shakespeare's Festive Comedy: A Study of Dramatic Form and Its Relation to Social Custom. Princeton, NJ: Princeton UP, 1959. Looks at the Christians' opulent festivity as challenged by Shylock's fiercely reductive attitude toward money.

Burckhardt, Sigurd. "The Merchant of Venice: The Gentle Bond." Shakespearean Meanings. Princeton, NJ: Princeton UP, 1968. 206–89. Examines the importance of various kinds of bonds in The Merchant of Venice.

Cohen, Walter. "The Merchant of Venice and the Possibilities of Historical Criticism." English Literary History 49 (1982): 765–89. Explores the play's theatrical artifice as reflecting economic conflicts in early modern Europe.

Danson, Lawrence. The Harmonies of "The Merchant of Venice." New Haven, CT: Yale UP, 1978. Describes the play's conflicts in detail and argues for their satisfactory resolution.

Engle, Lars. "Money and Moral Luck in The Merchant of Venice." Shakespearean Pragmatism: Market of His Time. Chicago: U of Chicago P, 1993. 77–106. Reads The Merchant of Venice through the lens of late twentieth-century ethical philosophy.

Gross, Kenneth. Shylock Is Shakespeare. Chicago: U of Chicago P, 2006. Analyzes Shakespeare's personal connection to Shylock.

Lewalski, Barbara. "Biblical Allusion and Allegory in The Merchant of Venice." Shakespeare Quarterly 13 (1962): 327–43. Looks at Shakespeare's use of biblical typology.

Lupton, Julia Reinhard. "Merchants of Venice, Circles of Citizenship." Citizen-Saints: Shakespeare and Political Theology. Chicago: U of Chicago P, 2005. 75–101. Explores Judaism and citizenship in early modern Venice.

Maus, Katharine Eisaman. *Being and Having in Shakespeare*. Oxford: Oxford UP, 2013. Chapters 3 and 4. Traces the flow of wealth in the play's marriages, friendships, and business relationships.

Newman, Karen. "Portia's Ring: Unruly Women and the Structure of Exchange in *The Merchant of Venice*." *Shakespeare Quarterly* 38 (1987): 19–33. Looks at how Portia, as gift-giver, occupies a position of power usually coded as masculine.

Shapiro, James. *Shakespeare and the Jews*. New York: Columbia UP, 1996. Examines anti-Semitism in Shakespeare's time.

Shell, Marc. "'The Wether and the Ewe': Verbal Usury in *The Merchant of Venice*." *Kenyon Review* 1.4 (1979): 65–92. Analyzes exchange and redemption in *The Merchant of Venice*, focusing particularly on Shylock's story of Laban and Jacob.

Wilson, Luke. "Drama and Marine Insurance in Shakespeare's London." *The Law in Shakespeare*. Ed. Constance Jordan and Karen Cunningham. London: Palgrave Macmillan, 2007. 127–42. Looks at some of the legal complexities of the play in the context of Shakespeare's time.

FILMS

The Merchant of Venice. 1973. Dir. John Sichel. UK. 131 min. Laurence Olivier as Shylock.

The Merchant of Venice. 1980. Dir. Jack Gold. UK. 157 min. Textually faithful but stilted. Gemma Jones is a chilly, calculating Portia.

The Merchant of Venice. 2001. Dir. Trevor Nunn. UK. 141 min. The film version of an acclaimed Royal National Theatre production, set in Europe between the world wars. Vividly acted, with many interesting directorial choices. Henry Goodman's Shylock is especially memorable.

The Merchant of Venice. 2004. Dir. Michael Radford. UK. 131 min. Al Pacino as Shylock, Lynn Collins as Portia. Sumptuous period costumes and sets. This production emphasizes the disquieting aspects of the play, not only the Venetians' anti-Semitism but the struggle between Portia and Antonio over Bassanio's allegiance.

TEXTUAL INTRODUCTION

The first known edition of *The Merchant of Venice* was published in 1600 and called on its title page, rather flamboyantly, "The most excellent / Historie of the *Merchant / of Venice. /* With the extreame crueltie of *Shylocke* the Iewe / towards the sayd Merchant, in cutting a iust pound / of his flesh: and the obtayning of *Portia /* by the choyce of three / chests. / *As it hath beene diuers times acted by the Lord / Chamberlaine his Servants.*" This edition, known as the First Quarto or Q1, is remarkably well printed by the standards of the time and is used as the textual basis of most modern editions of the play, including this one. The next quarto edition that we know of, Q2, appeared in 1619 as one of the so-called "Pavier quartos"—a collection of nine Shakespeare plays published for Thomas Pavier by William Jaggard, who would go on to publish the Shakespeare First Folio in 1623. The date on Q2's title page was, however, spurious: it claimed to have been produced in 1600—the same year as Q1. Perhaps Jaggard was trying to get around the Stationers' Company restrictions in publishing Q2 with its fictitious date; in any case, he published the play again in the Shakespeare First Folio (F) four years later. Q2 and F are not significantly better printed than Q1, though they do correct a few Q1 misprints and supply a few additional stage directions. As is common among Shakespeare quartos, neither Q1 nor Q2 contains act and scene divisions. F helpfully divides the play into acts; the scene divisions in this edition are derived from later editorial tradition, which assumed that a scene ended when the stage was cleared.

The most interesting textual issue in relation to *The Merchant of Venice* is the vexed matter of speech prefixes. In Shakespeare's time, quarto playtexts were typically printed without cast lists, and there was no convention requiring that a speech prefix remain constant through the course of the play. As a result we sometimes experience confusion about who is speaking. Take the vexed matter of Antonio and Bassanio's friends whose names begin with "S." How many are there and what are their names? *"Salerio," "Salanio," "Solanio," "Salarino," "Salaryno," "Salario," "Sal.," "Sol.," "Sola.," "Sala."*—all of these forms occur in the First Quarto version, and they are by no means used consistently. At some points, one of these seemingly interchangeable characters is indicated in the stage directions as entering, but the actual speech prefixes that follow name another. A case can be made for three characters rather than two—Salerio, Solanio, and Salarino—but even then, they are not differentiated in the quarto with anything approaching consistency. This edition follows most previous editions in boiling all the "S" names down to two: Salerio and Solanio.

A slightly different problem exists for Lancelet the clown, whose name in most editions of the play has been Launcelot or Lancelot. In stage directions and speech prefixes to Q1, Q2, and F, he is variously called *"Lancelet"* or *"Clown,"* but he is never called "Launcelot" or "Lancelot." *The Norton Shakespeare* restores what we believe is his original name, which can mean "little lance" or "little knife"—an interesting choice of name in a play that centers on Shylock's knife.

The name of Shylock the Jew is even more problematic. Sometimes in Q1 prefixes he is *"Shylock"* and sometimes he is *"Jew."* At one point in act 4, Portia addresses him, "Is your name Shylock?" and he answers, "Shylock is my name," but the speech prefix before this answer calls him *"Jew."* The speech prefix *"Jew"* is especially prevalent at points in the play in which the action resonates with traditional anti-Semitic stereotypes (see Digital Edition TC 3, 1.3.26). By looking in the Digital Edition at each textual variant associated with Shylock's name, users of *The Norton Shakespeare* will be able to trace the substitutions of *"Jew"* for *"Shylock"* over the course of the play. Q2 switches several of the *"Jew"* prefixes back to *"Shylock"* or *"Shy.,"* but in F all of these follow Q1 and use *"Jew."* Like so many other textual variants in Shakespeare, this one remains mysterious in terms of its possible motivation: it could go back to Shakespeare's own manuscript, or have been introduced during the copying or printing of the play. Some bibliographers believe that the original speech prefix was *"Jew"* throughout, and that the speech prefix *"Shylock"* was only introduced because of type shortages in the printing house. But that hypothesis seems unlikely: the argument depends on assumptions about the way early texts were printed that are not supported by subsequent research on the way printing jobs were typically managed in a printing house. Here, as so often in Shakespeare, we view the lost "original" through so many veils of mediation that the author's intentions cannot reliably be recovered.

LEAH S. MARCUS

PERFORMANCE NOTE

With its controversial subjects, uncertain genre, and multiple subplots, *The Merchant of Venice* presents unique challenges to theater companies that undertake to perform it. Perhaps foremost among these challenges is deciding just how much of the play to perform. *Merchant* is stocked with robust roles, each with unsavory elements, so what is kept or cut can decisively influence which story is told and which character emerges at its center. One production may work to sanitize the Venetians and heighten Shylock's savagery, steering the play toward a less adulterated comic resolution; another may emphasize the Christians' cruelty in order to intensify Shylock's tragic situation, thus overshadowing the comic ending in Belmont. Both can work, and that neither choice wholly occludes aspects of the other is one of the play's strengths and a source of tension and engagement for audiences. In orchestrating the balance between comic and tragic elements, directors also must decide on issues such as the centrality of Antonio, whose sadness is never explicitly revisited, and whether to present Shylock as eager to assimilate, mirroring Antonio's bearing and behavior, or to emphasize his foreignness and isolation.

Each of the play's first six scenes initiates a new subplot featuring a new character. *Merchant* therefore requires an unusually strong and versatile ensemble, one that can maintain interest while plot threads and protagonists vie for primacy. Similar vying is apparent within the characters too. Shylock and Antonio are tender one moment and vicious the next. Portia must be charming even in condescension, as winning when seeking mercy as she is severe when showing none. These characters thrive on ambivalences, so a further challenge in production is to reconcile extremes credibly, yet without dulling their edges. The characterizations of lesser roles are relevant too. Lancelet can either sport with or torment Jessica about her conversion in 3.5; Morocco can invite mockery or move audiences to sympathize with the plights of foreigners. And Salerio and Solanio stand in for Venetians at large, so how they parody Shylock and respond to his complaints will affect the audience's judgment of its comic heroes, and investment in its tragic one.

BRETT GAMBOA

The Comical History of the Merchant of Venice

[THE PERSONS OF THE PLAY

At Venice:
DUKE of Venice
ANTONIO, a merchant of Venice
BASSANIO, friend to Antonio and suitor to Portia
LORENZO ⎫
GRAZIANO ⎬ friends to Antonio and Bassanio
SALERIO ⎥
SOLANIO ⎭
SERVINGMAN to Antonio
LEONARDO, servant to Bassanio
SHYLOCK, a Jewish moneylender
JESSICA, daughter to Shylock
TUBAL, another Jew
LANCELET, a clown, servant to Shylock and then to Bassanio
GOBBO, father to Lancelet
Magnificoes of Venice
Jailer

At Belmont:
PORTIA, an heiress
NERISSA, attending on Portia
BALTHAZAR ⎫
MESSENGER ⎥
MUSICIANS ⎬ servants to Portia
STEFANO ⎥
Servitor ⎭
Prince of MOROCCO ⎫
Prince of ARAGON ⎬ suitors to Portia]

1.1

Enter ANTONIO, SALERIO, *and* SOLANIO.[1]

ANTONIO   In sooth° I know not why I am so sad.   *truth*
It wearies me, you say it wearies you,
But how I caught it, found it, or came by it,
What stuff 'tis made of, whereof it is born,
5   I am to learn;°   *have yet to discover*
And such a want-wit° sadness makes of me   *dullard*
That I have much ado to know myself.
SALERIO   Your mind is tossing on the ocean,
There where your argosies° with portly° sail   *merchant ships / stately*
10   Like signors° and rich burghers on the flood   *lords*
Or, as it were, the pageants[2] of the sea,

1.1 Location: Venice.
1. TEXTUAL COMMENT Stage directions and speech-prefix abbreviations in early editions of *Merchant* leave it unclear whether there are two or three nearly interchangeable friends whose names all begin with "S." See Digital Edition TC 1.
2. Movable stages used by itinerant actors or in parades.

Do over-peer° the petty traffickers   *tower over*
That curtsy[3] to them, do them reverence,
As they fly by them with their woven wings.

15   SOLANIO   Believe me, sir, had I such venture° forth,   *a risky undertaking*
The better part of my affections would
Be with my hopes abroad. I should be still°   *always*
Plucking the grass to know where sits the wind,
Peering in maps for ports and piers and roads,°   *open harbors*
20   And every object that might make me fear
Misfortune to my ventures, out of doubt,
Would make me sad.

   SALERIO   My wind cooling my broth
Would blow me to an ague° when I thought   *make me shiver*
What harm a wind too great might do at sea.
25   I should not see the sandy hourglass run
But I should think of shallows and of flats°   *shoals*
And see my wealthy Andrew[4] dock in sand,
Vailing her high top° lower than her ribs   *Lowering her topmast*
To kiss her burial.° Should I go to church   *burial place*
30   And see the holy edifice of stone
And not bethink me straight° of dangerous rocks   *immediately think*
Which, touching but my gentle vessel's side,
Would scatter all her spices on the stream,
Enrobe the roaring waters with my silks,
35   And, in a word, but even now° worth this°   *moments ago / so much*
And now worth nothing? Shall I have the thought
To think on this, and shall I lack the thought
That such a thing bechanced° would make me sad?   *having occurred*
But tell not me; I know Antonio
40   Is sad to think upon his merchandise.

   ANTONIO   Believe me, no. I thank my fortune for it:
My ventures are not in one bottom° trusted,   *ship*
Nor to one place,° nor is my whole estate   *destination*
Upon the fortune of this present year;
45   Therefore my merchandise makes me not sad.

   SOLANIO   Why, then, you are in love.

   ANTONIO   Fie, fie!

   SOLANIO   Not in love neither? Then let us say you are sad
Because you are not merry; and 'twere as easy
For you to laugh and leap and say you are merry
50   Because you are not sad. Now, by two-headed Janus,[5]
Nature hath framed strange fellows in her time:
Some that will evermore peep through their eyes[6]
And laugh like parrots° at a bagpiper,[7]   *(screeching loudly)*
And other of such vinegar aspect°   *sour looks*
55   That they'll not show their teeth in way of smile
Though Nestor[8] swear the jest be laughable.

         Enter BASSANIO, LORENZO, *and* GRAZIANO.
Here comes Bassanio, your most noble kinsman,
Graziano, and Lorenzo. Fare ye well!

---

3. By bobbing on the waves or by lowering their flags in salute.
4. Name of a Spanish galleon captured by the English at Cádiz in 1596.
5. Roman god with faces looking both forward and backward.
6. Eyes almost shut by violent laughter.
7. Whose music was considered woeful.
8. Sober, elderly Greek hero in *The Iliad*.

We leave you now with better company.[9]

60 SALERIO   I would have stayed till I had made you merry
If worthier friends had not prevented me.

ANTONIO   Your worth is very dear in my regard.
I take it your own business calls on you,
And you embrace th'occasion to depart.

65 SALERIO   Good morrow, my good lords.

BASSANIO   Good signors both, when shall we laugh?°   make merry together
Say, when?
You grow exceeding strange!° Must it be so?   reserved

SALERIO   We'll make our leisures to attend on° yours.   suit

Exeunt SALERIO *and* SOLANIO.

LORENZO   My lord Bassanio, since you have found Antonio,
70 We two will leave you; but at dinnertime
I pray you have in mind where we must meet.

BASSANIO   I will not fail you.

GRAZIANO   You look not well, Signor Antonio.
You have too much respect upon the world:°   anxiety about business
75 They lose it that do buy it with much care.
Believe me, you are marvelously changed.

ANTONIO   I hold the world but as the world, Graziano—
A stage where every man must play a part
And mine a sad one.

GRAZIANO   Let me play the fool—
80 With mirth and laughter let old[1] wrinkles come,
And let my liver[2] rather heat with wine
Than my heart cool with mortifying[3] groans.
Why should a man whose blood is warm within
Sit like his grandsire cut in alabaster,[4]
85 Sleep when he wakes, and creep into the jaundice[5]
By being peevish? I tell thee what, Antonio,
I love thee, and 'tis my love that speaks:
There are a sort of men whose visages
Do cream and mantle[6] like a standing° pond,   stagnant
90 And do a willful stillness entertain
With purpose to be dressed in an opinion°   a reputation
Of wisdom, gravity, profound conceit—°   judgment
As who should say, "I am Sir Oracle,
And when I ope my lips let no dog bark."
95 O my Antonio, I do know of these
That therefore only are reputed wise
For saying nothing, when I am very sure
If they should speak would almost damn those ears
Which, hearing them, would call their brothers fools.[7]
100 I'll tell thee more of this another time.
But fish not with this melancholy bait
For this fool gudgeon,° this opinion.   tiny, easily caught fish

---

9. PERFORMANCE COMMENT The play never explicitly revisits the source of Antonio's sadness. In productions, directors often imply that it results from an unrequited romantic attachment to Bassanio. See Digital Edition PC 1.
1. Accompanying old age; abundant.
2. The liver was considered the seat of passion.
3. Deadly (groans were believed to drain blood from the heart).

4. Stone from which tomb effigies were carved.
5. Thought to result from too much yellow bile, a bodily substance associated with irritability.
6. *cream and mantle*: grow a scum; that is, assume a fixed countenance.
7. *would . . . fools*: alluding to Matthew 5:22: "And whosoever shall say to his brother . . . , fool, shall be in danger of hellfire."

Come, good Lorenzo. [*to* ANTONIO *and* BASSANIO] Fare ye well
    awhile.
I'll end my exhortation after dinner.
105 LORENZO   Well, we will leave you then till dinnertime.
    I must be one of these same dumb° wise men,   *mute*
    For Graziano never lets me speak.
GRAZIANO   Well, keep me company but two years more—
    Thou shalt not know the sound of thine own tongue!
110 ANTONIO   Fare you well! I'll grow a talker for this gear.[8]
GRAZIANO   Thanks i'faith, for silence is only commendable
    In a neat's° tongue dried and a maid not vendible.[9]   *an ox's*
                          Exeunt [LORENZO *and* GRAZIANO].
ANTONIO   It is that—anything now.
BASSANIO   Graziano speaks an infinite deal of nothing, more
115 than any man in all Venice. His reasons° are as two grains of   *sensible remarks*
    wheat hid in two bushels of chaff: you shall seek all day ere
    you find them, and when you have them they are not worth
    the search.
ANTONIO   Well, tell me now—what lady is the same
120 To whom you swore a secret pilgrimage
    That you today promised to tell me of?
BASSANIO   'Tis not unknown to you, Antonio,
    How much I have disabled mine estate
    By something showing a more swelling port°   *extravagant lifestyle*
125 Than my faint means would grant continuance.°   *allow to continue*
    Nor do I now make moan to be abridged°   *reduced*
    From such a noble rate;° but my chief care   *style*
    Is to come fairly off from the great debts
    Wherein my time, something too prodigal,
130 Hath left me gaged.° To you, Antonio,   *pledged*
    I owe the most in money and in love,
    And from your love I have a warranty°   *sanction*
    To unburden all my plots and purposes
    How to get clear of all the debts I owe.
135 ANTONIO   I pray you, good Bassanio, let me know it,
    And if it stand, as you yourself still do,
    Within the eye of honor, be assured
    My purse, my person, my extremest means
    Lie all unlocked to your occasions.°   *requirements*
140 BASSANIO   In my school days, when I had lost one shaft,
    I shot his° fellow of the selfsame flight°   *its / size and weight*
    The selfsame way, with more advisèd° watch,   *careful*
    To find the other forth; and by adventuring° both,   *hazarding*
    I oft found both. I urge this childhood proof
145 Because what follows is pure innocence.
    I owe you much, and like a willful youth
    That which I owe is lost; but if you please
    To shoot another arrow that self° way   *same*
    Which you did shoot the first, I do not doubt,
150 As I will watch the aim, or° to find both,   *either*
    Or bring your latter hazard° back again   *risk*
    And thankfully rest debtor for the first.

---

8. *for this gear:* as a result of your talk.   9. Sellable—that is, marriageable.

ANTONIO   You know me well, and herein spend but° time   *only lose*
To wind about my love with circumstance;°   *circumlocution*
155 And out of doubt you do me now more wrong
In making question of my uttermost[1]
Than if you had made waste of all I have.
Then do but say to me what I should do
That, in your knowledge, may by me be done,
160 And I am pressed unto° it—therefore speak.   *obliged to do*
BASSANIO   In Belmont is a lady richly left,°   *left a fortune*
And she is fair, and fairer than that word,
Of wondrous virtues. Sometimes° from her eyes   *At times*
I did receive fair speechless messages.
165 Her name is Portia, nothing undervalued
To[2] Cato's daughter, Brutus' Portia.[3]
Nor is the wide world ignorant of her worth,
For the four winds blow in from every coast
Renownèd suitors; and her sunny locks
170 Hang on her temples like a golden fleece,
Which makes her seat of Belmont Colchis' strand,[4]
And many Jasons come in quest of her.
O my Antonio, had I but the means
To hold a rival place with one of them,
175 I have a mind presages me such thrift°   *prosperity*
That I should questionless be fortunate.
ANTONIO   Thou know'st that all my fortunes are at sea:
Neither have I money nor commodity°   *goods*
To raise a present sum. Therefore go forth—
180 Try what my credit can in Venice do;
That shall be racked° even to the uttermost   *stretched*
To furnish thee to Belmont to fair Portia.
Go presently inquire, and so will I,
Where money is; and I no question make
185 To have it of my trust or for my sake.[5]   *Exeunt.*

1.2
Enter PORTIA *with her waiting woman,* NERISSA.
PORTIA   By my troth,° Nerissa, my little body is a-weary of this   *faith*
great world.
NERISSA   You would be,[1] sweet madam, if your miseries were
in the same abundance as your good fortunes are. And yet,
5   for aught I see, they are as sick that surfeit with too much as
they that starve with nothing. It is no mean° happiness, there-   *slight*
fore, to be seated in the mean:° superfluity comes sooner   *middle / sooner gets*
by° white hairs, but competency° lives longer.   *moderate estate*
PORTIA   Good sentences,° and well pronounced.   *aphorisms*
10   NERISSA   They would be better if well followed.
PORTIA   If to do were as easy as to know what were good to do,
chapels had been churches and poor men's cottages princes'
palaces. It is a good divine° that follows his own instruc-   *clergyman*
tions. I can easier teach twenty what were good to be done

1. In doubting that I would do my utmost to help you.
2. *nothing . . . / To:* no less worthy than.
3. Roman matron famous for heroic fidelity to her husband; a character in *Julius Caesar.*
4. Coast of Colchis, where in classical mythology

Jason won the Golden Fleece.
5. *of . . . sake:* because of my creditworthiness or as a personal favor.
1.2 Location: Belmont.
1. You would have reason to be weary.

15   than to be one of the twenty to follow mine own teaching.
        The brain may devise laws for the blood,° but a hot temper[2]   *passion*
        leaps o'er a cold decree: such a hare is madness, the youth,
        to skip o'er the meshes° of good counsel, the cripple.[3] But   *snares*
        this reasoning is not in the fashion° to choose me a husband.   *of a kind*
20   O me! The word "choose"! I may neither choose who I would
        nor refuse who I dislike; so is the will° of a living daughter   *wish*
        curbed by the will° of a dead father. Is it not hard, Nerissa,   *testament*
        that I cannot choose one nor refuse none?
        NERISSA   Your father was ever virtuous, and holy men at their
25   death have good inspirations; therefore the lottery that he
        hath devised in these three chests of gold, silver, and lead,
        whereof who chooses his meaning chooses you, will no doubt
        never be chosen by any rightly but one who you shall rightly
        love. But what warmth is there in your affection towards any
30   of these princely suitors that are already come?
        PORTIA   I pray thee, over-name them, and as thou namest
        them I will describe them and, according to my description,
        level° at my affection.   *guess*
        NERISSA   First, there is the Neapolitan prince.
35   PORTIA   Ay, that's a colt[4] indeed! For he doth nothing but talk
        of his horse, and he makes it a great appropriation° to his   *augmentation*
        own good parts° that he can shoe him himself. I am much   *own abilities*
        afeared my lady, his mother, played false with a smith.
        NERISSA   Then is there the County Palatine.[5]
40   PORTIA   He doth nothing but frown—as who should say,
        "An° you will not have me, choose."° He hears merry tales   *If / do as you wish*
        and smiles not. I fear he will prove the weeping philosopher[6]
        when he grows old, being so full of unmannerly° sadness in   *immoderate*
        his youth. I had rather be married to a death's head with a
45   bone in his mouth than to either of these. God defend me
        from these two!
        NERISSA   How say you by the French lord, Monsieur Le Bon?
        PORTIA   God made him, and therefore let him pass for a man.
        In truth I know it is a sin to be a mocker, but he—why he hath
50   a horse better than the Neapolitan's, a better bad habit of
        frowning than the Count Palatine: he is every man in no man.
        If a throstle° sing he falls straight° a-capering; he will fence   *thrush / immediately*
        with his own shadow. If I should marry him, I should marry
        twenty husbands. If he would despise me, I would forgive
55   him; for if he love me to madness, I shall never requite him.
        NERISSA   What say you, then, to Falconbridge, the young baron
        of England?
        PORTIA   You know I say nothing to him, for he understands-
        not me nor I him: he hath neither Latin, French, nor Italian,
60   and you will come into the court and swear that I have a
        poor pennyworth in the English. He is a proper° man's pic-   *handsome*
        ture, but alas! Who can converse with a dumb show?° How   *pantomime*
        oddly he is suited! I think he bought his doublet° in Italy, his   *upper garment*
        round hose[7] in France, his bonnet° in Germany, and his   *hat*
65   behavior everywhere.

2. An impetuous disposition.   5. Count possessing royal powers.
3. Because wisdom is imagined as elderly.   6. Heracleitus, a melancholy Greek philosopher.
4. Foolish young man. Neapolitans were excellent   7. Puffed breeches.
horsemen.

NERISSA   What think you of the Scottish lord, his neighbor?[8]

PORTIA   That he hath a neighborly charity in him, for he borrowed a box of the ear of the Englishman and swore he
would pay him again when he was able. I think the French-
70 man became his surety and sealed under for another.[9]

NERISSA   How like you the young German, the Duke of Sax-
ony's nephew?

PORTIA   Very vilely in the morning when he is sober, and most
vilely in the afternoon when he is drunk. When he is best,
75 he is a little worse than a man, and when he is worst, he
is little better than a beast. An the worst fall that ever fell,
I hope I shall make shift° to go without him.   *manage*

NERISSA   If he should offer° to choose, and choose the right   *endeavor*
casket, you should refuse to perform your father's will if you
80 should refuse to accept him.

PORTIA   Therefore, for fear of the worst, I pray thee set a deep
glass of Rhenish wine° on the contrary casket; for if the dev- *white German wine*
il be within and that temptation without, I know he will
choose it. I will do anything, Nerissa, ere I will be married
85 to a sponge!

NERISSA   You need not fear, lady, the having any of these
lords. They have acquainted me with their determinations,
which is, indeed, to return to their home and to trouble you
with no more suit, unless you may be won by some other sort°   *way*
90 than your father's imposition,° depending on the caskets.   *conditions*

PORTIA   If I live to be as old as Sibylla,[1] I will die as chaste as
Diana unless I be obtained by the manner of my father's will.
I am glad this parcel of wooers are so reasonable, for there is
not one among them but I dote on his very absence, and I
95 pray God grant them a fair departure.

NERISSA   Do you not remember, lady, in your father's time, a
Venetian—a scholar and a soldier—that came hither in
company of the Marquess of Montferrat?

PORTIA   Yes, yes—it was Bassanio; as I think, so was he called.

100 NERISSA   True, madam. He of all the men that ever my foolish
eyes looked upon was the best deserving a fair lady.

PORTIA   I remember him well, and I remember him worthy of
thy praise.
        Enter STEFANO.
How now? What news?

105 STEFANO   The four strangers seek for you, madam, to take
their leave; and there is a forerunner come from a fifth, the
Prince of Morocco, who brings word the Prince his master
will be here tonight.

PORTIA   If I could bid the fifth welcome with so good heart as
110 I can bid the other four farewell, I should be glad of his
approach. If he have the condition° of a saint and the com-   *character*
plexion of a devil,[2] I had rather he should shrive me° than *absolve me of my sins*

---

8. TEXTUAL COMMENT "Scottish" in the 1601 Q was
changed to "other" in the 1624 F edition; after King
James of Scotland came to the English throne in
1603, playwrights who ridiculed Scotland could find
themselves in trouble. See Digital Edition TC 2.
9. The Frenchman vouched for the Scot's payment
(of a box on the ear) and promised to add another

himself (referring to France's frequent promises to
help the Scots against the English).
1. In classical mythology, the Cumaean Sibyl asked
Apollo for as many years of life as the grains of sand
she held in her hand; she forgot to ask for eternal
youth.
2. Devils were imagined as black.

wive me. Come, Nerissa. —Sirrah, go before. Whiles we shut
the gate upon one wooer, another knocks at the door.

Exeunt.

1.3

Enter BASSANIO *with* SHYLOCK *the Jew.*

SHYLOCK   Three thousand ducats[1]—well.

BASSANIO   Ay, sir—for three months.

SHYLOCK   For three months—well.

BASSANIO   For the which, as I told you, Antonio shall be bound.°   *contractually*

5   SHYLOCK   Antonio shall become bound—well.   *responsible*

BASSANIO   May you stead° me? Will you pleasure me? Shall I   *accommodate*
know your answer?

SHYLOCK   Three thousand ducats for three months, and Antonio bound.

10   BASSANIO   Your answer to that?

SHYLOCK   Antonio is a good man.

BASSANIO   Have you heard any imputation to the contrary?

SHYLOCK   Ho, no, no, no, no: my meaning in saying he is a
good man is to have you understand me that he is suffi-

15   cient.[2] Yet his means are in supposition:° he hath an argosy   *doubt*
bound to Tripoli, another to the Indies. I understand, more-
over, upon the Rialto,[3] he hath a third at Mexico, a fourth
for England, and other ventures he hath squandered abroad.
But ships are but boards, sailors but men; there be land rats

20   and water rats, water thieves and land thieves—I mean
pirates. And then there is the peril of waters, winds, and
rocks. The man is, notwithstanding, sufficient. Three thousand ducats: I think I may take his bond.

BASSANIO   Be assured you may.

25   SHYLOCK   I will be assured[4] I may; and that I may be assured,
I will bethink me. May I speak with Antonio?[5]

BASSANIO   If it please you to dine with us.

SHYLOCK   Yes—to smell pork, to eat of the habitation which
your prophet the Nazarite[6] conjured the devil into? I will

30   buy with you, sell with you, talk with you, walk with you,
and so following. But I will not eat with you, drink with you,
nor pray with you.

Enter ANTONIO.

What news on the Rialto? Who is he comes here?

BASSANIO   This is Signor Antonio.

35   SHYLOCK [*aside*]   How like a fawning publican[7] he looks!
I hate him for he is a Christian,
But more for that in low simplicity[8]
He lends out money gratis° and brings down   *free*
The rate of usance° here with us in Venice.   *interest*

40   If I can catch him once upon the hip,[9]
I will feed fat the ancient grudge I bear him.
He hates our sacred nation,° and he rails,   *(the Jews)*

1.3 Location: Street in Venice.
1. Gold coins. The sum is very large.
2. *sufficient:* of adequate wealth.
3. Merchants' exchange in Venice.
4. Sure (but Shylock uses the word to mean "given financial guarantees").
5. TEXTUAL COMMENT In early printed texts the speech prefix for Shylock varies over the course of the play; sometimes he is "Shylock," and other times

he is "Jew." See Digital Edition TC 3.
6. Jesus, who cast devils into a herd of swine.
7. Tax collector; he robs me, but now, like the publican in Luke 18:10–14 who prays to Jesus for mercy, tries to ingratiate himself because he wants a favor.
8. In meek honesty; in base folly.
9. *upon the hip:* at a disadvantage (wrestling terminology).

Even there where merchants most do congregate,
On me, my bargains, and my well-won thrift,°   *profit*
45 Which he calls interest. Cursed be my tribe
If I forgive him.
BASSANIO   Shylock, do you hear?
SHYLOCK   I am debating of my present store°   *supply of money*
And, by the near guess of my memory,
I cannot instantly raise up the gross°   *total*
50 Of full three thousand ducats. What of that?
Tubal, a wealthy Hebrew of my tribe,
Will furnish me. But soft;° how many months   *wait*
Do you desire? —Rest you fair, good signor,
Your worship was the last man in our mouths.[1]
55 ANTONIO   Shylock, albeit I neither lend nor borrow
By taking nor by giving of excess,
Yet to supply the ripe° wants of my friend   *urgent*
I'll break a custom. —Is he yet possessed°   *informed*
How much ye would?
SHYLOCK   Ay, ay—three thousand ducats.
60 ANTONIO   And for three months.
SHYLOCK   I had forgot: three months. You told me so.
Well, then, your bond. And let me see, but hear you—
Methoughts you said you neither lend nor borrow
Upon advantage.°   *interest*
ANTONIO   I do never use it.
65 SHYLOCK   When Jacob grazed his uncle Laban's sheep,
This Jacob from our holy Abram was—
As his wise mother wrought in his behalf—
The third possessor; ay, he was the third[2]—
ANTONIO   And what of him? Did he take interest?
70 SHYLOCK   No, not take interest—not, as you would say,
Directly interest. Mark what Jacob did:
When Laban and himself were compromised°   *agreed*
That all the eanlings° which were streaked and pied°   *lambs / spotted*
Should fall as Jacob's hire, the ewes, being rank,°   *in heat*
75 In end of autumn turnèd to the rams;
And when the work of generation° was   *mating*
Between these woolly breeders in the act,
The skillful shepherd peeled me certain wands,[3]
And in the doing of the deed of kind°   *nature*
80 He stuck them up before the fulsome ewes,
Who then, conceiving, did in eaning° time   *lambing*
Fall° particolored lambs; and those were Jacob's.   *Deliver*
This was a way to thrive, and he was blest;
And thrift is blessing, if men steal it not.
85 ANTONIO   This was a venture, sir, that Jacob served for[4]—
A thing not in his power to bring to pass,
But swayed and fashioned by the hand of heaven.
Was this inserted to make interest good?[5]
Or is your gold and silver ewes and rams?
90 SHYLOCK   I cannot tell; I make it breed as fast.

---

1. We were just mentioning you.
2. After Abraham and Isaac; his mother, Rebecca, helped him cheat his brother Esau of his birthright. The story of Laban's sheep is told in Genesis 30:25–43.
3. Stripped part of the bark off some sticks ("me" is colloquial).
4. This was a speculative enterprise on which Jacob staked his wages as a servant.
5. Was this brought up to defend taking interest?

But note me, signor—
ANTONIO   —Mark you this, Bassanio:
The devil can cite scripture for his purpose.
An evil soul producing holy witness
Is like a villain with a smiling cheek,
95   A goodly apple rotten at the heart.
Oh, what a goodly outside falsehood hath!
SHYLOCK   Three thousand ducats—'tis a good round sum.
Three months from twelve—then let me see the rate.
ANTONIO   Well, Shylock, shall we be beholden to you?
100 SHYLOCK   Signor Antonio, many a time and oft
In the Rialto you have rated° me   *berated*
About my moneys and my usances.
Still° have I borne it with a patient shrug,   *Always*
For suff'rance is the badge[6] of all our tribe.
105   You call me "misbeliever," "cut-throat dog,"
And spit upon my Jewish gabardine,°   *long coat*
And all for use of that which is mine own.
Well, then, it now appears you need my help.
Go to, then: you come to me and you say,
110   "Shylock, we would have moneys": you say so—
You that did void your rheum° upon my beard   *spit*
And foot me as you spurn° a stranger cur   *contemptuously kick*
Over your threshold. Moneys is your suit.
What should I say to you? Should I not say,
115   "Hath a dog money? Is it possible
A cur can lend three thousand ducats?" Or
Shall I bend low and in a bondman's° key,   *slave's*
With bated breath and whispering humbleness,
Say this: "Fair sir, you spit on me on Wednesday last;
120   You spurned me such a day; another time
You called me dog, and for these courtesies
I'll lend you thus much moneys"?
ANTONIO   I am as like to call thee so again—
To spit on thee again, to spurn thee, too.
125   If thou wilt lend this money, lend it not
As to thy friends, for when did friendship take
A breed[7] for barren metal of his friend?
But lend it rather to thine enemy,
Who, if he break,° thou mayst with better face   *fail to repay*
Exact the penalty.
130 SHYLOCK   Why, look you, how you storm!
I would be friends with you and have your love,
Forget the shames that you have stained me with,
Supply your present wants and take no doit°   *small coin*
Of usance for my moneys—and you'll not hear me.
This is kind[8] I offer.
135 BASSANIO   This were° kindness.   *would be*
SHYLOCK   This kindness will I show:
Go with me to a notary; seal me there
Your single bond[9] and, in a merry sport,

---

6. For enduring insult is the characteristic.
7. Offspring (interest); alluding to an ancient argument that it was unnatural to use money to "breed," or make, more money.

8. Benevolent; natural (but perhaps with the covert suggestion "in kind").
9. Bond signed by the debtor alone (Antonio) without additional guarantors.

If you repay me not, on such a day
140 In such a place, such sum or sums as are
Expressed in the condition, let the forfeit°   *penalty*
Be nominated for an equal° pound   *Be stipulated as an exact*
Of your fair flesh, to be cut off and taken
In what part of your body pleaseth me.
145 ANTONIO   Content, in faith. I'll seal to such a bond
And say there is much kindness in the Jew.
BASSANIO   You shall not seal to such a bond for me;
I'll rather dwell in my necessity.°   *remain in need*
ANTONIO   Why, fear not, man: I will not forfeit it.
150 Within these two months—that's a month before
This bond expires—I do expect return
Of thrice three times the value of this bond.
SHYLOCK   O father Abram, what these Christians are,
Whose own hard dealings teaches them suspect
155 The thoughts of others! Pray you, tell me this:
If he should break his day, what should I gain
By the exaction of the forfeiture?
A pound of man's flesh taken from a man
Is not so estimable,° profitable neither,   *valuable*
160 As flesh of muttons, beefs, or goats. I say
To buy his favor I extend this friendship.
If he will take it, so; if not, adieu,
And for my love I pray you wrong me not.
ANTONIO   Yes, Shylock, I will seal unto this bond.
165 SHYLOCK   Then meet me forthwith at the notary's.
Give him direction for this merry bond,
And I will go and purse the ducats straight;
See to my house, left in the fearful° guard   *doubtful*
Of an unthrifty knave; and presently
I'll be with you.   *Exit.*
170 ANTONIO   Hie thee,° gentle Jew!   *Hurry*
The Hebrew will turn Christian—he grows kind.
BASSANIO   I like not fair terms and a villain's mind.
ANTONIO   Come on—in this there can be no dismay;
My ships come home a month before the day.   *Exeunt.*

2.1

*Enter [the Prince of] MOROCCO, a tawny Moor all in
white, and three or four followers accordingly,*[1] *with
PORTIA, NERISSA, and their train.*

MOROCCO   Mislike me not for my complexion,
The shadowed livery° of the burnished sun,   *servant's uniform*
To whom I am a neighbor and near bred.°   *close kin*
Bring me the fairest creature northward born,
5 Where Phoebus'° fire scarce thaws the icicles,   *the sun god's*
And let us make incision for your love
To prove whose blood is reddest[2]—his or mine.
I tell thee, lady, this aspect° of mine   *countenance*
Hath feared° the valiant; by my love I swear   *frightened*
10 The best regarded virgins of our clime

2.1 Location: Belmont.   2. Red blood was considered a sign of valor.
1. Of similar complexion and dress.

Have loved it too. I would not change this hue
Except to steal your thoughts, my gentle queen.
PORTIA   In terms of choice I am not solely led
By nice direction° of a maiden's eyes.   *fastidious guidance*
15   Besides, the lott'ry of my destiny
Bars me the right of voluntary choosing.
But if my father had not scanted° me,   *limited*
And hedged° me by his wit° to yield myself   *restricted / wisdom*
His wife who wins me by that means I told you,
20   Yourself, renownèd prince, then stood as fair³
As any comer I have looked on yet
For my affection.
MOROCCO   Even for that I thank you.
Therefore, I pray you, lead me to the caskets
To try my fortune. By this scimitar
25   That slew the Sophy° and a Persian prince,   *Shah of Persia*
That won three fields of Sultan Suleiman,°   *Turkish ruler*
I would o'er-stare the sternest eyes that look,
Outbrave the heart most daring on the earth,
Pluck the young sucking cubs from the she-bear;
30   Yea, mock the lion when 'a° roars for prey,   *he*
To win the lady. But alas the while,
If Hercules and Lychas° play at dice   *Hercules' servant*
Which is the better man, the greater throw
May turn by fortune from the weaker hand—
35   So is Alcides° beaten by his rage⁴   *Hercules*
And so may I, blind Fortune leading me,
Miss that which one unworthier may attain
And die with grieving.
PORTIA   You must take your chance
And either not attempt to choose at all,
40   Or swear before you choose, if you choose wrong
Never to speak to lady afterward
In way of marriage. Therefore be advised.°   *careful*
MOROCCO   Nor will not. Come, bring me unto my chance.
PORTIA   First forward to the temple; after dinner
Your hazard shall be made.
45   MOROCCO   Good fortune, then,
To make me blest or cursèd'st among men.   *Exeunt.*

2.2
Enter [LANCELET,] *the clown, alone.*¹
LANCELET   Certainly, my conscience will serve° me to run   *allow*
from this Jew, my master. The fiend is at mine elbow and
tempts me, saying to me, "Gobbo, Lancelet Gobbo, good
Lancelet" or "good Gobbo" or "good Lancelet Gobbo, use your
5   legs, take the start,° run away." My conscience says, "No,   *begone*
take heed, honest Lancelet; take heed, honest Gobbo," or,
as aforesaid, "honest Lancelet Gobbo, do not run, scorn
running with thy heels."° Well, the most courageous fiend   *indignantly (with pun)*

---

3. Seemed as attractive; stood as good a chance.
4. Often amended to "page."
2.2 Location: Venice.
1. TEXTUAL COMMENT In early editions, just as Shy-

lock is often called "*Jew*" in speech prefixes and stage
directions, Lancelet is often called "*Clown*." Both his
first and his last names vary somewhat in Q1, Q2, and
F. See Digital Edition TC 4 and TC 5.

bids me pack: "Fia!"° says the fiend. "Away!" says the fiend,   *Away*

10 "for the heavens rouse up a brave mind," says the fiend,
"and run!" Well, my conscience, hanging about the neck of
my heart, says very wisely to me, "My honest friend Lancelet, being an honest man's son," or rather, "an honest woman's son"—for indeed my father did something smack,

15 something grow to; he had a kind of taste.² Well, my conscience says, "Lancelet, budge not." "Budge," says the fiend.
"Budge not," says my conscience. "Conscience," say I, "you
counsel well." "Fiend," say I, "you counsel well." To be ruled
by my conscience I should stay with the Jew my master, who

20 —God bless the mark³—is a kind of devil. And to run away
from the Jew, I should be ruled by the fiend, who—saving
your reverence—is the devil himself. Certainly the Jew is
the very devil incarnation.° And in my conscience, my con-   *(for "incarnate")*
science is but a kind of hard conscience to offer to counsel

25 me to stay with the Jew. The fiend gives the more friendly
counsel: I will run. Fiend, my heels are at your commandment; I will run!

    Enter old GOBBO *with a basket.*

GOBBO   Master young man—you, I pray you—which is the
way to Master Jew's?

30 LANCELET   O heavens! This is my true-begotten father, who,
being more than sand-blind—high gravel-blind⁴—knows me
not. I will try confusions⁵ with him.

GOBBO   Master young gentleman, I pray you, which is the way
to Master Jew's?

35 LANCELET   Turn up on your right hand at the next turning,
but at the next turning of all on your left. Marry, at the very
next turning turn of no hand, but turn down indirectly to
the Jew's house.

GOBBO   By God's sonties,° 'twill be a hard way to hit! Can you   *saints*

40 tell me whether one Lancelet that dwells with him dwell
with him or no?

LANCELET   Talk you of young Master⁶ Lancelet? —Mark me
now; now will I raise the waters.⁷ —Talk you of young Master Lancelet?

45 GOBBO   No "Master," sir, but a poor man's son. His father,
though I say't, is an honest, exceeding poor man and, God
be thanked, well to live.⁸

LANCELET   Well, let his father be what 'a° will, we talk of   *he*
young Master Lancelet.

50 GOBBO   Your worship's friend and Lancelet, sir.

LANCELET   But, I pray you, ergo,° old man, ergo, I beseech   *therefore*
you, talk you of young Master Lancelet?

GOBBO   Of Lancelet, an't° please your mastership.   *if it*

LANCELET   Ergo, Master Lancelet! Talk not of Master Lance-

55 let, father,⁹ for the young gentleman, according to fates and
destinies and such odd sayings, the sisters three° and such   *the Fates*

---

2. *my father . . . taste:* that is, my father was licentious.
3. Conventional apology before a rude remark, like "saving your reverence."
4. Lancelet's coinage for a degree of blindness between sand-blind (partly blind) and stone-blind.

5. Lancelet's version of "try conclusions" (experiment).
6. "Master" was only applied to gentlemen's sons.
7. Start something; bring on tears.
8. Well-to-do (contradicts the previous line).
9. Customary address to an old man.

branches of learning, is indeed deceased, or as you would
say in plain terms, gone to heaven.

GOBBO   Marry, God forbid! The boy was the very staff of my
60   age, my very prop!

LANCELET   Do I look like a cudgel or a hovel post,° a staff or a   *shed post*
prop? Do you know me, father?

GOBBO   Alack the day! I know you not, young gentleman; but
I pray you tell me: is my boy, God rest his soul, alive or dead?

65   LANCELET   Do you not know me, father?

GOBBO   Alack, sir, I am sand-blind. I know you not.

LANCELET   Nay, indeed, if you had your eyes you might fail
of the knowing me: it is a wise father that knows his own
child.[1] Well, old man, I will tell you news of your son. Give
70   me your blessing. Truth will come to light; murder cannot
be hid long; a man's son may, but in the end truth will out.

GOBBO   Pray you, sir, stand up. I am sure you are not Lancelet, my boy.

LANCELET   Pray you, let's have no more fooling about it, but
75   give me your blessing. I am Lancelet—your boy that was,
your son that is, your child that shall be.

GOBBO   I cannot think you are my son.

LANCELET   I know not what I shall think of that, but I am
Lancelet, the Jew's man; and I am sure Margery, your wife,
80   is my mother.

GOBBO   Her name is Margery, indeed. I'll be sworn if thou be
Lancelet, thou art mine own flesh and blood. Lord, worshipped might He be, what a beard hast thou got![2] Thou
hast got more hair on thy chin than Dobbin my fill-horse°   *cart horse*
85   has on his tail.

LANCELET   It should seem then that Dobbin's tail grows backward.[3] I am sure he had more hair of his tail than I have of
my face when I last saw him.

GOBBO   Lord, how art thou changed! How dost thou and thy
90   master agree?° I have brought him a present; how 'gree you   *get along*
now?

LANCELET   Well, well. But for mine own part, as I have set up
my rest[4] to run away, so I will not rest till I have run some
ground. My master's a very Jew.[5] Give him a present?—give
95   him a halter!° I am famished in his service. You may tell°   *noose / count*
every finger I have with my ribs. Father, I am glad you are
come. Give me° your present to one Master Bassanio, who,   *Give*
indeed, gives rare new liveries.° If I serve not him, I will run   *servants' uniforms*
as far as God has any ground. Oh, rare fortune! Here comes
100   the man: to him, father, for I am a Jew if I serve the Jew any
longer.

Enter BASSANIO *with* [LEONARDO *and*] *a follower or two.*

BASSANIO   You may do so, but let it be so hasted° that supper   *hurried*
be ready at the farthest° by five of the clock. See these let-   *latest*
ters delivered, put the liveries to making, and desire° Gra-   *tell*
105   ziano to come anon° to my lodging.   *at once*

---

1. Transposing the proverb "A wise child knows his
own father."
2. Gobbo mistakes Lancelet's hair for a beard.
3. Gets shorter; grows from the wrong end.

4. As I have definitely determined (phrase in the
card game primero meaning "risk everything").
5. Cruel, grasping person; Hebrew. *a very:* an absolute.

LANCELET   To him, father!

GOBBO   God bless your worship.

BASSANIO   Gramercy.° Wouldst thou aught° with me?   *Many thanks / anything*

GOBBO   Here's my son, sir, a poor boy.

110   LANCELET   Not a poor boy, sir, but the rich Jew's man that
would, sir, as my father shall specify.

GOBBO   He hath a great infection,° sir, as one would say, to   *(for "affection"; wish)*
serve.

LANCELET   Indeed the short and the long is, I serve the Jew

115   and have a desire as my father shall specify.

GOBBO   His master and he, saving your worship's reverence,
are scarce cater-cousins.°   *close friends*

LANCELET   To be brief, the very truth is that the Jew, having
done me wrong, doth cause me, as my father, being I hope

120   an old man, shall fructify° unto you—   *(for "certify")*

GOBBO   I have here a dish of doves that I would bestow upon
your worship, and my suit is—

LANCELET   In very brief, the suit is impertinent° to myself, as   *(for "pertinent")*
your worship shall know by this honest old man and, though

125   I say it, though old man, yet poor man, my father—

BASSANIO   One speak for both: what would you?

LANCELET   Serve you, sir.

GOBBO   That is the very defect° of the matter, sir.   *(for "effect")*

BASSANIO   I know thee well; thou hast obtained thy suit.

130   Shylock thy master spoke with me this day
And hath preferred thee, if it be preferment[6]
To leave a rich Jew's service to become
The follower of so poor a gentleman.

LANCELET   The old proverb[7] is very well parted between my

135   master Shylock and you, sir: you have the grace of God, sir,
and he hath enough.

BASSANIO   Thou speak'st it well. —Go, father, with thy son.
—Take leave of thy old master and inquire
My lodging out. —Give him a livery

140   More guarded° than his fellows'. See it done.   *decorated*

LANCELET   Father, in. I cannot get a service—no! I have ne'er
a tongue in my head. Well, if any man in Italy have a fairer
table[8] which doth offer to swear upon a book[9]—I shall have
good fortune. Go to—here's a simple° line of life; here's a   *unremarkable (ironic)*

145   small trifle of wives. Alas, fifteen wives is nothing! Eleven
widows and nine maids is a simple coming in[1] for one man,
and then to scape drowning thrice, and to be in peril of my
life with the edge of a featherbed.[2] Here are simple scapes!
Well, if Fortune be a woman, she's a good wench, for this

150   gear.° Father, come. I'll take my leave of the Jew in the twin-   *matter*
kling.   *Exit* [LANCELET *the*] *clown* [*with old* GOBBO].

BASSANIO   I pray thee, good Leonardo, think on this.
These things being bought and orderly bestowed,°   *stowed on ship*
Return in haste, for I do feast tonight

155   My best esteemed acquaintance. Hie thee; go!

6. And has recommended you, if it be advancement.
7. "The grace of God is gear enough."
8. Palm (Lancelet reads the lines of his palm to predict the future).

9. To tell the truth (referring to the practice of taking an oath with the palm on the Bible).
1. A scanty income; an easy sexual entrance.
2. Alluding to a sexual adventure.

LEONARDO   My best endeavors shall be done herein.
          Enter GRAZIANO.
GRAZIANO   Where's your master?
LEONARDO   Yonder, sir, he walks.   *Exit.*
GRAZIANO   Signor Bassanio!
BASSANIO   Graziano!
GRAZIANO   I have suit to you.
BASSANIO   You have obtained it.
160 GRAZIANO   You must not deny me. I must go with you to
          Belmont.
BASSANIO   Why, then you must; but hear thee, Graziano:
          Thou art too wild, too rude and bold of voice—
          Parts° that become thee happily enough   *Attributes*
          And in such eyes as ours appear not faults.
165   But where thou art not known, why there they show
          Something too liberal.° Pray thee, take pain   *unrestrained*
          To allay with some cold drops of modesty
          Thy skipping spirit, lest through thy wild behavior
          I be misconstered° in the place I go to,   *misconstrued*
          And lose my hopes.
170 GRAZIANO   Signor Bassanio, hear me.
          If I do not put on a sober habit,°   *behavior; clothing*
          Talk with respect, and swear but now and then,
          Wear prayer books in my pocket, look demurely,
          Nay, more—while grace is saying, hood mine eyes
175   Thus with my hat,³ and sigh, and say "Amen"—
          Use all the observance of civility,
          Like one well studied in a sad ostent°   *solemn appearance*
          To please his grandam,° never trust me more.°   *grandmother / again*
BASSANIO   Well, we shall see your bearing.
180 GRAZIANO   Nay, but I bar tonight—you shall not gauge me
          By what we do tonight.
BASSANIO   No, that were pity!
          I would entreat you rather to put on
          Your boldest suit of mirth, for we have friends
          That purpose merriment. But fare you well;
185   I have some business.
GRAZIANO   And I must to Lorenzo and the rest;
          But we will visit you at supper time.   *Exeunt.*

2.3
          Enter JESSICA *and* [LANCELET] *the clown.*
JESSICA   I am sorry thou wilt leave my father so;
          Our house is hell, and thou, a merry devil,
          Didst rob it of some taste of tediousness.
          But fare thee well; there is a ducat for thee.
5   And, Lancelet, soon at supper shalt thou see
          Lorenzo, who is thy new master's guest.
          Give him this letter; do it secretly,
          And so farewell. I would not have my father
          See me in talk with thee.
10 LANCELET   Adieu! Tears exhibit° my tongue, most beautiful   *(for "inhibit")*
          pagan, most sweet Jew. If a Christian do not play the knave

---

3. Hats were worn at meals but taken off for grace.   2.3 Location: Shylock's house in Venice.

and get thee, I am much deceived. But adieu! These foolish
drops do something drown my manly spirit. Adieu!   [*Exit.*]
JESSICA   Farewell, good Lancelet.
15   Alack, what heinous sin is it in me
To be ashamed to be my father's child!
But though I am a daughter to his blood
I am not to his manners.° O Lorenzo,   *behavior*
If thou keep promise, I shall end this strife—
20   Become a Christian and thy loving wife.   *Exit.*

2.4

Enter GRAZIANO, LORENZO, SALERIO, *and* SOLANIO.

LORENZO   Nay, we will slink away in° supper time,   *during*
Disguise us at my lodging, and return
All in an hour.
GRAZIANO   We have not made good preparation.
5   SALERIO   We have not spoke us yet of° torchbearers.   *not yet arranged for*
SOLANIO   'Tis vile unless it may be quaintly ordered,°   *cleverly managed*
And better in my mind not undertook.
LORENZO   'Tis now but four of clock; we have two hours
To furnish us.
Enter LANCELET [*with a letter*].
Friend Lancelet, what's the news?
10   LANCELET   An° it shall please you to break up° this, it shall   *If / open*
seem to signify.
LORENZO   I know the hand: in faith, 'tis a fair hand,
And whiter than the paper it writ on
Is the fair hand that writ.
GRAZIANO   Love news, in faith.
LANCELET   By your leave, sir—
15   LORENZO   Whither goest thou?
LANCELET   Marry, sir, to bid my old master the Jew to sup
tonight with my new master the Christian.
LORENZO   Hold°—here, take this. Tell gentle Jessica   *Wait*
I will not fail her; speak it privately. *Exit* [LANCELET *the*] *clown.*
20   Go, gentlemen.
Will you prepare you for this masque tonight?
I am provided of a torchbearer.
SALERIO   Ay, marry, I'll be gone about it straight.°   *immediately*
SOLANIO   And so will I.
LORENZO   Meet me and Graziano
25   At Graziano's lodging some hour hence.
SALERIO   'Tis good we do so. *Exit* [*with* SOLANIO].
GRAZIANO   Was not that letter from fair Jessica?
LORENZO   I must needs tell thee all: she hath directed
How I shall take her from her father's house,
30   What gold and jewels she is furnished with,
What page's suit she hath in readiness.
If e'er the Jew her father come to heaven,
It will be for his gentle daughter's sake;
And never dare misfortune cross her foot
35   Unless she° do it under this excuse: *(misfortune)*
That she° is issue° to a faithless Jew.   *(Jessica) / offspring*

2.4 Location: Street in Venice.

Come, go with me; peruse this as thou goest.
Fair Jessica shall be my torchbearer.　　　　　　　*Exeunt.*

2.5

Enter [SHYLOCK *the*] *Jew and his man that*
was°[, LANCELET] *the clown.*　　　　　　　　　　　　　*former servant*

SHYLOCK　Well, thou shalt see, thy eyes shall be thy judge,
　　The difference of old Shylock and Bassanio.
　　—[*He calls.*] What, Jessica! —Thou shalt not gourmandize°　　*overeat*
　　As thou hast done with me. —[*He calls.*] What, Jessica!
5　　—And sleep, and snore, and rend apparel out.°　　　　　*wear out clothes*
　　—[*He calls.*] Why, Jessica, I say!
LANCELET　　　　　　　　　　　　　Why, Jessica!
SHYLOCK　Who bids thee call? I do not bid thee call.
LANCELET　Your worship was wont to tell me I could do noth-
　　ing without bidding.
　　　　　　Enter JESSICA.
10　JESSICA　Call you? What is your will?
SHYLOCK　I am bid forth to supper, Jessica.
　　There are my keys. But wherefore° should I go?　　　　*why*
　　I am not bid for love—they flatter me—
　　But yet I'll go in hate to feed upon
15　　The prodigal Christian. Jessica, my girl,
　　Look to my house. I am right loath° to go;　　　　　*very unwilling*
　　There is some ill a-brewing towards my rest,
　　For I did dream of moneybags tonight.°　　　　　　　*last night*
LANCELET　I beseech you, sir, go. My young master doth expect
20　　your reproach.°　　　　　　　　　　　　　　*(for "approach")*
SHYLOCK　So do I his.
LANCELET　And they have conspired together. I will not say
　　you shall see a masque, but if you do, then it was not for
　　nothing that my nose fell a-bleeding on Black Monday° last　　*Easter Monday*
25　　at six o'clock i'th' morning, falling out that year on Ash
　　Wednesday was four year in th'afternoon.[1]
SHYLOCK　What, are there masques? Hear you me, Jessica:
　　Lock up my doors, and when you hear the drum
　　And the vile squealing of the wry-necked[2] fife,
30　　Clamber not you up to the casements then,
　　Nor thrust your head into the public street
　　To gaze on Christian fools with varnished° faces;　　　*painted; masked*
　　But stop my house's ears—I mean my casements.
　　Let not the sound of shallow fopp'ry° enter　　　　　　*frivolity*
35　　My sober house. By Jacob's staff[3] I swear
　　I have no mind of feasting forth° tonight;　　　　　*away from home*
　　But I will go. —Go you before me, sirrah.
　　Say I will come.
LANCELET　　　　　　I will go before, sir.
　　—Mistress, look out at window for all this[4]—
40　　There will come a Christian by
　　Will be worth a Jewess' eye.　　　　　　　　　　[*Exit.*]
SHYLOCK　What says that fool of Hagar's offspring?[5] Ha?

2.5 Location: Outside Shylock's house.
1. Lancelet mocks Shylock's superstition.
2. Fifes were played with the head turned sideways.
3. See Genesis 32:10 and Hebrews 11:21.
4. *for all this*: despite Shylock's instructions.

5. That despicable gentile. Hagar, Abraham's gentile
servant, bore him a son, Ishmael; she and her child
were cast out after the birth of Abraham's legitimate
son, Isaac.

JESSICA His words were "Farewell, mistress," nothing else.
SHYLOCK The patch° is kind enough, but a huge feeder, *fool*
45 Snail-slow in profit,° and he sleeps by day *proficiency*
More than the wildcat. Drones hive not with me;
Therefore I part with him, and part with him
To one that I would have him help to waste
His borrowed purse. Well, Jessica, go in.
50 Perhaps I will return immediately.
Do as I bid you; shut doors after you.
Fast bind, fast find:[6]
A proverb never stale in thrifty mind. *Exit.*
JESSICA Farewell, and if my fortune be not crossed,
55 I have a father, you a daughter, lost. *Exit.*

2.6
Enter the Masquers GRAZIANO *and* SALERIO.
GRAZIANO This is the penthouse[1] under which Lorenzo
Desired us to make stand.
SALERIO His hour is almost past.
GRAZIANO And it is marvel he outdwells his hour,
5 For lovers ever run before the clock.
SALERIO Oh, ten times faster Venus' pigeons[2] fly
To seal love's bonds new made than they are wont
To keep obligèd° faith unforfeited.° *pledged / unbroken*
GRAZIANO That ever holds°: who riseth from a feast *remains true*
10 With that keen appetite that he sits down?
Where is the horse that doth untread° again *retrace*
His tedious measures with the unbated fire
That he did pace them first? All things that are
Are with more spirit chasèd than enjoyed.
15 How like a younker or a prodigal[3]
The scarfèd bark° puts from her native bay, *streamer-bedecked ship*
Hugged and embracèd by the strumpet wind;
How like the prodigal doth she return
With over-weathered ribs° and ragged sails, *weatherbeaten timbers*
20 Lean, rent,° and beggared by the strumpet wind! *torn*
        Enter LORENZO.
SALERIO Here comes Lorenzo; more of this hereafter.
LORENZO Sweet friends, your patience for my long abode°; *delay*
Not I but my affairs have made you wait.
When you shall please to play the thieves for wives,
25 I'll watch° as long for you then. Approach. *wait*
Here dwells my father° Jew. —How? Who's within? *father-in-law*
        [*Enter*] JESSICA *above*[, *dressed like a boy*].
JESSICA Who are you? Tell me for more certainty,
Albeit I'll swear that I do know your tongue.
LORENZO Lorenzo, and thy love.
30 JESSICA Lorenzo, certain, and my love indeed;
For who love I so much? And now who knows
But you, Lorenzo, whether I am yours?
LORENZO Heaven and thy thoughts are witness that thou art.
JESSICA Here—catch this casket. It is worth the pains.

6. Something firmly secured will remain fastened.
2.6 Location: Scene continues.
1. Projecting roof of an upper story.

2. Doves that drew the love goddess's chariot.
3. See Luke 15:11–31. *younker:* fashionable youth;
junior seaman.

35 I am glad 'tis night—you do not look on me—
For I am much ashamed of my exchange.°   *change of clothes*
But love is blind, and lovers cannot see
The pretty° follies that themselves commit.   *ingenious*
For if they could, Cupid himself would blush
40 To see me thus transformèd to a boy.
LORENZO   Descend, for you must be my torchbearer.
JESSICA   What? Must I hold a candle to my shames?
They in themselves, good sooth,° are too, too light.°   *in truth / clear; wanton*
Why, 'tis an office of discovery,⁴ love,
And I should be obscured.
45 LORENZO   So are you, sweet,
Even in the lovely garnish° of a boy.   *dress*
But come at once,
For the close° night doth play the runaway,°   *secret / steals away*
And we are stayed° for at Bassanio's feast.   *waited*
50 JESSICA   I will make fast the doors, and gild myself
With some more ducats, and be with you straight. [*Exit above.*]
GRAZIANO   Now by my hood, a gentle° and no Jew.   *gentile; gentle person*
LORENZO   Beshrew° me, but I love her heartily;   *Evil befall*
For she is wise, if I can judge of her;
55 And fair she is, if that mine eyes be true;
And true she is, as she hath proved herself.
And therefore like herself—wise, fair, and true—
Shall she be placèd in my constant soul.
        Enter JESSICA [*below*].
What, art thou come? On, gentlemen, away.
60 Our masquing mates by this time for us stay.
        Exeunt [LORENZO, JESSICA, *and* SALERIO].
    Enter ANTONIO.
ANTONIO   Who's there?
GRAZIANO   Signor Antonio?
ANTONIO   Fie, fie, Graziano—where are all the rest?
'Tis nine o'clock; our friends all stay for you.
No masque tonight; the wind is come about.
65 Bassanio presently° will go aboard.   *immediately*
I have sent twenty out to seek for you.
GRAZIANO   I am glad on't. I desire no more delight
Than to be under sail and gone tonight.   *Exeunt.*

2.7
    Enter PORTIA *with* [*the Prince of*] MOROCCO *and*
    both their trains.
PORTIA   Go, draw aside the curtains and discover°   *reveal*
The several caskets to this noble prince.
—Now make your choice.
MOROCCO   This first of gold, who° this inscription bears: *which*
5 "Who chooseth me shall gain what many men desire."
The second, silver, which this promise carries:
"Who chooseth me shall get as much as he deserves."
This third, dull lead, with warning all as blunt:¹
"Who chooseth me must give and hazard all he hath."

---

4. (Torchbearing) is a task of disclosure.   1. Plainly spoken; not sharp (with play on "dull lead").
2.7 Location: Belmont.

10　How shall I know if I do choose the right?
PORTIA　The one of them contains my picture, Prince.
　　　If you choose that, then I am yours withal.°　　　　　　　*with it*
MOROCCO　Some god direct my judgment. Let me see.
　　　I will survey th'inscriptions back again.
15　What says this leaden casket?
　　　"Who chooseth me must give and hazard all he hath."
　　　Must give for what? For lead—hazard for lead?
　　　This casket threatens; men that hazard all
　　　Do it in hope of fair advantages.
20　A golden mind stoops not to shows of dross;°　　　　　　*rubbish*
　　　I'll then nor° give nor hazard aught for lead.　　　　　*neither*
　　　What says the silver with her virgin hue?
　　　"Who chooseth me shall get as much as he deserves."
　　　As much as he deserves—pause there, Morocco,
25　And weigh thy value with an even° hand.　　　　　　　　*impartial*
　　　If thou beest rated by thy estimation
　　　Thou dost deserve enough, and yet enough
　　　May not extend so far as to the lady.
　　　And yet to be afeared of my deserving
30　Were but a weak disabling° of myself.　　　　　　　　*disparagement*
　　　As much as I deserve—why, that's the lady!
　　　I do in birth deserve her, and in fortunes,
　　　In graces, and in qualities of breeding;
　　　But more than these, in love I do deserve.
35　What if I strayed no farther but chose here?
　　　Let's see once more this saying graved in gold:
　　　"Who chooseth me shall gain what many men desire."
　　　Why, that's the lady! All the world desires her;
　　　From the four corners of the earth they come
40　To kiss this shrine, this mortal breathing saint.
　　　The Hyrcanian deserts[2] and the vasty° wilds　　　　　*vast*
　　　Of wide Arabia are as thoroughfares° now　　　　　　*main roads*
　　　For princes to come view fair Portia.
　　　The watery kingdom, whose ambitious head°　　　　　*(of a storm)*
45　Spits in the face of heaven, is no bar
　　　To stop the foreign spirits, but they come,
　　　As o'er a brook, to see fair Portia.
　　　One of these three contains her heavenly picture.
　　　Is't like° that lead contains her? 'Twere damnation　　*probable*
50　To think so base a thought. It° were too gross　　　　　*(lead)*
　　　To rib her cerecloth[3] in the obscure grave.
　　　Or shall I think in silver she's immured,°　　　　　　*enclosed*
　　　Being ten times undervalued to tried° gold?　　　　　*purified*
　　　Oh, sinful thought! Never so rich a gem
55　Was set in worse than gold. They have in England
　　　A coin that bears the figure of an angel[4]
　　　Stamped in gold, but that's insculped° upon.　　　　*engraved*
　　　But here an angel in a golden bed
　　　Lies all within. —Deliver me the key!
60　Here do I choose, and thrive I as I may.

2. Wild region south of the Caspian Sea.
3. To enclose her shroud (normally covered with a layer of lead).
4. The gold coin called angel had the figure of St. Michael on its face.

PORTIA There—take it, Prince, and if my form° lie there   *image*
    Then I am yours.
MOROCCO [*opening the golden casket*]
                    O hell! What have we here?
    A carrion death,° within whose empty eye   *A skull*
    There is a written scroll. I'll read the writing:
65   "All that glisters is not gold.
                Often have you heard that told.
                Many a man his life hath sold
                But my outside⁵ to behold.
                Gilded timber do worms enfold.°   *enclose*
70   Had you been as wise as bold,
                Young in limbs, in judgment old,
                Your answer had not been inscrolled.
                Fare you well; your suit is cold."
    Cold indeed and labor lost.
75 Then farewell, heat, and welcome, frost.
    Portia, adieu; I have too grieved a heart
    To take a tedious leave. Thus losers part.   *Exit* [*with his train*].
PORTIA A gentle riddance! Draw the curtains; go.
    Let all of his complexion choose me so.⁶   *Exeunt.*

2.8

Enter SALERIO *and* SOLANIO.

SALERIO Why, man, I saw Bassanio under sail.
    With him is Graziano gone along,
    And in their ship I am sure Lorenzo is not.
SOLANIO The villain Jew with outcries raised° the Duke,   *roused*
5   Who went with him to search Bassanio's ship.
SALERIO He came too late; the ship was under sail.
    But there the Duke was given to understand
    That in a gondola were seen together
    Lorenzo and his amorous Jessica.
10 Besides, Antonio certified the Duke
    They were not with Bassanio in his ship.
SOLANIO I never heard a passion° so confused,   *an outburst*
    So strange, outrageous, and so variable
    As the dog Jew did utter in the streets:
15 "My daughter, O my ducats, O my daughter!
    Fled with a Christian! O my Christian ducats!
    Justice, the law, my ducats, and my daughter!
    A sealèd bag—two sealèd bags of ducats—
    Of double ducats stolen from me by my daughter;
20 And jewels—two stones, two rich and precious stones¹
    Stolen by my daughter! Justice! Find the girl.
    She hath the stones upon her, and the ducats."
SALERIO Why, all the boys in Venice follow him
    Crying, "His stones, his daughter, and his ducats."
25 SOLANIO Let good Antonio look he keep his day,°   *repay his debt on time*

---

5. Gold; face that once covered the skull.
6. PERFORMANCE COMMENT Portia's final line is often cut from productions so as not to compromise her standing with audiences. Rescuing the play from its objectionable speeches is common in *Merchant* and

can affect the story and its generic balance considerably. See Digital Edition PC 2.
2.8 Location: Venice.
1. With the suggestion "testicles," taken up by the mocking boys in line 24.

Or he shall pay for this.
SALERIO   Marry, well remembered.
I reasoned° with a Frenchman yesterday   *conversed*
Who told me in the narrow seas° that part   *(English Channel)*
The French and English there miscarrièd°   *wrecked*
30   A vessel of our country richly fraught.°   *laden*
I thought upon Antonio when he told me
And wished in silence that it were not his.
SOLANIO   You were best to tell Antonio what you hear.
Yet do not suddenly, for it may grieve him.
35   SALERIO   A kinder gentleman treads not the earth.
I saw Bassanio and Antonio part.
Bassanio told him he would make some speed
Of his return; he answered, "Do not so;
Slubber not° business for my sake, Bassanio;   *Do not hastily perform*
40   But stay the very riping of the time.
And for the Jew's bond which he hath of me,
Let it not enter in your mind° of love.   *interrupt your thoughts*
Be merry and employ your chiefest thoughts
To courtship and such fair ostents° of love   *displays*
45   As shall conveniently° become you there."   *properly*
And even there, his eye being big with tears,
Turning his face, he put his hand behind him
And with affection wondrous sensible°   *obvious; heartfelt*
He wrung Bassanio's hand; and so they parted.
50   SOLANIO   I think he only loves the world for him.
I pray thee, let us go and find him out
And quicken his embracèd heaviness[2]
With some delight or other.
SALERIO   Do we so.   *Exeunt.*

2.9

Enter NERISSA *and a Servitor.*
NERISSA   Quick, quick, I pray thee, draw the curtain straight;°   *immediately*
The Prince of Aragon hath ta'en his oath
And comes to his election presently.°   *his choice at once*
Enter [the Prince of] ARAGON, *his train, and* PORTIA.
PORTIA   Behold, there stand the caskets, noble Prince.
5   If you choose that wherein I am contained
Straight shall our nuptial rites be solemnized;
But if you fail, without more speech, my lord,
You must be gone from hence immediately.
ARAGON   I am enjoined by oath to observe three things:
10   First, never to unfold to anyone
Which casket 'twas I chose; next, if I fail
Of the right casket, never in my life
To woo a maid in way of marriage; lastly,
If I do fail in fortune of my choice,
15   Immediately to leave you and be gone.
PORTIA   To these injunctions everyone doth swear
That comes to hazard° for my worthless self.   *gamble*
ARAGON   And so have I addressed° me. Fortune now   *prepared*
To my heart's hope! Gold, silver, and base lead.

---

2. And lighten the grief he embraces.   **2.9** Location: Belmont.

20   "Who chooseth me must give and hazard all he hath."
     You shall look fairer ere I give or hazard.
     What says the golden chest? Ha, let me see:
     "Who chooseth me shall gain what many men desire."
     What many men desire—that "many" may be meant
25   By° the fool multitude that choose by show,   *For*
     Not learning more than the fond° eye doth teach,   *foolish*
     Which pries not to th'interior but like the martlet°   *swallow*
     Builds in the weather° on the outward wall,   *open air*
     Even in the force and road of casualty.°   *mishap*
30   I will not choose what many men desire,
     Because I will not jump° with common spirits   *agree*
     And rank me with the barbarous multitudes.
     Why, then, to thee, thou silver treasure-house.
     Tell me once more what title thou dost bear:
35   "Who chooseth me shall get as much as he deserves."
     And well said, too, for who shall go about
     To cozen° fortune and be honorable   *cheat*
     Without the stamp° of merit? Let none presume   *official seal*
     To wear an undeservèd dignity.
40   Oh, that estates, degrees,° and offices   *social ranks*
     Were not derived° corruptly, and that clear honor   *gained*
     Were purchased° by the merit of the wearer!   *acquired*
     How many then should cover that stand bare;[1]
     How many be commanded that command;
45   How much low peasantry would then be gleaned°   *separated*
     From the true seed of honor; and how much honor
     Picked from the chaff and ruin of the times
     To be new varnished?° Well—but to my choice: *regain its luster*
     "Who chooseth me shall get as much as he deserves."
50   I will assume° desert: give me a key for this,   *claim*
     And instantly unlock my fortunes here.
                    [*He opens the silver casket.*]
     PORTIA   Too long a pause for that which you find there.
     ARAGON What's here—the portrait of a blinking idiot
     Presenting me a schedule?° I will read it.   *document*
55   How much unlike art thou to Portia!
     How much unlike my hopes and my deservings!
     "Who chooseth me shall have as much as he deserves"?
     Did I deserve no more than a fool's head?
     Is that my prize? Are my deserts no better?
60   PORTIA   To offend and judge are distinct offices,[2]
     And of opposèd natures.
     ARAGON   What is here?
     "The fire seven times tried° this;   *purified*
     Seven times tried that judgment is
     That did never choose amiss.
65   Some there be that shadows kiss;[3]
     Such have but a shadow's bliss.
     There be fools alive, iwis,°   *in truth*
     Silvered[4] o'er, and so was this.

---

1. Should wear hats who now stand bareheaded (before their social superiors).
2. To err and to judge are different functions.

3. Like Narcissus in classical mythology, a youth who fell in love with his own reflection.
4. Silver-haired (thus apparently wise).

Take what wife you will to bed,
70   I° will ever be your head.   (*the blinking idiot*)
So be gone; you are sped."°   *finished*
Still more fool I shall appear
By the time I linger here.
With one fool's head I came to woo,
75   But I go away with two.
Sweet, adieu; I'll keep my oath
Patiently to bear my wroth.°   *grief*

          [*Exit the Prince of* ARAGON *with his train.*]
PORTIA   Thus hath the candle singed the moth.
          Oh, these deliberate° fools—when they do choose   *careful*
80   They have the wisdom by their wit to lose!
NERISSA   The ancient saying is no heresy:
          Hanging and wiving goes by destiny.
PORTIA   Come, draw the curtain, Nerissa.

                    Enter MESSENGER.
MESSENGER   Where is my lady?
PORTIA   Here—what would my lord?
85 MESSENGER   Madam, there is alighted at your gate
          A young Venetian, one that comes before
          To signify th'approaching of his lord,
          From whom he bringeth sensible regreets:°   *tangible greetings*
          To wit, besides commends and courteous breath,
90   Gifts of rich value. Yet° I have not seen   *Until now*
          So likely° an ambassador of love.   *suitable*
          A day in April never came so sweet
          To show how costly° summer was at hand,   *lavish*
          As this fore-spurrer comes before his lord.
95 PORTIA   No more, I pray thee. I am half afeared
          Thou wilt say anon° he is some kin to thee,   *soon*
          Thou spend'st such high-day⁵ wit in praising him.
          Come, come, Nerissa, for I long to see
          Quick Cupid's post° that comes so mannerly.   *messenger*
100 NERISSA   Bassanio, Lord Love,° if thy will it be.   *Exeunt.*   *Cupid*

                            3.1
                [*Enter*] SOLANIO *and* SALERIO.
SOLANIO   Now, what news on the Rialto?
SALERIO   Why, yet it lives there unchecked¹ that Antonio hath
          a ship of rich lading wrecked on the narrow seas—the Good-
          wins² I think they call the place, a very dangerous flat, and
5   fatal, where the carcasses of many a tall ship lie buried, as they
          say, if my gossip Report° be an honest woman of her word.   *Dame Rumor*
SOLANIO   I would she were as lying a gossip in that as ever
          knapped° ginger or made her neighbors believe she wept for   *nibbled*
          the death of a third husband. But it is true, without any slips
10   of prolixity° or crossing the plain highway of talk, that the   *any wordy lies*
          good Antonio, the honest Antonio—oh, that I had a title
          good enough to keep his name company—
SALERIO   Come, the full stop.°   *period*

---

5. Holiday (fit for special occasions).   2. Goodwin Sands, where the Thames joins the sea.
3.1 Location: Venice.   "Goodwin" means "friend."
1. It circulates there without denial.

SOLANIO Ha, what sayest thou? Why the end is, he hath lost a
15 ship.
SALERIO I would it might prove the end of his losses.
    Enter SHYLOCK.
SOLANIO Let me say amen betimes lest the devil cross° my   *thwart*
    prayer, for here he comes in the likeness of a Jew.
    —How now, Shylock, what news among the merchants?
20 SHYLOCK You knew, none so well, none so well as you, of my
    daughter's flight.
SALERIO That's certain. I, for my part, knew the tailor that
    made the wings[3] she flew withal.
SOLANIO And Shylock, for his own part, knew the bird was
25   fledge,° and then it is the complexion° of them all to leave   *feathered / disposition*
    the dam.°   *mother (here, parent)*
SHYLOCK She is damned for it.
SALERIO That's certain, if the devil may be her judge.
SHYLOCK My own flesh and blood to rebel![4]
30 SOLANIO Out upon it, old carrion! Rebels it at these years?
SHYLOCK I say my daughter is my flesh and my blood.
SALERIO There is more difference between thy flesh and hers
    than between jet° and ivory; more between your bloods than   *black mineral*
    there is between red wine and Rhenish.° But tell us: do you   *white wine*
35   hear whether Antonio have had any loss at sea, or no?
SHYLOCK There I have another bad match:° a bankrupt, a   *bad deal*
    prodigal who dare scarce show his head on the Rialto, a beg-
    gar that was used to come so smug upon the mart! Let him
    look to his bond. He was wont to call me usurer; let him look
40   to his bond. He was wont to lend money for a° Christian   *out of*
    courtesy; let him look to his bond.
SALERIO Why, I am sure if he forfeit thou wilt not take his
    flesh. What's that good for?
SHYLOCK To bait fish withal.° If it will feed nothing else, it   *with*
45   will feed my revenge. He hath disgraced me and hindered me
    half a million, laughed at my losses, mocked at my gains,
    scorned my nation, thwarted my bargains, cooled my friends,
    heated mine enemies, and what's his reason? I am a Jew.
    Hath not a Jew eyes? Hath not a Jew hands, organs, dimen-
50   sions,° senses, affections, passions—fed with the same food,   *bodily form*
    hurt with the same weapons, subject to the same diseases,
    healed by the same means, warmed and cooled by the same
    winter and summer as a Christian is? If you prick us do we
    not bleed? If you tickle us do we not laugh? If you poison us
55   do we not die, and if you wrong us shall we not revenge? If we
    are like you in the rest, we will resemble you in that. If a Jew
    wrong a Christian, what is his° humility? Revenge! If a Chris-   *(the Christian's)*
    tian wrong a Jew, what should his sufferance° be by Christian   *patience*
    example? Why, revenge! The villainy you teach me I will exe-
60   cute, and it shall go hard but I will better the instruction.[5]
    Enter a SERVINGMAN *from* ANTONIO.

---

3. Playing on "wing," a decorative flap on the upper
sleeve.
4. Shylock means "my own offspring"; Solanio pretends he means "carnal appetite."
5. PERFORMANCE COMMENT Depending on the characterization of Shylock, the speech can be delivered

as a sympathetic plea for the Christians to recognize
the common humanity of all inhabitants of Venice or
as a justification for Shylock's imminent revenge on
Antonio. Actors often mingle aspects of both interpretations. See Digital Edition PC 3.

SERVINGMAN Gentlemen, my master Antonio is at his house
and desires to speak with you both.

SALERIO We have been up and down to seek him.
    Enter TUBAL.

SOLANIO Here comes another of the tribe; a third cannot be
65 matched° unless the devil himself turn Jew.   *found to match*
    Exeunt Gentlemen [—SALERIO, *and* SOLANIO—
                                    and SERVINGMAN].⁶

SHYLOCK How now, Tubal! What news from Genoa? Hast
thou found my daughter?

TUBAL I often came where I did hear of her, but cannot find her.

SHYLOCK Why, there, there, there, there—a diamond gone
70 cost me two thousand ducats in Frankfurt!⁷ The curse never
fell upon our nation till now. I never felt it till now: two
thousand ducats in that and other precious, precious jewels!
I would my daughter were dead at my foot and the jewels in
her ear! Would she were hearsed° at my foot and the ducats   *coffined*
75 in her coffin! No news of them? Why so? And I know not
what's spent in the search. Why, thou: loss upon loss, the
thief gone with so much, and so much to find the thief, and
no satisfaction, no revenge, nor no ill luck stirring but what
lights o'my shoulders, no sighs but o'my breathing, no tears
80 but o'my shedding.

TUBAL Yes, other men have ill luck too. Antonio, as I heard in
Genoa—

SHYLOCK What, what, what? Ill luck, ill luck?

TUBAL   —hath an argosy cast away coming from Tripoli.

85 SHYLOCK I thank God! I thank God! Is it true, is it true?

TUBAL I spoke with some of the sailors that escaped the
wreck.

SHYLOCK I thank thee, good Tubal. Good news, good news.
Ha, ha, heard in Genoa!

90 TUBAL Your daughter spent in Genoa, as I heard, one night
fourscore ducats.

SHYLOCK Thou stick'st a dagger in me; I shall never see my
gold again! Fourscore ducats at a sitting, fourscore ducats!

TUBAL There came divers of Antonio's creditors in my com-
95 pany to Venice that swear he cannot choose but break.°   *go bankrupt*

SHYLOCK I am very glad of it. I'll plague him; I'll torture him. I
am glad of it.

TUBAL One of them showed me a ring that he had of your
daughter for a monkey.

100 SHYLOCK Out upon her; thou torturest me, Tubal! It was my
turquoise; I had it of Leah when I was a bachelor. I would
not have given it for a wilderness of monkeys.

TUBAL But Antonio is certainly undone.

SHYLOCK Nay, that's true, that's very true. Go, Tubal, fee° me   *hire*
105 an officer; bespeak him a fortnight before. I will have the
heart of him if he forfeit, for were he out of Venice I can
make what merchandise° I will. Go, Tubal, and meet me at   *drive what bargains*
our synagogue. Go, good Tubal; at our synagogue, Tubal.
                                                Exeunt.

6. TEXTUAL COMMENT The stage direction implies   considered "gentlemen." See Digital Edition TC 6.
that the Jewish characters, Shylock and Tubal, are not   7. Site of a jewel market.

3.2

Enter BASSANIO, PORTIA, [NERISSA,] GRAZIANO,
[MUSICIANS,] *and all their trains.*

PORTIA   I pray you, tarry; pause a day or two
  Before you hazard, for in choosing° wrong   *if you choose*
  I lose your company.[1] Therefore forbear a while.
  There's something tells me—but it is not love—
5 I would not lose you; and you know yourself
  Hate counsels not in such a quality.°   *way*
  But lest you should not understand me well—
  And yet a maiden hath no tongue but thought—
  I would detain you here some month or two
10 Before you venture for me. I could teach you
  How to choose right, but then I am forsworn;
  So° will I never be. So may you miss me,[2]   *(forsworn)*
  But if you do, you'll make me wish a sin—
  That I had been forsworn. Beshrew your eyes!
15 They have o'erlooked° me and divided me.   *bewitched*
  One half of me is yours, the other half yours—
  Mine own I would say—but if mine, then yours,
  And so all yours. Oh, these naughty° times   *evil*
  Puts bars between the owners and their rights—
20 And so, though yours, not yours. Prove it so,
  Let fortune go to hell for it, not I.[3]
  I speak too long, but 'tis to peise° the time,   *extend*
  To eke° it and to draw it out in length   *augment*
  To stay° you from election.°   *delay / choosing*
BASSANIO   Let me choose.
25 For as I am I live upon the rack.[4]
PORTIA   Upon the rack, Bassanio? Then confess
  What treason there is mingled with your love.
BASSANIO   None but that ugly treason of mistrust,°   *uncertainty*
  Which makes me fear° th'enjoying of my love.   *doubt*
30 There may as well be amity and life
  'Tween snow and fire, as treason and my love.
PORTIA   Ay, but I fear you speak upon the rack,
  Where men, enforcèd, do speak anything.
BASSANIO   Promise me life, and I'll confess the truth.
PORTIA   Well, then, confess and live.
35 BASSANIO   Confess and love
  Had been the very sum of my confession.
  Oh, happy torment when my torturer
  Doth teach me answers for deliverance!°   *release*
  But let me to my fortune and the caskets.
40 PORTIA   Away, then. I am locked in one of them;
  If you do love me, you will find me out.
  Nerissa and the rest, stand all aloof.
  Let music sound while he doth make his choice.
  Then if he lose, he makes a swanlike end,[5]

3.2 Location: Belmont.
1. PERFORMANCE COMMENT In productions the intermission often falls just before 3.2, and directors sometimes use the entrance to suggest that Bassanio has been in Belmont for some time before the action resumes. Consequently, Bassanio's and Portia's entrance may suggest a full-blown romance, raising the stakes for the impending casket choice. See Digital Edition PC 4.
2. Fail to attain me.
3. *Prove . . . I:* If it turns out thus, let it be fortune's fault, not mine (for breaking my oath).
4. Instrument of torture used on traitors.
5. The swan was thought to sing only once, just before its death.

45   Fading in music. That the comparison
       May stand more proper, my eye shall be the stream
       And watery deathbed for him. He may win,
       And what is music then? Then music is
       Even as the flourish° when true subjects bow   *fanfare*
50   To a new-crowned monarch. Such it is
       As are those dulcet sounds in break of day
       That creep into the dreaming bridegroom's ear
       And summon him to marriage.[6] Now he goes,
       With no less presence° but with much more love   *dignity*
55   Than young Alcides when he did redeem
       The virgin tribute paid by howling Troy
       To the sea monster.[7] I stand for sacrifice;
       The rest aloof are the Dardanian° wives   *Trojan*
       With blearèd° visages come forth to view   *weepy*
60   The issue° of th'exploit. Go, Hercules!   *outcome*
       Live thou,° I live! With much, much more dismay   *If you live*
       I view the fight than thou that mak'st the fray.
          A song, the whilst BASSANIO *comments on the caskets to*
          himself.[8]

FIRST MUSICIAN   Tell me where is fancy° bred: *love; infatuation*
              Or° in the heart or in the head;   *Whether*
65   How begot, how nourishèd?
              Reply, reply!
SECOND MUSICIAN   It is engend'red in the eye,[9]
              With gazing fed; and fancy dies
              In the cradle[1] where it lies.
70   Let us all ring fancy's knell.
              I'll begin it: Ding dong, bell.
ALL   Ding, dong, bell.
BASSANIO   So may the outward shows be least themselves.[2]
       The world is still° deceived with ornament.   *continually*
75   In law, what plea so tainted and corrupt
       But, being seasoned with a gracious voice,
       Obscures the show of evil? In religion,
       What damnèd error but some sober brow
       Will bless it and approve° it with a text,   *prove*
80   Hiding the grossness with fair ornament?
       There is no vice so simple° but assumes   *unalloyed; stupid*
       Some mark of virtue on his° outward parts,   *its*
       How many cowards, whose hearts are all as false
       As stairs of sand, wear yet upon their chins
85   The beards of Hercules and frowning Mars,
       Who, inward searched,° have livers white as milk;[3]   *examined*
       And these assume but valor's excrement[4]
       To render them redoubted.° Look on beauty,   *feared*
       And you shall see 'tis purchased by the weight,°   *(like cosmetics)*
90   Which therein works a miracle in nature,

6. It was customary to play music under a bride-groom's window on the morning of his wedding.
7. Alcides (Hercules) saved the Trojan princess Hesione when she was to be sacrificed to a sea monster, not because he loved her but to win two horses her father offered as a reward.
8. TEXTUAL COMMENT Early editions of the play do not indicate who sings the song or whether "All" in line 72 refers to all Portia's servants, or only to the musicians. See Digital Edition TC 7.

9. Love was imagined to enter through the eyes. TEXTUAL COMMENT The spelling "engendred" in early editions emphasizes the rhyme with "bred," "head," and "nourishèd" (the last pronounced as a three-syllable word). See Digital Edition TC 8.
1. In infancy, in the eyes (?).
2. Least express the truth.
3. Lily-livered (the liver was considered the seat of courage).
4. External attribute; hair (the beard).

Making them lightest° that wear most of it.   *most licentious*
So are those crispèd,° snaky golden locks,   *curled*
Which maketh such wanton gambols with the wind
Upon supposèd fairness,° often known   *beauty*
95   To be the dowry° of a second head—   *endowment (in a wig)*
The skull that bred them in the sepulcher.
Thus ornament is but the guilèd° shore   *beguiling*
To a most dangerous sea, the beauteous scarf
Veiling an Indian° beauty—in a word,   *a swarthy (pejorative)*
100   The seeming truth which cunning times put on
To entrap the wisest. Therefore, then, thou gaudy gold,
Hard food for Midas,[5] I will none of thee.
Nor none of thee, thou pale and common drudge°   *laborer (in coins)*
'Tween man and man. But thou! Thou meager lead,
105   Which rather threaten'st than dost promise aught,
Thy paleness moves me more than eloquence,
And here choose I—joy be the consequence!
PORTIA   How all the other passions fleet to air—
As° doubtful thoughts and rash-embraced despair   *Such as*
110   And shudd'ring fear and green-eyed jealousy!
O Love, be moderate, allay thy ecstasy,
In measure rein thy joy, scant° this excess.[6]   *lessen*
I feel too much thy blessing; make it less
For fear I surfeit!
BASSANIO [*opening the leaden casket*]
                What find I here?
115   Fair Portia's counterfeit!° What demigod[7]   *likeness*
Hath come so near creation? Move these eyes,
Or whether, riding on the balls of mine,°   *my eyes*
Seem they in motion? Here are severed lips,
Parted with sugar breath; so sweet a bar
120   Should sunder such sweet friends. Here in her hairs
The painter plays the spider and hath woven
A golden mesh t'entrap the hearts of men
Faster than gnats in cobwebs. But her eyes—
How could he see to do them? Having made one,
125   Methinks it should have power to steal both his
And leave itself unfurnished.° Yet look—how far   *unaccompanied*
The substance of my praise doth wrong this shadow°   *portrait*
In underprizing° it, so far this shadow   *understating*
Doth limp behind the substance.° Here's the scroll,   *real thing (Portia)*
130   The continent° and summary of my fortune: *container*
         "You that choose not by the view
         Chance as fair° and choose as true.   *Gamble as luckily*
         Since this fortune falls to you,
         Be content and seek no new.
135   If you be well pleased with this,
         And hold your fortune for your bliss,
         Turn you where your lady is
         And claim her with a loving kiss."
A gentle scroll! Fair lady, by your leave—
         [*He kisses her.*]

---

5. Everything King Midas touched, including his   6. Synonym for "interest" or "usury."
food, turned to gold.   7. Supernaturally gifted painter.

140   I come by note to give[8] and to receive.
    Like one of two contending in a prize°   *contest*
    That thinks he hath done well in people's eyes—
    Hearing applause and universal shout,
    Giddy in spirit, still gazing in a doubt
145   Whether those peals of praise be his° or no—   *for him*
    So, thrice-fair lady, stand I even so,
    As doubtful whether what I see be true
    Until confirmed, signed, ratified by you.
    PORTIA   You see me, Lord Bassanio, where I stand,
150   Such as I am. Though for myself alone
    I would not be ambitious in my wish
    To wish myself much better, yet for you
    I would be trebled twenty times myself—
    A thousand times more fair, ten thousand times
155   More rich; that only to stand high in your account°   *estimation*
    I might in virtues, beauties, livings,° friends   *possessions*
    Exceed account. But the full sum of me
    Is sum of something, which to term in gross°   *to describe fully*
    Is an unlessoned girl, unschooled, unpracticed;
160   Happy° in this: she is not yet so old   *Fortunate*
    But she may learn; happier than this:
    She is not bred so dull but she can learn;
    Happiest of all is that her gentle spirit
    Commits itself to yours to be directed
165   As from her lord, her governor, her king.
    Myself and what is mine to you and yours
    Is now converted.° But° now, I was the lord   *transferred / Just*
    Of this fair mansion, master of my servants,
    Queen o'er myself; and even now, but now,
170   This house, these servants, and this same myself
    Are yours, my lord's. I give them with this ring,
    Which when you part from, lose, or give away,
    Let it presage the ruin of your love
    And be my vantage to exclaim on you.[9]
175   BASSANIO   Madam, you have bereft me of all words.
    Only my blood speaks to you in my veins;
    And there is such confusion in my powers°   *faculties*
    As after some oration fairly spoke
    By a beloved prince, there doth appear
180   Among the buzzing, pleasèd multitude—
    Where every something, being blent° together,   *blended*
    Turns to a wild° of nothing save of joy   *chaos*
    Expressed and not expressed. But when this ring
    Parts from this finger, then parts life from hence:
185   Oh, then be bold to say° Bassanio's dead.   *say confidently*
    NERISSA   My lord and lady, it is now our time,
    That have stood by and seen our wishes prosper,
    To cry good joy, good joy, my lord and lady!
    GRAZIANO   My lord Bassanio and my gentle lady,
190   I wish you all the joy that you can wish,
    For I am sure you can wish none from me.[1]

---

8. I come by written authorization to give a kiss; to   9. And be my opportunity to reproach you.
give myself.   1. You do not need my good wishes.

And when your honors mean to solemnize
The bargain of your faith, I do beseech you
Even at that time I may be married too.
195 BASSANIO With all my heart, so° thou canst get a wife.   *if*
GRAZIANO I thank your lordship, you have got me one.
My eyes, my lord, can look as swift as yours.
You saw the mistress; I beheld the maid.
You loved, I loved; for intermission°   *delay*
200 No more pertains to me, my lord, than you.
Your fortune stood upon the caskets there,
And so did mine, too, as the matter falls.
For wooing here until I sweat again,°   *repeatedly*
And swearing till my very roof° was dry   *(of his mouth)*
205 With oaths of love, at last, if promise² last,
I got a promise of this fair one here
To have her love, provided that your fortune
Achieved her mistress.
PORTIA   Is this true, Nerissa?
NERISSA Madam, it is, so you stand pleased withal.
210 BASSANIO And do you, Graziano, mean good faith?
GRAZIANO Yes, faith, my lord.
BASSANIO Our feast shall be much honored in your marriage.
GRAZIANO We'll play° with them the first boy for a thousand ducats.   *wager*
NERISSA What, and stake down?³
215 GRAZIANO No, we shall ne'er win at that sport and stake down!
    Enter LORENZO, JESSICA, *and* SALERIO [*as*] *a messenger*
        from Venice.
But who comes here? Lorenzo and his infidel?
What, and my old Venetian friend Salerio?
BASSANIO Lorenzo and Salerio, welcome hither,
If that the youth of my new interest° here   *position*
220 Have power° to bid you welcome. By your leave,   *Gives me the right*
I bid my very° friends and countrymen,   *true*
Sweet Portia, welcome.
PORTIA So do I, my lord; they are entirely welcome.
LORENZO I thank your honor. For my part, my lord,
225 My purpose was not to have seen you here,
But meeting with Salerio by the way
He did entreat me past all saying nay
To come with him along.
SALERIO   I did, my lord,
And I have reason for it. Signor Antonio
Commends him° to you.   *Sends greeting*
    [*He gives* BASSANIO *a letter.*]
230 BASSANIO   Ere I ope his letter
I pray you tell me how my good friend doth.
SALERIO Not sick, my lord, unless it be in mind;
Nor well, unless in mind: his letter there
Will show you his estate.°   *situation*
    [BASSANIO *opens*] *the letter.*
235 GRAZIANO Nerissa, cheer yond stranger; bid her welcome.
Your hand, Salerio; what's the news from Venice?

2. Nerissa's, to wed Graziano.
3. Put the money down now (Graziano follows with a bawdy joke on "flaccid penis").

How doth that royal° merchant, good Antonio?   *princely*
I know he will be glad of our success.
We are the Jasons: we have won the fleece.
240 SALERIO I would you had won the fleece° that he hath lost.   *(punning on "fleets")*
PORTIA There are some shrewd° contents in yond same paper   *evil*
That steals the color from Bassanio's cheek—
Some dear friend dead, else nothing in the world
Could turn° so much the constitution   *change*
245 Of any constant° man. What, worse and worse?   *resolute*
With leave, Bassanio—I am half yourself,
And I must freely have the half of anything
That this same paper brings you.
     BASSANIO   O sweet Portia,
Here are a few of the unpleasant'st words
250 That ever blotted paper. Gentle lady,
When I did first impart my love to you,
I freely told you all the wealth I had
Ran in my veins—I was a gentleman—
And then I told you true. And yet, dear lady,
255 Rating myself at nothing, you shall see
How much I was a braggart. When I told you
My state° was nothing, I should then have told you   *wealth*
That I was worse than nothing; for indeed
I have engaged° myself to a dear friend,   *pledged*
260 Engaged my friend to his mere° enemy,   *utter*
To feed my means. Here is a letter, lady,
The paper° as the body of my friend,   *(ripped open)*
And every word in it a gaping wound
Issuing lifeblood. But is it true, Salerio?
265 Hath all his ventures failed? What, not one hit,°   *success*
From Tripoli, from Mexico and England,
From Lisbon, Barbary, and India,
And not one vessel scape the dreadful touch
Of merchant-marring rocks?
     SALERIO   Not one, my lord.
270 Besides, it should appear that if he had
The present° money to discharge° the Jew,   *ready / pay*
He° would not take it. Never did I know   *(Shylock)*
A creature that did bear the shape of man
So keen° and greedy to confound° a man.   *eager / destroy*
275 He plies the Duke at morning and at night,
And doth impeach the freedom of the state[4]
If they deny him justice. Twenty merchants,
The Duke himself, and the magnificoes°   *Venetian magnates*
Of greatest port° have all persuaded° with him,   *dignity / argued*
280 But none can drive him from the envious° plea   *malicious*
Of forfeiture, of justice, and his bond.
JESSICA When I was with him I have heard him swear
To Tubal and to Chus, his countrymen,
That he would rather have Antonio's flesh
285 Than twenty times the value of the sum
That he did owe him; and I know, my lord,
If law, authority, and power deny not,

---

4. Accuse the state of not preserving commercial liberty.

It will go hard with poor Antonio.

PORTIA   Is it your dear friend that is thus in trouble?

290   BASSANIO   The dearest friend to me, the kindest man,
The best-conditioned° and unwearied spirit   *best-natured*
In doing courtesies, and one in whom
The ancient Roman honor more appears
Than any that draws breath in Italy.

295   PORTIA   What sum owes he the Jew?

BASSANIO   For me, three thousand ducats.

PORTIA   What, no more?
Pay him six thousand and deface° the bond;   *destroy*
Double six thousand and then treble that,
Before a friend of this description

300   Shall lose a hair through Bassanio's fault.
First go with me to church and call me wife,
And then away to Venice to your friend.
For never shall you lie by Portia's side
With an unquiet soul. You shall have gold

305   To pay the petty debt twenty times over.
When it is paid, bring your true friend along.
My maid Nerissa and myself meantime
Will live as maids and widows. Come, away,
For you shall hence upon your wedding day.

310   Bid your friends welcome; show a merry cheer;°   *countenance*
Since you are dear° bought, I will love you dear.°   *expensively / dearly*
But let me hear the letter of your friend.

BASSANIO [*reads*]   "Sweet Bassanio, my ships have all miscarried; my creditors grow cruel; my estate is very low; my bond

315   to the Jew is forfeit; and since in paying it, it is impossible I
should live, all debts are cleared between you and I if I might
but see you at my death. Notwithstanding, use your pleasure;°   *follow your wishes*
if your love do not persuade you to come, let not my letter."

PORTIA   O love, dispatch all business and be gone!

320   BASSANIO   Since I have your good leave to go away,
I will make haste; but till I come again
No bed shall e'er be guilty of my stay,
Nor rest be interposer twixt us twain.   *Exeunt.*

3.3

Enter [SHYLOCK] *the Jew and* [SOLANIO] *and* ANTONIO
and the Jailer.

SHYLOCK   Jailer, look to him; tell not me of mercy.
This is the fool that lent out money gratis.
Jailer, look to him.

ANTONIO   Hear me yet, good Shylock—

SHYLOCK   I'll have my bond; speak not against my bond.

5   I have sworn an oath that I will have my bond.
Thou called'st me dog before thou hadst a cause;
But since I am a dog, beware my fangs.
The Duke shall grant me justice. —I do wonder,
Thou naughty° jailer, that thou art so fond°   *wicked / foolish*

10   To come abroad° with him at his request.   *outside*

ANTONIO   I pray thee, hear me speak.

3.3 Location: Street in Venice.

SHYLOCK I'll have my bond; I will not hear thee speak.
　　I'll have my bond, and therefore speak no more.
　　I'll not be made a soft and dull-eyed° fool,　　　　　　　　　*gullible*
15　To shake the head, relent and sigh, and yield
　　To Christian intercessors. Follow not.
　　I'll have no speaking; I will have my bond.
　　　　　　　　　　　　　　　　Exit [SHYLOCK *the*] *Jew.*
SOLANIO It is the most impenetrable cur
　　That ever kept° with men.　　　　　　　　　　　　　　*lived*
ANTONIO　　　　　　　　　　Let him alone.
20　I'll follow him no more with bootless° prayers.　　　　　　*fruitless*
　　He seeks my life; his reason well I know:
　　I oft delivered° from his forfeitures　　　　　　　　　　*saved*
　　Many that have at times made moan to me;
　　Therefore he hates me.
SOLANIO　　　　　　　　　I am sure the Duke
25　Will never grant this forfeiture to hold.
ANTONIO The Duke cannot deny° the course of law,　　　　　*prevent*
　　For the commodity that strangers[1] have
　　With us in Venice, if it be denied,
　　Will much impeach the justice of the state,
30　Since that the trade and profit of the city
　　Consisteth of all nations. Therefore go.
　　These griefs and losses have so bated° me　　　　　　　*diminished*
　　That I shall hardly spare a pound of flesh
　　Tomorrow to my bloody creditor.
35　Well, jailer, on! Pray God Bassanio come
　　To see me pay his debt, and then I care not.　　　*Exeunt.*

3.4

Enter PORTIA, NERISSA, LORENZO, JESSICA, *and*
[BALTHAZAR,] *a man of Portia's.*
LORENZO Madam, although I speak it in your presence,
　　You have a noble and a true conceit°　　　　　　　　　*conception*
　　Of godlike amity, which appears most strongly
　　In bearing thus the absence of your lord.
5　But if you knew to whom you show this honor,
　　How true a gentleman you send relief,
　　How dear a lover° of my lord your husband,　　　　　　*friend*
　　I know you would be prouder of the work
　　Than customary bounty can enforce you.[1]
10　PORTIA I never did repent for doing good,
　　Nor shall not now; for in companions
　　That do converse and waste° the time together,　　*spend (not pejorative)*
　　Whose souls do bear an equal yoke of love,
　　There must needs be a like proportion
15　Of lineaments, of manners, and of spirit;
　　Which makes me think that this Antonio,
　　Being the bosom lover of my lord,
　　Must needs be like my lord. If it be so,
　　How little is the cost I have bestowed
20　In purchasing the semblance of my soul[2]

1. For the trading privileges that foreigners have (including Jews).
3.4 Location: Belmont.

1. Than ordinary generosity permits you.
2. In redeeming the likeness of my Bassanio (Antonio).

From out the state of hellish cruelty!
This comes too near the praising of myself;
Therefore no more of it. Hear other things:
Lorenzo, I commit into your hands

25 The husbandry° and manage of my house   *care*
Until my lord's return. For mine own part,
I have toward heaven breathed a secret vow
To live in prayer and contemplation,
Only attended by Nerissa here,

30 Until her husband and my lord's return.
There is a monastery two miles off,
And there we will abide. I do desire you
Not to deny this imposition,°   *decline this charge*
The which my love and some necessity
Now lays upon you.

35 LORENZO   Madam, with all my heart
I shall obey you in all fair commands.
PORTIA   My people do already know my mind
And will acknowledge you and Jessica
In place of Lord Bassanio and myself.

40 So fare you well till we shall meet again.
LORENZO   Fair thoughts and happy hours attend on you!
JESSICA   I wish your ladyship all heart's content.
PORTIA   I thank you for your wish, and am well pleased
To wish it back on you. Fare you well, Jessica!
                    Exeunt [LORENZO *and* JESSICA].

45 Now, Balthazar,
As I have ever found thee honest true,
So let me find thee still: take this same letter
And use thou all th'endeavor of a man
In speed to Padua; see thou render this

50 Into my cousin's hands, Doctor Bellario,
And look what notes and garments he doth give thee.
Bring them, I pray thee, with imagined° speed   *all imaginable*
Unto the traject,° to the common° ferry   *ferry / public*
Which trades° to Venice. Waste no time in words,   *goes back and forth*

55 But get thee gone; I shall be there before thee.
BALTHAZAR   Madam, I go with all convenient° speed.   [*Exit.*]   *due*
PORTIA   Come on, Nerissa. I have work in hand
That you yet know not of. We'll see our husbands
Before they think of us!

NERISSA   Shall they see us?

60 PORTIA   They shall, Nerissa, but in such a habit°   *garb*
That they shall think we are accomplishèd°   *equipped*
With that we lack.° I'll hold thee any wager   *(i.e., penises)*
When we are both accoutred like young men
I'll prove the prettier fellow of the two,

65 And wear my dagger with the braver grace,
And speak between the change of man and boy
With a reed° voice, and turn two mincing steps   *piping*
Into a manly stride, and speak of frays
Like a fine bragging youth, and tell quaint° lies   *elaborate*

70 How honorable ladies sought my love,
Which I denying, they fell sick and died—
I could not do withal!° Then I'll repent   *help it*

And wish, for all that, that I had not killed them;
And twenty of these puny lies I'll tell,
75   That men shall swear I have discontinued° school   *been out of*
Above° a twelve-month. I have within my mind   *At least*
A thousand raw tricks of these bragging Jacks,°   *fellows*
Which I will practice.
NERISSA   Why, shall we turn to[3] men?
PORTIA   Fie, what a question's that,
80   If thou wert near a lewd interpreter!
But come, I'll tell thee all my whole device°   *plan*
When I am in my coach, which stays for us
At the park gate; and therefore haste away,
For we must measure twenty miles today.   *Exeunt.*

3.5
Enter [LANCELET the] clown and JESSICA.

LANCELET   Yes, truly, for look you, the sins of the father are
to be laid upon the children; therefore, I promise you, I fear°   *fear for*
you. I was always plain with you, and so now I speak my agi-
tation° of the matter. Therefore be o'good cheer, for truly I   *(for "cogitation")*
5   think you are damned. There is but one hope in it that can
do you any good, and that is but a kind of bastard hope
neither.
JESSICA   And what hope is that, I pray thee?
LANCELET   Marry, you may partly hope that your father got
10   you not, that you are not the Jew's daughter.
JESSICA   That were a kind of bastard hope indeed—so the sins
of my mother should be visited upon me!
LANCELET   Truly, then, I fear you are damned both by father
and mother; thus when I shun Scylla, your father, I fall into
15   Charybdis, your mother.[1] Well, you are gone° both ways.   *doomed*
JESSICA   I shall be saved by my husband.[2] He hath made me a
Christian.
LANCELET   Truly, the more to blame he! We were Christians
enough before, e'en as many as could well live one by
20   another.[3] This making of Christians will raise the price of
hogs; if we grow all to be pork eaters, we shall not shortly
have a rasher° on the coals for money.°   *bacon strip / any price*
Enter LORENZO.
JESSICA   I'll tell my husband, Lancelet, what you say—here he
comes!
25   LORENZO   I shall grow jealous of you shortly, Lancelet, if you
thus get my wife into corners.
JESSICA   Nay, you need not fear us, Lorenzo. Lancelet and I
are out.° He tells me flatly there's no mercy for me in heaven   *quarreling*
because I am a Jew's daughter; and he says you are no good
30   member of the commonwealth, for in converting Jews to
Christians you raise the price of pork.
LORENZO   I shall answer° that better to the commonwealth   *explain*

---

3. Turn into (with bawdy suggestion).
3.5 Location: Portia's garden in Belmont.
1. Scylla was a mythological sea monster, Charybdis
a whirlpool in the Strait of Messina. Mariners had to
avoid both, a proverbially difficult task.

2. "The unbelieving wife is sanctified by the husband" (1 Corinthians 7:14).
3. *well . . . another:* reside next door to one another;
earn a living off one another.

than you can the getting up of the negro's belly: the Moor[4] is
with child by you, Lancelet!

35 LANCELET   It is much that the Moor should be more than
reason,[5] but if she be less than an honest° woman she is   *a chaste*
indeed more than I took her for.

LORENZO   How every fool can play upon the word! I think the
best grace of wit will shortly turn into silence, and discourse

40 grow commendable in none only but parrots. Go in, sirrah;
bid them prepare for dinner.

LANCELET   That is done, sir; they have all stomachs.°   *appetites*

LORENZO   Goodly Lord! What a wit snapper are you! Then bid
them prepare dinner!

45 LANCELET   That is done too, sir; only "cover"[6] is the word.

LORENZO   Will you cover then, sir?

LANCELET   Not so, sir, neither; I know my duty.

LORENZO   Yet more quarreling with occasion![7] Wilt thou show
the whole wealth of thy wit in an instant? I pray thee under-

50 stand a plain man in his plain meaning: go to thy fellows,
bid them cover the table, serve in the meat, and we will
come in to dinner.

LANCELET   For the table,° sir, it shall be served in; for the   *meal*
meat, sir, it shall be covered;[8] for your coming in to dinner,

55 sir, why let it be as humors and conceits° shall govern.   *whims and notions*

Exit [LANCELET *the*] *clown.*

LORENZO   O dear discretion, how his words are suited![9]
The fool hath planted in his memory
An army of good words, and I do know
A many fools that stand in better place,

60 Garnished° like him, that for a tricksy word   *Provided (with words)*
Defy the matter.° How cheer'st thou,[1] Jessica?   *Refuse to talk sense*
And now, good sweet, say thy opinion:
How dost thou like the Lord Bassanio's wife?

JESSICA   Past all expressing. It is very meet°   *proper*

65 The Lord Bassanio live an upright life,
For, having such a blessing in his lady,
He finds the joys of heaven here on earth.
And if on earth he do not mean it, it
Is reason he should never come to heaven.

70 Why, if two gods should play some heavenly match
And on the wager lay two earthly women
And Portia one, there must be something else
Pawned° with the other, for the poor rude world   *Wagered*
Hath not her fellow.

LORENZO   Even such a husband

75 Hast thou of me as she is for wife.

JESSICA   Nay, but ask my opinion, too, of that!

LORENZO   I will anon;° first let us go to dinner.   *soon*

JESSICA   Nay, let me praise you while I have a stomach.°   *an appetite; desire*

LORENZO   No, pray thee, let it serve for table talk—

---

4. Apparently an African woman of Portia's
household.
5. Should be bigger than is reasonable (punning on
"more/Moor").
6. Set the table; but Lancelet puns on "cover" as
meaning "put on the hat."

7. Playing on words whenever possible.
8. Served in covered dishes (playfully or unconsciously reversing Lorenzo's instructions).
9. Adapted to the occasion. *dear discretion:* precious
discrimination (ironic).
1. How are you?

80   Then howsoe'er° thou speak'st, 'mong other things   *however*
    I shall digest° it.   *ingest; analyze*

JESSICA   Well, I'll set you forth.²   *Exeunt.*

4.1

Enter the DUKE, *the Magnificoes,* ANTONIO, BASSANIO,
[SALERIO,] *and* GRAZIANO.

DUKE   What, is Antonio here?

ANTONIO   Ready, so please your grace.

DUKE   I am sorry for thee. Thou art come to answer
    A stony adversary, an inhuman wretch,
5   Uncapable of pity, void and empty
    From any dram° of mercy.   *trace*

ANTONIO   I have heard
    Your grace hath ta'en great pains to qualify°   *alleviate*
    His rigorous course; but since he stands obdurate,
    And that no lawful means can carry me
10   Out of his envy's° reach, I do oppose   *malice's*
    My patience to his fury and am armed°   *prepared*
    To suffer with a quietness of spirit
    The very tyranny° and rage of his.   *cruelty*

DUKE   Go one, and call the Jew into the court.

15 SALERIO   He is ready at the door; he comes, my lord.

    Enter SHYLOCK.

DUKE   Make room and let him stand before our° face.   *(the royal "we")*
    Shylock, the world thinks, and I think so too,
    That thou but leadest this fashion° of thy malice   *sustain the pretense*
    To the last hour of act;° and then, 'tis thought,   *brink of performance*
20   Thou'lt show thy mercy and remorse° more strange°   *compassion / extraordinary*
    Than is thy strange apparent cruelty.
    And where thou now exacts the penalty,
    Which is a pound of this poor merchant's flesh,
    Thou wilt not only lose° the forfeiture,   *waive*
25   But, touched with human gentleness and love,
    Forgive a moiety° of the principal,   *part*
    Glancing an eye of pity on his losses
    That have of late so huddled° on his back—   *piled*
    Enough to press a royal merchant down
30   And pluck commiseration of this state's,
    From brassy° bosoms and rough hearts of flints,   *unfeeling*
    From stubborn Turks and Tartars never trained
    To offices° of tender courtesy.   *acts*
    We all expect a gentle answer, Jew.

35 SHYLOCK   I have possessed° your grace of what I purpose,   *informed*
    And by our holy Sabbath have I sworn
    To have the due and forfeit of my bond.
    If you deny it, let the danger° light   *damage*
    Upon your charter and your city's freedom!
40   You'll ask me why I rather choose to have
    A weight of carrion flesh than to receive
    Three thousand ducats. I'll not answer that,
    But say it is my humor.° Is it answered?   *caprice*

2. I'll serve you up (like a dinner); I'll extol you.   **4.1** Location: The Venetian court

What if my house be troubled with a rat
45 And I be pleased to give ten thousand ducats
To have it baned?° What, are you answered yet?   *poisoned*
Some men there are love not a gaping pig;[1]
Some that are mad if they behold a cat;
And others, when the bagpipe sings i'th' nose,
50 Cannot contain their urine; for affection,°   *impulse*
Masters of passion, sways it to the mood
Of what it likes or loathes. Now for your answer:
As there is no firm reason to be rendered
Why he° cannot abide a gaping pig,   *one man*
55 Why he° a harmless necessary cat,   *another*
Why he° a woolen bagpipe, but of force°   *yet another / necessarily*
Must yield to such inevitable shame
As to offend, himself being offended;
So can I give no reason, nor I will not,
60 More than a lodged° hate and a certain loathing   *settled*
I bear Antonio, that I follow thus
A losing° suit against him. Are you answered?   *An unprofitable*
BASSANIO   This is no answer, thou unfeeling man,
To excuse the current of thy cruelty!
65 SHYLOCK   I am not bound to please thee with my answers.
BASSANIO   Do all men kill the things they do not love?
SHYLOCK   Hates any man the thing he would not kill?
BASSANIO   Every offense is not a hate at first.
SHYLOCK   What, wouldst thou have a serpent sting thee twice?
70 ANTONIO   I pray you, think you question° with the Jew.   *dispute*
You may as well go stand upon the beach
And bid the main flood bate his° usual height;   *high tide reduce its*
You may as well use question with the wolf
Why he hath made the ewe bleat for the lamb;
75 You may as well forbid the mountain of pines
To wag their high tops and to make no noise
When they are fretten° with the gusts of heaven;   *fretted; agitated*
You may as well do anything most hard
As seek to soften that than which what's harder—
80 His Jewish heart. Therefore, I do beseech you,
Make no more offers, use no farther means,
But with all brief and plain conveniency°   *suitability*
Let me have judgment and the Jew his will.
BASSANIO   For thy three thousand ducats here is six.
85 SHYLOCK   If every ducat in six thousand ducats
Were in six parts, and every part a ducat,
I would not draw° them. I would have my bond.   *take*
DUKE   How shalt thou hope for mercy, rend'ring none?
SHYLOCK   What judgment shall I dread, doing no wrong?
90 You have among you many a purchased slave,
Which like your asses and your dogs and mules
You use in abject and in slavish parts°   *roles*
Because you bought them. Shall I say to you,
"Let them be free; marry them to your heirs!
95 Why sweat they under burdens? Let their beds

---

1. Roasted pig with its mouth propped open.

Be made as soft as yours, and let their palates
Be seasoned with such viands"?° You will answer,   *food*
"The slaves are ours." So do I answer you:
The pound of flesh which I demand of him
100 Is dearly bought, 'tis mine, and I will have it.
If you deny me, fie upon your law:
There is no force in the decrees of Venice.
I stand for judgment. Answer! Shall I have it?
DUKE   Upon° my power I may dismiss this court   *In accordance with*
105 Unless Bellario, a learned doctor
Whom I have sent for to determine° this,   *resolve*
Come here today.
SALERIO   My lord, here stays without°   *waits outside*
A messenger with letters from the doctor,
New come from Padua.
110 DUKE   Bring us the letters. Call the messenger.
BASSANIO   Good cheer, Antonio! What, man, courage yet!
The Jew shall have my flesh, blood, bones and all,
Ere thou shalt lose for me one drop of blood!
ANTONIO   I am a tainted wether° of the flock,   *castrated ram*
115 Meetest for death.° The weakest kind of fruit   *Most fit for slaughter*
Drops earliest to the ground, and so let me.
You cannot better be employed, Bassanio,
Than to live still and write mine epitaph.
          Enter NERISSA *[disguised as Bellario's messenger].*
DUKE   Come you from Padua, from Bellario?
120 NERISSA   From both, my lord. Bellario greets your grace.
          [She presents a letter.]
BASSANIO   Why dost thou whet thy knife so earnestly?
SHYLOCK   To cut the forfeiture from that bankrupt there.
GRAZIANO   Not on thy sole, but on thy soul, harsh Jew,
Thou mak'st thy knife keen. But no metal can—
125 No, not the hangman's° ax—bear° half the keenness   *executioner's / have*
Of thy sharp envy.° Can no prayers pierce thee?   *malice*
SHYLOCK   No, none that thou hast wit enough to make.
GRAZIANO   Oh, be thou damned, inexecrable dog,
And for thy life° let justice be accused.   *for allowing you to live*
130 Thou almost mak'st me waver in my faith—
To hold opinion with Pythagoras²
That souls of animals infuse themselves
Into the trunks of men. Thy currish spirit
Governed a wolf who hanged for human slaughter;³
135 Even from the gallows did his fell soul fleet°   *his cruel soul flit*
And, whilst thou layest in thy unhallowed dam,
Infused itself in thee; for thy desires
Are wolvish, bloody, starved, and ravenous.
SHYLOCK   Till thou canst rail the seal from off my bond
140 Thou but offend'st° thy lungs to speak so loud.   *hurt*
Repair thy wit, good youth, or it will fall
To cureless° ruin. I stand here for law.   *incurable*
DUKE   This letter from Bellario doth commend

---

2. Greek philosopher who believed in the transmigration of souls.
3. In Elizabethan times, animals were tried and hanged for wrongdoing; possibly an allusion to the 1594 execution of the Jewish physician Lopez (Latin *lupus,* "wolf").

A young and learned doctor to our court.
Where is he?

145 NERISSA   He attendeth here hard by
To know your answer whether you'll admit him.

DUKE   With all my heart. Some three or four of you
Go give him courteous conduct° to this place;   escort
[*Exeunt some Magnificoes.*]
Meantime the court shall hear Bellario's letter:

150 [*He reads.*] "Your grace shall understand that at the receipt
of your letter I am very sick, but in the instant that your
messenger came, in loving visitation was with me a young
doctor of Rome; his name is Balthazar. I acquainted him
with the cause in controversy between the Jew and Antonio

155 the merchant. We turned o'er many books together. He is
furnished with my opinion which, bettered with his own
learning—the greatness whereof I cannot enough commend—
comes with him at my importunity to fill up° your grace's   answer
request in my stead. I beseech you, let his lack of years be

160 no impediment to let him lack° a reverend estimation; for I   keep him from having
never knew so young a body with so old a head. I leave him
to your gracious acceptance, whose trial shall better publish his commendation."[4]

Enter PORTIA [*disguised as*] Balthazar[*, attended by*
Magnificoes].

You hear the learn'd Bellario, what he writes;

165 And here, I take it, is the doctor come.
Give me your hand; come you from old Bellario?

PORTIA   I did, my lord.

DUKE   You are welcome; take your place.
Are you acquainted with the difference°   dispute

170 That holds this present question[5] in the court?

PORTIA   I am informed throughly° of the cause.°   thoroughly / case
Which is the merchant here and which the Jew?[6]

DUKE   Antonio and old Shylock, both stand forth.

PORTIA   Is your name Shylock?

SHYLOCK   Shylock is my name.

175 PORTIA   Of a strange nature is the suit you follow,
Yet in such rule° that the Venetian law   order
Cannot impugn you as you do proceed.
—You stand within his danger,° do you not?   power to harm

ANTONIO   Ay, so he says.

PORTIA   Do you confess the bond?

ANTONIO   I do.

180 PORTIA   Then must the Jew be merciful.

SHYLOCK   On what compulsion must I? Tell me that.

PORTIA   The quality of mercy is not strained;°   compelled
It droppeth as the gentle rain from heaven
Upon the place beneath. It is twice blest:

185 It blesseth him that gives and him that takes.
'Tis mightiest in the mightiest; it becomes

---

4. Whose performance ("trial") shall better make
known his worth.
5. That is now being tried.
6. PERFORMANCE COMMENT Portia's inability to distinguish Antonio from Shylock is surprising given both
that Jews in other Renaissance plays appear to have

been marked by dress, hair color, or physiognomy and
that *Merchant* refers to Shylock's distinctive dress at
1.3.106–11. Stage traditions vary, with some Shylocks
eager to assimilate and others equally intent on not
fitting in. See Digital Edition PC 5.

The thronèd monarch better than his crown.
His scepter shows the force of temporal power,
The attribute to° awe and majesty   *of*
190 Wherein doth sit the dread and fear of kings.
But mercy is above this sceptered sway;
It is enthronèd in the hearts of kings;
It is an attribute to God himself,
And earthly power doth then show likest° God's   *most like*
195 When mercy seasons° justice. Therefore, Jew,   *moderates*
Though justice be thy plea, consider this—
That in the course of justice none of us
Should see salvation. We do pray for mercy,
And that same prayer° doth teach us all to render   *(the Lord's Prayer)*
200 The deeds of mercy. I have spoke thus much
To mitigate the justice of thy plea,°   *your demand for justice*
Which if thou follow, this strict court of Venice
Must needs give sentence 'gainst the merchant there.
SHYLOCK My deeds upon my head![7] I crave the law,
205 The penalty and forfeit of my bond.
PORTIA Is he not able to discharge the money?
BASSANIO Yes, here I tender it for him in the court—
Yea, twice the sum; if that will not suffice,
I will be bound to pay it ten times o'er
210 On forfeit of my hands, my head, my heart.
If this will not suffice, it must appear
That malice bears down° truth. And I beseech you—   *overwhelms*
Wrest once° the law to your authority;   *For once twist*
To do a great right do a little wrong
215 And curb this cruel devil of his will.
PORTIA It must not be. There is no power in Venice
Can alter a decree establishèd.
'Twill be recorded for a precedent,
And many an error by the same example
220 Will rush into the state. It cannot be.
SHYLOCK A Daniel come to judgment! Yea, a Daniel![8]
O wise young judge, how I do honor thee!
PORTIA I pray you, let me look upon the bond.
SHYLOCK Here 'tis, most reverend doctor, here it is.
225 PORTIA Shylock, there's thrice thy money offered thee.
SHYLOCK An oath, an oath, I have an oath in heaven
Shall I lay perjury upon my soul?
Not, not for Venice!
PORTIA   Why, this bond is forfeit,
And lawfully by this the Jew may claim
230 A pound of flesh to be by him cut off
Nearest the merchant's heart. Be merciful—
Take thrice thy money; bid me tear the bond!
SHYLOCK When it is paid according to the tenor.°   *condition*
It doth appear you are a worthy judge;
235 You know the law; your exposition
Hath been most sound. I charge you by the law

---

7. The Jewish crowd at Jesus' trial cried, "His blood be on us, and on our children" (Matthew 27:25).
8. In the Apocrypha, the youth Daniel judges the case of Susanna, accused of inchastity by the Elders; he rescues her and convicts them.

Whereof you are a well-deserving pillar,
Proceed to judgment. By my soul I swear
There is no power in the tongue of man
240   To alter me! I stay° here on my bond.   *insist*
ANTONIO   Most heartily I do beseech the court
To give the judgment.
PORTIA   Why, then, thus it is:
You must prepare your bosom for his knife.
SHYLOCK   O noble judge, O excellent young man!
245   PORTIA   For the intent and purpose of the law
Hath full relation to⁹ the penalty,
Which here appeareth due upon the bond.
SHYLOCK   'Tis very true. O wise and upright judge,
How much more elder art thou than thy looks!
PORTIA   Therefore lay bare your bosom.
250   SHYLOCK   Ay—his breast.
So says the bond, doth it not, noble judge?
"Nearest his heart"; those are the very words.
PORTIA   It is so. Are there balance° here   *scales*
To weigh the flesh?
SHYLOCK   I have them ready.
255   PORTIA   Have by some surgeon, Shylock, on your charge,°   *expense*
To stop his wounds lest he do bleed to death.
SHYLOCK   Is it so nominated in the bond?
PORTIA   It is not so expressed, but what of that?
'Twere good you do so much for charity.
260   SHYLOCK   I cannot find it; 'tis not in the bond.
PORTIA   You, merchant, have you anything to say?
ANTONIO   But little. I am armed and well prepared.
Give me your hand, Bassanio; fare you well.
Grieve not that I am fallen to this for you,
265   For herein Fortune shows herself more kind
Than is her custom: it is still her use°   *commonly her habit*
To let the wretched man outlive his wealth,
To view with hollow eye and wrinkled brow
An age of poverty; from which lingering penance
270   Of such misery doth she cut me off.
Commend me to your honorable wife:
Tell her the process° of Antonio's end;   *tale*
Say how I loved you; speak me fair° in death.   *well of me*
And when the tale is told, bid her be judge
275   Whether Bassanio had not once a love.
Repent but you° that you shall lose your friend   *Sorrow only*
And he repents not that he pays your debt;
For if the Jew do cut but deep enough,
I'll pay it instantly with all my heart.
280   BASSANIO   Antonio, I am married to a wife
Which is as dear to me as life itself;
But life itself, my wife, and all the world
Are not with me esteemed above thy life.
I would lose all—ay, sacrifice them all
285   Here to this devil—to deliver you.
PORTIA   Your wife would give you little thanks for that

---

9. Is entirely in agreement with.

If she were by to hear you make the offer.
GRAZIANO   I have a wife who I protest I love—
I would she were in heaven so she could
290   Entreat some power to change this currish Jew.
NERISSA   'Tis well you offer it behind her back;
The wish would make else an unquiet house.
SHYLOCK   These be the Christian husbands! I have a daughter—
Would any of the stock of Barabbas[1]
295   Had been her husband rather than a Christian!
We trifle° time; I pray thee, pursue° sentence.   waste / proceed with
PORTIA   A pound of that same merchant's flesh is thine:
The court awards it and the law doth give it.
SHYLOCK   Most rightful judge!
300   PORTIA   And you must cut this flesh from off his breast:
The law allows it and the court awards it.
SHYLOCK   Most learned judge, a sentence! —Come, prepare!
PORTIA   Tarry a little. There is something else:
This bond doth give thee here no jot of blood.
305   The words expressly are "A pound of flesh."
Take then thy bond, take thou thy pound of flesh;
But in the cutting it, if thou dost shed
One drop of Christian blood, thy lands and goods
Are by the laws of Venice confiscate
310   Unto the state of Venice.
GRAZIANO   O upright judge! Mark, Jew! O learned judge!
SHYLOCK   Is that the law?
PORTIA   Thyself shall see the act;
For as thou urgest justice, be assured
Thou shalt have justice more than thou desir'st.
315   GRAZIANO   O learned judge! Mark, Jew, a learned judge!
SHYLOCK   I take this offer then; pay the bond thrice
And let the Christian go.
BASSANIO   Here is the money.
PORTIA   Soft°—   Not so fast
The Jew shall have all justice! Soft, no haste—
320   He shall have nothing but the penalty.
GRAZIANO   O Jew, an upright judge, a learned judge!
PORTIA   Therefore prepare thee to cut off the flesh.
Shed thou no blood, nor cut thou less nor more
But just° a pound of flesh. If thou tak'st more   exactly
325   Or less than a just pound, be it but so much
As makes it light or heavy in the substance°   weight
Or the division° of the twentieth part   fraction
Of one poor scruple°—nay, if the scale do turn   tiny weight
But in the estimation° of a hair—   amount
330   Thou diest and all thy goods are confiscate.
GRAZIANO   A second Daniel, a Daniel, Jew!
Now, infidel, I have you on the hip![2]
PORTIA   Why doth the Jew pause? Take thy forfeiture!
SHYLOCK   Give me my principal and let me go.
335   BASSANIO   I have it ready for thee; here it is.
PORTIA   He hath refused it in the open court.

---

1. Thief whom the Jews asked Pilate to set free   2. At a disadvantage (see 1.3.40).
instead of Jesus (Mark 15:6–15).

He shall have merely justice and his bond.

GRAZIANO   A Daniel, still say I; a second Daniel!
I thank thee, Jew, for teaching me that word.

340   SHYLOCK   Shall I not have barely° my principal?   *even*

PORTIA   Thou shalt have nothing but the forfeiture
To be so taken at thy peril, Jew.

SHYLOCK   Why, then, the devil give him good of it!
I'll stay no longer question.[3]

PORTIA   Tarry, Jew—

345   The law hath yet another hold on you.
It is enacted in the laws of Venice
If it be proved against an alien
That by direct or indirect attempts
He seek the life of any citizen,

350   The party 'gainst the which he doth contrive°   *plot*
Shall seize one half his goods; the other half
Comes to the privy coffer° of the state;   *private treasury*
And the offender's life lies in° the mercy   *at*
Of the Duke only, 'gainst all other voice.

355   In which predicament I say thou stand'st:
For it appears by manifest proceeding
That indirectly, and directly too,
Thou hast contrived against the very life
Of the defendant; and thou hast incurred

360   The danger° formerly by me rehearsed.°   *penalty / described*
Down, therefore, and beg mercy of the Duke.

GRAZIANO   Beg that thou mayst have leave to hang thyself!
And yet, thy wealth being forfeit to the state,
Thou hast not left the value of a cord;

365   Therefore thou must be hanged at the state's charge.°   *expense*

DUKE   That thou shalt see the difference of our spirit,
I pardon thee thy life before thou ask it.
For half thy wealth, it is Antonio's;
The other half comes to the general state,

370   Which humbleness may drive° unto a fine.   *reduce*

PORTIA   Ay, for the state, not for Antonio.[4]

SHYLOCK   Nay, take my life and all, pardon not that.
You take my house when you do take the prop
That doth sustain my house; you take my life

375   When you do take the means whereby I live.[5]

PORTIA   What mercy can you render him, Antonio?

GRAZIANO   A halter° gratis—nothing else, for God's sake!   *hangman's noose*

ANTONIO   So please my lord the Duke, and all the court,
To quit the fine for one half of his goods

380   I am content, so he will let me have
The other half in use,[6] to render it
Upon his death unto the gentleman
That lately stole his daughter.

---

3. I'll press my case no further.
4. With respect to the state's half, not Antonio's.
5. "He that taketh away his neighbor's living, slayeth him" (Ecclesiastes 34:22).
6. Antonio's conditions are unclear, because "quit" in line 379 (requite) could mean "pardon" or "make him pay," and "in use" (line 381) could mean either

"in trust" or "for my own purposes." But the arrangements for Shylock's property later in the scene suggest that Antonio succeeds in getting Shylock's penalty reduced: Shylock retains half of his wealth, and Antonio holds the other half in trust for Jessica and Lorenzo until Shylock dies, at which point they inherit the whole estate.

Two things provided more: that for this favor
385 He presently° become a Christian;   *immediately*
The other, that he do record a gift
Here in the court of all he dies possessed
Unto his son Lorenzo and his daughter.
DUKE   He shall do this or else I do recant°   *withdraw*
390 The pardon that I late pronouncèd here.
PORTIA   Art thou contented, Jew? What dost thou say?
SHYLOCK   I am content.[7]
PORTIA   Clerk, draw a deed of gift.
SHYLOCK   I pray you, give me leave to go from hence;
I am not well. Send the deed after me
And I will sign it.
395 DUKE   Get thee gone, but do it.
GRAZIANO   In christening shalt thou have two godfathers.
Had I been judge, thou shouldst have had ten more°   *(to constitute a jury)*
To bring thee to the gallows, not to the font.

                                     Exit [SHYLOCK].

DUKE   —Sir, I entreat you home with me to dinner.
400 PORTIA   I humbly do desire your grace of pardon.
I must away this night toward Padua,
And it is meet° I presently set forth.   *proper*
DUKE   I am sorry that your leisure serves you not.°   *you haven't the time*
Antonio, gratify° this gentleman,   *reward*
405 For in my mind you are much bound to him.

                        Exeunt DUKE *and his train.*

BASSANIO   Most worthy gentleman, I and my friend
Have by your wisdom been this day acquitted
Of grievous penalties, in lieu whereof
410 Three thousand ducats due unto the Jew
We freely cope° your courteous pains withal.   *repay*
ANTONIO   And stand indebted over and above
In love and service to you evermore.
PORTIA   He is well paid that is well satisfied;
And I, delivering you, am satisfied,
415 And therein do account myself well paid.
My mind was never yet more mercenary.
I pray you, know me when we meet again.
I wish you well, and so I take my leave.
BASSANIO   Dear sir, of force° I must attempt you further.   *necessity*
420 Take some remembrance of us as a tribute,
Not as fee. Grant me two things, I pray you:
Not to deny me, and to pardon me.°   *excuse my urging*
PORTIA   You press me far, and therefore I will yield.
Give me your gloves; I'll wear them for your sake.
425 And for your love I'll take this ring from you.
Do not draw back your hand; I'll take no more,
And you, in love, shall not deny me this!
BASSANIO   This ring, good sir, alas—it is a trifle;
I will not shame myself to give you this!

7. PERFORMANCE COMMENT An audience that wel-   farthest, can undercut the joyful resolution to Anto-
comes Antonio's deliverance is often made uncom-   nio's trial and overshadow the fifth act. See Digital
fortable by the exaction of these penalties against   Edition PC 6.
Shylock. How far the Venetians go, and who goes

430 PORTIA   I will have nothing else but only this,
And now, methinks, I have a mind to it!
BASSANIO   There's more depends on this° than on the value.   *involved here*
The dearest ring in Venice will I give you,
And find it out by proclamation.
435 Only for this, I pray you, pardon me.
PORTIA   I see, sir, you are liberal in offers.
You taught me first to beg, and now, methinks,
You teach me how a beggar should be answered.
BASSANIO   Good sir, this ring was given me by my wife,
440 And when she put it on she made me vow
That I should neither sell nor give nor lose it.
PORTIA   That 'scuse serves many men to save their gifts;
An if° your wife be not a madwoman,   *An if = If*
And know how well I have deserved this ring,
445 She would not hold out enemy forever
For giving it to me. Well, peace be with you.
                    Exeunt [PORTIA *and* NERISSA].
ANTONIO   My lord Bassanio, let him have the ring.
Let his deservings and my love withal
Be valued 'gainst your wife's commandment.
450 BASSANIO   Go, Graziano, run and overtake him.
Give him the ring and bring him, if thou canst,
Unto Antonio's house. Away, make haste!   *Exit* GRAZIANO.
Come, you and I will thither presently,
And in the morning early will we both
455 Fly toward Belmont. Come, Antonio.   *Exeunt.*

4.2

Enter [PORTIA *and*] NERISSA [*still in disguise*].
PORTIA   Inquire the Jew's house out; give him this deed,[1]
And let him sign it. We'll away tonight
And be a day before our husbands home.
This deed will be well welcome to Lorenzo!
                    Enter GRAZIANO.
5 GRAZIANO   Fair sir, you are well o'erta'en:
My lord Bassanio, upon more advice,°   *further thought*
Hath sent you here this ring, and doth entreat
Your company at dinner.
PORTIA   That cannot be.
His ring I do accept most thankfully,
And so I pray you tell him. Furthermore,
10 I pray you show my youth old Shylock's house.
GRAZIANO   That will I do.
NERISSA   Sir, I would speak with you.
[*to* PORTIA] I'll see if I can get my husband's ring,
Which I did make him swear to keep forever.
15 PORTIA   Thou mayst, I warrant. We shall have old° swearing   *lots of*
That they did give the rings away to men;
But we'll outface them and outswear them too.
Away, make haste! Thou know'st where I will tarry.
NERISSA   Come, good sir, will you show me to this house?
                    [*Exeunt.*]

4.2 Location: Street in Venice.   1. Mentioned in 4.1.392 and 394.

5.1

Enter LORENZO *and* JESSICA.

LORENZO   The moon shines bright. In such a night as this,
When the sweet wind did gently kiss the trees
And they did make no noise, in such a night
Troilus methinks mounted the Trojan walls
5   And sighed his soul toward the Grecian tents
Where Cressid lay that night.[1]

JESSICA   In such a night
Did Thisbe fearfully o'ertrip the dew,
And saw the lion's shadow ere himself,
And ran dismayed away.[2]

LORENZO   In such a night
10   Stood Dido with a willow in her hand
Upon the wild sea banks and waft her love
To come again to Carthage.[3]

JESSICA   In such a night
Medea gathered the enchanted herbs
That did renew old Aeson.[4]

LORENZO   In such a night
15   Did Jessica steal° from the wealthy Jew   escape; rob
And with an unthrift° love did run from Venice   a spendthrift
As far as Belmont.

JESSICA   In such a night
Did young Lorenzo swear he loved her well,
Stealing her soul with many vows of faith,
And ne'er a true one.

20   LORENZO   In such a night
Did pretty Jessica, like a little shrew,
Slander her love, and he forgave it her.

JESSICA   I would out-night you did nobody come,
But hark—I hear the footing° of a man.   footsteps

Enter [STEFANO,] *a messenger.*

25   LORENZO   Who comes so fast in silence of the night?

STEFANO   A friend.

LORENZO   A friend? What friend? Your name, I pray you, friend?

STEFANO   Stefano is my name, and I bring word
My mistress will before the break of day
30   Be here at Belmont. She doth stray about
By holy crosses° where she kneels and prays   roadside shrines
For happy wedlock hours.

LORENZO   Who comes with her?

STEFANO   None but a holy hermit and her maid.
I pray you, is my master yet returned?

35   LORENZO   He is not, nor we have not heard from him.
But go we in, I pray thee, Jessica,
And ceremoniously let us prepare

5.1 Location: Belmont.
1. Troilus was a Trojan prince whose lover, Cressida, forsook him for the Greek Diomedes after she was sent from Troy to the Greek camp. See *Troilus and Cressida.*
2. Thisbe, going at night to meet her lover, Pyramus, was frightened by a lion and fled. Pyramus, assuming she was dead, killed himself; when she found his body, Thisbe committed suicide too. The story is dramatized by "the rude mechanicals" in *A Midsummer Night's Dream.*
3. Dido, Queen of Carthage, was abandoned by her lover, the Trojan hero Aeneas. *willow:* emblem of forsaken love. *waft:* waved to.
4. Medea was a sorceress who loved Jason and helped him win the Golden Fleece; she magically restored Aeson, Jason's father, to youth.

Some welcome for the mistress of the house.
            Enter [LANCELET *the*] *clown.*
 LANCELET Sola, sola! Wo ha, ho sola, sola!⁵
40 LORENZO Who calls?
 LANCELET Sola! Did you see Master Lorenzo and Mistress
  Lorenzo? Sola, sola!
 LORENZO Leave hallooing, man! Here!
 LANCELET Sola! Where, where?
45 LORENZO Here!
 LANCELET Tell him there's a post° come from my master,   *messenger*
  with his horn full of good news. My master will be here ere
  morning.   [*Exit.*]
 LORENZO Sweet soul, let's in and there expect° their coming. *await*
50 And yet, no matter. Why should we go in?
 My friend Stefano, signify,° I pray you,   *announce*
 Within the house, your mistress is at hand,
 And bring your music forth into the air. [*Exit* STEFANO.]
 —How sweet the moonlight sleeps upon this bank.
55 Here will we sit and let the sounds of music
 Creep in our ears. Soft stillness and the night
 Become the touches⁶ of sweet harmony.
 Sit, Jessica. Look how the floor of heaven
 Is thick inlaid with patens° of bright gold;   *disks*
60 There's not the smallest orb which thou behold'st
 But in his motion like an angel sings,
 Still° choiring to the young-eyed⁷ cherubim.   *Continually*
 Such harmony⁸ is in immortal souls,
 But whilst this muddy vesture of decay°   *this mortal body*
65 Doth grossly close it° in, we cannot hear it.° *(the soul) / (the music)*
 —Come, ho! And wake Diana⁹ with a hymn.
    [*Enter* MUSICIANS.]
 With sweetest touches pierce your mistress'° ear   *(Portia's)*
 And draw her home with music.
    [MUSICIANS] *play music.*
 JESSICA I am never merry when I hear sweet music.
70 LORENZO The reason is, your spirits are attentive;
 For do but note a wild and wanton herd
 Or race° of youthful and unhandled colts   *group*
 Fetching mad bounds, bellowing, and neighing loud,
 Which is the hot condition of their blood:
75 If they but hear perchance a trumpet sound,
 Or any air of music touch their ears,
 You shall perceive them make a mutual° stand,   *simultaneous*
 Their savage eyes turned to a modest gaze
 By the sweet power of music. Therefore the poet¹
80 Did feign that Orpheus drew° trees, stones, and floods, *allured*
 Since naught so stockish,° hard, and full of rage   *stolid*
 But music for the time doth change his nature.
 The man that hath no music in himself,
 Nor is not moved with concord of sweet sounds,
85 Is fit for treasons, stratagems,° and spoils;° *plots / plunder*

---

5. Imitating a messenger's horn.
6. Suit the notes (literally, the fingering of a stringed instrument).
7. Keen-sighted.

8. The music of the spheres.
9. Goddess of the moon and of chastity.
1. Ovid, in *Metamorphoses* 10, tells the story of Orpheus, a legendary musician.

The motions of his spirit are dull as night,
And his affections° dark as Erebus.° *inclinations / hell*
Let no such man be trusted! Mark the music.

Enter PORTIA *and* NERISSA.

PORTIA   That light we see is burning in my hall;
90   How far that little candle throws his beams!
So shines a good deed in a naughty° world. *an evil*
NERISSA   When the moon shone we did not see the candle.
PORTIA   So doth the greater glory dim the less.
A substitute° shines brightly as a king *deputy*
95   Until a king be by, and then his state
Empties itself as doth an inland brook
Into the main of waters.° Music, hark! *the ocean*
NERISSA   It is your music, madam, of the house.
PORTIA   Nothing is good, I see, without respect;° *reference to context*
100   Methinks it sounds much sweeter than by day.
NERISSA   Silence bestows that virtue on it, madam.
PORTIA   The crow doth sing as sweetly as the lark
When neither is attended;² and I think
The nightingale, if she should sing by day
105   When every goose is cackling, would be thought
No better a musician than the wren.
How many things by season seasoned are³
To their right praise and true perfection!
Peace! How the moon sleeps with Endymion⁴
And would not be awaked.
110   LORENZO   That is the voice,
Or I am much deceived, of Portia.
PORTIA   He knows me as the blind man knows the cuckoo—
By the bad voice!
LORENZO   Dear lady, welcome home!
PORTIA   We have been praying for our husbands' welfare,
115   Which speed,° we hope, the better for our words. *Who prosper*
Are they returned?
LORENZO   Madam, they are not yet,
But there is come a messenger before
To signify their coming.
PORTIA   Go in, Nerissa.
Give order to my servants that they take
120   No note at all of our being absent hence
— Nor you, Lorenzo —Jessica, nor you.
        [*Trumpet sounds.*]
LORENZO   Your husband is at hand. I hear his trumpet.
We are no telltales, madam; fear you not.
PORTIA   This night, methinks, is but the daylight sick;
125   It looks a little paler. 'Tis a day
Such as the day is when the sun is hid.

Enter BASSANIO, ANTONIO, GRAZIANO, *and their followers.*

BASSANIO   We should hold day with the Antipodes,
If you would walk in absence of the sun.⁵

---

2. Is listened to; is accompanied.
3. *by season . . . are*: by proper time are adapted.
4. In classical mythology, a shepherd beloved of the moon goddess, who caused him to sleep forever.

5. *We . . . sun*: We would share daylight with the other side of the world (Antipodes) if you habitually walked when the sun was gone (implying "such is your radiance").

PORTIA   Let me give light, but let me not be light;°   *unfaithful*
130   For a light wife doth make a heavy° husband,   *sad*
      And never be Bassanio so for me—
      But God sort° all. You are welcome home, my lord.   *decide*
BASSANIO   I thank you, madam. Give welcome to my friend.
      This is the man; this is Antonio
135   To whom I am so infinitely bound.
PORTIA   You should in all° sense be much bound to him,   *every*
      For, as I hear, he was much bound for you.
ANTONIO   No more than I am well acquitted° of.   *freed*
PORTIA   Sir, you are very welcome to our house.
140   It must appear in other ways than words;
      Therefore I scant this breathing courtesy.⁶
GRAZIANO [*to* NERISSA]   By yonder moon I swear you do me wrong.
      In faith, I gave it to the judge's clerk.
      Would he were gelt° that had it, for my part,   *gelded; castrated*
145   Since you do take it, love, so much at heart!
PORTIA   A quarrel, ho! Already? What's the matter?
GRAZIANO   About a hoop of gold, a paltry ring
      That she did give me, whose posy° was   *motto*
      For all the world like cutler's poetry
150   Upon a knife: "Love me and leave me not."
NERISSA   What, talk you of the posy or the value?
      You swore to me when I did give it you
      That you would wear it till your hour of death
      And that it should lie with you in your grave.
155   Though not for me, yet for your vehement oaths,
      You should have been respective° and have kept it.   *careful*
      Gave it a judge's clerk! No, God's my judge,
      The clerk will ne'er wear hair on 's face that had it!
GRAZIANO   He will an if he live to be a man.
160   NERISSA   Ay, if a woman live to be a man!
GRAZIANO   Now, by this hand, I gave it to a youth—
      A kind of boy, a little scrubbèd° boy,   *stunted*
      No higher than thyself—the judge's clerk,
      A prating° boy that begged it as a fee.   *chattering*
165   I could not for my heart deny it him.
PORTIA   You were to blame—I must be plain with you—
      To part so slightly with your wife's first gift,
      A thing stuck on with oaths upon your finger
      And so riveted with faith unto your flesh.
170   I gave my love a ring and made him swear
      Never to part with it; and here he stands.
      I dare be sworn for him he would not leave° it,   *part with*
      Nor pluck it from his finger, for the wealth
      That the world masters.° Now, in faith, Graziano,   *possesses*
175   You give your wife too unkind a cause of grief;
      An 'twere to me I should be mad at it.
BASSANIO [*aside*]   Why, I were best to cut my left hand off
      And swear I lost the ring defending it!
GRAZIANO   My lord Bassanio gave his ring away
180   Unto the judge that begged it, and indeed
      Deserved it, too. And then the boy, his clerk,

---

6. I make brief this verbal welcome.

That took some pains in writing, he begged mine;
And neither man nor master would take aught
But the two rings.

PORTIA   What ring gave you, my lord?
185   Not that, I hope, which you received of me.

BASSANIO   If I could add a lie unto a fault,
I would deny it; but you see my finger
Hath not the ring upon it. It is gone.

PORTIA   Even so void is your false heart of truth.
190   By heaven, I will ne'er come in your bed
Until I see the ring!

NERISSA   Nor I in yours
Till I again see mine!

BASSANIO   Sweet Portia,
If you did know to whom I gave the ring,
If you did know for whom I gave the ring,
195   And would conceive for what I gave the ring,
And how unwillingly I left the ring
When naught would be accepted but the ring,
You would abate the strength of your displeasure.

PORTIA   If you had known the virtue° of the ring,   *power*
200   Or half her worthiness that gave the ring,
Or your own honor to contain° the ring,   *retain*
You would not then have parted with the ring.
What man is there so much unreasonable,
If you had pleased to have defended it
205   With any terms of zeal, wanted° the modesty°   *would lack / moderation*
To urge° the thing held as a ceremony?°   *insist on / sacred symbol*
Nerissa teaches me what to believe:
I'll die for't, but some woman had the ring!

BASSANIO   No, by my honor, madam. By my soul,
210   No woman had it, but a civil doctor,°   *doctor of civil law*
Which did refuse three thousand ducats of me
And begged the ring, the which I did deny him,
And suffered° him to go displeased away—   *permitted*
Even he that had held up the very life
215   Of my dear friend. What should I say, sweet lady?
I was enforced to send it after him.
I was beset with shame and courtesy;
My honor would not let ingratitude
So much besmear it. Pardon me, good lady,
220   For by these blessed candles of the night,
Had you been there, I think you would have begged
The ring of me to give the worthy doctor!

PORTIA   Let not that doctor e'er come near my house.
Since he hath got the jewel that I loved,
225   And that which you did swear to keep for me,
I will become as liberal° as you: *generous; licentious*
I'll not deny him anything I have—
No, not my body nor my husband's bed!
Know° him I shall; I am well sure of it.   *(with sexual suggestion)*
230   Lie not a night from home; watch me like Argus.[7]

---

7. Mythical many-eyed monster.

If you do not, if I be left alone,
Now by mine honor, which is yet mine own,
I'll have that doctor for mine bedfellow.

NERISSA And I his clerk. Therefore, be well advised
235 How you do leave me to mine own protection!

GRAZIANO Well, do you so. Let not me take him, then;
For if I do, I'll mar the young clerk's pen.°   (with sexual suggestion)

ANTONIO I am th'unhappy subject of these quarrels.

PORTIA Sir, grieve not you; you are welcome notwithstanding.

240 BASSANIO Portia, forgive me this enforcèd wrong,
And in the hearing of these many friends
I swear to thee—even by thine own fair eyes
Wherein I see myself—

PORTIA   Mark you but that?
In both my eyes he doubly sees himself—
245 In each eye one. Swear by your double° self,   twofold; deceitful
And there's an oath of credit!8

BASSANIO   Nay, but hear me.
Pardon this fault, and by my soul I swear
I never more will break an oath with thee.

ANTONIO I once did lend my body for his wealth,
250 Which but for him that had your husband's ring
Had quite miscarried. I dare be bound again,
My soul upon the forfeit, that your lord
Will never more break faith advisedly.°   intentionally

PORTIA Then you shall be his surety:° give him this,   guarantor of a loan
255 And bid him keep it better than the other.

ANTONIO Here, Lord Bassanio, swear to keep this ring.

BASSANIO By heaven, it is the same I gave the doctor!

PORTIA I had it of him. Pardon me, Bassanio,
For by this ring the doctor lay with me.

260 NERISSA And pardon me, my gentle Graziano,
For that same "scrubbèd boy," the doctor's clerk,
In lieu of° this last night did lie with me.   In exchange for

GRAZIANO Why, this is like the mending of highways
In summer, where the ways are fair enough!9
265 What, are we cuckolds ere we have deserved it?

PORTIA Speak not so grossly. You are all amazed.°   confused
Here is a letter; read it at your leisure.
It comes from Padua from Bellario.
There you shall find that Portia was the doctor,
270 Nerissa there her clerk. Lorenzo here
Shall witness I set forth as soon as you
And even but now returned. I have not yet
Entered my house. Antonio, you are welcome,
And I have better news in store for you
275 Than you expect. Unseal this letter soon.
There you shall find three of your argosies
Are richly come to harbor suddenly.
You shall not know by what strange accident
I chancèd on this letter.

ANTONIO   I am dumb!°   dumbstruck

---

8. An oath to be believed (ironic).   9. *where . . . enough:* when repair is not required.

280 BASSANIO   Were you the doctor and I knew you not?
GRAZIANO   Were you the clerk that is to make me cuckold?
NERISSA   Ay, but the clerk that never means to do it,
   Unless he live until he be a man.
BASSANIO   Sweet doctor, you shall be my bedfellow.
285   When I am absent, then lie with my wife.
ANTONIO   Sweet lady, you have given me life and living,°   *possessions*
   For here I read for certain that my ships
   Are safely come to road.°   *harbor*
PORTIA   How now, Lorenzo!
   My clerk hath some good comforts too for you.
290 NERISSA   Ay, and I'll give them him without a fee.
   There do I give to you and Jessica
   From the rich Jew a special deed of gift,
   After his death of all he dies possessed of.
LORENZO   Fair ladies, you drop manna in the way
   Of starvèd people.
295 PORTIA   It is almost morning,
   And yet I am sure you are not satisfied
   Of these events at full. Let us go in,
   And charge us there upon interrogatories,[1]
   And we will answer all things faithfully.
300 GRAZIANO   Let it be so. The first interrogatory
   That my Nerissa shall be sworn on is
   Whether till the next night she had rather stay,
   Or go to bed now, being two hours to day.
   But were the day come, I should wish it dark
305   Till I were couching° with the doctor's clerk.   *lying*
   Well, while I live I'll fear no other thing
   So sore as keeping safe Nerissa's ring.°   *Exeunt.*[2] *(with sexual suggestion)*

---

1. And question us under oath.
2. PERFORMANCE COMMENT While Graziano's speech suggests a cheerful resolution, the final exit or tableau offers several possibilities for directors to influence an audience's interpretation of the action and comment on the futures of its principals. See Digital Edition PC 7.

Much Ado About Nothing

There are certain foods whose sweet deliciousness relies upon an undertone of bitterness. The bitterness by itself would be unpalatable; the sweetness alone would be cloying. Everything depends on the way the tastes are braided together, either in nature or by a skilled chef. *Much Ado About Nothing,* first published in 1600 and probably written in 1598, is precisely such a food. The play weaves together two stories: the benevolent luring of the quarreling Beatrice and Benedict into mutual declarations of love, and the villainous luring of Claudio into the mistaken belief that his fiancée, Hero, is unchaste. For the former plot, there seems to be no specific source, though Shakespeare would have encountered stories of scorners of love who fall in love (including Chaucer's *Troilus and Criseyde*). For the story of the virtuous lady falsely accused, sources abound, including Ludovico Ariosto's wonderful version in Canto V of *Orlando Furioso* (1516, translated into English by Sir John Harington in 1591) and Matteo Bandello's twenty-second *Novella* (1554, translated into French by François de Belleforest in 1574). Shakespeare probably knew these and other versions, both dramatic and nondramatic, among them a tragic retelling by Edmund Spenser in Book II of *The Faerie Queene* (1590). By deftly intertwining the two plots, *Much Ado About Nothing* mingles lightheartedness with a certain haunting sadness.

Sadness is a recurrent undertone in Shakespeare's earlier comedies: *The Comedy of Errors* opens with a condemned man's lament, *The Merchant of Venice* is darkened by Antonio's melancholy and Shylock's bitter rage, and *Love's Labor's Lost* (which features in Biron and Rosaline a pair of sparring lovers who strikingly anticipate Benedict and Beatrice) ends with a death. In several later comedies, most notably *Measure for Measure,* the darkness is so intensified as to make the term "comedy" seem a problem. But in *Much Ado About Nothing* Shakespeare creates a balance of laughter, longing, and pain that he equals only in two other great romantic comedies from the same period, *As You Like It* and *Twelfth Night, or What You Will.* The titles of all three plays convey an impression of easy, festive wit, a magical effortlessness that is in fact the product of extraordinary discipline and skill.

This cunning use of effort to produce the effect of effortlessness can be understood in the light of Baldassare Castiglione's famous courtesy manual *The Book of the Courtier* (1528). Castiglione's book, published in an English translation in 1561, depicts a witty and sophisticated group of men and women who, in several extended conversations, discuss the qualities that must be possessed by the ideal courtier. The courtier, as they envisage him, must be equally adept at making war and making love. He must be able to assist the Prince and to dance elegantly, to grasp the subtleties of diplomacy and to sing in a pleasant, unaffected voice, to engage in philosophical speculation and to tell amusing after-dinner stories. In similar fashion, court ladies must be at once modest and spirited, chaste and slyly knowing, unspoiled and elegant. These are, in less idealized and rarefied form, the social roles that Benedict and Beatrice are called upon to play. They are roles that demand exceptionally versatile actors.

Such courtly performances, Castiglione's conversationalists acknowledge, risk seeming stilted and artificial; they will be successful only if they appear entirely spontaneous and natural. However carefully they prepare their parts, courtiers should hide all signs of study and rehearsal. To achieve grace, they must practice what Castiglione calls *sprezzatura,* a cultivated nonchalance. *Sprezzatura* is a technique for the manipulation of appearance, for masking the hard work that underlies successful performances. This masking is an open secret: others know that you are masking, but they must keep this knowledge suspended in the belief that it is a breach of decorum to acknowledge their own knowledge.

The society of *The Book of the Courtier* lives with other open secrets. Dark forces lie just outside the charmed circle of delightful lords and ladies: war, arbitrary power, the high risk of betrayal and double-dealing, the commodification of women, the grinding labor to which the great mass of human beings are condemned. The courtier's artful refusal to acknowledge any of these forces could be a mode of escapism, but Castiglione is alert to reality's harsh demands. For him, fashioning the self is a means not of withdrawing from a treacherous world, but of operating successfully within it.

Like Castiglione's *Courtier, Much Ado About Nothing* (whose title suggests the playwright's own mastery of *sprezzatura*) is pervasively concerned with social performance that seems at once spontaneous and calculated. Beatrice and Benedict, at the play's center, are both exquisitely self-conscious, but their self-consciousness takes the paradoxical form of a jaunty indifference to conventional niceties, an almost reckless exuberance that masks a heightened sensitivity to the social currents in which they swim.

By contrast, Don John, the bastard brother, characterizes himself from the start as a radically antisocial creature: "I had rather be a canker in a hedge than a rose in his grace. And it better fits my blood to be disdained of all than to fashion a carriage to rob love from any" (1.3.22–24). These are the sentiments of the outsider, one who, like the bastard Edmund in *King Lear,* is not properly part of the family and kinship network, and they are sufficient, in this play, to account for Don John's relentless, curiously disinterested villainy. He is a man who refuses to "fashion a carriage"—to observe the appropriate code of manners—and this refusal is itself a sign of rebellion. For manners are the lived texture of social life in *Much Ado,* not in the sense of a compulsory set of rules but rather in the sense of an evolving awareness of mutual obligation and interconnectedness.

There is, to be sure, something like compulsion in the obligations and pressures within which the men and women of *Much Ado* live, but the play frustrates any attempt to strip away the fabric of graciousness, apparent choice, and pretended spontaneity with which the compulsions are dressed. An exchange in the comedy's opening moments exemplifies the perfect balance between obligation and will that governs the play's vision of social life. Leonato, the Governor of Messina, is informed by letter of the imminent arrival of Don Pedro of Aragon. (Sicily was ruled for centuries by Spanish viceroys and governors.) Entertainment must be provided at once, and Don Pedro's first words call attention to the pressure of compulsory courtesy: "Good Signor Leonato, are you come to meet your trouble! The fashion of the world is to avoid cost, and you encounter it." It is obviously the fashion of the world to apologize in just this way for imposition, and such an apology calls for an equally conventional denial that any trouble is involved. Leonato duly produces such a denial, a particularly gracious and well-turned one: "Never came trouble to my house in the likeness of your grace. For trouble being gone, comfort should remain, but when you depart from me, sorrow abides and happiness takes his leave." Don Pedro responds to this exquisite compliment with an elegantly modified renewal of his first words and then a polite turn toward Leonato's daughter, Hero: "You embrace your charge too willingly. I think this is your daughter?" (1.1.77–85).

In a strict calculation of power politics, these words are meaningless: they posture emptily above the "real" social exchange, which involves the obligation of the civilian authority toward the military authority (as it happens, a foreign military) at the close of a successful campaign. But such a view neglects the importance of graceful social performance, performance whose ease signals the elite status of the speakers and tacitly acknowledges the possibility of failure or refusal. With a ceremonial greeting such as this, the possibility may seem merely theoretical, but in fact it comes to hover over the entire play (whose main plot is in effect formally initiated by Don Pedro's polite notice of Leonato's daughter). By the fifth act, after Don Pedro's officer Claudio has publicly humiliated and repudiated his intended bride, all courtesy has withered away, and only bitterness and recrimination exist between the gracious host and his princely guest.

Dogberry's zany sleuthing resolves the crisis, but the crucial point is that there is nothing absolute and automatic about the code of manners. Social rituals are vulnerable to disruption and misunderstanding, and this vulnerability underscores the importance of consciously keeping up appearances, patrolling social perimeters, and fabricating civility. In Casti-

A night watchman. From Thomas Dekker, *The Bellman of London* (1608).

glione's world, a high premium is placed on the concealment of the labor expended in this fabrication, but Shakespeare's comedy gives us glimpses in the frequent references to the support staff and attentiveness involved in entertainment: "Where is my cousin your son? Hath he provided this music?" (1.2.1–2); "Being entertained for a perfumer—as I was smoking a musty room . . ." (1.3.47–48); "The revelers are entering, brother. Make good room" (2.1.71–72). Social labor is still more visible in the diverse kinds of discourse in which the characters participate or to which they refer: greeting, entertainment, embassy, formal letter, conjuration, courtship, epigraph, sonneteering, gossip, legal deposition, aggressive wit, formal denunciation, ritualized apology.

Each of these forms of speech requires a display of skill and hence confers a measure of the honor or shame to which the characters of *Much Ado About Nothing* are intensely attuned. Honor and shame are particularly social emotions, the emotions of those who exist in a world of watching and being watched. "Nothing" in Shakespeare's time was pronounced "noting": this is a play obsessed with characters noting other characters. Hence the special force of *masking,* where the serious business of watching is playfully disrupted by disguise, and hence too the crucial significance of those scenes in which Beatrice and Benedict think they are noting others but are in reality being noted (and tricked). Sensitivity to the possibility of being shamed—which includes being laughed at, rejected, insulted, dishonored, humiliated, and so forth—is never far from the characters of *Much Ado*. It extends from Leonato, who thinks that death is the fairest cover for his daughter's public humiliation; to Benedict, whose intellectual and sexual endurance is ridiculed by Beatrice when he ducks out of their first exchange with "a jade's trick" (1.1.118); to Dogberry, who longs to be writ down an ass. At its core is intense male anxiety about female infidelity, manifested in the constant nervous jokes about cuckoldry and played on viciously by Don John. "If I see anything tonight why I should not marry her," Claudio tells Don John, "tomorrow in the congregation, where I should wed, there will I shame her." Don Pedro promises to join with his friend "to disgrace her" (3.2.104–08).

Honor and shame, as the play develops them, are closely bound up with linguistic performance. Language is society's way of being intimately present in the individual; the characters may adjust to that social presence, may like Beatrice and Benedict playfully resist it, may like Dogberry distort it unintentionally, but the shared codes of language are more powerful than any individual.

Close attention to the language of *Much Ado About Nothing* begins with the observation that the comedy is written largely, though not entirely, in prose, a medium far more familiar to modern audiences than the blank verse that dominates many of Shakespeare's plays. (A relevant contrast would be to *Romeo and Juliet*, which shares some of the comedy's preoccupations with social pressure and the disruptive power of love, but is written largely, though not entirely, in exceptionally intense poetry.) There are moments of verse in *Much Ado*, such as Leonato's ghastly expression of hope in act 4 that his shamed daughter will die, but these quickly give way to the looser, more irregular rhythms of prose. This prose, however, is of a kind to which we are no longer accustomed. Modern prose tends by design to be rather plain and colorless; Elizabethan prose is often playful, rhetorically inventive, and richly metaphorical. *Much Ado About Nothing* at once plays elaborate prose games and pokes fun at them, as when Benedict complains that lovesick Claudio "was wont to speak plain and to the purpose, like an honest man and a soldier; and now is he turned orthography. His words are a very fantastical banquet: just so many strange dishes" (2.3.17–20). Shakespeare was certainly capable of writing what we would regard as clear, uncluttered prose: "I learn in this letter that Don Pedro of Aragon comes this night to Messina" (1.1.1–2). But he could also produce astonishing rhetorical effects:

> She told me, not thinking I had been myself, that I was the Prince's jester; that I was duller than a great thaw—huddling jest upon jest with such impossible con- veyance upon me that I stood like a man at a mark with a whole army shooting at me. She speaks poniards and every word stabs. If her breath were as terrible as her terminations, there were no living near her; she would infect to the north star. I would not marry her though she were endowed with all that Adam had left him before he transgressed. She would have made Hercules have turned spit, yea, and have cleft his club to make the fire, too. (2.1.216–26)

The wonderful improvisational piling up of images, each at once subtly linked to the preceding one and yet swerving in a new direction, captures the movement of Benedict's mind: the rush of genuine anger and hurt feelings mingled with the impulse to turn his pain into a comically misogynistic performance to entertain Don Pedro (a performance that, ironically, confirms the charge—that he is the Prince's jester—that originally stung him).

Linguistic performance is the social equivalent of the performance in warfare that is both alluded to and conspicuously excluded from the play's action. Language is vio- lence, and language is the alternative to violence: the play entertains both hypotheses and plays them off against each other. "There is a kind of merry war betwixt Signor Benedict and her," says Leonato of his niece. "They never meet but there's a skirmish of wit between them" (1.1.49–51). If words are the agents of civility, they are also dan- gerous weapons: "Thy slander hath gone through and through her heart / And she lies buried with her ancestors"; "God knows, I loved my niece, / And she is dead, slandered to death by villains" (5.1.68–69, 87–88). What we glimpse in the symbolic murder of Hero is not only the maligning power of slander, but also the aggressive potential of even polite or playful speech. The "merry war" between Beatrice and Benedict leaves scars.

The more one attends to the language of *Much Ado About Nothing*, the more its whiplash merriment seems saturated with violence. In the lighthearted opening scene alone, there are almost constant comic references to war, plague, betrayal, heresy, burning at the stake, blinding, hanging, spying, poisoning. To be sure, the horrors are not themselves realized dramatically in the play; they are present as mere jokes. Nonetheless, they are present, recalled again and again by the constant threat of disaster, by symbolic death, by public shaming. Even in the tidal rush of the comic resolution, amid the marriages, the music, and the dance, Benedict's final words— the final words of the play—deliberately call attention to the violence that the language has continually, if obliquely, registered. Informed of Don John's capture,

Lovers sparring with torches. From George Wither, *A Collection of Emblems* (1635).

Benedict declares, "Think not on him till tomorrow. I'll devise thee brave punishments for him. Strike up, pipers!" [MUSICIANS *play. They all] dance [and exeunt]* (5.4.123–24).

Viewed in the light of the close, with its conspicuous deferral of torture, but only until tomorrow, the play does not simply transform human misery and violence into wit, but rather addresses itself to the ways in which society manages to endure, to reproduce, to avoid immersion in its own destructive element, to dance. It does so by conscious and unconscious deferral, by the manipulation of appearances, by the deployment of illusions that are known by at least some of its members (the worst and the best) to be illusions.

Illusions are tricks and deceptions, but they are also the social fictions men and women live by. Claudio and Hero exist in the play almost entirely in and as such fictions: their emotions seem less something they possess inwardly than something constructed for them out of the appropriate conventions and rituals. A more complex manifestation in the play of the primacy of illusion is the relation between Beatrice and Benedict. The plot to trick the celebrated skirmishers into marriage originates with Don Pedro, who promises, if Leonato, Hero, and Claudio cooperate with him, to "fashion" the match (2.1.324). The key to his success is his ability to mobilize the social code of shame and honor to which Beatrice and Benedict are bound and to use this code as a means to discipline—to shape into a plot that will culminate in marriage—the powerful chafing between them. For both Beatrice and Benedict, the force that pushes them toward declarations of love and hence toward marriage vows is as much hearing themselves criticized by their friends as hearing that the other is desperately in love. "Can this be true?" asks Beatrice, her ears burning. "Stand I condemned for pride and scorn so much?" (3.1.107–08). "I hear how I am censured," Benedict declares, resolving that he "must not seem proud" (2.3.198–99, 202).

The conspiratorial fabrication of appearances so as to manipulate the code of shame and honor has the odd effect of establishing a link between the socially approved practices of Don Pedro and the wicked practices of Don John, his bastard brother. Shakespeare seems to go out of his way to call attention to this link: moments after Don Pedro undertakes to "fashion" the affection between Beatrice and Benedict, the villainous Borachio declares that he "will so fashion the matter that Hero shall be absent" and hence can be impersonated by Margaret (2.2.39–40). In effect, the play's term for the social system in which all the characters—evil as well as virtuous—are involved is "fashion." Shakespeare deftly uses the term as both noun and verb—that is, both to designate the images (including the fashionable costumes) that elicit emotions and to describe the process that shapes these images.

Fashion is closely related not only to image but also to verbal style, which in the aesthetics of the period was regarded as a kind of dress. "The body of your discourse," laughs Benedict, "is sometime guarded with fragments, and the guards are but slightly basted on neither" (1.1.242–44). The pervasiveness of fashion allows the possibility of drastic deception, but it is also society's redemptive principle. The movement of the play is not so much the unmasking of fraud to reveal the true, virtuous essence within as it is the refashioning, after a dangerous illusion, of the proper image and the appropriate words: "Sweet Hero," cries Claudio after his eyes have been opened to the deception, "now thy image doth appear / In the rare semblance that I loved it first" (5.1.236–37).

The fashioning with which the play is concerned complicates any simple opposition between authentic inner feelings and social norms. This is, after all, a plot that features a wooing by masked proxy instead of direct wooing, a theatrical ritual of remorse instead of remorse, a declaration of love based upon a set of illusions and motivated by the fear of shame. Near the play's close, we see Benedict struggling to compose the required sonnet to Beatrice—an entirely conventional exercise performed to fulfill the theatrical role in which he has been cast ("myself in love"). And in the final moments, when the deception is revealed, it is this exercise, rather than any feelings of the heart, that confirms the match. "I'll be sworn upon't, that he loves her," declares Claudio:

> For here's a paper written in his hand,
> A halting sonnet of his own pure brain,
> Fashioned to Beatrice.
>
> (5.4.85–88)

When a similar sonnet by Beatrice is produced, Benedict cries, "A miracle! Here's our own hands against our hearts" (5.4.91–92).

Many readers of the play, and most performers, have tried to reverse this formulation: Beatrice and Benedict's conversations may be hostile, the interpretation goes, but in their hearts they are, and have long been, deeply in love. Beatrice seems to refer to an earlier time when she had given her heart to Benedict and had evidently been disappointed: "once before he won it of me with false dice" (2.1.248). If they do not declare their love, it is because they are too defensive or, alternatively, too wise to play society's conventional game. In a world of pervasive conventionality and social control, one clever way to insist upon some spontaneity and hence to achieve some authenticity is to quarrel. Perhaps. But what if we do not dismiss their own words? What if we take the conspiracy against them seriously? Beatrice and Benedict would in that case not "love" each other from the start; it would not at all be clear that they love each other, entirely independent of social manipulation, at the close. They are, at least to some extent, tricked into marriage; without the pressure that moves them to professions of love, they would have remained unmarried. Beatrice and Benedict constantly tantalize us with the possibility of an identity quite different from that of Claudio and Hero, an identity deliberately fashioned to resist the constant pressure of society. But that pressure finally prevails. Marriage is a social conspiracy.

If such a view seems ultimately too unsentimental to be tenable in a romantic comedy, it nonetheless makes possible the brilliant scene in which Benedict asks what he can do to prove his love for Beatrice, and Beatrice replies, "Kill Claudio" (4.1.285). Similarly, it helps to account for the laughter provoked by the disillusioned exchange very near the play's close: "Do not you love me?" "Why, no, no more than reason". (5.4.74). In both cases, where we might expect tender words, we get the opposite. If we feel nonetheless that romantic love triumphs in the end, we do so in effect because we—audience and readers—participate in the conspiracy to gull the pair into marriage by insisting that they love each other more than reason. In doing so, we confer upon the general restoration of civility at the play's close something more deeply pleasurable.

Benedict and Beatrice have rational arguments, grounded in the gender politics of their world, for remaining single. Benedict knows that a married man must put his honor at risk by entrusting it to a woman, while Beatrice knows that a married woman must put her integrity at risk by submitting herself to a man: "Would it not grieve a woman to be overmastered with a piece of valiant dust?" (2.1.51–52). Even when they are manipulated into declaring their love, they cannot settle into the language of conventional courtship: "Thou and I are too wise," Benedict tells Beatrice, "to woo peaceably" (5.2.60). Their union at the close is a triumph of folly over the "wisdom" of the single life, a triumph that recalls Erasmus's *Praise of Folly,* where love is said to be possible only because men and women are induced to put aside their reason and plunge into saving foolishness. Why should they do so? The answer is that it is better to live in illusion than in social isolation and that, as Benedict says, "the world must be peopled" (2.3.213).

In most productions of the play, audiences are made to feel that submission to the discipline of love and marriage—"Taming my wild heart" (3.1.112), as Beatrice so wonderfully puts it—is a magnificent release of love and energy. Shakespeare had already experimented with comparable themes in *The Taming of the Shrew,* but Petruccio's conquest of Katherina seems, at least for many modern viewers, too brutal to accept without a lingering sense of constriction and loss. What keeps the conclusion of *Much Ado About Nothing* from appearing brittle or bitter is a sense that the triumph of illusion is life-affirming, a sense that the friction between Beatrice and Benedict can be turned into mutual pleasure.

A man trapped in the yoke of matrimony. From Henry Peacham, *Minerva Britanna* (1612).

If the Claudio/Hero plot and the Beatrice/Benedict plot are two ways in which Shakespeare's comedy shows the saving necessity of illusion, there is a third manifestation: the illusion that evil manifests itself as Don John—that is, in a supremely incompetent and finally impotent form—and that, although it fools clear-eyed and sophisticated observers like Don Pedro, it may be exposed by a bumbling idiot like Dogberry. Some years later, Shakespeare returned to a ruthlessly disillusioned version of the same story, the lover tricked into believing that his beloved has been unfaithful, and called it not *Much Ado About Nothing* but *Othello*.

STEPHEN GREENBLATT

SELECTED BIBLIOGRAPHY

Berger, Harry, Jr. "Against the Sink-a-Pace: Sexual and Family Politics in *Much Ado About Nothing.*" *Shakespeare Quarterly* 33 (1982): 302–13. Characterizes Messina's gender conventions in terms of virtue, constancy, reputation, deception, and fashion.

Berry, Ralph. *Shakespeare's Comedies: Explorations in Form.* Princeton, NJ: Princeton UP, 1972. 154–74. Argues that by focusing on the difficult reconciliation of sensory experience and judgment, *Much Ado About Nothing* explores the limits of knowledge.

Cook, Carol. "'The Sign and Semblance of Her Honor': Reading Gender Difference in *Much Ado About Nothing.*" *PMLA* 101.2 (1986): 186–202. Explores how the play presents the polysemous threat of women in a world where men are the manipulators and interpreters of signs.

Everett, Barbara. "*Much Ado About Nothing*: The Unsociable Comedy." *English Comedy.* Ed. Michael Cordner, Peter Holland, and John Kerrigan. New York: Cambridge UP, 1994. 68–84. Discusses how Shakespeare's realistic portrait of love in society typically mixes its comic nothings with serious concerns.

Gay, Penny. "*Much Ado About Nothing*: A Kind of Merry War." *As She Likes It: Shakespeare's Unruly Women.* London: Routledge, 1994. 143–77. Presents performance history since the 1950s, spotlighting representations of Beatrice and Benedict.

Howard, Jean. "Renaissance Antitheatricality and the Politics of Gender and Rank in *Much Ado About Nothing.*" *Shakespeare Reproduced: The Text in History and Ideology.* Ed. Jean E. Howard and Marion F. O'Connor. New York: Methuen, 1987. 163–87. Argues that *Much Ado About Nothing* supports Elizabethan ideology, condemning marginal social groups through accusations of illegitimate theatrical practice.

Moisan, Thomas. "Deforming Sources: Literary Antecedents and Their Traces in *Much Ado About Nothing.*" *Shakespeare Studies* 31 (2003): 165–83. Examines how the play's furtive and ambivalent relationship to its sources reflects its depiction of character, politics, power, and representation.

Myhill, Nova. "Spectatorship in/of *Much Ado About Nothing.*" *Studies in English Literature* 39.2 (1999): 291–311. Considers how *Much Ado About Nothing*'s unreliable "notings" challenge the theater audience's assumptions of omniscience and invulnerability.

Salingar, Leo. "Borachio's Indiscretion: Some Noting about *Much Ado.*" *The Italian World of English Renaissance Drama: Cultural Exchange and Intertextuality.* Ed. Michele Marrapodi. London: Associated UP, 1998. 225–38. Looks at *Much Ado* as a bittersweet masquerade of social ambiguity and false communications.

Traugott, John. "Creating a Rational Rinaldo: A Study in the Mixture of the Genres of Comedy and Romance in *Much Ado About Nothing.*" *Genre* 15 (1982): 157–81. Shows how comedy and romance contaminate and purify each other, one becoming ennobled and the other cured of cruelty.

MUSIC AND FILMS

Berlioz, Hector. *Béatrice et Bénédict*. Recommended recording: Baker, Allen, Davis, LSO arkivmusic.com. Typically lush operatic reimagining that leaves out the Don John subplot to focus on the gradual, eventually ecstatic union of Beatrice and Benedict.

Much Ado About Nothing. 1993. Dir. Kenneth Branagh. UK/USA. 111 min. Festive romp set in sunny country-house Italy. With Kenneth Branagh and Emma Thompson. (See also Branagh, *"Much Ado About Nothing": Screenplay, Introduction, and Notes on the Making of the Movie* [New York: Norton, 1993].)

Much Ado About Nothing. 2013. Dir. Joss Whedon. USA. 109 min. Benedict slips from Beatrice's bed at the opening of this black-and-white recasting of the play in contemporary Southern California. With Amy Acker as Beatrice, Alexis Denisof as Benedict, and Nathan Fillion as Dogberry.

TEXTUAL INTRODUCTION

The text of *Much Ado About Nothing* is one of the most exciting in the Shakespeare canon because of the opportunity it gives us to see the playwright at work. The play was published once during Shakespeare's lifetime, in London in 1600 by Andrew Wise and William Aspley. This edition, a small quarto (or Q), formed the basis of the text printed in 1623 in the First Folio (F). *The Norton Shakespeare* is based on Q because this text was probably printed from Shakespeare's own working papers. There are several places where we can see that the text from which the printer was working was not the final state of the play. It opens, for example, with an entrance for Innogen, who is described as Leonato's wife. Leonato's wife also enters at the beginning of 2.1, but Innogen does not speak on any occasion and is never referred to again. Leonato's brother is not named in the dialogue until 5.1.92, but is introduced first as *"an old man brother to Leonato"* (1.2.0) and then in speech prefixes and stage directions as *"Brother"* until 5.4, when he becomes *"old man."* Similarly, Prince John is called *"Bastard."* This suggests that Shakespeare was thinking of character-types when he started work on the play and developed the characters' personalities as he went along. Stage directions are adequate for a reader but would not be sufficiently precise for an acting company. In act 5, for example, we have *two or three [Attendants]* (5.4.33), *three or four [Attendants]* (5.3.0), and *Constables* (5.1.195), but are not told the precise number of actors on stage. Although the play is set in Messina, in Sicily, which at the time Shakespeare was writing was part of the Spanish Kingdom of Aragon, the Prince is at first called *"Peter"* before Shakespeare settles into calling him *"Pedro."*

The most complex scenes textually are those involving Dogberry, Verges, and the officers of the watch (3.3, 3.5, 4.2, and 5.1). The number of watchmen, or constables, is not specified. Verges is called the *"Headborough,"* or local constable, in the entrance to 3.5 only. A Sexton appears in 4.2 together with a Town Clerk who, like Innogen, is a ghost character who never speaks: he may be the same as the Sexton. All this suggests that Shakespeare was picturing the characters from a small-town administration as he developed the plot. In 4.2 we come even closer to Shakespeare's creative process, when the speeches for Dogberry's role are labeled *"Kemp,"* for Will Kemp, the comic actor who played this part, and at 4.2.4 *"Andrew,"* meaning a clown's role. Verges's speeches are labeled *"Cowley"* or *"Couley,"* which again was the name of an actor, Richard Cowley. Shakespeare here had in his mind's eye the roles as they would appear on stage, impersonated by his colleagues in the Lord Chamberlain's Men, and these slips of the pen allow us to be certain that the text that we are reading is unusually close to Shakespeare's own draft.

The publishers of the play made their entry in the Stationers' Register on August 23, 1600, giving them the right to print both *Much Ado About Nothing* and *2 Henry IV*. Less than three weeks earlier, on August 4, 1600, the Stationers Company had recorded that *Much Ado* was to be "stayed," or withheld from publishing, but the reason for this is not known.

Wise and Aspley contracted out the production of the book, in quarto format, to the printer Valentine Sims, who also printed *2 Henry IV*. The same compositor set both texts; *Much Ado* was probably printed after *2 Henry IV*. On the first and last pages of sheet G, scenes 4.1 and 4.2, the text is crowded on the page, which suggests that the compositor made a slight error in "casting off" his copy and had too much material. Charlton Hinman argued that *Much Ado* was printed by page rather than by forme (see Glossary) and that the crowded page reflected the actual layout of Shakespeare's papers, but Hinman's studies cannot be fully replicated and it is more likely that Q was printed by formes in the normal way. Several of the textual problems, especially in the Dogberry scenes (e.g., 4.2.61), are apparently the result of the state of Shakespeare's papers and the need to crowd the page.

While sheets D, E, F and G were being printed, some corrections, or "press variants," were made. One surviving copy, Qu, preserves the uncorrected readings, which mostly affect spelling and punctuation.

TRUDI DARBY

TEXTUAL BIBLIOGRAPHY

Ferguson, W. Craig. "The Compositors of *Henry IV, Part 2, Much Ado About Nothing, The Shoemakers' Holiday,* and *The First Part of the Contention.*" *Studies in Bibliography* 13 (1960): 20–31.

Hazel Smith, John. "The Composition of the Quarto of *Much Ado About Nothing.*" *Studies in Bibliography* 16 (1963): 10–27.

Hinman, Charlton. *Much Ado About Nothing.* Shakespeare Quarto Facsimiles No. 15. Oxford: Clarendon, 1971.

PERFORMANCE NOTE

Much Ado About Nothing is rare among Shakespeare's plays for having its star characters, Beatrice and Benedict, occupy places of secondary importance in the main plot. Consequently, productions must address the need for the sparring couple to command the audience's attention without overwhelming the play, either by marginalizing the courtship and eventual union of Claudio and Hero or by rendering Dogberry's comedy, or Don John's villainy, distracting or superfluous. Beatrice and Benedict require actors of considerable versatility: alternating sarcastic banter with moments of humble self-reflection, each graduates from episodes of screwball comedy to solemn expressions of love and fidelity. It can therefore be challenging for productions to succeed on each of these fronts without eclipsing the subplots or obscuring their purposes. Productions must also decide, crucially, whether Beatrice and Benedict's verbal banter is lighthearted or acerbic, the result of genuine distaste or of a need to mask their affections for one another. Benedict often makes his attraction to Beatrice legible to the audience from the start, while Beatrice shows perfect indifference; other productions emphasize Beatrice's account of a failed romance with Benedict to suggest her lingering affection. Either choice complicates their exchanges throughout the play.

Productions must also consider the transition from the lighthearted comedy of the play's first half to the tragic events of the second, determining whether to foreshadow the sobering divisions to come by emphasizing such things as Don Pedro's rejection by Beatrice or Don John's exclusion from his brother's circle. Other prominent staging considerations include the degree of credibility necessary for the deceptions of onstage audiences; whether to introduce Margaret in scenes that highlight her role in Hero's ruin; and the delivery and aftermath of Beatrice's notorious challenge to Benedict: "Kill Claudio" (4.1.285).

Brett Gamboa

Much Ado About Nothing

[THE PERSONS OF THE PLAY

PEDRO, Prince of Aragon
JOHN, illegitimate half-brother to Pedro
BENEDICT ⎫ accompanying Pedro
CLAUDIO ⎭
BORACHIO ⎫ accompanying John
CONRAD ⎭
MESSENGER
LORD

LEONATO, Governor of Messina
Innogen, wife to Leonato
ANTHONY, brother to Leonato
HERO, daughter to Leonato
BEATRICE, niece to Leonato
BALTHASAR ⎫
MARGARET ⎬ members of Leonato's household
URSULA ⎭
BOY
FRIAR
MUSICIANS
Kinsmen
Attendants

DOGBERRY, a Constable in charge of the WATCH
VERGES, the Headborough
SEXTON
FIRST WATCHMAN
SECOND WATCHMAN
WATCHMEN
Town Clerk]

1.1

Enter LEONATO *Governor of Messina,* Innogen *his wife,*
HERO *his daughter, and* BEATRICE *his niece, with a*
MESSENGER.[1]

LEONATO   I learn in this letter that Don Pedro of Aragon comes
this night to Messina.
MESSENGER   He is very near by this. He was not three leagues
off when I left him.
5   LEONATO   How many gentlemen have you lost in this action?°   *campaign*
MESSENGER   But few of any sort,° and none of name.°   *rank / distinction*
LEONATO   A victory is twice itself when the achiever brings
home full numbers. I find here that Don Pedro hath bestowed
much honor on a young Florentine called Claudio.

1.1 Location: Messina (a city in Sicily). Before the
house of Leonato.
1. TEXTUAL COMMENT Innogen is a ghost, or silent,
character: she never speaks, although she appears
twice in the play. See Digital Edition TC 1.

10 MESSENGER   Much deserved on his part, and equally remembered° by Don Pedro. He hath borne himself beyond the promise of his age, doing in the figure of a lamb the feats of a lion. He hath indeed better bettered° expectation than you must expect of me to tell you how.

15 LEONATO   He hath an uncle here in Messina will be very much glad of it.

MESSENGER   I have already delivered him letters, and there appears much joy in him, even so much that joy could not show itself modest° enough without a badge° of bitterness.°

20 LEONATO   Did he break out into tears?

MESSENGER   In great measure.

LEONATO   A kind° overflow of kindness.° There are no faces truer than those that are so washed. How much better is it to weep at joy than to joy at weeping!

25 BEATRICE   I pray you, is Signor Mountanto[2] returned from the wars or no?

MESSENGER   I know none of that name, lady. There was none such in the army of any sort.

LEONATO   What is he that you ask for, niece?

30 HERO   My cousin means Signor Benedict of Padua.[3]

MESSENGER   Oh, he's returned, and as pleasant° as ever he was.

BEATRICE   He set up his bills° here in Messina and challenged Cupid at the flight,[4] and my uncle's fool,° reading the challenge, subscribed for Cupid and challenged him at the bird-

35 bolt.[5] I pray you, how many hath he killed and eaten in these wars? But how many hath he killed? For indeed, I promised to eat all of his killing.

LEONATO   Faith, niece, you tax° Signor Benedict too much. But he'll be meet° with you, I doubt it not.

40 MESSENGER   He hath done good service, lady, in these wars.

BEATRICE   You had musty victual, and he hath holp° to eat it. He is a very valiant trencher-man.° He hath an excellent stomach.°

MESSENGER   And a good soldier too, lady.

BEATRICE   And a good soldier to a lady. But what is he to a lord?

45 MESSENGER   A lord to a lord, a man to a man, stuffed° with all honorable virtues.

BEATRICE   It is so indeed. He is no less than a stuffed man.° But for the stuffing—well, we are all mortal.[6]

LEONATO   You must not, sir, mistake my niece. There is a kind

50 of merry war betwixt Signor Benedict and her. They never meet but there's a skirmish of wit between them.

BEATRICE   Alas, he gets nothing by that. In our last conflict, four of his five wits[7] went halting° off, and now is the whole man governed with one. So that if he have wit enough to keep

55 himself warm, let him bear it for a difference between himself and his horse, for it is all the wealth that he hath left: to be known a reasonable creature. Who is his companion now? He hath every month a new sworn brother.

rewarded

exceeded

moderate / show / grief

natural / tenderness

entertaining
public notices
jester

abuse
even

helped
hearty eater / appetite

well furnished

mannequin

limping

MESSENGER   Is't possible?

60   BEATRICE   Very easily possible. He wears his faith° but as the   *loyalty*
fashion of his hat: it ever changes with the next block.[8]

MESSENGER   I see, lady, the gentleman is not in your books.°   *favor*

BEATRICE   No. An° he were, I would burn my study. But I pray   *If*
you, who is his companion? Is there no young squarer° now   *boisterous quarreler*

65   that will make a voyage with him to the devil?

MESSENGER   He is most in the company of the right noble
Claudio.

BEATRICE   O Lord! He will hang upon him like a disease. He is
sooner caught than the pestilence,° and the taker° runs   *plague / victim*

70   presently° mad. God help the noble Claudio. If he have caught   *immediately*
the Benedict it will cost him a thousand pound ere 'a° be cured.   *he*

MESSENGER   I will hold friends[9] with you, lady.

BEATRICE   Do, good friend.

LEONATO   You will never run mad,[1] niece.

75   BEATRICE   No, not till a hot January.

MESSENGER   Don Pedro is approached.

Enter Don PEDRO, CLAUDIO, BENEDICT, BALTHASAR,
and JOHN *the bastard.*

PEDRO   Good Signor Leonato, are you come to meet your
trouble! The fashion° of the world is to avoid cost, and you   *custom*
encounter° it.   *go to meet*

80   LEONATO   Never came trouble to my house in the likeness of
your grace. For trouble being gone, comfort should remain,
but when you depart from me, sorrow abides and happiness
takes his leave.

PEDRO   You embrace your charge° too willingly. I think this is   *duty*

85   your daughter?

LEONATO   Her mother hath many times told me so.

BENEDICT   Were you in doubt, sir, that you asked her?

LEONATO   Signor Benedict, no, for then were you a child.[2]

PEDRO   You have it full,[3] Benedict. We may guess by this what

90   you are, being a man. Truly, the lady fathers herself.[4] Be
happy, lady, for you are like an honorable father.

[He talks aside with LEONATO.*]*

BENEDICT   If Signor Leonato be her father, she would not have
his head[5] on her shoulders for all Messina, as like him as she is.

BEATRICE   I wonder that you will still° be talking, Signor Bene-   *always*

95   dict. Nobody marks you.

BENEDICT   What! My dear Lady Disdain! Are you yet living?

BEATRICE   Is it possible Disdain should die while she hath
such meet° food to feed it as Signor Benedict? Courtesy   *suitable*
itself must convert° to Disdain if you come in her presence.   *turn*

100   BENEDICT   Then is Courtesy a turncoat. But it is certain I am
loved of° all ladies, only you excepted, and I would I could   *by*
find in my heart that I had not a hard heart, for truly I love
none.

BEATRICE   A dear happiness to women; they would else have

105   been troubled with a pernicious suitor. I thank God and my

---

8. Newest mold for a hat; fashion.
9. I will stay on good terms.
1. "Catch the Benedict."
2. Implying facetiously that if he hadn't been a child

at the time Benedict might have cuckolded Leonato.
3. Your sarcasm is fully repaid.
4. She shows by her looks who her father is.
5. The head of an old man.

cold blood, I am of your humor° for that. I had rather hear
my dog bark at a crow than a man swear he loves me.

disposition

BENEDICT God keep your ladyship still in that mind. So some
gentleman or other shall scape a predestinate° scratched

escape an inevitable

110 face.

BEATRICE Scratching could not make it worse, an 'twere such
a face as yours were.

BENEDICT Well, you are a rare parrot teacher.[6]

BEATRICE A bird of my tongue is better than a beast of yours.[7]

115 BENEDICT I would my horse had the speed of your tongue and
so good a continuer.[8] But keep your way,° o'God's name. I

carry on

have done.

BEATRICE You always end with a jade's trick.[9] I know you of
old.

120 PEDRO [*finishing his conversation*] That is the sum of all,
Leonato. —Signor Claudio and Signor Benedict! My dear
friend Leonato hath invited you all. I tell him we shall stay
here at the least a month, and he heartily prays some occasion may detain us longer. I dare swear he is no hypocrite

125 but prays from his heart.

LEONATO If you swear, my lord, you shall not be forsworn. [*to*
JOHN] Let me bid you welcome, my lord, being° reconciled to

since you are

the Prince your brother. I owe you all duty.

JOHN I thank you. I am not of many words, but I thank you.

130 LEONATO [*to* PEDRO] Please it your grace lead on?

PEDRO Your hand, Leonato, we will go together.[1]

Exeunt all but BENEDICT *and* CLAUDIO.

CLAUDIO Benedict, didst thou note the daughter of Signor
Leonato?

BENEDICT I noted her not,[2] but I looked on her.

135 CLAUDIO Is she not a modest young lady?

BENEDICT Do you question me as an honest man should do,
for my simple true judgment? Or would you have me speak
after my custom, as being a professed tyrant to° their sex?

pitiless critic of

CLAUDIO No, I pray thee, speak in sober judgment.

140 BENEDICT Why, i'faith, methinks she's too low° for a high

short

praise, too brown for a fair praise, and too little for a great
praise. Only this commendation I can afford her, that were
she other than she is, she were unhandsome; and being no
other but as she is, I do not like her.

145 CLAUDIO Thou thinkest I am in sport.° I pray thee tell me

jest

truly how thou lik'st her.

BENEDICT Would you buy her, that you inquire after her?

CLAUDIO Can the world buy such a jewel?

BENEDICT Yea, and a case to put it into. But speak you this

150 with a sad° brow? Or do you play the flouting jack, to tell us

serious

---

6. Chatterer (repetitive, like one who teaches a parrot to speak).
7. A bird with my powers of speech is better than a
dumb beast who, like you, has none.
8. And had your staying power ("continuer," in
horsemanship, means "stayer").

9. A trick worthy of a badly trained horse (here,
dropping out of a race).
1. We will walk out hand in hand (and thus avoid
taking precedence).
2. I paid her no special attention.

Cupid is a good hare-finder, and Vulcan a rare carpenter?[3]
Come, in what key shall a man take° you to go° in the song?   *understand / join*

CLAUDIO   In mine eye she is the sweetest lady that ever I
looked on.

155   BENEDICT   I can see yet without spectacles, and I see no such
matter. There's her cousin, an she were not possessed with a
fury, exceeds her as much in beauty as the first of May doth
the last of December. But I hope you have no intent to turn
husband, have you?

160   CLAUDIO   I would scarce trust myself, though I had sworn the
contrary, if Hero would be my wife.

BENEDICT   Is't come to this? In faith, hath not the world one
man but he will wear his cap with suspicion?[4] Shall I never
see a bachelor of threescore again? Go to,° i'faith. An thou   *Go on*

165   wilt needs thrust thy neck into a yoke, wear the print of it
and sigh away Sundays.[5] Look, Don Pedro is returned to
seek you.

     Enter PEDRO.

PEDRO   What secret hath held you here that you followed not
to Leonato's?

170   BENEDICT   I would your grace would constrain me to tell.

PEDRO   I charge thee on thy allegiance.

BENEDICT   You hear, Count Claudio? I can be secret as a dumb°   *mute*
man, I would have you think so, but on my allegiance—mark
you this, on my allegiance—he is in love. "With who?" Now

175   that is your grace's part. Mark how short his answer is:
"With Hero, Leonato's short daughter."

CLAUDIO   If this were so, so were it uttered.[6]

BENEDICT   Like the old tale, my lord, "It is not so, nor 'twas
not so."[7] But indeed, God forbid it should be so.

180   CLAUDIO   If my passion change not shortly, God forbid it
should be otherwise.

PEDRO   Amen, if you love her, for the lady is very well
worthy.

CLAUDIO   You speak this to fetch me in,° my lord.   *trick me*

185   PEDRO   By my troth, I speak my thought.

CLAUDIO   And in faith, my lord, I spoke mine.

BENEDICT   And by my two faiths and troths,[8] my lord, I spoke
mine.

CLAUDIO   That I love her, I feel.

190   PEDRO   That she is worthy, I know.

BENEDICT   That I neither feel how she should be loved, nor
know how she should be worthy, is the opinion that fire cannot melt out of me. I will die in it at the stake.

PEDRO   Thou wast ever an obstinate heretic in the despite° of   *contempt*
200   beauty.

---

3. *play . . . carpenter:* spout praises contrary to fact
and intended satirically. Blind Cupid is poorly suited
to the sharp-sighted sport of hunting hares, while Vulcan, the god of fire, was an excellent ("rare") blacksmith, not a carpenter. *flouting jack:* mocking rogue.
4. *but . . . suspicion:* who will not be suspected of
wearing his cap in order to hide a cuckold's horns
(conventional sign of a wife's infidelity).
5. *thrust . . . Sundays:* take on the burdens and tedium

of marriage, when you might be enjoying yourself as a
bachelor.
6. *so . . . uttered:* This is how Benedict would tell it.
7. In an English fairy tale (a variant on the Blue-
beard story), a man suspected by his bride-to-be of
having killed his former wives denies his guilt with
the refrain Benedict quotes.
8. His loyalty to both Don Pedro and Claudio and,
jokingly, his duplicity.

CLAUDIO   And never could maintain his part° but in the force   *argument*
of his will.[9]
BENEDICT   That a woman conceived me, I thank her; that she
brought me up, I likewise give her most humble thanks. But
205   that I will have a recheat winded in my forehead, or hang
my bugle in an invisible baldric,[1] all women shall pardon
me. Because I will not do them the wrong to mistrust any,[2]
I will do myself the right to trust none. And the fine° is (for   *conclusion*
the which I may go the finer[3]), I will live a bachelor.
210   PEDRO   I shall see thee, ere I die, look pale with love.
BENEDICT   With anger, with sickness, or with hunger, my
lord, not with love. Prove° that ever I lose more blood with   *If you prove*
love than I will get again with drinking,[4] pick out mine eyes
with a ballad-maker's[5] pen and hang me up at the door of a
215   brothel house for the sign of blind Cupid.[6]
PEDRO   Well, if ever thou dost fall from this faith, thou wilt
prove a notable argument.°   *subject of talk*
BENEDICT   If I do, hang me in a bottle like a cat and shoot at
me,[7] and he that hits me, let him be clapped on the shoulder
220   and called Adam.[8]
PEDRO   Well, as time shall try.° In time the savage bull doth   *prove*
bear the yoke.[9]
BENEDICT   The savage bull may, but if ever the sensible°   *rational*
Benedict bear it, pluck off the bull's horns and set them in
225   my forehead. And let me be vilely painted, and in such great
letters as they write, "Here is good horse to hire," let them
signify under my sign, "Here you may see Benedict, the
married man."
CLAUDIO   If this should ever happen, thou wouldst be horn-
230   mad.[1]
PEDRO   Nay, if Cupid have not spent all his quiver in Venice,[2]
thou wilt quake for this shortly.
BENEDICT   I look for an earthquake[3] too, then.
PEDRO   Well, you will temporize with the hours.[4] In the mean-
235   time, good Signor Benedict, repair° to Leonato's. Commend   *go*
me to him, and tell him I will not fail him at supper, for
indeed he hath made great preparation.
BENEDICT   I have almost matter° enough in me for such an   *intelligence*
embassage.° And so I commit you—   *errand*
240   CLAUDIO   To the tuition[5] of God. From my house, if I had it—

---

9. Through prideful obstinacy rather than reason.
1. *But . . . baldric:* But that I should wear a cuckold's
horns. A recheat was a call sounded ("winded") on a
horn to recall the hounds. A baldric was a belt to hold
a horn ("bugle"); it was invisible, a sign of the cuckold's ignorance.
2. Because I do not wish to wrong women by sus-
pecting any of infidelity.
3. I may dress better (because he will have more
money to spare).
4. *lose . . . drinking:* alluding to the belief that sighing like a lover caused the blood to evaporate, and
drinking wine renewed it.
5. Popular love poet or satirist.
6. A painted sign, such as might hang before a brothel.
7. *hang . . . me:* Cats in baskets ("bottles") were com-

mon Elizabethan targets for recreational archery.
8. Perhaps Adam Bell, a celebrated archer.
9. Proverbial; here, apparently a variation on a line
from Thomas Kyd's *Spanish Tragedy* (ca. 1587): "In
time the savage bull sustains the yoke" (2.1.3).
1. Furious; raving like a wild beast (referring to the
rage of a cuckolded husband).
2. Venice was famous in Shakespeare's time for its
beautiful courtesans. *spent all his quiver:* used all his
arrows, with sexual innuendo.
3. An earthquake would be as unlikely as my quak-
ing with love.
4. You will soften as time passes; with perhaps a bawdy
pun on "hours," "whores" (pronounced similarly).
5. Protection (Claudio and Don Pedro parody a conventional formula for ending a letter).

PEDRO   The sixth of July, your loving friend, Benedict.

BENEDICT   Nay, mock not, mock not. The body of your discourse is sometime guarded with fragments,[6] and the guards
are but slightly basted on,[7] neither. Ere you flout° old ends°   *mock / clichés*
245   any further, examine your conscience. And so I leave you.

                                                                Exit.

CLAUDIO   My liege, your highness now may do me good.

PEDRO   My love is thine to teach. Teach it but how,
And thou shalt see how apt it is to learn
Any hard lesson that may do thee good.

250   CLAUDIO   Hath Leonato any son, my lord?

PEDRO   No child but Hero. She's his only heir.
Dost thou affect° her, Claudio?   *love*

CLAUDIO   O my lord,
When you went onward on this ended action,°   *campaign*
I looked upon her with a soldier's eye
255   That liked, but had a rougher task in hand
Than to drive liking to the name of love.
But now I am returned and that° war thoughts   *now that*
Have left their places vacant—in their rooms
Come thronging soft and delicate desires,
260   All prompting me how fair young Hero is,
Saying, I liked her ere I went to wars—

PEDRO   Thou wilt be like a lover presently°   *shortly*
And tire the hearer with a book of words.°   *lover's set speeches*
If thou dost love fair Hero, cherish it,
265   And I will break° with her and with her father,   *speak*
And thou shalt have her. Was't not to this end
That thou began'st to twist° so fine a story?   *spin*

CLAUDIO   How sweetly you do minister to love
That know love's grief by his complexion!°   *by its appearance*
270   But lest my liking might too sudden seem,
I would have salved° it with a longer treatise.   *smoothed*

PEDRO   What need the bridge much broader than the flood?°   *river*
The fairest grant is the necessity.[8]
Look, what° will serve is fit. 'Tis once,° thou lovest,   *whatever / In brief*
275   And I will fit thee with the remedy.
I know we shall have reveling° tonight.   *festivity; masked ball*
I will assume thy part° in some disguise   *role*
And tell fair Hero I am Claudio,
And in her bosom I'll unclasp my heart[9]
280   And take her hearing prisoner with the force
And strong encounter of my amorous tale.
Then after, to her father will I break,
And the conclusion is, she shall be thine.
In practice let us put it presently.   *Exeunt.*

---

6. *The body . . . fragments:* The substance (also punning on the dressmaker's "bodice") of what you say is
sometimes ornamented ("guarded") with odds and
ends ("fragments") such as you are mocking me for
using.

7. And the decorative phrases are barely relevant.
8. The best gift is something that is truly needed.
9. And I will privately reveal to her my feelings (as if
I were you).

1.2

Enter LEONATO *and an old man* [ANTHONY], *brother
to* LEONATO.

LEONATO   How now, brother? Where is my cousin° your son?   *kinsman (nephew)*
Hath he provided this music?
ANTHONY   He is very busy about it. But brother, I can tell you
strange news that you yet dreamt not of.
5 LEONATO   Are they° good?   *(the news)*
ANTHONY   As the event stamps them.[1] But they have a good
cover; they show well outward. The Prince and Count Clau-
dio, walking in a thick pleached[2] alley in mine orchard,°   *garden*
were thus much overheard by a man of mine. The Prince
10 discovered° to Claudio that he loved my niece, your daugh-   *revealed*
ter, and meant to acknowledge it this night in a dance. And
if he found her accordant,° he meant to take the present   *consenting*
time by the top[3] and instantly break° with you of it.   *speak*
LEONATO   Hath the fellow any wit° that told you this?   *intelligence*
15 ANTHONY   A good sharp fellow. I will send for him, and question him yourself.
           [*Enter Attendants.*][4]
LEONATO   No, no. We will hold it as a dream till it appear°   *manifest*
itself. But I will acquaint my daughter withal,° that she may   *with it*
be the better prepared for an answer if, peradventure,° this   *by chance*
20 be true. Go you and tell her of it. [*to Attendants*] Cousins,
you know what you have to do. Oh, I cry you mercy,[5] friend.
Go you with me, and I will use your skill. Good cousin, have
a care this busy time.   *Exeunt.*

1.3

Enter Sir JOHN *the bastard, and* CONRAD
his companion.

CONRAD   What the good year, my lord! Why are you thus out
of measure[1] sad?
JOHN   There is no measure in the occasion that breeds. Therefore the sadness is without limit.
5 CONRAD   You should hear reason.
JOHN   And when I have heard it, what blessing brings it?
CONRAD   If not a present° remedy, at least a patient suffer-   *immediate*
ance.
JOHN   I wonder that thou, being as thou sayest thou art, born
10 under Saturn,[2] goest about to apply a moral medicine to a
mortifying mischief.° I cannot hide what I am. I must be sad   *deadly sickness*
when I have cause and smile at no man's jests; eat when I
have stomach° and wait for no man's leisure; sleep when I   *appetite*
am drowsy and tend on° no man's business; laugh when I am   *attend to*
15 merry and claw° no man in his humor.°   *flatter / mood*

1.2 Location: Leonato's house.
1. As good as the outcome ("event") proves ("stamps")
them. The image is of news bound in a book with a
handsome cover.
2. Enclosed by trees with intertwining boughs.
3. He meant to seize the opportunity. (Time is proverbially bald except for the "top," or forelock.)
4. The attendants are evidently engaged in preparations for the reveling (2.1). "Cousins" (line 20) may
refer to dependents in Leonato's household.

5. I beg your pardon (perhaps because he has not
initially recognized one of the attendants, or
because he has bumped into him). Leonato's reference to "skill" suggests that he might be talking to a
musician.
1.3 Location: Scene continues.
1. *What the good year:* What the devil. *out of measure:*
disproportionately.
2. Born when Saturn was in the ascendant (therefore "saturnine," meaning melancholy).

CONRAD Yea, but you must not make the full show of this till
you may do it without controlment.° You have of late stood out°   restraint / rebelled
against your brother, and he hath ta'en you newly into his
grace,° where it is impossible you should take true root but   favor
20   by the fair weather that you make yourself. It is needful that
you frame the season for your own harvest.

JOHN I had rather be a canker° in a hedge than a rose³ in his   wild rose; weed
grace. And it better fits my blood° to be disdained of all than   disposition
to fashion° a carriage° to rob love from any. In this, though I   affect; feign / behavior
25   cannot be said to be a flattering honest man, it must not be
denied but I am a plain-dealing villain. I am trusted with a
muzzle and enfranchised with a clog;⁴ therefore I have
decreed° not to sing in my cage. If I had my mouth, I would   determined
bite. If I had my liberty, I would do my liking. In the mean-
30   time, let me be that I am, and seek not to alter me.

CONRAD Can you make no use of your discontent?

JOHN I make all use of it, for I use it only.

    Enter BORACHIO.⁵

Who comes here? What news, Borachio?

BORACHIO I came yonder from a great supper. The Prince
35   your brother is royally entertained by Leonato, and I can
give you intelligence of an intended marriage.

JOHN Will it serve for any model° to build mischief on? What   ground plan
is he for a fool⁶ that betroths himself to unquietness?

BORACHIO Marry,⁷ it is your brother's right hand.

40 JOHN Who? The most exquisite Claudio?

BORACHIO Even he.

JOHN A proper squire!⁸ And who? And who? Which way looks
he?

BORACHIO Marry, one Hero, the daughter and heir of
45   Leonato.

JOHN A very forward March-chick.⁹ How came you to this?

BORACHIO Being entertained for a perfumer¹—as I was smok-
ing° a musty room—comes me the Prince and Claudio, hand   perfuming
in hand, in sad° conference. I whipped me behind the arras°   serious / wall hanging
50   and there heard it agreed upon that the Prince should woo
Hero for himself, and, having obtained her, give her to
Count Claudio.

JOHN Come, come, let us thither. This may prove food to my
displeasure.° That young start-up° hath all the glory of my   hatred / upstart
55   overthrow. If I can cross² him any way, I bless myself every
way. You are both sure,° and will assist me?   reliable

CONRAD To the death, my Lord.

JOHN Let us to the great supper. Their cheer is the greater
that° I am subdued. Would the cook were o'my mind!³ Shall   since
60   we go prove° what's to be done?   find out

BORACHIO We'll wait° upon your lordship.   *Exeunt.*   attend

---

3. Cultivated rose.
4. I am trusted by being muzzled (in other words, not
trusted at all) and given my freedom with a clog (a
heavy block of wood attached to an animal or man as
a restraint).
5. The name derives from the Spanish for "drunkard" or "wine bottle."
6. What kind of fool is he.

7. By the Virgin Mary (a mild oath).
8. A fine young lover (ironic).
9. Precocious youngster, like a bird hatched early in
the season.
1. Being hired to burn sweet herbs (to mask unpleasant domestic odors).
2. Thwart (punning on "make the sign of the cross").
3. *o'my mind:* inclined to poison the food.

2.1

Enter LEONATO, *his brother* [ANTHONY], *his wife,*
HERO *his daughter, and* BEATRICE *his niece,* [URSULA,
MARGARET,] *and a kinsman.*

LEONATO Was not Count John here at supper?

ANTHONY I saw him not.

BEATRICE How tartly° that gentleman looks! I never can see   *sour*
him, but I am heartburned[1] an hour after.

5 HERO He is of a very melancholy disposition.

BEATRICE He were° an excellent man that were made just in   *would be*
the midway between him and Benedict. The one is too like
an image° and says nothing, and the other too like my lady's   *a statue*
eldest son,[2] evermore tattling.°   *chattering*

10 LEONATO Then half Signor Benedict's tongue in Count John's
mouth, and half Count John's melancholy in Signor Benedict's face—

BEATRICE With a good leg and a good foot, uncle, and money
enough in his purse, such a man would win any woman in

15 the world, if 'a° could get her goodwill.   *he*

LEONATO By my troth, niece, thou wilt never get thee a husband if thou be so shrewd° of thy tongue.   *shrewish*

ANTHONY In faith, she's too curst.°   *sharp-tongued*

BEATRICE Too curst is more[3] than curst. I shall lessen God's

20 sending that way, for it is said, "God sends a curst cow short
horns,[4] but to a cow too curst, he sends none."

LEONATO So, by being too curst, God will send you no horns?

BEATRICE Just,° if he send me no husband,[5] for the which   *Just so*
blessing I am at him upon my knees every morning and eve-

25 ning. Lord, I could not endure a husband with a beard on
his face. I had rather lie in the woolen![6]

LEONATO You may light on a husband that hath no beard.

BEATRICE What should I do with him? Dress him in my
apparel and make him my waiting-gentlewoman? He that

30 hath a beard is more than a youth, and he that hath no
beard is less than a man; and he that is more than a youth is
not for me, and he that is less than a man, I am not for him.
Therefore, I will even take sixpence in earnest of the bear-
ward and lead his apes into hell.[7]

35 LEONATO Well, then, go you into hell?

BEATRICE No, but° to the gate, and there will the devil meet   *only*
me, like an old cuckold with horns on his head, and say,
"Get you to heaven, Beatrice, get you to heaven! Here's no
place for you maids." So deliver I up my apes and away to

40 Saint Peter for the heavens.[8] He shows me where the bachelors[9] sit, and there live we, as merry as the day is long.

ANTHONY [*to* HERO] Well, niece, I trust you will be ruled by
your father.

2.1 Location: Leonato's house.
1. I suffer from heartburn, caused by Don John's tart
looks.
2. That is, a spoiled child.
3. By one, punning on "too/two."
4. Proverbial: God makes sure that the vicious
("curst") have little power to do harm.
5. That is, if God sent her a husband, she would cuckold him.

6. Sleep between rough blankets (without sheets).
7. *take . . . hell:* take advance payment from the bear-
keeper (who trained bears for the popular sport of
bearbaiting and who usually had charge of other animals); leading apes into hell was the proverbial fate
of old maids.
8. Peter is gatekeeper of heaven. *for the heavens:* as
far as heaven is concerned.
9. Unwed men or women.

BEATRICE   Yes, faith. It is my cousin's duty to make curtsy and
45   say, "Father, as it please you." But yet, for all that, cousin, let
him be a handsome fellow or else make another curtsy and
say, "Father, as it please me."
LEONATO   Well, niece, I hope to see you one day fitted with a
husband.
50   BEATRICE   Not till God make men of some other metal than
earth. Would it not grieve a woman to be overmastered
with° a piece of valiant dust? To make an account of her life   *by*
to a clod of wayward marl?° No, uncle, I'll none. Adam's   *clay*
sons are my brethren, and, truly, I hold it a sin to match in
55   my kindred.[1]
LEONATO   Daughter, remember what I told you. If the Prince
do solicit you in that kind,[2] you know your answer.
BEATRICE   The fault will be in the music, cousin, if you be not
wooed in good time. If the Prince be too important,° tell   *importunate*
60   him there is measure[3] in everything, and so dance out the
answer. For hear me, Hero: wooing, wedding, and repenting is as a Scotch jig, a measure, and a cinquepace.[4] The
first suit° is hot and hasty like a Scotch jig and full as fantas-   *courtship*
tical; the wedding, mannerly° modest as a measure, full of   *graciously*
65   state and ancientry;° and then comes Repentance, and with   *old-fashioned decorum*
his bad legs falls into the cinquepace, faster and faster, till
he sink into his grave.
LEONATO   Cousin, you apprehend passing° shrewdly.   *understand more than*
BEATRICE   I have a good eye, uncle. I can see a church by
70   daylight.[5]
LEONATO   The revelers are entering, brother. Make good
room.
        Enter Prince PEDRO, CLAUDIO, *and* BENEDICT, *and*
        BALTHASAR, *and Don* JOHN[, *and* BORACHIO,
        wearing masks].
PEDRO   Lady, will you walk about with your friend?[6]
HERO   So you walk softly, and look sweetly, and say nothing, I
75   am yours for the walk, and especially when I walk away.
PEDRO   With me in your company.
HERO   I may say so when I please.
PEDRO   And when please you to say so?
HERO   When I like your favor,° for God defend the lute should   *face*
80   be like the case.[7]
PEDRO   My visor° is Philemon's roof. Within the house is   *mask*
Jove.[8]
HERO   Why, then, your visor should be thatched.[9]
PEDRO   Speak low, if you speak love.
        [*They step aside.*]

---

1. *match in my kindred:* marry incestuously.
2. *in that kind:* that is, to marry him.
3. Moderation (punning on the name of a slow, stately dance [line 62] and continuing the link between dancing and wooing "in good time" [line 59]).
4. A lively five-step dance.
5. That is, see what's in front of me.
6. *friend:* often used to mean "lover." *walk about:* take a turn (apparently a term in dancing).
7. God forbid your face should be as unappealing as your mask.
8. The peasant Philemon and his wife, Baucis, entertained Jove, disguised, in their humble cottage (Ovid, *Metamorphoses* 8).
9. According to Golding, Philemon's roof was "thatched all with straw"; Hero means that the mask should be fitted with false hair or beard.

85 BALTHASAR [*to* MARGARET] Well, I would you did like me.[1]

MARGARET So would not I, for your own sake, for I have
many ill° qualities.   *bad*

BALTHASAR Which is one?

MARGARET I say my prayers aloud.

90 BALTHASAR I love you the better. The hearers may cry
"Amen."

MARGARET God match me with a good dancer.

BALTHASAR Amen.

MARGARET And God keep him out of my sight when the
95   dance is done. Answer, clerk![2]

BALTHASAR No more words. The clerk is answered.

URSULA [*to* ANTHONY] I know you well enough. You are Signor
Anthonio.

ANTHONY At a word,° I am not.   *In short*

100 URSULA I know you by the waggling of your head.

ANTHONY To tell you true, I counterfeit him.

URSULA You could never do him so ill-well[3] unless you were
the very man. Here's his dry hand up and down.[4] You are he!
You are he!

105 ANTHONY At a word, I am not.

URSULA Come, come, do you think I do not know you by your
excellent wit? Can virtue° hide itself? Go to! Mum,° you are   *excellence / Be quiet*
he. Graces will appear, and there's an end.[5]

BEATRICE [*to* BENEDICT] Will you not tell me who told
110   you so?

BENEDICT No, you shall pardon me.

BEATRICE Nor will you not tell me who you are?

BENEDICT Not now.

BEATRICE That I was disdainful, and that I had my good wit
115   out of the *Hundred Merry Tales*?[6] Well, this was Signor
Benedict that said so.

BENEDICT What's he?

BEATRICE I am sure you know him well enough.

BENEDICT Not I, believe me.

120 BEATRICE Did he never make you laugh?

BENEDICT I pray you, what is he?

BEATRICE Why, he is the Prince's jester. A very dull fool, only
his° gift is in devising impossible° slanders. None but liber-   *his only / unbelievable*
tines delight in him, and the commendation is not in his
125   wit, but in his villainy,° for he both pleases men and angers   *rudeness*
them. And then they laugh at him and beat him. I am sure
he is in the fleet.° I would he had boarded me.[7]   *company (of dancers)*

BENEDICT When I know the gentleman, I'll tell him what you
say.

---

1. TEXTUAL COMMENT In the original quarto, lines 85, 88, and 90 are spoken by Benedict, but because various problems arise in staging the scene when Benedict speaks the lines, editors have traditionally reassigned them to Balthasar. See Digital Edition TC 2.
2. That is, say "Amen" again. The parish clerk led the

responses in church services.
3. *do him so ill-well*: mime his imperfections so ably.
4. His wrinkled hand exactly.
5. And that is all there is to be said.
6. A famously bad joke-book, first published in 1526.
7. Assaulted me like a ship.

130 BEATRICE   Do, do. He'll but break a comparison[8] or two on
me, which, peradventure,° not marked, or not laughed at,   *perhaps*
strikes him into melancholy. And then there's a partridge
wing saved, for the fool will eat no supper that night. We
must follow the leaders.°   *leaders in the dance*
135 BENEDICT   In every good thing.
BEATRICE   Nay, if they lead to any ill I will leave them at the
next turning.

        [*They*] *dance* [*and all but* JOHN, CLAUDIO, *and*
                        BORACHIO] *exeunt.*

JOHN [*to* BORACHIO]   Sure, my brother is amorous on Hero
and hath withdrawn her father to break° with him about it.   *speak*
140 The ladies follow her, and but one visor° remains.   *(man wearing a) mask*
BORACHIO   And that is Claudio. I know him by his bearing.
JOHN [*to* CLAUDIO]   Are not you Signor Benedict?
CLAUDIO   You know me well. I am he.
JOHN   Signor, you are very near my brother in his love.° He is   *favor*
145 enamored on Hero. I pray you, dissuade him from her. She
is no equal for his birth. You may do the part of an honest
man in it.
CLAUDIO   How know you he loves her?
JOHN   I heard him swear his affection.
150 BORACHIO   So did I too, and he swore he would marry her
tonight.
JOHN   Come, let us to the banquet.°   *after-dinner sweets*

       Exeunt JOHN *and* BORACHIO. CLAUDIO *remains.*

CLAUDIO   Thus answer I in name of Benedict
But hear these ill news with the ears of Claudio.
155 'Tis certain° so. The Prince woos for himself.   *certainly*
Friendship is constant in all other things
Save in the office° and affairs of love.   *business*
Therefore all° hearts in love use their own tongues.   *let all*
Let every eye negotiate for itself
160 And trust no agent. For beauty is a witch
Against whose charms faith° melteth into blood.°   *loyalty / passion*
This is an accident of hourly proof[9]
Which I mistrusted° not. Farewell, therefore, Hero.   *suspected*

      Enter BENEDICT.

BENEDICT   Count Claudio?
165 CLAUDIO   Yea, the same.
BENEDICT   Come, will you go with me?
CLAUDIO   Whither?
BENEDICT   Even to the next willow[1] about your own business,
County.° What fashion will you wear the garland° of? About   *Count / (of willow)*
170 your neck, like an usurer's chain?[2] Or under your arm, like a
lieutenant's scarf?[3] You must wear it one° way, for the Prince   *some*
hath got your Hero.
CLAUDIO   I wish him joy of her.

---

8. He'll only try out, or "crack," a satirical comparison (as one "breaks" a lance).
9. An occurrence demonstrated every hour; a common event.

1. Symbol of unrequited love.
2. A gold chain worn by a moneylender.
3. A sash draped across the chest.

BENEDICT   Why, that's spoken like an honest drover;° so they   *cattle dealer*
175   sell bullocks. But did you think the Prince would have
served you thus?
CLAUDIO   I pray you, leave me.
BENEDICT   Ho, now! You strike like the blind man. 'Twas the
boy that stole your meat, and you'll beat the post.[4]
180   CLAUDIO   If it° will not be, I'll leave you.   *Exit.*   *(your departure)*
BENEDICT   Alas, poor hurt fowl! Now will he creep into
sedges.[5] But that my lady Beatrice should know me and not
know me! The Prince's fool? Hah! It may be I go under that
title because I am merry. Yea, but so I am apt to do myself
185   wrong. I am not so reputed. It is the base, though bitter,
disposition of Beatrice that puts the world into her person
and so gives me out.[6] Well, I'll be revenged as I may.
Enter [PEDRO] the Prince.
PEDRO   Now signor, where's the Count? Did you see him?
BENEDICT   Troth, my lord, I have played the part of Lady
190   Fame.° I found him here as melancholy as a lodge in a war-   *Lady Rumor*
ren.[7] I told him, and I think I told him true, that your grace
had got the goodwill of this young lady, and I offered him
my company to a willow tree, either to make him a garland,
as being forsaken, or to bind him up a rod,° as being worthy   *bundle of sticks*
195   to be whipped.
PEDRO   To be whipped? What's his fault?
BENEDICT   The flat° transgression of a schoolboy, who, being   *stupid*
overjoyed with finding a birds' nest, shows it his companion,
and he steals it.
200   PEDRO   Wilt thou make a trust a transgression? The transgression is in the stealer.
BENEDICT   Yet it had not been amiss the rod had been made,
and the garland, too. For the garland he might have worn
himself, and the rod he might have bestowed on you, who,
205   as I take it, have stolen his birds' nest.
PEDRO   I will but teach them to sing and restore them to the
owner.
BENEDICT   If their singing answer your saying, by my faith,
you say honestly.[8]
210   PEDRO   The lady Beatrice hath a quarrel to° you. The gentle-   *with*
man that danced with her told her she is much wronged by
you.
BENEDICT   Oh, she misused° me past the endurance of a block!   *abused*
An oak but with one green leaf on it[9] would have answered
215   her. My very visor began to assume life and scold with her.
She told me, not thinking I had been myself, that I was the
Prince's jester; that I was duller than a great thaw[1]—huddling
jest upon jest with such impossible conveyance° upon me   *speed*

---

4. Probably alluding to a folktale, which existed in various forms, of a boy who robbed and played a trick on his blind master. *post:* pillar (with play on Benedict as the "post," or messenger, who bears bad news).
5. *creep into sedges:* hide to nurse his wounds, as an injured bird crawls into the tall grass along a riverbank.
6. It is Beatrice's low but sarcastic disposition that

makes her believe the whole world is of her opinion and represents me accordingly.
7. A burrow in a rabbit warren. (The rabbit was a traditional symbol of melancholy.)
8. If they sing as you say they will—if you have wooed Hero for Claudio—then you are talking honorably.
9. An oak with barely any life remaining in it.
1. When the muddy roads kept everyone at home.

that I stood like a man at a mark° with a whole army shoot-   target
220 ing at me. She speaks poniards° and every word stabs. If her   daggers
breath were as terrible as her terminations,° there were no   expressions
living near her; she would infect to the north star.[2] I would
not marry her though she were endowed with all that Adam
had left him° before he transgressed. She would have made   (the whole world)
225 Hercules have turned spit, yea, and have cleft his club to
make the fire, too.[3] Come, talk not of her. You shall find her
the infernal Ate° in good apparel. I would to God some   goddess of discord
scholar would conjure[4] her, for certainly, while she is here a
man may live as quiet in hell as in a sanctuary, and people
230 sin upon purpose because they would go thither. So indeed
all disquiet, horror, and perturbation follows° her.   attends upon
            Enter CLAUDIO *and* BEATRICE[, HERO, *and* LEONATO].
PEDRO   Look! Here she comes.
BENEDICT   Will your grace command me any service to the
world's end? I will go on the slightest errand now to the
235 Antipodes° that you can devise to send me on. I will fetch   other side of the world
you a tooth-picker,° now, from the furthest inch of Asia;   toothpick
bring you the length of Prester John's foot; fetch you a hair
off the great Cham's beard; do you any embassage to the
pigmies,[5] rather than hold three words' conference with this
240 harpy.[6] You have no employment for me?
PEDRO   None, but to desire your good company.
BENEDICT   O God, sir! Here's a dish I love not. I cannot
endure my Lady Tongue.   *Exit.*
PEDRO   Come, lady, come! You have lost the heart of Signor
245 Benedict.
BEATRICE   Indeed, my lord, he lent it me awhile, and I gave
him use° for it: a double heart for his single one. Marry,   interest
once before he won it of° me with false dice. Therefore your   from
grace may well say I have lost it.[7]
250 PEDRO   You have put him down, lady. You have put him down.[8]
BEATRICE   So I would not he should do me, my lord, lest I
should prove the mother of fools. I have brought Count Claudio, whom you sent me to seek.
PEDRO   Why, how now, Count? Wherefore are you sad?
255 CLAUDIO   Not sad, my lord.
PEDRO   How then? Sick?
CLAUDIO   Neither, my lord.
BEATRICE   The Count is neither sad, nor sick, nor merry, nor
well, but civil,° Count, civil as an orange,[9] and something°   serious / somewhat
260 of that jealous complexion.[1]

2. Thought to be the remotest star.
3. The Amazon Omphale made Hercules, a Greek
hero, wear her clothes and spin; Benedict imagines
an even greater humiliation and more menial duty—
turning the spit.
4. Conjure the evil spirits out of, or supernaturally
consign to hell. *scholar:* learned person (who could
speak Latin, the language of exorcism).
5. *Prester John's . . . pigmies:* all distant, fantastic figures. In legend, Prester John ruled in Ethiopia, while
the Great Cham (Kublai Khan) reigned in Mongolia,
and a race of dwarfs was said to inhabit the mountains of India.
6. Mythical creature with the face and body of a
woman and the wings and claws of a bird of prey.
7. PERFORMANCE COMMENT How and to whom Beatrice discloses her past romantic attachment to Benedict can influence the tone of a production. See
Digital Edition PC 1.
8. Humiliated him. (Beatrice, in reply, puns on the
physical sense of "put down".)
9. Punning on "Seville," famous for its bitter oranges.
1. Yellow (the traditional color of jealousy).

PEDRO   I'faith, lady, I think your blazon° to be true; though   *formal description*
I'll be sworn, if he be so, his conceit° is false. Here, Claudio,   *imagined idea*
I have wooed in thy name, and fair Hero is won. I have
broke° with her father, and his goodwill obtained. Name the   *negotiated*
265   day of marriage, and God give thee joy.
LEONATO   Count, take of me my daughter, and with her my
fortunes. His grace hath made the match, and all grace say
amen to it.[2]
BEATRICE   Speak, Count. 'Tis your cue.
270   CLAUDIO   Silence is the perfectest herald of joy. I were but
little happy if I could say how much. Lady, as you are mine,
I am yours. I give away myself for you and dote upon the
exchange.
BEATRICE [*to* HERO]   Speak, cousin! Or if you cannot, stop his
275   mouth with a kiss and let not him speak neither.
PEDRO   In faith, lady, you have a merry heart.
BEATRICE   Yea, my lord, I thank it. Poor fool, it keeps on the
windy° side of care. My cousin tells him in his ear that he is   *windward; safe*
in her heart.
280   CLAUDIO   And so she doth, cousin.
BEATRICE   Good Lord, for alliance![3] Thus goes everyone to
the world but I, and I am sunburnt.[4] I may sit in a corner
and cry, "Heigh ho, for a husband!"[5]
PEDRO   Lady Beatrice, I will get you one.
285   BEATRICE   I would rather have one of your father's getting.°   *begetting*
Hath your grace ne'er a° brother like you? Your father got   *no*
excellent husbands, if a maid could come by them.
PEDRO   Will you have me, lady?
BEATRICE   No, my lord, unless I might have another for work-
290   ing days. Your grace is too costly to wear every day. But I
beseech your grace, pardon me. I was born to speak all
mirth and no matter.°[6]   *substance*
PEDRO   Your silence most offends me, and to be merry best
becomes you. For out o'question, you were born in a merry
295   hour.
BEATRICE   No, sure, my lord, my mother cried. But then there
was a star danced, and under that was I born. Cousins, God
give you joy.
LEONATO   Niece, will you look to those things I told you of?
300   BEATRICE   I cry you mercy,° uncle. [*to* PEDRO] By your grace's   *I beg your pardon*
pardon.   *Exit* BEATRICE.
PEDRO   By my troth, a pleasant-spirited lady.
LEONATO   There's little of the melancholy element in her, my
lord. She is never sad° but when she sleeps, and not ever°   *serious / not always*
305   sad then. For I have heard my daughter say she hath often
dreamt of unhappiness and waked herself with laughing.
PEDRO   She cannot endure to hear tell of a husband.

---

2. May God, the source of all grace, confirm it.
3. Kinship through marriage. (Claudio has just addressed Beatrice as one of the family.)
4. Unattractive, and therefore unlikely to marry. (Suntans, like dark complexions, were unfashionable.) *goes . . . to the world:* gets married.

5. Title of a ballad; probably a catchphrase in Shakespeare's time.
6. PERFORMANCE COMMENT Don Pedro's marriage offer, and Beatrice's quick refusal, can be played sincerely or as repartee. See Digital Edition PC 2.

LEONATO   Oh, by no means. She mocks all her wooers out of
suit.°   *wooing (her)*
310 PEDRO   She were an excellent wife for Benedict.
LEONATO   O Lord! My lord, if they were but a week married
they would talk themselves mad.
PEDRO   County Claudio, when mean you to go to church?
CLAUDIO   Tomorrow, my lord. Time goes on crutches till Love
315 have all his rites.
LEONATO   Not till Monday, my dear son, which is hence a just
seven-night. And a time too brief, too, to have all things
answer° my mind.°   *match / wishes*
PEDRO   Come, you shake the head at so long a breathing,° but   *interval*
320 I warrant° thee, Claudio, the time shall not go dully by us. I   *assure*
will, in the interim, undertake one of Hercules' labors,[7]
which is, to bring Signor Benedict and the lady Beatrice into
a mountain of affection, th'one with th'other. I would fain°   *gladly*
have it a match, and I doubt not but to fashion it, if you
325 three will but minister such assistance as I shall give you
direction.
LEONATO   My lord, I am for you, though it cost me ten nights'
watchings.°   *staying awake*
CLAUDIO   And I, my lord.
330 PEDRO   And you too, gentle Hero?
HERO   I will do any modest office,° my lord, to help my cousin   *task*
to a good husband.
PEDRO   And Benedict is not the unhopefullest° husband that   *least promising*
I know. Thus far can I praise him. He is of a noble strain,° of   *descent*
335 approved° valor, and confirmed honesty.° [*to* HERO] I will   *proven / honor*
teach you how to humor your cousin, that she shall fall in
love with Benedict. [*to* CLAUDIO *and* LEONATO] And I, with
your two helps, will so practice on° Benedict that in despite   *trick*
of his quick wit and his queasy stomach,° he shall fall in love   *qualms (about love)*
340 with Beatrice. If we can do this, Cupid is no longer an
archer. His glory shall be ours, for we are the only love gods.
Go in with me, and I will tell you my drift.°   *Exeunt.*   *scheme*

2.2

Enter JOHN *and* BORACHIO.

JOHN   It is so. The Count Claudio shall marry the daughter of
Leonato.
BORACHIO   Yea, my lord. But I can cross° it.   *thwart*
JOHN   Any bar, any cross, any impediment will be medicinable°   *therapeutic*
5   to me. I am sick in displeasure to him, and whatsoever comes
athwart his affection ranges evenly with mine.[1] How canst
thou cross this marriage?
BORACHIO   Not honestly, my lord, but so covertly that no dishonesty shall appear in me.
10   JOHN   Show me briefly how.
BORACHIO   I think I told your lordship, a year since, how
much I am in the favor of Margaret, the waiting-
gentlewoman to Hero.

---

7. Hercules performed twelve tasks, or labors, of   1. Whatever frustrates his wishes conforms with
extraordinary difficulty.   mine.
2.2 Location: Scene continues.

JOHN I remember.

15 BORACHIO I can, at any unseasonable instant° of the night,   *any time whatever*
appoint° her to look out at her lady's chamber window.   *arrange with*

JOHN What life is in that to be the death of this marriage?

BORACHIO The poison of that lies in you to temper.° Go you   *concoct*
to the Prince your brother. Spare not to tell him that he

20 hath wronged his honor in marrying the renowned Claudio,
whose estimation° do you mightily hold up,° to a contami-   *reputation / defend*
nated stale,° such a one as Hero.   *prostitute*

JOHN What proof shall I make of that?

BORACHIO Proof enough to misuse° the Prince, to vex° Clau-   *deceive / torment*

25 dio, to undo Hero, and kill Leonato. Look you for any other
issue?°   *result*

JOHN Only to despite° them I will endeavor anything.   *Merely to spite*

BORACHIO Go, then. Find me a meet hour to draw Don Pedro
and the Count Claudio alone. Tell them that you know that

30 Hero loves me. Intend° a kind of zeal both to the Prince and   *Pretend*
Claudio, as in° love of your brother's honor, who hath made   *as if for*
this match, and his friend's reputation, who is thus like to
be cozened with the semblance of a maid,[2] that you have discovered thus. They will scarcely believe this without trial.°   *proof*

35 Offer them instances, which shall bear no less likelihood
than to see me at her chamber window; hear me call Margaret, Hero; hear Margaret term me, Claudio;[3] and bring them
to see this the very night before the intended wedding. For in
the meantime, I will so fashion the matter that Hero shall be

40 absent, and there shall appear such seeming truth of Hero's
disloyalty that jealousy shall be called assurance,[4] and all
the preparation° overthrown.   *wedding preparation*

JOHN Grow this° to what adverse issue it can, I will put it in   *Let this lead*
practice. Be cunning in the working this,° and thy fee is a   *of this*

45 thousand ducats.°   ⸿   *gold coins*

BORACHIO Be you constant in the accusation, and my cunning
shall not shame me.

JOHN I will presently go learn their day of marriage.

Exeunt.

2.3

Enter BENEDICT *alone.*

BENEDICT Boy!

[*Enter* BOY.]

BOY Signor?

BENEDICT In my chamber window lies a book. Bring it hither
to me, in the orchard.

5 BOY I am here already,[1] sir.

BENEDICT I know that, but I would have thee hence, and here
again.

Exit [BOY].

---

2. To be cheated with the mere appearance of a
virgin.
3. TEXTUAL COMMENT Most editors assume an error
in the Quarto here and emend to "Borachio," but this
edition follows the Quarto. See Digital Edition TC 3.

4. That suspicion shall be called certainty.
2.3 Location: Leonato's garden.
1. That is, it's as good as done. (Benedict takes him
literally.)

I do much wonder that one man, seeing how much another
man is a fool when he dedicates his behaviors to love, will,
10 after he hath laughed at such shallow follies in others, become
the argument° of his own scorn by falling in love; and such   *subject*
a man is Claudio. I have known when there was no music
with him but the drum and the fife, and now had he rather
hear the tabor and the pipe.[2] I have known when he would
15 have walked ten mile afoot to see a good armor,° and now will   *suit of armor*
he lie ten nights awake, carving° the fashion of a new dou-   *designing*
blet.° He was wont° to speak plain and to the purpose, like   *jacket / accustomed*
an honest man and a soldier; and now is he turned orthogra-
phy.[3] His words are a very fantastical° banquet: just so many   *poetic*
20 strange dishes. May I be so converted and see° with these   *still see*
eyes? I cannot tell; I think not. I will not be sworn but love
may transform me to an oyster; but I'll take my oath on it, till
he have made an oyster of me, he shall never make me such
a fool. One woman is fair, yet I am well; another is wise, yet
25 I am well; another virtuous, yet I am well. But till all graces
be in one woman, one woman shall not come in my grace.°   *favor*
Rich she shall be, that's certain; wise, or I'll none;[4] virtuous,
or I'll never cheapen° her; fair, or I'll never look on her; mild,   *bargain for*
or come not near me; noble, or not I for an angel;[5] of good
30 discourse, an excellent musician, and her hair shall be of
what color it please God. Ha! The Prince and Monsieur Love!
I will hide me in the arbor.

     Enter Prince [PEDRO], LEONATO, CLAUDIO. [MUSICIANS
     play within.][6]

PEDRO   Come, shall we hear this music?
CLAUDIO   Yea, my good lord. How still the evening is,
35 As° hushed on purpose to grace harmony!   *As if*
PEDRO   See you where Benedict hath hid himself?
CLAUDIO   Oh, very well, my lord. The music ended,°   *Once the music is over*
  We'll fit the kid-fox with a pennyworth.[7]

     Enter BALTHASAR *with* [*the* MUSICIANS].

PEDRO   Come, Balthasar, we'll hear that song again.
40 BALTHASAR   Oh, good my lord, tax° not so bad a voice   *task*
  To slander music any more than once.
PEDRO   It is the witness still of excellency,
  To put a strange face on his own perfection.[8]
  I pray thee, sing, and let me woo° no more.   *cajole*
45 BALTHASAR   Because you talk of wooing[9] I will sing,
  Since many a wooer doth commence his suit
  To her he thinks not worthy. Yet he woos,
  Yet will he swear he loves.
PEDRO   Nay, pray thee, come,

---

2. The drum and fife were used by the military; the tabor (a small drum) and pipe were used in social festivities.
3. Become overelaborate in his speech.
4. I'll have none (of her).
5. Not I, though she be an angel (punning on coins: an angel was worth 10 shillings, and a noble 6 shillings 8 pence).
6. TEXTUAL COMMENT The cues for music in the Quarto edition are somewhat confusing and require editorial intervention. Examining the original cues

and how editors revise them can help readers think about how musical performance is staged in this play. See Digital Edition TC 4.
7. We'll give our young cub more than he bargained for. *kid-fox:* apparently refers to a young fox; this is the only listed usage in the *OED.*
8. *It is the witness . . . perfection:* It is always the mark of great skill to deny its own proficiency.
9. Because you put it in terms of wooing (and so are likely to continue to flatter me insincerely).

Or if thou wilt hold longer argument,
Do it in notes.°   *music*

50 BALTHASAR   Note this before my notes:
There's not a note of mine that's worth the noting.

PEDRO   Why, these are very crochets[1] that he speaks:
Note notes, forsooth, and nothing.[2]

BENEDICT [*aside*]   Now, divine air, now is his soul ravished. Is
55 it not strange that sheeps' guts[3] should hale° souls out of men's   *drag*
bodies? Well, a horn[4] for my money, when all's done.

The Song.

BALTHASAR [*sings*]   Sigh no more, ladies, sigh no more.
           Men were deceivers ever,
           One foot in sea, and one on shore,
           To one thing constant never.
60   Then sigh not so, but let them go,
           And be you blithe and bonny,°   *beautiful*
           Converting all your sounds of woe,
           Into hey nonny nonny.

65   Sing no more ditties, sing no more
           Of dumps[5] so dull and heavy,
           The fraud of men was ever so,
           Since summer first was leafy,
           Then sigh not so, &c.

70 PEDRO   By my troth, a good song.

BALTHASAR   And an ill singer, my lord.

PEDRO   Ha! No, no, faith, thou sing'st well enough for a shift.°   *to make do*

BENEDICT [*aside*]   An° he had been a dog that should have   *If*
howled thus they would have hanged him, and I pray God
75 his bad voice bode no mischief. I had as lief° have heard the   *gladly*
night raven,° come what plague could have come after it.   *bird of ill omen*

PEDRO   Yea, marry,[6] dost thou hear, Balthasar? I pray thee,
get us some excellent music, for tomorrow night we would
have it at the lady Hero's chamber window.

80 BALTHASAR   The best I can, my lord.

PEDRO   Do so. Farewell.   *Exit* BALTHASAR.
Come hither, Leonato. What was it you told me of today,
that your niece Beatrice was in love with Signor Benedict?

CLAUDIO [*aside*]   Oh, ay, stalk on, stalk on. The fowl sits.[7] [*He
85 raises his voice.*] I did never think that lady would have loved
any man.

LEONATO   No, nor I neither. But most wonderful° that she   *astounding*
should so dote on Signor Benedict, whom she hath in all
outward behaviors seemed ever to abhor.

90 BENEDICT [*aside*]   Is't possible? Sits the wind in that corner?

LEONATO   By my troth, my lord, I cannot tell what to think of
it. But that she loves him with an enraged° affection, it is   *violent*
past the infinite° of thought.   *furthest bounds*

---

1. Whimsies; quarter notes (in music).
2. *Note . . . nothing:* Get on with your singing, and nothing else. ("Nothing" and "noting" sounded the same in Elizabethan pronunciation. Compare the same play on words in the comedy's title.)
3. Used to string musical instruments.
4. Military or hunting horn.
5. Melancholy tunes or moods.
6. A mild oath. (Don Pedro is continuing the speech interrupted by Benedict's aside.)
7. *stalk . . . sits:* go on quietly. Our prey has alighted.

PEDRO   Maybe she doth but counterfeit.

95   CLAUDIO   Faith, like° enough.   *likely*

LEONATO   O God! Counterfeit? There was never counterfeit of passion came so near the life of passion as she discovers° it.   *exhibits*

PEDRO   Why? What effects of passion shows she?

100   CLAUDIO   [*aside*]   Bait the hook well. This fish will bite.

LEONATO   What effects, my lord? She will sit you[8]— [*to* CLAUDIO] You heard my daughter tell you how.

CLAUDIO   She did indeed.

PEDRO   How? How, I pray you? You amaze me. I would have
105   thought her spirit had been invincible against all assaults of affection.

LEONATO   I would have sworn it had, my lord, especially against Benedict.

BENEDICT   [*aside*]   I should think this a gull,° but that the   *trick*
110   white-bearded fellow speaks it. Knavery cannot, sure, hide himself in such reverence.

CLAUDIO   [*aside*]   He hath ta'en th'infection. Hold° it up.   *Keep*

PEDRO   Hath she made her affection known to Benedict?

LEONATO   No, and swears she never will. That's her torment.

115   CLAUDIO   'Tis true indeed, so your daughter says. "Shall I," says she, "that have so oft encountered him with scorn, write to him that I love him?"

LEONATO   This says she now when she is beginning to write to him. For she'll be up twenty times a night, and there will
120   she sit in her smock° till she have writ a sheet of paper. My   *slip*
daughter tells us all.

CLAUDIO   Now you talk of a sheet of paper, I remember a pretty jest your daughter told us of.

LEONATO   Oh, when she had writ it and was reading it over,
125   she found Benedict and Beatrice between the sheet.

CLAUDIO   That.

LEONATO   Oh, she tore the letter into a thousand halfpence;°   *small pieces*
railed at herself, that she should be so immodest to write to one that she knew would flout° her. "I measure him," says   *jeer at*
130   she, "by my own spirit. For I should flout him if he writ to me, yea, though I love him, I should."

CLAUDIO   Then down upon her knees she falls, weeps, sobs, beats her heart, tears her hair, prays, curses, "Oh, sweet Benedict! God give me patience."

135   LEONATO   She doth indeed. My daughter says so. And the ecstasy° hath so much overborne her that my daughter is   *passion*
sometime afeard she will do a desperate outrage° to herself.   *injury*
It is very true.

PEDRO   It were good that Benedict knew of it by some other, if
140   she will not discover° it.   *reveal*

CLAUDIO   To what end? He would make but a sport of it and torment the poor lady worse.

PEDRO   An he should, it were an alms° to hang him. She's an   *charitable deed*
excellent sweet lady, and, out of all suspicion,° she is virtuous.   *doubt*

---

8. She will sit down (i.e., weak with lovesickness).

145 CLAUDIO And she is exceeding wise—
 PEDRO In everything but in loving Benedict.
 LEONATO O my lord! Wisdom and blood° combating in so   *passion*
  tender a body, we have ten proofs to one that blood hath the
  victory. I am sorry for her, as I have just cause, being her
150 uncle and her guardian.
 PEDRO I would she had bestowed this dotage° on me. I would *infatuation*
  have daffed[9] all other respects° and made her half myself. I *considerations*
  pray you, tell Benedict of it, and hear what 'a° will say.   *he*
 LEONATO Were it good, think you?
155 CLAUDIO Hero thinks surely she will die. For, she says, she
  will die if he love her not; and she will die ere she make her
  love known; and she will die if he woo her, rather than she
  will bate° one breath of her accustomed crossness.° *abate / contrariness*
 PEDRO She doth well. If she should make tender° of her love, *make an offer*
160 'tis very possible he'll scorn it. For the man, as you know all,
  hath a contemptible° spirit.   *contemptuous*
 CLAUDIO He is a very proper° man.   *handsome*
 PEDRO He hath, indeed, a good outward happiness.[1]
 CLAUDIO Before God, and in my mind, very wise.
165 PEDRO He doth, indeed, show some sparks that are like wit.
 CLAUDIO And I take him to be valiant.
 PEDRO As Hector,[2] I assure you. And in the managing of
  quarrels you may say he is wise, for either he avoids them
  with great discretion, or undertakes them with a most
170 Christianlike fear.
 LEONATO If he do fear God, 'a must necessarily keep peace. If
  he break the peace, he ought to enter into a quarrel with
  fear and trembling.
 PEDRO And so will he do, for the man doth fear God, howso-
175 ever it seems not in him by some large° jests he will make. *improper*
  Well, I am sorry for your niece. Shall we go seek Benedict
  and tell him of her love?
 CLAUDIO Never tell him, my lord. Let her wear it out with
  good counsel.°   *advice*
180 LEONATO Nay, that's impossible. She may wear her heart out
  first.
 PEDRO Well, we will hear further of it by° your daughter. Let *from*
  it cool the while. I love Benedict well, and I could wish he
  would modestly examine himself to see how much he is
185 unworthy so good a lady.
 LEONATO My lord, will you walk? Dinner is ready.
 CLAUDIO [*aside*] If he do not dote on her upon this, I will
  never trust my expectation.°   *predictions*
 PEDRO [*aside*] Let there be the same net spread for her, and
190 that must your daughter and her gentlewomen carry.° The *manage*
  sport will be, when they hold one an opinion of another's
  dotage, and no such matter.[3] That's the scene that I would
  see, which will be merely a dumb show.[4] Let us send her to
  call him in to dinner.   [*Exeunt.* BENEDICT *remains.*]

---

9. Set aside or cast off.
1. He is well endowed with looks and bearing.
2. The noblest and bravest Trojan warrior in Homer's *Iliad*.

3. *when . . . matter:* when each believes that the other is madly in love, without any basis in fact.
4. Pantomime (because words for once will fail them).

195 BENEDICT This can be no trick. The conference was sadly
borne.° They have the truth of this from Hero. They seem to   *seriously conducted*
pity the lady; it seems her affections have their full bent.[5]
Love me? Why, it must be requited. I hear how I am censured. They say I will bear myself proudly if I perceive the
200 love come from her. They say, too, that she will rather die
than give any sign of affection. I did never think to marry. I
must not seem proud. Happy are they that hear their detrac-
tions and can put them to mending.° They say the lady is   *amending*
fair. 'Tis a truth; I can bear them witness. And virtuous? 'Tis
205 so, I cannot reprove° it. And wise, but for loving me. By my   *contradict*
troth, it is no addition to her wit,[6] nor no great argument of
her folly, for I will be horribly in love with her. I may chance
have some odd quirks° and remnants of wit broken on° me   *quips / cracked against*
because I have railed so long against marriage; but doth not
210 the appetite alter? A man loves the meat in his youth that he
cannot endure in his age. Shall quips, and sentences,° and   *epigrams*
these paper bullets of the brain awe a man from the career°   *swift course*
of his humor?° No, the world must be peopled. When I said   *liking*
I would die a bachelor, I did not think I should live till I were
215 married.
       Enter BEATRICE.
Here comes Beatrice. By this day, she's a fair lady. I do spy
some marks of love in her.
BEATRICE Against my will, I am sent to bid you come in to
dinner.
220 BENEDICT Fair Beatrice, I thank you for your pains.
BEATRICE I took no more pains for those thanks than you
take pains to thank me. If it had been painful, I would not
have come.
BENEDICT You take pleasure, then, in the message?
225 BEATRICE Yea, just so much as you may take upon a knife's
point and choke a daw withal.° You have no stomach,° signor?   *jackdaw with / appetite*
Fare you well.   *Exit.*
BENEDICT Hah! "Against my will, I am sent to bid you come
in to dinner." There's a double meaning in that. "I took no
230 more pains for those thanks than you took pains to thank me":
that's as much as to say, any pains that I take for you is as easy
as thanks. If I do not take pity of her, I am a villain. If I do not
love her, I am a Jew.[7] I will go get her picture.[8]   *Exit.*

3.1

Enter HERO *and two gentlewomen,* MARGARET
    and URSULA.
HERO Good Margaret, run thee to the parlor.
There shalt thou find my cousin Beatrice
Proposing° with the Prince and Claudio.   *Talking*
Whisper her ear,° and tell her I and Ursula   *(in her ear)*
5 Walk in the orchard, and our whole discourse
Is all of her. Say that thou overheard'st us,

---

5. Are stretched to the limit (like a bent bow).
6. No additional proof of her intelligence.
7. That is, lacking in Christian charity (an anti-
Semitic stereotype).

8. *get her picture:* have her portrait painted (for a
love locket) or sketch it himself.
3.1 Location: Leonato's garden.

And bid her steal into the pleachèd[1] bower
Where honeysuckles, ripened by the sun,
Forbid the sun to enter, like favorites
10 Made proud by princes, that advance their pride
Against that power that bred it.[2] There will she hide her
To listen° our propose.° This is thy office.   *hear / conversation*
Bear thee well in it, and leave us alone.
MARGARET   I'll make her come, I warrant you, presently. [*Exit.*]
15 HERO   Now, Ursula, when Beatrice doth come,
As we do trace° this alley up and down   *pace*
Our talk must only be of Benedict.
When I do name him, let it be thy part
To praise him more than ever man did merit.
20 My talk to thee must be how Benedict
Is sick in love with Beatrice. Of this matter
Is little Cupid's crafty arrow made
That only wounds by hearsay.[3] Now begin,
For look where Beatrice like a lapwing[4] runs
25 Close by the ground to hear our conference.
            Enter BEATRICE.
URSULA [*aside to* HERO]   The pleasantest angling is to see the fish
Cut with her golden oars the silver stream
And greedily devour the treacherous bait.
So angle we for Beatrice, who even now
30 Is couchèd° in the woodbine coverture.[5]   *hidden*
Fear you not my part of the dialogue.
HERO [*aside to* URSULA]   Then go we near her, that her ear lose
            nothing
Of the false sweet bait that we lay for it.
[*aloud*] No, truly, Ursula, she is too disdainful.
35 I know her spirits are as coy° and wild   *disdainful; shy*
As haggards° of the rock.   *wild female hawks*
URSULA   But are you sure
That Benedict loves Beatrice so entirely?
HERO   So says the Prince and my new trothèd lord.
URSULA   And did they bid you tell her of it, madam?
40 HERO   They did entreat me to acquaint her of it,
But I persuaded them, if they loved Benedict,
To wish him wrestle with affection
And never to let Beatrice know of it.
URSULA   Why did you so? Doth not the gentleman
45 Deserve as full° as fortunate a bed   *fully*
As ever Beatrice shall couch upon?
HERO   O God of love! I know he doth deserve
As much as may be yielded to a man.
But nature never framed a woman's heart
50 Of prouder stuff than that of Beatrice.
Disdain and scorn ride sparkling in her eyes,
Misprizing° what they look on, and her wit   *Despising*
Values itself so highly that to her

---

1. Screened by intertwining branches.
2. *that advance . . . it:* who presumptuously oppose the power that created them.
3. Wounds by rumor or gossip.
4. Peewit, a bird that scuttles along the ground.
5. The honeysuckle arbor.

	All matter else seems° weak. She cannot love,	*Other topics seem*
55	Nor take no shape nor project of affection,[6]	
	She is so self-endeared.	
	URSULA Sure, I think so,	
	And therefore, certainly, it were not good	
	She knew his love, lest she'll make sport at it.	
	HERO Why, you speak truth. I never yet saw man,	
60	How° wise, how noble, young, how rarely° featured,	*However / splendidly*
	But she would spell him backward.[7] If fair-faced,	
	She would swear the gentleman should be her sister;	
	If black,° why, nature, drawing of an antic,°	*dark / buffoon*
	Made a foul blot;° if tall, a lance ill-headed;	*error*
65	If low, an agate[8] very vilely cut;	
	If speaking, why, a vane blown with all winds;	
	If silent, why, a block movèd with° none.	*by*
	So turns she every man the wrong side out,	
	And never gives to truth and virtue that	
70	Which simpleness° and merit purchaseth.°	*integrity / deserve*
	URSULA Sure, sure, such carping is not commendable.	
	HERO No, not to be so odd and from all fashions,[9]	
	As Beatrice is, cannot be commendable.	
	But who dare tell her so? If I should speak,	
75	She would mock me into air. Oh, she would laugh me	
	Out of myself; press me to death with wit.[1]	
	Therefore let Benedict, like covered fire,	
	Consume away in sighs;[2] waste inwardly.	
	It were a better death than die with mocks,	
80	Which is as bad as die with tickling.	
	URSULA Yet tell her of it; hear what she will say.	
	HERO No. Rather I will go to Benedict	
	And counsel him to fight against his passion.	
	And truly, I'll devise some honest° slanders	*harmless*
85	To stain my cousin with. One doth not know	
	How much an ill word may empoison liking.	
	URSULA Oh, do not do your cousin such a wrong!	
	She cannot be so much without true judgment,	
	Having so swift and excellent a wit	
90	As she is prized° to have, as to refuse	*esteemed*
	So rare a gentleman as Signor Benedict.	
	HERO He is the only man of Italy,	
	Always excepted my dear Claudio.	
	URSULA I pray you, be not angry with me, madam.	
95	Speaking my fancy, Signor Benedict,	
	For shape, for bearing, argument,[3] and valor,	
	Goes foremost in report through Italy.	
	HERO Indeed, he hath an excellent good name.	
	URSULA His excellence did earn it ere he had it.	
100	When are you married, madam?	

---

6. *Nor take . . . affection:* Nor form the image or even the concept of love.
7. She would speak of his virtues as faults.
8. Tiny figures were carved in agates and used as seals or in rings.
9. *from all fashions:* contrary to normal behavior.
1. Crushing weights were loaded upon accused crim-

inals who refused to enter a plea. Hero suggests that she will be silenced with mockery ("laugh me / Out of myself") and then mocked for her silence ("press me to death with wit").
2. Each sigh was said to draw a drop of blood from the heart.
3. Intellect and rhetorical skill.

HERO   Why, every day! Tomorrow![4] Come, go in.
I'll show thee some attires and have thy counsel
Which is the best to furnish° me tomorrow.   *grace*
URSULA [*aside to* HERO]   She's limed,[5] I warrant you. We have
caught her, madam.
105 HERO [*aside to* URSULA]   If it prove so, then loving goes by haps.°   *chance*
Some Cupid kills with arrows, some with traps.
                                   [*Exeunt* HERO *and* URSULA.]
BEATRICE   What fire is in mine ears?[6] Can this be true?
Stand I condemned for pride and scorn so much?
Contempt, farewell, and maiden pride, adieu!
110 No glory lives behind the back of such.[7]
And Benedict, love on. I will requite thee,
Taming my wild heart to thy loving hand.[8]
If thou dost love, my kindness° shall incite thee   *reciprocal love*
To bind our loves up in a holy band.°   *marriage*
115 For others say thou dost deserve, and I
Believe it better than reportingly.°   *Exit.*   *as mere rumor*

3.2

Enter Prince [PEDRO], CLAUDIO, BENEDICT,
and LEONATO.

PEDRO   I do but stay till your marriage be consummate, and
then go I toward Aragon.
CLAUDIO   I'll bring° you thither, my lord, if you'll vouchsafe° me.   *accompany / allow*
PEDRO   Nay. That would be as great a soil in the new gloss of
5   your marriage as to show a child his new coat and forbid
him to wear it. I will only be bold with° Benedict for his   *ask*
company, for from the crown of his head to the sole of his
foot, he is all mirth. He hath twice or thrice cut Cupid's
bowstring, and the little hangman° dare not shoot at him.   *rogue; executioner*
10   He hath a heart as sound as a bell, and his tongue is the
clapper: for what his heart thinks, his tongue speaks.
BENEDICT   Gallants, I am not as I have been.
LEONATO   So say I. Methinks you are sadder.°   *more serious*
CLAUDIO   I hope he be in love.
15   PEDRO   Hang him, truant! There's no true drop of blood in
him, to be truly touched with love. If he be sad, he wants°   *lacks*
money.
BENEDICT   I have the toothache.[1]
PEDRO   Draw° it.   *Extract*
20   BENEDICT   Hang it.
CLAUDIO   You must hang it first and draw it afterwards.[2]
PEDRO   What? Sigh for the toothache?
LEONATO   Where is but a humor[3] or a worm.
BENEDICT   Well, everyone can master a grief but he that has it.
25   CLAUDIO   Yet, say I, he is in love.

---

4. From tomorrow on, I shall be a married woman
every day.
5. Snared with birdlime, a glue spread on branches
to catch birds.
6. Proverbially, if others were talking about you elsewhere, your ears would burn.
7. No one praises such people behind their backs.
8. In falconry, the bird is tamed by the hand of the

falconer. There is also a pun on "heart/hart."
3.2 Location: Leonato's house.
1. Toothaches supposedly plagued lovers.
2. *hang it:* a mild expletive (like "darn it"). Claudio
plays on the notion of hanging criminals, who were
then cut down and "drawn" (disemboweled).
3. Poisonous fluid in the body (which, along with
worms, was thought to be the cause of toothache).

PEDRO   There is no appearance of fancy° in him, unless it be   *love*
a fancy that he hath to strange disguises, as to be a Dutch-
man today, a Frenchman tomorrow; or in the shape of two
countries at once, as a German from the waist downward,
30   all slops,° and a Spaniard from the hip upward, no doublet.⁴   *baggy breeches*
Unless he have a fancy to this foolery, as it appears he hath,
he is no fool for fancy, as you would have it appear he is.⁵
CLAUDIO   If he be not in love with some woman, there is no
believing old° signs. 'A° brushes his hat o'mornings. What   *time-honored / He*
35   should that bode?
PEDRO   Hath any man seen him at the barber's?
CLAUDIO   No. But the barber's man hath been seen with him,
and the old ornament of his cheek hath already stuffed tennis balls.⁶
40   LEONATO   Indeed, he looks younger than he did, by the loss of
a beard.
PEDRO   Nay, 'a rubs himself with civet.° Can you smell him   *perfume*
out⁷ by that?
CLAUDIO   That's as much as to say, the sweet youth's in love.
45   PEDRO   The greatest note of it is his melancholy.
CLAUDIO   And when was he wont to wash⁸ his face?
PEDRO   Yea, or to paint himself? For the which, I hear what
they say of him.
CLAUDIO   Nay, but his jesting spirit, which is now crept into a
50   lute string, and now governed by stops.⁹
PEDRO   Indeed, that tells a heavy tale for him. Conclude, conclude! He is in love.
CLAUDIO   Nay, but I know who loves him.
PEDRO   That would I know too. I warrant, one that knows him
55   not.
CLAUDIO   Yes, and his ill conditions,¹ and in despite of all,
dies for him.
PEDRO   She shall be buried with her face upwards.²
BENEDICT   Yet is this no charm for the toothache. [*to* LEONATO]
60   Old signor, walk aside with me. I have studied eight or nine
wise words to speak to you, which these hobbyhorses° must   *clowns*
not hear.   [*Exeunt* BENEDICT *and* LEONATO.]
PEDRO   For° my life, to break° with him about Beatrice.   *Upon / speak*
CLAUDIO   'Tis even so. Hero and Margaret³ have by this° played   *by now*
65   their parts with Beatrice, and then the two bears will not
bite one another when they meet.
                    Enter JOHN *the bastard.*
JOHN   My lord and brother, God save you.
PEDRO   Good e'en,° brother.   *Good evening*
JOHN   If your leisure served, I would speak with you.
70   PEDRO   In private?

---

4. His doublet is covered with a Spanish cloak.
5. Unless he enjoys dressing up foolishly, as it seems
he does, he is not in love, as you believe.
6. Benedict has shaved off his beard. Tennis balls
were stuffed with hair.
7. Detect his secret (with play on literal "smell").
8. When was he accustomed to use cosmetic washes
on (compare "paint" in following line).
9. Frets on a lute's fingerboard; restraints. (Lutes
were associated with lovers' serenades.)

1. *Yes . . . conditions:* I.e., You're mistaken; she does
know him and his bad qualities.
2. That is, in Benedict's arms, where she will die
(Elizabethan slang for "have an orgasm") in the act of
love; perhaps a joking reversal of the idea that as one
responsible for her own fate, she should be buried,
like a suicide, with her face downward.
3. Ursula and Hero played the trick on Beatrice with
help from Margaret.

JOHN   If it please you. Yet Count Claudio may hear, for what I
    would speak of concerns him.
PEDRO   What's the matter?
JOHN [*to* CLAUDIO]   Means your lordship to be married
75   tomorrow?
PEDRO   You know he does.
JOHN   I know not that, when he knows what I know.
CLAUDIO   If there be any impediment, I pray you discover° it.   *reveal*
JOHN   You may think I love you not. Let that appear hereafter
80   and aim better at° me by that I now will manifest. For my   *think better of*
    brother, I think he holds you well,° and in dearness° of heart *in high respect / affection*
    hath holp° to effect your ensuing marriage. Surely, suit ill   *helped*
    spent, and labor ill bestowed.
PEDRO   Why, what's the matter?
85 JOHN   I came hither to tell you. And circumstances short-
    ened,° for she has been too long a-talking of,[4] the lady is   *put simply*
    disloyal.°   *unfaithful*
CLAUDIO   Who? Hero?
JOHN   Even she. Leonato's Hero, your Hero, every man's Hero.
90 CLAUDIO   Disloyal?
JOHN   The word is too good to paint out° her wickedness. I   *fully describe*
    could say she were worse. Think you of a worse title, and I
    will fit her to it. Wonder not till further warrant.° Go but   *evidence*
    with me tonight. You shall see her chamber window entered,
95   even the night before her wedding day. If you love her, then
    tomorrow wed her; but it would better fit your honor to
    change your mind.
CLAUDIO   May this be so?
PEDRO   I will not think it.
100 JOHN   If you dare not trust that you see, confess not that you
    know.[5] If you will follow me, I will show you enough; and
    when you have seen more and heard more, proceed accord-
    ingly.
CLAUDIO   If I see anything tonight why I should not marry her,
105   tomorrow in the congregation, where I should wed, there will
    I shame her.
PEDRO   And as I wooed for thee to obtain her, I will join with
    thee to disgrace her.
JOHN   I will disparage her no farther till you are my wit-
110   nesses. Bear it coldly° but till midnight, and let the issue   *calmly*
    show itself.
PEDRO   Oh, day untowardly turned!°   *miserably changed*
CLAUDIO   Oh, mischief strangely thwarting!
JOHN   Oh, plague right well prevented! So will you say when
115   you have seen the sequel.   [*Exeunt.*]

---

4. For we have already talked about her too much.   5. If you won't risk seeing for yourself, don't claim to
know.

3.3

Enter DOGBERRY *and* [VERGES] *his compartner° with*   *fellow officer*
the WATCH.[1]

DOGBERRY   Are you good men and true?

VERGES   Yea, or else it were pity but they should suffer salvation,[2] body and soul.

DOGBERRY   Nay, that were a punishment too good for them if
5   they should have any allegiance° in them, being chosen for   *(for "disloyalty")*
the Prince's watch.

VERGES   Well, give them their charge,° neighbor Dogberry.   *instructions*

DOGBERRY   First, who think you the most desertless° man to   *(for "deserving")*
be Constable?[3]

10   FIRST WATCHMAN   Hugh Oatcake, sir, or George Seacoal, for
they can write and read.

DOGBERRY   Come hither, neighbor Seacoal. God hath blessed
you with a good name.[4] To be a well-favored° man is the gift   *good-looking*
of fortune, but to write and read comes by nature.

15   SECOND WATCHMAN   Both which, Master Constable—

DOGBERRY   You have. I knew it would be your answer. Well,
for your favor,° sir, why, give God thanks and make no boast   *looks*
of it. And for your writing and reading, let that appear when
there is no need of such vanity. You are thought here to be
20   the most senseless° and fit man for the Constable of the   *(for "sensible")*
watch: therefore, bear you the lantern. This is your charge.
You shall comprehend all vagrom[5] men. You are to bid any
man stand,° in the Prince's name.   *stop*

SECOND WATCHMAN   How if 'a° will not stand?   *he*

25   DOGBERRY   Why, then, take no note of him, but let him go
and presently° call the rest of the watch together, and thank   *immediately*
God you are rid of a knave.

VERGES   If he will not stand when he is bidden, he is none of
the Prince's subjects.

30   DOGBERRY   True, and they are to meddle with none but the
Prince's subjects. You shall also make no noise in the streets;
for, for the watch to babble and to talk is most tolerable° and   *(for "intolerable")*
not to be endured.

A WATCHMAN   We will rather sleep than talk. We know what
35   belongs° to a watch.[6]   *is appropriate*

DOGBERRY   Why, you speak like an ancient° and most quiet   *experienced*
watchman, for I cannot see how sleeping should offend.
Only have a care that your bills[7] be not stolen. Well, you are
to call at all the alehouses and bid those that are drunk, get
40   them to bed.

A WATCHMAN   How if they will not?

3.3 Location: A street.
1. Watchmen who patrolled the streets, proclaiming
the hour and performing police duties. "Verges"
probably alludes to a "verge," or wand of office, carried by officials.
2. For "damnation." (Verges and Dogberry repeatedly say the opposite of what they mean.)
3. The leader of the watch. (Dogberry himself is the
parish constable.)
4. Sea coal from Newcastle was known for its high

quality (thus the "good name").
5. For "vagrant." *comprehend:* for "apprehend."
6. TEXTUAL COMMENT As with the other scenes
involving Dogberry and the watch, the speech prefixes in this scene show clear signs of being work in
progress and need editorial intervention. Examining
how editors revise the original speech prefixes provides insight into Shakespeare's creative process. See
Digital Edition TC 5.
7. Weapons (long shafts with blades or ax heads).

DOGBERRY   Why, then, let them alone till they are sober. If they make you not then the better answer, you may say they are not the men you took them for.

45 A WATCHMAN   Well, sir.

DOGBERRY   If you meet a thief, you may suspect him, by virtue of your office, to be no true° man. And for such kind of men, the less you meddle or make° with them, why, the more is° for your honesty.   *honest / have to do / the better it is*

50 A WATCHMAN   If we know him to be a thief, shall we not lay hands on him?

DOGBERRY   Truly, by your office you may, but I think they that touch pitch will be defiled.[8] The most peaceable way for you, if you do take a thief, is to let him show himself what he

55 is and steal out of your company.

VERGES   You have been always called a merciful man, partner.

DOGBERRY   Truly, I would not hang a dog by my will, much more° a man who hath any honesty in him.   *(for "less")*

VERGES   If you hear a child cry in the night, you must call to

60 the nurse and bid her still° it.   *calm*

A WATCHMAN   How if the nurse be asleep and will not hear us?

DOGBERRY   Why, then, depart in peace and let the child wake her with crying. For the ewe that will not hear her lamb when it baas will never answer a calf° when he bleats.   *blockhead*

65 VERGES   'Tis very true.

DOGBERRY   This is the end of the charge. You, Constable, are to present° the Prince's own person.[9] If you meet the Prince in the night, you may stay° him.   *represent / stop*

VERGES   Nay, by'r Lady, that I think 'a cannot.

70 DOGBERRY   Five shillings to one on't with any man that knows the statutes, he may stay him. Marry, not without° the Prince be willing. For, indeed, the watch ought to offend no man, and it is an offense to stay a man against his will.   *unless*

VERGES   By'r Lady, I think it be so.

75 DOGBERRY   Hah, ah, hah! Well, masters, good night. An there be any matter of weight chances,[1] call up me. Keep your fellows' counsels, and your own, and good night. [*to* VERGES] Come, neighbor.

A WATCHMAN   Well, masters, we hear our charge. Let us go sit

80 here upon the church bench till two, and then all to bed.

DOGBERRY   One word more, honest neighbors. I pray you, watch about Signor Leonato's door, for the wedding being there tomorrow there is a great coil° tonight. Adieu! Be vigilant,° I beseech you.   *to-do, bustle / (for "vigilant")*

            Exeunt [DOGBERRY *and* VERGES].

          Enter BORACHIO *and* CONRAD.

85 BORACHIO   What, Conrad!

A WATCHMAN [*aside*]   Peace, stir not.

BORACHIO   Conrad, I say!

CONRAD   Here, man. I am at thy elbow.

---

8. A proverbial saying, derived from the Apocryphal book of Ecclesiasticus (13:1). *pitch*: tar.
9. Dogberry presents a parodic version of the notion that the monarch's authority was in theory separable from his person (others could represent that authority when he was physically absent).
1. *An . . . chances*: If anything important happens.

	BORACHIO Mass,° and my elbow itched!² I thought there would	*By the mass*
90	a scab³ follow.	
	CONRAD I will owe thee an answer for that. And now, forward with thy tale.	
	BORACHIO Stand thee close then under this penthouse,° for it	*overhanging structure*
	drizzles rain, and I will, like a true drunkard, utter⁴ all to thee.	
95	A WATCHMAN [*aside*] Some treason, masters. Yet stand close.°	*keep hidden*
	BORACHIO Therefore, know, I have earned of Don John a thousand ducats.	
	CONRAD Is it possible that any villainy should be so dear?°	*valuable*
	BORACHIO Thou shouldst rather ask if it were possible any	
100	villainy should be so rich. For when rich villains have need of poor ones, poor ones may make what price they will.	
	CONRAD I wonder at it.	
	BORACHIO That shows thou art unconfirmed.° Thou knowest	*inexperienced*
	that the fashion of a doublet, or a hat, or a cloak is nothing	
105	to⁵ a man.	
	CONRAD Yes; it is apparel.	
	BORACHIO I mean the fashion.	
	CONRAD Yes; the fashion is the fashion.	
	BORACHIO Tush! I may as well say, the fool's the fool. But	
110	seest thou not what a deformed° thief⁶ this fashion is?	*deforming*
	A WATCHMAN [*aside*] I know that Deformed. 'A° has been a	*He*
	vile thief this seven year. 'A goes up and down° like a gentle-	*struts here and there*
	man. I remember his name.	
	BORACHIO Didst thou not hear somebody?	
115	CONRAD No. 'Twas the vane on the house.	
	BORACHIO Seest thou not, I say, what a deformed thief this	
	fashion is? How giddily 'a turns about all the hot bloods°	*dandies*
	between fourteen and five-and-thirty, sometimes fashion-	
	ing them like Pharaoh's soldiers in the reechy° painting,⁷	*grimy*
120	sometime like god Bel's⁸ priests in the old church window,	
	sometime like the shaven Hercules⁹ in the smirched worm-	
	eaten tapestry, where his codpiece¹ seems as massy as his club?	
	CONRAD All this I see, and I see that the fashion wears out	
	more apparel than the man.² But art not thou thyself giddy	
125	with the fashion too, that thou hast shifted³ out of thy tale	
	into telling me of the fashion?	
	BORACHIO Not so, neither. But know that I have tonight wooed	
	Margaret, the lady Hero's gentlewoman, by the name of Hero.	
	She leans me° out at her mistress' chamber window; bids me	*leans*
130	a thousand times good night. I tell this tale vilely. I should	
	first tell thee how the Prince, Claudio, and my master, planted,	

---

2. Proverbially, itching elbows alerted you against shady company.
3. Contemptible person; punning on a literal "scab."
4. The drunken Borachio alludes to the Latin tag *in vino veritas* ("in wine there is truth").
5. Tells us nothing about (but Conrad takes him to mean "means nothing to").
6. Used here to mean "rogue"—but also that keeping up with fashion robs men of their money.
7. Perhaps refers to a painting of the fleeing Israelites pursued by Pharaoh's army.

8. Bel (Baal) was a Babylonian god who had seventy priests. His story, told in the biblical Apocrypha, is sometimes depicted in stained-glass windows.
9. Probably referring to the story of Omphale (compare 2.1.225), or perhaps confusing Hercules with Samson.
1. Pouch, often stuffed and ornamented, worn over a man's breeches, covering the genitals.
2. *fashion . . . man*: fashions change before clothes wear out.
3. Punning on "changed clothes."

and placed, and possessed[4] by my master Don John, saw afar
off in the orchard this amiable° encounter.   *loving*

CONRAD And thought they Margaret was Hero?

135 BORACHIO Two of them did: the Prince and Claudio. But the
devil my master knew she was Margaret. And partly by his
oaths which first possessed them; partly by the dark night
which did deceive them; but chiefly by my villainy, which did
confirm any slander that Don John had made—away went

140 Claudio enraged; swore he would meet her as he was appointed
next morning at the temple;° and there, before the whole   *church*
congregation, shame her with what he saw o'er night and
send her home again without a husband.

FIRST WATCHMAN We charge you, in the Prince's name, stand!

145 SECOND WATCHMAN Call up the right[5] Master Constable! We
have here recovered the most dangerous piece of lechery[6]
that ever was known in the commonwealth.

FIRST WATCHMAN And one Deformed is one of them. I know
him. 'A wears a lock.[7]

150 CONRAD Masters! Masters!

SECOND WATCHMAN You'll be made bring Deformed forth, I
warrant you.

CONRAD Masters!

A WATCHMAN Never speak, we charge you. Let us obey° you   *(for "compel")*
155 to go with us.

BORACHIO We are like to prove a goodly° commodity, being   *fine (ironic)*
taken up of these men's bills.[8]

CONRAD A commodity in question,[9] I warrant you. [*to the*
WATCH] Come, we'll obey you.   *Exeunt.*

3.4

Enter HERO, *and* MARGARET, *and* URSULA.

HERO Good Ursula, wake my cousin Beatrice and desire her
to rise.

URSULA I will, lady.

HERO And bid her come hither.

5 URSULA Well.°   [*Exit* URSULA.]   *Very well*

MARGARET Troth, I think your other rebato° were better.   *stiffly wired collar*

HERO No, pray thee, good Meg, I'll wear this.

MARGARET By my troth, 's° not so good, and I warrant° your   *it's / am sure*
cousin will say so.

10 HERO My cousin's a fool and thou art another. I'll wear none
but this.

MARGARET I like the new tire° within excellently, if the hair   *headdress with wig*
were a thought browner. And your gown's a most rare° fash-   *splendid*
ion, i'faith. I saw the Duchess of Milan's gown that they

15 praise so.

HERO Oh, that exceeds,° they say.   *surpasses all*

4. Informed; but perhaps also controlled (as by the
devil).
5. Respectfully, as in "right worshipful."
6. For "treachery." *recovered:* for "discovered."
7. A "lovelock," or curl of hair, worn by courtiers.
8. *being . . . bills:* a multiple pun: after we have been

hoisted on their halberds (weapons); been arrested
on their warrants; been obtained on credit ("taken
up") in exchange for their bonds ("bills").
9. Of doubtful value; about to be judicially
interrogated.
3.4 Location: Leonato's house.

MARGARET By my troth, 's but a nightgown° in respect of   *dressing gown*
  yours. Cloth o'gold and cuts, and laced with silver, set with
  pearls, down sleeves, side sleeves, and skirts round, under-
20 borne with a bluish tinsel.[1] But for a fine, quaint,° graceful,   *elegant*
  and excellent fashion, yours is worth ten on't.
HERO God give me joy to wear it, for my heart is exceeding
  heavy.
MARGARET 'Twill be heavier soon by the weight of a man.
25 HERO Fie upon thee! Art not ashamed?
MARGARET Of what, lady? Of speaking honorably? Is not
  marriage honorable in° a beggar? Is not your lord honorable   *even in*
  without marriage? I think you would have me say, saving
  your reverence,[2] "a husband." An° bad thinking do not wrest°   *If / pervert*
30 true speaking, I'll offend nobody. Is there any harm in "the
  heavier for a husband"? None, I think, an it be the right
  husband and the right wife; otherwise, 'tis light° and not   *licentious*
  heavy.
          Enter BEATRICE.
  Ask my lady Beatrice else. Here she comes.
35 HERO Good morrow, coz.
BEATRICE Good morrow, sweet Hero.
HERO Why, how now? Do you speak in the sick tune?
BEATRICE I am out of all other tune, methinks.
MARGARET Clap's° into "Light o'love"; that goes without a   *Let us shift*
40 burden.[3] Do you sing it, and I'll dance it.
BEATRICE Ye light o'love with your heels?[4] Then if your hus-
  band have stables enough, you'll see he shall lack no bairns.[5]
MARGARET Oh, illegitimate construction![6] I scorn that with
  my heels.[7]
45 BEATRICE 'Tis almost five o'clock, cousin. 'Tis time you were
  ready,° by my troth. I am exceeding ill, heigh-ho.   *dressed*
MARGARET For a hawk, a horse,[8] or a husband?
BEATRICE For the letter that begins them all: H.[9]
MARGARET Well, an you be not turned Turk,[1] there's no more
50 sailing by the star.[2]
BEATRICE What means the fool, trow?°   *I wonder*
MARGARET Nothing, I, but God send everyone their heart's
  desire.
HERO These gloves the Count sent me—they are an excellent
55 perfume.[3]
BEATRICE I am stuffed,[4] cousin, I cannot smell.
MARGARET A maid, and stuffed! There's goodly catching of cold.

---

1. *Cloth . . . tinsel:* made of silk or woolen cloth interwoven with gold thread, with ornamental slashes
("cuts") showing the fabric beneath, and decorated
with silver embroidery or lace and with pearls; with
fitted ("down") sleeves and another pair that hung
open from the shoulder; trimmed at the hem or fully
lined ("underborne") with another kind of metallic
fabric.
2. A polite expression of apology (as if "husband" were
an offensive term).
3. Bass part (for a man's voice), with play on heavy
"weight of a man." "Light o' Love" was a popular tune.
4. *Ye . . . heels:* Your dancing toys with love? ("Light-
heeled" was slang for "promiscuous.")
5. Punning on "barns." *bairns:* children.

6. A multiple pun: forced interpretation; making of
bastards; illegal building (of stables and barns).
7. I kick that away (reject it).
8. Responding to Beatrice's ostentatious sigh as a
hunting cry.
9. Punningly: "ache" was pronounced in the same
way.
1. If you have not reneged (on your vows against marriage). "To turn Turk" is, in the Christian proverb, to
become a renegade (by going over to the enemy, the
Muslim Turks).
2. No more navigating by the polestar. (No truths
can be trusted from now on.)
3. Perfumed gloves were fashionable.
4. In the nose; Margaret follows with an obscene pun.

BEATRICE Oh, God help me! God help me! How long have
you professed apprehension?°   *claimed to be witty*
60 MARGARET Ever since you left it. Doth not my wit become me
rarely?°   *excellently*
BEATRICE It is not seen enough. You should wear it in your
cap.[5] By my troth, I am sick.
MARGARET Get you some of this distilled *carduus benedictus*[6]
65 and lay it to your heart. It is the only thing for a qualm.°   *sudden faintness*
HERO There thou prickest her with a thistle.
BEATRICE *Benedictus?* Why *benedictus?* You have some moral[7]
in this *benedictus.*
MARGARET Moral? No, by my troth, I have no moral mean-
70 ing. I meant plain holy thistle. You may think, perchance,°   *perhaps*
that I think you are in love. Nay, by'r Lady, I am not such a
fool to think what I list;° nor I list not to think what I can;   *please*
nor, indeed, I cannot think, if I would think my heart out of
thinking, that you are in love, or that you will be in love, or
75 that you can be in love. Yet Benedict was such another,[8] and
now is he become a man. He swore he would never marry,
and yet now, in despite of his heart, he eats his meat without
grudging.[9] And how you may be converted I know not, but
methinks you look with your eyes as other women do.
80 BEATRICE What pace is this that thy tongue keeps?
MARGARET Not a false gallop.[1]
Enter URSULA.
URSULA Madam, withdraw. The Prince, the Count, Signor
Benedict, Don John, and all the gallants of the town are come
to fetch you to church.
85 HERO Help to dress me, good coz, good Meg, good Ursula.
[*Exeunt.*]

3.5

Enter LEONATO, *and* [DOGBERRY] *the Constable, and*
[VERGES] *the Headborough.*°   *local constable*
LEONATO What would you with me, honest neighbor?
DOGBERRY Marry, sir, I would have some confidence° with you,   *(for "conference")*
that discerns° you nearly.   *(for "concerns")*
LEONATO Brief,° I pray you, for you see it is a busy time with me.   *Be brief*
5 DOGBERRY Marry, this it is, sir.
VERGES Yes, in truth it is, sir.
LEONATO What is it, my good friends?
DOGBERRY Goodman° Verges, sir, speaks a little off the   *(commoner's title)*
matter.° An old man, sir, and his wits are not so blunt° as,   *subject / (for "sharp")*
10 God help, I would desire they were. But, in faith, honest as
the skin between his brows.
VERGES Yes. I thank God, I am as honest as any man living
that is an old man and no honester than I.
DOGBERRY Comparisons are odorous.° Palabras,[1] neighbor   *(for "odious")*
15 Verges!

---

5. Like the coxcomb of a professional fool.
6. Holy thistle, or blessed thistle (a medicinal herb
good for the heart).
7. Hidden meaning (with ensuing pun on "no moral"
as "immoral").
8. Benedict was once an enemy of love.

9. Nonetheless, he has a perfectly good appetite.
1. Not a canter. (I am not speaking at a false pace.)
3.5 Location: Scene continues.
1. Be brief (from a Spanish expression, *pocas pal-abras*, meaning "few words").

LEONATO   Neighbors, you are tedious.[2]

DOGBERRY   It pleases your worship to say so, but we are the
poor Duke's officers.° But truly, for mine own part, if I were   *the Duke's poor officers*
as tedious as a king, I could find in my heart to bestow it all
20   of your worship.

LEONATO   All thy tediousness on me, ah?

DOGBERRY   Yea, an 'twere a thousand pound more than 'tis,
for I hear as good exclamation[3] on your worship as of any
man in the city. And though I be but a poor man, I am glad
25   to hear it.

VERGES   And so am I.

LEONATO   I would fain° know what you have to say.   *gladly*

VERGES   Marry, sir, our watch tonight, excepting your worship's
presence,[4] ha' ta'en a couple of as arrant knaves as any in
30   Messina.

DOGBERRY   A good old man, sir; he will be talking. As they
say, "When the age is in, the wit is out,"[5] God help us. It is a
world to see.[6] Well said, i'faith, neighbor Verges. Well, God's
a good man. An° two men ride of a horse, one must ride   *If*
35   behind. An honest soul, i'faith, sir, by my troth he is, as ever
broke bread.[7] But God is to be worshipped. All men are not
alike. Alas, good neighbor.

LEONATO   Indeed, neighbor, he comes too short of you.

DOGBERRY   Gifts that God gives.

40   LEONATO   I must leave you.

DOGBERRY   One word, sir! Our watch, sir, have indeed comprehended two aspitious[8] persons, and we would have them
this morning examined before your worship.

LEONATO   Take their examination yourself and bring it me.
45   I am now in great haste, as it may appear unto you.

DOGBERRY   It shall be suffigance.°   *(nonsense word for*
                                                    "sufficient")
LEONATO   Drink some wine ere you go. Fare you well.

[*Enter* MESSENGER.]

MESSENGER   My lord, they stay° for you, to give your daughter   *wait*
to her husband.

50   LEONATO   I'll wait upon them. I am ready.

[*Exeunt* LEONATO *and* MESSENGER.]

DOGBERRY   Go, good partner, go get you to Francis Seacoal.[9]
Bid him bring his pen and inkhorn to the jail. We are now to
examination° these men.   *(for "examine")*

VERGES   And we must do it wisely.

55   DOGBERRY   We will spare for no wit, I warrant you. Here's that°   *that which*
shall drive some of them to a *non come*.[1] Only get the learned
writer to set down our excommunication,° and meet me at   *(for "examination")*
the jail.   [*Exeunt*.]

---

2. Dogberry takes it to mean "rich."
3. Properly, "accusation"; but Dogberry probably
intends "acclamation."
4. For "respecting your worship's presence": an apology for speaking what might displease.
5. Dogberry's version of the proverb "When the wine
is in, the wit is out."
6. Dogberry seems to mean "a strange world"; the
expression normally meant "wonderful to behold."

7. Dogberry strings together three proverbial sentences, all of which are remembered correctly but
irrelevantly.
8. For "suspicious." *comprehended*: for "apprehended."
9. Refers to the Sexton in 4.2, not the George Seacoal of the watch in 3.3.
1. For "nonplus" (bewilderment); perhaps confused
by Dogberry with *non compos mentis* (insane).

4.1

Enter [PEDRO *the*] *Prince,* [JOHN *the*] *Bastard,*
LEONATO, FRIAR, CLAUDIO, BENEDICT, HERO, *and*
BEATRICE.[1]

LEONATO   Come, Friar Francis, be brief. Only to the plain
form of marriage, and you shall recount their particular
duties afterward.

FRIAR [*to* CLAUDIO]   You come hither, my lord, to marry this
5   lady?

CLAUDIO   No.

LEONATO   To be married to her, Friar. You come to marry her.

FRIAR [*to* HERO]   Lady, you come hither to be married to this
Count?

10   HERO   I do.

FRIAR   If either of you know any inward° impediment why   secret
you should not be conjoined, I charge you on your souls to
utter it.

CLAUDIO   Know you any, Hero?

15   HERO   None, my lord.

FRIAR   Know you any, Count?

LEONATO   I dare make his answer. "None!"

CLAUDIO   Oh, what men dare do! What men may do! What men
daily do, not knowing what they do!

20   BENEDICT   How now? Interjections? Why, then, some be of
laughing, as, "ah, ha, he."[2]

CLAUDIO   Stand thee by, Friar. [*to* LEONATO] Father, by your leave,
Will you with free and unconstrainèd° soul   uncompelled
Give me this maid, your daughter?

25   LEONATO   As freely, son, as God did give her me.

CLAUDIO   And what have I to give you back, whose worth
May counterpoise° this rich and precious gift?   equal

PEDRO   Nothing, unless you render her again.°   give her back

CLAUDIO   Sweet Prince, you learn° me noble thankfulness.   teach

30   There, Leonato, take her back again.
Give not this rotten orange to your friend.
She's but the sign° and semblance of her honor.   mere appearance
Behold, how like a maid she blushes here!
Oh, what authority and show of truth

35   Can cunning sin cover itself withal!°   with
Comes not that blood° as modest evidence   blush
To witness° simple virtue? Would you not swear,   testify to
All you that see her, that she were a maid
By these exterior shows? But she is none.

40   She knows the heat of a luxurious° bed.   lustful
Her blush is guiltiness, not modesty.

LEONATO   What do you mean, my lord?

CLAUDIO   Not to be married;
Not to knit my soul to an approvèd° wanton.   proven

LEONATO   Dear my lord, if you, in your own proof,°   endeavor

45   Have vanquished the resistance of her youth

4.1 Location: A church.
1. PERFORMANCE COMMENT Margaret is notably
absent from this scene; some stage directors choose
to include her. See Digital Edition PC 3.

2. Benedict alludes to a passage in William Lily's
Latin grammar, used in all Elizabethan schools:
"Some [interjections] are of laughing; as Ha ha he"
(1567 edition).

And made defeat of her virginity—
CLAUDIO   I know what you would say. If I have known her,
You will say, she did embrace me as a husband,
And so extenuate the forehand sin.[3]
50   No, Leonato,
I never tempted her with word too large°   immodest
But, as a brother to his sister, showed
Bashful sincerity and comely love.
HERO   And seemed I ever otherwise to you?
55   CLAUDIO   Out on thee,[4] seeming! I will write against it.
You seem to me as Dian in her orb,[5]
As chaste as is the bud ere it be blown.°   blossom
But you are more intemperate in your blood°   passion
Than Venus or those pampered animals
60   That rage in savage sensuality.
HERO   Is my lord well, that he doth speak so wide?°   wildly
LEONATO   Sweet prince, why speak not you?
PEDRO   What should I speak?
  I stand dishonored, that have gone about°   tried
  To link my dear friend to a common stale.°   prostitute
65   LEONATO   Are these things spoken, or do I but dream?
JOHN   Sir, they are spoken, and these things are true.
BENEDICT   This looks not like a nuptial.
HERO   "True"? O God!
CLAUDIO   Leonato, stand I here?
  Is this the Prince? Is this the Prince's brother?
70   Is this face Hero's? Are our eyes our own?
LEONATO   All this is so. But what of this, my lord?
CLAUDIO   Let me but move° one question to your daughter,   put
And by that fatherly and kindly° power   natural
That you have in her, bid her answer truly.
75   LEONATO   I charge thee do so, as thou art my child.
HERO   Oh, God defend me! How am I beset!
  What kind of catechizing[6] call you this?
CLAUDIO   To make you answer truly to your name.[7]
HERO   Is it not Hero? Who can blot that name
  With any just reproach?
80   CLAUDIO   Marry, that can Hero.
  "Hero" itself[8] can blot out Hero's virtue.
  What man was he talked with you yesternight
  Out at your window betwixt twelve and one?
  Now if you are a maid, answer to this.
85   HERO   I talked with no man at that hour, my lord.
PEDRO   Why, then are you no maiden. Leonato,
  I am sorry you must hear. Upon mine honor,
  Myself, my brother, and this grievèd° Count   wronged
  Did see her, hear her, at that hour last night
90   Talk with a ruffian at her chamber window;
  Who hath, indeed, most like a liberal° villain,   loose-tongued

3. And so excuse the sin of having sex before marriage ("the forehand sin").
4. A curse; "thee" could refer to Hero or "seeming"
(putting on a false show).
5. Diana (Roman goddess of chastity and of the
moon) in her orbit, or sphere of activity.

6. A catechism is a set of formal questions and
answers used to teach church doctrine.
7. To make you admit that you are what you have
been called.
8. The name (or reputation) of Hero.

Confessed the vile encounters they have had
A thousand times in secret.
JOHN   Fie, fie, they are
Not to be named, my lord; not to be spoke of.
95   There is not chastity enough in language
Without offense to utter them. Thus, pretty lady,
I am sorry for thy much misgovernment.°   ample misconduct
CLAUDIO   O Hero! What a Hero hadst thou been,
If half thy outward graces had been placed
100 About thy thoughts and counsels of thy heart!
But fare thee well. Most foul, most fair, farewell!
Thou pure impiety and impious purity.
For° thee I'll lock up all the gates of love,   Because of
And on my eyelids shall conjecture° hang   suspicion
105 To turn all beauty into thoughts of harm;
And never shall it more be gracious.°   attractive
LEONATO   Hath no man's dagger here a point for me?
BEATRICE   Why, how now, cousin? Wherefore sink you down?
JOHN   Come, let us go. These things come thus to light
Smother her spirits° up.   [Exeunt PEDRO, CLAUDIO,   vital forces
                                    and JOHN.]
110 BENEDICT   How doth the lady?
BEATRICE   Dead, I think. Help, uncle!
Hero! Why, Hero! Uncle! Signor Benedict! Friar!
LEONATO   O Fate! Take not away thy heavy hand.
Death is the fairest cover for her shame
That may be wished for.
115 BEATRICE   How now? Cousin Hero?
FRIAR   Have comfort, lady.
LEONATO   Dost thou look up?
FRIAR   Yea, wherefore should she not?
LEONATO   Wherefore? Why, doth not every earthly thing
Cry shame upon her? Could she here deny
120 The story that is printed in her blood?°   blush
Do not live, Hero. Do not ope thine eyes.
For did I think thou wouldst not quickly die—
Thought I thy spirits were stronger than thy shame—
Myself would on the rearward° of reproaches   in the wake
125 Strike at thy life. Grieved I, I had but one?
Chid I for that at frugal nature's frame?°   plan
Oh, one too much by thee. Why had I one?
Why ever wast thou lovely in my eyes?
Why had I not with charitable hand
130 Took up a beggar's issue at my gates,
Who, smirchèd thus° and mired with infamy,   (as you are)
I might have said, "No part of it is mine.
This shame derives itself from unknown loins."
But mine, and mine I loved, and mine I praised,
135 And mine that I was proud on,° mine so much   of
That I myself was to myself not mine[9]
Valuing of her—why, she—oh, she is fallen
Into a pit of ink, that the wide sea

9. That I cared nothing for myself in comparison.

Hath drops too few to wash her clean again
140 And salt too little which may season give[1]
To her foul tainted flesh.
BENEDICT   Sir, sir, be patient.
For my part, I am so attired in wonder
I know not what to say.
BEATRICE   Oh, on my soul, my cousin is belied.°   *slandered*
145 BENEDICT   Lady, were you her bedfellow last night?
BEATRICE   No, truly, not; although until last night
I have this twelvemonth been her bedfellow.
LEONATO   Confirmed, confirmed! Oh, that is stronger made
Which was before° barred up with ribs of iron.   *already*
150 Would the two princes lie, and Claudio lie,
Who loved her so that, speaking of her foulness,
Washed it with tears? Hence from her. Let her die.
FRIAR   Hear me a little,
For I have only silent been so long
155 And given way unto this course of fortune[2]
By noting of the lady.[3] I have marked
A thousand blushing apparitions
To start into her face; a thousand innocent shames
In angel whiteness beat away those blushes;
160 And in her eye there hath appeared a fire
To burn the errors° that these princes hold   *(like heretics)*
Against her maiden truth. Call me a fool,
Trust not my reading nor my observations,
Which with experimental seal doth warrant
165 The tenor of my book;[4] trust not my age,
My reverence, calling, nor divinity,
If this sweet lady lie not guiltless here,
Under some biting error.
LEONATO   Friar, it cannot be.
Thou seest that all the grace that she hath left
170 Is that she will not add to her damnation
A sin of perjury. She not denies it.
Why seek'st thou then to cover with excuse
That which appears in proper° nakedness?   *true*
FRIAR   Lady, what man is he you are accused of?
175 HERO   They know that do accuse me. I know none.
If I know more of any man alive
Than that which maiden modesty doth warrant,
Let all my sins lack mercy. O my father!
Prove you that any man with me conversed
180 At hours unmeet,° or that I yesternight   *improper*
Maintained the change° of words with any creature,   *exchange*
Refuse° me, hate me, torture me to death.   *Disown*
FRIAR   There is some strange misprision° in the princes.   *misunderstanding*

1. Give renewal. (Salt is a preservative for meat.)
2. TEXTUAL COMMENT The Quarto sets lines 153–55
as prose, but it is likely that this was a result of error
by the printer. This edition follows editorial tradition
in printing the lines as poetry. See Digital Edition
TC 6.

3. *By . . . lady:* So I could observe, or because I was
observing, Hero.
4. *Which . . . book:* Which guarantees, with the confirmation of experience, the truth of the conclusions
I have drawn from my study.

BENEDICT   Two of them have the very bent of° honor,   *are wholly devoted to*

185   And if their wisdoms be misled in this

       The practice° of it lives in John the bastard,   *trickery*

       Whose spirits toil in frame of° villainies.   *in plotting*

LEONATO   I know not. If they speak but truth of her,

       These hands shall tear her. If they wrong her honor,

190   The proudest of them shall well hear of it.

       Time hath not yet so dried this blood of mine,

       Nor age so ate up my invention,°   *ingenuity*

       Nor fortune made such havoc of my means,°   *wealth*

       Nor my bad life reft° me so much of friends,   *deprived*

195   But they shall find awaked in such a kind°   *manner*

       Both strength of limb and policy° of mind,   *cunning*

       Ability in means and choice of friends,

       To quit me of[5] them throughly.°   *thoroughly*

FRIAR   Pause awhile,

       And let my counsel sway you in this case.

200   Your daughter here the princes left for dead.

       Let her awhile be secretly kept in,

       And publish° it that she is dead indeed.   *announce*

       Maintain a mourning ostentation,°   *formal display*

       And on your family's old monument°   *burial vault*

205   Hang mournful epitaphs, and do all rites

       That appertain unto a burial.

LEONATO   What shall become of this? What will this do?

FRIAR   Marry, this well carried° shall on her behalf   *managed*

       Change slander to remorse.° That is some good.   *pity*

210   But not for that dream I on this strange course,

       But on° this travail look for greater birth.[6]   *from*

       She dying, as it must be so maintained,

       Upon the instant that she was accused,

       Shall be lamented, pitied, and excused

215   Of° every hearer. For it so falls out   *By*

       That what we have, we prize not to the worth°   *full value*

       Whiles we enjoy it. But being lacked and lost,

       Why, then we rack[7] the value. Then we find

       The virtue that possession would not show us

220   Whiles it was ours. So will it fare with Claudio.

       When he shall hear she died upon° his words   *as a result of*

       Th'idea° of her life shall sweetly creep   *The image*

       Into his study of imagination,°   *reverie*

       And every lovely organ° of her life   *aspect*

225   Shall come appareled in more precious habit,

       More moving delicate and full of life,

       Into the eye and prospect° of his soul   *vision*

       Than when she lived indeed. Then shall he mourn,

       If ever love had interest in his liver,[8]

230   And wish he had not so accusèd her.

       No, though he thought his accusation true.

       Let this be so, and doubt not but success°   *what follows*

       Will fashion the event° in better shape   *result*

---

5. To be avenged upon.
6. Look for a more important consequence (with pun on "travail" as "labor pains" as well as "effort").
7. Stretch (as on a rack, an instrument of torture).
8. Thought of as the seat of passions, including love.

Than I can lay it down in likelihood.
235 But if all aim but this be leveled false,[9]
The supposition of the lady's death
Will quench the wonder of her infamy.
And if it sort° not well, you may conceal her   turn out
As best befits her wounded reputation,
240 In some reclusive° and religious life,   cloistered
Out of all eyes, tongues, minds, and injuries.°   calumny
BENEDICT   Signor Leonato, let the Friar advise you.
And though you know my inwardness° and love   close friendship
Is very much unto the Prince and Claudio,
245 Yet, by mine honor, I will deal in this
As secretly and justly as your soul
Should with your body.
LEONATO   Being that I flow in° grief,   Since I am flooded by
The smallest twine° may lead me.   thread
FRIAR   'Tis well consented. Presently away,°   Let's leave immediately
250 For to strange sores, strangely they strain the cure.[1]
Come, lady, die to live. This wedding day
Perhaps is but prolonged.° Have patience and endure.   postponed
                 Exeunt [all but BEATRICE *and* BENEDICT].
BENEDICT   Lady Beatrice, have you wept all this while?
BEATRICE   Yea, and I will weep a while longer.
255 BENEDICT   I will not desire that.
BEATRICE   You have no reason. I do it freely.
BENEDICT   Surely, I do believe your fair cousin is wronged.
BEATRICE   Ah, how much might the man deserve of me that
would right her!
260 BENEDICT   Is there any way to show such friendship?
BEATRICE   A very even° way, but no such friend.   clear
BENEDICT   May a man do it?
BEATRICE   It is a man's office, but not yours.
BENEDICT   I do love nothing in the world so well as you. Is not
265 that strange?
BEATRICE   As strange as the thing I know not. It were as pos-
sible for me to say I loved nothing so well as you. But believe
me not. And yet I lie not. I confess nothing, nor I deny noth-
ing. I am sorry for my cousin.
270 BENEDICT   By my sword, Beatrice, thou lovest me.
BEATRICE   Do not swear and eat it.[2]
BENEDICT   I will swear by it that you love me, and I will make
him eat it that says I love not you.
BEATRICE   Will you not eat your word?
275 BENEDICT   With no sauce that can be devised to it. I protest°   affirm
I love thee.
BEATRICE   Why, then, God forgive me.
BENEDICT   What offense, sweet Beatrice?
BEATRICE   You have stayed me in a happy hour.[3] I was about
280 to protest I loved you.
BENEDICT   And do it with all thy heart.

9. But if we miss our aim in all but this.
1. Shakespeare's version of the proverb "A desperate
disease must have a desperate cure." *strange:* extreme,
extraordinary. *sores:* sicknesses. *strain:* employ something beyond its usual use.

2. Eat your words; go back on your oath. Benedict
takes it to mean his sword (as does F: "swear by it and
eat it").
3. You have stopped me at a fortunate moment.

BEATRICE   I love you with so much of my heart that none is
left to protest.
BENEDICT   Come, bid me do anything for thee.
285 BEATRICE   Kill Claudio.[4]
BENEDICT   Ha! Not for the wide world.
BEATRICE   You kill me to deny° it. Farewell.   *by refusing*
BENEDICT   Tarry, sweet Beatrice.
BEATRICE   I am gone, though I am here. There is no love in
290 you. Nay, I pray you, let me go.
BENEDICT   Beatrice.
BEATRICE   In faith, I will go.
BENEDICT   We'll be friends first.
BEATRICE   You dare easier be friends with me than fight with
295 mine enemy.
BENEDICT   Is Claudio thine enemy?
BEATRICE   Is 'a not approved in the height[5] a villain that hath
slandered, scorned, dishonored my kinswoman? Oh, that I
were a man! What, bear her in hand[6] until they come to take
300 hands and then with public accusation, uncovered° slander,   *barefaced*
unmitigated rancor—O God, that I were a man! I would eat
his heart in the marketplace.
BENEDICT   Hear me, Beatrice.
BEATRICE   Talk with a man out at a window? A proper saying!°   *A likely story*
305 BENEDICT   Nay, but Beatrice—
BEATRICE   Sweet Hero! She is wronged. She is slandered. She
is undone.
BENEDICT   Beatrice!
BEATRICE   Princes and counties! Surely a princely testimony. A
310 goodly count![7] Count Comfit!° A sweet gallant, surely! Oh,   *Sugarplum*
that I were a man for his sake! Or that I had any friend would
be a man for my sake! But manhood is melted into curtsies,
valor into compliment, and men are only turned into tongue,
and trim° ones, too. He is now as valiant as Hercules that°   *fine (ironic) / who*
315 only tells a lie and swears it. I cannot be a man with° wishing.   *by*
Therefore I will die a woman with grieving.
BENEDICT   Tarry, good Beatrice. By this hand, I love thee.
BEATRICE   Use it for my love some other way than swearing
by it.
320 BENEDICT   Think you in your soul the Count Claudio hath
wronged Hero?
BEATRICE   Yea, as sure as I have a thought or a soul.
BENEDICT   Enough; I am engaged.° I will challenge him. I will   *pledged*
kiss your hand, and so I leave you. By this hand, Claudio
325 shall render me a dear account.° As you hear of me, so think   *pay me dearly*
of me. Go comfort your cousin. I must say she is dead; and
so farewell.   [*Exeunt.*]

---

4. PERFORMANCE COMMENT In performance, this
line can be delivered with gravity or for comic effect.
See Digital Edition PC 4.
5. Is he not proved in the highest degree.

6. *bear her in hand:* lead her on with false hopes.
7. Story, tale (with plays on "count" as a legal indictment and as Claudio's title).

4.2

Enter the Constables [DOGBERRY, VERGES, *the* SEXTON],
BORACHIO *and the Town Clerk, in gowns*[1][, *the*
WATCH, *and* CONRAD].

DOGBERRY   Is our whole dissembly° appeared?   *(for "assembly")*
VERGES   Oh, a stool and a cushion for the Sexton.
SEXTON   Which be the malefactors?[2]
DOGBERRY   Marry, that am I and my partner.
5   VERGES   Nay, that's certain. We have the exhibition° to examine.   *(for "commission")*
SEXTON   But which are the offenders that are to be examined?
   Let them come before Master Constable.
DOGBERRY   Yea, marry, let them come before me. What is your
   name, friend?
10   BORACHIO   Borachio.
DOGBERRY   Pray write down, "Borachio." Yours, sirrah?[3]
CONRAD   I am a gentleman, sir, and my name is Conrad.
DOGBERRY   Write down, "Master Gentleman Conrad." Masters, do you serve God?
15   CONRAD *and* BORACHIO   Yea, sir, we hope.
DOGBERRY   Write down that they hope they serve God. And
   write "God" first, for God defend° but God should go before[4]   *forbid*
   such villains. Masters, it is proved already that you are little
   better than false knaves, and it will go near to be thought so
20   shortly. How answer you for yourselves?
CONRAD   Marry, sir, we say we are none.
DOGBERRY   A marvelous witty° fellow, I assure you. But I will   *clever*
   go about with° him. Come you hither, sirrah! A word in your   *outwit*
   ear, sir. I say to you, it is thought you are false knaves.
25   BORACHIO   Sir, I say to you, we are none.
DOGBERRY   Well, stand aside. Fore God, they are both in a tale.°   *telling the same story*
   Have you writ down that they are none?
SEXTON   Master Constable, you go not the way to examine.
   You must call forth the watch that are their accusers.
30   DOGBERRY   Yea, marry, that's the eftest° way. Let the watch   *(nonsense word*
   come forth. —Masters, I charge you in the Prince's name,   *for "aptest")*
   accuse these men.
FIRST WATCHMAN   This man said, sir, that Don John the Prince's
   brother was a villain.
35   DOGBERRY   Write down, "Prince John a villain." Why, this is
   flat perjury:[5] to call a prince's brother "villain."
BORACHIO   Master Constable.
DOGBERRY   Pray thee, fellow, peace! I do not like thy look, I
   promise thee.
40   SEXTON   What heard you him say else?
SECOND WATCHMAN   Marry, that he had received a thousand
   ducats of Don John for accusing the lady Hero wrongfully.
DOGBERRY   Flat burglary° as ever was committed.   *(for "perjury")*

4.2 Location: A prison or hearing room in Messina.
1. Constables wore black gowns. The Sexton is presumably Francis Seacoal (3.5.51). Q's direction calls
him the town clerk, an office more appropriate to his
function in the scene than sexton, with which, however, it seems often to have been combined.

2. Dogberry seems to mistake "malefactors" for "factors," or agents.
3. Contemptuous, since "sirrah" is used to address
inferiors, provoking Conrad's claim to be a gentleman.
4. (Punningly) take precedence over.
5. Perhaps a mistake for "treachery" or "slander."

VERGES Yea, by mass,[6] that it is.

45 SEXTON What else, fellow?

FIRST WATCHMAN And that Count Claudio did mean upon°   *on the basis of*
his words to disgrace Hero before the whole assembly, and
not marry her.

DOGBERRY Oh! Villain, thou wilt be condemned into everlast-

50 ing redemption° for this.   *(for "damnation")*

SEXTON What else?

FIRST WATCHMAN *and* SECOND WATCHMAN This is all.

SEXTON And this is more, masters, than you can deny. Prince
John is this morning secretly stolen away. Hero was in this

55 manner accused; in this very manner refused; and upon the
grief of this, suddenly died. Master Constable, let these men
be bound and brought to Leonato's. I will go before and
show him their examination.   [*Exit.*]

VERGES Come, let them be opinioned.° Let them be in the   *(for "pinioned")*

60 hands of—

CONRAD [*pointing to* DOGBERRY] Coxcomb![7]

DOGBERRY God's° my life, where's the Sexton? Let him write   *God save*
down, "The Prince's officer, Coxcomb!" Come, bind them.
—Thou naughty varlet.°   *wicked knave*

65 CONRAD Away! You are an ass. You are an ass.

DOGBERRY Dost thou not suspect° my place? Dost thou not   *(for "respect")*
suspect my years? Oh, that he were here to write me down
an ass! But masters, remember that I am an ass. Though it
be not written down, yet forget not that I am an ass. No,

70 thou villain, thou art full of picty,° as shall be proved upon   *(for "impiety")*
thee by good witness. I am a wise fellow, and which is more,
an officer, and which is more, a householder, and which is
more, as pretty a piece of flesh[8] as any is in Messina, and
one that knows the law, go to, and a rich fellow enough, go

75 to, and a fellow that hath had losses,[9] and one that hath two
gowns and everything handsome about him. Bring him
away. Oh, that I had been writ down an ass!   *Exeunt.*

5.1

Enter LEONATO *and his brother* [ANTHONY].

ANTHONY If you go on thus you will kill yourself,
And 'tis not wisdom thus to second° grief   *assist*
Against yourself.

LEONATO   I pray thee, cease thy counsel,
Which falls into mine ears as profitless

5 As water in a sieve. Give not me counsel,
Nor let no comforter delight mine ear
But such a one whose wrongs do suit° with mine.   *match*
Bring me a father that so loved his child,
Whose joy of° her is overwhelmed like mine,   *in*

10 And bid him speak of patience.
Measure his woe the length and breadth of mine,
And let it answer every strain° for strain—   *intense hardship*

---

6. "By the mass," a common oath.
7. This is an emendation of a corrupt passage, given
in Q as part of the previous speech.
8. *as pretty . . . flesh:* as fine (or gallant) a mortal

man.
9. *hath had losses:* was once richer.
5.1 Location: Near Leonato's house.

As thus for thus, and such a grief for such—
In every lineament, branch, shape, and form.[1]
15   If such a one will smile and stroke his beard,
And sorrow, wag, cry "Hem!" when he should groan[2]—
Patch° grief with proverbs, make misfortune drunk   *Mend*
With candle-wasters[3]—bring him yet to me,
And I of him will gather patience.
20   But there is no such man. For, brother, men
Can counsel and speak comfort to that grief
Which they themselves not feel. But tasting it,
Their counsel turns to passion which before
Would give preceptial° medicine to rage,   *precepts as*
25   Fetter strong madness in a silken thread,
Charm ache with air° and agony with words.   *breath*
No, no! 'Tis all men's office° to speak patience   *business*
To those that wring° under the load of sorrow,   *writhe*
But no man's virtue nor sufficiency°   *ability*
30   To be so moral° when he shall endure   *moralizing*
The like himself. Therefore give me no counsel.
My griefs cry louder than advertisement.°   *advice*
ANTHONY Therein do men from children nothing differ.
LEONATO I pray thee, peace! I will be flesh and blood.
35   For there was never yet philosopher
That could endure the toothache patiently,
However they have writ the style of gods
And made a push at chance and sufferance.[4]
ANTHONY Yet bend° not all the harm upon yourself.   *direct*
40   Make those that do offend you suffer too.
LEONATO There thou speak'st reason. Nay, I will do so.
My soul doth tell me Hero is belied,
And that shall Claudio know. So shall the Prince
And all of them that thus dishonor her.
        Enter Prince [PEDRO] *and* CLAUDIO.
45   ANTHONY Here comes the Prince and Claudio hastily.
PEDRO Good e'en,° good e'en.   *evening*
CLAUDIO   Good day to both of you.
LEONATO Hear you, my lords?
PEDRO   We have some haste, Leonato.
LEONATO Some haste, my lord? Well, fare you well, my lord.
Are you so hasty now? Well, all is one.°   *no matter*
50   PEDRO Nay, do not quarrel with us, good old man.
ANTHONY If he could right himself with quarreling
Some of us° would lie low.   *(Don Pedro and Claudio)*
CLAUDIO   Who wrongs him?
LEONATO Marry, thou dost wrong me, thou dissembler, thou![5]
Nay, never lay thy hand upon thy sword.
I fear thee not.

1. Leonato moves from the outline of the body to its integral whole. *lineament:* outline. *branch:* limb. *shape:* appearance. *form:* entire body.
2. TEXTUAL COMMENT *wag, cry "Hem!":* talk animatedly, clear his throat (as if about to make a speech). This somewhat baffling line, perhaps reflecting Leonato's anguish, has puzzled editors, who have proposed many emendations. See Digital Edition TC 7.
3. *make misfortune . . . candle-wasters:* forget about misfortune through tedious philosophy. *drunk:* insensible. *candle-wasters:* philosophers; burners of midnight oil (and their works).
4. *writ . . . sufferance:* written as if they transcended human passion, and expressed themselves scornfully about (said "push" to) bad luck and suffering. *push:* equivalent here to "pish," a noise of disdain.
5. "Thou," which in early modern English is less formal than "you," is used contemptuously here.

55	CLAUDIO Marry, beshrew° my hand	*curse*
	If it should give your age such cause of fear.	
	In faith, my hand meant nothing to⁶ my sword.	
	LEONATO Tush, tush, man! Never fleer° and jest at me.	*sneer; mock*
	I speak not like a dotard nor a fool	
60	As under privilege of age to brag	
	What I have done, being young, or what would do,	
	Were I not old. Know, Claudio, to thy head,°	*face*
	Thou hast so wronged mine innocent child and me	
	That I am forced to lay my reverence by,	
65	And with gray hairs and bruise of many days	
	Do challenge thee to trial of a man.°	*(a duel)*
	I say thou hast belied mine innocent child.	
	Thy slander hath gone through and through her heart	
	And she lies buried with her ancestors,	
70	Oh! in a tomb where never scandal slept	
	Save this of hers, framed° by thy villainy.	*created*
	CLAUDIO My villainy?	
	LEONATO Thine, Claudio, thine I say.	
	PEDRO You say not right, old man.	
	LEONATO My lord, my lord!	
	I'll prove it on his body if he dare,	
75	Despite his nice fence⁷ and his active practice,	
	His May of youth and bloom of lustihood.°	*virility*
	CLAUDIO Away! I will not have to do with you.	
	LEONATO Canst thou so daff me?° Thou hast killed my child.	*brush me off*
	If thou kill'st me, boy, thou shalt kill a man.	
80	ANTHONY He shall kill two of us, and men indeed.	
	But that's no matter. Let him kill one first.	
	Win me and wear me!⁸ Let him answer me.°	*(in a duel)*
	Come, follow me, boy! Come, sir boy, come follow me,	
	Sir boy! I'll whip you from your foining fence.⁹	
85	Nay, as I am a gentleman, I will.	
	LEONATO Brother!	
	ANTHONY Content yourself.° God knows, I loved my niece,	*Don't interfere*
	And she is dead, slandered to death by villains	
	That dare as well answer a man indeed	
90	As I dare take a serpent by the tongue.	
	Boys, apes,° braggarts, jacks,° milksops!	*fools / knaves*
	LEONATO Brother Anthony!	
	ANTHONY Hold you content. What, man! I know them, yea,	
	And what they weigh, even to the utmost scruple.°	*1/24 ounce*
95	Scambling, outfacing, fashion-monging boys¹	
	That lie, and cog,° and flout,° deprave,° and slander,	*cheat / mock / defame*
	Go anticly,° and show outward hideousness,²	*outlandishly dressed*
	And speak of half a dozen dang'rous words,	
	How they might hurt their enemies, if they durst.	
	And this is all.	
100	LEONATO But brother Anthony.	

---

6. My hand had no designs upon.
7. His nimble fencing (said contemptuously).
8. A form of challenge: let him beat me and only then boast of it.
9. Thrusting position in fencing (Anthony probably

means that he will compel Claudio to close with him in the duel, or that he will literally take a whip to him).
1. *Scambling . . . boys:* Quarrelsome, insolent, faddish boys.
2. A fearsome exterior.

ANTHONY   Come, 'tis no matter.
　　Do not you meddle. Let me deal in this.
PEDRO   Gentlemen both, we will not wake° your patience.　　　　　*test*
　　My heart is sorry for your daughter's death,
105　　But on my honor, she was charged with nothing
　　But what was true and very full of proof.
LEONATO   My lord, my lord!
PEDRO　　　　　　　　　　　I will not hear you.
LEONATO   No? Come, brother, away. I will be heard.
ANTHONY   And shall, or some of us will smart for it.

　　　　　　　Exeunt LEONATO *and* ANTHONY.

110　PEDRO   See, see! Here comes the man we went to seek.

　　　　　　Enter BENEDICT.

CLAUDIO   Now, signor, what news?
BENEDICT   Good day, my lord.
PEDRO   Welcome, signor. You are almost come to part almost
　　a fray.
115　CLAUDIO   We had liked to have had° our two noses snapped　　*We nearly had*
　　off with° two old men without teeth.　　　　　　　　　　　　*by*
PEDRO   Leonato and his brother. What thinkest thou? Had we
　　fought, I doubt° we should have been too young for them.　　*suspect*
BENEDICT   In a false quarrel there is no true valor. I came to
120　seek you both.
CLAUDIO   We have been up and down to seek thee, for we are
　　high proof° melancholy and would fain have it beaten away.　　*to a high degree*
　　Wilt thou use thy wit?
BENEDICT   It is in my scabbard. Shall I draw it?
125　PEDRO   Dost thou wear thy wit by thy side?
CLAUDIO   Never any did so, though very many have been beside
　　their wit.° I will bid thee draw as we do the minstrels:[3] draw　　*out of their minds*
　　to pleasure us.
PEDRO   As I am an honest man, he looks pale. Art thou sick,
130　or angry?
CLAUDIO   What, courage, man! What though care killed a cat?[4]
　　Thou hast mettle° enough in thee to kill care.　　　　　　　*spirit; courage*
BENEDICT   Sir, I shall meet your wit in the career.° An you　　*at full gallop*
　　charge° it against me, I pray you, choose another subject.　　*aim*
135　CLAUDIO   Nay, then, give him another staff.° This last was broke　　*lance*
　　'cross.[5]
PEDRO   By this light, he changes° more and more. I think he　　*changes color*
　　be angry indeed.
CLAUDIO   If he be, he knows how to turn his girdle.[6]
140　BENEDICT   [*to* CLAUDIO]   Shall I speak a word in your ear?
CLAUDIO   God bless° me from a challenge!　　　　　　　　　　*protect*
BENEDICT   [*aside to* CLAUDIO]   You are a villain. I jest not. I will
　　make it good how you dare, with what° you dare, and when　　*whatever weapon*
　　you dare. Do me right,[7] or I will protest° your cowardice.　　*proclaim*
145　You have killed a sweet lady, and her death shall fall heavy
　　on you. Let me hear from you.

---

3. *draw . . . minstrels:* draw a sword, the way a min-
strel is bidden to draw a bow across his musical
instrument.
4. Proverbial (compare "Curiosity killed the cat").
5. Was snapped in the middle, like a badly handled

lance. (Claudio is mocking Benedict's attempt at wit.)
6. A colloquialism of uncertain derivation, possibly meaning "let him get on with it" or "that's his
problem."
7. Give me satisfaction.

CLAUDIO [*aside to* BENEDICT] Well, I will meet you, so I may
    have good cheer.
PEDRO What? A feast? A feast?
150 CLAUDIO I'faith, I thank him, he hath bid me to a calf's head
    and a capon, the which if I do not carve most curiously,° say   *daintily*
    my knife's naught.° Shall I not find a woodcock[8] too?   *useless*
BENEDICT Sir, your wit ambles[9] well. It goes easily.
PEDRO I'll tell thee how Beatrice praised thy wit the other
155   day. I said thou hadst a fine wit. "True," said she, "a fine little
    one." "No," said I, "a great wit." "Right," says she, "a great
    gross one." "Nay," said I, "a good wit." "Just," said she, "it
    hurts nobody." "Nay," said I, "the gentleman is wise." "Cer-
    tain," said she, "a wise gentleman."[1] "Nay," said I, "he hath the
160   tongues."° "That I believe," said she, "for he swore a thing to   *knows several languages*
    me on Monday night which he forswore on Tuesday morning.
    There's a double tongue. There's two tongues." Thus did she
    an hour together trans-shape° thy particular virtues, yet at   *distort*
    last she concluded, with a sigh, thou wast the properest° man   *handsomest*
165   in Italy.
CLAUDIO For the which she wept heartily and said she cared
    not.
PEDRO Yea, that she did. But yet, for all that, and if she did
    not hate him deadly, she would love him dearly. The old man's
170   daughter told us all.
CLAUDIO All, all, and moreover, God saw him when he was
    hid in the garden.[2]
PEDRO But when shall we set the savage bull's horns on the
    sensible Benedict's head?
175 CLAUDIO Yea, and text underneath, "Here dwells Benedict
    the married man"?[3]
BENEDICT Fare you well, boy. You know my mind. I will leave
    you now to your gossip-like° humor. You break° jests as brag-   *old-womanish / crack*
    garts do their blades,[4] which, God be thanked, hurt not. My
180   lord, for your many courtesies I thank you. I must discon-
    tinue your company. Your brother the bastard is fled from
    Messina. You have among you killed a sweet and innocent
    lady. For my lord Lackbeard there, he and I shall meet, and
    till then, peace be with him.   [*Exit.*]
185 PEDRO He is in earnest.
CLAUDIO In most profound earnest, and I'll warrant you, for
    the love of Beatrice.
PEDRO And hath challenged thee?
CLAUDIO Most sincerely.
190 PEDRO What a pretty thing man is, when he goes in his dou-
    blet and hose and leaves off his wit![5]

8. The calf's head, capon, and woodcock were variet-
ies of food that also symbolize stupidity.
9. Moves slowly (in other words, it does not gallop as
a quick wit would).
1. A phrase often used ironically to mean "an old
fool."
2. Allusion to Genesis 3:8 (Adam attempting to hide
from God in the Garden of Eden); contains a half-
hidden reference to the trick played on Benedict in

the garden.
3. Claudio and Don Pedro recall that Benedict joked
that if he ever fell in love, his friends could set horns
in his forehead, have his picture painted, and title it
"Benedict, the married man" (1.1.223–28).
4. Braggarts secretly dent their swords to make it
appear that they have been dealing fierce blows.
5. When he puts on fine clothes but forgets to wear
his brain.

CLAUDIO He is then a giant to an ape, but then is an ape a
doctor to such a man.[6]

195 PEDRO But soft you,° let me be. Pluck up,° my heart, and be *wait / Collect yourself*
sad.° Did he not say my brother was fled?   *serious*

Enter Constables [DOGBERRY *and* VERGES], CONRAD,
and BORACHIO.

DOGBERRY Come you, sir, if justice cannot tame you she shall
ne'er weigh more reasons[7] in her balance.° Nay, and you be a   *scales*
cursing hypocrite once,° you must be looked to.   *even once*

200 PEDRO How now, two of my brother's men bound? Borachio
one?

CLAUDIO Hearken after° their offense, my lord.   *Inquire into*

PEDRO Officers, what offense have these men done?

DOGBERRY Marry, sir, they have committed false report.
Moreover, they have spoken untruths. Secondarily, they are
205 slanders.° Sixth and lastly, they have belied a lady. Thirdly,   *(for "slanderers")*
they have verified° unjust things. And to conclude, they are   *affirmed as true*
lying knaves.

PEDRO First I ask thee, what they have done? Thirdly I ask
thee, what's their offense? Sixth and lastly, why they are
210 committed?° And to conclude, what you lay to their charge?   *held on arrest*

CLAUDIO Rightly reasoned and in his own division.° And by   *logical organization*
my troth, there's one meaning well suited.[8]

PEDRO [*to* CONRAD *and* BORACHIO] Who have you offended,
masters, that you are thus bound to your answer?[9] This
215 learned Constable is too cunning to be understood. What's
your offense?

BORACHIO Sweet Prince, let me go no farther to mine answer.°   *trial; account*
Do you hear me, and let this Count kill me. I have deceived
even your very eyes. What your wisdoms could not discover
220 these shallow fools have brought to light, who in the night
overheard me confessing to this man how Don John, your
brother, incensed° me to slander the lady Hero; how you were   *incited*
brought into the orchard and saw me court Margaret in
Hero's garments; how you disgraced her when you should
225 marry her. My villainy they have upon record, which I had
rather seal° with my death than repeat over to my shame. The   *confirm; end*
lady is dead upon mine and my master's false accusation, and
briefly, I desire nothing but the reward of a villain.

PEDRO [*to* CLAUDIO] Runs not this speech like iron through
230 your blood?

CLAUDIO I have drunk poison whiles he uttered it.

PEDRO [*to* BORACHIO] But did my brother set thee on to this?

BORACHIO Yea, and paid me richly for the practice° of it.   *execution*

PEDRO He is composed and framed° of treachery   *made up*
235 And fled he is upon this villainy.

CLAUDIO Sweet Hero, now thy image doth appear
In the rare semblance° that I loved it first.   *likeness*

---

6. Such a man is much bigger than an ape, but an
ape is a learned man ("doctor") compared with him.
7. Legal cases. Also, "reason" was pronounced like
"raisin," producing a comic image here.

8. Dressed in several different costumes (with play
on legal "suit").
9. Required to respond (punning on "bound over for
trial" and "bound with ropes").

DOGBERRY Come, bring away the plaintiffs.° By this time our   *(for "defendants")*
    Sexton hath reformed° Signor Leonato of the matter. And   *(for "informed")*
240   masters, do not forget to specify, when time and place shall
    serve, that I am an ass.
VERGES Here! Here comes master Signor Leonato, and the
    Sexton too.
                Enter LEONATO, *his brother* [ANTHONY], *and*
                the SEXTON.
LEONATO Which is the villain? Let me see his eyes,
245   That when I note another man like him
    I may avoid him. Which of these is he?
BORACHIO If you would know your wronger, look on me.
LEONATO Art thou the slave that with thy breath hast killed
    Mine innocent child?
BORACHIO   Yea, even I alone.
250 LEONATO No, not so, villain. Thou beliest thyself.
    Here stand a pair of honorable men;
    A third is fled that had a hand in it.
    I thank you, princes, for my daughter's death.
    Record it with your high and worthy deeds.
255   'Twas bravely done, if you bethink you of it.
CLAUDIO I know not how to pray your patience,
    Yet I must speak. Choose your revenge yourself.
    Impose° me to what penance your invention   *Subject*
    Can lay upon my sin. Yet sinned I not
    But in mistaking.
260 PEDRO   By my soul, nor I.
    And yet, to satisfy this good old man
    I would bend under any heavy weight
    That he'll enjoin me to.
LEONATO I cannot bid you bid my daughter live;
265   That were impossible. But I pray you both,
    Possess° the people in Messina here   *Inform*
    How innocent she died, and if your love
    Can labor aught in sad invention,[1]
    Hang her an epitaph upon her tomb
270   And sing it to her bones. Sing it tonight.
    Tomorrow morning, come you to my house,
    And since you could not be my son-in-law,
    Be yet my nephew. My brother hath a daughter,
    Almost the copy of my child that's dead,
275   And she alone is heir to both of us.[2]
    Give her the right you should have given her cousin,
    And so dies my revenge.
CLAUDIO   O noble sir!
    Your over-kindness doth wring tears from me.
    I do embrace your offer, and dispose
280   For henceforth° of poor Claudio.   *For the future*
LEONATO Tomorrow then I will expect your coming.
    Tonight I take my leave. This naughty° man   *evil*
    Shall face to face be brought to Margaret,

1. Can produce anything in the way of sad art.
2. Shakespeare (or Leonato) has apparently forgotten Anthony's son mentioned at 1.2.1.

Who, I believe, was packed° in all this wrong,   *confederate*
285   Hired to it by your brother.
       BORACHIO   No, by my soul, she was not,
       Nor knew not what she did when she spoke to me,
       But always hath been just and virtuous
       In anything that I do know by° her.   *of*
290   DOGBERRY   Moreover, sir, which indeed is not under white
       and black, this plaintiff[3] here, the offender, did call me
       "ass." I beseech you, let it be remembered in his punish-
       ment. And also, the watch heard them talk of one Deformed.
       They say he wears a key in his ear and a lock hanging by it,[4]
295   and borrows money in God's name, the which he hath used°   *done habitually*
       so long and never paid that now men grow hard-hearted and
       will lend nothing for God's sake.[5] Pray you, examine him
       upon that point.
       LEONATO   I thank thee for thy care and honest pains.
300   DOGBERRY   Your worship speaks like a most thankful and rev-
       erend youth, and I praise God for you.
       LEONATO   [*giving money to* DOGBERRY]   There's for thy pains.
       DOGBERRY   God save the foundation.[6]
       LEONATO   Go. I discharge thee of thy prisoner, and I thank
305   thee.
       DOGBERRY   I leave an arrant knave with your worship, which I
       beseech your worship to correct yourself[7] for the example of
       others. God keep your worship. I wish your worship well.
       God restore you to health. I humbly give you leave to depart,
310   and if a merry meeting may be wished, God prohibit° it.   *(for "permit")*
       Come, neighbor.   [*Exeunt* DOGBERRY *and* VERGES.]
       LEONATO   Until tomorrow morning, lords, farewell.
       ANTHONY   Farewell, my lords. We look for you tomorrow.
       PEDRO   We will not fail.
       CLAUDIO   Tonight I'll mourn with Hero.
315   LEONATO   Bring you these fellows on. We'll talk with Margaret,
       How her acquaintance grew with this lewd° fellow.   *worthless*
                                                    Exeunt.

                                    5.2
                 Enter BENEDICT *and* MARGARET.
       BENEDICT   Pray thee, sweet mistress Margaret, deserve well
       at my hands by helping me to the speech of Beatrice.
       MARGARET   Will you then write me a sonnet in praise of my
       beauty?
5   BENEDICT   In so high a style, Margaret, that no man living
       shall come over[1] it. For in most comely truth, thou deservest it.
       MARGARET   To have no man come over me? Why, shall I
       always keep below stairs?[2]

---

3. For "defendant." *under white and black:* in writing.
4. Dogberry's garbled recollection of the lovelock mentioned at 3.3.149.
5. "In God's name" and "for God's sake" were phrases
used by beggars.
6. A conventional response to alms from a charitable
foundation.
7. Dogberry wishes Leonato himself to punish ("cor-

rect") Borachio, but accidentally says that Leonato
should be punished.
5.2 Location: Near Leonato's house or in his garden.
1. Surpass; climb over (punning on "stile": steps over
a fence). Margaret humorously takes "come over" in a
sexual sense.
2. In the servants' quarters (and therefore never as a
"mistress").

BENEDICT   Thy wit is as quick as the greyhound's mouth.³ It
10   catches.

MARGARET   And yours as blunt as the fencer's foils,⁴ which hit
but hurt not.

BENEDICT   A most manly wit, Margaret. It will not hurt a woman.
And so, I pray thee, call Beatrice. I give thee the bucklers.⁵

15   MARGARET   Give us the swords. We have bucklers of our own.

BENEDICT   If you use them, Margaret, you must put in the
pikes with a vice,° and they are dangerous weapons for maids.   *screw*

MARGARET   Well, I will call Beatrice to you, who I think hath
legs.   *Exit* MARGARET.

20   BENEDICT   And therefore will come.⁶

[*Sings.*]   The god of love
That sits above,
And knows me, and knows me,
How pitiful I deserve.⁷

25   I mean in singing. But in loving, Leander the good swimmer,
Troilus the first employer of panders,⁸ and a whole book full
of these quondam carpet-mongers⁹ whose names yet run
smoothly in the even road of a blank verse—why, they were
never so truly turned over and over° as my poor self in love.   *head over heels*

30   Marry, I cannot show it in rhyme. I have tried. I can find out
no rhyme to "lady" but "baby"; an innocent° rhyme. For   *childish*
"scorn," "horn"; a hard¹ rhyme. For "school," "fool"; a babbling rhyme; very ominous endings. No, I was not born under
a rhyming planet,² nor I cannot woo in festival terms.°   *fancy rhetoric*

Enter BEATRICE.

35   Sweet Beatrice, wouldst thou come when I called thee?

BEATRICE   Yea, signor, and depart when you bid me.

BENEDICT   Oh, stay but till then.

BEATRICE   "Then" is spoken. Fare you well now. And yet, ere I
go, let me go with that° I came, which is with knowing what   *what*

40   hath passed between you and Claudio.

BENEDICT   Only foul words, and thereupon I will kiss thee.

BEATRICE   Foul words is but foul wind, and foul wind is but
foul breath, and foul breath is noisome.° Therefore I will   *foul-smelling*
depart unkissed.

45   BENEDICT   Thou hast frighted the word out of his° right sense,°   *its / meaning; wits*
so forcible is thy wit. But I must tell thee plainly, Claudio
undergoes° my challenge, and either I must shortly hear   *is subject to*
from him, or I will subscribe° him a coward. And I pray thee,   *proclaim*
now tell me, for which of my bad parts didst thou first fall in

50   love with me?

BEATRICE   For them all together, which maintained so poli-
tic° a state of evil that they will not admit any good part to   *cunningly governed*

3. Your wit picks things up as easily as a hunting dog
with its mouth.
4. Practice rapiers, capped at the tip.
5. Benedict offers to surrender by giving up the
bucklers: shields with spikes ("pikes") in the center.
Margaret bawdily interprets this as the female sexual
organ.
6. A popular question and answer of the time was
"How came you hither?" "On my legs."
7. How greatly I deserve pity (but Benedict takes it
as "how pitifully small my deserts are"). These four
lines are the beginning of a popular sentimental

ballad.
8. Troilus, loving Cressida, employed her uncle Pandarus as go-between. Leander swam the Hellespont
nightly to be with his love, Hero.
9. Knights of long ago ("quondam") who avoided
military service and spent their time in ladies' car-
peted boudoirs.
1. Disagreeable, because horns were associated with
cuckoldry.
2. At a time when the stars would influence me to
become a poet.

intermingle with them. But for which of my good parts did
you first suffer° love for me?   feel

55 BENEDICT Suffer love! A good epithet.° I do suffer° love indeed,   expression / suffer from
for I love thee against my will.

BEATRICE In spite of your heart, I think. Alas, poor heart! If
you spite it for my sake, I will spite it for yours, for I will
never love that which my friend hates.

60 BENEDICT Thou and I are too wise to woo peaceably.

BEATRICE It appears not in this confession.³ There's not one
wise man among twenty that will praise himself.

BENEDICT An old, an old instance,° Beatrice, that lived in the   maxim
time of good neighbors.⁴ If a man do not erect in this age his
65 own tomb ere he dies, he shall live no longer in monument°   remembrance
than the bell rings and the widow weeps.

BEATRICE And how long is that, think you?

BENEDICT Question?⁵ Why, an hour in clamor° and a quarter   ringing
in rheum.° Therefore is it most expedient for the wise, if Don   tears
70 Worm, his conscience,⁶ find no impediment to the contrary,
to be the trumpet of his own virtues, as I am to myself. So
much for praising myself, who I myself will bear witness is
praiseworthy. And now tell me, how doth your cousin?

BEATRICE Very ill.

75 BENEDICT And how do you?

BEATRICE Very ill too.

BENEDICT Serve God, love me, and mend.° There will I leave   recover
you, too, for here comes one in haste.

       Enter URSULA.

URSULA Madam, you must come to your uncle. Yonder's old
80 coil° at home. It is proved my lady Hero hath been falsely   great disturbance
accused, the Prince and Claudio mightily abused,° and Don   deceived
John is the author of all, who is fled and gone. Will you
come presently?

BEATRICE Will you go hear this news, signor?

85 BENEDICT I will live in thy heart, die⁷ in thy lap, and be buried
in thy eyes. And moreover, I will go with thee to thy uncle's.
                                                                    Exeunt.

                              5.3
       Enter CLAUDIO, *Prince* [PEDRO, *a* LORD], *and three or*
       four [Attendants] *with tapers*¹ [and a MUSICIAN].²

CLAUDIO Is this the monument° of Leonato?   family tomb

LORD It is, my lord.
       [*He reads the*] *epitaph.*
       "Done to death by slanderous tongues
       Was the Hero that here lies.
5   Death, in guerdon° of her wrongs,   recompense
       Gives her fame which never dies.

3. Since it is not wise to claim to be wise.
4. In the good old days, when neighbors praised each
other.
5. Is that the question?
6. Facetious way of referring to the proverbial gnaw-
ing "worm of conscience."
7. With the common Elizabethan connotation of
orgasm.

5.3 Location: A churchyard.
1. Candles or torches carried in token of penitence.
2. TEXTUAL COMMENT Q does not give an entry for a
Musician at the beginning of this scene, which
means it is not clear who sings the song "Pardon,
goddess of the night." To solve the problem, this edition calls for a Musician to enter here. See Digital
Edition TC 8.

So the life that died with° shame   *from*
Lives in death with glorious fame."
[*He hangs up the scroll.*]
Hang thou there upon the tomb,
10   Praising her when I am dead.
CLAUDIO   Now, music, sound and sing your solemn hymn.
                                    Song.
MUSICIAN [*sings*]   Pardon, goddess of the night,[3]
                Those that slew thy virgin knight.[4]
                For the which, with songs of woe,
15   Round about her tomb they go.
                Midnight, assist our moan!
                Help us to sigh and groan
                Heavily, heavily.
                Graves, yawn and yield your dead!
20   Till death be utterèd,°   *fully lamented*
                Heavily, heavily.[5]
LORD   Now unto thy bones, goodnight!
        Yearly will I do this rite.
PEDRO   Good morrow, masters. Put your torches out.
25   The wolves have preyed,[6] and look, the gentle day,
        Before the wheels of Phoebus,[7] round about
        Dapples the drowsy East with spots of gray.
        Thanks to you all, and leave us. Fare you well.
CLAUDIO   Good morrow, masters. Each his several° way.   *separate*
30 PEDRO   Come! Let us hence, and put on other weeds!°   *garments*
        And then to Leonato's we will go.
CLAUDIO   And Hymen now with luckier issue speed 's[8]
        Than this° for whom we rendered up this woe.   *Exeunt.*   *this woman*

5.4

Enter LEONATO, BENEDICT, MARGARET, URSULA,
Old Man [ANTHONY], FRIAR, HERO.
FRIAR   Did I not tell you she was innocent?
LEONATO   So are the Prince and Claudio, who accused her
        Upon° the error that you heard debated.   *Because of*
        But Margaret was in some fault for this,
5   Although against her will,° as it appears   *unintentionally*
        In the true course of all the question.°   *investigation*
ANTHONY   Well, I am glad that all things sorts° so well.   *turn out*
BENEDICT   And so am I, being else by faith° enforced   *my pledge*
        To call young Claudio to a reckoning for it.
10 LEONATO   Well, daughter, and you gentlewomen all,
        Withdraw into a chamber by yourselves,
        And when I send for you, come hither masked.
        The Prince and Claudio promised by this hour

---

3. Diana, Roman goddess of the moon and patroness
of virgins.
4. Hero (imagined as a knight, or follower, of Diana).
5. TEXTUAL COMMENT In F, the final line of the song
reads "Heavenly, heavenly." Although this edition follows Q, it is interpretively rewarding to consider F's

variant. See Digital Edition TC 9.
6. Have finished preying (for the night has passed).
7. The sun god's chariot wheels.
8. And may Hymen (Greek god of marriage) grant us
more favorable results.
5.4 Location: Leonato's house.

	To visit me. You know your office,° brother.	*task*
15	You must be father to your brother's daughter,	
	And give her to young Claudio. *Exeunt ladies.*	
	ANTHONY Which I will do with confirmed° countenance.	*serious*
	BENEDICT Friar, I must entreat your pains, I think.	
	FRIAR To do what, signor?	
20	BENEDICT To bind me or undo° me; one of them.	*ruin; unbind*
	Signor Leonato, truth it is, good signor,	
	Your niece regards me with an eye of favor.	
	LEONATO That eye my daughter lent her— 'tis most true.	
	BENEDICT And I do with an eye of love requite her.	
25	LEONATO The sight whereof I think you had from me,	
	From Claudio, and the Prince. But what's your will?	
	BENEDICT Your answer, sir, is enigmatical.	
	But for my will: my will is,° your goodwill	*is that*
	May stand with ours, this day to be conjoined	
30	In the state of honorable marriage	
	In which, good Friar, I shall desire your help.	
	LEONATO My heart is with your liking.	
	FRIAR And my help.	
	Here comes the Prince and Claudio.	

Enter Prince [PEDRO], *and* CLAUDIO, *and two or
three* [Attendants].

	PEDRO Good morrow to this fair assembly.	
35	LEONATO Good morrow, Prince. Good morrow, Claudio.	
	We here attend you. Are you yet° determined	*still*
	Today to marry with my brother's daughter?	
	CLAUDIO I'll hold my mind° were she an Ethiope.[1]	*intention*
	LEONATO Call her forth, brother. Here's the Friar ready.	

[*Exit* ANTHONY.]

40	PEDRO Good morrow, Benedict. Why, what's the matter	
	That you have such a February face?	
	So full of frost, of storm and cloudiness?	
	CLAUDIO I think he thinks upon the savage bull.[2]	
	Tush, fear not, man! We'll tip thy horns with gold,	
45	And all Europa° shall rejoice at thee	*Europe*
	As once Europa did at lusty Jove,	
	When he would play the noble beast in love.[3]	
	BENEDICT Bull Jove, sir, had an amiable° low.	*amorous*
	And some such strange bull leaped your father's cow	
50	And got a calf° in that same noble feat	*begot a blockhead*
	Much like to you, for you have just his bleat.	

Enter Brother [ANTHONY], HERO, BEATRICE,
MARGARET, URSULA[, *the women masked*].

	CLAUDIO For this I owe you.[4] Here comes other reck'nings.°	*accounts to settle*
	Which is the lady I must seize upon?	
	LEONATO This same is she, and I do give you her.	
55	CLAUDIO Why then, she's mine. Sweet, let me see your face.	
	LEONATO No, that you shall not, till you take her hand	
	Before this Friar and swear to marry her.	
	CLAUDIO Give me your hand before this holy Friar.	

---

1. In other words, black and therefore, according to
the Elizabethan racist stereotype, ugly.
2. Continuing the teasing of 5.1.173.
3. In Greek mythology, Jove took the form of a bull

to carry off the princess Europa, who, according to
the poet Ovid, decked the bull's horns with flowers.
4. I will pay you back later (for the insults).

I am your husband, if you like of me.°   *like me*

60 HERO [*taking off her mask*]   And when I lived I was your other
    wife,
    And when you loved, you were my other husband.

CLAUDIO   Another Hero?

HERO   Nothing certainer.
    One Hero died defiled,° but I do live,   *slandered*
    And surely as I live, I am a maid.

65 PEDRO   The former Hero? Hero that is dead?

LEONATO   She died, my lord, but whiles her slander lived.

FRIAR   All this amazement can I qualify.°   *lessen*
    When after that the holy rites are ended,
    I'll tell you largely° of fair Hero's death.   *in full*

70   Meantime, let wonder° seem familiar,°   *marvels / commonplace*
    And to the chapel let us presently.

BENEDICT   Soft and fair,° Friar. Which is Beatrice?   *Wait a minute*

BEATRICE   I answer to that name. What is your will?

BENEDICT   Do not you love me?

BEATRICE   Why, no, no more than reason.

75 BENEDICT   Why, then, your uncle, and the Prince, and Claudio
    Have been deceived. They swore you did.

BEATRICE   Do not you love me?

BENEDICT   Troth, no, no more than reason.

BEATRICE   Why, then, my cousin, Margaret, and Ursula
    Are much deceived, for they did swear you did.

80 BENEDICT   They swore that you were almost sick for me.

BEATRICE   They swore that you were well-nigh dead for me.

BENEDICT   'Tis no such matter. Then you do not love me?

BEATRICE   No, truly, but in friendly recompense.

LEONATO   Come, cousin. I am sure you love the gentleman.

85 CLAUDIO   And I'll be sworn upon't, that he loves her.
    For here's a paper written in his hand,
    A halting sonnet of his own pure brain,
    Fashioned° to Beatrice.   *Addressed*

HERO   And here's another,
    Writ in my cousin's hand, stolen from her pocket,

90   Containing her affection unto Benedict.

BENEDICT   A miracle! Here's our own hands against our
    hearts.[5] Come, I will have thee. But by this light, I take thee
    for pity.

BEATRICE   I would not deny you. But by this good day, I yield
95   upon great persuasion, and partly to save your life. For I was
    told you were in a consumption.

LEONATO   Peace! [*He gives her hand to* BENEDICT.] I will stop
    your mouth.
            [BENEDICT *kisses* BEATRICE.]

PEDRO   How dost thou, Benedict the married man?

100 BENEDICT   I'll tell thee what, Prince. A college of wit-crackers[6]
    cannot flout° me out of my humor. Dost thou think I care   *jeer*
    for a satire or an epigram? No. If a man will be beaten with

---

5. Our own handwritten testimony contradicts the
indifference we claim to feel in our hearts (or proves
our hearts to be guilty of loving).

6. *a college of wit-crackers*: a whole assembly of
wise-guys.

brains, 'a shall wear nothing handsome about him.[7] In brief,
since I do purpose° to marry, I will think nothing to any   *intend*
105   purpose that the world can say against it. And therefore
never flout at me for what I have said against it; for man is a
giddy thing, and this is my conclusion. For thy part, Claudio, I did think to have beaten thee. But in that thou art
like° to be my kinsman, live unbruised, and love my cousin.   *likely*
110 CLAUDIO I had well hoped thou wouldst have denied Beatrice, that I might have cudgeled thee out of thy single life to
make thee a double-dealer;° which out of question thou wilt   *married man; adulterer*
be, if my cousin do not look exceeding narrowly° to thee.   *closely*
BENEDICT Come, come! We are friends. Let's have a dance
115   ere we are married, that we may lighten our own hearts and
our wives' heels.
      [*Enter* MUSICIANS.]
LEONATO We'll have dancing afterward.
BENEDICT First, of my word! Therefore play music. Prince,
thou art sad. Get thee a wife! Get thee a wife! There is no
120   staff more reverend than one tipped with horn.[8]
      Enter MESSENGER.
MESSENGER My lord, your brother John is ta'en in flight
And brought with armed men back to Messina.
BENEDICT Think not on him till tomorrow. I'll devise thee
brave° punishments for him. Strike up, pipers!   *fine*
      [MUSICIANS *play. They all*] *dance* [*and exeunt*].

---

7. No, if a man is easily injured by ridicule, he will
never even dare to dress well (since that would provoke attention).
8. A final allusion to the cuckold's horns.

The Merry Wives of Windsor

"The first act of the *Merry Wives* alone contains more life and reality than all German literature." So wrote Friedrich Engels to Karl Marx, his fellow German revolutionary and coauthor with Engels of the *Manifesto of the Communist Party*. Perhaps what he admired in *The Merry Wives of Windsor* (1599) is the dramatization of the middle class as it is being formed out of social tensions and verbal distinctions. Probably Engels also shared the enthusiasm of centuries of theater audiences for the play's elaborate intrigues and stage business. Certainly, this is Shakespeare's most middle-class play in subject matter, setting, and outlook. It is also his most farcical, more so even than early works like *The Comedy of Errors* and *The Taming of the Shrew*. Farce and intrigue establish the comic tone that informs the play's ultimate good-humored reconciliation. They also provide the plot mechanisms through which the characters' self-interest is forged into a social unity where hierarchy, though not eliminated, is temporarily suspended. The fusion of these two elements— the theatrical and the social—produces the play's distinctiveness.

The Merry Wives celebrates the playful but chaste behavior of the titular characters, Mistress Page and Mistress Ford, each married to a prosperous burgher. Mistress Page delivers the overt message: "Wives may be merry and yet honest too" (4.2.92),* where "honest" means sexually faithful to one's husband. Master Page's easy and—from a sexual perspective—justified trust of his wife provides a norm from which Master Ford's irrational jealousy of his wife deviates. The two women's plot against Sir John Falstaff, their would-be seducer, is also designed to dupe and cure Ford. In the subplot, the love marriage between Fenton, the impoverished gentleman, and the Pages' daughter Anne—beneath him socially but above him financially— arguably is also assimilable to citizen values.

The play's time and place reinforce this sense of middle-class community. They create the impression of life in an English provincial town at the moment of the work's first performance. Although *The Comedy of Errors* and *The Merchant of Venice* depict prosperous citizens below the aristocracy, those characters live abroad, in the past, or both. By contrast, *The Merry Wives* retains a contemporary, domestic, and nonaristocratic feel unique in Shakespeare. This feel is not uniform, however. The play refers back to the early fifteenth century, and the closest analogue and most likely source for the main plot are from the Italian writer Ser Giovanni Fiorentino's *Il Pecorone* (1558). This plot and the primary subplot also draw on ancient Roman comedy, medieval farce, and Renaissance Italian drama. Finally, the play includes characters from above and below the middle class. Yet the historical allusions don't evoke a bygone era, the foreign traditions are reworked into English stereotypes, and the upper- and lower-class figures ultimately underscore middle-class inclusiveness.

The play ironizes nearly every character's claim to social standing. Slender's pretensions to gentility are mocked from beginning to end. In the opening scene, his uncle, Justice Shallow, acts not to preserve the peace but to undermine it. Similarly ineffectual are the pacifying efforts of the Welsh parson, Sir Hugh Evans, who agrees to a duel with another foreigner, the well-to-do French Doctor Caius. Most of these characters, moreover, derive their authority from the outside—the church or the royal court.

*All quotations are taken from the edited text of the Folio, printed here. The Digital Edition includes edited texts of both the Folio and the Quarto.

Cuckold, his unfaithful wife, and the seducer. From *Roxburghe Ballads* (seventeenth century).

A different kind of conflict pits the wealthy citizens against their social superiors. Page rejects the love suit of Fenton, and Falstaff is abused—in act 5 functioning as a scapegoat against whom the townspeople can unite. This antagonism between citizen and gentleman is given a financial twist appropriate to the dominant ethos of the play. Page believes that Fenton is motivated by money rather than love, a charge that Fenton tells Anne was originally—but is no longer—true:

> I found thee of more value
> Than stamps in gold or sums in sealèd bags,
> And 'tis the very riches of thyself
> That now I aim at.
>
> (3.4.15–18)

Free of romantic concerns, Falstaff's seductions are motivated perhaps by lust and certainly by profit, metaphorically figured as mercantile imperialist treasure. Of Mistress Page he exclaims: "She bears the purse too. She is a region in Guiana, all gold and bounty. I will be cheaters to them both, and they shall be exchequers to me. They shall be my East and West Indies, and I will trade to them both. . . . Sail like my pinnace to these golden shores" (1.3.58–61, 70).

The conclusion resolves this conflict. Page and his wife, although at cross-purposes with each other, each try to marry Anne off to an unsuitable partner. But having been outwitted, both accept their daughter's marriage with good humor. This incorporation of Fenton is extended by Mistress Page to Falstaff as well. Her act reveals the generosity of the citizens' world. The marriage of Fenton to Anne—the main accomplishment of the play, with the exception of the simultaneous duping of Falstaff and curing of Ford—reconciles the middle class with their social betters. Both plots raise the fear of mercenary, sexually threatening aristocratic interlopers only to dispel the concern—because of the predator's comic incompetence or the falseness of the suspicion. Even though the play's language highlights Fenton's lofty rank—he alone speaks primarily in blank verse—he too becomes part of the community. Similarly, the climactic tricking of Falstaff draws on the court masque. But this theatrical form, in which courtiers become the actors, is here recast in a popular, festive mode.

The concluding scene in the fuller Folio text also includes a compliment to the Order of the Garter uttered in blank verse—to reflect the elevated subject matter—by Mistress Quickly disguised as the Queen of Fairies (5.5.52–73). The Order of the Garter was an aristocratic fraternity under the patronage of the Queen that inducted new members at Windsor Castle. This passage has the effect of placing the town of Windsor under the protection of the castle of Windsor, just as the town's Garter Inn evokes the castle's more elevated Order of the Garter. *The Merry Wives* also shares the names of several characters with the two parts of *Henry IV* and with *Henry V*—Falstaff, Mistress Quickly, Shallow, Pistol, Bardolph, Nim. Fenton supposedly "kept company with the wild Prince and Poins" (3.2.64), an allusion to the future Henry V and one of his companions in the *Henry IV* plays. But though the names are the same, the characters are not. The easily duped Falstaff of Windsor lacks the indomitable comic resourcefulness he repeatedly demonstrates in the history plays. Still, the political associations lend a national, monarchical aspect to the more circumscribed events of *The Merry Wives*. The effect is contradictory: royal power is asserted in its absence, but the town's middling sort come to stand for all of England.

The play's generalizing force is further enhanced by an indebtedness to popular culture unusual even for Shakespeare. In keeping with its social milieu, *The Merry Wives* has a far higher percentage of prose than does any other Shakespearean work. Much of it satirically reproduces the language of proverb and cliché; Master Slender and Mistress Quickly in particular depend on language that verges on the meaningless. Shallow's words to Page convey vague goodwill and ineptitude: "Master Page, I am glad to see you. Much good do it your good heart. . . . and I thank you always with my heart, la, with my heart. . . . Sir, I thank you, by yea and no, I do" (1.1.67–72). Similarly, Quickly unleashes a barrage of weakly communicative phrasing that somehow enables her to connect with almost all the other characters: "nobody but has his fault," "the very yea and the no," "that's neither here nor there," "What the goodyear," "thereby hangs a tale," "an honest maid as ever broke bread," "Out upon't" (1.4.12, 84–85, 94–95, 108, 132, 133–34, 147).

The Merry Wives also brings onstage a considerable number of lower-class characters. These are not the clowns and fools of the more aristocratic romantic comedies, but servants: John and Robert, who work for the Fords; Simple, who waits on Slender; John Rugby and Mistress Quickly, who belong to Caius's household; and Falstaff's hangers-on—Bardolph, Pistol, and Nim. In the final scene, when the children of Windsor dress as fairies to punish Falstaff, they mobilize a popular rural belief, evidently shared by their victim, in mischievous immortal spirits who prey upon local inhabitants. Falstaff's insults and injuries—suffocation, dunking in the river, beating, and pinching—belong to the popular tradition of knockabout physical stage action in farce and shaming rituals of the time.

Yet the play's relationship to the lower classes, as to the upper, is mixed. Mistress Quickly is treated with contemptuous condescension. More important, Falstaff and his followers, despite Falstaff's elite connections, engage in the lawlessness that the prosperous middle class of the time attributed to the poor. As the play opens, Shallow charges Falstaff with various crimes, among them stealing his deer. Falstaff then directs his penchant for poaching to the merry wives—unsuccessfully— until he himself becomes the hunted and symbolically cuckolded deer at play's end. Thus, the Pages and Fords define themselves against the social strata both above and below them. This position is modified in the final scene, but only by celebrating a popular culture whose superstitions are viewed with nostalgia but without credulity.

Windsor's sense of community depends in addition on cheerfully casual ethnocentrism. Hostility to foreigners is part of the throwaway language of the play (especially the Host's): "base Hungarian wight," "Base Phrygian Turk," "Flemish drunkard," "Cathayan," "Ethiopian," "Francisco," "Castalian king urinal," "Anthropophaginian" (cannibal), "Bohemian Tartar" (1.3.18, 78; 2.1.19, 127; 2.3.24, 29; 4.5.8, 16). Ford

Elizabeth I and the Knights of the Garter. Engraved by Michael Gheeraerts the Elder (1576).

trades in similar stereotypes: "I will rather trust a Fleming with my butter, Parson Hugh the Welshman with my cheese, an Irishman with my aqua-vitae bottle, or a thief to walk my ambling gelding, than my wife with herself" (2.2.267–70). The same effect is produced by the obscure, satirical treatment of Germans and of a particular German duke, who is accused of horse stealing in the fragmentary third plot of the play, Caius and Evans's revenge on the Host (4.3, 4.5.60–76).

But the chauvinism of *The Merry Wives* appears most prominently in the fractured English of the French Caius and Welsh Evans themselves, and in the good-humored ridicule it evokes. Evans "makes fritters of English" (5.5.134); he and Caius "hack our English" (3.1.68). Their marked accents, as well as Caius's frequent reversion to French, foreground their foreignness. The Host thwarts their silly decision to duel out of affection for the two men and perhaps out of hostility to this aristocratic practice. Their intention and their inability to execute it intensify the other characters' sense of English middle-class superiority. This sense is clear in the First Folio (1623), which the present (print) edition follows. But it is even more consistently emphasized in the 1602 First Quarto, for which see the Digital Edition. (For more on the differences between the Folio and Quarto, see the Textual Introduction.) Nonetheless, the Welshman is more integrated into Windsor life than the truly foreign Frenchman is. At least Evans attempts to make peace; he teaches Latin to one child and prepares others for the final trick on Falstaff; and he participates in the punishment and criticism of the fat intruder. By contrast, Caius instigates a duel, seeks a loveless marriage, and is then duped.

As the title reveals, however, the play's conflicts are fought mainly in terms of gender. But the meaning of these conflicts is unclear. Is the wives' triumph over Falstaff's sexual adventuring and Ford's jealousy a victory for *middle-class* women, for middle-class *women,* for both? The play celebrates the wives' autonomy, their merriness—a merriness, however, that protects their husbands' wealth.

But not entirely. First, the wives, through their self-discipline and disciplining of

others, define the social norm and are given increasingly broad authority to enforce it. Their household tasks—not least laundering—become metaphors for larger projects: Falstaff is dumped in the river to cleanse him of his sins, and Mistress Quickly as the Queen of Fairies orders elves to "scour" Windsor Castle (5.5.58). Second, though Page contrasts his liberal attitude toward his wife with Ford's misogyny, Mistress Page's scheming against her husband's plans for their daughter's marriage reveals that female self-assertion does not necessarily dovetail with male desire. In this sense, Ford's fears are justified, Page's confidence undermined. Neither parent prevails, though a woman does: Anne replicates her parents' companionate marriage, but against their will, by choosing her own husband.

Mistress Quickly's language produces a view of gender and sexuality less tied to middle-class norms. Although that language's sexual innuendo often escapes the speaker herself, she is not alone in her heedless punning. Evans evinces a comparable obliviousness to the sexual implications of his words, an obliviousness that Quickly's comic misunderstandings during the Latin lesson (4.1) reveal. Evans, who doubles as Windsor's schoolmaster, quizzes young William Page on Latin grammar as it was taught in the first school years, asking his pupil for the plural possessive (or "genitive case") of the word for "this" ("of these"). Mistress Quickly comments uncomprehendingly: what she overlooks in her own speech she detects in a language she cannot understand.

> WILLIAM   Genitive case?
> EVANS   Ay.
> WILLIAM   Genitive, *horum, harum, horum.*
> MISTRESS QUICKLY   Vengeance of Jenny's case! Fie on her,
>   never name her, child, if she be a whore!
>
> (4.1.51–55)

Here, "genitive" suggests "generative" or even "genital" as well as "Jenny"; "case" is slang for "vagina"; and *"horum,"* a genitive plural, evokes the more obvious "whore."

The scene counterposes Latin and English, literacy and illiteracy, middle class and lower, man and woman.

This is not an isolated moment. Earlier, the language of grammar, here too allied to translation, is sexualized when Falstaff announces his intention to seduce Mistress Ford:

> FALSTAFF   I can construe the action of her familiar style, and
> the hardest voice of her behavior, to be Englished rightly, is "I
> am Sir John Falstaff's."
> PISTOL   He hath studied her will, and translated her will—out of
> honesty, into English.
>
> (1.3.39–43)

A different pattern of sexual allusion emerges when Falstaff is trapped in Ford's house on his second assignation with Mistress Ford, and the wives have him escape disguised as the "Aunt of Brentford." Although Ford does not detect the trick, he does spew out a torrent of hostile rhetoric—"A witch, a quean, an old cozening quean!" he begins (4.2.150)—before beating up someone he believes to be an old woman. But of course the woman is Falstaff, whose transvestite outfit anticipates the conclusion of *The Merry Wives*. Although neither the Folio nor the Quarto is consistent enough about the colors the characters wear at the end of the play to make clear how Fenton fools the other suitors and elopes with Anne, the central trick is unambiguous. "I came yonder at Eton to marry Mistress Anne Page, and she's a great lubberly boy!" Slender laments. "If I had been married to him, for all he was in woman's apparel, I would not have had him" (5.5.167–68, 174–75). Caius is even more entangled in the deception. "Vere is Mistress Page? By gar, I am cozened! I ha' married *un garçon*, a boy, *un paysan*, by gar! A boy . . ." (5.5.184–85).

This is not the first such sexual tease. Earlier, Ford complains of the intimacy between the merry wives: "I think if your husbands were dead, you two would marry." The charge of what we would now call homosexuality is rejected. "Be sure of that— two other husbands," Mistress Page replies (3.2.11–13). Similarly, the ending entertains the option of man–boy sexual relations only to punish Anne's foolish suitors. Like adultery and financially motivated arranged marriages, these are deviations from the romantic and sexual norm, whose literal issue is emphasized by the unusual prominence of children in the play.

Yet the cross-dressing conclusion points self-referentially beyond the fiction to the actors producing it. Shakespeare wrote for a transvestite theater in which boys performed female parts. The audience might note the distance between the Queen of Fairies—a flattering allusion to Queen Elizabeth—and Mistress Quickly, the fictional character playing the doubly fictional part. It might register the real boy actor impersonating these two fictional figures. And at the very end, Slender and Caius are not alone in their predicament: Fenton, too, goes off with a boy dressed as a girl. This conclusion simultaneously celebrates and subverts the theatrical illusion. Renaissance accounts praise the lifelike persuasiveness of the best boy actors who impersonated women. Here, the boy gets the girl just as the audience would wish, at the very moment Shakespeare reminds it that it has believed in the very falsehood accepted by some of the play's more foolish characters. This belief in turn links up with the many challenges to the normative heterosexuality apparently embodied by the merry wives—the linguistic suggestiveness, the almost complete absence of romantic or sexual attachment between man and woman, the various hints of homosocial bonding or homoerotic desire.

Something similar applies to the setting of this dramaturgical brazenness, Windsor Forest itself. As Shallow's charge that Falstaff has "killed my deer" suggests (1.1.95), the forest is contested space. But though it is a real place, it is also an invented one. The fairies who haunt it are just children performing a play. The story of Herne the Hunter, "with great ragged horns" (4.4.28), is not taken seriously by the perpetrators

A "skimmington," a public rite of humiliation for domestic disorder.
From *English Customs* (1628).

of the trick. The natural world is given its meaning by human activity within it. The effect is to equate the horned Falstaff first with Herne and then with the oak tree around which Herne supposedly walks. The fairy children circle Falstaff, and as they prepare to burn his fingers, Evans asks of him: "Will this wood take fire?" (5.5.86). Earlier in the scene, Falstaff calls himself "a woodman" (5.5.24). And his name not only alludes to his sexual failure but also fits with his decision to lie down in terror (5.5.45 SD), while its second syllable suggests the material of which he is made. He is the oak in the royal forest felled by the townspeople asserting their (uncertain) rights to Crown land.

This final scene, like *The Merry Wives* as a whole, is socially suggestive and visually funny. Much of the play's pleasure arises from the physical comedy of plot and counterplot—Caius discovering Simple in his closet, Ford in disguise urging Falstaff to seduce his wife, Caius and Evans unknowingly preparing for solo duels, Falstaff repeatedly escaping Ford only to suffer still greater humiliation, the deluded would-be bridegrooms stealing off with the wrong fairies. This effective stage business helps explain the work's success both in the theater and in operatic adaptation (especially Verdi's *Falstaff*, 1893).

Particularly at the end, however, stage business also settles the subplot in a way that unravels the logic of the main plot. The revenge on Falstaff brings together a socially and verbally heterogeneous, often antagonistic group—the merry wives and their servants, their husbands, Evans, Mistress Quickly, and the children of Windsor. Yet the result is not the expected expulsion of the predatory courtier by a unified town but the undoing of nearly all positions of superiority.

The mechanism for this anti-scapegoating outcome is the decision by the Fords and Pages to subject Falstaff to one more humiliation. Though they are confident that he no longer poses a threat, perhaps they believe he needs to make amends to the whole town. Thus, the main plot, in which Falstaff and Ford are fooled by the wives, is balanced by the subplot, in which the fun at the expense of Caius and Slender is less important than the thwarting of the Pages, who have plotted against each other and must endure the humbling reversal of having Ford and Falstaff lecture them. As Falstaff says: "I am glad, though you have ta'en a special stand to strike at me, that your arrow hath glanced" (5.5.210–11). Even Anne acknowledges fault: "Pardon, good father. —Good my mother, pardon!" (line 192). Similarly, in the fragmentary third plot the Host fools Evans and Caius, only to have these two rivals unite to exact revenge from him.

The pattern is that of the duper duped. The renunciation of plotting and hostility by a compromised group of characters produces a moral leveling. The hierarchies and conflicts that separate man from woman, parent from child, sexual normality from sexual deviancy, town from Crown, Englishman from foreigner, upper class from middle class, and middle class from lower are resolved—or evaded—through a good-natured, universal inclusiveness. The middle class is a more encompassing category than at the beginning of the play. Its strength lies in its cheerful capacity to absorb all comers despite the efforts of most of the leading characters, its ability to fashion a unity felt to be more profound than the conflicts dividing the town. When Mistress Page invites the other characters to "laugh this sport o'er by a country fire" (5.5.218), she incorporates within the play an experience the play itself has provided to its audience.

Earlier, however, Ford has disguised himself as Broom ostensibly to aid Falstaff in seducing Mistress Ford, so that he, Broom, will be able to commit adultery with her in turn. Thus, when Ford, undisguised, concludes *The Merry Wives* by informing Falstaff that Broom will in fact sleep with Mistress Ford, we may see either a witty assertion of marital fidelity or a tacit acknowledgment that there is pleasure only in the violation of that norm.

Walter Cohen

SELECTED BIBLIOGRAPHY

Goldberg, Jonathan. "What Do Women Want? *The Merry Wives of Windsor.*" *Criticism* 51 (2009): 367–83. Argues that the play actually undermines the apparently normative heterosexuality embodied by the merry wives, instead presenting homosocial triangles, hostility between the sexes, and same-sex desire.

Helgerson, Richard. "Language Lessons: Linguistic Colonialism, Linguistic Postcolonialism, and the Early Modern English Nation." *Yale Journal of Criticism* 11 (1998): 289–99. Explores Latin versus English versus marginal dialects as colonizing and colonized languages.

Kegl, Rosemary. "'The Adoption of Abominable Terms': Middle Classes, Merry Wives, and the Insults That Shape Windsor." *The Rhetoric of Concealment: Figuring Gender and Class in Renaissance Literature.* Ithaca, NY: Cornell UP, 1994. 77–125. Examines the language of class and gender hierarchy, with attention to issues of ethnocentrism.

Korda, Natasha. *Shakespeare's Domestic Economies: Gender and Property in Early Modern England.* Philadelphia: U of Pennsylvania P, 2002. 76–110. Emphasizes the merry wives' disciplining and self-disciplining management of their households, behavior ratified at the national level through the concluding role of the Queen of Fairies.

Lamb, Mary Ellen. *The Popular Culture of Shakespeare, Spenser, and Jonson.* New York: Routledge, 2006. 125–59. Sees the play's middling sort as defining themselves against both dissolute aristocrats and the criminal poor, both exemplified by Falstaff, with the final scene combining contempt and nostalgia for a popular culture.

Nardizzi, Vin. "Felling Falstaff in Windsor Park." *Ecocritical Shakespeare.* Ed. Lynn Bruckner and Dan Brayton. Farnham, Surrey: Ashgate, 2011. 123–38. Emphasizes, in the final scene, the identification of Falstaff with Herne's oak, whose felling establishes a tenuously unified middle-class community.

Parker, Patricia. "*The Merry Wives of Windsor* and Shakespearean Translation." *Modern Language Quarterly* 52 (1991): 225–61. Focuses on the scene of Latin instruction (4.1) as integral to the play, revealing links between language and sexuality.

Theis, Jeffrey. "The 'ill-kill'd' Deer: Poaching and Social Order in *The Merry Wives of Windsor.*" *Texas Studies in Literature and Language* 43 (2001): 46–73. Argues that the play draws on the class issue of poaching—literally in the opening of the play, metaphorically in Falstaff's sexual designs on the merry wives.

Wall, Wendy. *Staging Domesticity: Household Work and English Identity in Early Modern Drama.* Cambridge: Cambridge UP, 2002. 90–95, 112–26. Places female domesticity (especially cleaning) at the center of local and national community, connecting it to proper English speech, the fabricated popular culture of fairies, and the monarchy.

Zucker, Adam. *The Places of Wit in Early Modern English Comedy.* Cambridge: Cambridge UP, 2011. 23–53. Treats Windsor Forest in the final scene as a socially contested real place and a creation of the townspeople, who show similar social and linguistic mastery throughout the play.

FILM

The Merry Wives of Windsor. 1982. Dir. David Hugh Jones. UK. 170 min. A BBC production with Ben Kingsley as Ford and Judy Davis as Mistress Ford.

TEXTUAL INTRODUCTION

The Merry Wives of Windsor was entered in the Stationers' Register in two separate entries for January 18, 1602 (here modernized):

> JOHN BUSBY   Entered for his copy under the hand of Master
> Seton a book called An excellent and pleasant conceited
> comedy of Sir John Falstaff and the merry wives of Windsor.
> [6 pence]
>
> ARTHUR JOHNSON   Entered for his copy by assignment from John
> Busby, a book called an excellent and pleasant conceited
> comedy of Sir John Falstaff and the merry wives of Windsor.
> [6 pence]

The reassignment of copyright to produce the printed book was legal and not infrequent among printers. Johnson sold the book "at his shop in Paul's Churchyard at the sign of the Flower-de-luce and the Crown" (title page), but he subcontracted the printing from Thomas Creede, who published many plays between 1594 and 1638.

Normally, the earliest printed text of a play is considered authoritative, but in this case scholars have regarded the 1602 First Quarto (Q1) as a "bad quarto" because of its differences from the 1623 Folio: it is 40 percent shorter, with markedly different treatments of the Anne/Fenton romance plot and of the resolutions of act 5. For a long time, scholars believed Q1 to represent a "memorial reconstruction"—a recollected or reported version of the play, based on a performance and published without the theatrical owner's permission. In 1910, W. W. Greg deduced that the actor who played the Host of the Garter must have pirated the material, largely because Q1 accurately reflects F in most of the Host's lines and those of characters in scenes with him but tends to be sketchy elsewhere. Falstaff's lines are also represented fairly accurately, and possibly the actor playing Falstaff participated in the memorial reconstruction. Like the tradition—invented by John Dennis in 1702 and accepted by various editors since 1709—that Queen Elizabeth asked Shakespeare to write a play about Falstaff in love, theories about Q1 in relation to F have a life of their own. Scholars long accepted Greg's theory, but recently critics have doubted that memorial reconstruction is an adequate explanation for certain anomalies in Q1. Some have argued that Q1 is either a performance-based abridgment or an authorized revision of an even earlier text that eventually became the F version. The differences between the *Merry Wives* texts are not surprising considering the twenty-one-year gap between the printed books. Certainly, Q1 remains the only version printed in Shakespeare's lifetime. Very likely Q1 was performed as well as read; it was reprinted as Q2 in 1619 virtually without change.

Q1 is an important witness to performance practice, which is visible especially in stage directions not present in F. It offers a vivid report of how actors moved on the stage, including entrances and exits, and demonstrates how characters responded to lines with actions (as in the buck-basket scenes and the final scene in Windsor Forest). The Q1 text is more accurate in giving Ford's "alias" as "Brook," a word on which puns and politics depend, rather than F's "Broom," and does not try to hide the jokes about German courtiers. Q1's language tends to be more racy and colloquial, typical of plays printed before the laws against profanity came into force (1606). Q1 has fewer scenes, and they are sequenced differently from F, which transposes the last two scenes of act 3 and adds the first four scenes of act 5. Robin, Falstaff's page, has no lines in Q, and William Page has no role and no Latin lesson; the sole "Garter" reference is to the name of the inn where Falstaff lodges. Windsor references are rare in Q, but the play's energetic representation of middle-class town life establishes *The Merry Wives* as Shakespeare's only citizen comedy.

The 1623 F text is the scribe Ralph Crane's transcription, showing his characteristic division into acts and scenes, use of parentheses and hyphens, and massed entries at the head of each scene. F's text is considerably different and much longer than Q's; nevertheless, approximately five hundred lines of Q find no exact counterpart in F. Q also offers other changes—often delightful rhetorical expansions—that suggest a different overall concept. F's curious omissions and errors include the absence of Q scene 8's "Give me thy hand terrestrial" (3.1.90–91), required by the Host's rhetorical balance; the muddle of speech prefixes in F 4.2.46–58, which assign Mistress Ford two speeches in a row; and the grammatically flawed "him" in F 4.3.5 instead of Q scene 14's "them" (line 5), referring to gentlemen meeting the German duke. F fails to indicate which boy wears which color in the boy-brides sequence of 5.5. The exits and re-entrances for Mistress Ford, Mistress Page, and Falstaff in F 4.2 are not as straightforward as in Q. F notably inserts Pistol in the Herne's Oak entertainment of 5.5, although, in Q and apparently in F as well, Pistol had left Windsor by mid-play.

Textual scholars disagree about which version is the original. Most editors reject the undocumented theory of an urtext and point out that there is no proof that plays were abridged for touring. F may be a version presented at court, possibly as entertainment for a Garter Feast at Windsor Castle between 1597 and 1601; current scholarship dates the play 1599, shortly before *Henry V*. Alternatively, F may have been revised from Q for James's court or for the Garter Feast in 1604, with an elaboration of the fairy queen episode into something like a court masque. Thus, Q might have developed into F through rewriting and improvisation, perhaps by Shakespeare and/or other actors, several times by 1623. Since Shakespeare retired from the stage around 1613 and died in 1616, he may have had no hand in later accretions to the text, the authority of which would then depend on the theatrical traditions of the King's Men.

Helen Ostovich

Textual Bibliography

Grav, Peter. "Money Changes Everything: Quarto and Folio *The Merry Wives of Windsor* and the Case for Revision." *Comparative Drama* 40.2 (2006): 217–40.

Greg, W. W., ed. *Shakespeare's "Merry Wives of Windsor," 1602*. Oxford: Clarendon, 1911.

Johnson, Gerald D. "*The Merry Wives of Windsor*, Q1: Provincial Touring and Adapted Texts." *Shakespeare Quarterly* 38.2 (1987): 154–65.

PERFORMANCE NOTE

Unlike most plays by Shakespeare, *The Merry Wives of Windsor* seems to yield limited rewards to directorial interpretation and ingenuity. Attempts to add tension by darkening the tone of what is essentially "revenge" comedy or to create psychological depth in characters distinguished from one another by their linguistic particularities and cartoonish excesses can actually sap the strength of this play—the essence of which lies precisely in caricature, farce, and the vibrancy and resilience of Falstaff, its central character. Productions sometimes make travesties of Falstaff and Ford, though at the risk of damaging their credibility as "straight men," thereby lessening the stakes of the embarrassments they suffer at the hands of the merry wives. Falstaff's challenge to the actor is to be both the butt of jokes and the play's best joker, distinguished as much for his lordly manner as for his low behavior. Likewise, the Ford actor must invite both condescension and empathy, his irrational jealousy not wholly occluding his humanity.

Though Ford and Falstaff suffer stinging embarrassments during the first four acts, the tone can change in act 5, when Falstaff appears as Herne the Hunter. The fairies' appearance and the subsequent masque present opportunities not only for spectacle and invention, but also for introducing realistic brutality and even terror, depending on how roughly the fairies "pinch the unclean knight" (4.4.54) and how dark and sinister the forest appears. Depending on the production's approach, Falstaff can share in the couples' spirit of forgiveness and reconciliation at play's end, or he can remain ostracized and humiliated, like Shylock or Malvolio at the conclusions of *The Merchant of Venice* and *Twelfth Night*, respectively. The fact that the farce persists until so late in the play can intensify the effect of such a turn. Productions must further decide whether Falstaff pursues the two wives purely for money or for lust as well; how to stage his exit from Ford's house in a buck-basket; how to clarify Evans and Caius's plot to revenge themselves on the Host; and how perceptible characters such as Mistress Quickly and Anne Page are during the masque.

BRETT GAMBOA

The Merry Wives of Windsor

[THE PERSONS OF THE PLAY

Justice SHALLOW
SLENDER, nephew to Justice Shallow
SIMPLE, servant to Slender

Master PAGE
MISTRESS PAGE
ANNE Page
WILLIAM Page

Master FORD
MISTRESS FORD
Two SERVANTS in the Ford household

HOST of the Garter Inn
Sir Hugh EVANS
Doctor CAIUS
MISTRESS QUICKLY, housekeeper to Caius
John RUGBY, servant to Caius

Sir John FALSTAFF
PISTOL
BARDOLPH
NIM
ROBIN, Falstaff's boy

Master FENTON
Boys, dressed like FAIRIES]

1.1 (Q 1)

Enter Justice SHALLOW, SLENDER, *[and]*
Sir[1] *Hugh* EVANS.

SHALLOW Sir Hugh, persuade me not. I will make a Star
Chamber° matter of it. If he were twenty Sir John Falstaffs,   *high court*
he shall not abuse Robert Shallow, esquire.°   *(just below a knight)*
SLENDER In the county of Gloucester, justice of peace and
5   quorum.[2]
SHALLOW Ay, cousin° Slender, and *custalorum*.   *kinsman (here, nephew)*
SLENDER Ay, and *ratolorum*[3] too; and a gentleman born, Mas-
ter Parson, who writes himself *Armigero*° in any bill, war-   *esquire; arms bearer*
rant, quittance,° or obligation—*Armigero*!   *discharge from debt*
10 SHALLOW Ay, that I do, and have done any time these three
hundred years.

1.1 Location: A street, later moving to the entrance
to Page's house.
1. *Justice:* justice of the peace (line 4), a local judge.
Sir: clergyman's honorary title, not indicating knighthood, as it does with Falstaff (line 2). As 4.1 reveals,
Evans is also the town's schoolmaster.

2. Designating justices who could try a felon if a sufficient number of them (two or more) were present.
3. *"Custalorum"* (line 6) and *"ratolorum"* are blunders for *custos rotulorum* ("keeper of the rolls"), the
principal justice in a county; perhaps a play on "rat."

SLENDER   All his successors gone before him hath done't, and
all his ancestors that come after him may. They may give the
dozen white luces° in their coat.°   *pike / coat of arms*
15   SHALLOW   It is an old coat.
EVANS   The dozen white louses do become an old coat[4] well. It
agrees well passant.[5] It is a familiar° beast to man and signi-   *familial; too intimate*
fies love.
SHALLOW   The luce is the fresh fish; the salt fish is an old cod.[6]
20   SLENDER   I may quarter,[7] coz.°   *kinsman*
SHALLOW   You may, by marrying.
EVANS   It is marring indeed, if he quarter it.
SHALLOW   Not a whit.
EVANS   Yes, py'r Lady.° If he has a quarter of your coat, there is   *by our Lady (Mary)*
25   but three skirts° for yourself, in my simple conjectures, but   *coattails*
that is all one. If Sir John Falstaff have committed dispar-
agements unto you, I am of the church and will be glad to
do my benevolence to make atonements and compromises
between you.
30   SHALLOW   The council[8] shall hear it. It is a riot.
EVANS   It is not meet° the council hear a riot; there is no fear   *fitting that*
of Got in a riot. The council, look you, shall desire to hear
the fear of Got, and not to hear a riot. Take your 'visements
in that.°   *Be advised*
35   SHALLOW   Ha! O'my life, if I were young again, the sword
should end it.
EVANS   It is petter that friends is the sword, and end it.[9] And
there is also another device in my prain, which peradventure prings goot discretions with it. There is Anne Page,
40   which is daughter to Master George Page, which is pretty
virginity.
SLENDER   Mistress Anne Page? She has brown hair and speaks
small° like a woman.   *in a soprano voice*
EVANS   It is that fery person for all the 'orld, as just as you will
45   desire, and seven hundred pounds of moneys, and gold and
silver, is° her grandsire upon his death's-bed—Got deliver to   *did*
a joyful resurrections—give, when she is able to overtake
seventeen years old. It were a goot motion,° if we leave our   *plan*
pribbles and prabbles,° and desire a marriage between Mas-   *raving and squabbles*
50   ter Abraham° and Mistress Anne Page.   *(Slender)*
SLENDER   Did her grandsire leave her seven hundred pound?
EVANS   Ay, and her father is make her a petter penny.°   *will give much more*
SLENDER   I know the young gentlewoman. She has good gifts.°   *qualities*
EVANS   Seven hundred pounds and possibilities° is goot gifts.   *financial prospects*

---

4. Cod; scrotum. Evans, in what is meant to be a stereotypical Welsh accent, often pronounces "t" for
"d," "p" for "b," and "f" for "v" and omits initial "w."
"Louses" is Evans's comic error for "luces" (line 14), a
term from heraldry, the branch of knowledge concerned with the right to bear arms, with family pedi-
grees, and with coats of arms. (See also "Armigero"
and "coat," lines 8–9, 15–16.) The error is set up by
the two meanings of "old coat" (noble lineage, worn-
out clothing), and Evans's pronunciation then provokes further uncomprehending wordplay by Shallow
(line 19).
5. Walking, looking to the right with the right paw

raised (heraldic); surpassingly. The heraldic image is
absurd for a fish, only slightly less so for a louse.
6. Perhaps a joke involving Evans's pronunciation
("louses/luces"; "coat/cod"). *fresh:* freshwater, unpre-
served. *salt:* saltwater, salt-cured, obscene.
7. I may add another (family's) coat to one of the four
parts of my heraldic arms (for instance, through marriage); but in Evans's reply, cut up in quarters.
8. Star Chamber (lines 1–2); but Evans understands
it as "church council."
9. The intervention of friends should end the
dispute.

55 SHALLOW   Well, let us see honest Master Page. Is Falstaff there?
    EVANS   Shall I tell you a lie? I do despise a liar, as I do despise
    one that is false, or as I despise one that is not true. The
    knight Sir John is there, and I beseech you be ruled by your
    well-willers.° I will peat the door for Master Page.   *well-wishers*
    [*He knocks on the door.*]
60 —What ho? Got pless your house here!
    PAGE [*within*]   Who's there?
    EVANS   Here is Got's plessing and your friend, and Justice
    Shallow, and here young Master Slender, that peradventures
    shall tell you another tale,° if matters grow to your likings.   *(a marriage proposal)*
    [*Enter Master* PAGE.]
65 PAGE   I am glad to see your worships well. I thank you for my
    venison, Master Shallow.
    SHALLOW   Master Page, I am glad to see you. Much good do it
    your good heart. I wished your venison better; it was ill°   *ineptly; unlawfully*
    killed—how doth good Mistress Page?—and I thank you
70 always with my heart, la,° with my heart.   *indeed*
    PAGE   Sir, I thank you.
    SHALLOW   Sir, I thank you, by yea and no,° I do.   *(almost meaningless)*
    PAGE   I am glad to see you, good Master Slender.
    SLENDER   How does your fallow° greyhound, sir? I heard say   *light-brown*
75 he was outrun on Cotswold.°   *the Cotswold hills*
    PAGE   It could not be judged, sir.
    SLENDER   You'll not confess, you'll not confess!°   *(that the dog lost)*
    SHALLOW [*to* SLENDER]   That he will not. 'Tis your fault,° 'tis   *You're in the wrong*
    your fault. [*to* PAGE] 'Tis a good dog.
80 PAGE   A cur, sir.
    SHALLOW   Sir, he's a good dog and a fair dog. Can there be
    more said? He is good and fair. Is Sir John Falstaff here?
    PAGE   Sir, he is within, and I would I could do a good office
    between you.
85 EVANS   It is spoke as a Christians ought to speak.
    SHALLOW   He hath wronged me, Master Page.
    PAGE   Sir, he doth in some sort confess it.
    SHALLOW   If it be confessed, it is not redressed. Is not that so,
    Master Page? He hath wronged me, indeed he hath, at a
90 word° he hath. Believe me, Robert Shallow, esquire, saith   *in short*
    he is wronged.
    PAGE   Here comes Sir John.
        [*Enter Sir John* FALSTAFF, BARDOLPH, NIM,
            and PISTOL.]
    FALSTAFF   Now, Master Shallow, you'll complain of me to the
    King?
95 SHALLOW   Knight, you have beaten my men, killed my deer,
    and broke open my lodge.°   *keeper's house*
    FALSTAFF   But not kissed your keeper's daughter?
    SHALLOW   Tut, a pin.° This shall be answered.   *trifling comment*
    FALSTAFF   I will answer it straight: I have done all this. That
100 is now answered.
    SHALLOW   The council shall know this.
    FALSTAFF   'Twere better for you if it were known in counsel.°   *kept secret*
    You'll be laughed at.
    EVANS   *Pauca verba,*° Sir John, good worts.   *Few words*

105 FALSTAFF Good worts?° Good cabbage! —Slender, I broke   *words; cabbage*
your head. What matter° have you against me?   *complaint*
SLENDER Marry, sir, I have matter in my head against you,
and against your coney-catching° rascals, Bardolph, Nim,   *swindling*
and Pistol.
110 BARDOLPH You Banbury cheese.°   *thin (like Slender)*
SLENDER Ay, it is no matter.
PISTOL How now, Mephistopheles?[1]
SLENDER Ay, it is no matter.
NIM Slice, I say, *pauca, pauca*! Slice, that's my humor.[2]
115 SLENDER [*to* SHALLOW] Where's Simple, my man? Can you
tell, cousin?
EVANS Peace, I pray you. Now let us understand. There is
three umpires in this matter, as I understand; that is, Mas-
ter Page (*fidelicet*° Master Page), and there is myself (*fideli-*   *namely*
120 *cet* myself), and the three party is (lastly and finally) mine
Host of the Garter.°   *(a Windsor inn)*
PAGE We three to hear it and end it between them.
EVANS Fery goot. I will make a prief of it in my notebook, and
we will afterwards 'ork upon the cause with as great dis-
125 creetly as we can.
FALSTAFF Pistol.
PISTOL He hears with ears.
EVANS The tevil and his tam!° What phrase is this? He hears   *dam (mother)*
with ear? Why, it is affectations.
130 FALSTAFF Pistol, did you pick Master Slender's purse?
SLENDER Ay, by these gloves, did he—or I would I might never
come in mine own great chamber° again else—of seven   *hall; bedroom*
groats in mill sixpences and two Edward shovelboards[3] that
cost me two shilling and two pence apiece of Ed Miller, by
135 these gloves.
FALSTAFF Is this true, Pistol?
EVANS No, it is false, if it° is a pickpurse.   *he*
PISTOL Ha, thou mountain foreigner!° Sir John and master   *Welshman*
mine,
I combat challenge of this latten bilbo.[4]
140 Word of denial in thy *labras*° here,   *lips*
Word of denial! Froth and scum, thou liest!
SLENDER [*pointing to* NIM] By these gloves, then 'twas he.
NIM Be advised, sir, and pass good humors.° I will say marry   *behave properly*
trap with you,[5] if you run the nut hook's humor on me.[6]
145 That is the very note° of it.   *fact*
SLENDER [*indicating* BARDOLPH] By this hat, then he in the
red face° had it, for though I cannot remember what I did   *(Bardolph)*

---

1. The devil in Christopher Marlowe's *Dr. Faustus*,
perhaps played as a thin, gaunt character.
2. "Slice" takes up the Banbury cheese insult (line
110) and may command Slender to cut off his remarks,
to stick to few words ("*pauca*"). Nim's temperament
("humor") is to slice Slender with his sword. Nim's
use of "humor" as an almost meaningless verbal tic
pokes fun at the contemporary comedy of humors,
written by Ben Jonson and others.
3. *groat*: four-penny coin. *mill sixpences*: new coins
that may have been worth more than their face value.

Edward shovelboards: old shillings. Shallow has paid
over twice their face value because of their use in the
game of shovel board.
4. A sword (from Bilbao, Spain, where fine swords
known for their elasticity were produced) made of
"latten"—brass or a brasslike, yellow mixed metal;
probably alluding to Slender's cowardice and thinness.
5. Get lost; go play a children's game (?). *humors*:
Nim's verbal tic, again almost meaningless.
6. If you act like a constable in accusing me.

when you made me drunk, yet I am not altogether an ass.

FALSTAFF What say you, Scarlet and John?[7]

150 BARDOLPH Why, sir, for my part, I say the gentleman had
drunk himself out of his five sentences.

EVANS It is "his five senses." Fie, what the ignorance is!

BARDOLPH And being fap,° sir, was, as they say, cashiered,°   drunk / kicked out
and so conclusions passed the careers.[8]

155 SLENDER Ay, you spake in Latin[9] then too. But 'tis no matter.
I'll ne'er be drunk whilst I live again, but in honest, civil,
godly company, for° this trick. If I be drunk, I'll be drunk   on account of
with those that have the fear of God, and not with drunken
knaves.

160 EVANS So Got 'udge me,° that is a virtuous mind.   judge

FALSTAFF You hear all these matters denied, gentlemen, you
hear it.
      [Enter MISTRESS FORD, MISTRESS PAGE, and her
      daughter ANNE with wine.][1]

PAGE Nay, daughter, carry the wine in. We'll drink within.
                                                [Exit ANNE.]

SLENDER O heaven! This is Mistress Anne Page.

165 PAGE How now, Mistress Ford?

FALSTAFF Mistress Ford, by my troth, you are very well met.
By your leave, good mistress.
      [Sir John kisses MISTRESS FORD.]

PAGE Wife, bid these gentlemen welcome. —Come, we have
a hot venison pasty to° dinner. Come, gentlemen, I hope we   pie for
170 shall drink down all unkindness.
                                    [Exeunt all but SLENDER.]

SLENDER I had rather than forty shillings I had my book of
songs and sonnets here.[2]
      [Enter SIMPLE.]
How now, Simple, where have you been? I must wait on
myself, must I? You have not the book of riddles about you,
175 have you?

SIMPLE Book of riddles? Why, did you not lend it to Alice
Shortcake upon Allhallowmas last, a fortnight afore
Michaelmas?[3]
      [Enter SHALLOW and EVANS.]

SHALLOW Come, coz, come, coz, we stay° for you. A word   wait
180 with you, coz. [He draws SLENDER aside.] Marry,° this, coz: Indeed
there is as 'twere a tender,° a kind of tender, made afar   (marriage) proposal
off° by Sir Hugh here. Do you understand me?   indirectly
                                                          (with Falstaff)
SLENDER Ay, sir, you shall find me reasonable.° If it be so, I
shall do that that is reason.

185 SHALLOW Nay, but understand me.

SLENDER So I do, sir.

---

7. Robin Hood's accomplices, Will Scarlet and Little
John; alluding to Bardolph's complexion.
8. Things got out of hand; he misinterpreted
things.
9. Slender can't understand Bardolph's slang and so
assumes it must be Latin.
1. TEXTUAL COMMENT For the stage directions and
stage action in lines 161–70, see Digital Edition TC 1

(Folio edited text).
2. Probably Richard Tottel's Miscellany (1557), an
out-of-date collection of love poetry on whose quot-
able quotes Slender wishes to draw in wooing Anne
Page.
3. Allhallowmas, or All Saints' Day (November 1), is
actually over a month after Michaelmas, September 29.

EVANS   Give ear to his motions.° Master Slender, I will descrip-   *proposals*
tion the matter to you, if you be capacity of it.
SLENDER   Nay, I will do as my cousin Shallow says. I pray you,
190   pardon me. He's a justice of peace in his country,° simple°   *district / humble; foolish*
though I stand here.
EVANS   But that is not the question. The question is concerning your marriage.
SHALLOW   Ay, there's the point, sir.
195   EVANS   Marry, is it, the very point of it—to Mistress Anne
Page.
SLENDER   Why, if it be so, I will marry her, upon any reason-
able demands.°   *requests*
EVANS   But can you affection the 'oman? Let us command to
200   know that of your mouth, or of your lips, for divers philosophers hold that the lips is parcel° of the mouth. Therefore,   *part and parcel*
precisely, can you carry your good will to the maid?
SHALLOW   Cousin Abraham Slender, can you love her?
SLENDER   I hope, sir, I will do as it shall become one that would
205   do reason.
EVANS   Nay, Got's lords and his ladies, you must speak possit-
able,° if you can carry her your desires towards her.   *positively*
SHALLOW   That you must. Will you, upon good dowry, marry
her?
210   SLENDER   I will do a greater thing than that upon your request,
cousin, in° any reason.   *within*
SHALLOW   Nay, conceive° me, conceive me, sweet coz! What I   *understand*
do is to pleasure you, coz. Can you love the maid?
SLENDER   I will marry her, sir, at your request. But if there be
215   no great love in the beginning, yet heaven may decrease° it   *(for "increase")*
upon better acquaintance, when we are married and have
more occasion to know one another. I hope upon familiarity
will grow more content. But if you say marry her, I will marry
her. That I am freely dissolved° and dissolutely.   *(for "resolved")*
220   EVANS   It is a fery discretion answer, save the faul'° is in the   *fault*
'ord dissolutely. The 'ort is, according to our meaning, reso-
lutely. His meaning is good.
SHALLOW   Ay, I think my cousin meant well.
SLENDER   Ay, or else I would I might be hanged, la.
[*Enter* ANNE *Page.*]
225   SHALLOW   Here comes fair Mistress Anne. —Would I were
young for your sake, Mistress Anne.
ANNE   The dinner is on the table. My father desires your wor-
ships' company.
SHALLOW   I will wait on him, fair Mistress Anne.
230   EVANS   Od's° plessed will, I will not be absence at the grace.   *God's*
[*Exeunt* SHALLOW *and* EVANS.]
ANNE [*to* SLENDER]   Will't please your worship to come in, sir?
SLENDER   No, I thank you, forsooth, heartily. I am very well.
ANNE   The dinner attends° you, sir.   *awaits*
SLENDER   I am not a-hungry, I thank you, forsooth. [*to* SIM-
235   PLE] Go, sirrah, for all you are my man, go wait upon my
cousin Shallow.   [*Exit* SIMPLE.]
A justice of peace sometime may be beholden to his friend
for a man. I keep but three men and a boy yet, till my mother

be dead. But what though?° Yet I live like a poor gentleman   *what of it*
240 born.
ANNE   I may not go in without your worship. They will not sit
     till you come.
SLENDER   I'faith, I'll eat nothing. I thank you as much as
     though I did.
245 ANNE   I pray you, sir, walk in.
SLENDER   I had rather walk here, I thank you. I bruised my
     shin th'other day with playing at sword and dagger with a
     master of fence°—three venies° for a dish of stewed prunes⁴—   *fencing / bouts*
     and, by my troth, I cannot abide the smell of hot meat° since.   *food; prostitutes*
        [*Dogs bark within.*]
250 Why do your dogs bark so? Be there bears i'th' town?
ANNE   I think there are, sir. I heard them talked of.
SLENDER   I love the sport° well, but I shall as soon quarrel at⁵   *bearbaiting*
     it as any man in England. You are afraid if you see the bear
     loose, are you not?
255 ANNE   Ay, indeed, sir.
SLENDER   That's meat and drink° to me now. I have seen   *everyday fare*
     Sackerson⁶ loose twenty times, and have taken him by the
     chain. But, I warrant you, the women have so cried and
     shrieked at it that it passed.° But women indeed cannot   *surpassed description*
260 abide 'em. They are very ill-favored° rough things.   *ugly*
        [*Enter* PAGE.]
PAGE   Come, gentle Master Slender, come. We stay for you.
SLENDER   I'll eat nothing, I thank you, sir.
PAGE   By cock and pie,° you shall not choose,° sir. Come, come.   *(mild oath) / you must*
SLENDER   Nay, pray you lead the way.
265 PAGE   Come on, sir.
SLENDER   Mistress Anne, yourself shall go first.
ANNE   Not I, sir. Pray you keep on.°   *go on*
SLENDER   Truly I will not go first, truly, la. I will not do you
     that wrong.
270 ANNE   I pray you, sir.
SLENDER   I'll rather be unmannerly than troublesome. You do
     yourself wrong, indeed, la.
        Exeunt [SLENDER *first,* PAGE *and* ANNE *following*].

1.2 (Q 2)

Enter EVANS *and* SIMPLE.

EVANS   Go your ways, and ask of° Doctor Caius' house which   *concerning*
     is the way. And there dwells one Mistress Quickly, which is
     in the manner of his nurse, or his dry-nurse,° or his cook, or   *housekeeper*
     his laundry, his washer, and his wringer.
5 SIMPLE   Well, sir.
EVANS   Nay, it is petter yet. Give her this letter, for it is a 'oman
     that altogethers acquaintance° with Mistress Anne Page;   *is well acquainted*
     and the letter is to desire and require her to solicit your mas-
     ter's desires, to Mistress Anne Page. I pray you, begone.
        [*Exit* SIMPLE.]
10 I will make an end of my dinner; there's pippins° and cheese   *apples*
     to come.   *Exit.*

───────────

4. Also slang for "prostitute."   6. Famous bear used in bearbaiting.
5. Object to dispute.   1.2 Location: Scene continues.

1.3 (Q 3)

Enter FALSTAFF, HOST [*of the Garter*], BARDOLPH, NIM,
PISTOL[, *and the boy* ROBIN].

FALSTAFF   Mine Host of the Garter.

HOST   What says my bully rook?° Speak scholarly and wisely.   *fine fellow*

FALSTAFF   Truly, mine Host, I must turn away some of my
followers.

5   HOST   Discard, bully Hercules, cashier.° Let them wag.° Trot,   *dismiss / go their ways*
trot.

FALSTAFF   I sit° at ten pounds a week.   *lodge*

HOST   Thou'rt an emperor—Caesar, kaiser, and vizier.[1] I will
entertain° Bardolph. He shall draw, he shall tap.° Said I   *employ / tend bar*
10   well, bully Hector?[2]

FALSTAFF   Do so, good mine Host.

HOST   I have spoke. Let him follow. [*to* BARDOLPH] Let me see
thee froth[3] and live. I am at a word.° Follow.   [*Exit.*]   *I mean what I say*

FALSTAFF   Bardolph, follow him. A tapster is a good trade. An
15   old cloak makes a new jerkin;° a withered servingman a   *jacket*
fresh tapster. Go, adieu.

BARDOLPH   It is a life that I have desired. I will thrive.   [*Exit.*]

PISTOL   O base Hungarian wight,[4] wilt thou the spigot wield?

NIM   He was gotten in drink.[5] Is not the humor conceited?°   *idea witty*

20   FALSTAFF   I am glad I am so acquit of this tinderbox.[6] His thefts
were too open. His filching was like an unskillful singer: he
kept not time.

NIM   The good humor° is to steal at a minute's rest.°   *trick / within a minute*

PISTOL   Convey, the wise it call. Steal? Foh, a fico[7] for the
25   phrase!

FALSTAFF   Well, sirs, I am almost out at heels.°   *destitute*

PISTOL   Why, then, let kibes° ensue.   *sore heels*

FALSTAFF   There is no remedy. I must coney-catch,° I must   *swindle*
shift.°   *live by my wits*

30   PISTOL   Young ravens must have food.

FALSTAFF   Which of you know Ford of this town?

PISTOL   I ken the wight.° He is of substance good.°   *know the man / well-off*

FALSTAFF   My honest lads, I will tell you what I am about.°   *up to; in girth*

PISTOL   Two yards and more.

35   FALSTAFF   No quips now, Pistol. Indeed I am in the waist two
yards about, but I am now about no waste. I am about thrift.
Briefly, I do mean to make love to Ford's wife. I spy entertainment[8] in her. She discourses, she carves,[9] she gives the
leer of invitation. I can construe[1] the action of her familiar
40   style, and the hardest voice of her behavior, to be Englished
rightly, is "I am Sir John Falstaff's."

1.3 Location: The Garter Inn.
1. *vizier:* Turkish viceroy. *Caesar:* the name of Julius
Caesar became a title, "emperor."
2. Greatest of the Trojans who fought in the Trojan
War. Similarly, Hercules (line 5) was the most famous
hero of classical mythology.
3. *froth:* cheat the customer—by putting a good head
on the beer (to give short measure).
4. Hungry, contemptible man.
5. Begotten when his parents were drunk (thought to
make one cowardly).
6. Alluding to Bardolph's red complexion and irascible temper. *acquit:* rid.

7. An abusive insult usually accompanied by the gesture of showing the thumb pushed between index
and middle fingers: historically, "fig" (Spanish); allu-
sively, "female genitals."
8. Provision of food, drink, and lodging; ability to
give sexual pleasure.
9. Perhaps: acts courteously; gestures broadly with
her hands; shows pleasing skill in carving meat—
hence, somewhere between ordinary friendliness and
sexual enticement.
1. Interpret (beginning a grammatical pun that
includes "style," "voice," "Englished," and "translated,"
lines 40, 42).

PISTOL   He hath studied her will, and translated her will²—
    out of honesty,° into English.   *chastity*
NIM   The anchor is deep.³ Will that humor pass?°   *phrase pass muster*
45   FALSTAFF   Now, the report° goes, she has all the rule of her   *rumor*
    husband's purse. He hath legions of angels.°   *gold coins*
PISTOL   As many devils entertain,° and to her, boy,° say I.   *employ / (hunting cry)*
NIM   The humor rises. It is good—humor me the angels!⁴
FALSTAFF   I have writ me here a letter to her, and here another
50   to Page's wife, who even now gave me good eyes too, exam-
    ined my parts° with most judicious oeillades:° sometimes the   *sexual capacity / ogling*
    beam of her view gilded my foot, sometimes my portly belly.
PISTOL   Then did the sun on dunghill shine.
NIM   I thank thee for that humor.
55   FALSTAFF   Oh, she did so course° o'er my exteriors, with such   *travel*
    a greedy intention, that the appetite of her eye did seem to
    scorch me up like a burning-glass.⁵ Here's another letter to
    her. She bears the purse too. She is a region in Guiana,⁶ all
    gold and bounty. I will be cheaters⁷ to them both, and they
60   shall be exchequers to me. They shall be my East and West
    Indies, and I will trade to them both. [*He gives a letter to*
    PISTOL.] Go, bear thou this letter to Mistress Page; [*giving a*
    letter to NIM] and thou this to Mistress Ford. We will thrive,
    lads, we will thrive!
65   PISTOL [*returning the letter*]   Shall I Sir Pandarus of Troy⁸
    become,
    And by my side wear steel?° Then Lucifer take all.   *And remain a soldier*
NIM [*returning the letter*]   I will run no base humor. Here,
    take the humor-letter. I will keep the 'havior of reputation.⁹
FALSTAFF [*to* ROBIN]   Hold,° sirrah, bear you these letters   *Take these*
70   tightly;°   *safely*
    Sail like my pinnace° to these golden shores.   *small, fast boat*
    [*to* PISTOL *and* NIM] Rogues, hence, avaunt!° Vanish like   *begone*
    hailstones, go!
    Trudge, plod away i'th' hoof,° seek shelter, pack!°   *on foot / be off*
    Falstaff will learn the honor of the age,
    French thrift, you rogues—myself and skirted page.¹
                  [*Exeunt* FALSTAFF *and* ROBIN.]
75   PISTOL   Let vultures gripe° thy guts, for gourd and fulham²   *seize*
    holds,°   *are profitable*
    And high and low beguiles the rich and poor!
    Tester° I'll have in pouch° when thou shalt lack,   *Sixpence / purse*
    Base Phrygian Turk!³

2. Intention; sexual desires; legal document (thought
of as written in Latin).
3. That's a deep plot; you're out of your depth (?).
4. Perhaps: the plot develops; it's good. Get the
money. (Here, as elsewhere in Nim's speech, "humor"
means whatever the context demands.)
5. Glass lens used to concentrate the sun's rays and
so start a fire.
6. South American country famed for its unexploited
wealth and fertility, as were the East and West Indies
(lines 60–61).
7. Escheaters, officers of the Exchequer (or Treasury; line 60) responsible for estates that fell forfeit
and so came to the Crown; deceivers, robbers.
8. Pandarus is the aristocrat who, as Troy is besieged
by the Greeks, serves as go-between (or pander) in

the affair between Troilus and Cressida, Pandarus's
niece. Shakespeare's *Troilus and Cressida* is several
years later than *The Merry Wives*.
9. I will behave respectfully.
1. Suggesting that French gentlemen were thought
to retain few, though well-dressed, followers. *skirted:*
wearing a coat with full tails.
2. *gourd and fulham:* false dice and loaded dice—
loaded "high" to produce a four, five, or six, or "low"
to produce a one, two, or three. See line 76.
3. Terms of abuse. The Turks, Europe's main military foe, were Muslims and hence considered infi-
dels. The Phrygians, early inhabitants of what is now
Turkey, were conquered by Europeans; to the classical Greeks, "Phrygian" was equivalent to "slave."

NIM   I have operations° which be humors of revenge.   *plans*
PISTOL   Wilt thou revenge?
80 NIM   By welkin° and her star.   *the sky (poetic)*
PISTOL   With wit or steel?
NIM   With both the humors, I!
I will discuss° the humor of this love to Ford.   *disclose*
PISTOL   And I to Page shall eke° unfold   *also (archaic)*
How Falstaff, varlet vile,
85 His dove will prove,° his gold will hold,   *test; sample*
And his soft couch defile.
NIM   My humor shall not cool. I will incense Ford to deal
with poison; I will possess him with yellowness,⁴ for this
revolt of mine° is dangerous. That is my true humor.   *(against Falstaff)*
90 PISTOL   Thou art the Mars of malcontents.⁵
I second thee. Troop on!   *Exeunt.*

1.4 (Q 4)

Enter MISTRESS QUICKLY [*and*] SIMPLE.

MISTRESS QUICKLY   What,° John Rugby!   *(a summoning call)*
[*Enter John* RUGBY.]
I pray thee go to the casement and see if you can see my
master, Master Doctor Caius, coming. If he do, i'faith, and
find anybody in the house, here will be an old° abusing of   *will be lots of*
5   God's patience and the King's English.
RUGBY   I'll go watch.
MISTRESS QUICKLY   Go, and we'll have a posset¹ for't soon at
night,° in faith, at the latter end of a sea-coal² fire.   *toward nightfall*
[*Exit* RUGBY.]
An honest, willing, kind fellow, as ever servant shall come in
10 house withal,° and, I warrant you, no telltale, nor no breed-   *with*
bate.° His worst fault is that he is given to prayer; he is   *troublemaker*
something peevish° that way—but nobody but has his fault.   *foolish*
But let that pass. Peter Simple you say your name is?
SIMPLE   Ay, for fault° of a better.   *lack*
15 MISTRESS QUICKLY   And Master Slender's your master?
SIMPLE   Ay, forsooth.
MISTRESS QUICKLY   Does he not wear a great round beard like
a glover's paring knife?
SIMPLE   No, forsooth. He hath but a little wee face with a
20 little yellow beard, a Cain-colored° beard.   *yellow or reddish*
MISTRESS QUICKLY   A softly-sprighted° man, is he not?   *meek-spirited*
SIMPLE   Ay, forsooth. But he is as tall a man of his hands as
any is, between this and his head.³ He hath fought with a
warrener.°   *gamekeeper*
25 MISTRESS QUICKLY   How, say you? Oh, I should remember him.
Does he not hold up his head, as it were, and strut in his gait?
SIMPLE   Yes, indeed, does he.

---

4. Fill him with jealousy. (An inconsistency: in 2.1,   1. Restorative drink of hot milk curdled with wine
Nim goes to Page and Pistol to Ford, who is pos-   or ale.
sessed with yellowness.)   2. Coal brought by sea.
5. Most warlike rebel (Mars was the Roman god of war).   3. But he is as brave a man as any is around here.
1.4 Location: Dr. Caius's house.

MISTRESS QUICKLY Well, heaven send Anne Page no worse
fortune! Tell Master Parson Evans I will do what I can for
30   your master. Anne is a good girl, and I wish—
        [*Enter* RUGBY.]
RUGBY Out, alas, here comes my master!   [*Exit.*]
MISTRESS QUICKLY We shall all be shent.° Run in here, good   *scolded*
    young man. Go into this closet.
        [SIMPLE *steps into the closet.*]
        [*aside*] He will not stay long. —[*loudly*] What, John Rugby?
35   John? What, John, I say!
        [*Enter* RUGBY.]
        [*loudly*] Go, John, go inquire for my master. I doubt° he be   *suspect*
    not well, that he comes not home.   [*Exit* RUGBY.]
        [*Sings.*]   And down, down, a'down-a (etc.).
        [*Enter Doctor* CAIUS.]
CAIUS Vat is you sing? I do not like dese toys.° Pray you, go   *frivolous tunes*
40   and vetch me in my closet, *une boîte en vert*; a box, a green-a
    box. *Tu entends*° vat I speak? A green-a box.   *Do you hear*
MISTRESS QUICKLY Ay, forsooth, I'll fetch it you. [*aside*] I am
    glad he went not in himself. If he had found the young man,
    he would have been horn-mad.°   *mad as a bull*
        [*She fetches the box from the closet.*]
45 CAIUS *Fe, fe, fe, fe! Ma foi, il fait fort chaud! Je m'en vais à la*
    cour—la grande affaire.[4]
MISTRESS QUICKLY Is it this, sir?
CAIUS *Oui, mets-la à ma* pocket.[5] *Dépêche*, quickly! Vere is
    dat knave, Rugby?
50 MISTRESS QUICKLY [*calling*] What, John Rugby! John!
        [*Enter* RUGBY.]
RUGBY Here, sir.
CAIUS You are John Rugby, and you are Jack° Rugby. Come,   *(connotes knavery)*
    take-a your rapier, and come after my heel to the court.
RUGBY 'Tis ready, sir, here in the porch.
        [*He fetches the rapier.*]
55 CAIUS By my trot,° I tarry too long. Od's me,° *qu'ai-j'oublié?*[6]   *troth / God save me*
    Dere is some simples[7] in my closet dat I vill not for the varld
    I shall leave behind.
        [*He goes to the closet.*]
MISTRESS QUICKLY [*aside*] Ay me, he'll find the young man
    there, and be mad.
60 CAIUS [*discovering* SIMPLE] Oh, *diable*,° *diable!* Vat is in my   *devil*
    closet? Villainy! *Larron!*° —Rugby, my rapier.   *Thief*
MISTRESS QUICKLY Good master, be content.
CAIUS Wherefore shall I be content-a?
MISTRESS QUICKLY The young man is an honest man.
65 CAIUS What shall de honest man do in my closet? Dere is no
    honest man dat shall come in my closet.
MISTRESS QUICKLY I beseech you be not so phlegmatic.[8] Hear
    the truth of it. He came of an errand to me from Parson Hugh.

---

4. French: By my faith, it is very hot. I am going to
court—important business. (The French in this
scene is translated only when Caius fails to do so
himself.)
5. Yes, put it in my pocket.

6. What have I forgotten?
7. Medicines composed of one herb or constituent;
unknown to Caius, also the character's name.
8. Cold and dull (Quickly's mistake for the opposite
temperament—choleric, or angry).

CAIUS Vell.

70 SIMPLE Ay, forsooth, to desire her to—

MISTRESS QUICKLY Peace, I pray you.

CAIUS [*to* MISTRESS QUICKLY] Peace-a your tongue! [*to* SIMPLE]
Speak-a your tale.

SIMPLE To desire this honest gentlewoman, your maid, to

75 speak a good word to Mistress Anne Page for my master in
the way of marriage.

MISTRESS QUICKLY This is all, indeed, la, but I'll ne'er put my
finger in the fire, an need not.[9]

CAIUS Sir Hugh send-a you? —Rugby, *baille*° me some paper.   *bring*

80 [*to* SIMPLE] Tarry you a little-a while.

    [RUGBY *brings paper. The doctor writes.*]

MISTRESS QUICKLY [*aside to* SIMPLE] I am glad he is so quiet.
If he had been thoroughly moved,° you should have heard   *really angered*
him so loud and so melancholy!° But notwithstanding, man,   *(for "choleric"?)*
I'll do you your master what good I can. And the very yea

85 and the no is, the French doctor, my master—I may call him
my master, look you, for I keep his house, and I wash, wring,
brew, bake, scour, dress meat° and drink, make the beds,   *prepare food*
and do all myself—

SIMPLE 'Tis a great charge° to come under one body's hand.   *burden; (sexual)*

90 MISTRESS QUICKLY Are you advised o'that?° You shall find it a   *You're telling me*
great charge, and to be up early and down late. But notwith-
standing—to tell you in your ear, I would have no words of
it—my master himself is in love with Mistress Anne Page.
But notwithstanding that I know Anne's mind, that's neither

95 here nor there.

CAIUS [*giving the letter to* SIMPLE] You, jack'nape,° give-a this   *idiot*
letter to Sir Hugh. By gar,° it is a shallenge. I will cut his   *God*
troat in de park, and I will teach a scurvy jackanape priest
to meddle or make°—you may be gone. It is not good you   *interfere*

100 tarry here. By gar, I will cut all his two stones.° By gar, he   *testicles*
shall not have a stone to throw at his dog.   [*Exit* SIMPLE.]

MISTRESS QUICKLY Alas, he speaks but for his friend.

CAIUS It is no matter-a ver° dat. Do not you tell-a me dat I   *for*
shall have Anne Page for myself? By gar, I vill kill de jack-

105 priest!° And I have appointed mine Host of de Jarteer° to   *knave-priest / Garter*
measure our weapon.° By gar, I will myself have Anne Page.   *to referee*

MISTRESS QUICKLY Sir, the maid loves you, and all shall be
well. We must give folks leave to prate. What the goodyear!°   *What the devil*

CAIUS Rugby, come to the court with me. [*to* MISTRESS

110 QUICKLY] By gar, if I have not Anne Page, I shall turn your
head out of my door. —Follow my heels, Rugby.

MISTRESS QUICKLY You shall have An°—   *Anne; an*

    [*Exit* CAIUS *with* RUGBY.]

fool's head of your own. No, I know Anne's mind for that.
Never a woman in Windsor knows more of Anne's mind than

115 I do, nor can do more than I do with her, I thank heaven.

FENTON [*within*] Who's within there, ho?

MISTRESS QUICKLY Who's there, I trow?° —Come near° the   *wonder / Enter*
house, I pray you.

    [*Enter* FENTON.]

---

9. I'll never put myself in danger by getting involved if I don't have to.

FENTON   How now, good woman, how dost thou?

120 MISTRESS QUICKLY   The better that it pleases your good worship to ask!

FENTON   What news? How does pretty Mistress Anne?

MISTRESS QUICKLY   In truth, sir, and she is pretty, and hon-
est,° and gentle,° and one that is your friend. I can tell you   *chaste / well-bred*
125 that by the way, I praise heaven for it.

FENTON   Shall I do any good,° think'st thou? Shall I not lose   *make any progress*
my suit?

MISTRESS QUICKLY   Troth, sir, all is in His hands above. But
notwithstanding, Master Fenton, I'll be sworn on a book°   *a Bible*
130 she loves you. Have not your worship a wart above your eye?

FENTON   Yes, marry, have I. What of that?

MISTRESS QUICKLY   Well, thereby hangs a tale. Good faith, it
is such another Nan!¹ But, I detest,° an honest maid as ever   *(for "protest")*
broke bread.° We had an hour's talk of that wart. I shall   *ate (proverbial)*
135 never laugh but in that maid's company. But, indeed, she is
given too much to allicholy° and musing. But for you—   *(for "melancholy")*
well—go to!°   *come, come*

FENTON   Well, I shall see her today. Hold, there's money for
thee. Let me have thy voice in my behalf. If thou seest her
140 before me, commend me—

MISTRESS QUICKLY   Will I? I'faith, that we will. And I will tell
your worship more of the wart the next time we have confi-
dence,° and of other wooers.   *private talk*

FENTON   Well, farewell. I am in great haste now.

145 MISTRESS QUICKLY   Farewell to your worship.   [*Exit* FENTON.]
Truly an honest gentleman. But Anne loves him not. For I
know Anne's mind as well as another° does.—Out upon't,²   *anyone else*
what have I forgot?   *Exit.*

2.1 (Q 5)

Enter MISTRESS PAGE [*reading of a letter*].

MISTRESS PAGE   What, have I scaped love letters in the holiday
time° of my beauty, and am I now a subject for them? Let me   *heyday*
see: "Ask me no reason why I love you, for though Love use
Reason for his precisian, he admits him not for his coun-
5 selor.¹ You are not young; no more am I. Go to, then, there's
sympathy.° You are merry; so am I. Ha, ha, then there's more   *agreement*
sympathy. You love sack,° and so do I. Would you desire bet-   *Spanish wine*
ter sympathy? Let it suffice thee, Mistress Page, at the least
if the love of soldier can suffice, that I love thee. I will not say
10 'pity me'—'tis not a soldier-like phrase—but I say 'love me':
By me, thine own true knight,
By day or night,
Or any kind of light,
With all his might,
15 For thee to fight.
John Falstaff."
What a Herod of Jewry° is this? Oh, wicked, wicked world!   *bragging stage villain*
One that is well-nigh worn to pieces with age, to show him-

1. Nan (Anne) is such an extraordinary (or lively) one.
2. Expression of dismay.
2.1 Location: Outside Page's house.

1. Though Love employs Reason to make strong
arguments, or preach, on Love's behalf (a "precisian"
was a puritan), Love will not accept Reason's advice.

self a young gallant? What an unweighed° behavior hath this   *unbalanced*
20 Flemish° drunkard pickèd, with the devil's name,° out of my *(proverbially drunk) / aid*
conversation,° that he dares in this manner assay° me?   *conduct / proposition*
Why, he hath not been thrice in my company. What should
I say° to him? I was then frugal of my mirth. Heaven for-   *should I have said*
give me! Why, I'll exhibit° a bill in the parliament for the   *introduce*
25 putting down² of men. How shall I be revenged on him?
For revenged I will be, as sure as his guts are made of
puddings!°   *gut-encased sausages*
[*Enter* MISTRESS FORD.]
MISTRESS FORD Mistress Page, trust me, I was going to your
house.
30 MISTRESS PAGE And, trust me, I was coming to you. You look
very ill.
MISTRESS FORD Nay, I'll ne'er believe that. I have° to show to   *have something*
the contrary.
MISTRESS PAGE Faith, but you do, in my mind.
35 MISTRESS FORD Well, I do then. Yet I say I could show you to
the contrary. O Mistress Page, give me some counsel.
MISTRESS PAGE What's the matter, woman?
MISTRESS FORD O woman, if it were not for one trifling respect,°   *consideration*
I could come to such honor!°   *rank*
40 MISTRESS PAGE Hang the trifle, woman; take the honor. What
is it? Dispense with trifles. What is it?
MISTRESS FORD If I would but go to hell for an eternal
moment or so, I could be knighted.³
MISTRESS PAGE What? Thou liest! Sir Alice Ford? These
45 knights will hack,° and so thou shouldst not alter the article   *(military); (sexual?)*
of thy gentry.°   *terms of your station*
MISTRESS FORD We burn daylight.° Here, read, read. Perceive   *waste time*
how I might be knighted. [*She gives a letter to* MISTRESS PAGE,
who reads it.] I shall think the worse of fat men, as long as I
50 have an eye to make difference of° men's liking.° And yet he   *judge among / looks*
would not swear, praised women's modesty, and gave such
orderly and well-behaved reproof to all uncomeliness,° that I   *improper behavior*
would have sworn his disposition would have gone to° the   *accorded with*
truth of his words. But they do no more adhere and keep
55 place together than the hundred psalms to the tune of
"Greensleeves."° What tempest, I trow, threw this whale,   *(popular love song)*
with so many tuns° of oil in his belly, ashore at Windsor?   *casks*
How shall I be revenged on him? I think the best way
were to entertain him with hope till the wicked fire of lust
60 have melted him in his own grease. Did you ever hear the
like?
MISTRESS PAGE Letter for letter, but that the name of Page
and Ford differs. [*She shows her own letter.*] To thy great
comfort in this mystery of ill opinions,⁴ here's the twin
65 brother of thy letter. But let thine inherit first, for I protest
mine never shall. I warrant he hath a thousand of these letters, writ with blank space for different names—sure,
more, and these are of the second edition. He will print

---

2. *putting down:* suppression; perhaps also an   3. Dubbed a knight; sexually provided with a knight.
unconscious sexual suggestion that men are to be put   4. Falstaff's unfounded and hence mysterious belief
down for the purpose of intercourse.   that the wives are promiscuous.

them, out of doubt,° for he cares not what he puts into the   *undoubtedly*
70   press[5] when he would put us two. I had rather be a giantess
and lie under Mount Pelion.[6] Well, I will find you twenty
lascivious turtles[7] ere one chaste man.

MISTRESS FORD [*comparing the two letters*] Why, this is the
very same: the very hand, the very words! What doth he think
75   of us?

MISTRESS PAGE Nay, I know not. It makes me almost ready to
wrangle° with mine own honesty.° I'll entertain° myself like   *argue / chastity / treat*
one that I am not acquainted withal,° for sure, unless he   *with*
know some strain in me that I know not myself, he would
80   never have boarded[8] me in this fury.

MISTRESS FORD Boarding, call you it? I'll be sure to keep him
above deck.

MISTRESS PAGE So will I. If he come under my hatches, I'll
never to sea again. Let's be revenged on him. Let's appoint
85   him a meeting, give him a show of comfort° in his suit, and   *encouragement*
lead him on with a fine-baited° delay, till he hath pawned   *temptingly alluring*
his horses to mine Host of the Garter.[9]

MISTRESS FORD Nay, I will consent to act any villainy against
him that may not sully the chariness° of our honesty. Oh,   *scrupulous integrity*
90   that my husband saw this letter! It would give eternal food
to his jealousy.

[*Enter* MASTER FORD *with* PISTOL, *and* MASTER PAGE
with NIM.]

MISTRESS PAGE Why, look where he comes, and my goodman°   *husband*
too. He's as far from jealousy as I am from giving him cause,
and that, I hope, is an unmeasurable distance.
95 MISTRESS FORD You are the happier woman.

MISTRESS PAGE Let's consult together against this greasy
knight. Come hither.

[*They talk aside.*]

FORD Well, I hope it be not so.

PISTOL Hope is a curtal° dog in some affairs.   *an unreliable*
100   Sir John affects° thy wife.   *loves; aims at*

FORD Why, sir, my wife is not young.

PISTOL He woos both high and low, both rich and poor,
Both young and old, one with another,° Ford.   *indiscriminately*
He loves the gallimaufry,° Ford. Perpend.°   *mixture / Consider*
105 FORD Love my wife?

PISTOL With liver° burning hot. Prevent—   *(seat of the passions)*
Or go thou like Sir Actaeon,[1]
He, with Ringwood[2] at thy heels.
Oh, odious is the name!
110 FORD What name, sir?

PISTOL The horn,° I say. Farewell.   *(of a cuckold)*
Take heed, have open eye, for thieves do foot°   *walk; (sexual)*

---

5. Printing press; what he presses sexually.
6. The giants were the Titans, who in Greek mythology rebelled against the Olympian gods and were punished by being buried under Mt. Pelion.
7. Turtledoves (proverbially true to their mates).
8. Nautical metaphor: accosted; sexually entered.
9. See note to 4.3.11. The plot does not develop in exactly the way anticipated: Ford supplies Sir John

with funds, so at first he doesn't have to pawn his horses to raise money for his courting.
1. In Greek mythology, Actaeon was turned into a stag and consequently was hunted and killed by his own dogs. The stag, in particular its horns, was considered an emblem of the cuckold, the man whose wife was unfaithful to him.
2. Supposed name of one of Actaeon's dogs.

By night. Take heed, ere summer comes, or cuckoo
Birds[3] do sing. —Away, Sir Corporal Nim!
115 —Believe it, Page, he speaks sense.   [*Exit.*]
FORD [*aside*]   I will be patient. I will find out° this.   *investigate*
NIM [*to* PAGE]   And this is true. I like not the humor of lying.
He hath wronged me in some humors: I should° have borne   *was supposed to*
the humored letter to her. But I have a sword, and it shall
120 bite upon my necessity.° He loves your wife. There's the short   *when I need it to*
and the long. My name is Corporal Nim. I speak, and I
avouch 'tis true. My name is Nim, and Falstaff loves your
wife. Adieu. I love not the humor of bread and cheese.[4] Adieu.
                              [*Exit.*]
PAGE [*aside*]   The humor of it, quoth 'a?° Here's a fellow   *he*
125 frights English out of his° wits.   *its*
FORD [*aside*]   I will seek out Falstaff.
PAGE [*aside*]   I never heard such a drawling, affecting° rogue.   *affectedly speaking*
FORD [*aside*]   If I do find° it—well.   *ascertain*
PAGE [*aside*]   I will not believe such a Cathayan,° though the   *Chinese; scoundrel*
130 priest o'th' town commended him for° a true man.   *as*
FORD [*aside*]   'Twas a good sensible fellow. Well.
         [MISTRESS PAGE *and* MISTRESS FORD *come forward.*]
PAGE   How now, Meg?
MISTRESS PAGE   Whither go you, George? Hark you.
         [*They talk apart.*]
MISTRESS FORD   How now, sweet Frank? Why art thou
135 melancholy?
FORD   I melancholy? I am not melancholy. Get you home, go.
MISTRESS FORD   Faith, thou hast some crochets° in thy head.   *strange notions*
—Now, will you go, Mistress Page?
MISTRESS PAGE   Have with you.° —You'll come to dinner,   *I'm coming*
140 George?
         [*Enter* MISTRESS QUICKLY.]
[*aside to* MISTRESS FORD] Look who comes yonder. She shall
be our messenger to this paltry knight.
MISTRESS FORD [*aside to* MISTRESS PAGE]   Trust me, I thought
on her. She'll fit it.°   *fit the part*
145 MISTRESS PAGE [*to* MISTRESS QUICKLY]   You are come to see my
daughter Anne?
MISTRESS QUICKLY   Ay, forsooth, and I pray how does good
Mistress Anne?
MISTRESS PAGE   Go in with us and see. We have an hour's talk
150 with you.   [*Exeunt* MISTRESS PAGE, MISTRESS FORD, *and*
                              MISTRESS QUICKLY.]
PAGE   How now, Master Ford?
FORD   You heard what this knave told me, did you not?
PAGE   Yes, and you heard what the other told me?
FORD   Do you think there is truth in them?
155 PAGE   Hang 'em, slaves! I do not think the knight would offer°   *attempt*
it. But these that accuse him in his intent towards our wives

3. The cuckoo's habit of leaving its eggs to be hatched
by others made it the emblem of cuckolders and made
the sound of its call a taunt to cuckolds. Its song is
prevalent in late spring, after the mating season.

4. Nim's meager fare as Falstaff's retainer, or as now
unemployed; a popular name for wood sorrel, an edi-
ble plant also known as cuckoo-bread or cuckoo-
cheese—hence, an allusion to cuckolding.

are a yoke° of his discarded men—very rogues, now they be   *pair*
out of service.

160 FORD Were they his men?

PAGE Marry, were they.

FORD I like it never the better for that. Does he lie° at the   *lodge*
Garter?

PAGE Ay, marry, does he. If he should intend this voyage
toward my wife, I would turn her loose to him, and what he
165 gets more of her than sharp words, let it lie on my head.[5]

FORD I do not misdoubt° my wife, but I would be loath to   *mistrust*
turn them together. A man may be too confident. I would
have nothing lie on my head. I cannot be thus satisfied.

  [*Enter* HOST.]

PAGE Look where my ranting Host of the Garter comes.
170 There is either liquor in his pate, or money in his purse,
when he looks so merrily. —How now, mine Host?

HOST How now, bully rook?° Thou'rt a gentleman.   *fine fellow*

  [*Enter* SHALLOW.]

Cavaliero[6] Justice, I say.

SHALLOW I follow, mine Host, I follow. —Good even° and   *day*
175 twenty,° good Master Page. Master Page, will you go with us?   *twenty times over*
We have sport in hand.

HOST Tell him, Cavaliero Justice. Tell him, bully rook.

SHALLOW Sir, there is a fray to be fought, between Sir Hugh,
the Welsh priest, and Caius, the French doctor.

180 FORD Good mine Host o'th' Garter, a word with you.

HOST What say'st thou, my bully rook?

  [*They talk aside.*]

SHALLOW [*to* PAGE] Will you go with us to behold it? My
merry Host hath had the measuring of their weapons;° and I   *has been named referee*
think hath appointed them contrary° places. For, believe   *different*
185 me, I hear the parson is no jester. Hark, I will tell you what
our sport shall be.

  [*They talk aside.*]

HOST Hast thou° no suit against my knight, my guest cavaliero?   *Are you sure you have*

FORD None, I protest. But I'll give you a pottle of burned°   *two quarts of heated*
sack to give me recourse° to him, and tell him my name is   *access*
190 Broom[7]—only for a jest.

HOST My hand, bully. Thou shalt have egress and regress—
said I well? And thy name shall be Broom. It is a merry
knight. [*to* SHALLOW *and* PAGE] Will you go, mijn'heers?°   *gentlemen (Dutch)*

SHALLOW Have with you, mine Host.

195 PAGE I have heard the Frenchman hath good skill in his rapier.

SHALLOW Tut, sir. I could have told you more. In these times
you stand on distance: your passes, stoccados,[8] and I know
not what. 'Tis the heart, Master Page, 'tis here,° 'tis here. I   *like this (?)*
have seen the time, with my long sword,[9] I would have made
200 you four tall° fellows skip like rats.   *valiant*

---

5. Let it be my responsibility (but Ford hears an allusion to the cuckold's horns).
6. Gallant gentleman (comic).
7. Q: Brook; F: Broom. "Brooke" was the family
name of Lord Cobham, who had objected to the
characterization of his ancestor Oldcastle in *1 Henry*

IV. The name was changed to "Falstaff." Presumably,
another such objection led to the shift from "Brook"
to "Broom." See the Textual Introduction.
8. *In . . . stoccados:* Today, people rely on the distance between duelists—lunges, thrusts.
9. Obsolete, heavy weapon.

HOST   Here, boys, here, here. Shall we wag?°   *go*
PAGE   Have with you. I had rather hear them scold than fight.
         [Exeunt HOST *and* SHALLOW *with* PAGE.]
FORD   Though Page be a secure° fool and stands so firmly on   *an overconfident*
    his wife's frailty, yet I cannot put off my opinion so easily. She
205 was in his company at Page's house, and what they made°   *got up to*
    there, I know not. Well, I will look further into't, and I have a
    disguise to sound¹ Falstaff. If I find her honest, I lose° not my   *waste*
    labor. If she be otherwise, 'tis labor well bestowed.   *Exit.*

2.2 (Q 6)
       Enter FALSTAFF *[and]* PISTOL.
FALSTAFF   I will not lend thee a penny.
PISTOL *[drawing his sword]*   Why, then, the world's mine oyster,
    Which I with sword will open.
FALSTAFF   Not a penny. I have been content, sir, you should
5 lay my countenance to pawn.¹ I have grated upon° my good   *harassed*
    friends for three reprieves for you and your coach-fellow°   *companion*
    Nim, or else you had looked through the grate° like a gemini°   *prison bars / pair*
    of baboons. I am damned in hell for swearing to gentlemen
    my friends you were good soldiers and tall fellows. And when
10 Mistress Bridget lost the handle of her fan,² I took't° upon   *swore*
    mine honor thou hadst it not.
PISTOL   Didst not thou share? Hadst thou not fifteen pence?
FALSTAFF   Reason,° you rogue, reason. Think'st thou I'll endan-   *With good reason*
    ger my soul gratis?° At a word, hang no more about me; I am   *for free*
15 no gibbet° for you. Go, a short knife and a throng,° to your   *gallows / thrust*
    manor of Pict-hatch, go.³ You'll not bear a letter for me, you
    rogue? You stand upon your honor. Why, thou unconfinable
    baseness, it is as much as I can do to keep the terms of my
    honor precise.° Ay, ay, I myself sometimes, leaving the fear of   *pure*
20 heaven on the left hand⁴ and hiding mine honor in my neces-
    sity, am fain to shuffle, to hedge, and to lurch;⁵ and yet you,
    rogue, will ensconce° your rags, your cat-a-mountain° looks,   *hide / wildcat*
    your red-lattice° phrases, and your bold-beating° oaths under *alehouse / very bold (?)*
    the shelter of your honor? You will not do it? You?
25 PISTOL *[sheathing his sword]*   I do relent. What would thou
      more of man?
      [Enter ROBIN.]
ROBIN   Sir, here's a woman would speak with you.
FALSTAFF   Let her approach.
      [Enter MISTRESS QUICKLY.]
MISTRESS QUICKLY   Give your worship good morrow.
FALSTAFF   Good morrow, goodwife.
30 MISTRESS QUICKLY   Not so, an't please your worship.
FALSTAFF   Good maid, then.
MISTRESS QUICKLY   I'll be sworn, as my mother was the first
    hour I was born.

---

1. To plumb the depths of.
2.2 Location: The Garter Inn.
1. Exploit my reputation (as surety for borrowing money, etc.).
2. Fans were often made with handles of precious metal or ivory.
3. Pickpockets used a short knife to cut purse strings

in a crowd. Pict-hatch was an area of London infamous for its thieves and prostitutes—hence, an unlikely locale for a "manor" (with a possible pun on "manner," or habits).
4. Disregarding the fear of God.
5. Am obliged to cheat, be devious, and steal.

FALSTAFF I do believe the swearer.[6] What° with me?   *What do you want?*

35 MISTRESS QUICKLY Shall I vouchsafe[7] your worship a word or
two?

FALSTAFF Two thousand, fair woman, and I'll vouchsafe thee
the hearing.

MISTRESS QUICKLY There is one Mistress Ford, sir—I pray,
40 come a little nearer this ways.
[*She draws* FALSTAFF *aside.*]
I myself dwell with Master Doctor Caius.

FALSTAFF Well, on. Mistress Ford, you say.

MISTRESS QUICKLY Your worship says very true. I pray your
worship, come a little nearer this ways.

45 FALSTAFF I warrant thee, nobody hears. [*He gestures at* PIS-
TOL *and* ROBIN.] Mine own people,° mine own people.   *(Pistol and Robin)*

MISTRESS QUICKLY Are they so? Heaven bless them and make
them his servants.

FALSTAFF Well, Mistress Ford—what of her?

50 MISTRESS QUICKLY Why, sir, she's a good creature. Lord,
Lord, your worship's a wanton! Well, heaven forgive you,
and all of us, I pray—

FALSTAFF Mistress Ford—come, Mistress Ford—

MISTRESS QUICKLY Marry, this is the short and the long of it.
55 You have brought her into such a canaries° as 'tis wonderful.   *(for "quandaries")*
The best courtier of them all, when the court lay° at Wind-   *resided*
sor, could never have brought her to such a canary. Yet there
has been knights, and lords, and gentlemen, with their
coaches, I warrant you, coach after coach, letter after letter,
60 gift after gift, smelling so sweetly, all musk, and so rustling,
I warrant you, in silk and gold, and in such alligant° terms,   *(for "elegant")*
and in such wine and sugar° of the best and the fairest that   *flattery*
would have won any woman's heart, and, I warrant you, they
could never get an eye-wink of her. I had myself twenty
65 angels° given me this morning, but I defy° all angels in any   *coins (as bribe) / despise*
such sort, as they say, but in the way of honesty. And, I war-
rant you, they could never get her so much as sip on a cup
with the proudest of them all, and yet there has been earls—
nay, which is more, pensioners[8]—but I warrant you, all is
70 one with her.

FALSTAFF But what says she to me? Be brief, my good she-
Mercury.°   *female messenger*

MISTRESS QUICKLY Marry, she hath received your letter, for
the which she thanks you a thousand times, and she gives
75 you to notify° that her husband will be absence from his   *note*
house between ten and eleven.

FALSTAFF Ten and eleven.

MISTRESS QUICKLY Ay, forsooth, and then you may come and
see the picture, she says, that you wot° of. Master Ford her   *know*
80 husband will be from home. Alas, the sweet woman leads an
ill life with him. He's a very jealousy man. She leads a very
frampold° life with him, good heart.   *disagreeable*

---

6. Quickly thinks she is asserting her virginity, but
by confusing the proverbs "as good a maid as her
mother" and "as innocent as a newborn babe," she
actually claims the opposite. Falstaff expresses his
belief in what she has literally, but unintentionally,
said.
7. Grant (error for "be vouchsafed, or granted, by").
8. Gentlemen of the royal bodyguard.

FALSTAFF Ten and eleven. Woman, commend me to her. I
will not fail her.

85 MISTRESS QUICKLY Why, you say well. But I have another
messenger° to your worship. Mistress Page hath her hearty   *(for "message")*
commendations to you too, and, let me tell you in your ear,
she's as fartuous° a civil modest wife, and one, I tell you,   *(for "virtuous"); farting*
that will not miss you° morning nor evening prayer, as any is   *miss*
90 in Windsor, whoe'er be the other, and she bade me tell your
worship that her husband is seldom from home, but she hopes
there will come a time. I never knew a woman so dote upon a
man. Surely I think you have charms,° la—yes, in truth!   *magic powers*

FALSTAFF Not I, I assure thee. Setting the attraction of my
95 good parts° aside, I have no other charms.   *sexual capacities*

MISTRESS QUICKLY Blessing on your heart for't.

FALSTAFF But I pray thee, tell me this: has Ford's wife and
Page's wife acquainted each other how they love me?

MISTRESS QUICKLY That were a jest indeed! They have not so
100 little grace, I hope. That were a trick indeed! But Mistress
Page would desire you to send her your little page, of all
loves.° Her husband has a marvelous infection to⁹ the little   *for love's sake*
page, and truly Master Page is an honest man. Never a wife
in Windsor leads a better life than she does. Do what she will,
105 say what she will, take all, pay all, go to bed when she list,° rise   *wants*
when she list, all is as she will. And truly she deserves it, for if
there be a kind woman in Windsor, she is one. You must send
her your page, no remedy.

FALSTAFF Why, I will.

110 MISTRESS QUICKLY Nay, but do so then, and, look you, he may
come and go between you both. And in any case have a nay-
word,° that you may know one another's mind, and the boy   *password*
never need to understand anything, for 'tis not good that
children should know any wickedness. Old folks, you know,
115 have discretion, as they say, and know the world.

FALSTAFF Fare thee well, commend me to them both. There's
my purse—I am yet thy debtor. —Boy, go along with this
woman.   [*Exit* MISTRESS QUICKLY *with* ROBIN.]
[*aside*] This news distracts° me.   *bewilders (with joy)*

120 PISTOL [*aside*] This punk° is one of Cupid's carriers.°   *whore / messengers*
Clap on° more sails! Pursue! Up with your sights!   *Set*
Give fire! She is my prize,° or ocean whelm° them all. [*Exit.*]   *booty / overwhelm*

FALSTAFF Say'st thou so, old Jack?° Go thy ways. I'll make   *(addressing himself)*
more of thy old body than I have done. Will they yet look
125 after° thee? Wilt thou, after the expense of so much money,   *desire*
be now a gainer? Good body, I thank thee. Let them say 'tis
grossly° done; so it be fairly° done, no matter.   *crudely / successfully*
[*Enter* BARDOLPH *with a cup of sack.*]

BARDOLPH Sir John, there's one Master Broom below would
fain° speak with you, and be acquainted with you; and hath   *be pleased to*
130 sent your worship a morning's draught of sack.

FALSTAFF Broom is his name?

BARDOLPH Ay, sir.

---

9. For "affection for."

FALSTAFF   Call him in.   [*Exit* BARDOLPH.]
[*He drinks sack.*] Such Brooms are welcome to me, that
135   o'erflows such liquor.¹ Aha, Mistress Ford and Mistress Page,
have I encompassed° you? Go to, *via!*°   *outwitted / On with it*
[*Enter* FORD *disguised like Broom, ushered in
by* BARDOLPH.]
FORD   Bless you, sir.
FALSTAFF   And you, sir. Would you speak with me?
FORD   I make bold to press with so little preparation° upon   *prior notice*
140   .you.
FALSTAFF   You're welcome. What's your will? Give us leave,
drawer.°   [*Exit* BARDOLPH.]   *Leave us, bartender*
FORD   Sir, I am a gentleman that have spent much. My name
is Broom.
145   FALSTAFF   Good Master Broom, I desire more acquaintance
of you.
FORD   Good Sir John, I sue for yours—not to charge you,° for   *(with an expense)*
I must let you understand I think myself in better plight for
a lender than you are;² the which hath something° embold-   *somewhat*
150   ened me to this unseasoned° intrusion. For they say if money   *ill-timed*
go before, all ways do lie open.
FALSTAFF   Money is a good soldier, sir, and will on.°   *get on*
FORD   Troth, and I have a bag of money here troubles me. If
you will help to bear it, Sir John, take all, or half, for easing
155   me of the carriage.°   *burden of carrying it*
FALSTAFF   Sir, I know not how I may deserve to be your porter.
FORD   I will tell you, sir, if you will give me the hearing.
FALSTAFF   Speak, good Master Broom. I shall be glad to be
your servant.
160   FORD   Sir, I hear you are a scholar—I will be brief with you—
and you have been a man long known to me, though I had
never so good means as desire to make myself acquainted
with you. I shall discover° a thing to you, wherein I must   *reveal*
very much lay open mine own imperfection. But, good Sir
165   John, as you have one eye upon my follies, as you hear them
unfolded, turn another into the register° of your own, that I   *catalog*
may pass with a reproof the easier, sith° you yourself know   *since*
how easy it is to be such an offender.
FALSTAFF   Very well, sir, proceed.
170   FORD   There is a gentlewoman in this town—her husband's
name is Ford.
FALSTAFF   Well, sir.
FORD   I have long loved her and, I protest° to you, bestowed   *declare*
much on her; followed her with a doting observance;°   *attentiveness*
175   engrossed° opportunities to meet her; fee'd° every slight   *collected / purchased*
occasion that could but niggardly give me sight of her; not
only bought many presents to give her, but have given largely°   *bountifully*
to many to know what she would have given.° Briefly, I have   *would like to be given*
pursued her as love hath pursued me, which hath been on
180   the wing of all occasions. But, whatsoever I have merited,

---

1. Q's "Brook" produces wordplay with "o'erflows,"   housecleaning.
lost here. See also 3.5.30–31. But Ford's pseudonym   2. I am more able to undertake a risk, an obligation,
of "Broom" in F connects with the play's emphasis on   or a pledge ("plight") as a lender than you are.

either in my mind, or in my means, meed° I am sure I have   *recompense*
received none, unless experience be a jewel that I have purchased at an infinite rate,° and that hath taught me to say   *cost*
this:

185 Love like a shadow flies, when substance Love pursues,
Pursuing that that flies, and flying what pursues.[3]

FALSTAFF   Have you received no promise of satisfaction at her
hands?

FORD   Never.

190 FALSTAFF   Have you importuned her to such a purpose?

FORD   Never.

FALSTAFF   Of what quality was your love, then?

FORD   Like a fair house, built on another man's ground, so
that I have lost my edifice by mistaking the place where I

195 erected it.

FALSTAFF   To what purpose have you unfolded this to me?

FORD   When I have told you that, I have told you all. Some say
that, though she appear honest° to me, yet in other places   *chaste*
she enlargeth° her mirth so far that there is shrewd° con- *gives rein to / malicious*

200 struction made of her. Now, Sir John, here is the heart of my
purpose: you are a gentleman of excellent breeding, admira-
ble discourse, of great admittance,[4] authentic in your place°   *of respectable rank*
and person, generally allowed° for your many warlike, court- *universally approved*
like, and learned preparations.°   *accomplishments*

205 FALSTAFF   O sir!

FORD   Believe it, for you know it. There is money. [*He offers
money.*] Spend it, spend it, spend more, spend all I have—only
give me so much of your time in exchange of it as to lay an
amiable° siege to the honesty of this Ford's wife. Use your art   *amorous*

210 of wooing; win her to consent to you. If any man may, you
may as soon as any.

FALSTAFF   Would it apply well to the vehemency of your affection that I should win what you would enjoy? Methinks you
prescribe to yourself very preposterously.

215 FORD   Oh, understand my drift. She dwells so securely° on *relies so confidently*
the excellency of her honor that the folly of my soul dares
not present itself. She is too bright to be looked against.°   *at*
Now, could I come to her with any detection° in my hand,   *accusation*
my desires had instance° and argument to commend them-   *precedent*

220 selves. I could drive her then from the ward° of her purity,   *defense*
her reputation, her marriage vow, and a thousand other her°   *of her*
defenses, which now are too too strongly embattled against
me. What say you to't, Sir John?

FALSTAFF   Master Broom, [*accepting the money*] I will first

225 make bold with your money. Next, give me your hand. [*They
shake hands.*] And last, as I am a gentleman, you shall, if you
will, enjoy Ford's wife.

FORD   O good sir!

FALSTAFF   I say you shall.

---

3. *Love . . . what pursues:* Like a shadow, love pursues a physical object ("substance")/person/money
that flees, and flees a physical object/person/money
that pursues.
4. Having qualities ensuring ready admittance into
high society.

230 FORD Want° no money, Sir John, you shall want none. — *Lack*

FALSTAFF Want no Mistress Ford, Master Broom, you shall want none. I shall be with her, I may tell you, by her own appointment. Even as you came in to me, her assistant, or go-between, parted from me. I say I shall be with her

235 between ten and eleven, for at that time the jealous rascally knave her husband will be forth.° Come you to me at night; you shall know how I speed.° — *away* / *do*

FORD I am blest in your acquaintance. Do you know Ford, sir?

240 FALSTAFF Hang him, poor cuckoldly knave, I know him not. Yet I wrong him to call him poor. They say the jealous wittolly° knave hath masses of money, for the° which his wife seems to me well favored.° I will use her as the key of the cuckoldly rogue's coffer, and there's my harvest-home.° — *willingly cuckolded* / *due to* / *good-looking* / *profitable harvest*

245 FORD I would you knew Ford, sir, that you might avoid him if you saw him.

FALSTAFF Hang him, mechanical salt-butter[5] rogue! I will stare him out of his wits. I will awe him with my cudgel: it shall hang like a meteor° o'er the cuckold's horns. Master — *an (ill-omened) comet*

250 Broom, thou shalt know I will predominate over the peasant, and thou shalt lie with his wife. Come to me soon at night. Ford's a knave, and I will aggravate his style.[6] Thou, Master Broom, shalt know him for knave and cuckold. Come to me soon at night.   [*Exit.*]

255 FORD What a damned epicurean° rascal is this? My heart is ready to crack with impatience. Who says this is improvident° jealousy? My wife hath sent to him, the hour is fixed, the match is made. Would any man have thought this? See the hell of having a false woman! My bed shall be abused, my — *sensual* / *baseless*

260 coffers ransacked, my reputation gnawn at, and I shall not only receive this villainous wrong, but stand under° the adoption of abominable terms, and by him that does me this wrong. Terms! Names! Amaimon sounds well; Lucifer, well; Barbason, well; yet they are devils' additions,° the names of — *have to put up with* / *names*

265 fiends. But cuckold? Wittol? Cuckold? The devil himself hath not such a name. Page is an ass, a secure ass; he will trust his wife, he will not be jealous! I will rather trust a Fleming with my butter, Parson Hugh the Welshman with my cheese, an Irishman with my aqua-vitae° bottle, or a thief to walk my — *whiskey*

270 ambling gelding, than my wife with herself. Then she plots, then she ruminates, then she devises; and what they think in their hearts they may effect, they will break their hearts but they will effect. Heaven be praised for my jealousy! Eleven o'clock the hour. I will prevent this, detect my wife, be

275 revenged on Falstaff, and laugh at Page. I will about it. Better three hours too soon than a minute too late. Fie, fie, fie! Cuckold, cuckold, cuckold.   *Exit.*

---

5. *mechanical salt-butter:* lower-class cheap-living; Flemish salt butter was less expensive than domestic butter. 6. Increase (irritate) his titles (by adding the title of "cuckold" to Ford's name).

2.3 (Q 7)

Enter [Doctor] CAIUS *[and his man]* RUGBY.

CAIUS   Jack Rugby.

RUGBY   Sir.

CAIUS   Vat is the clock, Jack?

RUGBY   'Tis past the hour, sir, that Sir Hugh promised to meet.

5   CAIUS   By gar, he has save his soul, dat he is no come. He has
pray his pible well, dat he is no come. By gar, Jack Rugby, he
is dead already, if he be come.

RUGBY   He is wise, sir. He knew your worship would kill him
if he came.

10   CAIUS   *[drawing his rapier]*   By gar, de herring is no dead so[1] as
I vill kill him. Take your rapier, Jack. I vill tell you how I vill
kill him.

RUGBY   Alas, sir, I cannot fence.

CAIUS   Villain, take your rapier.

15   RUGBY   Forbear. Here's company.
[CAIUS *sheathes his rapier.*]
[*Enter* SHALLOW, PAGE, *the* HOST *of the Garter,
and* SLENDER.]

HOST   Bless thee, bully Doctor.

SHALLOW   Save you, Master Doctor Caius.

PAGE   Now, good Master Doctor.

SLENDER   Give you good morrow, sir.

20   CAIUS   Vat be all you one, two, tree, four, come for?

HOST   To see thee fight, to see thee foin,° to see thee traverse,[2]   thrust
to see thee here, to see thee there, to see thee pass thy punto,
thy stock, thy reverse, thy distance, thy montant.[3] Is he dead,
my Ethiopian?° Is he dead, my Francisco?° Ha, bully? What   black man / Frenchman
25   says my Aesculapius, my Galen, my heart of elder,[4] ha? Is he
dead, bully stale?[5] Is he dead?

CAIUS   By gar, he is de coward jack-priest° of de vorld. He is   knave-priest
not show his face.

HOST   Thou art a Castalian king urinal,[6] Hector of Greece,°   (*error for "Troy"*)
30   my boy.

CAIUS   I pray you bear witness that me have stay six or seven,
two, tree hours for him, and he is no come.

SHALLOW   He is the wiser man, Master Doctor. He is a curer
of souls, and you a curer of bodies. If you should fight, you go
35   against the hair° of your professions. Is it not true, Master   grain
Page?

PAGE   Master Shallow, you have yourself been a great fighter,
though now a man of peace.

SHALLOW   Bodykins,° Master Page, though I now be old and   By God's dear body
40   of the peace, if I see a sword out, my finger itches to make
one.° Though we are justices, and doctors, and churchmen,   join in
Master Page, we have some salt° of our youth in us. We are   vigor
the sons of women, Master Page.

2.3 Location: Windsor Park (east of Windsor).
1. Not so dead (from the proverbial simile "dead as a
herring").
2. Move backward and forward.
3. *pass . . . montant:* use your thrust with the sword
point, your thrust, your backhand sword blow, your skill
in keeping at the right distance, your upward thrust.
4. Replacing "heart of oak"; as the elder is a soft,

low-growing tree, this is an insult disguised as a compliment. Aesculapius was the classical god of medicine. Galen was a physician of ancient Greece.
5. Decoy or dupe; wine or urine (often used for medical diagnosis).
6. Urine bottle. *Castalian:* of the spring Castalia, which
was sacred to the Muses; "cast-stale-ian" (one who
diagnoses by inspecting urine); Castilian (Spanish).

PAGE   'Tis true, Master Shallow.

45 SHALLOW   It will be found so, Master Page. Master Doctor
Caius, I am come to fetch you home. I am sworn of the
peace. You have showed yourself a wise physician, and Sir
Hugh hath shown himself a wise and patient churchman.
You must go with me, Master Doctor.

50 HOST   Pardon, guest° Justice. [*to* CAIUS] A word, Monsieur   *(at the Host's inn)*
Mockwater.[7]

CAIUS   Mockvater? Vat is dat?

HOST   Mockwater, in our English tongue, is valor, bully.

CAIUS   By gar, then I have as much mockvater as de Englishman.

55 Scurvy jack-dog° priest! By gar, me vill cut his ears.   *mongrel*

HOST   He will clapperclaw thee tightly,° bully.   *maul thee soundly*

CAIUS   Clapper-de-claw? Vat is dat?

HOST   That is, he will make thee amends.

CAIUS   By gar, me do look° he shall clapper-de-claw me, for,   *anticipate*

60 by gar, me vill have it.

HOST   And I will provoke him to't, or let him wag.°   *run away*

CAIUS   Me tank you for dat.

HOST   And moreover, bully— [*aside to the others*] but first, Master Guest and Master Page, and eke° Cavaliero Slender, go you   *also*

65 through the town to Frogmore.°   *(village near Windsor)*

PAGE [*aside to* HOST]   Sir Hugh is there, is he?

HOST [*aside to* PAGE]   He is there. See what humor he is in,
and I will bring the doctor about by the fields. Will it do well?

SHALLOW [*aside to* HOST]   We will do it.

70 PAGE, SHALLOW, SLENDER [*to* CAIUS]   Adieu, good Master
Doctor.   [*Exeunt all but the* HOST *and Doctor* CAIUS;
                                RUGBY *waits aside.*]

CAIUS   By gar, me vill kill de priest, for he speak for a jacka-
nape° to Anne Page.   *on behalf of an idiot*

HOST   Let him die. Sheathe thy impatience; throw cold water

75 on thy choler. Go about the fields with me through Frogmore.
I will bring thee where Mistress Anne Page is, at a farmhouse
a-feasting, and thou shalt woo her. Cried game![8] Said I well?

CAIUS   By gar, me tank you vor dat. By gar, I love you. And I
shall procure-a you de good guest: de earl, de knight, de lords,

80 de gentlemen, my patients.

HOST   For the which I will be thy adversary[9] toward Anne
Page. Said I well?

CAIUS   By gar, 'tis good. Vell said.

HOST   Let us wag, then.

85 CAIUS   Come at my heels, Jack Rugby.   *Exeunt.*

3.1 (Q 8)

Enter EVANS [*with a Bible in one hand and a rapier in
the other, and*] SIMPLE [*carrying Evans' gown*].

EVANS   I pray you now, good Master Slender's servingman and
friend Simple by your name, which way have you looked for
Master Caius, that calls himself doctor of physic?°   *medicine*

---

7. Implying that Caius's diagnoses from urine are
quackery, or that Caius is sterile (water being semen)
and so lacking in valor.
8. The chase is on.

9. The Host again makes a joke at the expense of
Caius, who understands "adversary" as "advocate."
3.1 Location: In fields near Frogmore.

SIMPLE   Marry, sir, the Petty Ward, the Park Ward,[1] every
5   way—Old Windsor way[2] and every way but the town way.

EVANS   I most fehemently desire you, you will also look that
way.

SIMPLE   I will, sir.   [*Exit.*]

EVANS   Pless my soul! How full of cholers° I am, and trempling   *anger*
10   of mind! I shall be glad if he have deceived me. How melan-
cholies I am! I will knog° his urinals about his knave's cos-   *knock*
tard,° when I have good opportunities for the 'ork.° Pless my   *head / work*
soul!
[*Sings.*]   To shallow rivers to whose falls
15   Melodious birds sings madrigals.
      There will we make our peds of roses,
      And a thousand fragrant posies.[3]
      To shallow—
Mercy on me, I have a great dispositions to cry.
20   [*Sings.*]   Melodious birds sing madrigals.—
      When as I sat in Pabylon[4]—
      And a thousand vagrant posies.
      To shallow, etc.
      [*Enter* SIMPLE.]

SIMPLE   Yonder he° is coming, this way, Sir Hugh.   *(Caius)*
25   EVANS   He's welcome.
[*Sings.*]   To shallow rivers to whose falls—
Heaven prosper the right. What weapons is° he?   *has*

SIMPLE   No weapons, sir. There comes my master, Master Shallow, and another gentleman, from Frogmore, over the stile,
30   this way.

EVANS   Pray you give me my gown—or else keep it in your arms.
[*He seems to read his Bible.*]
[*Enter* PAGE, SHALLOW, *and* SLENDER.]

SHALLOW   How now, Master Parson? Good morrow, good Sir
Hugh. Keep a gamester from the dice and a good student
from his book, and it is wonderful.
35   SLENDER [*aside*]   Ah, sweet Anne Page.

PAGE   Save you, good Sir Hugh.

EVANS   Pless you from° his mercy sake, all of you.   *for*

SHALLOW   What? The sword and the word?° Do you study them   *the Bible*
both, Master Parson?
40   PAGE   And youthful still in your doublet and hose,[5] this raw
rheumatic day!

EVANS   There is reasons and causes for it.

PAGE   We are come to you to do a good office, Master Parson.

EVANS   Fery well. What is it?
45   PAGE   Yonder is a most reverend gentleman who, belike,° hav-   *probably*
ing received wrong by some person, is at most odds with his
own gravity and patience that ever you saw.

SHALLOW   I have lived fourscore years and upward. I never
heard a man of his place, gravity, and learning so wide of his
50   own respect.[6]

1. Toward the Little Park and the Great Park.
2. Toward Old Windsor (a village near Shakespeare's Windsor).
3. Somewhat misrecalled lines from "Come live with me and be my love," a song by Christopher Marlowe.
4. Evans inserts the first line of a metrical version of

Psalm 137 (with "I" for "we"), which describes the weeping of the exiled Israelites in Babylon.
5. Close-fitting jacket and tights—that is, without a cloak.
6. Indifferent to his own good reputation.

EVANS What is he?
PAGE I think you know him: Master Doctor Caius, the
renowned French physician.
EVANS Got's will and his passion of my heart! I had as lief°   *as much wished*
55 you would tell me of a mess of porridge.°   *thick soup*
PAGE Why?
EVANS He has no more knowledge in Hibbocrates[7] and Galen,
and he is a knave besides—a cowardly knave as you would
desires to be acquainted withal.
60 PAGE [*to* SHALLOW] I warrant° you, he's the man should fight
with him.
SLENDER [*aside*] O sweet Anne Page!
SHALLOW [*to* PAGE] It appears so by his weapons. Keep them
asunder—here comes Doctor Caius.
[*Enter the* HOST, CAIUS, *and* RUGBY.]
[CAIUS *and* EVANS *offer to fight.*]
65 PAGE Nay, good Master Parson, keep in your weapon.
SHALLOW So do you, good Master Doctor.
HOST Disarm them, and let them question.°   *debate*
[PAGE *and* SHALLOW *take their weapons.*]
Let them keep their limbs whole and hack our English.
CAIUS [*aside to* EVANS] I pray you, let-a me speak a word with
70 your ear. [*aloud*] Vherefore vill you not meet-a me?
EVANS [*aside to* CAIUS] Pray you use your patience. [*aloud*] In
good time.
CAIUS By gar, you are de coward, de jack-dog, john-ape!
EVANS [*aside to* CAIUS] Pray you let us not be laughingstocks
75 to other men's humors. I desire you in friendship, and I will
one way or other make you amends. [*aloud*] I will knog your
urinal about your knave's cogscomb!°   *coxcomb; head*
CAIUS *Diable!*° Jack Rugby, mine Host de Jarteer, have I not   *Devil*
stay for him to kill him? Have I not? At de place I did
80 appoint?
EVANS As I am a Christians soul, now look you, this is the place
appointed! I'll be judgment° by mine Host of the Garter.   *judged*
HOST Peace, I say, Gallia and Gaul, French and Welsh, soul-
curer and body-curer![8]
85 CAIUS Ay, dat is very good, excellent.
HOST Peace, I say. Hear mine Host of the Garter. Am I politic?°   *devious*
Am I subtle?° Am I a machiavel?[9] Shall I lose my doctor? No,   *crafty*
he gives me the potions and the motions.°   *bowel movements*
parson, my priest, my Sir Hugh? No, he gives me the prov-
90 erbs and the no-verbs.[1] [*to* CAIUS] Give me thy hand terrestrial.° [*to* EVANS] Give me thy hand celestial—so! Boys of   *(as bodily curer)*
art,° I have deceived you both: I have directed you to wrong   *learning*
places. Your hearts are mighty, your skins are whole, and let
burned sack be the issue!° [*to* SHALLOW *and* PAGE] Come, lay   *outcome*
95 their swords to pawn.[2] [*to* EVANS *and* CAIUS] Follow me, lads
of peace, follow, follow, follow!   [*Exit.*]

---

7. Hippocrates (ancient Greek physician).
8. *Gallia and Gaul:* Wales and France. TEXTUAL
COMMENT For the possible stage business that accompanies the three paired addresses to the two antago-
nists, see Digital Edition TC 2 (Folio edited text).
9. Follower of Niccolò Machiavelli, Italian political

theorist reviled by the Elizabethans, who was held to
epitomize the "politic" and "subtle."
1. Prohibitions; verbal errors (the Welshman's misuse of standard English).
2. As a pledge; because they are not needed.

SHALLOW   Trust me, a mad° host! Follow, gentlemen, follow.   *wildly exuberant*
                            [*Exeunt* SHALLOW *and* PAGE.]
SLENDER   O sweet Anne Page!   [*Exit.*]
CAIUS   Ha, do I perceive dat? Have you make-a de sot° of us,   *fool*
100   ha, ha?
EVANS   This is well. He has made us his vlowting-stog.³ I desire
    you that we may be friends, and let us knog our prains
    together to be revenge on this same scall,° scurvy, cogging   *scabby*
    companion,° the Host of the Garter.   *cheating rogue*
105   CAIUS   By gar, with all my heart. He promise to bring me where
    is Anne Page. By gar, he deceive me too.
EVANS   Well, I will smite his noddles.° Pray you, follow.   *head*
                                        [*Exeunt.*]

3.2 (Q 9)
Enter MISTRESS PAGE [*and*] ROBIN.

MISTRESS PAGE   Nay, keep your way,° little gallant. You were   *go on*
    wont° to be a follower,° but now you are a leader. Whether   *accustomed / servant*
    had you rather:° lead mine eyes, or eye your master's heels?   *Which would you prefer*
ROBIN   I had rather, forsooth, go before you like a man than
5   follow him° like a dwarf.   *(Falstaff)*
MISTRESS PAGE   Oh, you are a flattering boy! Now I see you'll
    be a courtier.
            [*Enter* FORD.]
FORD   Well met, Mistress Page. Whither go you?
MISTRESS PAGE   Truly, sir, to see your wife. Is she at home?
10   FORD   Ay, and as idle as she may hang together for want¹ of
    company. I think if your husbands were dead, you two would
    marry.
MISTRESS PAGE   Be sure of that—two other husbands.
FORD [*indicating* ROBIN]   Where had you this pretty weather-
15   cock?°   *(Robin)*
MISTRESS PAGE   I cannot tell what the dickens his name is my
    husband had him of.° —What do you call your knight's   *got him from*
    name, sirrah?
ROBIN   Sir John Falstaff.
20   FORD   Sir John Falstaff?
MISTRESS PAGE   He, he. I can never hit on 's name. There is
    such a league° between my goodman° and he! Is your wife at   *friendship / husband*
    home indeed?
FORD   Indeed she is.
25   MISTRESS PAGE   By your leave, sir, I am sick till I see her.
                                    [*Exit with* ROBIN.]
FORD   Has Page any brains? Hath he any eyes? Hath he any
    thinking? Sure they sleep—he hath no use of them! Why, this
    boy will carry a letter twenty mile as easy as a cannon will
    shoot point-blank twelve score.² He pieces out° his wife's   *increases*
30   inclination. He gives her folly motion and advantage.³ And
    now she's going to my wife, and Falstaff's boy with her. A
    man may hear this shower sing in the wind°—and Falstaff's   *hear trouble brewing*

---

3. Flouting-stock (laughingstock).
3.2 Location: A street in Windsor.
1. And as bored as she can stand to be without falling apart, for lack.

2. Will shoot straight 240 yards.
3. He gives her lust ("folly") prompting and
opportunity.

boy with her! Good plots they are laid, and our revolted°   *disloyal*
wives share damnation together. Well, I will take him,° then   *catch him by surprise*
35   torture my wife, pluck the borrowed veil of modesty from
the so-seeming Mistress Page, divulge° Page himself for a   *reveal*
secure° and willful Actaeon,° and to these violent proceed-   *overconfident / cuckold*
ings all my neighbors shall cry aim.° [*A clock strikes.*] The   *shall applaud*
clock gives me my cue, and my assurance bids me search.
40   There I shall find Falstaff. I shall be rather praised for this
than mocked, for it is as positive as the earth is firm that Falstaff is there. I will go.
      [*Enter* PAGE, SHALLOW, SLENDER, HOST, EVANS,
        CAIUS, *and* RUGBY.]
SHALLOW, PAGE, SLENDER, HOST, EVANS, CAIUS   Well met, Master Ford.
45 FORD   Trust me, a good knot!° I have good cheer° at home,   *group / food and drink*
and I pray you all go with me.
SHALLOW   I must excuse myself, Master Ford.
SLENDER   And so must I, sir. We have appointed to dine with
Mistress Anne, and I would not break with° her for more   *break my word to*
50   money than I'll speak of.
SHALLOW   We have lingered about° a match between Anne   *delayed in concluding*
Page and my cousin Slender, and this day we shall have our
answer.
SLENDER   I hope I have your good will, Father Page.
55 PAGE   You have, Master Slender. I stand wholly for you, but
my wife, Master Doctor, is for you altogether.
CAIUS   Ay, be gar, and de maid is love-a me. My nursh-a°   *housekeeper*
Quickly tell me so mush.
HOST   What say you to young Master Fenton? He capers,° he   *leaps in dancing*
60   dances, he has eyes of youth. He writes verses, he speaks
holiday,° he smells April and May. He will carry't,° he will   *gaily / succeed*
carry't, 'tis in his buttons,° he will carry't!   *youth*
PAGE   Not by my consent, I promise you. The gentleman is of
no having,° he kept company with the wild prince and Poins.[4]   *property*
65   He is of too high a region;° he knows too much.[5] No, he shall   *rank*
not knit a knot in° his fortunes with the finger of my sub-   *strengthen*
stance.° If he take her, let him take her simply.° The wealth I   *wealth / without dowry*
have waits on my consent, and my consent goes not that way.
FORD   I beseech you heartily, some of you go home with me to
70   dinner. Besides your cheer you shall have sport: I will show
you a monster.° Master Doctor, you shall go. So shall you,   *(Falstaff)*
Master Page, and you, Sir Hugh.
SHALLOW   Well, fare you well. [*aside to* SLENDER] We shall
have the freer wooing at Master Page's.
                     [*Exit with* SLENDER.]
75 CAIUS   Go home, John Rugby. I come anon.   [*Exit* RUGBY.]
HOST   Farewell, my hearts. I will to my honest knight Falstaff
and drink canary° with him.   *Canary Islands wine*
FORD [*aside*]   I think I shall drink in pipe-wine first with him.

---

4. Prince Hal (the future Henry V) and Poins (line   than Fenton's, companions.
64) in *1* and *2 Henry IV*—actually Falstaff's, rather   5. *knows too much:* is too sophisticated and courtly.

I'll make him dance.[6] [*aloud*] Will you go, gentles?°   *gentlemen*
80 PAGE, CAIUS, *and* EVANS Have with you° to see this monster!   *We are coming*

Exeunt.

3.3 (Q 10)

Enter MISTRESS FORD [*and*] MISTRESS PAGE.

MISTRESS FORD [*calling*] What, John! What, Robert!
MISTRESS PAGE Quickly, quickly! Is the buck-basket°—   *laundry basket*
MISTRESS FORD I warrant.° —What, Robert, I say.   *I'm sure it is*
MISTRESS PAGE Come, come, come!

[*Enter two* SERVANTS *and a great buck-basket.*]

5   MISTRESS FORD Here, set it down.
MISTRESS PAGE Give your men the charge.° We must be brief.   *instructions*
MISTRESS FORD [*to the* SERVANTS] Marry, as I told you before,
John and Robert, be ready here hard by in the brewhouse
and, when I suddenly call you, come forth and without any
10 pause or staggering take this basket on your shoulders. That
done, trudge with it in all haste, and carry it among the
whitsters° in Datchet Mead,[1] and there empty it in the   *linen bleachers*
muddy ditch close by the Thames' side.
MISTRESS PAGE [*to the* SERVANTS] You will do it?
15 MISTRESS FORD [*to* MISTRESS PAGE] I ha' told them over and
over. They lack no direction.° [*to the* SERVANTS] Begone, and   *instructions*
come when you are called.   [*Exeunt* SERVANTS.]

[*Enter* ROBIN.]

MISTRESS PAGE Here comes little Robin.
MISTRESS FORD How now, my cyas-musket,° what news with   *young sparrow hawk*
20 you?
ROBIN My master Sir John is come in at your back door, Mistress Ford, and requests your company.
MISTRESS PAGE You little Jack-a-Lent,° have you been true to us?   *Lenten puppet*
ROBIN Ay, I'll be sworn! My master knows not of your being
25 here, and hath threatened to put me into everlasting liberty
if I tell you of it,° for he swears he'll turn me away.[2]   *(Falstaff's visit)*
MISTRESS PAGE Thou'rt a good boy. This secrecy of thine shall
be a tailor to thee, and shall make thee a new doublet and
hose. I'll go hide me.
30 MISTRESS FORD Do so. [*to* ROBIN] Go tell thy master I am alone.

[*Exit* ROBIN.]

—Mistress Page, remember you your cue.
MISTRESS PAGE I warrant thee. If I do not act it, hiss me.

[*Exit.*]

MISTRESS FORD Go to, then. We'll use this unwholesome
humidity,° this gross watery pumpkin. We'll teach him to   *body fluids*
35 know turtles from jays.[3]

[*Enter* FALSTAFF.]

---

6. *drink . . . dance:* make it uncomfortable for Falstaff. Pipe wine is wine from the cask, with a pun on
"the whine of musical pipes," which are played for a
dance. Ford also puns on "canary" (line 77), which is
also a dance. Drinking becomes a metaphor for
Ford's intention to make Falstaff dance to his tune.

3.3 Location: Ford's house.
1. Meadow situated between Windsor Little Park
and the Thames.
2. He'll dismiss me.
3. Gaudy birds: hence, flirtatious women. *turtles:*
turtledoves, proverbially faithful.

FALSTAFF Have I caught thee, my heavenly jewel? Why, now
 let me die,° for I have lived long enough. This is the period°   *(death); (orgasm) / end*
 of my ambition. Oh, this blessed hour!
MISTRESS FORD O sweet Sir John.
40 FALSTAFF Mistress Ford, I cannot cog,° I cannot prate, Mis-   *lie*
 tress Ford. Now shall I sin in my wish: I would thy husband
 were dead. I'll speak it before the best lord—I would make
 thee my lady.
MISTRESS FORD I, your lady, Sir John? Alas, I should be a piti-
45 ful lady.
FALSTAFF Let the court of France show me such another. I
 see how thine eye would emulate the diamond. Thou hast
 the right arched beauty of the brow that becomes the ship-
 tire, the tire-valiant, or any tire of Venetian admittance.[4]
50 MISTRESS FORD A plain kerchief, Sir John. My brows become
 nothing else, nor that well neither.
FALSTAFF Thou art a tyrant° to say so. Thou wouldst make an   *(punning on "tire")*
 absolute° courtier, and the firm fixture of thy foot would give   *a perfect*
 an excellent motion to thy gait in a semicircled farthingale.[5]
55 I see what thou wert° if fortune thy foe were not, nature thy   *would be*
 friend.° Come, thou canst not hide it.   *nature being thy friend*
MISTRESS FORD Believe me, there's no such thing in me.
FALSTAFF What made me love thee? Let that persuade thee.
 There's something extraordinary in thee. Come, I cannot cog
60 and say thou art this and that, like a-many of these lisping
 hawthorn buds° that come like women in men's apparel and   *young perfumed wooers*
 smell like Bucklersbury[6] in simple time.[7] I cannot, but I love
 thee, none but thee; and thou deserv'st it.
MISTRESS FORD Do not betray° me, sir. I fear you love Mistress   *deceive*
65 Page.
FALSTAFF Thou mightst as well say I love to walk by the Coun-
 ter gate,° which is as hateful to me as the reek of a limekiln.[8]   *debtors' prison*
MISTRESS FORD Well, heaven knows how I love you, and you
 shall one day find it.
70 FALSTAFF Keep in that mind. I'll deserve it.
MISTRESS FORD Nay, I must tell you, so you do, or else I could
 not be in that mind.
   [*Enter* ROBIN.]
ROBIN Mistress Ford, Mistress Ford, here's Mistress Page at
 the door, sweating and blowing° and looking wildly, and   *puffing*
75 would needs speak with you presently!°   *immediately*
FALSTAFF She shall not see me. I will ensconce me behind the
 arras.°   *wall curtain*
MISTRESS FORD Pray you do so. She's a very tattling woman.
   [FALSTAFF *stands behind the arras.*]
   [*Enter* MISTRESS PAGE.]
 —What's the matter? How now?
80 MISTRESS PAGE O Mistress Ford, what have you done? You're
 shamed, you're overthrown, you're undone forever!

---

4. Fancifully extravagant headdresses ("tires"), the
"ship-tire" in the form of a ship, that were acceptable
in Venice. "Tire" is from "attire."
5. Skirt shaped with covered hoops at the back.
6. London street where herbs were sold.

7. Summer (when medicinal herbs, or "simples,"
were available).
8. *reek of a limekiln*: smoke of a furnace used to produce lime by heating limestone.

MISTRESS FORD   What's the matter, good Mistress Page?

MISTRESS PAGE   Oh, welladay,° Mistress Ford, having an honest   *alas*
man to° your husband, to give him such cause of suspicion!   *as*

85 MISTRESS FORD   What cause of suspicion?

MISTRESS PAGE   What cause of suspicion? Out upon you!° How   *(a reproach)*
am I mistook in you!

MISTRESS FORD   Why, alas, what's the matter?

MISTRESS PAGE   Your husband's coming hither, woman, with
90 all the officers in Windsor, to search for a gentleman that he
says is here now in the house, by your consent, to take an ill
advantage of his absence. You are undone.

MISTRESS FORD   'Tis not so, I hope.

MISTRESS PAGE   Pray heaven it be not so, that you have such a
95 man here. But 'tis most certain your husband's coming with
half Windsor at his heels to search for such a one. I come
before to tell you. If you know yourself clear,° why, I am glad   *innocent*
of it. But if you have a friend° here, convey, convey him out!   *lover*
Be not amazed,° call all your senses to you, defend your   *bewildered*
100 reputation, or bid farewell to your good° life forever.   *respectable*

MISTRESS FORD   What shall I do? There is a gentleman, my
dear friend, and I fear not mine own shame so much as his
peril. I had rather than a thousand pound he were out of the
house.

105 MISTRESS PAGE   For shame, never stand° "you had rather" and   *waste time over*
"you had rather"! Your husband's here at hand. Bethink you
of some conveyance.° In the house you cannot hide him. Oh,   *trick; transport*
how have you deceived me! Look, here is a basket. If he be of
any reasonable stature, he may creep in here and throw foul
110 linen upon him, as if it were going to bucking.° Or it is whit-   *washing*
ing° time—send him by your two men to Datchet Mead.   *bleaching*

MISTRESS FORD   He's too big to go in there: what shall I do?

FALSTAFF [*rushing forward*]   Let me see't, let me see't, oh, let
me see't! I'll in, I'll in. —Follow your friend's counsel—I'll in!

115 MISTRESS PAGE   What, Sir John Falstaff? [*aside to him*] Are
these your letters, knight?

FALSTAFF [*aside to her*]   I love thee. Help me away! Let me
creep in here. I'll never—
     [*Sir John goes into the basket; they put clothes
     over him.*]

MISTRESS PAGE [*to* ROBIN]   Help to cover your master, boy.
120 —Call your men, Mistress Ford. [*aside to* FALSTAFF] You dissembling knight!

MISTRESS FORD   What John, Robert! John!
     [*Enter the two* SERVANTS.]
Go, take up these clothes here, quickly. Where's the cowl-
staff?° Look how you drumble!° Carry them to the laun-   *basket pole / dawdle*
125 dress in Datchet Mead. Quickly, come.
     [SERVANTS *carry the basket away.*]
     [*Enter* FORD, PAGE, CAIUS, EVANS *to meet it.*]

FORD [*to the gentlemen*]   Pray you come near. If I suspect
without cause, why then make sport at me, then let me be
your jest—I deserve it. [*to* SERVANTS] How now? Whither
bear you this?

130 SERVANTS   To the laundress, forsooth.

MISTRESS FORD Why, what have you to do° whither they bear
it? You were best° meddle with buck-washing.⁹ | *to do with*
(sarcastic)

FORD Buck? I would I could wash myself of the buck! Buck,
buck, buck, ay, buck! I warrant you, buck! And of the season

135 too, it shall appear.

[*Exeunt* SERVANTS *with the buck-basket and* ROBIN.]

Gentlemen, I have dreamed tonight;° I'll tell you my dream. | *last night*
Here, here, here be my keys, ascend° my chambers, search, | *go up to*
seek, find out! I'll warrant we'll unkennel° the fox. Let me | *dislodge*
stop this way° first. [*He locks the door.*] So, now uncase! | *passage*

140 PAGE Good Master Ford, be contented. You wrong yourself
too much.

FORD True, Master Page. —Up, gentlemen, you shall see
sport anon. Follow me, gentlemen.   [*Exit.*]

EVANS This is fery fantastical humors and jealousies.

145 CAIUS By gar, 'tis no the fashion of France. It is not jealous in
France.

PAGE Nay, follow him, gentlemen. See the issue of his search.

[*Exeunt all the gentlemen.*]

MISTRESS PAGE Is there not a double excellency in this?

MISTRESS FORD I know not which pleases me better, that my

150 husband is deceived, or Sir John.

MISTRESS PAGE What a taking° was he in, when your husband | *panic*
asked who was in the basket!

MISTRESS FORD I am half afraid he will have need of wash-
ing.¹ So throwing him into the water will do him a benefit.

155 MISTRESS PAGE Hang him, dishonest rascal! I would all of the
same strain were in the same distress.

MISTRESS FORD I think my husband hath some special suspicion of Falstaff's being here, for I never saw him so gross in
his jealousy till now.

160 MISTRESS PAGE I will lay a plot to try° that, and we will yet | *test*
have more tricks with Falstaff. His dissolute disease will | *be cured by*
scarce obey° this medicine. | *rotten flesh*

MISTRESS FORD Shall we send that foolish carrion,° Mistress
Quickly, to him, and excuse his throwing into the water, and

165 give him another hope, to betray him to another punishment?

MISTRESS PAGE We will do it. Let him be sent for tomorrow
eight o'clock to have amends.

[*Enter* FORD, PAGE, CAIUS, *and* EVANS.]

FORD I cannot find him. Maybe the knave bragged of that he
could not compass.° | *accomplish*

170 MISTRESS PAGE [*aside to* MISTRESS FORD] Heard you that?

MISTRESS FORD You use me well, Master Ford, do you?

FORD Ay, I do so.

MISTRESS FORD Heaven make you better than your thoughts.

FORD Amen.

175 MISTRESS PAGE You do yourself mighty wrong, Master Ford.

FORD Ay, ay, I must bear it.

EVANS If there be anypody in the house, and in the cham-
bers, and in the coffers, and in the presses,° heaven forgive | *large recessed cupboards*
my sins at the day of judgment!

---

9. Washing that needs bleaching (but Ford thinks of
"buck" as "stag," the horned cuckold, and as a verb
meaning "to copulate").
1. Fear will have made him urinate.

180 CAIUS Begar, nor I too. There is nobodies.
　　　PAGE Fie, fie, Master Ford, are you not ashamed? What spirit,
　　　　　what devil suggests this imagination? I would not ha' your
　　　　　distemper in this kind for the wealth of Windsor Castle.
　　　FORD 'Tis my fault, Master Page. I suffer for it.
185 EVANS You suffer for a pad conscience. Your wife is as honest
　　　　　a 'omans as I will desires among five thousand, and five hun-
　　　　　dred too.
　　　CAIUS By gar,° I see 'tis an honest woman.　　　　　　　　　　　*By God*
　　　FORD Well, I promised you a dinner. Come, come, walk in
190 　　　the park. I pray you pardon me. I will hereafter make known
　　　　　to you why I have done this. —Come, wife. Come, Mistress
　　　　　Page. I pray you pardon me, pray heartily pardon me.
　　　PAGE Let's go in, gentlemen, [*aside to* CAIUS *and* EVANS] but,
　　　　　trust me, we'll mock him. —[*aloud*] I do invite you tomorrow
195 　　　morning to my house to breakfast. After, we'll a-birding°　　*go bird hunting*
　　　　　together. I have a fine hawk for² the bush. Shall it be so?
　　　FORD Anything.
　　　EVANS If there is one, I shall make two in the company.
　　　CAIUS If there be one, or two, I shall make-a the turd.
200 FORD Pray you go, Master Page.
　　　　　　　　　　　　[*Exeunt all but* EVANS *and* CAIUS.]
　　　EVANS I pray you now, remembrance tomorrow on the lousy
　　　　　knave, mine Host.³
　　　CAIUS Dat is good, by gar—with all my heart!
　　　EVANS A lousy knave, to have his gibes and his mockeries.
　　　　　　　　　　　　　　　　　　　　　　　　　　　Exeunt.

3.4 (Q 12)
Enter FENTON [*and*] ANNE *Page.*
　　　FENTON I see I cannot get thy father's love;
　　　　　Therefore no more turn me to him, sweet Nan.
　　　ANNE Alas, how then?
　　　FENTON　　　　　　　Why, thou must be thyself.°　　　　*in charge of yourself*
　　　　　He doth object I am too great of birth
5　　　　And that, my state being galled with° my expense,　　*estate being hurt by*
　　　　　I seek to heal it only by his wealth.
　　　　　Besides these, other bars he lays before me—
　　　　　My riots past, my wild societies°—　　　　　　　　　*companionships*
　　　　　And tells me 'tis a thing impossible
10　　　　I should love thee but as a property.
　　　ANNE Maybe he tells you true.
　　　FENTON No, heaven so speed° me in my time to come!　　*as heaven may prosper*
　　　　　Albeit I will confess thy father's wealth
　　　　　Was the first motive that I wooed thee, Anne,
15　　　　Yet wooing thee, I found thee of more value
　　　　　Than stamps in gold° or sums in sealèd bags,　　　*stamped gold coins*
　　　　　And 'tis the very riches of thyself
　　　　　That now I aim at.
　　　ANNE　　　　　　　Gentle Master Fenton,¹
　　　　　Yet seek my father's love, still seek it, sir.

2. For driving birds into.　　　　　　　　　　3.4 Location: Outside Page's house.
3. A cryptic reference to the "revenge" proposal at　　1. For a very different handling of this moment, see
3.1.101–04.　　　　　　　　　　　　　　　　Q 12.11–31.

20   If opportunity and humblest suit
      Cannot attain it, why then—
              [*Enter* SHALLOW, SLENDER, *and* MISTRESS QUICKLY.]
                          Hark you hither.
              [*She whispers to him aside.*]
SHALLOW Break their talk, Mistress Quickly. My kinsman
      shall speak for himself.
SLENDER I'll make a shaft or a bolt on't.[2] 'Slid,° 'tis but   *By God's eyelid*
25   venturing.
              [MISTRESS QUICKLY *approaches* ANNE.]
SHALLOW Be not dismayed.
SLENDER No, she shall not dismay me. I care not for that, but
      that I am afeared.
MISTRESS QUICKLY [*to* ANNE] Hark ye, Master Slender would
30   speak a word with you.
ANNE I come to him. [*aside to* FENTON] This is my father's
      choice.
      Oh, what a world of vile ill-favored° faults   *ugly*
      Looks handsome in three hundred pounds a year!°   *(moderate wealth)*
              [ANNE *moves toward* SHALLOW *and* SLENDER.]
MISTRESS QUICKLY [*drawing* FENTON *aside*] And how does
35   good Master Fenton? Pray you, a word with you.
SHALLOW She's coming. To her, coz! O boy, thou hadst a
      father°—   *be manly; you're manly*
SLENDER I had a father, Mistress Anne; my uncle can tell you
      good jests of him. —Pray you, uncle, tell Mistress Anne the
40   jest how my father stole two geese out of a pen, good uncle.
SHALLOW Mistress Anne, my cousin loves you.
SLENDER Ay, that I do, as well as I love any woman in
      Gloucestershire.
SHALLOW He will maintain you like a gentlewoman.
45 SLENDER Ay, that I will, come cut and long tail,° under the   *no matter what*
      degree° of a squire.   *in the rank*
SHALLOW He will make you a hundred and fifty pounds
      jointure.°   *widowhood settlement*
ANNE Good Master Shallow, let him woo for himself.
50 SHALLOW Marry, I thank you for it. I thank you for that good
      comfort. [*withdrawing*] —She calls you, coz. I'll leave you.
ANNE Now, Master Slender.
SLENDER Now, good Mistress Anne.
ANNE What is your will?
55 SLENDER My will? 'Od's heartlings,° that's a pretty jest indeed.   *By God's little hearts*
      I ne'er made my will yet, I thank heaven. I am not such a
      sickly creature, I give heaven praise.
ANNE I mean, Master Slender, what would you with me?
SLENDER Truly, for mine own part, I would little or nothing
60   with you. Your father and my uncle hath made motions.° If it   *proposals*
      be my luck, so; if not, happy man be his dole.[3] They can tell
      you how things go better than I can. You may ask your father.
      Here he comes.
              [*Enter* PAGE *and* MISTRESS PAGE.]

---

2. I'll do it one way or another (with possible sexual   3. Good luck to the successful suitor.
connotation).

PAGE   Now, Master Slender. —Love him, daughter Anne.
65   Why, how now? What does Master Fenton here?
       [*to* FENTON] You wrong me, sir, thus still to haunt my house.
       I told you, sir, my daughter is disposed of.
FENTON   Nay, Master Page, be not impatient.
MISTRESS PAGE   Good Master Fenton, come not to my child.
PAGE   She is no match for you.
70 FENTON   Sir, will you hear me?
PAGE   No, good Master Fenton.
       —Come, Master Shallow. Come, son Slender, in.
       —Knowing my mind, you wrong me, Master Fenton.
                    [*Exit* PAGE *with* SHALLOW *and* SLENDER.]
MISTRESS QUICKLY [*aside to* FENTON]   Speak to Mistress Page.
75 FENTON   Good Mistress Page, for that° I love your daughter   *because*
       In such a righteous fashion as I do,
       Perforce,° against all checks,° rebukes, and manners,   *Of necessity / reproofs*
       I must advance the colors° of my love   *military banners*
       And not retire. Let me have your good will.
80 ANNE   Good mother, do not marry me to yond fool.
MISTRESS PAGE   I mean it not. I seek you a better husband.
MISTRESS QUICKLY   That's my master, Master Doctor.
ANNE   Alas, I had rather be set quick i'th' earth°   *half-buried alive*
       And bowled to death with turnips!
85 MISTRESS PAGE [*to* ANNE]   Come, trouble not yourself. —Good
          Master Fenton,
       I will not be your friend, nor enemy.
       My daughter will I question how she loves you,
       And, as I find her, so am I affected.°   *inclined*
       Till then, farewell, sir. She must needs go in,
90   Her father will be angry.
FENTON   Farewell, gentle Mistress. Farewell, Nan.
                      [*Exeunt* MISTRESS PAGE *and* ANNE.]
MISTRESS QUICKLY   This is my doing now. "Nay," said I, "will
       you cast away your child on a fool and a physician? Look on
       Master Fenton." This is my doing.
95 FENTON   I thank thee, and I pray thee, [*handing her a ring*]
          once° tonight   *at some time*
       Give my sweet Nan this ring. [*He gives her money.*] There's
          for thy pains.
MISTRESS QUICKLY   Now heaven send thee good fortune!
                                              [*Exit* FENTON.]
       A kind heart he hath. A woman would run through fire and
       water for such a kind heart. But yet I would my master had
100   Mistress Anne, or I would Master Slender had her. Or, in
       sooth, I would Master Fenton had her. I will do what I can
       for them all three, for so I have promised, and I'll be as good
       as my word, but speciously⁴ for Master Fenton. Well, I must
       of° another errand to Sir John Falstaff from my two mis-   *run*
105   tresses. What a beast am I to slack° it!   *Exit.*   *to be remiss in*

----

4. *speciously:* error for "specially," but Quickly's mistake inadvertently reveals the truth that she is playing falsely with Fenton.

3.5 (Q 11)

Enter FALSTAFF.

FALSTAFF   Bardolph, I say!

[*Enter* BARDOLPH.]

BARDOLPH   Here, sir.

FALSTAFF   Go, fetch me a quart of sack. Put a toast° in't.   *piece of hot toast*

[*Exit* BARDOLPH.]

Have I lived to be carried in a basket like a barrow° of   *wheelbarrow*
5   butcher's offal?° And to be thrown in the Thames? Well, if I   *waste meat*
be served such another trick, I'll have my brains ta'en out and
buttered,¹ and give them to a dog for a New Year's gift. The
rogues slighted° me into the river with as little remorse as   *slid; dumped scornfully*
they would have drowned a blind bitch's° puppies, fifteen   *bitch's blind*
10   i'th' litter. And you may know by my size that I have a kind
of alacrity in sinking. If the bottom were as deep as hell, I
should down.° I had been drowned but that the shore was   *reach the bottom*
shelvy° and shallow: a death that I abhor. For the water   *made of sandbanks*
swells a man, and what a thing should I have been when I
15   had been swelled! I should have been a mountain of mummy.°   *dead flesh*

[*Enter* BARDOLPH *with sack.*]

BARDOLPH   Here's Mistress Quickly, sir, to speak with you.

FALSTAFF   Come, let me pour in some sack to the Thames
water, for my belly's as cold as if I had swallowed snowballs
for pills to cool the reins.° [*He drinks.*] Call her in.   *kidneys*
20   BARDOLPH   Come in, woman.

[*Enter* MISTRESS QUICKLY.]

MISTRESS QUICKLY   By your leave, I cry you mercy.² Give your
worship good morrow.

FALSTAFF [*to* BARDOLPH]   Take away these chalices. Go, brew°   *prepare*
me a pottle° of sack finely.   *two quarts*
25   BARDOLPH   With eggs, sir?

FALSTAFF   Simple of itself.° I'll no pullet°-sperm in my brewage.   *Pure / young hen*

[*Exit* BARDOLPH.]

—How now?

MISTRESS QUICKLY   Marry, sir, I come to your worship from
Mistress Ford.

30   FALSTAFF   Mistress Ford? I have had Ford enough. I was
thrown into the ford; I have my belly full of ford.

MISTRESS QUICKLY   Alas the day, good heart, that was not her
fault. She does so take on with her men; they mistook their
erection.³

35   FALSTAFF   So did I mine, to build upon a foolish woman's
promise.

MISTRESS QUICKLY   Well, she laments, sir, for it, that it would
yearn° your heart to see it. Her husband goes this morning   *grieve*
a-birding; she desires you once more to come to her, between
40   eight and nine. I must carry her word° quickly. She'll make   *your reply*
you amends, I warrant you.

FALSTAFF   Well, I will visit her. Tell her so, and bid her think
what a man is. Let her consider his frailty, and then judge of
my merit.

3.5 Location: The Garter Inn.   3. Quickly means that Mistress Ford "does take on"
1. "Buttered" brains may have meant "foolish."   (scold) her servants, who misunderstood her direction,
2. *I cry you mercy:* Excuse me.   but there's an obvious, unintentional sexual pun.

45 MISTRESS QUICKLY I will tell her.

  FALSTAFF Do so. Between nine and ten, say'st thou?

  MISTRESS QUICKLY Eight and nine, sir.

  FALSTAFF Well, be gone. I will not miss° her.   *fail*

  MISTRESS QUICKLY Peace be with you, sir.   *[Exit.]*

50 FALSTAFF I marvel I hear not of Master Broom; he sent me

   word to stay° within. I like his money well. Oh, here he comes. *wait for him*

    [Enter FORD *disguised as Broom.]*

  FORD Bless you, sir.

  FALSTAFF Now, Master Broom, you come to know what hath

   passed between me and Ford's wife.

55 FORD That indeed, Sir John, is my business.

  FALSTAFF Master Broom, I will not lie to you. I was at her

   house the hour she appointed me.

  FORD And sped you,° sir?   *did you succeed*

  FALSTAFF Very ill-favoredly,° Master Broom.   *badly*

60 FORD How so, sir? Did she change her determination?

  FALSTAFF No, Master Broom, but the peaking cornuto° her *sneaking cuckold*

   husband, Master Broom, dwelling in a continual 'larum° of *alarm*

   jealousy, comes me° in the instant of our encounter, after we *comes*

   had embraced, kissed, protested, and, as it were, spoke the

65   prologue of our comedy; and at his heels, a rabble of his

   companions, thither provoked and instigated by his distem-

   per, and, forsooth, to search his house for his wife's love.

  FORD What? While you were there?

  FALSTAFF While I was there.

70 FORD And did he search for you and could not find you?

  FALSTAFF You shall hear. As good luck would have it, comes

   in one Mistress Page, gives intelligence of Ford's approach,

   and in her invention, and Ford's wife's distraction, they con-

   veyed me into a buck-basket.

75 FORD A buck-basket?

  FALSTAFF Yes. A buck-basket. Rammed me in with foul shirts

   and smocks, socks, foul stockings, greasy napkins,° that,° *cloths / so that*

   Master Broom, there was the rankest compound of villain-

   ous smell that ever offended nostril.

80 FORD And how long lay you there?

  FALSTAFF Nay, you shall hear, Master Broom, what I have

   suffered to bring this woman to evil for your good. Being

   thus crammed in the basket, a couple of Ford's knaves, his

   hinds,° were called forth by their mistress to carry me in the *servants (pejorative)*

85   name of foul clothes to Datchet Lane. They took me on their

   shoulders; met the jealous knave their master in the door,

   who asked them once or twice what they had in their basket!

   I quaked for fear lest the lunatic knave would have searched

   it. But fate, ordaining he should be a cuckold, held° his hand. *held back*

90   Well, on went he for a search, and away went I for foul

   clothes. But mark the sequel, Master Broom. I suffered the

   pangs of three several° deaths: first, an intolerable fright, to *different*

   be detected with° a jealous rotten bellwether;[4] next, to be *by*

   compassed like a good bilbo in the circumference of a peck,[5]

---

4. Leader of the flock, with a bell around its neck and a horn like a cuckold's on its head.
5. To be bent double (encompassed) like a flexible sword from Bilbao; see note to 1.1.139) in the cramped space of a laundry basket (in a receptacle holding a peck, or a quarter of a bushel).

95   hilt to point, heel to head; and then, to be stopped° in like a
     strong distillation° with stinking clothes that fretted[6] in their
     own grease. Think of that—a man of my kidney°—think of
     that, that am as subject to heat as butter; a man of continual
     dissolution° and thaw. It was a miracle to scape suffocation.
100 And in the height of this bath—when I was more than half
     stewed in grease, like a Dutch dish—to be thrown into the
     Thames and cooled, glowing hot, in that surge like a
     horseshoe! Think of that—hissing hot—think of that, Master
     Broom!
105 FORD   In good sadness,° sir, I am sorry that for my sake you
     have suffered all this. My suit then is desperate. You'll under-
     take her no more?
     FALSTAFF   Master Broom, I will be thrown into Etna,° as I have
     been into Thames, ere I will leave her thus. Her husband is
110 this morning gone a-birding. I have received from her another
     embassy° of meeting. Twixt eight and nine is the hour, Mas-
     ter Broom.
     FORD   'Tis past eight already, sir.
     FALSTAFF   Is it? I will then address me to my appointment.
115 Come to me at your convenient leisure, and you shall know
     how I speed. And the conclusion shall be crowned with your
     enjoying her. Adieu. You shall have her, Master Broom.
     Master Broom, you shall cuckold Ford.   [Exit.]
     FORD   Hum! Ha! Is this a vision? Is this a dream? Do I sleep?
120 Master Ford, awake! Awake, Master Ford! There's a hole
     made in your best coat,[7] Master Ford. This 'tis to be married;
     this 'tis to have linen and buck-baskets! Well, I will proclaim
     myself what I am. I will now take° the lecher. He is at my
     house. He cannot scape me. 'Tis impossible he should. He
125 cannot creep into a halfpenny purse, nor into a pepperbox.
     But lest the devil that guides him should aid him, I will
     search impossible places. Though what I am I cannot avoid;
     yet to be what I would not shall not make me tame. If I have
     horns to make one mad, let the proverb go with me. I'll be
130 horn-mad.[8]   Exit.

4.1[1]

Enter MISTRESS PAGE, MISTRESS QUICKLY, [*and*]
WILLIAM.

     MISTRESS PAGE   Is he at Master Ford's already, think'st thou?
     MISTRESS QUICKLY   Sure he is by this,° or will be presently,°
     but truly he is very courageous° mad about his throwing into
     the water. Mistress Ford desires you to come suddenly.°
5   MISTRESS PAGE   I'll be with her by and by.° I'll but bring my
     young man here to school. Look where his master comes;
     'tis a playing day, I see.
        [*Enter* EVANS.]
     How now, Sir Hugh, no school today?
     EVANS   No. Master Slender is let° the boys leave° to play.
10   MISTRESS QUICKLY   Blessing of his heart!

Right-margin glosses:

95 *stoppered*
96 *liquid*
97 *constitution*
99 *melting*
105 *seriousness*
108 *Sicilian volcano*
111 *message*
123 *catch*

4.1
2 *now / immediately*
3 *(for "ragingly")*
4 *at once*
5 *right away*
9 *asked that / be allowed*

---

6. Fermented.
7. Proverbial for "Your reputation is spoiled."
8. I'll be as furious as a horned animal in breeding

season; furious to be a cuckold.
4.1 Location: Outdoors.
1. This scene is not present in Q.

MISTRESS PAGE Sir Hugh, my husband says my son profits nothing in the world[2] at his book. I pray you, ask him some questions in his accidence.°   *Latin grammar*

EVANS Come hither, William. Hold up your head, come.

15 MISTRESS PAGE Come on, sirrah. Hold up your head. Answer your master—be not afraid.

EVANS William, how many numbers is in nouns?

WILLIAM Two.°   *(singular and plural)*

MISTRESS QUICKLY Truly, I thought there had been one num-
20 ber more, because they say " 'od's 'ouns."[3]

EVANS Peace your tattlings. —What is "fair," William?

WILLIAM *Pulcher.*

MISTRESS QUICKLY Polecats?° There are fairer things than   *Smelly animals; whores*
polecats, sure.

25 EVANS You are a very simplicity 'oman. I pray you, peace.
—What is *lapis*, William?

WILLIAM A stone.

EVANS And what is a stone, William?

WILLIAM A pebble.

30 EVANS No, it is *lapis.* I pray you remember in your prain.

WILLIAM *Lapis.*

EVANS That is a good William. What is he, William, that does lend articles?

WILLIAM Articles are borrowed of the pronoun, and be thus
35 declined: *singulariter nominativo, hic, haec, hoc.*[4]

EVANS *Nominativo, hig, hag, hog.*[5] Pray you, mark: *genitivo,*°   *genitive*
huius. Well, what is your accusative case?

WILLIAM *Accusativo, hinc.*°   *(for "hunc")*

EVANS I pray you, have your remembrance, child. *Accusativo,*
40 *hing, hang, hog.*

MISTRESS QUICKLY Hang-hog[6] is Latin for bacon, I warrant you.

EVANS Leave your prabbles, 'oman. —What is the focative°   *vocative; (obscene)*
case, William?

45 WILLIAM Oh . . . *vocativo* . . . oh—

EVANS Remember, William, focative is *caret.*[7]

MISTRESS QUICKLY And that's a good root.

EVANS 'Oman, forbear.

MISTRESS PAGE [*to* MISTRESS QUICKLY] Peace.

50 EVANS What is your genitive case plural, William?

WILLIAM Genitive case?

EVANS Ay.

WILLIAM Genitive, *horum, harum, horum.*

MISTRESS QUICKLY Vengeance of° Jenny's case! Fie on her,   *A plague on*
55 never name her, child, if she be a whore![8]

EVANS For shame, 'oman.

MISTRESS QUICKLY You do ill to teach the child such words.

---

2. My son fails to improve.
3. God's wounds; three is an odd ('od's) number.
4. William recites by memory from his textbook. *Singulariter nominativo* is "in the nominative singular" (in which William gives the masculine, feminine, and neuter forms of the pronoun "this").
5. The pronunciation in Evans's accent.
6. Alluding to the saying "Hog is not bacon until it be hanged."

7. Missing. Quickly understands "carrot," whose slang sense "penis" is supported by a suggestion of "fuck" in "focative."
8. *Jenny's case . . . whore:* "Genitive" is perhaps misunderstandable as Latin for "generative" or even "genital"—as well as "Jenny"; "case" is understood by Quickly to mean "situation" and also the slang term for "vagina."

[*to* MISTRESS PAGE] He teaches him to hick and to hack;
which they'll do fast enough of themselves, and to call
60   whore'm. [*to* EVANS] Fie upon you![9]
EVANS   'Oman, art thou lunatics? Hast thou no understand-
ings for thy cases, and the numbers of the genders? Thou art
as foolish Christian creatures as I would desires.
MISTRESS PAGE [*to* MISTRESS QUICKLY]   Prithee, hold thy peace.
65   EVANS   Show me now, William, some declensions of your
pronouns.
WILLIAM   Forsooth, I have forgot.
EVANS   It is *qui, que, quod;* if you forget your *quis,* your *ques,*
and your *quods,*[1] you must be preeches.° Go your ways and   *flogged*
70   play, go.
MISTRESS PAGE   He is a better scholar than I thought he was.
EVANS   He is a good sprag° memory. Farewell, Mistress Page.   *sprack (lively)*
MISTRESS PAGE   Adieu, good Sir Hugh.   [*Exit* EVANS.]
Get you home, boy.   [*Exit* WILLIAM.]
75   Come, we stay too long.
          Exeunt [MISTRESS PAGE *and* MISTRESS QUICKLY].

4.2 (Q 13)
Enter FALSTAFF [*and*] MISTRESS FORD.
FALSTAFF   Mistress Ford, your sorrow hath eaten up my sufferance.[1] I see you are obsequious° in your love, and I pro-   *devoted*
fess requital to a hair's breadth,° not only, Mistress Ford, in   *in full*
the simple office of love, but in all the accoutrement, com-
5   pliment, and ceremony of it. But are you sure of your husband now?
MISTRESS FORD   He's a-birding, sweet Sir John.
MISTRESS PAGE [*within*]   What ho, gossip° Ford! What ho!   *friend*
MISTRESS FORD   Step into the chamber, Sir John.
       [*Enter* MISTRESS PAGE.]
10   MISTRESS PAGE   How now, sweetheart, who's at home besides
yourself?
MISTRESS FORD   Why, none but mine own people.°   *servants*
MISTRESS PAGE   Indeed?
MISTRESS FORD   No, certainly. [*aside to her*] Speak louder.
15   MISTRESS PAGE [*loudly*]   Truly, I am so glad you have nobody
here.
MISTRESS FORD   Why?
MISTRESS PAGE   Why, woman, your husband is in his old lines°   *role*
again. He so takes on° yonder with my husband, so rails   *raves*
20   against all married mankind, so curses all Eve's daughters,°   *women*
of what complexion° soever, and so buffets himself on the   *temperament*
forehead, crying, "Peer out,[2] peer out!" that any madness I
ever yet beheld seemed but tameness, civility, and patience
to this his distemper he is in now. I am glad the fat knight is
25   not here.

---

9. *to hick and to hack:* to hiccup (from drinking) and slash to pieces (perhaps sexual). TEXTUAL COMMENT On Quickly's misunderstanding of Latin as English in this scene, see Digital Edition TC 3 (Folio edited text).
1. Possibly pronounced as "keys, case, cods," with "keys" a euphemism for "penis," "case" a term for

"vagina," and "cods" slang for "testicles."
4.2 Location: Ford's house.
1. Your sorrow has made the memory of my suffering disappear.
2. Emerge (addressed to imagined cuckold's horns).

MISTRESS FORD Why, does he talk of him?

MISTRESS PAGE Of none but him, and swears he was carried
out, the last time he searched for him, in a basket. Protests
to my husband he is now here, and hath drawn him and the
30 rest of their company from their sport to make another
experiment° of his suspicion. But I am glad the knight is not   trial
here. Now he shall see his own foolery.

MISTRESS FORD How near is he, Mistress Page?

MISTRESS PAGE Hard by, at street end. He will be here anon.

35 MISTRESS FORD I am undone. The knight is here.

MISTRESS PAGE Why, then you are utterly shamed, and he's
but a dead man. What a woman are you? Away with him,
away with him! Better shame than murder.

MISTRESS FORD Which way should he go? How should I
40 bestow° him? Shall I put him into the basket again?   dispose of
[Enter FALSTAFF.]

FALSTAFF No, I'll come no more i'th' basket. May I not go out
ere he come?

MISTRESS PAGE Alas, three of Master Ford's brothers watch
the door with pistols, that none shall issue out. Otherwise
45 you might slip away ere he came. But what make you° here?   are you doing

FALSTAFF What shall I do? I'll creep up into the chimney.

MISTRESS FORD[3] There they always use to discharge their
birding-pieces.°   bird guns

MISTRESS PAGE Creep into the kiln-hole.°   oven

50 FALSTAFF Where is it?

MISTRESS FORD He will seek there, on my word! Neither press,°   cupboard
coffer, chest, trunk, well, vault, but he hath an abstract° for   a list
the remembrance of such places, and goes to them by his
note. There is no hiding you in the house.

55 FALSTAFF I'll go out then.

MISTRESS FORD If you go out in your own semblance, you die,
Sir John—unless you go out disguised.

MISTRESS PAGE How might we disguise him?

MISTRESS FORD Alas the day, I know not. There is no wom-
60 an's gown big enough for him. Otherwise he might put on a
hat, a muffler,° and a kerchief, and so escape.   face scarf

FALSTAFF Good hearts, devise something! Any extremity rather
than a mischief.°   calamity

MISTRESS FORD My maid's aunt, the fat woman of Brentford,[4]
65 has a gown above.

MISTRESS PAGE On my word, it will serve him. She's as big as
he is! And there's her thrummed° hat and her muffler too.   fringed
Run up, Sir John.

MISTRESS FORD Go, go, sweet Sir John. Mistress Page and I
70 will look° some linen for your head.   look for

MISTRESS PAGE Quick, quick! We'll come dress you straight.
Put on the gown the while.   [Exit FALSTAFF.]

---

3. TEXTUAL COMMENT For the assigning of speeches
to Mistresses Ford and Page in this scene, see Digital
Edition TC 4 (Folio edited text).
4. Gillian of Brentford, a scurrilous comic figure,
perhaps historically based, best known for her will,
in which she supposedly "bequeathed a score of farts
amongst her friends" (Thomas Nashe, prologue to his
Summer's Last Will and Testament). Brentford was a
village halfway between Windsor and London.

MISTRESS FORD   I would my husband would meet him in this
shape! He cannot abide the old woman of Brentford; he
75   swears she's a witch, forbade her my house, and hath threatened to beat her.

MISTRESS PAGE   Heaven guide him to thy husband's cudgel,
and the devil guide his cudgel afterwards.

MISTRESS FORD   But is my husband coming?

80   MISTRESS PAGE   Ay, in good sadness,° is he, and talks of the   in all seriousness
basket, too, howsoever⁵ he hath had intelligence.°   information

MISTRESS FORD   We'll try° that, for I'll appoint my men to carry   test
the basket again, to meet him at the door with it, as they did
last time.

85   MISTRESS PAGE   Nay, but he'll be here presently. Let's go dress
him like the witch of Brentford.

MISTRESS FORD   I'll first direct my men what they shall do
with the basket. Go up. I'll bring linen for him straight.°   immediately

MISTRESS PAGE   Hang him, dishonest° varlet, we cannot mis-   lewd
90   use him enough.
We'll leave a proof by that which we will do,
Wives may be merry and yet honest° too.   chaste
We do not act that° often jest and laugh;   misbehave who
'Tis old, but true: "Still swine eats all the draff."⁶
    [Exeunt MISTRESS FORD and MISTRESS PAGE.]
    [Enter the two SERVANTS with MISTRESS FORD.]

95   MISTRESS FORD   Go, sirs, take the basket again on your shoulders. Your master is hard at° door. If he bid you set it down,   close to the
obey him. Quickly, dispatch.   [Exit.]

FIRST SERVANT   Come, come, take it up.

SECOND SERVANT   Pray heaven it be not full of knight again.

100   FIRST SERVANT   I hope not. I had lief° as bear so much lead.   I would rather
    [Enter FORD, PAGE, EVANS, CAIUS, and SHALLOW.]

FORD   Ay, but if it prove true, Master Page, have you any way
then to unfool me again?⁷ [to SERVANTS] Set down the basket, villains. —Somebody call my wife. [to SERVANTS] Youth
in a basket!° Oh, you panderly rascals! [to his guests] There's   Fortunate lover
105   a knot,° a ging,° a pack, a conspiracy against me! Now shall   group / gang
the devil be shamed.° —What, wife, I say! Come, come forth!   truth be known
Behold what honest clothes you send forth to bleaching.

PAGE   Why, this passes,° Master Ford. You are not to go loose   goes beyond all bounds
any longer; you must be pinioned.

110   EVANS   Why, this is lunatics. This is mad as a mad dog.

SHALLOW   Indeed, Master Ford, this is not well, indeed.
    [Enter MISTRESS FORD.]

FORD   So say I too, sir. —Come hither, Mistress Ford, Mistress
Ford, the honest woman, the modest wife, the virtuous creature, that hath the jealous fool to° her husband. I suspect   for
115   without cause, mistress, do I?

MISTRESS FORD   Heaven be my witness, you do, if you suspect
me in any dishonesty.

FORD   Well said, brazen-face, hold it out!° [He kicks the bas-   keep it up
ket.] Come forth, sirra.

---

5. By whatever means.
6. Proverbial: "The quiet swine eats all the hogwash."
In other words, quietness conceals sexual immorality
(whereas playfulness is innocent; see line 92).

7. Page has evidently accused Ford of making a fool
of himself; Ford wants to know if Page will withdraw
the charge if Ford is proved correct in his suspicions.

[*He opens the basket and begins to toss out
    the laundry.*]

120 PAGE This passes.

MISTRESS FORD Are you not ashamed? Let the clothes alone.

FORD [*into the basket*] I shall find you anon.

EVANS 'Tis unreasonable! Will you take up your wife's clothes?
    Come, away.

125 FORD Empty the basket, I say.

MISTRESS FORD Why, man, why?

FORD Master Page, as I am a man, there was one conveyed
    out of my house yesterday in this basket. Why may not he be
    there again? In my house I am sure he is. My intelligence° is   information
130 true. My jealousy is reasonable. Pluck me out all the linen!

MISTRESS FORD If you find a man there, he shall die a flea's
    death.[8]

PAGE Here's no man.

SHALLOW By my fidelity, this is not well, Master Ford. This
135 wrongs you.°   *You shame yourself*

EVANS Master Ford, you must pray, and not follow the imagi-
    nations of your own heart. This is jealousies.

FORD Well, he's not here I seek for.

PAGE No, nor nowhere else but in your brain.

140 FORD Help to search my house this one time. If I find not
    what I seek, show no color° for my extremity.° Let me for-   *excuse / excesses*
    ever be your table-sport.° Let them say of me, "As jealous as   *laughingstock*
    Ford, that searched a hollow walnut for his wife's leman."°   *lover*
    Satisfy me once more! Once more search with me!

    [*Exeunt the* SERVANTS *with the refilled basket.*]

145 MISTRESS FORD [*calling*] What ho, Mistress Page, come you
    and the old woman down. My husband will come into the
    chamber.

FORD Old woman? What old woman's that?

MISTRESS FORD Why, it is my maid's aunt of Brentford.

150 FORD A witch, a quean, an old cozening quean!° Have I not   *cheating hussy*
    forbid her my house? She comes of errands, does she? We are
    simple men, we do not know what's brought to pass under
    the profession° of fortune-telling. She works by charms, by   *claim*
    spells, by th' figure,[9] and such daubery° as this is beyond our   *trickery*
155 element.° We know nothing. Come down, you witch, you hag   *knowledge*
    you, come down, I say!

MISTRESS FORD Nay, good sweet husband! —Good gentle-
    men, let him not strike the old woman.

    [*Enter* MISTRESS PAGE *bringing* FALSTAFF *disguised
        as an old woman.*]

MISTRESS PAGE Come, Mother Pratt.° Come, give me your   *Buttocks*
160 hand.

FORD I'll prat° her! [FORD *beats* FALSTAFF *with a cudgel.*] Out   *beat; trick*
    of my door, you witch, you rag, you baggage, you polecat, you
    runion,° out, out! I'll conjure you! I'll fortune tell you!   *contemptible woman*

    [*Exit* FALSTAFF, *running.*]

8. Anyone hiding there must be insignificantly small.
9. Astrological or magical diagrams, or wax effigies used by witches.

MISTRESS PAGE   Are you not ashamed? I think you have killed
165   the poor woman.

MISTRESS FORD   Nay, he will do it. [*to* FORD] 'Tis a goodly credit
for you.

FORD   Hang her, witch!

EVANS   By yea and no, I think the 'oman is a witch indeed. I
170   like not when a 'oman has a great peard; I spy a great peard
under his muffler.

FORD   Will you follow, gentlemen? I beseech you, follow. See
but the issue° of my jealousy. If I cry out° thus upon no trail,   *outcome / bark*
never trust me when I open° again.   *start barking*

175   PAGE   Let's obey his humor° a little further. Come, gentlemen.   *indulge him*
          [*Exeunt* FORD, PAGE, EVANS, CAIUS, *and* SHALLOW.]

MISTRESS PAGE   Trust me, he beat him most pitifully.

MISTRESS FORD   Nay, by the mass, that he did not. He beat
him most unpitifully, methought.

MISTRESS PAGE   I'll have the cudgel hallowed and hung o'er
180   the altar. It hath done meritorious service.

MISTRESS FORD   What think you? May we, with the warrant of
womanhood and the witness of a good conscience, pursue
him with any further revenge?

MISTRESS PAGE   The spirit of wantonness is sure scared out of
185   him. If the devil have him not in fee simple with fine and
recovery, he will never, I think, in the way of waste attempt us
again.[1]

MISTRESS FORD   Shall we tell our husbands how we have
served him?

190   MISTRESS PAGE   Yes, by all means, if it be but to scrape the
figures° out of your husband's brains! If they can find in   *fantasies*
their hearts the poor unvirtuous fat knight shall be any further afflicted, we two will still be the ministers.

MISTRESS FORD   I'll warrant they'll have him publicly shamed,
195   and methinks there would be no period° to the jest should   *conclusion*
he not be publicly shamed.

MISTRESS PAGE   Come, to the forge with it, then shape it! I
would not have things cool.   *Exeunt.*

4.3 (Q 14)

Enter HOST *and* BARDOLPH.

BARDOLPH   Sir, the German desires to have three of your horses.
The Duke himself will be tomorrow at court, and they° are   *(the Germans)*
going to meet him.

HOST   What duke should that be, comes° so secretly? I hear   *who comes*
5   not of him in the court. Let me speak with the gentlemen.
They speak English?

BARDOLPH   Ay, sir! I'll call them to you.

HOST   They shall have my horses, but I'll make them pay. I'll
sauce them.° They have had my houses a week at command.[1]   *make them pay dearly*
10   I have turned away my other guests. They must come off,° I'll   *pay up*
sauce them. Come.[2]   *Exeunt.*

---

1. Legal terms: If the devil doesn't absolutely own
him, he won't try to despoil us (sexually and economically) again.
4.3 Location: The Garter Inn.
1. They have had my inn at their disposal for a week.
2. The German duke is fiction, part of a plot whereby

Caius and Evans revenge themselves on the Host.
The exact details are obscure. A scene or more may
have been censored in which Caius and Evans, or
some other characters, disguised themselves as Germans and duped the Host. Evidently, Sir John also
parts with his horses: see 5.5.108–09 and 2.1.86.

4.4 (Q 15)

Enter PAGE, FORD, MISTRESS PAGE, MISTRESS FORD,
and EVANS.

EVANS 'Tis one of the best discretions of a 'oman¹ as ever I
did look upon.

PAGE And did he send you both these letters at an instant?°   *at the same time*

MISTRESS PAGE Within a quarter of an hour.

5 FORD Pardon me, wife. Henceforth do what thou wilt.
I rather will suspect the sun with° cold   *of*
Than thee with wantonness. Now doth thy honor stand,
In him that was of late an heretic,
As firm as faith.

PAGE   'Tis well, 'tis well, no more.

10 Be not as extreme in submission as in offense,
But let our plot go forward. Let our wives
Yet once again—to make us public sport—
Appoint a meeting with this old fat fellow
Where we may take him and disgrace him for it.

15 FORD There is no better way than that they spoke of.

PAGE How? To send him word they'll meet him in the park at
midnight? Fie, fie, he'll never come.

EVANS You say he has been thrown in the rivers, and has
been grievously peaten as an old 'oman. Methinks there

20 should be terrors in him that he should not come! Methinks
his flesh is punished. He shall have no desires.

PAGE So think I too.

MISTRESS FORD Devise but how you'll use° him when he comes,   *treat*
And let us two devise to bring him thither.

25 MISTRESS PAGE There is an old tale goes that Herne the
Hunter,
Sometime° a keeper here in Windsor Forest,   *Once*
Doth all the winter time, at still midnight,
Walk round about an oak, with great ragged° horns,   *jagged*
And there he blasts° the tree, and takes° the cattle,   *blights / bewitches*

30 And makes milch kine° yield blood, and shakes a chain   *dairy cattle*
In a most hideous and dreadful manner.
You have heard of such a spirit, and well you know
The superstitious idle-headed eld°   *people of olden times*
Received and did deliver to our age

35 This tale of Herne the Hunter for a truth.

PAGE Why, yet there want not° many that do fear   *are*
In deep of night to walk by this Herne's oak.
But what of this?

MISTRESS FORD   Marry, this is our device:
That Falstaff at that oak shall meet with us.

40 PAGE Well, let it not be doubted but he'll come,
And, in this shape, when you have brought him thither,
What shall be done with him? What is your plot?

MISTRESS PAGE That likewise have we thought upon, and
thus:
Nan Page, my daughter, and my little son,

45 And three or four more of their growth,° we'll dress   *size*
Like urchins,° ouphes,° and fairies, green and white,   *goblins / elf children*

4.4 Location: Ford's house.   1. Mistress Page is one of the most discreet women.

With rounds of waxen tapers° on their heads   *crowns of candles*
And rattles in their hands. Upon a sudden,
As Falstaff, she, and I are newly met,
50   Let them from forth a sawpit² rush at once
With some diffusèd° song. Upon their sight   *disordered*
We two, in great amazèdness, will fly.
Then let them all encircle him about,
And fairy-like to pinch the unclean knight,
55   And ask him why that hour of fairy revel,
In their so sacred paths, he dares to tread
In shape profane.
FORD   And till he tell the truth,
Let the supposèd fairies pinch him sound°   *soundly*
And burn him with their tapers.
MISTRESS PAGE   The truth being known,
60   We'll all present ourselves, dishorn the spirit,
And mock him home to Windsor.
FORD   The children must
Be practiced well to this, or they'll ne'er do't.
EVANS   I will teach the children their behaviors, and I will be
like a jackanapes° also, to burn the knight with my taber.   *tame monkey; trickster*
65   FORD   That will be excellent. I'll go buy them vizards.°   *masks*
MISTRESS PAGE   My Nan shall be the queen of all the fairies,
Finely attired in a robe of white.
PAGE [*aside*]   That silk³ will I go buy, and in that time
Shall Master Slender steal my Nan away
70   And marry her at Eton.⁴ [*aloud*] Go send to Falstaff straight.
FORD   Nay, I'll to him again in name of Broom.
He'll tell me all his purpose. Sure, he'll come.
MISTRESS PAGE   Fear not you that. Go get us properties°   *props*
And tricking° for our fairies.   *costumes*
75   EVANS   Let us about it! It is admirable pleasures and ferry hon-
est knaveries.   [*Exeunt* EVANS, FORD, *and* PAGE.]
MISTRESS PAGE   Go, Mistress Ford,
Send quickly to Sir John to know his mind.
                              [*Exit* MISTRESS FORD.]
I'll to the doctor. He hath my good will,
80   And none but he, to marry with Nan Page.
That Slender, though well landed,° is an idiot;   *owning much land*
And he° my husband best of all affects.°   *him / likes most*
The doctor is well moneyed, and his friends
Potent at court. He, none but he, shall have her,
85   Though twenty thousand worthier come to crave her.
                                        [*Exit.*]

4.5 (Q 16)

Enter [*the*] HOST [*and*] SIMPLE.

HOST   What wouldst thou have, boor? What, thickskin?° Speak,   *dullard*
breathe, discuss; brief, short, quick, snap!
SIMPLE   Marry, sir, I come to speak with Sir John Falstaff
from Master Slender.

---

2. A pit over which wood was sawed.   4. Across the Thames from Windsor.
3. A sign of Page's financial means.   4.5 Location: The Garter Inn.

5 HOST   There's his chamber, his house, his castle, his standing
       bed and truckle bed.¹ 'Tis² painted about with the story of
       the prodigal,° fresh and new. Go, knock, and call. He'll speak   *prodigal son (Luke 15)*
       like an Anthropophaginian° unto thee. Knock, I say!   *cannibal*
   SIMPLE   There's an old woman, a fat woman, gone up into his
10   chamber. I'll be so bold as stay, sir, till she come down. I come
       to speak with her, indeed.
   HOST   Ha? A fat woman? The knight may be robbed. I'll call.
       —Bully knight! Bully Sir John! Speak from thy lungs mili-
       tary! Art thou there? It is thine Host, thine Ephesian,° calls.   *mate*
15 FALSTAFF [*within*]   How now, mine Host?
   HOST   Here's a Bohemian Tartar tarries° the coming down of   *Here a savage awaits*
       thy fat woman. Let her descend, bully, let her descend! My
       chambers are honorable. Fie! Privacy?° Fie!   *secret goings-on*
           [*Enter* FALSTAFF.]
   FALSTAFF   There was, mine Host, an old fat woman even now
20   with me, but she's gone.
   SIMPLE   Pray you, sir, was't not the wise woman° of Brentford?   *woman skilled in magic*
   FALSTAFF   Ay, marry, was it, mussel shell.° What would you   *empty head (?); gaper (?)*
       with her?
   SIMPLE   My master, sir, my Master Slender, sent to her, seeing
25   her go through the streets, to know, sir, whether one Nim,
       sir, that beguiled° him of a chain, had the chain or no.   *cheated*
   FALSTAFF   I spake with the old woman about it.
   SIMPLE   And what says she, I pray, sir?
   FALSTAFF   Marry, she says that the very same man that
30   beguiled Master Slender of his chain cozened° him of it.   *tricked*
   SIMPLE   I would I could have spoken with the woman herself.
       I had other things to have spoken with her too from him.
   FALSTAFF   What are they? Let us know.
   HOST   Ay, come! Quick!
35 SIMPLE   I may not conceal° them, sir.   *(for "reveal")*
   HOST   Conceal them, or thou diest.
   SIMPLE   Why, sir, they were nothing but about Mistress Anne
       Page, to know if it were my master's fortune to have her
       or no.
40 FALSTAFF   'Tis, 'tis his fortune.
   SIMPLE   What, sir?
   FALSTAFF   To have her or no. Go, say the woman told me so.
   SIMPLE   May I be bold to say so, sir?
   FALSTAFF   Ay, sir. Like who more bold?°   *As bold as they come*
45 SIMPLE   I thank your worship. I shall make my master glad
       with these tidings.   [*Exit.*]
   HOST   Thou art clerkly,° thou art clerkly, Sir John. Was there   *learned*
       a wise woman with thee?
   FALSTAFF   Ay, that there was, mine Host, one that hath taught
50   me more wit than ever I learned before in my life. And I paid
       nothing for it neither, but was paid° for my learning.   *thrashed*
           [*Enter* BARDOLPH *in filthy wet clothes.*]
   BARDOLPH   Out, alas, sir! Cozenage, mere° cozenage!   *utter*
   HOST   Where be my horses? Speak well of them, varletto.°   *varlet*

---

1. Trundle bed, which could be stored under the   2. The "it" in "'Tis" refers to either the wall hanging
larger standing bed.   or the bed hanging.

BARDOLPH   Run away with the cozeners! For so soon as I came
55   beyond Eton, they threw me off from behind one of them in
a slough of mire, and set spurs and away, like three German
devils, three Doctor Faustaffs![3]
HOST   They are gone but to meet the Duke, villain. Do not say
they be fled. Germans are honest men.
        [*Enter* EVANS.]
60   EVANS   Where is mine Host?
HOST   What is the matter, sir?
EVANS   Have a care of your entertainments.° There is a friend   guests
of mine come to town tells me there is three cozen°-Germans   related; cheating
that has cozened all the hosts of Reading, of Maidenhead, of
65   Colnbrook,° of horses and money. I tell you for good will, look   nearby villages
you. You are wise and full of gibes and vlouting-stocks,° and   laughingstocks
'tis not convenient° you should be cozened. Fare you well.   appropriate
                                                [*Exit.*]
        [*Enter* CAIUS.]
CAIUS   Vere is mine Host *de* Jarteer?
HOST   Here, Master Doctor, in perplexity and doubtful dilemma.
70   CAIUS   I cannot tell vat is dat, but it is tell-a me dat you make
grande préparation for a duke *de* Jamanie.° By my trot,° der   Germany / troth
is no duke that the court is know to come. I tell you for good
will. *Adieu.*   [*Exit.*]
HOST [*to* BARDOLPH]   Hue and cry,° villain! Go! [*to* FALSTAFF]   Raise the alarm
75   Assist me, knight! I am undone. [*to* BARDOLPH] Fly, run! Hue
and cry, villain! —I am undone.
                [*Exeunt* HOST *and* BARDOLPH.]
FALSTAFF   I would all the world might be cozened, for I have
been cozened and beaten too. If it should come to the ear of
the court how I have been transformed, and how my trans-
80   formation hath been washed and cudgeled, they would melt
me out of my fat, drop by drop, and liquor° fishermen's boots   grease
with me. I warrant they would whip me with their fine wits
till I were as crestfallen° as a dried pear. I never prospered   shriveled
since I forswore myself at primero.° Well, if my wind were   cards
85   but long enough,° I would repent.   (to list all my sins)
        [*Enter* MISTRESS QUICKLY.]
Now, whence come you?
MISTRESS QUICKLY   From the two parties, forsooth.
FALSTAFF   The devil take one party and his dam° the other, and   mother
so they shall be both bestowed. I have suffered more for their
90   sakes, more than the villainous inconstancy of man's disposition is able to bear.
MISTRESS QUICKLY   And have not they suffered? Yes, I war-
rant, speciously° one of them. Mistress Ford, good heart, is   (for "specially")
beaten black and blue, that you cannot see a white spot
95   about her.
FALSTAFF   What tell'st thou me of black and blue? I was beaten
myself into all the colors of the rainbow, and I was like to be
apprehended for the witch of Brentford! But that my admi-

3. Bardolph alludes to Marlowe's *Doctor Faustus,* throw them in "some lake of mud and dirt" (1616
whose titular hero makes a pact with the devil. In   Quarto; scene 13). In the following scene, the three
one scene, three devils are conjured to "horse" Ben-   appear muddy and, anticipating Falstaff's punishment,
volio, Frederick, and Martino on their backs and   with horns on their heads.

rable dexterity of wit, my counterfeiting the action of an old
100 woman, delivered me, the knave constable had set me i'th'
stocks—i'th' common stocks—for a witch!
MISTRESS QUICKLY   Sir, let me speak with you in your chamber.
You shall hear how things go and, I warrant, to your content.
Here is a letter will say somewhat. Good hearts, what ado
105 here is to bring you together! Sure, one of you does not serve
heaven well, that you are so crossed.°   thwarted
FALSTAFF   Come up into my chamber.   *Exeunt.*

4.6 (Q 17)
Enter FENTON [*and the*] HOST.
HOST   Master Fenton, talk not to me. My mind is heavy. I will
give over° all.   give up
FENTON   Yet hear me speak. Assist me in my purpose
And, as I am a gentleman, I'll give thee
5 A hundred pound in gold, more than your loss.
HOST   I will hear you, Master Fenton, and I will at the least
keep your counsel.°   secret
FENTON   From time to time, I have acquainted you
With the dear love I bear to fair Anne Page,
10 Who mutually hath answered my affection—
So far forth as herself might be her chooser¹—
Even to my wish. I have a letter from her
Of such contents as you will wonder at;
The mirth whereof, so larded with my matter,°   mixed with my concern
15 That neither singly can be manifested
Without the show of both. Fat Falstaff
Hath a great scene. The image° of the jest   idea
I'll show you here at large. Hark, good mine Host.
Tonight at Herne's Oak, just twixt twelve and one,
20 Must my sweet Nan present° the Fairy Queen.   play the part of
The purpose why is here—[*showing a letter*]—in which
disguise,
While other jests are something rank on foot,°   somewhat thick afoot
Her father hath commanded her to slip
Away with Slender and with him at Eton
25 Immediately to marry. She hath consented. Now, sir,
Her mother, even strong against that match
And firm for Doctor Caius, hath appointed
That he shall likewise shuffle her away,
While other sports are tasking of° their minds,   engaging
30 And at the dean'ry,² where a priest attends,
Straight marry her. To this her mother's plot
She, seemingly obedient, likewise hath
Made promise to the doctor. Now, thus it rests:°   things stand thus
Her father means she shall be all in white,
35 And in that habit,° when Slender sees his time   dress
To take her by the hand and bid her go,
She shall go with him. Her mother hath intended—
The better to denote her to the doctor,

4.6 Location: Scene continues.
1. Insofar as she might choose her own husband.
2. Residence of the dean (the head of the clergy on

the staff of certain churches); (loosely) a parsonage.
Here, Fenton refers to the deanery attached to St.
George's Chapel on the property of Windsor Castle.

For they must all be masked and vizarded—

40 That, quaint° in green, she shall be loose enrobed, *elegantly*

With ribbons pendent flaring° 'bout her head; *waving down*

And when the doctor spies his vantage ripe,

To pinch her by the hand, and on that token

The maid hath given consent to go with him.

45 HOST Which means she to deceive, father or mother?

FENTON Both, my good Host, to go along with me.

And here it rests, that you'll procure the vicar

To stay for me at church twixt twelve and one,

And, in the lawful name of° marrying, *name of lawful*

50 To give our hearts united ceremony.

HOST Well, husband° your device. I'll to the vicar. *manage well; (pun)*

Bring you the maid, you shall not lack a priest.

FENTON So shall I evermore be bound to thee.

Besides, I'll make a present° recompense. *immediate*

[FENTON *gives him money.*]

Exeunt [*severally*].

5.1

Enter FALSTAFF *and* MISTRESS QUICKLY.

FALSTAFF Prithee, no more prattling. Go. I'll hold.° —This *keep the appointment*

is the third time. I hope good luck lies in odd numbers.

—Away, go! —They say there is divinity° in odd numbers, *divine power*

either in nativity, chance, or death. —Away!

5 MISTRESS QUICKLY I'll provide you a chain, and I'll do what I

can to get you a pair of horns.

FALSTAFF Away, I say! Time wears!° Hold up your head and *passes*

mince.° [*Exit* MISTRESS QUICKLY.] *walk affectedly*

[*Enter* FORD *disguised as Broom.*]

How now, Master Broom? Master Broom, the matter will be

10 known tonight or never. Be you in the park about midnight

at Herne's Oak, and you shall see wonders.

FORD Went you not to her yesterday, sir, as you told me you

had appointed?

FALSTAFF I went to her, Master Broom, as you see,° like a *as I am now*

15 poor old man, but I came from her, Master Broom, like a

poor old woman. That same knave Ford, her husband, hath

the finest mad devil of jealousy in him, Master Broom, that

ever governed frenzy. I will tell you, he beat me grievously in

the shape of a woman—for in the shape of man, Master

20 Broom, I fear not Goliath with a weaver's beam,[1] because I

know also life is a shuttle.[2] I am in haste. Go along with me.

I'll tell you all, Master Broom. Since I plucked geese,° played *(child's prank)*

truant, and whipped top,° I knew not what 'twas to be beaten *spun a top*

till lately. Follow me. I'll tell you strange things of this knave

25 Ford, on whom tonight I will be revenged, and I will deliver

his wife into your hand. Follow. Strange things in hand,

Master Broom! Follow. *Exeunt.*

5.1 Location: The Garter Inn. 2. From Job 7:6: "My days are swifter than a weaver's

1. The biblical simile for Goliath's spear handle shuttle."

(1 Samuel 17:7).

5.2

Enter PAGE, SHALLOW, [*and*] SLENDER.

PAGE   Come, come. We'll couch° i'th' castle ditch till we see   *lie*
the light of our fairies. Remember, son Slender, my—

SLENDER   Ay, forsooth, I have spoke with her, and we have a nay-
word° how to know one another. I come to her in white and cry   *password*
5   "mum"; she cries "budget"°; and by that we know one another.   *mumbudget (silence)*

SHALLOW   That's good, too. But what needs either your "mum"
or her "budget"? The white will decipher her well enough.
—It hath struck ten o'clock.

PAGE   The night is dark. Light and spirits will become it well.
10   Heaven prosper our sport! No man means evil but the devil,
and we shall know him by his horns. Let's away. Follow me.

                                                          Exeunt.

5.3

Enter MISTRESS PAGE, MISTRESS FORD, [*and*] CAIUS.

MISTRESS PAGE   Master Doctor, my daughter is in green.
When you see your time, take her by the hand, away with
her to the deanery, and dispatch it quickly. Go before into
the park. We two must go together.

5   CAIUS   I know vat I have to do. Adieu.

MISTRESS PAGE   Fare you well, sir.   [*Exit* CAIUS.]
My husband will not rejoice so much at the abuse of Falstaff
as he will chafe at the doctor's marrying my daughter. But
'tis no matter. Better a little chiding than a great deal of
10   heartbreak.

MISTRESS FORD   Where is Nan now, and her troop of fairies,
and the Welsh devil, Hugh?

MISTRESS PAGE   They are all couched in a pit hard by Herne's
Oak with obscured lights which, at the very instant of Fal-
15   staff's and our meeting, they will at once display to the night.

MISTRESS FORD   That cannot choose but amaze° him.   *That is bound to frighten*

MISTRESS PAGE   If he be not amazed, he will be mocked. If he
be amazed, he will every way be mocked.

MISTRESS FORD   We'll betray him finely.

20   MISTRESS PAGE   Against such lewdsters and their lechery,
Those that betray them do no treachery.

MISTRESS FORD   The hour draws on. To the oak, to the oak!

                                                          Exeunt.

5.4

Enter EVANS *and* FAIRIES.

EVANS   Trib,° trib, fairies! Come, and remember your parts.   *Trip (move nimbly)*
Be pold, I pray you! Follow me into the pit and, when I give
the watch-'ords, do as I pid you. Come, come—trib, trib!

                                                          Exeunt.

5.5 (Q 18)

Enter FALSTAFF [*with a buck's head upon him*].

FALSTAFF   The Windsor bell hath struck twelve. The minute
draws on. Now the hot-blooded gods assist me! Remember,

5.2 Location: An approach to Windsor Park.   5.4 Location: Scene continues.
5.3 Location: Scene continues.   5.5 Location: Windsor Park.

Jove, thou wast a bull for thy Europa.[1] Love set on thy horns.
O powerful Love, that in some respects makes a beast a
man; in some other, a man a beast. You were also, Jupiter, a
swan for the love of Leda.[2] O omnipotent Love, how near
the god drew to the complexion of a goose! A fault done first
in the form of a beast—O Jove, a beastly fault!—and then
another fault in the semblance of a fowl. Think on't, Jove, a
foul fault! When gods have hot° backs, what shall poor men   *lustful*
do? For me, I am here a Windsor stag, and the fattest, I
think, i'th' forest. Send me a cool rut-time,° Jove, or who can   *mating season*
blame me to piss my tallow?[3] —Who comes here? My doe?

[*Enter* MISTRESS FORD.]

MISTRESS FORD   Sir John? Art thou there, my dear? My male
deer?

FALSTAFF   My doe with the black scut?° Let the sky rain pota-   *tail; pubic hair*
toes; let it thunder to the tune of "Greensleeves,"° hail   *popular love song*
kissing-comfits, and snow eringoes![4] Let there come a tem-
pest of provocation,° I will shelter me here.   *sexual incitement*

[*He clutches her.*]

[*Enter* MISTRESS PAGE.]

MISTRESS FORD   Mistress Page is come with me, sweet hart.°   *deer; (pun on "heart")*

FALSTAFF   Divide me like a bribed° buck, each a haunch. [*They*   *stolen*
sit on his lap.] I will keep my sides to myself, my shoulders for
the fellow of this walk,° and my horns° I bequeath your hus-   *woods keeper / (cuckold's)*
bands. Am I a woodman,[5] ha? Speak I like Herne the Hunter?
Why, now is Cupid a child of conscience. He makes restitu-
tion.° As I am a true spirit, welcome!   *repays my suffering*

[*There is a noise of horns.*]

MISTRESS PAGE   Alas, what noise?

MISTRESS FORD   Heaven forgive our sins!

FALSTAFF   What should this be?

MISTRESS FORD *and* MISTRESS PAGE   Away, away!

[*The two women run away.*]

FALSTAFF   I think the devil will not have me damned, lest the
oil that's in me should set hell on fire. He would never else
cross me thus.

Enter [MISTRESS QUICKLY *like the Queen of Fairies,*
PISTOL *as Hobgoblin,*[6] EVANS *like a satyr, and boys*
dressed like] FAIRIES [*carrying tapers, including*
ANNE *Page*].

MISTRESS QUICKLY   Fairies black, gray, green, and white,
You moonshine revelers and shades° of night,   *spirits*
You orphan heirs of fixèd destiny,[7]
Attend° your office° and your quality.°   *Perform / duty / calling*
Crier° Hobgoblin, make the fairy oyes.°   *Town crier / hear ye*

---

1. In classical mythology, Jupiter turned himself into
a bull and abducted Europa by swimming across the
sea with her on his back.
2. Jupiter turned himself into a swan in order to rape
Leda.
3. If I urinate or sweat away my fat (as stags were
thought to do at rutting time).
4. Candied roots of sea holly that, like sweet "pota-
toes" (lines 16–17), were considered an aphrodisiac.
kissing-comfits: breath sweeteners ("comfits" are

candies).
5. *Woodman:* hunter; lecher; wooden man.
6. Anne, who was assigned the part of the Queen of
Fairies at 4.4.66, is here replaced by Quickly, either as
part of the marital scheming or simply as an indication
that the boy actor who played Quickly also is to play
this role. Similarly, Hobgoblin may have been played
by Pistol or simply by the actor who played Pistol.
7. You parentless inheritors of fixed duties (?). (Fairies were supposed to be parentless.)

PISTOL Elves, list° your names. Silence, you airy toys!° *listen for / trifles*
40 Cricket,° to Windsor chimneys shalt thou leap. *(elf's name)*
Where fires thou find'st unraked° and hearths unswept, *(hence, likely to die out)*
There pinch the maids as blue as bilberry!° *blueberry*
Our radiant queen hates sluts and sluttery.° *dirtiness*
FALSTAFF [aside] They are fairies. He that speaks to them
shall die!
45 I'll wink° and couch.° No man their works must eye. *shut my eyes / lie down*
[FALSTAFF *lies down and covers his eyes.*]
EVANS Where's Bede?
[*Second boy steps forward.*]
Go you and, where you find a maid
That ere she sleep has thrice her prayers said,
Raise up° the organs of her fantasy;° *Stimulate / imagination*
Sleep she[8] as sound as careless° infancy. *carefree*
50 But those as° sleep and think not on their sins, *who*
Pinch them—arms, legs, backs, shoulders, sides, and shins.
MISTRESS QUICKLY About,° about!°[9] *To work*
Search Windsor Castle, elves, within and out.
Strew good luck, ouphes,° on every sacred room, *elves*
55 That it may stand till the perpetual doom° *Judgment Day*
In state° as wholesome as in state° 'tis fit, *condition / dignity*
Worthy° the owner and the owner it. *Worthy of*
The several chairs of order[1] look you scour
With juice of balm and every precious flower.
60 Each fair installment,° coat, and sev'ral crest,[2] *stall or seat*
With loyal blazon,[3] evermore be blest.
And nightly, meadow fairies, look you sing
Like to the Garter's compass,° in a ring. *circle*
Th'expressure° that it bears, green let it be, *image*
65 More fertile fresh than all the field to see,
And *Honi soit qui mal y pense*[4] write
In emerald tufts, flowers purple, blue, and white,
Like sapphire, pearl, and rich embroidery,
Buckled below fair knighthood's bending knee.
70 Fairies use flowers for their charactery.° *lettering*
Away, disperse! But till 'tis one o'clock,
Our dance of custom° round about the oak *customary dance*
Of Herne the Hunter let us not forget.
EVANS Pray you lock hand in hand; yourselves in order set;
75 And twenty glowworms shall our lanterns be
To guide our measure° round about the tree. *dance*
But stay! I smell a man of middle earth.° *a mortal*
FALSTAFF [aside] Heavens defend me from that Welsh fairy,
lest he transform me to a piece of cheese!
80 PISTOL [to FALSTAFF] Vile worm, thou wast o'erlooked° even *destined to evil*
in thy birth.

8. Though she is sleeping; may she sleep.
9. TEXTUAL COMMENT For this speech's courtly account of the Order of the Garter, given a more popular tone in Q, see Digital Edition TC 5 (Folio edited text).
1. The various stalls assigned, in St. George's Chapel, Windsor, to members of the Order of the Garter (a high dignity that the monarch conferred, marked by a garter worn below the knee).
2. *crest:* heraldic device on top of the helmet. *coat:* coat of arms displayed on the stall or seat.
3. *With loyal blazon:* Together with the coat of arms on a banner.
4. Evil to him who evil thinks (the motto of the Order of the Garter).

MISTRESS QUICKLY   With trial-fire touch me° his finger end.   *touch*
  If he be chaste, the flame will back descend
  And turn him to no pain. But if he start,
85 It is the flesh of a corrupted heart.
PISTOL   A trial, come!
EVANS   Come! Will this wood° take fire?[5]   *(Falstaff's fingers)*
  [*The* FAIRIES *variously burn Falstaff's fingers and
    then pinch him.*]
FALSTAFF [*startled*]   Oh, oh, oh!
MISTRESS QUICKLY   Corrupt, corrupt, and tainted in desire!
  About him, fairies, sing a scornful rhyme
90 And, as you trip, still° pinch him to your time.   *continually*
                    The Song.

FAIRIES [*sing*]
        Fie on sinful fantasy! Fie on lust and luxury!°   *lechery*
        Lust is but a bloody fire,° kindled with unchaste   *fire of the blood*
          desire,
        Fed in heart whose flames aspire°   *rise up*
        As thoughts do blow them higher and higher.
95   Pinch him, fairies, mutually.° Pinch him for his   *all together*
          villainy.
        Pinch him, and burn him, and turn him about,
        Till candles, and starlight, and moonshine be out!
  [*Here they pinch him, and sing about him, and the
    DOCTOR comes one way and steals away first boy in
    white.[6] And SLENDER another way he takes second boy
    in green. And FENTON steals Mistress ANNE, being in
    red. And a noise of hunting is made within: and all
    the FAIRIES run away. FALSTAFF pulls off his buck's
    head and rises up. And enter Master PAGE, Master
    FORD, and their wives MISTRESS PAGE and MISTRESS
    FORD, with Master SHALLOW.*]
PAGE [*to* FALSTAFF]   Nay, do not fly. I think we have watched
  you° now.   *caught you in the act*
  Will none but Herne the Hunter serve your turn?
100 MISTRESS PAGE [*to* PAGE]   I pray you, come, hold up° the jest   *prolong*
  no higher.°   *further*
  [*to* FALSTAFF] Now, good Sir John, how like you Windsor
    wives?
MISTRESS FORD   See you these, husband? [*She points to the
    buck-horns.*] Do not these fair yokes°   *horns*
  Become the forest better than the town?
FORD [*to* FALSTAFF]   Now, sir, who's a cuckold now? Master
105 Broom, Falstaff's a knave, a cuckoldly knave. Here are his
  horns, Master Broom. And, Master Broom, he hath enjoyed
  nothing of Ford's but his buck-basket, his cudgel, and twenty
  pounds of money, which must be paid to Master Broom. His
  horses are arrested° for it,[7] Master Broom.   *seized as security*

---

5. Here and elsewhere in the scene, Falstaff is almost equated with Herne's oak and hence treated like a piece of wood—as the second syllable of his name suggests. His entire name suggests his repeated sexual failures.

6. TEXTUAL COMMENT For the color-coding of the fairies in this SD, absent in F but present in Q, see Digital Edition TC 6 (Folio edited text).
7. See note to 4.3.11.

110 MISTRESS FORD   Sir John, we have had ill luck. We could never
       meet. I will never take you for my love again, but I will always
       count you my deer.

     FALSTAFF   I do begin to perceive that I am made an ass.

     FORD   Ay, and an ox too. Both the proofs are extant.[8]

115 FALSTAFF   And these are not fairies. I was three or four times
       in the thought they were not fairies, and yet the guiltiness of
       my mind, the sudden surprise of my powers,° drove the   (of reason)
       grossness of the foppery° into a received belief, in despite of   deceit
       the teeth of° all rhyme and reason, that they were fairies.   against

120   See now how wit may be made a Jack-a-Lent° when 'tis upon   butt
       ill employment.

     EVANS   Sir John Falstaff, serve Got and leave your desires,
       and fairies will not pince you.

     FORD   Well said, fairy Hugh.

125 EVANS   And leave you your jealousies too, I pray you.

     FORD   I will never mistrust my wife again, till thou art able to
       woo her in good English.

     FALSTAFF   Have I laid my brain in the sun and dried it, that it
       wants° matter to prevent so gross o'erreaching as this? Am I   lacks

130   ridden with° a Welsh goat too? Shall I have a coxcomb° of   harassed by / jester's cap
       frieze? 'Tis time I were choked with a piece of toasted cheese.[9]

     EVANS   Seese is not good to give putter; your belly is all putter.

     FALSTAFF   Seese and putter? Have I lived to stand at the taunt
       of one that makes fritters of English? This is enough to be

135   the decay of lust and late-walking° through the realm.   (for sexual purposes)

     MISTRESS PAGE   Why, Sir John, do you think though° we would   even if
       have thrust virtue out of our hearts by the head and shoul-
       ders, and have given ourselves without scruple to hell, that
       ever the devil could have made you our delight?

140 FORD   What, a hodge-pudding?° A bag of flax?   sausage

     MISTRESS PAGE   A puffed° man?   inflated

     PAGE   Old, cold, withered, and of intolerable entrails?

     FORD   And one that is as slanderous as Satan?

     PAGE   And as poor as Job?

145 FORD   And as wicked as his wife?[1]

     EVANS   And given to fornications, and to taverns, and sack,
       and wine, and metheglins,° and to drinkings, and swear-   Welsh spiced drink
       ings, and starings? Pribbles and prabbles?°   Raving and squabbles

     FALSTAFF   Well, I am your theme. You have the start° of me. I   advantage

150   am dejected.° I am not able to answer the Welsh flannel.   humbled
       Ignorance itself is a plummet o'er me.[2] Use me as you will.

     FORD   Marry, sir, we'll bring you to Windsor to one Master
       Broom, that you have cozened of money, to whom you should
       have been° a pander. Over and above that° you have suffered,   intended to be / what

155   I think to repay that money will be a biting affliction.

---

8. "Ox" (fool, cuckold) is inspired by "yokes" (line 102).
The "proofs" are either the horns, which are "extant"
(existing), or the "ass" and the "ox."
9. "Welsh goat" (line 130) refers to the large number
of goats in Wales, "frieze" (line 131) to a coarse wool
made there, and "toasted cheese" to what was supposedly a favorite Welsh food.
1. Satan slanders Job (Job 1:9–11, 2:4–5); Job's wife
tempts him to curse God (2:9).

2. A "plummet" is a "plumb line," used for measuring
depths, with a pun on "plumbet," a woolen fabric and,
hence, connected with "Welsh flannel," one of Falstaff's names here for Evans (along with "Ignorance").
The ignorant Evans, the "Welsh flannel," is a woolen
fabric over Falstaff, by which Falstaff means that
even the ignorant Evans can plumb Falstaff's depths,
can see his true motives.

PAGE   Yet be cheerful, knight. Thou shalt eat a posset[3] tonight
at my house, where I will desire thee to laugh at my wife,
that now laughs at thee. Tell her Master Slender hath married her daughter.

160   MISTRESS PAGE [aside]   Doctors doubt that.° If Anne Page be   (expresses disbelief)
my daughter, she is, by this,° Doctor Caius' wife.   now
            Enter SLENDER.
SLENDER   Whoa, ho, ho, father Page!
PAGE   Son? How now? How now, son, have you dispatched?°   settled the business
SLENDER   Dispatched? I'll make the best in Gloucestershire
165   know on't°—would I were hanged, la, else!°   of it / otherwise
PAGE   Of what, son?
SLENDER   I came yonder at Eton to marry Mistress Anne
Page, and she's a great lubberly° boy! If it had not been i'th'   loutish
church, I would have swinged° him, or he should have   beaten
170   swinged me. If I did not think it had been Anne Page, would
I might never stir, and 'tis a postmaster's boy.°   stableboy
PAGE   Upon my life, then, you took the wrong.
SLENDER   What need you tell me that? I think so, when I took
a boy for a girl! If I had been married to him, for all° he was   even though
175   in woman's apparel, I would not have had him.
PAGE   Why, this is your own folly! Did not I tell you how you
should know my daughter by her garments?
SLENDER   I went to her in green, and cried "mum," and she cried
"budget," as Anne and I had appointed, and yet it was not
180   Anne, but a postmaster's boy.
MISTRESS PAGE [to PAGE]   Good George, be not angry. I knew
of your purpose; turned my daughter into white, and indeed
she is now with the doctor at the deanery, and there married.
            Enter CAIUS.
CAIUS   Vere is Mistress Page? By gar, I am cozened! I ha' mar-
185   ried *un garçon*, a boy, *un paysan*,° by gar! A boy, it is not Anne   a peasant
Page, by gar! I am cozened.
MISTRESS PAGE   Why? Did you take her in white?
CAIUS   Ay, by gar, and 'tis a boy! By gar, I'll raise all Windsor.
FORD   This is strange. Who hath got the right Anne?
190   PAGE   My heart misgives me. Here comes Master Fenton.
            [*Enter* FENTON *and* ANNE.]
How now, Master Fenton?
ANNE   Pardon, good father. —Good my mother, pardon!
PAGE   Now, mistress, how chance you went not with Master
Slender?
195   MISTRESS PAGE   Why went you not with Master Doctor, maid?
FENTON   You do amaze° her. Hear the truth of it.   confuse
You would have married her most shamefully
Where there was no proportion° held in love.   balance
The truth is, she and I, long since contracted,°   betrothed
200   Are now so sure° that nothing can dissolve° us.   united / separate
Th'offense is holy that she hath committed,
And this deceit loses the name of craft,
Of disobedience, or unduteous title,°   undutifulness
Since therein she doth evitate° and shun   avoid

---

3. Take a restorative drink of hot milk curdled with wine or ale.

205   A thousand irreligious cursèd hours
       Which forcèd marriage would have brought upon her.
    FORD [*to* PAGE *and* MISTRESS PAGE]   Stand not amazed. Here is
           no remedy.
       In love, the heavens themselves do guide the state:
       Money buys lands, and wives are sold by fate.
210 FALSTAFF   I am glad, though you have ta'en a special stand° to   *hunter's station*
       strike at me, that your arrow hath glanced.°   *missed*
    PAGE   Well, what remedy? —Fenton, heaven give thee joy. What
       cannot be eschewed must be embraced.
    FALSTAFF   When night-dogs run, all sorts of deer are chased.[4]
215 MISTRESS PAGE   Well, I will muse° no further. —Master Fenton,   *complain*
       Heaven give you many many merry days.
       Good husband, let us everyone go home,
       And laugh this sport o'er by a country fire,
       Sir John and all.
    FORD   Let it be so. Sir John,
220   To Master Broom you yet shall hold your word,
       For he tonight shall lie with Mistress Ford.   *Exeunt.*

---

4. When "dogs" (the failed suitors) run out of control at night, they may catch "all sorts of deer" (the disguised boys, rather than Anne). In other words, you can't control nocturnal intrigue.

As You Like It

Most of *As You Like It* occurs in a forest that Shakespeare transforms into a place for thought experiments, debates, and disguises. In the forest, time slows down. As one character famously says: "There's no clock in the forest" (3.2.278–79). As a result, those who live there or visit have the leisure to talk, sing, jest, and try out new social roles. In the spirit of serious play, *As You Like It* invites its characters and its audiences to suspend the rules of everyday existence and to imagine different realities. What could the world look like if, for example, women had the same freedoms as men? Or if rank did not matter in determining a person's worth? As a clown figure in the play says: "Much virtue in 'if'" (5.4.94). What if we could have the world "as [we] like it?" Shakespeare's title invites us to contemplate that very question. What do we like? What do we desire? And, by extension, how could the world be rearranged to accommodate those desires and wishes?

Because of its setting and its themes, *As You Like It* is usually called a pastoral comedy—that is, a comic play that juxtaposes (1) a corrupt world of the city or the court and (2) what is imagined as the simpler existence of the fields and forest. The pastoral mode had its origins in ancient Greece, where the poet Theocritus used rural settings and rustic shepherds to explore the pain of love and the harsh injustices of daily life. The Roman poet Virgil expanded this tradition, elaborating in particular the opposition between city and country life. In England, many of Shakespeare's contemporaries worked in pastoral forms, particularly Edmund Spenser, whose *Shepheardes Calender* (1579) was modeled on Virgil's *Eclogues,* and Sir Philip Sidney, whose vast prose romance *The Countess of Pembrokes Arcadia* was first published in revised form in 1590. These works often juxtaposed a corrupt court and rural innocence.

As a literary mode, pastoral can take many forms. There are pastoral lyrics, dialogues, prose romances, and dramas. Certain topics and situations, however, recur in many kinds of pastoral. Often, for example, people in flight from urban or courtly life temporarily retreat to the country, where, sometimes disguising themselves as shepherds, they converse with those native to the place. In this rural setting talk abounds. Characters complain about unresponsive lovers, hold singing contests, and debate the relative merits of country and court life, whether nature is improved or spoiled by art, and whether "gentleness" (meaning both "nobility" and "a virtuous nature") is a condition one can achieve or to which one must be born. The rural setting also affords the opportunity for serious social critique. The greed of landlords, the deceit of courtiers, and the corruption of the clergy are common topics of complaint.

The relationship of the "natural" to the "artificial" is a topic fundamental to pastoral; that is, are what human beings have made—cities, gardens, systems of social hierarchy—preferable to the simplicity and lack of artifice supposedly found in rural settings and communities? Such debates continue today, as we frequently long for simpler, slower lives but find it hard to wean ourselves from all the sophisticated conveniences of modern life. The choices weren't easier in the early modern period, when courts and cities had pleasures and attractions as well as vices and corruptions. Moreover, while pastoral frequently celebrates simplicity, it does so in a highly artful manner, drawing on conventions that have been part of the Western literary tradition for at least two thousand years; and the characters who most praise

First page of the *Gest of Robin Hood*, one of the most important sixteenth-century renditions of the Robin Hood legend.

rural life are frequently "just visiting" and playing an elaborate game of "let's pretend." Hence, many disguises are found in pastoral, where courtiers pose as rustic shepherds, men as women, women as men, and dukes as forest outlaws. As all those who take rural vacations know, however, retreating to a green world—even if one does not stay—can offer a much-needed change of perspective and an opportunity to see oneself and others in a new way, and perhaps to grow and change. This is, of course, the challenge facing the many courtly characters who end up in *As You Like It*'s green world.

In writing the play, Shakespeare fully embraced the serious concerns of pastoral while reveling in its potential for high-spirited fun. In the main action, a good ruler, Duke Senior, has been ousted from his throne by a usurping younger brother, Duke Frederick. The banished Duke takes refuge in the Forest of Arden, where he lives like Robin Hood with a band of loyal followers. When his daughter, Rosalind, companion to Frederick's daughter, Celia, is likewise banished, she disguises herself as a young man named Ganymede and also journeys to Arden. Celia, posing as a lowborn woman named Aliena, goes with her, as does Touchstone the Clown. A second line of action concerns two other brothers: Orlando, the youngest son, and Oliver, the oldest son of Sir Roland de Bois. The inheritor of his father's estate, Oliver treats Orlando cruelly, denying him the education befitting a gentleman. In danger both from Duke Frederick and from his brother, Orlando also flees to the forest, accompanied by Adam, a family servant who long ago had served Orlando's father. By act 2, all of these refugees from court life find themselves in a natural world, which, in spite of its considerable hardships, they prefer to the treachery of court. Arden, however, is not Edenic. There are lions and snakes in this pastoral retreat, and real shepherds like Corin who speak matter-of-factly about the hard and dirty labor that tending real sheep entails. But in Arden there is also time to mock infatuated lovers, to jest, and to sing. In fact, *As You Like It* contains more songs than any other Shakespearean play. In their song-filled green world, the characters hunt deer, tend sheep, and converse endlessly about exile, love, and other matters of the heart.

The broad outlines of the *As You Like It* story are taken from Thomas Lodge's enormously popular prose romance *Rosalynde,* written in 1586–87 and published in 1590, although Shakespeare also changed what he drew from Lodge. In *Rosalynde,* for example, the Duke Senior and Duke Frederick characters are not brothers, but in both the ducal and the Orlando-Oliver plots Shakespeare makes the enmity of brothers the principal sign of the corruption of "civilized" life. In Lodge, moreover, the father in the Orlando-Oliver plot does not follow the English custom of primogeniture, by which all property is settled on the oldest son; instead, he divides his property among his male offspring according to their merits. By having Oliver inherit almost everything, Shakespeare evokes an English social practice that caused great hardship to many younger brothers. Furthermore, Shakespeare's Orlando, unlike his counterpart in Lodge's story, writes exceptionally bad love poetry, contributing to the sense that love makes people foolish even as it exalts them. The court women are handled differently as well by Shakespeare: he reduces the Celia character's centrality and instead emphasizes Rosalind and her love affair with Orlando. Throughout, Shakespeare tempers the violence of Lodge's romance and elaborates its comic potential. In *Rosalynde*, for example, the exiled Duke defeats the usurper in battle, but Shakespeare's Frederick has a religious conversion and voluntarily relinquishes the dukedom. Shakespeare also added to Lodge's cast of characters. Oliver Martext, William, Audrey, Touchstone the Clown, and Jaques the melancholy satirist are all Shakespeare's creations. Jaques, in particular, adds a touch of caustic salt and Touchstone a dash of earthy realism to the play's exploration of competing value systems.

In fact, *As You Like It* is poised carefully on the razor's edge separating fantasy from harsh reality. Shakespeare's use of place is a case in point. Lodge's romance is set in the Forest of Ardennes, an ancient woodland comprising part of what are now France, Belgium, and Luxembourg. Shakespeare also uses a French setting, but in the First Folio (1623) this woodland is called the Forest of Arden, an anglicized spelling that also happens to be the name of an English forest near Shakespeare's birthplace in Warwickshire. This fortuitous overlapping of French and English place-names is indicative of the play's double vision. Overtly set in a fantastical foreign kingdom, *As You Like It* nonetheless alludes to places (such as the Forest of Arden), people (such as Robin Hood), and practices (such as primogeniture) native to Shakespeare's own England. Through the distancing artifice of pastoral, the play deals with problems close to home.

The Englishness of Shakespeare's *As You Like It* is enhanced by allusions to the popular folk hero Robin Hood. In the opening scene of *As You Like It*, Charles the wrestler reports that the banished Duke is "already in the forest of Arden, and a many merry men with him; and there they live like the old Robin Hood of England. They say many young gentlemen flock to him every day and fleet the time carelessly as they did in the golden world" (1.1.100–104). Shakespeare could count on his audience to know the story of Robin Hood, and its evocation carried certain associations. The legendary figure and his band of men stood not only for the community and brotherhood characteristic of the Golden Age and absent in modern life, but also for resistance to tyranny. The great forests of England were the king's own preserves. To kill the deer in those forests was a crime against the monarch. Yet Robin Hood lived in the forest, dined on the king's deer, and opposed King John's unjust reign. In the 1590s, many of those resisting the enclosure of farmland for sheep grazing took refuge in forest areas, and poaching the king's deer had long been one way by which the poor defied the law to feed themselves when food was short, as it often was because of bad harvests in the late 1590s.

As You Like It only obliquely alludes to this immediate social context, but act 1 depicts a world of injustice and social disorder that both motivates the flight to Arden and evokes the tradition of opposition to tyranny associated with Robin Hood. Orlando's situation speaks to the peculiarly English plight of younger brothers who, under the system of primogeniture, inherited little from their fathers and were often at the mercy of elder siblings. Oliver is a nightmare version of an eldest son: he deprives Orlando of a gentleman's education, connives with the Duke's professional wrestler to have his brother injured, and throws his father's old servant, Adam, out of the house. His cruelty is echoed by the tyranny of Duke Frederick. The play's opening scenes underscore the inhumanity and tyrannical willfulness in the court and in the household of old Sir Roland's eldest son. Less clear is whether this corruption stems from human institutions, particularly the system of primogeniture, or from the "naturally" evil natures of Frederick and Oliver. The play does not answer this or other thorny questions directly. In fact, it seems organized to provoke thought rather than to urge conclusions, and the ending does not so much lay out a plan for social reform as celebrate a utopian moment of forgiveness, reconciliation, and hope—the latter symbolized by the multiple marriages it energetically stages.

The play's most sustained examination of human folly focuses on the behavior of those who succumb to love. There are many lovers in Arden, and for almost none does the course of love run smooth. Lovesickness was a recognized malady in early modern culture, a condition that so disordered those who endured it that it could cause paleness, sighing, tears, fainting, melancholy, palpitations, and a host of other symptoms. In *As You Like It*, all lovers are slightly mad, and the play approaches their tribulations with a mixture of sympathy, detached amusement, and analytical curiosity. Shakespeare draws on the critical capacities of pastoral to explore the causes of lovers' unhappiness and to probe the surprisingly complex issue of what is natural in matters of love and sexual desire. In this regard, the play takes little for granted—neither the stability of gender difference nor the naturalness of heterosexuality nor the invariant nature of being in love.

Rosalind and Orlando are the play's most prominent lovers, and through their courtship the play explores the problems of loving well. Orlando, for example, loves by the book—that is, in imitation of the conventions employed by the fourteenth-century Italian poet Petrarch, whose love poems to a woman named Laura established one of the paradigmatic love rhetorics of Renaissance culture. Conventionally, the Petrarchan lover worships and idealizes a woman who is inaccessible to him, either because of her rank or because of her cold heart. He burns with passion; he wastes from despair; she does not respond. Orlando, rushing through the forest pinning bad love poems on trees, is a sendup of a Petrarchan lover. Touchstone makes fun of his verses; Rosalind, dressed as a man but pretending to be "Rosalind" in order to cure Orlando of his lovesickness, delights in showing how exaggerated and unrealistic are the Petrarchan lover's claims for the perfection of his mistress and the vastness of his suffering. As she caustically says to him, when he protests that he will die for his passion: "men have died from time to time, and worms have eaten them, but not for love" (4.1.92–94). She is equally hard on the idealization of women, insisting that real women can be fickle and bad-tempered as easily as they can seem like goddesses. One way to interpret Orlando and Rosalind's prolonged interactions is to see her slowly educating him in a more realistic and egalitarian approach to the relationship of man to woman than that offered by the Petrarchan tradition. Yet the self-mockery, realism, and genuine regard for the other that come to characterize their relationship are hardly in themselves natural behaviors, but ones in which Orlando must be tutored. Other critics argue that the lengthy byplay between Orlando and his "Rosalind" indicates Rosalind's desire to retain her maidenly independence as long as possible, since as a wife her freedom of speech and movement would in all likelihood be more curtailed than when she is cross-dressed as a saucy boy.

Rosalind and Orlando, however, are not the only lovers in the forest. There is also the mooning shepherd, Silvius, who believes no one has ever loved with his intensity, and his proud mistress, Phoebe, who thinks much too well of her own limited charms and throws herself quite inappropriately into the part of the disdainful Petrarchan mistress. As Rosalind informs her: "I must tell you friendly in your ear, / Sell when you can; you are not for all markets" (3.5.59–60). Even Touchstone, ever ready to puncture the romantic ravings of Orlando and Rosalind, Silvius and Phoebe, cannot escape love's call. Functioning as the clown figure often does, to provide a detached commentary on the action around him, Touchstone is nonetheless a participant as well as an observer. His "love" is about as natural—in the sense of urgently physical—and as far removed from Petrarchan idealizations as can be imagined. His intended, Audrey, does not know what "poetical" means, and Touchstone laments that she has such a rudimentary command of language that she often cannot understand what he says to her. And yet, as he confides to Jaques, "As the ox hath his bow, sir, the horse his curb, and the falcon her bells, so man hath his desires" (3.3.67–68)—that is, as each creature has some restraint placed on his movement, so a man's sexual desires constrain him to accommodate himself to a woman, even one like Audrey, and to the marriage yoke. If Orlando and Silvius live too much in the thrall of poetic idealizations, Touchstone and Audrey starkly reveal what love looks like when it is reduced to a matter of pure desire and when all artfulness, all poetry, and all sweet amorous delay are eschewed.

The delightful Rosalind, however, is the play's most intriguing lover. Her importance is signaled by the fact that she is given more lines to speak than any other female character in any of Shakespeare's plays. Articulate and witty, she is at once an observer and a critic of others and herself a full participant in the whirligig of love. In this, she resembles Touchstone the Clown and differs from the melancholy Jaques, who persistently catalogs the follies of others but holds back from full participation in the life around him. (Fittingly, Jaques remains in the forest at the end of the play, when most of the others return to their lives outside the pastoral retreat.) Rosalind is at the center of nearly everything that happens in As You Like It, and the complexity of her role is enhanced by the fact that for much of four acts she dresses like a man and successfully passes for one. In the 1590s, Shakespeare wrote a number of other comedies (The Two Gentlemen of Verona, The Merchant of Venice, Twelfth Night) in which women dress as men to protect themselves from danger, to pursue a lover, or temporarily to acquire the prerogatives of the socially dominant gender. Rosalind's is arguably the most complicated of these cases of cross-dressing because she not only passes as a man, but while in her male disguise plays the role of Rosalind in her forest encounters with Orlando. A woman disguised as a man thus makes her own identity into a fiction she performs!

Rosalind's complex cross-dressing has many consequences. For one thing, it makes problematic the "natural" gender distinctions that supposedly separate man from woman. In a literal sense, clothes here make the man—or woman. A doublet and hose and a swaggering demeanor effectively create the illusion of masculinity, and Rosalind uses her disguise to try on the privileges of the supposedly superior sex. Far from a passive object of Petrarchan adoration, she takes charge of her escape from Frederick's court and her encounters with Orlando in the forest. Typically, Renaissance women remained under the control of their fathers and mothers until marriage bequeathed them to the care of a husband. Rosalind's special circumstances—a father banished, an uncle who wants her gone from court—put her in an unusual situation. Her decision to cross-dress further sets her apart. Mobile, loquacious, and bossy, Rosalind confutes the idea that women are by nature passive, silent, and in need of masculine supervision. At the same time, she exhibits certain stereotypically "female" behavior: to Celia she confesses how much she is in love with Orlando, and when he is wounded she faints from seeing his blood on a cloth. The cross-dressed Rosalind keeps open the question of what a woman (or a man) "really" is.

To the question of how men and women differ, some Renaissance anatomical theory gave answers unlike those we now take for granted. According to Galen, an ancient Greek anatomist whose work on the body was widely influential in the early modern period, men and women had similar anatomical structures; women were simply less perfect than men, there having been less heat present when they were conceived. This meant, among other things, that women's genitalia were just like men's—with the vagina and ovaries corresponding to the penis and scrotum—except that they had not been pushed outside the body as men's had been. Because by this account male-female difference was less grounded in ideas of absolute bodily difference than is typical today, much emphasis was placed on behavioral differences and on distinctions of dress. Preachers enjoined women to be chaste, silent, and obedient and forbade them to wear the clothes of the opposite sex. In such a context, female cross-dressing, however playfully undertaken, always threatened to expose the artifice of gender distinctions by showing how easily one sex could assume the clothes and ape the behavior of the other.

The particularities of Rosalind's disguise, moreover, complicate her representation even further. When cross-dressed, Rosalind calls herself Ganymede, a name that had long-standing and unmistakable associations with homoerotic love. In Greek mythology, Ganymede was a beautiful boy whom Jove desired and whom he seized and carried to Mount Olympus to be cupbearer to the gods. A number of early modern paintings, woodcuts, and engravings depict the moment when Jove, in the

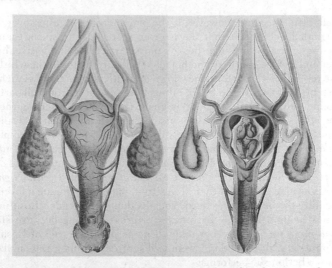

Typical sixteenth-century anatomy-book illustration of the female organs of generation.
Left: The vagina and uterus are almost indistinguishable from the male penis and
scrotum. *Right:* They have been cut open to reveal a tiny fetus in the uterus.
From Fritz Weindler, *Geschichte der Gynäkologisch-anatomischen Abbildung* (1908).
(Originally appeared in George Bartisch, *Kunstbuch*, 1575.)

form of an eagle, sweeps the boy away from earth and into the heavens. In Shakespeare's day, the word "Ganymede" commonly signified a young boy who was the
lover of another (usually older) man. Shakespeare could hardly have been unaware of
these associations when he had Rosalind choose this name as her alias. Consequently, when the cross-dressed heroine commands Orlando to woo his "Rosalind,"
he woos a figure who is dressed like a man and who bears a name signifying his status as a homoerotic love object. In performance, what the audience *sees* is one "man"
flirting with another, even while the audience *knows* that one of these "men" is a
woman. Provocatively, Shakespeare uses Orlando and Rosalind's encounters to over-
lay a story of male-female desire with traces of another tale of a man's love for a boy.

Long before *As You Like It* was penned, pastoral had been used to depict the
beauty of both male friendship and homoerotic love. Edmund Spenser, in the January Eclogue of *The Shepheardes Calender,* describes the passion of Hobbinol for
Colin Cloute, who in turn loves an unresponsive woman named Rosalind. Commenting on this passage, E.K., the anonymous annotator of *The Shepheardes Calender,*
drew on classical precedent to defend pederastic love (love of an older man for a
younger boy) as less dangerous than gynerastic love (love of man for woman). Since
women were generally considered men's intellectual and moral inferiors, love for a
woman was—so the argument went—less likely to be a rational passion than was
love for a boy or a man. In the 1580s, Richard Barnfield wrote a pastoral work called
The Affectionate Shepherd in which the male speaker celebrates his love for a beautiful young man named Ganymede.

Shakespeare is therefore not unique in introducing a Ganymede figure into the
pastoral landscape, though he does so with a difference. In *As You Like It,* Ganymede
is a disguise, a persona assumed and eventually discarded by Rosalind. As with much
else in this play, Shakespeare thus presents two opposing outcomes as simultaneously possible. For several acts, Orlando seems to pursue in one person both a boy
and a woman, but in the final scene Rosalind reassumes her female clothes and
Ganymede disappears, thus ending the play with an emphasis on the culmination of
male-female love in marriage. But this is not quite the whole story. On the Renaissance
stage, women's parts were played by boy actors. In the Epilogue, which Rosalind

Ganymede being abducted by Jupiter in the form of an eagle.
Woodcut by Virgil Solis. From *Metamorphosis Ovidii* . . . (1563).

speaks, she calls attention to this fact, making it clear that if Orlando has finally won his Rosalind, the two players who enact this union are a young boy and a man. Man has married woman; man has simultaneously embraced boy.

In *As You Like It*, other erotic possibilities flourish as well. The friendship between Rosalind and Celia, for example, is remarkably close. Charles the wrestler says: "never two ladies loved as they do" (1.1.98). Celia readily gives up her father, her fortune, and her position at the court to follow Rosalind to Arden, where the two women in effect set up household together. Although they are yoked in love like Juno's swans, from the beginning Celia is afraid that Rosalind does not love her as much as she loves Rosalind (1.2.6–11). Quite quickly, Rosalind's primary interest becomes her pursuit of Orlando. Yet in the midst of her love games with him, Rosalind also dallies with the ambitious and amorous Phoebe, who has taken the disguised Rosalind for a man. Overtly, Rosalind scorns Phoebe and directs her to love Silvius, but she also takes care to tell Phoebe where she lives (3.5.73–74) and encourages her attentions even while denying them. As with other relationships in the play, it is not altogether clear whom Phoebe really desires: is it the man she thinks she sees or the woman beneath? Though the play eventually deposits Rosalind, Celia, and Phoebe all within the circle of Hymen, the god of marriage, it does so only after raising the possibility of other erotic conjunctions, including woman's love for woman.

In part, *As You Like It* can play so freely with various erotic possibilities because in the early modern period people were not assumed, as they often are today, to have a fixed sexual identity—to *be*, that is, a lesbian or a heterosexual. Often, one could engage in a range of sexual practices without contradiction. Depending on life stage and social circumstance, a man might have sex with a dependent man, such as a servant, and with a woman, such as his wife. The point is that performing a specific sexual act did not presume—or guarantee—a particular sexual identity. And yet Shakespeare's comedy, like many others, also acknowledges the social weight that the early modern period placed on marriage, the institution through which political alliances were forged, property passed, and lineage established. As You Like It both celebrates and pokes fun at the social importance of marriage by having Hymen, god of marriage, appear onstage in the last act to preside over a veritable spate of betrothals—four, to be exact. As Jaques suggests (5.4.35–36), it is indeed as if the beasts were proceeding, two by two, into Noah's ark.

Besides yoking individual man to individual woman, marriage in this play helps to resolve seemingly intractable social problems. For example, Orlando's situation as younger brother is miraculously ameliorated through his marriage to Rosalind. As her husband, he becomes Duke Senior's heir, thus achieving a fortune equal to his gentle nature. Again, the play has things two ways at once. Duke Senior is restored to his dukedom, which confirms the prerogatives of older brothers, but Orlando does not have to suffer permanently the disadvantages of being a younger son. Primogeniture is simultaneously affirmed and circumvented. Moreover, when Oliver reforms, that reformation is sealed by his marriage to Celia, an indication that he now takes part in the communal life of his culture without the willful displays of indifference and selfishness that marked his earlier behavior.

Yet as this comedy celebrates marriage, it also registers a certain resistance to it and persistently maps alternative routings of desire. Rosalind registers that resistance when she complains of how avidly men court women before marriage and how indifferently they treat them afterward: "men are April when they woo, December when they wed" (4.1.127–28). Marriage, she implies, can dull a man's desire and lessen a woman's emotional power over him. It also, of course, made women legally subject to their husbands. When Rosalind doffs her man's disguise to become a wife, she relinquishes many kinds of freedom. But the play also records *men's* resistance to marriage, partly through its many cuckold jokes. These jokes acknowledge that marriage may not fully circumscribe or satisfy a woman's sexual desires, that a man's control of his wife's sexuality may be more fiction than fact, leaving him vulnerable to public mockery. As the Duke's men sing as they bring home a slaughtered deer:

> Take thou no scorn to wear the horn.
> It was a crest e'er thou wast born.
> Thy father's father wore it,
> And thy father bore it.
>
> (4.2.14–17)

The song transforms cuckold anxiety into entertainment, but it cannot erase that anxiety.

Consider, as well, the strange moment when Orlando comes across his brother, Oliver, lying asleep under an old oak. As Oliver sleeps, a female snake approaches his open mouth, threatening his life. Though the snake is frightened off, it is immediately replaced in this fantastic, dreamlike scenario by a hungry female lion with whom Orlando fights in order to save his brother's life (4.3.97–131). Twice, danger is represented in female form, and the reconciliation of the two brothers occurs only when Orlando spills his own blood to beat back these threats. In As You Like It, as marriage is both desired and feared, so the feminine is represented as both an attraction and a source of danger.

In pastoral, little is immune from critique. Yet the remarkable thing about As You Like It is that critique does not cancel affirmation. The play anatomizes court life and exposes its treachery, but many characters leave Arden to journey back to the court when Frederick has repented and the benevolent Duke Senior has returned to power. The play likewise dissects the problems of marriage, yet many marry at the end. Pastoral has a utopian as well as a critical dimension. The green world of shepherds holds traces of the simplicity of a lost Golden Age, and a sojourn in that world can prompt transformations in the everyday world to which the sojourners return. *As You Like It* is to a remarkable degree open to the infinite malleability of human beings and their social practices. A duke can become a forest outlaw and embrace the change; a tyrannical usurper can be touched by the words of a holy man, relinquish his power, and retire from the world. What men and women have marred, they may also mend.

It is through the heroine, however, that *As You Like It* offers its richest dramatization of a figure who plays endlessly with the limits and possibilities of her circumstances. This is true even in the Epilogue, when Rosalind, now in woman's clothing, steps forward to address the audience and solicit their applause. The persona of Ganymede cast aside, the heroine appears as the woman she "really" is. But it is precisely at this moment of closure that she breaks the dramatic frame to remind the audience of *another* reality: that "she" is played by a "he." Dressed like a woman but declaring she is not, this unpredictable figure, this he/she, continues to the end to defy the fixed identities and the exclusionary choices of the everyday world, offering instead a world of multiple possibilities and transformable identities, a world as perhaps we might come to like it.

Jean E. Howard

SELECTED BIBLIOGRAPHY

Colie, Rosalie L. "Perspectives on Pastoral: Romance, Comic and Tragic." *Shakespeare's Living Art.* Princeton, NJ: Princeton UP, 1974. 243–83. Analyzes the many pastoral conventions found in *As You Like It* and how they contribute to the play's perspectivism — that is, its juxtaposition of competing viewpoints.

Crane, Mary. "Theatrical Practice and the Ideologies of Status in *As You Like It*." *Shakespeare's Brain: Reading with Cognitive Theory.* Princeton, NJ: Princeton UP, 2001. 67–93. Examines how, through its emphasis on words like "villain" and "clown," *As You Like It* explores possibilities for upward and downward mobility in the world of the play and in the social world at large, including the theatrical community of which Shakespeare was a part.

Fisher, Will. "Home Alone: The Place of Women's Homoerotic Desire in Shakespeare's *As You Like It*." *Feminisms and Early Modern Texts: Essays for Phyllis Rackin.* Ed. Rebecca Anne Bach and Gwynne Kennedy. Selinsgrove, PA: Susquehanna UP, 2010. 99–118. Explores how Rosalind and Celia mimic aspects of heterosexual marriage, including a concern with acquiring property, and establish a household beyond the boundaries of masculine control.

Howard, Jean E. "Power and Eros: Crossdressing in Dramatic Representation and Theatrical Practice." *The Stage and Social Struggle in Early Modern England.* London: Routledge, 1994. 93–128. Examines cross-dressing as a convention through which *As You Like It* and other comedies explore the politics of early modern gender relations and the fluidity of sexual desire.

Marshall, Cynthia. "The Doubled Jaques and Constructions of Negation in *As You Like It*." *Shakespeare Quarterly* 49 (1998): 375–92. Argues that in *As You Like It* the repression of melancholia, registered as a trace in the figure of Jaques, allows for the release of the high spirits and verbal fireworks proper to comedy.

Montrose, Louis. "'The Place of a Brother' in *As You Like It*: Social Process and Comic Form." *Shakespeare Quarterly* 32 (1981): 28–54. Argues that in *As You Like It* the process of comedy repairs the negative consequences of primogeniture for younger sons as Orlando finds a surrogate father in Duke Senior and a fortune through marriage.

Theis, Jeffrey S. "Shakespeare's Green Plot: The Stage as Forest and the Forest as Stage in *As You Like It*." *Writing the Forest in Early Modern England: A Sylvan*

Pastoral Nation. Pittsburgh, PA: Duquesne UP, 2009. 35–89. Explores the forest of Arden as a malleable stage where characters experiment with new or altered social roles and test pastoral conventions.

Traub, Valerie. "The Homoerotics of Shakespearean Comedy." *Desire and Anxiety: Circulations of Sexuality in Shakespearean Drama*. London: Routledge, 1992. 117–44. Explores the role of the boy actor in the production and circulation of homoerotic desire and argues that *As You Like It* playfully refuses the binary distinction between the heteroerotic and the homoerotic.

Watson, Robert N. "As You Liken It: Simile in the Forest." *Back to Nature: The Green and the Real in the Late Renaissance*. Philadelphia: U of Pennsylvania P, 2006. 77–107. Argues for the importance of similes in *As You Like It* as they show humanity's attempts to comprehend and become one with a natural world from which it is fundamentally alienated.

Wilson, Richard. "Like the Old Robin Hood: *As You Like It* and the Enclosure Riots." *Will Power: Essays on Shakespearean Authority*. London: Harvester Wheatsheaf, 1993. 63–82. Connects *As You Like It* to the social disturbances and food shortages of the 1590s but argues that the play pulls back from lodging a radical critique of social injustice.

FILMS

As You Like It. 1936. Dir. Paul Czinner. UK. 96 min. This black-and-white film features Laurence Olivier, in his first Shakespeare performance on film, as the dashing but moody Orlando with Elisabeth Bergner as an insipid Rosalind. Charming woodland scenes in a significantly cut production.

As You Like It. 1978. Dir. Basil Coleman. UK. 150 min. Lively performances in this BBC-TV production by Helen Mirren as Rosalind, Angharad Rees as Celia, and Victoria Plucknett as Phoebe. Playing Jaques, Richard Pasco brings poignant understatement to the famous "seven ages of man" speech.

As You Like It. 2006. Dir. Kenneth Branagh. UK. 127 min. In this gorgeous production, the action is relocated from medieval France to nineteenth-century Japan. With Bryce Dallas Howard (Rosalind), David Oyelowo (Orlando), Rowola Garai (Celia), Brian Blessed (Duke Senior and Duke Frederick), and Alfred Molina (Touchstone).

TEXTUAL INTRODUCTION

The text of *As You Like It* presents few difficulties. There are no early quarto versions—at least none are known to have survived—and thus we have only one authoritative early text, that preserved in the First Folio (F). Unlike many other plays in the Folio, *As You Like It* is well printed by the standards of its time. It has a full set of act and scene divisions. It is fairly reliable in terms of speech prefixes and lineation that signals the difference between verse and prose. Its stage directions are spare but for the most part not problematic. One major difference between F and most modern editions is that, with one exception, throughout F in entrances, exits, and speech prefixes Touchstone is called only "*Clown*," a generic label that emphasizes his role as the play's official fool-figure rather than his individuality. Even in the one entrance that does give his name (at 2.4.0), he is referred to in F as "*Clowne, alias Touchstone*." Aside from that mention, the only way we know his name in F is that he is addressed as "Touchstone" three times by other characters (2.4.15, 3.2.11, and 3.2.40). In *The Norton Shakespeare*, in keeping with our faithfulness to the early texts on which the edition is based, we have followed F and identified this character as "*Clown*" rather than "*Touchstone*" in all speech prefixes. (See also Digital Edition TC 2.)

There are other small difficulties with casting, since the Folio does not include a list of "The Persons of the Play." For example, how many Lords attend on Duke Senior in the forest or on the usurping Duke Frederick at court? Does the Forest of Arden have "Foresters" in addition to the "Lords," or do the Lords simply function at times as foresters? The F stage direction at the beginning of 2.1 specifies the entrance of "*two or three Lords like Forresters,*" suggesting that in this scene the Lords simply habit themselves as foresters. But at the beginning of 4.2, the stage direction reads "*Enter Iaques and Lords, Forresters,*" leaving open the question of whether there are separate Foresters on stage. Here, the fluidity of the stage directions may tell us something about performance: how many Lords were in attendance and the extent to which some of them dressed as foresters would depend on the availability of extra actors for any given performance.

This edition does not preserve another "error" in the Folio—its use of male pronouns for female actors and persons. At several points, Rosalind is referred to as the "wrong" gender—most notably, in the final scene. Hymen in F seems to construct a tableau of same-sex marriage by inviting the Duke to "receive thy daughter" and Orlando so that he can "join his hand with his" (5.4.105), where we would expect "her hand with his." Since in Shakespeare's company women's parts were all played by men or boys, Hymen's speech gestures toward the sexual identity of the boy actor playing the part of Rosalind. In a play so rife with gender confusion, the mistake is perhaps not surprising, and most editors have emended one of the occurrences of "his" to "her." If this were the only case of pronoun gender confusion in the play, we might chalk it up to a printer's error, but similar errors, mostly in connection with Rosalind, occur at several other points in the text: see 1.1.95 (discussed in Digital Edition TC 1), 3.2.133, 5.2.17, and as a confirmation to the audience of the male identity of the youth playing her part, Rosalind's "Epilogue." *As You Like It* plays with gender confusion in hilarious, outrageously excessive ways, such as having a heroine who is a boy actor playing the part of a young woman who goes on to play the part of a young man who then enacts the part of the woman, Rosalind, he really "is" beneath his disguise. In such a dizzying array of possibilities for gender confusion, we should not be surprised to see a similar confusion in the play's language relating to gender identity, and we should not assume that it is an error on Shakespeare or someone else's part.

In this edition we have preserved a few wordings that are usually modernized in recent editions. For example, in Rosalind's derisive speech at 4.1.33, does she refer to Jaques as having "swum" in a "gondola," as the word is modernized in most recent editions, or in a "gundello," as here and in F? *The Norton Shakespeare* has kept the Folio reading on the grounds that it signals Rosalind's ridicule of Jaques (see Digital Edition TC 7). Added stage directions are usually implied by the play's language. For example, in 1.1.46, when Orlando responds to Oliver's attack, this edition adds "*He grabs* OLIVER *by the throat*" because Orlando states in his next speech: "Wert thou not my brother I would not take this hand from thy throat till this other [hand] had pulled out thy tongue." Stage directions are added in 3.3 to clarify that Jaques is not at first visible to the Clown and Audrey, and at 3.5 to clarify a speech in which Rosalind addresses alternately Silvius and Phoebe. Similarly, at several points F is confusing about speech prefixes. In 2.5.41–50, for example, three speeches in a row are attributed to "*Amiens*" with a song in between. Does he speak them all, and does he sing the song? In this edition he does, because that seems the most likely interpretation of the Folio speech prefixes.

LEAH S. MARCUS

PERFORMANCE NOTE

Shakespeare constantly sought to enrich the fundamental attraction of acting—namely, that actors clearly are, and as clearly are not, the characters they play. Rosalind is like every character in that she is represented by an actor, but she is unique in Shakespeare for portraying a second character that plays (represents) a version of the first, thus ultimately playing both characters and genders simultaneously. Productions of *As You Like It* often seek to extend the paradoxes of person and gender exemplified in Rosalind—for instance, by casting the Forest of Arden as an idyllic approximation of the court; by redeploying Duke Frederick, Le Beau, and Charles as Duke Senior, Jaques, and Amiens; or by indicating that Orlando is sexually attracted to the indeterminate figure Ganymede, thereby possibly posing a barrier to the play's generic resolution. These rich potential gender dynamics may explain why the play continues to inspire directors to employ all-male or all-female casts.

Even relative to other Shakespeare plays, *As You Like It* offers companies an unusual number and range of choices respecting characterization. Actors and directors must decide, for instance, whether Rosalind begins the play morose at her father's banishment or fierce before an unjust usurper, whether she passes easily as a boy or forever seems moments from discovery, whether she is confident in her hold on Orlando or continuously jealous and alert. Jaques can appear misanthropic or simply melancholy, while the merry men might seem at ease in their new lifestyle or merely to be smiling through their misery. Orlando, meanwhile, may present as a Petrarchan lover or as aggressive and immature; Touchstone the Clown can be a loyal confidante or a parasite; Corin, Silvius, Phoebe, and the other Arden dwellers can be attractive in their simplicity or tedious and filthy. Other considerations in performance include the relative heights of Rosalind and Celia; staging the wrestling and other set pieces; the depiction and mood of the Forest of Arden; and the ontological status of Hymen.

BRETT GAMBOA

As You Like It

[THE PERSONS OF THE PLAY

ROSALIND, daughter to the banished Duke Senior, later disguised as Ganymede
CELIA, daughter to Duke Frederick and cousin to Rosalind; later disguised as Aliena
ORLANDO, youngest son to Sir Roland de Bois
OLIVER, eldest son to Sir Roland de Bois
JAQUES DE BOIS, second son to Sir Roland de Bois
ADAM, servant to Oliver, later to Orlando
DENNIS, servant to Oliver

DUKE SENIOR, now living in exile
AMIENS
JAQUES
FIRST LORD ⎫
SECOND LORD ⎬ courtiers attending on Duke Senior
FIRST PAGE
SECOND PAGE ⎭

DUKE FREDERICK, younger brother to Duke Senior
Touchstone the CLOWN, court jester to Duke Frederick
CHARLES, wrestler attached to Duke Frederick's court
LE BEAU ⎫
FIRST LORD ⎬ courtiers attending on Duke Frederick
SECOND LORD ⎭

CORIN, an old shepherd
SILVIUS, a young shepherd, in love with Phoebe
PHOEBE, a shepherdess
WILLIAM, a countryman, in love with Audrey
AUDREY, a country wench
SIR OLIVER MARTEXT, a country vicar

HYMEN, god of marriage

Attendants, Musicians]

1.1

Enter ORLANDO *and* ADAM.

ORLANDO As I remember, Adam, it was upon this fashion bequeathed me by will: but poor° a thousand crowns¹ and, as thou say'st, charged° my brother on his blessing² to breed me° well—and there begins my sadness. My brother Jaques
5 he keeps at school° and report speaks goldenly of his profit. For my part, he keeps me rustically at home or, to speak more properly, stays° me here at home unkept.° For call you

only
he (my father) charged
bring me up
university

detains / uncared for

1.1 Location: The orchard of Oliver's house, in the vicinity of Duke Frederick's court in France.
1. Equivalent to about 25,000 English pounds in today's currency. Orlando's inheritance is worth twice as much as Adam's life savings (see 2.3.38).
2. On pain of losing his blessing.

673

that keeping for a gentleman of my birth that differs not
from the stalling of an ox? His horses are bred better: for
10 besides that they are fair with° their feeding, they are taught   *handsome because of*
their manège,[3] and to that end riders dearly° hired. But I,   *expensively*
his brother, gain nothing under him but growth, for the which
his animals on his dunghills are as much bound to him as I.
Besides this nothing that he so plentifully gives me, the some-
15 thing that nature gave me his countenance° seems to take   *conduct*
from me. He lets me feed with his hinds,° bars me[4] the place   *farmworkers*
of a brother, and as much as in him lies, mines my gentility
with my education.[5] This is it, Adam, that grieves me; and
the spirit of my father, which I think is within me, begins to
20 mutiny against this servitude. I will no longer endure it,
though yet I know no wise remedy how to avoid it.

     Enter OLIVER.

ADAM Yonder comes my master, your brother.
ORLANDO Go apart, Adam, and thou shalt hear how he will
shake me up.°   *insult me*
25 OLIVER Now, sir, what make you° here?   *are you doing*
ORLANDO Nothing. I am not taught to make anything.
OLIVER What mar you° then, sir?   *are you destroying*
ORLANDO Marry,[6] sir, I am helping you to mar that which God
made—a poor unworthy brother of yours—with idleness.
30 OLIVER Marry, sir, be better employed and be naught° awhile.   *get lost*
ORLANDO Shall I keep your hogs and eat husks with them?
What prodigal portion have I spent that I should come to
such penury?[7]
OLIVER Know you where you are, sir?
35 ORLANDO O sir, very well: here in your orchard.
OLIVER Know you before whom, sir?
ORLANDO Ay, better than him I am before knows me. I know
you are my eldest brother and, in the gentle condition of
blood, you should so know me.[8] The courtesy of nations[9]
40 allows you my better in that you are the first born, but the same
tradition takes not away my blood, were there twenty brothers
betwixt us. I have as much of my father in me as you, albeit I
confess your coming before me is nearer to his reverence.[1]
OLIVER What, boy?
     [*He attacks* ORLANDO.]
45 ORLANDO Come, come, elder brother—you are too young° in   *inexperienced*
this!
     [*He grabs* OLIVER *by the throat.*]
OLIVER Wilt thou lay hands on me, villain?°   *lowborn man; scoundrel*
ORLANDO I am no villain. I am the youngest son of Sir Roland
de Bois. He was my father, and he is thrice a villain that says
50 such a father begot villains. Wert thou not my brother I would
not take this hand from thy throat till this other had pulled
out thy tongue for saying so: thou hast railed on° thyself.   *abused*

---

3. Paces and actions of a trained horse.
4. Excludes me from.
5. Undermines my gentility by my (poor) education.
6. An oath, derived from the name of the Virgin
Mary.
7. Alluding to the biblical parable of the prodigal son
(Luke 15:11–32), who after squandering his share of
his father's fortune envied the swine he tended and

wished to eat their fodder.
8. And because of the noble blood that we share, you
should acknowledge me as a brother.
9. Customs of civil society. Referring to the English
system of primogeniture, which allowed for the transmission of all property to the eldest son.
1. Your being older than I am makes you more worthy of the respect that he commanded.

ADAM Sweet masters, be patient! For your father's remembrance, be at accord.

55 OLIVER Let me go, I say!

ORLANDO I will not till I please. You shall hear me. My father
charged you in his will to give me good education. You have
trained me like a peasant, obscuring and hiding from me
all gentleman-like qualities.° The spirit of my father grows   *accomplishments*
60 strong in me, and I will no longer endure it. Therefore allow
me such exercises° as may become a gentleman, or give me   *pursuits*
the poor allottery° my father left me by testament. With that   *portion*
I will go buy my fortunes.

OLIVER And what wilt thou do—beg when that is spent? Well,
65 sir, get you in. I will not long be troubled with you. You shall
have some part of your will. I pray you leave me.

ORLANDO I will no further offend you than becomes me for
my good.

OLIVER Get you with him, you old dog.

70 ADAM Is "old dog" my reward? Most true—I have lost my teeth
in your service. God be with my old master; he would not
have spoke such a word.   *Exeunt* ORLANDO [*and*] ADAM.

OLIVER Is it even so? Begin you to grow upon me?[2] I will physic
your rankness[3] and yet give no thousand crowns neither.
75 Holla, Dennis!
          Enter DENNIS.

DENNIS Calls your worship?

OLIVER Was not Charles, the duke's wrestler, here to speak
with me?

DENNIS So please you, he is here at the door and importunes
80 access to you.

OLIVER Call him in. 'Twill be a good way, and tomorrow the
wrestling is.   [*Exit* DENNIS.]
          Enter CHARLES.

CHARLES Good morrow to your worship.

OLIVER Good Monsieur Charles, what's the new news at the
85 new court?

CHARLES There's no news at the court, sir, but the old news:
that is, the old Duke is banished by his younger brother, the
new Duke; and three or four loving lords have put themselves
into voluntary exile with him, whose lands and revenues
90 enrich the new Duke; therefore he gives them good leave° to   *full permission*
wander.

OLIVER Can you tell if Rosalind, the Duke's daughter, be
banished with her father?

CHARLES Oh, no, for the Duke's daughter, her cousin, so loves
95 her, being ever from their cradles bred° together, that she[4]   *brought up*
would have followed her exile or have died to stay behind her.
She is at the court and no less beloved of her uncle than his
own daughter, and never two ladies loved as they do.

OLIVER Where will the old Duke live?

---

2. To grow so big you crowd upon me.
3. Remedy your overgrowth (as with vegetation);
apply a purgative to your diseased blood.
4. TEXTUAL COMMENT The Folio (F) prints "hee"

instead of "she," perhaps referring to the sex of the
boy actor who would have played Celia on the early
modern stage. See Digital Edition TC 1.

100 CHARLES They say he is already in the Forest of Arden,[5] and
a many merry men with him; and there they live like the old
Robin Hood[6] of England. They say many young gentlemen
flock to him every day and fleet° the time carelessly° as they   *pass / without worries*
did in the golden world.[7]

105 OLIVER What, you wrestle tomorrow before the new Duke?

CHARLES Marry, do I, sir, and I came to acquaint you with a
matter: I am given, sir, secretly to understand that your
younger brother Orlando hath a disposition to come in disguised against me to try a fall.° Tomorrow, sir, I wrestle for my   *bout*

110 credit,° and he that escapes me without some broken limb   *reputation*
shall acquit him well. Your brother is but young and tender,
and for your love I would be loath to foil° him, as I must for   *defeat*
my own honor, if he come in. Therefore, out of my love to you
I came hither to acquaint you withal,° that either you might   *with this*

115 stay° him from his intendment° or brook° such disgrace well   *keep / intent / endure*
as he shall run into, in that it is a thing of his own search° and   *seeking*
altogether against my will.

OLIVER Charles, I thank thee for thy love to me, which thou
shalt find I will most kindly requite. I had myself notice of

120 my brother's purpose herein, and have by underhand° means   *subtle*
labored to dissuade him from it, but he is resolute. I'll tell
thee, Charles, it° is the stubbornest young fellow of France: *(Orlando)*
full of ambition, an envious emulator of every man's good
parts,° a secret and villainous contriver against me, his natu-   *qualities*

125 ral brother. Therefore use thy discretion: I had as lief° thou   *willingly*
didst break his neck as his finger. And thou wert best look
to't, for if thou dost him any slight disgrace, or if he do not
mightily grace° himself on thee, he will practice° against   *win credit for / plot*
thee by poison, entrap thee by some treacherous device, and

130 never leave thee till he hath ta'en thy life by some indirect
means or other. For I assure thee, and almost with tears I
speak it, there is not one so young and so villainous this day
living. I speak but brotherly[8] of him, but should I anatomize°   *dissect; fully reveal*
him to thee as he is, I must blush and weep and thou must

135 look pale and wonder.

CHARLES I am heartily glad I came hither to you. If he come
tomorrow I'll give him his payment. If ever he go alone°   *walks without aid*
again, I'll never wrestle for prize more. And so God keep
your worship!

140 OLIVER Farewell, good Charles.   *Exit* [CHARLES].
Now will I stir this gamester.° I hope I shall see an end of   *(Orlando)*
him, for my soul—yet I know not why—hates nothing more
than he. Yet he's gentle,° never schooled and yet learned,   *of noble character*
full of noble device,° of all sorts enchantingly beloved,[9] and   *purposes*

145 indeed so much in the heart of the world, and especially of

---

5. TEXTUAL COMMENT F anglicizes the spelling of the
French Ardennes, the name of an ancient forest encompassing parts of France, Belgium, and Luxembourg,
thus evoking the English forest of Arden near Shakespeare's birthplace in Warwickshire. Some editions
emend "Arden" to "Ardennes." See Digital Edition TC 2.
6. A legendary English outlaw, associated with Not-
tingham's Sherwood Forest, who robbed from the

rich and gave his plunder to the poor.
7. Alluding to the classical myth of an earlier world
of perpetual spring, abundance, and ease from which
humankind had degenerated (Ovid, *Metamorphoses*
1). This golden world was often identified with a pastoral life.
8. In a manner proper to a brother.
9. Beloved of all ranks as if by enchantment.

my own people, who best know him, that I am altogether
misprized.° But it shall not be so long—this wrestler shall   *despised*
clear all.° Nothing remains but that I kindle° the boy   *fix everything*
thither,° which now I'll go about.   *Exit.*   *urge / (to the court)*

1.2
Enter ROSALIND *and* CELIA.

CELIA   I pray thee, Rosalind, sweet my coz,° be merry.   *cousin*
ROSALIND   Dear Celia, I show more mirth than I am mistress
of, and would you yet I were merrier? Unless you could
teach me to forget a banished father, you must not learn° me   *teach*
5   how to remember any extraordinary pleasure.
CELIA   Herein I see thou lov'st me not with the full weight
that I love thee. If my uncle, thy banished father, had banished thy uncle, the Duke my father, so° thou hadst been   *provided*
still with me I could have taught my love to take thy father
10 for mine. So wouldst thou if the truth of thy love to me were
so righteously tempered° as mine is to thee.   *properly constituted*
ROSALIND   Well, I will forget the condition of my estate° to   *circumstances*
rejoice in yours.
CELIA   You know my father hath no child but I, nor none is
15 like to have. And truly, when he dies, thou shalt be his heir;
for what he hath taken away from thy father, perforce° I will   *as a matter of course*
render thee again in affection. By mine honor I will, and
when I break that oath let me turn monster. Therefore, my
sweet Rose, my dear Rose, be merry.
20 ROSALIND   From henceforth I will, coz, and devise sports.°   *entertainments*
Let me see—what think you of falling in love?
CELIA   Marry, I prithee do—to make sport withal.° But love   *to provide amusement*
no man in good earnest, nor no further in sport neither than
with safety of a pure blush thou mayst in honor come off
25 again.[1]
ROSALIND   What shall be our sport then?
CELIA   Let us sit and mock the good housewife Fortune[2] from
her wheel, that her gifts may henceforth be bestowed
equally.
30 ROSALIND   I would we could do so, for her benefits are mightily misplaced, and the bountiful blind woman° doth most   *(Fortune)*
mistake in her gifts to women.
CELIA   'Tis true, for those that she makes fair she scarce
makes honest,° and those that she makes honest she makes   *chaste*
35 very ill-favoredly.°   *ugly*
ROSALIND   Nay, now thou goest from Fortune's office° to   *function*
Nature's: Fortune reigns in° gifts of the world, not in the   *presides over*
lineaments of Nature.[3]
Enter CLOWN.[4]

1.2 Location: The grounds of Duke Frederick's
court.
1. *than . . . again:* than, with the protection afforded
by your innocence ("pure blush"), you may honorably
escape ("come off again").
2. Referring to the blind goddess of classical mythology who directed human destiny with the movements
of her wheel, here likened to the mistress of a
household with a spinning wheel.

3. *lineaments of nature:* one's natural features.
4. TEXTUAL COMMENT Although most modern editions refer to this character as "Touchstone" from his
first entrance, it is only at the beginning of 2.4 that
the stage directions of F name him as such. He is
otherwise called only "*Clown*" in the stage directions
and speech prefixes of F, a designation that links him
with the stock fool-figures of other plays. See Digital
Edition TC 3.

CELIA   No, when Nature hath made a fair creature, may she
40   not by Fortune fall into the fire? Though Nature hath given
us wit to flout at Fortune, hath not Fortune sent in this fool
to cut off the argument?

ROSALIND   Indeed, there is Fortune too hard for Nature,
when Fortune makes Nature's natural° the cutter-off of   *fool*
45   Nature's wit.

CELIA   Peradventure° this is not Fortune's work neither, but   *Perhaps*
Nature's, who perceiveth our natural wits too dull to reason
of such goddesses, hath sent this natural for our whetstone.[5]
For always the dullness of the fool is the whetstone of the
50   wits. —How now, wit, whither wander you?[6]

CLOWN   Mistress, you must come away to your father.

CELIA   Were you made the messenger?

CLOWN   No, by mine honor, but I was bid to come for you.

ROSALIND   Where learned you that oath, fool?

55   CLOWN   Of a certain knight that swore by his honor they
were good pancakes and swore by his honor the mustard
was naught.° Now I'll stand to it° the pancakes were naught   *worthless / affirm*
and the mustard was good, and yet was not the knight
forsworn.°   *perjured*

60   CELIA   How prove you that in the great heap of your knowledge?

ROSALIND   Ay, marry, now unmuzzle your wisdom.

CLOWN   Stand you both forth now: stroke your chins and
swear by your beards that I am a knave.

65   CELIA   By our beards, if we had them, thou art.

CLOWN   By my knavery, if I had it, then I were. But if you
swear by that that is not you are not forsworn. No more was
this knight swearing by his honor, for he never had any; or if
he had, he had sworn it away before ever he saw those pancakes or that mustard.

CELIA   Prithee, who is't that thou mean'st?

CLOWN   One that old Frederick, your father, loves.

ROSALIND[7]   My father's love is enough to honor him enough.
Speak no more of him: you'll be whipped for taxation° one of   *slander*
75   these days.

CLOWN   The more pity that fools may not speak wisely what
wise men do foolishly.

CELIA   By my troth thou sayest true, for since the little wit
that fools have was silenced,[8] the little foolery that wise men
80   have makes a great show. Here comes Monsieur the Beau.

Enter LE BEAU.

ROSALIND   With his mouth full of news.

CELIA   Which he will put on° us as pigeons feed their young.   *force upon*

ROSALIND   Then shall we be news-crammed.[9]

---

5. Celia suggests the Clown's function by describing
him as a "whetstone" (a stone for sharpening tools), a
word that also plays on his name (a touchstone was a
stone that was used to test the purity of gold and silver). Touchstone tests and sharpens the wits of those
he encounters.
6. Alluding to the catchphrase "wandering wits."
7. TEXTUAL COMMENT Most modern editors assign
this speech to Celia on the grounds that she asked
the question to which the Clown has just responded

and because the Clown has referred to her father. F,
however, assigns this speech to Rosalind, who might
be asserting the preeminence of her father's love over
Frederick's. See Digital Edition TC 4.
8. This is a possible allusion to the Bishop of London's
order for the burning of satirical books in June 1599.
9. Forced to digest news, also suggesting "mews" as
meaning the cages in which pigeons were kept before
being fattened, or "crammed," for the table.

CELIA   All the better: we shall be the more marketable.°   *fit to be sold*
85   —Bonjour,° Monsieur Le Beau. What's the news?   *Good day*
LE BEAU   Fair princess, you have lost much good sport.
CELIA   Sport? Of what color?°   *kind*
LE BEAU   What color, madam? How shall I answer you?
ROSALIND   As wit and fortune will.°   *desire*
90   CLOWN   Or as the destinies decrees.
CELIA   Well said—that was laid on with a trowel.[1]
CLOWN   Nay, if I keep not my rank—[2]
ROSALIND   Thou losest thy old smell.
LE BEAU   You amaze° me, ladies. I would have told you of good   *confuse*
95   wrestling, which you have lost the sight of.
ROSALIND   Yet tell us the manner of the wrestling.
LE BEAU   I will tell you the beginning, and if it please your
ladyships, you may see the end. For the best is yet to do,°   *to come*
and here, where you are, they are coming to perform it.
100   CELIA   Well, the beginning? That is dead and buried.[3]
LE BEAU   There comes an old man and his three sons—
CELIA   I could match this beginning with an old tale.[4]
LE BEAU   —Three proper° young men, of excellent growth   *handsome*
and presence—
105   ROSALIND   With bills° on their necks: "Be it known unto all   *proclamations*
men by these presents"[5]—
LE BEAU   —The eldest of the three wrestled with Charles, the
Duke's wrestler, which Charles in a moment threw him and
broke three of his ribs, that there is little hope of life in him.
110   So he served the second and so the third. Yonder they lie,
the poor old man, their father, making such pitiful dole°   *mourning*
over them that all the beholders take his part with weeping.
ROSALIND   Alas!
CLOWN   But what is the sport, monsieur, that the ladies have
115   lost?
LE BEAU   Why, this that I speak of.
CLOWN   Thus men may grow wiser every day. It is the first
time that ever I heard breaking of ribs was sport for ladies.
CELIA   Or I, I promise thee.
120   ROSALIND   But is there any else° longs to see this broken   *anyone else who*
music[6] in his sides? Is there yet another dotes upon rib-
breaking? Shall we see this wrestling, cousin?
LE BEAU   You must if you stay here, for here is the place
appointed for the wrestling and they are ready to perform it.
125   CELIA   Yonder, sure, they are coming. Let us now stay and
see it.
    Flourish.[7] *Enter* DUKE [FREDERICK], LORDS, ORLANDO,
    CHARLES, *and Attendants.*

1. Bluntly; excessively. With a reference to a build-er's heavy application of mortar.
2. My status (as a jester). Rosalind then puns on the meaning of "rank" as "foul smelling."
3. *the beginning . . . buried*: Over and done with; gone. (Referring to the start of the wrestling, with a possible jab at Le Beau's longwindedness.)
4. *old tale*: Celia suggests that the motif of a father and his three sons is the starting point for many familiar folktales.
5. That is, by these legal documents—a legal phrase that appears at the start of formal documents, with a pun on "presence."
6. Literally, a musical composition for a variety of instruments; here, referring to the labored breathing caused by the broken ribs.
7. The sounding of horns or trumpets to signal the arrival of an important person.

DUKE FREDERICK Come on! Since the youth will not be
entreated,° his own peril on his forwardness.[8]   *persuaded (to desist)*
ROSALIND Is yonder the man?
130 LE BEAU Even he, madam.
CELIA Alas, he is too young! Yet he looks successfully.°   *as if he would do well*
DUKE FREDERICK How now, daughter and cousin[9]—are you
crept hither to see the wrestling?
ROSALIND Ay, my liege, so please you give us leave.
135 DUKE FREDERICK You will take little delight in it, I can tell
you: there is such odds° in the man. In pity of the challeng-   *superiority*
er's youth I would fain° dissuade him, but he will not be   *willingly*
entreated. Speak to him, ladies; see if you can move him.
CELIA Call him hither, good Monsieur Le Beau.
140 DUKE FREDERICK Do so. I'll not be by.
LE BEAU Monsieur the challenger, the princess calls for you.
ORLANDO I attend them with all respect and duty.
ROSALIND Young man, have you challenged Charles the
wrestler?
145 ORLANDO No, fair princess. He is the general challenger. I
come but in, as others do, to try with him the strength of my
youth.
CELIA Young gentleman, your spirits are too bold for your
years. You have seen cruel proof of this man's strength; if
150 you saw yourself with your eyes or knew yourself with your
judgment,[1] the fear° of your adventure would counsel you to   *danger*
a more equal enterprise. We pray you for your own sake to
embrace your own safety and give over this attempt.
ROSALIND Do, young sir. Your reputation shall not therefore
155 be misprized.° We will make it our suit to the Duke that the   *undervalued*
wrestling might not go forward.
ORLANDO I beseech you, punish me not with your hard
thoughts,° wherein I confess me much guilty to deny so fair   *displeasure*
and excellent ladies anything. But let your fair eyes and
160 gentle wishes go with me to my trial, wherein if I be foiled°   *defeated*
there is but one shamed that was never gracious;° if killed,   *in favor*
but one dead that is willing to be so. I shall do my friends no
wrong, for I have none to lament me; the world no injury, for
in it I have nothing. Only in the world I fill up a place, which
165 may be better supplied when I have made it empty.
ROSALIND The little strength that I have, I would it were with
you.
CELIA And mine to eke out° hers.   *add to*
ROSALIND Fare you well! Pray heaven I be deceived in you.
170 CELIA Your heart's desires be with you.
CHARLES Come, where is this young gallant that is so desirous to lie with his mother earth?[2]
ORLANDO Ready, sir, but his will° hath in it a more modest   *(sexual) desire*
working.°   *undertaking*
175 DUKE FREDERICK You shall try but one fall.

---

8. *his own . . . forwardness:* let the danger he encounters be blamed on his own rashness.
9. *cousin:* a term used to signify many kinship
relations.
1. If you used your discernment and judgment upon

yourself.
2. To fall to the ground. The words echo biblical
descriptions of the body's return to earth at death
and pun on "lie with" as slang for "have sexual relations with."

CHARLES No, I warrant your grace, you shall not entreat him
    to a second that have so mightily persuaded him from a first.
ORLANDO You mean to mock me after. You should not have
    mocked me before—but come your ways.°   *let's begin*
180 ROSALIND Now Hercules be thy speed,³ young man!
CELIA I would I were invisible, to catch the strong fellow by
    the leg.
           [CHARLES *and* ORLANDO] *wrestle.*
ROSALIND O excellent young man!
CELIA If I had a thunderbolt in mine eye, I can tell who
185   should down.
          Shout. [ORLANDO *throws* CHARLES.]
DUKE FREDERICK No more, no more!
ORLANDO Yes, I beseech your grace—I am not yet well
    breathed.°   *exercised*
DUKE FREDERICK How dost thou, Charles?
LE BEAU   He cannot speak, my lord.
DUKE FREDERICK Bear him away.
      ·   [*Attendants carry* CHARLES *off.*]
190   —What is thy name, young man?
ORLANDO Orlando, my liege, the youngest son of Sir Roland
    de Bois.
DUKE FREDERICK I would thou hadst been son to some man else.
    The world esteemed thy father honorable,
195   But I did find him still° mine enemy.   *always*
    Thou shouldst have better pleased me with this deed
    Hadst thou descended from another house.
    But fare thee well! Thou art a gallant youth.
    I would thou hadst told me of another father.
          Exeunt DUKE [FREDERICK, LORDS, *and* LE BEAU].
200 CELIA Were I my father, coz, would I do this?
ORLANDO I am more proud to be Sir Roland's son,
    His youngest son, and would not change that calling°   *title*
    To be adopted heir to Frederick.
ROSALIND My father loved Sir Roland as his soul,
205   And all the world was of my father's mind.
    Had I before known this young man his son
    I should have given him tears unto° entreaties   *as well as*
    Ere he should thus have ventured.
CELIA   Gentle° cousin,   *Noble; kind*
    Let us go thank him and encourage him.
210   My father's rough and envious° disposition   *spiteful*
    Sticks° me at heart. —Sir, you have well deserved.   *Stabs*
    If you do keep your promises in love
    But justly,° as you have exceeded all promise,   *to the same degree*
    Your mistress shall be happy.
ROSALIND   Gentleman,
    Wear this for me,
        [*giving him a chain from her neck*]
215   one out of suits° with fortune,   *favor*

---

3. May Hercules bring you luck. The phrase alludes to a mythological wrestling match in which Hercules,
whose name was synonymous with physical strength, vanquished Antaeus.

That could° give more but that her hand lacks means.   *would*
—Shall we go, coz?

CELIA   Ay. —Fare you well, fair gentleman.

ORLANDO   Can I not say I thank you? My better parts
Are all thrown down, and that which here stands up
220   Is but a quintain,[4] a mere lifeless block.

ROSALIND   He calls us back. My pride fell with my fortunes:
I'll ask him what he would. —Did you call, sir?
Sir, you have wrestled well and overthrown
More than your enemies.

CELIA   Will you go, coz?

225   ROSALIND   Have with you.° —Fare you well.   *I'll go with you*

Exeunt [CELIA, ROSALIND, *and* CLOWN].[5]

ORLANDO   What passion hangs these weights upon my tongue?
I cannot speak to her, yet she urged conference.°   *conversation*

Enter LE BEAU.

O poor Orlando, thou art overthrown!
Or° Charles or something weaker masters thee.   *Either*

230   LE BEAU   Good sir, I do in friendship counsel you
To leave this place. Albeit you have deserved
High commendation, true applause, and love,
Yet such is now the Duke's condition°   *state of mind*
That he misconsters° all that you have done.   *misconstrues*
235   The Duke is humorous:[6] what he is indeed
More suits° you to conceive than I to speak of.   *Is more fitting for*

ORLANDO   I thank you, sir, and pray you tell me this:
Which of the two was daughter of the Duke
That here was at the wrestling?

240   LE BEAU   Neither his daughter if we judge by manners,
But yet indeed, the taller is his daughter.[7]
The other is daughter to the banished Duke,
And here detained by her usurping uncle
To keep his daughter company, whose loves
245   Are dearer than the natural bond of sisters.
But I can tell you that of late this Duke
Hath ta'en displeasure 'gainst his gentle niece—
Grounded upon no other argument°   *reason*
But that the people praise her for her virtues
250   And pity her for her good father's sake—
And on my life, his malice 'gainst the lady
Will suddenly break forth. Sir, fare you well.
Hereafter, in a better world than this,
I shall desire more love and knowledge of you.

255   ORLANDO   I rest much bounden° to you. Fare you well.   *obliged*

[*Exit* LE BEAU.]

---

4. A wooden post used as a target in jousts and other
aristocratic sports. Orlando suggests that his reason
and speech (his "better parts") have been "thrown
down," or defeated, in his encounter with Rosalind,
leaving him standing speechless, like a post.
5. F marks only an exit for Rosalind here, but Celia
almost certainly accompanies her offstage. The Clown,
whose stage exit is not indicated in F, likely leaves
with Rosalind and Celia, rather than (as many editors
assume) with the Duke's party.

6. Moody. The term derives from Renaissance medical theory, which held that good mental and physical
health depended on the proper balance of four bodily
fluids, or humors.
7. TEXTUAL COMMENT Le Beau suggests here that
Celia is taller than Rosalind, but other moments in
the text (1.3.111; 4.3.86) indicate that Rosalind is the
taller of the two. Le Beau's mistake is characteristic
of his tendency to become easily confused. See Digital Edition TC 5.

Thus must I from the smoke into the smother—[8]
From tyrant duke unto a tyrant brother.
But heavenly Rosalind!   *Exit.*

1.3

Enter CELIA *and* ROSALIND.

CELIA   Why cousin, why Rosalind—Cupid have mercy![1] Not a
word?

ROSALIND   Not one to throw at a dog.

CELIA   No, thy words are too precious to be cast away upon
5   curs. Throw some of them at me; come, lame me with
reasons.[2]

ROSALIND   Then there were two cousins laid up, when the
one should be lamed with reasons and the other mad without any.

10 CELIA   But is all this for your father?

ROSALIND   No, some of it is for my child's father.[3] Oh, how
full of briars is this working-day world!

CELIA   They are but burrs, cousin, thrown upon thee in holiday foolery; if we walk not in the trodden paths our very
15   petticoats will catch them.

ROSALIND   I could shake them off my coat; these burrs are in
my heart.

CELIA   Hem[4] them away.

ROSALIND   I would try if I could cry "hem" and have him.

20 CELIA   Come, come—wrestle with thy affections.

ROSALIND   Oh, they take the part of a better wrestler than
myself.

CELIA   Oh, a good wish upon you:° you will try in time in   ° *good luck to you*
despite of a fall.[5] But turning these jests out of service,° let   *dismissing these jokes*
25   us talk in good earnest. Is it possible on such a sudden you
should fall into so strong a liking with old Sir Roland's youngest son?

ROSALIND   The Duke my father loved his father dearly.

CELIA   Doth it therefore ensue that you should love his son
30   dearly? By this kind of chase° I should hate him, for my   ° *logic*
father hated his father dearly; yet I hate not Orlando.

ROSALIND   No, faith, hate him not, for my sake.

CELIA   Why should I not? Doth he not deserve well?

Enter DUKE [FREDERICK] *with* LORDS.

ROSALIND   Let me love him for that, and do you love him
35   because I do. Look, here comes the Duke.

CELIA   With his eyes full of anger.

DUKE FREDERICK   Mistress, dispatch you with your safest haste[6]
And get you from our court.

ROSALIND   Me, uncle?

---

8. Out of the frying pan into the fire. *smother:* thick,
suffocating smoke.
1.3 Location: Duke Frederick's court.
1. May Cupid (god of love) be compassionate.
2. Throw so many reasons (for your silence) at me
that if they were stones, I would be made lame.
3. That is, for one who will be father to my child.

4. Cough, with a pun on "burrs" (lines 13, 16) as
meaning "something that sticks in your throat."
5. You are destined to wrestle with him eventually
even though it will cause you to fall, with a pun on
"fall" as "lapse from chastity."
6. Leave quickly, which is your best safety.

DUKE FREDERICK   You, cousin.
   Within these ten days if that thou beest found
40 So near our public court as twenty miles,
   Thou diest for it.
ROSALIND   I do beseech your grace,
   Let me the knowledge of my fault bear with me.
   If with myself I hold intelligence°   *I communicate*
   Or have acquaintance with mine own desires;
45 If that I do not dream or be not frantic°—   *insane*
   As I do trust I am not—then, dear uncle,
   Never so much as in a thought unborn
   Did I offend your highness.
DUKE FREDERICK   Thus do all traitors:
   If their purgation° did consist in words,   *exoneration*
50 They are as innocent as grace itself.
   Let it suffice thee that I trust thee not.
ROSALIND   Yet your mistrust cannot make me a traitor.
   Tell me whereon the likelihood depends.
DUKE FREDERICK   Thou art thy father's daughter—there's enough.
55 ROSALIND   So was I when your highness took his dukedom;
   So was I when your highness banished him.
   Treason is not inherited, my lord;
   Or if we did derive it from our friends,°   *relatives*
   What's that to me? My father was no traitor.
60 Then, good my liege, mistake me not so much
   To think my poverty is treacherous.
CELIA   Dear sovereign, hear me speak.
DUKE FREDERICK   Ay, Celia, we stayed° her for your sake;   *detained*
   Else had she with her father ranged° along.   *roamed*
65 CELIA   I did not then entreat to have her stay:
   It was your pleasure and your own remorse.°   *pity; sense of guilt*
   I was too young that time to value her,
   But now I know her: if she be a traitor,
   Why, so am I. We still° have slept together,   *always*
70 Rose at an instant,° learned, played, ate together,   *at the same moment*
   And wheresoe'er we went, like Juno's swans,
   Still we went coupled and inseparable.[7]
DUKE FREDERICK   She is too subtle° for thee, and her   *cunning*
      smoothness,
   Her very silence and her patience,
75 Speak to the people, and they pity her.
   Thou art a fool. She robs thee of thy name,°   *reputation; fame*
   And thou wilt show more bright and seem more virtuous
   When she is gone. Then open not thy lips.
   Firm and irrevocable is my doom,°   *judgment*
80 Which I have passed upon her: she is banished.
CELIA   Pronounce that sentence then on me, my liege.
   I cannot live out of her company.
DUKE FREDERICK   You are a fool. —You, niece, provide
      yourself:°   *make preparation*
   If you out-stay the time, upon mine honor

---

7. That is, yoked together inseparably like the swans that draw the chariot of Juno (queen of the gods). According to Ovid, swans were associated with Venus (goddess of love), not with Juno.

85　　And in the greatness of my word,[8] you die.

Exeunt DUKE [FREDERICK *and* LORDS].

CELIA　O my poor Rosalind, whither wilt thou go?

Wilt thou change° fathers? I will give thee mine.　　　　　　　　*exchange*

I charge thee, be not thou more grieved than I am.

ROSALIND　I have more cause.

CELIA　　　　　　　　　　　Thou hast not, cousin.

90　　Prithee, be cheerful. Know'st thou not the Duke

Hath banished me, his daughter?

ROSALIND　　　　　　　　That he hath not.

CELIA　No, hath not? Rosalind lacks then the love

Which teacheth thee that thou and I am one.

Shall we be sundered? Shall we part, sweet girl?

95　　No, let my father seek another heir.

Therefore devise with me how we may fly,

Whither to go and what to bear with us;

And do not seek to take your change upon you,[9]

To bear your griefs yourself and leave me out.

100　　For by this heaven, now at our sorrows pale,

Say what thou canst, I'll go along with thee.

ROSALIND　Why, whither shall we go?

CELIA　To seek my uncle in the Forest of Arden.

ROSALIND　Alas, what danger will it be to us,

105　　Maids as we are, to travel forth so far!

Beauty provoketh thieves sooner than gold.

CELIA　I'll put myself in poor and mean° attire　　　　　　　　*lowly*

And with a kind of umber[1] smirch my face;

The like do you. So shall we pass along

And never stir° assailants.　　　　　　　　　　　　　　　*provoke*

110　ROSALIND　　　　　　　　Were it not better

Because that I am more than common tall,

That I did suit° me all points° like a man:　　　　　　　*dress / ways*

A gallant curtal ax° upon my thigh,　　　　　　　　　*short sword*

A boar-spear[2] in my hand, and—in my heart

115　　Lie there what hidden woman's fear there will—

We'll have a swashing° and a martial outside,　　　　　　*swaggering*

As many other mannish cowards have

That do outface it with their semblances.[3]

CELIA　What shall I call thee when thou art a man?

120　ROSALIND　I'll have no worse a name than Jove's own page,

And therefore look you call me Ganymede.[4]

But what will you be called?

CELIA　Something that hath a reference to my state:

No longer Celia, but Aliena.°　　　　　　　　　　*"the estranged one"*

8. And in accordance with the power of my decree as Duke.

9. To bear alone the burden of your change of fortunes.

1. Brown pigment. Rubbing umber on their faces would give Rosalind and Celia the dark or sunburned complexion that in Elizabethan society marked the low social status of those who labored outside. Ladies wore masks to keep their complexions white. The text at 4.3.87 describes Celia as "browner" than Rosalind, suggesting that perhaps she is the only one of the two women to use the umber (or, possibly, that her hair is darker than Rosalind's).

2. A long-bladed spear used to impale boar.

3. Who brazenly defy the world with the mere appearance of bravery.

4. The name of a beautiful young man who, according to classical mythology, was so beloved by Jove (king of the gods) that Jove carried him off to heaven and made him his cupbearer. Also a slang term for a young man who sold his sexual services to or was kept by an older man.

125 ROSALIND But cousin, what if we assayed° to steal   *tried*
     The clownish fool out of your father's court—
     Would he not be a comfort to our travel?[5]
     CELIA He'll go along o'er the wide world with me.
     Leave me alone to woo him. Let's away
130 And get our jewels and our wealth together,
     Devise the fittest time and safest way
     To hide us from pursuit that will be made
     After my flight. Now go we in content
     To liberty and not to banishment.   *Exeunt.*

2.1

Enter DUKE SENIOR, AMIENS,[1] *and two or three* LORDS
like° Foresters.   *dressed as*

DUKE SENIOR Now, my co-mates and brothers in exile,
     Hath not old custom° made this life more sweet   *longstanding tradition*
     Than that of painted pomp?° Are not these woods   *artificial splendor*
     More free from peril than the envious court?
5 Here feel we not the penalty of Adam[2]—
     The season's difference,° as° the icy fang   *change / such as*
     And churlish° chiding of the winter's wind,   *rough*
     Which when it bites and blows upon my body
     Even till I shrink with cold, I smile and say,
10 "This is no flattery: these are counselors
     That feelingly° persuade me what I am."   *through my senses*
     Sweet are the uses° of adversity,   *benefits*
     Which like the toad, ugly and venomous,
     Wears yet a precious jewel in his head.[3]
15 And this our life exempt from public haunt°   *free from crowds*
     Finds tongues in trees, books in the running brooks,
     Sermons in stones, and good in everything.
     AMIENS I would not change it. Happy is your grace
     That can translate the stubbornness of fortune
20 Into so quiet and so sweet a style.
     DUKE SENIOR Come, shall we go and kill us venison?
     And yet it irks me the poor dappled fools,°   *innocent creatures*
     Being native burghers° of this desert° city,   *citizens / unpeopled*
     Should in their own confines,° with forkèd heads,°   *bounds / arrows*
     Have their round haunches gored.
25 FIRST LORD   Indeed, my lord,
     The melancholy Jaques[4] grieves at that,
     And in that kind° swears you do more usurp   *vein*
     Than doth your brother that hath banished you.
     Today my lord of Amiens and myself
30 Did steal behind him as he lay along°   *stretched out*
     Under an oak, whose antic° root peeps out   *old; oddly shaped*
     Upon the brook that brawls° along this wood,   *loudly flows*

---

5. F's spelling of "travel" as "travail" (suffering) emphasizes the hardship of the journey.
2.1 Location: The Forest of Arden.
1. The name of a town in northern France with which this character is perhaps associated.
2. In Genesis 3, Adam's punishment for disobeying God involved expulsion from Eden and the laying of a curse upon the earth. This was frequently interpreted as the end of the temperate climate associated with paradise.
3. The toad was popularly believed to be poisonous and to have in its head a jewel, the toadstone.
4. Jaques's name, usually pronounced with two syllables, puns on "jakes," the word for "privy" (toilet). He is a stock figure of the melancholic man prone to solitude and black thoughts because of an excess of black bile, one of the four humors.

To the which place a poor sequestered° stag   *cut off from the herd*
That from the hunter's aim had ta'en a hurt
35 Did come to languish. And indeed, my lord,
The wretched animal heaved forth such groans
That their discharge did stretch his leathern coat
Almost to bursting; and the big round tears
Coursed° one another down his innocent nose   *Pursued*
40 In piteous chase. And thus the hairy fool,
Much markèd of° the melancholy Jaques,   *observed by*
Stood on th'extremest verge° of the swift brook,   *farthest edge*
Augmenting it with tears.
DUKE SENIOR   But what said Jaques?
Did he not moralize° this spectacle?   *draw a moral from*
45 FIRST LORD   Oh, yes—into a thousand similes.
First, for his weeping into the needless° stream,   *needing no more water*
"Poor deer," quoth he, "thou mak'st a testament
As worldlings do, giving thy sum of more°   *your supplement*
To that which had too much." Then, being there alone,
50 Left and abandoned of° his velvet friend,[5]   *by*
"'Tis right," quoth he, "thus misery doth part°   *separate from*
The flux° of company." Anon° a careless[6] herd,   *flow / Just then*
Full of the pasture,° jumps along by him   *Full from grazing*
And never stays to greet him. "Ay," quoth Jaques,
55 "Sweep on, you fat and greasy citizens!
'Tis just the fashion: wherefore do you look
Upon that poor and broken bankrupt there?"
Thus most invectively he pierceth through
The body of country, city, court—
60 Yea, and of this our life—swearing that we
Are mere usurpers, tyrants, and what's worse°   *whatever is worse*
To fright the animals and to kill them up°   *off*
In their assigned and native dwelling place.
DUKE SENIOR   And did you leave him in this contemplation?
65 SECOND LORD   We did, my lord, weeping and commenting
Upon the sobbing deer.
DUKE SENIOR   Show me the place.
I love to cope° him in these sullen fits,   *contend with*
For then he's full of matter.°   *material for thought; pus*
FIRST LORD   I'll bring you to him straight.°   *immediately*
Exeunt.

2.2

Enter DUKE [FREDERICK] *with* LORDS.

DUKE FREDERICK   Can it be possible that no man saw them?
It cannot be! Some villains of my court
Are of consent and sufferance in this.[1]
FIRST LORD   I cannot hear of any that did see her.
5 The ladies, her attendants of her chamber,
Saw her abed, and in the morning early
They found the bed untreasured of their mistress.
SECOND LORD   My lord, the roynish° clown at whom so oft   *vulgar*

5. Smooth-coated companion. The phrase alludes both to the velvet covering the male deer's antlers and to an expensive fabric worn by the prosperous.

6. Carefree, unconcerned; thoughtless.
2.2 Location: Duke Frederick's court.
1. Have agreed to and tolerated this.

	Your grace was wont° to laugh is also missing.	accustomed
10	Hisperia, the princess' gentlewoman,	
	Confesses that she secretly o'erheard	
	Your daughter and her cousin much commend	
	The parts° and graces of the wrestler	qualities
	That did but lately foil the sinewy Charles;	
15	And she believes, wherever they are gone,	
	That youth is surely in their company.	

DUKE FREDERICK   Send to his brother.° Fetch that gallant   (Oliver)
hither.

If he° be absent, bring his brother° to me.   (Orlando) / (Oliver)
I'll make him find him. Do this suddenly,

20   And let not search and inquisition quail°   fail
To bring again° these foolish runaways.   Exeunt.   back

2.3
Enter ORLANDO *and* ADAM [*from different doors*].

ORLANDO   Who's there?

ADAM   What, my young master? O my gentle master,
O my sweet master, O you memory
Of old Sir Roland, why, what make you° here?   what are you doing
5   Why are you virtuous? Why do people love you?
And wherefore° are you gentle, strong, and valiant?   why
Why would you be so fond° to overcome   foolish
The bonny prizer° of the humorous° Duke?   robust champion / moody
Your praise is come too swiftly home before you.
10   Know you not, master, to some kind of men
Their graces° serve them but as enemies?   virtues
No more° do yours: your virtues, gentle master,   No better
Are sanctified and holy traitors to you.
Oh, what a world is this, when what is comely
15   Envenoms° him that bears it!   Poisons

ORLANDO   Why, what's the matter?

ADAM   O unhappy youth,
Come not within these doors. Within this roof
The enemy of all your graces lives.
Your brother—no, no brother, yet the son—
20   Yet not the son, I will not call him son—
Of him I was about to call his father—
Hath heard your praises, and this night he means
To burn the lodging where you use° to lie,   are accustomed
And you within it. If he fail of that
25   He will have other means to cut you off.
I overheard him and his practices.°   plots
This is no place;° this house is but a butchery.°   home / slaughterhouse
Abhor it, fear it, do not enter it!

ORLANDO   Why, whither, Adam, wouldst thou have me go?

30   ADAM   No matter whither, so you come not here.

ORLANDO   What, wouldst thou have me go and beg my food,
Or with a base and boisterous° sword enforce   violent
A thievish living on the common road?
This I must do or know not what to do.
35   Yet this I will not do, do how I can:

2.3 Location: Oliver's house.

I rather will subject me to the malice
Of a diverted blood[1] and bloody° brother.   *murderous*
ADAM   But do not so. I have five hundred crowns,[2]
The thrifty hire I saved[3] under your father,
40   Which I did store to be my foster nurse[4]
When service should in my old limbs lie lame°   *be lamely performed*
And unregarded age in corners thrown.°   *be thrown*
Take that, and he that doth the ravens feed,
Yea, providently caters for the sparrow,[5]
45   Be comfort to my age. Here is the gold.
All this I give you. Let me be your servant.
Though I look old, yet I am strong and lusty,°   *robust*
For in my youth I never did apply
Hot and rebellious° liquors in my blood,   *unhealthful*
50   Nor did not with unbashful forehead° woo   *bold countenance*
The means of weakness and debility.
Therefore my age is as a lusty winter:
Frosty but kindly.° Let me go with you.   *pleasant; benign*
I'll do the service of a younger man
55   In all your business and necessities.
ORLANDO   O good old man, how well in thee appears
The constant° service of the antique world,   *faithful*
When service sweat° for duty, not for meed!°   *labored / reward*
Thou art not for the fashion of these times,
60   Where none will sweat but for promotion
And having that, do choke their service up,°   *cease service*
Even with the having. It is not so with thee.
But poor old man, thou prun'st a rotten tree
That cannot so much as a blossom yield
65   In lieu of° all thy pains and husbandry.°   *In return for / gardening*
But come thy ways; we'll go along together
And ere we have thy youthful wages spent,
We'll light upon some settled low content.°   *humble contentment*
ADAM   Master, go on and I will follow thee
70   To the last gasp with truth and loyalty.
From seventeen years till now almost fourscore
Here lived I, but now live here no more.
At seventeen years many their fortunes seek,
But at fourscore it is too late a week.°   *a time*
75   Yet fortune cannot recompense me better
Than to die well and not my master's debtor.   *Exeunt.*

2.4

Enter ROSALIND *for*° Ganymede, CELIA *for Aliena, and*   *as*
CLOWN, *alias Touchstone.*
ROSALIND   O Jupiter,[1] how merry are my spirits!
CLOWN   I care not for my spirits if my legs were not weary.

1. Of a kinship diverted from its natural course.
2. Approximately 12,500 English pounds in today's currency.
3. The wages I thriftily saved.
4. Caretaker. A foster nurse was a woman hired to breast-feed and care for other people's children.
5. Alluding to various biblical passages (especially Luke 12:6 and 22–24 and Psalm 147:9) that characterize God as the caretaker of all creatures.
2.4 Location: The remainder of act 2 takes place in the Forest of Arden.
1. Another name for Jove, king of the gods in classical mythology and Ganymede's master.

ROSALIND   I could find in my heart to disgrace my man's
apparel and to cry like a woman, but I must comfort the
5   weaker vessel,° as doublet and hose[2] ought to show itself   *woman*
courageous to petticoat; therefore, courage, good Aliena!

CELIA   I pray you, bear with me; I cannot go no further.

CLOWN   For my part, I had rather bear with you than bear
you; yet I should bear no cross[3] if I did bear you, for I think
10   you have no money in your purse.

ROSALIND   Well, this is the Forest of Arden.[4]

CLOWN   Ay, now am I in Arden, the more fool I. When I was
at home I was in a better place, but travelers must be
content.

        Enter CORIN *and* SILVIUS.

15   ROSALIND   Ay, be so good, Touchstone.[5] Look you, who comes
here—a young man and an old in solemn talk.

CORIN   That is the way to make her scorn you still.

SILVIUS   O Corin, that thou knew'st how I do love her!

CORIN   I partly guess, for I have loved ere now.

20   SILVIUS   No, Corin, being old, thou canst not guess,
Though in thy youth thou wast as true a lover
As ever sighed upon a midnight pillow.
But if thy love were ever like to mine—
As sure I think did never man love so—
25   How many actions most ridiculous
Hast thou been drawn to by thy fantasy?°   *imagination*

CORIN   Into a thousand that I have forgotten.

SILVIUS   Oh, thou didst then never love so heartily.
If thou rememb'rest not the slightest folly
30   That ever love did make thee run into,
Thou hast not loved.
Or if thou hast not sat as I do now,
Wearing° thy hearer in thy mistress' praise,   *Wearying*
Thou hast not loved.
35   Or if thou hast not broke from company
Abruptly, as my passion now makes me,
Thou hast not loved.
O Phoebe, Phoebe, Phoebe!   *Exit.*

ROSALIND   Alas, poor shepherd! Searching of° thy wound,   *Probing*
40   I have by hard adventure° found mine own.   *unlucky chance*

CLOWN   And I mine. I remember when I was in love I broke
my sword upon a stone and bid him "Take that!" for coming
a-night to Jane Smile;[6] and I remember the kissing of her
batler[7] and the cow's dugs° that her pretty chapped hands   *udders*
45   had milked; and I remember the wooing of a peascod instead
of her, from whom I took two cods and, giving her them
again, said with weeping tears, "Wear these for my sake."[8]

2. That is, as manhood (signified by male attire,
close-fitting jacket and breeches).
3. Trouble; money—specifically, Elizabethan coins
stamped with the image of a cross.
4. PERFORMANCE COMMENT Production decisions
about representing the Forest of Arden involve set
design as well as the creation of an atmosphere. For
example, do Rosalind and Celia look upon their
arrival in Arden with wonder, or with fear? See Digital Edition PC 1.
5. F reads "be so good Touchstone." Most modern

editors emend to "be so, good Touchstone." In either
case, Rosalind is urging Touchstone to be content.
6. *I broke . . . Smile:* I struck a stone as though it were
a rival to me in my nocturnal visits to Jane Smile.
7. A wooden bat for beating clothes while washing
them.
8. *wooing . . . sake":* referring to English country
courtship rituals in which a pea pod ("peascod") and
its husks ("cods") were considered lucky gifts. "Peascod" and "cods" were also slang terms for male genitalia, suggesting the implicit sexual import of these gifts.

We that are true lovers run into strange capers; but as all is
mortal in nature, so is all nature in love mortal in folly.[9]

50 ROSALIND Thou speak'st wiser than thou art ware° of.　　　　　　　*aware*

CLOWN Nay, I shall ne'er be ware° of mine own wit till I　　　　　　*wary*
break my shins against it.

ROSALIND Jove, Jove! This shepherd's passion
Is much upon my fashion.°　　　　　　　　　　　　　　　　　*of my sort*

55 CLOWN And mine, but it grows something° stale with me.　　　　*somewhat*

CELIA I pray you, one of you question yond man
If he for gold will give us any food.
I faint almost to death.

CLOWN [*to* CORIN]　　　　　Holla, you clown!°　　　　　　*peasant; yokel*

ROSALIND Peace, fool—he's not thy kinsman.

CORIN Who calls?

CLOWN　　　　　Your betters, sir.

60 CORIN　　　　　　　　　　Else are they very wretched.

ROSALIND Peace, I say! —Good even° to you, friend.　　　　　　*evening*

CORIN And to you, gentle sir, and to you all.

ROSALIND I prithee, shepherd, if that love or gold
Can in this desert place buy entertainment,°　　　　　　*accommodation*

65 Bring us where we may rest ourselves and feed.
Here's a young maid with travel much oppressed,
And faints for succor.°　　　　　　　　　　　　*for lack of aid (food)*

CORIN　　　　　　Fair sir, I pity her
And wish, for her sake more than for mine own,
My fortunes were more able to relieve her.

70 But I am shepherd to another man
And do not shear the fleeces that I graze.
My master is of churlish° disposition　　　　　　　　　　　*miserly*
And little recks° to find the way to heaven　　　　　　　　　*thinks*
By doing deeds of hospitality.

75 Besides, his cot,° his flocks, and bounds of feed°　*cottage / grazing rights*
Are now on sale; and at our sheepcote° now,　　　　　　　*cottage*
By reason of his absence, there is nothing
That you will feed on. But what is, come see,
And in my voice[1] most welcome shall you be.

80 ROSALIND What° is he that shall buy his flock and pasture?　　*Who*

CORIN That young swain that you saw here but erewhile,°　　　*just now*
That little cares for buying anything.

ROSALIND I pray thee, if it stand with honesty,
Buy thou the cottage, pasture, and the flock,

85 And thou shalt have to pay° for it of us.　　　　　　　*the money to pay*

CELIA And we will mend° thy wages. I like this place　　　　　*improve*
And willingly could waste° my time in it.　　　　　　　　　*spend*

CORIN Assuredly the thing is to be sold.
Go with me: if you like upon report

90 The soil, the profit, and this kind of life,
I will your very faithful feeder° be　　　　　　　　　　　*servant*
And buy it with your gold right suddenly.　　　　*Exeunt.*

9. So all lovers show their humanity in their fool-　　1. And insofar as my authority stretches.
ishness.

2.5

Enter AMIENS, JAQUES, *and* [*other* LORDS].

Song.

AMIENS [*sings*]¹   Under the greenwood tree
Who loves to lie with me
And turn° his merry note   *tune*
Unto the sweet bird's throat:°   *voice*
5   Come hither, come hither, come hither.
Here shall he see
No enemy
But winter and rough weather.

JAQUES   More, more—I prithee, more!
10 AMIENS   It will make you melancholy, Monsieur Jaques.

JAQUES   I thank it. More, I prithee, more! I can suck melancholy out of a song as a weasel sucks eggs.² More, I prithee,
more!

AMIENS   My voice is ragged;° I know I cannot please you.   *harsh*
15 JAQUES   I do not desire you to please me, I do desire you to sing.
Come, more—another stanzo. Call you 'em stanzos?³

AMIENS   What you will, Monsieur Jaques.

JAQUES   Nay, I care not for their names;⁴ they owe me nothing.
Will you sing?
20 AMIENS   More at your request than to please myself.

JAQUES   Well, then, if ever I thank any man I'll thank you. But
that° they call compliment is like th'encounter of two dog-   *what*
apes;° and when a man thanks me heartily, methinks I have   *dog-faced baboons*
given him a penny and he renders me the beggarly thanks.⁵
25   Come, sing—and you that will not, hold your tongues.

AMIENS   Well, I'll end the song. —Sirs, cover the while.⁶ The
Duke will drink under this tree. —He hath been all this day
to look° you.   *searching for*

JAQUES   And I have been all this day to avoid him. He is too
30   disputable° for my company. I think of as many matters as   *argumentative*
he, but I give heaven thanks and make no boast of them.
Come, warble, come!

Song.

ALL (*together here*⁷)   Who doth ambition shun
And loves to live i'th' sun,
35   Seeking the food he eats
And pleased with what he gets:
Come hither, come hither, come hither.
Here shall he see, etc.

JAQUES   I'll give you a verse to this note° that I made yesterday   *tune*
40   in despite of my invention.⁸

[*He hands* AMIENS *a paper.*]

AMIENS   And I'll sing it. Thus it goes:

2.5
1. F does not indicate who sings this song. Traditionally, it has been assigned to Amiens, whose part may
have been played by Robert Armin, a clown who
joined Shakespeare's company in 1599 and who was
known for his fine singing voice.
2. *as a weasel sucks eggs*: referring to the belief that
weasels sucked the yolks out of birds' eggs.
3. A relatively new, and Italianate, word at the time

of the play's composition.
4. Punning on the legal sense of "names" as "signatures of borrowers."
5. Excessive thanks, like that given by a beggar.
6. Set the table in the meantime.
7. F's direction before this song reads: "Song. Altogether here."
8. Even though I have little power of creativity.

                    If it do come to pass
                    That any man turn ass,
                    Leaving his wealth and ease
45   A stubborn will to please,
                    Ducdame,[9] ducdame, ducdame:
                    Here shall he see
                    Gross fools as he
                    An if° he will come to me.   *If only*
50   What's that "ducdame"?
        JAQUES   'Tis a Greek[1] invocation to call fools into a circle. I'll
          go sleep if I can; if I cannot I'll rail against all the firstborn
          of Egypt.[2]
        AMIENS   And I'll go seek the Duke. His banquet[3] is prepared.
                                                               Exeunt.

                              2.6
                  Enter ORLANDO *and* ADAM.
        ADAM   Dear master, I can go no further. Oh, I die for food!
          Here lie I down and measure out my grave. Farewell, kind
          master.
        ORLANDO   Why, how now, Adam? No greater heart in thee?
5   Live a little, comfort° a little, cheer thyself a little. If this   *be comforted*
          uncouth° forest yield anything savage I will either be food   *wild*
          for it or bring it for food to thee. Thy conceit° is nearer death   *imagination*
          than thy powers. For my sake, be comfortable; hold death
          awhile at the arm's end. I will here be with thee presently,°   *soon*
10   and if I bring thee not something to eat, I will give thee
          leave to die; but if thou diest before I come thou art a
          mocker of my labor. Well said—thou look'st cheerily,° and   *cheerfully*
          I'll be with thee quickly. Yet thou liest in the bleak air.
          Come, I will bear thee to some shelter, and thou shalt not
15   die for lack of a dinner if there live anything in this desert.°   *uninhabited place*
          Cheerily, good Adam!   *Exeunt.*

                              2.7
        Enter DUKE SENIOR *and* LORD[s], *like° outlaws.*   *dressed as*
        DUKE SENIOR   I think he be transformed into a beast,
          For I can nowhere find him like° a man.   *in the shape of*
        FIRST LORD   My lord, he is but even now gone hence.
          Here was he merry, hearing of a song.
5   DUKE SENIOR   If he, compact of jars,° grow musical,   *full of discords*
          We shall have shortly discord in the spheres.[1]
          Go seek him; tell him I would speak with him.
                  Enter JAQUES.
        FIRST LORD   He saves my labor by his own approach.
        DUKE SENIOR   Why how now, monsieur, what a life is this
10   That your poor friends must woo your company?
          What? You look merrily.

9. A word of unknown meaning. Possibly a variation
on a Welsh phrase meaning "Come hither" or on a
Gypsy phrase meaning "I foretell."
1. "Greek" was used to signify anything unintelligible.
2. According to Exodus 11 and 12, the Hebrew God
caused the deaths of all firstborn Egyptian children
after Pharaoh would not let the Israelites leave his
country. Jaques may be vowing to denounce all first-

born sons, which would include Duke Senior.
3. A light meal of sweetmeats and wine.
2.7
1. Alluding to the Pythagorean belief that the earth
was the center of eight concentric spheres whose
movements created a heavenly harmony (the music
of the spheres) inaudible to humans.

JAQUES A fool, a fool! I met a fool i'th' forest—
A motley fool!² A miserable world!
As I do live by food, I met a fool,
15 Who laid him down and basked him in the sun,
And railed on Lady Fortune in good terms,
In good set° terms, and yet a motley fool.   *outspoken; rhetorical*
"Good morrow, fool," quoth I. "No, sir," quoth he,
"Call me not fool till heaven hath sent me fortune."³
20 And then he drew a dial⁴ from his poke,°   *pocket; pouch*
And looking on it with lackluster eye,
Says very wisely, "It is ten o'clock.
Thus we may see," quoth he, "how the world wags.°   *moves on*
'Tis but an hour ago since it was nine,
25 And after one hour more 'twill be eleven.
And so from hour to hour we ripe and ripe,
And then from hour to hour we rot and rot,
And thereby hangs a tale."⁵ When I did hear
The motley fool thus moral on the time,
30 My lungs began to crow like chanticleer°   *a rooster*
That fools should be so deep° contemplative;   *profoundly*
And I did laugh sans° intermission   *without*
An hour by his dial. O noble fool,
A worthy fool! Motley's the only wear.°   *garb worth wearing*
35 DUKE SENIOR What fool is this?
JAQUES O worthy fool! One that hath been a courtier
And says if ladies be but young and fair,
They have the gift to know it. And in his brain,
Which is as dry⁶ as the remainder° biscuit   *last*
40 After a voyage, he hath strange places° crammed   *sites; commonplaces*
With observation, the which he vents
In mangled forms. Oh, that I were a fool!
I am ambitious for a motley coat.
DUKE SENIOR Thou shalt have one.
JAQUES   It is my only suit,°   *request; costume*
45 Provided that you weed your better judgments
Of all opinion that grows rank° in them   *wild*
That I am wise. I must have liberty
Withal—as large a charter° as the wind   *license*
To blow on whom I please—for so fools have.
50 And they that are most gallèd° with my folly,   *vexed*
They most must laugh. And why, sir, must they so?
The why is plain as way to parish church:⁷
He that a fool doth very wisely hit
Doth very foolishly, although he smart,

---

2. Someone wearing "motley," the multicolored costume conventionally associated with fools and jesters.
3. Referring to the proverbial notion that fortune favored fools.
4. A portable sundial about the size of a napkin ring, or possibly an early version of the watch, which would have been carried in a pocket in the seventeenth century.
5. 'Tis . . . tale: the puns and sexual wordplay in these lines suggest a story of male sexual activity leading to debility: "hour" puns on "whore" (they were pronounced similarly); "ripe" means "to come of age sexually"; "rot" puns on "rut," which means "to have sex in an animal-like state of excitement"; and "tale" puns on "tail," slang for "penis." "And thereby hangs a tale" was an Elizabethan commonplace.
6. According to Renaissance medical theory, dry brains signified slow wits and strong memories.
7. plain . . . church: simple and easy to see, like the footpaths that often connected English parish churches with the surrounding rural areas.

55	Seem senseless of the bob.° If not,	*unaware of the taunt*
	The wise man's folly is anatomized°	*dissected; laid open*
	Even by the squand'ring glances° of the fool.	*random hits*
	Invest° me in my motley. Give me leave	*Dress; establish*
	To speak my mind, and I will through and through	
60	Cleanse the foul body of th'infected world	
	If they will patiently receive my medicine.	

DUKE SENIOR   Fie on thee! I can tell what thou wouldst do.

JAQUES   What, for a counter,[8] would I do but good?

DUKE SENIOR   Most mischievous foul sin in chiding sin:

65	For thou thyself hast been a libertine,°	*(sexually) unrestrained person*
	As sensual as the brutish sting° itself;	*lust*
	And all th'embossèd sores and headed evils[9]	
	That thou with license of free foot° hast caught	*travel*
	Wouldst thou disgorge° into the general world.	*vomit*
70	JAQUES Why, who cries out on pride°	*extravagance*
	That can therein tax° any private party?°	*blame / one person*
	Doth it not flow as hugely as the sea,	
	Till that the weary very means° do ebb?	*source itself*
	What woman in the city do I name	
75	When that I say the city woman bears	
	The cost° of princes on unworthy shoulders?	*costly attire*
	Who can come in and say that I mean her,	
	When such a one as she, such is her neighbor?	
	Or what is he of basest function°	*lowliest social status*
80	That says his bravery° is not on° my cost,	*fine attire / at*
	Thinking that I mean him, but therein suits	
	His folly to the mettle° of my speech?	*spirit*
	There then, how then, what then—let me see wherein	
	My tongue hath wronged him. If it do him right,°	*describe him justly*
85	Then he hath wronged himself. If he be free,°	*guiltless*
	Why then my taxing° like a wild goose flies—	*reproof*
	Unclaimed of any man. But who comes here?	

Enter ORLANDO [*with sword drawn*].

ORLANDO   Forbear and eat no more!

	JAQUES Why, I have ate° none yet.	*eaten*
90	ORLANDO Nor shalt not till necessity be served.	
	JAQUES Of what kind° should this cock come of?	*lineage; stock*

DUKE SENIOR   Art thou thus boldened, man, by thy distress?

Or else a rude despiser of good manners,

That in civility thou seem'st so empty?

95	ORLANDO You touched my vein° at first—the thorny point	*assessed my condition*
	Of bare distress hath ta'en from me the show	
	Of smooth civility. Yet am I inland bred,[1]	
	And know some nurture. But forbear, I say!	
	He dies that touches any of this fruit	
100	Till I and my affairs are answerèd.°	*satisfied*
	JAQUES An° you will not be answered with reason, I must die.	*If*
	DUKE SENIOR What would you have? Your gentleness° shall force	*gentility; kindness*
	More than your force move us to gentleness.	

---

8. In return for a coin of no value (normally used for reckoning sums).
9. Swollen sores and boils that have come to a head. Both were symptoms of venereal disease.

1. Brought up in a civilized way—that is, raised in the country's interior regions rather than near its supposedly savage borders.

ORLANDO I almost die for food, and let me have it.
105 DUKE SENIOR Sit down and feed, and welcome to our table.
ORLANDO Speak you so gently? Pardon me, I pray you.
     I thought that all things had been savage here,
     And therefore put I on the countenance
     Of stern commandment. But whate'er you are
110 That in this desert inaccessible
     Under the shade of melancholy boughs,
     Lose and neglect the creeping hours of time:
     If ever you have looked on better days,
     If ever been where bells have knolled° to church,   summoned
115 If ever sat at any good man's feast,
     If ever from your eyelids wiped a tear,
     And know what 'tis to pity and be pitied,
     Let gentleness my strong enforcement be,[2]
     In the which hope I blush and hide my sword.
120 DUKE SENIOR True it is that we have seen better days,
     And have with holy bell been knolled to church,
     And sat at good men's feasts and wiped our eyes
     Of drops that sacred pity hath engendered;
     And therefore, sit you down in gentleness
125 And take upon command° what help we have   at your will
     That to your wanting may be ministered.
ORLANDO Then but forbear your food a little while,
     Whiles like a doe I go to find my fawn
     And give it food. There is an old poor man,
130 Who after me hath many a weary step
     Limped in pure love; till he be first sufficed°—   satisfied
     Oppressed with two weak° evils, age and hunger—   enfeebling
     I will not touch a bit.
DUKE SENIOR   Go find him out,
     And we will nothing waste° till your return.   consume
135 ORLANDO I thank ye, and be blest for your good comfort!
                                               [Exit.]
DUKE SENIOR Thou seest we are not all alone unhappy:
     This wide and universal theater
     Presents more woeful pageants° than the scene   spectacles
     Wherein we play in.
JAQUES   All the world's a stage,
140 And all the men and women merely players.
     They have their exits and their entrances,
     And one man in his time plays many parts,
     His acts being seven ages. At first the infant,
     Mewling° and puking in the nurse's arms;   Crying
145 Then the whining schoolboy with his satchel
     And shining morning face, creeping like snail
     Unwillingly to school. And then the lover,
     Sighing like furnace,[3] with a woeful ballad
     Made to his mistress' eyebrow. Then a soldier,
150 Full of strange oaths and bearded like the pard,[4]
     Jealous in honor,[5] sudden and quick in quarrel,

---

2. Let natural kindness or gentility be what compels
your compassion.
3. Emitting sighs as a furnace emits smoke.

4. Leopard. The soldier's bristling mustache is compared to the leopard's whiskers.
5. Vigilant in matters of honor.

Seeking the bubble reputation
Even in the cannon's mouth. And then the justice,
In fair round belly with good capon[6] lined,°   *filled; stuffed*
155   With eyes severe and beard of formal cut,
Full of wise saws° and modern instances,°   *sayings / trite examples*
And so he plays his part. The sixth age shifts
Into the lean and slippered pantaloon,[7]
With spectacles on nose and pouch on side,
160   His youthful hose, well saved, a world too wide
For his shrunk shank;° and his big manly voice,   *calf*
Turning again toward childish treble, pipes
And whistles in his° sound. Last scene of all,   *its*
That ends this strange eventful history,
165   Is second childishness and mere° oblivion,   *complete*
Sans° teeth, sans eyes, sans taste, sans everything.   *Without*
        Enter ORLANDO [*carrying*] ADAM.
DUKE SENIOR   Welcome! Set down your venerable burden
  And let him feed.
ORLANDO   I thank you most for him.
ADAM   So had you need:
170   I scarce can speak to thank you for myself.
DUKE SENIOR   Welcome! Fall to; I will not trouble you
  As yet to question you about your fortunes.°   *circumstances*
  —Give us some music and, good cousin, sing.
               Song.
AMIENS [*sings*][8]   Blow, blow, thou winter wind.
175   Thou art not so unkind
         As man's ingratitude.
         Thy tooth is not so keen
         Because thou art not seen,
         Although thy breath be rude.°   *rough*
180   Heigh-ho, sing heigh-ho unto the green holly.[9]
         Most friendship is feigning, most loving mere folly.
         Then heigh-ho, the holly:
         This life is most jolly.

         Freeze, freeze, thou bitter sky
185   That dost not bite so nigh°   *closely*
         As benefits forgot.
         Though thou the waters warp,°   *cause to contract; freeze*
         Thy sting is not so sharp
         As friend remembered not.
190   Heigh-ho, sing, etc.

DUKE SENIOR   If that you were the good Sir Roland's son,
  As you have whispered faithfully you were,
  And as mine eye doth his effigies° witness   *likeness*
  Most truly limned° and living in your face,   *portrayed*
195   Be truly welcome hither. I am the Duke
  That loved your father. The residue of your fortune
  Go to my cave and tell me. —Good old man,

---

6. A cock, castrated and fattened as a delicacy (proverbially, a bribe for magistrates).
7. A foolish old man named after a figure in *commedia dell'arte*, Italian popular comedy.

8. Again, F does not indicate who sings this song. It
is usually assigned to Amiens.
9. The evergreen associated with English holiday
festivities.

Thou art right welcome, as thy master is.
—Support him by the arm. —Give me your hand,
200   And let me all your fortunes understand.   *Exeunt.*

3.1

Enter DUKE [FREDERICK], LORDS, *and* OLIVER.

DUKE FREDERICK   Not see him since? Sir, sir, that cannot be.
But were I not the better part made° mercy,   *composed of*
I should not seek an absent argument°   *subject*
Of my revenge, thou present. But look to it:
5   Find out thy brother, wheresoe'er he is.
Seek him with candle;° bring him dead or living   *diligently*
Within this twelvemonth, or turn° thou no more   *return*
To seek a living in our territory.
Thy lands and all things that thou dost call thine
10   Worth seizure do we seize into our hands
Till thou canst quit° thee by thy brother's mouth   *acquit*
Of what we think against thee.
OLIVER   Oh, that your highness knew my heart in this!
I never loved my brother in my life.
15   DUKE FREDERICK   More villain thou. —Well, push him out of
doors,
And let my officers of such a nature°   *whose job it is*
Make an extent° upon his house and lands.   *a writ of seizure*
Do this expediently° and turn° him going.   *Exeunt.*   *quickly / set*

3.2

Enter ORLANDO [*holding a sheaf of papers*].

ORLANDO   Hang there, my verse, in witness of my love.
And thou, thrice-crownèd queen of night,[1] survey
With thy chaste eye from thy pale sphere above
Thy huntress' name,° that my full life doth sway.°   *(Rosalind) / rule*
5   O Rosalind, these trees shall be my books,
And in their barks my thoughts I'll character,°   *inscribe*
That every eye which in this forest looks
Shall see thy virtue witnessed everywhere.
Run, run, Orlando—carve on every tree
10   The fair, the chaste and unexpressive° she!   *Exit.*[2]   *inexpressible*
Enter CORIN *and* CLOWN.

CORIN   And how like you this shepherd's life, Master Touchstone?
CLOWN   Truly, shepherd, in respect of° itself, it is a good life;   *with regard to*
but in respect that it is a shepherd's life, it is naught.° In   *worthless*
15   respect that it is solitary, I like it very well; but in respect that
it is private, it is a very vile life. Now in respect it is in the
fields, it pleaseth me well; but in respect it is not in the court,
it is tedious. As it is a spare° life, look you, it fits my humor°   *frugal / temperament*

3.1 Location: Duke Frederick's court.
3.2 Location: The remaining scenes of the play take place in the Forest of Arden.
1. The goddess who ruled on earth as Diana, patron of chastity and of the hunt; in the heavens as Cynthia, Phoebe, or Luna, goddess of the moon; and in the underworld as Hecate.
2. Orlando's appearance at lines 1–10 is self-

contained and could form a separate scene. However, the ensuing conversation between Corin and Touchstone appears to take place on the same spot where Orlando has just stood, making the action continuous. This edition, like F, makes Orlando's lines part of the longer scene involving Corin, Touchstone, and eventually Rosalind and others.

well; but as there is no more plenty in it, it goes much against
20   my stomach.° Hast any philosophy in thee, shepherd?   *inclination*

CORIN   No more but that I know the more one sickens, the
    worse at ease he is; and that he that wants° money, means,   *lacks*
    and content, is without three good friends; that the property
    of rain is to wet and fire to burn; that good pasture makes fat
25   sheep and that a great cause of the night is lack of the sun;
    that he that hath learned no wit by nature nor art may com-
    plain° of good breeding, or comes of a very dull kindred.   *lament his lack*

CLOWN   Such a one is a natural philosopher.[3] Wast ever in
    court, shepherd?

30 CORIN   No, truly.

CLOWN   Then thou art damned.

CORIN   Nay, I hope.

CLOWN   Truly thou art damned, like an ill-roasted egg all on
    one side.[4]

35 CORIN   For not being at court? Your reason?

CLOWN   Why if thou never wast at court thou never saw'st
    good manners.° If thou never saw'st good manners, then thy   *etiquette; morals*
    manners must be wicked, and wickedness is sin, and sin is
    damnation. Thou art in a parlous° state, shepherd!   *perilous*

40 CORIN   Not a whit, Touchstone—those that are good manners
    at the court are as ridiculous in the country as the behavior
    of the country is most mockable at the court. You told me
    you salute not at the court but° you kiss your hands. That   *unless*
    courtesy would be uncleanly if courtiers were shepherds.

45 CLOWN   Instance,° briefly; come, instance.   *An example*

CORIN   Why, we are still° handling our ewes, and their fells,° *constantly / skins*
    you know, are greasy.

CLOWN   Why, do not your courtiers' hands sweat? And is not
    the grease of a mutton as wholesome as the sweat of a man?
50   Shallow, shallow! A better instance, I say—come!

CORIN   Besides, our hands are hard.

CLOWN   Your lips will feel them the sooner. Shallow again—a
    more sounder instance, come!

CORIN   And they are often tarred over with the surgery of our
55   sheep,[5] and would you have us kiss tar? The courtiers' hands
    are perfumed with civet.[6]

CLOWN   Most shallow man, thou worm's meat in respect of° a *in comparison with*
    good piece of flesh, indeed! Learn of the wise and perpend:°   *consider*
    civet is of a baser birth than tar—the very uncleanly flux° of   *discharge*
60   a cat. Mend° the instance, shepherd.   *Improve*

CORIN   You have too courtly a wit for me; I'll rest.

CLOWN   Wilt thou rest damned? God help thee, shallow man!
    God make incision in thee: thou art raw.[7]

CORIN   Sir, I am a true laborer: I earn that° I eat, get° that I   *what / make*
65   wear, owe no man hate, envy no man's happiness, glad of
    other men's good, content with my harm;° and the greatest   *misfortune*
    of my pride is to see my ewes graze and my lambs suck.

---

3. A born philosopher; a philosopher who studies
natural phenomena; a fool.
4. *ill-roasted . . . side*: referring to the practice of
roasting eggs on a spit over a wood fire.
5. Referring to the practice of treating sheep wounds
with tar.

6. A musk-scented substance obtained from the anal
glands of certain cats.
7. Make a cut to let blood (and thus cure you of your
"raw"ness, or inexperience); make a cut to score you,
as raw meat was scored in preparation for cooking.

CLOWN   That is another simple° sin in you: to bring the ewes   *foolish; plain*
and the rams together and to offer° to get your living by the   *undertake*
70   copulation of cattle, to be bawd to a bellwether⁸ and to
betray a she-lamb of a twelvemonth to a crooked-pated old
cuckoldy ram,⁹ out of all reasonable match. If thou beest not
damned for this, the devil himself will have no shepherds.¹ I
cannot see else how thou shouldst scape.°   *escape*
75   CORIN   Here comes young Master Ganymede, my new mistress's brother.
          Enter ROSALIND[, *as Ganymede, reading a paper*].
ROSALIND   "From the east to western Inde,°   *Indies*
                No jewel is like Rosalind.
                Her worth, being mounted on the wind,
80   Through all the world bears Rosalind.
                All the pictures fairest lined°   *drawn*
                Are but black to° Rosalind.   *compared to*
                Let no face be kept in mind
                But the fair of Rosalind."
85   CLOWN   I'll rhyme you so eight years together, dinners and
suppers and sleeping-hours excepted; it is the right butter-
women's rank to market.²
ROSALIND   Out, fool!
CLOWN   For a taste:
90   If a hart° do lack a hind,°   *male deer / female deer*
                Let him seek out Rosalind.
                If the cat will after kind,°   *act naturally; mate*
                So, be sure, will Rosalind.
                Wintered garments must be lined,³
95   So must slender Rosalind.
                They that reap must sheaf and bind,
                Then to cart⁴ with Rosalind.
                Sweetest nut hath sourest rind:
                Such a nut is Rosalind.
100   He that sweetest rose will find
                Must find love's prick° and Rosalind.   *thorn; penis*
This is the very false gallop of verses.° Why do you infect   *way verses canter on*
yourself with them?
ROSALIND   Peace, you dull fool! I found them on a tree.
105   CLOWN   Truly, the tree yields bad fruit.
ROSALIND   I'll graft it with you° and then I shall graft it with   *(punning on "yew")*
a medlar:⁵ then it will be the earliest fruit i'th' country, for
you'll be rotten ere you be half ripe, and that's the right°   *true*
virtue of the medlar.

---

8. The leading sheep of a flock, who usually wore a bell.
9. Cuckolds, men whose wives were sexually unfaithful, supposedly wore horns to signify their shame. The ram may *make* cuckolds—that is, be lecherous. *crooked-pated*: with crooked horns.
1. It will be because the devil refuses to admit shepherds into hell.
2. *It . . . market:* The rhymes are truly like a stream of dairywomen going to market at the same time. Such women were proverbially talkative.
3. Clothes worn in winter must be stuffed with

material, with a pun on "lined" as meaning "copulated with," used especially of female animals. The implication is that "slender Rosalind" will be impregnated and thus grow larger.
4. A cart on which harvests were transported to the market; a cart on which women accused of prostitution or other forms of disorderly conduct were transported and exposed to public abuse.
5. A tree whose fruit was not ripe until it was so soft as to be rotten, with a pun on "meddler," one who meddles.

110   CLOWN   You have said—but whether wisely or no, let the forest
     judge.
          Enter CELIA [*as Aliena*] *with a writing.*
    ROSALIND   Peace! Here comes my sister reading—stand aside.
    CELIA   "Why should this a desert be—
          For it is unpeopled? No.
115   Tongues I'll hang on every tree
          That shall civil° sayings show: *civilized*
          Some, how brief the life of man
          Runs his erring° pilgrimage,   *wandering*
          That the stretching of a span
120   Buckles in his sum of age;[6]
          Some of violated vows
          Twixt the souls of friend and friend.
          But upon the fairest boughs,
          Or at every sentence end,
125   Will I Rosalinda write,
          Teaching all that read to know
          The quintessence of every sprite°   *spirit; soul*
          Heaven would in little show.[7]
          Therefore heaven nature charged
130   That one body should be filled
          With all graces wide enlarged:[8]
          Nature presently° distilled   *at once*
          Helen's cheek but not her heart,[9]
          Cleopatra's[1] majesty,
135   Atalanta's better part,[2]
          Sad Lucretia's modesty.[3]
          Thus Rosalind of many parts,
          By heavenly synod° was devised   *assembly*
          Of many faces, eyes, and hearts
140   To have the touches° dearest prized.   *traits*
          Heaven would that she these gifts should have,
          And I to live and die her slave."
    ROSALIND   O most gentle Jupiter! What tedious homily of love
     have you wearied your parishioners withal, and never cried,
145   "Have patience, good people."
    CELIA   How now? Back, friends. Shepherd, go off a little; go
     with him, sirrah.
    CLOWN   Come, shepherd, let us make an honorable retreat,
     though not with bag and baggage, yet with scrip and scrippage.[4]

---

6. *the stretching . . . age:* the width of an open hand (a "span") encompasses an entire lifetime. A comparison derived from verses appearing in Elizabethan prayer books.

7. In classical and medieval philosophy, the quintessence of a thing is its purest part or most essential characteristic. Orlando's poem suggests that heaven and nature have extracted all the best virtues of other women and embodied and portrayed them "in little"—that is, in only one person, Rosalind.

8. Graces that otherwise have been widely distributed.

9. The features, but not the false heart, of Helen of Troy. Supposedly, Helen's abduction by Paris from her husband, Menelaus, was the event that precipitated the Trojan War. In some accounts, Helen is blamed for her abduction and so could be said to have a false heart.

1. Queen of Egypt and the tragic heroine of Shakespeare's *Antony and Cleopatra*.

2. In Greek myth, Atalanta was a fleet-footed and chaste hunter who challenged her suitors to a race. She was only defeated when one of them dropped three golden apples, which she stopped to pick up. The reference here is possibly to her beauty or her speed, rather than her greed.

3. Lucretia killed herself to save her honor after being raped by Tarquin (a story told by Shakespeare in *The Rape of Lucrece*).

4. *though . . . scrippage:* though not with the belongings retained by an army in retreat, yet with a shepherd's pouch and its contents.

Exeunt [CLOWN *and* CORIN].

150 CELIA Didst thou hear these verses?

ROSALIND Oh, yes, I heard them all and more too, for some of them had in them more feet° than the verses would bear.   *metrical units*

CELIA That's no matter; the feet might bear° the verses.   *carry*

ROSALIND Ay, but the feet were lame and could not bear
155 themselves without° the verse, and therefore stood lamely in the verse.   *out of*

CELIA But didst thou hear without wondering how thy name should be° hanged and carved upon these trees?   *came to be*

ROSALIND I was seven of the nine days out of the wonder[5]
160 before you came; for look here what I found on a palm tree. I was never so be-rhymed since Pythagoras' time that I was an Irish rat,[6] which I can hardly remember.

CELIA Trow you° who hath done this?   *Can you imagine*

ROSALIND Is it a man?

165 CELIA And a chain, that you once wore, about his neck. Change you color?

ROSALIND I prithee, who?

CELIA O Lord, Lord—it is a hard matter for friends to meet, but mountains may be removed with° earthquakes and so   *moved by*
170 encounter.

ROSALIND Nay, but who is it?

CELIA Is it possible?

ROSALIND Nay, I prithee now with most petitionary vehemence, tell me who it is.

175 CELIA Oh, wonderful, wonderful, and most wonderful—wonderful and yet again wonderful, and after that out of all hooping![7]

ROSALIND Good my complexion![8] Dost thou think though I am caparisoned° like a man I have a doublet and hose in my   *dressed*
180 disposition? One inch of delay more is a South Sea of discovery.[9] I prithee, tell me who is it quickly, and speak apace.°   *quickly*
I would thou couldst stammer, that thou mightst pour this concealed man out of thy mouth as wine comes out of a narrow-mouthed bottle: either too much at once or none at
185 all. I prithee, take the cork out of thy mouth that I may drink thy tidings.

CELIA So you may put a man in your belly.°   *stomach; womb*

ROSALIND Is he of God's making? What manner of man? Is his head worth a hat or his chin worth a beard?

190 CELIA Nay, he hath but a little beard.

ROSALIND Why, God will send more if the man will be thankful. Let me stay° the growth of his beard if thou delay me   *wait for*
not the knowledge of his chin.

---

5. Referring to the proverbial "nine days' wonder," a novelty that caused amazement.
6. I was never so overwhelmed with rhyme since the days of the ancient Greeks, when I was an Irish rat. Alluding to Pythagoras's doctrine of the transmigration of souls and to the popular belief in England that Irish bards were capable of rhyming rats to death.
7. After that, beyond what can be contained, with a

pun on "whooping": beyond what all shouts of astonishment can express.
8. An expression of impatience. "Complexion" means "temperament," believed to be caused by the particular mixture of the four humors in one's body. Rosalind's meaning seems to be: Pay attention to my womanly temperament (which is impatient)!
9. More delay will seem as infinite as a voyage of discovery to the South Seas.

CELIA   It is young Orlando, that tripped up the wrestler's
195   heels and your heart both in an instant.
ROSALIND   Nay, but the devil take mocking: speak sad brow
    and true maid.[1]
CELIA   I'faith, coz, 'tis he.
ROSALIND   Orlando?
200 CELIA   Orlando!
ROSALIND   Alas the day! What shall I do with my doublet and
    hose? What did he when thou saw'st him? What said he?
    How looked he? Wherein went he?° What makes he here?   *What was he wearing?*
    Did he ask for me? Where remains he? How parted he with
205   thee? And when shalt thou see him again? Answer me in
    one word.
CELIA   You must borrow me Gargantua's[2] mouth first: 'tis a
    word too great for any mouth of this age's size. To say ay
    and no to these particulars is more than to answer in a
210   catechism.[3]
ROSALIND   But doth he know that I am in this forest and in
    man's apparel? Looks he as freshly as he did the day he
    wrestled?
CELIA   It is as easy to count atomies° as to resolve the proposi-   *specks (of dust)*
215   tions[4] of a lover. But take a taste of my finding him and relish
    it with good observance:[5] I found him under a tree, like a
    dropped acorn—
ROSALIND   It may well be called Jove's tree,[6] when it drops
    forth fruit.
220 CELIA   Give me audience, good madam.
ROSALIND   Proceed.
CELIA   There lay he, stretched along like a wounded knight—
ROSALIND   Though it be pity to see such a sight, it well
    becomes the ground.
225 CELIA   Cry "holla"° to the tongue, I prithee; it curvets° unsea-   *hold / leaps about*
    sonably. He was furnished° like a hunter—   *dressed*
ROSALIND   Oh, ominous: he comes to kill my heart![7]
CELIA   I would sing my song without a burden.° Thou bring'st   *refrain*
    me out of tune.
230 ROSALIND   Do you not know I am a woman? When I think I
    must speak. Sweet, say on.
                Enter ORLANDO *and* JAQUES.
CELIA   You bring me out.° Soft, comes he not here?   *make me lose the tune*
ROSALIND   'Tis he! Slink by and note him.
JAQUES   I thank you for your company, but good faith, I had as
235   lief° have been myself alone.   *as willingly*
ORLANDO   And so had I; but yet, for fashion sake, I thank you
    too for your society.
JAQUES   God b'wi' you,° let's meet as little as we can.   *Good-bye*

1. Speak seriously and as a virtuous woman or on your honor as a virgin.
2. A voracious giant famous in French folklore and from the writings of Rabelais.
3. A summary, in question-and-answer form, of basic tenets of religious doctrine. In Shakespeare's time, all members of the Church of England learned to recite such a catechism.
4. *resolve the propositions:* answer the questions.
5. And enhance its flavor by paying careful attention.
6. The oak was traditionally viewed as sacred to Jove, the god of thunder, and was said therefore to be often struck by lightning.
7. TEXTUAL COMMENT F reads "Hart" (a male deer). In the forest scenes, the pursuit of love (seeking hearts) is often compared to the hunting of deer. See Digital Edition TC 6.

ORLANDO   I do desire we may be better strangers.

240   JAQUES   I pray you, mar no more trees with writing love songs in their barks.

ORLANDO   I pray you, mar no more of my verses with reading them ill-favoredly.°   *unsympathetically*

JAQUES   Rosalind is your love's name?

245   ORLANDO   Yes, just.

JAQUES   I do not like her name.

ORLANDO   There was no thought of pleasing you when she was christened.

JAQUES   What stature is she of?

250   ORLANDO   Just as high as my heart.

JAQUES   You are full of pretty answers. Have you not been acquainted with goldsmiths' wives and conned them out of rings?[8]

ORLANDO   Not so. But I answer you right painted cloth,[9] from

255   whence you have studied your questions.

JAQUES   You have a nimble wit: I think 'twas made of Atalanta's heels.[1] Will you sit down with me, and we two will rail against our mistress, the world, and all our misery?

ORLANDO   I will chide no breather° in the world but myself,   *person*

260   against whom I know most faults.

JAQUES   The worst fault you have is to be in love.

ORLANDO   'Tis a fault I will not change for your best virtue. I am weary of you.

JAQUES   By my troth, I was seeking for a fool when I found

265   you.

ORLANDO   He is drowned in the brook. Look but in and you shall see him.

JAQUES   There I shall see mine own figure.

ORLANDO   Which I take to be either a fool or a cipher.[2]

270   JAQUES   I'll tarry no longer with you. Farewell, good Signor Love.

ORLANDO   I am glad of your departure. Adieu, good Monsieur Melancholy.   [*Exit* JAQUES.][3]

ROSALIND   I will speak to him like a saucy lackey,° and under   *insolent servant*

275   that habit° play the knave with him. —Do you hear, forester?   *guise; disguise*

ORLANDO   Very well. What would you?

ROSALIND   I pray you, what is't o'clock?

ORLANDO   You should ask me what time o'day. There's no clock in the forest.

280   ROSALIND   Then there is no true lover in the forest, else sigh-ing every minute and groaning every hour would detect° the   *reveal*

lazy foot of time as well as a clock.

ORLANDO   And why not the swift foot of time? Had not that been as proper?

8. Romantic verses were often inscribed on rings sold in shops managed by the wives of goldsmiths; with a pun on "rings" as a slang term for "vaginas."
9. I answer you in the style of the pithy sayings issu-ing from the mouths of figures in painted wall hang-ings (a popular and inexpensive form of interior decoration).
1. See note to 3.2.135.

2. A zero; punning on "figure" (line 268) as meaning "numeral."
3. Editors usually give Jaques an exit here, although none is indicated in F. It would not be out of charac-ter, however, for Jaques to remain onstage in the background during Orlando and Rosalind's exchange (as he does during Touchstone's courting of Audrey in 3.3) and to exit with them at the end of the scene.

285 ROSALIND   By no means, sir. Time travels in divers paces with
      divers persons. I'll tell you who Time ambles withal,° who   *with*
      Time trots withal, who Time gallops withal, and who he
      stands still withal.
ORLANDO   I prithee, who doth he trot withal?
290 ROSALIND   Marry, he trots hard° with a young maid between   *uncomfortably*
      the contract of her marriage and the day it is solemnized. If
      the interim be but a se'nnight,° Time's pace is so hard that it   *week*
      seems the length of seven year.
ORLANDO   Who ambles Time withal?
295 ROSALIND   With a priest that lacks Latin and a rich man that
      hath not the gout: for the one sleeps easily because he can-
      not study, and the other lives merrily because he feels no
      pain—the one lacking the burden of lean and wasteful°   *illness-inducing*
      learning, the other knowing no burden of heavy tedious
300   penury.° These Time ambles withal.   *poverty*
ORLANDO   Who doth he gallop withal?
ROSALIND   With a thief to the gallows, for though he go as
      softly° as foot can fall, he thinks himself too soon there.   *slowly*
ORLANDO   Who stays it still withal?
305 ROSALIND   With lawyers in the vacation, for they sleep
      between term⁴ and term and then they perceive not how
      Time moves.
ORLANDO   Where dwell you, pretty youth?
ROSALIND   With this shepherdess, my sister, here in the
310   skirts° of the forest like fringe upon a petticoat.   *edges*
ORLANDO   Are you native of this place?
ROSALIND   As the coney° that you see dwell where she is   *rabbit*
      kindled.°   *born*
ORLANDO   Your accent is something finer than you could pur-
315   chase° in so removed° a dwelling.   *acquire / remote*
ROSALIND   I have been told so of many. But indeed, an old
      religious uncle of mine taught me to speak, who was in his
      youth an inland man, one that knew courtship° too well, for   *court life; wooing*
      there he fell in love. I have heard him read many lectures
320   against it, and I thank God I am not a woman, to be touched
      with so many giddy offenses as he hath generally taxed their
      whole sex withal.
ORLANDO   Can you remember any of the principal evils that
      he laid to the charge of women?
325 ROSALIND   There were none principal; they were all like one
      another as halfpence are, every one fault seeming mon-
      strous till his fellow-fault came to match it.
ORLANDO   I prithee, recount some of them.
ROSALIND   No, I will not cast away my physic but° on those   *my medicine except*
330   that are sick. There is a man haunts the forest that abuses
      our young plants with carving "Rosalind" on their barks,
      hangs odes upon hawthorns and elegies on brambles—all,
      forsooth, deifying the name of Rosalind. If I could meet that
      fancy-monger,° I would give him some good counsel, for he   *dealer in love*
335   seems to have the quotidian⁵ of love upon him.

---

4. *term:* a limited period of time in which the courts   busy. Vacation came between terms.
were in session and when lawyers were therefore   5. Daily recurring fever said to be a sign of love.

ORLANDO   I am he that is so love-shaked. I pray you tell me
your remedy.

ROSALIND   There is none of my uncle's marks upon you. He
taught me how to know a man in love, in which cage of
340   rushes⁶ I am sure you are not prisoner.

ORLANDO   What were his marks?

ROSALIND   A lean cheek, which you have not; a blue eye⁷ and
sunken, which you have not; an unquestionable° spirit, which   *a taciturn*
you have not; a beard neglected, which you have not—but
345   I pardon you for that, for simply your having in beard° is   *such beard as you have*
a younger brother's revenue.⁸ Then your hose should be
ungartered, your bonnet unbanded,° your sleeve unbut-   *lacking a band*
toned, your shoe untied, and everything about you demonstrating a careless desolation. But you are no such man; you
350   are rather point-device° in your accoutrements, as loving   *extremely precise*
yourself than seeming the lover of any other.

ORLANDO   Fair youth, I would I could make thee believe I love.

ROSALIND   Me believe it? You may as soon make her that you
love believe it, which I warrant she is apter to do than to
355   confess she does: that is one of the points in the which
women still° give the lie to their consciences. But in good   *always*
sooth,° are you he that hangs the verses on the trees,   *truth*
wherein Rosalind is so admired?

ORLANDO   I swear to thee, youth, by the white hand of Rosa
360   lind, I am that he—that unfortunate he.

ROSALIND   But are you so much in love as your rhymes speak?

ORLANDO   Neither rhyme nor reason can express how much.

ROSALIND   Love is merely a madness and, I tell you, deserves
as well a dark house and a whip as madmen do;⁹ and the
365   reason why they° are not so punished and cured is that the   *(lovers)*
lunacy is so ordinary that the whippers are in love too. Yet I
profess curing it by counsel.

ORLANDO   Did you ever cure any so?

ROSALIND   Yes, one—and in this manner: he was to imagine
370   me his love, his mistress, and I set him every day to woo me.
At which time would I, being but a moonish° youth, grieve,   *changeable*
be effeminate,¹ changeable, longing and liking, proud, fan-
tastical,° apish,° shallow, inconstant, full of tears, full of   *capricious / affected*
smiles; for every passion something and for no passion truly
375   anything, as boys and women are for the most part cattle of
this color; would now like him, now loathe him, then enter-
tain him,° then forswear him, now weep for him, then spit   *treat him kindly*
at him; that I drave° my suitor from his mad humor of love   *drove*
to a living humor° of madness, which was to forswear the   *an actual condition*
380   full stream of the world and to live in a nook merely monastic.° *as a hermit*
And thus I cured him, and this way will I take upon me to
wash your liver² as clean as a sound sheep's heart, that there
shall not be one spot of love in't.

---

6. A prison easy to escape from.
7. An eye ringed with dark circles (suggesting insomnia).
8. Younger brothers traditionally received small inheritances; here, suggesting that Orlando's beard is likewise thin or small.
9. Confinement in a dark room and whipping, com-

mon treatments for insanity, were believed to rid the insane of the devils that possessed them.
1. Like a woman; sensual or self-indulgent; a term often used to deride men perceived as excessive in their sexual interest in women.
2. In Renaissance medical theory, the seat of the passions.

ORLANDO   I would not be cured, youth.

385 ROSALIND   I would cure you if you would but call me Rosalind
and come every day to my cot° and woo me.   *cottage*

ORLANDO   Now, by the faith of my love, I will. Tell me where
it is.

ROSALIND   Go with me to it and I'll show it you, and by the way
390 you shall tell me where in the forest you live. Will you go?

ORLANDO   With all my heart, good youth.

ROSALIND   Nay, you must call me Rosalind. —Come, sister,
will you go?   *Exeunt.*

3.3
Enter CLOWN [*and*] AUDREY; *and* JAQUES [*apart*].

CLOWN   Come apace, good Audrey. I will fetch up your goats,
Audrey. And how, Audrey—am I the man yet? Doth my simple
feature° content you?   *appearance*

AUDREY   Your features! Lord warrant° us, what features?   *defend*

5 CLOWN   I am here with thee and thy goats as the most capri-
cious° poet, honest Ovid, was among the Goths.[1]   *witty; lascivious*

JAQUES [*aside*]   Oh, knowledge ill-inhabited—worse than Jove
in a thatched house![2]

CLOWN   When a man's verses cannot be understood nor a
10 man's good wit seconded with° the forward child under-   *supported by*
standing, it strikes a man more dead than a great reckoning°   *tavern bill*
in a little room.[3] Truly, I would the gods had made thee
poetical.

AUDREY   I do not know what "poetical" is. Is it honest in deed
15 and word? Is it a true thing?

CLOWN   No, truly—for the truest poetry is the most feigning°   *imaginative; false*
and lovers are given to poetry; and what they swear in poetry
may be said, as lovers, they do feign.

AUDREY   Do you wish then that the gods had made me
20 poetical?

CLOWN   I do, truly. For thou swear'st to me thou art honest.°   *chaste*
Now if thou wert a poet I might have some hope thou didst
feign.

AUDREY   Would you not have me honest?

25 CLOWN   No, truly, unless thou wert hard-favored;° for honesty   *ugly*
coupled to beauty is to have honey a sauce to sugar.

JAQUES [*aside*]   A material° fool!   *full of matter or sense*

AUDREY   Well, I am not fair, and therefore I pray the gods
make me honest.

30 CLOWN   Truly, and to cast away honesty upon a foul slut were
to put good meat into an unclean dish.[4]

AUDREY   I am not a slut, though I thank the gods I am foul.[5]

CLOWN   Well, praised be the gods for thy foulness—sluttishness
may come hereafter. But be it as it may be, I will marry thee;

3.3
1. Punning on "goats / Goths," which were similarly
pronounced, and referring to the Roman poet's exile
among the Goths.
2. In *Metamorphoses* 8, Ovid tells how the king of
the gods was given shelter for a time in the humble
dwelling of Philemon and Baucis.
3. These lines have been taken to refer to the death

in 1593 of Christopher Marlowe, a contemporary
playwright, in a quarrel in a tavern over a bill.
4. The term "slut" was used to describe a woman of
dirty or untidy habits and appearance, as well as one
whose character and behavior were considered loose.
5. Ugly. Audrey apparently takes "foul" as a term of
praise.

35 and to that end I have been with Sir Oliver Martext, the
vicar of the next village, who hath promised to meet me in
this place of the forest and to couple us.

JAQUES [*aside*]   I would fain° see this meeting.   *gladly*

AUDREY   Well, the gods give us joy!

40 CLOWN   Amen. A man may, if he were of a fearful heart, stag-
ger° in this attempt: for here we have no temple but the wood,   *hesitate*
no assembly but horn-beasts.[6] But what though? Courage!
As horns are odious, they are necessary. It is said many a
man knows no end of his goods:[7] right—many a man has

45 good horns and knows no end of them. Well, that is the
dowry of his wife: 'tis none of his own getting.[8] Horns? Even
so. Poor men alone? No, no—the noblest deer hath them as
huge as the rascal.° Is the single man therefore blessed? No,   *young or lean deer*
as a walled town is more worthier than a village, so is the

50 forehead of a married man more honorable than the bare
brow of a bachelor. And by how much defense° is better   *skill in self-defense*
than no skill, by so much is a horn more precious than to
want.°   *to lack (one)*

      Enter SIR OLIVER MARTEXT.

Here comes Sir Oliver. —Sir Oliver Martext, you are well

55 met. Will you dispatch us here under this tree, or shall we
go with you to your chapel?

SIR OLIVER   Is there none here to give the woman?

CLOWN   I will not take her on gift of any man.

SIR OLIVER   Truly, she must be given, or the marriage is not

60 lawful.

JAQUES [*coming forward*]   Proceed, proceed. I'll give her.

CLOWN   Good even, good Master What-ye-call't. How do you,
sir? You are very well met. God 'ield you for your last com-
pany.[9] I am very glad to see you. Even a toy° in hand here,   *trifling matter*

65 sir. Nay, pray be covered.°   *replace your hat*

JAQUES   Will you be married, motley?

CLOWN   As the ox hath his bow,° sir, the horse his curb,[1] and   *yoke*
the falcon her bells,[2] so man hath his desires; and as pigeons
bill,° so wedlock would be nibbling.   *rub bill to bill*

70 JAQUES   And will you, being a man of your breeding, be married under a bush like a beggar? Get you to church and have
a good priest that can tell you what marriage is; this fellow
will but join you together as they join wainscot.° Then one   *wood paneling*
of you will prove a shrunk panel and, like green timber,

75 warp,° warp.   *go wrong; shrink*

CLOWN   I am not in the mind but° I were better to be married   *not sure but that*
of° him than of another; for he is not like to marry me well,   *by*
and not being well married it will be a good excuse for me
hereafter to leave my wife.

---

6. Horned beasts such as deer, goats, and the like
that inhabited the forest, with an allusion to the
horns of the cuckolded husband.
7. A proverbial expression suggesting a man so
wealthy he can't count all his money.
8. *'tis . . . getting:* he is not responsible for the horns;
he is not responsible for conceiving his children
(since his wife has been sexually unfaithful).

9. God yield you (a salutation meaning "May God
reward you") for your recent companionship.
1. A bit placed in the horse's mouth to control its
movements.
2. Bells attached to a falcon's legs before releasing
it for the hunt so that it might be easily reclaimed
afterward.

80 JAQUES Go thou with me
     And let me counsel thee.
    CLOWN Come, sweet Audrey—
     We must be married,° or we must live in bawdry.°   *(properly wed) / in sin*
     Farewell, good Master Oliver—not
85   "O sweet Oliver,
                  O brave Oliver,
                 Leave me not behind thee!"[3]
    but
                 Wind° away,   *Go*
90   Begone I say.
               I will not to wedding with thee.
    SIR OLIVER 'Tis no matter. Ne'er a fantastical knave of them
    all shall flout me out of my calling.   *Exeunt.*

3.4
Enter ROSALIND [*as Ganymede*] *and* CELIA [*as Aliena*].

    ROSALIND Never talk to me—I will weep!
    CELIA Do, I prithee, but yet have the grace to consider that
    tears do not become a man.
    ROSALIND But have I not cause to weep?
5   CELIA As good cause as one would desire; therefore, weep.
    ROSALIND His very hair is of the dissembling color.[1]
    CELIA Something° browner than Judas's; marry, his kisses are   *Somewhat*
    Judas's own children.
    ROSALIND I'faith, his hair is of a good color.
10 CELIA An excellent color: your chestnut was ever the only
    color.
    ROSALIND And his kissing is as full of sanctity as the touch of
    holy bread.[2]
    CELIA He hath bought a pair of cast° lips of Diana.[3] A nun of   *cast-off; sculpted*
15 winter's sisterhood° kisses not more religiously: the very ice   *devoted to coldness*
    of chastity is in them.
    ROSALIND But why did he swear he would come this morning
    and comes not?
    CELIA Nay, certainly there is no truth in him.
20 ROSALIND Do you think so?
    CELIA Yes, I think he is not a pickpurse nor a horse-stealer,
    but for his verity° in love—I do think him as concave° as a   *truthfulness / hollow*
    covered goblet or a worm-eaten nut.
    ROSALIND Not true in love?
25 CELIA Yes, when he is in, but I think he is not in.
    ROSALIND You have heard him swear downright he was.
    CELIA Was is not is. Besides, the oath of lover is no stronger
    than the word of a tapster:° they are both the confirmer of   *tavern-keeper*
    false reckonings. He attends° here in the forest on the Duke   *waits*
30 your father.
    ROSALIND I met the Duke yesterday and had much question°   *conversation*
    with him. He asked me of what parentage I was; I told him

---

3. Lines from a popular Elizabethan ballad.
3.4
1. Alluding to the tradition that Judas, the disciple
who betrayed Jesus, had red hair.

2. Referring to bread blessed after the Eucharist
during Christian religious services and distributed to
those who did not take Communion.
3. The goddess of chastity. See note to 3.2.2.

of as good as he, so he laughed and let me go. But what talk
we of fathers when there is such a man as Orlando?

35 CELIA   Oh, that's a brave° man: he writes brave verses, speaks   *splendid*
brave words, swears brave oaths, and breaks them bravely—
quite traverse,⁴ athwart the heart of his lover, as a puny°   *an unskilled*
tilter that spurs his horse but° on one side breaks his staff   *only*
like a noble goose.° But all's brave that youth mounts and   *fool*
40 folly guides. Who comes here?

Enter CORIN.

CORIN   Mistress and master, you have oft enquired
After the shepherd that complained of love,
Who you saw sitting by me on the turf,
Praising the proud disdainful shepherdess
That was his mistress.

45 CELIA   Well, and what of him?
CORIN   If you will see a pageant truly played
Between the pale complexion of true love
And the red glow of scorn and proud disdain,⁵
Go hence a little and I shall conduct you,
If you will mark° it.   *observe*

50 ROSALIND   Oh, come, let us remove.
The sight of lovers feedeth those in love.
Bring us to this sight and you shall say
I'll prove a busy actor in their play.   *Exeunt.*

3.5

Enter SILVIUS *and* PHOEBE.

SILVIUS   Sweet Phoebe, do not scorn me; do not, Phoebe.
Say that you love me not, but say not so
In bitterness. The common executioner,
Whose heart th'accustomed sight of death makes hard,
5 Falls not° the ax upon the humbled neck   *Does not let fall*
But first begs° pardon. Will you sterner be   *Without first begging*
Than he that dies and lives by bloody drops?

Enter ROSALIND [*as Ganymede*], CELIA [*as Aliena*],
and CORIN.

PHOEBE   I would not be thy executioner.
I fly thee, for I would not injure thee.
10 Thou tell'st me there is murder in mine eye.
'Tis pretty, sure, and very probable
That eyes, that are the frail'st and softest things,
Who shut their coward gates on atomies,°   *dust motes*
Should be called tyrants, butchers, murderers.
15 Now I do frown on thee with all my heart,
And if mine eyes can wound, now let them kill thee.
Now counterfeit to swoon; why now, fall down;
Or if thou canst not, oh, for shame, for shame,
Lie not to say mine eyes are murderers!
20 Now show the wound mine eye hath made in thee.
Scratch thee but with a pin and there remains
Some scar of it; lean upon a rush,

4. Crossways. The term from jousting was used to
designate the dishonorable practice of breaking one's
lance across, rather than directly against, an opponent's shield.

5. Referring to the paleness of Silvius, the true lover,
and the red cheeks of the disdainful Phoebe.

The cicatrice and capable impressure[1]
Thy palm some moment keeps. But now mine eyes,
25 Which I have darted at thee, hurt thee not;
Nor, I am sure, there is no force in eyes
That can do hurt.

SILVIUS   O dear Phoebe,
If ever—as that ever may be near—
You meet in some fresh cheek the power of fancy,°   *love*
30 Then shall you know the wounds invisible
That love's keen arrows make.

PHOEBE   But till that time
Come not thou near me. And when that time comes,
Afflict me with thy mocks; pity me not,
As till that time I shall not pity thee.

35 ROSALIND   And why, I pray you? Who might be your mother
That you insult, exult, and all at once°   *all in one breath*
Over the wretched? What though you have no beauty—
As, by my faith, I see no more in you
Than without candle may go dark to bed[2]—
40 Must you be therefore proud and pitiless?
Why, what means this? Why do you look on me?
I see no more in you than in the ordinary°   *common run*
Of nature's sale-work.° —'Ods my little life,[3]   *ready-made goods*
I think she means to tangle° my eyes too!   *entrap*
45 —No, faith, proud mistress, hope not after it;
'Tis not your inky brows, your black silk hair,
Your bugle° eyeballs, nor your cheek of cream   *like black glass beads*
That can entame my spirits to your worship.°   *the worship of you*
—You foolish shepherd, wherefore do you follow her
50 Like foggy south,° puffing with wind and rain?[4]   *south wind*
You are a thousand times a properer° man   *more attractive*
Than she a woman. 'Tis such fools as you
That makes the world full of ill-favored° children.   *ugly*
'Tis not her glass° but you that flatters her,   *mirror*
55 And out of you° she sees herself more proper   *from you (as mirror)*
Than any of her lineaments can show her.
—But mistress, know yourself: down on your knees
And thank heaven, fasting, for a good man's love.
For I must tell you friendly in your ear,
60 Sell when you can; you are not for all markets.
Cry the man mercy,° love him, take his offer.   *Beg his pardon*
Foul is most foul, being foul, to be a scoffer.[5]
—So take her to thee, shepherd. Fare you well.

PHOEBE   Sweet youth, I pray you, chide a year together.°   *without interruption*
65 I had rather hear you chide than this man woo.

ROSALIND   He's fallen in love with your foulness [*to* SILVIUS]
and she'll fall in love with my anger. If it be so, as fast as she
answers thee with frowning looks, I'll sauce° her with bitter   *sharply rebuke*
words. [*to* PHOEBE] Why look you so upon me?

70 PHOEBE   For no ill will I bear you.

3.5
1. The scarlike mark and the impression that the
skin receives.
2. *I see . . . bed:* I see you have not enough beauty to
light your way to bed without a candle.

3. An abbreviated version of the oath "God save my
life."
4. That is, with sighs and tears.
5. The ugly seem most ugly when they are abusive.

ROSALIND   I pray you, do not fall in love with me,
 For I am falser than vows made in wine.°   *when drinking*
 Besides, I like you not. If you will know my house,
 'Tis at the tuft of olives,° here hard by.   *olive trees*
75 Will you go, sister? Shepherd, ply her hard.°   *assail her vigorously*
 Come, sister. —Shepherdess, look on him better
 And be not proud: though all the world could see
 None could be so abused in sight as he.
 —Come, to our flock.
     Exeunt [ROSALIND, CELIA, *and* CORIN].[6]
80 PHOEBE   Dead shepherd,[7] now I find thy saw of might:° *your saying powerful*
 "Who ever loved that loved not at first sight?"
SILVIUS   Sweet Phoebe—
PHOEBE   Ha? What say'st thou, Silvius?
SILVIUS   Sweet Phoebe, pity me.
PHOEBE   Why, I am sorry for thee, gentle Silvius.
85 SILVIUS   Wherever sorrow is, relief would be.
 If you do sorrow at my grief in love,
 By giving love your sorrow and my grief
 Were both exterminèd.°   *Would both be ended*
PHOEBE   Thou hast my love—is not that neighborly?[8]
SILVIUS   I would have you.
90 PHOEBE   Why, that were covetousness.[9]
 Silvius, the time was that I hated thee,
 And yet it is not° that I bear thee love.   *it has not yet happened*
 But since that thou canst talk of love so well,
 Thy company, which erst° was irksome to me,   *formerly*
95 I will endure, and I'll employ thee too.
 But do not look for further recompense
 Than thine own gladness that thou art employed.
SILVIUS   So holy and so perfect is my love,
 And I in such a poverty of grace,[1]
100 That I shall think it a most plenteous crop
 To glean the broken ears° after the man   *(of corn)*
 That the main harvest reaps. Loose now and then
 A scattered° smile, and that I'll live upon.   *stray*
PHOEBE   Know'st thou the youth that spoke to me erewhile?
105 SILVIUS   Not very well, but I have met him oft,
 And he hath bought the cottage and the bounds°   *pastures*
 That the old Carlot once was master of.
PHOEBE   Think not I love him though I ask for him.
 'Tis but a peevish boy, yet he talks well.
110 But what care I for words? Yet words do well
 When he that speaks them pleases those that hear.
 It is a pretty youth—not very pretty—
 But sure, he's proud, and yet his pride becomes him.
 He'll make a proper° man. The best thing in him   *handsome*
115 Is his complexion; and faster than his tongue

---

6. F marks a single exit for Rosalind here, but it is
unlikely that Celia and Corin remain.
7. Referring to Christopher Marlowe, poet and playwright who died in 1593. Line 81 is taken from his
poem *Hero and Leander.*
8. With a reference to Romans 13:9: "Thou shalt love
thy neighbor as thyself."

9. With a reference to Exodus 20:17: "Thou shalt not
covet thy neighbor's house, thou shalt not covet thy
neighbor's wife, nor his manservant, nor his maid
servant, nor his ox, nor his ass, nor any thing that is
thy neighbor's."
1. And I so lacking in (your) favor.

Did make offense, his eye did heal it up.
He is not very tall, yet for his years he's tall.
His leg is but so-so, and yet 'tis well.
There was a pretty redness in his lip—
120 A little riper and more lusty red
Than that mixed in his cheek; 'twas just the difference
Betwixt the constant red and mingled damask.[2]
There be some women, Silvius, had they marked him
In parcels° as I did, would have gone near   *Item by item*
125 To fall in love with him. But for my part,
I love him not, nor hate him not, and yet
Have more cause to hate him than to love him.
For what had he to do to chide at me?
He said mine eyes were black and my hair black
130 And, now I am remembered, scorned at me.
I marvel why I answered not again.
But that's all one; omittance is no quittance.[3]
I'll write to him a very taunting letter,
And thou shalt bear it. Wilt thou, Silvius?
SILVIUS   Phoebe, with all my heart.
135 PHOEBE   I'll write it straight.°   *immediately*
The matter's in my head and in my heart.
I will be bitter with him and passing° short.   *extremely*
Go with me, Silvius.   *Exeunt.*

4.1

Enter ROSALIND [*as Ganymede*], CELIA [*as Aliena*],
and JAQUES.

JAQUES   I prithee, pretty youth, let me be better acquainted
with thee.
ROSALIND   They say you are a melancholy fellow.
JAQUES   I am so: I do love it better than laughing.
5 ROSALIND   Those that are in extremity of either are abominable fellows and betray themselves to every modern censure
worse than drunkards.
JAQUES   Why, 'tis good to be sad° and say nothing.   *serious*
ROSALIND   Why, then 'tis good to be a post.
10 JAQUES   I have neither the scholar's melancholy, which is
emulation;° nor the musician's, which is fantastical;° nor the   *envy / overly fanciful*
courtier's, which is proud; nor the soldier's, which is ambi-
tious; nor the lawyer's, which is politic; nor the lady's, which
is nice;° nor the lover's, which is all these; but it is a melan-   *fastidious*
15 choly of mine own, compounded of many simples,° extracted   *ingredients*
from many objects,° and indeed the sundry contemplation   *sights*
of my travels,[1] in° which by often° rumination wraps me in a   *upon / frequent*
most humorous° sadness.   *moody*
ROSALIND   A traveler? By my faith, you have great reason to
20 be sad! I fear you have sold your own lands to see other
men's; then to have seen much and to have nothing is to
have rich eyes and poor hands.

---

2. *constant . . . damask:* uniform red and a mixture
of red and white characteristic of certain kinds of
roses.
3. A proverbial expression meaning that a debt is not

canceled simply because one fails ("omits") to exact it.
4.1
1. The various thoughts arising during my travels,
with a pun on "travails," meaning "labors."

JAQUES   Yes, I have gained my experience.
    Enter ORLANDO.
ROSALIND   And your experience makes you sad. I had rather
25   have a fool to make me merry than experience to make me
    sad—and to travel for it too!
ORLANDO   Good day and happiness, dear Rosalind.
JAQUES   Nay then, God b'wi' you an° you talk in blank verse.   *if*
ROSALIND   Farewell, Monsieur Traveler. Look you lisp² and
30   wear strange° suits, disable° all the benefits of your own   *foreign / disparage*
    country, be out of love with your nativity,° and almost chide   *birthplace*
    God for making you that countenance you are; or I will scarce
    think you have swum in a gundello.³   [*Exit* JAQUES.]⁴
    Why, how now, Orlando, where have you been all this while?
35   You, a lover? An you serve me such another trick, never
    come in my sight more.
ORLANDO   My fair Rosalind, I come within an hour of my
    promise.
ROSALIND   Break an hour's promise in love? He that will
40   divide a minute into a thousand parts and break but a part
    of the thousand part of a minute in the affairs of love, it may
    be said of him that Cupid hath clapped him o'th' shoulder,
    but I'll warrant him heart-whole.⁵
ORLANDO   Pardon me, dear Rosalind.
45   ROSALIND   Nay, an you be so tardy, come no more in my sight.
    I had as lief° be wooed of a snail.   *as gladly*
ORLANDO   Of a snail?
ROSALIND   Ay, of a snail: for though he comes slowly, he car-
    ries his house on his head—a better jointure,° I think, than   *marriage settlement*
50   you make a woman. Besides, he brings his destiny with him.
ORLANDO   What's that?
ROSALIND   Why, horns, which such as you are fain to be
    beholden to your wives for.⁶ But he comes armed in his for-
    tune⁷ and prevents the slander of his wife.
55   ORLANDO   Virtue is no horn-maker, and my Rosalind is
    virtuous.
ROSALIND   And I am your Rosalind.
CELIA   It pleases him to call you so. But he hath a Rosalind of
    a better leer° than you.   *more attractive*
60   ROSALIND   Come—woo me, woo me, for now I am in a holiday
    humor and like enough to consent. What would you say to
    me now an I were your very, very Rosalind?
ORLANDO   I would kiss before I spoke.
ROSALIND   Nay, you were better speak first, and when you
65   were graveled° for lack of matter, you might take occasion to   *at a loss*
    kiss. Very good orators, when they are out,° they will spit;   *speechless*
    and for lovers lacking (God warn° us) matter, the cleanliest   *defend*
    shift° is to kiss.   *cleverest device*
ORLANDO   How if the kiss be denied?

---

2. Speak with an affected (foreign) accent.
3. TEXTUAL COMMENT Ridden in a gondola—that is,
seen Venice, a popular destination for English travelers. See Digital Edition TC 7.
4. F marks no exit for Jaques here, but he and Rosalind have formally parted, and Jaques enters with a

new group of characters at the beginning of 4.2.
5. Cupid has tapped him (as in an arrest) or wounded
him (with his arrow), but I'll guarantee he left his
heart intact.
6. An allusion to the cuckold's horns.
7. Equipped with the insignia of his destined future.

70 ROSALIND Then she puts you to entreaty, and there begins
　　new matter.
　ORLANDO Who could be out, being before his beloved mistress?
　ROSALIND Marry, that should you if I were your mistress, or I
　　should think my honesty ranker than my wit.[8]
75 ORLANDO What, of my suit?[9]
　ROSALIND Not out of your apparel, and yet out of your suit.
　　Am not I your Rosalind?
　ORLANDO I take some joy to say you are because I would be
　　talking of her.
80 ROSALIND Well, in her person, I say I will not have you.
　ORLANDO Then in mine own person, I die.
　ROSALIND No, faith, die by attorney.° The poor world is　　　　　*proxy*
　　almost six thousand years old,[1] and in all this time there was
　　not any man died in his own person, *videlicet*° in a love　　　　*namely*
85　cause. Troilus[2] had his brains dashed out with a Grecian
　　club; yet he did what he could to die before, and he is one of
　　the patterns of love. Leander,[3] he would have lived many a
　　fair year though Hero had turned nun, if it had not been for
　　a hot midsummer night; for, good youth, he went but forth
90　to wash him in the Hellespont and, being taken with the
　　cramp, was drowned, and the foolish chroniclers of that age
　　found° it was Hero of Sestos. But these are all lies: men　　　　*claimed*
　　have died from time to time, and worms have eaten them,
　　but not for love.
95 ORLANDO I would not have my right° Rosalind of this mind,　　　*true*
　　for I protest her frown might kill me.
　ROSALIND By this hand, it will not kill a fly. But come—now
　　I will be your Rosalind in a more coming-on° disposition,　　　*agreeable*
　　and ask me what you will, I will grant it.
100 ORLANDO Then love me, Rosalind.
　ROSALIND Yes, faith, will I—Fridays and Saturdays and all.
　ORLANDO And wilt thou have me?
　ROSALIND Ay, and twenty such.
　ORLANDO What sayest thou?
105 ROSALIND Are you not good?
　ORLANDO I hope so.
　ROSALIND Why, then, can one desire too much of a good thing?
　　—Come, sister, you shall be the priest and marry us.
　　—Give me your hand, Orlando. What do you say, sister?
110 ORLANDO Pray thee, marry us.
　CELIA I cannot say the words.
　ROSALIND You must begin, "Will you, Orlando,"—
　CELIA Go to![4] Will you, Orlando, have to wife this Rosalind?
　ORLANDO I will.
115 ROSALIND Ay, but when?
　ORLANDO Why now, as fast as she can marry us.

---

8. I would think my chastity was fouler than my
intelligence; with a pun on "out" (lines 66, 72) as
meaning "not permitted sexual entrance."
9. My petition. Orlando asks if he will be at a loss for
words ("out") in furthering his courtship ("suit").
Rosalind puns on "suit" as meaning "clothing."
1. Elizabethan divines generally dated the world's

creation somewhere around 4000 B.C.E.
2. The forsaken Trojan lover of Cressida, killed by
the Greek warrior Achilles.
3. In Greek mythology, the lover of Hero; he swam
the Hellespont nightly to visit her and was drowned.
4. An expression of mild impatience.

ROSALIND   Then you must say, "I take thee, Rosalind, for wife."

ORLANDO   I take thee, Rosalind, for wife.[5]

ROSALIND   I might ask you for your commission,° but I do take   *authority*
120 thee, Orlando, for my husband. There's a girl goes before°   *who anticipates*
the priest, and certainly a woman's thought runs before her
actions.

ORLANDO   So do all thoughts: they are winged.

ROSALIND   Now tell me how long you would have her after
125 you have possessed her.

ORLANDO   Forever and a day.

ROSALIND   Say "a day" without the "ever." No, no, Orlando: men
are April when they woo, December when they wed; maids are
May when they are maids, but the sky changes when they are
130 wives. I will be more jealous of thee than a Barbary cock-
pigeon[6] over his hen, more clamorous than a parrot against°   *in expectation of*
rain, more newfangled° than an ape, more giddy in my desires   *in love with novelty*
than a monkey. I will weep for nothing, like Diana in the
fountain,[7] and I will do that when you are disposed to be
135 merry. I will laugh like a hyen,° and that when thou art   *hyena*
inclined to sleep.

ORLANDO   But will my Rosalind do so?

ROSALIND   By my life, she will do as I do.

ORLANDO   Oh, but she is wise.

140 ROSALIND   Or else she could not have the wit to do this: the
wiser the waywarder. Make° the doors upon a woman's wit   *Close*
and it will out at the casement;° shut that and 'twill out at   *window frame*
the keyhole; stop that, 'twill fly with the smoke out at the
chimney.

145 ORLANDO   A man that had a wife with such a wit, he might
say, "Wit, whither wilt?"[8]

ROSALIND   Nay, you might keep that check° for it, till you met   *rebuke*
your wife's wit going to your neighbor's bed.

ORLANDO   And what wit could wit have to excuse that?

150 ROSALIND   Marry, to say she came to seek you there. You shall
never take her without her answer unless you take her without her tongue. Oh, that woman that cannot make her fault
her husband's occasion,[9] let her never nurse her child herself, for she will breed it like a fool.

155 ORLANDO   For these two hours, Rosalind, I will leave thee.

ROSALIND   Alas, dear love, I cannot lack thee two hours!

ORLANDO   I must attend the Duke at dinner. By two o'clock I
will be with thee again.

ROSALIND   Ay, go your ways, go your ways! I knew what you
160 would prove:° my friends told me as much, and I thought no   *turn out to be*
less. That flattering tongue of yours won me. 'Tis but one
cast away° and so, come, death! Two o'clock is your hour?   *one lover jilted*

ORLANDO   Ay, sweet Rosalind.

5. Performance Comment Some directors have
Orlando and Rosalind kiss here to seal their compact. Many productions suggest either that Orlando
recognizes Rosalind or that he experiences a same-sex
attraction to Ganymede. See Digital Edition PC 2.
6. An ornamental bird, traditionally an emblem of
jealousy. It was introduced into Europe from Asia by
Turks, whom Elizabethans associated with North
Africa's Barbary Coast. Turkish husbands were imag-

ined by the English to be excessively vigilant about
the sexual fidelity of their wives.
7. Referring to the figures of the goddess Diana used
as centerpieces for ornamental fountains in London
and elsewhere.
8. Wit, where would you go? A catchphrase
addressed to one who talks too much.
9. Who cannot make her error a means of putting
her husband in the wrong.

ROSALIND   By my troth, and in good earnest, and so God
165   mend me, and by all pretty oaths that are not dangerous—if
you break one jot of your promise or come one minute
behind your hour, I will think you the most pathetical°   *pathetic*
break-promise, and the most hollow lover, and the most
unworthy of her you call Rosalind that may be chosen out of
170   the gross° band of the unfaithful. Therefore beware my cen-   *entire*
sure and keep your promise!

ORLANDO   With no less religion° than if thou wert indeed my   *faith*
Rosalind. So, adieu.

ROSALIND   Well, Time is the old justice that examines all such
175   offenders, and let Time try.° Adieu.   *Exit* [ORLANDO].   *determine*

CELIA   You have simply misused° our sex in your love-prate: we   *completely slandered*
must have your doublet and hose plucked over your head and
show the world what the bird hath done to her own nest.

ROSALIND   O coz, coz, coz, my pretty little coz, that thou didst
180   know how many fathom deep I am in love! But it cannot be
sounded: my affection hath an unknown bottom, like the
Bay of Portugal.

CELIA   Or rather bottomless, that° as fast as you pour affec-   *so that*
tion in, it runs out.

185   ROSALIND   No, that same wicked bastard of Venus¹ that was
begot of thought, conceived of spleen,° and born of   *caprice*
madness—that blind rascally boy that abuses° everyone's   *deceives*
eyes because his own are out—let him be judge how deep I
am in love. I'll tell thee, Aliena, I cannot be out of the sight
190   of Orlando. I'll go find a shadow° and sigh till he come.   *shady place*

CELIA   And I'll sleep.   *Exeunt.*

4.2

Enter JAQUES *and* LORDS [*dressed as*] *foresters.*¹

JAQUES   Which is he that killed the deer?

FIRST LORD   Sir, it was I.

JAQUES   Let's present him to the Duke like a Roman conqueror.
And it would do well to set the deer's horns upon his head for
5   a branch° of victory. Have you no song, forester, for this   *wreath*
purpose?

SECOND LORD   Yes, sir.

JAQUES   Sing it. 'Tis no matter how it be in tune, so it make
noise enough.

Music. Song.

10   SECOND LORD [*sings*]²   What shall he have that killed the deer?
His leather skin and horns to wear.
Then sing him home. The rest shall bear°   *carry; sing*
This burden:°   *(the deer); refrain*
Take thou no scorn° to wear the horn.   *Do not disdain*
15   It was a crest³ e'er thou wast born.
Thy father's father wore it,
And thy father bore it.

---

1. Cupid, the son of Venus by her lover Mercury, not
by her husband, Vulcan.
4.2
1. F's stage direction—"*Enter Jaques and Lords,
Foresters*"—leaves ambiguous whether Jaques and

the lords are dressed as foresters or are accompanied
by them.
2. F does not assign this song to anyone. The stage
direction reads: "*Music. Song.*"
3. A coat of arms; a head ornament.

The horn, the horn, the lusty horn
Is not a thing to laugh to scorn.

Exeunt.

4.3

Enter ROSALIND [*as Ganymede*] *and* CELIA [*as Aliena*].

ROSALIND   How say you now, is it not past two o'clock? And
here much Orlando!

CELIA   I warrant you, with pure love and troubled brain, he
hath ta'en his bow and arrows and is gone forth to sleep.

Enter SILVIUS [*with a letter*].

5   Look who comes here.

SILVIUS   My errand is to you, fair youth.
My gentle Phoebe did bid me give you this.
I know not the contents, but as I guess
By the stern brow and waspish action

10   Which she did use as she was writing of it,
It bears an angry tenor. Pardon me.
I am but as a guiltless messenger.

ROSALIND [*reads*]   Patience herself would startle at this letter
And play the swaggerer.[1] Bear this, bear all!

15   She says I am not fair, that I lack manners;
She calls me proud and that she could not love me,
Were man as rare as phoenix.[2] 'Od's°° my will,   *God's*
Her love is not the hare that I do hunt!
Why writes she so to me? Well, shepherd, well—

20   This is a letter of your own device.

SILVIUS   No, I protest I know not the contents.
Phoebe did write it.

ROSALIND   Come, come—you are a fool
And turned° into the extremity of love.   *brought*
I saw her hand. She has a leathern hand,

25   A freestone°-colored hand. I verily did think   *yellow-brown limestone*
That her old gloves were on, but 'twas her hands.
She has a housewife's hand. But that's no matter.
I say she never did invent this letter;
This is a man's invention and his hand.

30   SILVIUS   Sure, it is hers.

ROSALIND   Why, 'tis a boisterous and a cruel style—
A style for challengers. Why, she defies me
Like Turk to Christian.[3] Women's gentle brain
Could not drop forth such giant rude invention,

35   Such Ethiope[4] words, blacker in their effect
Than in their countenance! Will you hear the letter?

SILVIUS   So please you, for I never heard it yet—
Yet heard too much of Phoebe's cruelty.

ROSALIND   She "Phoebes" me.[5] Mark how the tyrant writes:

4.3
1. *Patience . . . swaggerer*: even patience would be surprised by the contents of this letter and respond with defiance.
2. A legendary bird of Arabia, supposedly unique, which lived five hundred years, died in flames, and was reborn from its own ashes.
3. Alluding to medieval plays in which Turks and

Christians appeared as bitter enemies or to a common Elizabethan perception of the Turk as an enemy to the Christian countries of western Europe.
4. Ethiopian. In Elizabethan racial discourse, the term signified blackness and evil.
5. She addresses me as Phoebe would—that is, in a disdainful manner.

40   (*Reads.*) "Art thou god to shepherd turned,
                      That a maiden's heart hath burned?"
        —Can a woman rail thus?
        SILVIUS   Call you this railing?
        ROSALIND (*reads*) "Why, thy godhead laid apart,°   set aside
45   Warr'st thou with a woman's heart?"
        —Did you ever hear such railing?
                      "Whiles the eye of man did woo me,
                      That could do no vengeance° to me."   harm
        —Meaning me a beast.
50   "If the scorn of your bright eyne°   eyes
                      Have power to raise such love in mine,
                      Alack, in me what strange effect
                      Would they work in mild aspect?°   if they looked kindly
                      Whiles you chid me I did love:
55   How then might your prayers move?
                      He that brings this love to thee
                      Little knows this love in me;
                      And by him seal up thy mind,⁶
                      Whether that thy youth and kind°   nature
60   Will the faithful offer take
                      Of me and all that I can make.°   offer you
                      Or else by him my love deny,
                      And then I'll study how to die."
        SILVIUS   Call you this chiding?
65   CELIA   Alas, poor shepherd!
        ROSALIND   Do you pity him? No, he deserves no pity. —Wilt
          thou love such a woman? What, to make thee an instrument
          and play false strains upon thee? Not to be endured! Well,
          go your way to her, for I see love hath made thee a tame
70   snake, and say this to her: that if she love me, I charge her to
          love thee; if she will not, I will never have her unless thou
          entreat for her. If you be a true lover, hence and not a word,
          for here comes more company.   *Exit* SILVIUS.
                    Enter OLIVER.
        OLIVER   Good morrow, fair ones. Pray you, if you know,
75   Where in the purlieus° of this forest stands   outskirts
        A sheepcote fenced about with olive trees?
        CELIA   West of this place, down in the neighbor bottom:°   next valley
        The rank of osiers° by the murmuring stream,   row of willows
        Left on your right hand, brings you to the place.
80   But at this hour the house doth keep itself:
        There's none within.
        OLIVER   If that an eye may profit by a tongue,
        Then should I know you by description,
        Such garments and such years: "The boy is fair,
85   Of female favor,° and bestows° himself   appearance / behaves
        Like a ripe° sister; the woman low°   mature / short
        And browner than her brother." Are not you
        The owner of the house I did inquire for?
        CELIA   It is no boast, being asked, to say we are.
90   OLIVER   Orlando doth commend him to you both,

---

6. And by means of him (Silvius), send your thoughts to me (in a letter).

And to that youth he calls his Rosalind
He sends this bloody napkin.° Are you he?   *handkerchief*
ROSALIND   I am. What must we understand by this?
OLIVER   Some of my shame, if you will know of me
95 What man I am, and how and why and where
This handkerchief was stained.
CELIA   I pray you, tell it.
OLIVER   When last the young Orlando parted from you
He left a promise to return again
Within an hour; and pacing through the forest,
100 Chewing the food of sweet and bitter fancy,
Lo, what befell: he threw his eye aside,
And mark what object° did present itself.   *spectacle*
Under an old oak, whose boughs were mossed with age
And high top bald with dry antiquity,
105 A wretched, ragged man, o'ergrown with hair,
Lay sleeping on his back. About his neck
A green and gilded snake had wreathed itself,
Who with her head, nimble in threats, approached
The opening of his mouth. But suddenly,
110 Seeing Orlando, it unlinked° itself   *uncoiled*
And with indented° glides did slip away   *undulating*
Into a bush, under which bush's shade
A lioness with udders all drawn dry[7]
Lay couching, head on ground, with catlike watch
115 When that° the sleeping man should stir. For 'tis   *In readiness for when*
The royal disposition of that beast
To prey on nothing that doth seem as dead.
This seen, Orlando did approach the man,
And found it was his brother, his elder brother.
120 CELIA   Oh, I have heard him speak of that same brother,
And he did render him the most unnatural
That lived amongst men.
OLIVER   And well he might so do,
For well I know he was unnatural.
ROSALIND   But to Orlando: did he leave him there,
125 Food to the sucked and hungry lioness?
OLIVER   Twice did he turn his back and purposed so;
But kindness, nobler ever than revenge,
And nature, stronger than his just occasion,°   *fair opportunity*
Made him give battle to the lioness,
130 Who quickly fell before him, in which hurtling,°   *conflict*
From miserable slumber I awaked.
CELIA   Are you his brother?
ROSALIND   Was't you he rescued?
CELIA   Was't you that did so oft contrive° to kill him?   *plot*
OLIVER   'Twas I, but 'tis not I: I do not shame
135 To tell you what I was, since my conversion
So sweetly tastes, being the thing I am.
ROSALIND   But for° the bloody napkin?   *What about*
OLIVER   By and by.

---

7. Having been nursed dry, the lion would be ferociously hungry.

When from the first to last, betwixt us two,
Tears our recountments° had most kindly bathed—   *narratives*
140 As how I came into that desert place—
In brief, he led me to the gentle Duke,
Who gave me fresh array and entertainment,°   *hospitality*
Committing me unto my brother's love,
Who led me instantly unto his cave,
145 There stripped himself; and here upon his arm
The lioness had torn some flesh away,
Which all this while had bled; and now he fainted
And cried in fainting upon Rosalind.
Brief, I recovered° him, bound up his wound;   *revived*
150 And after some small space, being strong at heart,
He sent me hither, stranger as I am,
To tell this story, that you might excuse
His broken promise, and to give this napkin,
Dyed in this blood, unto the shepherd youth
155 That he in sport doth call his Rosalind.
          [ROSALIND *faints.*]
CELIA   Why, how now, Ganymede? Sweet Ganymede!
OLIVER   Many will swoon when they do look on blood.
CELIA   There is more in it. —Cousin Ganymede!
OLIVER   Look, he recovers.
ROSALIND   I would I were at home.
160 CELIA   We'll lead you thither.
          —I pray you, will you take him by the arm?
OLIVER   Be of good cheer, youth. You a man?
You lack a man's heart.
ROSALIND   I do so, I confess it.
Ah, sirrah, a body would think this was well counterfeited!
165 I pray you, tell your brother how well I counterfeited.
Heigh-ho!
OLIVER   This was not counterfeit: there is too great testimony
in your complexion that it was a passion of earnest.°   *a genuine fit*
ROSALIND   Counterfeit, I assure you.
170 OLIVER   Well, then, take a good heart and counterfeit to be a
man.
ROSALIND   So I do, but i'faith, I should have been a woman by
right.
CELIA   Come, you look paler and paler. Pray you, draw home-
175 wards. —Good sir, go with us.
OLIVER   That will I, for I must bear answer back
How you excuse my brother, Rosalind.
ROSALIND   I shall devise something; but I pray you, commend
my counterfeiting to him. Will you go?   *Exeunt.*

5.1

Enter CLOWN *and* AUDREY.
CLOWN   We shall find a time, Audrey. Patience, gentle Audrey!
AUDREY   Faith, the priest was good enough, for all the old
gentleman's° saying.   *(Jaques's)*
CLOWN   A most wicked Sir Oliver, Audrey, a most vile Mar-
5 text. But Audrey, there is a youth here in the forest lays claim
to you.

AUDREY Ay, I know who 'tis: he hath no interest in me° in the *no right to me*
world. Here comes the man you mean.
    Enter WILLIAM.

CLOWN It is meat and drink to me to see a clown,° by my *peasant; yokel*
10 troth. We that have good wits have much to answer for: we
shall be flouting; we cannot hold.° *refrain*

WILLIAM Good ev'n, Audrey.

AUDREY God ye° good ev'n, William. *God give you*

WILLIAM And good ev'n to you, sir.
    [*He takes off his hat.*]

15 CLOWN Good ev'n, gentle friend. Cover thy head,[1] cover thy
head—nay, prithee, be covered! How old are you, friend?

WILLIAM Five and twenty, sir.

CLOWN A ripe age. Is thy name William?

WILLIAM William, sir.

20 CLOWN A fair name. Wast born i'th' forest here?

WILLIAM Ay, sir, I thank God.

CLOWN "Thank God"—a good answer. Art rich?

WILLIAM Faith, sir, so-so.

CLOWN "So-so" is good, very good, very excellent good. And
25 yet it is not; it is but so-so. Art thou wise?

WILLIAM Ay, sir. I have a pretty wit.

CLOWN Why, thou say'st well. I do now remember a saying:
"The fool doth think he is wise, but the wise man knows
himself to be a fool." The heathen philosopher, when he had
30 a desire to eat a grape, would open his lips when he put it
into his mouth, meaning thereby that grapes were made to
eat and lips to open.[2] You do love this maid?

WILLIAM I do, sir.

CLOWN Give me your hand. Art thou learned?

35 WILLIAM No, sir.

CLOWN Then learn this of me: to have is to have. For it is a
figure in rhetoric° that drink, being poured out of a cup into *rhetorical commonplace*
a glass, by filling the one doth empty the other. For all your
writers do consent that *ipse* is he.[3] Now you are not *ipse*, for
40 I am he.

WILLIAM Which "he," sir?

CLOWN He, sir, that must marry this woman. Therefore, you
clown, abandon—which is in the vulgar "leave"—the
society—which in the boorish is "company"—of this
45 female—which in the common is "woman." Which together
is, abandon the society of this female or, clown, thou
perishest—or to thy better understanding, diest—or, to wit,
I kill thee: make thee away, translate thy life into death, thy
liberty into bondage. I will deal in poison with thee, or in
50 bastinado,° or in steel. I will bandy with thee in faction; I will *beating with a club*
o'errun thee with policy;[4] I will kill thee a hundred and fifty
ways. Therefore tremble and depart!

AUDREY Do, good William.

5.1
1. Evidently William has taken off his hat in a gesture of deference.
2. Touchstone's speech may be a response to William's gaping mouth.

3. For all authorities agree that *ipse* is translated as
"he himself." The Latin word was proverbially
applied to wooers who won the favor of their lovers.
4. I will contend ("bandy") with you in argument; I
will overwhelm you with craftiness.

WILLIAM   God rest you merry, sir.   *Exit.*
             Enter CORIN.

55   CORIN   Our master and mistress seeks you. Come away, away!
    CLOWN   Trip, Audrey, trip, Audrey! I attend, I attend.
                                          Exeunt.

5.2
Enter ORLANDO *and* OLIVER.

ORLANDO   Is't possible that on so little acquaintance you
    should like her? That but seeing, you should love her? And
    loving, woo? And wooing, she should grant? And will you
    persevere to enjoy her?

5   OLIVER   Neither call the giddiness° of it in question, the pov-   *foolish haste*
    erty of her, the small acquaintance, my sudden wooing, nor
    sudden consenting, but say with me, "I love Aliena." Say
    with her that she loves me. Consent with both, that we may
    enjoy each other. It shall be to your good, for my father's
10   house and all the revenue that was old Sir Roland's will I
    estate° upon you, and here live and die a shepherd.   *settle*
              Enter ROSALIND [*as Ganymede*].

ORLANDO   You have my consent. Let your wedding be tomor-
    row. Thither will I invite the Duke and all 's contented fol-
    lowers. Go you and prepare Aliena; for look you, here comes
15   my Rosalind.
ROSALIND   God save you, brother.
OLIVER   And you, fair sister.   [*Exit.*]
ROSALIND   O my dear Orlando, how it grieves me to see thee
    wear thy heart in a scarf!°   *sling*
20   ORLANDO   It is my arm.
ROSALIND   I thought thy heart had been wounded with the
    claws of a lion.
ORLANDO   Wounded it is, but with the eyes of a lady.
ROSALIND   Did your brother tell you how I counterfeited to
25   swoon when he showed me your handkerchief?
ORLANDO   Ay, and greater wonders than that.
ROSALIND   Oh, I know where you are. Nay, 'tis true. There was
    never anything so sudden but the fight of two rams and Cae-
    sar's thrasonical° brag of "I came, saw, and overcome."[1] For   *boastful*
30   your brother and my sister no sooner met but they looked,
    no sooner looked but they loved, no sooner loved but they
    sighed, no sooner sighed but they asked one another the
    reason, no sooner knew the reason but they sought the rem-
    edy. And in these degrees have they made a pair° of stairs   *flight*
35   to marriage, which they will climb incontinent° or else be   *hastily*
    incontinent[2] before marriage. They are in the very wrath of
    love° and they will together. Clubs cannot part them.   *heat of passion*
ORLANDO   They shall be married tomorrow, and I will bid the
    Duke to the nuptial. But oh, how bitter a thing it is to look
40   into happiness through another man's eyes! By so much the
    more shall I tomorrow be at the height of heart-heaviness by

---

5.2
1. Caesar's well-known announcement of military
victory, made famous as "I came, I saw, I overcame"
in Thomas North's translation of Plutarch's *Lives*
(1579).
2. Be sexually unrestrained.

how much I shall think my brother happy in having what he
wishes for.

ROSALIND   Why, then, tomorrow I cannot serve your turn[3] for
45   Rosalind?

ORLANDO   I can live no longer by thinking.

ROSALIND   I will weary you, then, no longer with idle talking.
Know of me then, for now I speak to some purpose, that I
know you are a gentleman of good conceit.° I speak not this   *understanding*
50   that you should bear a good opinion of my knowledge, inso-
much° I say I know you are. Neither do I labor for a greater   *inasmuch as*
esteem than may in some little measure draw a belief from
you, to do yourself good[4] and not to grace me. Believe then,
if you please, that I can do strange things. I have since I was
55   three year old conversed° with a magician most profound in   *associated*
his art, and yet not damnable.[5] If you do love Rosalind so
near the heart as your gesture° cries it out, when your brother   *behavior*
marries Aliena shall you marry her. I know into what straits
of fortune she is driven, and it is not impossible to me, if it
60   appear not inconvenient to you, to set her before your eyes
tomorrow—human as she is and without any danger.

ORLANDO   Speak'st thou in sober meanings?

ROSALIND   By my life, I do—which I tender° dearly, though I   *value*
say I am a magician. Therefore put you in your best array;
65   bid° your friends. For if you will be married tomorrow you   *invite*
shall, and to Rosalind if you will.

        Enter SILVIUS *and* PHOEBE.

Look, here comes a lover of mine and a lover of hers.

PHOEBE   Youth, you have done me much ungentleness°   *discourtesy*
To show the letter that I writ to you.

70   ROSALIND   I care not if I have. It is my study°   *objective*
To seem despiteful° and ungentle to you.   *contemptuous*
You are there followed by a faithful shepherd.
Look upon him, love him; he worships you.

PHOEBE   Good shepherd, tell this youth what 'tis to love.

75   SILVIUS   It is to be all made of sighs and tears,
And so am I for Phoebe.

PHOEBE   And I for Ganymede.

ORLANDO   And I for Rosalind.

ROSALIND   And I for no woman.

80   SILVIUS   It is to be all made of faith and service,
And so am I for Phoebe.

PHOEBE   And I for Ganymede.

ORLANDO   And I for Rosalind.

ROSALIND   And I for no woman.

85   SILVIUS   It is to be all made of fantasy,
All made of passion and all made of wishes,
All adoration, duty, and observance,°   *devotion*
All humbleness, all patience and impatience,
All purity, all trial, all observance,
90   And so am I for Phoebe.

---

3. Substitute for Rosalind; satisfy you sexually in
Rosalind's place.
4. *Neither . . . good:* Nor am I attempting to enhance
my reputation more than is necessary to persuade
you to do yourself some good.
5. That is, not meriting execution for heresy. Elizabethan statutes made certain forms of witchcraft and
black magic punishable by death.

PHOEBE   And so am I for Ganymede.

ORLANDO   And so am I for Rosalind.

ROSALIND   And so am I for no woman.

PHOEBE   If this be so, why blame you me to love you?

95 SILVIUS   If this be so, why blame you me to love you?

ORLANDO   If this be so, why blame you me to love you?

ROSALIND   Why do you speak too, "Why blame you me to love
you?"

ORLANDO   To her that is not here, nor doth not hear.

ROSALIND   Pray you, no more of this—'tis like the howling of
100   Irish wolves against the moon.[6] [to SILVIUS] I will help you
if I can. [to PHOEBE] I would love you if I could. Tomorrow
meet me all together. I will marry you if ever I marry woman,
and I'll be married tomorrow. [to ORLANDO] I will satisfy you
if ever I satisfied man, and you shall be married tomorrow.
105   [to SILVIUS] I will content you if what pleases you contents
you, and you shall be married tomorrow. [to ORLANDO] As
you love Rosalind, meet. [to SILVIUS] As you love Phoebe,
meet. And as I love no woman, I'll meet. So fare you well. I
have left you commands.

110 SILVIUS   I'll not fail, if I live.

PHOEBE   Nor I.

ORLANDO   Nor I.   *Exeunt.*

5.3

Enter CLOWN *and* AUDREY.

CLOWN   Tomorrow is the joyful day, Audrey; tomorrow will
we be married.

AUDREY   I do desire it with all my heart, and I hope it is no
dishonest° desire to desire to be a woman of the world.[1]   unchaste
5   Here come two of the banished Duke's pages.

Enter two PAGES.

FIRST PAGE   Well met, honest gentleman!

CLOWN   By my troth, well met! Come, sit, sit—and a song.

SECOND PAGE   We are for you.° Sit i'th' middle.   *That suits us*

FIRST PAGE   Shall we clap into't roundly, without hawking[2] or
10   spitting or saying we are hoarse—which are the only° pro-   *best; sole*
logues to a bad voice?

SECOND PAGE   I'faith, i'faith—and both in a tune° like two   *in unison*
gypsies on a horse.

Song.

PAGES [*sing*][3]   It was a lover and his lass,
15   With a hey and a ho and a hey nonny-no,
            That o'er the green cornfield° did pass   *field of wheat*
            In the springtime, the only pretty ring time,°   *time for weddings*
            When birds do sing, hey ding-a ding, ding,
            Sweet lovers love the spring.

---

6. That is, it is barbaric. The howling of wolves at the moon was a proverbial way of referring to an irrational or futile course of action. Irish wolves might be perceived as especially disorderly, for Ireland's abundance of wolves was for many Elizabethan writers a mark of that country's lack of civility.

5.3

1. A married woman.

2. Shall we begin energetically and at once, without clearing our throats?

3. F does not include this speech prefix, simply the world "song." This is one of the few Shakespeare songs for which contemporary music survives. It is set for a single voice with lute accompaniment in Thomas Morley's *First Book of Airs* (1600).

20   And therefore take° the present time,   seize
With a hey and a ho and a hey nonny-no,
For love is crownèd with the prime°   spring; perfection
In springtime, etc.

Between the acres of the rye,
25   With a hey and a ho and a hey nonny-no,
These pretty country folks would lie
In springtime, etc.

This carol they began that hour,
With a hey and a ho and a hey nonny-no,
30   How that a life was but a flower
In springtime, etc.[4]

CLOWN   Truly, young gentlemen, though there was no great
matter° in the ditty, yet the note was very untunable.[5]   sense
FIRST PAGE   You are deceived, sir. We kept time; we lost not
35   our time.
CLOWN   By my troth, yes. I count it but time lost to hear such
a foolish song. God b'wi' you and God mend your voices.
Come, Audrey.   Exeunt.

5.4

Enter DUKE SENIOR, AMIENS, JAQUES, ORLANDO,
OLIVER, [*and*] CELIA [*as Aliena*].
DUKE SENIOR   Dost thou believe, Orlando, that the boy
Can do all this that he hath promisèd?
ORLANDO   I sometimes do believe and sometimes do not,
As those that fear they hope[1] and know they fear.
Enter ROSALIND [*as Ganymede*], SILVIUS, *and* PHOEBE.
5   ROSALIND   Patience once more whiles our compact is urged.°   declared
You say if I bring in your Rosalind,
You will bestow her on Orlando here?
DUKE SENIOR   That would I, had I° kingdoms to give with her.   even if I had
ROSALIND   And you say you will have her when I bring her?
10   ORLANDO   That would I, were I of all kingdoms king.
ROSALIND   You say you'll marry me if I be willing?
PHOEBE   That will I, should I die the hour after.
ROSALIND   But if you do refuse to marry me,
You'll give yourself to this most faithful shepherd?
15   PHOEBE   So is the bargain.
ROSALIND   You say that you'll have Phoebe if she will?
SILVIUS   Though to have her and death were both one thing.
ROSALIND   I have promised to make all this matter even.°   smooth; right
Keep you your word, O Duke, to give your daughter;
20   You yours, Orlando, to receive his daughter.
Keep you your word, Phoebe, that you'll marry me
Or else, refusing me, to wed this shepherd.
Keep your word, Silvius, that you'll marry her
If she refuse me; and from hence I go
25   To make these doubts all even.

4. TEXTUAL COMMENT The order of these stanzas   5. Yet the music was disagreeable.
differs from that found in Morley's *First Book of Airs.*   **5.4**
See Digital Edition TC 8.   1. Fear that their hope will not be fulfilled.

Exeunt ROSALIND *and* CELIA.

DUKE SENIOR   I do remember in this shepherd boy
   Some lively° touches of my daughter's favor.°   *vivid / appearance*
ORLANDO   My lord, the first time that I ever saw him
   Methought he was a brother to your daughter.
30   But my good lord, this boy is forest-born
   And hath been tutored in the rudiments
   Of many desperate° studies by his uncle,   *dangerous*
   Whom he reports to be a great magician
   Obscurèd in the circle of this forest.[2]

Enter CLOWN *and* AUDREY.

35 JAQUES   There is, sure, another flood toward,° and these cou-   *at hand*
   ples are coming to the ark.[3] Here comes a pair of very
   strange beasts, which in all tongues are called fools.
CLOWN   Salutation and greeting to you all!
JAQUES   Good my lord, bid him welcome. This is the motley-
40 minded° gentleman that I have so often met in the forest.   *foolish-brained*
   He hath been a courtier, he swears.
CLOWN   If any man doubt that, let him put me to my purgation.[4] I have trod a measure,° I have flattered a lady, I have   *danced*
   been politic with my friend, smooth with mine enemy. I
45 have undone° three tailors, I have had four quarrels, and   *made bankrupt*
   like to have fought° one.   *came close to fighting*
JAQUES   And how was that ta'en up?°   *settled*
CLOWN   Faith, we met and found the quarrel was upon the
   seventh cause.
50 JAQUES   How seventh cause? Good my lord, like this fellow!
DUKE SENIOR   I like him very well.
CLOWN   God 'ield you, sir, I desire you of the like. I press
   in here, sir, amongst the rest of the country copulatives,[5] to
   swear and to forswear, according as marriage binds and
55 blood breaks:° a poor virgin, sir, an ill-favored thing, sir, but   *passion rebels*
   mine own; a poor humor° of mine, sir, to take that that no   *whim*
   man else will. Rich honesty° dwells like a miser, sir, in a   *chastity*
   poor house as your pearl in your foul oyster.
DUKE SENIOR   By my faith, he is very swift and sententious.°   *witty and wise*
60 CLOWN   According to the fool's bolt,[6] sir, and such dulcet
   diseases.°   *sweet afflictions*
JAQUES   But for the seventh cause—how did you find the
   quarrel on the seventh cause?
CLOWN   Upon a lie seven times removed —bear your body
65 more seeming,° Audrey —as thus, sir: I did dislike[7] the cut of   *becomingly*
   a certain courtier's beard; he sent me word if I said his beard
   was not cut well, he was in the mind it was. This is called
   the Retort Courteous. If I sent him word again it was not
   well cut, he would send me word he cut it to please himself.
70 This is called the Quip Modest. If again it was not well cut,

---

2. Concealed within the boundaries of this forest.
This may be a reference to the magic circle within
which magicians were supposed to be able to practice
their art safely.
3. Alluding to a biblical account in Genesis 7:2 in
which pairs of male and female animals shelter on
Noah's ark to escape the flood that covers the earth.

4. Let me be put to trial to clear myself (of the
charge of lying).
5. People who are about to copulate.
6. And his wittiness quickly disappears. The comment alludes to the proverb "A fool's bolt (or arrow) is
soon shot."
7. Show my dislike of.

he disabled° my judgment. This is called the Reply Churlish.   *disparaged*
If again it was not well cut, he would answer I spake not
true. This is called the Reproof Valiant. If again it was not
well cut, he would say I lie. This is called the Countercheck°   *Rebuff*
75 Quarrelsome, and so to Lie Circumstantial° and the Lie   *Indirect*
Direct.

JAQUES   And how oft did you say his beard was not well cut?

CLOWN   I durst go no further than the Lie Circumstantial;
nor he durst not give me the Lie Direct, and so we measured
80 swords[8] and parted.

JAQUES   Can you nominate° in order, now, the degrees of the   *name*
lie?

CLOWN   O sir, we quarrel in print, by the book,[9] as you have
books for good manners.[1] I will name you the degrees: the
85 first, the Retort Courteous; the second, the Quip Modest;
the third, the Reply Churlish; the fourth, the Reproof Valiant; the fifth, the Countercheck Quarrelsome; the sixth,
the Lie with Circumstance; the seventh, the Lie Direct. All
these you may avoid but the Lie Direct, and you may avoid
90 that too with an "if." I knew when seven justices could not take
up° a quarrel; but when the parties were met themselves,   *settle*
one of them thought but of an "if"—as, "if you said so then
I said so"—and they shook hands and swore brothers.° Your   *became sworn brothers*
"if" is the only peacemaker: much virtue in "if."

95 JAQUES   Is not this a rare fellow, my lord? He's as good at anything, and yet a fool.

DUKE SENIOR   He uses his folly like a stalkinghorse,[2] and
under the presentation° of that he shoots his wit.   *appearance*

    Enter HYMEN,[3] *[god of marriage,]* ROSALIND, *and*
    CELIA *[as themselves].*
    Still° music.   *Soft*

HYMEN   Then is there mirth in heaven
100 When earthly things, made even,°   *set right*
Atone° together.   *Are at one; unite*
Good Duke, receive thy daughter;
Hymen from heaven brought her—
Yea, brought her hither
105 That thou mightst join her hand with his,[4]
Whose heart within his bosom is.

ROSALIND *[to* DUKE SENIOR*]*   To you I give myself, for I am yours.
    [to ORLANDO*]* To you I give myself, for I am yours.

DUKE SENIOR   If there be truth in sight, you are my daughter.

110 ORLANDO   If there be truth in sight, you are my Rosalind.

PHOEBE   If sight and shape be true,
Why then my love adieu!

---

8. We checked that our swords were of the same
length (as was customary prior to a duel).
9. According to the rules as set down in books on the
etiquette of dueling. Touchstone's speech exposes
the absurd aspects of the elaborate codes of behavior
set forth in such books.
1. Elizabethan England witnessed an outpouring of
courtesy literature aimed at both social aspirants and
established courtiers.
2. A real or imitation horse used as a means of cam-

ouflage in hunting.
3. The god of marriage in classical mythology, conventionally depicted as a young man who carried a
veil and a bridal torch. PERFORMANCE COMMENT
Directors must decide whether to make Hymen a
heavenly deity or one of Rosalind's friends recruited
to help her. See Digital Edition PC 3.
4. TEXTUAL COMMENT F prints "his hand with his,"
here emended to "her hand with his." For the possible reasons for this, see Digital Edition TC 9.

ROSALIND I'll have no father if you be not he.
　—I'll have no husband if you be not he,
115　—Nor ne'er wed woman if you be not she.
HYMEN Peace, ho! I bar° confusion.　　　　　　　　　　　*forbid*
　'Tis I must make conclusion
　Of these most strange events.
　Here's eight that must take hands
120　To join in Hymen's bands°　　　　　　　　　　　*bonds of marriage*
　If truth hold true contents.[5]
　[*to* ROSALIND *and* ORLANDO.] You and you no cross° shall part.　　*adversity*
　[*to* CELIA *and* OLIVER] You and you are heart in heart.
　[*to* PHOEBE] You to his love must accord,°　　　　　　　*consent*
125　Or have a woman to° your lord.　　　　　　　　　　　*as*
　[*to* CLOWN *and* AUDREY] You and you are sure together,°　　*tightly bound*
　As the winter to foul weather.
　Whiles a wedlock hymn we sing,
　Feed° yourselves with questioning,　　　　　　　　　　*Satisfy*
130　That reason wonder may diminish
　How thus we met, and these things finish.
　　　　　　　　Song.
　　Wedding is great Juno's° crown.　　　　　　　*goddess of marriage*
　　O blessèd bond of board and bed!
　　'Tis Hymen peoples every town;
135　　High° wedlock then be honorèd.　　　　　　　　*Solemn*
　　Honor, high honor, and renown
　　To Hymen, god of every town.
DUKE SENIOR　O my dear niece, welcome thou art to me!
　Even daughter, welcome in no less degree.[6]
140 PHOEBE　I will not eat my word: now thou art mine,
　Thy faith my fancy° to thee doth combine.　　　　　　　*love*
　　Enter [JAQUES DE BOIS, *the*] *second brother.*
JAQUES DE BOIS　Let me have audience for a word or two.
　I am the second son of old Sir Roland,
　That bring these tidings to this fair assembly.
145　Duke Frederick, hearing how that every day
　Men of great worth resorted to this forest,
　Addressed a mighty power,° which were on foot　　　　　*army*
　In his own conduct,° purposely to take　　　　　*Under his command*
　His brother here and put him to the sword.
150　And to the skirts° of this wild wood he came,　　　　*outskirts*
　Where, meeting with an old religious man,
　After some question° with him, was converted　　　　*conversation*
　Both from his enterprise and from the world,
　His crown bequeathing to his banished brother
160　And all their lands restored to him[7] again
　That were with him exiled. This to be true
　I do engage° my life.　　　　　　　　　　　　*pledge*
DUKE SENIOR　　　　　Welcome, young man.
　Thou offer'st fairly° to thy brothers' wedding:　　　*You bring fine gifts*
　To one° his lands withheld and to the other°　　*(Oliver) / (Orlando)*

---

5. If truth is true; if truth please you.
6. Daughter, you are no less welcome.

7. Although F has "him," many modern editions emend to "them."

160   A land itself at large,[8] a potent° dukedom.   *powerful*
      First in this forest let us do° those ends   *accomplish*
      That here were well begun and well begot;°   *conceived*
      And after, every° of this happy number   *every one*
      That have endured shrewd° days and nights with us   *evil*
165   Shall share the good of our returnèd fortune,
      According to the measure of their states.°   *ranks*
      Meantime, forget this new-fall'n° dignity   *newly acquired*
      And fall into our rustic revelry.
      Play music, and you brides and bridegrooms all,
170   With measure heaped in joy to th' measures fall.[9]
    JAQUES   Sir, by your patience.° If I heard you rightly,   *with your permission*
      The duke hath put on a religious life
      And thrown into neglect the pompous° court?   *ceremonious*
    JAQUES DE BOIS   He hath.
175   JAQUES   To him will I: out of these convertites°   *converts*
      There is much matter to be heard and learned.
      [*to* DUKE SENIOR] You to your former honor I bequeath—
      Your patience and your virtue well deserves it;
      [*to* ORLANDO *and* ROSALIND] You to a love that your true faith
         doth merit,
180   [*to* OLIVER *and* CELIA] You to your land and love and great
         allies,°   *relatives*
      [*to* SILVIUS *and* PHOEBE] You to a long and well-deservèd bed,
      [*to* CLOWN *and* AUDREY] And you to wrangling, for thy loving
         voyage
      Is but for two months victualed.° So—to your pleasures!   *supplied with food*
      I am for other than for dancing measures.
185   DUKE SENIOR   Stay, Jaques, stay!
    JAQUES   To see no pastime, I! What you would have°   *like (from me)*
      I'll stay to know at your abandoned cave.   *Exit.*
    DUKE SENIOR   Proceed, proceed! We'll begin these rites,
      As we do trust they'll end in true delights.
         [*Dancing, then exeunt all but* ROSALIND.][1]

[*Epilogue.*]

190   ROSALIND   It is not the fashion to see the lady the epilogue,[2]
      but it is no more unhandsome than to see the lord the pro-
      logue. If it be true that good wine needs no bush,[3] 'tis true
      that a good play needs no epilogue. Yet to good wine they do
      use good bushes, and good plays prove the better by the help
195   of good epilogues.
         What a case° am I in, then, that am neither a good epi-   *plight; costume*
      logue nor cannot insinuate° with you in the behalf of a good   *ingratiate myself*
      play? I am not furnished like a beggar; therefore to beg will
      not become me. My way is to conjure° you, and I'll begin   *charge; bewitch*
200   with the women: I charge you, O women, for the love you

---

8. An entire country. As Rosalind's husband, Orlando is heir to the dukedom returned to Duke Senior.
9. With a measure of overflowing joy, begin your dances ("measures").
1. TEXTUAL COMMENT F indicates only a single exit for Duke Senior, but most editors assume that Rosalind remains alone onstage to deliver the Epilogue.

See Digital Edition TC 10.
Epilogue
2. In the vast majority of Elizabethan plays, the Epilogue is spoken by a male character.
3. Advertisement. The proverb derived from the practice of hanging a branch of ivy in tavern windows to indicate that wine was for sale.

bear to men, to like as much of this play as please you. And I charge you, O men, for the love you bear to women—as I perceive by your simpering, none of you hates them—that between you and the women, the play° may please. If I were a woman[4] I would kiss as many of you as had beards that pleased me, complexions that liked° me, and breaths that I defied° not. And I am sure, as many as have good beards or good faces or sweet breaths will for my kind offer, when I make curtsey, bid me farewell.°   *Exit.*

°*drama; love play*

°*pleased*
°*disdained*

°*(with applause)*

205

4. A pointed reference to the fact that women's roles in the Elizabethan theater were played by boys.

Twelfth Night

Shakespeare's contemporary Thomas Coryat wrote that he witnessed something quite remarkable when he went to the theater in Venice: "I saw women act, a thing that I never saw before." That an Englishman had to travel abroad to see women actors for the first time is not surprising. All the great women's roles in Elizabethan and Jacobean plays were written to be performed by trained adolescent boys, and boys played the female parts as well in all grammar school and university productions. But what struck Coryat in Venice was neither the gratifying naturalness of finally seeing women play women's parts nor the comparative inadequacy of English boy actors. Rather, he was impressed that the women actors managed to hold their own in representing the female sex: "They performed it," he writes, "with as good a grace, as ever I saw any masculine Actor."

Recent scholars have observed that there were in fact occasions in which audiences in England could have seen women performing: troupes from abroad, including women actors, occasionally toured England, and English women performed in the theatrical spectacles known as masques and in other entertainments. But in England, women did not perform on the public stage (the word "actress" had not yet entered the English language), and the remarks of Coryat and others suggest that their absence was rarely if ever lamented. The boy actors were evidently extraordinarily skillful, and the audiences were sufficiently immersed in the conventions both of theater and of social life in general to accept gesture, makeup, and above all dress as a convincing representation of femininity.

Twelfth Night, or What You Will, written for Shakespeare's all-male company, plays brilliantly with these conventions. The comedy depends on an actor's ability to transform himself, through costume, voice, and gesture, into a young gentlewoman, Viola, who transforms herself, through costume, voice, and gesture, into a young man, Cesario. The play's delicious complications follow from the emotional turbulence that Viola's transformation engenders. Shipwrecked on a strange coast and bereft of her twin brother, the disguised Viola finds a place in the service of the powerful Duke Orsino, with whom she promptly falls in love. Orsino is in love with Lady Olivia, a wealthy countess whose household includes, among its servants and dependents, a steward or house manager, a waiting-gentlewoman, a professional entertainer, and a down-at-the-heels, perpetually drunken uncle. When Orsino sends Cesario to help him woo the proud Olivia, Olivia not only rejects the Duke's suit but falls in love with his messenger. Discomfited to learn that she is the object of Olivia's love, Viola reflects on the plot's impassioned triangle:

> My master loves her dearly,
> And I, poor monster, fond as much on him.
> And she, mistaken, seems to dote on me.
> What will become of this?
>
> (2.2.32–35)

"Poor monster": in *Twelfth Night,* clothes do not simply reveal or disguise identity; they partly constitute identity—or so Viola playfully imagines—making her a strange, hybrid creature. To be sure, she understands perfectly well the narrow biological definition of her sex (though in the characteristically male-centered language of Shakespeare's culture, she phrases that definition in terms of what she "lack[s]" [3.4.272]). Yet there is something almost magical in this play about costume, so that even at the close, when identities have been sorted out and the couples happily matched, Orsino cannot bring himself to call his bride-to-be by her rightful name or to address her as a woman:

> Cesario, come—
> For so you shall be while you are a man—
> But when in other habits you are seen,
> Orsino's mistress and his fancy's queen.
>   (5.1.371–74)

It would have been simple for Shakespeare to devise a concluding scene in which Viola appears in women's "habits," but he goes out of his way to leave her in men's clothes and hence to disrupt with a delicate comic touch the return to the "normal." The transforming power of costume unsettles fixed categories of gender and social class; it allows characters to explore emotional territory that a culture officially hostile to same-sex desire and cross-class marriage would ordinarily have ruled out of bounds. Longing, intimacy, and desire do not conform comfortably to social norms. Formal speeches take on a startling intensity, service slides into aching love, friendship turns into self-abnegating adoration, the pursued becomes the pursuer. In *Twelfth Night*, conventional expectations repeatedly give way to a different way of perceiving the world.

Shakespeare wrote *Twelfth Night* around 1601. He had already written such comedies as *A Midsummer Night's Dream, Much Ado About Nothing,* and *As You Like It,* with their playful, subtly ironic investigations of the ways in which heterosexual couples precipitate from the murkier crosscurrents of male and female friendships; as interesting, perhaps, he had probably just recently completed *Hamlet,* with its unprecedented exploration of mourning, betrayal, antic humor, and tragic isolation. *Twelfth Night* would prove to be, in the view of many critics, both the most perfect and in some sense the last of the great festive comedies. Shakespeare returned to comedy later in his career, but always with more insistent overtones of bitterness, loss, and grief. There are dark notes in *Twelfth Night* as well: Olivia is in mourning for her brother; Viola thinks that her brother, too, is dead; Antonio believes that he has been betrayed by the man he loves; Orsino threatens to kill Cesario. Desire is repeatedly linked to frustration and loss. The servants who devote themselves tirelessly to pleasing the wealthy aristocrats on whose whims they depend anxiously compete with one another for signs of favor and live in fear of the contempt or indifference of their masters. But these notes are swept up in the current of sweet music that pervades the play, drawing the characters into a giddy, carnivalesque dance of illusion, disguise, folly, and clowning. And for at least the heroine, selfless devotion is magically rewarded, as the intimacy between master and trusted servant is transmuted into reciprocal love and desire.

The play's subtitle, *What You Will,* underscores the celebratory spirit associated with Twelfth Night, the Feast of the Epiphany (January 6), which in Elizabethan England marked the culminating night of the traditional Christmas revels. On Twelfth Night 1601, the Queen's guest of honor was a twenty-eight-year-old Italian nobleman, Don Virginio Orsino, Duke of Bracciano. Orsino wrote to his wife that he was entertained that night with "a mingled comedy, with pieces of music and dances." Since the company that performed was the Lord Chamberlain's Men—Shakespeare's company—it has been argued that the comedy was *Twelfth Night,* but there is no scholarly consensus on this hypothesis. The title, in any case, would for Shakespeare's contemporaries have conjured up a whole series of time-honored festivities associated with the midwinter season. A rigidly hierarchical social order that ordinarily demanded deference, sobriety, and strict obedience to authority temporarily gave way to raucous rituals of inversion: young boys were crowned for a day as bishops and carried through the streets in mock religious processions; abstemiousness was toppled by bouts of heavy drinking and feasting; the spirit of parody, folly, and misrule reigned briefly in places normally reserved for stern-faced moralists and sober judges.

That these festivities were associated with Christian holidays—the Epiphany marked the visit of the Three Kings to Bethlehem to worship the Christ child—did not altogether obscure the continuities with pagan winter rituals such as the Roman Saturnalia, with its comparably explosive release from everyday discipline into a disorderly realm of belly laughter and belly cheer. Puritans emphasized these continuities in launching a fierce attack on the Elizabethan festive calendar and its whole ethos, just as they attacked the theater for what they saw as its links with paganism, idleness, and sexual license. Elizabethan and Jacobean authorities in the church and the state had their own concerns about idleness and subversion, but they generally protected and patronized both festive ritual and theater on the grounds that these provided a valuable release from tensions that might otherwise prove dangerous. Sobriety, piety, and discipline were no doubt admirable virtues, but most human beings were not saints. "Dost thou think because thou art virtuous," the drunken Sir Toby asks the censorious steward Malvolio, "there shall be no more cakes and ale?" (2.3.106–08).

Fittingly, the earliest firm record of a performance of *Twelfth Night,* as noted in the diary of John Manningham, was "at our feast" in the Middle Temple (one of London's law schools) in February 1602. Manningham wrote observantly that the play was "much like the *Comedy of Errors,* or *Menaechmi* in Plautus, but most like and near to that in Italian called *Inganni.*" That is, *Twelfth Night* resembles Shakespeare's own earlier play on identical twins (along with that play's Roman source) and still more resembles a series of sixteenth-century Italian comedies built around the intertwining themes of love, fraud *(inganno),* and mistaken identity. Several of these comedies feature the plot device of a female twin who takes service as a page with the man she loves. Closest of these to Shakespeare's comedy is *Gl'Ingannati* (The Deceived), written for performance at Carnival time in Siena in 1531 and translated into French in 1543. It seems likely that Shakespeare knew this play or one that derived from it, and he may have picked up several details in addition to the overall plot line. But the tone of *Gl'Ingannati,* with its bawdy jokes about nuns and old men, its sly, sardonic servants, and its farcical intrigues, is far from *Twelfth Night*'s blend of melancholy and delight, its bittersweet mingling of divided and contradictory desires. Tellingly, in the Italian comedy, the heroine is all along plotting to win the love of the man she serves; she has disguised herself in order to dissuade him from wooing elsewhere. Viola's predicament—her attempt to serve Orsino even at the cost of her own deepest longings—represents a wholly different emotional register.

That predicament is not Shakespeare's invention; he found it, with many other elements of his plot, in an English story, Barnabe Riche's tale "Apollonius and Silla" in *Riche His Farewell to Military Profession* (1581), which was in turn based on French and Italian sources. Riche is too addicted to moralizing to explore his heroine's character with much subtlety, but he does underscore how painful it is for her to hide her feelings while acting as go-between, and hence he anticipates, if only woodenly, the mood that Shakespeare exquisitely captures in Viola's lines about one who "sat like Patience on a monument, / Smiling at grief" (2.4.111–12). There is less precedent, in Riche or in any of the known sources, for the aspect of *Twelfth Night* that Manningham found particularly memorable and that has continued to delight audiences: the gulling of Malvolio.

Malvolio (It. *male voglio*: "I wish ill") is explicitly linked to those among Shakespeare's contemporaries most hostile to the theater and to such holidays as Twelfth Night: "sometimes," says Lady Olivia's waiting-gentlewoman Maria, "he is a kind of puritan" (2.3.129). When we first see Malvolio, he is harshly critical of the Clown, who is attempting to win back Olivia's favor. "Unless you laugh and minister occasion to him," Malvolio sourly observes, "he is gagged" (1.5.78–79). Though ungenerous, the observation is canny, for comedy does seem to depend on a collaborative spirit from which Malvolio conspicuously excludes himself. He is a man without friends. More dangerously, he is a man in a socially dependent position with a gift for acquiring enemies, as he does when he tries to silence the noisy revelry of that classic carnivalesque

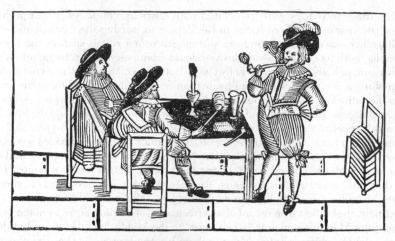

Gentlemen drinking and smoking. From Phillip Stubbes, *The Anatomy of Abuses* (1583).

threesome of a drunkard, a blockhead, and a professional fool: Olivia's uncle Sir Toby, his boon companion Sir Andrew Aguecheek, and the Clown.

Olivia remarks to Malvolio that he is "sick of self-love" (1.5.82), and it is this narcissism that his enemies exploit to undo him. When Malvolio finds Maria's forged letter, he is in the midst of a deliciously self-gratifying fantasy that he has married Olivia, a fantasy less of erotic bliss than of social domination. The dream of rising above his station fuels his credulous eagerness to interpret the letter according to his fondest wishes and to comply with its absurd suggestions for his festive dress and demeanor. This compliance, by making it seem to Olivia that he has gone mad, renders Malvolio vulnerable to a further humiliation. In a parody of the age's brutal "therapy" for insanity, he is clapped into a dark room and subjected to a mock exorcism. Finally, he suffers what is perhaps the cruelest punishment for someone who dreams that greatness will be thrust upon him: he is simply forgotten. When in the play's final moments he is released, Malvolio is in no mood to join in the general air of communal wonder and rejoicing. More alone than ever, he introduces into the comedy's resolution an extraordinary note of vindictive bitterness: "I'll be revenged on the whole pack of you" (5.1.364). Shakespeare does not hide the cruelty of the treatment to which Malvolio has been subjected—"He hath been most notoriously abused" (5.1.365), says Olivia— nor does he shrink from showing the audience other disagreeable qualities in Sir Toby and his companions. But while the close of the comedy seems to embrace these failings in a tolerant, bemused, aristocratic recognition of human folly, it can find no place for Malvolio's blend of puritanism and social climbing.

Malvolio is scapegoated for indulging in a fantasy that colors several of the key relationships in *Twelfth Night*: the fantasy of winning the hand of one of the noble and enormously wealthy aristocrats who reign over the social world of the play. The beautiful heiress Olivia, mistress of a great house, is a glittering prize that lures not only Malvolio but also the foolish Sir Andrew and the elegant, imperious Duke Orsino. In falling in love with the Duke's graceful messenger (and, as she thinks she has done, in marrying him), Olivia seems to have made precisely the kind of match that had fueled Malvolio's social-climbing imagination. As it turns out, the match is not between unequals: "Be not amazed," the Duke tells her when she realizes that she has married someone she scarcely knows. "Right noble is his blood" (5.1.254). The social order, then, has not been overturned: as in a carnival, when the disguises are removed, the revelers resume their "proper" socially and sexually approved positions.

Yet there is something decidedly improper about the perverse erotic excitement that the play discovers in disguise, displacement, indirection, and deferral, and something irreducibly strange about the marriages with which *Twelfth Night* ends. The drunken aristocrat Sir Toby has married the lady-in-waiting Maria as a reward for devising the plot against Malvolio. Olivia has entered into a "contract of eternal bond of love" (5.1.149) with someone whose actual identity is only revealed to her after the marriage ceremony. (In Riche's version of the story, she is pregnant and her marriage saves her from social disgrace; but Shakespeare omits this plot twist, thereby raising the tone but heightening the irrationality of the finale.) The strangeness of the bond between virtual strangers is matched by the strangeness of Orsino's instantaneous decision to marry his page Cesario—as soon as "he" can become Viola by changing into women's clothes. Only a few minutes earlier, in a fit of jealous rage at Olivia's love for Cesario, Orsino had threatened to kill "the lamb that I do love" (5.1.123); now he will wed that lamb.

Lutenist. By Jost Amman (1568).

The sudden transformation is prepared for in part by Orsino's passionate insistence that he loves the boy he intends to kill and in part by the earlier signs of intimacy between them: "I have," he tells Cesario, "unclasped / To thee the book even of my secret soul" (1.4.12–13). But this intimacy between master and servant has been formed around Orsino's grand passion for Olivia, a passion that is reiterated through virtually the entire play. The revelation at the play's climax—"One face, one voice, one habit, and two persons" (5.1.206)—forces a realignment of all the relationships. With Sebastian married to Olivia, Viola becomes Olivia's "sister" (or, as we would say, sister-in-law); and by marrying Viola, Orsino likewise makes Olivia his "sweet sister" (5.1.370). Orsino then will continue in a sense to "love" Olivia, but only through the bond of kinship formed by the linked twins—a strangely appropriate fate for someone who tried to woo by proxy!

That this solution does not seem entirely zany—that it seems a fit ending for a romantic comedy—depends on several key features in *Twelfth Night*'s emotional landscape. It is significant that Orsino's love for Olivia, though poetically intense, is detached from any direct personal encounter. Not only does her vow of a seven-year seclusion compel Orsino to delegate his passion to a messenger, but also this passion seems largely self-regarding and self-indulgent. His famous opening lines on the paradoxes of love—its close intertwining of fulfillment and decline, stealing and giving, freshness and decay—revolve around the contemplation less of the lady than of his own solitary, self-gratifying imagination: "So full of shapes is fancy / That it alone is high fantastical" (1.1.14–15). The play does not ridicule Orsino's aristocratic reveries, although they seem at moments like elegant versions of what is cruelly mocked in Malvolio, but it does invite the audience to treat them with a certain ironic detachment.

Orsino's love seems to circle all too readily back upon himself: he is fascinated by his role as melancholy lover. That self-absorption is not the only shape of passion is made clear by several contrasting figures, of whom the most selfless is the sea captain Antonio, consumed with desire for his friend Sebastian. In a play full of coy allusions to same-sex desire, Antonio's "willing love" (3.3.11) is the most explicit representation of passion as absolute devotion, a willingness to sacrifice everything in the service of the beloved. The mistaken belief that this devotion has been callously betrayed is one of the play's most poignant moments, a moment perhaps only partially redeemed by the manifest relief and joy with which the newly wed Sebastian greets his friend in the last act.

Intense, intimate bonding between men is a recurrent theme in Shakespeare's culture. (A comparable interest in female friendship is reflected in the love between Hermia and Helena in *A Midsummer Night's Dream* and Rosalind and Celia in *As You Like It*.) Shakespeare explores the pleasures and perils of male friendship in such plays as *The Two Gentlemen of Verona, The Merchant of Venice,* and *Much Ado About Nothing* and, most famously, in the sonnets to the fair young man whom he calls "the master-mistress of my passion" (Sonnet 20). Orsino expresses doubt that a woman can love with an intensity equal to a man's:

> There is no woman's sides
> Can bide the beating of so strong a passion
> As love doth give my heart. No woman's heart
> So big, to hold so much. They lack retention.
> (2.4.90–93)

It is perhaps this misogynistic belief (which the play proves to be utterly wrong) that conditions the only authentic emotional bond that we see Orsino forge, the bond with his devoted young servant Cesario. In conversation with Cesario, the haughty Duke manages for a few moments at least to escape from his languid self-absorption and express interest in someone else's thoughts and feelings: "What dost thou know?"; "And what's her history?"; "But died thy sister of her love, my boy?" (2.4.101, 106, 116). These simple questions, modest in themselves, are a marked departure from Orsino's usual manner of speech; they signal both a curiosity and a responsiveness that he does not manifest with anyone else. Part of the quirky delight of the play's resolution is to give to the union between Orsino and Viola something of the intimacy that had only seemed possible between men.

This resolution depends principally on the remarkable qualities of the play's central character, Viola. Like Antonio, Viola is prepared to sacrifice herself for her beloved: "And I most jocund, apt, and willingly," she tells Orsino, "To do you rest a thousand deaths would die" (5.1.125–26). But where Antonio experiences passion as tragic compulsion—he speaks of Sebastian's beauty as "witchcraft" drawing him into danger—Viola's spirit, as her word "jocund" suggests, is extraordinarily resilient. No sooner does she sadly observe that her brother must have perished in the shipwreck than she remarks, "Perchance he is not drowned" (1.2.5); no sooner does she find herself isolated and unprotected than she determines to serve Lady Olivia; and no sooner does she learn that this route is blocked than she resolves to disguise herself as a man and serve Orsino instead. Here and throughout the play, Viola seems to draw on an inward principle of hope. That principle, along with an improvisational boldness, an eloquent tongue, and a keen wit, enables her to keep afloat in an increasingly mad swirl of misunderstandings and cross-purposes.

Those misunderstandings, of course, are largely her creation in the sense that they mainly derive from a disguise that confounds the distinction between male and female. "they shall yet belie thy happy years / That say thou art a man," Orsino says to Cesario (1.4.29–30). The description that follows seems to imagine that boys begin almost as girls and only subsequently become males:

> Diana's lip
> Is not more smooth and rubious. Thy small pipe
> Is as the maiden's organ, shrill and sound,
> And all is semblative a woman's part.
> (1.4.30–33)

This perception of ambiguity, rooted in early modern ideas about sexuality and gender, is one of the elements that enabled a boy actor in this period convincingly to mime "a woman's part." According to one ancient anatomical tradition, contested but still highly influential in Shakespeare's time, sexual difference is not absolute: males and females share a single physiological structure whose differentiation only occurs over time. Such a theory implies a prolonged period of indistinction upon which *Twelfth Night* continually plays, and that helps to account for the emotional tangle that the cross-dressed Viola inspires.

Having, in her role as intermediary, aroused Olivia's love, Viola does not see how to disabuse the enamored Countess without abandoning the disguise. For all her lively resolution, she is passive in the face of the complexities she has engendered, counting on time and chance to sort out what she cannot: "O time, thou must untangle this, not I. / It is too hard a knot for me t'untie" (2.2.39–40). Perhaps this passivity, or more accurately this trust in time, is a form of wisdom in a world where everything seems topsy-turvy. If so, it is a wisdom that links Viola to the Clown, who exults at the play's close in what he calls "the whirligig of time" (5.1.363).

The Clown does not have a major part in the comedy's plot, but he shares with Viola a place at its imaginative center. A few years before the creation of *Twelfth Night*, the famous, boisterous clown Will Kemp quit Shakespeare's company in a huff and was replaced by Robert Armin, a comic actor of unusual sensitivity and subtlety. In paying handsome tribute to the Clown's intelligence, Viola seems to acknowledge Armin's special gift: "This fellow is wise enough to play the fool / And to do that well craves a kind of wit" (3.1.53–54). His wit often takes the form of a perverse literalism that slyly calls attention to the play's repeated confounding of such simple binaries as male and female, outside and inside, role and reality. The paradox of the wise fool, celebrated by Erasmus in his famous *Praise of Folly* (1509), is one that fascinated Shakespeare, who returned to it in plays as diverse as *As You Like It* and *King Lear*. More clearly than his equivalents elsewhere in Shakespeare's work, the Clown is a professional entertainer, paid for his services and finding employment now in one noble house and now in another. He can be unreliable, irresponsible, and importunate, but he also understands, as he teasingly shows Olivia, that it is foolish to bewail forever a loss that cannot be recovered. And he understands that it is important to take such pleasures as life offers and not to wait: "In delay there lies no plenty," he sings. "Then come kiss me, sweet and twenty. / Youth's a stuff will not endure" (2.3.48–50). There is in this wonderful song, as in all of his jests, a current of sadness. The Clown knows, as the refrain of the last of his songs puts it, that "the rain it raineth every day" (5.1.378). His counsel is for "present mirth" and "present laughter" (2.3.46). This is, of course, the advice of a fool. But do the Malvolios of the world have anything wiser to suggest?

STEPHEN GREENBLATT

SELECTED BIBLIOGRAPHY

Auden, W. H. "Music in Shakespeare." *The Dyer's Hand, and Other Essays.* New York: Random House, 1948. Analyzing songs from the plays, Auden reflects on music as a social exercise, dramatic convention, and supernatural signifier.

Callaghan, Dympna. "'And all is semblative a woman's part': Body Politics and *Twelfth Night*." *Shakespeare without Women: Representing Gender and Race on the Renaissance Stage.* New York: Routledge, 2000. 26–48. Argues that the misogynistic ridicule of Olivia's genitals in the Malvolio letter is an assertion of male control over the female body.

Gay, Penny. "*Twelfth Night*: Desire and Its Discontents." *As She Likes It: Shakespeare's Unruly Women.* London: Routledge, 1994. 17–47. Describes key postwar English stage productions.

Greenblatt, Stephen. "Fiction and Friction." *Shakespearean Negotiations: The Circulation of Social Energy in Renaissance England.* Berkeley: U of California P, 1988. 66–93. In light of contemporary anatomical theories, relates sexual chafing to verbal sparring and the generation of identity.

Malcolmson, Cristina. "'What You Will': Social Mobility and Gender in *Twelfth Night*." *The Matter of Difference: Materialist Feminist Criticism of Shakespeare*. Ed. Valerie Wayne. Ithaca, NY: Cornell UP, 1991. 29–57. Argues that *Twelfth Night* dramatizes the superiority of women to men in order to call into question the rigid structures of the traditional social order governing both gender and status.

Neely, Carol Thomas. *Distracted Subjects: Madness and Gender in Shakespeare and Early Modern Culture*. Ithaca, NY: Cornell UP, 2004. Asserts that *Twelfth Night*'s displaced erotic choices cohere with changing medical discourse about pathological female lovesickness.

Orgel, Stephen. *Impersonations: The Performance of Gender in Shakespeare's England*. Cambridge: Cambridge UP, 1996. Approaches paradoxes in English playacting practice through contemporary notions of gender construction and sexual desire.

Schalkwyk, David. "Love and Service in *Twelfth Night* and the Sonnets." *Shakespeare Quarterly* 56 (2005): 76–100. Explores how intimacy between masters and servants complicates and enriches depiction of love.

Schiffer, James, ed. *"Twelfth Night": New Critical Essays*. New York: Routledge, 2011. Presents fifteen contemporary essays covering a range of topics from performance history and editing to queer theory and social class.

Wells, Stanley, ed. *"Twelfth Night": Critical Essays*. New York: Garland, 1986. Twenty essays from the nineteenth century onward treat mainly formal and structural aspects and early twentieth-century productions.

FILMS

Twelfth Night [Dvenadsataia 'noch]. 1956. Dir. Y. Fried. USSR. 90 min. This Soviet version celebrates the triumph of carnivalesque optimism over turmoil.

Twelfth Night: Shakespeare: The Animated Tales. 1992. Dir. Marcia Muat. UK/Russia. 20 min. This animated version was produced in joint Welsh-Russian collaboration.

Twelfth Night. 1996. Dir. Trevor Nunn. UK. 134 min. With Ben Kingsley, Helena Bonham Carter, and Nigel Hawthorne. Romantic Celtic coastlines combine with a poignant musical score, a stuffy Malvolio, and a gravely wise Feste.

Twelfth Night. 2003. Dir. Tim Supple. UK. 125 min. Parminder Nagra as Viola. A contemporary, multicultural update.

She's the Man. 2006. Dir. Andy Fickman. USA. 105 min. An updated American high-school romantic comedy.

TEXTUAL INTRODUCTION

Twelfth Night was first printed in the First Folio of 1623, which thus serves as the only authority for its text. Though it was common for plays to be set by two compositors, the whole of *Twelfth Night* was set by the workman identifiable by his idiosyncratic habits of spelling and composition and known to scholars as Compositor B.

Of the twenty-one Folio pages (numbered 255 to 275, with 265 misnumbered as 273) that constitute *Twelfth Night*, only three show any evidence of proofreading, and none of the corrections on those pages is substantive. But even without proofreading, the text is unusually clean. There are appropriate act and scene divisions throughout (which have been followed for this edition). Except for act 3, the ends of acts are marked with "*Finis.*" Characters' entrances and exits are mostly noted and usually timely, and speech prefixes are generally correct. The accuracy of the presswork improves as it progresses, and what mistakes there are seem to be simple typos, misreading of the copy, or dropped or misattributed speech prefixes. In the original text at 1.3.88–89, Sir Toby Belch tells Sir Andrew Aguecheek nonsensically that his hair will not "coole my nature." Editors, emending the line to "curl by nature," infer that the compositor simply misread his copy. In 3.4.23–24, Malvolio clearly does not utter the line

"Why, how dost thou, man? What is the matter with thee?" and this edition, like others, attributes it to Olivia, though the speech might also belong to Maria. A more interesting case involves the famous speech in 2.5.126–28 in which Malvolio reads from the letter, "Some are born great, some achieve greatness, and some have greatness thrust upon 'em." The Folio text, however, begins the sequence with "Some are become great," which makes sense and therefore should not require emendation. But when Malvolio repeats the words of the letter to Olivia at 3.4.36–40, he uses the more familiar "Some are born great." Editors have adopted that reading as an emendation in the first instance, assuming both that the compositor misread his copy and that the sentence makes better sense as a progression from "born great" to "achieve greatness." Another mistake may be compositorial misremembering. At the entrance of Viola as Cesario in 1.5.155, the Folio text reads *Enter Violenta*, the name of a ghost character in *All's Well That Ends Well*, which Compositor B had just been working on. Perhaps, scholars have suggested, his copy text read *Vio.* and he supplied the spelling of that play's character. Such mistakes are both minor and relatively rare in *Twelfth Night*.

Even so, textual scholars debate what kind of manuscript Compositor B was working from—a theatrical promptbook (or transcript thereof) or a scribal copy not of playhouse origin but derived instead from Shakespeare's working papers. Theatrical manuscripts are said to be characterized by the occasional insertion of actors' names instead of characters' names—which does not occur in *Twelfth Night*—or by technical stage directions. These might include the direction "*Enter* VIOLA [*as Cesario*] *and* MALVOLIO *at several doors*" that opens act 2, scene 2; or the direction "MALVOLIO (*within*)" in act 4, scene 2; or even "*Clock strikes*" in act 3, scene 1.

But such evidence is too slight to prove a theatrical origin for the manuscript behind the Folio text of *Twelfth Night*. Instead, the manuscript shows signs of being the scribal transcript of authorial papers, often called "foul papers" from their supposed messiness. Evidence for this theory is the Latin explicit—such as *"Finis Actus Primus"*—that ends all of the acts but act 3. In a stage tradition of continuous action, as at the public theaters where *Twelfth Night* was first performed, such act-scene divisions would be considered merely decorative or editorial in nature rather than functional. But this evidence, too, is slight and conjectural, based on speculations about what features manuscripts of different origins should and should not have. The manuscript's evident tidiness suggests that it was a transcript, but its origins—theatrical, authorial, or other—will never be known. Since Shakespeare left behind no dramatic manuscripts and cannot have been involved with the printing of the First Folio, we will probably never know exactly what kind of manuscript provided the working copy for Compositor B, except that it was clearly in good shape and hence relatively easy for him to read.

More interesting is the question of when—in the sequence of printing the First Folio—*Twelfth Night* was printed. In the book's divisions by genre, the play is the penultimate of the Comedies—appearing between *All's Well That Ends Well* and *The Winter's Tale*. A blank page—itself highly unusual at a time when paper constituted the highest cost in publishing—comes between the end of *Twelfth Night* and the beginning of *Winter's Tale*, suggesting that *Twelfth Night* was originally intended to conclude the Comedies. Even more perplexing is that the printing—heretofore proceeding in an unbroken sequence—was interrupted before *Twelfth Night*, with Compositor B jumping ahead from the not-quite-finished *All's Well* to the Histories section. He then composed the whole of *King John* and part of *Richard II* before returning to complete *All's Well* and set type for *Twelfth Night*. There can have been no problem in securing the right to print the play. *Twelfth Night* was entered properly in the Stationers' Register and appeared in the Folio for the first time. Perhaps there was a delay in securing the manuscript—a scribe not having finished transcribing it. But an answer to that question would depend on knowing what kind of text the compositor was working from, and as discussed above, evidence for that too can never be conclusive.

GAIL KERN PASTER

PERFORMANCE NOTE

Given its evenhanded distribution of lines and variety of substantial secondary roles, *Twelfth Night* calls for an ensemble with extraordinary depth and versatility. Its casting challenges include finding at least six talented comic actors, as well as a credible pair of "twins" for Viola and Sebastian, but the most notable issue may be the absence of a clear male lead. Orsino's pursuit of Olivia is the plot's first matter of business; Toby Belch has the play's largest role; and Sebastian's marriage to Olivia and reunion with Viola are central concerns of the last act—yet none of the roles tends to dominate the audience's attention like those of Viola, Malvolio, and the Clown. Each production, then, must establish its particular balance between the three star parts—each capable of overshadowing the others as well as the production—while accommodating the play's repeated efforts to advance more traditional protagonists in their stead.

The uncertainty of the main plot and the absence of a clear male lead allow directors to tell starkly different stories without substantially altering the text. Whether a production exposes or understates Orsino's self-importance; whether Toby is a good-natured friend to Andrew or purely mercenary; whether Malvolio's tyranny or his tragedy is emphasized; whether Antonio's feud with Orsino and love for Sebastian are featured or downplayed—all are choices that can shift the play's focus as well as the audience's sense of allegiance. Productions must also address the tension created by the farcical below-stairs comedy that grows darker and more complicated than the play's genre anticipates. In recent years, directors have often explored the comedy's darker matter, both by intensifying Malvolio's (and sometimes Antonio's) plight and by accenting the strains of melancholy and cynicism that are potential in the Clown.

BRETT GAMBOA

Twelfth Night, or What You Will

[THE PERSONS OF THE PLAY

ORSINO, Duke of Illyria
VALENTINE }
CURIO   } members of Orsino's court

VIOLA, a shipwrecked lady from Messaline, later disguised as Cesario
CAPTAIN, rescuer of Viola
SEBASTIAN, twin brother to Viola
ANTONIO, sea captain, rescuer of Sebastian

Lady OLIVIA, a Countess
MARIA, waiting-gentlewoman to Olivia
MALVOLIO, steward to Olivia
FABIAN, member of Olivia's household
CLOWN, Olivia's jester, also called Feste
SIR TOBY Belch, kinsman to Olivia
SIR ANDREW Aguecheek, a visiting knight
PRIEST

FIRST OFFICER
SECOND OFFICER
SERVANTS
Lords, Sailors, Musicians, Attendants]

1.1

Enter ORSINO, *Duke of Illyria,* CURIO, *and other
Lords [with Musicians playing].*

ORSINO   If music be the food of love, play on.
　　Give me excess of it that, surfeiting,
　　The appetite may sicken and so die.
　　That strain again—it had a dying fall.°   *cadence*
5　Oh, it came o'er my ear like the sweet sound
　　That breathes upon a bank of violets,
　　Stealing and giving odor. Enough, no more!
　　'Tis not so sweet now as it was before.
　　O spirit of love, how quick and fresh° art thou   *lively and eager*
10　That, notwithstanding thy capacity
　　Receiveth as the sea,° naught enters there   *Receives without limit*
　　Of what validity° and pitch° soe'er,   *value / height; excellence*
　　But falls into abatement° and low price   *lesser value*
　　Even in a minute. So full of shapes is fancy°   *love; desire*
15　That it alone is high fantastical.°   *uniquely imaginative*
CURIO   Will you go hunt, my lord?
ORSINO　　　　　　　　　　　　　What, Curio?
CURIO　　　　　　　　　　　　　　　　　　The hart.

ORSINO   Why, so I do, the noblest that I have.[1]
Oh, when mine eyes did see Olivia first,
Methought she purged the air of pestilence.[2]
20   That instant was I turned into a hart,
And my desires, like fell° and cruel hounds,   *savage*
E'er since pursue me.[3]
　　　　Enter VALENTINE.
　　　　　　How now, what news from her?
VALENTINE   So please my lord, I might not be admitted,
But from her handmaid do return this answer:
25   The element itself, till seven years' heat,[4]
Shall not behold her face at ample° view,   *full*
But, like a cloistress,° she will veilèd walk   *nun*
And water once a day her chamber round
With eye-offending brine.° All this to season   *stinging tears*
30   A brother's dead love,[5] which she would keep fresh
And lasting in her sad remembrance.
ORSINO   Oh, she that hath a heart of that fine° frame   *exquisitely made*
To pay this debt of love but to a brother,
How will she love, when the rich golden shaft[6]
35   Hath killed the flock of all affections else°   *other emotions*
That live in her; when liver, brain, and heart,[7]
These sovereign thrones, are all supplied, and filled
Her sweet perfections[8] with one self° king!   *one and the same*
Away before me to sweet beds of flowers.
40   Love thoughts lie rich when canopied with bowers.
　　　　　　　　　　　　　　　Exeunt.

1.2

　　　Enter VIOLA, *a* CAPTAIN, *and Sailors.*
VIOLA[1]   What country, friends, is this?
CAPTAIN   This is Illyria, lady.
VIOLA   And what should I do in Illyria?
My brother, he is in Elysium.[2]
5   Perchance° he is not drowned. What think you, sailors?   *Perhaps*
CAPTAIN   It is perchance° that you yourself were saved.   *by chance*
VIOLA   Oh, my poor brother! And so perchance may he be.
CAPTAIN   True, madam. And, to comfort you with chance,[3]
Assure yourself, after our ship did split,
10   When you and those poor number saved with you
Hung on our driving boat,[4] I saw your brother,
Most provident in peril, bind himself
(Courage and hope both teaching him the practice)
To a strong mast that lived° upon the sea.   *remained afloat*

1.1 Location: Illyria, the Greek and Roman name for
the eastern Adriatic coast; probably not suggesting a
real country to Shakespeare's audience.
1. Orsino plays on "hart/heart."
2. Plague and other illnesses were thought to be
caused by bad air.
3. Alluding to the classical legend of Actaeon, who
was turned into a stag and hunted by his own hounds
for having seen the goddess Artemis naked.
4. The sky itself / for seven summers.
5. *All . . . love:* All this to preserve (by the salt of the
tears) the love of a dead brother.

6. Of Cupid's golden-tipped arrow, which caused
desire.
7. In Elizabethan psychology, these were the seats of
passion, intellect, and feeling.
8. *and filled . . . perfections:* and all her flawless qualities are governed by.
1.2 Location: The coast of Illyria.
1. Viola is not named in the dialogue until 5.1.231.
2. The heaven of classical mythology.
3. With what may have happened.
4. The ship's boat. *driving:* being driven by the
wind.

15   Where, like Arion[5] on the dolphin's back,
        I saw him hold acquaintance with the waves,
        So long as I could see.
        VIOLA [*giving him money*]   For saying so, there's gold.
        Mine own escape unfoldeth to° my hope,   *encourages*
        Whereto thy speech serves for authority°   *support*
20   The like of him.[6] Know'st thou this country?
        CAPTAIN   Ay, madam, well, for I was bred and born
        Not three hours' travel from this very place.
        VIOLA   Who governs here?
        CAPTAIN   A noble duke in nature, as in name.
25   VIOLA   What is his name?
        CAPTAIN   Orsino.
        VIOLA   Orsino. I have heard my father name him.
        He was a bachelor then.
        CAPTAIN   And so is now, or was so very late.°   *lately*
30   For but a month ago I went from hence,
        And then 'twas fresh in murmur° (as you know,   *newly rumored*
        What great ones do, the less will prattle of)
        That he did seek the love of fair Olivia.
        VIOLA   What's she?
35   CAPTAIN   A virtuous maid, the daughter of a count
        That died some twelvemonth since, then leaving her
        In the protection of his son, her brother,
        Who shortly also died. For whose dear love,
        They say, she hath abjured the sight
        And company of men.
40   VIOLA   Oh, that I served that lady,
        And might not be delivered° to the world   *revealed*
        Till I had made mine own occasion mellow°   *ripe (to be revealed)*
        What my estate° is.   *social rank*
        CAPTAIN   That were hard to compass,°   *achieve*
        Because she will admit no kind of suit,°   *petition*
45   No, not the Duke's.
        VIOLA   There is a fair behavior[7] in thee, Captain.
        And though that nature with a beauteous wall
        Doth oft close in pollution, yet of thee
        I will believe thou hast a mind that suits
50   With this, thy fair and outward character.[8]
        I prithee (and I'll pay thee bounteously)
        Conceal me what I am, and be my aid
        For such disguise as haply shall become
        The form of my intent.[9] I'll serve this duke.
55   Thou shalt present me as an eunuch[1] to him.
        It may be worth thy pains, for I can sing
        And speak to him in many sorts of music
        That will allow° me very worth his service.   *prove*

---

5. A legendary Greek musician who, in order to save himself from being murdered on a voyage, jumped overboard and was carried to land by a dolphin.
6. That he too has survived.
7. Outward appearance; conduct.
8. Appearance (suggesting moral qualities).

9. *as . . . intent:* that perhaps may be fitting to my purpose. *form:* shape.
1. Castrati (hence, "eunuchs") were prized as male sopranos; the disguise would have explained Viola's feminine voice. Viola (or perhaps Shakespeare) seems to have changed plans: she presents herself instead as a young page.

What else may hap, to time I will commit.
60   Only shape thou thy silence to my wit.°   *imagination; plan*
CAPTAIN   Be you his eunuch, and your mute[2] I'll be.
When my tongue blabs, then let mine eyes not see.
VIOLA   I thank thee. Lead me on.   *Exeunt.*

1.3

Enter SIR TOBY *and* MARIA.

SIR TOBY   What a plague means my niece to take the death of
her brother thus? I am sure care's an enemy to life.
MARIA   By my troth, Sir Toby, you must come in earlier a-nights.
Your cousin,[1] my lady, takes great exceptions to your ill
5   hours.
SIR TOBY   Why, let her except before excepted.[2]
MARIA   Ay, but you must confine yourself within the modest°   *moderate*
limits of order.
SIR TOBY   Confine! I'll confine myself no finer[3] than I am.
10   These clothes are good enough to drink in, and so be these
boots, too. An° they be not, let them hang themselves in their   *If*
own straps.
MARIA   That quaffing and drinking will undo you. I heard my
lady talk of it yesterday and of a foolish knight that you brought
15   in one night here to be her wooer.
SIR TOBY   Who, Sir Andrew Aguecheek?
MARIA   Ay, he.
SIR TOBY   He's as tall a man as any's[4] in Illyria.
MARIA   What's that to th' purpose?
20 SIR TOBY   Why, he has three thousand ducats a year.
MARIA   Ay, but he'll have but a year in all these ducats.[5] He's
a very° fool and a prodigal.   *an absolute*
SIR TOBY   Fie, that you'll say so! He plays o'th' viol-de-
gamboys,[6] and speaks three or four languages word for word
25   without book,° and hath all the good gifts of nature.   *from memory*
MARIA   He hath, indeed, almost natural.[7] For besides that he's
a fool, he's a great quarreler. And but that he hath the gift°   *talent; present*
of a coward to allay the gust° he hath in quarreling, 'tis   *gusto*
thought among the prudent he would quickly have the gift
30   of a grave.
SIR TOBY   By this hand, they are scoundrels and substractors[8]
that say so of him. Who are they?
MARIA   They that add, moreover, he's drunk nightly in your
company.
35 SIR TOBY   With drinking healths to my niece. I'll drink to her
as long as there is a passage in my throat and drink in
Illyria. He's a coward and a coistrel° that will not drink   *horse groom; lout*

---

2. In Turkish harems, eunuchs served as guards and were assisted by "mutes" (usually, servants whose tongues had been cut out).
1.3 Location: The Countess Olivia's house.
1. Term used generally of kinsfolk.
2. Playing on the legal jargon *exceptis excipiendis,* "with the previously stated exceptions." Sir Toby refuses to take Olivia's displeasure seriously.
3. Suggesting both "a refined manner of dress" and

"narrowly" (referring to his girth).
4. Any (man who) is. *tall:* brave; worthy. (Maria takes it in the modern sense of height.)
5. He'll spend his fortune in a year.
6. A facetious corruption of "viola da gamba," a bass viol held between the knees.
7. Idiots and fools were called "naturals."
8. Corruption of "detractors." (In reply, Maria puns on "substract" as "subtract.")

to my niece till his brains turn o'th' toe like a parish top.
What, wench! *Castiliano vulgo*,[9] for here comes Sir Andrew
40 Agueface.

       Enter SIR ANDREW *Aguecheek.*

SIR ANDREW   Sir Toby Belch. How now, Sir Toby Belch?

SIR TOBY   Sweet Sir Andrew.

SIR ANDREW   Bless you, fair shrew.[1]

MARIA   And you too, sir.

45 SIR TOBY   Accost, Sir Andrew, accost.[2]

SIR ANDREW   What's that?

SIR TOBY   My niece's chambermaid.[3]

SIR ANDREW   Good Mistress Accost, I desire better acquaintance.

MARIA   My name is Mary, sir.

50 SIR ANDREW   Good Mistress Mary Accost—

SIR TOBY   You mistake, knight. "Accost" is front° her, board   *confront*
her, woo her, assail[4] her.

SIR ANDREW   By my troth, I would not undertake[5] her in this
company.° Is that the meaning of "accost"?   *the audience*

55 MARIA   Fare you well, gentlemen.

SIR TOBY   An thou let part so,[6] Sir Andrew, would thou mightst
never draw sword again.

SIR ANDREW   An you part so, mistress, I would I might never
draw sword again. Fair lady, do you think you have fools in
60 hand?°   *to deal with*

MARIA   Sir, I have not you by th' hand.

SIR ANDREW   Marry, but you shall have, and here's my hand.

MARIA [*taking his hand*]   Now, sir, thought is free.[7] I pray you,
bring your hand to th' buttery bar,[8] and let it drink.

65 SIR ANDREW   Wherefore, sweetheart? What's your metaphor?

MARIA   It's dry,[9] sir.

SIR ANDREW   Why, I think so. I am not such an ass, but I can
keep my hand dry.[1] But what's your jest?

MARIA   A dry jest,[2] sir.

70 SIR ANDREW   Are you full of them?

MARIA   Ay, sir, I have them at my fingers' ends.[3] Marry, now
I let go your hand, I am barren.°   *Exit.*   *empty of jokes*

SIR TOBY   O knight, thou lack'st a cup of canary.[4] When did I
see thee so put down?[5]

75 SIR ANDREW   Never in your life, I think, unless you see canary
put me down. Methinks sometimes I have no more wit than

---

9. Variously interpreted, but may mean "Speak of the devil," since Castilians were considered devilish, and *vulgo* refers to the common tongue. *parish top:* parishes kept large tops that were spun by whipping them, for the parishioners' amusement and exercise.
1. Andrew possibly confuses "shrew" (ill-tempered woman) with "mouse," an endearment.
2. Address (her); originally a naval term meaning "go alongside; greet."
3. Lady-in-waiting; not a menial servant, but a gentlewoman in attendance on a great lady.
4. *board:* speak to; tackle. *assail:* greet (also nautical).
5. Take her on (with sexual implication).
6. If you let her go without protest or without bidding her farewell.

7. The customary retort to "Do you think I am a fool?"
8. Ledge on the half-door to a buttery or a wine cellar on which drinks were served.
9. Thirsty; but a dry hand was also thought to be a sign of impotence.
1. Alluding to the proverb "Even fools have enough wit to come in out of the rain."
2. A stupid joke (referring to Andrew's stupidity); an ironic quip; a joke about dryness.
3. Always ready; or "by th' hand" (line 61).
4. A sweet wine, like sherry, originally from the Canary Islands.
5. Defeated in repartee; "put down" with drink.

a Christian° or an ordinary man has. But I am a great eater   *an average man*
of beef,⁶ and I believe that does harm to my wit.
SIR TOBY   No question.
80 SIR ANDREW   An I thought that, I'd forswear it. I'll ride home
tomorrow, Sir Toby.
SIR TOBY   *Pourquoi,°* my dear knight?   *Why*
SIR ANDREW   What is *pourquoi?* Do, or not do? I would I had
bestowed that time in the tongues⁷ that I have in fencing,
85 dancing, and bearbaiting. Oh, had I but followed the arts.
SIR TOBY   Then hadst thou had an excellent head of hair.
SIR ANDREW   Why would that have mended° my hair?   *improved*
SIR TOBY   Past question, for thou seest it will not curl by
nature.⁸
90 SIR ANDREW   But it becomes me well enough, does't not?
SIR TOBY   Excellent, it hangs like flax on a distaff.⁹ And I hope
to see a housewife¹ take thee between her legs and spin it
off.²
SIR ANDREW   Faith, I'll home tomorrow, Sir Toby. Your niece
95 will not be seen. Or, if she be, it's four to one she'll none of
me. The Count himself here hard by woos her.
SIR TOBY   She'll none o'th' Count. She'll not match above her
degree,° neither in estate,³ years, nor wit. I have heard her   *social rank*
swear't. Tut, there's life in't,⁴ man.
100 SIR ANDREW   I'll stay a month longer. I am a fellow o'th' strangest mind i'th' world. I delight in masques and revels sometimes altogether.
SIR TOBY   Art thou good at these kickshawses,⁵ knight?
SIR ANDREW   As any man in Illyria, whatsoever he be, under
105 the degree of my betters, and yet I will not compare with an
old man.⁶
SIR TOBY   What is thy excellence in a galliard,⁷ knight?
SIR ANDREW   Faith, I can cut a caper.⁸
SIR TOBY   And I can cut the mutton to't.
110 SIR ANDREW   And I think I have the back-trick⁹ simply as strong
as any man in Illyria.
SIR TOBY   Wherefore are these things hid? Wherefore have
these gifts a curtain¹ before 'em? Are they like to take dust
like Mistress Mall's² picture? Why dost thou not go to church
115 in a galliard and come home in a coranto?³ My very walk
should be a jig. I would not so much as make water but in a
cinquepace.⁴ What dost thou mean? Is it a world to hide
virtues in? I did think by the excellent constitution of thy
leg, it was formed under the star of a galliard.⁵

6. Contemporary medicine held that beef dulled the intellect.
7. Foreign languages; Toby takes him to mean "curling tongs."
8. To contrast with Andrew's "arts" (line 85).
9. In spinning, flax would hang in long, thin, yellowish strings on the "distaff," a pole held between the knees.
1. Housewives spun flax; the pronunciation, "hus-wife," also suggests the meaning "prostitute."
2. Make him bald (as a result of venereal disease).
3. Status; possession.
4. Proverbial: "While there's life, there's hope."
5. Trifles; trivialities (from the French *quelque chose*).
6. An expert (perhaps a backhanded compliment).

7. A lively, complex dance, including the caper.
8. Leap. (Toby puns on the pickled flower buds used in a sauce served with mutton.)
9. Probably a dance movement, a kick of the foot behind the body (also suggesting sexual prowess, with later reference to "mutton" as "prostitute").
1. Used to protect paintings from dust.
2. Like "Moll[y]," "Mall" was a nickname for "Mary."
3. An even more rapid dance than the galliard.
4. Galliard, or, more properly, the steps joining the figures of the dance; punning on "cinque" pronounced as "sink," as in "sewer."
5. Astrological influences favorable to dancing.

120   SIR ANDREW   Ay, 'tis strong, and it does indifferent° well in a   *moderately*
        dun-colored[6] stock.° Shall we set about some revels?   *stocking*
        SIR TOBY   What shall we do else? Were we not born under
        Taurus?[7]
        SIR ANDREW   Taurus? That's sides and heart.
125   SIR TOBY   No, sir, it is legs and thighs. Let me see thee
        caper. [SIR ANDREW *dances a caper.*] Ha, higher! Ha, ha,
        excellent!   *Exeunt.*

1.4

Enter VALENTINE *and* VIOLA [*as Cesario*] *in man's attire.*[1]

VALENTINE   If the Duke continue these favors towards you,
        Cesario, you are like to be much advanced. He hath known
        you but three days, and already you are no stranger.
VIOLA   You either fear his humor° or my negligence that you   *moodiness*
5   call in question the continuance of his love. Is he incon-
        stant, sir, in his favors?
VALENTINE   No, believe me.
            Enter DUKE, CURIO, *and Attendants.*
VIOLA   I thank you. Here comes the Count.
ORSINO   Who saw Cesario, ho?
10   VIOLA   On your attendance,° my lord, here.   *Waiting at your service*
ORSINO [*to* CURIO *and Attendants*]   Stand you awhile aloof.°   *aside*
      —Cesario,
      Thou know'st no less, but all.° I have unclasped   *than everything*
      To thee the book even of my secret soul.
      Therefore, good youth, address thy gait° unto her,   *go*
15   Be not denied access, stand at her doors,
      And tell them, there thy fixèd foot shall grow°   *take root*
      Till thou have audience.
VIOLA   Sure, my noble lord,
      If she be so abandoned to her sorrow
      As it is spoke, she never will admit me.
20   ORSINO   Be clamorous and leap all civil bounds[2]
      Rather than make unprofited° return.   *unsuccessful*
VIOLA   Say I do speak with her, my lord, what then?
ORSINO   Oh, then unfold the passion of my love,
      Surprise[3] her with discourse of my dear° faith.   *heartfelt*
25   It shall become thee well to act my woes.
      She will attend it better in thy youth
      Than in a nuncio's° of more grave aspect.°   *messenger's / appearance*
VIOLA   I think not so, my lord.
ORSINO   Dear lad, believe it.
      For they shall yet belie thy happy years
30   That say thou art a man. Diana's lip
      Is not more smooth and rubious.° Thy small pipe°   *ruby red / voice*

---

6. TEXTUAL COMMENT The Folio's "dam'd color'd" does not make much sense as a modifier for stockings and has prompted a variety of emendations. For more on this issue, see Digital Edition TC 1.
7. The astrological sign of the bull was usually thought to govern the neck and throat (appropriate to heavy drinkers).

1.4 Location: Orsino's palace.
1. PERFORMANCE COMMENT How to stage Viola's first appearance in masculine attire is one of many important decisions related to twinning and cross-dressing in this play. For more, see Digital Edition PC 1.
2. All constraints of polite behavior.
3. Capture by unexpected attack (of military origin).

Is as the maiden's organ, shrill and sound,[4]
And all is semblative° a woman's part. [5]   *like*
I know thy constellation[6] is right apt
35   For this affair. —Some four or five, attend him,
All if you will. For I myself am best
When least in company. [*to* VIOLA] Prosper well in this,
And thou shalt live as freely as thy lord
To call his fortunes thine.

VIOLA   I'll do my best
40   To woo your lady. [*aside*] Yet a barful strife;[7]
Whoe'er I woo, myself would be his wife.   *Exeunt.*

1.5

Enter MARIA *and* CLOWN.

MARIA   Nay, either tell me where thou hast been, or I will not
open my lips so wide as a bristle may enter in° way of thy   *by*
excuse. My lady will hang thee for thy absence.

CLOWN   Let her hang me. He that is well hanged in this world
5   needs to fear no colors.[1]

MARIA   Make that good.°   *Explain that*

CLOWN   He shall see none to fear.

MARIA   A good lenten[2] answer. I can tell thee where that saying
was born, of "I fear no colors."

10   CLOWN   Where, good Mistress Mary?

MARIA   In the wars,[3] and that may you be bold to say in your
foolery.

CLOWN   Well, God give them wisdom that have it. And those
that are fools, let them use their talents.[4]

15   MARIA   Yet you will be hanged for being so long absent. Or to
be turned away,[5] is not that as good as a hanging to you?

CLOWN   Many a good hanging prevents a bad marriage.[6] And
for turning away, let summer bear it out.°   *make it endurable*

MARIA   You are resolute then?

20   CLOWN   Not so, neither, but I am resolved on two points.

MARIA   That if one break, the other will hold. Or if both break,
your gaskins fall.[7]

CLOWN   Apt in good faith, very apt. Well, go thy way. If Sir
Toby would leave drinking, thou wert as witty a piece of
25   Eve's flesh[8] as any in Illyria.

MARIA   Peace, you rogue, no more o'that. Here comes my lady.
Make your excuse wisely, you were best.°   *you had better*

Enter Lady OLIVIA *with* MALVOLIO° [*and Attendants*].   *"ill will"*

CLOWN   Wit,[9] an't° be thy will, put me into good fooling.   *if it*
Those wits that think they have thee do very oft prove fools,

---

4. High pitched and uncracked.
5. PERFORMANCE COMMENT Orsino's attention to feminine qualities in Cesario is particularly charged in performance. For more on the dramatic possibilities this moment affords, see Digital Edition PC 2.
6. Nature and abilities (as supposedly determined by the stars).
7. An undertaking full of impediments.
1.5 Location: Olivia's house.
1. Proverbial for "fear nothing." colors: worldly deceptions, with a pun on "collars" as "hangman's noose."
2. Thin or meager (like Lenten fare).
3. *In the wars:* "colors" in line 9 refers to military flags.
4. Alluding to the parable of the talents, Matthew

25. The comic implication is that a fool should strive to increase his measure of folly. Since "fool" and "fowl" had similar pronunciations, there may also be a play on "talents/talons."
5. Dismissed; also, perhaps, turned off or hanged.
6. *Many . . . marriage:* Proverbial. *hanging:* execution; sexual prowess.
7. Maria puns on "points" as the laces used to fasten gaskins—wide breeches—to a man's jacket.
8. A woman. The Clown may imply both that Maria and Toby would make a good match and that Maria is as witty as Toby is sober.
9. Intelligence, which is often contrasted with will.

30   and I that am sure I lack thee may pass for a wise man. For
what says Quinapalus?[1] "Better a witty fool than a foolish
wit." —God bless thee, lady.[2]

OLIVIA   Take the fool away.

CLOWN   Do you not hear, fellows? Take away the lady.

35 OLIVIA   Go to, you're a dry[3] fool. I'll no more of you. Besides,
you grow dishonest.°   *unreliable*

CLOWN   Two faults, madonna,° that drink and good counsel   *my lady*
will amend. For give the dry fool drink, then is the fool not
dry. Bid the dishonest man mend° himself; if he mend, he is   *reform*

40   no longer dishonest. If he cannot, let the botcher° mend him.   *tailor; cobbler*
Anything that's mended is but patched. Virtue that trans-
gresses is but patched with sin, and sin that amends is but
patched with virtue. If that this simple syllogism will serve,
so. If it will not, what remedy? As there is no true cuckold

45   but calamity, so beauty's a flower.[4] The lady bade, take away
the fool. Therefore I say again, take her away.

OLIVIA   Sir, I bade them take away you.

CLOWN   Misprision[5] in the highest degree. Lady, *Cucullus
non facit monachum.*[6] That's as much to say as I wear not

50   motley[7] in my brain. Good madonna, give me leave to prove
you a fool.

OLIVIA   Can you do it?

CLOWN   Dexteriously,° good madonna.   *Dexterously*

OLIVIA   Make your proof.

55 CLOWN   I must catechize[8] you for it, madonna. Good my mouse
of virtue,° answer me.   *My good virtuous mouse*

OLIVIA   Well, sir, for want of other idleness,° I'll bide° your   *pastime / await*
proof.

CLOWN   Good madonna, why mourn'st thou?

60 OLIVIA   Good fool, for my brother's death.

CLOWN   I think his soul is in hell, madonna.

OLIVIA   I know his soul is in heaven, fool.

CLOWN   The more fool, madonna, to mourn for your brother's
soul, being in heaven. Take away the fool, gentlemen.

65 OLIVIA   What think you of this fool, Malvolio? Doth he not
mend?[9]

MALVOLIO   Yes, and shall do, till the pangs of death shake
him. Infirmity° that decays the wise doth ever make the bet-   *(Old) age*
ter fool.[1]

70 CLOWN   God send you, sir, a speedy infirmity, for the better
increasing your folly. Sir Toby will be sworn that I am no
fox, but he will not pass his word for twopence that you are
no fool.

OLIVIA   How say you to that, Malvolio?

---

1. The Clown frequently invents his own authorities.
2. TEXTUAL COMMENT Editors sometimes mark this speech of the Clown's as an aside. But this apostrophe to wit, for a character as bold and outspoken as the Clown, does not seem to require this editorial intervention. For more on the issue of asides, see Digital Edition TC 2.
3. Dull, but the Clown interprets the term as "thirsty." *Go to*: an expression of impatience.
4. *As . . . flower*: In taking her vow (1.2.38–40), Olivia has wedded herself to calamity but must be

unfaithful, or let pass her moment of beauty.
5. Misapprehension; wrongful arrest.
6. The cowl does not make the monk (a Latin proverb).
7. The multicolored costume of a fool.
8. Question (as in catechism, which tests the orthodoxy of belief).
9. Improve, but Malvolio takes "mend" to mean "grow more foolish."
1. Make the fool more foolish.

75 MALVOLIO I marvel your ladyship takes delight in such a bar-
ren rascal. I saw him put down° the other day with an ordi-   *defeated in repartee*
nary fool that has no more brain than a stone. Look you
now, he's out of his guard° already. Unless you laugh and   *defenseless*
minister occasion² to him, he is gagged. I protest I take
80 these wise men that crow so at these set° kind of fools no   *artificial*
better than the fools' zanies.°   *stooges*
OLIVIA Oh, you are sick of self-love, Malvolio, and taste with
a distempered³ appetite. To be generous, guiltless, and of
free° disposition is to take those things for bird-bolts⁴ that   *magnanimous*
85 you deem cannon bullets. There is no slander in an allowed
fool, though he do nothing but rail, nor no railing in a
known discreet man, though he do nothing but reprove.
CLOWN Now Mercury endue thee with leasing,⁵ for thou
speak'st well of fools.
    Enter MARIA.
90 MARIA Madam, there is at the gate a young gentleman much
desires to speak with you.
OLIVIA From the Count Orsino, is it?
MARIA I know not, madam. 'Tis a fair young man and well
attended.
95 OLIVIA Who of my people hold him in delay?
MARIA Sir Toby, madam, your kinsman.
OLIVIA Fetch him off, I pray you. He speaks nothing but
madman.° Fie on him.   [*Exit* MARIA.]   *madman's talk*
—Go you, Malvolio. If it be a suit from the Count, I am sick
100 or not at home. What° you will to dismiss it. *Exit* MALVOLIO.   *Say whatever*
—Now you see, sir, how your fooling grows old,° and people   *stale*
dislike it.
CLOWN Thou hast spoke for us, madonna, as if thy eldest son
should be a fool. Whose skull Jove cram with brains, for—
105 here he comes—
    Enter SIR TOBY.
one of thy kin has a most weak *pia mater.*⁶
OLIVIA By mine honor, half drunk. What is he at the gate,
cousin?°   *kinsman*
SIR TOBY A gentleman.
110 OLIVIA A gentleman? What gentleman?
SIR TOBY 'Tis a gentleman here. [*He belches.*] A plague o'these
pickle herring! [*to* CLOWN] How now, sot?°   *fool; drunkard*
CLOWN Good Sir Toby.
OLIVIA Cousin, cousin, how have you come so early by this
115 lethargy?
SIR TOBY Lechery? I defy lechery. There's one° at the gate.   *someone*
OLIVIA Ay, marry, what is he?
SIR TOBY Let him be the devil an° he will, I care not. Give me   *if*
faith,⁷ say I. Well, it's all one.°   *Exit.*   *it doesn't matter*
120 OLIVIA What's a drunken man like, fool?
CLOWN Like a drowned man, a fool, and a madman. One

2. And give opportunity.
3. An unbalanced; a sick.
4. Blunt arrows for shooting birds.
5. May Mercury, the god of deception, endow you

with the talent of tactful lying.
6. Brain; or literally, the membrane enclosing it.
7. To defy the devil by faith alone.

draught above heat[8] makes him a fool, the second mads him, and a third drowns him.

125 OLIVIA   Go thou and seek the crowner° and let him sit o'[9] my   *coroner*
coz,° for he's in the third degree of drink. He's drowned. Go   *cousin; uncle*
look after him.

CLOWN   He is but mad yet, madonna, and the fool shall look
to the madman.   [*Exit.*]

Enter MALVOLIO.

MALVOLIO   Madam, yond young fellow swears he will speak
130 with you. I told him you were sick; he takes on him to
understand so much, and therefore° comes to speak with   *for that very reason*
you. I told him you were asleep; he seems to have a fore-
knowledge of that too, and therefore comes to speak with
you. What is to be said to him, lady? He's fortified against
135 any denial.

OLIVIA   Tell him he shall not speak with me.

MALVOLIO   He's been told so. And he says he'll stand at your
door like a sheriff's post,[1] and be the supporter to a bench,
but he'll speak with you.

140 OLIVIA   What kind o'man is he?

MALVOLIO   Why, of mankind.°   *like any other*

OLIVIA   What manner of man?

MALVOLIO   Of very ill manner. He'll speak with you, will you
or no.

145 OLIVIA   Of what personage° and years is he?   *appearance*

MALVOLIO   Not yet old enough for a man, nor young enough
for a boy; as a squash[2] is before 'tis a peascod, or a codling°   *an unripe apple*
when 'tis almost an apple. 'Tis with him in standing water°   *at the turn of the tide*
between boy and man. He is very well favored,° and he speaks   *handsome*
150 very shrewishly.° One would think his mother's milk were   *sharply*
scarce out of him.

OLIVIA   Let him approach. Call in my gentlewoman.

MALVOLIO   Gentlewoman, my lady calls.   *Exit.*

Enter MARIA.

OLIVIA   Give me my veil, come, throw it o'er my face.
155 We'll once more hear Orsino's embassy.

Enter VIOLA [*as Cesario*].[3]

VIOLA   The honorable lady of the house, which is she?

OLIVIA   Speak to me; I shall answer for her. Your will?

VIOLA   Most radiant, exquisite, and unmatchable beauty—I
pray you, tell me if this be the lady of the house, for I never
160 saw her. I would be loath to cast away° my speech. For   *waste*
besides that it is excellently well penned, I have taken great
pains to con° it. Good beauties, let me sustain no scorn. I   *memorize*
am very comptible° even to the least sinister usage.[4]   *sensitive*

OLIVIA   Whence came you, sir?

165 VIOLA   I can say little more than I have studied,[5] and that
question's out of my part. Good gentle one, give me modest°   *adequate*

---

8. One drink ("draught") beyond the quantity necessary to warm him.
9. *sit o':* hold an inquest for.
1. A decorative post set before a sheriff's door, as a
sign of authority.
2. An undeveloped pea pod.
3. TEXTUAL COMMENT The stage direction in F reads

"*Enter Violenta,*" so editors invariably emend to read
"*Viola.*" For discussion of how this mistake might have
happened, see Digital Edition TC 3 and the Textual
Introduction.
4. To the slightest discourteous treatment.
5. Learned by heart (a theatrical term).

assurance if you be the lady of the house, that I may proceed
in my speech.

OLIVIA   Are you a comedian?°   *an actor*

170   VIOLA   No, my profound heart.[6] And yet, by the very fangs of
malice, I swear I am not that I play. Are you the lady of the
house?

OLIVIA   If I do not usurp myself, I am.

VIOLA   Most certain, if you are she, you do usurp yourself. For

175   what is yours to bestow is not yours to reserve. But this is
from my commission.° I will on with my speech in your   *beyond my instructions*
praise, and then show you the heart of my message.

OLIVIA   Come to what is important in't. I forgive you° the   *excuse you from*
praise.

180   VIOLA   Alas, I took great pains to study it, and 'tis poetical.

OLIVIA   It is the more like to be feigned. I pray you keep it in.
I heard you were saucy at my gates, and allowed your
approach rather to wonder at you than to hear you. If you
be not mad,° be gone. If you have reason,° be brief. 'Tis not   *utterly mad / any sanity*

185   that time of moon with me to make one in so skipping a
dialogue.[7]

MARIA   Will you hoist sail, sir? Here lies your way.

VIOLA   No, good swabber, I am to hull[8] here a little longer.
—Some mollification for your giant,[9] sweet lady.

190   OLIVIA   Tell me your mind.

VIOLA   I am a messenger.[1]

OLIVIA   Sure you have some hideous matter to deliver, when
the courtesy° of it is so fearful. Speak your office.°   *introduction / business*

VIOLA   It alone concerns your ear. I bring no overture° of war,   *declaration*

195   no taxation of homage.[2] I hold the olive[3] in my hand. My
words are as full of peace as matter.°   *meaning*

OLIVIA   Yet you began rudely. What are you? What would you?

VIOLA   The rudeness that hath appeared in me have I learned
from my entertainment.° What I am, and what I would, are   *reception*

200   as secret as maidenhead.° To your ears, divinity; to any oth-   *virginity*
ers, profanation.

OLIVIA   Give us the place alone. We will hear this divinity.°   *religious discourse*
                    [*Exeunt* MARIA *and Attendants.*]
—Now sir, what is your text?[4]

VIOLA   Most sweet lady—

205   OLIVIA   A comfortable° doctrine, and much may be said of it.   *comforting*
Where lies your text?

VIOLA   In Orsino's bosom.

OLIVIA   In his bosom? In what chapter of his bosom?

VIOLA   To answer by the method,° in the first of his heart.   *in the same style*

210   OLIVIA   Oh, I have read it; it is heresy. Have you no more
to say?

VIOLA   Good madam, let me see your face.

---

6. My most wise lady; upon my soul.
7. *'Tis . . . dialogue:* I am not lunatic enough to take
part in so flighty a conversation. (Lunacy was thought
to be influenced by the phases of the moon.)
8. To lie unanchored with lowered sails. *swabber:* a
cleaner of boat decks.
9. Mythical giants guarded ladies; here, also mocking Maria's diminutive size. *Some . . . for:* Please

pacify.
1. From Orsino; Olivia pretends she understands her
to mean a king's messenger, or a messenger-at-arms,
employed on important state affairs.
2. Demand for dues paid to a superior.
3. Olive branch (as a symbol of peace).
4. Quotation (as a theme of a sermon, in keeping
with "divinity," "doctrine," "heresy," etc.).

OLIVIA   Have you any commission from your lord to negotiate
with my face? You are now out of° your text. But we will   *straying from*
215   draw the curtain and show you the picture. [*She unveils.*]
Look you, sir, such a one I was this present.[5] Is't not well
done?
VIOLA   Excellently done, if God did all.[6]
OLIVIA   'Tis in grain,° sir, 'twill endure wind and weather.   *genuine*
220   VIOLA   'Tis beauty truly blent,[7] whose red and white
Nature's own sweet and cunning° hand laid on.   *skillful*
Lady, you are the cruel'st she° alive   *woman*
If you will lead these graces to the grave
And leave the world no copy.[8]
225   OLIVIA   O sir, I will not be so hardhearted. I will give out divers schedules° of my beauty. It shall be inventoried and   *various inventories*
every particle and utensil labeled[9] to my will. As *item*, two
lips, indifferent° red; *item*, two gray eyes, with lids[1] to them;   *moderate*
item, one neck, one chin, and so forth. Were you sent hither
230   to praise° me?   *appraise; flatter*
VIOLA   I see you what you are, you are too proud.
But if° you were the devil, you are fair.   *Even if*
My lord and master loves you. Oh, such love
Could be but recompensed though[2] you were crowned
235   The nonpareil of beauty.°   *An unequaled beauty*
OLIVIA   How does he love me?
VIOLA   With adorations, fertile° tears,   *ever-flowing*
With groans that thunder love, with sighs of fire.
OLIVIA   Your lord does know my mind. I cannot love him.
240   Yet I suppose him virtuous, know him noble,
Of great estate, of fresh and stainless youth,
In voices well divulged,° free,° learned, and valiant,   *spoken of / generous*
And in dimension and the shape of nature[3]
A gracious person. But yet I cannot love him.
245   He might have took his answer long ago.
VIOLA   If I did love you in° my master's flame,°   *with / passion*
With such a suffering, such a deadly° life,   *deathlike*
In your denial I would find no sense.
I would not understand it.
OLIVIA   Why, what would you?
250   VIOLA   Make me a willow[4] cabin at your gate
And call upon my soul° within the house;   *(Olivia)*
Write loyal cantons of contemnèd° love   *songs of rejected*
And sing them loud even in the dead of night;
Halloo[5] your name to the reverberate° hills   *echoing*
255   And make the babbling gossip of the air[6]
Cry out, "Olivia!" Oh, you should not rest

5. Portraits usually gave the year of painting. "This present" was a term used to date letters.
6. If it is natural (without the use of cosmetics).
7. Blended, or mixed (of paints). Shakespeare uses the same metaphor in Sonnet 20, lines 1–2, and Viola's next lines recall Sonnet 11, lines 13–14. As Cesario, Viola is playing with established conventions of poetic courtship.
8. Viola means "child"; Olivia takes her to mean "list" or "inventory."
9. Every single part and article added as a codicil (parodying the legal language of a last will and testa-

ment).
1. Eyelids, but also punning on "pot lids" (punning on "utensil" as a household implement).
2. *Could . . . though:* Would have to be requited even if.
3. *dimension . . . shape of nature:* The two terms are synonymous, meaning "bodily form."
4. Traditional symbol of rejected love.
5. Shout; or perhaps "hallow," as in "bless."
6. For the love of Narcissus, the nymph Echo wasted away to a mere voice, only able to repeat whatever she heard spoken.

Between the elements of air and earth
But you should pity me.
OLIVIA　　　　　　　　　You might do much.
What is your parentage?
260 VIOLA　Above my fortunes, yet my state° is well.　　　　　　　　*social status*
I am a gentleman.
OLIVIA　　　　　　　　Get you to your lord.
I cannot love him. Let him send no more
Unless, perchance, you come to me again
To tell me how he takes it. Fare you well.
265 I thank you for your pains. Spend this for me.
　　　　[*She offers a purse.*]
VIOLA　I am no fee'd post,° lady. Keep your purse.　　　　　　　*hired messenger*
My master, not myself, lacks recompense.
Love make his heart of flint that you shall love,[7]
And let your fervor, like my master's, be
270 Placed in contempt. Farewell, fair cruelty.　　　　　　　　*Exit.*
OLIVIA　"What is your parentage?"
"Above my fortunes, yet my state is well.
I am a gentleman." I'll be sworn thou art.
Thy tongue, thy face, thy limbs, actions, and spirit
275 Do give thee five-fold blazon.[8] Not too fast. Soft,° soft,　　　　*Wait*
Unless the master were the man.[9] How now?
Even so quickly may one catch the plague?
Methinks I feel this youth's perfections
With an invisible and subtle stealth
280 To creep in at mine eyes. Well, let it be.
What ho, Malvolio!
　　　　Enter MALVOLIO.
MALVOLIO　　　　　　Here, madam, at your service.
OLIVIA　Run after that same peevish messenger,
The County's° man. He left this ring behind him,　　　　　　　*Count's*
Would I° or not. Tell him I'll none of it.　　　　　　　*Whether I wished it*
285 Desire him not to flatter with° his lord,　　　　　　　*encourage*
Nor hold him up with hopes. I am not for him.
If that the youth will come this way tomorrow,
I'll give him reasons for't. Hie thee,° Malvolio.　　　　　　　*Hurry*
MALVOLIO　Madam, I will.　　　　　　　*Exit.*
290 OLIVIA　I do I know not what, and fear to find
Mine eye too great a flatterer for my mind.[1]
Fate, show thy force. Ourselves we do not owe.°　　　　　　　*own*
What is decreed must be, and be this so.　　　　　　　[*Exit.*]

2.1

Enter ANTONIO *and* SEBASTIAN.

ANTONIO　Will you stay no longer? Nor will° you not that I go　　　*wish*
　with you?
SEBASTIAN　By your patience, no. My stars shine darkly over
　me. The malignancy of my fate[1] might perhaps distemper°　　　*infect*

---

7. *Love . . . love:* May love make the heart of the man
you love as hard as flint.
8. Formal description of a gentleman's coat of arms.
9. If Orsino were Cesario (*man:* servant).
1. My eye (through which love has entered my heart)

has seduced my reason.
2.1 Location: Near the coast of Illyria.
1. Evil influence of the stars; "malignancy" also signifies a deadly disease.

5   yours. Therefore I shall crave of you your leave that I may
bear my evils alone. It were a bad recompense for your love
to lay any of them on you.

ANTONIO   Let me yet know of you whither you are bound.

SEBASTIAN   No, sooth,° sir. My determinate° voyage is mere   *truly / destined*
10   extravagancy.° But I perceive in you so excellent a touch of   *idle wandering*
modesty° that you will not extort from me what I am willing   *politeness*
to keep in. Therefore it charges me in manners[2] the rather
to express° myself. You must know of me then, Antonio, my   *reveal*
name is Sebastian, which I called Roderigo. My father was
15   that Sebastian of Messaline[3] whom I know you have heard
of. He left behind him myself and a sister, both born in an°   *within the same*
hour. If the heavens had been pleased, would we had so
ended. But you, sir, altered that, for some hour before you
took me from the breach° of the sea was my sister drowned.   *surf*

20 ANTONIO   Alas the day!

SEBASTIAN   A lady, sir, though it was said she much resembled
me, was yet of many accounted beautiful. But though I
could not with such estimable° wonder overfar believe that,   *appreciative*
yet thus far I will boldly publish° her: she bore a mind that   *proclaim*
25   envy could not but call fair. She is drowned already, sir, with
salt water, though I seem to drown her remembrance again
with more.

ANTONIO   Pardon me, sir, your bad entertainment.[4]

SEBASTIAN   O good Antonio, forgive me your trouble.

30 ANTONIO   If you will not murder me[5] for my love, let me be
your servant.

SEBASTIAN   If you will not undo what you have done—that is,
kill him whom you have recovered°—desire it not. Fare ye   *rescued*
well at once. My bosom is full of kindness,° and I am yet° so   *tender emotion / still*
35   near the manners of my mother[6] that upon the least occa-
sion more mine eyes will tell tales of me.° I am bound to the   *betray my feelings*
Count Orsino's court. Farewell.   *Exit.*

ANTONIO   The gentleness° of all the gods go with thee.   *favor*
I have many enemies in Orsino's court,
40   Else would I very shortly see thee there.
But come what may, I do adore thee so
That danger shall seem sport, and I will go.   *Exit.*

2.2

Enter VIOLA *[as Cesario] and* MALVOLIO *at
several° doors.*   *separate*

MALVOLIO   Were not you e'en° now with the Countess Olivia?   *just*

VIOLA   Even now, sir. On° a moderate pace I have since arrived   *At*
but hither.°   *come only this far*

MALVOLIO [*giving her a ring*]   She returns this ring to you, sir.
5   You might have saved me my pains to have taken° it away   *by taking*
yourself. She adds, moreover, that you should put your lord

---

2. Therefore courtesy requires.
3. Possibly Messina, Sicily.
4. Your poor reception at my hands.
5. Murder him by insisting that they part.

6. So near woman's readiness to weep.
2.2 Location: Between Olivia's house and Orsino's
palace.

into a desperate assurance° she will none of him. And one　　　　*hopeless certainty*
thing more, that you be never so hardy° to come again in his　　　　*bold*
affairs unless it be to report your lord's taking of this.[1]
10　Receive it so.
VIOLA　She took the ring of me.[2] I'll none of it.
MALVOLIO　Come, sir, you peevishly threw it to her, and, her
will is, it should be so returned. [*He throws down the ring.*] If
it be worth stooping for, there it lies, in your eye.° If not, be　　　　*sight*
15　it his that finds it.　　　　　　　　　　　　　　　　*Exit.*
VIOLA [*picking up the ring*]　I left no ring with her. What means
　　this lady?
Fortune forbid my outside° have not charmed her.　　　　*appearance*
She made good view of° me, indeed so much　　　　*looked carefully at*
That methought her eyes had lost° her tongue,　　　　*made her lose*
20　For she did speak in starts distractedly.°　　　　*madly*
She loves me, sure. The cunning of her passion
Invites me in° this churlish messenger.　　　　*by means of*
None of my lord's ring? Why, he sent her none.
I am the man.[3] If it be so, as 'tis,
25　Poor lady, she were better love a dream.
Disguise, I see thou art a wickedness
Wherein the pregnant enemy[4] does much.
How easy is it for the proper false[5]
In women's waxen hearts to set their forms.[6]
30　Alas, our frailty is the cause, not we,
For such as we are made of, such we be.[7]
How will this fadge?° My master loves her dearly,　　　　*turn out*
And I, poor monster,[8] fond° as much on him.　　　　*dote*
And she, mistaken, seems to dote on me.
35　What will become of this? As I am man,
My state is desperate° for my master's love.　　　　*hopeless*
As I am woman, now, alas the day,
What thriftless° sighs shall poor Olivia breathe!　　　　*unprofitable*
O time, thou must untangle this, not I.
40　It is too hard a knot for me t'untie.　　　　　　　[*Exit.*]

2.3

Enter SIR TOBY *and* SIR ANDREW.

SIR TOBY　Approach, Sir Andrew. Not to be abed after midnight is to be up betimes,° and "*diluculo surgere*,"[1] thou　　　　*early*
know'st.
SIR ANDREW　Nay, by my troth,° I know not. But I know to be　　　　*faith*
5　up late is to be up late.
SIR TOBY　A false conclusion; I hate it as an unfilled can.° To　　　　*tankard*
be up after midnight and to go to bed then is early. So that
to go to bed after midnight is to go to bed betimes. Does not
our lives consist of the four elements?[2]

---

1. Reception of this rejection.
2. Viola pretends to believe Olivia's story. *of*: from.
3. The man with whom she has fallen in love.
4. The devil, who is always quick and ready ("pregnant") to deceive.
5. Handsome, but deceitful (men).
6. *In . . . forms*: To impress their images on women's
affections (as a seal stamps its image in wax).

7. For being made of frail flesh, we are frail.
8. Since she is both man and woman.
2.3 Location: Olivia's house.
1. Part of a Latin proverb, meaning "to rise at dawn
(is most healthy)."
2. The four elements, thought to make up all matter,
were earth, air, fire, and water.

10   SIR ANDREW   Faith, so they say. But I think it rather consists
of eating and drinking.

     SIR TOBY   Thou'rt a scholar. Let us therefore eat and drink.
—Marian, I say, a stoup° of wine!   *two-pint tankard*
         Enter CLOWN.

     SIR ANDREW   Here comes the fool, i'faith.

15   CLOWN   How now, my hearts. Did you never see the picture of
We Three?[3]

     SIR TOBY   Welcome, ass, now let's have a catch.[4]

     SIR ANDREW   By my troth, the fool has an excellent breast.° I   *singing voice*
had rather than forty shillings I had such a leg,° and so   *(for dancing)*

20   sweet a breath to sing, as the fool has. In sooth, thou wast in
very gracious fooling last night when thou spok'st of Pigrogromitus of the Vapians passing the equinoctial of Queubus.[5] 'Twas very good, i'faith. I sent thee sixpence for thy
leman.° Hadst it?   *sweetheart*

25   CLOWN   I did impeticos thy gratility.[6] For Malvolio's nose is
no whipstock. My lady has a white hand, and the Myrmidons are no bottle-ale houses.[7]

     SIR ANDREW   Excellent! Why, this is the best fooling when all
is done. Now, a song.

30   SIR TOBY   Come on, there is sixpence for you. Let's have a
song.

     SIR ANDREW   There's a testril[8] of me too. If one knight
give a—[9]

     CLOWN   Would you have a love song or a song of good life?

35   SIR TOBY   A love song, a love song.

     SIR ANDREW   Ay, ay. I care not for good life.

     CLOWN (*sings*)   O mistress mine, where are you roaming?
                     Oh, stay and hear, your true love's coming
                     That can sing both high and low.

40   Trip° no further, pretty sweeting.   *Go*
                     Journeys end in lovers meeting,
                     Every wise man's son doth know.[1]

     SIR ANDREW   Excellent good, i'faith.

     SIR TOBY   Good, good.

45   CLOWN [*sings*]   What is love? 'Tis not hereafter.
                     Present mirth hath present laughter.
                     What's to come is still° unsure.   *always*
                     In delay there lies no plenty,
                     Then come kiss me, sweet and twenty.°   *twenty times sweet*

50   Youth's a stuff will not endure.

     SIR ANDREW   A mellifluous voice, as I am true knight.

     SIR TOBY   A contagious breath.[2]

     SIR ANDREW   Very sweet and contagious, i'faith.

---

3. A trick picture portraying two fools' or asses'
heads, the third being that of the viewer.
4. A round: a simple song for several voices.
5. *Pigrogromitus . . . Queubus:* the Clown's mock
learning. *equinoctial:* equator of the astronomical
heavens.
6. Comic jargon for "impocket (or impetticoat) your
gratuity."
7. *for . . . houses:* Perhaps it is the sheer inscrutabil-
ity of the Clown's foolery that so impresses Sir
Andrew (lines 28–29). *whipstock:* handle of a whip.

bottle-ale houses: cheap taverns.
8. Sir Andrew's version of "tester" (sixpence).
9. In F, "give a" appears at the end of a justified line;
an omission is possible.
1. *O mistress . . . know:* The words are not certainly
Shakespeare's; they fit the tune of an instrumental
piece printed in Thomas Morley's *First Book of Consort Lessons* (1599). *wise man's son:* wise men were
thought to have foolish sons.
2. A catchy voice; with a play on "disease-causing
air."

SIR TOBY To hear by the nose, it is dulcet in contagion.[3] But
shall we make the welkin° dance indeed? Shall we rouse the   sky
night owl in a catch that will draw three souls out of one
weaver?[4] Shall we do that?

SIR ANDREW An° you love me, let's do't. I am dog° at a catch.   If / clever

CLOWN By'r lady, sir, and some dogs will catch well.

SIR ANDREW Most certain. Let our catch be "Thou knave."

CLOWN "Hold thy peace, thou knave,"[5] knight. I shall be constrained in't to call thee knave, knight.

SIR ANDREW 'Tis not the first time I have constrained one to
call me knave. Begin, fool. It begins, "Hold thy peace."

CLOWN I shall never begin if I hold my peace.

SIR ANDREW Good, i'faith. Come, begin.

> *Catch sung.*
> *Enter* MARIA.

MARIA What a caterwauling do you keep here! If my lady
have not called up her steward Malvolio and bid him turn
you out of doors, never trust me.

SIR TOBY My lady's a Cathayan,[6] we are politicians,° Malvolio's   schemers
a Peg-o-Ramsey,[7] and [*singing*] "Three merry men be we."
Am not I consanguineous?[8] Am I not of her blood? Tilly-
vally!° "Lady"! [*He sings.*] "There dwelt a man in Babylon,   Fiddlesticks
lady, lady."[9]

CLOWN Beshrew° me, the knight's in admirable fooling.   Curse

SIR ANDREW Ay, he does well enough if he be disposed, and
so do I too. He does it with a better grace, but I do it more
natural.[1]

SIR TOBY [*sings*] "O'the twelfth day of December"[2]—

MARIA For the love o'God, peace!

> *Enter* MALVOLIO.

MALVOLIO My masters, are you mad? Or what are you? Have
you no wit,° manners, nor honesty° but to gabble like tinkers   sense / decency
at this time of night? Do ye make an alehouse of my lady's
house, that ye squeak out your coziers'° catches without any   cobblers'
mitigation or remorse[3] of voice? Is there no respect of place,
persons, nor time in you?

SIR TOBY We did keep time, sir, in our catches. Sneck up!°   Go hang yourself

MALVOLIO Sir Toby, I must be round° with you. My lady bade   plainspoken
me tell you that, though she harbors you as her kinsman,
she's nothing allied to your disorders. If you can separate
yourself and your misdemeanors, you are welcome to the
house. If not, an it would please you to take leave of her,
she is very willing to bid you farewell.

SIR TOBY [*sings*] "Farewell, dear heart, since I must needs be
gone."[4]

---

3. If one could hear through the nose, the sound would be sweetly ("dulcet") infectious.

4. Weavers were traditionally addicted to psalm singing, so to move them with popular catches would be a great triumph. Music was said to be able to draw the soul from the body.

5. The words of the catch are "Hold thy peace, I prithee hold thy peace, thou knave." Each singer repeatedly calls the others knaves and tells them to stop singing.

6. A Cathayan (or Chinese); also, from travelers' tales, someone who misleads or exaggerates. (See T. Billings, "Caterwauling Cataians: The Genealogy of a Gloss," in SQ 54 [2003]: 1–28.)

7. Name of a dance and popular song; here, used contemptuously.

8. A blood relative of Olivia's. *"Three . . . we"*: a refrain from a popular song.

9. The opening and refrain of a popular song called "Constant Susanna."

1. Effortlessly; but unconsciously playing on "natural" as in "fool" or "idiot."

2. Snatch of a ballad; or possibly a drunken version of "twelfth day of Christmas"—that is, Twelfth Night.

3. Without any abating or softening.

4. Part of another song that Sir Toby and the Clown adapt for the occasion.

95 MARIA   Nay, good Sir Toby.

CLOWN [*sings*]   "His eyes do show his days are almost done."

MALVOLIO   Is't even so?

SIR TOBY [*sings*]   "But I will never die."

CLOWN [*sings*]   "Sir Toby, there you lie."

100 MALVOLIO   This is much credit to you.

SIR TOBY [*sings*]   "Shall I bid him go?"

CLOWN [*sings*]   "What an if° you do?"   *an if* = *if*

SIR TOBY [*sings*]   "Shall I bid him go, and spare not?"

CLOWN [*sings*]   "Oh, no, no, no, no, you dare not."

105 SIR TOBY   Out o'tune, sir, ye lie. [*to* MALVOLIO] Art any more
than a steward? Dost thou think because thou art virtuous,
there shall be no more cakes and ale?⁵

CLOWN   Yes, by Saint Anne, and ginger⁶ shall be hot i'th'
mouth, too.

110 SIR TOBY   Thou'rt i'th' right. [*to* MALVOLIO] Go, sir, rub your
chain with crumbs.⁷ —A stoup of wine, Maria.

MALVOLIO   Mistress Mary, if you prized my lady's favor
at anything more than contempt, you would not give
means° for this uncivil rule.° She shall know of it, by this   *drink / behavior*

115 hand.   *Exit.*⁸

MARIA   Go shake your ears!°   *(like an ass)*

SIR ANDREW   'Twere as good a deed as to drink when a man's
a-hungry to challenge him the field,° and then to break   *to a duel*
promise with him, and make a fool of him.

120 SIR TOBY   Do't, knight. I'll write thee a challenge, or I'll deliver
thy indignation to him by word of mouth.

MARIA   Sweet Sir Toby, be patient for tonight. Since the youth
of the Count's was today with my lady, she is much out of
quiet. For Monsieur Malvolio, let me alone with him. If I do

125 not gull him into a nay-word⁹ and make him a common rec-
reation,° do not think I have wit enough to lie straight in my   *sport; jest*
bed. I know I can do it.

SIR TOBY   Possess° us, possess us. Tell us something of him.   *Inform*

MARIA   Marry, sir, sometimes he is a kind of puritan.¹

130 SIR ANDREW   Oh, if I thought that, I'd beat him like a dog.

SIR TOBY   What, for being a puritan? Thy exquisite° reason,   *ingenious*
dear knight?

SIR ANDREW   I have no exquisite reason for't, but I have reason good enough.

135 MARIA   The devil a puritan that he is, or anything constantly
but a time-pleaser,° an affectioned° ass that cons state with-   *bootlicker / affected*
out book and utters it by great swaths.² The best persuaded
of himself³—so crammed, as he thinks, with excellencies—
that it is his grounds of faith° that all that look on him love   *his creed*

140 him. And on that vice in him will my revenge find notable
cause to work.

---

5. *cakes and ale*: traditionally associated with church
festivals, and therefore disliked by puritans.
6. Used to spice ale. *Saint Anne*: mother of the Virgin; the oath would be offensive to puritans who
attacked her cult.
7. Clean your steward's chain; mind your own business.
8. **Textual Comment** Although F has Malvolio exit
by himself here, some editors choose to have the
Clown exit here as well. For more on the implications

of this decision, see Digital Edition TC 4.
9. If I do not trick ("gull") him into making his name
a byword (for "dupe").
1. Could mean "morally strict and censorious," as
well as "a follower of the puritan religious faith."
2. *cons . . . swaths*: memorizes dignified and high-
flown language and utters it in great sweeps (like hay
falling under a scythe).
3. Having the highest opinion of himself.

SIR TOBY   What wilt thou do?

MARIA   I will drop in his way some obscure epistles of love,
wherein by the color of his beard, the shape of his leg, the
145   manner of his gait, the expressure° of his eye, forehead, and   *expression*
complexion he shall find himself most feelingly personated.°   *represented*
I can write very like my lady, your niece. On a forgotten°   *bygone*
matter we can hardly make distinction of our hands.°   *handwriting*

SIR TOBY   Excellent, I smell a device.

150   SIR ANDREW   I have't in my nose too.

SIR TOBY   He shall think by the letters that thou wilt drop that
they come from my niece, and that she's in love with him.

MARIA   My purpose is indeed a horse of that color.

SIR ANDREW   And your horse now would make him an ass.

155   MARIA   Ass,° I doubt not.   *(punning on "as")*

SIR ANDREW   Oh, 'twill be admirable.

MARIA   Sport royal, I warrant you. I know my physic° will work   *medicine*
with him. I will plant you two, and let the fool make a third,
where he shall find the letter. Observe his construction° of it.   *interpretation*
160   For this night, to bed, and dream on the event.° Farewell.   *outcome*

                                                  Exit.

SIR TOBY   Good night, Penthesilea.[4]

SIR ANDREW   Before me,[5] she's a good wench.

SIR TOBY   She's a beagle true bred, and one that adores me.
What o'that?

165   SIR ANDREW   I was adored once too.

SIR TOBY   Let's to bed, knight. Thou hadst need send for more
money.

SIR ANDREW   If I cannot recover° your niece, I am a foul way   *win*
out.°   *out of money*

170   SIR TOBY   Send for money, knight. If thou hast her not i'th'
end, call me cut.[6]

SIR ANDREW   If I do not, never trust me, take it how you will.

SIR TOBY   Come, come, I'll go burn some sack.[7] 'Tis too late to
go to bed now. Come, knight; come, knight.   *Exeunt.*

2.4

Enter DUKE, VIOLA [*as Cesario*], CURIO, *and others.*

ORSINO   Give me some music. Now good morrow,° friends.   *morning*
Now, good Cesario, but° that piece of song,   *just*
That old and antique° song we heard last night.   *quaint*
Methought it did relieve my passion° much,   *suffering*
5   More than light airs and recollected° terms°   *artificial / lyrics*
Of these most brisk and giddy-pacèd times.
Come, but one verse.

CURIO   He is not here, so please your lordship, that should sing it.

ORSINO   Who was it?

10   CURIO   Feste the jester,[1] my lord, a fool that the Lady Olivia's
father took much delight in. He is about the house.

---

4. Queen of the Amazons (a joke about Maria's small
size).
5. On my soul (a mild oath).
6. A dock-tailed horse; also, slang for "gelding" or for
"female genitals."
7. I'll go warm and spice some Spanish wine.
2.4 Location: Orsino's palace.

1. TEXTUAL COMMENT This is the only time in the
play that Olivia's household entertainer is ever given
a proper name, yet editorial tradition has often preferred "Feste" over any other speech prefix. This edition follows F and denominates him by his status and
profession as "Clown." For more on the issue of
speech prefixes and names, see Digital Edition TC 5.

ORSINO Seek him out and play the tune the while.

[Exit CURIO.]

Music plays.

—Come hither, boy. If ever thou shalt love,
In the sweet pangs of it remember me.

15 For such as I am, all true lovers are,
Unstaid° and skittish in all motions° else   *Unstable / emotions*
Save in the constant image of the creature
That is beloved. How dost thou like this tune?

VIOLA It gives a very echo to the seat
Where love is throned.²

20 ORSINO   Thou dost speak masterly.°   *expertly*
My life upon't, young though thou art, thine eye
Hath stayed upon some favor° that it loves.   *face*
Hath it not, boy?

VIOLA   A little, by your favor.°   *leave; face*

ORSINO What kind of woman is't?

VIOLA   Of your complexion.

25 ORSINO She is not worth thee then. What years, i'faith?

VIOLA About your years, my lord.

ORSINO Too old, by heaven. Let still° the woman take   *always*
An elder than herself. So wears° she to him,   *adapts*
So sways she level³ in her husband's heart.

30 For, boy, however we do praise ourselves,
Our fancies° are more giddy and unfirm,   *affections*
More longing, wavering, sooner lost and worn,°   *exhausted*
Than women's are.

VIOLA   I think° it well, my lord.   *believe*

ORSINO Then let thy love be younger than thyself,

35 Or thy affection cannot hold the bent.⁴
For women are as roses whose fair flower,
Being once displayed,° doth fall that very hour.   *opened*

VIOLA And so they are. Alas, that they are so,
To die even° when they to perfection grow!   *just*

Enter CURIO *and* CLOWN.

40 ORSINO [*to* CLOWN] O fellow, come, the song we had last night.
Mark it, Cesario, it is old and plain.
The spinsters° and the knitters in the sun   *spinners*
And the free° maids that weave their thread with bones⁵   *carefree*
Do use to chant it. It is silly sooth°   *simple truth*

45 And dallies with° the innocence of love,   *lingers lovingly on*
Like the old° age.   *golden*

CLOWN Are you ready, sir?

ORSINO Ay, prithee, sing.

Music. The Song.

CLOWN [*sings*] Come away,° come away, death,   *Come hither*

50 And in sad cypress⁶ let me be laid.
Fly away, fly away, breath,
I am slain by a fair cruel maid.

2. *It . . . throned:* It reflects the feelings of the heart.
3. So does she balance influence and affection.
4. Cannot remain at full stretch (like the tautness of a bowstring).
5. Spools made from bone on which lace (called "bone lace") was woven.
6. Cypress-wood coffin. Like yews, cypresses were emblematic of mourning.

My shroud of white stuck all with yew,°   *sprigs of yew*
Oh, prepare it.
55   My part of death, no one so true
Did share it.[7]
Not a flower, not a flower sweet
On my black coffin let there be strewn.
Not a friend, not a friend greet
60   My poor corpse where my bones shall be thrown.
A thousand thousand sighs to save,
Lay me, oh, where
Sad true lover never find my grave,
To weep there.

65 ORSINO [*giving money*]   There's for thy pains.
CLOWN   No pains, sir. I take pleasure in singing, sir.
ORSINO   I'll pay thy pleasure, then.
CLOWN   Truly, sir, and pleasure will be paid° one time or   *paid for*
another.
70 ORSINO   Give me now leave° to leave° thee.   *permission / dismiss*
CLOWN   Now the melancholy god[8] protect thee, and the tailor
make thy doublet of changeable taffeta,[9] for thy mind is a very
opal.[1] I would have men of such constancy put to sea, that their
business might be everything and their intent° everywhere, for   *destination*
75   that's it that always makes a good voyage of nothing.[2] Farewell.
Exit.

ORSINO   Let all the rest give place.°   [*Exeunt* CURIO *and others.*]   *withdraw*
Once more, Cesario,
Get thee to yond same sovereign cruelty.
Tell her my love, more noble than the world,
Prizes not quantity of dirty lands.
80   The parts° that Fortune hath bestowed upon her,[3]   *possessions*
Tell her I hold as giddily[4] as Fortune,
But 'tis that miracle and queen of gems
That nature pranks° her in attracts my soul.   *adorns*
VIOLA   But if she cannot love you, sir?
ORSINO   It cannot be so answered.
85 VIOLA   Sooth,° but you must.   *In truth*
Say that some lady, as perhaps there is,
Hath for your love as great a pang of heart
As you have for Olivia. You cannot love her.
You tell her so. Must she not then be answered?
90 ORSINO   There is no woman's sides
Can bide° the beating of so strong a passion   *withstand*
As love doth give my heart. No woman's heart
So big, to hold so much. They lack retention.°   *constancy*
Alas, their love may be called appetite,
95   No motion of the liver, but the palate,[5]

---

7. *My part . . . it:* No one has died so true to love as I.
8. Saturn (thought to control the melancholic).
9. Shot silk, whose color changes with the angle of
vision. *doublet:* close-fitting jacket.
1. An iridescent gemstone that changes color
depending on the angle from which it is seen.
2. *that's . . . nothing:* This fickle lack of direction can
make a voyage in the notoriously changeful sea carefree and consonant with one's desires.
3. TEXTUAL COMMENT F does not capitalize "for-

tune" in line 80, though "Fortune" does appear in the
very next line. Since the word seems to refer to the
allegorical figure of Fortuna, both instances have
been capitalized here. For more on the issue of capi-
talization, see Digital Edition TC 6.
4. Lightly (fortune being fickle).
5. *appetite . . . palate:* Appetite, like the palate, is easily sated and thus lacks the emotional depth and complexity of real love, whose seat is the liver. *motion:*
impulse.

That suffer surfeit, cloyment,° and revolt.°   *satiety / revulsion*
But mine is all as hungry as the sea
And can digest as much. Make no compare
Between that love a woman can bear me
And that I owe° Olivia.   *have for*
100   VIOLA   Ay, but I know—
ORSINO   What dost thou know?
VIOLA   Too well what love women to men may owe.
In faith, they are as true of heart as we.
My father had a daughter loved a man
105   As it might be perhaps, were I a woman,
I should your lordship.
ORSINO   And what's her history?
VIOLA   A blank, my lord. She never told her love
But let concealment, like a worm i'th' bud,
Feed on her damask[6] cheek. She pined in thought,
110   And, with a green and yellow° melancholy,   *pale and sallow*
She sat like Patience on a monument,[7]
Smiling at grief. Was not this love indeed?
We men may say more, swear more, but indeed
Our shows are more than will.[8] For still° we prove   *always*
115   Much in our vows, but little in our love.
ORSINO   But died thy sister of her love, my boy?
VIOLA   I am all the daughters of my father's house,
And all the brothers too, and yet I know not.
Sir, shall I to this lady?
ORSINO   Ay, that's the theme,
120   To her in haste. Give her this jewel. Say
My love can give no place, bide no denay.[9]   *Exeunt.*

2.5

Enter SIR TOBY, SIR ANDREW, *and* FABIAN.

SIR TOBY   Come thy ways,° Signior Fabian.   *Come along*
FABIAN   Nay, I'll come. If I lose a scruple° of this sport, let me   *miss a scrap*
    be boiled to death with melancholy.[1]
SIR TOBY   Wouldst thou not be glad to have the niggardly ras-
5   cally sheep-biter[2] come by some notable shame?
FABIAN   I would exult, man. You know he brought me out
    o'favor with my lady about a bearbaiting[3] here.
SIR TOBY   To anger him we'll have the bear again, and we will
    fool° him black and blue, shall we not, Sir Andrew?   *mock*
10   SIR ANDREW   An° we do not, it is pity of our lives.   *If*
        Enter MARIA [*with a letter*].
SIR TOBY   Here comes the little villain. How now, my metal of
    India?[4]
MARIA   Get ye all three into the box tree.°[5] Malvolio's coming   *hedge of boxwood*
    down this walk. He has been yonder i'the sun practicing

---

6. Pink and white, like a damask rose.
7. A memorial statue symbolizing patience.
8. Our displays of love are greater than our actual
feelings.
9. My love cannot be bated, nor tolerate refusal.
2.5 Location: Olivia's garden.
1. Melancholy was a cold humor; "boiled" puns on
"bile," the surplus of which produced melancholy.
2. Literally, a dog that attacks sheep; here, a mali-

cious sneak.
3. Puritans disapproved of blood sports like bearbaiting.
4. A woman worth her weight in gold.
5. PERFORMANCE COMMENT The exact onstage location where Toby, Andrew, and Fabian hide while spying
on Malvolio can make a significant difference in productions. For more, see Digital Edition PC 3.

15   behavior to his own shadow this half hour. Observe him, for
      the love of mockery, for I know this letter will make a con-
      templative° idiot of him. Close,° in the name of jesting!   *vacuous / Keep close; hide*
            [*The men hide. She places the letter.*]
      Lie thou there, for here comes the trout that must be caught
      with tickling.[6]   *Exit.*
            Enter MALVOLIO.
20   MALVOLIO   'Tis but fortune, all is fortune. Maria once told me
      she° did affect° me, and I have heard herself come thus   *(Olivia) / care for*
      near, that should she fancy,° it should be one of my complex-   *fall in love*
      ion. Besides, she uses me with a more exalted respect than
      anyone else that follows her. What should I think on't?
25   SIR TOBY   Here's an overweening rogue.
      FABIAN   Oh, peace! Contemplation makes a rare turkeycock[7]
      of him. How he jets° under his advanced° plumes!   *struts / raised*
      SIR ANDREW   'Slight,[8] I could so beat the rogue.
      SIR TOBY   Peace, I say.
30   MALVOLIO   To be Count Malvolio.
      SIR TOBY   Ah, rogue.
      SIR ANDREW   Pistol him, pistol him!
      SIR TOBY   Peace, peace.
      MALVOLIO   There is example° for't. The Lady of the Strachy   *precedent*
35   married the yeoman of the wardrobe.[9]
      SIR ANDREW   Fie on him, Jezebel.[1]
      FABIAN   Oh, peace, now he's deeply in. Look how imagination
      blows him.°   *puffs him up*
      MALVOLIO   Having been three months married to her, sitting
40   in my state°—   *chair of state*
      SIR TOBY   Oh, for a stone-bow[2] to hit him in the eye!
      MALVOLIO   Calling my officers° about me, in my branched[3]   *household attendants*
      velvet gown, having come from a daybed° where I have left   *couch*
      Olivia sleeping.
45   SIR TOBY   Fire and brimstone!
      FABIAN   Oh, peace, peace.
      MALVOLIO   And then, to have the humor of state[4] and, after a
      demure travel of regard,[5] telling them I know my place as I
      would they should do theirs, to ask for my kinsman Toby—
50   SIR TOBY   Bolts and shackles!
      FABIAN   Oh, peace, peace, peace! Now, now.
      MALVOLIO   Seven of my people with an obedient start make°   *go*
      out for him. I frown the while, and perchance wind up my
      watch, or play with my[6]—some rich jewel. Toby approaches,
55   curtsies° there to me—   *bows*
      SIR TOBY   Shall this fellow live?
      FABIAN   Though our silence be drawn from us with cars,[7] yet
      peace.

---

6. Flattery; trout can be caught by stroking them
under the gills.
7. Proverbially proud; they display their feathers like
peacocks.
8. By God's light (an oath).
9. Perhaps an allusion to a noblewoman who had
married her manservant, but there is no certain identification. *yeoman of the wardrobe:* keeper of clothes
and linen.
1. Biblical allusion to the proud wife of Ahab, king of
Israel.

2. A catapult, or a crossbow for stones.
3. Embroidered with branch patterns.
4. To adopt the grand air of exalted greatness.
5. After casting my eyes gravely about the room.
6. Malvolio momentarily forgets that he will have
abandoned his steward's chain; watches were an
expensive luxury at this time.
7. A prisoner might be tied to two carts or chariots
("cars") and pulled by horses in opposite directions to
extort information.

MALVOLIO   I extend my hand to him thus, quenching my famil-
60   iar smile with an austere regard of control.
SIR TOBY   And does not Toby take° you a blow o'the lips, then?   *give*
MALVOLIO   Saying, "Cousin Toby, my fortunes having cast me
   on your niece, give me this prerogative of speech."
SIR TOBY   What, what?
65   MALVOLIO   "You must amend your drunkenness."
SIR TOBY   Out, scab.
FABIAN   Nay, patience, or we break the sinews of our plot.
MALVOLIO   "Besides, you waste the treasure of your time with
   a foolish knight."
70   SIR ANDREW   That's me, I warrant you.
MALVOLIO   "One Sir Andrew."
SIR ANDREW   I knew 'twas I, for many do call me fool.
MALVOLIO [*seeing the letter*]   What employment° have we here?   *business*
FABIAN   Now is the woodcock near the gin.[8]
75   SIR TOBY   Oh, peace, and the spirit of humors intimate[9] reading aloud to him.
MALVOLIO [*picking up the letter*]   By my life, this is my lady's
   hand. These be her very c's, her u's, and her t's,[1] and thus
   makes she her great P's. It is in contempt of° question her   *beyond*
80   hand.
SIR ANDREW   Her c's, her u's, and her t's. Why that?
MALVOLIO   "To the unknown beloved, this and my good
   wishes"—her very phrases! By your leave, wax.[2] [*He opens the
   letter.*] Soft°—and the impressure her Lucrece[3] with which   *Wait*
85   she uses to seal.° 'Tis my lady! To whom should this be?   *habitually seals*
FABIAN   This wins him, liver and all.
MALVOLIO   "Jove knows I love,
      But who?
      Lips, do not move.
90   No man must know."
   "No man must know." What follows? The numbers altered.°   *meter changed*
   "No man must know." If this should be thee, Malvolio!
SIR TOBY   Marry, hang thee, brock.[4]
MALVOLIO   "I may command where I adore,
95   But silence, like a Lucrece knife,[5]
      With bloodless stroke my heart doth gore.
      M.O.A.I. doth sway my life."
FABIAN   A fustian° riddle.   *bombastic*
SIR TOBY   Excellent wench, say I.
100   MALVOLIO   "M.O.A.I. doth sway my life." Nay, but first let me
   see, let me see, let me see.
FABIAN   What dish o'poison has she dressed° him!   *prepared*
SIR TOBY   And with what wing the staniel checks at it.[6]
MALVOLIO   "I may command where I adore." Why, she may
105   command me. I serve her, she is my lady. Why, this is evident

8. Snare. *woodcock*: a proverbially foolish bird.
9. And may a capricious impulse suggest.
1. Malvolio unwittingly spells out "cut," slang for
"female genitals"; the meaning is compounded by
"great P's." In fact, these letters do not appear on the
outside of the letter.
2. *By . . . wax:* addressed to the sealing wax.

3. The figure of Lucrece, a Roman model of chastity,
is the device ("impressure") imprinted on the seal.
4. Badger (proverbially stinking).
5. The knife with which Lucrece killed herself after
she was raped.
6. And with what alacrity the sparrow hawk goes
after it.

to any formal capacity.° There is no obstruction in this. And   *normal intelligence*
the end—what should that alphabetical position° portend? If I   *arrangement*
could make that resemble something in me. Softly, "M.O.A.I."

SIR TOBY   Oh, ay,[7] make up that. He is now at a cold scent.

110 FABIAN   Sowter will cry upon't for all this, though it be as rank
as a fox.[8]

MALVOLIO   "M"—Malvolio. M—why, that begins my name.

FABIAN   Did not I say he would work it out? The cur is excellent at faults.[9]

115 MALVOLIO   M. But then there is no consonancy in the sequel.[1]
That suffers under probation.[2] A should follow, but O does.

FABIAN   And "O"[3] shall end, I hope.

SIR TOBY   Ay, or I'll cudgel him, and make him cry "Oh!"

MALVOLIO   And then "I" comes behind.

120 FABIAN   Ay, an you had any eye behind you, you might see
more detraction° at your heels than fortunes before you.   *defamation*

MALVOLIO   "M.O.A.I." This simulation° is not as the former.   *disguise; riddle*
And yet to crush° this a little, it would bow° to me, for every   *force / yield; point*
one of these letters are in my name. Soft, here follows prose.

125 "If this fall into thy hand, revolve.° In my stars° I am above   *consider / fortunes*
thee, but be not afraid of greatness. Some are born great,
some achieve greatness, and some have greatness thrust upon
'em.[4] Thy fates open their hands.° Let thy blood and spirit   *bestow gifts*
embrace them, and to inure° thyself to what thou art like° to   *accustom / likely*
130 be, cast thy humble slough[5] and appear fresh. Be opposite°   *contrary*
with a kinsman, surly with servants. Let thy tongue tang
arguments of state.[6] Put thyself into the trick of singularity.°   *Cultivate eccentricity*
She thus advises thee that sighs for thee. Remember who
commended thy yellow stockings and wished to see thee
135 ever cross-gartered.[7] I say remember, go to,[8] thou art made if
thou desir'st to be so. If not, let me see thee a steward still,
the fellow of servants, and not worthy to touch Fortune's
fingers. Farewell, she that would alter services[9] with thee,
the Fortunate Unhappy." Daylight and champaign discov-
140 ers[1] not more. This is open.° I will be proud, I will read   *clear*
politic° authors, I will baffle[2] Sir Toby, I will wash off gross   *political*
acquaintance, I will be point-device, the very man.[3] I do not
now fool myself to let imagination jade° me, for every reason   *trick*
excites to this—that my lady loves me! She did commend my
145 yellow stockings of late; she did praise my leg being cross-
gartered. And in this, she manifests herself to my love and
with a kind of injunction drives me to these habits° of her   *clothes*
liking. I thank my stars, I am happy. I will be strange,° stout,°   *aloof / proud*

---

7. *Oh, ay:* playing on "O.I."
8. "Sowter" (the name of a hound), having lost the scent, will start to bay loudly as he picks up the new, rank (stinking) smell of the fox. *though:* as though.
9. At picking up a scent after it is momentarily lost. A "fault" is a "cold scent" (line 109).
1. There is no consistency in what follows.
2. That weakens upon being put to the test.
3. As in the hangman's noose; the last letter of Malvolio's name; or "O" as a lamentation.
4. TEXTUAL COMMENT In F's version of this scene, this oft-quoted sentence begins differently, with "Some are become great." For more details, see Digital Edition TC 7.

5. A snake's old skin, which peels away.
6. Let your tongue ring out arguments of statecraft or politics.
7. An antiquated way of adjusting a garter—going once below the knee, crossing behind it, and knotting above the knee at the side.
8. An emphatic expression, like "I tell you."
9. Change places (of servant and mistress or master).
1. *champaign discovers:* open countryside reveals.
2. Term used to describe the formal unmaking of a knight; hence, "disgrace."
3. I will be in every detail the identical man (described in the letter).

150 in yellow stockings, and cross-gartered even with the swiftness of putting on. Jove and my stars be praised. Here is yet
a postscript: "Thou canst not choose but know who I am. If
thou entertainest° my love, let it appear in thy smiling. Thy | accept
smiles become thee well. Therefore in my presence still° smile, | constantly
dear my sweet, I prithee." Jove, I thank thee! I will smile, I
155 will do everything that thou wilt have me. *Exit.*

FABIAN I will not give my part of this sport for a pension of
thousands to be paid from the Sophy.° | Shah of Persia

SIR TOBY I could marry this wench for this device.

SIR ANDREW So could I too.

160 SIR TOBY And ask no other dowry with her, but such another jest.
Enter MARIA.

SIR ANDREW Nor I neither.

FABIAN Here comes my noble gull-catcher.° | trickster

SIR TOBY Wilt thou set thy foot o'my neck?

SIR ANDREW Or o'mine either?

165 SIR TOBY Shall I play my freedom at tray-trip[4] and become thy
bond slave?

SIR ANDREW I'faith, or I either?

SIR TOBY Why, thou hast put him in such a dream that, when
the image of it leaves him, he must run mad.

170 MARIA Nay, but say true: does it work upon him?

SIR TOBY Like aqua vitae° with a midwife. | spirits; liquor

MARIA If you will then see the fruits of the sport, mark his
first approach before my lady. He will come to her in yellow
stockings, and 'tis a color she abhors, and cross-gartered, a
175 fashion she detests. And he will smile upon her, which will
now be so unsuitable to her disposition, being addicted to a
melancholy as she is, that it cannot but turn him into a
notable contempt.[5] If you will see it, follow me.

SIR TOBY To the gates of Tartar,° thou most excellent devil | hell
180 of wit.

SIR ANDREW I'll make one° too. *Exeunt.* | go along

3.1

Enter VIOLA *[as Cesario] and* CLOWN *[with a tabor].*[1]

VIOLA Save° thee, friend, and thy music. Dost thou live by thy | God save
tabor?

CLOWN No, sir, I live by° the church. | near

VIOLA Art thou a churchman?

5 CLOWN No such matter, sir. I do live by[2] the church, for I do
live at my house, and my house doth stand by the church.

VIOLA So thou mayst say, the king lies by[3] a beggar if a beggar
dwell near him. Or the church stands° by thy tabor, if thy | is maintained
tabor stand by the church.

10 CLOWN You have said, sir. To see this age! A sentence° is but | saying
a chev'rel° glove to a good wit. How quickly the wrong side | kidskin
may be turned outward.

---

4. A game of dice in which the winner throws a three
("tray" is from the Spanish *tres*). *play:* wager.
5. A notorious object of contempt.
3.1 Location: Olivia's garden.
1. The dialogue demands only a tabor, but jesters
commonly played a pipe with one hand while tapping

a tabor (a small drum, hanging from the neck) with
the other.
2. Viola understands "by" to mean "earn my keep
through," but the Clown explains "by" as merely
"close to."
3. Lives near; punning on "goes to bed with."

VIOLA   Nay, that's certain. They that dally nicely° with words   *play subtly*
    may quickly make them wanton.[4]

15 CLOWN   I would therefore my sister had had no name, sir.

VIOLA   Why, man?

CLOWN   Why, sir, her name's a word, and to dally with that
    word might make my sister wanton. But, indeed, words are
    very rascals since bonds disgraced them.[5]

20 VIOLA   Thy reason, man?

CLOWN   Troth, sir, I can yield you none without words, and
    words are grown so false, I am loath to prove reason with them.

VIOLA   I warrant thou art a merry fellow and car'st for nothing.

CLOWN   Not so, sir, I do care for something. But in my con-
25   science, sir, I do not care for you. If that be to care for noth-
    ing, sir, I would it would make you invisible.

VIOLA   Art not thou the Lady Olivia's fool?

CLOWN   No indeed, sir, the Lady Olivia has no folly. She will
    keep no fool, sir, till she be married, and fools are as like hus-
30   bands as pilchers[6] are to herrings—the husband's the bigger.
    I am indeed not her fool, but her corrupter of words.

VIOLA   I saw thee late° at the Count Orsino's.   *lately*

CLOWN   Foolery, sir, does walk about the orb[7] like the sun. It
    shines everywhere. I would be sorry, sir, but the fool should
35   be as oft with your master as with my mistress.[8] I think I
    saw your wisdom[9] there.

VIOLA   Nay, an thou pass upon[1] me, I'll no more with thee.
    Hold, there's expenses for thee.
        [*She gives him a coin.*]

CLOWN   Now Jove in his next commodity° of hair send thee a   *shipment*
40   beard.

VIOLA   By my troth, I'll tell thee, I am almost sick for one,[2]
    though I would not have it grow on my chin. Is thy lady within?

CLOWN   Would not a pair of these have bred,[3] sir?

VIOLA   Yes, being kept together and put to use.[4]

45 CLOWN   I would play Lord Pandarus[5] of Phrygia, sir, to bring
    a Cressida to this Troilus.

VIOLA   I understand you, sir. 'Tis well begged.
        [*She gives him another coin.*]

CLOWN   The matter I hope is not great, sir, begging but a beg-
    gar. Cressida was a beggar.[6] My lady is within, sir. I will
50   conster° to them whence you come. Who you are and what   *explain*
    you would are out of my welkin. I might say "element," but
    the word is overworn.[7]   *Exit.*

---

4. Equivocal; the Clown puns on the meaning "unchaste."

5. Since legal contracts replaced a man's word of honor. ("Bonds" plays on "sworn statements" and "fetters," betokening criminality.)

6. Small fish similar to herring.

7. World; the sun was still believed to circle the earth.

8. I, the Clown, should visit master and mistress alike; Orsino should be called "fool" as often as Olivia.

9. *your wisdom:* a mocking title for Cesario.

1. If you express an opinion of; if you joke about.

2. Almost eager for a beard; almost pining for a man

(Orsino).

3. Would not a pair of coins such as these have multiplied (with possible pun on "be enough to buy bread").

4. *put to use:* invested to produce interest.

5. Go-between, or "pander," since the Clown needs a "mate" for his coin(s). Shakespeare dramatizes the story in *Troilus and Cressida.*

6. In asking for the "mate" to his Troilus coin, the Clown draws on a version of the story of Troilus and Cressida in which Cressida became a beggar.

7. "Welkin" (sky or air) is synonymous with one meaning of "element," used in what the Clown regards as the overworn phrase "out of my element."

VIOLA   This fellow is wise enough to play the fool
   And to do that well craves a kind of wit.°   *intelligence*
55   He must observe their mood on whom he jests,
   The quality of persons, and the time,
   And, like the haggard, check at every feather
   That comes before his eye.[8] This is a practice°   *skill*
   As full of labor as a wise man's art.
60   For folly that he wisely shows is fit,[9]
   But wise men, folly-fall'n, quite taint[1] their wit.
        Enter SIR TOBY *and* SIR ANDREW.

SIR TOBY   Save you, gentleman.

VIOLA   And you, sir.

SIR ANDREW   *Dieu vous garde,[2] monsieur.*

65 VIOLA   *Et vous aussi. Votre serviteur.[3]*

SIR ANDREW   I hope, sir, you are, and I am yours.

SIR TOBY   Will you encounter[4] the house? My niece is desirous
   you should enter, if your trade be to her.

VIOLA   I am bound to° your niece, sir. I mean, she is the list° of   *for / destination*
70   my voyage.

SIR TOBY   Taste° your legs, sir, put them to motion.   *Try*

VIOLA   My legs do better understand° me, sir, than I understand   *stand under*
   what you mean by bidding me taste my legs.

SIR TOBY   I mean, to go, sir, to enter.

75 VIOLA   I will answer you with gate and entrance, but we are
   prevented.°   *anticipated*
        Enter OLIVIA *and* [MARIA, *her*] *gentlewoman.*
   Most excellent accomplished lady, the heavens rain odors on
   you.

SIR ANDREW [*to* SIR TOBY]   That youth's a rare° courtier. "Rain   *an excellent*
80   odors," well.°   *well put*

VIOLA   My matter hath no voice,° lady, but to your own most   *must not be spoken*
   pregnant° and vouchsafed° ear.   *receptive / proffered*

SIR ANDREW [*to* SIR TOBY]   "Odors," "pregnant," and "vouchsafed." I'll get 'em all three all ready.[5]

85 OLIVIA   Let the garden door be shut, and leave me to my hearing.
        [*Exeunt* SIR TOBY, SIR ANDREW, *and* MARIA.]
   Give me your hand, sir.

VIOLA   My duty, madam, and most humble service.

OLIVIA   What is your name?

VIOLA   Cesario is your servant's name, fair princess.

90 OLIVIA   My servant, sir? 'Twas never merry world[6]
   Since lowly feigning° was called compliment.   *pretended humility*
   You're servant to the Count Orsino, youth.

VIOLA   And he is yours, and his must needs be yours.
   Your servant's servant is your servant, madam.

95 OLIVIA   For° him, I think not on him. For his thoughts,   *As for*
   Would they were blanks rather than filled with me.

---

8. *And . . . eye:* As a wild hawk ("haggard") must be
sensitive to its prey's disposition.
9. For folly that he skillfully displays is proper.
1. Discredit; spoil. *folly-fall'n:* fallen into folly.
2. God protect you (French).
3. And you also. (I am) your servant. (Sir Andrew's
awkward reply demonstrates that his French is

limited.)
4. Pedantry for "enter." (Toby mocks Viola's courtly
language.)
5. *I'll . . . ready:* I'll commit them all to memory for
later use.
6. *'Twas . . . world:* the proverbial "Things have never
been the same."

VIOLA   Madam, I come to whet your gentle thoughts
    On his behalf.
OLIVIA   Oh, by your leave,[7] I pray you.
    I bade you never speak again of him.
100   But would you undertake another suit,
    I had rather hear you to solicit that
    Than music from the spheres.[8]
VIOLA   Dear lady—
OLIVIA   Give me leave, beseech you. I did send,
    After the last enchantment you did here,
105   A ring in chase of you. So did I abuse°   deceive; dishonor
    Myself, my servant, and I fear me you.°   and, as I fear, you
    Under your hard construction[9] must I sit
    To force° that on you in a shameful cunning   For forcing
    Which you knew none of yours. What might you think?
110   Have you not set mine honor at the stake,
    And baited it with all th'unmuzzled thoughts[1]
    That tyrannous heart can think? To one of your receiving°   perception
    Enough is shown. A cypress,[2] not a bosom,
    Hides my heart. So let me hear you speak.
VIOLA   I pity you.
115 OLIVIA   That's a degree to° love.   toward
VIOLA   No, not a grece,° for 'tis a vulgar proof°   step / common experience
    That very oft we pity enemies.
OLIVIA   Why, then methinks 'tis time to smile again.[3]
    O world, how apt° the poor are to be proud!   ready
120   If one should be a prey, how much the better
    To fall before the lion than the wolf.[4]
        Clock strikes.
    The clock upbraids me with the waste of time.
    Be not afraid, good youth, I will not have you.
    And yet when wit and youth is come to harvest,
125   Your wife is like to reap a proper° man.   handsome; worthy
    There lies your way, due west.
VIOLA   Then westward ho![5]
    Grace and good disposition° attend your ladyship.   peace of mind
    You'll nothing, madam, to my lord by me?
OLIVIA   Stay. I prithee, tell me what thou[6] think'st of me?
130 VIOLA   That you do think you are not what you are.[7]
OLIVIA   If I think so, I think the same of you.[8]
VIOLA   Then think you right. I am not what I am.
OLIVIA   I would you were as I would have you be.
VIOLA   Would it be better, madam, than I am?
135   I wish it might, for now I am your fool.[9]

7. Permit me to interrupt (polite expression).
8. Exquisite music thought to be made by the planets as they moved, but inaudible to mortal ears.
9. Your unfavorable interpretation (of my behavior).
1. set . . . thoughts: as bears that were tied up at the stake and baited with dogs.
2. Veil of transparent silken gauze; the cypress tree was also emblematic of mourning.
3. Time to discard love's melancholy.
4. If . . . wolf: If I had to fall prey to love, it would have been better to succumb to the noble Orsino

than to the hard-hearted Cesario.
5. Thames watermen's cry to attract passengers for the court at Westminster from London.
6. Olivia changes from "you" to the familiar "thou."
7. In other words, that you think you are in love with a man, but in fact you are in love with a woman.
8. Olivia may think that Cesario has suggested that she is mad; or she may imply that she thinks that Cesario, despite his subordinate position, is noble.
9. You have made a fool of me.

OLIVIA [*aside*]   Oh, what a deal of scorn looks beautiful
In the contempt and anger of his lip!
A murd'rous guilt shows not itself more soon
Than love that would seem hid. Love's night is noon.[1]
140 —Cesario, by the roses of the spring,
By maidhood, honor, truth, and everything,
I love thee so that, maugre° all thy pride,   *despite*
Nor° wit nor reason can my passion hide.   *Neither*
Do not extort thy reasons from this clause,[2]
145 For that° I woo thou therefore hast no cause.   *That because*
But rather reason thus with reason fetter;[3]
Love sought is good, but given unsought is better.
VIOLA   By innocence I swear, and by my youth,
I have one heart, one bosom, and one truth,
150 And that no woman has, nor never none
Shall mistress be of it, save I alone,
And so adieu, good madam. Never more
Will I my master's tears to you deplore.°   *lament*
OLIVIA   Yet come again. For thou perhaps mayst move
155 That heart, which now abhors, to like his love.   *Exeunt.*

3.2

Enter SIR TOBY, SIR ANDREW, *and* FABIAN.
SIR ANDREW   No, faith, I'll not stay a jot longer.
SIR TOBY   Thy reason, dear venom,° give thy reason.   *venomous one*
FABIAN   You must needs yield your reason, Sir Andrew.
SIR ANDREW   Marry, I saw your niece do more favors to the
5 Count's servingman than ever she bestowed upon me. I saw't
i'th' orchard.°   *garden*
SIR TOBY   Did she see thee the while, old boy, tell me that?
SIR ANDREW   As plain as I see you now.
FABIAN   This was a great argument° of love in her toward you.   *proof*
10 SIR ANDREW   'Slight,° will you make an ass o'me?   *By God's light*
FABIAN   I will prove it legitimate, sir, upon the oaths of judgment and reason.
SIR TOBY   And they have been grand-jury men[1] since before
Noah was a sailor.
15 FABIAN   She did show favor to the youth in your sight only to
exasperate you, to awake your dormouse° valor, to put fire in   *meek; timid*
your heart and brimstone in your liver. You should then have
accosted her and, with some excellent jests, fire-new from
the mint,° you should have banged the youth into dumbness.   *newly minted*
20 This was looked for at your hand and this was balked.° The   *neglected*
double gilt[2] of this opportunity you let time wash off, and
you are now sailed into the north of my lady's opinion,[3]
where you will hang like an icicle on a Dutchman's[4] beard,
unless you do redeem it by some laudable attempt either of
25 valor or policy.°   *cunning*

---

1. Love, though attempting secrecy, still shines out
as bright as day.
2. Do not take the position that just because I woo
you, you are under no obligation to reciprocate.
3. But instead constrain your reasoning with this
argument.
3.2 Location: Olivia's house.

1. Grand-jury men were supposed to be good judges
of evidence.
2. Twice gilded, and as such, Sir Andrew's "golden
opportunity" to prove both love and valor.
3. Into Olivia's cold disfavor.
4. Perhaps an allusion to navigator Willem Barents,
who led an expedition to the Arctic in 1596–97.

SIR ANDREW An't° be any way, it must be with valor, for policy *If it*
I hate. I had as lief° be a Brownist as a politician.[5] *as soon*

SIR TOBY Why, then, build me thy fortunes upon the basis of
valor. Challenge me° the Count's youth to fight with him, *for me*
30   hurt him in eleven places. My niece shall take note of it, and,
assure thyself, there is no love-broker in the world can more
prevail in man's commendation with woman than report of
valor.

FABIAN There is no way but this, Sir Andrew.

35 SIR ANDREW Will either of you bear me a challenge to him?

SIR TOBY Go, write it in a martial hand. Be curst° and brief. It *sharp*
is no matter how witty, so it be eloquent and full of invention.° *imagination; untruth*
Taunt him with the license of ink.[6] If thou thou'st[7] him
some thrice, it shall not be amiss, and as many lies° as will *accusations of lying*
40   lie in thy sheet of paper, although the sheet were big enough
for the bed of Ware[8] in England, set 'em down, go about it.
Let there be gall[9] enough in thy ink, though thou write with
a goose-pen,[1] no matter. About it.

SIR ANDREW Where shall I find you?

45 SIR TOBY We'll call thee at the cubiculo.° Go. *little chamber*

Exit SIR ANDREW.

FABIAN This is a dear manikin° to you, Sir Toby. *puppet*

SIR TOBY I have been dear° to him, lad, some two thousand *costly*
strong or so.

FABIAN We shall have a rare letter from him. But you'll not
50   deliver't?

SIR TOBY Never trust me, then. And by all means stir on the
youth to an answer. I think oxen and wain-ropes[2] cannot hale° *drag*
them together. For Andrew, if he were opened and you find
so much blood in his liver[3] as will clog° the foot of a flea, I'll *weigh down*
55   eat the rest of th'anatomy.° *cadaver*

FABIAN And his opposite° the youth bears in his visage no *adversary*
great presage of cruelty.

Enter MARIA.

SIR TOBY Look where the youngest wren of mine comes.

MARIA If you desire the spleen° and will laugh yourselves into *a laughing fit*
60   stitches, follow me. Yon gull° Malvolio is turned heathen, a *fool*
very renegado.[4] For there is no Christian that means to be
saved by believing rightly can ever believe such impossible
passages of grossness.[5] He's in yellow stockings.

SIR TOBY And cross-gartered?

65 MARIA Most villainously,° like a pedant° that keeps a school *abominably / teacher*
i'th' church.[6] I have dogged him like his murderer. He does
obey every point of the letter that I dropped to betray him.
He does smile his face into more lines than is in the new

---

5. A schemer. A Brownist was a member of the puritan sect founded in 1581 by Robert Browne.
6. *license of ink*: freedom taken in writing, but not risked in conversation.
7. Call him "thou" (an insult to a stranger).
8. Famous Elizabethan bedstead, nearly eleven feet square, now in the Victoria and Albert Museum, London.
9. Oak gall, an ingredient in ink; bitterness or rancor.
1. A quill made of a goose feather. (The goose was

proverbially cowardly and foolish.)
2. Wagon ropes pulled by oxen.
3. Supposed to be the source of blood, which engendered courage.
4. Renegade (Spanish); a Christian converted to Islam.
5. Such patent absurdities (in the letter).
6. Because no schoolroom is available in a small rustic community.

70 map with the augmentation of the Indies.[7] You have not
seen such a thing as 'tis. I can hardly forbear hurling things
at him. I know my lady will strike him. If she do, he'll smile
and take't for a great favor.

SIR TOBY Come, bring us, bring us where he is.　　*Exeunt.*

3.3

Enter SEBASTIAN *and* ANTONIO.

SEBASTIAN I would not by my will have troubled you,
But, since you make your pleasure of your pains,
I will no further chide you.

ANTONIO I could not stay behind you. My desire,
5　More sharp than filèd steel, did spur me forth.
And not all° love to see you, though so much　　　　　　　*only*
As might have drawn one to a longer voyage,
But jealousy° what might befall your travel,　　　　　　*apprehension*
Being skill-less in° these parts which, to a stranger　　*unfamiliar to*
10　Unguided and unfriended, often prove
Rough and unhospitable. My willing love,
The rather° by these arguments of fear,　　　　　　　*more willingly*
Set forth in your pursuit.

SEBASTIAN　　　　　　　My kind Antonio,
I can no other answer make but thanks
15　And thanks. And ever oft,° good turns　　　　　　　*very often*
Are shuffled off° with such uncurrent[1] pay.　　　　*shrugged off*
But were my worth as is my conscience° firm,　*sense of indebtedness*
You should find better dealing. What's to do?
Shall we go see the relics° of this town?　　　　　　　*sights*
20　ANTONIO Tomorrow, sir. Best first go see your lodging.
SEBASTIAN I am not weary, and 'tis long to night.
I pray you, let us satisfy our eyes
With the memorials and the things of fame
That do renown this city.

ANTONIO　　　　　　　Would you'd pardon me.
25　I do not without danger walk these streets.
Once in a sea-fight 'gainst the Count his° galleys　　*(the Count's)*
I did some service, of such note indeed
That were I ta'en° here it would scarce be answered.[2]　*captured*
SEBASTIAN Belike° you slew great number of his people?　*Perhaps*
30　ANTONIO Th'offense is not of such a bloody nature,
Albeit the quality° of the time and quarrel　　　　　*circumstances*
Might well have given us bloody argument.°　　　*cause for bloodshed*
It might have since been answered in repaying
What we took from them, which for traffic's° sake　　*trade's*
35　Most of our city did. Only myself stood out,
For which, if I be lapsèd° in this place,　　　　　　　*caught*
I shall pay dear.

SEBASTIAN　　　　　Do not then walk too open.
ANTONIO It doth not fit me. Hold, sir, here's my purse.

---

7. Possibly refers to a map published in 1599 showing the East Indies more fully than in earlier maps
and crisscrossed by many rhumb lines.
3.3 Location: A street scene.

1. Out of currency; worthless.
2. It would be difficult for me to make reparation
(and thus my life would be in danger).

In the south suburbs at the Elephant[3]

40 Is best to lodge. I will bespeak our diet°   *order our meals*

Whiles you beguile° the time and feed your knowledge   *pass*

With viewing of the town. There shall you have me.

SEBASTIAN   Why I your purse?

ANTONIO   Haply° your eye shall light upon some toy°   *Perhaps / trifle*

45 You have desire to purchase, and your store,°   *resources*

I think, is not for idle markets,[4] sir.

SEBASTIAN   I'll be your purse-bearer and leave you

For an hour.

ANTONIO   To th'Elephant.

SEBASTIAN   I do remember.   *Exeunt.*

3.4

Enter OLIVIA *and* MARIA.

OLIVIA [*aside*]   I have sent after him. He says he'll come.

How shall I feast him? What bestow of° him?   *on*

For youth is bought more oft than begged or borrowed.[1]

I speak too loud.

5 —Where's Malvolio? He is sad,° and civil,°   *sober / respectful*

And suits well for a servant with my fortunes.

Where is Malvolio?

MARIA   He's coming, madam, but in very strange manner. He

is sure possessed,° madam.   *(by the devil); insane*

10 OLIVIA   Why, what's the matter? Does he rave?

MARIA   No, madam, he does nothing but smile. Your ladyship

were best to have some guard about you if he come, for sure

the man is tainted in 's wits.

OLIVIA   Go, call him hither.   [*Exit* MARIA.]

                        I am as mad as he,

15 If sad and merry madness equal be.

        Enter MALVOLIO [*with* MARIA].

How now, Malvolio?

MALVOLIO   Sweet lady, ho, ho.

OLIVIA   Smil'st thou? I sent for thee upon a sad occasion.°   *about a serious matter*

MALVOLIO   Sad, lady? I could be sad. This does make some

20 obstruction in the blood, this cross-gartering. But what of

that? If it please the eye of one, it is with me as the very true

sonnet° is: "please one, and please all."[2]   *song*

OLIVIA   Why, how dost thou, man? What is the matter with

thee?

25 MALVOLIO   Not black in my mind, though yellow[3] in my legs.

It did come to his hands, and commands shall be executed.

I think we do know the sweet Roman hand.°   *italic calligraphy*

OLIVIA   Wilt thou go to bed,[4] Malvolio?

MALVOLIO   To bed? "Ay, sweetheart, and I'll come to thee."[5]

30 OLIVIA   God comfort thee! Why dost thou smile so and kiss

thy hand so oft?

---

3. An inn with this name did in fact exist on Bankside, near the Globe. The area was notorious for its many brothels.

4. Not large enough to spend on luxuries.

3.4 Location: The garden of Olivia's house.

1. "Better to buy than to beg or borrow" was proverbial.

2. If I please one, I please all I care to please (words

of a popular bawdy ballad).

3. Black and yellow bile indicated choleric and melancholic dispositions, respectively. "Black and yellow" was the name of a popular song; to "wear yellow hose" was to be jealous.

4. In order to cure his madness with sleep.

5. A line from a popular song.

MARIA   How do you, Malvolio?

MALVOLIO   At your request. Yes, nightingales answer daws.[6]

MARIA   Why appear you with this ridiculous boldness before
35   my lady?

MALVOLIO   "Be not afraid of greatness." 'Twas well writ.

OLIVIA   What mean'st thou by that, Malvolio?

MALVOLIO   "Some are born great."

OLIVIA   Ha?

40   MALVOLIO   "Some achieve greatness."

OLIVIA   What say'st thou?

MALVOLIO   "And some have greatness thrust upon them."

OLIVIA   Heaven restore thee.

MALVOLIO   "Remember who commended thy yellow
45   stockings"—

OLIVIA   Thy yellow stockings?

MALVOLIO   "And wished to see thee cross-gartered."

OLIVIA   Cross-gartered?

MALVOLIO   "Go to. Thou art made, if thou desir'st to be so."

50   OLIVIA   Am I made?

MALVOLIO   "If not, let me see thee a servant still."

OLIVIA   Why, this is very midsummer madness.
        Enter SERVANT.

SERVANT   Madam, the young gentleman of the Count Orsi-
        no's is returned. I could hardly entreat him back. He attends
55   your ladyship's pleasure.

OLIVIA   I'll come to him.   [*Exit* SERVANT.]
        Good Maria, let this fellow be looked to. Where's my cousin
        Toby? Let some of my people have a special care of him. I
        would not have him miscarry° for the half of my dowry.   *come to harm*
                        Exeunt [OLIVIA *and* MARIA].

60   MALVOLIO   Oh, ho, do you come near° me now? No worse man   *appreciate*
        than Sir Toby to look to me. This concurs directly with the
        letter. She sends him on purpose that I may appear stubborn
        to him, for she incites me to that in the letter. "Cast thy
        humble slough," says she. "Be opposite with a kinsman, surly
65   with servants, let thy tongue tang with arguments of state,
        put thyself into the trick of singularity." And consequently°   *subsequently*
        sets down the manner how—as a sad face, a reverend car-
        riage, a slow tongue, in the habit of some sir of note,° and so   *gentleman*
        forth. I have limed[7] her. But it is Jove's doing, and Jove make
70   me thankful. And when she went away now—"let this fellow
        be looked to." "Fellow"![8] Not "Malvolio," nor after my degree,
        but "fellow." Why, everything adheres together, that no dram
        of a scruple, no scruple of a scruple,[9] no obstacle, no incred-
        ulous or unsafe circumstance—what can be said? Nothing
75   that can be can come between me and the full prospect of
        my hopes. Well, Jove, not I, is the doer of this, and he is to be
        thanked.
                Enter SIR TOBY, FABIAN, *and* MARIA.

SIR TOBY   Which way is he, in the name of sanctity? If all the

---

6. Shall I deign to reply to you? Yes, since even the
nightingale sings in response to the crowing of the
jackdaw.
7. Birds were caught by smearing sticky birdlime on
branches.

8. Malvolio takes the word to mean "companion."
9. *no dram . . . scruple:* both phrases mean "no scrap
of a doubt." *dram:* one-eighth of a fluid ounce. *scruple:* one-third of a dram.

devils of hell be drawn in little,[1] and Legion[2] himself pos-
80 sessed him, yet I'll speak to him.

FABIAN   Here he is, here he is. [*to* MALVOLIO] How is't with
you, sir? How is't with you, man?

MALVOLIO   Go off, I discard you. Let me enjoy my private.° Go   *privacy*
off.

85 MARIA   Lo, how hollow° the fiend speaks within him. Did not   *resonantly*
I tell you? Sir Toby, my lady prays you to have a care of him.

MALVOLIO   Ah ha, does she so?

SIR TOBY   Go to, go to. Peace, peace, we must deal gently with
him. Let me alone.° —How do you, Malvolio? How is't with   *Leave him to me*
90 you? What, man, defy the devil. Consider, he's an enemy to
mankind.

MALVOLIO   Do you know what you say?

MARIA   La° you, an you speak ill of the devil, how he takes it   *Look*
at heart. Pray God he be not bewitched.

95 FABIAN   Carry his water to th' wise woman.[3]

MARIA   Marry, and it shall be done tomorrow morning if I
live. My lady would not lose him for more than I'll say.

MALVOLIO   How now, mistress?

MARIA   O Lord.

100 SIR TOBY   Prithee, hold thy peace. This is not the way. Do you
not see you move° him? Let me alone with him.   *anger*

FABIAN   No way but gentleness, gently, gently. The fiend is
rough° and will not be roughly used.   *violent*

SIR TOBY   Why, how now, my bawcock?[4] How dost thou, chuck?

105 MALVOLIO   Sir.

SIR TOBY   Ay, biddy,° come with me. What, man, 'tis not for grav-   *hen*
ity° to play at cherry-pit[5] with Satan. Hang him, foul collier.[6]   *for a man of dignity*

MARIA   Get him to say his prayers, good Sir Toby. Get him to
pray.

110 MALVOLIO   My prayers, minx?°   *impertinent girl*

MARIA   No, I warrant you, he will not hear of godliness.

MALVOLIO   Go, hang yourselves all. You are idle° shallow things.   *foolish*
I am not of your element.° You shall know more hereafter.   *social sphere*
                                                        Exit.

SIR TOBY   Is't possible?

115 FABIAN   If this were played upon a stage now, I could condemn it as an improbable fiction.

SIR TOBY   His very genius° hath taken the infection of the   *spirit*
device,° man.   *trick*

MARIA   Nay, pursue him now, lest the device take air and taint.[7]

120 FABIAN   Why, we shall make him mad indeed.

MARIA   The house will be the quieter.

SIR TOBY   Come, we'll have him in a dark room and bound.[8] My
niece is already in the belief that he's mad. We may carry it

---

1. Be contracted into a small space (punning on
"painted in miniature").
2. Alluding to a scene of exorcism in Mark 5:8–9:
"For he [Jesus] said unto him, Come out of the man,
thou unclean spirit. And he asked him, What is thy
name? And he answered saying, My name is Legion:
for we are many."
3. *water*: urine (for medical diagnosis). *wise woman*:
local healer, "good witch."

4. Fine fellow (from the French *beau coq*, "fine bird").
5. A children's game in which cherrystones were
thrown into a hole.
6. Dirty coal man (the devil was supposed to be
black).
7. Spoil (like leftover food) by exposure to air; become
known (and thus ruined).
8. Customary treatments for madness.

thus° for our pleasure and his penance till our very pastime,   *continue the pretense*
125   tired out of breath, prompt us to have mercy on him. At which
time, we will bring the device to the bar[9] and crown thee for
a finder of madmen.[1] But see, but see.
    Enter SIR ANDREW.
FABIAN   More matter for a May morning.[2]
SIR ANDREW [*presenting a paper*] Here's the challenge. Read
130   it. I warrant there's vinegar and pepper in't.
FABIAN   Is't so saucy?
SIR ANDREW   Ay, is't. I warrant him. Do but read.
SIR TOBY   Give me. [*He reads.*] "Youth, whatsoever thou art,
thou art but a scurvy fellow."
135 FABIAN   Good and valiant.
SIR TOBY   "Wonder not, nor admire° not in thy mind why I do   *marvel*
call thee so, for I will show thee no reason for't."
FABIAN   A good note, that keeps you from the blow of the law.[3]
SIR TOBY   "Thou com'st to the Lady Olivia, and in my sight she
140   uses thee kindly. But thou liest in thy throat.° That is not   *deeply*
the matter I challenge thee for."
FABIAN   Very brief and to exceeding good sense—less.[4]
SIR TOBY   "I will waylay thee going home, where if it be thy
chance to kill me—"
145 FABIAN   Good.
SIR TOBY   "Thou kill'st me like a rogue and a villain."
FABIAN   Still you keep o'th' windy side[5] of the law. Good.
SIR TOBY   "Fare thee well, and God have mercy upon one of
our souls. He may have mercy upon mine, but my hope is
150   better,[6] and so look to thyself. Thy friend, as thou usest him,
and thy sworn enemy, Andrew Aguecheek."
SIR TOBY   If this letter move° him not, his legs cannot. I'll   *provoke*
give't him.
MARIA   You may have very fit occasion for't. He is now in some
155   commerce° with my lady, and will by and by depart.   *conversation*
SIR TOBY   Go, Sir Andrew, scout me° for him at the corner of   *look out*
the orchard like a bumbaily.[7] So soon as ever thou seest him,
draw and, as thou draw'st, swear horrible. For it comes to
pass oft that a terrible oath, with a swaggering accent sharply
160   twanged off, gives manhood more approbation° than ever   *credit*
proof° itself would have earned him. Away.   *trial*
SIR ANDREW   Nay, let me alone for swearing.[8]   *Exit.*
SIR TOBY   Now will not I deliver his letter. For the behavior of
the young gentleman gives him out to be of good capacity°   *ability*
165   and breeding. His employment between his lord and my
niece confirms no less. Therefore, this letter, being so excellently ignorant, will breed no terror in the youth. He will
find it comes from a clodpoll.° But, sir, I will deliver his   *blockhead*
challenge by word of mouth, set upon Aguecheek a notable

---

9. Into the open court (to be judged).
1. *finder of madmen:* one of a jury "finding," or declaring, a man to be mad.
2. More pastime fit for a holiday.
3. That protects you from a charge of a breach of peace.
4. F's "sence-lesse" appears to use the hyphen to signal an aside.

5. To windward (and therefore safe, not exposed to the law's blasts).
6. *my hope is better:* Andrew means that he expects to survive, but he ineptly implies that he expects to be damned.
7. A petty sheriff's officer employed to arrest debtors.
8. Have no doubts as to my swearing ability.

170   report of valor, and drive the gentleman—as I know his
      youth will aptly receive it[9]—into a most hideous opinion of
      his rage, skill, fury, and impetuosity. This will so fright
      them both that they will kill one another by the look, like
      cockatrices.[1]
          Enter OLIVIA *and* VIOLA [*as Cesario*].

175   FABIAN   Here he comes with your niece. Give them way° till   *Stand aside*
      he take leave and presently after him.
   SIR TOBY   I will meditate the while upon some horrid message
      for a challenge.   [*Exeunt* SIR TOBY, MARIA, *and* FABIAN.]
   OLIVIA   I have said too much unto a heart of stone
180   And laid mine honor too unchary° on't.   *carelessly*
      There's something in me that reproves my fault,
      But such a headstrong potent fault it is
      That it but mocks reproof.
   VIOLA   With the same 'havior that your passion bears[2]
185   Goes on my master's griefs.
   OLIVIA   Here, wear this jewel[3] for me. 'Tis my picture.
      Refuse it not. It hath no tongue to vex you.
      And I beseech you come again tomorrow.
      What shall you ask of me that I'll deny,
190   That honor, saved, may upon asking give?[4]
   VIOLA   Nothing but this: your true love for my master.
   OLIVIA   How with mine honor may I give him that
      Which I have given to you?
   VIOLA   I will acquit you.[5]
   OLIVIA   Well, come again tomorrow. Fare thee well.
195   A fiend like thee might bear my soul to hell.   [*Exit.*]
          Enter SIR TOBY *and* FABIAN.
   SIR TOBY   Gentleman, God save thee.
   VIOLA   And you, sir.
   SIR TOBY   That defense thou hast, betake thee to't. Of what
      nature the wrongs are thou hast done him I know not, but
200   thy intercepter, full of despite,° bloody as the hunter, attends°   *defiance / awaits*
      thee at the orchard end. Dismount thy tuck,[6] be yare° in thy   *prompt*
      preparation, for thy assailant is quick, skillful, and deadly.
   VIOLA   You mistake, sir, I am sure. No man hath any quarrel
      to me. My remembrance° is very free and clear from any   *memory*
205   image of offense done to any man.
   SIR TOBY   You'll find it otherwise, I assure you. Therefore, if
      you hold your life at any price, betake you to your guard. For
      your opposite° hath in him what youth, strength, skill, and   *opponent*
      wrath can furnish man withal.
210   VIOLA   I pray you, sir, what is he?
   SIR TOBY   He is knight dubbed with unhatched[7] rapier and on
      carpet consideration,[8] but he is a devil in private brawl.
      Souls and bodies hath he divorced three, and his incense-

---

9. As I know his inexperience will readily believe the
report.
1. Basilisks; mythical creatures supposed to be able
to kill at a glance.
2. *'havior . . . bears*: behavior that characterizes your
lovesickness.
3. Jeweled ornament; here, a brooch or a locket with
Olivia's picture.

4. That honor may grant without compromising
itself.
5. I will release you from your promise.
6. Draw your rapier.
7. Unhacked, or undented; never used in battle.
8. A "carpet knight" obtained his title through connections at court rather than valor on the battlefield.

ment at this moment is so implacable that satisfaction can
215 be none but by pangs of death and sepulcher. "Hob, nob,"[9] is
his word,° "give't or take't."   *motto*

VIOLA   I will return again into the house and desire some con-
duct° of the lady. I am no fighter. I have heard of some kind   *escort*
of men that put quarrels purposely on others to taste° their   *test*
220 valor. Belike this is a man of that quirk.

SIR TOBY   Sir, no. His indignation derives itself out of a very
competent° injury. Therefore, get you on and give him his   *sufficient*
desire. Back you shall not to the house, unless you under-
take that° with me which with as much safety you might   *(a duel)*
225 answer him. Therefore on, or strip your sword stark naked.
For meddle° you must, that's certain, or forswear to wear   *engage in a duel*
iron about you.[1]

VIOLA   This is as uncivil as strange. I beseech you do me this
courteous office, as to know of° the knight what my offense   *ascertain from*
230 to him is. It is something of my negligence, nothing of my
purpose.

SIR TOBY   I will do so. Signor Fabian, stay you by this gentleman till my return.   *Exit.*

VIOLA   Pray you, sir, do you know of this matter?

235 FABIAN   I know the knight is incensed against you even to a
mortal arbitrament,° but nothing of the circumstance more.   *deadly duel*

VIOLA   I beseech you, what manner of man is he?

FABIAN   Nothing of that wonderful promise to read him by his
form[2] as you are like to find him in the proof of his valor. He
240 is indeed, sir, the most skillful, bloody, and fatal opposite that
you could possibly have found in any part of Illyria. Will you
walk towards him? I will make your peace with him, if I can.

VIOLA   I shall be much bound to you for't. I am one that had
rather go with Sir Priest[3] than Sir Knight. I care not who
245 knows so much of my mettle.°   *Exeunt.*   *disposition*
        Enter SIR TOBY *and* SIR ANDREW.

SIR TOBY   Why, man, he's a very devil. I have not seen such a
virago.[4] I had a pass° with him, rapier, scabbard, and all, and   *fencing bout*
he gives me the stuck-in[5] with such a mortal motion that it
is inevitable. And on the answer,° he pays you as surely as   *return hit*
250 your feet hits the ground they step on. They say he has been
fencer to the Sophy.°   *Shah of Persia*

SIR ANDREW   Pox on't, I'll not meddle with him.

SIR TOBY   Ay, but he will not now be pacified. Fabian can
scarce hold him yonder.

255 SIR ANDREW   Plague on't, an° I thought he had been valiant   *if*
and so cunning in fence, I'd have seen him damned ere I'd
have challenged him. Let him let the matter slip and I'll give
him my horse, gray Capilet.

SIR TOBY   I'll make the motion.° Stand here, make a good show   *offer*
260 on't. This shall end without the perdition of souls.° [*aside*]   *loss of lives*
Marry, I'll ride your horse as well as I ride you.
        Enter FABIAN *and* VIOLA [*as Cesario*].

---

9. Have or have not ("all or nothing").
1. Or forfeit your right to wear a sword.
2. *Nothing . . . form:* From his outward appearance,
you cannot perceive him to be as remarkable.

3. Priests were often addressed as "sir."
4. A woman warrior (suggesting great ferocity with a
feminine appearance).
5. The thrust (from the Italian *stoccata*).

[*aside to* FABIAN] I have his horse to take up° the quarrel. I   *settle*
have persuaded him the youth's a devil.
FABIAN [*aside*] He is as horribly conceited⁶ of him, and pants
265 and looks pale as if a bear were at his heels.
SIR TOBY There's no remedy, sir, he will fight with you for 's
oath sake. Marry, he hath better bethought him of his quarrel, and he finds that now scarce to be worth talking of.
Therefore, draw for the supportance of his vow. He protests
270 he will not hurt you.
VIOLA [*aside*] Pray God defend me. A little thing would make
me tell them how much I lack of a man.
FABIAN Give ground if you see him furious.
SIR TOBY Come, Sir Andrew, there's no remedy. The gentleman
275 will for his honor's sake have one bout with you. He cannot by
the duello° avoid it. But he has promised me, as he is a gentle-   *code of dueling*
man and a soldier, he will not hurt you. Come on, to't.
SIR ANDREW [*drawing his sword*] Pray God he keep his oath.
          Enter ANTONIO.
VIOLA [*drawing her sword*] I do assure you 'tis against my will.
280 ANTONIO [*drawing his sword*] Put up your sword. If this young
          gentleman
Have done offense, I take the fault on me.
If you offend him, I for him defy you.
SIR TOBY You, sir? Why, what are you?
ANTONIO One, sir, that for his love dares yet do more
285 Than you have heard him brag to you he will.
SIR TOBY [*drawing his sword*] Nay, if you be an undertaker,⁷
I am for you.
          Enter OFFICERS.
FABIAN O good Sir Toby, hold. Here come the officers.
SIR TOBY [*to* ANTONIO] I'll be with you anon.
290 VIOLA [*to* SIR ANDREW] Pray, sir, put your sword up, if you please.
SIR ANDREW Marry, will I, sir. And for that° I promised you, I'll   *as for that*
be as good as my word. He will bear you easily and reins well.
FIRST OFFICER This is the man; do thy office.
SECOND OFFICER Antonio, I arrest thee at the suit of Count
295 Orsino.
ANTONIO You do mistake me, sir.
FIRST OFFICER No, sir, no jot. I know your favor° well,   *face*
Though now you have no sea cap on your head.
—Take him away. He knows I know him well.
300 ANTONIO I must obey. [*to* VIOLA] This comes with seeking you.
But there's no remedy, I shall answer° it.   *answer for*
What will you do now my necessity
Makes me to ask you for my purse? It grieves me
Much more for what I cannot do for you
305 Than what befalls myself. You stand amazed,
But be of comfort.
SECOND OFFICER   Come, sir, away.
ANTONIO I must entreat of you some of that money.
VIOLA What money, sir?

---

6. He has as terrifying an idea.   7. One who would take upon himself a task (here, a
                                                    challenge).

For the fair kindness you have showed me here,
310 And part° being prompted by your present trouble,   *in part*
Out of my lean and low ability
I'll lend you something. My having is not much.
I'll make division of my present° with you.   *ready money*
Hold, there's half my coffer.
    [*She offers him money.*]
ANTONIO   Will you deny me now?
315 Is't possible that my deserts to you
Can lack persuasion?[8] Do not tempt my misery,
Lest that it make me so unsound° a man   *morally weak*
As to upbraid you with those kindnesses
That I have done for you.
VIOLA   I know of none,
320 Nor know I you by voice or any feature.
I hate ingratitude more in a man
Than lying, vainness, babbling drunkenness,
Or any taint of vice whose strong corruption
Inhabits our frail blood.
ANTONIO   Oh, heavens themselves!
325 SECOND OFFICER   Come, sir, I pray you go.
ANTONIO   Let me speak a little. This youth that you see here,
I snatched one half out of the jaws of death,
Relieved him with such sanctity° of love,   *great devotion*
And to his image,[9] which methought did promise
330 Most venerable worth,[1] did I devotion.
SECOND OFFICER   What's that to us? The time goes by. Away!
ANTONIO   But oh, how vile an idol proves this god!
Thou hast, Sebastian, done good feature° shame.   *physical beauty*
In nature there's no blemish but the mind.
335 None can be called deformed but the unkind.
Virtue is beauty, but the beauteous evil
Are empty trunks, o'er-flourished[2] by the devil.
FIRST OFFICER   The man grows mad, away with him. —Come,
    come, sir.
ANTONIO   Lead me on.   *Exeunt* [ANTONIO *and* OFFICERS].
340 VIOLA [*aside*]   Methinks his words do from such passion fly
That he believes himself. So do not I.[3]
Prove true, imagination, oh, prove true,
That I, dear brother, be now ta'en for you.
SIR TOBY   Come hither, knight; come hither, Fabian. We'll
345 whisper o'er a couplet or two of most sage saws.°   *sayings; maxims*
    [*They step aside.*]
VIOLA   He named Sebastian. I my brother know
Yet living in my glass.° Even such and so   *mirror*
In favor° was my brother, and he went   *appearance*
Still° in this fashion, color, ornament,   *Always*
350 For him I imitate. Oh, if it prove,
Tempests are kind, and salt waves fresh in love!   [*Exit.*]

---

8. *Is't . . . persuasion:* Is it possible that my past kindness can fail to persuade you?
9. Appearance (with a play on "religious icon").
1. *did . . . worth:* was worthy of veneration.

2. Chests decorated with carving or painting; beautified bodies.
3. *So do not I:* I do not entirely believe the passionate
hope (for my brother's rescue) that is arising in me.

SIR TOBY   A very dishonest° paltry boy, and more a coward *dishonorable*
    than a hare. His dishonesty appears in leaving his friend
    here in necessity and denying him. And for his cowardship,
355   ask Fabian.
FABIAN   A coward, a most devout coward, religious in it.
SIR ANDREW   'Slid,° I'll after him again, and beat him. *By God's eyelid*
SIR TOBY   Do, cuff him soundly, but never draw thy sword.
SIR ANDREW   An I do not—   [*Exit.*]
360 FABIAN   Come, let's see the event.° *outcome*
SIR TOBY   I dare lay any money, 'twill be nothing yet.° *after all*

                                  Exeunt.

4.1

Enter SEBASTIAN *and* CLOWN.

CLOWN   Will you° make me believe that I am not sent for you? *Are you trying to*
SEBASTIAN   Go to, go to, thou art a foolish fellow. Let me be
    clear° of thee. *rid*
CLOWN   Well held out,° i'faith. No, I do not know you, nor I *kept up*
5   am not sent to you by my lady to bid you come speak with
    her, nor your name is not Master Cesario, nor this is not my
    nose neither. Nothing that is so, is so.
SEBASTIAN   I prithee vent° thy folly somewhere else. Thou *utter; excrete*
    know'st not me.
10 CLOWN   "Vent my folly." He has heard that word of some great
    man and now applies it to a fool. "Vent my folly." I am afraid
    this great lubber° the world will prove a cockney.° —I prithee *lout / sissy*
    now, ungird thy strangeness[1] and tell me what I shall vent to
    my lady? Shall I vent to her that thou art coming?
15 SEBASTIAN   I prithee, foolish Greek,° depart from me. There's *buffoon*
    money for thee. If you tarry longer, I shall give worse
    payment.
CLOWN   By my troth, thou hast an open hand. These wise men
    that give fools money get themselves a good report,° after *reputation*
20   fourteen years' purchase.[2]

Enter SIR ANDREW, SIR TOBY, *and* FABIAN.

SIR ANDREW   Now, sir, have I met you again. There's for you.
    [*He strikes* SEBASTIAN.]
SEBASTIAN   Why, there's for thee, and there, and there. [*He
    strikes* SIR ANDREW.] Are all the people mad?
SIR TOBY   Hold, sir, or I'll throw your dagger o'er the house.
25 CLOWN   This will I tell my lady straight.° I would not be in *straightaway*
    some of your coats for twopence.   [*Exit.*]
SIR TOBY   Come on, sir, hold.
SIR ANDREW   Nay, let him alone. I'll go another way to work
    with him. I'll have an action of battery° against him, if there *a lawsuit for assault*
30   be any law in Illyria. Though I struck him first, yet it's no
    matter for that.
SEBASTIAN   [*to* SIR TOBY]   Let go thy hand.
SIR TOBY   Come, sir, I will not let you go. Come, my young
    soldier, put up your iron. You are well fleshed.[3] Come on.

4.1 Location: Near Olivia's house.
1. *I . . . strangeness:* Stop pretending not to know me.
(The Clown mocks Sebastian's affected language.)
2. *after . . . purchase:* at a high price. The purchase

price of land was normally twelve times its annual
rent.
3. Experienced in combat. Hunting hounds were said
to be "fleshed" after being fed part of their first kill.

35   SEBASTIAN   I will be free from thee. [*He draws his sword.*] What
        wouldst thou now? If thou dar'st tempt me further, draw thy
        sword.
      SIR TOBY   What, what? [*He draws his sword.*] Nay, then, I must
        have an ounce or two of this malapert° blood from you.   *impudent*
          Enter OLIVIA.
40   OLIVIA   Hold, Toby, on thy life, I charge thee hold!
      SIR TOBY   Madam.
      OLIVIA   Will it be ever thus? Ungracious wretch,
      Fit for the mountains and the barbarous caves
      Where manners ne'er were preached, out of my sight!
45   Be not offended, dear Cesario.
      —Rudesby,° be gone.   *Ruffian*
         [*Exeunt* SIR TOBY, SIR ANDREW, *and* FABIAN.]
                I prithee, gentle friend,
      Let thy fair wisdom, not thy passion, sway
      In this uncivil and unjust extent°   *assault*
      Against thy peace. Go with me to my house,
50   And hear thou there how many fruitless pranks
      This ruffian hath botched up,° that thou thereby   *clumsily contrived*
      Mayst smile at this. Thou shalt not choose but go.
      Do not deny. Beshrew° his soul for me,   *Curse*
      He started one poor heart of mine in thee.[4]
55   SEBASTIAN [*aside*]   What relish° is in this? How runs the   *task; meaning*
        stream?
      Or° I am mad, or else this is a dream.   *Either*
      Let fancy° still my sense in Lethe[5] steep.   *imagination*
      If it be thus to dream, still let me sleep.
      OLIVIA   Nay, come, I prithee. Would thou'dst be ruled by me!
      SEBASTIAN   Madam, I will.
60   OLIVIA   Oh, say so, and so be.   *Exeunt.*

4.2

Enter MARIA [*carrying a costume*] *and* CLOWN.

      MARIA   Nay, I prithee put on this gown and this beard. Make
      him believe thou art Sir Topas[1] the curate. Do it quickly. I'll
      call Sir Toby the whilst.°   [*Exit.*]   *in the meantime*
      CLOWN   Well, I'll put it on, and I will dissemble[2] myself in't.
5   [*He puts on gown and beard.*] And I would I were the first
      that ever dissembled in such a gown. I am not tall enough to
      become the function well[3] nor lean enough to be thought a
      good student.° But to be said° an honest man and a good   *(of divinity)* / *reputed*
      housekeeper° goes as fairly as[4] to say a careful man and a   *host*
10   great scholar. The competitors° enter.   *associates*
          Enter SIR TOBY [*and* MARIA].
      SIR TOBY   Jove bless thee, Master Parson.

---

4. *He . . . thee:* By attacking Sebastian, Sir Toby frightened Olivia, who has exchanged hearts with Sebastian.
started: an allusion to hunting, creating a pun on
"hart/heart."
5. The mythical river of oblivion.
4.2 Location: Olivia's house, where Malvolio will be
found "in a dark room and bound" (3.4.122).

1. The comical hero of Chaucer's *Rime of Sir Topas*.
Also alluding to the mineral topaz, which was thought
to have special curative qualities for insanity.
2. Disguise; with a subsequent play on "lie."
3. To grace the priestly office. *tall:* stout, rather than
of great height.
4. *goes as fairly as:* sounds as well as.

CLOWN   *Bonos dies,*[5] Sir Toby. For, as the old hermit of Prague[6]
that never saw pen and ink very wittily° said to a niece of King   *intelligently*
Gorboduc,° "That that is, is." So I, being Master Parson, am   *legendary British king*
15   Master Parson. For what is "that" but "that," and "is" but "is"?
SIR TOBY   To him, Sir Topas.
CLOWN   What ho, I say, peace in this prison!
SIR TOBY   The knave counterfeits well. A good knave.
MALVOLIO (*within*)[7]   Who calls there?
20   CLOWN   Sir Topas the curate, who comes to visit Malvolio the
lunatic.
MALVOLIO   Sir Topas, Sir Topas, good Sir Topas, go to my lady.
CLOWN   Out, hyperbolical fiend,[8] how vexest thou this man!
Talkest thou nothing but of ladies?
25   SIR TOBY [*aside*]   Well said, Master Parson.
MALVOLIO   Sir Topas, never was man thus wronged. Good Sir
Topas, do not think I am mad. They have laid me here in
hideous darkness.
CLOWN   Fie, thou dishonest Satan. I call thee by the most
30   modest° terms, for I am one of those gentle ones that will   *mildest*
use the devil himself with courtesy. Say'st thou that house°   *room*
is dark?
MALVOLIO   As hell, Sir Topas.
CLOWN   Why, it hath bay windows transparent as barricadoes
35   and the clerestories[9] toward the south-north are as lustrous
as ebony.[1] And yet complainest thou of obstruction?
MALVOLIO   I am not mad, Sir Topas. I say to you this house is
dark.
CLOWN   Madman, thou errest. I say there is no darkness but
40   ignorance, in which thou art more puzzled than the Egyp-
tians in their fog.[2]
MALVOLIO   I say this house is as dark as ignorance, though
ignorance were as dark as hell. And I say there was never
man thus abused. I am no more mad than you are. Make the
45   trial of it in any constant question.°   *logical discussion*
CLOWN   What is the opinion of Pythagoras[3] concerning wild
fowl?
MALVOLIO   That the soul of our grandam might haply° inhabit   *perhaps*
a bird.
50   CLOWN   What think'st thou of his opinion?
MALVOLIO   I think nobly of the soul and no way approve his
opinion.
CLOWN   Fare thee well. Remain thou still in darkness. Thou
shalt hold th'opinion of Pythagoras ere I will allow of thy
55   wits,° and fear to kill a woodcock[4] lest thou dispossess the   *certify your sanity*
soul of thy grandam. Fare thee well.
MALVOLIO   Sir Topas, Sir Topas.

5. Good day (false Latin).
6. Probably an invented authority.
7. PERFORMANCE COMMENT Malvolio's prison has
taken many different forms onstage. For examples
as well as information on how the scene may have
been performed on Shakespeare's stages, see Digital
Edition PC 4.
8. The Clown treats Malvolio as a man possessed by
vehement ("hyperbolical") evil spirits.
9. Upper windows, usually in a church or great hall.

barricadoes: barricades (subsequent paradoxes are
equivalent to "as clear as mud").
1. A dense and naturally dull black wood.
2. One of the plagues of Egypt was a "black darkness"
lasting for three days (Exodus 10:21–23).
3. An ancient Greek philosopher who held that
the same soul could successively inhabit different
creatures.
4. A traditionally stupid bird.

SIR TOBY My most exquisite Sir Topas.

CLOWN Nay, I am for all waters.[5]

60 MARIA Thou mightst have done this without thy beard and gown; he sees thee not.

SIR TOBY To him in thine own voice and bring me word how thou find'st him. I would we were well rid of this knavery. If he may be conveniently delivered, I would he were, for I am 65 now so far in offense with my niece that I cannot pursue with any safety this sport to the upshot.° Come by and by to *climax; limit* my chamber.   *Exeunt* [SIR TOBY *and* MARIA].

CLOWN [*sings*][6] "Hey, Robin, jolly Robin,
              Tell me how thy lady does."

70 MALVOLIO Fool.

CLOWN [*sings*] "My lady is unkind, pardie."[7]

MALVOLIO Fool.

CLOWN [*sings*] "Alas, why is she so?"

MALVOLIO Fool, I say.

75 CLOWN [*sings*] "She loves another." Who calls, ha?

MALVOLIO Good fool, as ever thou wilt deserve well at my hand, help me to a candle, and pen, ink, and paper. As I am a gentleman, I will live to be thankful to thee for't.

CLOWN Master Malvolio?

80 MALVOLIO Ay, good fool.

CLOWN Alas, sir, how fell you besides° your five wits?[8]   *out of*

MALVOLIO Fool, there was never man so notoriously° abused.   *outrageously* I am as well in my wits, fool, as thou art.

CLOWN But as well? Then you are mad indeed, if you be no 85 better in your wits than a fool.

MALVOLIO They have here propertied me,[9] keep me in darkness, send ministers to me—asses—and do all they can to face me[1] out of my wits.

CLOWN Advise you° what you say. The minister is here. [*He   *Be careful* 90 disguises his voice.*] Malvolio, Malvolio, thy wits the heavens restore. Endeavor thyself to sleep, and leave thy vain bibble-babble.

MALVOLIO Sir Topas.

CLOWN [*as Sir Topas*] Maintain no words with him, good fel-95 low. [*as himself*] Who I, sir? Not I, sir. God buy you,° good   *God be with you* Sir Topas. [*as Sir Topas*] Marry, amen. [*as himself*] I will, sir, I will.

MALVOLIO Fool, fool, fool, I say.

CLOWN Alas, sir, be patient. What say you, sir? I am shent°   *scolded* 100 for speaking to you.

MALVOLIO Good fool, help me to some light and some paper. I tell thee I am as well in my wits as any man in Illyria.

CLOWN Well-a-day,° that you were, sir.   *Alas*

MALVOLIO By this hand, I am. Good fool, some ink, paper, and 105 light. And convey what I will set down to my lady. It shall advantage thee more than ever the bearing of letter did.

---

5. I am able to turn my hand to anything.
6. The Clown's song, which makes Malvolio aware of his presence, is traditional. There is a version by Sir Thomas Wyatt.
7. A corruption of the French *pardieu*, "by God."

8. Usually regarded as common sense, fantasy, memory, judgment, and imagination.
9. Treated me as a piece of property.
1. *face me:* brazenly construe me as.

CLOWN   I will help you to't. But tell me true, are you not mad
    indeed, or do you but counterfeit?
MALVOLIO   Believe me, I am not, I tell thee true.
110   CLOWN   Nay, I'll ne'er believe a madman till I see his brains. I
    will fetch you light, and paper, and ink.
MALVOLIO   Fool, I'll requite it in the highest degree. I prithee,
    be gone.
CLOWN [sings]   I am gone, sir, and anon, sir,
115   I'll be with you again,
          In a trice, like to the old Vice,[2]
          Your need to sustain.
          Who with dagger of lath,
          In his rage and his wrath,
120   Cries, "Aha" to the devil,
          Like a mad lad,
          "Pare thy nails, dad.
          Adieu, goodman[3] devil."   *Exit.*

4.3

Enter SEBASTIAN.
SEBASTIAN   This is the air, that is the glorious sun.
    This pearl she gave me, I do feel't and see't,
    And though 'tis wonder that enwraps me thus,
    Yet 'tis not madness. Where's Antonio then?
5   I could not find him at the Elephant.
    Yet there he was,° and there I found this credit,°   *had been / report*
    That he did range the town to seek me out.
    His counsel now might do me golden service
    For, though my soul disputes well with my sense[1]
10   That this may be some error but no madness,
    Yet doth this accident and flood of fortune
    So far exceed all instance,° all discourse,°   *precedent / reasoning*
    That I am ready to distrust mine eyes
    And wrangle with my reason that persuades me
15   To any other trust° but that I am mad—   *belief*
    Or else the lady's mad. Yet if 'twere so,
    She could not sway° her house, command her followers,   *rule*
    Take and give back affairs and their dispatch[2]
    With such a smooth, discreet, and stable bearing
20   As I perceive she does. There's something in't
    That is deceivable.° But here the lady comes.   *deceptive*
        Enter OLIVIA *and* PRIEST.
OLIVIA   Blame not this haste of mine. If you mean well,
    Now go with me and with this holy man
    Into the chantry by.° There, before him   *nearby chapel*
25   And underneath that consecrated roof,
    Plight me the full assurance of your faith,[3]
    That my most jealous° and too doubtful soul   *anxious*
    May live at peace. He shall conceal it
    Whiles° you are willing it shall come to note,   *Until*

---

2. A stock comic figure in the old morality plays; the
Vice often carried a wooden dagger.
3. Yeoman; a title given to one not of gentle birth,
hence a parting insult to Malvolio.

4.3 Location: Near Olivia's house.
1. For though my reason and my sense both concur.
2. Undertake business and ensure that it is carried out.
3. Enter into the solemn contract of betrothal.

30   What° time we will our celebration keep   *At which*
       According to my birth.° What do you say?   *rank*
   SEBASTIAN   I'll follow this good man and go with you
       And, having sworn truth, ever will be true.
   OLIVIA   Then lead the way, good father, and heavens so shine,
35   That they may fairly note° this act of mine.   *Exeunt.*   *look favorably upon*

5.1
Enter CLOWN *and* FABIAN.

   FABIAN   Now, as thou lov'st me, let me see his letter.
   CLOWN   Good Master Fabian, grant me another request.
   FABIAN   Anything.
   CLOWN   Do not desire to see this letter.
5   FABIAN   This is to give a dog and in recompense desire my dog
       again.[1]

Enter DUKE, VIOLA [*as Cesario*], CURIO, *and Lords.*

   ORSINO   Belong you to the Lady Olivia, friends?
   CLOWN   Ay, sir, we are some of her trappings.°   *ornaments*
   ORSINO   I know thee well. How dost thou, my good fellow?
10   CLOWN   Truly, sir, the better for my foes and the worse for my
       friends.
   ORSINO   Just the contrary, the better for thy friends.
   CLOWN   No, sir, the worse.
   ORSINO   How can that be?
15   CLOWN   Marry, sir, they praise me and make an ass of me.
       Now my foes tell me plainly, I am an ass. So that by my foes,
       sir, I profit in the knowledge of myself, and by my friends I
       am abused.° So that, conclusions to be as kisses, if your four   *deceived*
       negatives make your two affirmatives,[2] why then, the worse
20   for my friends and the better for my foes.
   ORSINO   Why, this is excellent.
   CLOWN   By my troth, sir, no. Though it please you to be one of
       my friends.
   ORSINO   Thou shalt not be the worse for me. There's gold.
25   CLOWN   But° that it would be double dealing,[3] sir, I would you   *Except for the fact*
       could make it another.
   ORSINO   Oh, you give me ill counsel.
   CLOWN   Put your grace in your pocket,[4] sir, for this once, and
       let your flesh and blood obey it.[5]
30   ORSINO   Well, I will be so much a sinner to° be a double dealer.   *as to*
       There's another.
   CLOWN   *Primo, secundo, tertio*[6] is a good play,° and the old   *game*
       saying is, the third pays for all.[7] The triplex,° sir, is a good   *triple time in music*
       tripping measure, or the bells of Saint Bennet,[8] sir, may put
35   you in mind. One, two, three.

5.1 Location: Before Olivia's house.
1. Perhaps a reference to an anecdote, recorded in
John Manningham's diary, in which Queen Elizabeth
requested a dog, and the donor, when granted a wish in
return, asked for the dog back.
2. *conclusions . . . affirmatives:* As in grammar, a double negative can make an affirmative (and therefore
four negatives can make two affirmatives); so when a
coy girl is asked for a kiss, her four refusals can be
construed as "yes, yes."
3. A duplicity; a double donation.

4. Set aside (pocket up) your virtue; also (with a play
on the customary form of address for a duke, "your
grace"), reach into your pocket and grace me with
another coin.
5. Let your normal human instincts (as opposed to
grace) follow the "ill counsel" (line 27).
6. First, second, third (Latin); perhaps an allusion to
a dice throw or a child's game.
7. Third time lucky (proverbial).
8. A London church, across the Thames from the
Globe, was known as St. Bennet Hithe.

ORSINO   You can fool no more money out of me at this throw.°   *throw of the dice*
   If you will let your lady know I am here to speak with her
   and bring her along with you, it may awake my bounty
   further.
40 CLOWN   Marry, sir, lullaby to your bounty till I come again. I
   go, sir, but I would not have you to think that my desire of
   having is the sin of covetousness. But, as you say, sir, let
   your bounty take a nap, I will awake it anon.   *Exit.*
          Enter ANTONIO *and* OFFICERS.
VIOLA   Here comes the man, sir, that did rescue me.
45 ORSINO   That face of his I do remember well.
   Yet, when I saw it last, it was besmeared
   As black as Vulcan⁹ in the smoke of war.
   A baubling° vessel was he captain of,   *trifling*
   For shallow draught and bulk unprizeable,¹
50   With which such scatheful° grapple did he make   *destructive*
   With the most noble bottom° of our fleet   *ship*
   That very envy° and the tongue of loss°   *even enmity / the losers*
   Cried fame and honor on him. What's the matter?
FIRST OFFICER   Orsino, this is that Antonio
55   That took the Phoenix and her fraught from Candy.²
   And this is he that did the Tiger board
   When your young nephew Titus lost his leg.
   Here in the streets, desperate of shame and state,³
   In private brabble° did we apprehend him.   *brawl*
60 VIOLA   He did me kindness, sir, drew on my side,⁴
   But in conclusion put strange speech upon° me.   *spoke strangely to*
   I know not what 'twas but distraction.°   *if not insanity*
ORSINO   Notable° pirate, thou saltwater thief,   *Notorious*
   What foolish boldness brought thee to their mercies,
65   Whom thou in terms so bloody and so dear°   *dire*
   Hast made thine enemies?
ANTONIO   Orsino, noble sir,
   Be pleased that I shake off these names you give me.
   Antonio never yet was thief or pirate,
   Though I confess, on base° and ground enough,   *foundation*
70   Orsino's enemy. A witchcraft drew me hither.
   That most ingrateful boy there by your side
   From the rude sea's enraged and foamy mouth
   Did I redeem. A wrack past hope he was.
   His life I gave him and did thereto add
75   My love without retention° or restraint,   *reservation*
   All his in dedication. For his sake
   Did I expose myself, pure° for his love,   *only*
   Into the danger of this adverse° town,   *hostile*
   Drew to defend him when he was beset;
80   Where, being apprehended, his false cunning,
   Not meaning to partake with me in danger,
   Taught him to face me out of his acquaintance⁵
   And grew a twenty years' removèd thing

9. Blacksmith of the Roman gods.
1. Of no value because of its small size. *draught:*
water displaced by a vessel.
2. Candia, capital of Crete.
3. *desperate . . . state:* recklessly oblivious of the danger

to his honor and his position (as a free man and public
enemy).
4. Drew his sword in my defense.
5. To brazenly deny my acquaintance.

While one would wink,[6] denied me mine own purse,
85   Which I had recommended° to his use   *consigned*
Not half an hour before.

VIOLA   How can this be?

ORSINO   When came he to this town?

ANTONIO   Today, my lord. And, for three months before,
No int'rim, not a minute's vacancy,°   *interval*
90   Both day and night did we keep company.

            Enter OLIVIA *and Attendants.*

ORSINO   Here comes the countess. Now heaven walks on
    earth.
—But for thee, fellow. Fellow, thy words are madness.
Three months this youth hath tended upon me.
But more of that anon. [*to* FIRST OFFICER] Take him aside.

95   OLIVIA   What would my lord, but that he may not have,[7]
Wherein Olivia may seem serviceable?
—Cesario, you do not keep promise with me.

VIOLA   Madam?

ORSINO   Gracious Olivia.

OLIVIA   What do you say, Cesario? —Good my lord.

100   VIOLA   My lord would speak, my duty hushes me.

OLIVIA   If it be aught° to the old tune, my lord,   *anything*
It is as fat and fulsome° to mine ear   *gross and offensive*
As howling after music.

ORSINO   Still so cruel?

OLIVIA   Still so constant, lord.

105   ORSINO   What, to perverseness? You uncivil lady,
To whose ingrate and unauspicious° altars   *unfavorable*
My soul the faithful'st off'rings have breathed out
That e'er devotion tendered, what shall I do?

OLIVIA   Even what it please my lord that shall become° him.   *be fitting for*

110   ORSINO   Why should I not, had I the heart to do it
Like to th'Egyptian thief at point of death
Kill what I love?[8]—A savage jealousy
That sometime savors nobly.° But hear me this.   *of nobility*
Since you to non-regardance° cast my faith,   *oblivion*
115   And that I partly know the instrument
That screws° me from my true place in your favor,   *wrenches*
Live you the marble-breasted tyrant still.
But this your minion,° whom I know you love   *darling*
And whom, by heaven I swear, I tender° dearly,   *regard*
120   Him will I tear out of that cruel eye
Where he sits crownèd in his master's spite.[9]
Come, boy, with me. My thoughts are ripe in mischief.
I'll sacrifice the lamb that I do love
To spite a raven's heart within a dove.

125   VIOLA   And I most jocund,° apt,° and willingly   *cheerfully / readily*
To do you rest a thousand deaths would die.

OLIVIA   Where goes Cesario?

---

6. *And . . . wink:* In the wink of an eye, pretended we had been estranged for twenty years.
7. Except that which he may not have (my love).
8. In Heliodorus of Emesa's *Ethiopica,* a Greek prose romance translated into English in 1569 and popular in Shakespeare's day, the Egyptian robber chief Thyamis tries to kill his captive Chariclea, whom he loves, when he is in danger from a rival band.
9. To the mortification of his master.

VIOLA   After him I love
More than I love these eyes, more than my life,
More by all mores[1] than e'er I shall love wife.
130 If I do feign, you witnesses above,
Punish my life for tainting of my love.
OLIVIA Ay me detested, how am I beguiled?
VIOLA Who does beguile you? Who does do you wrong?
OLIVIA Hast thou forgot thyself? Is it so long?
Call forth the holy father.   [*Exit Attendant.*]
135 ORSINO [*to* VIOLA]   Come, away.
OLIVIA Whither, my lord? Cesario, husband, stay.
ORSINO Husband?
OLIVIA   Ay, husband. Can he that deny?
ORSINO Her husband, sirrah?[2]
VIOLA   No, my lord, not I.
OLIVIA Alas, it is the baseness of thy fear
140 That makes thee strangle thy propriety.[3]
Fear not, Cesario, take thy fortunes up.
Be that thou know'st thou art, and then thou art
As great as that° thou fear'st.   *him whom*
  Enter PRIEST.
       Oh, welcome, Father.
Father, I charge thee by thy reverence
145 Here to unfold—though lately we intended
To keep in darkness what occasion° now   *necessity*
Reveals before 'tis ripe—what thou dost know
Hath newly passed between this youth and me.
PRIEST A contract of eternal bond of love,
150 Confirmed by mutual joinder° of your hands,   *joining*
Attested by the holy close° of lips,   *meeting*
Strengthened by interchangement of your rings,
And all the ceremony of this compact
Sealed in my function[4] by my testimony.
155 Since when, my watch hath told me, toward my grave
I have traveled but two hours.
ORSINO O thou dissembling cub! What wilt thou be
When time hath sowed a grizzle on thy case?[5]
Or will not else thy craft° so quickly grow   *craftiness*
160 That thine own trip shall be thine overthrow?[6]
Farewell and take her, but direct thy feet
Where thou and I henceforth may never meet.
VIOLA My lord, I do protest.
OLIVIA   Oh, do not swear.
Hold little° faith though thou hast too much fear. *Preserve some*
  Enter SIR ANDREW.
165 SIR ANDREW For the love of God, a surgeon! Send one
presently° to Sir Toby.   *immediately*
OLIVIA What's the matter?

---

1. More beyond all comparison.
2. Contemptuous form of address to an inferior.
3. That makes you deny your identity (as my husband).
4. Ratified by priestly authority.

5. A gray hair ("grizzle") on your hide (sustaining the metaphor of "cub").
6. That your attempt to trip someone else will be the cause of your downfall.

SIR ANDREW   He's broke° my head across, and has given Sir   *cut*
Toby a bloody coxcomb[7] too. For the love of God, your help!

170   I had rather than forty pound I were at home.

OLIVIA   Who has done this, Sir Andrew?

SIR ANDREW   The Count's gentleman, one Cesario. We took
him for a coward, but he's the very devil incardinate.[8]

ORSINO   My gentleman Cesario?

175   SIR ANDREW   Odd's lifelings,° here he is. You broke my head   *By God's little lives*
for nothing, and that that I did, I was set on to do't by Sir
Toby.

VIOLA   Why do you speak to me? I never hurt you.
You drew your sword upon me without cause,

180   But I bespake you fair[9] and hurt you not.

       Enter SIR TOBY *and* CLOWN.

SIR ANDREW   If a bloody coxcomb be a hurt, you have hurt
me. I think you set nothing by° a bloody coxcomb. Here   *think nothing of*
comes Sir Toby halting.° You shall hear more, but if° he had *limping / if only*
not been in drink, he would have tickled° you othergates° *chastised / in other ways*

185   than he did.

ORSINO   How now, gentleman? How is't with you?

SIR TOBY   That's all one.° He's hurt me, and there's th'end on't.   *No matter*
[*to* CLOWN] Sot,° didst see Dick Surgeon, sot?   *Fool; drunkard*

CLOWN   Oh, he's drunk, Sir Toby, an hour agone. His eyes were

190   set[1] at eight i'th' morning.

SIR TOBY   Then he's a rogue, and a passy-measures pavan.[2] I
hate a drunken rogue.

OLIVIA   Away with him! Who hath made this havoc with them?

SIR ANDREW   I'll help you, Sir Toby, because we'll be dressed[3]

195   together.

SIR TOBY   Will you help? An ass-head and a coxcomb,° and a   *fool*
knave, a thin-faced knave, a gull!°   *dupe*

OLIVIA   Get him to bed, and let his hurt be looked to.

       Enter SEBASTIAN.

SEBASTIAN   I am sorry, madam, I have hurt your kinsman.

200   But, had it been the brother of my blood,
I must have done no less with wit and safety.[4]
You throw a strange regard upon me,° and by that   *regard me strangely*
I do perceive it hath offended you.
Pardon me, sweet one, even for the vows

205   We made each other but so late ago.

ORSINO   One face, one voice, one habit, and two persons—
A natural perspective,[5] that is and is not.

SEBASTIAN   Antonio, O my dear Antonio,
How have the hours racked and tortured me

210   Since I have lost thee!

ANTONIO   Sebastian are you?

SEBASTIAN   Fear'st thou° that, Antonio?   *Do you doubt*

---

7. Head; also, a fool's cap, which resembles the crest
of a cock.
8. Sir Andrew's blunder for "incarnate" (in the flesh).
9. But I spoke courteously to you.
1. Closed (as the sun sets).
2. A variety of the slow dance known as "pavane"

(from the Italian *passamezzo pavana*). Sir Toby may
think its swaying movements suggest drunkenness.
3. We'll have our wounds dressed.
4. With any sense of my welfare.
5. An optical illusion produced by nature (rather
than by a mirror or a "perspective glass").

ANTONIO   How have you made division of yourself?
    An apple cleft in two is not more twin
    Than these two creatures. Which is Sebastian?
215 OLIVIA   Most wonderful!°   *full of wonder*
SEBASTIAN   Do I stand there? I never had a brother,
    Nor can there be that deity° in my nature   *divine power*
    Of here and everywhere.° I had a sister   *Of omnipresence*
    Whom the blind waves and surges have devoured.
220   Of charity,° what kin are you to me?   *Please*
    What countryman? What name? What parentage?
VIOLA   Of Messaline. Sebastian was my father;
    Such a Sebastian was my brother too.
    So went he suited[6] to his watery tomb.
225   If spirits can assume both form and suit,°   *appearance and dress*
    You come to fright us.
SEBASTIAN   A spirit I am indeed,
    But am in that dimension grossly clad
    Which from the womb I did participate.[7]
    Were you a woman, as the rest goes even,°   *the rest suggests*
230   I should my tears let fall upon your cheek
    And say, thrice welcome, drownèd Viola.
VIOLA   My father had a mole upon his brow.
SEBASTIAN   And so had mine.
VIOLA   And died that day when Viola from her birth
235   Had numbered thirteen years.
SEBASTIAN   Oh, that record is lively[8] in my soul.
    He finished indeed his mortal act
    That day that made my sister thirteen years.
VIOLA   If nothing lets° to make us happy both   *hinders*
240   But this my masculine usurped attire,
    Do not embrace me till each circumstance
    Of place, time, fortune do cohere and jump°   *agree*
    That I am Viola. Which to confirm,
    I'll bring you to a captain in this town
245   Where lie my maiden weeds,° by whose gentle help   *clothes*
    I was preserved to serve this noble count.
    All the occurrence of my fortune since
    Hath been between this lady and this lord.
SEBASTIAN   So comes it, lady, you have been mistook.
250   But Nature to her bias drew in that.[9]
    You would have been contracted° to a maid.   *betrothed*
    Nor are you therein, by my life, deceived:
    You are betrothed both to a maid and man.[1]
ORSINO   Be not amazed. Right noble is his blood.
255   If this be so, as yet the glass seems true,[2]
    I shall have share in this most happy wrack.
    —Boy, thou hast said to me a thousand times,
    Thou never shouldst love woman like to me.

---

6. Dressed just like you he went.
7. *But . . . participate:* But I am clad, like all mortals, in the flesh in which I was born.
8. The memory of that is vivid.
9. But Nature followed her inclination. (The image is from the game of bowls, in which players use a ball with an off-centered weight that causes it to curve away from a straight course.)
1. *maid and man:* a man who is a virgin.
2. *the glass seems true:* the "natural perspective" (line 207) continues to seem real.

VIOLA   And all those sayings will I overswear,°   *swear again*
260   And all those swearings keep as true in soul
         As doth that orbèd continent³ the fire
         That severs day from night.
ORSINO   Give me thy hand,
         And let me see thee in thy woman's weeds.
VIOLA   The captain that did bring me first on shore
265   Hath my maid's garments. He upon some action°   *legal charge*
         Is now in durance° at Malvolio's suit,   *prison*
         A gentleman and follower of my lady's.
OLIVIA   He shall enlarge° him. [*to Attendant*] Fetch Malvolio   *release*
         hither.
         And yet, alas, now I remember me,
270   They say, poor gentleman, he's much distract.°   *insane*
                    Enter CLOWN *with a letter and* FABIAN.
         A most extracting° frenzy of mine own   *distracting*
         From my remembrance clearly banished his.
         How does he, sirrah?
CLOWN   Truly, madam, he holds Beelzebub at the stave's end⁴
275   as well as a man in his case may do. He's here writ a letter to
         you. I should have given't you today morning. But, as a mad-
         man's epistles are no gospels,⁵ so it skills° not much when they   *matters*
         are delivered.
OLIVIA   Open't, and read it.
280 CLOWN   Look then to be well edified, when the fool delivers°   *speaks the words of*
         the madman. [*He reads.*] "By the Lord, madam—"
OLIVIA   How now, art thou mad?
CLOWN   No, madam, I do but read madness. An your ladyship
         will have it as it ought to be, you must allow *vox.*⁶
285 OLIVIA   Prithee, read i'thy right wits.
CLOWN   So I do, madonna. But to read his right wits⁷ is to
         read thus. Therefore, perpend,° my princess, and give ear.   *pay attention*
OLIVIA [*taking the letter and giving it to* FABIAN]   Read it you,
         sirrah.
290 FABIAN (*reads*)   "By the Lord, madam, you wrong me, and the
         world shall know it. Though you have put me into darkness
         and given your drunken cousin rule over me, yet have I the
         benefit of my senses as well as your ladyship. I have your own
         letter that induced me to the semblance I put on, with the
295   which I doubt not but to do myself much right or you much
         shame. Think of me as you please. I leave my duty a little
         unthought of, and speak out of my injury.⁸
                                    The madly used Malvolio."
OLIVIA   Did he write this?
300 CLOWN   Ay, madam.
ORSINO   This savors not much of distraction.°   *insanity*
OLIVIA   See him delivered.° Fabian, bring him hither.   *released*
                                    [*Exit* FABIAN.]

---

3. Referring to either the sun or the sphere within which the sun was thought to be fixed.
4. He holds the devil (who threatens to possess him) at a distance (proverbial).
5. Gospel truths. *epistles:* letters (playing on the sense

of apostolic accounts of Christ in the New Testament).
6. The appropriate voice (Latin).
7. To accurately represent his mental state.
8. I neglect the formality I owe you as your servant and speak as an injured person.

My lord, so please you, these things further thought on,
To think me as well a sister as a wife,[9]
305   One day shall crown th'alliance[1] on't, so please you,
Here at my house and at my proper cost.°   *own expense*

ORSINO   Madam, I am most apt° t'embrace your offer.   *ready*
[*to* VIOLA]   Your master quits° you and, for your service   *releases*
          done him
So much against the mettle° of your sex,   *disposition*
310   So far beneath your soft and tender breeding,
And since you called me master for so long,
Here is my hand. You shall from this time be
Your master's mistress.

OLIVIA   A sister, you are she.
          Enter [FABIAN *with*] MALVOLIO.

ORSINO   Is this the madman?

OLIVIA   Ay, my lord, this same.
315   —How now, Malvolio?

MALVOLIO   Madam, you have done me wrong, notorious wrong.

OLIVIA   Have I, Malvolio? No.

MALVOLIO [*handing her a letter*]   Lady, you have. Pray you
          peruse that letter.
You must not now deny it is your hand.°   *handwriting*
320   Write from° it if you can, in hand or phrase,   *differently from*
Or say, 'tis not your seal, not your invention.°   *composition*
You can say none of this. Well, grant it then,
And tell me, in the modesty of honor,[2]
Why you have given me such clear lights° of favor,   *signs*
325   Bade me come smiling and cross-gartered to you,
To put on yellow stockings, and to frown
Upon Sir Toby and the lighter° people.   *lesser*
And, acting° this in an obedient hope,   *upon doing*
Why have you suffered me to be imprisoned,
330   Kept in a dark house, visited by the priest,
And made the most notorious geck° and gull   *fool*
That e'er invention° played on? Tell me, why?   *trickery*

OLIVIA   Alas, Malvolio, this is not my writing,
Though I confess much like the character.°   *handwriting*
335   But out of question, 'tis Maria's hand.
And, now I do bethink me, it was she
First told me thou wast mad, then cam'st° in smiling,   *you came*
And in such forms which here were presupposed°   *previously suggested*
Upon thee in the letter. Prithee, be content.
340   This practice hath most shrewdly passed[3] upon thee,
But, when we know the grounds and authors of it,
Thou shalt be both the plaintiff and the judge
Of thine own cause.

FABIAN   Good madam, hear me speak,
And let no quarrel nor no brawl to come
345   Taint the condition of this present hour,
Which I have wondered° at. In hope it shall not,   *marveled*
Most freely I confess myself and Toby
Set this device against Malvolio here,

9. To think as well of me as a sister-in-law as you
would have thought of me as a wife.
1. The impending double-marriage ceremony.
2. Tell me with the propriety that becomes a
noblewoman.
3. This trick has most mischievously played.

Upon° some stubborn and uncourteous parts°   *Because / behavior*
350 We had conceived against him.[4] Maria writ
The letter at Sir Toby's great importance,°   *importunity*
In recompence whereof he hath married her.
How with a sportful malice it was followed°   *followed through*
May rather pluck on° laughter than revenge,   *incite*
355 If that the injuries be justly weighed
That have on both sides passed.
OLIVIA [*to* MALVOLIO] Alas, poor fool, how have they baffled°   *disgraced*
 thee!
CLOWN Why, some are born great, some achieve greatness,
 and some have greatness thrown upon them. I was one, sir, in
360 this interlude,° one Sir Topas, sir. But that's all one. "By the   *comedy*
 Lord, fool, I am not mad." But do you remember, "Madam, why
 laugh you at such a barren rascal. An you smile not, he's
 gagged." And thus the whirligig° of time brings in his revenges.   *spinning top*
MALVOLIO I'll be revenged on the whole pack of you. [*Exit.*]
365 OLIVIA He hath been most notoriously abused.
ORSINO Pursue him and entreat him to a peace.
           [*Exit Attendant.*]
He hath not told us of the captain yet.
When that is known, and golden time convents,°   *summons; is convenient*
A solemn combination shall be made
370 Of our dear souls. Meantime, sweet sister,
We will not part from hence.° Cesario, come—   *(Olivia's house)*
For so you shall be while you are a man—
But when in other habits you are seen,
Orsino's mistress and his fancy's° queen.   *love's; imagination's*
        Exeunt [*all but* CLOWN].
375 CLOWN (*sings*) When that I was and a little tiny boy,
    With hey, ho, the wind and the rain,
    A foolish thing was but a toy,
    For the rain it raineth every day.

    But when I came to man's estate,
380   With hey, ho, etc.
    'Gainst knaves and thieves men shut their gate,
    For the rain, etc.

    But when I came, alas, to wive,
    With hey, ho, etc.
385   By swaggering could I never thrive,
    For the rain, etc.

    But when I came unto my beds,
    With hey, ho, etc.
    With tosspots° still had drunken heads,   *drunkards*
390   For the rain, etc.

    A great while ago the world begun,
    Hey, ho, etc.
    But that's all one, our play is done,
    And we'll strive to please you every day. [*Exit.*]

---

4. *We . . . him:* To which we took exception.

Troilus and Cressida

Audiences or readers who come to *Troilus and Cressida* (written 1601–02) from the *Iliad* are in for a shock. Where Homer sings of heroic conflict culminating in the epic battle between Hector and Achilles, Shakespeare gives center stage to a love story that, like the events of the Trojan War itself, he treats skeptically. Where Homer finds tragic grandeur in the events he portrays, Shakespeare sees only carnage, a carnage unrelieved by the romantic plot, which ends—and indeed, arguably, begins—in disillusionment. This unfamiliar recasting of traditional material produces a modern, dark view of sexuality and politics.

Shakespeare knew Homer through George Chapman's *Seven Books of the Iliads of Homer* (1598) and perhaps through earlier English and French translations. (The frontispiece from Chapman's *Homer* suggests the era's standard view of the Trojan War; see p. 1983.) Moreover, the English monarchy had long traced its lineage back to Troy. For the titular figures and core narrative, Shakespeare almost certainly drew on Geoffrey Chaucer's *Troilus and Criseyde* (1380s), which views the central relationship through the code of courtly love and produces an aristocratic medieval tragedy from the failure of that love. Shakespeare was also indebted to a range of other texts: classical (Virgil's *Aeneid*, Ovid's *Metamorphoses*, perhaps several plays of Euripides), medieval (John Lydgate's *Troy Book*, early fifteenth century), and Renaissance (probably including Robert Greene's *Euphues His Censure to Philautus*, 1587). In *Doctor Faustus* (1592?), a tragedy that broadly influenced Shakespeare, Christopher Marlowe's titular figure lovingly apostrophizes Helen of Troy: "Was this the face that launched a thousand ships, / And burned the topless towers of Ilium?" And in 1599, a London theatrical company apparently performed Thomas Dekker and Henry Chettle's *Troilus and Cressida*, but only a fragmentary list of little more than stage entrances and exits survives today. The lost drama may have covered the same territory as *Troilus and Cressida* from an epic, didactic, and sentimental perspective to which Shakespeare's company, perceiving the commercial opportunities of a rival work on the topic, stingingly replied.

Troilus and Cressida achieves ironic effect by self-consciously retelling a familiar story. The lovers swear oaths of fidelity that, as audience members but not the characters realize, anticipate their quite different literary reputations. Cressida's uncle, the go-between Pandarus, provides a summary: "If ever you prove false one to another, . . . let all pitiful goers-between be called to the world's end after my name: call them all panders. Let all constant men be Troiluses, all false women Cressids, and all brokers-between panders" (3.2.185–90).* Pandarus's initial neutrality ("If ever you prove false one to another") reverts to the traditional sexual double standard, a shift predictive of the outcome and already voiced in the lovers' immediately preceding speeches, where only Cressida's faithfulness is in question.

Similarly, the military plot recalls attention to the very different Homeric version. Achilles is outfought by Hector and must appeal to the Trojan's chivalric generosity: "Pause if thou wilt" (5.6.14). Achilles then treacherously employs his soldiers, the Myrmidons, to ambush and kill Hector:

---

*All quotations are taken from the edited text of the Folio, printed here. The Digital Edition includes edited texts of both the Folio and the Quarto.

> HECTOR I am unarmed. Forgo this vantage, Greek.
> ACHILLES Strike, fellows, strike; this is the man I seek.
> . . . .
>
> On, Myrmidons, cry you all amain:
> "Achilles hath the mighty Hector slain!"
>
> (5.9.9–14)

The passage both deflates the epic account and explains how that false account arose in the first place. It thus reconciles conflicting interpretations while propelling a movement toward increasing bitterness.

The play equally breaks with the drama Shakespeare composed in the first half of his career. The romantic comedies from *Two Gentlemen of Verona* to *Twelfth Night* focus on romantic attachment and conclude in marriage. *Troilus and Cressida* moves from extramarital sex to infidelity, recriminations, deception, self-deception, venereal disease, and despair. The English history plays from *2 Henry VI* to *Henry V* usually turn on martial action in defense of the state. But *Troilus and Cressida* questions the moral legitimacy of war, viewed as an arena of mindless brutality.

The play's negativity is partly anticipated in the sources. The *Iliad* mixes nostalgic admiration for warrior culture with an awareness of human suffering. Robert Henryson's *Testament of Cresseid* (late fifteenth century) punishes Cressida's infidelity by the infliction of leprosy, and William Caxton's *Recuyell of the Historyes of Troye* (the first English printed book, about 1474) has a jaundiced view of the Trojan War. Similarly, Shakespeare's earlier comedies and histories hint at the dyspeptic vision of *Troilus and Cressida*.

More important, contemporary London stage practice provides a suggestive context. The children's theaters that reopened in 1599 popularized misogynistic dramatic satire, to which *Troilus and Cressida* responds. The play arguably participates in the battle of rival playwrights at the turn of the century, known as the Poets' War. The ridiculous figure of Ajax may satirize Ben Jonson, whose drama had criticized Shakespeare's works. And the railing Thersites perhaps points to John Marston, the most vituperative satiric playwright. Within Shakespeare's own oeuvre, *Troilus and Cressida*'s tone anticipates the so-called problem plays, *Measure for Measure* and *All's Well That Ends Well*. Further, beginning in 1599 with *Julius Caesar*, Shakespeare initiated a decade-long appropriation of classical history in which, generally, Rome is the subject of tragedy, Greece of satire. But satire and especially a disgust with women, sexuality, and the diseased body are important throughout Shakespeare's tragic period (1599–1608).

Finally, because the play is heterogeneous in tone, it sometimes connects with sunnier motifs in Shakespeare's earlier work. Troilus's initial state echoes the comically extravagant romantic excess in which Duke Orsino begins *Twelfth Night*. When asked by an attendant whether he will hunt the "hart" (deer, with a pun on "heart," line 16), the Duke explains that when he first saw Olivia, he was

> turned into a hart,
> And my desires, like fell and cruel hounds,
> E'er since pursue me.
>
> (1.1.20–22)

Lovesick Troilus also renounces the hunt:

> Why should I war without the walls of Troy
> That find such cruel battle here within?
> Each Trojan that is master of his heart,
> Let him to field. Troilus, alas, hath none.
>
> (1.1.2–5)

This opening follows the Prologue's military exposition and is succeeded by scenes of sexual comedy, cynical politics, satiric abuse, and perverse idealism. By the time any

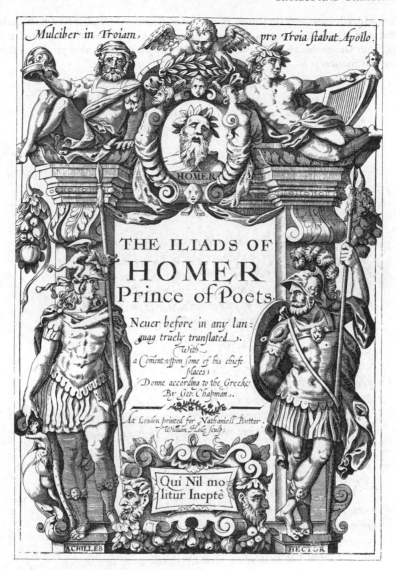

Mulciber in Troiam,   pro Troia ſtabat Apollo.

HOMER

THE ILIADS OF
HOMER
Prince of Poets.

Neuer before in any lan=
guag truely tranſlated.
With
a Coment vppon ſome of his chiefe
ſlaces;
Donne according to the Greeke
Br. Geo: Chapman.

At London printed for Nathaniell Butter.
William Hole ſculp:

Qui Nil mo=
litur Ineptè

ACHILLES   HECTOR

Title page of the *Iliad* of Homer in George Chapman's translation (1611?). Shakespeare probably used the less complete 1598 edition.

of these perspectives is repeated, one-third of the play is over. *Troilus and Cressida* thus presents multiple views: it is formally hybrid.

Hence, even though ironic disillusionment becomes increasingly pervasive, it does not subsume other perspectives. Accordingly, the nature of the work has always provoked disagreement. Early seventeenth-century references label it variously a history, a comedy, and a tragedy. By adding satire to the list, twentieth-century critics intensified the uncertainty. Although Shakespeare's career is marked by formal mixing, by the violation of neoclassical norms that separated comedy from tragedy, *Troilus and Cressida* represents an extreme. The play never adopts a consistent outlook in dismantling central aristocratic narrative forms—medieval chivalric romance and classical epic.

This disorientation extends to particular scenes. In 5.2, one of Shakespeare's most celebrated forays into eavesdropping, Diomedes and Cressida have an assignation,

Troilus and Ulysses secretly watch them, Thersites covertly observes both pairs of figures, and the audience sees all five characters. Cressida's behavior elicits judgments from Diomedes and especially from Cressida herself; it also produces the following commentary:

> ULYSSES   Cressid was here but now.
> TROILUS Let it not be believed, for womanhood.
>   Think, we had mothers; do not give advantage
>   To stubborn critics, apt without a theme

This prefatory epistle (continued on the facing page) was added to the second state of the 1609 Quarto of *Troilus and Cressida* (Qc). It is not found in the first state (Qu) or in the First Folio (F).

For deprivation, to square the general sex
By Cressid's rule. Rather, think this not Cressid.
ULYSSES What hath she done, Prince, that can soil our mothers?
TROILUS Nothing at all, unless that this were she.
THERSITES Will he swagger himself out on 's own eyes?

(5.2.128–36)

Troilus oscillates between misogynistic generalization and idealistic denial of Cressida's infidelity, Ulysses rejects extrapolation from individual to gender, and Thersites ridicules Troilus's willful blindness. Not only does staged action diverge from commentary on that action; one commentary is also at odds with the next. This pattern suggests that the play's view is broader than Thersites'. But what is that view? Although the audience occupies a privileged position, it must synthesize incompatible

THE EPISTLE.

much as will make you thinke your testerne well bestowd) but for so much worth, as euen poore I know to be stuft in it. It deserues such a labour, as well as the best Commedy in Terence or Plautus. And beleeue this, that when hee is gone, and his Commedies out of sale, you will scramble for them, and set vp a new English Inquisition. Take this for a warning, and at the perrill of your pleasures losse, and Iudgements, refuse not, nor like this the lesse, for not being sullied, with the smoaky breath of the multitude; but thanke fortune for the scape it hath made amongst you. Since by the grand possessors wills I beleeue you should haue prayd for them rather then beene prayd. And so I leaue all such to bee prayd for (for the states of their wits healths) that will not praise it

Vale.

perspectives. Multiple eavesdropping onstage opens up an infinite regress that extends to the spectators, thereby undermining interpretive certainty. This uncertainty holds throughout *Troilus and Cressida*.

The play's philosophical rationales for even the most trivial actions intensify this effect. Characters disagree with one another and with themselves in the sense that their words diverge from their deeds. The linkage of policy questions to foundational principles thus highlights the practical irrelevance of those principles. Further, since there is almost no fighting until act 5, the play relies on talk and on decisions about how—or even whether—to prosecute the war. In the meeting of the Greek leaders (1.3), Ulysses treats Achilles' defection from the war as a disruption of "degree" (1.3.82)—of a hierarchically ordered world—by mere power. His speech, the most famous in the play, has often been read as Shakespeare's own orthodox credo.

The dramatic context undermines this judgment, however. Ulysses' humanely conservative political vision sits oddly with the manipulative scheme he immediately proposes to return Achilles to the fray. Similarly, Ulysses complains that Patroclus amuses Achilles by satirically impersonating other Greek leaders. To illustrate, he reproduces Patroclus's performances, thereby ridiculing Agamemnon and Nestor. And his own satiric voice is repeatedly heard, especially about Ajax. In this, the play echoes events of the previous dozen years, in which puritan satirical attacks on the official Church of England were answered, with the approval of the bishops, by satires on the satirists. As such, it dramatizes a cynical world antithetical to the norms of trust that are necessary, early modern political theorists argued, in any reasonably functioning society.

Slippage from lofty precept to dubious behavior also marks the corresponding Trojan council (2.2). Arguing that it is worth returning Helen to the Greeks to achieve peace, Hector asserts, "Every tithe soul 'mongst many thousand dismes [souls] / Hath been as dear as Helen" (2.2.19–20). This claim leads to a debate with Troilus:

> HECTOR   Brother, she [Helen] is not worth what she doth cost
>   The holding.
> TROILUS   What's aught but as 'tis valued?
> HECTOR   But value dwells not in particular will;
>   It holds his estimate and dignity
>   As well wherein 'tis precious of itself
>   As in the prizer.
>
>   (2.2.51–56)

In response to Troilus's subjective view, then, Hector offers an equally weighty, objective standard of value. Hector's disabused view of Helen differs from at least three other positions staked out in the play. It is more bitterly refracted when Paris asks who deserves her more, "Myself or Menelaus" (4.1.55). Diomedes replies:

> He merits well to have her that doth seek her,
> Not making any scruple of her soilure,
> With such a hell of pain and world of charge;
> And you as well to keep her that defend her,
> Not palating the taste of her dishonor,
> With such a costly loss of wealth and friends.
>   (4.1.56–61)

Accordingly, Helen is branded a "whore" by both Diomedes and Thersites (4.1.67, 2.3.65) before that term is attached to Cressida. Misogyny thus fuses with the play's dominant anti-war sentiment.

Second, when the Greek leaders snub Achilles to get him to fight, Ulysses tells the shaken warrior that value consists not in merit but in reputation—almost the opposite of Hector's position. Characteristically, the play provides no resolution to this implicit disagreement. And third, Troilus himself is undeterred by Hector's argument. Now appealing not to subjective attribution of value but to constancy of purpose, he rejects returning Helen to end the war:

> I take today a wife, and my election
> Is led on in the conduct of my will,
> . . . .
> . . . How may I avoid,
> Although my will distaste what it elected,
> The wife I chose? There can be no evasion
> To blench from this and to stand firm by honor.
> (2.2.61–68)

Troilus's defense of marital commitment unwittingly militates against his own position, however. Helen is Menelaus's wife, not Paris's, and Troilus himself gives no thought to marrying Cressida. Even Hector, the play's noblest character, cannot act on his words. Claiming that to keep Helen is self-destructive and immoral, he wins the debate with Troilus (and Paris). But partly inspired by desire for chivalric glory, he collapses intellectually, agreeing to fight for Trojan "dignities," the very aristocratic honor he had just scorned.

The romantic plot also holds contradictory outlooks in tension. Reacting against earlier criticism that identified with Troilus, recent discussions look skeptically at the male lover and sympathetically at the woman who apparently betrays him. Troilus has a mundane goal: "Her bed is India: there she lies, a pearl" (1.1.95). This sensual motivation turns Cressida into an object of exchange. The jarring juxtaposition ironizes the idealized image of love he articulates elsewhere: the metaphor parallels the businesslike enterprise of seduction in which Pandarus is instrumental. When Troilus calls himself "skill-less as unpracticed infancy" and "simpler than the infancy of truth" (1.1.12, 3.2.157), he continues his self-regarding rhetoric, distancing himself from his own sexually aggressive behavior and arguably imagining sexual intercourse between adults as the relationship between infant and mother. Troilus fears a subsequent letdown: "that the will is infinite and the execution confined, that the desire is boundless and the act a slave to limit" (3.2.75–76). Disappointment is Cressida's anxiety as well, although her concern is male inconstancy: "Yet hold I off. Women are angels, wooing; / Things won are done, joy's soul lies in the doing" (1.2.264–65). Cressida's ambivalence turns on the conviction, embedded in gender inequality, that female sexual surrender cools male ardor. She acts out of multiple motives—love and sexual desire, vulnerability, fear of betrayal, the possibility of self-betrayal from the need to protect herself, and the tendency to understand herself as others define her.

The play validates her worries. She has been abandoned by her father, and her remaining relative seeks to send her to bed with Troilus. Following their first and only night together, the lovers' common fear is realized. Troilus cheerfully gets up to leave, over Cressida's objections. The news that she will be swapped for Antenor—will become an object of exchange—elicits her passionate refusal but Troilus's immediate resignation. Although her reference to "the merry Greeks" (4.4.55) arouses Troilus's jealousy, Cressida interprets his renewed passion as further devaluation of her. Upon her arrival in the enemy camp, she is kissed by the Greek leaders in a scene that may reveal everything from her wantonness to near gang rape. Reunited with a father who delivers her to Diomedes, she acts with characteristic ambiguity, perhaps combining ambivalence, a sense of entrapment, desperation, weakness, desire, and manipulation.

But one should not simply reverse Troilus's self-understanding, seeing him as victimizer and Cressida as victim. The play offers competing interpretations without privileging any of them. In a way, this uncertainty does not matter. Troilus and Cressida's relationship is a zero-sum game: however one explains their behavior, the effect is to undermine ideals that have been overrated all along.

Ambiguity and degradation also mark the military climax. Hector compounds his

The friendly chivalric combat between two noble kinsmen, Hector and Ajax. From Geffrey Whitney, *A Choice of Emblems* (1586).

failure in the Trojan council by disastrous chivalric generosity. Driven by honor, he insists on fighting, although he is warned not to and the fate of Troy hangs on his health. Ulysses, Ajax, and Troilus remark on his habit of sparing a defeated foe. This habit depends on the assumption, despite clear evidence to the contrary, that others operate similarly. Thus, when Hector disarms before Achilles comes upon him, he proves an easy target. With this implicit judgment of Hector, the play universalizes its critique. The result is near moral vacuum. Although aristocratic norms retain some of their former appeal, the struggle to live by them is scarcely worth the effort. The play may thus gesture toward the political crisis at the end of Elizabeth's reign, highlighted by the execution of the Earl of Essex, whose ambitious factionalism (perhaps echoed in Achilles) and chivalric competitiveness (perhaps exemplified by Hector) more generally marked the behavior of competing groups of courtiers who sought royal favor.

The systematic ambiguity of *Troilus and Cressida* is intensified by the early publishing history of the play. (See the Textual Introduction.) The First Quarto emphasizes Troilus, Cressida, and Pandarus on the title page and is prefaced by an anonymous prose epistle that defines the work as a comedy. (See the facsimile reproduction of the epistle, pp. 1984–85, and the transcription in the Digital Edition of Q.) The First Folio version is called a tragedy and lacks the epistle, instead introducing the play by a verse Prologue that ignores the lovers while focusing on the Trojan War itself, treated in heroic terms. In other words, the two texts set up antithetical expectations for their readers.

The Quarto's satiric thrust and the epistle's claim that the work was never performed in a public theater have given rise to the theory that it was composed for elite private performance—possibly at one of the Inns of Court (law schools) or at Cambridge. This view, often supported by emphasis on the play's Latinate language, legal references, and philosophical argument, is unsupported by contemporary documents and is at odds with Shakespeare's normal practice. Possibly, however, *Troilus and Cressida* was relatively unsuccessful at the Globe; probably it was influenced by the Inns of Court; possibly it was performed there, at Cambridge, or in both locales. Whatever the truth, the debate about the nature and location of the early audience reproduces the generic ambiguity of *Troilus and Cressida*: coterie performance implies satire; the public stage, tragedy.

This uncertainty troubled neoclassical writers. In 1679, John Dryden removed "that heap of rubbish" that detracted from tragedy. His Cressida remains true to Troilus but commits suicide, and Achilles kills off Troilus. Dryden's adaptation was occasionally staged between 1679 and 1734. Thereafter, *Troilus and Cressida* went unperformed until 1898. Especially in the last fifty years, however, its incompatible meanings and bitter view of love and war have made it popular. Just as Shakespeare's history plays were mobilized to support patriotic sentiment, *Troilus and Cressida* has given expression to anti-war views—on the eve of both world wars, repeatedly during the Vietnam War in the 1960s and 1970s, and more recently with reference to the

Middle East. Consequently, Thersites sometimes becomes the play's central spokesman; Ulysses, advocate of traditional hierarchy, is ironized. Similarly, feminist-inspired sympathy for Cressida leads to depreciation of Troilus.

But does the play offer positive values, even if they cannot be openly articulated? The ceremonial exchanges between the rival military leaders suggest the lure of homosocial bonding, which simultaneously excludes women and drives men back into battle. Performances since the 1960s have frequently been sensitive to this motif. Hector challenges "the fair'st of Greece," by which he means not a woman but a man, and indeed a man who will "dare avow her [the man's mistress's] beauty and her worth / In other arms than hers" (1.3.262, 268–69). Ulysses resorts to similar wordplay when trying to persuade Achilles to overcome heterosexual love: "And better would it fit Achilles much / To throw down Hector than Polyxena" (3.3.206–07).

An ambivalent imagistic pattern connecting women, effeminacy, and sexual deviation comes closest to providing a countervision to this heroic ethos. Cassandra interrupts the Trojan council with prophecies of doom, a tactic she repeats—again unsuccessfully—in seconding Andromache's efforts to prevent Hector's fatal return to combat. Priam sums up the primarily female argument for inaction, telling Hector, "go back. / Thy wife hath dreamt, thy mother hath had visions, / Cassandra doth foresee" (5.3.62–64). Paris reports, "I would fain have armed today, but my Nell [Helen] would not have it so" (3.1.126–27). And Achilles' love for Polyxena keeps him sidelined: "Fall Greeks, fail fame, honor or go or stay, / My major vow lies here; this I'll obey" (5.1.38–39).

The warriors internalize the female perspective. Troilus cannot fight because his love for Cressida makes him "weaker than a woman's tear, / . . . Less valiant than the virgin in the night" (1.1.9–11). Here, sexual desire works against the instrumental use of women to further men's relations with one another. Only temporarily, however, The dispatch of Cressida to the Greek camp, ending her relationship with Troilus, partly counterbalances the earlier flight of Helen from the Greeks to the Trojans that establishes the (hostile) connection between the two groups of warriors in the first place. But Troilus's womanliness is a general phenomenon. Ajax calls the play's leading satirist "Mistress Thersites" (2.1.32). Hector opens his attack on the war by asserting: "There is no lady . . . / More ready to cry out, 'Who knows what follows?' / Than Hector is" (2.2.11–14).

Achilles has "a woman's longing, / . . . / To see great Hector in his weeds of peace" (3.3.237–39). Thersites, when faced in battle with "A bastard son of Priam's," makes an illogical, if life-saving, argument: "I am a bastard too. I love bastards! . . . Take heed, the quarrel's most ominous to us: if the son of a whore fight for a whore, he tempts judgment" (5.8.8–13). Here, Thersites' cowardice evokes a sexually illegitimate brotherhood opposed to meaningless slaughter. Finally, Patroclus is loathed as "an effeminate man" (3.3.217); he tells Achilles, owing to their enforced leisure:

> I stand condemned for this;
> They think my little stomach to the war
> And your great love to me restrains you thus.
> (3.3.218–20)

What "they think" may be true. Thersites calls Patroclus "Achilles' brach" (bitch hound, 2.1.108), later describing him as "Achilles' male varlet . . . his masculine whore" (5.1.14–16). The death of "My sweet Patroclus" (5.1.32) causes Achilles to break his vow and seek revenge, just as the loss of Cressida turns Troilus toward savagery. In a play about the most famous war in Western literature, opposition to battle brings disgrace. But in such moments—moments of sexual, romantic, or familial intimacy rooted in female or homoerotic experience—an alternative to both aristocratic values and their ironic deflation can be glimpsed.

WALTER COHEN

SELECTED BIBLIOGRAPHY

Charnes, Linda. "The Two Party System in *Troilus and Cressida*." *A Companion to Shakespeare's Works*. Vol. 4: *The Poems, Problem Comedies, Late Plays*. Ed. Richard Dutton and Jean E. Howard. Oxford: Blackwell, 2003. 302–15. Argues that the play begins from, rather than moves toward, disillusionment, with the characters accordingly exhibiting cynical idealism—passionate avowal of causes in which they don't believe.

Gil, Daniel Juan. "At the Limits of the Social World: Fear and Pride in *Troilus and Cressida*." *Shakespeare Quarterly* 52 (2001): 336–59. Investigates the contradiction between aristocratic, lineage-based relations and universalist, modern ones, focusing on the consequent disruption by sexuality of standard homosocial bonds, in which men use women to establish connections with other men.

Grady, Hugh. *Shakespeare's Universal Wolf: Studies in Early Modern Reification*. Oxford: Clarendon, 1996. 58–94. Argues that, philosophically, the play negates all value, seeing a world, from which it dissents, dominated by desire, power, capital, and instrumental reason unlinked to ethics.

James, Heather. *Shakespeare's Troy: Drama, Politics, and the Translation of Empire*. New York: Cambridge UP, 1997. 85–118. Explores Shakespeare's refusal to choose among alternative versions of the Troy legend, some of which trace a direct lineage from the Trojan to the English monarchy, the result being a conflicted play rooted in the late Elizabethan crisis.

Navitsky, Joseph. "Scurrilous Jests and Retaliatory Abuse in Shakespeare's *Troilus and Cressida*." *English Literary Renaissance* 42 (2012): 3–31. Argues that Ulysses' satiric response to Achilles' satire on the Greek leaders parallels the official clerical response to satire on the late Elizabethan church—in both instances thereby undermining the very values ostensibly being defended.

Scott, William O. "Risk, Distrust, and Ingratitude in Shakespeare's *Troilus and Cressida*." *Studies in English Literature* 52 (2012): 345–62. Contrasts Hobbes's understanding of the political basis of contractual trust with the cynical world of both the military and the sexual plots.

Shirley, Frances A., ed. *Troilus and Cressida*. New York: Cambridge UP, 2005. Presents a performance history, followed by a text of the play with notes on staging from various productions.

Traub, Valerie. *Desire and Anxiety: Circulations of Sexuality in Shakespearean Drama*. London: Routledge, 1992. 72–87. Connects militarism, sexual desire, and disease (syphilis) in the play—articulated by Thersites and Pandarus, projected onto Helen and especially Cressida, countered by bawdy, and undercut by homoeroticism.

Weimann, Robert. *Author's Pen and Actor's Voice: Playing and Writing in Shakespeare's Theatre*. Ed. Helen Higbee and William West. Cambridge: Cambridge UP, 2000. 62–70. Understands the play's "bifold authority" as a contrast between word and action, between mimetic performance and onstage commentary about it, and between performed and printed versions of the play.

Yachnin, Paul. "'The Perfection of Ten': Populuxe Art and Artisanal Value in *Troilus and Cressida*." *Shakespeare Quarterly* 56 (2005): 306–27. Sees *Troilus and Cressida* as an upscale, deluxe satire performed by a popular, artisan acting company whose need to win audience approval informs the play's debates about value and reputation.

FILM

Troilus and Cressida. 1981. Dir. Jonathan Miller. UK. 190 min. Relatively conservative BBC production that steers clear of homoeroticism but offers a spirited, rather than a debased, Cressida and effectively exploits television's resources by using both broad background shots and intimate close-ups.

TEXTUAL INTRODUCTION

Witnessing Cressida's interaction with Diomedes late in this play, Troilus cannot understand what he is seeing; thus, he famously laments that "This is and is not Cressid" (5.2.146). The same indeterminacy haunts the textual dimension of *Troilus and Cressida*, for every aspect of its printing history gives at least two alternatives, resulting in fundamental uncertainties that make this one of the most unsolvable textual puzzles in the Shakespearean canon.

First, there are two entries in the Stationers' Register. The earlier is dated February 7, 1603, when James Roberts entered "the Booke of Troilus and Cresseda as acted by the Lord Chamberlain's Men." Six years later, on January 28, 1609, Richard Bonion and Henry Walley (or Walleys) entered their copy of "the history of Troylus and Cressida." These entries suggest that Roberts gained the right to print but never undertook the financial risk of doing so, later selling the play to Bonion and Walley, who went on to publish *Troilus* in quarto form in 1609.

The resulting Quarto exists in two "states." Bonion and Walley engaged George Eld, who also printed Shakespeare's sonnets, as the printer for *Troilus*. The work commenced with a title page identifying the play as "The Historie of Troylus and Cresseida, As it was acted by the Kings Maiesties seruants at the Globe." However, this title page was replaced by another that says nothing about performance and adds a reference to "the conceited wooing of Pandarus Prince of Licia." A new epistle to the reader identifies the play as a comedy and claims that it has never been performed or "clapper-clawd with the palmes of the vulgar." Aside from the first three pages, the rest of the text is identical, yet the initial differences between the two states lead to a variety of questions: Was the play performed by Shakespeare's company? If so, was the performance at the Globe or somewhere else? If it was performed, why does the epistle claim otherwise? These questions about performance and printing history are inevitably tied to other issues, such as *Troilus*'s genre: Was it written as a history, a comedy, a satire, or, as it may seem, a tragedy?

No scholarly consensus has satisfactorily solved these problems, though one popular suggestion is that the play was written (or else revised) for a performance somewhere other than the Globe, such as the Inns of Court or Cambridge. This theory perhaps accounts for the contradictory claims about performance and may explain the satirical tone of the play. Unfortunately, however, there is no solid evidence for this claim. Furthermore, it is unlikely that Shakespeare would have gone to the trouble of writing a play not intended for performance, so unless there were problems with its political content—some scholars have suggested dangerous connections to the Essex rebellion—surely the King's (or Chamberlain's) Men would have attempted a performance at one or more venues. Nevertheless, the length of the play, as well as the second-issue title page and epistle, may suggest that the Quarto was intended for the reading public.

Even the 1623 Folio text tells an ambiguous story. *Troilus* was originally planned as part of the tragedies section, to be placed after *Romeo and Juliet*, and the printing was begun with this arrangement. After the first few pages, however, William Jaggard, the printer of the Folio, stopped the printing and canceled these pages, leaving a space in the tragedies section that *Timon of Athens* was selected to fill. Later, Jaggard apparently achieved or regained the right to print *Troilus*, placing it hurriedly between the histories and tragedies and inserting a Prologue not present in the previous version; *Troilus* did not even make it into the table of contents (the "Catalogue") of the Folio because of its late addition. The most insistent mystery about the Folio printing is the origin of the text from which it was printed. During the initial attempt to print *Troilus*, the Folio compositors were clearly using the Quarto as their base text, but after those pages were canceled and the printing resumed, they were also consulting another text of unknown origin.

The discrepancies between the Quarto and Folio texts are many: five thousand minor variants, but five hundred substantive ones. In most cases, both readings are viable. Despite theories that attribute variants to author, scribes, compositors, theatrical annotation, or revision, no explanation has been agreed upon. Arguments have been made that both texts derive from Shakespeare's foul papers or from transcriptions of them, yet no evidence conclusively proves that one text has earlier origins than the other. In the absence of any consensus about the relationship between these texts, *Troilus* emerges as one of the most compelling case studies for a two-text edition. Undoubtedly, many hands (those of actors, scribes, compositors, annotators) were involved in creating these two versions, yet too often previous editors have based their theories about their chosen base text on assumptions about certain readings being "better" or "more Shakespearean." However, allowing these two versions to stand as discrete examples of *Troilus* obviates the need for such adjudication. A close analysis reveals that the Folio version is more tragic and the Quarto more satiric, but the differences also offer performance alternatives that lend some weight to theories that these two versions were designed for different performances and venues.

The base text for the present printed edition is the Folio. This decision is not predicated upon assumptions about its aesthetic superiority or closeness to Shakespeare's intentions. Instead, the Folio is chosen because it was printed later and its provenance draws not just upon the Quarto but upon other sources as well. It also provides a somewhat expanded text, though we cannot know whether the additional passages and alterations of the Folio resulted from revisions by Shakespeare or by the theatrical companies. Revision does not ensure that the resulting play is necessarily "better"; nonetheless, one of the few certainties is that *Troilus* was a particularly volatile and indeterminate play from its inception, and the Folio text does the better job of illustrating this phenomenon.

GRETCHEN E. MINTON

PERFORMANCE NOTE

The sprawling, often stagnant plot of *Troilus and Cressida,* combined with its generic uncertainty, makes it one of Shakespeare's most difficult plays to produce. Directors can adapt the play so as to make it more uniformly tragic or satiric, and many strive to increase its relevance by substituting modern national or racial groups for the Trojans and Greeks. Yet actors are still challenged to facilitate engagement with characters that, in comparison to the heroic figures on which they are based, often appear distressingly inconsistent, obtuse, or morally deficient. They must also sustain interest in romantic and martial subplots amid scathing internal critiques of love and war, without allowing satire to eclipse Troilus's humanity or prevent audiences from becoming emotionally invested in his situation. Multiple passages of tortured syntax and drawn-out debate, meanwhile, make for a text that is unusually tricky to elucidate, as does the play's dubious and contested (non-)ending. Yet for all its challenges, *Troilus* can succeed brilliantly when directors recognize that fragmentation and irresolution lie at the heart of its dramatic logic.

Pandarus, Thersites, and Cressida, the main sources of dramatic interest and energy, are cases in point. The play seems to work best when audiences are in equal measure charmed and repulsed by each character, finding Pandarus as sentimental as he is sleazy; Thersites as fascinating, and convincing, as he is vile; and Cressida both wholly sympathetic and blameworthy. The potential for productive contradiction is there across the *dramatis personae*: Diomedes can be both chivalrous and menacing; Achilles the height of masculinity and an effeminate lover to Patroclus; Ulysses a moral compass and a trickster. Productions can even complicate Troilus's proverbial constancy, arguing Cressida's status as a tragic figure by implying that her indiscretions are forced by Troilus's jealousy and ready assent to her exchange for Antenor. Why Cressida yields to Diomedes is always a crucial consideration for productions, as is whether to stress the comparison between Pandarus (in wooing Cressida) and Ulysses (in wooing Achilles to battle). Other considerations include the casting of the Prologue (Pandarus and Thersites, "choral" presences throughout, are regular choices) and staging the many instances of onstage voyeurism (especially 5.2).

BRETT GAMBOA

The Tragedy of Troilus and Cressida

Trojans:
PRIAM, King of Troy
HECTOR
PARIS
HELENUS, a priest 〉 sons to Priam and Hecuba
DEIPHOBUS
TROILUS
Margarelon the BASTARD, illegitimate son to Priam
CASSANDRA, a prophetess, daughter to Priam and Hecuba
ANDROMACHE, wife to Hector
AENEAS 〉 Trojan commanders
Antenor
CALCHAS, a Trojan priest
CRESSIDA, daughter to Calchas
PANDARUS, uncle to Cressida
MAN (Alexander), servant to Cressida
Troilus' BOY
TROILUS' MAN
SERVANT to Paris
Attendants, Soldiers, Musicians, Trumpeter

Greeks:
AGAMEMNON, general of the Greek forces
MENELAUS, brother to Agamemnon
HELEN, wife to Menelaus, living in Troy with Paris
NESTOR
ULYSSES
ACHILLES 〉 Greek commanders
AJAX
DIOMEDES
PATROCLUS, companion to Achilles
THERSITES, a scurrilous fool
SERVANT to Diomedes
MYRMIDONS
Servants, Soldiers, Attendants, Trumpeter

PROLOGUE]

The Prologue
[*Enter the* PROLOGUE *in armor.*][1]
PROLOGUE   In Troy, there lies the scene. From isles of Greece

Prologue
1. TEXTUAL COMMENT In armor (see line 23); perhaps referring to Ben Jonson's prologue to *Poetaster* (1601), where an armed figure defends Jonson's embattled reputation among playwrights. The Prologue first appeared in F. See Digital Edition TC 1 (Folio edited text) for its textual history and its differences from the opening of Q. For the epistle prefacing the second state of Q, see the facsimile on pp. 1984–85, as well as the electronic version of Q and Digital Edition TC 1 (Quarto edited text) for that text. See also the Textual Introduction.

The princes orgulous, their high blood chafed,[2]
Have to the port of Athens sent their ships,
Fraught° with the ministers and instruments   *Weighted down*
5   Of cruel war. Sixty and nine that wore
Their crownets° regal from th'Athenian bay   *coronets*
Put forth toward Phrygia,[3] and their vow is made
To ransack Troy, within whose strong immures°   *fortifications*
The ravished° Helen, Menelaus' queen,   *kidnapped (sexual)*
10   With wanton Paris sleeps—and that's the quarrel.°   *(petty) cause of complaint*
To Tenedos° they come,   *island near Troy*
And the deep-drawing barks[4] do there disgorge
Their warlike freightage. Now on Dardan[5] plains
The fresh and yet unbruisèd Greeks do pitch
15   Their brave pavilions.° Priam's six-gated city—   *finely arrayed tents*
Dardan, and Timbria, Helias, Chetas, Troien,
And Antenorides—with massy staples°   *bolt holes*
And corresponsive and fulfilling bolts
Spar up the sons of Troy.[6]
20   Now expectation, tickling skittish° spirits   *excitable*
On one and other side, Trojan and Greek,
Sets all on hazard.° And hither am I come,   *at stake*
A Prologue armed, but not in confidence
Of author's pen or actor's voice,[7] but suited
25   In like conditions as our argument,[8]
To tell you, fair beholders, that our play
Leaps o'er the vaunt° and firstlings of those broils,   *preliminaries*
Beginning in the middle,[9] starting thence away
To what may be digested in a play.
30   Like or find fault, do as your pleasures are,
Now good or bad, 'tis but the chance of war.   [*Exit.*]

1.1 (Q 1.1)

Enter PANDARUS *and* TROILUS.

TROILUS   Call here my varlet;° I'll unarm again.   *page (of genteel birth)*
Why should I war without° the walls of Troy   *outside*
That° find such cruel battle here within?°   *Who / in myself*
Each Trojan that is master of his heart,
5   Let him to field. Troilus, alas, hath none.[1]
PANDARUS   Will this gear° ne'er be mended?   *affair*
TROILUS   The Greeks are strong, and skillful to their
strength,[2]
Fierce to their skill, and to their fierceness valiant;
But I am weaker than a woman's tear,

2. The princes proud, their noble blood heated.
3. The region around Troy (now northwestern Turkey).
4. Boats riding deeply in the water (because they are heavily laden).
5. Trojan. Dardanus was the mythical founder of the city.
6. The sons of Troy shut up the six-gated city. (But the inverted syntax also suggests that the city, whose six gates the Prologue has just named, shuts in "the sons of Troy.")
7. *not . . . voice:* not confident of success at writing or acting.
8. *suited . . . argument:* dressed appropriately for our subject.
9. On the model of epic poetry in the Homeric tradi-

tion and as recommended by the ancient Latin poet Horace in his *Art of Poetry.* Despite the play's classical subject matter, the double plot and generic hybridity deviate from what Renaissance critics understood to be classical dramatic norms. But the play comes close to observing two of the three supposedly Aristotelian unities (of time, place, and action) by compressing events after act 1, scene 2, into little more than forty-eight hours and by restricting the scene to Troy and its immediate surroundings.
1.1 Location: Troy.
1. Has no heart for battle (having lost his heart to Cressida).
2. And as skilled as they are strong.

10 Tamer than sleep, fonder° than ignorance,   *sillier*
  Less valiant than the virgin in the night,
  And skill-less as unpracticed infancy.
  PANDARUS Well, I have told you enough of this. For my part,
  I'll not meddle nor make° no farther. He that will have a *be involved (proverbial)*
15 cake out of the wheat must needs tarry° the grinding.   *wait for*
  TROILUS Have I not tarried?
  PANDARUS Ay, the grinding, but you must tarry the bolting.° *sifting*
  TROILUS Have I not tarried?
  PANDARUS Ay, the bolting, but you must tarry the leav'ning.
20 TROILUS Still have I tarried.
  PANDARUS Ay, to the leavening, but here's yet in the word° *(tarry)*
  hereafter the kneading, the making of the cake, the heating
  of the oven, and the baking—nay, you must stay the cooling
  too, or you may chance to burn your lips.
25 TROILUS Patience herself, what goddess e'er she be,
  Doth lesser blench at sufferance³ than I do.
  At Priam's royal table do I sit,
  And when fair Cressid comes into my thoughts—
  So, traitor,⁴ "when she comes"? When is she thence?
30 PANDARUS Well, she looked yesternight fairer than ever I saw
  her look, or any woman else.
  TROILUS I was about to tell thee: when my heart,
  As wedgèd° with a sigh, would rive° in twain,   *divided / tear apart*
  Lest Hector or my father should perceive me,
35 I have, as when the sun doth light a storm,
  Buried this sigh in wrinkle of a smile,
  But sorrow that is couched° in seeming gladness   *concealed*
  Is like that mirth fate turns to sudden sadness.
  PANDARUS An° her hair were not somewhat darker than   *If*
40 Helen's⁵—well, go to,° there were no more comparison *say no more*
  between the women. But, for my part, she is my kinswoman; I
  would not, as they term it, praise° her, but I would somebody *compliment; appraise*
  had heard her talk yesterday as I did. I will not dispraise your
  sister Cassandra's wit, but—
45 TROILUS O Pandarus, I tell thee, Pandarus,
  When I do tell thee there my hopes lie drowned,
  Reply not in how many fathoms deep
  They lie indrenched. I tell thee I am mad
  In Cressid's love; thou answer'st she is fair,
50 Pour'st in the open ulcer of my heart
  Her eyes, her hair, her cheek, her gait, her voice;
  Handlest in thy discourse—oh, that her hand,⁶
  In whose comparison all whites are ink
  Writing their own reproach, to° whose soft seizure° *compared to / grasp*
55 The cygnet's down is harsh, and spirit of sense⁷
  Hard as the palm of plowman. This thou tell'st me,
  As true° thou tell'st me, when I say I love her.   *Truly*
  But saying thus, instead of oil and balm,

---

3. Shies away less from suffering. (Troilus presumably means more, not "lesser.")
4. Troilus considers himself a "traitor" to Cressida for ever forgetting her.
5. Pandarus shows the standard Elizabethan hostility to dark hair or a dark complexion.

6. *Handlest . . . hand:* You treat in your discussion—Oh, that hand of hers. (Troilus's use of "handlest" reminds him of Cressida's hand.)
7. The quintessential medium of feeling or touch that conveyed sense impressions from body to mind.

Thou lay'st in every gash that love hath given me
60   The knife that made it.
PANDARUS   I speak no more than truth.
TROILUS   Thou dost not speak so much.
PANDARUS   Faith, I'll not meddle in't. Let her be as she is. If
      she be fair, 'tis the better for her; an she be not, she has the
      mends° in her own hands.   *cure (cosmetics)*
65   TROILUS   Good Pandarus—how now, Pandarus?
PANDARUS   I have had my labor for my travail,° ill thought on   *my pains as payment*
      of her, and ill thought on of you, gone between and between,
      but small thanks for my labor.
TROILUS   What, art thou angry, Pandarus? What, with me?
70   PANDARUS   Because she's kin to me, therefore she's not so fair
      as Helen; an she were not kin to me, she would be as fair on
      Friday as Helen is on Sunday.[8] But what care I? I care not
      an she were a blackamoor—'tis all one to me.
TROILUS   Say I she is not fair?
75   PANDARUS   I do not care whether you do or no. She's a fool to
      stay behind her father;[9] let her to the Greeks, and so I'll tell
      her the next time I see her. For my part, I'll meddle nor make
      no more i'th' matter.
TROILUS   Pandarus—
80   PANDARUS   Not I.
TROILUS   Sweet Pandarus—
PANDARUS   Pray you, speak no more to me. I will leave all as
      I found it, and there an end.   *Exit.*
          Sound alarum.°   *trumpet call to arms*
TROILUS   Peace, you ungracious clamors, peace, rude
      sounds!
85   Fools on both sides. Helen must needs be fair
      When with your blood you daily paint° her thus.   *daub (as with rouge)*
      I cannot fight upon this argument;°   *on these grounds*
      It is too starved a subject° for my sword.   *too weak a reason*
      But Pandarus—O gods, how do you plague me!
90   I cannot come to Cressid but by Pandar,
      And he's as tetchy to be° wooed to woo   *touchy about being*
      As she is stubborn, chaste against all suit.
      Tell me, Apollo, for thy Daphne's love,[1]
      What Cressid is, what Pandar, and what we.
95   Her bed is India:[2] there she lies, a pearl.
      Between our Ilium° and where she resides   *(Priam's palace)*
      Let it be called the wild and wand'ring flood,
      Ourself the merchant, and this sailing Pandar
      Our doubtful° hope, our convoy,° and our bark.   *uncertain / escort*
          Alarum. Enter AENEAS.
100 AENEAS   How now, Prince Troilus? Wherefore not afield?
TROILUS   Because not there. This woman's answer sorts,°   *is fitting*
      For womanish it is to be from thence.
      What news, Aeneas, from the field today?

---

8. *An . . . Sunday:* If she weren't my kinswoman
(with the result that my praise seems biased), she'd
be as beautiful in everyday dress as Helen is in her
finest clothes.
9. She's a fool not to leave with her father, Calchas, a
prophet who deserted to the Greeks, having foreseen
their victory.
1. For your love of Daphne. Daphne was a nymph
who prayed (successfully) to be turned into a bay tree
to escape the advances of Apollo, god of poetry.
2. Source of jewels, precious metals, exotic spices,
and rich fabrics.

AENEAS   That Paris is returnèd home, and hurt.
TROILUS   By whom, Aeneas?
105 AENEAS   Troilus, by Menelaus.
TROILUS   Let Paris bleed—'tis but a scar to scorn;
   Paris is gored with Menelaus' horn.[3]
         Alarum.
AENEAS   Hark, what good sport is out of town° today.   *outside Troy*
TROILUS   Better at home, if "would I might" were "may."[4]
110   But to the sport abroad—are you bound thither?
AENEAS   In all swift haste.
TROILUS   Come, go we then together.
                                               Exeunt.

1.2 (Q 1.2)

Enter CRESSIDA *and her* MAN.

CRESSIDA   Who were those went by?
MAN   Queen Hecuba and Helen.
CRESSIDA   And whither go they?
MAN   Up to the eastern tower,
   Whose height commands as subject all the vale,°   *valley*
   To see the battle. Hector, whose patience
5   Is as a virtue fixed,° today was moved.°   *unwavering / angry*
   He chides Andromache and struck his armorer,
   And, like as there were husbandry in war,
   Before the sun rose[1] he was harnessed light,°   *in lightweight armor*
   And to the field goes he, where every flower
10   Did as a prophet weep° what it foresaw   *Was wet with dew at*
   In Hector's wrath.
CRESSIDA   What was his cause of anger?
MAN   The noise° goes this: there is among the Greeks   *rumor*
   A lord of Trojan blood, nephew° to Hector;   *relation*
   They call him Ajax.
CRESSIDA   Good,° and what of him?   *Well*
15 MAN   They say he is a very man *per se*° and stands alone.°   *unique man / is preeminent*
CRESSIDA   So do all men, unless they are drunk, sick, or have
   no legs.
MAN   This man, lady, hath robbed many beasts of their partic-
   ular additions:° he is as valiant as the lion, churlish as the   *characteristics*
20   bear, slow as the elephant—a man into whom nature hath so
   crowded humors[2] that his valor is crushed into folly, his folly
   sauced with discretion. There is no man hath a virtue that he
   hath not a glimpse° of, nor any man an attaint° but he carries   *hint / a flaw*
   some stain of it. He is melancholy without cause and merry
25   against the hair;° he hath the joints of everything, but every-   *against the grain*
   thing so out of joint that he is a gouty Briareus, many hands
   and no use; or purblinded Argus, all eyes and no sight.[3]

---

3. *'tis . . . horn:* it's just a trivial wound (or a wound
given in return for Paris's scorn of Menelaus): Paris is
wounded by the emblem of the cuckold (having
seduced Helen, Menelaus's wife).
4. If what I wished for (an affair with Cressida) were
what I could actually have.
1.2 Location: Troy.
1. *like . . . rose:* as if there were prudent management
in war as in agriculture, where the conscientious
laborer gets up before dawn. The comparison continues with "field" and "flower" (line 9).
2. Peculiarities. Humors were the four main bodily
fluids, which were believed to determine a person's
temperament.
3. He is put together with everything, but so badly
that he is a giant (Briareus), whose hundred hands are
ruined by gout, or totally blind Argus, whose hundred
eyes Juno deprived of sight because he fell asleep
guarding Io.

CRESSIDA But how should this man that makes me smile
make Hector angry?

30 MAN They say he yesterday coped° Hector in the battle and   *engaged*
struck him down, the disdain° and shame whereof hath ever   *indignation*
since kept Hector fasting and waking.

    Enter PANDARUS.

CRESSIDA Who comes here?

MAN Madam, your uncle Pandarus.

35 CRESSIDA Hector's a gallant man.

MAN As may be in the world, lady.

PANDARUS What's that? What's that?

CRESSIDA Good morrow, uncle Pandarus.

PANDARUS Good morrow, cousin° Cressid. What do you talk   *relation*
40 of? —Good morrow, Alexander. —How do you, cousin? When
were you at Ilium?

CRESSIDA This morning, uncle.

PANDARUS What were you talking of when I came? Was Hector armed and gone ere ye came to Ilium? Helen was not up,
45 was she?

CRESSIDA Hector was gone, but Helen was not up.

PANDARUS E'en so. Hector was stirring early.

CRESSIDA That were we talking of, and of his anger.

PANDARUS Was he angry?

50 CRESSIDA So he° says here.   *(Alexander)*

PANDARUS True, he was so. I know the cause too; he'll lay
about him today, I can tell them that.

    [*He dismisses Cressida's* MAN.]

And there's Troilus will not come far behind him; let them
take heed of Troilus, I can tell them that too.

55 CRESSIDA What, is he angry too?

PANDARUS Who, Troilus? Troilus is the better man of the two.

CRESSIDA O Jupiter, there's no comparison!

PANDARUS What, not between Troilus and Hector? Do you
know a man if you see him?

60 CRESSIDA Ay, if I ever saw him before and knew him.[4]

PANDARUS Well, I say Troilus is Troilus.°   *(that special man)*

CRESSIDA Then you say as I say, for I am sure he is not Hector.

PANDARUS No, nor Hector is not Troilus in some degrees.°   *respects*

CRESSIDA 'Tis just to each of them: he is himself.

65 PANDARUS Himself? Alas, poor Troilus, I would he were.

CRESSIDA So he is.

PANDARUS Condition I had gone barefoot to India.[5]

CRESSIDA He is not Hector.

PANDARUS Himself? No, he's not himself; would 'a° were   *he*
70 himself. Well, the gods are above; time must friend or end.°   *befriend or kill him*
Well, Troilus, well. I would my heart were in her body. No,
Hector is not a better man than Troilus.

CRESSIDA Excuse me.[6]

PANDARUS He is elder.

75 CRESSIDA Pardon me, pardon me.

---

4. Here and in the following lines, Cressida obsti-
nately takes Pandarus's figurative language literally.
Recognized him; met an ideal man; saw him from the
front ("before") and had sexual intercourse with

("knew") him.
5. If I'd gone barefoot (on pilgrimage) to India—an
impossibility.
6. Cressida disagrees, as in line 68.

PANDARUS　Th'other's not come to't.° You shall tell me another　*his prime; intercource*
tale when th'other's come to't. Hector shall not have his will[7]
this year.
CRESSIDA　He shall not need it if he have his own.
80　PANDARUS　Nor his qualities.
CRESSIDA　No matter.
PANDARUS　Nor his beauty.
CRESSIDA　'Twould not become him; his own's better.
PANDARUS　You have no judgment, niece. Helen herself swore
85　th'other day that Troilus, for a brown favor[8]—for so 'tis, I
must confess—not brown neither—
CRESSIDA　No, but brown.
PANDARUS　Faith, to say truth, brown and not brown.
CRESSIDA　To say the truth, true and not true.
90　PANDARUS　She praised his complexion above Paris'.
CRESSIDA　Why, Paris hath color enough.
PANDARUS　So he has.
CRESSIDA　Then Troilus should° have too much. If she praised　*must therefore*
him above, his° complexion is higher than his;° he having　*(Troilus's) / (Paris's)*
95　color enough, and the other higher, is too flaming a praise for
a good complexion. I had as lief Helen's golden tongue had
commended Troilus for a copper nose.[9]
PANDARUS　I swear to you I think Helen loves him better than
Paris.
100　CRESSIDA　Then she's a merry Greek[1] indeed.
PANDARUS　Nay, I am sure she does. She came to him th'other
day into the compassed° window—and you know he has not　*bay*
past three or four hairs on his chin—
CRESSIDA　Indeed, a tapster's° arithmetic may soon bring his　*the simplest*
105　particulars therein to a total.
PANDARUS　Why, he is very young, and yet will he within three
pound lift as much as his brother Hector.
CRESSIDA　Is he so young a man and so old a lifter?°　*so practiced a thief*
PANDARUS　But to prove to you that Helen loves him: she
110　came and puts me° her white hand to his cloven chin—　*puts me = puts*
CRESSIDA　Juno have mercy! How came it cloven?
PANDARUS　Why, you know 'tis dimpled. I think his smiling
becomes him better than any man in all Phrygia.
CRESSIDA　Oh, he smiles valiantly.
115　PANDARUS　Does he not?
CRESSIDA　Oh, yes, an 'twere a cloud in autumn.[2]
PANDARUS　Why, go to then! But to prove to you that Helen
loves Troilus—
CRESSIDA　Troilus will stand to the proof[3] if you'll prove it so.
120　PANDARUS　Troilus? Why, he esteems her no more than I esteem
an addle° egg.　*a rotten*
CRESSIDA　If you love an addle egg as well as you love an idle
head, you would eat chickens i'th' shell.[4]

7. Troilus's resolve; Troilus's sexual desire.
8. Notwithstanding his (unfashionably) dark or
tanned face.
9. Red nose, caused by drinking; perhaps also an artificial nose, made necessary by the ravages of syphilis.
1. Slang for a reveler or wanton, implying good fellowship and superficiality; here, appropriately applied
to Helen and more generally to the Greeks, at least as
they treat Cressida.
2. As if he were a rain cloud.
3. Will uphold the proof; will have an erection.
4. An addled egg often resulted from the chick dying
during hatching.

PANDARUS   I cannot choose but laugh to think how she tick-
125   led his chin—indeed, she has a marvelous white hand, I
    must needs confess.
CRESSIDA   Without the rack.°   *being tortured*
PANDARUS   And she takes upon her to spy a white hair on his
    chin.
130 CRESSIDA   Alas, poor chin; many a wart is richer.°   *(in hairs)*
PANDARUS   But there was such laughing. Queen Hecuba
    laughed that° her eyes ran o'er.   *so much that*
CRESSIDA   With millstones.[5]
PANDARUS   And Cassandra laughed.
135 CRESSIDA   But there was more temperate fire under the pot of
    her eyes.[6] Did her eyes run o'er too?
PANDARUS   And Hector laughed.
CRESSIDA   At what was all this laughing?
PANDARUS   Marry,[7] at the white hair that Helen spied on Troi-
140   lus' chin.
CRESSIDA   An't had been a green hair I should have laughed
    too.
PANDARUS   They laughed not so much at the hair as at his
    pretty° answer.   *witty*
145 CRESSIDA   What was his answer?
PANDARUS   Quoth she, "Here's but two and fifty hairs on your
    chin, and one of them is white."
CRESSIDA   This is her question.
PANDARUS   That's true, make no question of that. "Two and
150   fifty hairs," quoth he, "and one white. That white hair is my
    father and all the rest are his sons.[8]" "Jupiter!" quoth she,
    "Which of these hairs° is Paris, my husband?" "The forked[9]   *pun on "heirs"*
    one," quoth he, "pluck't out and give it him." But there was
    such laughing, and Helen so blushed, and Paris so chafed,°   *(was) so irritated*
155   and all the rest so laughed, that it passed.°   *surpassed description*
CRESSIDA   So let it now, for it has been a great while going by.
PANDARUS   Well, cousin, I told you a thing yesterday. Think
    on't.
CRESSIDA   So I do.
160 PANDARUS   I'll be sworn 'tis true; he will weep you an 'twere°   *for you as if he were*
    a man born in April.°   *month of showers*
CRESSIDA   And I'll spring up in his tears an 'twere° a nettle   *as if I were*
    against° May.   *anticipating*
         Sound a retreat.
PANDARUS   Hark, they are coming from the field. Shall we
165   stand up here and see them as they pass toward Ilium, good
    niece? Do, sweet niece Cressida.
CRESSIDA   At your pleasure.
PANDARUS   Here, here, here's an excellent place! Here we may

---

5. A hard-hearted person was proverbially said to weep millstones rather than tears. Cressida doesn't think the story is particularly funny.
6. Cassandra's tears are "more temperate" because she was associated with mournful, doom-laden prophecy. Cressida imagines tears of laughter as a pot boiling over.

7. An oath based on the name of the Virgin Mary; here, meaning "Why," elsewhere "Indeed."
8. Priam reputedly had fifty sons. The "forked" hair (line 152) apparently counts as two.
9. Like a cuckold's horns, thereby suggesting Helen's unfaithfulness to Paris.

see most bravely.° I'll tell you them all by their names as they | *very finely*
170 pass by, but mark Troilus above the rest.
Enter AENEAS [*and passes over the stage*].
CRESSIDA Speak not so loud.
PANDARUS That's Aeneas. Is not that a brave° man? He's one | *splendid; courageous*
of the flowers° of Troy, I can tell you. But mark Troilus; you | *finest men*
shall see anon.
175 CRESSIDA Who's that?
Enter Antenor [*and passes over the stage*].
PANDARUS That's Antenor. He has a shrewd wit, I can tell
you, and he's a man good enough. He's° one o'th' soundest | *He has*
judgments in Troy whosoever,° and a proper man of person.[1] | *of any man*
When comes Troilus? I'll show you Troilus anon. If he see
180 me, you shall see him nod at me.
CRESSIDA Will he give you the nod?
PANDARUS You shall see.
CRESSIDA If he do, the rich shall have more.[2]
Enter HECTOR [*and passes over the stage*].
PANDARUS That's Hector—that, that, look you that, there's a
185 fellow! —Go thy way, Hector! —There's a brave man, niece.
O brave Hector! Look how he looks—there's a countenance.
Is't not a brave man?
CRESSIDA O brave man!
PANDARUS Is 'a° not? It does a man's heart good. Look you | *he*
190 what hacks are on his helmet; look you yonder, do you see?
Look you there, there's no jesting; laying on, take't off who
will,[3] as they say; there be hacks!
CRESSIDA Be those with swords?
Enter PARIS [*and passes over the stage*].
PANDARUS Swords, anything, he cares not an the devil come
195 to him, it's all one.° By God's lid,° it does one's heart good. | *the same / eyelid*
Yonder comes Paris, yonder comes Paris! Look ye yonder,
niece, is't not a gallant° man too, is't not? Why, this is brave | *fine*
now. Who said he came hurt home today? He's not hurt.
Why, this will do Helen's heart good now, ha? Would I could
200 see Troilus now; you shall° Troilus anon. | *shall see*
CRESSIDA Who's that?
Enter HELENUS [*and passes over the stage*].
PANDARUS That's Helenus. I marvel where Troilus is. That's
Helenus. I think he went not forth today. That's Helenus.
CRESSIDA Can Helenus fight, uncle?
205 PANDARUS Helenus? No. Yes, he'll fight indifferent° well. I | *fairly*
marvel where Troilus is. Hark, do you not hear the people
cry "Troilus"? Helenus is a priest.
CRESSIDA What sneaking fellow comes yonder?
Enter TROILUS [*and passes over the stage*].
PANDARUS Where? Yonder? That's Deiphobus. 'Tis Troilus!
210 There's a man, niece. Hem! Brave Troilus, the prince of
chivalry!

1. Is a good-looking man.
2. If Troilus acknowledges Pandarus with a nod, this will make Pandarus even more of a noddy, a fool. "Give you the nod" (line 181) implies both personal

recognition and recognition of folly.
3. There's hard fighting, denials notwithstanding (with sexual wordplay: "laying on" versus "take't off").

CRESSIDA   Peace, for shame, peace.

PANDARUS   Mark him, note him. O brave Troilus! Look well
upon him, niece. Look you how his sword is bloodied and
215   his helm more hacked than Hector's, and how he looks, and
how he goes.° O admirable youth! He ne'er saw three-and-   *walks*
twenty. —Go thy way, Troilus, go thy way. —Had I a sister
were a grace⁴ or a daughter a goddess, he should take his
choice. O admirable man! Paris? Paris is dirt to him, and I
220   warrant Helen to change° would give money to boot.   *exchange*

      Enter common Soldiers [and pass over the stage].

CRESSIDA   Here come more.

PANDARUS   Asses, fools, dolts; chaff and bran, chaff and bran;
porridge° after meat. I could live and die i'th' eyes of Troilus.   *soup*
Ne'er look, ne'er look, the eagles are gone; crows and daws,°   *jackdaws; fools*
225   crows and daws. I had rather be such a man as Troilus than
Agamemnon and all Greece.

CRESSIDA   There is among the Greeks Achilles, a better man
than Troilus.

PANDARUS   Achilles? A drayman,° a porter, a very camel.   *cart driver*
230 CRESSIDA   Well, well.

PANDARUS   "Well, well"? Why, have you any discretion? Have
you any eyes? Do you know what a man is? Is not birth,°   *lineage*
beauty, good shape, discourse,° manhood, learning, gentle-   *eloquence*
ness,° virtue, youth, liberality, and so forth the spice and salt   *gentility*
235   that seasons a man?

CRESSIDA   Ay, a minced⁵ man, and then to be baked with no
date in the pie, for then the man's date's out.⁶

PANDARUS   You are such another woman!° One knows not at   *like other women*
what ward you lie.⁷

240 CRESSIDA   Upon my back to defend my belly,⁸ upon my wit to
defend my wiles, upon my secrecy° to defend mine honesty,⁹   *privacy; genitals*
my mask to defend my beauty,° and you to defend all these.   *(from sun)*
And at all these wards I lie, at a thousand watches.¹

PANDARUS   Say one of your watches.

245 CRESSIDA   Nay, I'll watch you for that, and that's one of the
chiefest of them, too.² If I cannot ward what I would not
have hit,° I can watch you for° telling how I took the blow—   *(sexually) / from*
unless it swell past hiding,° and then it's past watching.   *(from pregnancy)*

      Enter [Troilus'] BOY.

PANDARUS   You are such another!

250 BOY   Sir, my lord would instantly speak with you.

PANDARUS   Where?

BOY   At your own house.

PANDARUS   Good boy, tell him I come.   *[Exit BOY.]*

---

4. The three Graces were goddesses of beauty and charm.
5. Affected (punning on "mincemeat" to suggest the multiple ingredients of Troilus and thus beginning to develop Pandarus's "spice and salt" metaphor); also hints at impotence.
6. The man is flavorless; out of date; past his sexual prime; not in female genitalia.
7. One doesn't know what position of defense in fencing ("ward") you adopt. (A man doesn't know how to deal with you.)

8. Vagina. Lying on one's back is not, of course, the obvious way to defend one's virginity.
9. Reputation.
1. Ways of guarding; hours of the night; the duties of a watchman (playing on "watch" and "ward," line 243); devotional exercises (line 244). "Watch" as a verb is also implied: observe (line 245); prevent (lines 246–47); worry (line 248).
2. Presumably the immediately preceding phrase is one of her chief devotional exercises.

I doubt° he be hurt. Fare ye well, good niece.   *fear*
255   CRESSIDA   Adieu, uncle.
    PANDARUS   I'll be with you, niece, by and by.
    CRESSIDA   To bring, uncle?
    PANDARUS   Ay, a token from Troilus.
    CRESSIDA   By the same token you are a bawd.°   *pander; pimp*

Exit PANDARUS.

260   Words, vows, gifts, tears, and love's full sacrifice
    He offers in another's enterprise,
    But more in Troilus thousandfold I see
    Than in the glass° of Pandar's praise may be.   *mirror*
    Yet hold I off. Women are angels, wooing;°   *when men woo them*
265   Things won are done, joy's soul lies in the doing.
    That she beloved° knows naught that knows not this: *A woman who is loved*
    Men prize the thing ungained more than it is.°   *is worth*
    That she was never yet that ever knew
    Love got so sweet as when desire did sue.[3]
270   Therefore this maxim out of° love I teach: *taken from*
    Achievement is command; ungained, beseech.[4]
    Then though my heart's contents[5] firm love doth bear,
    Nothing of that shall from mine eyes appear.   *Exit.*

1.3 (Q 1.3)

Sennet.° Enter AGAMEMNON, NESTOR, ULYSSES,   *Fanfare*
DIOMEDES, MENELAUS, *with others.*
  AGAMEMNON   Princes, what grief hath set the jaundice° on   *sickliness*
    your cheeks?
    The ample proposition that hope makes
    In all designs begun on earth below
    Fails in the promised largeness; checks° and disasters   *obstacles*
5   Grow in the veins[1] of actions highest reared,
    As knots by the conflux° of meeting sap   *confluence*
    Infect the sound pine and divert his° grain,   *its*
    Tortive° and errant,° from his course of growth.   *Contorted / straying*
    Nor, princes, is it matter new to us
10   That we come short of our suppose° so far,   *intention*
    That after seven years' siege yet Troy walls stand,
    Sith° every action that hath gone before,   *Since*
    Whereof we have record, trial did draw
    Bias and thwart,[2] not answering° the aim   *living up to*
15   And that unbodied figure° of the thought   *theoretical design*
    That gave't surmisèd shape. Why, then, you princes,
    Do you with cheeks abashed behold our works
    And think them shame which are indeed naught else
    But the protractive trials of great Jove
20   To find persistive constancy in men,
    The fineness of which metal° is not found   *hard substance; mettle*

---

3. *That . . . sue:* No woman has ever known making love with a man to be as sweet as when it is still desired for the first time.
4. Once a woman yields, the man controls her; what the man doesn't have, he must plead for.
5. *contents:* con-tents'—happiness; con'tents—substance.

1.3 Location: The Greek camp outside Troy.
1. It is assumed that trees have veins through which sap flows.
2. *trial . . . thwart:* the act of attempting the deed ("action") called it into being crookedly and in a manner at odds with the purpose.

In Fortune's love? For then the bold and coward,
The wise and fool, the artist° and unread,   *learned*
The hard and soft seem all affined° and kin.   *related*
25 But in the wind and tempest of her frown,
Distinction, with a loud and powerful fan,
Puffing at all, winnows the light away,[3]
And what hath mass or matter by itself
Lies rich in virtue and unminglèd.
30 NESTOR   With due observance of° thy godly seat,°   *respect to / throne*
Great Agamemnon, Nestor shall apply°   *explain*
Thy latest words. In the reproof of° chance   *rebuff by; rebuttal of*
Lies the true proof of men. The sea being smooth,
How many shallow bauble° boats dare sail   *toy*
35 Upon her patient breast, making their way
With those of nobler bulk!
But let the ruffian Boreas° once enrage   *north wind*
The gentle Thetis,[4] and anon behold
The strong-ribbed bark through liquid mountains cut,
40 Bounding between the two moist elements°   *(water and air)*
Like Perseus' horse.° Where's then the saucy° boat   *(winged Pegasus) / bold*
Whose weak untimbered sides but even° now   *just*
Co-rivaled greatness? Either to harbor fled,
Or made a toast for Neptune.[5] Even so
45 Doth valor's show and valor's worth divide
In storms of fortune, for in her° ray and brightness   *(fortune's)*
The herd hath more annoyance by the breese°   *gadfly*
Than by the tiger. But when the splitting wind
Makes flexible the knees° of knotted° oaks   *tough timber / gnarled*
50 And flies flee under shade, why then the thing of courage,°   *brave person*
As roused with rage, with rage doth sympathize,[6]
And with an accent tuned in selfsame key
Retires° to chiding fortune.   *Returns*
ULYSSES   Agamemnon,
Thou great commander, nerve° and bone of Greece,   *sinew*
55 Heart of our numbers,° soul and only spirit,   *troops*
In whom the tempers and the minds of all
Should be shut up,° hear what Ulysses speaks.   *encapsulated*
Besides the applause° and approbation,   *approval*
The which [*to* AGAMEMNON] most mighty for thy place and
sway,°   *position and power*
60 [*to* NESTOR] And thou most reverend for thy stretched-out
life,
I give to both your speeches, which were such
As Agamemnon and the hand of Greece
Should hold up high in brass;° and such again   *record permanently*
As venerable Nestor, hatched[7] in silver,
65 Should, with a bond of air strong as the axletree[8]
On which the heavens ride, knit all Greeks' ears

3. The comparison is to light, dry chaff blown away from grain.
4. Sea goddess (mother of Achilles); here, standing for the sea.
5. Morsel of toasted bread, floated in wine, for the god of the sea.
6. Himself enraged, behaves like the raging storm.

7. Etched with parallel lines, as if inlaid with precious metal (alluding to Nestor's white hair and beard, or his wrinkled face).
8. *bond of air*: persuasive rhetoric. *axletree*: the axis on which the universe was imagined to revolve, earth being at the center.

To his experienced tongue—yet let it please both,
Thou great, and wise, to hear Ulysses speak.
AGAMEMNON   Speak, prince of Ithaca, and be't of less expect⁹

70   That matter needless, of importless burden,°   *irrelevant meaning*
Divide thy lips than we are confident
When rank° Thersites opes his mastic° jaws   *rancid / abusive*
We shall hear music, wit, and oracle.
ULYSSES   Troy, yet upon his basis,° had been down   *still standing*
75   And the great Hector's sword had lacked a master
But for these instances:°   *causes*
The specialty° of rule hath been neglected;   *rights and duties*
And look how many Grecian tents do stand
Hollow° upon this plain, so many hollow° factions.   *Empty / false*
80   When that the general is not like the hive
To whom the foragers° shall all repair,   *food collectors*
What honey is expected? Degree° being vizarded,°   *Rank / concealed*
Th'unworthiest shows as fairly in the mask.
The heavens themselves, the planets, and this center°   *(the earth)*
85   Observe degree, priority, and place,
Insisture,° course, proportion, season, form,   *Fixity*
Office,° and custom, in all line of order.   *Function*
And therefore is the glorious planet Sol¹
In noble eminence enthroned and sphered°   *placed in orbit*
90   Amidst the other,° whose med'cinable² eye   *remaining planets*
Corrects the ill aspects° of planets evil   *looks; influence*
And posts,° like the commandment of a king,   *hastens*
Sans° check to good and bad.³ But when the planets   *Without*
In evil mixture to disorder wander,⁴
95   What plagues and what portents, what mutiny,
What raging of the sea, shaking of earth,
Commotion in the winds, frights, changes,° horrors,   *political strife*
Divert and crack, rend and deracinate°   *uproot*
The unity and married calm of states
100 Quite from their fixure! Oh, when degree is shaked,
Which is the ladder° to all high designs,   *(literal sense of "degree")*
The enterprise is sick. How could communities,
Degrees in schools,° and brotherhoods° in cities,   *Academic rank / guilds*
Peaceful commerce from dividable shores,°   *lands separated by sea*
105 The primogenitive° and due of birth,   *inheritance by oldest son*
Prerogative of age, crowns, scepters, laurels,
But by degree stand in authentic place?
Take but degree away, untune that string,
And hark what discord follows: each thing meets
110 In mere oppugnancy;° the bounded waters   *total antagonism*
Should lift their bosoms higher than the shores
And make a sop° of all this solid globe;   *lump of soaked bread*
Strength should be lord of imbecility,°   *weakness*
And the rude son should strike his father dead;

9. *expect:* likelihood. TEXTUAL COMMENT For the significance of this short speech's presence here, but
not in Q, see Digital Edition TC 2 (Folio edited text).
1. In the Ptolemaic system, the sun was thought to
be a planet revolving around the earth.
2. Curative. The eyes were thought to see by emitting rays—like the sun. Kings sometimes claimed an
ability to cure similar to that attributed to the sun.
3. *good and bad:* promotion of the good and preven-
tion of the bad.
4. The word "planets" means "wanderers," referring
to their apparently erratic course, as seen from earth.
evil mixture: wicked coupling.

115   Force should be right—or rather, right and wrong,

Between whose endless jar justice resides,[5]

Should lose their names, and so should justice too.

Then everything includes itself in° power,   *comes down to*

Power into will,° will into appetite,°   *egotism / lust*

120   And appetite, an universal wolf,

So doubly seconded with will and power,

Must make perforce an universal prey,°   *seizing*

And last eat up himself. Great Agamemnon,

This chaos, when degree is suffocate,

125   Follows the choking.

And this neglection of degree is it

That by a pace goes backward in a purpose

It hath to climb.[6] The general's disdained

By him one step below, he by the next,

130   That next by him beneath—so every step,

Exampled by the first pace that is sick

Of his superior, grows to an envious fever

Of pale and bloodless emulation.°   *sick rivalry*

And 'tis this fever that keeps Troy on foot,°   *standing*

135   Not her own sinews. To end a tale of length,

Troy in our weakness lives, not in her strength.

NESTOR   Most wisely hath Ulysses here discovered°   *revealed*

The fever whereof all our power is sick.

AGAMEMNON   The nature of the sickness found, Ulysses,

140   What is the remedy?

ULYSSES   The great Achilles, whom opinion° crowns   *consensus*

The sinew and the forehand° of our host,°   *strongest / army*

Having his ear full of his airy° fame,   *lofty; insubstantial*

Grows dainty of° his worth and in his tent   *too conscious of*

145   Lies mocking our designs. With him Patroclus,

Upon a lazy bed, the livelong day

Breaks scurrile° jests,   *scurrilous*

And with ridiculous and awkward action°—   *gesture*

Which, slanderer, he "imitation" calls—

150   He pageants° us. Sometime, great Agamemnon,   *mimics*

Thy topless deputation° he puts on,   *supreme rank*

And, like a strutting player whose conceit

Lies in his hamstring[7] and doth think it rich

To hear the wooden dialogue and sound

155   Twixt his stretched footing and the scaffoldage,[8]

Such to-be-pitied and o'er-wrested seeming°   *pitiful imitation*

He acts thy greatness in. And when he speaks

'Tis like a chime a-mending, with terms unsquared,[9]

Which from the tongue of roaring Typhon[1] dropped

160   Would seem hyperboles. At this fusty° stuff   *stale; bombastic*

The large Achilles, on his pressed° bed lolling,   *(by Achilles' weight)*

From his deep chest laughs out a loud applause,

---

5. Justice stands between the clashing ("jar") of the opposing contenders.

6. *That . . . climb*: That drops back step by step when it intends to climb.

7. *whose . . . hamstring*: whose brains are in his thighs.

8. *To hear . . . scaffoldage*: To hear the sound of his long, powerful strides (and dull speech?) on the plat-

form stage.

9. Like bells being repaired (or tuned), with ill-fitting expressions.

1. Monster with a hundred heads, each uttering the cry of a different beast; eventually buried by Jupiter under (and so associated with) a volcano.

	Cries, "Excellent! 'Tis Agamemnon just.°	*exactly*
	Now play me Nestor—'hem'° and stroke thy beard	*(as in "ahem")*
165	As he being dressed to° some oration."	*preparing for*
	That's done as near as the extremest ends	
	Of parallels, as like as Vulcan and his wife,²	
	Yet god° Achilles still cries, "Excellent!	*semidivine (ironic)*
	'Tis Nestor right. Now play him me, Patroclus,	
170	Arming to answer in° a night alarm."	*respond to*
	And then, forsooth, the faint° defects of age	*weak*
	Must be the scene of mirth: to cough and spit,	
	And, with a palsy fumbling on his gorget,°	*throat armor*
	Shake in and out the rivet.° And at this sport	*fastening bolt*
175	Sir Valor dies,° cries, "Oh, enough, Patroclus,	*(laughing)*
	Or give me ribs of steel! I shall split all	
	In pleasure of my spleen."° And in this fashion	*(seat of mirth)*
	All our abilities, gifts, natures, shapes,	
	Severals and generals of grace exact,³	
180	Achievements, plots, orders, preventions,°	*precautions*
	Excitements° to the field, or speech for truce,	*Urgings*
	Success or loss, what is or is not, serves	
	As stuff for these two to make paradoxes.°	*absurdities*

NESTOR   And in the imitation of these twain—

185	Who, as Ulysses says, opinion crowns	
	With an imperial voice—many are infect:°	*infected*
	Ajax is grown self-willed and bears his head	
	In such a rein,° in full as proud a place	*So high*
	As broad Achilles, and keeps° his tent like him;	*stays within*
190	Makes factious° feasts; rails on° our state of war,	*divisive / complains about*
	Bold as an oracle; and sets Thersites,	
	A slave whose gall° coins slanders like a mint,	*rancor*
	To match us in comparisons with dirt,	
	To weaken and discredit our exposure,°	*exposed position*
195	How rank° soever rounded in with° danger.	*densely / hemmed in by*

ULYSSES   They tax° our policy and call it cowardice,   *criticize*

	Count wisdom as no member of the war,	
	Forestall prescience,° and esteem no act	*advance planning*
	But that of hand.° The still and mental parts	*brute force*
200	That do contrive how many hands shall strike	
	When fitness° calls them on, and know by measure	*the right moment*
	Of their observant toil the enemy's weight°—	*power*
	Why, this hath not a finger's dignity!	
	They call this bed-work, mapp'ry,° closet-war,	*mere mapping; planning*
205	So that the ram that batters down the wall	
	For the great swing and rudeness of his poise⁴	
	They place before° his hand that made the engine°	*exalt above / (the ram)*
	Or those that with the fineness° of their souls	*subtlety*
	By reason guide his execution.°	*the ram's use*

210   NESTOR   Let this be granted, and Achilles' horse

---

2. *as near . . . wife:* as closely as the ends of parallel lines (which, since they are equidistant, never meet), and as the ugly, limping god Vulcan, the smith, resembles his beautiful wife, Venus. Ulysses is stressing how bad the acting is, while at the same time covertly belittling Agamemnon and Nestor.
3. Supreme merits, possessed individually and in common.
4. Because of the impetus and violence of its impact.

Makes many Thetis' sons.[5]
  Tucket.°   *Trumpet call*
AGAMEMNON   What trumpet? Look, Menelaus.
MENELAUS   From Troy.
  Enter AENEAS [*with a Trumpeter*].
AGAMEMNON   What would you fore° our tent?   *before*
AENEAS   Is this great Agamemnon's tent, I pray you?
215 AGAMEMNON   Even this.
AENEAS   May one that is a herald and a prince
  Do a fair message to his kingly ears?
AGAMEMNON   With surety° stronger than Achilles' arm   *security*
  Fore all the Greekish heads, which with one voice
220 Call Agamemnon head and general.
AENEAS   Fair leave and large° security. How may   *generous*
  A stranger to those most imperial looks
  Know them from eyes of other mortals?
AGAMEMNON   How?
AENEAS   Ay, I ask that I might waken reverence
225 And on the cheek be ready with a blush
  Modest as morning when she coldly eyes
  The youthful Phoebus.[6]
  Which is that god in office, guiding men?
  Which is the high and mighty Agamemnon?
230 AGAMEMNON   This Trojan scorns us, or the men of Troy
  Are ceremonious courtiers.
AENEAS   Courtiers as free,° as debonair,° unarmed,   *generous / gracious*
  As bending° angels—that's their fame in peace—   *ministering*
  But when they would seem soldiers they have galls,[7]
235 Good arms, strong joints, true swords, and, Jove's accord,°   *Jove willing*
  Nothing° so full of heart.° But peace, Aeneas,   *No one / courage*
  Peace, Trojan, lay thy finger on thy lips;
  The worthiness of praise distains° his worth   *stains*
  If that the praised himself bring the praise forth.
240 But what the repining° enemy commends,   *grudging*
  That breath fame blows; that praise, sole pure,° transcends.   *the only pure kind*
AGAMEMNON   Sir, you of Troy, call you yourself Aeneas?
AENEAS   Ay, Greek,° that is my name.   *cheater (slang)*
AGAMEMNON   What's your affair, I pray you?
245 AENEAS   Sir, pardon, 'tis for Agamemnon's ears.
AGAMEMNON   He hears naught privately that comes from
    Troy.
AENEAS   Nor I from Troy come not to whisper him.
  I bring a trumpet to awake his ear,
  To set his sense on the attentive bent,
  And then to speak.
250 AGAMEMNON   Speak frankly° as the wind;   *freely*
  It is not Agamemnon's sleeping hour.
  That thou shalt know, Trojan, he is awake,
  He tells thee so himself.
AENEAS   Trumpet,° blow loud!   *Trumpeter*

---

5. *Let . . . sons:* If this is true, then Achilles' horse is
worth many Achilleses. Thetis was the mother of
Achilles.
6. *Modest . . . Phoebus:* Modest as Aurora, the blush-

ing dawn personified, when she coldly eyes Apollo,
the sun god ("youthful" because it is early morning).
7. But when it is time for them to be warriors, their
courageous tempers do not tolerate mistreatment.

Send thy brass voice through all these lazy tents,
255 And every Greek of mettle, let him know
What Troy means fairly shall be spoke aloud.
          [*Sound trumpet.*]
We have, great Agamemnon, here in Troy
A prince called Hector—Priam is his father—
Who in this dull and long-continued truce
260 Is rusty grown. He bade me take a trumpet
And to this purpose speak: "Kings, princes, lords,
If there be one amongst the fair'st of Greece
That holds his honor higher than his ease,
That seeks his praise more than he fears his peril,
265 That knows his valor and knows not his fear,
That loves his mistress more than in confession
With truant vows to her own lips he loves,[8]
And dare avow her beauty and her worth
In other arms than hers,° to him this challenge.   armor; Hector's arms
270 Hector in view of Trojans and of Greeks
Shall make it good, or do his best to do it:
He hath a lady wiser, fairer, truer
Than ever Greek did compass° in his arms,   hold
And will tomorrow with his trumpet call
275 Midway between your tents and walls of Troy
To rouse a Grecian that is true in love.
If any come, Hector shall honor him;
If none, he'll say in Troy when he retires
The Grecian dames are sunburnt° and not worth   not fair-skinned
280 The splinter° of a lance." Even so much.   breaking; fragment
AGAMEMNON   This shall be told our lovers, Lord Aeneas.
     If none of them have soul in such a kind,
     We left them all at home. But we are soldiers,
     And may that soldier a mere recreant° prove   coward
285 That means not, hath not,[9] or is not in love.
     If then one is, or hath, or means to be,
     That one meets Hector; if none else, I'll be he.
NESTOR   Tell him of Nestor, one that was a man
     When Hector's grandsire sucked. He is old now,
290 But if there be not in our Grecian mold°   character; model
     One noble man that hath one spark of fire
     To answer for his love, tell him from me
     I'll hide my silver beard in a gold beaver°   helmet's face guard
     And in my vambrace° put this withered brawn,°   forearm armor / arm
295 And, meeting him, will tell him that my lady
     Was fairer than his grandam and as chaste
     As may be in the world. His youth in flood,°   Despite his youth
     I'll pawn this truth with my three drops of blood.
AENEAS   Now heavens forbid such scarcity of youth!
300 ULYSSES   Amen.
AGAMEMNON   Fair Lord Aeneas, let me touch° your hand;   shake
     To our pavilion shall I lead you first.
     Achilles shall have word of this intent,

___

8. *That loves . . . loves:* Who will declare his love   promises.
with stronger proof (deeds) than unreliable, private   9. Who does not aim (to be), has never been.

So shall each lord of Greece from tent to tent.
305 Yourself shall feast with us before you go
And find the welcome of a noble foe.

Exeunt. ULYSSES *and* NESTOR *remain.*

ULYSSES   Nestor!
NESTOR   What says Ulysses?
ULYSSES   I have a young conception in my brain;
310 Be you my time¹ to bring it to some shape.
NESTOR   What is't?
ULYSSES   This 'tis:

Blunt wedges rive° hard knots; the seeded pride	*split*
That hath to this maturity blown° up	*swelled*
315 In rank° Achilles must or° now be cropped	*overgrown / either*
Or, shedding,° breed a nursery of like evil	*dropping its seed*
To over-bulk° us all.	*overrun*

NESTOR   Well, and how?
ULYSSES   This challenge that the gallant Hector sends,
However it is spread in general name,
320 Relates in purpose only to Achilles.

NESTOR The purpose is perspicuous° even as substance°	*easy to see / wealth*
Whose grossness little characters sum up;²	
And in the publication make no strain³	
But that Achilles, were his brain as barren	
325 As banks of Libya°—though, Apollo knows,	*the Sahara Desert*
'Tis dry° enough—will with great speed of judgment,	*infertile; empty*
Ay, with celerity, find Hector's purpose	
Pointing on him.°	*himself*

ULYSSES   And wake him to the answer, think you?

330 NESTOR Yes, 'tis most meet.° Who may you else oppose	*fitting*
That can from Hector bring his honor off	
If not Achilles? Though't be a sportful combat,	
Yet in this trial much opinion° dwells,	*reputation*
For here the Trojans taste our dear'st repute	
335 With their fin'st palate. And trust to me, Ulysses,	
Our imputation° shall be oddly poised⁴	*reputation*
In this wild° action, for the success,	*uncontrollable*
Although particular, shall give a scantling	
Of good or bad unto the general;⁵	
340 And in such indexes,° although small pricks	*tables of contents*
To° their subsequent volumes, there is seen	*Compared to*
The baby figure of the giant mass	
Of things to come at large. It is supposed	
He that meets Hector issues from our choice,	
345 And choice, being mutual act of all our souls,	
Makes merit her election° and doth boil,	*grounds of choice*
As 'twere from forth us all, a man distilled	
Out of our virtues; who miscarrying,°	*should he lose*
What heart from hence receives the conqu'ring part	

---

1. *conception . . . time:* The primary meaning (unfolding of a plan) metaphorically extended to pregnancy's onset and gestation period, the latter associated with the male and aged Nestor, who is oddly connected with this female and ordinarily youthful activity, presumably because he embodies the passage of time.

2. Whose size is reckoned by small figures (on paper).
3. And, with the announcement, do not doubt.
4. Disproportionately judged.
5. *the success . . . general:* the outcome, although relating only to one person, shall serve as an example of the whole army's abilities.

<table>
<tr><td>350</td><td>To steel a strong opinion to themselves!⁶
Which entertained, limbs are his instruments
In no less working than are swords and bows
Directive by the limbs.⁷</td><td></td></tr>
</table>

350 To steel a strong opinion to themselves!⁶
    Which entertained, limbs are his instruments
    In no less working than are swords and bows
    Directive by the limbs.⁷
ULYSSES   Give pardon to my speech:
    Therefore 'tis meet° Achilles meet not Hector.   *appropriate*
355 Let us, like merchants, show our foulest wares
    And think perchance they'll sell; if not,
    The luster of the better yet to show°   *not yet shown*
    Shall show the better. Do not consent
    That ever Hector and Achilles meet,
360 For both our honor and our shame in this
    Are dogged with two strange followers.°   *unpleasant effects*
NESTOR   I see them not with my old eyes; what are they?
ULYSSES   What glory our Achilles shares° from Hector,   *gains*
    Were he not proud, we all should wear° with him.   *share*
365 But he already is too insolent,
    And we were better parch in Afric sun
    Than in the pride and salt° scorn of his eyes   *bitter*
    Should he scape Hector fair. If he were foiled,
    Why, then we did our main opinion° crush   *common reputation*
370 In taint of° our best man. No, make a lott'ry,   *In the dishonor of*
    And by device let blockish° Ajax draw   *blockheaded*
    The sort° to fight with Hector. Among ourselves   *lot*
    Give him allowance° as the worthier man,   *acknowledgment*
    For that will physic the great Myrmidon,⁸
375 Who broils in° loud applause, and make him fall°   *is excited by / lower*
    His crest that prouder than blue Iris⁹ bends.
    If the dull brainless Ajax come safe off,
    We'll dress him up in voices;° if he fail,   *sing his praises*
    Yet go we under our opinion still
380 That we have better men. But hit or miss,
    Our project's life° this shape of sense° assumes: *success / rationale*
    Ajax employed plucks down Achilles' plumes.
NESTOR   Now, Ulysses, I begin to relish thy advice,
    And I will give a taste of it forthwith
385 To Agamemnon. Go we to him straight.°   *immediately*
    Two curs shall tame each other; pride alone
    Must tar the mastiffs on,¹ as 'twere° their bone.   *Exeunt.*   *if it were*

2.1 (Q 2.1)

Enter AJAX *and* THERSITES.

AJAX   Thersites!
THERSITES   Agamemnon. How° if he had boils, full,° all over,   *What / (of pus)*
    generally?
AJAX   Thersites!
5 THERSITES   And those boils did run—say so—did not the gen-
    eral run?¹ Were not that a botchy core?°   *an ulcerous center*

---

6. *What . . . themselves:* What motivation will the Trojans get from this to make them feel more confident (with a play on "steel" = "steal")!
7. *Which . . . limbs:* Assuming that this confidence ("strong opinion") is received from the victory, the soldiers' limbs become the mechanisms ("instruments") of that confidence in the same way that swords and bows are subject to direction by the limbs themselves.

8. Will give medicine to (purge) Achilles, who led the Myrmidons.
9. Goddess of the rainbow; blue flower.
2.1 Location: The Greek camp.
1. *And . . . run:* And if those boils ran—let's say— wouldn't the general (Agamemnon, the whole army) have running sores (flee from battle)?

AJAX Dog!

THERSITES Then there would come some matter° from him. I   *pus; sense*
see none now.

10 AJAX Thou bitch-wolf's son, canst thou not hear? Feel, then.
        [*He*] *strikes* [THERSITES].

THERSITES The plague of Greece upon thee, thou mongrel[2]
beef-witted° lord!   *dumb as an ox*

AJAX Speak, then, you finewed'st leaven,[3] speak. I will beat[4]
thee into handsomeness.°   *decency; good looks*

15 THERSITES I shall sooner rail thee into wit and holiness; but I
think thy horse will sooner con° an oration than thou learn   *memorize*
a prayer without book.° Thou canst strike, canst thou? A red   *by heart*
murrain o'thy jade's[5] tricks!

AJAX Toadstool,[6] learn me° the proclamation!   *instruct me (about)*

20 THERSITES Dost thou think I have no sense,° thou strik'st me   *feeling*
thus?

AJAX The proclamation!

THERSITES Thou art proclaimed a fool, I think.

AJAX Do not, porcupine,[7] do not; my fingers itch°—   *(to hit you)*

25 THERSITES I would thou didst itch from head to foot and I
had the scratching of thee. I would make thee the loathsom'st
scab in Greece.

AJAX I say, the proclamation.

THERSITES Thou grumblest and railest every hour on Achil-
30 les, and thou art as full of envy at his greatness as Cerberus
is at Proserpina's[8] beauty, ay, that° thou bark'st at him.   *so much so that*

AJAX Mistress[9] Thersites!

THERSITES Thou shouldst strike him.°   *(Achilles)*

AJAX Cobloaf!°   *Small crusty loaf*

35 THERSITES He would pun° thee into shivers° with his fist, as   *pound / pieces*
a sailor breaks a biscuit.

AJAX [*striking him*] You whoreson cur!

THERSITES Do, do.°   *Go on*

AJAX Thou stool° for a witch!   *privy*

40 THERSITES Ay, do, do, thou sodden-witted° lord. Thou hast no   *boiled-brained*
more brain than I have in mine elbows—an asinego° may   *little ass*
tutor thee. Thou scurvy-valiant ass! Thou art here but to
thresh° Trojans, and thou art bought and sold[1] among those of   *harvest*
any wit like a barbarian slave. If thou use° to beat me, I will   *continue*
45 begin at thy heel and tell what thou art by inches, thou thing
of no bowels,° thou.   *with no pity*

AJAX You dog!

THERSITES You scurvy lord!

AJAX [*striking him*] You cur!

50 THERSITES Mars his idiot!° Do, rudeness; do, camel, do, do!   *God of war's jester*
        Enter ACHILLES *and* PATROCLUS.

---

2. Ajax's mother was Trojan; hence, he was of mixed
breed, "mongrel."
3. *leaven:* fermenting agent, causing dough to rise.
finewed'st: moldiest. Hence, Ajax accuses Thersites of
being a pollutant.
4. Punning on the pounding of bread dough.
5. A bloody plague on your bad-tempered worn-out
horse's (woman's).
6. Toadstools were once thought to be a toad's poisonous excrement (stool).

7. The porcupine's sharp quills were emblematic of
the satirist (here, Thersites).
8. Cerberus was the monstrous three-headed dog who
guarded the gate of Hades. Proserpina was Queen of
Hades and wife of Pluto, god of the underworld.
9. Because a woman's only weapon was thought to be
her tongue, because Thersites is a coward, or because
he is believed to be homosexual.
1. You are traded like goods—hence, treated as an
object, treated contemptuously.

ACHILLES Why, how now, Ajax? Wherefore do you this?
—How now, Thersites? What's the matter, man?
THERSITES You see him there, do you?
ACHILLES Ay, what's the matter?
55 THERSITES Nay, look upon him.
ACHILLES So I do. What's the matter?
THERSITES Nay, but regard him well.
ACHILLES Well, why I do so.
THERSITES But yet you look not well upon him,[2] for whosom-
60 ever you take him to be, he is Ajax.°   *a jakes = toilet*
ACHILLES I know that, fool.
THERSITES Ay, but that fool knows not himself.[3]
AJAX Therefore I beat thee.[4]
THERSITES Lo,° lo, lo, lo, what modicums of wit he utters.   *Behold (sarcastic)*
65 His evasions have ears thus long.[5] I have bobbed° his brain   *thumped*
more than he has beat my bones; I will° buy nine sparrows   *can*
for a penny, and his *pia mater*° is not worth the ninth part of   *brain*
a sparrow. This lord, Achilles—Ajax, who wears his wit in
his belly and his guts in his head—I'll tell you what I say of
70 him.
ACHILLES What?
THERSITES I say, this Ajax—
ACHILLES [*holding* AJAX *back*] Nay, good Ajax.
THERSITES Has not so much wit—
75 ACHILLES Nay, I must hold° you.   *restrain*
THERSITES As will stop the eye of Helen's needle,[6] for whom
he comes to fight.
ACHILLES Peace, fool.
THERSITES I would have peace and quietness, but the fool°   *(Ajax)*
80 will not: he there, that he,° look you there.   *(I mean Ajax)*
AJAX O thou damned cur, I shall—
ACHILLES Will you set your wit to° a fool's?   *against*
THERSITES No, I warrant you, for a fool's will shame it.
PATROCLUS Good words,° Thersites.   *Speak with restraint*
85 ACHILLES What's the quarrel?
AJAX I bade the vile owl[7] go learn me the tenor of the procla-
mation, and he rails upon me.
THERSITES I serve thee not.
AJAX Well, go to, go to.
90 THERSITES I serve here voluntary.°   *as a volunteer*
ACHILLES Your last service was sufferance, 'twas not volun-
tary. No man is beaten voluntary. Ajax was here the voluntary, and you as under an impress.[8]
THERSITES E'en so; a great deal of your wit too lies in your
95 sinews, or else there be liars. Hector shall have a great catch
if he knock out either of your brains; he were as good° crack   *might as well*
a fusty° nut with no kernel.   *rotten*

---

2. Thersites is probably feigning amazement that Achilles can look at Ajax and yet not see what a fool he is; but he may also mean that Achilles does not do well to favor ("look . . . upon") him.
3. Thersites deliberately understands Achilles' line without the intended comma: "I know that fool" (Ajax), rather than "I know that [fact], fool."
4. Ajax thinks Thersites is calling himself (rather than Ajax) a "fool" who does not know himself.
5. His efforts to dodge witty rejoinders are like an ass's—hence, asinine.
6. "Eye" perhaps alludes to "vagina"; "needle" is also obscene. *stop:* fill.
7. The owl is associated with evil portent.
8. As a conscript; being hit as though with a stamp (by Ajax).

ACHILLES   What, with me too, Thersites?

THERSITES   There's Ulysses and old Nestor, whose wit was
100   moldy ere your grandsires had nails on their toes, yoke you
like draft-oxen and make you plow up the war.°   *(pun on ware = crops)*

ACHILLES   What, what?

THERSITES   Yes, good sooth: To,° Achilles! To, Ajax! To—   *(urging on the oxen)*

AJAX   I shall cut out your tongue.

105   THERSITES   'Tis no matter; I shall speak as much as thou
afterwards.

PATROCLUS   No more words, Thersites.

THERSITES   I will hold my peace when Achilles' brach° bids   *bitch*
me, shall I?

110   ACHILLES   There's for you, Patroclus.

THERSITES   I will see you hanged like clodpolls° ere I come   *blockheads*
any more to your tents; I will keep where there is wit stirring
and leave the faction of fools.   *Exit.*

PATROCLUS   A good riddance.

115   ACHILLES   [*to* AJAX]   Marry, this, sir, is proclaimed through all
our host:
That Hector by the fifth hour° of the sun   *11 A.M.*
Will with a trumpet twixt our tents and Troy
Tomorrow morning call some knight to arms
That hath a stomach,° and such a one that dare   *an appetite for combat*
120   Maintain—I know not what. 'Tis trash. Farewell.

AJAX   Farewell. Who shall answer him?

ACHILLES   I know not; 'tis put to lott'ry. Otherwise,
He knew his man.   [*Exeunt* ACHILLES *and* PATROCLUS.]

AJAX   Oh, meaning you? I will go learn more of it.   *Exit.*

2.2 (Q 2.2)

Enter PRIAM, HECTOR, TROILUS, PARIS, *and* HELENUS.

PRIAM   After so many hours, lives, speeches spent,
Thus once again says Nestor from the Greeks:
"Deliver Helen, and all damage else—
As° honor, loss of time, travail,° expense,   *Such as / hard labor*
5   Wounds, friends, and what else dear° that is consumed   *beloved; costly*
In hot digestion of this cormorant° war—   *rapacious*
Shall be struck off."° Hector, what say you to't?   *expunged*

HECTOR   Though no man lesser fears the Greeks than I
As far as touches my particular,°   *own concerns*
10   Yet, dread Priam,
There is no lady of more softer bowels,°   *compassion*
More spongy to suck in° the sense of fear,   *able to absorb*
More ready to cry out, "Who knows what follows?"
Than Hector is. The wound° of peace is surety°—   *danger / false confidence*
15   Surety secure—but modest doubt° is called   *precaution*
The beacon of the wise, the tent° that searches   *surgical probe*
To th' bottom of the worst. Let Helen go.
Since the first sword was drawn about this question
Every tithe soul 'mongst many thousand dismes
20   Hath been as dear as Helen[1]—I mean of ours.

2.2 Location: The palace in Troy.
1. *Every . . . Helen:* Every soul taken to pay the tithe
(a tenth of one's goods, paid as a tax), among many
thousand "dismes" (tenths; tithes paid, through soldiers' deaths), has been as valuable as Helen.

If we have lost so many tenths of ours
To guard a thing not ours, nor worth to us,
Had it our name, the value of one ten,[2]
What merit's in that reason which denies
The yielding of her up?
25 TROILUS   Fie, fie, my brother!
Weigh you the worth and honor of a king
So great as our dread father in a scale
Of common ounces? Will you with counters° sum   *worthless chips*
The past-proportion of his infinite[3]
30 And buckle in a waist most fathomless[4]
With spans° and inches so diminutive   *nine inches*
As fears and reasons?° Fie, for godly shame!   *(pun on "raisins")*
HELENUS   No marvel though you bite so sharp at reasons,
You are so empty of them. Should not our father
35 Bear the great sway of his affairs with reasons
Because your speech hath none that tell him so?
TROILUS   You are for dreams and slumbers, brother priest.
You fur your gloves with reason;[5] here are your reasons:
You know an enemy intends you harm,
40 You know a sword employed is perilous,
And reason flies the object of all harm.°   *any sight of danger*
Who marvels then, when Helenus beholds
A Grecian and his sword, if he do set
The very wings of reason to his heels
45 And fly like chidden Mercury[6] from Jove,
Or like a star disorbed?° Nay, if we talk of reason   *a shooting star*
Let's shut our gates and sleep. Manhood and honor
Should have hare° hearts would they but fat their thoughts   *timid*
With this crammed° reason. Reason and respect°   *fattened / deliberation*
50 Makes livers° pale and lustihood° deject.   *courage / energy*
HECTOR   Brother, she is not worth what she doth cost
The holding.°   *To keep*
TROILUS   What's aught but as 'tis valued?[7]
HECTOR   But value dwells not in particular will;°   *individual desire*
It holds his° estimate and dignity   *its*
55 As well wherein 'tis precious of itself
As in the prizer. 'Tis mad idolatry
To make the service° greater than the god,   *the devotion paid*
And the will dotes that is inclineable
To what infectiously itself affects
60 Without some image of th'affected merit.[8]
TROILUS   I take today a wife, and my election°   *choice*
Is led on in the conduct° of my will,   *under the guidance*
My will enkindled by mine eyes and ears,

	Two traded° pilots twixt the dangerous shores	*experienced*
65	Of will and judgment. How may I avoid,	
	Although my will distaste what it elected,	
	The wife I chose? There can be no evasion	
	To blench° from this and to stand firm by honor.	*shy away*
	We turn not back° the silks upon° the merchant	*don't return / to*
70	When we have spoiled them, nor the remainder viands°	*uneaten food*
	We do not throw in unrespective° sieve	*undiscriminating*
	Because we now are full. It was thought meet°	*appropriate that*
	Paris should do some vengeance on the Greeks.	
	Your breath of full consent bellied° his sails;	*swelled*
75	The seas and winds, old wranglers,° took a truce	*opponents*
	And did him service. He touched the ports desired,	
	And for an old aunt whom the Greeks held captive⁹	
	He brought a Grecian queen,° whose youth and freshness	*(pun on quean = whore?)*
	Wrinkles Apollo's and makes stale the morning.¹	
80	Why keep we her? The Grecians keep our aunt.	
	Is she worth keeping? Why, she is a pearl	
	Whose price hath launched above a thousand ships²	
	And turned crowned kings to merchants.	
	If you'll avouch 'twas wisdom Paris went—	
85	As you must needs, for you all cried "Go, go!"—	
	If you'll confess he brought home noble prize—	
	As you must needs, for you all clapped your hands	
	And cried "Inestimable!"—why do you now	
	The issue° of your proper° wisdoms rate°	*result / own / berate*
90	And do a deed that Fortune never did:³	
	Beggar the estimation⁴ which you prized	
	Richer than sea and land? Oh, theft most base	
	That° we have stol'n what we do fear to keep!	*In that*
	But thieves unworthy of a thing so stol'n	
95	That in their country did them that disgrace	
	We fear to warrant in our native place.⁵	

CASSANDRA [*within*]　　Cry, Trojans, cry!⁶

PRIAM　　　　　　　　　　What noise? What shriek is this?

TROILUS　'Tis our mad sister; I do know her voice.

CASSANDRA [*within*]　　Cry, Trojans!

| 100 | HECTOR　It is Cassandra. | |

Enter CASSANDRA⁷ *with her hair about her ears.*

CASSANDRA　Cry, Trojans, cry! Lend me ten thousand eyes
And I will fill them with prophetic tears.

HECTOR　Peace, sister, peace.

	CASSANDRA　Virgins and boys, mid-age and wrinkled old,°	*old people*
105	Soft infancy that nothing can° but cry,	*can do*
	Add to my clamor. Let us pay betimes°	*in advance*

---

9. Hesione, Priam's sister, kidnapped by the Greeks; "aunt" is also slang for "whore." The "vengeance" (line 73) is for the kidnapping.
1. Helen's "youth and freshness" by comparison make Apollo's (hence, also the sun's) "youth and freshness" seem old, and rosy dawn seem dried out (but also, unintentionally on Troilus's part, sluttish).
2. A well-worn phrase even when Marlowe used it in *Doctor Faustus*: "Was this the face that launched a thousand ships?" Here, given a mercantile turn.
3. And act more erratically than Fortune.

4. (Why do you) deem worthless the valued object?
5. *That . . . place*: (We Trojans) who in Greece dishonored the Greeks but back home are afraid to stand up for what we did.
6. TEXTUAL COMMENT On the timing of Cassandra's entrance and her appearance when she enters, see Digital Edition TC 3 (Folio edited text).
7. Apollo gave Cassandra the gift of prophecy to win her love, but because she rejected his wooing, he cursed her by causing her prophecies to be disregarded.

A moiety° of that mass° of moan to come.   *portion / sum*
Cry, Trojans, cry! Practice your eyes with tears.°   *Learn to weep*
Troy must not be, nor goodly Ilium stand;
110 Our firebrand[8] brother, Paris, burns us all.
Cry, Trojans, cry—a Helen and a woe!
Cry, cry! Troy burns, or else let Helen go.   *Exit.*
HECTOR   Now, youthful Troilus, do not these high strains
Of divination in our sister work
115 Some touches of remorse? Or is your blood
So madly hot that no discourse of reason
Nor fear of bad success° in a bad cause   *outcome*
Can qualify° the same?   *moderate*
TROILUS   Why brother Hector,
We may not think the justness of each act
120 Such and no other than event doth form it,[9]
Nor once deject° the courage of our minds   *reduce*
Because Cassandra's mad. Her brainsick raptures
Cannot distaste° the goodness of a quarrel   *make distasteful*
Which hath our several honors all engaged
125 To make it gracious.° For my private part,   *righteous; successful*
I am no more touched° than all Priam's sons,   *implicated*
And Jove forbid there should be done amongst us
Such things as might offend the weakest spleen
To fight for and maintain.[1]
130 PARIS   Else might the world convince° of levity   *convict*
As well my undertakings as your counsels.
But I attest° the gods: your full consent   *call to witness*
Gave wings to my propension° and cut off   *leaning*
All fears attending on so dire a project—
135 For what, alas, can these my single arms?°   *can my arms do alone*
What propugnation° is in one man's valor   *defense*
To stand the push° and enmity of those   *thrust*
This quarrel would excite?° Yet I protest,   *incite to battle*
Were I alone to pass° the difficulties   *endure*
140 And had as ample power as I have will,
Paris should ne'er retract what he hath done,
Nor faint in the pursuit.
PRIAM   Paris, you speak
Like one besotted° on your sweet delights: *drunk*
You have the honey still, but these the gall,
145 So° to be valiant is no praise at all.   *In such circumstances*
PARIS   Sir, I propose not merely to myself°   *for my own benefit*
The pleasures such a beauty brings with it,
But I would have the soil of her fair rape[2]
Wiped off in honorable keeping her.
150 What treason were it to the ransacked° queen,   *carried off as plunder*
Disgrace to your great worths, and shame to me
Now to deliver her possession up
On terms of base compulsion! Can it be

8. When pregnant with Paris, Hecuba dreamed of giving birth to a firebrand.
9. *We . . . it:* We must not judge the "justness" of our cause only by the results.
1. *And Jove . . . maintain:* We ("Priam's sons") shouldn't undertake something unless even the least courageous of us is willing to fight to defend it.
2. The defilement (of Helen or Paris, or both) resulting from her proper (also, beautiful) abduction (also, sexual violation).

That so degenerate a strain° as this   *an impulse*
155 Should once set footing in your generous° bosoms?   *noble*
There's not the meanest spirit on our party
Without a heart to dare or sword to draw
When Helen is defended, nor none so noble
Whose life were ill bestowed or death unfamed
160 Where Helen is the subject. Then, I say,
Well may we fight for her whom we know well
The world's large spaces cannot parallel.
HECTOR   Paris and Troilus, you have both said well,
And on the cause and question now in hand
165 Have glozed,° but superficially—not much   *commented*
Unlike young men whom Aristotle thought
Unfit to hear moral philosophy.[3]
The reasons you allege do more conduce
To the hot passion of distempered blood
170 Than to make up a free determination
Twixt right and wrong, for pleasure and revenge
Have ears more deaf than adders[4] to the voice
Of any true decision. Nature craves
All dues be rendered to their owners: now
175 What nearer debt in all humanity
Than wife is to the husband? If this law
Of nature be corrupted through affection,°   *lust*
And that great minds, of partial° indulgence   *through prejudiced*
To their benumbèd° wills, resist the same,°   *dulled / (law of nature)*
180 There is a law in each well-ordered nation
To curb those raging appetites that are
Most disobedient and refractory.°   *stubborn*
If Helen then be wife to Sparta's king,
As it is known she is, these moral laws
185 Of nature and of nation speak aloud
To have her back returned. Thus to persist
In doing wrong extenuates not wrong,
But makes it much more heavy. Hector's opinion
Is this in way of° truth. Yet ne'ertheless,   *with respect to*
190 My sprightly° brethren, I propend° to you   *spirited / incline*
In resolution to keep Helen still,
For 'tis a cause that hath no mean dependence
Upon our joint and several° dignities.   *separate*
TROILUS   Why, there you touch the life of our design!
195 Were it not glory that we more affected°   *desired*
Than the performance of our heaving spleens,°   *acting on our anger*
I would not wish a drop of Trojan blood
Spent more in her defense. But, worthy Hector,
She is a theme of honor and renown,
200 A spur to valiant and magnanimous° deeds,   *noble*
Whose present courage may beat down our foes
And fame in time to come canonize° us;   *future fame glorify*
For I presume brave Hector would not lose

---

3. Political philosophy. This is an anachronistic reference to Aristotle's *Nicomachean Ethics* 1.3.
4. Adders were proverbially deaf. See Psalms 58:4–5:

"like the deaf adder that stoppeth his ear. Which heareth not the voice of the enchanter, though he be most expert in charming."

So rich advantage of a promised glory
205 As smiles upon the forehead° of this action   *countenance*
For° the wide world's revenue.   *in return for*
HECTOR   I am yours,
You valiant offspring of great Priamus.
I have a roisting° challenge sent amongst   *boisterous*
The dull and factious nobles of the Greeks
210 Will° strike amazement to their drowsy spirits.   *That will*
I was advertised their great general slept[5]
Whilst emulation° in the army crept;   *jealous rivalry*
This, I presume, will wake him.   *Exeunt.*

2.3 (Q 2.3)

Enter THERSITES *alone.*

THERSITES   How now, Thersites? What, lost in the labyrinth
of thy fury? Shall the elephant Ajax carry it° thus? He beats   *get away with it*
me, and I rail at him. Oh, worthy satisfaction. Would it were
otherwise: that I could beat him whilst he railed at me.
5 'Sfoot,° I'll learn to conjure and raise devils, but I'll see   *God's foot*
some issue of my spiteful execrations.[1] Then there's Achil-
les, a rare engineer.[2] If Troy be not taken till these two
undermine it, the walls will stand till they fall of themselves. O thou great thunder-darter of Olympus, forget that
10 thou art Jove, the king of gods; and Mercury, lose all the
serpentine craft of thy caduceus,[3] if thou take not that little,
little—less than little—wit from them that they have, which
short-armed ignorance[4] itself knows is so abundant° scarce   *manifestly*
it will not in circumvention deliver a fly from a spider with-
15 out drawing the massy irons and cutting the web.[5] After
this, the vengeance on the whole camp, or rather the bone-
ache,° for that, methinks, is the curse dependent° on those   *syphilis / impending*
that war for a placket.[6] I have said my prayers, and devil
Envy say "Amen." —What ho! My lord Achilles!

Enter PATROCLUS *[at the opening of the tent].*

20 PATROCLUS   Who's there? Thersites. Good Thersites, come in
and rail.   *[PATROCLUS withdraws.]*
THERSITES   If I could have remembered a gilt counterfeit thou
wouldst not have slipped out of my contemplation[7]—but it is
no matter. Thyself upon thyself;[8] the common curse of man-
25 kind, folly and ignorance, be thine in great revenue.° Heaven   *amounts*
bless° thee from a tutor, and discipline come not near thee.   *save*
Let thy blood° be thy direction° till thy death; then, if she   *lust / guide*
that lays thee out says thou art a fair corpse, I'll be sworn
and sworn upon't, she never shrouded any but lazars.° Amen.   *lepers; sick bodies*
    [Enter PATROCLUS.*]*

---

5. I was told that Achilles (Agamemnon?) slept.
2.3 Location: The Greek camp, outside Achilles' tent.
1. *but I'll . . . execrations:* in order to get tangible results
from my contemptuous (or, unintended, "malicious")
curses.
2. Constructor of military earthworks and machines.
3. Mercury's emblem, a rod entwined by snakes.
Known for "craft," Mercury was the patron of thieves.
4. "Short-armed" because most things are beyond its
grasp.

5. *it will not . . . web:* it will use excessive, brute force.
Circumvention: craftiness. *irons:* swords.
6. Petticoat; woman; woman's genitalia (obscene).
7. If I could have remembered a fake gold coin
(worthless Patroclus), you wouldn't have been forgotten (punning on "slip," a counterfeit coin) in my
devout meditation (which focused on Ajax and Achilles, but only to curse them).
8. To be Patroclus is the worst possible fate—hence,
Thersites' curse on him is to be himself.

30 —Where's Achilles?
PATROCLUS What, art thou devout? Wast thou in a prayer?
THERSITES Ay, the heavens hear me.
     Enter ACHILLES.
ACHILLES Who's there?
PATROCLUS Thersites, my lord.
35 ACHILLES Where? Where? —Art thou come? Why, my cheese,°   *digestive aid*
     my digestion, why hast thou not served thyself in to my table
     so many meals? Come, what's Agamemnon?
THERSITES Thy commander, Achilles. Then tell me, Patro-
     clus, what's Achilles?
40 PATROCLUS Thy lord, Thersites. Then tell me, I pray thee,
     what's thyself?
THERSITES Thy knower, Patroclus. Then tell me, Patroclus,
     what art thou?
PATROCLUS Thou mayst tell that know'st.
45 ACHILLES Oh, tell, tell.
THERSITES I'll decline the whole question:[9] Agamemnon com-
     mands Achilles, Achilles is my lord, I am Patroclus' knower,
     and Patroclus is a fool.
PATROCLUS You rascal!
50 THERSITES Peace, fool, I have not done.
ACHILLES He is a privileged man.[1] Proceed, Thersites.
THERSITES Agamemnon is a fool, Achilles is a fool, Thersites
     is a fool, and, as aforesaid, Patroclus is a fool.
ACHILLES Derive this,° come.   *Show your reasoning*
55 THERSITES Agamemnon is a fool to offer to command Achil-
     les, Achilles is a fool to be commanded of Agamemnon,
     Thersites is a fool to serve such a fool, and Patroclus is a fool
     positive.°   *absolute*
PATROCLUS Why am I a fool?
60 THERSITES Make that demand to the Creator; it suffices me
     thou art. Look you, who comes here?
     Enter [at a distance] AGAMEMNON, ULYSSES, NESTOR,
          DIOMEDES, AJAX, *and* CALCHAS.
ACHILLES Patroclus, I'll speak with nobody. Come in with
     me, Thersites.   *Exit.*
THERSITES Here is such patchery,° such juggling,° and such   *foolery / deception*
65 knavery. All the argument is a cuckold and a whore—a good
     quarrel to draw[2] emulous° factions and bleed to death upon.   *envious*
     Now the dry serpigo° on the subject, and war and lechery   *skin disease*
     confound all!   *[Exit.]*
AGAMEMNON Where is Achilles?
70 PATROCLUS Within his tent, but ill-disposed,° my lord.   *unwell; bad-tempered*
AGAMEMNON Let it be known to him that we are here.
     He shent° our messengers, and we lay by   *shamed*
     Our appertainments,° visiting of him.   *rights of rank*
     Let him be told so, lest perchance he think
75 We dare not move the question of our place°   *assert our authority*
     Or know not what we are.

---

9. I'll recite in order the entire subject under investigation. "The words decline," "Derive" (line 54), and
"positive" (line 58) are all grammatical terms.

1. An acknowledged fool could speak with impunity.
2. Attract to itself, like a magnet; extract, like a
sword; tear to pieces; drag to execution.

PATROCLUS   I shall so say to him.   [*Exit.*]
ULYSSES   We saw him at the opening of his tent;
    He is not sick.
AJAX   Yes, lion-sick,° sick of proud heart. You may call it mel-   *sick with pride*
80 ancholy³ if you will favor the man, but, by my head, it is
    pride. But why? Why? Let him show us the cause. —A word,
    my lord.
           [AJAX *takes* AGAMEMNON *aside.*]
NESTOR   What moves Ajax thus to bay at him?
ULYSSES   Achilles hath inveigled° his fool from him.   *enticed away*
85 NESTOR   Who, Thersites?
ULYSSES   He.
NESTOR   Then will Ajax lack matter,⁴ if he have lost his
    argument.°   *subject matter*
ULYSSES   No, you see he is his argument that has his argu-
90 ment:⁵ Achilles.
NESTOR   All the better; their fraction° is more our wish than   *division*
    their faction.° But it was a strong counsel that a fool could   *joint rebellion*
    disunite.°   *(ironic)*
ULYSSES   The amity that wisdom knits not° folly may easily   *is not created by*
95 untie.   *wisdom*
           Enter PATROCLUS.
    Here comes Patroclus.
NESTOR   No Achilles with him.
ULYSSES   The elephant hath joints, but none for courtesy.⁶
    His legs are legs for necessity, not for flexure.°   *bending*
100 PATROCLUS   Achilles bids me say he is much sorry
    If anything more than your sport and pleasure
    Did move your greatness and this noble state°   *company*
    To call upon him. He hopes it is no other
    But for your health and your digestion sake—
    An after-dinner's breath.°   *exercise*
105 AGAMEMNON   Hear you, Patroclus:
    We are too well acquainted with these answers,
    But his evasion, winged thus swift with scorn,
    Cannot out-fly° our apprehensions.°   *escape / understanding*
    Much attribute° he hath, and much the reason   *reputation*
110 Why we ascribe it to him. Yet all his virtues,
    Not virtuously of his own part beheld,°   *performed by him*
    Do in our eyes begin to lose their gloss—
    Yea, and like fair fruit in an unwholesome dish
    Are like to rot untasted. Go and tell him
115 We came to speak with him, and you shall not sin
    If you do say we think him over-proud
    And under-honest, in self-assumption° greater   *his own opinion*
    Than in the note of judgment. And worthier° than himself   *one(s) worthier*
    Here tends° the savage strangeness° he puts on,   *waits on / aloofness*
120 Disguise the holy strength of their command,

---

3. A fashionable philosophical malady.
4. Something to say; sense; pus.
5. Achilles is the person who is Ajax's argument.
Since Achilles has taken Thersites (who used to be
Ajax's object of derision) as the object of his derision,

Ajax has transferred his scorn from Thersites to
Achilles.
6. The elephant's supposed lack of knee joints made
it resemble a proud, unbowing man.

And underwrite in an observing kind°   submit compliantly to
His humorous predominance[7]—yea, watch
His pettish lines,° his ebbs, his flows, as if   sulky behavior
The passage and whole carriage° of this action   means and ends
125 Rode on his tide. Go tell him this, and add
That if he overhold° his price so much   overestimate
We'll none of him, but let him, like an engine
Not portable, lie under this report:
"Bring action hither; this cannot go to war.
130 A stirring° dwarf we do allowance give   bustling
Before a sleeping giant." Tell him so.
PATROCLUS   I shall, and bring his answer presently.°   [Exit.]   immediately
AGAMEMNON   In second voice° we'll not be satisfied.   By proxy (Patroclus)
We come to speak with him. —Ulysses, enter you.

                                                                    Exit ULYSSES.

135 AJAX   What is he more than another?
AGAMEMNON   No more than what he thinks he is.[8]
AJAX   Is he so much? Do you not think he thinks himself a
better man than I am?
AGAMEMNON   No question.
140 AJAX   Will you subscribe his thought and say he is?
AGAMEMNON   No, noble Ajax. You are as strong, as valiant, as
wise, no less noble, much more gentle, and altogether more
tractable.
AJAX   Why should a man be proud? How doth pride grow? I
145 know not what it is.
AGAMEMNON   Your mind is the clearer, Ajax, and your virtues
the fairer. He that is proud eats up himself; pride is his own
glass,° his own trumpet, his own chronicle, and whatever   its own mirror
praises itself but in the deed devours the deed in the praise.[9]

                         Enter ULYSSES.

150 AJAX   I do hate a proud man as I hate the engendering° of   mating
toads.
NESTOR [aside]   Yet he loves himself; is't not strange?
ULYSSES   Achilles will not to the field tomorrow.
AGAMEMNON   What's his excuse?
ULYSSES   He doth rely on none,
155 But carries on the stream of his dispose°   disposition
Without observance or respect of any,
In will peculiar and in self-admission.[1]
AGAMEMNON   Why will he not upon our fair request
Untent his person and share the air with us?
160 ULYSSES   Things small as nothing, for request's sake only,[2]
He makes important. Possessed° he is with greatness,   Bewitched
And speaks not to himself but with a pride
That quarrels at self-breath.[3] Imagined worth
Holds in his blood such swoll'n and hot discourse

---

7. His idiosyncratic assumption of superiority; the
domination of one particular "humor" (temperament)—
pride.
8. He's the only one with a high opinion of him; he's
worth as much as he thinks he is.
9. Whatever self-praise arises except from silently
performing the noble deed itself destroys the deed by

the act of praising it.
1. In self-will and in acknowledgment of only his
own authority.
2. Merely because they are asked for.
3. And . . . self-breath: Achilles is not even satisfied
with what he himself has to say in praise of his merits; he is too proud to talk even to himself.

165   That twixt his mental and his active parts
    Kingdomed Achilles[4] in commotion° rages   *insurrection*
    And batters 'gainst himself. What should I say?
    He is so plaguy proud that the death-tokens of it[5]
    Cry, "No recovery!"
    AGAMEMNON   Let Ajax go to him.
170   —Dear lord, go you and greet him in his tent;
    'Tis said he holds you well and will be led
    At your request a little from himself.°   *from his self-conceit*
    ULYSSES   O Agamemnon, let it not be so.
    We'll consecrate the steps that Ajax makes
175   When they go from Achilles. Shall the proud lord
    That bastes his arrogance with his own seam[6]
    And never suffers matter° of the world   *the affairs*
    Enter his thoughts, save° such as do revolve   *except*
    And ruminate° himself? Shall he be worshipped   *turn on*
180   Of that° we hold an idol more than he?   *By one who*
    No, this thrice-worthy and right valiant lord
    Must not so stale his palm° nobly acquired,   *sully his honor*
    Nor by my will assubjugate° his merit,   *reduce to subjection*
    As amply titled as Achilles' is,
185   By going to Achilles.
    That were to enlard his fat-already pride
    And add more coals to Cancer[7] when he burns
    With entertaining great Hyperion.°   *the sun*
    This lord go to him? Jupiter forbid,
190   And say in thunder: "Achilles, go to him!"
    NESTOR [*aside*]   Oh, this is well; he rubs the vein of him.°   *stirs up Ajax*
    DIOMEDES [*aside*]   And how his silence drinks up this
        applause.
    AJAX   If I go to him, with my armèd fist
    I'll pash° him o'er the face.   *smash*
    AGAMEMNON   Oh, no, you shall not go.
195   AJAX   An 'a° be proud with me, I'll feeze° his pride.   *If he / take care of*
       Let me go to him.
    ULYSSES   Not for the worth that hangs upon our quarrel.°   *(with Troy)*
    AJAX   A paltry, insolent fellow.
    NESTOR [*aside*]   How he describes himself.
200   AJAX   Can he not be sociable?
    ULYSSES [*aside*]   The raven chides blackness.
    AJAX   I'll let his humors blood.[8]
    AGAMEMNON [*aside*]   He will be the physician that should be
       the patient.
205   AJAX   An all men were o'my mind—
    ULYSSES [*aside*]   Wit would be out of fashion.
    AJAX   'A should not bear it so; 'a should eat swords[9] first. Shall
       pride carry it?
    NESTOR [*aside*]   An 'twould, you'd carry half.

---

4. Achilles' body is imagined as a state at civil war.
5. He is so annoyingly (diseasedly) proud that the fatal signs of plague.
6. Fat; appearance (punning on "seam" as "seem"). Achilles is accused of feeding self-flattery to his already inflated arrogance.
7. And add fuel to the fire. Cancer is the sign of the zodiac that begins on June 21—hence, a symbol of summer heat.
8. I'll cure his illness (pride) by bloodletting, as a doctor would do to get rid of surplus humors.
9. He wouldn't carry on so; he would be defeated in combat (eat his words).

210 ULYSSES [*aside*] 'A would have ten shares.[1]
AJAX I will knead him, I'll make him supple;° he's not yet   *compliant*
    through warm.°   *warm all through*
NESTOR [*aside*] Farce° him with praises—pour in, pour in;   *Stuff; sauce*
    his ambition is dry.°   *thirsty*
215 ULYSSES [*to* AGAMEMNON] My lord, you feed too much on
    this dislike.
NESTOR Our noble general, do not do so.
DIOMEDES You must prepare to fight without Achilles.
ULYSSES Why, 'tis this naming of him° doth him harm.   *(as our sole hope)*
    Here is a man°—but 'tis before his face;°   *(Ajax) / he's present*
    I will be silent.
220 NESTOR   Wherefore should you so?
    He is not emulous,° as Achilles is.   *hungry for praise*
ULYSSES Know the whole world,° he is as valiant.   *May the whole world know*
AJAX A whoreson dog that shall palter° thus with us.   *deal evasively*
    Would he were a Trojan!
225 NESTOR What a vice were it in Ajax now—
ULYSSES If he were proud.
DIOMEDES   Or covetous of praise.
ULYSSES Ay, or surly borne.
DIOMEDES   Or strange,° or self-affected.°   *aloof / egotistical*
ULYSSES [*to* AJAX] Thank the heavens, lord, thou art of sweet
    composure.°   *temperament*
    Praise him that got thee, she that gave thee suck;
230 Famed be thy tutor, and thy parts of nature°   *natural attributes*
    Thrice-famed beyond, beyond all erudition;[2]
    But he that disciplined thy arms to fight,
    Let Mars divide eternity in twain
    And give him half; and for thy vigor,
235 Bull-bearing Milo[3] his addition° yield   *reputation*
    To sinewy Ajax. I will not praise thy wisdom,°   *(ironic)*
    Which, like a bourn, a pale, a shore, confines[4]
    Thy spacious and dilated° parts. Here's Nestor,   *ample; famous*
    Instructed by the antiquary° times;   *ancient*
240 He must, he is, he cannot but be wise.
    But pardon, father Nestor, were your days
    As green[5] as Ajax' and your brain so tempered,°   *composed*
    You should not have the eminence of° him,   *be superior to*
    But be as° Ajax.   *equal to*
AJAX   Shall I call you father?°   *guide*
ULYSSES Ay, my good son.
245 DIOMEDES   Be ruled by him, Lord Ajax.
ULYSSES There is no tarrying here; the hart Achilles
    Keeps thicket.[6] Please it our general°   *(Agamemnon)*
    To call together all his state° of war.   *council*
    Fresh kings° are come to Troy; tomorrow   *Reinforcements*
250 We must with all our main of power° stand fast.   *utmost strength*
    And here's a lord—come knights from east to west°   *the whole world*

1. Probably alluding to the ten shares into which the
assets of Shakespeare's company, the Lord Chamberlain's Men, were divided—hence, everything.
2. Ajax's glory exceeds anything scholars might say
about it. Also, ironic: learning constitutes no part of it.
3. Famous Greek athlete who bore a four-year-old
bull on his shoulders.
4. Which like a boundary, a fence, a shore, marks
the extent of (probably ironic).
5. Young, fresh; immature; gullible.
6. Stays concealed (at home).

And cull their flower,[7] Ajax shall cope° the best.   *match*
AGAMEMNON   Go we to counsel. Let Achilles sleep;
Light boats may sail swift, though greater hulks draw
   deep.[8]   *Exeunt.*

3.1 (Q 3.1)

Music sounds within. Enter PANDARUS *and a*
SERVANT[, *meeting*].

PANDARUS   Friend, you, pray you, a word: do not you follow
   the young Lord Paris?
SERVANT   Ay, sir, when he goes before me.
PANDARUS   You depend upon him,° I mean.   *serve him*
5 SERVANT   Sir, I do depend upon the Lord.°   *God; Paris*
PANDARUS   You depend upon a noble gentleman; I must needs
   praise him.
SERVANT   The Lord be praised!
PANDARUS   You know me, do you not?
10 SERVANT   Faith, sir, superficially.
PANDARUS   Friend, know me better: I am the Lord Pandarus.
SERVANT   I hope I shall know your honor better.[1]
PANDARUS   I do desire it.
SERVANT   You are in the state of grace?[2]
15 PANDARUS   Grace? Not so, friend; "honor" and "lordship" are
   my titles. What music is this?
SERVANT   I do but partly know, sir; it is music in parts.
PANDARUS   Know you the musicians?
SERVANT   Wholly, sir.
20 PANDARUS   Who play they to?
SERVANT   To the hearers, sir.
PANDARUS   At whose pleasure, friend?
SERVANT   At mine, sir, and theirs that love music.
PANDARUS   Command, I mean, friend.
25 SERVANT   Who shall I command, sir?
PANDARUS   Friend, we understand not one another: I am too
   courtly, and thou art too cunning. At whose request do
   these men play?
SERVANT   That's to't° indeed, sir. Marry, sir, at the request of   *to the point*
30 Paris, my lord, who's there in person, with him the mortal°   *living; fatal*
   Venus, the heart-blood of beauty, love's invisible soul.°   *(made visible)*
PANDARUS   Who, my cousin Cressida?
SERVANT   No, sir, Helen—could you not find out that by her
   attributes?
35 PANDARUS   It should seem, fellow, that thou hast not seen the
   lady Cressida. I come to speak with Paris from the Prince
   Troilus; I will make a complimental° assault upon him, for   *courteous*
   my business seethes.°   *boils; is pressing*

---

7. And choose their best men.
8. We will progress more swiftly without Achilles (perhaps alluding to the success of "light" English ships
against the "greater hulks" of the Spanish Armada).
Doubly ironic: Ajax is hardly a "light boat," and the
Greeks are associated with "deep-drawing" boats in
the Prologue (line 12).
3.1 Location: Troy's palace.
1. I hope to get to know you better. I hope to learn of
an improvement in your spiritual health. The double

meaning here is typical of the servant's playful
mockery of Pandarus, which partly contrasts Pandarus's secular concerns with more important, albeit
anachronistic, Christian ones.
2. Theologically (deliberately misunderstanding Pandarus's "desire" in line 13 as a wish for moral improvement rather than social acquaintance). Pandarus
proceeds to misunderstand "grace" as the status of
being called "your grace" (a duke's title).

SERVANT Sodden business? There's a stewed[3] phrase indeed.
Enter PARIS *and* HELEN[, *with Attendants*].

40 PANDARUS Fair be to you, my lord, and to all this fair company. Fair desires in all fair measure fairly guide them— especially to you, fair Queen: fair thoughts be your fair pillow.

HELEN Dear lord, you are full of fair words.

45 PANDARUS You speak your fair pleasure, sweet Queen. Fair prince, here is good broken music.[4]

PARIS You have broke° it, cousin,[5] and by my life you shall   *interrupted*
make it whole again; you shall piece it out° with a piece of   *repair it*
your performance.° —Nell, he is full of harmony.   *performed by you*

50 PANDARUS Truly, lady, no.

HELEN O sir!

PANDARUS Rude,° in sooth; in good sooth, very rude.   *Unskilled; unmusical*

PARIS Well said, my lord; well, you say so in fits.[6]

PANDARUS I have business to my lord, dear Queen. —My lord,
55 will you vouchsafe me a word?

HELEN Nay, this shall not hedge° us out; we'll hear you sing,   *keep*
certainly.

PANDARUS Well, sweet Queen, you are pleasant with° me.   *teasing*
But marry, thus, my lord: my dear lord and most esteemed
60 friend, your brother Troilus—

HELEN My lord Pandarus, honey-sweet lord—

PANDARUS Go to, sweet Queen, go to! —commends himself most affectionately to you.

HELEN You shall not bob° us out of our melody. If you do, our   *swindle*
65 melancholy[7] upon your head.

PANDARUS Sweet Queen, sweet Queen, that's a sweet Queen, i'faith—

HELEN And to make a sweet lady sad is a sour offense.

PANDARUS Nay, that shall not serve your turn, that shall it
70 not in truth, la. Nay, I care not for such words, no, no.
—And, my lord, he desires you that, if the King call for him
at supper, you will make his excuse.

HELEN My lord Pandarus?

PANDARUS What says my sweet Queen, my very, very sweet
75 Queen?

PARIS What exploit's in hand? Where sups he tonight?

HELEN Nay, but my lord—

PANDARUS What says my sweet Queen? My cousin will fall out with you.[8]

80 HELEN [*to* PARIS] You must not° know where he sups.   *are not supposed to*

PARIS With my disposer[9] Cressida.

PANDARUS No, no, no such matter; you are wide.° Come, your   *off target*
disposer° is sick.   *(Cressida)*

---

3. "Stewed" (overdone, literally and metaphorically; associated with stews, or brothels) puns on "sodden," which means "boiled" (picking up on "seethes," line 38); is stupid; is drunk; is being treated for venereal disease.
4. Music for instruments of different kinds—for example, strings and woodwind.
5. Kinsman (used especially by sovereigns to noblemen, whether or not related).
6. In sections of music (fits and starts; spasms of laughter).
7. May our "melancholy" mood (supposedly cured by music) be.
8. *What . . . you:* If you (Helen) keep interrupting, my "cousin" Paris (as in line 47) will be angry with you; if you keep inquiring about private affairs, my "cousin" Cressida will be angry with you.
9. Of uncertain meaning but perhaps suggesting that Paris is at Cressida's service, that Cressida can do what she likes with Troilus and Paris.

PARIS Well, I'll make excuse.°   *(for Troilus)*
85 PANDARUS Ay, good my lord. Why should you say Cressida?
No, your poor disposer's sick.
PARIS I spy[1]—
PANDARUS You spy? What do you spy? *[to an Attendant]*
Come, give me an instrument. Now, sweet Queen—
90 HELEN Why, this is kindly done!
PANDARUS My niece is horribly in love with a thing you have,
sweet Queen.
HELEN She shall have it, my lord, if it be not my lord Paris.
PANDARUS He? No, she'll none of him; they two are twain.°   *estranged*
95 HELEN Falling in[2] after falling out° may make them three.   *arguing*
PANDARUS Come, come, I'll hear no more of this. I'll sing you
a song now.
HELEN Ay, ay, prithee now; by my troth, sweet lord, thou hast
a fine forehead.[3]
100 PANDARUS Ay, you may, you may.°   *(go on)*
HELEN Let thy song be love: "This love will undo us all."
O Cupid, Cupid, Cupid!
PANDARUS Love? Ay, that it shall,° i'faith.   *(be); (undo us)*
PARIS Ay, good now:° "Love, love, nothing but love . . ."   *please*
105 PANDARUS In good troth, it° begins so.   *the song; love*
[*Sings.*] Love, love, nothing but love, still° more: *always*
For oh, love's bow shoots buck and doe.°   *male and female*
The shaft° confounds, not that it wounds,   *arrow; penis*
But tickles still the sore.[4]
110 These lovers cry "Oh! Oh!" they die;°   *perish; have an orgasm*
Yet that which seems the wound to kill°   *mortal wound*
Doth turn "Oh! Oh!" to "Ha ha he!",[5]
So dying love lives still.
"Oh! Oh!" awhile, but "Ha ha ha!"
115 "Oh! Oh!" groans out for "Ha ha ha!"
—Heigh-ho!
HELEN In love, i'faith, to the very tip of the nose.
PARIS He eats nothing but doves,° love, and that breeds hot   *emblem of true love*
blood, and hot blood begets hot thoughts, and hot thoughts
120 beget hot deeds, and hot deeds is love.
PANDARUS Is this the generation° of love: hot blood, hot   *genealogy; source*
thoughts, and hot deeds? Why, they are vipers. Is love a gen-
eration of vipers?[6]
[*Alarum.*]
Sweet lord, who's afield today?
125 PARIS Hector, Deiphobus, Helenus, Antenor, and all the gal-
lantry of Troy. I would fain have° armed today, but my Nell   *like to have*
would not have it so. How chance my brother Troilus went
not?
HELEN He hangs the lip° at something. —You know all, Lord   *looks despondent*
130 Pandarus.
PANDARUS Not I, honey-sweet Queen. I long to hear how they
sped today. —You'll remember your brother's excuse?

1. I understand what's going on between Troilus and
Cressida (alluding to a child's game).
2. "Falling in" sexually, so as to produce a child.
3. Impudence; modesty; sign of male beauty; hint of
cuckoldry.

4. Wound; four-year-old buck.
5. Turns pain to joy; turns ecstasy to derision.
6. Anachronistic allusion to a biblical phrase—for
instance, the "generation of vipers" in Matthew 23:33,
promising damnation.

PARIS   To a hair.°   *Exactly*
PANDARUS   Farewell, sweet Queen.
135 HELEN   Commend me to your niece.
PANDARUS   I will, sweet Queen.   [*Exit.*]
        Sound a retreat.
PARIS   They're come from field. Let us to Priam's hall
        To greet the warriors. Sweet Helen, I must woo you
        To help unarm our Hector. His stubborn buckles
140   With these, your white enchanting fingers, touched,
        Shall more obey than to the edge of steel°   *sword blade*
        Or force of Greekish sinews. You shall do more
        Than all the island kings:° disarm great Hector.   *Greek lords*
HELEN   'Twill make us proud to be his servant, Paris.
145   Yea, what he shall receive of us in duty
        Gives us more palm in° beauty than we have—   *fame for*
        Yea, overshines ourself.
        Sweet, above thought I love thee!⁷   *Exeunt.*

3.2 (Q 3.2)
        Enter PANDARUS *and* TROILUS' MAN[, *meeting*].
PANDARUS   How now, where's thy master? At my cousin
        Cressida's?
TROILUS' MAN   No, sir, he stays for you to conduct him thither.
        Enter TROILUS.
PANDARUS   Oh, here he comes. —How now, how now?
5   TROILUS   Sirrah, walk off.   [*Exit* TROILUS' MAN.]
PANDARUS   Have you seen my cousin?
TROILUS   No, Pandarus. I stalk about her door
        Like a strange° soul upon the Stygian banks,   *newly arrived*
        Staying for waftage.¹ Oh, be thou my Charon
10   And give me swift transportation to those fields²
        Where I may wallow° in the lily-beds   *roll around*
        Proposed for° the deserver. O gentle Pandarus,   *Promised to*
        From Cupid's shoulder pluck his painted° wings   *brightly colored*
        And fly with me to Cressid!
15 PANDARUS   Walk here i'th' orchard;° I'll bring her straight.   *garden*
                                                              Exit.
TROILUS   I am giddy; expectation whirls me round.
        Th'imaginary relish° is so sweet   *pleasant anticipation*
        That it enchants my sense. What will it be
        When that the wat'ry° palates taste indeed   *watering*
20   Love's thrice-repurèd nectar?³ Death, I fear me,
        Swooning destruction, or some joy too fine,°   *exquisite*
        Too subtle-potent, and too sharp in sweetness°   *(musically)*
        For the capacity of my ruder powers.
        I fear it much, and I do fear besides
25   That I shall lose distinction in° my joys,   *power to distinguish among*
        As doth a battle° when they charge on heaps°   *an army / en masse*

---

7. TEXTUAL COMMENT For the different implications of Q's attribution of this line to Paris, where it ends with "her" rather than "thee," see Digital Edition TC 4 (Folio edited text).
3.2 Location: Cressida's garden.
1. Waiting to be ferried across. The dead were car-
ried across the river Styx into the underworld by the ferryman Charon.
2. The Elysian Fields, which were reserved for the blessed dead ("the deserver," line 12).
3. Thrice-purified drink of the gods (giving immortality).

The enemy flying.
    Enter PANDARUS.

PANDARUS   She's making her ready; she'll come straight.° You   *immediately*
   must be witty° now; she does so blush and fetches her wind°   *clever; sane / breath*
30   so short, as if she were 'fraid with a sprite.[4] I'll fetch her. It
   is the prettiest villain;° she fetches her breath so short as a   *peasant (affectionate)*
   new-ta'en° sparrow.   *Exit.*   *just-captured*
TROILUS   Even such a passion doth embrace my bosom:
   My heart beats thicker° than a feverous pulse,   *faster*
35   And all my powers do their bestowing° lose   *function*
   Like vassalage at unawares° encount'ring   *vassals unexpectedly*
   The eye of majesty.
    Enter PANDARUS *and* CRESSIDA[, *veiled*].
PANDARUS   Come, come, what need you blush? Shame's a baby.
   —Here she is now; swear the oaths now to her that you have
40   sworn to me. [CRESSIDA *draws back*.] —What, are you gone
   again? You must be watched ere you be made tame,[5] must
   you? Come your ways, come your ways; an you draw backward we'll put you i'th' thills.[6] —Why do you not speak to
   her? —Come, draw this curtain, and let's see your picture.[7]
45   [*He unveils her.*] Alas, the day! How loath you are to offend
   daylight; an 'twere dark you'd close° sooner. —So, so, rub on,   *agree; unite*
   and kiss the mistress.[8] [TROILUS *kisses her*.] How now, a kiss in
   fee-farm?° Build there, carpenter; the air° is sweet. Nay, you *land tenure / her breath*
   shall fight your hearts out ere I part you, the falcon as the
50   tercel,[9] for° all the ducks i'th' river. Go to, go to.   *I'd bet*
TROILUS   You have bereft me of all words, lady.
PANDARUS   Words pay no debts; give her deeds. But she'll
   bereave you o'th' deeds° too if she call your activity° in ques- *wear you out / virility*
   tion. [*They kiss.*] What, billing° again? Here's "In witness   *kissing*
55   whereof the parties interchangeably[1]—" Come in, come in;
   I'll go get a fire.°   [*Exit.*]   *(for the bedroom)*
CRESSIDA   Will you walk in, my lord?
TROILUS   O Cressida, how often have I wished me thus!
CRESSIDA   Wished, my lord? The gods grant—O my lord—
60 TROILUS   What should they grant? What makes this pretty
   abruption?° What too curious dreg° espies my sweet lady in *pause / speck of dirt*
   the fountain of our love?
CRESSIDA   More dregs than water, if my fears have eyes.
TROILUS   Fears make devils of cherubim;° they never see truly. *predict the worst*
65 CRESSIDA   Blind fear, that seeing° reason leads, finds safer   *clear-sighted*
   footing than blind reason, stumbling without fear. To fear
   the worst oft cures the worse.
TROILUS   Oh, let my lady apprehend no fear; in all Cupid's
   pageant there is presented no monster.
70 CRESSIDA   Nor nothing monstrous neither?
TROILUS   Nothing but our undertakings° when we vow to weep   *promises*

---

4. Frightened by a ghost.
5. Hawks were kept awake at night to tame them.
6. If you back away, we'll back you, like a horse, into
the shafts of a cart.
7. Cressida's face is veiled. Pictures were curtained
for protection against light and dust.
8. Metaphor from the game of bowls: keep on course,

and touch gently the master ball (a small ball at which
bowls were aimed).
9. The female hawk as (eagerly as) the male.
1. A garbled version of a betrothal; also, a contractual legal formula completed by the words "have set
their hands and seals."

seas, live in fire, eat rocks, tame tigers, thinking it harder for
our mistress to devise imposition enough° than for us to   *a big enough challenge*
undergo any difficulty imposed. This is the monstrosity in
75   love, lady: that the will is infinite and the execution confined,
that the desire is boundless and the act° a slave to limit.   *(sex) act*

CRESSIDA   They say all lovers swear more performance than
they are able, and yet reserve an ability that they never perform, vowing more than the perfection of ten° and discharg-   *(lovers)*
80   ing less than the tenth part of one. They that have the voice
of lions and the act of hares—are they not monsters?

TROILUS   Are there such? Such are not we. Praise us as we are
tasted,° allow° us as we prove. Our head shall go bare till   *tested / praise*
merit crown it. No perfection in reversion shall have a praise
85   in present;[2] we will not name desert° before his° birth, and,   *mention merit / its*
being born, his addition° shall be humble. Few words to fair   *title*
faith.[3] Troilus shall be such to Cressid as what envy can say
worst shall be a mock for his truth,[4] and what truth can
speak truest not truer[5] than Troilus.

90 CRESSIDA   Will you walk in, my lord?

        Enter PANDARUS.

PANDARUS   What, blushing still? Have you not done talking
yet?

CRESSIDA   Well, uncle, what folly° I commit I dedicate to you.   *whatever indiscretion*

PANDARUS   I thank you for that. If my lord get a boy of you,
95   you'll give him me. Be true to my lord; if he flinch,° chide   *(sexually)*
me for it.

TROILUS   You know now your hostages:° your uncle's word and   *pledges*
my firm faith.

PANDARUS   Nay, I'll give my word for her too. Our kindred,
100   though they be long ere they are wooed, they are constant
being won. They are burrs, I can tell you—they'll stick where
they are thrown.°   *laid (sexual)*

CRESSIDA   Boldness comes to me now and brings me heart.
Prince Troilus, I have loved you night and day
105   For many weary months.

TROILUS   Why was my Cressid then so hard to win?

CRESSIDA   Hard to seem won; but I was won, my lord,
With the first glance that ever—pardon me:
If I confess much you will play the tyrant.
110   I love you now, but not, till now, so much
But I might master it. In faith, I lie;
My thoughts were like unbridled children grown
Too headstrong for their mother. See, we fools!
Why have I blabbed? Who shall be true to us°   *(women)*
115   When we are so unsecret to ourselves?°   *betray ourselves*
But though I loved you well, I wooed you not,
And yet, good faith, I wished myself a man,
Or that we women had men's privilege
Of speaking first. Sweet, bid me hold my tongue,
120   For in this rapture I shall surely speak

---

2. We won't count our chickens before they're
hatched.
3. Brevity goes with honesty (proverbial).

4. *as . . . truth:* that envy's most malicious comment
on Troilus can only be to mock him for constancy.
5. *not truer:* could not be more reliable.

The thing I shall repent. See, see, your silence,
Coming° in dumbness, from my weakness draws   (forward)
My soul of counsel° from me. Stop my mouth.   most secret thoughts
TROILUS   And shall, albeit sweet music issues thence.
        [*He kisses her.*]
125 PANDARUS   Pretty, i'faith.
CRESSIDA   My lord, I do beseech you, pardon me.
    'Twas not my purpose thus to beg a kiss.
    I am ashamed. O heavens, what have I done?
    For this time will I take my leave, my lord.
130 TROILUS   Your leave, sweet Cressid?
PANDARUS   Leave? An you take leave till tomorrow morning—
CRESSIDA   Pray you, content you.°   be quiet
TROILUS   What offends you, lady?
CRESSIDA   Sir, mine own company.
TROILUS   You cannot shun yourself.
CRESSIDA   Let me go and try.
135   I have a kind of self resides with you,
    But an unkind° self that itself will leave   unnatural
    To be another's fool. Where is my wit?
    I would be gone; I speak I know not what.
TROILUS   Well know they what they speak that speaks so
    wisely.
140 CRESSIDA   Perchance, my lord, I show more craft° than love   cunning
    And fell so roundly° to a large° confession   openly / full
    To angle for° your thoughts. But you are wise,   fish for
    Or else you love not,⁶ for to be wise and love
    Exceeds man's might: that dwells with gods above.
145 TROILUS   Oh, that I thought it could be in a woman—
    As if it can, I will presume in° you—   it to be in
    To feed for aye° her lamp and flames of love,   forever
    To keep her constancy in plight° and youth,   as when first pledged
    Outliving beauty's outward° with a mind   exterior
150   That doth renew swifter than blood° decays;   passion
    Or that persuasion could but thus convince me
    That my integrity and truth to you
    Might be affronted° with the match and weight°   met / same amount
    Of such a winnowed⁷ purity in love—
155   How were I then uplifted! But alas,
    I am as true as truth's simplicity°   truth itself
    And simpler° than the infancy of truth.   more naive
CRESSIDA   In that I'll war° with you.   compete
TROILUS   Oh, virtuous fight
    When right with right wars who shall be most right!
160   True swains in love shall in the world to come
    Approve° their truths by Troilus: when their rhymes,   Attest
    Full of protest,° of oath and big compare,°   protestation / comparison
    Wants° similes, truth tired with iteration°—   Lack / repetition
    As true as steel, as plantage to the moon,⁸
165   As sun to day, as turtle° to her mate,   turtledove

6. Alternative explanations for why he has made no   light chaff).
"large confession" (line 141).   8. Plants were supposed to be affected in growth by
7. Grain is "winnowed" (separated from worthless   the moon.

As iron to adamant,° as earth to th' center[9]— *a magnet*
Yet, after all comparisons of truth,
As truth's authentic author to be cited,
"As true as Troilus" shall crown up the verse
And sanctify the numbers.° *verses*

170 CRESSIDA   Prophet may you be.
If I be false, or swerve a hair from truth,
When time is old and hath forgot itself,
When water drops have worn the stones of Troy,
And blind oblivion swallowed cities up,
175 And mighty states characterless are grated° *are ground up unrecorded*
To dusty nothing, yet let memory,
From false° to false among false maids in love, *falsehood*
Upbraid my falsehood. When they've said, "As false
As air, as water, as wind, as sandy earth,
180 As fox to lamb, as wolf to heifer's calf,
Pard° to the hind, or stepdame to her son"— *Panther; leopard*
Yea, let them say, to stick the heart° of falsehood, *hit the bullseye*
"As false as Cressid."
PANDARUS Go to, a bargain made. Seal it, seal it! I'll be the
185 witness. Here I hold your hand, here my cousin's.[1] If ever
you prove false one to another, since I have taken such pains
to bring you together, let all pitiful goers-between be called
to the world's end after my name: call them all panders. Let
all constant men be Troiluses, all false women Cressids, and
190 all brokers-between° panders. Say "Amen." *pimps*
TROILUS Amen.
CRESSIDA Amen.
PANDARUS Amen. Whereupon I will show you a chamber,
which bed, because it shall not speak of your pretty encoun-
195 ters, press it to death.[2] Away!
                    [*Exeunt* TROILUS *and* CRESSIDA.]
And Cupid grant all tongue-tied maidens° here *male or female virgins*
Bed, chamber, and pander to provide this gear.° *Exit.* *equipment*

3.3 (Q 3.3)
Flourish. Enter ULYSSES, DIOMEDES, NESTOR,
AGAMEMNON, [AJAX,] MENELAUS, *and* CALCHAS.[1]
CALCHAS Now, princes, for the service I have done you
Th'advantage° of the time prompts me aloud *opportunity*
To call for recompense. Appear it° to your mind *Let it appear*
That, through the sight I bear in things to come,
5 I have abandoned Troy, left my possession,° *belongings*
Incurred a traitor's name, exposed myself
From certain and possessed conveniences
To doubtful fortunes, sequest'ring° from me all *divorcing*
That time, acquaintance, custom, and condition° *position*
10 Made tame° and most familiar to my nature, *accustomed*
And here to do you service am become

---

9. The earth's surface to the earth's center, or axis.
1. Taking hands before a witness could be regarded
as a (civil) marriage.
2. Customary punishment for an accused person

who remained silent and would not plead.
3.3 Location: The Greek camp.
1. Calchas is Cressida's father, a Trojan priest siding
with the Greeks.

As new into the world, strange, unacquainted.
I do beseech you, as in way of taste,°   *a foretaste*
To give me now a little benefit

15 Out of those many registered in promise°   *many promised things*
Which you say live to come° in my behalf.   *wait to be fulfilled*

AGAMEMNON   What wouldst thou of us, Trojan? Make
    demand.

CALCHAS   You have a Trojan prisoner called Antenor,
    Yesterday took; Troy holds him very dear.

20 Oft have you—often have you thanks therefore°—   *for it*
Desired my Cressid in right great exchange,²
Whom Troy hath still denied; but this Antenor
I know is such a wrest³ in their affairs
That their negotiations° all must slack,   *affairs of state*

25 Wanting his manage,° and they will almost   *guidance*
Give us a prince of blood,° a son of Priam,   *a royal prince*
In change of° him. Let him be sent, great princes,   *exchange for*
And he shall buy my daughter, and her presence
Shall quite strike off° all service I have done   *annul*
In most accepted° pain.   *willingly undertaken*

30 AGAMEMNON   Let Diomedes bear him,
And bring us Cressid hither. Calchas shall have
What he requests of us. Good Diomed,
Furnish you fairly° for this interchange;   *Completely ready yourself*
Withal° bring word if Hector will tomorrow   *At the same time*

35 Be answered in his challenge. Ajax is ready.

DIOMEDES   This shall I undertake, and 'tis a burden
    Which I am proud to bear.

            Exeunt [DIOMEDES *and* CALCHAS].
      Enter ACHILLES *and* PATROCLUS *in* [*the opening of*]
      their tent.

ULYSSES   Achilles stands i'th' entrance of his tent.
Please it our general to pass strangely° by him,   *aloofly*

40 As if he were forgot; and, princes all,
Lay negligent and loose° regard upon him.   *casual*
I will come last; 'tis like he'll question me
Why such unplausive° eyes are bent, why turned, on him.   *unapproving*
If so, I have derision medicinable°   *health-giving scorn*

45 To use° between your strangeness and his pride   *act as intermediary*
Which his own will shall have desire to drink.
It may do good: pride hath no other glass
To show itself but pride,⁴ for supple knees°   *bowing and scraping*
Feed arrogance and are the proud man's fees.°   *expected reward*

50 AGAMEMNON   We'll execute your purpose and put on
A form° of strangeness as we pass along;   *An appearance*
So do each lord, and either greet him not
Or else disdainfully, which shall shake him more
Than if not looked on. I will lead the way.

     [*They file past Achilles' tent.*]

55 ACHILLES   What, comes the general to speak with me?
You know my mind: I'll fight no more 'gainst Troy.

---

2. In return for someone important.
3. Tuning key for a stringed instrument (hence,
probably related to "slack," line 24); peg for tighten-

ing a surgical ligature.
4. *pride . . . pride:* a proud person recognizes excessive pride only when shown it in others.

AGAMEMNON What says Achilles? Would he aught with us?

NESTOR Would you, my lord, aught with the general?

ACHILLES No.

60 NESTOR Nothing, my lord.

AGAMEMNON The better. [*Exeunt* AGAMEMNON *and* NESTOR.]

ACHILLES Good day, good day.

MENELAUS How do you, how do you? [*Exit.*]

ACHILLES What? Does the cuckold scorn me?

65 AJAX How now, Patroclus?

ACHILLES Good morrow, Ajax.

AJAX Ha?

ACHILLES Good morrow.

AJAX Ay, and good next day too. *Exit.*

[ULYSSES *remains behind, reading.*]

70 ACHILLES What mean these fellows? Know they not
　　　　　Achilles?

PATROCLUS They pass by strangely; they were used to bend,
　　　To send their smiles before them to Achilles,
　　　To come as humbly as they used° to creep   　　　　　*are accustomed*
　　　To holy altars.

ACHILLES 　　　　　What, am I poor° of late?   　　　　　*insignificant*

75 'Tis certain, greatness, once fall'n out with fortune,
　　　Must fall out with men too. What the declined° is   　　　*man who has sunk in life*
　　　He shall as soon read in the eyes of others
　　　As feel in his own fall, for men, like butterflies,
　　　Show not their mealy° wings but to the summer;   　　　　　*powdery*

80 And not a man,° for being simply man,   　　　　　*no man*
　　　Hath any honor but honored for⁵ those honors
　　　That are without° him, as place, riches, and favor⁶—   　　　*external to*
　　　Prizes of accident° as oft as merit,   　　　　　*that come by chance*
　　　Which, when they fall, as being slippery standers,°   　　　*on an uncertain base*

85 The love that leaned on them, as slippery too,
　　　Doth one° pluck down another, and together   　　　　　*The one doth*
　　　Die in the fall. But 'tis not so with me:
　　　Fortune and I are friends. I do enjoy
　　　At ample point° all that I did possess,   　　　　　*Fully*

90 Save° these men's looks, who do, methinks, find out   　　　*Except*
　　　Something not worth in me such rich beholding°   　　　　　*attention*
　　　As they have often given. Here is Ulysses;
　　　I'll interrupt his reading.
　　　—How now, Ulysses?

ULYSSES 　　　　　Now, great Thetis' son!

ACHILLES What are you reading?

95 ULYSSES 　　　　　A strange fellow here
　　　Writes me that man, how dearly ever parted,°   　　　*however valuably endowed*
　　　How much in having, or without or in,⁷
　　　Cannot make boast to have that which he hath,
　　　Nor feels not what he owes,° but by reflection°—   　　　*owns / how others respond*

100 As when his virtues, shining upon others,
　　　Heat them, and they retort° that heat again   　　　　　*cast back*
　　　To the first giver.

ACHILLES 　　　　　This is not strange, Ulysses.

---

5. *but honored for:* except.
6. Position, wealth, and popularity (or looks).

7. However much he possesses, either externally or internally.

The beauty that is borne here in the face
The bearer knows not, but commends itself,
105   Not going from itself, but eye to eye opposed,
Salutes each other with each other's form;[8]
For speculation° turns not to itself   *sight*
Till it hath traveled and is mirrored there,
Where it may see itself. This is not strange at all.
110 ULYSSES   I do not strain at° the position°—   *question / thesis*
It is familiar—but at the author's drift,
Who in his circumstance expressly° proves   *in detail explicitly*
That no man is the lord of anything,
Though in and of him there is much consisting,°   *value*
115   Till he communicate his parts° to others;   *qualities*
Nor doth he of himself know them for aught°   *as valuable*
Till he behold them formed in th'applause
Where they are extended, who° like an arch° reverb'rate   *(the applauders) / a vault*
The voice again, or, like a gate of steel
120   Fronting° the sun, receives and renders back   *Facing*
His figure° and his heat. I was much rapt in this,   *Its appearance*
And apprehended here immediately
The unknown Ajax. Heavens, what a man is there!
A very horse that has he knows not what.°   *doesn't know himself*
125   Nature, what things there are
Most abject in regard and dear in use;°   *Despised but useful*
What things again most dear in the esteem
And poor in worth! Now shall we see tomorrow
An act that very° chance doth throw upon him.   *pure*
130   Ajax renowned? O heavens, what some men do,
While some men leave to do!°   *leave undone*
How some men° creep in° skittish Fortune's hall   *(like Ajax) / sneak into*
Whiles others play the idiots in her eyes;[9]
How one man° eats into another's° pride   *(Ajax) / (Achilles')*
135   While pride is fasting in his wantonness![1]
To see these Grecian lords—why, even already
They clap the lubber° Ajax on the shoulder   *lout*
As if his foot were on brave Hector's breast
And great Troy shrinking.°   *cowering; declining*
ACHILLES   I do believe it,
140   For they passed by me as misers do by beggars,
Neither gave to me good word nor look.
What, are my deeds forgot?
ULYSSES   Time hath, my lord, a wallet at° his back   *satchel on*
Wherein he puts alms for oblivion,
145   A great-sized monster[2] of ingratitudes.
Those scraps are good deeds past
Which are devoured as fast as they are made,
Forgot as soon as done. Perseverance, dear my lord,
Keeps honor bright. To have done° is to hang   *rely on past deeds*

---

8. *but commends . . . form:* unless it commends itself (to others), since it is unable to leave itself, but two eyes (in two people), looking at each other, can show both people their images.
9. While others (like Achilles) foolishly squander the opportunity provided by Fortune's attention.

1. While the second man in effect starves his pride, and hence his reputation, through his conceitedness.
2. *alms for oblivion:* feats that won't be remembered. Traditionally, if you wore your satchel behind you, it contained your vices, which you in this way forgot. *monster:* time or, more likely, oblivion.

150	Quite out of fashion, like a rusty mail,°	coat of armor
	In monumental mock'ry.° Take the instant way,	a useless monument
	For honor travels in a strait so narrow	
	Where one but goes abreast;° keep then the path,	must go single file
	For emulation hath a thousand sons	
155	That one by one pursue. If you give way	
	Or hedge aside from the direct forthright,°	straightforward path
	Like to an entered tide° they all rush by	a tide that has entered
	And leave you hindmost;	
	Or like a gallant horse fall'n in first rank	
160	Lie there for pavement to the abject rear,°	worthless rearguard
	O'er-run and trampled on. Then what they do in present,	
	Though less than yours in past, must o'er-top yours;	
	For Time is like a fashionable host	
	That slightly shakes his parting guest by th' hand	
165	And, with his arms outstretched as he would° fly,	as if he wanted to
	Grasps in the comer. The welcome ever smiles,	
	And farewells goes out sighing. Oh, let not virtue seek	
	Remuneration for the thing it was,	
	For beauty, wit,	
170	High birth, vigor of bone,° desert in service,°	strength / worthy service
	Love, friendship, charity are subjects all	
	To envious and calumniating Time.	
	One touch of nature° makes the whole world kin,°	natural fault / similar
	That all with one consent praise newborn gauds,°	toys; (pun on "gods")
175	Though they are made and molded of things past,	
	And give to dust that is a little gilt°	gilded
	More laud than gilt o'er-dusted.°	older treasures
	The present eye praises the present object.	
	Then marvel not, thou great and complete man,	
180	That all the Greeks begin to worship Ajax,	
	Since things in motion sooner catch the eye	
	Than what not stirs. The cry° went out on thee,	approval
	And still it might, and yet it may again,	
	If thou wouldst not entomb thyself alive	
185	And case° thy reputation in thy tent,	shut up
	Whose glorious deeds but in these fields of late	
	Made emulous missions 'mongst the gods themselves[3]	
	And drove great Mars to faction.°	to take sides

ACHILLES   Of this my privacy
   I have strong reasons.

ULYSSES   But 'gainst your privacy

190	The reasons are more potent and heroical.	
	'Tis known, Achilles, that you are in love	
	With one of Priam's daughters.°	(Polyxena)

ACHILLES   Ha, known?

ULYSSES   Is that a wonder?

195	The providence that's in a watchful state[4]	
	Knows almost every grain of Pluto's gold,[5]	
	Finds bottom in th'uncomprehensive° deeps,	unimaginable

---

3. Caused the gods to join the fight on both sides in
an effort to match Achilles.
4. Government foresight is compared to divine

"providence"—perhaps ironically.
5. That is, the gold of Pluto, god of the underworld
(regularly identified with Plutus, god of wealth).

Keeps place with thought,° and, almost like the gods,   *Stays on top of things*
Do thoughts unveil in their dumb cradles.[6]
200   There is a mystery (with whom relation°   *report*
Durst never meddle) in the soul of state
Which hath an operation more divine
Than breath or pen can give expressure° to.   *expression*
All the commerce° that you have had with Troy   *dealings*
205   As perfectly is ours as yours,[7] my lord.
And better would it fit Achilles much
To throw down° Hector than Polyxena.   *(in war); (in love)*
But it must grieve young Pyrrhus,° now at home,   *(Achilles' son)*
When Fame shall in our islands sound her trump,
210   And all the Greekish girls shall tripping sing:
"Great Hector's sister did Achilles win,
But our great Ajax bravely beat down him!"°   *(Hector)*
Farewell, my lord. I as your lover° speak;   *good friend*
The fool slides o'er the ice that you should break.[8]   [*Exit.*]
215 PATROCLUS   To this effect, Achilles, have I moved you.
A woman impudent° and mannish grown   *immodest*
Is not more loathed than an effeminate° man   *cowardly*
In time of action. I stand condemned for this;
They think my little stomach to° the war   *appetite for*
220   And your great love to me restrains you thus.
Sweet, rouse yourself, and the weak wanton Cupid
Shall from your neck unloose his amorous fold,°   *embrace*
And, like a dewdrop from the lion's mane,
Be shook to airy air.
225 ACHILLES   Shall Ajax fight with Hector?
PATROCLUS   Ay, and perhaps receive much honor by him.
ACHILLES   I see my reputation is at stake;
My fame is shrewdly gored.°   *severely wounded*
PATROCLUS   Oh, then beware;
Those wounds heal ill that men do give themselves.
230   Omission to do what is necessary
Seals a commission to a blank of danger,[9]
And danger, like an ague, subtly taints
Even then when we sit idly in the sun.[1]
ACHILLES   Go call Thersites hither, sweet Patroclus.
235   I'll send the fool to Ajax and desire him
T'invite the Trojan lords after the combat
To see us here unarmed. I have a woman's longing,
An appetite that I am sick withal,°   *with*
To see great Hector in his weeds° of peace,   *garments*
240   To talk with him and to behold his visage,
Even to my full of view.°   *in full view*
       Enter THERSITES.
          A labor saved.
THERSITES   A wonder.

---

6. *Do . . . cradles:* Discovers thoughts before they are spoken.
7. Is as well known to us (the other Greek leaders) as to you.
8. Perhaps: Ajax (the fool) can get away with what would be damaging to you; or, Ajax is engaged in superficial action, whereas only you can initiate real combat.
9. Gives danger free rein (literally, provides danger with a blank warrant to fill in as it pleases).
1. *danger . . . sun:* danger, like a fever, insidiously weakens (causes shivering) even when one is sitting in the sun. *ague:* fever; chills.

ACHILLES What?

THERSITES Ajax goes up and down the field, asking for
245 himself.[2]

ACHILLES How so?

THERSITES He must° fight singly tomorrow with Hector, and   is to
is so prophetically proud of an heroical cudgeling° that he   (by Hector)
raves in saying nothing.

250 ACHILLES How can that be?

THERSITES Why, he stalks up and down like a peacock, a
stride and a stand;° ruminates like an hostess that hath no   walking, then stopping
arithmetic but her brain to set down her reckoning;[3] bites
his lip with a politic regard,° as who should say, "There were   judicious expression
255 wit in his head, an 'twould out"°—and so there is, but it lies if it would only come out
as coldly in him as fire in a flint, which will not show with-
out knocking.° The man's undone forever, for if Hector   striking (into flame)
break not his neck i'th' combat he'll break't himself in vain-
glory. He knows not me; I said, "Good morrow, Ajax," and he
260 replies, "Thanks, Agamemnon." What think you of this man
that takes me for the general? He's grown a very land-fish,°   unnatural creature
languageless, a monster. A plague of opinion! A man may
wear it on both sides like a leather jerkin.[4]

ACHILLES Thou must be my ambassador to him, Thersites.

265 THERSITES Who, I? Why, he'll answer nobody. He professes
not answering;° speaking is for beggars. He wears his tongue   refuses to respond
in 's arms. I will put on° his presence. Let Patroclus make   imitate
his demands to me; you shall see the pageant of Ajax.

ACHILLES To him, Patroclus. Tell him I humbly desire the val-
270 iant Ajax to invite the most valorous Hector to come unarmed
to my tent, and to procure safe-conduct for his person of° the   for Hector from
magnanimous and most illustrious six-or-seven-times-
honored captain-general of the Grecian army, Agamemnon,
et cetera. Do this.

275 PATROCLUS Jove bless great Ajax!

THERSITES Hum!

PATROCLUS I come from the worthy Achilles—

THERSITES Ha?

PATROCLUS Who most humbly desires you to invite Hector to
280 his tent—

THERSITES Hum!

PATROCLUS And to procure safe-conduct from Agamemnon.

THERSITES Agamemnon?

PATROCLUS Ay, my lord.

285 THERSITES Ha?

PATROCLUS What say you to't?

THERSITES God b'wi' you,° with all my heart.   (dismissive)

PATROCLUS Your answer, sir.

THERSITES If tomorrow be a fair day, by eleven o'clock it will
290 go one way or other; howsoever, he shall pay for me ere° he   pay dearly before
has me.

---

2. Punning on "Ajax" and "a jakes" (a toilet), the point
presumably being that Ajax is so terrified by battle, he
cannot help relieving himself.
3. Like the hostess at an inn whose mathematical

ineptitude makes it hard for her to work out the bill.
4. A plague on conceit (or reputation)! One can wear
it either way (conceit or reputation) like a reversible
jacket (but it's still the same pride).

PATROCLUS Your answer, sir.

THERSITES Fare you well, with all my heart.

ACHILLES Why, but he is not in this tune,° is he?   *mood*

295 THERSITES No, but he's out o'tune thus. What music will be
in him when Hector has knocked out his brains I know not,
but I am sure none, unless the fiddler Apollo get his sinews
to make catlings⁵ on.

ACHILLES Come, thou shalt bear a letter to him straight.

300 THERSITES Let me carry another to his horse, for that's the
more capable° creature.   *intelligent*

ACHILLES My mind is troubled like a fountain stirred,
And I myself see not the bottom of it.

                    [*Exeunt* ACHILLES *and* PATROCLUS.]

THERSITES Would the fountain of your mind were clear

305 again, that I might water an ass at it. I had rather be a tick in
a sheep than such a valiant ignorance.°   [*Exit.*]   *puffed-up fool*

4.1 (Q 4.1)

Enter at one door AENEAS *with a torch, at another*
PARIS, DEIPHOBUS, *Antenor,* DIOMEDES *the Grecian,*
with torches.

PARIS See, ho! Who is that there?

DEIPHOBUS It is the Lord Aeneas.

AENEAS Is the Prince there in person?
Had I so good occasion to lie long

5 As you, Prince Paris, nothing but heavenly business
Should rob my bedmate of my company.

DIOMEDES That's my mind too. Good morrow, Lord Aeneas.

PARIS A valiant Greek, Aeneas; take his hand.
Witness the process of your speech¹ wherein

10 You told how Diomed, in a whole week by days,°   *every day*
Did haunt you in the field.

AENEAS   Health to you, valiant sir,
During all question of° the gentle truce,   *conversations during*
But when I meet you armed, as black defiance
As heart can think or courage execute.

15 DIOMEDES The one and other Diomed embraces.
Our bloods are now in calm, and so long, health;
But when contention and occasion meets,°   *it's time to fight*
By Jove, I'll play the hunter for thy life
With all my force, pursuit, and policy.°   *cunning*

20 AENEAS And thou shalt hunt a lion that will fly
With his face backward.² In humane gentleness,
Welcome to Troy. Now, by Anchises' life,
Welcome indeed! By Venus'³ hand, I swear
No man alive can love in such a sort°   *to such an extent*

25 The thing he means to kill more excellently.

DIOMEDES We sympathize.° Jove, let Aeneas live—   *feel the same*
If to my sword his fate be not the glory—

---

5. Instrument strings made of catgut.
4.1 Location: A street in Troy.
1. *Witness . . . speech:* As the thrust of your narrative
made clear (that he is valiant).
2. In the imagery of heraldry for chivalric combat, a

lion walking and looking back over his shoulder; also,
Aeneas will still fight even as he retreats.
3. Anchises and Venus, the goddess of love, were
Aeneas's parents.

A thousand complete courses of the sun,
But in mine emulous honor[4] let him die
30 With every joint a wound, and that tomorrow.
AENEAS   We know each other well.
DIOMEDES   We do, and long to know each other worse.
PARIS   This is the most despiteful'st gentle greeting,
The noblest hateful love, that e'er I heard of.
35 —What business, lord, so early?
AENEAS   I was sent for to the King, but why I know not.
PARIS   His purpose meets you:° it was to bring this Greek   *I'll tell you why*
To Calchas' house, and there to render him,
For the enfreed Antenor, the fair Cressid.
40 Let's have your company, or, if you please,
Haste there before us. [*aside to* AENEAS] I constantly° do   *firmly*
   think—
Or rather call my thought a certain knowledge—
My brother Troilus lodges there tonight.
Rouse him and give him note of our approach,
45 With the whole quality° whereof. I fear   *cause*
We shall be much unwelcome.
AENEAS [*aside to* PARIS]   That I assure you.
Troilus had rather Troy were borne to Greece
Than Cressid borne from Troy.
PARIS [*aside to* AENEAS]   There is no help;
The bitter disposition of the time
50 Will have it so. —On, lord; we'll follow you.
AENEAS   Good morrow, all.   *Exit.*
PARIS   And tell me, noble Diomed, faith, tell me true,
Even in the soul of sound good fellowship:
Who in your thoughts merits fair Helen most,
Myself or Menelaus?
55 DIOMEDES   Both alike.
He merits well to have her that doth seek her,
Not making any scruple of her soilure,°   *issue of her dishonor*
With such a hell of pain and world of charge;°   *expense*
And you as well to keep her that defend her,
60 Not palating the taste of° her dishonor,   *Not even tasting*
With such a costly loss of wealth and friends.
He like a puling° cuckold would drink up   *whining*
The lees and dregs of a flat tamèd piece;[5]
You like a lecher out of whorish loins
65 Are pleased to breed out your inheritors.°   *produce your heirs*
Both merits poised,° each weighs no less nor more,   *weighed in the scales*
But he as he: which heavier for a whore?[6]
PARIS   You are too bitter to° your countrywoman.   *(given that Helen is)*
DIOMEDES   She's bitter to her country. Hear me, Paris:
70 For every false drop in her bawdy veins
A Grecian's life hath sunk; for every scruple°   *tiny unit of weight*
Of her contaminated carrion° weight   *putrid*
A Trojan hath been slain. Since she could speak
She hath not given so many good words breath

4. If his death will increase my honor.   6. But one the same as the other: which more deserves
5. Of a stale insipid (penetrated) cask of wine (woman).   (is made sadder by) the whore?

75   As for her Greeks and Trojans suffered death.
      PARIS   Fair Diomed, you do as chapmen° do: *merchants*
          Dispraise the thing that you desire to buy.
          But we in silence hold this virtue well:
          We'll not commend what we intend to sell.[7]
80   Here lies our way.   *Exeunt.*

4.2a (Q 4.2)

Enter TROILUS *and* CRESSIDA.

TROILUS   Dear, trouble not yourself; the morn is cold.
CRESSIDA   Then, sweet my lord, I'll call mine uncle down.
      He shall unbolt the gates.
TROILUS   Trouble him not.
      To bed, to bed. Sleep kill those pretty eyes
5   And give as soft attachment° to thy senses   *imprisonment*
      As infants empty of all thought.
CRESSIDA   Good morrow, then.
TROILUS   I prithee now, to bed.
CRESSIDA   Are you aweary of me?
TROILUS   O Cressida! But that the busy day,
10   Waked by the lark, hath roused the ribald° crows,   *offensively noisy*
      And dreaming night will hide our eyes no longer,
      I would not from thee.
CRESSIDA   Night hath been too brief.
TROILUS   Beshrew the witch! With venomous wights[1] she
          stays
      As hideously as hell, but flies° the grasps of love   *flees*
15   With wings more momentary-swift than thought.
      You will catch cold and curse me.
CRESSIDA   Prithee, tarry; you men will never tarry.
      O foolish Cressid! I might have still held off,
      And then you would have tarried. —Hark, there's one up.
20   PANDARUS *(within)* What's° all the doors open here?   *Why are*
TROILUS   It is your uncle.
                Enter PANDARUS.
CRESSIDA   A pestilence on him! Now will he be mocking;
      I shall have such a life!
PANDARUS   How now, how now? How go° maidenheads? Hear   *What's the price of*
25   you, maid: where's my cousin Cressid?[2]
CRESSIDA   Go hang yourself, you naughty mocking uncle.
      You bring me to do°—and then you flout me too.   *have sex*
PANDARUS   To do what, to do what? Let her say what. What
          have I brought you to do?
30   CRESSIDA   Come, come, beshrew° your heart; you'll ne'er be   *curses on*
          good,
      Nor suffer others.°   *let others be good*

---

7. Possibly: we don't intend to bargain for Helen and so won't praise her. But this is not what Paris says. If Diomed belittles Helen because he wants to buy her back (line 77), Paris as potential seller ought to negotiate by praising her. But he won't praise what he's trying to sell (line 79). The problem in interpreting this passage is that he won't consider giving, or selling, Helen back.

4.2a Location: Cressida's house.
1. Curse the night! With evil people (who are hateful to one another).
2. Pandarus pretends not to recognize Cressida, now that she is no longer a virgin. It is possible that he addresses her as "maid" because she is wearing a veil, which suggests a modesty appropriate to virgins.

PANDARUS Ha, ha! Alas, poor wretch. Ah, poor *chipochia*°— *clitoris; vagina*
has't not slept tonight? Would he not, a naughty man, let it
sleep? A bugbear° take him! *goblin*
35 CRESSIDA Did not I tell you? Would he were knocked i'th'
head.° *killed*
One knocks.
Who's that at door? Good uncle, go and see.
—My lord, come you again into my chamber.
You smile and mock me, as if I meant naughtily.
TROILUS Ha, ha!
40 CRESSIDA Come, you are deceived; I think of no such thing.
Knock.
How earnestly they knock! Pray you, come in.
I would not for half Troy have you seen here.
Exeunt [TROILUS *and* CRESSIDA].
PANDARUS Who's there? What's the matter? Will you beat
down the door? How now, what's the matter?
[*Enter* AENEAS.]
45 AENEAS Good morrow, lord, good morrow.
PANDARUS Who's there? My lord Aeneas? By my troth, I knew
you not. What news with you so early?
AENEAS Is not Prince Troilus here?
PANDARUS Here? What should he do here?
50 AENEAS Come, he is here, my lord; do not deny him. It doth
import° him much to speak with me. *concern*
PANDARUS Is he here, say you? 'Tis more than I know, I'll be
sworn. For my own part, I came in late. What should he do
here?
55 AENEAS Whoa, nay then! Come, come, you'll do him wrong
ere you're ware.° You'll be so true to him to be false to him.° *aware / as to harm him*
Do not you know of him, but yet go fetch him hither. Go.
[*Exit* PANDARUS.][3]
Enter TROILUS.
TROILUS How now, what's the matter?
AENEAS My lord, I scarce have leisure to salute you,
60 My matter is so rash.° There is at hand *urgent*
Paris your brother, and Deiphobus,
The Grecian Diomed, and our Antenor
Delivered to us, and for him° forthwith, *(Antenor)*
Ere the first sacrifice, within this hour,
65 We must give up to Diomed's hand
The lady Cressida.
TROILUS Is it concluded so?
AENEAS By Priam and the general state° of Troy. *council*
They are at hand and ready to effect it.
TROILUS How my achievements mock me!
70 I will go meet them. And, my lord Aeneas,
We° met by chance—you did not find me here. *(Pretend that) we*
AENEAS Good, good, my lord; the secrets of nature
Have not more gift in taciturnity. *Exeunt.*

---

3. Editors usually keep him on and have Cressida enter alone at what is the beginning of 4.2b in this edition.

4.2b (Q 4.2)[1]

Enter PANDARUS *and* CRESSIDA.

PANDARUS   Is't possible? No sooner got but lost? The devil
take Antenor! The young prince will go mad. A plague upon
Antenor! I would they had broke 's neck.

CRESSIDA   How now? What's the matter? Who was here?

5   PANDARUS   Ah, ah!

CRESSIDA   Why sigh you so profoundly? Where's my lord?
Gone? Tell me, sweet uncle, what's the matter?

PANDARUS   Would I were as deep under the earth as I am
above.

10   CRESSIDA   O the gods, what's the matter?

PANDARUS   Prithee, get thee in. Would thou hadst ne'er been
born! I knew thou wouldst be his death. Oh, poor gentleman. A plague upon Antenor!

CRESSIDA   Good uncle, I beseech you, on my knees I beseech

15   you: what's the matter?

PANDARUS   Thou must be gone, wench, thou must be gone.
Thou art changed° for Antenor; thou must to thy father and   exchanged
be gone from Troilus. 'Twill be his death, 'twill be his bane;
he cannot bear it.

20   CRESSIDA   O you immortal gods, I will not go!

PANDARUS   Thou must.

CRESSIDA   I will not, uncle. I have forgot my father.
I know no touch of consanguinity—
No kin, no love, no blood, no soul so near me

25   As the sweet Troilus. O you gods divine,
Make Cressid's name the very crown° of falsehood   height
If ever she leave Troilus. Time, force, and death,
Do to this body what extremity you can,
But the strong base and building of my love

30   Is as the very center of the earth,
Drawing all things to it. I will go in and weep—

PANDARUS   Do, do.

CRESSIDA   Tear my bright hair and scratch my praisèd
cheeks,
Crack my clear voice with sobs, and break my heart

35   With sounding "Troilus." I will not go from Troy.   *Exeunt.*

4.3 (Q 4.3)

Enter PARIS, TROILUS, AENEAS, DEIPHOBUS, *Antenor,*
and DIOMEDES.

PARIS   It is great morning,° and the hour prefixed°   broad daylight / arranged
Of her delivery to this valiant Greek
Comes fast upon. Good my brother Troilus,
Tell you the lady what she is to do
And haste her to the purpose.

5   TROILUS   Walk into her house.
[*aside to* PARIS] I'll bring her to the Grecian presently,°   immediately
And to his hand, when I deliver her,

4.2b Location: Scene continues.
1. Textual Comment For the rationale behind the
partial scene division here, the thematic implica-

tions, and the difference from Q, see Digital Edition
TC 5 (Folio edited text).
4.3 Location: Outside Cressida's house.

Think it an altar, and thy brother Troilus
A priest there off'ring to it his heart.

10 PARIS [*aside to* TROILUS] I know what 'tis to love,
And would,° as I shall pity, I could help.   *wish*
—Please you walk in, my lords.   *Exeunt.*

4.4 (Q 4.4)

Enter PANDARUS *and* CRESSIDA.

PANDARUS Be moderate, be moderate.
CRESSIDA Why tell you me of moderation?
The grief is fine,° full, perfect that I taste,   *undiluted*
And no less in a sense° as strong   *in a manner*
5 As that which causeth it.° How can I moderate it?   *(her love)*
If I could temporize with° my affection,   *bargain with*
Or brew° it to a weak and colder palate,°   *dilute / taste*
The like allayment° could I give my grief.   *dilution*
My love admits no qualifying dross,°   *modifying impurity*
10 No more° my grief in such a precious loss.   *Any more than does*
      Enter TROILUS.
PANDARUS Here, here, here he comes—a sweet duck.
CRESSIDA O Troilus, Troilus!
PANDARUS What a pair of spectacles° is here! Let me embrace   *sights*
too. "O heart," as the goodly saying is:
15   "O heart, heavy heart,
      Why sighest thou without breaking?"
      Where he answers again:
      "Because thou canst not ease thy smart
      By friendship nor by speaking."
20 There was never a truer rhyme. Let us cast away nothing,
for we may live to have need of such a verse. We see it, we
see it. How now, lambs?
TROILUS Cressid, I love thee in so strange° a purity   *unusual*
That the blest gods, as° angry with my fancy,°   *as if / love*
25 More bright in zeal than the devotion which
Cold lips blow to their deities, take thee from me.
CRESSIDA Have the gods envy?
PANDARUS Ay, ay, ay, ay—'tis too plain a case.
CRESSIDA And is it true that I must go from Troy?
TROILUS A hateful truth.
30 CRESSIDA   What, and from Troilus too?
TROILUS From Troy and Troilus.
CRESSIDA   Is't possible?
TROILUS And suddenly°—where injury of° chance   *immediately / injurious*
Puts back° leave-taking, jostles roughly by°   *Prevents / past*
All time of pause, rudely beguiles° our lips   *deprives*
35 Of all rejoindure,° forcibly prevents   *joining again; reply*
Our locked embrasures, strangles our dear vows
Even in the birth of our own laboring breath°—   *(as in childbirth)*
We two, that with so many thousand sighs
Did buy each other, must poorly sell ourselves
40 With the rude brevity and discharge of one.°   *(sigh)*

4.4 Location: Inside Cressida's house.

Injurious time now with a robber's haste
Crams his rich thievery up he knows not how.[1]
As many farewells as be stars in heaven,
With distinct breath and consigned° kisses to them,   *ratifying*
He fumbles up° into a loose adieu   *clumsily combines*
And scants us with a single famished kiss,
Distasting[2] with the salt of broken° tears.   *interrupted*
AENEAS *(within)* My lord, is the lady ready?
TROILUS Hark, you are called. Some say the Genius° so   *guardian spirit*
Cries "Come!" to him that instantly must die.
[*to* PANDARUS] Bid them have patience; she shall come anon.
PANDARUS Where are my tears? Rain to lay this wind,° or my   *allay my sighs*
 heart will be blown up by the root.   [*Exit.*]
CRESSIDA I must then to the Grecians?
TROILUS   No remedy.
CRESSIDA A woeful Cressid 'mongst the merry Greeks.[3]
 When shall we see again?
TROILUS Hear me, my love: Be thou but true of heart—
CRESSIDA I true? How now, what wicked deem° is this?   *thought*
TROILUS Nay, we must use expostulation° kindly,   *conversation*
For it° is parting from us.   *the opportunity*
I speak not "Be thou true" as fearing thee—
For I will throw my glove to° Death himself   *challenge*
That there's no maculation° in thy heart—   *stain of infidelity*
But "Be thou true" say I to fashion in°   *introduce*
My sequent° protestation: Be thou true,   *following*
And I will see thee.
CRESSIDA Oh, you shall be exposed, my lord, to dangers
As infinite as imminent, but I'll be true.
TROILUS And I'll grow friend with danger. Wear this sleeve.[4]
CRESSIDA And you this glove. When shall I see you?
TROILUS I will corrupt the Grecian sentinels
To° give thee nightly visitation.   *In order that I may*
But yet be true.
CRESSIDA   O heavens, "Be true" again?
TROILUS Hear why I speak it, love:
The Grecian youths are full of quality,
Their loving well composed with gifts of nature,
Flowing and swelling o'er with arts° and exercise.°   *education / practice*
How novelties may move, and parts with person,°   *talent and good looks*
Alas, a kind of godly° jealousy—   *divinely sanctioned*
Which, I beseech you, call a virtuous sin—
Makes me afraid.
CRESSIDA   O heavens, you love me not!
TROILUS Die I a villain then.
In this I do not call your faith° in question   *fidelity*
So mainly° as my merit:[5] I cannot sing,   *much*
Nor heel the high lavolt, nor sweeten talk,[6]
Nor play at subtle games—fair virtues all,

---

1. Compresses his stolen goods (farewell kisses) into a short period, in disorganized fashion, distractedly.
2. Made distasteful.
3. Common phrase for licentious revelers; here, also meant literally.
4. Often detachable in Elizabethan dress.

5. Deserts; good works, deserving of salvation (picking up the religious language of the preceding lines, especially "faith," line 83).
6. Nor dance the "lavolt" (which involved spectacular jumps), nor flatter.

To which the Grecians are most prompt and pregnant;°   *ready*
But I can tell that in each grace of these
There lurks a still and dumb-discoursive° devil   *silently communicating*
90   That tempts most cunningly. But be not tempted.
CRESSIDA   Do you think I will?
TROILUS   No, but something may be done that we will not,°   *do not want; do not will*
And sometimes we are devils to ourselves
When we will tempt the frailty of our powers,
95   Presuming on their changeful potency.°   *unreliable strength*
AENEAS *(within)*   Nay, good my lord!
TROILUS   Come, kiss, and let us part.
PARIS *(within)*   Brother Troilus!
TROILUS   Good brother, come you hither,
And bring Aeneas and the Grecian with you.
CRESSIDA   My lord, will you be true?
100   TROILUS   Who, I? Alas, it is my vice, my fault.
Whiles others fish with craft° for great opinion,°   *guile / reputation*
I with great truth catch mere simplicity;[7]
Whilst some with cunning gild their copper crowns,°   *coins; heads*
With truth and plainness I do wear° mine bare.   *dress; erode*
105   Fear not my truth; the moral° of my wit   *maxim*
Is "plain and true"—there's all the reach of it.
        Enter [DIOMEDES, AENEAS, PARIS, DEIPHOBUS,
        and Antenor].
Welcome, Sir Diomed. Here is the lady
Which for Antenor we deliver you.
At the port,° lord, I'll give her to thy hand,   *gate of the city*
110   And by the way possess° thee what she is.   *instruct*
Entreat° her fair, and by my soul, fair Greek,   *Treat*
If e'er thou stand at mercy of my sword,
Name Cressid and thy life shall be as safe
As Priam is in Ilium.
DIOMEDES   Fair lady Cressid,
115   So please you, save the thanks this prince expects.[8]
The luster in your eye, heaven in your cheek
Pleads your fair usage,° and to Diomed   *treatment*
You shall be mistress and command him wholly.
TROILUS   Grecian, thou dost not use me courteously
120   To shame the seal of my petition to thee
I'praising her. I tell thee, lord of Greece:
She is as far high-soaring o'er thy praises
As thou unworthy to be called her servant.[9]
I charge thee, use her well, even for my charge,°   *simply at my command*
125   For, by the dreadful Pluto, if thou dost not,
Though the great bulk Achilles be thy guard,
I'll cut thy throat.
DIOMEDES   Oh, be not moved,° Prince Troilus.   *angry*
Let me be privileged by my place and message
To be a speaker free; when I am hence
130   I'll answer to my lust.° And know, my lord,   *do as I please*
I'll nothing do on charge°—to her own worth   *command*

---

7. Am known for complete sincerity (innocence).   for the good treatment I will give you.
8. *save . . . expects:* you won't need to thank Troilus   9. Like "mistress" (line 118), a cliché of courtly love.

She shall be prized; but that° you say "Be't so,"   *simply because*
I'll speak it in my spirit and honor: "No."
TROILUS   Come to the port. I'll tell thee, Diomed,
135   This brave° shall oft make thee to hide thy head.   *boast*
—Lady, give me your hand, and as we walk
To our own selves bend we our needful talk.
          [*Exeunt* TROILUS, CRESSIDA, *and* DIOMEDES.]
       Sound trumpet.
PARIS   Hark, Hector's trumpet!
AENEAS   How have we spent this morning!
The Prince must think me tardy and remiss
140   That swore to ride before him in the field.
PARIS   'Tis Troilus' fault. Come, come, to field with him.
DEIPHOBUS   Let us make ready straight.
AENEAS   Yea, with a bridegroom's fresh alacrity
Let us address° to tend on Hector's heels.   *prepare*
145   The glory of our Troy doth this day lie
On his fair worth and single chivalry.   *Exeunt.*

4.5a (Q 4.5)

Enter AJAX *armed,* ACHILLES, PATROCLUS,
AGAMEMNON, MENELAUS, ULYSSES, NESTOR[, *and*
a Trumpeter, with others*].

AGAMEMNON   Here art thou in appointment° fresh and fair,   *equipment*
Anticipating time.[1] With starting° courage   *bounding*
Give with thy trumpet a loud note to Troy,
Thou dreadful° Ajax, that the appallèd air   *causing fear*
5   May pierce the head of the great combatant
And hale° him hither.   *draw*
AJAX   Thou, trumpet,° there's my purse.   *Trumpeter*
Now crack thy lungs and split thy brazen pipe;°   *trumpet; windpipe*
Blow, villain,° till thy spherèd bias° cheek   *servant / puffed-out*
Out-swell the colic of puffed Aquilon.[2]
10   Come, stretch thy chest and let thy eyes spout blood—
Thou blowest for Hector.
         [*Trumpet sounds.*]
ULYSSES   No trumpet answers.
ACHILLES   'Tis but early days.°   *early in the day*
     [*Enter* DIOMEDES *and* CRESSIDA.]
AGAMEMNON   Is not yon Diomed, with Calchas' daughter?
ULYSSES   'Tis he; I ken° the manner of his gait: *recognize*
15   He rises on the toe. That spirit of his
In aspiration lifts him from the earth.
AGAMEMNON   Is this the lady Cressid?
DIOMEDES   Even she.
AGAMEMNON   Most dearly welcome to the Greeks, sweet lady.
     [AGAMEMNON *kisses her.*][3]
NESTOR   Our general doth salute you with a kiss.
20   ULYSSES   Yet is the kindness but particular;°   *from only one of us*

4.5a Location: Between the Greek camp and Troy.
1. Ajax has not waited for Hector to appear with his
challenge.
2. Outswells the intestinal pain (from bloating) of
the north wind (Aquilon). (Winds on contemporary

maps were represented as human heads blowing.)
3. PERFORMANCE COMMENT For the importance of
how the ensuing kisses are performed (respectful, lustful), see Digital Edition PC 1.

'Twere better she were kissed in general.
NESTOR   And very courtly counsel; I'll begin.
　　　[NESTOR *kisses her.*]
　　So much for Nestor.
ACHILLES   I'll take that winter° from your lips, fair lady.　　　　　　(*Nestor's old age*)
　　　[ACHILLES *kisses her.*]
25　Achilles bids you welcome.
MENELAUS   I had good argument° for kissing once—　　　　　　　(*Helen*)
PATROCLUS   But that's no argument for kissing now,
　　For thus popped° Paris in his hardiment.[4]　　　　　　　　　　　*thrust in*
　　　[PATROCLUS *kisses her.*]
ULYSSES   Oh, deadly gall and theme of all our scorns,
30　For which we lose our heads to gild his horns.°　　　　　　　*cuckold's horns*
PATROCLUS   The first was Menelaus' kiss, this mine.
　　　[PATROCLUS *kisses her again.*]
　　Patroclus kisses you.
MENELAUS　　　　　　　　Oh, this is trim.°　　　　　　　　　　*excellent*
PATROCLUS   Paris and I kiss evermore° for him.°　　　　　　*always / (Menelaus)*
MENELAUS   I'll have my kiss, sir. Lady, by your leave—
35　CRESSIDA   In kissing do you render or receive?
MENELAUS   Both take and give.
CRESSIDA　　　　　　　　　I'll make my match to live,°　　　　　*bet my life*
　　The kiss you take is better than you give;
　　Therefore, no kiss.
MENELAUS   I'll give you boot:° I'll give you three for one.　　　　*profit*
40　CRESSIDA   You are an odd[5] man; give even or give none.
MENELAUS   An odd man, lady? Every man is odd.
CRESSIDA   No, Paris is not, for you know 'tis true
　　That you are odd and he is even° with you.　　　　　　　*has gotten even*
MENELAUS   You fillip me o'th' head.[6]
CRESSIDA　　　　　　　　　No, I'll be sworn.
45　ULYSSES   It were no match, your nail against his horn.[7]
　　May I, sweet lady, beg a kiss of you?
CRESSIDA   You may.
ULYSSES　　　　　　　I do desire it.
CRESSIDA　　　　　　　　　　Why, beg then.
ULYSSES   Why then, for Venus' sake, give me a kiss
　　When Helen is a maid again and his.°　　　　　　　　　　*(Menelaus's)*
50　CRESSIDA   I am your debtor; claim it when 'tis due.
ULYSSES   Never's my day,° and then a kiss of you.　　　　　　*the due date*
DIOMEDES   Lady, a word: I'll bring you to your father.
NESTOR   A woman of quick sense.°　　　　　　　*intelligence; sexuality*
ULYSSES　　　　　　　　　Fie, fie upon her!
　　There's a language in her eye, her cheek, her lip—
55　Nay, her foot speaks; her wanton spirits look out°　　　　　*are exposed*
　　At every joint and motive° of her body.　　　　　　　　*moving limb*
　　Oh, these encounterers,° so glib of tongue,　　　　　*flirtatious women*
　　That give a coasting° welcome ere it comes　　　　　　*an indirect*
　　And wide unclasp the tables° of their thoughts　　　　　　*tablets*
60　To every tickling° reader. Set them down°　　　　　*lustful / Mark them*

4. Bold hardness; erection.
5. *odd* (lines 40–43): strange; unique; left out; single (lacking a partner); opposite of "even" (line 43).
6. You tease me about being a cuckold (literally, you flick your fingernail on my head).

7. No contest, Cressida's fingernail against Menelaus's cuckold's horn (which is far harder and for Ulysses therefore justifies Cressida's denial that she's tapping him on the head).

For sluttish spoils of opportunity°   *As easy sexual prey*
And daughters of the game.°   *prostitutes*
      Exeunt [DIOMEDES *and* CRESSIDA].
  Flourish. Enter all of Troy: HECTOR [*armed*], PARIS,
    AENEAS, [TROILUS,] HELENUS, *and Attendants.*
ALL   The Trojans' trumpet!°   *(Trojan strumpet)*
AGAMEMNON   Yonder comes the troop.
AENEAS   Hail, all you state° of Greece. What shall be done°   *noblemen / rewarded*
65   To him that victory commands? Or do you purpose
     A victor shall be known? Will you° the knights   *Do you wish that*
     Shall to the edge of all extremity°   *death*
     Pursue each other or shall be divided
     By any voice or order of the field?[8]
     Hector bade ask.
70 AGAMEMNON   Which way would Hector have it?
AENEAS   He cares not; he'll obey conditions.°   *your choice*
AGAMEMNON   'Tis done like Hector—but securely° done, *too boldly*
     A little proudly and great deal disprizing°   *underestimating*
     The knight opposed.
AENEAS   —If not Achilles, sir,
     What is your name?
75 ACHILLES   If not Achilles, nothing.
AENEAS   Therefore Achilles. But whate'er, know this:
     In the extremity of great and little,
     Valor and pride excel themselves in Hector—
     The one° almost as infinite as all,   *(valor)*
80   The other° blank as nothing. Weigh him well,   *(pride)*
     And that which looks like pride is courtesy.
     This Ajax is half made of Hector's blood,[9]
     In love whereof half Hector stays at home;
     Half heart, half hand, half Hector comes to seek
85   This blended knight, half Trojan and half Greek.
ACHILLES   A maiden° battle, then? Oh, I perceive you.   *bloodless*
     [*Enter* DIOMEDES.]
AGAMEMNON   Here is Sir Diomed. Go, gentle knight,
     Stand by our Ajax. As you and Lord Aeneas
     Consent° upon the order° of their fight,   *Decide / terms*
90   So be it—either to the uttermost,
     Or else a breath.°   *bout of exercise*
     [*Exeunt* HECTOR, AJAX, AENEAS, *and* DIOMEDES.]
          The combatants being kin
     Half stints their strife before their strokes begin.
ULYSSES   They are opposed already.[1]
AGAMEMNON   What Trojan is that same that looks so heavy?°   *sorrowful*
95 ULYSSES   The youngest son of Priam,
     A true knight; they call him Troilus.[2]
     Not yet mature, yet matchless firm of word,
     Speaking in deeds, and deedless in his tongue;°   *not boastful*
     Not soon provoked, nor, being provoked, soon calmed;

---

8. By any umpire or rules of combat?
9. Ajax was Priam's nephew.
1. TEXTUAL COMMENT For possible differences
between the staging of the combat in F and in
Q—offstage in F, onstage in Q—see Digital Edition

TC 6 (Folio edited text).
2. TEXTUAL COMMENT For the possible link between
the repetition of "they call him Troilus" (lines 96, 108)
and the different staging possibilities of this scene, see
Digital Edition TC 7 (Folio edited text).

100	His heart and hand both open and both free,°		*generous*
	For what he has he gives, what thinks he shows,		
	Yet gives he not till judgment guide his bounty,°		*generosity*
	Nor dignifies an impare° thought with breath;		*uneven; unfit; harmful*
	Manly as Hector, but more dangerous,		
105	For Hector in his blaze of wrath subscribes°		*relents*
	To tender objects, but he in heat of action		
	Is more vindicative° than jealous love.		*vindictive*
	They call him Troilus and on him erect		
	A second hope, as fairly built as Hector.		
110	Thus says Aeneas, one that knows the youth		
	Even to his inches and with private soul[3]		
	Did in great Ilium thus translate° him to me.		*describe*

    Alarum.

AGAMEMNON   They are in action.

NESTOR   Now, Ajax, hold thine own!

115 TROILUS   Hector, thou sleep'st; awake thee!

AGAMEMNON   His blows are well disposed. There, Ajax!

                                           [Exeunt.]

4.5b (Q 4.5)[1]

[Enter HECTOR and AJAX, fighting, with AENEAS and DIOMEDES attempting to stop them.] Trumpets cease.

DIOMEDES   You must no more.

AENEAS   Princes, enough, so please you.

AJAX   I am not warm yet; let us fight again.

DIOMEDES   As Hector pleases.

HECTOR   Why, then will I no more.

	Thou art, great lord, my father's sister's son,		
5	A cousin-german° to great Priam's seed.		*first cousin*
	The obligation of our blood forbids		
	A gory emulation° twixt us twain.		*competition*
	Were thy commixtion° Greek and Trojan so°		*blending / such*
	That thou couldst say: "This hand is Grecian all,		
10	And this is Trojan; the sinews of this leg		
	All Greek, and this all Troy; my mother's blood		
	Runs on the dexter° cheek, and this sinister°		*right / left*
	Bounds in my father's," by Jove multipotent,°		*most powerful*
	Thou shouldst not bear from me a Greekish member°		*part of the body*
15	Wherein my sword had not impressure made		
	Of our rank° feud. But the just gods gainsay°		*heated / prohibit*
	That any drop thou borrowed'st from thy mother,		
	My sacred aunt, should by my mortal sword		
	Be drained. Let me embrace thee, Ajax.		
20	By him that thunders,° thou hast lusty arms!		*(Jupiter)*
	Hector would have them fall upon him thus.°		*in an embrace*
	Cousin, all honor to thee.		

AJAX   I thank thee, Hector.

	Thou art too gentle and too free a man.		
	I came to kill thee, cousin, and bear hence		
25	A great addition° earnèd in thy death.		*title*

---

3. *Even . . . soul:* In utmost detail and in confidence.
4.5b Location: Scene continues.
1. TEXTUAL COMMENT Most modern editions do not

mark a scene break here; this affects the numbering of the following lines. See Digital Edition TC 6 (Folio edited text).

HECTOR   Not Neoptolemus[2] so mirable°—   *wonderful*
On whose bright crest° Fame with her loud'st oyez°   *helmet / hear ye*
Cries, "This is he!"—couldst promise to himself
A thought of added honor torn from Hector.
30 AENEAS   There is expectance here from both the sides
What further you will do.
HECTOR   We'll answer it:
The issue° is embracement. Ajax, farewell.   *conclusion*
AJAX   If I might in entreaties find success,
As seld° I have the chance, I would desire   *seldom*
35 My famous cousin to our Grecian tents.
DIOMEDES   'Tis Agamemnon's wish, and great Achilles
Doth long to see unarmed the valiant Hector.
HECTOR   Aeneas, call my brother Troilus to me
And signify this loving interview
40 To the expecters of our Trojan part;°   *awaiting Trojans*
Desire them home.° —Give me thy hand, my cousin;   *to go home*
I will go eat with thee and see your knights.
        Enter AGAMEMNON *and the rest*[: ULYSSES, TROILUS,
        ACHILLES, MENELAUS, *and* NESTOR].
AJAX   Great Agamemnon comes to meet us here.
HECTOR   The worthiest of them° tell me name by name—   *(the Greeks)*
45 But for Achilles, mine own searching eyes
Shall find him by his large and portly size.
AGAMEMNON   Worthy of arms! As welcome as to° one   *as you can be to*
That would be rid of such an enemy.
But that's no welcome. Understand more clear:
50 What's past and what's to come is strewed with husks
And formless ruin of oblivion;
But in this extant° moment, faith and troth,   *present*
Strained purely from all hollow bias-drawing,[3]
Bids thee with most divine integrity,
55 From heart of very heart, great Hector, welcome.
HECTOR   I thank thee, most imperious° Agamemnon.   *imperial*
AGAMEMNON [*to* TROILUS]   My well-famed lord of Troy, no
    less to you.
MENELAUS   Let me confirm my princely brother's greeting:
You brace° of warlike brothers, welcome hither.   *pair*
HECTOR   Who must we answer?
60 AENEAS   The noble Menelaus.
HECTOR   Oh, you, my lord. By Mars his° gauntlet, thanks.   *Mars's*
Mock not that I affect° th'untraded° oath: *choose / unfamiliar*
Your quondam° wife swears still by Venus' glove.[4]   *former*
She's well, but bade me not commend her to you.
65 MENELAUS   Name her not now, sir; she's a deadly theme.
HECTOR   Oh, pardon, I offend.
NESTOR   I have, thou gallant Trojan, seen thee oft,
Laboring for destiny,[5] make cruel way
Through ranks of Greekish youth; and I have seen thee,
70 As hot as Perseus,° spur thy Phrygian steed;   *(on winged Pegasus)*

2. Achilles' son Pyrrhus (but Shakespeare may have
thought Neoptolemus was Achilles' surname).
3. Freed from all insincerity and indirectness.
4. *Venus' glove:* contrasting with Mars's gauntlet and

alluding to Venus's adultery with Mars; possibly with
an obscene innuendo.
5. Doing the Fates' work for them.

And seen thee scorning forfeits and subduements[6]
When thou hast hung° thy advancèd sword i'th' air,   *kept high*
Not letting it decline° on the declined,°   *fall / fallen*
That I have said unto my standers by,
75   "Lo, Jupiter is yonder, dealing life."[7]
And I have seen thee pause and take thy breath
When that a ring of Greeks have hemmed thee in
Like an Olympian° wrestling. This have I seen,   *a god*
But this thy countenance, still° locked in steel,   *always*
80   I never saw till now. I knew thy grandsire[8]
And once fought with him; he was a soldier good,
But by great Mars, the captain of us all,
Never like thee. Let an old man embrace thee,
And, worthy warrior, welcome to our tents.
85 AENEAS   'Tis the old Nestor.
HECTOR   Let me embrace thee, good old chronicle°   *record of history*
    That hast so long walked hand in hand with time.
    Most reverend Nestor, I am glad to clasp thee.
NESTOR   I would my arms could match thee in contention°   *in battle*
90   As they contend with thee in courtesy.
HECTOR   I would they could.
NESTOR   Ha?
    By this white beard, I'd fight with thee tomorrow.
    Well, welcome, welcome. I have seen the time.[9]
95 ULYSSES   I wonder now how yonder city stands
    When we have here her base and pillar by us.
HECTOR   I know your favor,° Lord Ulysses, well.   *face*
    Ah, sir, there's many a Greek and Trojan dead
    Since first I saw yourself and Diomed
100   In Ilium on your Greekish embassy.
ULYSSES   Sir, I foretold you then what would ensue.
    My prophecy is but half his journey yet,
    For yonder walls that pertly front your town,
    Yon towers whose wanton° tops do buss° the clouds,   *reckless; (sexual) / kiss*
    Must kiss their own feet.
105 HECTOR   I must not believe you.
    There they stand yet, and modestly I think
    The fall of every Phrygian stone will cost
    A drop of Grecian blood. The end crowns all,
    And that old common arbitrator, Time,
    Will one day end it.
110 ULYSSES   So to him we leave it.
    Most gentle and most valiant Hector, welcome.
    After the general, I beseech you next
    To feast with me and see me at my tent.
ACHILLES   I shall forestall thee, Lord Ulysses, thou.[1]
115   —Now, Hector, I have fed mine eyes on thee;
    I have with exact view perused° thee, Hector,   *minutely looked over*
    And quoted° joint by joint.   *taken note*
HECTOR   Is this Achilles?

6. Scorning those whose lives might have been forfeit and (possible) conquests.
7. Giving life being the gods' prerogative.
8. Laomedon, builder of Troy's walls.
9. That is, the time when I could have met you in

combat. (Nestor takes Hector's "I would they could,"
line 91, as a put-down.)
1. Insulting use of the second person familiar—
"thee" (Ulysses), "thou" (Hector).

ACHILLES   I am Achilles.
HECTOR   Stand fair,° I prithee; let me look on thee.   *open to view*
ACHILLES   Behold thy fill.
120   HECTOR   Nay, I have done already.
ACHILLES   Thou art too brief. I will the second time,
   As° I would buy thee, view thee limb by limb.   *As though*
HECTOR   Oh, like a book of sport° thou'lt read me o'er;   *hunting manual*
   But there's more in me than thou understand'st.
125   Why dost thou so oppress² me with thine eye?
ACHILLES   Tell me, you heavens, in which part of his body
   Shall I destroy him—whether there, or there, or there—
   That I may give the local wound a name
   And make distinct the very breach whereout
130   Hector's great spirit flew. Answer me, heavens.
HECTOR   It would discredit the blest gods, proud man,
   To answer such a question. Stand again;°   *Let me look again*
   Think'st thou to catch my life so pleasantly°   *easily*
   As to prenominate° in nice° conjecture   *name in advance / exact*
   Where thou wilt hit me dead?
135   ACHILLES   I tell thee, yea.
HECTOR   Wert thou the oracle to tell me so,
   I'd not believe thee. Henceforth guard thee well,
   For I'll not kill thee there, nor there, nor there,
   But, by the forge that stithied° Mars his helm,   *forged*
140   I'll kill thee everywhere—yea, o'er and o'er.
   You wisest Grecians, pardon me this brag;
   His insolence draws folly from my lips,
   But I'll endeavor deeds to match these words,
   Or may I never—
AJAX   Do not chafe thee,° cousin.   *get angry*
145   And you, Achilles, let these threats alone
   Till accident or purpose bring you to't.
   You may every day enough of Hector
   If you have stomach.° The general state, I fear,   *appetite*
   Can scarce entreat you to be odd with him.³
150   HECTOR   I pray you, let us see you in the field.
   We have had pelting° wars since you refused   *paltry*
   The Grecians' cause.
ACHILLES   Dost thou entreat me, Hector?
   Tomorrow do I meet thee, fell as death.
   Tonight, all friends.
HECTOR   Thy hand upon that match.
155   AGAMEMNON   First, all you peers of Greece, go to my tent—
   There in the full convive you.° Afterwards,   *feast together*
   As Hector's leisure and your bounties shall
   Concur together, severally entreat° him.   *individually invite*
   Beat loud the taborins,° let the trumpets blow,   *small drums*
160   That this great soldier may his welcome know.
       [*Trumpets and drums.*]
             Exeunt [*all but* TROILUS *and* ULYSSES].
TROILUS   My lord Ulysses, tell me, I beseech you,

---

2. Molest; in heraldry, place a perpendicular or diagonal stripe across an animal (continuing the metaphor of Hector as a hunted animal from "book of sport,"
line 123).
3. I fear that the Greek leaders can hardly get you to oppose him.

In what place of the field doth Calchas keep?° reside
ULYSSES   At Menelaus' tent, most princely Troilus.
There Diomed doth feast with him tonight,
165   Who neither looks on heaven nor on earth,
But gives all gaze and bent° of amorous view inclination
On the fair Cressid.
TROILUS   Shall I, sweet lord, be bound to thee so much,
After we part from Agamemnon's tent,
To bring me thither?
170   ULYSSES   You shall command me, sir.
As gentle° tell me: of what honor was Just as courteously
This Cressida in Troy? Had she no lover there
That wails her absence?
TROILUS   O sir, to such as boasting show their scars° brag of past wounds
175   A mock is due. Will you walk on, my lord?
She was beloved, she loved, she is and doth;
But still sweet love is food for Fortune's tooth.   *Exeunt.*

5.1 (Q 5.1)

Enter ACHILLES *and* PATROCLUS.
ACHILLES   I'll heat his blood with Greekish wine tonight,
Which with my scimitar I'll cool° tomorrow. expose to air
Patroclus, let us feast him to the height.
PATROCLUS   Here comes Thersites.
     Enter THERSITES.
ACHILLES   How now, thou core° of envy, (of an ulcer)
5   Thou crusty batch¹ of nature, what's the news?
THERSITES   Why, thou picture° of what thou seem'st and idol mere image
of idiot-worshippers, here's a letter for thee.
ACHILLES   From whence, fragment?° scrap of leftovers
THERSITES   Why, thou full dish of fool,² from Troy.
[ACHILLES *stands aside to read the letter.*]
10   PATROCLUS   Who keeps the tent now?³
THERSITES   The surgeon's box, or the patient's wound.
PATROCLUS   Well said, adversity.° And what need these tricks? perversity
THERSITES   Prithee be silent, boy; I profit not by thy talk.
Thou art thought to be Achilles' male varlet.° servant; lover
15   PATROCLUS   Male varlet, you rogue? What's that?
THERSITES   Why, his masculine whore. Now the rotten diseases of the south, guts-griping, ruptures, catarrhs, loads
o'gravel i'th' back, lethargies, cold palsies,⁴ and the like, take
and take again such preposterous discoveries.° revealed sodomy
20   PATROCLUS   Why, thou damnable box of envy, thou, what
mean'st thou to curse thus?
THERSITES   Do I curse thee?
PATROCLUS   Why, no,⁵ you ruinous butt,° you whoreson indis- leaky tub
tinguishable cur.° formless beast

5.1. Location: The Greek camp, near Achilles' tent.
1. You scab-encrusted (bad-tempered) boil.
2. Punning on the name of a dessert, probably clotted cream or egg custard.
3. Who stays in the tent now? Thersites can no longer taunt Achilles for remaining indoors. But Thersites deliberately mistakes Patroclus to mean the surgeon's probe or lint used to clean a wound.
4. These may be separate diseases, but they can nearly

all be symptoms of venereal disease. *south:* referring to the arrival of venereal disease in Europe after the Crusades and its association with Italy, particularly Naples. *guts-griping:* colic. *ruptures:* hernias. *catarrhs:* nose or throat infections. *loads . . . back:* kidney stones. *lethargies:* inertia. *palsies:* paralysis.
5. Sarcastic, since Thersites obviously is cursing him; also, perhaps denying the charge of homosexuality.

25   THERSITES   No? Why art thou then exasperate,° thou idle   *irritated*
        immaterial skein of sleaved silk, thou green sarcenet flap[6] for
        a sore eye,[7] thou tassel of a prodigal's purse, thou? Ah, how
        the poor world is pestered with such waterflies°—diminutives   *tiny, flashy insects*
        of nature.
30   PATROCLUS   Out, gall!
    THERSITES   Finch egg!°   *small, gaudy egg*
    ACHILLES *[coming forward]*   My sweet Patroclus, I am
        thwarted quite
    From my great purpose in tomorrow's battle.
    Here is a letter from Queen Hecuba,
35   A token from her daughter, my fair love,
    Both taxing° me and gaging° me to keep   *reproving / binding*
    An oath that I have sworn. I will not break it.
    Fall Greeks, fail fame, honor or° go or stay,   *either*
    My major vow lies here; this I'll obey.
40   Come, come, Thersites; help to trim° my tent.   *decorate*
    This night in banqueting must all be spent.
    Away, Patroclus.   *Exeunt [ACHILLES and PATROCLUS].*
  THERSITES   With too much blood° and too little brain, these   *passion*
    two may run mad, but if with too much brain and too little
45   blood they do, I'll be a curer of madmen.[8] Here's° Agamem-   *Take*
    non, an honest fellow enough, and one that loves quails,° but   *(as food); prostitutes*
    he has not so much brain as earwax; and the goodly transfor-
    mation of Jupiter there, his brother—the bull,[9] the primitive°   *archetypal*
    statue and oblique° memorial of cuckolds, a thrifty shoeing-   *perverse*
50   horn in a chain, hanging at his brother's leg[1]—to what form
    but that° he is should wit larded with malice and malice   *other than what*
    farced° with wit turn him to?° To an ass were nothing—he is   *stuffed / transform*
    both ass and ox; to an ox were nothing—he is both ox and ass.   *him into*
    To be a dog, a mule, a cat, a fitchew,[2] a toad, a lizard, an owl,
55   a puttock,° or a herring without a roe° I would not care, but to *small hawk / of no value*
    be Menelaus I would conspire against destiny. Ask me not
    what I would be if I were not Thersites, for I care not to be°   *wouldn't mind being*
    the louse of a lazar, so[3] I were not Menelaus. Hey-day, spirits
    and fires![4]
        Enter HECTOR, [TROILUS,] AJAX, AGAMEMNON,
        [MENELAUS,] ULYSSES, NESTOR, DIOMEDES, with lights.
  AGAMEMNON   We go wrong, we go wrong.
60   AJAX   No, yonder 'tis,
    There where we see the light.
  HECTOR   I trouble you.
  AJAX   No, not a whit.
        Enter ACHILLES.
  ULYSSES   Here comes himself° to guide you.   *the man himself*
  ACHILLES   Welcome, brave Hector; welcome, princes all.
  AGAMEMNON   So now, fair prince of Troy, I bid good night.

---

6. *thou idle . . . flap:* you insubstantial fine silk thread, you immature patch of silk fabric.
7. Possible symptom of venereal disease.
8. Paradoxes and improbabilities: Achilles and Patroclus going mad from excess intellect and insufficient passion, and Thersites curing them.
9. Jupiter made himself into a bull to rape Europa; but Menelaus is bull-like for almost the opposite reason—he has the horns of a cuckold.

1. A convenient tool (the shoehorn, suggested by the cuckold's horn, was sometimes worn on "a chain") available to serve Agamemnon; also, always underfoot.
2. Polecat (proverbially lecherous and stinking).
3. The louse of a leper, as long as.
4. The Greeks approach with torches, suggesting night; Thersites imagines them to be light-bearing spirits.

65   Ajax commands the guard to tend on you.

HECTOR   Thanks and good night to the Greeks' general.

MENELAUS   Good night, my lord.

HECTOR   Good night, sweet Lord Menelaus.

THERSITES [*aside*]   Sweet draft!⁵ "Sweet," quoth 'a?° Sweet sink,°   *he / cesspool*

70   sweet sewer.

ACHILLES   Good night and welcome, both at once, to those

    That go or tarry.

AGAMEMNON   Good night.   [*Exeunt* AGAMEMNON *and*

                        MENELAUS.]

ACHILLES   Old Nestor tarries—and you too, Diomed,

75   Keep Hector company an hour or two.

DIOMEDES   I cannot, lord; I have important business,

    The tide° whereof is now. —Good night, great Hector.   *time*

HECTOR   Give me your hand.   [*Exit* DIOMEDES.]

ULYSSES [*aside to* TROILUS]   Follow his torch; he goes to

    Calchas' tent.

    I'll keep you company.

80 TROILUS   Sweet sir, you honor me.

                  [*Exeunt* TROILUS *and* ULYSSES.]

HECTOR   And so good night.

ACHILLES   Come, come, enter my tent.

        Exeunt [ACHILLES, HECTOR, AJAX, *and* NESTOR].

THERSITES   That same Diomed's a false-hearted rogue, a most

    unjust knave. I will no more trust him when he leers° than I   *smiles*

    will a serpent when he hisses. He will spend his mouth and

85   promise like Babbler the hound, but when he performs

    astronomers foretell it—that it is prodigious; there will come

    some change.⁶ The sun borrows of the moon⁷ when Diomed

    keeps his word. I will rather leave to see Hector than not to

    dog him.⁸ They say he keeps a Trojan drab° and uses the   *whore*

90   traitor Calchas his° tent. I'll after. Nothing but lechery—all   *Calchas's*

    incontinent varlets!   *Exit*.

5.2 (Q 5.2)

    Enter DIOMEDES.

DIOMEDES   What, are you up here, ho? Speak!

CALCHAS [*within*]   Who calls?

DIOMEDES   Diomed. Calchas, I think. Where's your daughter?

CALCHAS [*within*]   She comes to you.

    Enter TROILUS *and* ULYSSES [*at a distance, and after*

    them, THERSITES].

5 ULYSSES   Stand where the torch may not discover° us.   *disclose*

    Enter CRESSIDA.

TROILUS   Cressid comes forth to him.

DIOMEDES   How now, my charge?

CRESSIDA   Now, my sweet guardian, hark, a word with you.

    [*She whispers to him.*]

---

5. Drink; team of beasts used for pulling wagons; cesspool, toilet.
6. *He will . . . change:* He will bark and "promise" (that there is prey) like a hound that is noisy (quarrelsome), even when off the scent, but when he actually "performs" (acts in good faith, keeps his word), astronomers make predictions on that basis: it is such a rare event that they consider it an ominous warning of a cosmic happening (often indicative of massive political upheaval).
7. It was well known that the moon's light was merely a reflection of the sun's.
8. I'll stop seeing Hector rather than give up tailing Diomedes.
5.2 Location: Outside Calchas's tent.

TROILUS Yea, so familiar?

ULYSSES She will sing any man at first sight.[1]

10 THERSITES And any man may sing her, if he can take her clef;
she's noted.[2]

DIOMEDES Will you remember?

CRESSIDA Remember? Yes.

DIOMEDES Nay, but do then,

15 And let your mind be coupled with your words.

TROILUS What should she remember?

ULYSSES List!°   *Listen*

CRESSIDA Sweet honey Greek, tempt me no more to folly.°   *promiscuity*

THERSITES Roguery!

20 DIOMEDES Nay, then.

CRESSIDA I'll tell you what—

DIOMEDES Faugh, faugh, come, tell a pin;° you are a forsworn—   *tell me nothing*

CRESSIDA In faith, I cannot.° What would you have me do?   *(do as I promised)*

THERSITES A juggling trick, to be secretly open.[3]

25 DIOMEDES What did you swear you would bestow on me?

CRESSIDA I prithee do not hold me to mine oath;
Bid me do anything but that, sweet Greek.

DIOMEDES Good night.

TROILUS Hold, patience.

30 ULYSSES How now, Trojan?

CRESSIDA Diomed—

DIOMEDES No, no, good night. I'll be your fool no more.

TROILUS Thy better must.°   *(be Cressida's fool)*

CRESSIDA Hark, one word in your ear.

35 TROILUS Oh, plague and madness!

ULYSSES You are moved, Prince. Let us depart, I pray you,
Lest your displeasure should enlarge itself
To wrathful terms. This place is dangerous,
The time right deadly; I beseech you, go.

TROILUS Behold, I pray you.

40 ULYSSES   Nay, good my lord, go off.
You flow° to great distraction. Come, my lord.   *rise; flood*

TROILUS I pray thee, stay.

ULYSSES   You have not patience; come.

TROILUS I pray you, stay. By hell and hell-torments,
I will not speak a word.

DIOMEDES   And so good night.

CRESSIDA Nay, but you part in anger.

45 TROILUS   Doth that grieve thee?
Oh, withered truth!

ULYSSES   Why, how now, lord?

TROILUS   By Jove,
I will be patient.

CRESSIDA   Guardian? Why, Greek—

DIOMEDES Faugh, faugh, adieu, you palter.°   *equivocate*

CRESSIDA In faith, I do not. Come hither once again.

50 ULYSSES You shake, my lord, at something; will you go?

1. As in sight-reading of music; Cressida does not
need to know the man beforehand to play (upon) him.
2. *if . . . noted:* if he can find her musical key (also,
her cleft, or pudenda). She's like music written down;
she's note-orious.
3. *juggling:* often meant sexual dexterity. *open:* public; available for sexual intercourse.

You will break out.

TROILUS　　　　　　　She strokes his cheek!

ULYSSES　　　　　　　　　　　　Come, come.

TROILUS　Nay, stay. By Jove, I will not speak a word.

There is between my will and all offenses°　　　　　　*any bad deeds*

A guard° of patience. Stay a little while.　　　　　　　　*barrier*

55　THERSITES　How the devil Luxury° with his fat rump and　　*Lust*

potato⁴ finger tickles these together. Fry, lechery, fry!⁵

DIOMEDES　But will you, then?

CRESSIDA　In faith I will, la; never trust me else.

DIOMEDES　Give me some token for the surety of it.

60　CRESSIDA　I'll fetch you one.　　　　　　　　　　*Exit.*

ULYSSES　You have sworn patience.

TROILUS　　　　　　　　　　Fear me not, sweet lord.

I will not be myself, nor have cognition°　　　　　　　　*awareness*

Of what I feel. I am all patience.

　　　　　Enter CRESSIDA [*with Troilus' sleeve*].

THERSITES　Now the pledge, now, now, now!

65　CRESSIDA　Here, Diomed, keep this sleeve.

　　　　　[*She gives him the sleeve.*]

TROILUS　O beauty, where is thy faith?

ULYSSES　　　　　　　　　　My lord—

TROILUS　I will be patient; outwardly I will.

CRESSIDA　You look upon that sleeve; behold it well.

He loved me—O false wench! Give't me again.

　　　　　[*She takes it back from him.*]

70　DIOMEDES　Whose was't?

CRESSIDA　It is no matter, now I have't again.

I will not meet with you tomorrow night.

I prithee, Diomed, visit me no more.

THERSITES　Now she sharpens.⁶ Well said, whetstone!

DIOMEDES　I shall have it.

CRESSIDA　　　　　　　What, this?

75　DIOMEDES　　　　　　　　　Ay, that.

CRESSIDA　O all you gods! Oh, pretty, pretty pledge.

Thy master now lies thinking in his bed

Of thee and me, and sighs, and takes my glove,

And gives memorial° dainty kisses to it,　　　　　　　*in remembrance*

As I kiss thee.

　　　　　[*As she is kissing the sleeve,* DIOMEDES *takes it from*
　　　　　her; she tries to get it back.]

80　DIOMEDES　　　　　Nay, do not snatch it from me.

CRESSIDA　He that takes that takes my heart withal.

DIOMEDES　I had your heart before; this follows it.

TROILUS　I did swear patience.

CRESSIDA　You shall not have it, Diomed, faith, you shall not.

85　I'll give you something else.

DIOMEDES　I will have this. Whose was it?

CRESSIDA　It is no matter.

DIOMEDES　Come, tell me whose it was.

CRESSIDA　'Twas one that loved me better than you will.

---

4. The Spanish, or sweet, potato was thought to be　　5. In the fires of lust and of hell.
an aphrodisiac.　　　　　　　　　　　　　　　　　6. Becomes harsh; whets his desire.

But now you have it, take it.
90 DIOMEDES   Whose was it?
CRESSIDA   By all Diana's waiting-women⁷ yond,
    And by herself, I will not tell you whose.
DIOMEDES   Tomorrow will I wear it on my helm
    And grieve° his spirit that dares not challenge it.   *afflict*
95 TROILUS   Wert thou the devil and wor'st it on thy horn
    It should be challenged.
CRESSIDA   Well, well, 'tis done, 'tis past—and yet it is not;
    I will not keep my word.
DIOMEDES   Why then, farewell;
    Thou never shalt mock Diomed again.
100 CRESSIDA   You shall not go. One cannot speak a word
    But it straight starts you.°   *makes you run off*
DIOMEDES   I do not like this fooling.
THERSITES   Nor I, by Pluto, but that that likes not you° pleases   *that which you dislike*
    me best.
DIOMEDES   What, shall I come? The hour?
105 CRESSIDA   Ay, come. O Jove, do come! I shall be plagued.⁸
DIOMEDES   Farewell till then.
CRESSIDA   Good night. I prithee, come.
                                                Exit [DIOMEDES].
    Troilus, farewell. One eye yet looks on thee,
    But with my heart the other eye° doth see.°   *(pun on "I")* / *(Diomedes)*
    Ah, poor our° sex! This fault in us I find: *our poor*
110 The error of our eye directs our mind.
    What error° leads must err—oh, then conclude: *wandering*
    Minds swayed by eyes are full of turpitude.   *Exit.*
THERSITES   A proof of strength she could not publish more,⁹
    Unless she say, "My mind is now turned whore."
ULYSSES   All's done, my lord.
TROILUS   It is.
115 ULYSSES   Why stay we then?
TROILUS   To make a recordation to my soul
    Of every syllable that here was spoke.
    But if I tell how these two did co-act,
    Shall I not lie in publishing a truth,
120 Sith yet there is a credence in my heart,
    An esperance° so obstinately strong,   *hope*
    That doth invert th'attest° of eyes and ears,   *reverse the testimony*
    As if those organs had deceptious° functions,   *deceptive*
    Created only to calumniate?
    Was Cressid here?
125 ULYSSES   I cannot conjure,° Trojan.   *produce a ghost*
TROILUS   She was not, sure.
ULYSSES   Most sure she was.
TROILUS   Why, my negation hath no taste of madness.
ULYSSES   Nor mine, my lord: Cressid was here but now.
TROILUS   Let it not be believed, for° womanhood.   *for the sake of*
130 Think, we had mothers; do not give advantage

---

7. The stars (Diana being the goddess of the moon
and, ironically, of chastity).
8. Vexed; teased (but also alluding to her eventual
fate in late medieval narrative, as a leper). See the

Introduction.
9. She could not make a strong proof known more
clearly.

To stubborn critics, apt without a theme
For deprivation,[1] to square the general sex
By Cressid's rule.[2] Rather, think this not Cressid.
ULYSSES What hath she done, Prince, that can soil our
    mothers?
135 TROILUS Nothing at all, unless that this were she.
THERSITES Will he swagger himself out on 's own eyes?[3]
TROILUS This she? No, this is Diomed's Cressida.
    If beauty have a soul, this is not she;
    If souls guide vows, if vows are sanctimony,°   *sacred things*
140 If sanctimony° be the gods' delight,   *sanctity*
    If there be rule in unity itself,°   *unity is indivisible*
    This is not she. Oh, madness of discourse°   *reason*
    That cause[4] sets up with and against itself—
    Bifold authority, where reason can revolt
145 Without perdition and loss assume all reason
    Without revolt.[5] This is and is not Cressid.
    Within my soul there doth conduce° a fight   *come together*
    Of this strange nature, that a thing inseparate°   *indivisible*
    Divides more wider than the sky and earth,
150 And yet the spacious breadth of this division
    Admits no orifex° for a point as subtle°   *orifice / fine*
    As Ariachne's[6] broken woof° to enter.   *weaving thread*
    Instance,° O instance, strong as Pluto's gates: *Evidence*
    Cressid is mine, tied with the bonds of heaven.
155 Instance, O instance, strong as heaven itself:
    The bonds of heaven are slipped, dissolved, and loosed,
    And with another knot, five-finger-tied,[7]
    The fractions° of her faith, orts° of her love,   *pieces / leftover scraps*
    The fragments, scraps, the bits, and greasy relics
160 Of her o'er-eaten° faith are bound to Diomed.   *eaten-away; surfeited*
ULYSSES May worthy Troilus be half attached
    With that which here his passion doth express?[8]
TROILUS Ay, Greek, and that shall be divulgèd well
    In characters as red as Mars his° heart   *Mars's*
165 Inflamed with Venus. Never did young man fancy°   *love*
    With so eternal and so fixed a soul.
    Hark, Greek: as much as I do Cressida love,
    So much by weight hate I her Diomed.
    That sleeve is mine that he'll bear in his helm;
170 Were it a casque° composed by Vulcan's[9] skill,   *helmet*
    My sword should bite it. Not the dreadful spout
    Which shipmen do the hurricano° call,   *waterspout*

1. Depriving women of their reputation.
2. *to square . . . rule:* to measure all women by the standard of Cressida.
3. Will he bluster himself out of (the evidence of) his own eyes?
4. Case; plea (where, here, defendant and plaintiff are one).
5. *Bifold . . . revolt:* Perhaps: Divided authority, where reason can revolt (belief in the testimony of the senses) can revolt against itself (by claiming that this is not in fact Cressida) without being accused of loss of reason ("perdition"); and where loss of reason (inability to trust the senses), without rebelling against reason, can lay claim to being the highest form of reason precisely because the sensual evidence, which ought to be the highest form of reason, lies (because this cannot be Cressida).
6. A conflation of Arachne the weaver, turned into a spider by Athena for overweening pride in her work, and Ariadne, who gave Theseus a ball of thread to mark his way out of the Labyrinth of her father.
7. United by human hands (Cressida's and Diomedes'), as opposed to "the bonds of heaven" (line 154); evilly consummated (alluding to the devil's five fingers, symbolizing the steps to lechery).
8. *May . . . express:* Can worthy Troilus be even half as affected as he seems to be?
9. Smith of the gods, Vulcan made armor for various classical heroes, most notably Achilles.

	Constringèd° in mass by the almighty sun,	*Drawn together*
	Shall dizzy° with more clamor Neptune's ear	*stun*
175	In his descent than shall my prompted° sword	*eager*
	Falling on Diomed.	

THERSITES   He'll tickle it for his concupy!¹

TROILUS   O Cressid! O false Cressid—false, false, false!
Let all untruths stand by° thy stainèd name,   *be compared with*
And they'll seem glorious.

180   ULYSSES   Oh, contain yourself;
Your passion draws ears hither.
                    Enter AENEAS.

AENEAS   I have been seeking you this hour, my lord.
Hector by this° is arming him in Troy.   *by this time*
Ajax, your guard, stays to conduct you home.

185   TROILUS   Have° with you, Prince. —My courteous lord, adieu.   *I shall come*
[*aside*] Farewell, revolted fair, and Diomed,
Stand fast and wear a castle° on thy head.   *strong defense*

ULYSSES   I'll bring you to the gates.

TROILUS   Accept distracted thanks.
                    Exeunt TROILUS, AENEAS, *and* ULYSSES.

THERSITES   Would I could meet that rogue Diomed; I would
190   croak like a raven,² I would bode, I would bode.° Patroclus   *foretell evil*
will give me anything for the intelligence° of this whore—   *secret information*
the parrot will not do more for an almond³ than he for a
commodious drab.° Lechery, lechery, still wars and lechery;   *willing whore*
nothing else holds fashion. A burning devil° take them!   *venereal disease*
                                                              [*Exit.*]

5.3 (Q 5.3)
Enter HECTOR *and* ANDROMACHE.

ANDROMACHE   When was my lord so much ungently
        tempered
To stop his ears against admonishment?
Unarm, unarm, and do not fight today.

HECTOR   You train° me to offend you; get you gone.   *teach*
5   By the everlasting gods, I'll go.

ANDROMACHE   My dreams will sure prove ominous to the day.°   *true omens of the day*

HECTOR   No more, I say.
                    Enter CASSANDRA.

CASSANDRA   Where is my brother Hector?

ANDROMACHE   Here, sister, armed and bloody in intent.
Consort° with me in loud and dear° petition;   *Join / earnest*
10   Pursue we him on knees, for I have dreamt
Of bloody turbulence, and this whole night
Hath nothing been but shapes and forms of slaughter.

CASSANDRA   Oh, 'tis true.

HECTOR   Ho! Bid my trumpet sound!

CASSANDRA   No notes of sally, for the heavens, sweet brother.

15   HECTOR   Begone, I say; the gods have heard me swear.

CASSANDRA   The gods are deaf to hot and peevish° vows;   *headstrong*
They° are polluted off'rings, more abhorred   *(Rash vows)*

---

1. (Probably) Troilus will "tickle" (beat [ironic]) Diomedes' helmet for his lust (his concubine).
2. Proverbially, birds of ill omen.
3. *the parrot . . . almond:* proverbial for a brainless
passion for a trivial delicacy.
5.3 Location: Priam's palace.

Than spotted livers° in the sacrifice. · ruined offerings
ANDROMACHE Oh, be persuaded; do not count it holy[1]

20 To hurt by being just°—it is as lawful, · true to your vow
For we would° give much, to use violent thefts, · Because we want to
And rob in the behalf of charity.
CASSANDRA It is the purpose that makes strong the vow,
But vows to every purpose must not° hold. · do not have to
Unarm, sweet Hector.

25 HECTOR   Hold you still,° I say. · Stop it
Mine honor keeps the weather of° my fate; · counts for more than
Life every man holds dear, but the dear° man · worthy
Holds honor far more precious-dear than life.
          Enter TROILUS.
How now, young man, mean'st thou to fight today?

30 ANDROMACHE Cassandra, call my father° to persuade. · father-in-law
                    Exit CASSANDRA.
HECTOR No, faith, young Troilus, doff thy harness,° youth. · disarm
I am today i'th' vein of° chivalry; · mood for
Let grow thy sinews till their knots be strong,
And tempt not yet the brushes° of the war. · encounters

35 Unarm thee, go, and doubt thou not, brave boy,
I'll stand today for thee and me and Troy.
TROILUS Brother, you have a vice of mercy in you
Which better fits a lion[2] than a man.
HECTOR What vice is that? Good Troilus, chide me for it.

40 TROILUS When many times the captive° Grecian falls, · miserable
Even in the fan and wind of your fair sword,[3]
You bid them rise and live.
HECTOR Oh, 'tis fair play.
TROILUS   Fool's play, by heaven, Hector.
HECTOR How now? How now?
TROILUS   For th' love of all the gods,

45 Let's leave the hermit Pity with our mothers,
And when we have our armors buckled on,
The venomed vengeance ride upon our swords,
Spur them to ruthful° work, rein them from ruth.° · woeful / pity
HECTOR Fie, savage, fie!
TROILUS   Hector, then 'tis wars.° · then it's a true war

50 HECTOR Troilus, I would not have you fight today.
TROILUS Who should withhold me?
Not fate, obedience, nor the hand of Mars
Beck'ning with fiery truncheon[4] my retire;
Not Priamus and Hecuba on knees,

55 Their eyes o'er-gallèd° with recourse° of tears; · sore / repeated flow
Nor you, my brother, with your true sword drawn
Opposed to hinder me, should stop my way,
But by my ruin.
          Enter PRIAM *and* CASSANDRA.
CASSANDRA Lay hold upon him, Priam. Hold him fast.

1. TEXTUAL COMMENT For the differences between this passage (lines 19–28) and the equivalent lines in Q, see Digital Edition TC 8 (Folio edited text).
2. Lions were said not to attack any animal that submitted to them.
3. The rapidly moving sword is like a fan, blowing his enemies down before he reaches them.
4. Staff of office (carried by the marshal of a formal combat).

60   He is thy crutch. Now if thou lose thy stay,°   *prop*
      Thou on him leaning, and all Troy on thee,
      Fall all together.
    PRIAM   Come, Hector, come; go back.
      Thy wife hath dreamt, thy mother hath had visions,
      Cassandra doth foresee, and I myself
65   Am like a prophet suddenly enrapt°   *inspired*
      To tell thee that this day is ominous.
      Therefore, come back.
    HECTOR   Aeneas is afield,
      And I do stand engaged to many Greeks,
      Even in the faith of valor,° to appear   *warrior's honor*
      This morning to them.
70   PRIAM   Ay, but thou shalt not go.
    HECTOR   I must not break my faith.
      You know me dutiful; therefore, dear sir,
      Let me not shame respect,° but give me leave   *duty to a parent*
      To take that course by your consent and voice
75   Which you do here forbid me, royal Priam.
    CASSANDRA   O Priam, yield not to him!
    ANDROMACHE   Do not, dear father.
    HECTOR   Andromache, I am offended with you.
      Upon the love you bear me, get you in.   *Exit* ANDROMACHE.
    TROILUS   This foolish, dreaming, superstitious girl
      Makes all these bodements.°   *warnings*
80   CASSANDRA   Oh, farewell, dear Hector.
      Look how thou diest, look how thy eye turns pale,
      Look how thy wounds do bleed at many vents!
      Hark, how Troy roars, how Hecuba cries out,
      How poor Andromache shrills her dolor forth.
85   Behold: distraction, frenzy, and amazement,
      Like witless antics,° one another meet,   *buffoons*
      And all cry, "Hector, Hector's dead! O Hector!"
    TROILUS   Away, away.
    CASSANDRA   Farewell—yes, soft.° Hector, I take my leave; *wait a moment*
90   Thou dost thyself and all our Troy deceive.   *Exit.*
    HECTOR   You are amazed, my liege, at her exclaim.°   *outcry*
      Go in and cheer the town. We'll forth and fight,
      Do deeds of praise, and tell you them at night.
    PRIAM   Farewell. The gods with safety stand about thee.
                [*Exeunt* HECTOR *and* PRIAM *separately.*]
         Alarum.
95   TROILUS   They are at it, hark! Proud Diomed, believe:
      I come to lose my arm or win my sleeve.
          Enter PANDARUS.
    PANDARUS   Do you hear, my lord? Do you hear?
    TROILUS   What now?
    PANDARUS   Here's a letter come from yond poor girl.
100   TROILUS   Let me read.
          [TROILUS *reads the letter.*]
    PANDARUS   A whoreson phthisic,° a whoreson rascally phthisic *consumptive cough*
    so troubles me, and the foolish fortune of this girl, and what
    one thing, what another, that I shall leave you one o'these
    days. And I have a rheum° in mine eyes too, and such an *watery discharge*

105   ache in my bones° that, unless a man were cursed, I cannot   *(suggesting syphilis)*
    tell what to think on't. —What says she there?

TROILUS   Words, words, mere words, no matter from the
      heart—
    Th'effect° doth operate another way.   *Her action*
    [*He tears the letter.*]
    Go, wind, to wind, there turn and change together.[5]
110   My love with words and errors° still she feeds,   *lies*
    But edifies another with her deeds.

PANDARUS   Why, but hear you!

TROILUS   Hence, broker-lackey!° Ignomy° and shame   *pimp / Ignominy*
    Pursue thy life, and live aye with thy name.

                          Exeunt [*separately*].[6]

5.4 (Q 5.4)

Alarum. Enter THERSITES [*in the midst of an*]
excursion.°   *advancing troops*

THERSITES   Now they are clapper-clawing° one another; I'll   *thrashing*
    go look on. That dissembling abominable varlet, Diomed,
    has got that same scurvy, doting, foolish young knave's
    sleeve of Troy° there in his helm. I would fain see them   *Trojan knave's sleeve*
5   meet,[1] that that same young Trojan ass that loves the whore
    there might send that Greekish whore-masterly villain with
    the sleeve back to the dissembling luxurious drab of a sleeve-
    less errand.[2] O'th' t'other side, the policy° of those crafty   *statecraft; scheming*
    swearing rascals—that stale old mouse-eaten dry cheese,
10   Nestor, and that same dog-fox,° Ulysses—is not proved   *crafty one*
    worth a blackberry.° They set me up° in policy that mongrel   *proved worthless / set up*
    cur, Ajax, against that dog of as bad a kind, Achilles; and
    now is the cur Ajax prouder than the cur Achilles and will
    not arm today, whereupon the Grecians began to proclaim
15   barbarism,[3] and policy grows into an ill opinion.[4]

        Enter DIOMEDES[*, followed by*] TROILUS.

    Soft! Here comes sleeve and th'other.

TROILUS   Fly not, for shouldst thou take the river Styx,[5]
    I would swim after.

DIOMEDES   Thou dost miscall retire;°   *mistake my retreat*
    I do not fly, but advantageous care°   *tactical caution*
20   Withdrew me from the odds of multitude.
    Have at thee!

THERSITES   Hold thy whore, Grecian! Now for thy whore, Tro-
    jan! Now the sleeve, now the sleeve!

        [*Exeunt* TROILUS *and* DIOMEDES, *fighting.*]
      Enter HECTOR.

---

5. Go, empty words, into the breeze: there, along with the air, toss about ("turn" was often used of sexual infidelity).
6. TEXTUAL COMMENT See Digital Edition TC 9 (Folio edited text) for the textual and associated generic problems raised by lines 112–14, which are absent from the comparable point in Q but are repeated at F 5.11.32–34 and appear, similarly, at Q 5.11.31–33.
5.4 Location: The rest of the play takes place on the battlefield.

1. *fain see them meet:* rejoice to have them fight.
2. To the lying, lecherous slut on a pointless errand (punning on the actual sleeve).
3. Began to set up ignorance (or anarchy) in author- ity ("barbarism" being normally contrasted with "Greek"-ness).
4. *policy . . . opinion:* statecraft (or, more negatively, cunning) gets a bad reputation.
5. Even if you should enter the river of the under- world (as prey go into the water hoping to make the hunter lose the scent).

HECTOR   What art thou, Greek? Art thou for Hector's match?
25   Art thou of blood° and honor?   *nobility*
THERSITES   No, no, I am a rascal, a scurvy railing knave, a
   very filthy rogue.
HECTOR   I do believe thee. Live.[6]   [*Exit.*]
THERSITES   God-a-mercy° that thou wilt believe me, but a   *Thank God*
30   plague break thy neck for frighting me! What's become of
   the wenching rogues? I think they have swallowed one
   another. I would laugh at that miracle—yet, in a sort, lechery eats itself. I'll seek them.   *Exit.*

5.5 (Q 5.5)
Enter DIOMEDES *and* [SERVANT].

DIOMEDES   Go, go, my servant, take thou Troilus' horse;
   Present the fair steed to my lady Cressid.
   Fellow, commend my service to her beauty;
   Tell her I have chastised the amorous Trojan
   And am her knight by proof.°   *(of deeds)*
5   SERVANT   I go, my lord.   [*Exit.*]
Enter AGAMEMNON.

AGAMEMNON   Renew, renew! The fierce Polydamas
   Hath beat down Menon; bastard Margarelon
   Hath Doreus prisoner
   And stands colossus-wise, waving his beam°   *spearshaft*
10   Upon the pashèd° corpses of the kings   *smashed*
   Epistrophus and Cedius. Polyxenes is slain,
   Amphimacus and Thoas deadly hurt,
   Patroclus ta'en or slain, and Palamedes
   Sore hurt and bruised. The dreadful sagittary[1]
15   Appalls our numbers.° Haste we, Diomed,   *soldiers*
   To reinforcement, or we perish all.
Enter NESTOR [*and others*].

NESTOR   Go bear Patroclus' body to Achilles,
   And bid the snail-paced Ajax arm for shame.
                                                      [*Exeunt some.*]
   There is a thousand Hectors in the field:
20   Now here he fights on Galathe his horse,
   And there lacks work; anon he's there afoot,
   And there they fly or die like scalèd schools[2]
   Before the belching° whale; then is he yonder,   *spouting*
   And there the strawy Greeks, ripe for his edge,°   *sword blade*
25   Fall down before him like the mower's swath.
   Here, there, and everywhere he leaves and takes,[3]
   Dexterity so obeying appetite
   That what he will he does, and does so much
   That proof° is called impossibility.   *his achievement*
Enter ULYSSES.

30   ULYSSES   Oh, courage, courage, princes! Great Achilles
   Is arming, weeping, cursing, vowing vengeance.
   Patroclus' wounds have roused his drowsy blood,

---

6. Here, Hector is at once contemptuous and merciful.
5.5
1. A legendary centaurlike beast, armed with bow
and arrows.
2. Scaly (armor-clad) schools of fish.
3. He spares and kills; possibly, he "leaves" the dead
and "takes" on the living.

Together with his mangled Myrmidons,
That noseless, handless, hacked, and chipped come to him,
35 Crying on° Hector. Ajax hath lost a friend   *Complaining of*
And foams at mouth, and he is armed and at it,
Roaring for Troilus, who hath done today
Mad and fantastic execution,
Engaging and redeeming of° himself   *Risking and saving*
40 With such a careless force and forceless care,°   *effortless diligence*
As if that luck, in very spite of cunning,°   *his foes' skill*
Bade him win all.
      Enter AJAX.
AJAX   Troilus, thou coward Troilus!   *Exit.*
DIOMEDES   Ay, there, there!   *Exit.*
NESTOR   So, so, we draw together.°   *join forces*
      Enter ACHILLES.
ACHILLES   Where is this Hector?
45 Come, come, thou boy-queller, show thy face;
Know what it is to meet Achilles angry.
Hector! Where's Hector? I will none but Hector.   *Exeunt.*

5.6 (Q 5.6)

      Enter AJAX.
AJAX   Troilus, thou coward Troilus, show thy head!
      Enter DIOMEDES.
DIOMEDES   Troilus, I say! Where's Troilus?
AJAX   What wouldst thou?
DIOMEDES   I would correct° him.   *chastise*
AJAX   Were I the general
Thou shouldst have my office
5 Ere° that correction. —Troilus, I say! What, Troilus!   *Before you should have*
      Enter TROILUS.
TROILUS   O traitor Diomed! Turn thy false face, thou traitor,
And pay the life thou owest me for my horse.
DIOMEDES   Ha, art thou there?
AJAX   I'll fight with him alone. Stand, Diomed.
10 DIOMEDES   He is my prize; I will not look upon.°   *be a spectator*
TROILUS   Come, both you cogging° Greeks, have at you both!   *cheating*
      Enter HECTOR.
      Exit TROILUS[, *fighting with* AJAX *and* DIOMEDES].
HECTOR   Yea, Troilus! Oh, well fought, my youngest brother!
      Enter ACHILLES.
ACHILLES   Now do I see thee; have at thee, Hector!
      [*They fight, and* ACHILLES *is subdued.*]
HECTOR   Pause if thou wilt.
15 ACHILLES   I do disdain thy courtesy, proud Trojan.
Be happy that my arms are out of use;°   *practice*
My rest and negligence befriends thee now,
But thou anon shalt hear of me again,
Till when, go seek thy fortune.   *Exit.*
HECTOR   Fare thee well.
20 I would have been much more a fresher man
Had I expected thee.
      Enter TROILUS.
          How now, my brother?
TROILUS   Ajax hath ta'en° Aeneas. Shall it be?   *taken captive*

No, by the flame of yonder glorious heaven,
He shall not carry him. I'll be ta'en too,
25 Or bring him off.° Fate, hear me what I say: rescue Aeneas
I reck° not though thou end my life today.   *Exit.*   care
    Enter one in armor.
HECTOR   Stand, stand, thou Greek. Thou art a goodly mark.°   target
No? Wilt thou not? I like thy armor well;
I'll frush° it and unlock the rivets all,   smash
But I'll be master of it.   [*Exit one in armor.*]
30   Wilt thou not, beast, abide?
Why, then, fly on; I'll hunt thee for thy hide.   *Exit.*

5.7 (Q 5.7)

    Enter ACHILLES *with* MYRMIDONS.
ACHILLES   Come here about me, you my Myrmidons.
Mark what I say: attend me where I wheel;°   range
Strike not a stroke, but keep yourselves in breath,
And when I have the bloody Hector found
5 Empale° him with your weapons round about;   Fence in
In fellest° manner execute your arms.   fiercest
Follow me, sirs, and my proceedings eye;
It is decreed Hector the great must die.   *Exeunt.*

5.8 (Q 5.8)

    Enter THERSITES, [*watching*] MENELAUS *and*
    PARIS [*fight*].
THERSITES   The cuckold and the cuckold-maker are at it. Now,
bull! Now, dog! 'Loo, Paris,[1] 'loo! Now, my double-henned
sparrow![2] 'Loo Paris, 'loo. The bull has the game°—'ware°   *is winning / beware*
horns, ho!   *Exeunt* PARIS *and* MENELAUS.
    Enter BASTARD [*Margarelon*].
5 BASTARD   Turn, slave, and fight.
THERSITES   What art thou?
BASTARD   A bastard son of Priam's.
THERSITES   I am a bastard too. I love bastards! I am a bastard
begot, bastard instructed, bastard in mind, bastard in valor,
10 in everything illegitimate. One bear will not bite another,
and wherefore should one bastard? Take heed, the quarrel's
most ominous to us: if the son of a whore fight for a whore,
he tempts judgment. Farewell, bastard.   [*Exit.*]
BASTARD   The devil take thee, coward!   *Exit.*

5.9 (Q 5.9)

    Enter HECTOR.
HECTOR   Most putrifièd core,[1] so fair without,
Thy goodly armor thus hath cost thy life.
Now is my day's work done; I'll take good breath.
Rest, sword, thou hast thy fill of blood and death.

5.8
1. *'Loo:* Halloo (shout to encourage dogs chasing game
or in bullbaiting). *Paris:* the character; Paris Garden,
site of bullbaiting.
2. Paris is meek as a "sparrow" and "double-henned"

in possessing both Helen and a rejected wife.
5.9
1. Pun on French *corps* ("body"); hence, the "corpse"
of the fallen Greek.

[He disarms.]
Enter ACHILLES *and his* MYRMIDONS.

5 ACHILLES Look, Hector, how the sun begins to set,
How ugly night comes breathing at his heels.
Even with the vail[2] and dark'ning of the sun
To close the day up, Hector's life is done.
HECTOR I am unarmed. Forgo this vantage, Greek.
10 ACHILLES Strike, fellows, strike; this is the man I seek.
[They kill HECTOR.*]*
So, Ilium, fall thou. Now, Troy, sink down—
Here lies thy heart, thy sinews, and thy bone.
On, Myrmidons, cry you all amain:°   *with full force*
"Achilles hath the mighty Hector slain!"
Retreat [sounded].
15 Hark, a retreat upon our Grecian part.
[Another retreat sounded.]
A MYRMIDON The Trojan trumpets sounds the like, my lord.
ACHILLES The dragon wing of night o'erspreads the earth
And stickler°-like the armies separates.   *referee (in combat)*
My half-supped° sword that frankly° would have fed,   *half-satisfied / freely*
20 Pleased with this dainty bait,° thus goes to bed.   *snack*
[He sheathes his sword.]
Come, tie his body to my horse's tail;
Along the field I will the Trojan trail.   *Exeunt.*

5.10 (Q 5.10)

Sound retreat. Enter AGAMEMNON, AJAX, MENELAUS,
NESTOR, DIOMEDES, *and the rest, marching.*
Shout [within].
AGAMEMNON Hark, hark, what shout is that?
NESTOR Peace, drums.
SOLDIERS *[within]* Achilles, Achilles! Hector's slain!
    Achilles!
DIOMEDES The bruit° is Hector's slain, and by Achilles.   *report*
5 AJAX If it be so, yet bragless let it be;
Great Hector was a man as good as he.
AGAMEMNON March patiently along. Let one be sent
To pray Achilles see us at our tent.
If in his death the gods have us befriended,
10 Great Troy is ours, and our sharp° wars are ended. *Exeunt.*   *fierce*

5.11 (Q 5.11)

Enter AENEAS, PARIS, *Antenor, and* DEIPHOBUS.
AENEAS Stand ho! Yet are we masters of the field.
Never go home; here starve we out the night.[1]
Enter TROILUS.
TROILUS Hector is slain.
ALL   Hector? The gods forbid!
TROILUS He's dead, and at the murderer's horse's tail

---

2. At the same time as the setting.
5.11
1. Wait in discomfort; outlast, kill by starvation (the night being imagined as a city under siege). TEXTUAL

COMMENT For the different consequences of attributing this line to Aeneas, here, or to Troilus, in Q, see Digital Edition TC 10 (Folio edited text).

5   In beastly sort° dragged through the shameful field.   *manner*
       Frown on, you heavens; effect your rage with speed.
       Sit, gods, upon your thrones and smile at Troy.
       I say at once: let your brief plagues be mercy,[2]
       And linger not our sure destructions on.
10 AENEAS   My lord, you do discomfort all the host.°   *army*
     TROILUS   You understand me not that tell me so.
       I do not speak of flight, of fear, of death,
       But dare all imminence that gods and men
       Address their dangers in.[3] Hector is gone.
15   Who shall tell Priam so, or Hecuba?
       Let him that will a screech-owl aye° be called   *voice of doom always*
       Go into Troy and say there, "Hector's dead."
       There is a word° will Priam turn to stone,   *sentence that*
       Make wells and Niobes[4] of the maids and wives,
20   Cold statues of the youth, and, in a word,
       Scare Troy out of itself. But march away.
       Hector is dead; there is no more to say.
       Stay yet, you vile abominable tents
       Thus proudly pitched upon our Phrygian plains.
25   Let Titan° rise as early as he dare,   *sun god Hyperion*
       I'll through and through you. And thou great-sized
          coward,°   *(Achilles)*
       No space of earth shall sunder our two hates.
       I'll haunt thee like a wicked° conscience still°   *guilty / continually*
       That moldeth goblins swift as frenzy's thoughts.[5]
30   Strike a free march to Troy, with comfort° go;   *this one comfort*
       Hope of revenge shall hide our inward woe.
                    Enter PANDARUS.
     PANDARUS   But hear you, hear you!
     TROILUS   Hence, broker-lackey! [*He strikes him.*] Ignomy and
          shame
       Pursue thy life and live aye with thy name.
                              Exeunt [*all but* PANDARUS].
35 PANDARUS   A goodly medicine for mine aching bones. Oh,
       world, world, world! Thus is the poor agent despised. O trai-
       tors and bawds, how earnestly are you set a-work,° and how   *to work*
       ill requited. Why should our endeavor be so desired and the
       performance so loathed? What verse for it? What instance°   *traditional saying*
40   for it? Let me see:
          Full merrily the humble-bee doth sing,
          Till he hath lost his honey and his sting;
          And, being once subdued in armèd tail,[6]
          Sweet honey and sweet notes together fail.
45   Good traders in the flesh, set this in your painted cloths:[7]
       As many as be here of panders' hall,°   *guild hall*
       Your eyes, half out,[8] weep out at Pandar's fall.
       Or if you cannot weep, yet give some groans,

---

2. Be mercifully quick in destruction.
3. *But . . . in:* But dare all impending danger that gods and men prepare for me.
4. Mythical Queen of Thebes, who wept so much at the murder of her children by the gods that the gods turned her into a statue that flowed with water.
5. Generates evil spirits (in the mind) as quickly as

frenzy produces mad "thoughts."
6. And having lost his sting: alluding to impotence caused by venereal disease.
7. Inexpensive substitutes for tapestries, often including moralistic inscriptions.
8. Half-blinded by venereal disease.

Though not for me, yet for your aching bones.°   *(from syphilis)*
50   Brethren and sisters of the hold-door trade,°   *Pimps and bawds*
     Some two months hence my will shall here be made.[9]
     It should be now, but that my fear is this:
     Some gallèd goose of Winchester would hiss.[1]
     Till then I'll sweat[2] and seek about for eases,
55   And at that time bequeath you my diseases.   *Exit.*

9. The word "here" is possibly a reference to the stage of the Globe and hence the promise of a sequel that never materialized; it has also been taken to refer to an Inn of Court, where young men studied law, a plausible place to make a "will" and thus hypothesized by some scholars to be the location of the first performance. See the Introduction.

1. A prostitute or customer afflicted with venereal disease, from the diocese of Winchester (which had jurisdiction over Southwark, home of both the brothels and the Globe), would disapprove—of the will and/or the play.
2. Usual treatment for venereal disease.

Measure for Measure

A young man is in grave trouble with the law, and his beautiful sister goes to the magistrate to plead for mercy. The magistrate offers to remit the penalty if the sister will sleep with him. It is an old story in more ways than one. Shakespeare knew several sixteenth-century versions: the Italian Giovanbattista Giraldi Cinthio produced both prose and dramatic renderings, and in 1578 the English playwright George Whetstone published *Promos and Cassandra*, the most important source for *Measure for Measure*. Shakespeare's play was first performed in 1603 or 1604, though the text we have is probably derived from a revival staged in 1621 and likely contains some material by the younger playwright Thomas Middleton.

In the mid-to-late 1590s and the first years of the seventeenth century, Shakespeare wrote a series of comedies that explore complex issues of sex, marriage, and personal identity. *Measure for Measure* is the last play in this group. Its tone, themes, and methods of characterization veer close to tragedy, the genre that largely, though not exclusively, preoccupied Shakespeare in the years immediately following. Many critics, therefore, classify *Measure for Measure* as a "problem" comedy. The designation attests both to the difficult moral issues that the play confronts and to the boldness with which it stretches—some would say shatters—the normal limits of comic form. In *Measure for Measure*, Shakespeare considers the often-vexed relationship between civic life and human passion, and between religious commitment and the conduct of secular affairs. Is it possible or advisable to regulate sexual behavior through the courts? How do religious convictions affect the experience of sexual desire? These concerns resonate in an era like our own, characterized by a lack of consensus in religion and in sexual mores, by widespread transformations in the institution of marriage, and by debates over the extent to which the state ought to monitor the sexual behavior of citizens.

The play's distinctiveness becomes evident almost immediately. In act 1, scene 2, Claudio and his pregnant lover, Juliet, appear in the custody of the Provost, being led away to prison. Their crime is premarital sex; the penalty, for Claudio at least, is death. Claudio's initial description of his plight is quite remarkable:

> LUCIO   Why, how now, Claudio? Whence comes this restraint?
> CLAUDIO   From too much liberty, my Lucio, liberty.
>   As surfeit is the father of much fast,
>   So every scope by the immoderate use
>   Turns to restraint. Our natures do pursue,
>   Like rats that raven down their proper bane,
>   A thirsty evil, and when we drink, we die.
>
> (1.2.113–19)

Claudio likens his passion for his beloved to a rat's craving for poison: compulsive, irrational, and self-destructive. Excessive indulgence, or "surfeit," inevitably brings regret and punishment in its train. Claudio sounds as if he is describing the most arrant kind of lust, although, as he will subsequently explain, he is actually "precontracted" to Juliet—bound by a promise of marriage that many in Renaissance England saw as providing conjugal privileges. (Shakespeare himself may have subscribed to this view, since his wife gave birth to their daughter five months after their wedding. More pertinent, the Duke, in his guise as a friar, affirms that the precontract sanctions

Mariana's intimacy with Angelo later in the play.) It is interesting, however, that neither Claudio nor Juliet argues that their devotion to each other mitigates their guilt. Instead, they admit that they have committed "fornication," a severely condemnatory term that conflates all kinds of sex outside of marriage under the same rubric, recognizing no difference between long-term relationships and sheerest promiscuity.

As the play continues, it becomes clear that Claudio's imagery of suicidal animalism, havoc, and pollution is not merely the consequence of his immediate agitation, but expresses a profound assumption of the society in which he lives. For his sister, Isabella, sexual intercourse is "what I abhor to name" (3.1.101). The Duke deplores Pompey's "filthy vice" and Juliet's "most offenseful act." The wise Escalus acknowledges Claudio's "error" even as he attempts to alleviate his punishment. Few doubt that human sexuality is an essentially sordid matter, a sign of degradation rather than a means of creativity or love. Occasional glimpses of an alternative vision—Lucio's brief, radiant analogy between Juliet's pregnancy and agricultural fertility, for instance—by their very rarity reinforce the prevailing pessimism.

Such austere views of human sexuality have ancient roots. When the Duke calls Vienna's sex laws "needful bits and curbs to headstrong jades" (1.3.20), he recalls an image from Plato, who compared the desiring part of the soul to a useful but refractory horse, which the rational part of the soul needs to keep strictly bridled and under firm control. When Isabella refers to erotic desire as a "natural guiltiness" (2.2.140), she draws upon a traditional Christian connection between sexuality and original sin, the disobedience committed by Adam and Eve in the Garden of Eden and passed on to all their offspring as a kind of intrinsic pollution.

To say that a view is traditional, however, is not to say that it is inevitable. What makes sexuality so troublesome in this particular play? In Shakespeare's earlier, more optimistic comedies, the prospect of heterosexual consummation usually seems automatically to entail marriage, so that the weddings with which the plays conclude seem to follow spontaneously from the eroticism that fuels the plot. By marrying and establishing a family, the young couples satisfy their mutual yearning for one another as well as their community's demand for clear kinship structures and for orderly means of transferring property to "legitimate" members of a new generation. In *Measure for Measure*, however, the link between heterosexual desire and marriage seems to have snapped. Claudio and Juliet defer their wedding day; Angelo abandons Mariana; Lucio refuses to support his child or marry the mother. Prostitution flourishes. Rampant promiscuity makes syphilis a familiar ailment and a standard topic for nervous jokes.

Charioteer with two galloping horses. From Geffrey Whitney, *A Choice of Emblems* (1586).

Once carnal desire comes unhinged from the institution of marriage, it begins to seem subversive of personal and civic order. And if one believes that one's sexuality is intrinsically antisocial and depraved, then complete sexual renunciation might seem the wisest course. In *Measure for Measure*, the morally ambitious characters—the Duke, Angelo, and Isabella—initially assume that their virtue is tied up with, perhaps even identical with, their chastity. "Believe not that the dribbling dart of love / Can pierce a complete bosom," the Duke boasts to the Friar (1.3.2–3). Angelo attempts to protect his reputation for austerity even as he hopelessly compromises his scruples in secret. Isabella believes that sleeping with Angelo will defile her forever, even if she does so in order to save her brother's life.

The value of celibacy is endorsed by characters who do not themselves aspire to such high standards of conduct. Lucio is a libertine, but he believes that Isabella's intention to enter a nunnery renders her "a thing enskied and sainted" (1.4.35). Likewise, Pompey admits that his life as a pimp "does stink in some sort, sir" (3.1.282). A few of those who cannot be chaste themselves are, like Claudio, capable of moments of shame or self-loathing; others, like Lucio, shruggingly accept their lack of saintliness. The Vienna of *Measure for Measure* is full of people unlikely to be enlisted for projects of social or spiritual improvement: the moronic Elbow, the impenitent Pompey, the unregenerate Bawd, the "gravel-hearted" Barnardine, the heedless First and Second Gentlemen, the gullible Froth. These people are part of the commonwealth, subject to the law. They are willy-nilly part, too, of a Roman Catholic Church that aspires—as the Church of England did as well in Shakespeare's day—to include the entire community. Should the laws of this community reflect its stringent ideals or the actual behavior of most of its members? Throughout *Measure for Measure*, those who aspire to belong to a principled moral elite deplore the weaknesses of the reprobate. At the same time, because the rascals are so vividly memorable, the play also suggests that moral failure is often at least as humanly compelling as moral excellence is—at least moral excellence defined in the narrow, self-denying terms that prevail in Vienna.

For the intransigent majority unable or unwilling to control the horses of lust, the "needful bits and curbs" of which the Duke speaks (1.3.20) impose an external system of repression. Such a system would not have been unfamiliar to Shakespeare's original audience. Courts administered by the Church of England prosecuted many sexual infractions: among them fathering or giving birth to a bastard, committing adultery or bigamy, deserting a spouse, reneging on a wedding engagement, or groundlessly accusing others of such transgressions. Convicted individuals could be fined, whipped, displayed in the marketplace, or made to announce their sins in church. (Thus, Claudio and Juliet are paraded about the streets of Vienna before being taken to prison, to humiliate them and to serve as an example for others.) Repeat offenders were excommunicated, or cast out of the church.

Underlying such proceedings was the assumption, as in *Measure for Measure,* that morality could and should be legislated; that the sexual conduct of individuals was the business of the entire community. Indeed, in the early seventeenth century, when Shakespeare was writing *Measure for Measure,* an increasingly powerful group of Puritans, or "precisians," argued that the church courts' punishments were far too mild. Threats of disgrace and excommunication failed to deter the worst offenders, who had no reputation to lose and were unlikely to fret at their exclusion from church. Moreover, shaming punishments worked less well in the increasingly busy, heterogeneous neighborhoods of Jacobean London than they had in the smaller rural communities for which they were originally designed.

In *Measure for Measure,* the repeated characterization of Angelo as "precise" associates him with the rigorists of Shakespeare's time; and since Viennese justice treats Claudio more strictly than it does professionals in the sex trade, the question of what constitutes adequate severity is certainly at issue. Perhaps, then, the play constitutes Shakespeare's reflection on an issue of contemporary concern: what would happen if, as some argued, sexual misconduct could be punished with death? At the same time, Shakespeare carefully distinguishes the world of his play from that of seventeenth-century England, most obviously by making Vienna a Roman Catholic city peopled with the nuns and friars who had been eliminated from Protestant England over half a century earlier. For despite obvious connections between *Measure for Measure* and some of the issues of its own day, Shakespeare's play hardly constitutes a clear policy recommendation.

In *Measure for Measure,* Angelo's disastrous career suggests one possible effect of strict sexual self-denial: that the habits of restraint can themselves provoke sexual excitement. Rigid and self-righteous, Angelo seems not to have experienced the violence of desire until Isabella's first visit on behalf of her brother awakens his appetite:

> What's this, what's this? Is this her fault or mine?
> The tempter or the tempted, who sins most, ha?
> Not she, nor doth she tempt. But it is I
> That, lying by the violet in the sun,
> Do as the carrion does, not as the flower,
> Corrupt with virtuous season.

> (2.2.165–70)

Like Claudio, Angelo thinks of passion in terms of death and decay, but the resemblance between the two men ends there. Angelo imagines himself as tainted meat rotting all the faster under the very sun that gives life to innocent, lovely things. What ought to improve Angelo—his keen appreciation for the presence of virtue—makes him worse.

Angelo is sexually aroused by prohibition. Mariana loves him, and his relationship with her breaches no social norms; he discards her. Isabella is ostentatiously pristine, and her nun's habit marks her as taboo; he finds her irresistible. In order to extract pleasure from the encounter, however, Angelo must force himself to remain

Poor Clare nun. From Jost Amman, *Cleri totius Romanae ecclesiae subjecti* (1585).

aware of the principles he attempts so flagrantly to violate. If he rationalized his behavior or blamed it on Isabella, he would lose the nearly sensual luxury of self-hatred. Therefore, the lucidity with which Angelo analyzes his own motives leads not to penitence or self-restraint, but to an increasing recklessness. His inclination to categorize all sexual conduct as transgressive actually makes his offense easier to commit. Propositioning Isabella in their second meeting together, he tells her: "I have begun, / And now I give my sensual race the rein" (2.4.156–57). Angelo explains why he cannot govern himself with the same image of horsemanship that the Duke used to underscore the necessity of control. Once embarked on the "sensual race," Angelo imagines, there is no alternative to utter abandon.

For Isabella, however, sleeping with Angelo is out of the question. Some modern critics have found her defiance heroic, others chilling or selfish. Probably in Shakespeare's time she elicited a similarly mixed response. Shakespeare alters his source story considerably to expand Isabella's role and to specify its implications more exactly. In Whetstone's *Promos and Cassandra,* the sister has no plans to enter a convent, and she eventually goes to bed with the deputy in order to save her brother's life. For Isabella, by contrast, virginity is a principled choice, not an accident of youth. The vow of lifelong, religiously dedicated chastity she plans to take is a matter about which Shakespeare's contemporaries had conflicting feelings. One effect of England's break with the Catholic Church had been a spectacular change in official attitudes toward celibacy. While Catholics honored sexual renunciation and demanded that their clergy remain chaste, Protestants discouraged veneration of the Virgin Mary, abolished convents and monasteries, and urged clergy to marry. Despite these alterations, however, a powerful appreciation for virginity and belief in its semimagical powers persisted in Reformation England. The effect of Shakespeare's innovations on Whetstone, then, is both to heighten the ambivalence of the story and to focus the moral spotlight on Isabella's convictions and the choices that follow from them.

Isabella believes that she would damn herself by sleeping with Angelo.

> Better it were a brother died at once
> Than that a sister by redeeming him
> Should die forever.
>   (2.4.103–05)

Is she right? There is a long tradition of considering such questions. St. Augustine, the most influential Christian writer on sexual morality, insists that since sin is a property of the will, not a physical state, persons who are forced to perform sexual acts are blameless. Chastity, he argues, is a state of mind. In that case, the fate of Isabella's body is possibly independent of, and irrelevant to, the fate of her soul. Perhaps, in fact, by acquiescing to Angelo, Isabella would perform an act of charity, generously sacrificing her own preferences for Claudio's benefit. However, female "virtue" has traditionally been defined in physical as well as mental terms, so that chastity, the spiritual attitude, is hard to separate from virginity, the bodily condition. Moreover, Isabella is not the victim of forcible rape; she must, as Angelo says, "fit her consent" to his proposal. Does that consent, however reluctant, contaminate her with his sin? Quite possibly. Would it permanently unsuit her for her religious vocation? Quite possibly. Clearly, it is reasonable, then, for Isabella to be cautious; and no one, says Augustine, is obliged to put him- or herself in eternal peril merely in order to save the life of another person.

Since, however, Shakespeare characteristically translates sweeping moral questions into scrupulously personal terms, apparently reasonable general maxims do not entirely suffice to explain Isabella's motives. On the one hand, her obstinacy seems justified after the fact, when Angelo decides to execute Claudio, because clearly her capitulation would not have saved her brother's life. On the other hand, Isabella's obsession with her own purity seems excessive, especially in 3.1, when it manifests itself in gross insensitivity to her plaintive, terrified brother. Moreover, her fervent yearning for constraint, like Angelo's, seems luridly tinged with sadomasochism.

> were I under the terms of death,
> Th'impression of keen whips I'd wear as rubies,
> And strip myself to death as to a bed
> That longing have been sick for, ere I'd yield
> My body up to shame.
>
> (2.4.97–101)

At such moments, Isabella seems not to be exterminating or transcending her own sexuality, but redirecting it in ways of which she is not entirely conscious. She not only shares Angelo's assumption that the sexual act is a defilement, but like him she finds discipline exciting. With all our disapproval of Angelo's abuse of power and our sympathy with Isabella's indignation, we can still see how the conflict between them arises as much from their similarities as from their differences.

Isabella's difficulty is hard to resolve because it is unclear how much her chastity is worth. Is it more valuable than her brother's life? Is it more valuable than her own life, which she would throw down for Claudio, she claims, "as frankly as a pin" (3.1.105)? Is it only fair, as Angelo claims, to yield him her body as compensation for overlooking Claudio's offense, or is "lawful mercy . . . nothing kin to foul redemption" (2.4.109–10)? Shakespeare provides no answer to these questions, but the conflict they produce yields the play's most vividly realized interactions. As the title suggests, *Measure for Measure* is obsessed with problems of equivalence, asking us to reflect on which things are commensurable to, or equal in value to, or might be substituted for, which other things. We see this preoccupation in the opening scene in which Angelo takes over as the Duke's deputy, in Angelo's proposal that Isabella vindicate Claudio by committing his sin herself, in the bed trick that replaces Isabella with Mariana, in the Provost's exchange of Ragozine's head for Claudio's. Even the most apparently trivial comic interchanges persistently echo the concern with equivalence, proportionality, and relative priority: the Gentlemen argue about whether they are cut from lists or velvet; Pompey and Abhorson debate the relative standing of bawd and hangman.

Questions of equivalence seem to underlie the very possibility of justice, even the possibility of any ethical thinking. A wrongdoer ought, we feel, either to make adequate restitution for his or her misdeeds or to suffer in rough proportion to the anguish he or she has caused. Who can assess those penalties, who is subject to them, and how rigorous they ought to be—these become pressing issues again and again in *Measure for Measure*. Shakespeare takes the title of the play from Jesus' Sermon on the Mount: "Judge not, that ye be not judged. For with what judgment you judge, you shall be judged, and with what measure you mete, it shall be meted unto you again" (Matthew 7:1–2). The Bible passage is a complex one: even while assuring believers that ultimately, strict justice will be served, Jesus advises believers not to pass judgment at all. What would it mean to "judge not" in practical terms, given that some kind of justice system seems necessary for an orderly society?

In sexual matters, problems of just equivalence are especially murky, because there is no consensus regarding how apparently straightforward bodily acts ought to be interpreted. Angelo compares Claudio's offense to murder and counterfeiting; Lucio thinks it is trivial, "a game of tick-tack" (1.2.178). What seem to be the same actions can be evaluated in wildly different ways, depending on one's frame of reference: to the abstemious Angelo, Claudio's behavior looks like gross debauchery, while to the Bawd's dissolute patrons, it looks positively restrained. Motives alter what seem to be the same actions, so that we are inclined to regard Claudio more leniently than Lucio, who abandoned his mistress after making her pregnant. So do outcomes: the bed trick means that Angelo, intending to commit an impermissible act, in fact performs a licit one, unknowingly laying the groundwork for his pardon in the final scene.

The commitment of several characters to a Christian religious vocation further complicates the possibility of establishing some consensus about proper equivalence. Isabella, especially, assumes that spiritual goods like honor and purity are infinitely more important than secular, visible possessions. In her system of values, a promise of ardent prayer constitutes the most potent bribe she can offer Angelo, beside which gold is barren and trivial. Isabella's counterintuitive otherworldliness is central to Christianity, a religion founded on the spectacularly lopsided substitution of the blameless Christ for sinful humanity in the system of God's justice. But since such religious convictions are not subject to the verification of the senses, they are open to challenge by those more firmly attached to the things of this world. For Claudio, any fate seems better than death. His hierarchy of priorities is different from Isabella's.

How are such drastic discrepancies between the various characters' moral and social outlooks to be reconciled? The agent for bringing order and justice is Duke Vincentio, a concealed authority who learns everybody's secrets in the course of the play. Far from providing an authoritative solution to the play's ethical impasse, however, the Duke has elicited almost as much controversy as Isabella. Some critics see him as a version of God, "like power divine," as Angelo declares in the final scene (5.1.371). Some have suggested that the Duke was meant to compliment the diffident King James I, who at the time of the play's first performance had recently ascended the English throne after the death of his extroverted predecessor, Elizabeth I. More skeptical critics see the Duke as a schemer who foists his dirty work onto political subordinates and meddles impudently, even sacrilegiously, with the lives of his subjects.

Controversy over the Duke's role perhaps reflects the fact that the task he needs to accomplish requires him to wield two ordinarily distinct forms of power. The problems of Measure for Measure can be solved only by someone who can obtain access to the concealed realm of motives and intentions, a privilege usually reserved for a confessor. But merely knowing such information will not bring practical redress of injustice. So at the same time, unlike a clergyman, the Duke must retain the secular ruler's ability to mandate changes in the world. A prince disguised as a friar, the Duke bridges, however unsteadily, the gap between power and knowledge. His sweeping authority conveniently enables him to impose a resolution.

There are limits, however, even to Vincentio's power. Not even a duke can sequester erotic fervor from the cruelty and disorder with which it seems, in this play, to be so intimately and insidiously allied. Not even a duke can make passion tractable. The best he can manage is to introduce his subjects to some socially sanctioned medium between celibacy and abandon. Marriage in Measure for Measure is thus patently not a happy aspiration but a stopgap measure imposed on reluctant or noncommittal individuals, for whom the alternative in several cases is death. Indeed, Lucio, forthright as usual, complains that marriage is a worse fate than hanging; the others are distinctly muted in their response to the Duke's nuptial stratagems. Claudio and Juliet are given no lines in which to celebrate their reunion; nor do we hear that Angelo, who claims to "crave death more willingly than mercy" (5.1.480), is grateful to be preserved as Mariana's husband. Isabella remains silent in the face of the Duke's unexpected proposal of marriage, leaving it an open question whether she is overwhelmed with joy or gripped with horror. Does the Duke provide her with a socially and personally satisfying alternative to the cloister, or does he, from Isabella's point of view, merely recapitulate Angelo's harassment?

The pro forma quality of the coupling with which Measure for Measure concludes suggests that marital union is not, finally, the resolution toward which the play most convincingly moves. In quick succession, the Duke's trial in the last scene rehearses the normal outcome of Isabella's complaint—her condemnation and

Angelo's exoneration—and then demonstrates that in this instance, almost miraculously, Angelo's secret vice will be made manifest after all. But this disclosure does not end the play, for the Duke's plan demands that Isabella plead for Angelo's life "against all sense" (5.1.436), as the Sermon on the Mount commands her to do. The simple asceticism of the flesh with which *Measure for Measure* begins is displaced at last by a more subtle and exacting asceticism of the spirit, as Isabella renounces the hunger for vengeance in favor of a forgiveness that goes very much against the grain. Only this principled willingness to overlook injury and tolerate difference, the play seems to imply, can still the jostling among heterogeneous moral perspectives that endlessly complicate life in Vienna.

KATHARINE EISAMAN MAUS

SELECTED BIBLIOGRAPHY

Adelman, Janet. "Bed Tricks: On Marriage as the End of Comedy in *All's Well That Ends Well* and *Measure for Measure*." *Shakespeare's Personality*. Ed. Norman H. Holland, Sidney Homan, and Bernard J. Paris. Berkeley: U of California P, 1989. 151–74. Explores sexuality as defilement and marriage as punishment in *Measure for Measure*.

Beckwith, Sara. "Medieval Penance, Reformation Repentance, and *Measure for Measure*." *Reading the Medieval in Early Modern England*. Ed. Gordon McMullan and David Matthews. Cambridge: Cambridge UP, 2007. 193–204. Examines changing ways of thinking about confession, repentance, and the role of church and state, as reflected in *Measure for Measure*.

Bennett, Josephine Waters. *"Measure for Measure" as Royal Entertainment*. New York: Columbia UP, 1966. An examination of the play as it reflects James I's court, political philosophy, and royal persona.

Bloom, Harold, ed. *William Shakespeare's "Measure for Measure."* New York: Chelsea House, 1987. An anthology of critical essays.

Engle, Lars. "*Measure for Measure* and Modernity: The Problem of the Skeptic's Authority." *Shakespeare and Modernity: Early Modern to Millennium*. Ed. Hugh Grady. New York: Routledge, 2000. 85–104. Discusses ethical relativism and difficulties of judgment.

Jowett, John. "*Measure for Measure*: A Genetic Text." *Thomas Middleton: The Collected Works*. Oxford: Clarendon, 2007. 1542–85. Makes the case that Middleton revised *Measure for Measure* in 1621 and analyzes the significance of the changes he may have introduced.

Maus, Katharine Eisaman. "Sexual Secrecy in *Measure for Measure*." *Inwardness and Theater in the English Renaissance*. Chicago: U of Chicago P, 1995. 157–81. Examines sexual privacy as a challenge for legal supervision and as the grounds for character in *Measure for Measure*.

Shell, Marc. *The End of Kinship: "Measure for Measure," Incest, and the Ideal of Universal Siblinghood*. Stanford: Stanford UP, 1988. An analysis of proper and improper exchanges in the Christian world of *Measure for Measure*, in which everyone is a brother or sister to everyone else.

Shuger, Debora Kuller. *Political Theologies in Shakespeare's England: The Sacred and the State in "Measure for Measure."* New York: Palgrave, 2001. Argues that *Measure for Measure* shows the intimate connection between problems of governance and religion in early modern Europe.

Wheeler, Richard P. *Shakespeare's Development and The Problem Comedies: Turn and Counter-Turn*. Berkeley: U of California P, 1981. 1–33; 92–153. Offers a detailed psychoanalytic interpretation.

FILM

Measure for Measure. 1979. Dir. Desmond Davis. UK. This BBC-TV production features nuanced performances from the entire ensemble, particularly Tim Pigott-Smith (Angelo), Kenneth Colley (Duke), Kate Nelligan (Isabella), and Frank Middlemass (Pompey).

TEXTUAL INTRODUCTION

Measure for Measure was first printed in the 1623 First Folio. It is one of a group of plays occurring at the start of the Folio, including *The Tempest,* for which there is reason to think that the printers were working not from Shakespeare's own papers directly but from a now-lost transcript prepared by the professional scribe Ralph Crane. All subsequent printings derive from the Folio, which is the sole authoritative text for this play.

There are some internal inconsistencies, of which the clearest example occurs in 1.2, where the Bawd seems suddenly to forget the news that she has told everyone about Claudio's misfortune. These loose ends suggest revision of some sort. Furthermore, the song that appears in 4.1 also appears, in a more complete version, in *Rollo Duke of Normandy, or The Bloody Brother,* a play by John Fletcher, Philip Massinger, and possibly others, first performed around 1617; this fact might suggest that revision of *Measure for Measure* took place later than 1603–04, when it was first performed. The most developed version of this theory, put forward by the Oxford editors of *Measure for Measure* and articulated at greater length in the 2007 edition of Thomas Middleton's *Collected Works,* is that the play as we have it is a version substantially revised by Middleton for performance by the King's Men after Shakespeare's death. The Middleton theory remains unproven but persuasive.

If the Middleton hypothesis is correct, then there might be an argument for offering an edition of the play that attempts to purge it of its later revisions and return it to something like the state in which it might have existed in 1604. However, such an edition would be highly conjectural, because the play is only known through the 1623 version. Instead, the text of *Measure for Measure* offered here follows closely that of the First Folio, resisting the temptation to restructure the text we have so as to resolve apparent inconsistencies such as that noted in 1.2. In accordance with the policy of the edition as a whole, it also retains the character names in the forms favored by the First Folio: thus, CLOWN and BAWD are found in this edition as speech prefixes rather than POMPEY and MISTRESS OVERDONE.

Measure for Measure contains a number of passages that are so difficult to interpret that editors have suspected the text has become corrupt, either through mistakes in manuscript copying or through errors made by the compositors. Over the centuries, a large critical literature has built up around these cruces, as they are called, the most famous of which is perhaps the "brakes of ice / brakes of vice" passage (2.1.39). Each crux has attracted different attempts to make sense of it as it stands, as well as competing emendations that attempt to diagnose and correct errors in the text.

In making decisions about which emendations or explanations to adopt in each case, this edition is one of the first to be able to use the computer database *Early English Books Online,* which searches an electronic full-text database of (currently) around 30,000 early modern texts. For instance, *EEBO* finds hitherto unnoticed examples of Shakespeare's contemporaries using metaphorical phrases such as "brakes of vanity" or "brakes of sensuality." The same search currently finds no other instances of "brakes of" being followed by a word relating to ice. That result has informed this edition's decision to prefer the emendation "brakes of vice" at 2.1.39. *EEBO* similarly underpins decisions about the other cruces, as well as informing the three entirely new emendations offered in this text at 2.4.75, 4.1.53, and 4.4.24. For further details, see Digital Edition TC 3 and TC 8.

MATTHEW STEGGLE

TEXTUAL BIBLIOGRAPHY

Murphy, Andrew, ed. A *Concise Companion to Shakespeare and the Text*. Chichester: Wiley-Blackwell, 2010.
Shakespeare, William. *Measure for Measure*. Ed. Mark Eccles. New York: MLA, 1980.
Stewart, Alan. *Shakespeare's Letters*. Oxford: Oxford UP, 2008.

PERFORMANCE NOTE

Productions of *Measure for Measure* can convince audiences that any of the play's three leads—the Duke of Vienna, Isabella, or Angelo—occupies its central position, and each role can be played so as to deserve sympathy or condemnation, so performances can feel revelatory even to those already intimately familiar with the play. Whatever balance is struck among attention to the Duke's motives for abandoning authority, Isabella's moral dilemmas regarding sin and self-sacrifice, and Angelo's decline under the influence of power, each production must decide whether its Duke will appear more as a benevolent savior or a machiavel, whether Isabella performs piety or lives it, and whether Angelo is a victim of temptation or a vicious hypocrite. Productions must also determine how Isabella will react to the Duke's proposal and whether to indicate any romantic chemistry between the two beforehand.

Like its characters, the play's contrasting settings of state and street accommodate widely different interpretations. In some productions, a totalitarian government oppresses an attractive and pleasure-loving populace, often with signs of institutional control in the form of prison gates and crucifixes looming large. In others, benign leaders toil on behalf of a city wholly devoted to its own dissolution. Religion can be an oppressive or a vitalizing force, according to the production's emphasis on the prudery and self-righteousness of the nobles or the vulgarity of the masses. To these ends, many directors have opted for a Victorian setting that complements church and state efforts to legislate morality, while others have taken the play's illicit expressions of sexuality as grounds to portray Vienna as one big red light district.

BRETT GAMBOA

Measure for Measure

Vincentio, DUKE of Vienna
ANGELO, the deputy
ESCALUS, an ancient lord
CLAUDIO, a young gentleman
JULIET, beloved of Claudio
ISABELLA, sister to Claudio
LUCIO, a fantastic°   *an impulsive eccertric*
Two other like GENTLEMEN
FROTH, a foolish gentleman
Mistress Overdone, a BAWD
Pompey, her tapster, the CLOWN
The PROVOST
ELBOW, a simple constable
A JUSTICE
ABHORSON, an executioner
BARNARDINE, a dissolute prisoner
MARIANA, betrothed to Angelo
A BOY, Mariana's servant
FRIAR Thomas
Friar PETER
Francisca, a NUN
MESSENGER
SERVANTS
Varrius, a lord
Lords, Officers, Citizens

1.1

     Enter DUKE, ESCALUS, [and] Lords.[1]
DUKE   Escalus.
ESCALUS My lord.
DUKE   Of government the properties to unfold°   *explain*
    Would seem in me to affect° speech and discourse,   *love; show off*
5   Since I am put° to know that your own science°   *obliged / knowledge*
    Exceeds in that the lists° of all advice   *limits*
    My strength can give you. Then no more remains
    But that, to° your sufficiency,° as your worth is able,   *rely on / ability*
    And let them[2] work. The nature of our people,
10 Our city's institutions, and the terms°   *procedures*
    For common justice, you're as pregnant° in   *expert*
    As art° and practice hath enrichèd any   *learning*
    That we remember. There is our commission,
    From which we would not have you warp.°   *deviate*

1.1 Location: The play takes place in Vienna. Some scene locations can merely be inferred. This scene may be set in the Duke's palace.
1. TEXTUAL COMMENT In the Folio (F) text, the Duke is called "Vincentio" only in the cast list; stage directions and speech prefixes refer to him as "Duke." See Digital Edition TC 1 for a discussion on the different implications of these ways of referring to this character.
2. The referent of "them" is unclear. Perhaps a line is missing.

[*He gives* ESCALUS *a paper.*]
                                 Call hither,

15   I say bid come before us, Angelo.
What figure of us, think you, he will bear?[3]
For you must know, we have with special soul°   *deliberation*
Elected° him our absence to supply:°   *Chosen / make up for*
Lent him our terror, dressed him with our love,
20   And given his deputation° all the organs°   *deputyship / instruments*
Of our own power. What think you of it?
  ESCALUS   If any in Vienna be of worth
To undergo° such ample grace° and honor,   *sustain / favor*
It is Lord Angelo.
          Enter ANGELO.
  DUKE   Look where he comes.
25   ANGELO   Always obedient to your grace's will,
I come to know your pleasure.
  DUKE   Angelo,
There is a kind of character[4] in thy life
That to th'observer doth thy history°   *life story*
Fully unfold. Thyself and thy belongings°   *endowments*
30   Are not thine own so proper° as to waste   *exclusively*
Thyself upon thy virtues, they on thee.
Heaven doth with us as we with torches do,
Not light them for themselves. For if our virtues
Did not go forth of° us, 'twere all alike   *from*
35   As if we had them not.[5] Spirits are not finely touched
But to fine issues,[6] nor nature never lends
The smallest scruple° of her excellence,   *bit*
But like a thrifty goddess she determines°   *ordains*
Herself the glory of a creditor,
40   Both thanks and use.° But I do bend° my speech   *interest / direct*
To one that can my part in him advertise.°   *make known*
Hold,[7] therefore, Angelo.
In our remove be thou at full ourself.
Mortality° and mercy in Vienna   *Power to kill*
45   Live in thy tongue and heart. Old Escalus,
Though first in question, is thy secondary.[8]
Take thy commission.
  ANGELO   Now, good my lord,
Let there be some more test made of my mettle°   *punning on "metal"*
Before so noble and so great a figure
Be stamped upon it.
50   DUKE   No more evasion.
We have with a leavened° and preparèd choice   *fermented (mature)*
Proceeded to you; therefore take your honors.
      [*He gives* ANGELO *a paper.*]
Our haste from hence is of so quick condition
That it prefers itself and leaves unquestioned[9]
55   Matters of needful value. We shall write to you,

---

3. How do you think he will represent me (with the royal plural)? Angelo is imagined bearing his ruler's image like a coin; compare "mettle" (metal) in line 48.
4. Handwriting; engraved pattern.
5. *Heaven . . . not:* similarly, Jesus, in Matthew 5:14–16, tells his followers not to hide their light under a bushel.
6. *Spirits . . . issues:* Spirits are not made fine except to do fine deeds.
7. Silence; take (this commission).
8. Though first to be addressed, is your subordinate.
9. That it takes precedence and leaves unconsidered.

As time and our concernings° shall importune,°   *affairs / demand*
How it goes with us, and do look° to know   *expect*
What doth befall you here. So fare you well.
To th' hopeful execution do I leave you
Of your commissions.
60 ANGELO   Yet give leave, my lord,
That we may bring you something° on the way.   *some distance*
DUKE   My haste may not admit° it.   *permit*
Nor need you, on mine honor, have to do
With¹ any scruple. Your scope is as mine own,
65 So to enforce or qualify° the laws   *mitigate*
As to your soul seems good. Give me your hand.
I'll privily away. I love the people,
But do not like to stage me° to their eyes.   *display myself*
Though it do well,° I do not relish well   *is politically useful*
70 Their loud applause and aves° vehement,   *salutations*
Nor do I think the man of safe discretion°   *sound judgment*
That does affect° it. Once more, fare you well.   *desire*
ANGELO   The heavens give safety to your purposes!
ESCALUS   Lead forth and bring you back in happiness!
75 DUKE   I thank you. Fare you well.²   *Exit.*
ESCALUS   I shall desire you, sir, to give me leave
To have free° speech with you, and it concerns me   *frank*
To look into the bottom of my place.³
A power I have, but of what strength and nature
80 I am not yet instructed.°   *informed*
ANGELO   'Tis so with me. Let us withdraw together,
And we may soon our satisfaction have
Touching that point.
ESCALUS   I'll wait upon° your honor.   *Exeunt.*   *accompany*

1.2

*Enter LUCIO, and two other GENTLEMEN.*¹
LUCIO   If the Duke with the other dukes come not to compo-
sition° with the king of Hungary, why then all the dukes fall   *agreement*
upon° the King.   *attack*
FIRST GENTLEMAN   Heaven grant us its peace, but not the king
5   of Hungary's!
SECOND GENTLEMAN   Amen.
LUCIO   Thou conclud'st like the sanctimonious pirate, that went to
sea with the ten commandments but scraped° one out of   *erased*
the table.°   *tablet*
10 SECOND GENTLEMAN   Thou shalt not steal?
LUCIO   Ay, that he razed.
FIRST GENTLEMAN   Why, 'twas a commandment to command
the captain and all the rest from their functions. They put forth
to steal! There's not a soldier of us all that, in the thanksgiving
15   before meat,° do relish the petition well that prays for peace.   *food*
SECOND GENTLEMAN   I never heard any soldier dislike° it.   *express aversion to*

---

1. *have to do / With:* worry about.
2. PERFORMANCE COMMENT The part of the Duke
presents many challenges to the actor; for a discussion
of the options in performance, see Digital Edition PC 1.
3. To examine my duties thoroughly.

1.2. Location: A street or public place.
1. TEXTUAL COMMENT Various inconsistencies in this
scene suggest textual corruption or, perhaps, a revision that is not completely thorough. See Digital Edition TC 2.

LUCIO   I believe thee, for I think thou never wast where grace
was said.
SECOND GENTLEMAN   No, a dozen times at least.
20   FIRST GENTLEMAN   What? In meter?
LUCIO   In any proportion,° or in any language.   *meter*
FIRST GENTLEMAN   I think, or in any religion!
LUCIO   Ay, why not? Grace is grace, despite of all controversy.² [*to*
     FIRST GENTLEMAN] As, for example, thou thyself art a wicked
25   villain, despite of all grace.
FIRST GENTLEMAN   Well, there went but a pair of shears
between us.³
LUCIO   I grant, as there may between the lists° and the velvet.   *selvages*
Thou art the list.
30   FIRST GENTLEMAN   And thou the velvet. Thou art good velvet;
thou'rt a three-piled⁴ piece, I warrant thee. I had as lief° be a   *had rather*
list of an English kersey° as be piled, as thou art piled,⁵ for a   *wool cloth*
French velvet. Do I speak feelingly° now?   *to the point; painfully*
LUCIO   I think thou dost, and indeed with most painful feeling°   *conviction*
35   of thy speech. I will, out of thine own confession, learn to begin°   *drink to*
thy health, but, whilst I live, forget to drink after thee.°   *(to avoid infection)*
FIRST GENTLEMAN   I think I have done myself wrong,° have I   *laid myself open to that*
not?
SECOND GENTLEMAN   Yes, that thou hast, whether thou art
40   tainted or free.°   *sick or well*
     Enter BAWD.
LUCIO   Behold, behold, where Madam Mitigation° comes. I   *(of sexual desire)*
have purchased as many diseases under her roof as come
to—
SECOND GENTLEMAN   To what, I pray?
45   LUCIO   Judge.°   *Guess*
SECOND GENTLEMAN   To three thousand dolors° a year.   *pains; dollars*
FIRST GENTLEMAN   Ay, and more.
LUCIO   A French crown° more.   *coin; syphilitic sore*
FIRST GENTLEMAN   Thou art always figuring° diseases in me,   *imagining*
50   but thou art full of error. I am sound.°   *healthy*
LUCIO   Nay, not, as one would say, healthy, but so sound° as   *resounding*
things that are hollow. Thy bones are hollow.⁶ Impiety° has   *Wickedness*
made a feast of thee.
FIRST GENTLEMAN [*to* BAWD]   How now? Which of your hips
55   has the most profound sciatica?⁷
BAWD   Well, well. There's one yonder arrested and carried to
prison was worth five thousand of you all.
SECOND GENTLEMAN   Who's that, I pray thee?
BAWD   Marry,° sir, that's Claudio, Signor Claudio.   *By the Virgin Mary*
60   FIRST GENTLEMAN   Claudio to prison? 'Tis not so.
BAWD   Nay, but I know 'tis so. I saw him arrested, saw him

2. Referring to the religious controversy over
whether human beings are saved by divine grace or
by good works. *grace:* divine favor; prayer before a
meal.
3. We are cut from the same cloth.
4. Very plush; full of rectal sores (a symptom of
syphilis). Lucio accuses the First Gentleman of being
a "list," a selvage or edging of inferior cloth; the Gentleman retorts that he'd rather be a plain selvage

than an expensively "piled" velvet like Lucio. Lucio
then uses the Gentleman's knowledge of "piles" to
score a point against him.
5. Ruined; made bald (a sign of syphilis, the "French
pox"). Syphilitic sores were covered with velvet
patches.
6. Syphilis causes bones to become brittle.
7. Ache in the sciatic vein of the hip, associated with
venereal disease.

carried away, and which is more, within these three days his
head to be chopped off.

LUCIO But, after° all this fooling, I would not have it so. Art
65 thou sure of this?

BAWD I am too sure of it, and it is for getting Madam Julietta
with child.

LUCIO Believe me, this may be. He promised to meet me two
hours since, and he was ever precise in promise-keeping.

70 SECOND GENTLEMAN Besides, you know, it draws° something
near to the speech we had to such a purpose.

FIRST GENTLEMAN But most of all agreeing with the proclamation.

LUCIO Away, let's go learn the truth of it.
                    Exeunt [LUCIO *and the* GENTLEMEN].

BAWD Thus, what with the war, what with the sweat,° what
75 with the gallows, and what with poverty, I am custom-
shrunk.°
                Enter [*Pompey the*] CLOWN.
—How now? What's the news with you?

CLOWN Yonder man is carried to prison.

BAWD Well, what has he done?

80 CLOWN A woman.

BAWD But what's his offense?

CLOWN Groping for trouts in a peculiar river.

BAWD What? Is there a maid with child by him?

CLOWN No, but there's a woman with maid by him. You have
85 not heard of the proclamation, have you?

BAWD What proclamation, man?

CLOWN All houses in the suburbs[8] of Vienna must be plucked°
down.

BAWD And what shall become of those in the city?

90 CLOWN They shall stand for seed.[9] They had gone down too,
but that a wise burgher put in° for them.

BAWD But shall all our houses of resort in the suburbs be
pulled down?

CLOWN To the ground, mistress.

95 BAWD Why, here's a change indeed in the commonwealth!
What shall become of me?

CLOWN Come, fear not you. Good counselors° lack no clients. Though you change your place, you need not change
your trade. I'll be your tapster° still. Courage, there will be
100 pity taken on you; you that have worn your eyes almost out
in the service,[1] you will be considered.°
                [*A noise within.*]

BAWD What's to do° here, Thomas tapster?[2] Let's withdraw.
                Enter PROVOST,° CLAUDIO, JULIET,[3] *Officers,* LUCIO,
                and [*the*] *two* GENTLEMEN.

CLOWN Here comes Signor Claudio, led by the Provost to
prison, and there's Madam Juliet.
                [*Exeunt* BAWD *and* CLOWN.]

Glosses (right margin):
despite
approaches
plague
short on customers
torn
citizen interceded
attorneys
bartender
recompensed
the matter
jailer

8. London brothels ("houses") were located outside
the city walls, where civic authorities had difficulty
controlling them.
9. Grain for the next crop; semen.
1. "Eye" was slang for "female genital"; blindness is
another symptom of syphilis.
2. Stock name for a tapster.
3. Claudio and Juliet are perhaps wearing white
sheets of penance; such public humiliations were
common punishments for sexual transgressions.

105 CLAUDIO Fellow, why dost thou show me thus to th' world?
　　　Bear me to prison, where I am committed.
　　PROVOST I do it not in evil disposition,
　　　But from Lord Angelo by special charge.
　　CLAUDIO Thus can the demigod Authority
110　Make us pay down for our offense by weight.°　　　　　　　　*fully*
　　　The words of° heaven; on whom it will, it will,[4]　　　*judgment of*
　　　On whom it will not, so; yet still 'tis just.
　　LUCIO Why, how now, Claudio? Whence comes this restraint?
　　CLAUDIO From too much liberty,° my Lucio, liberty.　　　*looseness*
115　As surfeit is the father of much fast,°　　　*gluttony precedes fasting*
　　　So every scope° by the immoderate use　　　　　　　　*freedom*
　　　Turns to restraint. Our natures do pursue,
　　　Like rats that raven° down their proper bane,°　　　*devour / poison*
　　　A thirsty evil, and when we drink, we die.
120　LUCIO If I could speak so wisely under an arrest, I would
　　　send for certain of my creditors.[5] And yet, to say the truth, I
　　　had as lief have the foppery° of freedom as the morality of　　　*folly*
　　　imprisonment. What's thy offense, Claudio?
　　CLAUDIO What but to speak of would offend again.
125　LUCIO What, is't murder?
　　CLAUDIO No.
　　LUCIO Lechery?
　　CLAUDIO Call it so.
　　PROVOST Away, sir, you must go.
　　CLAUDIO　　　　　　　　　　　One word, good friend.
130　[*to* LUCIO] Lucio, a word with you.
　　LUCIO A hundred, if they'll do you any good. Is lechery so
　　　looked after?
　　CLAUDIO Thus stands it with me: upon a true contract[6]
　　　I got possession of Julietta's bed.
135　You know the lady. She is fast° my wife,　　　*nearly; entirely*
　　　Save that we do the denunciation° lack　　　　　　　*declaration*
　　　Of outward order.° This we came not to,　　　*public ceremony*
　　　Only for propagation° of a dower　　　　　　　　*enlargement*
　　　Remaining in the coffer of her friends,°　　　　　　*relatives*
140　From whom we thought it meet° to hide our love　　　*appropriate*
　　　Till time had made them for° us. But it chances　　*favorably disposed to*
　　　The stealth of our most mutual° entertainment　　*reciprocal; intimate*
　　　With character too gross° is writ on Juliet.　　　*writing too large*
　　LUCIO With child, perhaps?
　　CLAUDIO　　　　　　　　　　Unhappily, even so.
145　And the new deputy now for the Duke,
　　　Whether it be the fault and glimpse° of newness,　　　*glitter*
　　　Or whether that the body public be
　　　A horse whereon the governor doth ride,
　　　Who, newly in the seat, that it may know
150　He can command, lets it straight° feel the spur—　　　*immediately*
　　　Whether the tyranny be in his place°　　　　　　　　*office*

---

4. Paul has God say in Romans 9:15: "I will have mercy
on him, to whom I will show mercy: and will have compassion on him, on whom I will have compassion."
5. Who, Lucio implies, would have him arrested for
nonpayment of debts.
6. A secret plighting of troth, as opposed to public nup-

tials; in seventeenth-century England, such a contract
could constitute legal marriage if made in the present
tense ("I marry you" rather than "I will marry you") and
followed by sexual consummation. The nature of the
contract between Claudio and Juliet is unclear.

	Or in his eminence that fills it up,	
	I stagger in.° But this new governor	*hesitate to say*
	Awakes me all the enrolled° penalties	*recorded*
155	Which have like unscoured armor hung by th' wall	
	So long that nineteen zodiacs° have gone round	*years*
	And none of them been worn; and, for a name,°	*reputation*
	Now puts the drowsy and neglected act	
	Freshly on me. 'Tis surely for a name.	

160 LUCIO I warrant° it is. And thy head stands so tickle° on thy   *I'm sure / insecurely*
shoulders that a milkmaid, if she be in love, may sigh it off.[7]
Send after the Duke, and appeal to him.

CLAUDIO I have done so, but he's not to be found.
I prithee, Lucio, do me this kind service:

165	This day my sister should the cloister enter	
	And there receive her approbation.°	*become a novice*
	Acquaint her with the danger of my state,	
	Implore her, in my voice, that she make friends	
	To the strict deputy, bid herself assay° him.	*try*
170	I have great hope in that, for in her youth	
	There is a prone° and speechless dialect,	*eager; submissive*
	Such as move men. Beside, she hath prosperous art°	*skill*
	When she will play with reason and discourse,	
	And well she can persuade.	

175 LUCIO I pray she may, as well for the encouragement of the
like,° which else would stand under grievous imposition,° as   *those like you / burden*
for the enjoying of thy life, who I would be sorry should be
thus foolishly lost at a game of tick-tack.[8] I'll to her.

CLAUDIO I thank you, good friend Lucio.

LUCIO Within two hours.

180 CLAUDIO   Come, officer, away.   *Exeunt.*

1.3

Enter DUKE *and* FRIAR *Thomas.*

DUKE No, holy father, throw away that thought.

	Believe not that the dribbling[1] dart of love	
	Can pierce a complete° bosom. Why I desire thee	*an invulnerable*
	To give me secret harbor hath a purpose	
5	More grave and wrinkled° than the aims and ends	*(suggesting aged wisdom)*
	Of burning youth.	

FRIAR   May your grace speak of it?

DUKE My holy sir, none better knows than you

	How I have ever loved the life removed,°	*retired*
	And held in idle price° to haunt assemblies	*thought it frivolous*
10	Where youth and cost, witless bravery° keeps.	*pointless ostentation*
	I have delivered to Lord Angelo,	
	A man of stricture° and firm abstinence,	*self-restraint*
	My absolute power and place here in Vienna,	
	And he supposes me traveled to Poland;	
15	For so I have strewed it in the common ear,°	*ears of common people*

7. That a milkmaid's lovesick sigh may blow it off (with wordplay on "maidenhead").
8. A kind of backgammon scored by placing pegs into holes; with sexual innuendo.

1.3 Location: A friar's cell.
1. Inadequate, like an arrow shot without sufficient force.

And so it is received.° Now, pious sir,   *believed*
You will demand of me why I do this.
FRIAR   Gladly, my lord.
DUKE   We have strict statutes and most biting laws,
20   The needful bits and curbs to headstrong jades,°   *horses*
Which for this fourteen years we have let slip,°   *slide*
Even like an o'ergrown lion in a cave
That goes not out to prey. Now, as fond° fathers,   *doting*
Having bound up the threatening twigs of birch
25   Only to stick it in their children's sight
For terror, not to use, in time the rod
More mocked than feared becomes; so our decrees,
Dead to infliction,° to themselves are dead,   *Never inflicted*
And liberty plucks justice by the nose,[2]
30   The baby beats the nurse, and quite athwart
Goes all decorum.
FRIAR   It rested in° your grace   *remained possible for*
To unloose this tied-up justice when you pleased,
And it in you more dreadful would have seemed
Than in Lord Angelo.
DUKE   I do fear, too dreadful.
35   Sith° 'twas my fault to give the people scope,   *Since*
'Twould be my tyranny to strike and gall° them   *chafe*
For what I bid them do. For we bid this be done,
When evil deeds have their permissive pass°   *unhindered passage*
And not the punishment. Therefore indeed, my father,
40   I have on Angelo imposed the office,
Who may in th'ambush° of my name strike home,   *under cover*
And yet my nature never in the fight
To do in slander.° And to behold his sway°   *To permit slander / rule*
I will, as 'twere a brother of your order,
45   Visit both prince° and people. Therefore, I prithee,   *ruler*
Supply me with the habit, and instruct me
How I may formally in person bear°   *behave in character*
Like a true friar. More reasons for this action
At our more leisure shall I render you.
50   Only this one: Lord Angelo is precise,°   *puritanical*
Stands at a guard with envy,° scarce confesses   *on guard against desire*
That his blood flows or that his appetite
Is more to bread than stone. Hence shall we see
If power change purpose, what our seemers be.   *Exit.*

1.4

Enter ISABELLA *and Francisca, a* NUN.
ISABELLA   And have you nuns no farther privileges?
NUN   Are not these large° enough?   *generous*
ISABELLA   Yes, truly; I speak not as desiring more,
But rather wishing a more strict restraint
5   Upon the sisterhood, the votarists of Saint Clare.
LUCIO (*within*)   Ho! Peace be in this place.
ISABELLA   Who's that which calls?
NUN   It is a man's voice. Gentle Isabella,

---

2. Licentiousness insults the administration of law.
1.4 Location: A convent of St. Clare, an order known for austere discipline.

Turn you the key, and know° his business of° him.   *find out / from*
10   You may, I may not: you are yet unsworn.
      When you have vowed, you must not speak with men
      But in the presence of the prioress.
      Then, if you speak, you must not show your face,
      Or if you show your face, you must not speak.
15   He calls again. I pray you, answer him.
                [ISABELLA *opens the door.*]
      ISABELLA Peace and prosperity! Who is't that calls?
                [*Enter* LUCIO.]
      LUCIO   Hail, virgin, if you be, as those cheek-roses°   *glowing cheeks*
              Proclaim you are no less. Can you so stead° me   *help*
              As bring me to the sight of Isabella,
20   A novice of this place, and the fair sister
              To her unhappy° brother Claudio?   *unfortunate*
      ISABELLA Why "her unhappy brother," let me ask?
              The rather for I now must make you know
              I am that Isabella and his sister.
25   LUCIO   Gentle and fair, your brother kindly greets you.
              Not to be weary° with you, he's in prison.   *tedious*
      ISABELLA Woe me! For what?
      LUCIO   For that which, if myself might be his judge,
              He should receive his punishment in thanks.
30   He hath got his friend° with child.   *lover*
      ISABELLA Sir, make me not your story.°   *don't tell me tales*
      LUCIO   'Tis true.
              I would not, though 'tis my familiar° sin   *habitual*
              With maids to seem the lapwing[1] and to jest,
              Tongue far from heart, play with all virgins so.
35   I hold you as a thing enskied° and sainted   *placed in heaven*
              By your renouncement, an immortal spirit,
              And to be talked with in sincerity,
              As with a saint.
      ISABELLA You do blaspheme the good in mocking me.
40   LUCIO   Do not believe it. Fewness° and truth, 'tis thus.   *In few words*
              Your brother and his lover have embraced.
              As those that feed, grow full; as blossoming time
              That from the seedness° the bare fallow° brings   *sowing / plowland*
              To teeming foison;° even so her plenteous womb   *abundance*
45   Expresseth his full tilth° and husbandry.[2]   *tillage*
      ISABELLA Someone with child by him? My cousin Juliet?
      LUCIO   Is she your cousin?
      ISABELLA Adoptedly,° as school-maids change° their names   *By choice / exchange*
              By vain° though apt affection.   *foolish*
      LUCIO   She it is.
      ISABELLA Oh, let him marry her.
50   LUCIO   This is the point.
              The Duke is very strangely gone from hence;
              Bore many gentlemen, myself being one,
              In hand and hope of action.[3] But we do learn,
              By those that know the very nerves° of state,   *sinews (innermost secrets)*
55   His giving-out° were of an infinite distance   *What he proclaimed*

---

1. A bird that cries alarm when far from its nest, a
common figure for deception.
2. Cultivation (punning on "husband").

3. *Bore . . . action:* Deceived us into hoping for some
military action.

From his true-meant design. Upon° his place   *In*
And with full line° of his authority   *extent*
Governs Lord Angelo, a man whose blood
Is very snow-broth,° one who never feels   *melted snow*
60 The wanton stings and motions° of the sense   *stimulants and impulses*
But doth rebate° and blunt his natural edge   *dull*
With profits of the mind, study and fast.
He, to give fear to use° and liberty,   *custom*
Which have for long run by the hideous law
65 As mice by lions, hath picked out an act°   *a statute*
Under whose heavy° sense your brother's life   *oppressive*
Falls into forfeit. He arrests him on it,
And follows close the rigor of the statute
To make him an example. All hope is gone
70 Unless you have the grace by your fair prayer
To soften Angelo. And that's my pith° of business   *essence*
Twixt you and your poor brother.
ISABELLA   Doth he so
Seek his life?
LUCIO   Has censured° him already,   *sentenced*
And, as I hear, the Provost hath a warrant
For 's execution.
75 ISABELLA   Alas! What poor
Ability's in me to do him good?
LUCIO   Assay the power you have.
ISABELLA   My power? Alas, I doubt.
LUCIO   Our doubts are traitors
And makes us lose the good we oft might win,
80 By fearing to attempt. Go to Lord Angelo,
And let him learn to know, when maidens sue
Men give like gods, but when they weep and kneel,
All their petitions are as freely theirs
As° they themselves would owe° them.   *As if / were to own*
ISABELLA   I'll see what I can do.
85 LUCIO   But speedily.
ISABELLA   I will about it straight,°   *immediately*
No longer staying but to give the mother°   *Mother Superior*
Notice of my affair.° I humbly thank you.   *business*
Commend me to my brother. Soon at night
90 I'll send him certain word of my success.°   *fortune (good or bad)*
LUCIO   I take my leave of you.
ISABELLA   Good sir, adieu.[4]   *Exeunt.*

2.1
Enter ANGELO, ESCALUS, *a* JUSTICE, *and Servants.*
ANGELO   We must not make a scarecrow of the law,
Setting it up to fear° the birds of prey   *frighten*
And let it keep one shape till custom make it
Their perch and not their terror.
ESCALUS   Ay, but yet
5 Let us be keen, and rather cut a little
Than fall and bruise to death. Alas, this gentleman

---

4. **Performance Comment** Isabella's sexuality, and
the degree to which she is aware of it, has been variously imagined in different productions; for a discussion of the options in performance, see Digital
Edition PC 2.
2.1 Location: The court of justice.

Whom I would save had a most noble father.
Let but your honor know—
Whom I believe to be most strait° in virtue—   *rigorous*
10 That in the working of your own affections,°   *passions*
Had time cohered with place, or place with wishing,
Or that the resolute acting of your blood°   *desire*
Could have attained th'effect° of your own purpose, *fulfillment*
Whether you had not sometime in your life
15 Erred in this point which now you censure° him, *condemn in*
And pulled the law upon you.
ANGELO 'Tis one thing to be tempted, Escalus,
Another thing to fall. I not° deny   *do not*
The jury passing on the prisoner's life
20 May in the sworn twelve have a thief or two
Guiltier than him they try. What's open° made to justice, *evident*
That justice seizes. What knows the laws¹
That thieves do pass on thieves? 'Tis very pregnant,° *clear*
The jewel that we find, we stoop and take't,
25 Because we see it; but what we do not see
We tread upon and never think of it.
You may not so extenuate his offense
For° I have had such faults; but rather tell me   *Because*
When I, that censure him, do so offend,
30 Let mine own judgment pattern out° my death, *give precedent for*
And nothing come in partial.° Sir, he must die. *no allowances be made*
   Enter PROVOST.
ESCALUS Be it as your wisdom will.
ANGELO   Where is the Provost?
PROVOST Here, if it like your honor.
ANGELO   See that Claudio
Be executed by nine tomorrow morning.
35 Bring him his confessor, let him be prepared,
For that's the utmost of his pilgrimage.° [*Exit* PROVOST.] *life's journey*
ESCALUS [*aside*] Well, heaven forgive him, and forgive us all!
Some rise by sin, and some by virtue fall.
Some run from brakes of vice,² and answer none,° *not at all*
40 And some condemnèd for a fault alone.° *single imperfection*
   Enter ELBOW, FROTH, CLOWN, [*and*] *Officers.*
ELBOW Come, bring them away. If these be good people in a
commonweal, that do nothing but use their abuses° in com- *do their bad deeds*
mon houses,° I know no law. Bring them away. *brothels*
ANGELO How now, sir, what's your name? And what's the matter?
45 ELBOW If it please your honor, I am the poor Duke's constable,
and my name is Elbow. I do lean° upon justice, sir, and do *depend*
bring in here before your good honor two notorious benefac-
tors.³
ANGELO Benefactors? Well! What benefactors are they? Are
50 they not malefactors?
ELBOW If it please your honor, I know not well what they are.
But precise⁴ villains they are, that I am sure of, and void of all
profanation° in the world that good Christians ought to have. *(for "reverence")*

---

1. What does the law know; who knows what law.
2. *brakes*: thickets. TEXTUAL COMMENT F has "brakes of Ice," a famous crux; often amended as here. For a fuller discussion of the textual problem, and for a suggestion about how the mistake might have occurred, see Digital Edition TC 3.
3. Elbow comically misuses words; here he means "malefactors," criminals.
4. Elbow means "precious"; "precise" (morally scrupulous) is elsewhere applied to Angelo.

ESCALUS   This comes off° well! Here's a wise officer.   *turns out*

55   ANGELO   Go to. What quality° are they of? [*to* ELBOW] Elbow is   *rank*
     your name? Why dost thou not speak, Elbow?

CLOWN   He cannot, sir. He's out at elbow.[5]

ANGELO [*to* CLOWN]   What are you, sir?

ELBOW   He, sir? A tapster, sir, parcel bawd.° One that serves a   *part-time pimp*
60   bad woman, whose house, sir, was, as they say, plucked down
     in the suburbs. And now she professes a hothouse,° which I   *pretends to run a sauna*
     think is a very ill house, too.

ESCALUS   How know you that?

ELBOW   My wife, sir, whom I detest° before heaven and your honor—   *(for "protest")*

65   ESCALUS   How? Thy wife?

ELBOW   Ay, sir, whom I thank heaven is an honest woman—

ESCALUS   Dost thou detest her therefore?

ELBOW   I say, sir, I will detest myself also, as well as she, that
     this house, if it be not a bawd's house, it is pity of her life,° for   *a great pity*
70   it is a naughty° house.   *wicked*

ESCALUS   How dost thou know that, constable?

ELBOW   Marry, sir, by my wife, who, if she had been a woman
     cardinally° given, might have been accused in fornication,   *(for "carnally")*
     adultery, and all uncleanliness there.

75   ESCALUS   By the woman's means?

ELBOW   Ay, sir, by Mistress Overdone's means; but as she° spit   *(Elbow's wife)*
     in his° face, so she defied him.   *(the Clown's)*

CLOWN   Sir, if it please your honor, this is not so.

ELBOW   Prove it before these varlets° here, thou honorable   *villains*
80   man, prove it.

ESCALUS [*to* ANGELO]   Do you hear how he misplaces?°   *confuses his words*

CLOWN   Sir, she came in great with child, and longing, saving
     your honor's reverence,° for stewed prunes,[6] sir; we had but   *excuse the expression*
     two in the house, which at that very distant° time stood, as   *(for "instant")*
85   it were in a fruit dish,[7] a dish of some threepence; your hon-
     ors have seen such dishes—they are not china dishes, but
     very good dishes.

ESCALUS   Go to, go to. No matter for the dish, sir.

CLOWN   No, indeed, sir, not of° a pin; you are therein in the   *worth*
90   right, but to the point. As I say, this Mistress Elbow, being,
     as I say, with child, and being great-bellied, and longing, as
     I said, for prunes; and having but two in the dish, as I said,
     Master Froth here, this very man, having eaten the rest, as I
     said, and, as I say, paying for them very honestly —for, as
95   you know, Master Froth, I could not give you threepence
     again.°   *in change*

FROTH   No, indeed.

CLOWN   Very well. You being then, if you be remembered,
     cracking the stones of the foresaid prunes—

100   FROTH   Ay, so I did indeed.

CLOWN   Why, very well! I telling you then, if you be remembered,
     that such a one, and such a one, were past cure of the thing
     you wot of,[8] unless they kept very good diet, as I told you—

---

5. Ragged; perplexed at the sound of his name. The Clown loves to play on the double meanings of words.
6. Commonly served in brothels; also suggesting "testicles" in the series of double-entendres that follows.
7. Slang term for "female genital."
8. Euphemism for syphilis. *wot:* know.

FROTH All this is true.

105 CLOWN Why, very well then—

ESCALUS Come, you are a tedious fool! To the purpose: what
was done to Elbow's wife that he hath cause to complain of?
Come me° to what was done to her.   *Get*

CLOWN Sir, your honor cannot come to that yet.[9]

110 ESCALUS No, sir, nor I mean it not.°   *I don't mean that*

CLOWN Sir, but you shall come to it, by your honor's leave.
And I beseech you, look into° Master Froth here, sir, a man   *consider*
of fourscore pound a year,[1] whose father died at Hallow-
mas° —was't not at Hallowmas, Master Froth?   *Nov. 1, All Saints' Day*

115 FROTH All Hallow Eve.°   *Halloween*

CLOWN Why, very well! I hope here be truths. He, sir, sitting,
as I say, in a lower° chair, sir —'twas in the Bunch of Grapes,[2]   *reclining?*
[*to* FROTH] where indeed you have a delight to sit, have you
not?

120 FROTH I have so, because it is an open room[3] and good for
winter.

CLOWN Why, very well then. I hope here be truths.

ANGELO This will last out a night in Russia
When nights are longest there. I'll take my leave,

125 And leave you to the hearing of the cause,°   *case*
Hoping you'll find good cause to whip them all.

ESCALUS I think no less. Good morrow to your lordship.

                                                Exit ANGELO.

[*to* CLOWN] Now, sir, come on. What was done to Elbow's
wife, once more?

130 CLOWN Once, sir? There was nothing done to her once.

ELBOW [*to* ESCALUS] I beseech you, sir, ask him what this
man did to my wife.

CLOWN [*to* ESCALUS] I beseech your honor, ask me.

ESCALUS [*to* CLOWN] Well, sir, what did this gentleman to her?

135 CLOWN I beseech you, sir, look in this gentleman's face. Good
Master Froth, look upon his honor, 'tis for a good purpose.
Doth your honor mark° his face?   *note*

ESCALUS Ay, sir, very well.

CLOWN Nay, I beseech you, mark it well.

140 ESCALUS Well, I do so.

CLOWN Doth your honor see any harm in his face?

ESCALUS Why, no.

CLOWN I'll be supposed° upon a book,° his face is the worst   *(for "deposed") / Bible*
thing about him. Good, then, if his face be the worst thing

145 about him, how could Master Froth do the constable's wife
any harm? I would know that of your honor.

ESCALUS He's in the right. Constable, what say you to it?

ELBOW First, an it like° you, the house is a respected[4] house;   *if it please*
next, this is a respected fellow; and his mistress is a respected

150 woman.

CLOWN By this hand, sir, his wife is a more respected person
than any of us all.

---

9. Taking "done" in the sexual sense, the Clown pretends shock at Escalus's salaciousness.
1. Eighty pounds was a low income for a gentleman.
The father's recent death means that Froth has just

come into his inheritance.
2. A room in a tavern.
3. A public room (where fires were kept burning).
4. For "suspected."

ELBOW Varlet, thou liest, thou liest, wicked varlet! The time
is yet to come that she was ever respected with man, woman,
155   or child.

CLOWN Sir, she was respected with him before he married with
her.

ESCALUS [*aside*] Which is the wiser here, Justice or Iniquity?
—Is this true?

160   ELBOW O thou caitiff, O thou varlet, O thou wicked Hannibal![5] I respected with her before I was married to her? [*to*
ESCALUS] If ever I was respected with her, or she with me,
let not your worship think me the poor Duke's officer. [*to*
CLOWN] Prove this, thou wicked Hannibal, or I'll have mine
165   action of battery° on thee.   *(for "slander")*

ESCALUS If he took° you a box o'th' ear, you might have your   *struck*
action of slander too.

ELBOW Marry, I thank your good worship for it. What is't your
worship's pleasure I shall do with this wicked caitiff?°   *knave*

170   ESCALUS Truly, officer, because he hath some offenses in him
that thou wouldst discover° if thou couldst, let him continue   *expose*
in his courses° till thou know'st what they are.   *conduct*

ELBOW Marry, I thank your worship for it. —Thou seest, thou
wicked varlet now, what's come upon thee. Thou art to con-
175   tinue now, thou varlet, thou art to continue.

ESCALUS [*to* FROTH] Where were you born, friend?

FROTH Here in Vienna, sir.

ESCALUS Are you of fourscore pounds a year?

FROTH Yes, an't please you, sir.

180   ESCALUS So. [*to* CLOWN] What trade are you of, sir?

CLOWN A tapster, a poor widow's tapster.

ESCALUS Your mistress' name?

CLOWN Mistress Overdone.

ESCALUS Hath she had any more than one husband?

185   CLOWN Nine, sir. Overdone by the last.[6]

ESCALUS Nine? [*to* FROTH] Come hither to me, Master Froth.
Master Froth, I would not have you acquainted with tap-
sters. They will draw you,[7] Master Froth, and you will hang
them.° Get you gone, and let me hear no more of you.   *get them hanged*

190   FROTH I thank your worship. For mine own part, I never
come into any room in a taphouse, but I am drawn in.

ESCALUS Well, no more of it, Master Froth. Farewell.

                                    [*Exit* FROTH.]

Come you hither to me, Master Tapster. What's your name,
Master Tapster?

195   CLOWN Pompey.

ESCALUS What else?

CLOWN Bum, sir.

ESCALUS Troth, and your bum is the greatest thing about you,
so that in the beastliest sense, you are Pompey the Great.[8]

200   Pompey, you are partly a bawd, Pompey, howsoever you color
it in being a tapster, are you not? Come, tell me true, it shall
be the better for you.

---

5. Blunder for "cannibal"; also, both Hannibal and
Pompey were famous generals of ancient times.
6. She takes her name from Overdone, her last husband; her last husband wore her out.

7. Get you beer; steal your substance; convey you to
execution.
8. The Roman general Pompey was surnamed "the
Great."

CLOWN   Truly, sir, I am a poor fellow that would live.

ESCALUS   How would you live, Pompey? By being a bawd?
205   What do you think of the trade, Pompey? Is it a lawful trade?

CLOWN   If the law would allow it, sir.

ESCALUS   But the law will not allow it, Pompey, nor it shall   *nor shall it*
        not° be allowed in Vienna.

CLOWN   Does your worship mean to geld and splay all the
210   youth of the city?

ESCALUS   No, Pompey.

CLOWN   Truly, sir, in my poor opinion, they will to't then. If
        your worship will take order° for the drabs° and the knaves,   *measures / whores*
        you need not to fear the bawds.

215   ESCALUS   There is pretty orders beginning, I can tell you. It is
        but heading° and hanging.   *beheading*

CLOWN   If you head and hang all that offend that way but for
        ten year together, you'll be glad to give out a commission°   *an order*
        for more heads. If this law hold° in Vienna ten year, I'll rent   *remain*
220   the fairest house in it after threepence a bay.⁹ If you live to
        see this come to pass, say Pompey told you so.

ESCALUS   Thank you, good Pompey, and in requital of° your   *return for*
        prophecy, hark you: I advise you let me not find you before me
        again upon any complaint whatsoever, no, not for° dwelling   *even for*
225   where you do. If I do, Pompey, I shall beat you to your tent
        and prove a shrewd Caesar to you.¹ In plain dealing, Pom-
        pey, I shall have you whipped. So for this time, Pompey, fare
        you well.

CLOWN   I thank your worship for your good counsel; [*aside*]
230   but I shall follow it as the flesh and fortune shall better deter-
        mine. Whip me? No, no, let carman° whip his jade.°   *cart driver / horse*
        The valiant heart's not whipped out of his trade.

                                            Exit [*guarded*].

ESCALUS   Come hither to me, Master Elbow. —Come hither,
        Master Constable. How long have you been in this place of
235   constable?

ELBOW   Seven year and a half, sir.

ESCALUS   I thought, by the readiness in the office, you had
        continued in it some time. You say seven years together.

ELBOW   And a half, sir.

240   ESCALUS   Alas, it hath been great pains to you. They do you
        wrong to put you so oft upon't. Are there not men in your ward
        sufficient° to serve it?   *fit*

ELBOW   Faith, sir, few of any wit in such matters. As they are
        chosen, they are glad to choose me for them; I do it for some
245   piece of money, and go through withal.

ESCALUS   Look° you bring me in the names of some six or   *See that*
        seven, the most sufficient of your parish.

ELBOW   To your worship's house, sir?

ESCALUS   To my house. Fare you well.

                                        [*Exeunt* ELBOW *and Officers*.]

9. Townhouse rental fees were based on the number   1. Julius Caesar defeated Pompey in 48 B.C.E. *shrewd:*
of front windows ("bays").   harsh.

250 —What's o'clock, think you?
JUSTICE Eleven, sir.
ESCALUS I pray you home to dinner with me.²
JUSTICE I humbly thank you.
ESCALUS It grieves me for the death of Claudio,
255 But there's no remedy.
JUSTICE Lord Angelo is severe.
ESCALUS   It is but needful.
Mercy is not itself that oft looks so;
Pardon is still° the nurse of second woe.   *always*
But yet, poor Claudio! There is no remedy.
260 Come, sir.   *Exeunt.*

2.2

Enter PROVOST [*and*] SERVANT.

SERVANT He's hearing of a cause.° He will come straight.° I'll   *case / right away*
tell him of you.
PROVOST Pray you, do.   [*Exit* SERVANT.]
                            I'll know
His pleasure; maybe he will relent. Alas,
5 He° hath but as offended in a dream.   *(Claudio)*
All sects,° all ages smack° of this vice, and he   *kinds of people / partake*
To die for't?
            Enter ANGELO.
ANGELO   Now, what's the matter, Provost?
PROVOST Is it your will Claudio shall die tomorrow?
ANGELO Did not I tell thee yea? Hadst thou not order?
Why dost thou ask again?
10 PROVOST   Lest I might be too rash.
Under your good correction, I have seen
When after execution, judgment hath
Repented o'er his doom.°   *sentence*
ANGELO   Go to; let that be mine.°   *my concern*
Do you your office, or give up your place,
And you shall well be spared.°   *easily be done without*
15 PROVOST   I crave your honor's pardon.
What shall be done, sir, with the groaning Juliet?
She's very near her hour.°   *(of childbirth)*
ANGELO   Dispose of her
To some more fitter place, and that with speed.
            [*Enter* SERVANT.]
SERVANT Here is the sister of the man condemned
Desires access to you.
20 ANGELO   Hath he a sister?
PROVOST Ay, my good lord, a very virtuous maid,
And to be shortly of a sisterhood,
If not already.
ANGELO   Well, let her be admitted.   [*Exit* SERVANT.]
—See you the fornicatress be removed.
25 Let her have needful, but not lavish means.
There shall be order° for't.   *written direction*
            Enter LUCIO *and* ISABELLA.

___

2. Dinner was served at midday. *pray:* invite.   2.2 Location: A room in the court of justice.

PROVOST	Save your honor.	
ANGELO [*to* PROVOST] Stay a little while. [*to* ISABELLA] You're		
	welcome; what's your will?	
ISABELLA I am a woeful suitor to your honor,		
	Please° but your honor hear me.	*If it please*
ANGELO	Well, what's your suit?	

30 ISABELLA   There is a vice that most I do abhor
And most desire should meet the blow of justice;
For which I would not plead, but that I must;
For which I must not plead, but that I am
At war 'twixt will and will not.

ANGELO   Well, the matter?

35 ISABELLA   I have a brother is condemned to die.
I do beseech you, let it be his fault,°   *his fault be condemned*
And not my brother.

PROVOST [*aside*]   Heaven give thee moving graces.°   *the gift of persuasion*

ANGELO   Condemn the fault and not the actor° of it?   *doer*
Why, every fault's condemned ere it be done.

40 Mine were the very cipher of a function
To fine° the faults, whose fine° stands in record,   *condemn / penalty*
And let go by° the actor.   *leave unpunished*

ISABELLA   Oh, just but severe law!
I had a brother then. Heaven keep your honor.

LUCIO [*aside to* ISABELLA]   Give't not o'er° so. To him again,   *Don't give up*
entreat him,

45 Kneel down before him, hang upon° his gown.   *cling to*
You are too cold. If you should need a pin,
You could not with more tame a tongue desire it;
To him, I say.

ISABELLA   Must he needs° die?   *necessarily*

ANGELO   Maiden, no remedy.

50 ISABELLA   Yes. I do think that you might pardon him,
And neither heaven nor man grieve at the mercy.

ANGELO   I will not do't.

ISABELLA   But can you if you would?

ANGELO   Look, what° I will not, that I cannot do.   *Whatever*

ISABELLA   But might you do't and do the world no wrong,

55 If so your heart were touched with that remorse°   *pity*
As mine is to him?

ANGELO   He's sentenced. 'Tis too late.

LUCIO [*aside to* ISABELLA]   You are too cold.

ISABELLA   Too late? Why, no. I that do speak a word
May call° it again. Well, believe this: *retract*

60 No ceremony° that to great ones 'longs,   *symbolic accessory*
Not the king's crown, nor the deputed sword,
The marshal's truncheon, nor the judge's robe
Become them with one half so good a grace
As mercy does.

65 If he had been as you, and you as he,
You would have slipped like him, but he like you
Would not have been so stern.

ANGELO   Pray you be gone.

ISABELLA   I would to heaven I had your potency°   *power*
And you were Isabel. Should it then be thus?

70 No. I would tell what 'twere to be a judge,

And what a prisoner.

LUCIO [*aside to* ISABELLA]   Ay, touch him:[1] there's the vein.°   *that's the style*

ANGELO   Your brother is a forfeit of the law,
And you but waste your words.

ISABELLA   Alas, alas.
Why, all the souls that were, were forfeit[2] once,
75   And He that might the vantage° best have took   *advantage*
Found out° the remedy.[3] How would you be   *Procured*
If He, which is the top° of judgment, should   *highest pattern or source*
But judge you as you are? Oh, think on that,
And mercy then will breathe within your lips
Like man new made.°   *renewed by faith*

80   ANGELO   Be you content, fair maid.°   *(with play on "new made")*
It is the law, not I, condemn your brother.
Were he my kinsman, brother, or my son,
It should be thus with him. He must die tomorrow.

ISABELLA   Tomorrow? Oh, that's sudden. Spare him, spare him.
85   He's not prepared for death. Even for our kitchens
We kill the fowl of season.° Shall we serve heaven   *at the proper time*
With less respect than we do minister
To our gross selves? Good, good my lord, bethink you:
Who is it that hath died for this offense?
There's many have committed it.

90   LUCIO [*aside to* ISABELLA]   Ay, well said.

ANGELO   The law hath not been dead, though it hath slept.
Those many had not dared to do that evil
If the first that did th'edict infringe
Had answered for his deed. Now 'tis awake,
95   Takes note of what is done, and like a prophet
Looks in a glass° that shows what future evils   *mirror*
Either new,° or by remissness new-conceived   *unripe*
And so in progress to be hatched and born,
Are now to have no successive degrees,[4]
But ere they live to end.

100   ISABELLA   Yet show some pity.

ANGELO   I show it most of all when I show justice,
For then I pity those I do not know
Which a dismissed° offense would after gall,°   *Whom a pardoned / hurt*
And do him right that answering° one foul wrong   *paying for*
105   Lives not to act another. Be satisfied
Your brother dies tomorrow; be content.

ISABELLA   So you must be the first that gives this sentence,
And he, that suffers. Oh, it is excellent
To have a giant's strength, but it is tyrannous
To use it like a giant.

110   LUCIO [*aside to* ISABELLA]   That's well said.

ISABELLA   Could great men thunder
As Jove[5] himself does, Jove would never be quiet,
For every pelting° petty officer   *paltry*
Would use his heaven for thunder, nothing but thunder.
115   Merciful heaven!

---

1. Influence him; but perhaps Isabella touches Angelo's arm or garment here.
2. Lost (as a result of Adam and Eve's disobedience).
3. By saving all humankind in the person of Christ.
4. Future stages of development.
5. King of the Roman gods, whose weapon was the thunderbolt.

Thou rather with thy sharp and sulphurous° bolt *fiery*
Splits the unwedgeable and gnarlèd oak
Than the soft myrtle. But man, proud man,
Dressed in a little brief authority,
120 Most ignorant of what he's most assured—
His glassy° essence—like an angry ape⁶ *fragile; illusory*
Plays such fantastic tricks before high heaven
As makes the angels weep, who with our spleens⁷
Would all themselves laugh mortal.
125 LUCIO [*aside to* ISABELLA] Oh, to him, to him, wench,° he *girl*
will relent.
He's coming,° I perceive't. *yielding*
PROVOST [*aside*]   Pray heaven she win him!
ISABELLA We cannot weigh our brother with ourself.⁸
Great men may jest with saints; 'tis wit in them,
But in the less,° foul profanation. *ordinary people*
130 LUCIO [*aside to* ISABELLA] Thou'rt i'th' right, girl, more o'that.
ISABELLA That in the captain's but a choleric word
Which in the soldier is flat blasphemy.
LUCIO [*aside to* ISABELLA] Art advised o'that?° More on't! *So you know about that*
ANGELO Why do you put° these sayings upon me? *impose*
135 ISABELLA Because authority, though it err like others,
Hath yet a kind of medicine in itself
That skins the vice o'th' top.⁹ Go to your bosom,
Knock there, and ask your heart what it doth know
That's like my brother's fault; if it confess
140 A natural guiltiness such as is his,
Let it not sound a thought upon your tongue
Against my brother's life.
ANGELO [*aside*]   She speaks, and 'tis such sense° *sound advice*
That my sense breeds° with it. —Fare you well. *desire increases*
ISABELLA Gentle my° lord, turn back. *My gracious*
145 ANGELO I will bethink me.° Come again tomorrow. *consider*
ISABELLA Hark how I'll bribe you. Good my lord, turn back.
ANGELO How! Bribe me?
ISABELLA Ay, with such gifts that° heaven shall share with° you. *as / apportion to*
LUCIO [*aside*] You had marred all, else.
150 ISABELLA Not with fond° shekels of the testèd° gold, *foolish / refined*
Or stones° whose rate° are either rich or poor *jewels / value*
As fancy values them, but with true prayers
That shall be up at heaven and enter there
Ere sunrise, prayers from preservèd° souls, *protected*
155 From fasting maids, whose minds are dedicate
To nothing temporal.
ANGELO   Well, come to me tomorrow.
LUCIO [*to* ISABELLA] Go to;° 'tis well; away. *Come on*
ISABELLA   Heaven keep your honor¹ safe.
ANGELO [*aside*] Amen.
For I am that way going to temptation,
Where prayers cross.° *corrupt; frustrate*

---

6. A figure of grotesque mimicry.
7. Thought to be the seat of laughter.
8. We cannot judge others as we judge ourselves.
9. That causes a skin to grow over the sore.

1. Isabella calls Angelo "your honor" as a term of respect; Angelo understands the phrase as referring to his virtue.

160 ISABELLA   At what hour tomorrow
     Shall I attend your lordship?
    ANGELO   At any time fore noon.
    ISABELLA   Save° your honor.   *God save (a farewell)*
                [*Exeunt* ISABELLA, LUCIO, *and* PROVOST.]
    ANGELO   From thee, even from thy virtue.
165   What's this, what's this? Is this her fault or mine?
     The tempter or the tempted, who sins most, ha?
     Not she, nor doth she tempt. But it is I
     That, lying by the violet in the sun,
     Do as the carrion does, not as the flower,
170   Corrupt with virtuous season.° Can it be   *Rot in fine weather*
     That modesty may more betray our sense°   *seduce our appetite*
     Than woman's lightness?° Having waste ground enough,   *licentiousness*
     Shall we desire to raze the sanctuary
     And pitch° our evils there? Oh, fie, fie, fie!   *hurl; set up*
175   What dost thou, or what art thou, Angelo?
     Dost thou desire her foully for those things
     That make her good? Oh, let her brother live:
     Thieves for their robbery have authority
     When judges steal themselves. What, do I love her,
180   That I desire to hear her speak again
     And feast upon her eyes? What is't I dream on?
     O cunning enemy,° that to catch a saint°   *(Satan) / holy person*
     With saints dost bait thy hook. Most dangerous
     Is that temptation that doth goad us on
185   To sin in loving virtue. Never could the strumpet
     With all her double vigor,° art and nature,   *twofold power*
     Once stir my temper,° but this virtuous maid   *excite me*
     Subdues me quite. Ever till now
     When men were fond,° I smiled and wondered how.   *Exit.*   *infatuated*

2.3

Enter DUKE [*disguised as a friar*] *and* PROVOST.
    DUKE   Hail to you, Provost, so I think you are.
    PROVOST   I am the Provost. What's your will, good Friar?
    DUKE   Bound by my charity and my blessed order,
     I come to visit the afflicted spirits
5   Here in the prison.[1] Do me the common right°   *right of all clerics*
     To let me see them and to make me know
     The nature of their crimes, that I may minister
     To them accordingly.
    PROVOST   I would do more than that, if more were needful.
               Enter JULIET.
10   Look, here comes one, a gentlewoman of mine,°   *in my care*
     Who, falling in the flaws° of her own youth,   *faults; gusts of passion*
     Hath blistered her report.° She is with child,   *reputation*
     And he that got° it, sentenced; a young man   *begot*
     More fit to do another such offense
15   Than die for this.

2.3 Location: The prison.
1. Echoing 1 Peter 3:19: "He . . . went, and preached unto the spirits that were in prison."

DUKE   When must he die?

PROVOST   As I do think, tomorrow.
   [*to* JULIET] I have provided for you. Stay a while,
   And you shall be conducted.

DUKE   Repent you, fair one, of the sin you carry?

20 JULIET   I do, and bear the shame most patiently.

DUKE   I'll teach you how you shall arraign° your conscience   *accuse*
   And try your penitence, if it be sound
   Or hollowly put on.

JULIET   I'll gladly learn.

DUKE   Love you the man that wronged you?

25 JULIET   Yes, as I love the woman that wronged him.

DUKE   So then it seems your most offenseful act
   Was mutually committed.

JULIET   Mutually.

DUKE   Then was your sin of heavier° kind than his.   *graver*

JULIET   I do confess it and repent it, Father.

30 DUKE   'Tis meet° so, daughter, but lest you do repent   *appropriate*
   As that° the sin hath brought you to this shame,   *Because*
   Which sorrow is always toward ourselves, not heaven,
   Showing we would not spare heaven² as we love it
   But as we stand in fear—

35 JULIET   I do repent me as it is an evil,
   And take the shame with joy.

DUKE   There rest.°   *remain*
   Your partner, as I hear, must die tomorrow,
   And I am going with instruction to him.
   Grace go with you. *Benedicite.*°   *Exit.*   *Bless you*

40 JULIET   Must die tomorrow? O injurious love,
   That respites me a life³ whose very comfort
   Is still a dying horror.

PROVOST   'Tis pity of° him.   *Exeunt.*   *for*

2.4

Enter ANGELO.

ANGELO   When I would pray and think, I think and pray
   To several° subjects. Heaven hath my empty words,   *different*
   Whilst my invention,° hearing not my tongue,   *imagination*
   Anchors on Isabel. Heaven in my mouth,
5 As if I did but only chew his name,
   And in my heart the strong and swelling evil
   Of my conception.¹ The state° whereon I studied   *statecraft; dignity*
   Is like a good thing being often read,
   Grown feared° and tedious. Yea, my gravity   *disliked*
10 Wherein, let no man hear me, I take pride,
   Could I with boot° change for an idle plume²   *advantage*
   Which the air beats for vain. O place,° O form,°   *rank / formality*
   How often dost thou with thy case,° thy habit,°   *appearance / dress*

---

2. Relieve heaven from distress.
3. Pregnant women were spared the death penalty, at least until after childbirth.
2.4 Location: A room in the court of justice.

1. *the strong . . . conception:* the wickedness of my idea; original sin, inherited through the parents.
2. A frivolous feather, as worn in the hats of rakish youths.

Wrench awe from fools and tie the wiser souls
15 To thy false seeming! Blood, thou art blood.[3]
Let's write "good angel"[4] on the devil's horn;
'Tis not the devil's crest.°   *heraldic device*
[*Enter* SERVANT.]
                    How now? Who's there?
SERVANT One Isabel, a sister, desires access to you.
ANGELO Teach her the way.   [*Exit* SERVANT.]
                    O heavens!
20 Why does my blood thus muster° to my heart,   *crowd*
Making both it unable° for itself   *weak*
And dispossessing all my other parts
Of necessary fitness?
So play° the foolish throngs with one that swoons: *act*
25 Come all to help him, and so stop the air
By which he should revive; and even so
The general subject° to a well-wished king   *common people*
Quit their own part° and in obsequious fondness°   *place / foolish love*
Crowd to his presence, where their untaught° love   *ignorant*
Must needs appear offense.
          Enter ISABELLA.
30   —How now, fair maid?
ISABELLA I am come to know your pleasure.
ANGELO [*aside*] That you might know[5] it would much better
    please me
Than to demand° what 'tis. [*to* ISABELLA] Your brother cannot live. *ask*
ISABELLA Even so.° Heaven keep your honor.[6]   *So be it*
35 ANGELO Yet may he live a while, and it may be
As long as you or I; yet he must die.
ISABELLA Under your sentence?
ANGELO   Yea.
ISABELLA When, I beseech you? That in his reprieve
Longer or shorter, he may be so fitted°   *prepared*
40 That his soul sicken not.
ANGELO Ha! Fie, these filthy vices! It were as good
To pardon him that hath from nature stolen
A man already made,[7] as to remit°   *excuse*
Their saucy sweetness that do coin heaven's image
45 In stamps that are forbid.[8] 'Tis all as easy
Falsely° to take away a life true° made   *Wrongly / legitimately*
As to put metal[9] in restrainèd° means   *forbidden*
To make a false one.
ISABELLA 'Tis set down so in heaven, but not in earth.
50 ANGELO Say you so? Then I shall pose° you quickly.   *ask*
Which had you rather, that the most just law
Now took your brother's life, or to redeem him
Give up your body to such sweet uncleanness
As she that he hath stained?
ISABELLA   Sir, believe this:

---

3. That is, basic passions cannot be eradicated (contrasts with 1.4.56–62).
4. With pun on Angelo's name.
5. With pun on "carnal knowledge."
6. A form of farewell.
7. *hath . . . made*: has committed murder.

8. *coin . . . forbid*: counterfeit God's image (by begetting illegitimate children).
9. Variant spelling of "mettle" (spirit). Some people thought the child's spirit was conveyed in his or her father's semen.

55   I had rather give my body than my soul.

ANGELO   I talk not of your soul. Our compelled sins
Stand more for number than for account.[1]

ISABELLA   How say you?

ANGELO   Nay, I'll not warrant that,[2] for I can speak
Against the thing I say. Answer to this:

60   I, now the voice of the recorded law,
Pronounce a sentence on your brother's life.
Might there not be a charity in sin
To save this brother's life?

ISABELLA   Please° you to do't,   *If it please*
I'll take it as a peril to my soul

65   It is no sin at all, but charity.

ANGELO   Pleased you to do't, at peril of your soul,
Were equal poise° of sin and charity.   *balance*

ISABELLA   That I do beg his life, if it be sin,
Heaven let me bear it. You granting of° my suit,   *Supposing you grant*

70   If that be sin, I'll make it my morn prayer
To have it added to the faults of mine,
And nothing of your answer.

ANGELO   Nay, but hear me.
Your sense pursues not mine.[3] Either you are ignorant
Or seem so craftily, and that's not good.

75 ISABELLA   Let it be ignorant, and in nothing good,
But graciously° to know I am no better.   *by God's grace*

ANGELO   Thus wisdom wishes to appear most bright
When it doth tax° itself, as these black masks[4]   *reprove*
Proclaim an enshield° beauty ten times louder   *a shielded*

80   Than beauty could, displayed. But mark me.
To be received° plain, I'll speak more gross.°   *understood / clearly*
Your brother is to die.

ISABELLA   So.°   *Yes*

ANGELO   And his offense is so, as it appears,
Accountant° to the law upon that pain.°   *Accountable / penalty*

ISABELLA   True.

85 ANGELO   Admit° no other way to save his life   *Suppose*
—As I subscribe not° that, nor any other,   *agree to neither*
But in the loss of question[5]—that you, his sister,
Finding yourself desired of such a person
Whose credit with the judge, or own great place,°   *rank*

90   Could fetch your brother from the manacles
Of the all-binding law; and that there were
No earthly mean to save him but that either
You must lay down the treasures of your body
To this supposed,° or else to let him suffer;   *supposed man*

95   What would you do?

ISABELLA   As much for my poor brother as myself;
That is, were I under the terms° of death,   *sentence*
Th'impression of keen whips I'd wear as rubies,
And strip myself to death as to a bed

---

1. *Our . . . account:* Sins we are forced to commit fill
out the list but are not held against us.
2. I'll not guarantee that to be true.
3. You don't follow my meaning; your desire is not
aroused by mine.
4. Worn at court entertainments.
5. For the sake of discussion.

100   That longing have been sick for, ere I'd yield
       My body up to shame.
    ANGELO   Then must your brother die.
    ISABELLA   And 'twere the cheaper way.
       Better it were a brother died at once
       Than that a sister by redeeming him
105   Should die forever.°   *be eternally damned*
    ANGELO   Were not you then as cruel as the sentence
       That you have slandered so?
    ISABELLA   Ignomy in ransom and free pardon
       Are of two houses;° lawful mercy   *different families*
110   Is nothing kin to foul redemption.
    ANGELO   You seemed of late to make the law a tyrant,
       And rather proved° the sliding of your brother   *argued*
       A merriment than a vice.
    ISABELLA   Oh, pardon me, my lord, it oft falls out
115   To have what we would° have, we speak not what we mean.   *wish to*
       I something° do excuse the thing I hate   *to some extent*
       For his advantage that I dearly love.
    ANGELO   We are all frail.[6]
    ISABELLA   Else° let my brother die,   *Otherwise*
       If not a fedary° but only he   *confederate*
120   Owe and succeed thy weakness.[7]
    ANGELO   Nay, women are frail too.
    ISABELLA   Ay, as the glasses° where they view themselves,   *mirrors*
       Which are as easy broke as they make forms.
       Women? Help, heaven! Men their creation° mar   *origin*
125   In profiting by them. Nay, call us ten times frail,
       For we are soft as our complexions are
       And credulous to false prints.[8]
    ANGELO   I think it well,°   *agree completely*
       And from this testimony of your own sex
       —Since I suppose we are made to be no stronger
130   Than faults may shake our frames—let me be bold:°   *presumptuous*
       I do arrest° your words. Be that you are,   *seize upon*
       That is, a woman; if you be more,° you're none.   *(that is, better)*
       If you be one, as you are well expressed°   *shown to be*
       By all external warrants,° show it now   *evidence*
135   By putting on the destined livery.[9]
    ISABELLA   I have no tongue° but one. Gentle my lord,   *speech*
       Let me entreat you speak the former language.
    ANGELO   Plainly conceive, I love you.
    ISABELLA   My brother did love Juliet,
140   And you tell me that he shall die for't.
    ANGELO   He shall not, Isabel, if you give me love.
    ISABELLA   I know your virtue hath a license[1] in't
       Which seems a little fouler than it is,
       To pluck on° others.   *test; mislead*
    ANGELO   Believe me on mine honor,

---

6. Echoing Ecclesiastes 8:5: "We are all worthy blame."
7. Own and inherit the weakness under discussion, or the weakness that you possess.
8. And receptive to false impressions; referring to

Angelo's counterfeiting imagery, lines 44ff.
9. That is, by accepting women's sexual destiny and subjection to men. *livery:* servant's uniform.
1. Liberty to seem licentious.

145 My words express my purpose.
  ISABELLA   Ha! Little honor, to be much believed,
  And most pernicious purpose. Seeming, seeming!
  I will proclaim° thee, Angelo, look for't.   *denounce*
  Sign me a present° pardon for my brother,   *an immediate*
150 Or with an outstretched throat I'll tell the world aloud
  What man thou art.
  ANGELO   Who will believe thee, Isabel?
  My unsoiled name, th'austereness of my life,
  My vouch° against you, and my place i'th' state,   *attestation*
  Will so your accusation overweigh
155 That you shall stifle in your own report°   *story; reputation*
  And smell of calumny. I have begun,
  And now I give my sensual race the rein.
  Fit thy consent to my sharp appetite,
  Lay by all nicety and prolixious° blushes   *coyness and excessive*
160 That banish what they sue for. Redeem thy brother
  By yielding up thy body to my will,
  Or else he must not only die the death,
  But thy unkindness° shall his death draw out   *unnaturalness*
  To lingering sufferance.° Answer me tomorrow,   *torment*
165 Or by the affection° that now guides me most,   *passion*
  I'll prove a tyrant to him. As for you,
  Say what you can; my false o'erweighs your true.   *Exit.*
  ISABELLA   To whom should I complain? Did I tell this,
  Who would believe me? Oh, perilous mouths,
170 That bear in them one and the selfsame tongue
  Either of condemnation or approof,°   *approval*
  Bidding the law make curtsy° to their will,   *submit*
  Hooking both right and wrong to th'appetite,
  To follow as it draws! I'll to my brother.
175 Though he hath fallen by prompture° of the blood,   *instigation*
  Yet hath he in him such a mind of honor
  That had he twenty heads to tender° down   *pay*
  On twenty bloody blocks, he'd yield them up
  Before his sister should her body stoop
180 To such abhorred pollution.
  Then, Isabel, live chaste, and brother, die;
  More than our brother is our chastity.
  I'll tell him yet of Angelo's request,
  And fit his mind to death for his soul's rest.   *Exit.*

3.1
Enter DUKE [*disguised as a friar*], CLAUDIO, *and* PROVOST.
  DUKE   So then you hope of pardon from Lord Angelo?
  CLAUDIO   The miserable have no other medicine
  But only hope.
  I've hope to live, and am prepared to die.
5 DUKE   Be absolute° for death; either death or life   *resolved*
  Shall thereby be the sweeter. Reason thus with life:
  If I do lose thee, I do lose a thing
  That none but fools would keep. A breath thou art,
  Servile to all the skyey influences[1]

3.1 Location: The prison.   1. Subject to all the influences of the heavenly bodies.

10   That dost this habitation where thou keep'st°   *lives*
     Hourly afflict. Merely° thou art death's fool,°   *Utterly / dupe*
     For him thou labor'st by thy flight to shun,
     And yet runn'st toward him still.° Thou art not noble,   *always*
     For all th'accommodations° that thou bear'st   *material comforts*
15   Are nursed by baseness.[2] Thou'rt by no means valiant,
     For thou dost fear the soft and tender fork°   *forked tongue*
     Of a poor worm.° Thy best of rest is sleep,   *snake*
     And that thou oft provok'st,° yet grossly fear'st   *summons*
     Thy death, which is no more. Thou art not thyself,°   *self-contained*
20   For thou exists on many a thousand grains
     That issue out of dust.° Happy thou art not,   *grow from the ground*
     For what thou hast not, still thou striv'st to get,
     And what thou hast, forget'st. Thou art not certain,°   *stable*
     For thy complexion° shifts to strange effects   *temperament*
25   After° the moon. If thou art rich, thou'rt poor,[3]   *Following*
     For like an ass whose back with ingots bows,
     Thou bear'st thy heavy riches but a journey,
     And death unloads thee. Friend hast thou none.
     For thine own bowels° which do call thee sire,   *offspring*
30   The mere effusion° of thy proper° loins,   *very emission / own*
     Do curse the gout, serpigo,° and the rheum°   *skin disease / congestion*
     For ending thee no sooner. Thou hast nor youth, nor age,
     But as it were an after-dinner's sleep
     Dreaming on both, for all thy blessèd youth
35   Becomes as agèd° and doth beg the alms°   *as if old / for money*
     Of palsied eld;° and when thou art old and rich,   *old people*
     Thou hast neither heat,° affection, limb,° nor beauty   *desire / strength*
     To make thy riches pleasant. What's in this
     That bears the name of life? Yet in this life
40   Lie hid more thousand° deaths; yet death we fear,   *a thousand more*
     That makes these odds° all even.   *irregularities*
    CLAUDIO   I humbly thank you.
     To sue° to live, I find I seek to die,   *ask*
     And seeking death find life.[4] Let it come on.
          Enter ISABELLA.
    ISABELLA   What ho! Peace here, grace, and good company.
45   PROVOST   Who's there? Come in; the wish deserves a welcome.
    DUKE [*to* CLAUDIO]   Dear sir, ere long I'll visit you again.
    CLAUDIO   Most holy sir, I thank you.
    ISABELLA   My business is a word or two with Claudio.
    PROVOST   And very welcome. Look, signor, here's your sister.
50   DUKE [*aside to* PROVOST]   Provost, a word with you.
    PROVOST   As many as you please.
    DUKE   Bring me to hear them speak where I may be concealed.
                     [*Exeunt* DUKE *and* PROVOST.]
    CLAUDIO   Now, sister, what's the comfort?
    ISABELLA   Why,
55   As all comforts are: most good, most good indeed.

---

2. Are grown from plants and animals; made by lower-class people.
3. From Revelation 3:17: "For thou sayest, I am rich and increased with goods, and have need of nothing, and knowest not how thou art wretched and misera-ble, and poor, and blind, and naked."
4. Echoing Matthew 16:25: "For whosoever will save his life, shall lose it: and whosoever shall lose his life for my sake, shall find it."

Lord Angelo, having affairs to heaven,
Intends you for his swift ambassador,
Where you shall be an everlasting ledger.°   *resident ambassador*
Therefore your best appointment° make with speed;   *preparation*
Tomorrow you set on.°   *forward*

60 CLAUDIO   Is there no remedy?
    ISABELLA   None but such remedy as, to save a head,
    To cleave a heart in twain.
    CLAUDIO   But is there any?
    ISABELLA   Yes, brother, you may live.
    There is a devilish mercy in the judge,
65 If you'll implore it, that will free your life,
    But fetter you till death.
    CLAUDIO   Perpetual durance?°   *imprisonment*
    ISABELLA   Ay, just,° perpetual durance; a restraint,   *exactly so*
    Though all the world's vastidity° you had,   *vastness*
    To a determined scope.⁵
    CLAUDIO   But in what nature?
70 ISABELLA   In such a one as, you consenting to't,
    Would bark⁶ your honor from that trunk° you bear   *body; tree trunk*
    And leave you naked.
    CLAUDIO   Let me know the point.
    ISABELLA   Oh, I do fear thee, Claudio, and I quake
    Lest thou a feverous° life shouldst entertain,°   *feverish / cherish*
75 And six or seven winters more respect°   *esteem*
    Than a perpetual honor. Dar'st thou die?
    The sense° of death is most in apprehension,°   *awareness / anticipation*
    And the poor beetle that we tread upon
    In corporal sufferance° finds a pang as great   *bodily suffering*
    As when a giant dies.
80 CLAUDIO   Why give you me this shame?
    Think you I can a resolution fetch°   *derive*
    From flow'ry° tenderness? If I must die,   *florid*
    I will encounter darkness as a bride
    And hug it in mine arms.
85 ISABELLA   There spake my brother; there my father's grave
    Did utter forth a voice. Yes, thou must die.
    Thou art too noble to conserve a life
    In base appliances.° This outward-sainted deputy,   *ignoble means*
    Whose settledᵛ visage and deliberate word   *composed*
90 Nips youth i'th' head,⁷ and follies doth enew°   *drive into hiding*
    As falcon doth the fowl, is yet a devil.
    His filth within being cast,⁸ he would appear
    A pond as deep as hell.
    CLAUDIO   The precise⁹ Angelo?
    ISABELLA   Oh, 'tis the cunning livery of hell,
95 The damn'dest body to invest° and cover   *dress*
    In precise guards!° Dost thou think, Claudio,   *trimmings*
    If I would yield him my virginity

---

5. Constricted space (by the awareness of the means by which he had been saved).
6. Strip off, like bark from a tree.
7. As a hawk kills a bird.
8. Cleaned out; measured; vomited.

9. TEXTUAL COMMENT F has the nonsense word "prenzie" here and in line 96; some editors emend (as here) to "precise," others to "princely" or "priestly." See Digital Edition TC 4.

Thou mightst be freed?

CLAUDIO   O heavens, it cannot be.

ISABELLA   Yes, he would give't thee, from this rank offense,
100   So to offend him still.[1] This night's the time
         That I should do what I abhor to name,
         Or else thou diest tomorrow.

CLAUDIO   Thou shalt not do't.

ISABELLA   Oh, were it but my life,
         I'd throw it down for your deliverance
         As frankly° as a pin.   *freely*

105 CLAUDIO   Thanks, dear Isabel.

ISABELLA   Be ready, Claudio, for your death tomorrow.

CLAUDIO   Yes. Has he affections in him,
         That thus can make him bite the law by th' nose°   *flout the law*
         When he would force it? Sure it is no sin,
110   Or of the deadly seven[2] it is the least.

ISABELLA   Which is the least?

CLAUDIO   If it were damnable, he being so wise,
         Why would he for the momentary trick°   *trifle*
         Be perdurably fined?° O Isabel—   *eternally punished*

115 ISABELLA   What says my brother?

CLAUDIO   Death is a fearful thing.

ISABELLA   And shamèd life a hateful.

CLAUDIO   Ay, but to die, and go we know not where,
         To lie in cold obstruction° and to rot,   *congealment*
120   This sensible warm motion° to become   *conscious warm body*
         A kneaded clod; and the delighted° spirit   *expansive; released*
         To bathe in fiery floods or to reside
         In thrilling° region of thick-ribbèd ice,   *bitterly cold*
         To be imprisoned in the viewless° winds   *unseeing; invisible*
125   And blown with restless violence round about
         The pendent° world, or to be worse than worst   *hanging in space*
         Of those that lawless and incertain thought[3]
         Imagine howling—'tis too horrible!
         The weariest and most loathèd worldly life
130   That age, ache, penury, and imprisonment
         Can lay on nature, is a paradise
         To what we fear of death.

ISABELLA   Alas, alas.

CLAUDIO   Sweet sister, let me live.
         What sin you do to save a brother's life,
135   Nature dispenses with° the deed so far   *excuses*
         That it becomes a virtue.

ISABELLA   O you beast!
         O faithless coward, O dishonest wretch!
         Wilt thou be made a man° out of my vice?   *given life*
         Is't not a kind of incest to take life
140   From thine own sister's shame? What should I think?
         Heaven shield° my mother played my father fair,   *forbid*
         For such a warpèd slip of wilderness°   *shoot of wild stock*

---

1. *give't thee . . . still:* grant you freedom in return for
his foul sin, so that you might continue offending him.
2. Seven deadly sins (pride, lechery, envy, anger,
covetousness, gluttony, and sloth).
3. Of those whom unbridled and dubious conjecture.

Ne'er issued from his blood. Take my defiance;°　　　　　*rejection*
Die, perish! Might but my bending down
145　Reprieve thee from thy fate, it should proceed.
I'll pray a thousand prayers for thy death,
No word to save thee.
CLAUDIO　Nay, hear me, Isabel—
ISABELLA　　　　　　　　　Oh, fie, fie, fie!
Thy sin's not accidental,° but a trade.°　　　　　*casual / habit*
150　Mercy to thee would prove itself a bawd.[4]
'Tis best that thou diest quickly.
CLAUDIO　Oh, hear me, Isabella—
　　　　[*Enter* DUKE, *disguised as a friar.*]
DUKE　Vouchsafe a word, young sister, but one word.
ISABELLA　What is your will?
155　DUKE　Might you dispense with your leisure,° I would by and　　　*spare the time*
by have some speech with you. The satisfaction I would
require is likewise your own benefit.
ISABELLA　I have no superfluous leisure; my stay must be stolen out of other affairs. But I will attend° you a while.　　　*await*
160　DUKE　[*aside to* CLAUDIO]　Son, I have overheard what hath
passed between you and your sister. Angelo had never the
purpose to corrupt her; only he hath made an assay° of her　　　*a trial*
virtue, to practice his judgment with the disposition of
natures. She, having the truth of honor° in her, hath made　　　*chastity*
165　him that gracious° denial which he is most glad to receive. I　　　*virtuous*
am confessor to Angelo, and I know this to be true; there-
fore prepare yourself to death. Do not satisfy your resolu-
tion° with hopes that are fallible. Tomorrow you must die.　　　*buck yourself up*
Go to your knees and make ready.
170　CLAUDIO　Let me ask my sister pardon. I am so out of love with
life that I will sue to be rid of it.
DUKE　Hold you there.° Farewell.　　　　[*Exit* CLAUDIO.]　　*Remain so resolved*
　　　　　　　　　　　　　　Provost, a word with you.
　　　　[*Enter* PROVOST.]
PROVOST　What's your will, father?
DUKE　That now you are come, you will be gone. Leave me a
175　while with the maid. My mind° promises with my habit,° no　　*intention / friar's gown*
loss shall touch her by my company.
PROVOST　In good time.°　　　　　　　　　　*Exit.*　　　*Very well*
DUKE　The hand that hath made you fair hath made you good.
The goodness[5] that is cheap in beauty makes beauty brief in
180　goodness, but grace,° being the soul of your complexion,°　　*virtue / constitution*
shall keep the body of it ever fair. The assault that Angelo
hath made to you, fortune hath conveyed to my understand-
ing; and but that frailty hath examples° for his falling, I　　　*precedents*
should wonder at Angelo. How will you do to content this
185　substitute° and to save your brother?　　　　　　*deputy*
ISABELLA　I am now going to resolve him. I had rather my
brother die by the law than my son should be unlawfully born.
But oh, how much is the good Duke deceived in Angelo! If

---

4. By facilitating sinful behavior.
5. The goodness that is little valued by the beautiful makes beauty short-lived.

190 ever he return, and I can speak to him, I will open my lips in
vain or discover° his government.[6]   *expose*

DUKE   That shall not be much amiss. Yet, as the matter now
stands, he will avoid° your accusation: he "made trial of you"   *quash*
only. Therefore fasten your ear on my advisings; to the love
I have in doing good a remedy presents itself. I do make
195 myself believe that you may most uprighteously do a poor
wronged lady a merited benefit; redeem your brother from
the angry law; do no stain to your own gracious person; and
much please the absent Duke, if peradventure he shall ever
return to have hearing of this business.

200 ISABELLA   Let me hear you speak farther. I have spirit to do
anything that appears not foul in the truth of my spirit.

DUKE   Virtue is bold, and goodness never fearful. Have you
not heard speak of Mariana, the sister of Frederick, the
great soldier who miscarried° at sea?   *perished*
205 ISABELLA   I have heard of the lady, and good words went with
her name.

DUKE   She should this Angelo have married; was affianced to
her oath, and the nuptial appointed;° between which time of   *wedding day set*
the contract and limit° of the solemnity, her brother Freder-   *date*
210 ick was wrecked at sea, having in that perished vessel the
dowry of his sister. But mark how heavily this befell to the
poor gentlewoman. There she lost a noble and renowned
brother, in his love toward her ever most kind and natural;
with him, the portion and sinew° of her fortune, her mar-   *mainstay*
215 riage dowry; with both, her combinate° husband, this well-   *betrothed*
seeming Angelo.

ISABELLA   Can this be so? Did Angelo so leave her?

DUKE   Left her in her tears, and dried not one of them with
his comfort; swallowed° his vows whole, pretending° in her   *retracted / alleging*
220 discoveries of dishonor;° in few, bestowed her on her own   *unchastity*
lamentation, which she yet wears for his sake; and he, a
marble° to her tears, is washed with them but relents not.   *impervious*

ISABELLA   What a merit were it in death to take this poor
maid from the world! What corruption in this life, that it
225 will let this man live? But how out of this can she avail?°   *profit*

DUKE   It is a rupture that you may easily heal, and the cure of
it not only saves your brother, but keeps you from dishonor
in doing it.

ISABELLA   Show me how, good father.

230 DUKE   This forenamed maid hath yet in her the continuance
of her first affection.° His unjust unkindness, that in all rea-   *passion*
son should have quenched her love, hath, like an impedi-
ment in the current, made it more violent and unruly. Go you
to Angelo, answer his requiring with a plausible obedience,
235 agree with his demands to the point.° Only refer yourself to   *exactly*
this advantage: first, that your stay with him may not be long;
that the time may have all shadow° and silence in it; and the   *darkness*
place answer to convenience. This being granted in course,
and now follows all: we shall advise this wronged maid to
240 stead up° your appointment, go in your place. If the encoun-   *fulfill*

6. Conduct; mode of governing.

ter acknowledge itself° hereafter, it may compel him to her   *becomes known*
recompense. And here, by this is your brother saved, your
honor untainted, the poor Mariana advantaged, and the cor-
rupt deputy scaled.[7] The maid will I frame° and make fit for   *prepare*
245   his attempt. If you think well to carry this as you may, the
doubleness of the benefit defends the deceit from reproof.
What think you of it?

ISABELLA   The image of it gives me content already, and I
trust it will grow to a most prosperous perfection.°   *completion*
250   DUKE   It lies much in your holding up. Haste you speedily to
Angelo. If for this night he entreat you to his bed, give him
promise of satisfaction. I will presently to Saint Luke's.
There at the moated grange° resides this dejected[8] Mariana.   *country house*
At that place call upon me, and dispatch° with Angelo that it   *settle*
255   may be quickly.

ISABELLA   I thank you for this comfort. Fare you well, good
father.   *Exit.*

        Enter ELBOW, CLOWN, *and Officers.*[9]

ELBOW   Nay, if there be no remedy for it, but that you will
needs° buy and sell men and women like beasts, we shall   *you must*
260   have all the world drink brown and white bastard.°   *sweet wine (with pun)*

DUKE   O heavens, what stuff is here?

CLOWN   'Twas never merry world since of two usuries[1] the
merriest was put down, and the worser allowed by order of
law[2] a furred gown° to keep him warm; and furred with fox   *(worn by usurers)*
265   and lambskins, too, to signify that craft,° being richer than   *cunning*
innocency, stands for the facing.[3]

ELBOW   Come your way, sir. Bless you, good Father Friar.[4]

DUKE   And you, good brother father. What offense hath this
man made you, sir?

270   ELBOW   Marry, sir, he hath offended the law; and, sir, we take
him to be a thief too, sir; for we have found upon him, sir, a
strange picklock,° which we have sent to the deputy.   *skeleton key*

DUKE   Fie, sirrah, a bawd,° a wicked bawd!   *pimp*
The evil that thou causest to be done,
275   That is thy means to live. Do thou but think
What 'tis to cram a maw or clothe a back
From such a filthy vice; say to thyself,
From their abominable and beastly touches
I drink, I eat, array° myself, and live.   *dress*
280   Canst thou believe thy living is a life,
So stinkingly depending?° Go mend, go mend.   *dependent*

CLOWN   Indeed, it does stink in some sort, sir, but yet, sir, I
would prove—

DUKE   Nay, if the devil have given thee proofs for sin
285   Thou wilt prove° his. Take him to prison, officer.   *prove to be*
Correction° and instruction must both work   *Punishment*
Ere this rude° beast will profit.°   *barbarous / improve*

---

7. Overreached; weighed (and found wanting).
8. Depressed; rejected.
9. The rest of the scene takes place on the street.
Some editors begin a new scene here, though the
Duke remains onstage.
1. Lending of money at interest; prostitution.

2. A statute of 1570 allowed interest of 10 percent or
less.
3. Is used to trim the garment; displays itself to the
world.
4. Absurd, since "friar" means "brother"; hence the
Duke's reply.

ELBOW   He must before the deputy, sir, he has given him
warning. The deputy cannot abide a whoremaster. If he be a
290   whoremonger, and comes before him, he were as good go a
mile on his errand.[5]
DUKE   That° we were all, as some would seem to be,   *Would that*
Free from our faults, as faults from seeming free!°   *free from seeming*
ELBOW   His neck will come to° your waist—a cord,[6] sir.   *end up like*
Enter LUCIO.
295   CLOWN   I spy comfort, I cry bail! Here's a gentleman, and a
friend of mine.
LUCIO   How now, noble Pompey? What, at the wheels of Caesar? Art thou led in triumph?[7] What, is there none of Pygmalion's images[8] newly made woman to be had now, for
300   putting the hand in the pocket and extracting clutched?[9]
What reply, ha? What sayest thou to this tune, matter, and
method?[1] Is't not drowned i'th' last rain,[2] ha? What sayest
thou, trot?° Is the world as it was, man? Which is the way? Is   *bawd*
it sad and few words? Or how? The trick° of it?   *style*
305   DUKE   Still° thus and thus; still worse!   *Always*
LUCIO   How doth my dear morsel, thy mistress? Procures she
still? Ha?
CLOWN   Troth, sir, she hath eaten up° all her beef,° and she is   *worn out / prostitutes*
herself in the tub.[3]
310   LUCIO   Why, 'tis good! It is the right of it, it must be so. Ever
your fresh whore and your powdered[4] bawd, an unshunned°   *unavoidable*
consequence; it must be so. Art going to prison, Pompey?
CLOWN   Yes, faith, sir.
LUCIO   Why, 'tis not amiss, Pompey. Farewell. Go say I sent
315   thee thither. For debt, Pompey, or how?
ELBOW   For being a bawd, for being a bawd.
LUCIO   Well, then, imprison him. If imprisonment be the due
of a bawd, why, 'tis his right. Bawd is he doubtless, and of
antiquity° too, bawd born.° Farewell, good Pompey. Com-   *long standing / at birth*
320   mend me to the prison, Pompey; you will turn good hus-
band° now, Pompey; you will keep the house.   *householder*
CLOWN   I hope, sir, your good worship will be my bail?
LUCIO   No, indeed will I not, Pompey, it is not the wear.° I will   *fashion*
pray, Pompey, to increase your bondage; if you take it not
325   patiently, why, your mettle° is the more. Adieu, trusty Pom-   *spirit; shackles*
pey. Bless you, Friar.
DUKE   And you.
LUCIO   Does Bridget paint° still, Pompey, ha?   *use cosmetics*
ELBOW   Come your ways, sir, come.
330   CLOWN   You will not bail me then, sir?
LUCIO   Then, Pompey, nor now. What news abroad,° Friar?   *in the world*
What news?

---

5. *he were . . . errand:* he would be better doing anything rather than that.
6. Encircled by a rope, as the friar's cord encircles
his waist.
7. After Roman victories, vanquished generals were
paraded behind the chariot wheels of their
conquerors.
8. In classical legend, the sculptor Pygmalion fell in
love with one of his statues, who was given life by

Venus, the goddess of love; with a play on "become a
woman" (lose one's virginity).
9. Clenched, with money for bail.
1. This style, topic, and sequence of thought.
2. Overwhelmed with recent misfortune.
3. Pickling tub for preserving ("powdering") beef;
sweating tub for curing venereal disease.
4. Pickled; covered with cosmetic powder.

ELBOW   Come your ways, sir, come.

LUCIO   Go to kennel, Pompey,[5] go.

[*Exeunt* ELBOW, CLOWN, *and Officers.*]

335   What news, Friar, of the Duke?

DUKE   I know none. Can you tell me of any?

LUCIO   Some say he is with the Emperor of Russia; other
some,° he is in Rome; but where is he, think you? ⟶ *some others*

DUKE   I know not where, but wheresoever, I wish him well.

340 LUCIO   It was a mad fantastical trick° of him to steal from the ⟶ *eccentric caprice*
state and usurp the beggary he was never born to. Lord Angelo
dukes it° well in his absence; he puts transgression to't.[6] ⟶ *plays the Duke*

DUKE   He does well in't.

LUCIO   A little more lenity to lechery would do no harm in
345   him. Something too crabbed° that way, Friar. ⟶ *Somewhat too harsh*

DUKE   It is too general a vice, and severity must cure it.

LUCIO   Yes, in good sooth, the vice is of a great° kindred, it is ⟶ *an extensive; powerful*
well allied;° but it is impossible to extirp° it quite, Friar, till ⟶ *connected / extirpate*
eating and drinking be put down. They say this Angelo was
350   not made by man and woman after this downright[7] way of
creation. Is it true, think you?

DUKE   How should he be made then?

LUCIO   Some report a sea-maid° spawned him; some, that he ⟶ *mermaid*
was begot between two stockfishes.° But it is certain that ⟶ *dried fish*
355   when he makes water, his urine is congealed ice; that I know
to be true. And he is a motion generative,[8] that's infallible.° ⟶ *certain*

DUKE   You are pleasant,° sir, and speak apace.° ⟶ *merry / unrestrainedly*

LUCIO   Why, what a ruthless thing is this in him, for the rebellion of a codpiece[9] to take away the life of a man? Would the
360   Duke that is absent have done this? Ere he would have
hanged a man for the getting° a hundred bastards, he would ⟶ *begetting*
have paid for the nursing a thousand. He had some feeling of
the sport, he knew the service,° and that instructed him to ⟶ *(of prostitution)*
mercy.

365 DUKE   I never heard the absent Duke much detected° for ⟶ *accused*
women; he was not inclined that way.

LUCIO   O sir, you are deceived.

DUKE   'Tis not possible.

LUCIO   Who, not the Duke? Yes, your beggar of fifty, and his
370   use° was to put a ducat in her clack-dish.[1] The Duke had ⟶ *custom*
crotchets° in him. He would be drunk, too, that let me inform ⟶ *odd notions*
you.

DUKE   You do him wrong, surely.

LUCIO   Sir, I was an inward° of his. A shy fellow was the Duke, ⟶ *intimate*
375   and I believe I know the cause of his withdrawing.

DUKE   What, I prithee, might be the cause?

LUCIO   No, pardon. 'Tis a secret must be locked within the
teeth and the lips. But this I can let you understand, the
greater file of the subject° held the Duke to be wise. ⟶ *majority of the people*
380 DUKE   Wise? Why, no question but he was.

---

5. "Pompey" was a common name for a dog.
6. He prosecutes lawbreaking vigorously.
7. In accordance with this straightforward.

8. An impotent puppet.
9. Padded pouch worn over a man's breeches.
1. Begging bowl (with sexual innuendo).

LUCIO   A very superficial, ignorant, unweighing° fellow.   *injudicious*

DUKE   Either this is envy° in you, folly, or mistaking. The very   *malice*
stream° of his life, and the business he hath helmed,° must   *course / steered*
upon a warranted need° give him a better proclamation.°   *necessarily / reputation*

385   Let him be but testimonied° in his own bringings forth,°   *proven / public actions*
and he shall appear to the envious a scholar, a statesman,
and a soldier. Therefore you speak unskillfully,° or, if your   *ignorantly*
knowledge be more, it is much darkened in your malice.

LUCIO   Sir, I know him, and I love him.

390   DUKE   Love talks with better knowledge, and knowledge with
dearer love.

LUCIO   Come, sir. I know what I know.

DUKE   I can hardly believe that, since you know not what you
speak. But if ever the Duke return, as our prayers are he

395   may, let me desire you to make your answer before him. If it
be honest you have spoke, you have courage to maintain it. I
am bound to call upon° you, and I pray you, your name.   *accuse*

LUCIO   Sir, my name is Lucio, well known to the Duke.

DUKE   He shall know you better, sir, if I may live to report you.

400   LUCIO   I fear you not.

DUKE   Oh, you hope the Duke will return no more, or you
imagine me too unhurtful an opposite.° But indeed I can do   *adversary*
you little harm. You'll forswear this again.°   *at another time*

LUCIO   I'll be hanged first. Thou art deceived in me, Friar. But

405   no more of this. Canst thou tell if Claudio die tomorrow, or
no?

DUKE   Why should he die, sir?

LUCIO   Why? For filling a bottle with a tundish.° I would the   *funnel (with innuendo)*
Duke we talk of were returned again. This ungenitured

410   agent° will unpeople the province with continency. Sparrows[2]   *sexless deputy*
must not build in his house eaves, because they are lecher-   *(proverbially lustful)*
ous. The Duke yet would have dark deeds darkly answered;°   *secretly requited*
he would never bring them to light. Would he were returned.
Marry, this Claudio is condemned for untrussing.° Farewell,   *undoing his leggings*

415   good Friar, I prithee pray for me. The Duke, I say to thee
again, would eat mutton on Fridays.[3] He's now past it, and yet
I say to thee he would mouth° with a beggar, though she   *kiss*
smelt° brown bread and garlic.[4] Say that I said so! Farewell.   *smelled of*
                                                             Exit.

DUKE   No might, nor greatness in mortality°   *mortal existence*

420   Can censure scape.° Back-wounding calumny[5]   *escape censure*
The whitest virtue strikes. What king so strong,
Can tie the gall° up in the slanderous tongue?   *rancor*
But who comes here?

Enter ESCALUS, PROVOST, BAWD[, *and Officers*].

ESCALUS   Go, away with her to prison.

425   BAWD   Good my lord, be good to me; your honor is accounted
a merciful man, good my lord.

---

2. Sparrows were proverbially lustful.   4. The food of the poor.
3. *mutton:* prostitute (slang); it was forbidden to eat   5. *Back-wounding calumny:* slander ("calumny") is
meat on Fridays.   cowardly because it is not said to the victim's face.

ESCALUS Double and treble admonition,[6] and still forfeit in
the same kind!° This would make mercy swear[7] and play the   *way*
tyrant.

430 PROVOST A bawd of eleven years' continuance, may it please
your honor.

BAWD My lord, this is one Lucio's information° against me.   *accusation*
Mistress Kate Keepdown was with child by him in the
Duke's time, he promised her marriage. His child is a year
435 and a quarter old come Philip and Jacob.[8] I have kept it
myself, and see how he goes about° to abuse° me.   *out of his way / injure*

ESCALUS That fellow is a fellow of much license. Let him be
called before us. Away with her to prison, go to, no more
words.   [*Exeunt* BAWD *and Officers.*]

440 Provost, my brother° Angelo will not be altered: Claudio   *colleague*
must die tomorrow. Let him be furnished with divines and
have all charitable preparation.[9] If my brother wrought by°   *acted according to*
my pity, it should not be so with him.

PROVOST So please you, this friar hath been with him and
445 advised him for th'entertainment° of death.   *acceptance*

ESCALUS Good even, good father.

DUKE Bliss and goodness on you.

ESCALUSLUS Of whence are you?

DUKE Not of this country, though my chance° is now   *fortune*
450 To use it for my time.° I am a brother   *dwell here at present*
Of gracious order, late come from the See°   *Vatican*
In special business from his Holiness.

ESCALUS What news abroad i'th' world?

DUKE None, but that there is so great a fever on goodness that
455 the dissolution of it must cure it.[1] Novelty is only in request,°   *alone in demand*
and it is as dangerous to be aged in° any kind of course, as it   *habituated to*
is virtuous to be constant in any undertaking. There is
scarce truth° enough alive to make societies secure, but   *honesty; loyalty*
security[2] enough to make fellowships° accursed. Much   *partnerships*
460 upon° this riddle runs the wisdom of the world. This news is   *According to*
old enough, yet it is every day's news. I pray you, sir, of what
disposition was the Duke?

ESCALUS One that above all other strifes contended especially
to know himself.[3]

465 DUKE What pleasure was he given to?

ESCALUS Rather rejoicing to see another merry, than merry
at anything which professed° to make him rejoice. A gentle-   *attempted*
man of all temperance. But leave we him to his events,° with   *affairs*
a prayer they may prove prosperous, and let me desire to
470 know° how you find Claudio prepared. I am made to under-   *ask*
stand that you have lent him visitation.°   *visited him*

6. Exceeding that recommended by Paul in Titus
3:10: "Reject him that is an heretic, after once or
twice admonition."
7. Varying the proverbial "make a saint swear."
8. May 1 was the Feast of St. Philip and St. James
(Jacob), but also the time of sexually licentious May
Day festivities, when the child was presumably
conceived.

9. Spiritual preparation enjoined by Christian
charity.
1. *there is . . . it:* that is, goodness is so sick that only
death will "cure" it.
2. Financial bonds liable to forfeit; blind trustful-
ness. *societies:* association with others.
3. "Know thyself" was proverbial advice.

DUKE He professes to have received no sinister measure° from   *unjust treatment*
  his judge, but most willingly humbles himself to the deter-
  mination° of justice. Yet had he framed° to himself, by the   *sentence / imagined*
475   instruction of his frailty, many deceiving promises of life,
  which I by my good leisure° have discredited to him, and   *gradually*
  now is he resolved to die.
ESCALUS You have paid the heavens your function, and the
  prisoner the very debt of your calling.[4] I have labored for the
480   poor gentleman to the extremest shore° of my modesty, but   *utmost limit*
  my brother justice have I found so severe that he hath forced
  me to tell him, he is indeed Justice.[5]
DUKE If his own life answer° the straitness° of his proceeding, *correspond to / strictness*
  it shall become him well; wherein if he chance to fail he hath
485   sentenced° himself.   *condemned*
ESCALUS I am going to visit the prisoner. Fare you well.
DUKE Peace be with you.   *Exit* ESCALUS.
  He who the sword of heaven[6] will bear
  Should be as holy as severe;
490   Pattern in himself to know,
  Grace to stand, and virtue, go;[7]
  More nor less to others paying
  Than by self-offenses° weighing.   *his own offenses*
  Shame to him whose cruel striking
495   Kills for faults of his own liking;
  Twice treble shame on Angelo
  To weed my vice[8] and let his grow.
  Oh, what may man within him hide,
  Though angel on the outward side?
500   How may likeness made in crimes,[9]
  Making practice on the times,
  To draw with idle spiders' strings
  Most ponderous and substantial things?[1]
  Craft against vice I must apply.
505   With Angelo tonight shall lie
  His old betrothèd, but despisèd;
  So disguise shall by th' disguisèd[2]
  Pay with falsehood false exacting,
  And perform an old contracting.   *Exit.*

4.1

Enter MARIANA *and* BOY *singing.*
BOY [*sings*] Take, oh, take those lips away
       That so sweetly were forsworn,°   *perjured*
       And those eyes, the break of day,
       Lights° that do mislead° the morn;   *Suns / falsely guide*

---

4. You have repaid the heavens for giving you your
vocation, and given the prisoner all he can expect of
a friar.
5. Absolute justice personified.
6. The authority of a ruler, conferred by God.
7. When to stand firm, and when to take action (?).
8. The Duke speaks as a representative sinner.
9. How can the similarity between Claudio's and
Angelo's offenses . . . (see also note 1).
1. *To draw . . . things:* the law was proverbially compared to a spider's web, which caught small insects

but which large insects could break through. *idle:*
ineffectual. TEXTUAL COMMENT The text of 500–503
is clearly corrupt, but it is not clear how to fix it, so *The
Norton Shakespeare* prints the passage as it appears in
F. For a discussion of the problem, see Digital Edition
TC 5.
2. Mariana, "disguised" as Isabella.
4.1 Location: Mariana's house. Probably Mariana
and the Boy are "discovered" by drawing back a curtain to reveal the characters within an alcove at the
back of the stage.

5   But my kisses bring again, bring again,°   *return*
               Seals of love, but sealed in vain, sealed in vain.
         Enter DUKE [*disguised as a friar*].
MARIANA   Break off thy song and haste thee quick away.
               Here comes a man of comfort whose advice
               Hath often stilled my brawling° discontent.   [*Exit* BOY.]   *clamorous*

10   —I cry you mercy,° sir, and well could wish   *beg your pardon*
               You had not found me here so musical.
               Let me excuse me, and believe me so:°   *in this*
               My mirth it much displeased, but pleased my woe.[1]
DUKE   'Tis good, though music oft hath such a charm°   *magic spell*

15   To make bad good° and good provoke to harm.   *bad appear good*
               I pray you tell me, hath anybody inquired for me here today?
               Much upon° this time have I promised here to meet.   *At about*
MARIANA   You have not been inquired after. I have sat here
               all day.
         Enter ISABELLA [*carrying two keys*].
20 DUKE   I do constantly° believe you. The time is come even   *assuredly*
               now. I shall crave your forbearance° a little. Maybe I will   *departure; patience*
               call upon you anon for some advantage to yourself.
MARIANA   I am always bound to you.   *Exit.*
DUKE [*to* ISABELLA]   Very well met, and welcome.
25   What is the news from this good deputy?
ISABELLA   He hath a garden circummured° with brick,   *walled about*
               Whose western side is with a vineyard backed,
               And to that vineyard is a planchèd° gate   *made of planks*
               That makes his opening with this bigger key.
30   This other doth command a little door
               Which from the vineyard to the garden leads.
               There have I made my promise
               Upon the heavy° middle of the night   *In the gloomy*
               To call upon him.
35 DUKE   But shall you on your knowledge° find this way?   *with this information*
ISABELLA   I have ta'en a due and wary note upon't.
               With whispering and most guilty diligence,
               In action all of precept,° he did show me   *With explanatory gestures*
               The way twice o'er.
DUKE   Are there no other tokens°   *signs*
40   Between you 'greed concerning her observance?[2]
ISABELLA   No. None but only a repair° i'th' dark,   *journey to the place*
               And that I have possessed° him my most° stay   *informed / longest*
               Can be but brief, for I have made him know
               I have a servant comes with me along
45   That stays upon° me, whose persuasion is   *waits for*
               I come about my brother.
DUKE   'Tis well borne up.°   *maintained*
               I have not yet made known to Mariana
               A word of this. —What ho, within, come forth!
         Enter MARIANA.
               I pray you be acquainted with this maid.
50   She comes to do you good.
ISABELLA   I do desire the like.

---

1. The music drove away mirth but nurtured   2. That she (Mariana) must observe.
melancholy.

DUKE Do you persuade yourself° that I respect you?   *believe*
MARIANA Good friar, I know you do, and have so found it.
DUKE Take then this your companion° by the hand,   *partner*
55 Who hath a story ready for your ear.
I shall attend your leisure,° but make haste,   *wait until you are ready*
The vaporous night approaches.
MARIANA Will't please you walk aside?
                         [*Exeunt* MARIANA *and* ISABELLA.]
DUKE O place° and greatness! Millions of false° eyes   *rank / misjudging*
60 Are stuck° upon thee. Volumes of report°   *fixed / rumors*
Run with their false and most contrarious quest°   *misguided inquiry*
Upon thy doings. Thousand escapes° of wit   *sallies*
Make thee the father° of their idle dream°   *subject / fantasy*
And rack[3] thee in their fancies.
                         Enter MARIANA *and* ISABELLA.
                                        —Welcome, how agreed?
65 ISABELLA She'll take the enterprise upon her, father,
If you advise it.
DUKE   It is not my consent,
But my entreaty too.
ISABELLA   Little have you to say
When you depart from him, but soft and low,
"Remember now my brother."
MARIANA   Fear me not.[4]
70 DUKE Nor, gentle daughter, fear you not at all.
He is your husband on a precontract.°   *formal betrothal*
To bring you thus together 'tis no sin,
Sith that° the justice of your title to him   *Since*
Doth flourish° the deceit. Come, let us go;   *give propriety to*
75 Our corn's to reap, for yet our tilth's° to sow.   *Exeunt.*   *tilled land*

                                        4.2
                         Enter PROVOST *and* CLOWN.
PROVOST Come hither, sirrah. Can you cut off a man's head?
CLOWN If the man be a bachelor, sir, I can. But if he be a
married man, he's his wife's head,[1] and I can never cut off a
woman's head.[2]
5 PROVOST Come, sir, leave me° your snatches,° and yield me a   *stop / quips*
direct answer. Tomorrow morning are to die Claudio and
Barnardine. Here is in our prison a common executioner
who in his office lacks a helper. If you will take it on you to
assist him, it shall redeem you from your gyves.° If not, you   *fetters*
10 shall have your full time of imprisonment and your deliver-
ance with an unpitied° whipping, for you have been a noto-   *unmerciful*
rious bawd.
CLOWN Sir, I have been an unlawful bawd time out of mind,
but yet I will be content to be a lawful hangman. I would be
15 glad to receive some instruction from my fellow partner.
PROVOST What ho, Abhorson! Where's Abhorson there?
                         Enter ABHORSON.
ABHORSON Do you call, sir?

3. Misrepresent (literally, "torture by stretching").
4. Rely upon me; but the Duke takes "fear" in its
modern sense.
4.2 Location: The prison.

1. Alluding to Paul's doctrine that "the husband is
the wife's head," Ephesians 5:23.
2. Playing on "married woman's maidenhead," an
improbability.

PROVOST Sirrah, here's a fellow will help you tomorrow in
your execution. If you think it meet, compound with him by
20 the year,³ and let him abide here with you; if not, use him
for the present and dismiss him. He cannot plead his esti-
mation° with you; he hath been a bawd.   *reputation*

ABHORSON A bawd, sir? Fie upon him, he will discredit our
mystery.⁴

25 PROVOST Go to, sir, you weigh equally. A feather will turn the
scale.   *Exit.*

CLOWN Pray, sir, by your good favor°—for surely, sir, a good   *permission*
favor° you have, but that you have a hanging look⁵—do you   *face*
call, sir, your occupation a mystery?

30 ABHORSON Ay, sir, a mystery.

CLOWN Painting,⁶ sir, I have heard say, is a mystery; and your
whores, sir, being members of my occupation, using painting,
do prove my occupation a mystery. But what mystery there
should be in hanging, if I should be hanged I cannot imagine.

35 ABHORSON Sir, it is a mystery.

CLOWN Proof.

ABHORSON Every true man's apparel fits your thief.⁷

CLOWN If it be too little for your thief, your true man thinks
it big enough.° If it be too big for your thief, your thief   *a big enough loss*
40 thinks it little enough.° So, every true man's apparel fits   *a small enough gain*
your thief.

Enter PROVOST.

PROVOST Are you agreed?

CLOWN Sir, I will serve him, for I do find your hangman is a
more penitent trade than your bawd. He doth oftener ask
45 forgiveness.⁸

PROVOST You, sirrah, provide your block and your ax tomorrow,
four o'clock.

ABHORSON Come on, bawd, I will instruct thee in my trade.
Follow.

50 CLOWN I do desire to learn, sir. And I hope, if you have
occasion to use me for your own turn, you shall find me
yare.° For truly, sir, for your kindness, I owe you a good   *skillful; eager*
turn.⁹

PROVOST Call hither Barnardine and Claudio.

[*Exeunt* ABHORSON *and* CLOWN.]

55 Th'one has my pity, not a jot the other,
Being a murderer, though he were my brother.

Enter CLAUDIO.

Look, here's the warrant, Claudio, for thy death.
'Tis now dead midnight, and by eight tomorrow
Thou must be made immortal. Where's Barnardine?

60 CLAUDIO As fast locked up in sleep as guiltless labor
When it lies starkly° in the traveler's° bones.   *stiffly / worker's*
He will not wake.

---

3. Settle regular terms of employment with him.
4. Profession, requiring specialized skills and training.
5. Downcast expression; hangman's face.
6. Artist's occupation; use of cosmetics.
7. Abhorson implies that the thief assumes the character of an honest man by stealing his clothing; he

also suggests an analogy between the thief and the hangman, who was awarded the clothes of his victims.
8. Executioners customarily asked forgiveness of their victims before killing them.
9. Favor; turning off the scaffold.

PROVOST   Who can do good on him?
  Well, go prepare yourself. [*Knocking within.*] But hark,
    what noise?
  Heaven give your spirits comfort.   [*Exit* CLAUDIO.]
  [*Knocking within.*]
                         By and by!
65 I hope it is some pardon or reprieve
  For the most gentle Claudio.
       Enter DUKE [*disguised as a friar*].
                  Welcome, Father.
DUKE   The best and wholesom'st spirits of the night
  Envelop you, good Provost! Who called here of late?
PROVOST   None since the curfew[1] rung.
70 DUKE   Not Isabel?
PROVOST   No.
DUKE   They will, then, ere't be long.
PROVOST   What comfort is for Claudio?
DUKE   There's some in hope.
75 PROVOST   It is a bitter° deputy.   *cruel*
DUKE   Not so, not so. His life is paralleled
  Even with the stroke and line[2] of his great justice.
  He doth with holy abstinence subdue
  That in himself which he spurs on his power
80 To qualify° in others. Were he mealed° with that   *moderate / stained*
  Which he corrects, then were he tyrannous,
  But this being so, he's just. [*Knocking within.*] Now are they
    come.   [*Exit* PROVOST.]
  This is a gentle provost. Seldom-when°   *Rarely*
  The steelèd° jailer is the friend of men.   *hard-hearted*
      [*Enter* PROVOST. *Knocking within.*]
85 How now? What noise? That spirit's possessed with haste
  That wounds th'unresisting postern° with these strokes.   *unyielding door*
PROVOST   There he° must stay until the officer   *(the messenger)*
  Arise to let him in. He° is called up.   *(the officer)*
DUKE   Have you no countermand for Claudio yet,
90 But he must die tomorrow?
PROVOST   None, sir, none.
DUKE   As near the dawning, Provost, as it is,
  You shall hear more ere morning.
PROVOST   Haply°   *Perhaps*
  You something know, yet I believe there comes
  No countermand. No such example° have we.   *precedent*
95 Besides, upon the very siege° of justice   *seat*
  Lord Angelo hath to the public ear
  Professed the contrary.
      Enter a MESSENGER.
DUKE   This is his lordship's man.
PROVOST   And here comes Claudio's pardon.[3]

---

1. Evening bell, rung at 9:00 P.M.
2. Exact course; also suggesting ax blows and hanging ropes.
3. TEXTUAL COMMENT Some editors have argued that the end of line 97 makes more sense coming from the Provost and that the Duke ought to utter the following line. The Norton text retains the F speech prefixes. For an account of the problem, see Digital Edition TC 6.

MESSENGER My lord hath sent you this note, and by me this
100 further charge: that you swerve not from the smallest article
of it, neither in time, matter, or other circumstance. Good
morrow, for as I take it, it is almost day.
PROVOST I shall obey him.   [*Exit* MESSENGER.]
DUKE This is his pardon purchased by such sin
105 For which the pardoner himself is in.
Hence hath offense his° quick celerity   *its*
When it is born in high authority.
When vice makes mercy, mercy's so extended
That for the fault's love[4] is th'offender friended.°   *befriended*
110 —Now, sir, what news?
PROVOST I told you: Lord Angelo, belike thinking me remiss
in mine office, awakens me with this unwonted putting on,°   *urging*
methinks strangely, for he hath not used° it before.   *practiced*
DUKE Pray you, let's hear.
115 PROVOST [*reads the letter*][5] "Whatsoever you may hear to the
contrary, let Claudio be executed by four of the clock, and in
the afternoon Barnardine. For my better satisfaction, let me
have Claudio's head sent me by five. Let this be duly performed with a thought that more depends on it than we
120 must yet deliver.° Thus fail not to do your office, as you will   *make known*
answer it at your peril." What say you to this, sir?
DUKE What is that Barnardine who is to be executed in
th'afternoon?
PROVOST A Bohemian born, but here nursed up and bred, one
125 that is a prisoner nine years old.°   *nine years a prisoner*
DUKE How came it that the absent Duke had not either deliv-
ered him to his liberty or executed him? I have heard it was
ever his manner to do so.
PROVOST His friends still° wrought reprieves for him, and   *continually*
130 indeed his fact° till now in the government of Lord Angelo   *crime*
came not to an undoubtful° proof.   *a certain*
DUKE It is now apparent?
PROVOST Most manifest, and not denied by himself.
DUKE Hath he borne himself penitently in prison? How
135 seems he to be touched?°   *affected*
PROVOST A man that apprehends death no more dreadfully
but as a drunken sleep; careless, reckless, and fearless of
what's past, present, or to come; insensible of mortality, and
desperately mortal.[6]
140 DUKE He wants° advice.   *needs*
PROVOST He will hear none. He hath evermore had the liberty of the prison. Give him leave to escape hence, he would
not. Drunk many times a day, if not many days entirely°   *continuously*
drunk. We have very oft awaked him, as if to carry him to
145 execution, and showed him a seeming warrant for it. It hath
not moved him at all.
DUKE More of him anon. There is written in your brow, Provost, honesty and constancy. If I read it not truly, my ancient
skill beguiles me; but in the boldness° of my cunning,° I will   *confidence / skill*

---

4. For love of the fault.
5. TEXTUAL COMMENT In F, it is unclear who reads
the letter aloud; modern editors assign it to the Pro-

vost. The Textual Comment explores the significance
of the ambiguity. See Digital Edition TC 7.
6. Reckless of death, and in a state of mortal sin.

150   lay myself in hazard.[7] Claudio, whom here you have warrant
       to execute, is no greater forfeit to the law than Angelo who
       hath sentenced him. To make you understand this in a mani-
       fested effect,° I crave but four days' respite, for the which you   *clear demonstration*
       are to do me both a present° and a dangerous courtesy.°   *an immediate / favor*
155   PROVOST   Pray, sir, in what?
       DUKE   In the delaying death.
       PROVOST   Alack, how may I do it? Having the hour limited,
       and an express command, under penalty, to deliver his head
       in the view of Angelo? I may make my case as Claudio's to
160   cross° this in the smallest.   *oppose*
       DUKE   By the vow of mine order, I warrant you. If my instruc-
       tions may be your guide, let this Barnardine be this morning
       executed, and his head borne to Angelo.
       PROVOST   Angelo hath seen them both and will discover° the   *discern*
165   favor.
       DUKE   Oh, death's a great disguiser, and you may add to it.
       Shave the head, and tie the beard, and say it was the desire
       of the penitent to be so bared before his death; you know the
       course is common. If anything fall to you upon° this more   *as a result of*
170   than thanks and good fortune, by the saint whom I profess,[8]
       I will plead against it with my life.
       PROVOST   Pardon me, good Father; it is against my oath.
       DUKE   Were you sworn to the Duke, or to the deputy?
       PROVOST   To him and to his substitutes.
175   DUKE   You will think you have made no offense, if the Duke
       avouch° the justice of your dealing?   *vouch for*
       PROVOST   But what likelihood is in that?
       DUKE   Not a resemblance,° but a certainty. Yet since I see you   *likelihood*
       fearful that neither my coat,° integrity, nor persuasion can   *religious garb*
180   with ease attempt you,° I will go further than I meant, to   *win you over*
       pluck all fears out of you. Look you, sir, here is the hand and
       seal of the Duke. You know the character,° I doubt not, and   *handwriting*
       the signet is not strange to you.
       PROVOST   I know them both.
185   DUKE   The contents of this is the return of the Duke. You
       shall anon° over-read it at your pleasure, where you shall   *right away*
       find within these two days he will be here. This is a thing
       that Angelo knows not, for he this very day receives letters
       of strange tenor, perchance of the Duke's death, perchance
190   entering into some monastery, but by chance nothing of
       what is writ.° Look, th'unfolding star[9] calls up the shepherd.   *written here*
       Put not yourself into amazement° how these things should   *perplexity*
       be; all difficulties are but easy when they are known. Call
       your executioner, and off with Barnardine's head. I will
195   give him a present shrift[1] and advise him for a better
       place. Yet° you are amazed, but this° shall absolutely   *Still / (the letter)*
       resolve you.° Come away, it is almost clear dawn.   *Exeunt.*   *free you from doubt*

---

7. I will bet on it; I will put myself in peril.   safely release the sheep from the fold).
8. The patron saint of my order.   1. An immediate confession.
9. Morning star (which tells the shepherd he may

4.3

Enter CLOWN.

CLOWN   I am as well acquainted here as I was in our house of
profession.¹ One would think it were Mistress Overdone's
own house, for here be many of her old customers. First,
here's young Master Rash. He's in for a commodity² of brown
5   paper and old ginger, nine score and seventeen pounds, of
which he made five marks ready money.³ Marry, then gin-
ger⁴ was not much in request, for the old women were all
dead.⁵ Then is there here one Master Caper,° at the suit of   *fashionable dance*
Master Three-pile⁶ the mercer,° for some four suits of   *cloth dealer*
10   peach-colored satin which now peaches° him a beggar. Then   *impeaches; declares*
have we here young Dizzy, and young Master Deep-vow,
and Master Copper-spur, and Master Starve-lackey⁷ the
rapier and dagger man,⁸ and young Drop-heir⁹ that killed
lusty Pudding,° and Master Forthright the tilter,° and brave   *Stuffed Guts / fencer*
15   Master Shoe-tie the great traveler,¹ and wild Half-can that
stabbed Pots,² and I think forty more, all great doers in our
trade, and are now "for the Lord's sake."³

Enter ABHORSON.

ABHORSON   Sirrah, bring Barnardine hither.

CLOWN   Master Barnardine, you must rise⁴ and be hanged,
20   Master Barnardine.

ABHORSON   What ho, Barnardine!

BARNARDINE [*within*]   A pox o'your throats! Who makes that
noise there? What are you?

CLOWN   Your friends, sir—the hangman. You must be so
25   good, sir, to rise and be put to death.

BARNARDINE [*within*]   Away, you rogue, away, I am sleepy.

ABHORSON   Tell him he must awake, and that quickly too.

CLOWN   Pray, Master Barnardine, awake till you are executed
and sleep afterwards.

30   ABHORSON   Go in to him and fetch him out.

CLOWN   He is coming, sir, he is coming. I hear his straw rustle.

Enter BARNARDINE.

ABHORSON   Is the ax upon the block, sirrah?

CLOWN   Very ready, sir.

BARNARDINE   How now, Abhorson? What's the news with you?

35   ABHORSON   Truly, sir, I would desire you to clap into⁵ your
prayers, for look you, the warrant's come.

BARNARDINE   You rogue, I have been drinking all night. I am
not fitted for't.

CLOWN   Oh, the better, sir. For he that drinks all night and is
40   hanged betimes° in the morning, may sleep the sounder all   *early*
the next day.

Enter DUKE [*disguised as a friar*].

4.3 Location: Scene continues.
1. Religious house ("nunnery" was slang for "brothel").
2. To evade the statutory limit on interest, usurers
would give borrowers part of their loan in practically
worthless "commodities," which they were supposed
to sell for ready money. *He's in for*: He's in for falling
into debt over.
3. Rash paid 197 pounds for the "commodity," a very
large sum, and sold it for about 3.3 pounds.
4. Used to make warming tonics.
5. Presumably victims of the 1603 plague, men-

tioned earlier by Mistress Overdone.
6. Richest sort of velvet.
7. One who fails to feed his servants.
8. Suggesting a reputation for brawling.
9. With a pun on dropping hair, a sign of syphilis.
1. Observer of foreign fashions (probably ironic).
2. Suggesting drinking cups.
3. The cry of prisoners begging from the prison grate.
Prisoners had to pay for their own food and lodging.
4. Get out of bed; mount the scaffold.
5. Immediately begin; join your hands for.

ABHORSON   Look you, sir, here comes your ghostly° father. Do   *spiritual*
we jest now, think you?

DUKE   Sir, induced by my charity, and hearing how hastily
45   you are to depart, I am come to advise you, comfort you, and
pray with you.

BARNARDINE   Friar, not I. I have been drinking hard all night,
and I will have more time to prepare me, or they shall beat
out my brains with billets.° I will not consent to die this day,   *thick sticks*
50   that's certain.

DUKE   O sir, you must, and therefore I beseech you look
forward on the journey you shall go.

BARNARDINE   I swear I will not die today for any man's persuasion.

DUKE   But hear you—

55   BARNARDINE   Not a word. If you have anything to say to me,
come to my ward,° for thence will not I today.   *Exit.*   *cell*
      Enter PROVOST.

DUKE   Unfit to live or die! O gravel° heart.   *(i.e., hard)*
After him, fellows, bring him to the block.
      [*Exeunt* POMPEY *and* ABHORSON.]

PROVOST   Now, sir, how do you find the prisoner?

60   DUKE   A creature unprepared, unmeet° for death,   *unfit*
And to transport° him in the mind he is   *execute (euphemistic)*
Were damnable.

PROVOST   Here in the prison, father,
There died this morning of a cruel fever
One Ragozine, a most notorious pirate,

65   A man of Claudio's years, his beard and head
Just of his color. What if we do omit°   *disregard*
This reprobate till he were well inclined,
And satisfy the deputy with the visage
Of Ragozine, more like to Claudio?

70   DUKE   Oh, 'tis an accident that heaven provides.
Dispatch it presently. The hour draws on
Prefixed° by Angelo. See this be done,   *Designated in advance*
And sent according to command, whiles I
Persuade this rude° wretch willingly to die.   *uncivilized*

75   PROVOST   This shall be done, good Father, presently,
But Barnardine must die this afternoon.
And how shall we continue° Claudio,   *maintain*
To save me from the danger that might come
If he were known alive?

DUKE   Let this be done:

80   Put them in secret holds,° both Barnardine   *cells*
And Claudio.
Ere twice the sun hath made his journal° greeting   *daily*
To yonder generation,⁶ you shall find
Your safety manifested.

PROVOST   I am your free dependent.°   *willing servant*

85   DUKE   Quick, dispatch, and send the head to Angelo.
      Exit PROVOST.
Now will I write letters to Angelo⁷—
The Provost he shall bear them—whose contents

---

6. That is, the people outside the prison.
7. "Angelo" may be an error for "Varrius," whom the Duke meets outside the city in 4.5.

Shall witness to him I am near at home,
And that by great injunctions° I am bound   *for compelling reasons*
90   To enter publicly. Him I'll desire
To meet me at the consecrated fount
A league below the city, and from thence,
By cold gradation° and well-balanced form,   *deliberate degrees*
We shall proceed with Angelo.
        Enter PROVOST [*with a severed head*].
95   PROVOST   Here is the head. I'll carry it myself.
      DUKE   Convenient° is it. Make a swift return,   *Suitable*
For I would commune° with you of such things   *confer*
That want no ear but yours.
      PROVOST   I'll make all speed.   *Exit.*
      ISABELLA (*within*)   Peace, ho, be here!
100   DUKE   The tongue of Isabel. She's come to know
If yet her brother's pardon be come hither.
But I will keep her ignorant of her good,
To make her heavenly comforts of° despair   *out of*
When it is least expected.
        Enter ISABELLA.
105   ISABELLA   Ho, by your leave!
      DUKE   Good morning to you, fair and gracious daughter.
      ISABELLA   The better given me° by so holy a man.   *so greeted*
Hath yet the deputy sent my brother's pardon?
      DUKE   He hath released him, Isabel, from the world.
110   His head is off and sent to Angelo.
      ISABELLA   Nay, but it is not so.
      DUKE   It is no other.
Show your wisdom, daughter, in your close° patience.   *silent*
      ISABELLA   Oh, I will to° him, and pluck out his eyes!   *will go to*
      DUKE   You shall not be admitted to his sight.
115   ISABELLA   Unhappy Claudio, wretched Isabel,
Injurious world, most damnèd Angelo!
      DUKE   This nor° hurts him, nor profits you a jot.   *neither*
Forbear it therefore; give your cause° to heaven.   *grievance*
Mark what I say, which you shall find
120   By every syllable a faithful verity.
The Duke comes home tomorrow. Nay, dry your eyes.
One of our convent, and his confessor,
Gives me this instance.° Already he hath carried   *indication*
Notice to Escalus and Angelo,
125   Who do prepare to meet him at the gates
There to give up their power. If you can, pace° your wisdom   *train to walk*
In that good path that I would wish it go,
And you shall have your bosom° on this wretch,   *desire*
Grace° of the Duke, revenges to your heart,   *Favor*
And general honor.
130   ISABELLA   I am directed by you.
      DUKE [*giving* ISABELLA *a letter*]   This letter then to Friar Peter
         give;
'Tis that he sent me of the Duke's return.
Say, by this token, I desire his company
At Mariana's house tonight. Her cause and yours
135   I'll perfect° him withal, and he shall bring you   *fully instruct*
Before the Duke, and to the head of° Angelo   *and directly to*

Accuse him home and home.° For my poor self,   *to the utmost*
I am combinèd° by a sacred vow   *bound*
And shall be absent. Wend you° with this letter;   *Depart*
140   Command these fretting° waters from your eyes   *agitated; corrosive*
With a light heart; trust not my holy order
If I pervert° your course. —Who's here?   *lead astray*
      Enter LUCIO.

LUCIO   Good even.° —Friar, where's the Provost?   *evening*
DUKE   Not within, sir.
145 LUCIO   O pretty Isabella, I am pale at mine heart to see thine
    eyes so red; thou must be patient. I am fain to dine and sup
    with water and bran;[8] I dare not for my head fill my belly.
    One fruitful° meal would set me to't.[9] But they say the Duke   *plentiful*
    will be here tomorrow. By my troth, Isabel, I loved thy
150   brother. If the old fantastical° Duke of dark corners° had *capricious / secret places*
    been at home, he had lived.
DUKE   Sir, the Duke is marvelous° little beholden to your   *remarkably*
    reports, but the best is, he lives not° in them.   *is not to be found*
LUCIO   Friar, thou knowest not the Duke so well as I do: he's
155   a better woodman[1] than thou tak'st him for.
DUKE   Well, you'll answer° this one day. Fare ye well.   *account for*
LUCIO   Nay, tarry, I'll go along with thee. I can tell thee pretty
    tales of the Duke.
DUKE   You have told me too many of him already, sir, if they
160   be true. If not true, none were enough.
LUCIO   I was once before him for getting a wench with child.
DUKE   Did you such a thing?
LUCIO   Yes, marry did I. But I was fain to forswear it. They
    would else° have married me to the rotten medlar.[2]   *otherwise*
165 DUKE   Sir, your company is fairer° than honest. Rest you well. *more speciously pleasant*
LUCIO   By my troth, I'll go with thee to the lane's end. If
    bawdy talk offend you, we'll have very little of it. Nay, Friar,
    I am a kind of burr, I shall stick.   *Exeunt.*

4.4

      Enter ANGELO *and* ESCALUS.

ESCALUS   Every letter he hath writ hath disvouched other.°   *repudiated the others*
ANGELO   In most uneven and distracted manner. His actions
    show much like to madness. Pray heaven his wisdom be not
    tainted.° And why meet him at the gates and reliver° our   *impaired / hand over*
5   authorities there?
ESCALUS   I guess not.
ANGELO   And why should we proclaim it in an hour before his
    entering, that if any crave redress of injustice they should
    exhibit° their petitions in the street?   *present*
10 ESCALUS   He shows his reason for that: to have a dispatch° of   *prompt settlement*
    complaints, and to deliver us from devices° hereafter, which   *contrivances*
    shall then have no power to stand against us.
ANGELO   Well, I beseech you, let it be proclaimed betimes°   *early*
    i'th' morn. I'll call you at your house. Give notice to such
15   men of sort and suit° as are to meet him.   *rank and retinue*

---

8. Diet thought to suppress lust.   2. Kind of pear eaten when rotten; slang for
9. Would incite me to lechery.   "prostitute."
1. Hunter (literally, of game; here, of women).   4.4 Location: Vienna.

ESCALUS I shall, sir. Fare you well.   *Exit.*

ANGELO   Good night.

This deed unshapes° me quite, makes me unpregnant°   destroys / unready
And dull to all proceedings. A deflowered maid,
20 And by an eminent body[1] that enforced°   exerted; raped
The law against it? But that her tender shame
Will not proclaim against her maiden loss,°   loss of virginity
How might she tongue° me? Yet reason dares her no,[2]   reproach
For my authority bears so far credent bulk[3]
25 That no particular° scandal once can touch   private; single
But it confounds° the breather. He should have lived,   confutes; overthrows
Save that his riotous youth with dangerous sense°   sensibility; sensuality
Might in the times to come have ta'en revenge
By° so receiving a dishonored life   Because of
30 With ransom of such shame. Would yet he had lived.
Alack, when once our grace we have forgot,
Nothing goes right. We would, and we would not.   *Exit.*

4.5
Enter DUKE *[as himself] and Friar* PETER.

DUKE   These letters at fit time deliver me.
The Provost knows our purpose and our plot.
The matter being afoot, keep° your instruction   observe
And hold you ever to our special drift,°   purpose
5 Though sometimes you do blench° from this to that   swerve
As cause doth minister.° Go call at Flavius' house   serve
And tell him where I stay. Give the like notice
To Valencius, Rowland, and to Crassus,
And bid them bring the trumpets° to the gate.   trumpeters
But send me Flavius first.
10 PETER   It shall be speeded well.°   quickly done
Enter Varrius.
DUKE   I thank thee, Varrius, thou hast made good haste.
Come, we will walk.° There's other of our friends   withdraw
Will greet us here anon, my gentle° Varrius.   *Exeunt.*   noble

4.6
Enter ISABELLA *and* MARIANA.

ISABELLA   To speak so indirectly° I am loath.   evasively
I would say the truth, but to accuse him so—
That is your part, yet I am advised to do it,
He says, to veil full purpose.
MARIANA   Be ruled by him.
5 ISABELLA   Besides, he tells me that if peradventure
He speak against me on the adverse side
I should not think it strange, for 'tis a physic°   medicine
That's bitter to sweet end.
Enter [Friar] PETER.
MARIANA   I would Friar Peter—

---

1. Person (also suggesting the physical body).
2. Makes her dare not.
3. Sustains such massive credibility. TEXTUAL COMMENT The F text reads "For my Authoritie bears of a credent bulke," which probably involves a printing error. *The Norton Shakespeare* emends the passage; for a justification of this change, see Digital Edition TC 8.
4.5 Location: Outside the city.
4.6 Location: A street near the city gates.

10 ISABELLA Oh, peace, the friar is come.
  PETER Come. I have found you out a stand° most fit   place
     Where you may have such vantage° on the Duke   advantageous position
     He shall not pass you. Twice have the trumpets sounded.[1]
     The generous° and gravest citizens   noble
15   Have hent° the gates, and very near upon   reached
     The Duke is entering. Therefore hence, away!   *Exeunt.*

<h2 style="text-align:center">5.1</h2>

[Flourish.] Enter DUKE, *Varrius, Lords,* ANGELO, ESCALUS,
     LUCIO, [PROVOST, *Officers, and] Citizens at several doors.*
  DUKE *[to* ANGELO] My very worthy cousin,° fairly met.   *fellow nobleman*
     [to ESCALUS] Our old and faithful friend, we are glad to see you.
  ANGELO *and* ESCALUS Happy return be to your royal grace.
  DUKE Many and hearty thankings to you both.
5   *[to* ANGELO] We have made inquiry of you, and we hear
     Such goodness of your justice that our soul
     Cannot but yield you forth to public thanks,
     Forerunning more requital.°   *greater reward*
  ANGELO You make my bonds° still greater.   *obligations*
10 DUKE Oh, your desert speaks loud, and I should wrong it
     To lock it in the wards° of covert bosom   *prison cells*
     When it deserves with characters° of brass   *letters*
     A forted° residence 'gainst the tooth of time   *fortified*
     And razure° of oblivion. Give me your hand   *erasure*
15   And let the subject° see, to make them know   *people*
     That outward courtesies would fain proclaim
     Favors that keep° within. —Come, Escalus,   *dwell*
     You must walk by us on our other hand;
     And good supporters[1] are you.
        Enter [Friar] PETER *and* ISABELLA.
20 PETER Now is your time.
     Speak loud, and kneel before him.
  ISABELLA Justice, O royal Duke! vail your regard°   *look down*
     Upon a wronged—I would fain° have said a maid.   *like to*
     O worthy prince, dishonor not your eye
25   By throwing it on any other object
     Till you have heard me in my true complaint
     And given me justice, justice, justice, justice.
  DUKE Relate your wrongs: in what, by whom? Be brief.
     Here is Lord Angelo shall give you justice.
     Reveal yourself° to him.   *(your complaint)*
30 ISABELLA   O worthy Duke,
     You bid me seek redemption of the devil.
     Hear me yourself, for that which I must speak
     Must either punish me, not being believed,
     Or wring redress from you.
35   Hear me, oh, hear me, here.
  ANGELO My lord, her wits I fear me are not firm.
     She hath been a suitor to me for her brother
     Cut off° by course of justice.   *Executed*

---

1. The third flourish will signal the Duke's arrival.
5.1 Location: The city gates.

1. Attendants; in heraldry, "supporters" are figures
depicted beside a shield, holding it up.

ISABELLA   By course of justice!

40   ANGELO   And she will speak most bitterly and strange.

       ISABELLA   Most strange, but yet most truly will I speak.

       That Angelo's forsworn, is it not strange?

       That Angelo's a murderer, is't not strange?

       That Angelo is an adulterous thief,

45   An hypocrite, a virgin-violator,

       Is it not strange and strange?

       DUKE   Nay, it is ten times strange.

       ISABELLA   It is not truer he is Angelo

       Than this is all as true as it is strange.

50   Nay, it is ten times true, for truth is truth

       To th'end of reck'ning.[2]

       DUKE   Away with her. Poor soul,

       She speaks this in th'infirmity of sense.

       ISABELLA   O prince, I conjure° thee, as thou believ'st   *appeal to*

       There is another comfort than this world,

55   That thou neglect me not with that opinion

       That I am touched with madness. Make not impossible

       That which but seems unlike.° 'Tis not impossible   *unlikely*

       But° one the wicked'st caitiff° on the ground   *That / villain*

       May seem as shy,° as grave, as just, as absolute°   *reserved / perfect*

60   As Angelo. Even so may Angelo

       In all his dressings, caracts,[3] titles, forms,°   *formalities*

       Be an arch-villain. Believe it, royal prince.

       If he be less, he's nothing, but he's more,

       Had I more name for badness.

       DUKE   By mine honesty,

65   If she be mad, as I believe no other,

       Her madness hath the oddest frame° of sense,   *shape*

       Such a dependency° of thing on thing,   *connected sequence*

       As e'er I heard in madness.

       ISABELLA   O gracious Duke,

       Harp not on that, nor do not banish reason

70   For inequality,[4] but let your reason serve

       To make the truth appear where it seems hid

       And hide the false seems° true.   *that seems*

       DUKE   Many that are not mad

       Have sure more lack of reason. What would you say?

       ISABELLA   I am the sister of one Claudio,

75   Condemned upon the act of° fornication   *decree against*

       To lose his head, condemned by Angelo.

       I, in probation of a sisterhood,

       Was sent to by my brother; one Lucio

       As° then the messenger—   *Being*

80   LUCIO   That's I, an't like your grace.

       I came to her from Claudio and desired her

       To try her gracious fortune with Lord Angelo

       For her poor brother's pardon.

       ISABELLA   That's he indeed.

---

2. *for truth . . . reck'ning:* echoing 1 Ezra 4:38: "But truth doth abide, and is strong forever, and liveth and reigneth for ever and ever." *reck'ning:* day of reckoning.

3. Signs (of office).

4. Difference in rank (between Isabella and Angelo); discrepancy (between my report and what seems true).

DUKE   You were not bid to speak.
LUCIO   No, my good lord,
   Nor wished to hold my peace.
85 DUKE   I wish you now then.
   Pray you take note of it, and when you have
   A business for yourself, pray heaven you then
   Be perfect.
LUCIO   I warrant° your honor.   *assure*
DUKE   The warrant's⁵ for yourself. Take heed to't.
90 ISABELLA   This gentleman told somewhat of my tale.
LUCIO   Right.
DUKE   It may be right, but you are i'the wrong
   To speak before your time. [*to* ISABELLA] Proceed.
ISABELLA   I went
   To this pernicious caitiff deputy—
DUKE   That's somewhat madly spoken.
95 ISABELLA   Pardon it,
   The phrase is to the matter.°   *appropriate*
DUKE   Mended again. The matter; proceed.
ISABELLA   In brief, to set the needless process by⁶—
   How I persuaded, how I prayed and kneeled,
100 How he refelled° me, and how I replied,   *repelled*
   For this was of much length—the vile conclusion
   I now begin with grief and shame to utter.
   He would not but by gift of my chaste body
   To his concupiscible° intemperate lust   *desirous*
105 Release my brother; and after much debatement,
   My sisterly remorse confutes° mine honor,   *overcomes*
   And I did yield to him. But the next morn betimes,
   His purpose surfeiting,° he sends a warrant   *having been satisfied*
   For my poor brother's head.
DUKE   This is most likely!
110 ISABELLA   Oh, that it were as like° as it is true.   *probable*
DUKE   By heaven, fond° wretch, thou know'st not what thou   *foolish*
      speak'st,
   Or else thou art suborned against his honor
   In hateful practice.° First, his integrity   *conspiracy*
   Stands without blemish. Next, it imports no reason°   *makes no sense*
115 That with such vehemency he should pursue
   Faults proper° to himself. If he had so offended,   *belonging*
   He would have weighed thy brother by himself
   And not have cut him off. Someone hath set you on.°   *incited you*
   Confess the truth, and say by whose advice
   Thou cam'st here to complain.
120 ISABELLA   And is this all?
   Then, O you blessed ministers° above,   *angels*
   Keep me in patience, and with ripened time
   Unfold the evil which is here wrapped up
   In countenance!⁷ Heaven shield your grace from woe,
125 As I thus wrongèd hence unbelievèd go.
DUKE   I know you'd fain be gone. An officer!
   To prison with her!

---

5. That is, for arrest, punning on the verb in line 88.   7. In false appearance; in royal favor.
6. To skip unnecessary parts of the story.

[*An Officer arrests* ISABELLA.] Shall we thus permit
A blasting° and a scandalous breath to fall   *blighting*
On him so near us? This needs must be a practice.°   *conspiracy*
130 Who knew of your intent and coming hither?
ISABELLA   One that I would were here, Friar Lodowick.[8]
[*Exit, guarded.*]
DUKE   A ghostly father, belike! Who knows that Lodowick?
LUCIO   My lord, I know him; 'tis a meddling friar.
I do not like the man. Had he been lay, my lord,
135 For certain words he spake against your grace
In your retirement I had swinged° him soundly.   *beat*
DUKE   Words against me? This'° a good friar belike.   *This is*
And to set on this wretched woman here
Against our substitute! Let this friar be found.
140 LUCIO   But yesternight, my lord, she and that friar,
I saw them at the prison. A saucy friar,
A very scurvy fellow.
PETER   Blessed be your royal grace!
I have stood by, my lord, and I have heard
Your royal ear abused. First hath this woman
145 Most wrongfully accused your substitute,
Who is as free from touch or soil with her
As she from one ungot.°   *not yet begotten*
DUKE   We did believe no less.
Know you that Friar Lodowick that she speaks of?
PETER   I know him for a man divine and holy,
150 Not scurvy, nor a temporary meddler[9]
As he's reported by this gentleman,
And on my trust, a man that never yet
Did, as he vouches,° misreport your grace.   *asserts*
LUCIO   My lord, most villainously, believe it.
155 PETER   Well, he in time may come to clear himself,
But at this instant he is sick, my lord,
Of a strange fever. Upon his mere° request,   *Solely at his*
Being come to knowledge that there was complaint
Intended 'gainst Lord Angelo, came I hither
160 To speak as from his mouth what he doth know
Is true and false, and what he with his oath
And all probation° will make up full clear   *proof*
Whensoever he's convented.° First, for this woman,   *summoned*
To justify° this worthy nobleman   *vindicate*
165 So vulgarly and personally accused,
Her shall you hear disprovèd to her eyes,
Till she herself confess it.
DUKE   Good Friar, let's hear it.
[*Exit Friar* PETER.]
—Do you not smile at this, Lord Angelo?
O heaven, the vanity of wretched fools.
170 Give us some seats. Come, cousin Angelo,
In this I'll be impartial; be you judge
Of your own cause.[1]

---

8. Evidently the Duke's name when in disguise.
9. Meddler in temporal matters.

1. Ironically recalling the principle that no one ought to judge his or her own cause.

[*The* DUKE *and* ANGELO *sit.*]
Enter [*Friar* PETER *with*] MARIANA[, *veiled*].
Is this the witness, Friar?
First, let her show her face, and after, speak.
MARIANA   Pardon, my lord, I will not show my face
175   Until my husband bid me.
DUKE   What, are you married?
MARIANA   No, my lord.
DUKE   Are you a maid?°   *au unmarried woman; a virgin*
MARIANA   No, my lord.
180   DUKE   A widow, then?
MARIANA   Neither, my lord.
DUKE   Why, you are nothing then: neither maid, widow, nor wife?
LUCIO   My lord, she may be a punk,° for many of them are   *prostitute*
neither maid, widow, nor wife.
185   DUKE   Silence that fellow! I would° he had some cause to prat-   *wish*
tle for himself.°   *(in his own defense)*
LUCIO   Well, my lord.
MARIANA   My lord, I do confess I ne'er was married,
And I confess besides I am no maid.
190   I have known² my husband, yet my husband
Knows not that ever he knew me.
LUCIO   He was drunk, then, my lord; it can be no better.
DUKE   For the benefit of silence, would thou wert so too.
LUCIO   Well, my lord.
195   DUKE   This is no witness for Lord Angelo.
MARIANA   Now I come to't, my lord.
She that accuses him of fornication
In selfsame manner doth accuse my husband,
And charges him, my lord, with such a time
200   When I'll depose° I had him in mine arms   *testify*
With all th'effect° of love.   *manifestations*
ANGELO   Charges she more than me?
MARIANA   Not that I know.
DUKE   No? You say your husband.
205   MARIANA   Why, just,° my lord, and that is Angelo,   *just so*
Who thinks he knows that he ne'er knew my body,
But knows, he thinks, that he knows Isabel's.
ANGELO   This is a strange abuse!° Let's see thy face.   *imposture*
MARIANA   My husband bids me, now I will unmask.
210   This is that face, thou cruel Angelo,
Which once thou swor'st was worth the looking on.
This is the hand which with a vowed contract
Was fast belocked in thine. This is the body
That took away the match° from Isabel,   *assignation*
215   And did supply° thee at thy garden-house   *satisfy*
In her imagined person.
DUKE   Know you this woman?
LUCIO   Carnally, she says.
DUKE   Sirrah, no more.
220   LUCIO   Enough, my lord.
ANGELO   My lord, I must confess I know this woman,
And five years since there was some speech of marriage

2. Had sexual intercourse with.

Betwixt myself and her, which was broke off,
Partly for that her promised proportions°   *dowry*
225 Came short of composition,° but in chief   *the agreed sum*
For that her reputation was disvalued°   *discredited*
In levity.° Since which time of five years   *For wantonness*
I never spake with her, saw her, nor heard from her
Upon my faith and honor.

MARIANA [*kneeling*]   Noble prince,
230 As there comes light from heaven and words from breath,
As there is sense° in truth and truth in virtue,   *significance*
I am affianced this man's wife as strongly
As words could make up vows. And, my good lord,
But Tuesday night last gone, in 's garden-house
235 He knew me as a wife. As this is true,
Let me in safety raise me from my knees,
Or else forever be confixèd° here   *fixed firmly*
A marble monument.³

ANGELO   I did but smile till now.
240 Now, good my lord, give me the scope° of justice;   *extent*
My patience here is touched.° I do perceive   *irritated*
These poor informal° women are no more   *disorderly*
But instruments° of some more mightier member°   *agents / power*
That sets them on. Let me have way, my lord,
To find this practice out.

245 DUKE   Ay, with my heart,
And punish them to your height of pleasure.
Thou foolish friar, and thou, pernicious woman,
Compact with° her that's gone, think'st thou thy oaths,   *In league with*
Though they would swear down each particular saint,
250 Were testimonies against his worth and credit
That's sealed in approbation?° You, Lord Escalus,   *ratified by proof*
Sit with my cousin; lend him your kind pains
To find out this abuse, whence 'tis derived.
There is another friar that set them on.
255 Let him be sent for.

PETER   Would he were here, my lord, for he indeed
Hath set the women on to this complaint.
Your provost knows the place where he abides,
And he may fetch him.

DUKE   Go, do it instantly.   [*Exit* PROVOST.]
260 —And you, my noble and well-warranted cousin,
Whom it concerns to hear this matter forth,°   *out*
Do with your injuries as seems you best
In any chastisement. I for a while
Will leave you, but stir not you till you have
265 Well determined° upon these slanderers.   *Passed judgment*

ESCALUS   My lord, we'll do it throughly.°   *Exit* [DUKE].   *thoroughly*
[ESCALUS *sits in the Duke's place.*]
Signior Lucio, did not you say you knew that Friar Lodowick
to be a dishonest person?

LUCIO   *Cucullus non facit monachum.*⁴ Honest in nothing but

---

3. TEXTUAL COMMENT F leaves it unclear exactly
when, in this scene, Mariana kneels and when she
gets up again, so the modern editor must decide

where to insert stage directions. For a justification of
the Norton editor's decision, see Digital Edition TC 9.
4. The hood does not make the monk (proverbial).

270   in his clothes, and one that hath spoke most villainous
    speeches of the Duke.

ESCALUS   We shall entreat you to abide here till he come and
    enforce° them against him. We shall find this friar a notable   *urge*
    fellow.

275 LUCIO   As any in Vienna, on my word.

ESCALUS   Call that same Isabel here once again, I would
    speak with her. [*to* ANGELO] Pray you, my lord, give me leave
    to question. You shall see how I'll handle her.

LUCIO   Not better than he, by her own report.

280 ESCALUS   Say you?

LUCIO   Marry, sir, I think if you handled her privately she
    would sooner confess. Perchance publicly she'll be ashamed.

                  Enter ISABELLA [*guarded*].

ESCALUS   I will go darkly° to work with her.   *privately; soberly*

LUCIO   That's the way, for women are light[5] at midnight.

285 ESCALUS   Come on, mistress, here's a gentlewoman denies all
    that you have said.

              Enter DUKE [*disguised as a friar*] *and* PROVOST.

LUCIO   My lord, here comes the rascal I spoke of, here, with
    the Provost.

ESCALUS   In very good time. Speak not you to him till we call
290   upon you.

LUCIO   Mum.

ESCALUS   Come, sir, did you set these women on to slander Lord
    Angelo? They have confessed you did.

DUKE   'Tis false.

295 ESCALUS   How? Know you where you are?

DUKE   Respect to your great place; and let the devil
    Be sometime honored for his burning throne.[6]
    Where is the Duke? 'Tis he should hear me speak.

ESCALUS   The Duke's in° us, and we will hear you speak.   *The Duke's power is vested in*
300   Look you speak justly.°   *accurately*

DUKE   Boldly, at least. [*to* ISABELLA *and* MARIANA] But, O
      poor souls,
    Come you to seek the lamb here of the fox?
    Good night to your redress. Is the Duke gone?
    Then is your cause gone too. The Duke's unjust
305   Thus to retort° your manifest appeal°   *cast back / accusation*
    And put your trial in the villain's mouth
    Which here you come to accuse.

LUCIO   This is the rascal, this is he I spoke of.

ESCALUS   Why, thou unreverend and unhallowed° friar,   *impious*
310   Is't not enough thou hast suborned these women
    To accuse this worthy man, but in foul mouth,
    And in the witness of his proper° ear,   *own*
    To call him villain, and then to glance° from him   *ricochet*
    To th' Duke himself, to tax° him with injustice?   *reproach*
315   Take him hence! To th' rack with him. We'll touse° you   *tear*
    Joint by joint, but we will know his[7] purpose.

---

5. Licentious; exploiting the unintentional sexual
suggestion of Escalus's "go darkly to work."
6. *let . . . throne*: that is, the devil, too, seated on his

throne in hell, seems a figure of honor.
7. The friar's; the confusion of pronouns suggests
Escalus's fury.

What? Unjust?

DUKE   Be not so hot. The Duke dare
No more stretch this finger of mine than he
Dare rack his own. His subject am I not,
320 Nor here provincial.[8] My business in this state
Made me a looker-on here in Vienna,
Where I have seen corruption boil and bubble
Till it o'errun the stew:° laws for all faults,   *cauldron; brothel*
But faults so countenanced that the strong statutes
325 Stand like the forfeits[9] in a barber's shop,
As much in mock as mark.

ESCALUS   Slander to th' state! Away with him to prison.

ANGELO   What can you vouch against him, Signor Lucio? Is
this the man you did tell us of?

330 LUCIO   'Tis he, my lord. Come hither, Goodman Bald-pate.[1]
Do you know me?

DUKE   I remember you, sir, by the sound of your voice.[2] I met
you at the prison, in the absence of the Duke.

LUCIO   Oh, did you so? And do you remember what you said of
335 the Duke?

DUKE   Most notedly, sir.

LUCIO   Do you so, sir? And was the Duke a fleshmonger,° a   *whoremaster*
fool, and a coward, as you then reported him to be?

DUKE   You must, sir, change persons with me, ere you make
340 that my report. You indeed spoke so of him, and much more,
much worse.

LUCIO   O thou damnable fellow! Did I not pluck thee by the
nose° for thy speeches?   *(gesture of contempt)*

DUKE   I protest I love the Duke as I love myself.

345 ANGELO   Hark how the villain would close[3] now after his trea-
sonable abuses.

ESCALUS   Such a fellow is not to be talked withal. Away with
him to prison. Where is the Provost? Away with him to
prison! Lay bolts° enough upon him. Let him speak no more.   *fetters*
350 Away with those giglets° too, and with the other confederate   *strumpets*
companion.[4]

        [*The* PROVOST *attempts to lead the* DUKE *away.*]

DUKE   Stay, sir, stay a while.

ANGELO   What, resists he? Help him, Lucio.

LUCIO   Come, sir, come, sir, come, sir. Faugh,° sir! Why, you   *(expression of disgust)*
355 bald-pated lying rascal, you must be hooded, must you? Show
your knave's visage, with a pox to you. Show your sheep-
biting face,[5] and be hanged an hour.[6] Will't not off?

        [LUCIO *pulls off the Duke's hood.*]

DUKE   Thou art the first knave that e'er mad'st a duke.
—First, Provost, let me bail these gentle three.
360 [*to* LUCIO] Sneak not away, sir, for the friar and you

---

8. Subject to local ecclesiastical authorities.
9. Jocular list of penalties for minor infractions.
1. "Mr. Bald-head." "Goodman" was a form of address for a man below the rank of gentleman; friars shaved their heads.
2. The friar's hood presumably covers his face so that he cannot see Lucio.

3. Conclude; hide himself; come to a settlement.
4. Fellow (contemptuous).
5. Like the wolf in sheep's clothing.
6. Jocular way of saying "be hanged." Animals were sometimes executed like human beings for destroying life or property.

Must have a word anon. [*to Officers*] Lay hold on him!
LUCIO   This may prove worse than hanging.
DUKE [*to* ESCALUS]   What you have spoke, I pardon. Sit you down,
　　We'll borrow place° of him. [*to* ANGELO] Sir, by your leave.　　　　　*seat; office*
　　　　[*The* DUKE *takes Angelo's seat.*]
365　Hast thou or° word, or wit, or impudence,　　　　　　　　　　　　　*either*
　　That yet can do thee office?° If thou hast,　　　　　　　　　　　　*service*
　　Rely upon it till my tale be heard,
　　And hold no longer out.
ANGELO　　　　　　　　　　O my dread lord,
　　I should be guiltier than my guiltiness
370　To think I can be undiscernible
　　When I perceive your grace like power divine
　　Hath looked upon my passes.[7] Then, good prince,
　　No longer session° hold upon my shame,　　　　　　　　　　　　　*inquiry*
　　But let my trial be mine own confession.
375　Immediate sentence then and sequent° death　　　　　　　　　　*thereafter*
　　Is all the grace I beg.
DUKE　　Come hither, Mariana.
　　　　　[MARIANA *rises.*]
　　Say, wast thou e'er contracted to this woman?
ANGELO　　I was, my lord.
380　DUKE　　Go, take her hence, and marry her instantly.
　　—Do you the office, Friar, which consummate,°　　　　　　　　　*finished*
　　Return him here again. —Go with him, Provost.
　　　　Exeunt [ANGELO, MARIANA, *Friar* PETER, *and* PROVOST].
ESCALUS　　My lord, I am more amazed at his dishonor
　　Than at the strangeness of it.°　　　　　　　　　　　　*(the situation)*
DUKE　　　　　　　　Come hither, Isabel.
385　Your friar is now your prince. As I was then
　　Advertising° and holy to your business,　　　　　　　　　　　　*Attentive*
　　Not changing heart with habit, I am still
　　Attorneyed° at your service.　　　　　　　　　　*Engaged as advocate*
ISABELLA　　　　　　　　Oh, give me pardon
　　That I, your vassal, have employed and pained°　　　　　　　　*troubled*
　　Your unknown sovereignty.
390　DUKE　　　　　　　　You are pardoned, Isabel.
　　And now, dear maid, be you as free° to us.　　　　　　　　　　*generous*
　　Your brother's death I know sits at your heart,
　　And you may marvel why I obscured myself
　　Laboring to save his life, and would not rather
395　Make rash remonstrance° of my hidden power　　　　　　　*demonstration*
　　Than let him so be lost. O most kind maid,
　　It was the swift celerity of his death,
　　Which I did think with slower foot came on,
　　That brained° my purpose. But peace be with him!　　　　　　*killed*
400　That life is better life past fearing death,
　　Than that which lives to fear. Make it your comfort,
　　So happy is your brother.
　　　　Enter ANGELO, MARIANA, [*Friar*] PETER, *and* PROVOST.
ISABELLA　　　　　　　　I do, my lord.
DUKE　　For this new-married man approaching here,

---

7. Actions, trespasses; recalling Job 34:21: "For his eyes are upon the ways of man, and he seeth all his goings."

	Whose salt° imagination yet hath wronged	salacious
405	Your well-defended honor, you must pardon	
	For Mariana's sake. But as he adjudged° your brother,	condemned
	Being criminal in double violation	
	Of sacred chastity and of promise-breach,	
	Thereon dependent for your brother's life,	
410	The very mercy° of the law cries out	Even the merciful aspect
	Most audible even from his proper° tongue:	its own
	"An Angelo for Claudio, death for death.	
	Haste still° pays haste, and leisure° answers leisure;	always / deliberation
	Like doth quit° like, and measure still for measure."[8]	requite
415	Then, Angelo, thy fault's thus manifested	
	Which, though° thou wouldst deny, denies thee vantage.°	even if / (i.e., clemency)
	We do condemn thee to the very block	
	Where Claudio stooped to death, and with like haste.	
	Away with him.	

MARIANA   O my most gracious lord,
440   I hope you will not mock me with a husband.

DUKE   It is your husband mocked you with a husband.
        Consenting to the safeguard of your honor
        I thought your marriage fit, else imputation°   censure
        For that he knew you might reproach your life
425   And choke your good to come.° For his possessions,   ruin your prospects
        Although by confiscation they are ours,[9]
        We do instate and widow you° withal   give you widow's rights
        To buy you a better husband.

MARIANA   O my dear lord,
        I crave no other nor no better man.

430   DUKE   Never crave him, we are definitive.°   resolute

MARIANA [kneeling]   Gentle my liege—

DUKE   You do but lose your labor.
        Away with him to death. [to LUCIO] Now, sir, to you—

MARIANA   O my good lord! Sweet Isabel, take my part.
        Lend me your knees, and all my life to come
435   I'll lend you all my life to do you service.

DUKE   Against all sense you do importune her.
        Should she kneel down in mercy of this fact,°   crime
        Her brother's ghost his pavèd bed° would break   stone-covered grave
        And take her hence in horror.

MARIANA   Isabel!
440   Sweet Isabel, do yet but kneel by me.
        Hold up your hands, say nothing, I'll speak all.
        They say best men are molded out of faults,
        And for the most,° become much more the better   most part
        For being a little bad. So may my husband.
445   O Isabel, will you not lend a knee?

DUKE   He dies for Claudio's death.

ISABELLA [kneeling]   Most bounteous sir,
        Look, if it please you, on this man condemned
        As if my brother lived. I partly think
        A due sincerity governed his deeds

---

8. TEXTUAL COMMENT The F punctuation leaves it unclear at what point the Duke stops quoting "the law" and begins speaking in his own person; for the signifi-

cance of this ambiguity, see Digital Edition TC 10.
9. Because a felon's property was forfeit to the Crown.

450   Till he did look on me. Since it is so,
        Let him not die. My brother had but justice,
        In that he did the thing for which he died.
        For Angelo, his act did not o'ertake his bad intent
        And must be buried° but as an intent   *(i.e., forgotten)*
455   That perished by the way. Thoughts are no subjects,¹
        Intents but merely thoughts.
    MARIANA   Merely, my lord.
    DUKE   Your suit's unprofitable. Stand up, I say.
            [MARIANA *and* ISABELLA *rise.*]
        I have bethought me of another fault.
        Provost, how came it Claudio was beheaded
        At an unusual hour?
460   PROVOST   It was commanded so.
    DUKE   Had you a special warrant for the deed?
    PROVOST   No, my good lord. It was by private message.
    DUKE   For which I do discharge you of your office.
        Give up your keys.
    PROVOST   Pardon me, noble lord.
465   I thought it was a fault but knew it not,
        Yet did repent me after more advice,°   *deliberation*
        For° testimony whereof one in the prison   *As*
        That should by private order else° have died   *otherwise*
        I have reserved alive.
470   DUKE   What's he?
    PROVOST   His name is Barnardine.
    DUKE   I would thou hadst done so by Claudio.
        Go fetch him hither, let me look upon him.   [*Exit* PROVOST.]
    ESCALUS   I am sorry one so learnèd and so wise
475   As you, Lord Angelo, have still° appeared,   *always*
        Should slip so grossly both in the heat of blood
        And lack of tempered judgment afterward.
    ANGELO   I am sorry that such sorrow I procure,°   *cause*
        And so deep sticks it in my penitent heart
480   That I crave death more willingly than mercy.
        'Tis my deserving, and I do entreat it.
           Enter PROVOST, BARNARDINE, CLAUDIO [*muffled*],°   *with his face wrapped*
           and JULIET.
    DUKE   Which is that Barnardine?
    PROVOST   This, my lord.
    DUKE   There was a friar told me of this man.
        Sirrah, thou art said to have a stubborn soul
485   That apprehends no further than this world,
        And squar'st° thy life according. Thou'rt condemned,   *frames*
        But for those earthly faults,² I quit° them all,   *pardon*
        And pray thee take this mercy to provide
        For better times to come. Friar, advise him,
490   I leave him to your hand. What muffled fellow's that?
    PROVOST   This is another prisoner that I saved,
        Who should have died when Claudio lost his head,
        As like almost to Claudio as himself.
           [*Claudio's disguise is removed.*]

---

1. Thoughts are not subject to prosecution.   2. Offenses subject to earthly punishment.

DUKE [*to* ISABELLA]   If he be like your brother, for his sake
495   Is he pardoned, and for your lovely sake
Give me your hand, and say you will be mine,[3]
He is my brother° too—but fitter time for that.   (*as a brother-in-law*)
By this Lord Angelo perceives he's safe:
Methinks I see a quick'ning in his eye.
500   Well, Angelo, your evil quits° you well.   *recompenses*
Look that you love your wife, her worth worth° yours.   *being equal to*
I find an apt remission° in myself,   *inclination to mercy*
And yet here's one in place° I cannot pardon.   *present*
[*to* LUCIO] You, sirrah, that knew me for a fool, a coward,
505   One all of luxury,° an ass, a madman;   *lasciviousness*
Wherein have I so deserved of you
That you extol me thus?
LUCIO   'Faith, my lord, I spoke it but according to the trick.° If   *fashion*
you will hang me for it you may, but I had rather it would
510   please you I might be whipped.
DUKE   Whipped first, sir, and hanged after.
Proclaim it, Provost, round about the city,
If any woman wronged by this lewd fellow—
As I have heard him swear himself there's one
515   Whom he begot with child—let her appear,
And he shall marry her. The nuptial finished,
Let him be whipped and hanged.
LUCIO   I beseech your highness, do not marry me to a whore.
Your highness said even now I made you a duke. Good my
520   lord, do not recompense me in making me a cuckold.
DUKE   Upon mine honor thou shalt marry her.
Thy slanders I forgive, and therewithal
Remit thy other forfeits.° Take him to prison,   *punishments*
And see our pleasure herein executed.
525   LUCIO   Marrying a punk, my lord, is pressing to death,[4] whip-
ping, and hanging.
DUKE   Slandering a prince deserves it.
—She, Claudio, that you wronged, look you restore.[5]
—Joy to you, Mariana. —Love her, Angelo;
530   I have confessed her,° and I know her virtue.   *heard her confession*
—Thanks, good friend Escalus, for thy much goodness,
There's more behind° that is more gratulate.°   *to come / gratifying*
—Thanks, Provost, for thy care and secrecy;
We shall employ thee in a worthier place.
535   —Forgive him, Angelo, that brought you home
The head of Ragozine for Claudio's—
Th'offense pardons itself. Dear Isabel,
I have a motion° much imports your good,   *proposal*
Whereto if you'll a willing ear incline,
540   What's mine is yours, and what is yours is mine.
So bring° us to our palace, where we'll show   *accompany*
What's yet behind that's meet° you all should know.   *suitable*
[*Exeunt.*]

---

3. PERFORMANCE COMMENT It is not clear from
Shakespeare's text how Isabella responds to the
Duke's proposal of marriage; for some performance
options, see Digital Edition PC 3.

4. Executing by crushing under heavy weights.
5. To her good name, by marrying her publicly and
being a good husband.

All's Well That Ends Well

In innumerable old folktales, an unknown or lowborn young man of great courage, intelligence, or expertise addresses himself to a serious peril: a dragon no one can slay, a riddle no one can solve, a wound no one can cure. The grateful recipient of his aid—a king or mighty duke—rewards the youth with marriage to a princess who would ordinarily be far above his station. *All's Well That Ends Well* retells this popular tale of fantastic upward mobility, but with the genders reversed: the resourceful young quester is female, the marital prize male. Shakespeare did not invent the reversal; he adapted his plot from a story in Boccaccio's *Decameron* that is itself a retelling of a traditional tale. But *All's Well That Ends Well* considerably heightens the heroine's risk-taking initiative, making Helen's adventures in the first two acts correspond more precisely, in sexually transposed form, to the masculine pattern.

Even today, this reversal makes the story seem problematic. In the customary version, no one inquires into the feelings of the noblewoman who is the champion's prize. But in *All's Well*, when a man becomes a reward, he reacts with astonished anger:

> BERTRAM My wife, my liege? I shall beseech your highness:
> In such a business give me leave to use
> The help of mine own eyes.
> KING   Know'st thou not, Bertram,
> What she has done for me?
> BERTRAM   Yes, my good lord,
> But never hope to know why I should marry her.
> (2.3.104–08)

After the wedding ceremony, Bertram flees without consummating the union. He leaves behind a letter detailing for Helen two apparently impossible conditions she must satisfy before he will consider her his wife: "When thou canst get the ring upon my finger, which never shall come off, and show me a child begotten of thy body that I am father to, then call me husband" (3.2.53–55).

Folklorists have traced the second part of the play, in which Helen ingeniously fulfills Bertram's stipulations, to yet another old tale, that of the "clever wench" who ultimately wins a reluctant husband's affection by turning his recalcitrance to her own benefit. In Helen's case, however, her "unfeminine" audacity both before and after her wedding has repelled some commentators. Others have expressed doubts about Helen's bed trick, wherein she secretly substitutes herself for another woman and becomes pregnant by the spouse who thinks he loathes her. How, they wonder, could such a maneuver possibly convert anyone, much less Bertram, into a loving husband?

The gender reversals in the plot of *All's Well That Ends Well*, then, make the difference in conventional expectations for men and women vividly clear. The deviations from comic norms in *All's Well* might be taken as reflecting badly on the hero and heroine. At the same time, these deviations implicitly challenge conventional gender roles, making them seem artificial and restrictive. The generic uneasiness of the play has led some critics to classify it as a "problem comedy," a category that also includes *Measure for Measure* and sometimes *Troilus and Cressida*. Editors conjecture that all three plays were written between 1602 and

1607, a period in which Shakespeare was largely preoccupied with tragedy: *Hamlet, Othello, King Lear, Timon of Athens, Macbeth,* and *Antony and Cleopatra* are roughly contemporaneous compositions. The "problem comedies" often seem closer in theme and tone to these tragedies than to the sunnier romantic comedies Shakespeare wrote in the 1590s.

Nonetheless, *All's Well* has obvious connections to Shakespeare's earlier achievements. In *The Merchant of Venice, As You Like It,* and *Much Ado About Nothing,* Shakespeare had gradually developed the dramatic possibilities of an articulate, assertive, and sympathetic heroine. Helen is recognizably one of this company: generally beloved by those around her, premaritally chaste but intensely sexual, tenacious in pursuit of the man she desires. Bertram is likewise a version of a standard Shakespearean type: the immature youth who finds aggressively "masculine" enterprises like hunting or war emotionally easier to negotiate than the complications of heterosexual intimacy. Bertram's predecessors include the unwilling Adonis in *Venus and Adonis,* the naive Claudio in *Much Ado About Nothing,* the edgily unself-conscious Hotspur of *1 Henry IV,* and the narcissistic young man of the sonnets. Both Helen and Bertram, however, "push the envelope" of their generic type. No previous comic heroine need show herself as relentless as Helen in pursuing her man. And Bertram is surely the most perfidious, and the most thoroughly disgraced, of Shakespeare's callow males. His initial protest at being married off against his will does not seem unreasonable. Yet his objections to Helen seem purely snobbish and his contemptuous treatment of her entirely unwarranted. As the play continues he subjects Diana, the woman he claims to love, to even worse treatment, breaking his promises to her and then defaming her reputation.

In its portrayal of older characters, too, *All's Well* seems to develop out of Shakespeare's previous romantic plays. In much Greek and Roman comedy, parents or parent surrogates attempt to hinder their children's sexual happiness, and as a young playwright Shakespeare adhered to this ancient convention. In *A Midsummer Night's Dream* and *Romeo and Juliet,* written in the mid-1590s, parents are killjoys who block the glorious passions of youth out of mere peevishness. But in *The Merchant of Venice,* written a year or two later, Shylock's paternal possessiveness contrasts with the wise policy of Portia's father, whose strict constraints upon his daughter's marital options in fact ensure her happiness. In *Much Ado About Nothing* (1598), the sexually anxious young couples seem incapable of forming heterosexual pairs without the intervention of elders and friends. In *All's Well That Ends Well,* the marriage between Helen and Bertram is unthinkable without the support of the Countess and the King; the match is also roundly endorsed by the elderly courtier Lafeu. If the oldsters are culpable, it is for pushing the young people together prematurely, not for keeping them apart.

Arguably, this change in perspective is a consequence of Shakespeare's own aging. By the time he wrote *All's Well,* he was the father of two marriageable daughters, and surviving records indicate that he had strong opinions about the men they wed. At any rate, the role of family members in Shakespeare's romantic plays becomes more benign, even essential for the pairing-off with which the comedies conclude; by the time of the late romances, in fact, the primary dramatic emphasis tends to be less on the young couple than on their parents. Seen in such a light, *All's Well* marks an important transition in the generational dynamics of Shakespearean comedy.

At the same time, the expanded role of family and friends in "making a match" seems to reflect an increasing pessimism about sex. In both *All's Well* and *Measure for Measure,* mutual desire fails to flower spontaneously between eligible bachelors and maidens. Moreover, even when desire is somehow kindled, its relationship to the institution of lifelong monogamy seems difficult. In *All's Well,* erotic passion burns hottest not when it is gratified but when its goal is still unattained. Bertram wants Diana only so long as she rebuffs him:

> Madding my eagerness with her restraint,
> As all impediments in fancy's course
> Are motives of more fancy.
>
> (5.3.212–14)

Once he imagines he has deflowered her, he deserts her without compunction. Bertram behaves reprehensibly, and yet Helen's more steadfast love, too, seems at least in part an effect of distance and difficulty. In act 1, she declares Bertram to be a "bright particular star," fascinating although inaccessible, and perhaps *because* inaccessible. The obstacles Bertram places in the way of their union seem to make him all the more precious in Helen's eyes and to stimulate her extraordinary efforts to win his affections. But the more resolutely she strives to catch him, the more difficult it becomes to imagine her content with him once he is caught.

In sexual matters, apparently, as soon as one gets what one thinks one wants, it no longer seems so intensely appealing. "Success" brings disillusion in its train. In *All's Well,* this unfortunate arrangement is reflected in passages and episodes that oscillate painfully between imagined extremes of distance and intimacy. In act 2, Helen frets about the social gap that separates her from Bertram: he seems too alien for her. But when the Countess pleads that Helen consider her a "mother," Helen suffers a paroxysm of anxiety on the opposite count: that she and Bertram may be all too closely allied. "God's mercy, maiden," exclaims the Countess, "does it curd thy blood / To say I am thy mother?" (1.3.134–35). Helen's hysterical overreaction suggests that she fears being "too close" at the same time she fears being "too remote." Later in *All's Well,* the bed trick rehearses, in another key, a similar paradox of intimacy and distance. Fleeing his home and a spouse closely associated with his upbringing, Bertram lusts after a foreign woman. But this foreigner turns out, unbeknownst to him, to be interchangeable with his own wife.

Thus the fundamental structure of sexual desire seems inimical to a durably happy marriage, but marriage nonetheless remains the only socially approved arena for sexual expression. Caught in this dilemma, lovers simply cannot be trusted to make proper arrangements among themselves. The community therefore assumes a new prominence in initiating and regulating marriages. In *All's Well,* two means of such regulation are central to the plot. The first is the institution of wardship, a remnant of the feudal system. Minors who inherited estates automatically fell into the care of their feudal superiors: the King in Bertram's case. The guardian's powers included the right to specify a marriage partner of suitable social rank for the "ward." The ward could not refuse the match except by forfeiting much of his property; thus the tense exchange in 2.3 between Bertram and the King about Helen's qualifications in this respect.

Another form of external pressure is brought to bear upon Bertram at the end of the play, when Helen once again appeals to the King to enforce her claim. The hearing that ensues resembles those of the ecclesiastical courts, judicial bodies that settled complaints of sexual misconduct in early modern England. The conflicting testimony of Diana and Bertram painfully recalls the proceedings of the "bawdy courts," as they were popularly known: interminable prosecutions and counterprosecutions for premarital fornication, breach of promise, adultery, child support, and sexual slander—cases in which, as here, evidence was often hard to come by and truth difficult to unearth.

In the early seventeenth century, both wardship and the judicial regulation of sexual conduct were topics of considerable controversy. Some people fiercely resented any meddling in their domestic and sexual affairs, but others wanted the courts to monitor such behavior even more aggressively. Likewise, some attacked wardship on the grounds that guardians often trampled on the personal inclinations of the ward, while others argued that young heirs and heiresses required close supervision to prevent their seduction by unscrupulous gold diggers. In both cases, the point at issue is whether sexual conduct is an essentially personal matter or a

Drummers before an encampment. From
Geffrey Whitney, *A Choice of Emblems* (1586).

matter for public concern. By making both the custom of wardship and the procedures of the bawdy courts crucial to the plot of *All's Well*, Shakespeare seems to endorse the assumption upon which both institutions are premised: that individuals are not competent to manage their own sexual lives, and that stern legal measures are required to coerce the likes of Bertram into matrimony.

A comedy normally depicts the progress of young lovers toward marriage, and in *All's Well* Bertram's stubborn resistance to his generically mandated fate has important consequences. The protagonists of almost all comedies undergo some kind of suffering in the middle acts of the play, but that suffering is overcome. The happy ending retrospectively makes the hardships that preceded it seem worthwhile; conversely, pain validates and gives an appropriate significance to the concluding felicities. Despite its cheerful once-and-for-all title, *All's Well That Ends Well* does not conform to this timeworn pattern. Instead, the play constantly derails narrative expectations and promises endings that turn out to be mirages. Helen cures the King and weds Bertram, but the story is not yet over. She must then encounter Bertram somehow (whether by accident or design is unclear) and arrange to bed him. Then she must make sure she is pregnant; then she must return to France to beg justice of the King. The action continues past the point where one would expect it to terminate, again and again requiring the expenditure of additional effort and ingenuity on Helen's part. Early in act 5, even the King turns out to be surprisingly difficult to locate: Helen, Diana, and Diana's widowed mother arrive at Marseilles only to find that the court has just removed to Roussillon.

Helen's stamina is not demanded of the other characters, but they, too, persist willy-nilly after one might have expected them to subside, and they resurface after one might have expected them to vanish. The King is preparing for his own death when Helen's arrival returns him to the life he had resigned himself to losing. Later, Bertram believes that by fleeing Italy for France he has left Helen behind; similarly, returning to France from Italy, he forsakes Diana. But the two women decline to evaporate. They reappear together in a scene that begins with the King announcing that "the nature of [Bertram's] great offense is dead" (5.3.23), then revives and exacerbates his offense, then declares it buried once more.

These aborted endings, continual deferrals, unanticipated reemergences, and surprising persistences inevitably make the actual end of the play seem rather arbitrary. Eventually it becomes hard to credit the permanence of any resolution, any happy ending. When, in the play's final lines, the King blithely promises Diana her choice of husbands from among his stable of remaining wards, *All's Well* may seem not to be drawing to a close, but merely to be forecasting its own reiteration. The play's open-endedness has generated both dismay and appreciation, depending on the temperament of the critic and, often, on his or her convictions about literary form. Those who prefer celebratory and romantic modes often find the play's lack of convincing closure a disturbing flaw. Those who find the happy endings of most comedies wishful and unrealistic tend to applaud Shakespeare's eschewal of easy answers.

Once again, *All's Well*'s apparent noncompliance with "normal" comic practice implicitly suggests limitations inherent in the comic forms it forsakes. At the beginning of 2.4, when Helen asks the Clown whether the Countess is well, he replies that "she is not well," despite the fact that "she's very well and wants nothing i'th' world." To the baffled Helen, the Clown goes on to explain that he does not consider the Countess well because "she's not in heaven, whither God send her quickly." In the Clown's mind, only the dead are happy, a notion that gives a distinctly uncomical twist to the concept of ending well. Consciously or not, the Clown echoes a long tradition of classical and Christian thought that emphasizes the misery of this world and defers true happiness until after death. In 4.3, the First Lord Dumaine relates this apparently

Occasion with her forelock. From Geffrey Whitney, *A Choice of Emblems* (1586). She must be taken "by the forward top"—that is, at the moment when she presents herself; the back of her head is bald to signify that once she is past, she can no longer be grasped. See *All's Well That Ends Well* 5.3.39.

inevitable misery to the intransigence of human passions, an intransigence imagined in the Christian tradition in terms of original sin. "As we are ourselves, what things are we!" (lines 19–20). Only divine grace can remedy the defects of human nature in general and of human sexuality in particular. Only another world can offer the prospect of true, lasting felicity. But comedy is a secular mode, lacking the means to represent heaven or divine intervention, and to that extent its happy endings must be partial or temporary. *All's Well* is not unique among Shakespearean comedies in gesturing beyond the mundane, imperfect world with which plays are necessarily concerned, to an ideal world that cannot be directly represented in the theater. Lorenzo's discussion of the music of the spheres in *The Merchant of Venice* and Isabella's acute conviction of divine mentorship in *Measure for Measure* likewise have the effect of implicitly contrasting the limited bliss of comic endings with an unlimited, indescribable counterpart.

But although absolute fulfillment may be impossible in this world, relative improvements are surely feasible. In *All's Well,* it seems that a community can constructively intervene to correct, at least provisionally, some of the grosser imperfections of individuals. In act 4, Bertram acknowledges that he has misjudged Paroles and at the end of the play begs pardon for his behavior, finally promising to love his wife "ever, ever, dearly" (5.3.310). These apparent changes of heart are not motivated by an instinctive sense of regret for his past actions or by a spontaneous upwelling of love for Helen. Rather, the vigorous efforts of his mother, his king, his friends, and his wife force Bertram onto the path that seems best for him whether he likes it or not. Those critics who find his apparent reformation at the end of the play unconvincing are often those skeptical of whether this kind of social pressure will suffice to rescue Bertram from himself. If, however, we are to believe that Bertram is salvageable, as the play implies, then we must acknowledge the effectiveness of the community's efforts to rectify him.

Obviously, a society can have these beneficial effects on its more wayward members only if its moral intuitions are fundamentally sound, and only if its coercive resources have the potential to induce heartfelt, lasting change. The King can force

Bertram to marry Helen and to acknowledge the legitimacy of the child in her womb. But such decrees will ensure Bertram's *love* of Helen only if his inner convictions somehow follow from, or develop out of, his external submission to the King's commands. How actual—not merely apparent—compliance might be achieved is suggested in a speech in which the King warmly remembers Bertram's father, the late Count Roussillon. The old Count, according to the King, adhered to a traditional aristocratic code: he was careful to speak no more than he was willing to defend with his sword. Thought, word, and deed were thus inextricable. The King characterizes this inextricability as "honor," for honor and its corollary, shame, bridge the gap between external behavior and private states of mind, internalizing social scruples so that the aristocrat behaves well even in the absence of obvious incentives or punishments. At best, honor is thus a "clock to itself," a self-regulating mechanism. Only when that clock fails to function properly—as it fails in Bertram's case—must the same results be compelled by clumsier, more obviously extrinsic means.

In his comments on the old Count, the King claims that the up-and-coming generation has an insufficiently vivid conception of honor and its importance:

> Such a man
> Might be a copy to these younger times,
> Which followed well would demonstrate them now
> But goers backward.
>
> (1.2.45–48)

The danger of such a regression is embodied in Paroles, whose name means "words." Paroles exhibits all the superficial signs of courtiership—wit, lavish dress, a familiarity with military and courtly jargons—without any of the real skills or virtues those signs are supposed to indicate. Paroles endangers the social processes by which the world of *All's Well* is imagined to operate, estranging externals from inner substance and subversively demonstrating limitations in the courtly code of honor. He is tightly connected to Bertram, not merely through their friendship but by similarities in their circumstances. The staged drum trick on Paroles coincides temporally with the unstageable bed trick on Bertram, and there are clear thematic parallels as well: both victims are blind, morally as well as literally, to plots perpetrated by close acquaintances masquerading as strangers.

Still, Paroles' menace should not be overestimated. Everyone except Bertram sees through him instantly, and Bertram's inability to discern Paroles' pretenses is a telling mark of his immaturity. Once Bertram finally recognizes that Paroles is a "counterfeit model," moreover, he recoils violently from his former friend and adviser. Bertram may be gauche and inattentive, but he recognizes gross cowardice when he sees it, and in that rudimentary recognition of the difference between honorable and dishonorable conduct may lay the groundwork for his improvement.

Paroles, then, both incarnates Bertram's flaws and diminishes Bertram's culpability. "Your son was misled with a snipped taffeta fellow there," opines Lafeu indignantly to the Countess, "whose villainous saffron would have made all the unbaked and doughy youth of a nation in his color" (4.5.1–3). If, in the world of *All's Well,* good associates and benign forms of institutional duress can maneuver Bertram in the right direction, then bad associates and bad customs likewise have the power to exacerbate his worst impulses. On the other hand, unlike a sterner and more principled character, the "unbaked" Bertram retains the capacity to be reformed, like a lump of dough, despite his unpromising shape.

In less obvious ways, Paroles' presence in *All's Well* also deflects criticism from Helen. Helen's marital plans involve, as she herself admits, quite startling social ambitions. Marrying Bertram will elevate her from the relatively large gentry class to a tiny elite at the pinnacle of the social pyramid. In a hierarchically stratified society where people are supposed to "know their places," such aspirations might well seem disruptive. But Paroles, a cruder and less principled social climber, helps clarify the actually *conservative* nature of Helen's desires. In marked contrast to the craven Paroles, Helen is willing to certify her words with her body as honorable aristocrats are supposed to do, proposing to sacrifice life and reputation if her promises to cure the King prove empty. Helen's conviction that words must suit actions, that her tongue must obey her hand, marks her as "noble" despite her lack of material resources, and gains her the respect of the older members of the nobility, such as the King, the Countess, and Lafeu. Thus marriage to Bertram seems to remedy an unaccountable lapse in the proper social order, rather than to create a breach in that order.

Left deliberately vague is what relationship, if any, merit really has with birth. On the one hand, Helen's excellence seems to belie her humble origins; on the other hand, although both Helen and Diana are poor, it is carefully specified that they are not "base" persons of artisan or peasant stock. Their gentility, however modest, seems

Foppish camp follower. Peter Flötner (mid-sixteenth century).

to lend their upward mobility a respectability that Paroles' attempts at self-promotion can never possess. Paroles thus draws off criticism that Helen might otherwise attract for violating class boundaries. Similarly, his presence in the play serves partially to allay criticism of Helen's sexual transgressiveness: his boastful inaction is so obviously worse than Helen's vigorous but possibly "unfeminine" enterprise that once again he seems an instructive example that tells in Helen's favor.

Although Paroles functions as a scapegoat of sorts, at the end of the play he does not suffer the scapegoat's usual cruel fate. After his disgrace, his dramatic function as corrupter of Bertram and foil to Helen is evidently complete, and we might imagine that we have seen the last of him. But like so many other characters in *All's Well,* good and bad, Paroles has a surprising durability. "Simply the thing I am," he declares, "shall make me live" (4.3.316–17). Like Helen and Diana, he reappears in the final scenes, reinserting himself, in a reduced capacity, into a world that had scorned him. The partial, incremental improvement promised by the conclusion of *All's Well That Ends Well* may from some points of view seem disappointing. But its pessimism inspires a certain tolerance, a forbearance that allows even the ridiculous or debased to find a home.

KATHARINE EISAMAN MAUS

SELECTED BIBLIOGRAPHY

Donaldson, Ian. "*All's Well That Ends Well*: Shakespeare's Play of Endings." *Essays in Criticism* 27 (1977): 34–55. Discusses the play's preoccupation with endings and its problematic final scene.

Harris, Jonathan Gil. "All Swell That End Swell: Dropsy, Phantom Pregnancy, and the Sound of Deconception in *All's Well That Ends Well*." *Renaissance Drama* 35 (2006): 169–89. Swollen bodies: the King's illness, Paroles' empty inflation, Helen's pregnancy.

Hodgdon, Barbara. "The Making of Virgins and Mothers: Sexual Signs, Substitute Scenes, and Doubled Presences in *All's Well That Ends Well*." *Philological Quarterly* 66 (1987): 47–72. Examines the character of Helen, as Shakespeare develops it from the source story in Boccaccio's *Decameron*.

Huston, J. Dennis. "'Some Stain of Soldier': The Functions of Paroles in *All's Well That Ends Well*." *Shakespeare Quarterly* 21 (1970): 431–38. Compares Paroles with Helen.

Parker, Patricia. "*All's Well That Ends Well*: Increase and Multiply." *Creative Imitation: New Essays on Renaissance Literature in Honor of Thomas M. Greene*. Ed. David Quint, Margaret Ferguson, G. W. Pigman, and Wayne Rebhorn. Binghamton, NY: Medieval and Renaissance Texts and Studies, 1992. 355–90. Looks at linguistic and sexual deferral and displacement as the key to abundance in the play.

Schwarz, Kathryn. "'My Intents Are Fixed': Constant Will in *All's Well That Ends Well*." *Shakespeare Quarterly* 58 (2007): 200–27. Argues that Helen's admirable but disconcerting constancy shows how male privilege is contingent upon the active support of the women subjected to it.

Sullivan, Garrett. "'Be This Sweet Helen's Knell, and Now Forget Her': Forgetting, Memory, and Identity in *All's Well That Ends Well*." *Shakespeare Quarterly* 50 (1999): 51–69. Analyzes how the forgetfulness associated with sexual desire both threatens and produces identity in *All's Well That Ends Well*.

Traister, Barbara Howard. "'Doctor She': Healing and Sex in *All's Well That Ends Well*." *A Companion to Shakespeare's Works, IV: Poems, Problem Comedies, Late Plays*. Blackwell Companions to Literature and Culture 20. Ed. Richard Dutton and Jean E. Howard. Malden, MA: Blackwell, 2003. 333–47. Looks at Helen as lovesick physician.

Wheeler, Richard P. "Imperial Love and the Dark House: *All's Well That Ends Well*." *Shakespeare's Development and the Problem Comedies: Turn and Counter-Turn*. Berkeley: U of California P, 1981. 35–91. Offers a detailed psychoanalytic reading.

Zitner, Sheldon P. *All's Well That Ends Well*. Boston: Twayne, 1989. Stage and reception histories as well as critical commentary on the play.

Film

All's Well That Ends Well. 1981. Dir. Elijah Moshinsky. UK. 142 min. From BBC-TV. An elegant production, with sets and lighting that recall the paintings of Vermeer and Caravaggio. Compelling performances from Angela Down (Helen), Celia Johnson (Countess), Donald Sinden (King), and Ian Charleson (Bertram).

TEXTUAL INTRODUCTION

The only text of *All's Well That Ends Well* is that in the Folio. It was set primarily by Compositor B, but pages V3 recto and verso were set by Compositor D and V4 recto and verso by Compositor C. The play is divided into acts, but scenes are not numbered. Since division into acts occurred only once the King's Men started acting at the Blackfriars, this division may, if the play is from as late as 1607 rather than the traditional date of 1604–05 or earlier, anticipate the move. Otherwise the divisions may have been imposed later, either for a performance or for printing.

The text of *All's Well That Ends Well* offers a number of notorious difficulties. Aside from some verbal cruxes, these include variation in the names of characters, confusion of the two lords eventually identified as the brothers Dumaine, and some unusually worded stage directions. Initially, the Countess of Roussillon is called *"Mother"*; in the course of the play she is also identified as *"Countess," "Old Countess," "Lady,"* and *"Old Lady."* Her son is sometimes *"Count Roussillon,"* sometimes *"Roussillon,"* sometimes *"Bertram"*; Lafeu is *"Lord Lafeu," "Old Lafeu,"* and *"Old Lord"*; Helen is *"Helena"* once in dialogue and several times in stage directions. More troublesome is the confusion of the *"two French Lords,"* as they are called in the Folio's opening stage direction to 5.3, or *"the two Frenchmen"* (3.1.0 SD), or *"the Frenchmen, as at first"* (3.6.0 SD), or *"the two French Captaines"* (4.3.0 SD). We learn they are brothers only at 3.6.98 and that their name is Dumaine only at 4.3.172. In speech prefixes they are sometimes identified as *"1. Lo. G."* and *"2. Lo. E."* (1.2), sometimes differentiated only with numbers, e.g., *"1 Lord"* (3.1), sometimes with such abbreviated terms as *"French E."* (3.1), *"Cap. G.,"* or *"Cap. E."* (3.6). More important, the parts of the two characters seem to have become confused. The difficulties begin at the end of 3.6, when *"Cap. E."* has been urging Bertram to allow him to surprise Paroles. As Captain E. (in this edition called *"Second Lord Dumaine"*) says he will "go look my twigs"—presumably meaning that he will leave to prepare the ambush—Bertram responds, "Your brother, he shall go along with me," and *"Cap. G."* (or *"First Lord Dumaine"*) says, "As't please your lordship, I'll leave you." Captain E. remains with Bertram, who offers to "show [him] the lass [he] spoke of," i.e., Diana (3.6.96–102). Later, at 4.3.14–15, E. accordingly tells G. the details of how Bertram "hath perverted a young gentlewoman." Nevertheless, in Folio 4.1, it is E., not G., who leads the capture of Paroles. At the beginning of 4.3, E. reports to Bertram on Paroles' behavior once captured, but in the rest of 4.3 it is G. who leads the interrogation.

Different explanations have been offered for these variations. Traditionally it has been thought that they reflect Shakespeare's developing vision of his characters or their roles at particular moments (e.g., "mother"), and hence that these variations indicate that the play was set from Shakespeare's "foul papers" or working draft. The lack of consistency, along with the confusion over the French "lords Dumaine," perhaps suggests that there may have been interruptions in the writing during which Shakespeare lost track of the titles he had earlier given some characters. Changes of speech prefix within certain scenes—for example, the switch from *"Coun."* to *"Old Cou."* in 1.3 from lines 113 to 152—may indicate that some sections where new speech prefixes appear were additions originally written on separate sheets or in the margin.

Further support for the idea of interrupted composition comes from a number of stage directions in which what seem to be private notations have crept into the text. Two striking examples are F 2.3.181 SD, *"Parolles and Lafew stay behind, commenting of this wedding,"* and F 3.6.0, *"Enter Count Rossillion and the Frenchmen, as at first."* "Commenting of this wedding" and "as at first" are not directions that would be visible on the stage, and they can perhaps be understood as Shakespeare's notes to himself.

On the other hand, certain textual oddities have been attributed to collaboration. Laurie Maguire and Emma Smith propose that the play was written by Shakespeare and Thomas Middleton soon after their joint work on *Timon of Athens*. The play would thus date from 1606–07—a suggestion made on other grounds by scholars including McDonald P. Jackson and accepted in the *Norton Shakespeare* chronology—and collaboration might also explain the "notes to author" style of some of the stage directions, the variation in character names, and the confusion of the two French lords. Maguire and Smith find Middleton's hand in certain scenes (1.1, 1.3, 2.1, 2.3, 4.1, 4.3, and 5.3) or parts of scenes—for instance, at the switch of speech prefixes in 1.3. They cite a variety of characteristics of Middleton's style in sections of *All's Well*, including the high proportion of rhyming lines; characteristic contractions, exclamations, and vocabulary; and numerous blank verse lines with multisyllabic endings. They also argue that F's *"gentle Astringer"* (cf. 5.1.6 SD) is a misreading of *"a gentleman, a stranger."* That his subsequent speech prefixes are *"Gent.,"* they argue, suggests Middleton's habit "of introducing a character with a generic or status marker in the stage direction" but using "a specific name in speech-prefixes." Brian Vickers and Marcus Dahl have, however, re-argued the case for Shakespeare alone, and performance scholars have pointed out that the "Gentleman austringer" (or hawk-trainer) could usefully be differentiated from other courtiers onstage; this edition retains the base-text identification for the character.

For a Folio-only play, *All's Well* offers a number of issues of perhaps surprising complexity and resonance for the textual scholar. The knotty questions of author-ship, style, and habits of composition that underpin the debate over the play's authorship suggest that there is a great deal of work yet to be done before the play's textual circumstances and place in the Shakespeare canon are convincingly understood.

SUZANNE GOSSETT

TEXTUAL BIBLIOGRAPHY

Jackson, MacDonald P. "Spurio and the Date of *All's Well That Ends Well.*" *Notes and Queries* 48 (2001): 298–99.

Maguire, Laurie, and Emma Smith. "Many Hands: A New Shakespeare Collabora-tion?" *TLS* 20 April 2012: 13–15.

Vickers, Brian, and Marcus Dahl. "What is infirm . . . 'All's Well That Ends Well': An Attribution Rejected." *TLS* 11 May 2012: 14.

PERFORMANCE NOTE

Productions of *All's Well That Ends Well* must address the play's central problem: that Helen succeeds in regaining a husband who seems unworthy of her. Many productions aim to resolve the problem by creating a fairy-tale atmosphere, increasing thereby the audience's genre-based support for the marriage and softening Bertram's faults. Oth-ers, instead, undercut the comedy by exploiting the play's emphases on age and infir-mity, war and death, accentuating the troubled marriage and possibly overshadowing Bertram's reformation. Each production must decide whether Helen recognizes Ber-tram's deficiencies or whether she remains cheerfully unaware of what belies her good fortune. In either case, productions must balance her resilience, charm, and cleverness with her melancholy reflections.

Several related considerations influence the audience's allegiances. Most notable is whether Bertram abandons Helen wholly out of contempt and pride or because he is tempted from her by Paroles and the glories of war. One Countess may interrogate Helen (in 1.3) for misplaced affection, while another shows her satisfaction through-out; one Widow may eagerly help Helen trick Bertram into bed, while another appears wholly mercenary; the marriageable lords whom Helen passes over in favor of Bertram can appear either eager or terrified at the prospect of being chosen. The character of Paroles also influences the comedy and its resolution. Directors must decide whether his interrogation and its aftermath lean more toward comic comeup-pance or tragic humiliation, and if the latter, how the end for Paroles plays against the relatively easy road to forgiveness made available to Bertram. Other consider-ations in performance include whether to stage the "bed trick"; whether Helen appears visibly pregnant in the final scene; and whether Bertram seems sincere or reluctant in reconciling himself to marriage with Helen.

BRETT GAMBOA

All's Well That Ends Well

[THE PERSONS OF THE PLAY

In Roussillon:
COUNTESS of Roussillon
BERTRAM, Count of Roussillon, son to the Countess
HELEN, ward to the Countess
Rinaldo, STEWARD to the Countess
Lavache the CLOWN, servant to the Countess
PAROLES, companion to Bertram
LAFEU, a French lord
PAGE

At the French court:
KING
Four young LORDS
FIRST LORD DUMAINE
SECOND LORD DUMAINE

In Florence:
DUKE
WIDOW
DIANA, daughter to Widow
MARIANA, neighbor to Widow

SOLDIERS
GENTLEMAN austringer°   *falconer*
ATTENDANTS
SERVANTS]

1.1

Enter young BERTRAM, *Count of Roussillon, his*
mother [*the Dowager* COUNTESS], *and* HELEN, *Lord*
LAFEU, *all in black.*[1]

COUNTESS In delivering my son from me, I bury a second
husband.[2]
BERTRAM And I in going, madam, weep o'er my father's death
anew. But I must attend° his majesty's command, to whom I   *heed*
5   am now in ward,[3] evermore in subjection.
LAFEU You shall find of the King a husband,° madam; you, sir,   *patron*
a father. He that so generally° is at all times good must of   *universally*
necessity hold° his virtue to you, whose worthiness would stir   *uphold*
it up where it wanted° rather than lack it where there is such   *was lacking*
10   abundance.
COUNTESS What hope is there of his majesty's amendment?°   *improvement*

1.1 Location: Bertram's palace in Roussillon, in
southeast France.
1. TEXTUAL COMMENT The way the characters are
referred to in stage directions and speech prefixes in
the Folio text varies significantly; for the significance
of these variations, see Digital Edition TC 1.

2. Giving up my son grieves me as much as my husband's death (playing on "deliver" as "give birth").
3. Upon the old Count's death, the King becomes
guardian of Bertram's estate until he comes of age. A
guardian could arrange his ward's marriage, provided the match was with a social equal.

LAFEU   He hath abandoned his physicians,[4] madam, under
whose practices he hath persecuted time with hope[5] and
finds no other advantage in the process but only the losing
of hope by time.

COUNTESS   This young gentlewoman had a father—oh, that
"had," how sad a passage° 'tis!—whose skill was almost as   *expression; passing away*
great as his honesty;° had it° stretched so far, would have   *integrity / (his skill)*
made nature immortal, and death should have play for lack
of work. Would for the King's sake he were living: I think it
would be the death of the King's disease.

LAFEU   How called you the man you speak of, madam?

COUNTESS   He was famous, sir, in his profession, and it was
his great right to be so: Gerard de Narbonne.[6]

LAFEU   He was excellent indeed, madam; the King very lately
spoke of him admiringly and mourningly. He was skillful
enough to have lived still, if knowledge could be set up
against mortality.

BERTRAM   What is it, my good lord, the King languishes of?

LAFEU   A fistula,° my lord.   *abscess (often anal)*

BERTRAM   I heard not of it before.

LAFEU   I would it were not notorious.° [*He indicates* HELEN.]   *known to everyone*
Was this gentlewoman the daughter of Gerard de Narbonne?

COUNTESS   His sole child, my lord, and bequeathed to my
overlooking.[7] I have those hopes of her good that her edu-
cation° promises her dispositions she inherits, which   *upbringing*
makes fair gifts° fairer.[8] For where an unclean mind car-   *abilities*
ries virtuous qualities,° there commendations go with   *acquired skills*
pity:° they are virtues and traitors, too.[9] In her they are the   *mingle with regret*
better for their simpleness;° she derives° her honesty and   *purity / inherits*
achieves her goodness.

LAFEU   Your commendations, madam, get from her tears.

COUNTESS   'Tis the best brine a maiden can season° her praise   *preserve (as with salt)*
in. The remembrance of her father never approaches her
heart but the tyranny of her sorrows takes all livelihood°   *liveliness*
from her cheek. —No more of this, Helena: go to, no more,
lest it be rather thought you affect° a sorrow than to have—   *make a show of*

HELEN   I do affect a sorrow, indeed, but I have it, too.

LAFEU   Moderate lamentation is the right of the dead, excessive grief the enemy to the living.

COUNTESS   If the living be not enemy to the grief, the excess
makes it soon mortal.°   *fatal*

BERTRAM   Madam, I desire your holy wishes.°   *blessing*

LAFEU   How understand we that?[1]

COUNTESS   Be thou blest, Bertram, and succeed thy father
In manners° as in shape. Thy blood and virtue[2]   *behavior*
Contend for empire in thee, and thy goodness
Share with thy birthright. Love all, trust a few,

---

4. Playing on the usual "his physicians have abandoned him" (given up hope of his cure).
5. Afflicted his days by hoping for a cure.
6. Town just north of Roussillon.
7. Guardianship (Helen is the Countess's ward, as
Bertram is the King's).
8. TEXTUAL COMMENT Editors often add a semicolon
after "promises," but *The Norton Shakespeare* does

not for reasons explained in Digital Edition TC 2.
9. Because the skills are used for evil purposes.
1. TEXTUAL COMMENT Possibly a misplaced line;
possibly Lafeu thinks Bertram's interruption discourteous. For a fuller discussion, see Digital Edition TC 3.
2. (May) your noble birth and acquired goodness.

Do wrong to none. Be able° for thine enemy   *a match for*
60 Rather in power than use,[3] and keep thy friend
  Under thy own life's key.[4] Be checked° for silence   *criticized*
  But never taxed for speech.° What heaven more will *rebuked for chatter*
  That thee may furnish° and my prayers pluck down,   *embellish*
  Fall on thy head. [*to* LAFEU] Farewell, my lord.
65 'Tis an unseasoned° courtier. Good my lord,   *immature*
  Advise him.

 LAFEU   He cannot want the best
  That shall attend his love.[5]

 COUNTESS Heaven bless him! —Farewell, Bertram.

 BERTRAM The best wishes that can be forged° in your *fashioned*
70 thoughts be servants to you.°   [*Exit* COUNTESS.] *assist you*
  [*to* HELEN] Be comfortable° to my mother, your mistress, *comforting*
  and make much of her.

 LAFEU Farewell, pretty lady, you must hold the credit° of your *uphold the reputation*
  father.   [*Exeunt* BERTRAM *and* LAFEU.]
75 HELEN Oh, were that all! I think not on my father,
  And these great tears grace his remembrance more
  Than those I shed for him.[6] What was he like?
  I have forgot him. My imagination
  Carries no favor° in't but Bertram's.   *face; liking; love token*
80 I am undone. There is no living, none,
  If Bertram be away. 'Twere all one
  That° I should love a bright particular star   *It is just as if*
  And think to wed it, he is so above me.
  In his bright radiance and collateral[7] light
85 Must I be comforted, not in his sphere.
  Th'ambition in my love thus plagues itself:
  The hind° that would be mated by the lion   *doe*
  Must die for love. 'Twas pretty, though a plague,
  To see him every hour, to sit and draw
90 His archèd brows, his hawking° eye, his curls,   *sharp*
  In our heart's table°—heart too capable° *drawing table / receptive*
  Of every line and trick° of his sweet favor!°   *trait / face*
  But now he's gone, and my idolatrous fancy°   *love*
  Must sanctify his relics.[8] Who comes here?

     Enter PAROLES.

95 One that goes with him. I love him for his sake,
  And yet I know him a notorious liar,
  Think him a great way° fool, solely° a coward. *mostly a / completely*
  Yet these fixed evils sit so fit in him°   *fit him so well*
  That they take place[9] when virtue's steely bones°   *rigid severity*
100 Looks bleak i'th' cold wind withal. Full oft we see
  Cold wisdom waiting on superfluous folly.

 PAROLES Save° you, fair queen.   *God save*

 HELEN And you, monarch.

 PAROLES No.

105 HELEN And no.

---

3. By having power, rather than using it.
4. *keep . . . key:* safeguard your friend's life as you do
your own.
5. *He . . . love:* He will not lack the best advice my
affection for him can supply.
6. *grace . . . him:* are a better tribute to my father

than those (few) tears I actually shed for him.
7. Rotating in a separate orbit (in Ptolomaic
astronomy).
8. Must worship what reminds me of him.
9. Take precedence.

PAROLES   Are you meditating on virginity?

HELEN   Ay. You have some stain° of soldier in you; let me ask   *tinge*
you a question. Man is enemy to virginity: how may we
barricado° it against him?   *barricade*

110   PAROLES   Keep him out.

HELEN   But he assails, and our virginity, though valiant in the
defense, yet is weak. Unfold to us some warlike resistance.

PAROLES   There is none. Man setting down before° you will   *laying siege to*
undermine you and blow you up.[1]

115   HELEN   Bless our poor virginity from underminers and
blowers-up! Is there no military policy° how virgins might   *strategy*
blow up men?

PAROLES   Virginity being blown down, man will quicklier be
blown up.° Marry,[2] in blowing him down again, with the   *have an erection*

120   breach yourselves made you lose your city. It is not politic°   *expedient*
in the commonwealth of nature to preserve virginity. Loss
of virginity is rational increase,[3] and there was never virgin
got° till virginity was first lost. That° you were made of is   *begotten / What*
mettle° to make virgins. Virginity, by being once lost, may   *substance*

125   be ten times found;° by being ever kept, it is ever lost. 'Tis   *reproduced tenfold*
too cold a companion: away with't!

HELEN   I will stand for't° a little, though therefor I die a virgin.   *defend it*

PAROLES   There's little can be said in't:° 'tis against the rule of   *for it*
nature. To speak on the part of virginity is to accuse your

130   mothers, which is most infallible disobedience. He that
hangs himself is a virgin.[4] Virginity murders itself and
should be buried in highways out of all sanctified limit,[5] as a
desperate offendress against nature. Virginity breeds mites
much like a cheese,[6] consumes itself to the very paring, and

135   so dies with feeding his own stomach.° Besides, virginity is   *pride*
peevish, proud, idle, made of self-love—which is the most
inhibited° sin in the canon.° Keep it not; you cannot choose   *prohibited / scriptures*
but lose by't. Out with't:[7] within t'one year it will make itself
two, which is a goodly increase, and the principal[8] itself not

140   much the worse. Away with't!

HELEN   How might one do, sir, to lose it to her own liking?

PAROLES   Let me see. Marry, ill, to like him that ne'er it likes.[9]
'Tis a commodity will lose the gloss with lying:° the longer   *remaining idle*
kept, the less worth. Off with't while 'tis vendible;° answer   *salable*

145   the time of request.[1] Virginity, like an old courtier, wears
her cap out of fashion, richly suited° but unsuitable,° just   *dressed / inappropriate*
like the brooch and the toothpick, which wear not now.[2]
Your date° is better in your pie and your porridge than in   *fruit; age*
your cheek, and your virginity, your old virginity, is like one

150   of our French withered pears:[3] it looks ill, it eats drily—
marry, 'tis a withered pear. It was formerly better, marry, yet
'tis a withered pear. Will you anything with it?

---

1. *undermine you*: dig tunnels under you (to plant
explosives). *blow you up*: punning on "inflate," "make
you pregnant."
2. By Mary (a mild oath).
3. *rational increase*: judicious growth in the human
("rational") population.
4. A suicide, like a virgin, is a self-destroyer.
5. Consecrated ground (in which suicides were
denied burial).

6. Cheese was thought to generate spontaneously
the mites that fed on it.
7. Get rid of it; put it out at interest.
8. Original investment (the woman's body).
9. To please him who doesn't appreciate virginity.
1. Respond to demand (greatest in youth).
2. Which are no longer in fashion.
3. Dried pears (suggesting aged female genitals).

HELEN   Not my virginity yet[4]—
　　　There° shall your master have a thousand loves,　　　　　　(At court)
155　A mother, and a mistress, and a friend,
　　　A phoenix,[5] captain, and an enemy,
　　　A guide, a goddess, and a sovereign,
　　　A counselor, a traitress, and a dear.
　　　His humble ambition, proud humility;
160　His jarring concord, and his discord dulcet;[6]
　　　His faith, his sweet disaster, with a world
　　　Of pretty fond adoptious christendoms
　　　That blinking Cupid gossips.[7] Now shall he—
　　　I know not what he shall. God send him well.
165　The court's a learning place, and he is one—
PAROLES   What one, i'faith?
HELEN　　　　　　　　　　　—That I wish well. 'Tis pity—
PAROLES   What's pity?
HELEN   —That wishing well had not a body in't
　　　Which might be felt,° that we the poorer born,　　　　　　perceived
170　Whose baser stars do shut us up in wishes,[8]
　　　Might with effects of them follow our friends
　　　And show what we alone must° think, which never　　　　　must only
　　　Returns us thanks.°　　　　　　　　　　　　　　　Wins us gratitude
　　　　　　　Enter PAGE.
PAGE   Monsieur Paroles, my lord calls for you.　　　　　　[Exit.]
175　PAROLES   Little Helen, farewell. If I can remember thee, I will
　　　think of thee at court.
HELEN   Monsieur Paroles, you were born under a charitable
　　　star.
PAROLES   Under Mars,[9] I.
180　HELEN   I especially think under Mars.
PAROLES   Why under Mars?
HELEN   The wars hath so kept you under, that you must needs
　　　be born under Mars.
PAROLES   When he was predominant.°　　　　　　　　in the ascendant
185　HELEN   When he was retrograde,[1] I think rather.
PAROLES   Why think you so?
HELEN   You go so much backward when you fight.
PAROLES   That's for advantage.°　　　　　　　　　　tactical gain
HELEN   So is running away when fear proposes the safety. But
190　the composition° that your valor and fear makes in you is a　　truce; mixture
　　　virtue of a good wing,[2] and I like the wear° well.　　　habit; fashion
PAROLES   I am so full of businesses I cannot answer thee
　　　acutely. I will return perfect courtier, in the which my
　　　instruction shall serve to naturalize° thee, so thou wilt be　　familiarize
195　capable of a courtier's counsel and understand what advice
　　　shall thrust upon thee; else thou diest in thine unthankfulness,

---

4. Not with *my* virginity: not my virginity *yet* (but
soon).
5. The mythical phoenix was a one-of-a-kind bird;
hence, marvelous, unique being.
6. Harmonious (all these oxymorons were typical of
courtly love poetry).
7. *pretty . . . gossips:* foolish nicknames given when
blind Cupid is godfather at a christening.

8. Whose less elevated destinies confine us merely to
wishing.
9. The planet was identified with the god of war.
1. Retreating (said of a planet's apparent movement
relative to the zodiac).
2. *of a good wing:* that is, rapid in flight; also, with
large shoulder flaps. Paroles is foppishly dressed.

and thine ignorance makes thee away.° Farewell. When   *puts an end to you*
thou hast leisure, say thy prayers; when thou hast none,
remember thy friends.[3] Get thee a good husband, and use°   *treat*
200   him as he uses thee. So farewell.   [*Exit.*]
HELEN   Our remedies oft in ourselves do lie
Which we ascribe to heaven. The fated° sky   *destiny-ordaining*
Gives us free scope, only doth backward pull
Our slow designs when we ourselves are dull.°   *sluggish*
205   What power is it which mounts my love so high,[4]
That makes me see and cannot feed mine eye?
The mightiest space in fortune nature brings
To join like likes and kiss like native things.[5]
Impossible be strange° attempts to those   *unusual*
210   That weigh their pains in sense[6] and do suppose
What hath been cannot be. Who ever strove
To show her merit that did miss° her love?   *fail to achieve*
The King's disease—my project may deceive me,
But my intents are fixed and will not leave me.   *Exit.*

1.2

Flourish cornetts.°   *Wind-instrument fanfare*
Enter the KING *of France with letters and diverse*
ATTENDANTS[, *including the two* LORDS DUMAINE].[1]
KING   The Florentines and Sienese are by th'ears,°   *quarreling*
Have fought with equal fortune and continue
A braving° war.   *defiant; gallant*
FIRST LORD DUMAINE   So 'tis reported, sir.
KING   Nay, 'tis most credible. We here receive it
5   A certainty, vouched from our cousin Austria,[2]
With caution that the Florentine will move° us   *entreat*
For speedy aid, wherein our dearest friend°   *(the Duke of Austria)*
Prejudicates° the business and would seem   *Prejudges*
To have us make denial.
FIRST LORD DUMAINE   His love and wisdom,
10   Approved° so to your majesty, may plead   *Proven*
For amplest credence.
KING   He hath armed° our answer,   *hardened*
And Florence is denied before he comes.
Yet for our gentlemen that mean to see
The Tuscan service, freely have they leave
To stand on either part.°   *fight on either side*
15   SECOND LORD DUMAINE   It well may serve
A nursery to[3] our gentry, who are sick°   *pining*
For breathing° and exploit.   *exercise*
KING   What's he comes here?
Enter BERTRAM, LAFEU, *and* PAROLES.

---

3. Unclear: perhaps, Say your prayers when you have
the chance, and when you're too busy, rely on your
friends instead.
4. Which elevates my love to so lofty an object.
5. *The mightiest . . . things:* Natural affect brings
persons greatly distant in rank together as if they
were similar and conjoins them as if they had a common origin.

6. Who vividly imagine the difficulties.
1.2 Location: The King's court at Paris.
1. TEXTUAL COMMENT The roles of the two Lords
Dumaine are unclear in the original text. See Digital
Edition TC 4.
2. My kinsman, the Duke of Austria.
3. As a training school for.

FIRST LORD DUMAINE   It is the Count Roussillon, my good lord,
Young Bertram.
KING   Youth, thou bear'st thy father's face.
20 Frank° nature, rather curious° than in haste,   *Generous / meticulous*
Hath well composed thee. Thy father's moral parts°   *qualities*
Mayst thou inherit too. Welcome to Paris!
BERTRAM   My thanks and duty are your majesty's.
KING   I would I had that corporal soundness now
25 As when thy father and myself, in friendship,
First tried our soldiership. He did look far°   *see deeply*
Into the service° of the time and was   *military service*
Discipled of° the bravest. He lasted long,   *Followed by; taught by*
But on us both did haggish° age steal on   *witchlike; malevolent*
30 And wore us out of act.° It much repairs me   *action*
To talk of your good father. In his youth
He had the wit which I can well observe
Today in our young lords, but they may jest
Till their own scorn return to them unnoted[4]
35 Ere they can hide their levity in honor.[5]
So like a courtier,° contempt nor bitterness   *paradigm of courtesy*
Were in his pride° or sharpness;[6] if they were,   *self-esteem*
His equal had awaked them,[7] and his honor,
Clock to itself,° knew the true minute when   *Self-regulating*
40 Exception° bid him speak, and at this time   *Disapproval*
His tongue obeyed his hand.[8] Who were below him,
He used as creatures of another place[9]
And bowed his eminent top° to their low ranks,   *head*
Making them proud of his humility;
45 In their poor praise he humbled.[1] Such a man
Might be a copy° to these younger times,   *model*
Which followed well would demonstrate them now
But goers backward.°   *backsliders*
BERTRAM   His good remembrance, sir,
Lies richer in your thoughts than on his tomb.
50 So in approof° lives not his epitaph   *confirmation*
As in your royal speech.
KING   Would I were with him! He would always say—
Methinks I hear him now; his plausive° words   *praiseworthy*
He scattered not in ears, but grafted them[2]
55 To grow there and to bear—"Let me not live"—
This his good melancholy oft began
On the catastrophe° and heel of pastime   *end*
When it was out°—"Let me not live," quoth he,   *finished*
"After my flame lacks oil, to be the snuff[3]
60 Of younger spirits, whose apprehensive° senses   *quick*
All but new things disdain; whose judgments are
Mere fathers of their garments;[4] whose constancies°   *loyalties*

---

4. *they may . . . unnoted:* their ridicule merely rebounds upon them, ignored by others.
5. Before they can compensate for their frivolity with noble acts.
6. Keenness of wit.
7. *if they were . . . them:* if ever he spoke bitterly or contemptuously, it was to a social equal.
8. He said no more than he would back up with action.
9. He treated as people of a higher station.

1. He willingly humbled himself to praise their poor selves.
2. He did not strew (words) superficially among his hearers (like seed), but planted them permanently (as twigs of fruit trees are grafted to a tree trunk).
3. Burned upper wick, which if not trimmed keeps the lower part from burning properly.
4. *whose judgments . . . garments:* whose mental prowess creates only new clothes.

Expire before their fashions." This he wished.
I after him do after° him wish too,   *in harmony with*
65   Since I nor wax nor honey can bring home,
I quickly were dissolvèd° from my hive   *removed*
To give some laborers room.
SECOND LORD DUMAINE   You're loved, sir;
They that least lend it you° shall lack° you first.   *grant you love / miss*
KING   I fill a place, I know't. How long is't, Count,
70   Since the physician at your father's died?
He was much famed.
BERTRAM   Some six months since, my lord.
KING   If he were living, I would try him yet.
—Lend me an arm. —The rest have worn me out
With several applications.° Nature and sickness   *various treatments*
75   Debate it at their leisure.⁵ Welcome, Count;
My son's no dearer.
BERTRAM   Thank your majesty.   *Flourish. Exeunt.*

1.3
Enter COUNTESS, STEWARD, *and* CLOWN.
COUNTESS   I will now hear. What say you of this gentlewoman?
STEWARD   Madam, the care I have had to even your content¹
I wish might be found in the calendar° of my past endeavors,   *record*
for then we wound our modesty and make foul the clearness
5   of our deservings, when of ourselves we publish° them.   *advertise*
COUNTESS   What does this knave here? [*to* CLOWN] Get you
gone, sirrah! The complaints I have heard of you I do not all
believe. 'Tis my slowness that I do not, for I know you lack
not folly to commit them, and have ability enough to make
10   such knaveries yours.
CLOWN   'Tis not unknown to you, madam, I am a poor fellow.
COUNTESS   Well, sir?
CLOWN   No, madam, 'tis not so well that I am poor, though
many of the rich are damned. But if I may have your lady-
15   ship's good will to go to the world,° Isbel the woman° and I   *marry / maidservant*
will do as we may.²
COUNTESS   Wilt thou needs be a beggar?
CLOWN   I do beg your good will in this case.
COUNTESS   In what case?
20   CLOWN   In Isbel's case and mine own. Service is no heritage,³
and I think I shall never have the blessing of God till I have
issue o'my body. For they say bairns° are blessings.   *children*
COUNTESS   Tell me thy reason why thou wilt marry.
CLOWN   My poor body, madam, requires it; I am driven on by
25   the flesh, and he must needs go that the devil drives.
COUNTESS   Is this all your worship's reason?
CLOWN   Faith, madam, I have other holy reasons,⁴ such as they
are.

---

5. Argue over my condition at length.
1.3 Location: Roussillon.
1. To meet your desires.
2. Will do our best (with sexual pun on "do").
3. A servant has little to leave his children (prover-

bial; with sexual pun on "service").
4. Other motives sanctified by the marriage ceremony; with puns on "holy" ("hole-y") and "reasons"
("raisings").

COUNTESS   May the world know them?

30   CLOWN   I have been, madam, a wicked creature, as you and
all flesh and blood are, and indeed I do marry that I may
repent.[5]

COUNTESS   Thy marriage sooner than thy wickedness.

CLOWN   I am out o'friends, madam, and I hope to have friends
35   for my wife's sake.

COUNTESS   Such friends are thine enemies, knave.

CLOWN   You're shallow,° madam, in great friends, for the   *a superficial judge*
knaves come to do that for me which I am aweary of. He
that ears° my land spares my team and gives me leave to in°   *plows / harvest*
40   the crop. If I be his cuckold, he's my drudge. He that com-
forts my wife is the cherisher of my flesh and blood; he that
cherishes my flesh and blood loves my flesh and blood; he
that loves my flesh and blood is my friend; *ergo*, he that
kisses my wife is my friend. If men could be contented to be
45   what they are,° there were no fear in marriage, for young   *(cuckolds)*
Chairbonne the puritan and old Poisson the papist,[6]
howsome'er their hearts are severed in religion, their heads
are both one:° they may jowl° horns together like any deer   *identical / bump*
i'th' herd.[7]

50   COUNTESS   Wilt thou ever be a foul-mouthed and calumnious
knave?

CLOWN   A prophet I, madam, and I speak the truth the next°   *most direct*
way.
   [*Sings.*]   For I the ballad will repeat,
55   Which men full true shall find:
      "Your marriage comes by destiny,
      Your cuckoo sings by kind."[8]

COUNTESS   Get you gone, sir; I'll talk with you more anon.

STEWARD   May it please you, madam, that he bid Helen come
60   to you. Of her I am to speak.

COUNTESS   Sirrah, tell my gentlewoman I would speak with
her—Helen, I mean.

CLOWN [*sings*]   "Was this fair face the cause," quoth she,[9]
      "Why the Grecians sackèd Troy,
65   Fond° done, done fond, was this[1] King Priam's joy?"   *Foolishly; lovingly*
      With that she sighèd as she stood, *bis*°   *(repeat)*
      And gave this sentence° then: *maxim*
      "Among nine bad if one be good,
      Among nine bad if one be good,
70   There's yet one good in ten."

COUNTESS   What, one good in ten? You corrupt[2] the song,
sirrah.

CLOWN   One good woman in ten, madam, which is a purify-
ing o'th' song. Would God would serve the world so all the

---

5. That I may make my illicit sexual activity lawful
(but alluding to the proverb "Marry in haste and
repent at leisure").
6. *chair bonne*: good meat (French). *poisson*: fish.
Catholics ate fish on fast days, but puritans rejected
the custom.
7. Cuckolds were supposed to have horns in their
foreheads.
8. *by kind*: according to its nature (the cuckoo's song

was supposed to mock cuckolds).
9. The Clown is reminded of the "fair face" of Helen
of Troy, the most famous cuckold maker. *she*: probably Hecuba, wife of Priam and mother of Paris, Hel-
en's lover.
1. *this*: probably refers to Paris.
2. Debase (the original presumably had "one bad in
ten," referring to Paris, Priam's only bad son).

75   year, we'd find no fault with the tithe woman[3] if I were the
     parson. One in ten, quoth 'a?° An° we might have a good   *did he say / If*
     woman born but or every blazing star° or at an earthquake,   *comet*
     'twould mend the lottery° well. A man may draw his heart   *improve the odds*
     out ere 'a pluck[4] one.
80   COUNTESS   You'll be gone, sir knave, and do as I command you?
     CLOWN   That man should be at woman's command, and yet
     no hurt done! Though honesty be no puritan,[5] yet it will do
     no hurt;° it will wear the surplice of humility over the black   *harm*
     gown of a big heart.[6] I am going, forsooth. The business is
85   for Helen to come hither.   *Exit.*
     COUNTESS   Well, now.
     STEWARD   I know, madam, you love your gentlewoman
     entirely.
     COUNTESS   Faith, I do. Her father bequeathed her to me, and
90   she herself, without other advantage,[7] may lawfully make title
     to° as much love as she finds. There is more owing her than is   *claim*
     paid, and more shall be paid her than she'll demand.
     STEWARD   Madam, I was very late° more near her than I think   *recently*
     she wished me. Alone she was, and did communicate to her-
95   self her own words to her own ears. She thought, I dare vow
     for her, they touched not any stranger sense.[8] Her matter°   *subject*
     was, she loved your son. Fortune, she said, was no goddess,
     that had put such difference betwixt their two estates;° Love   *social stations*
     no god, that would not extend his might only where qualities
100 were level;[9] Dian° no queen of virgins, that would suffer her *Diana, goddess of chastity*
     poor knight surprised[1] without rescue in the first assault
     or ransom afterward. This she delivered in the most bitter
     touch° of sorrow that e'er I heard virgin exclaim in, which I   *strain*
     held my duty speedily to acquaint you withal, sithence° in   *since*
105 the loss that may happen, it concerns you something to
     know it.
     COUNTESS   You have discharged this honestly. Keep it to your-
     self. Many likelihoods informed me of this before, which
     hung so tottering in the balance that I could neither believe
110 nor misdoubt.° Pray you leave me. Stall° this in your bosom,   *doubt / Enclose*
     and I thank you for your honest care. I will speak with you
     further anon.   *Exit* STEWARD.
          Enter HELEN.
     COUNTESS [*aside*]   Even so it was with me when I was young.
     If ever we are nature's, these° are ours. This thorn   *(love pangs)*
115 Doth to our rose of youth rightly belong;
     Our blood° to us, this to our blood is born: *passions*
     It is the show° and seal of nature's truth   *sign*
     Where love's strong passion is impressed in youth.
     By our remembrances of days forgone,
120 Such were our faults, or° then we thought them none.   *although*
     Her eye is sick on't;° I observe her now.   *with it*

---

3. One-tenth of the parish produce was tithed to the church.
4. Before he draws (as from a lottery).
5. Though my honest self is not morally strict.
6. *it will wear . . . heart:* that is, the Clown will conceal his pride under apparent meekness. Some Puritan ministers obeyed English ecclesiastical law by wearing the surplice, or priestly garment, but with a black Calvinist gown underneath.
7. Even without any interest accrued (Helen being regarded as the "principal" bequeathed by her father).
8. Any other person's hearing.
9. Would not exercise his power except where rank was equal.
1. Would allow her poor devotee to be captured.

HELEN　What is your pleasure, madam?

COUNTESS　　　　　　　　　You know, Helen,
　I am a mother to you.

HELEN　Mine honorable mistress.

COUNTESS　　　　　　　　Nay, a mother.
125　Why not a mother? When I said "a mother"
　Methought you saw a serpent. What's in "mother"
　That you start at it? I say I am your mother,
　And put you in the catalogue of those
　That were enwombèd mine. 'Tis often seen
130　Adoption strives with nature, and choice breeds
　A native slip to us from foreign seeds.[2]
　You ne'er oppressed me with a mother's groan,°　　　　　*(in childbirth)*
　Yet I express to you a mother's care.
　God's mercy, maiden, does it curd thy blood
135　To say I am thy mother? What's the matter,
　That this distempered° messenger of wet,°　　　　*disturbed / rain; tears*
　The many-colored Iris,[3] rounds thine eye?
　Why? That you are my daughter?

HELEN　　　　　　　　　　That I am not.

COUNTESS　I say I am your mother.

HELEN　　　　　　　　　Pardon, madam.
140　The Count Roussillon cannot be my brother:
　I am from humble, he from honored name;
　No note° upon my parents, his all noble.　　　　　　*distinction*
　My master, my dear lord he is, and I
　His servant live and will his vassal die.
　He must not be my brother.

145　COUNTESS　　　　　　　　Nor I your mother?

HELEN　You are my mother, madam; would you were—
　So° that my lord your son were not my brother—　　　*Provided*
　Indeed my mother! Or were you both our mothers°　　*mother of us both*
　I care no more for than I do for heaven,
150　So I were not his sister. Can 't no other
　But, I your daughter, he must be my brother?

COUNTESS　Yes, Helen, you might be my daughter-in-law.
　God shield you mean it not![4] "Daughter" and "mother"
　So strive upon your pulse. What, pale again?
155　My fear hath catched your fondness!° Now I see　　　*love; folly*
　The mystery of your loneliness and find
　Your salt tears' head;° now to all sense 'tis gross:°　*source / obvious*
　You love my son. Invention[5] is ashamed
　Against° the proclamation of thy passion　　　　　*In the face of*
160　To say thou dost not. Therefore tell me true,
　But tell me then 'tis so, for look, thy cheeks
　Confess it t'one to th'other, and thine eyes
　See it so grossly shown in thy behaviors
　That in their kind° they speak it. Only sin　　　*after their fashion*
165　And hellish obstinacy tie thy tongue,
　That truth should be suspected.° Speak, is't so?　　*doubted*

---

2. *choice . . . seeds:* a twig chosen from foreign seed
becomes, once engrafted, part of our plant.
3. Goddess of rainbows (Helen's tear-filled eyes are
iridescent).
4. PERFORMANCE COMMENT The actor playing the

Countess might pitch this speech as a stern prohibition or as a teasing fake-scolding; there are also a
variety of ways Helen might respond. For a fuller
discussion, see Digital Edition PC 1.
5. (Your) capacity to invent excuses.

If it be so, you have wound a goodly clew;[6]
If it be not, forswear't.° Howe'er,° I charge thee,   *deny it / In any case*
As heaven shall work in me for thine avail,°   *benefit*
To tell me truly.
170 HELEN   Good madam, pardon me.
COUNTESS   Do you love my son?
HELEN   Your pardon, noble mistress.
COUNTESS   Love you my son?
HELEN   Do not you love him, madam?
COUNTESS   Go not about;[7] my love hath in't a bond
Whereof the world takes note.° Come, come: disclose   *society recognizes*
175 The state of your affection, for your passions
Have to the full appeached.°   *informed against you*
HELEN   Then I confess
Here on my knee, before high heaven and you,
That before you° and next unto high heaven,   *even more than I love you*
I love your son.
180 My friends° were poor but honest; so's my love.   *relatives*
Be not offended, for it hurts not him
That he is loved of me; I follow him not
By any token° of presumptuous suit,°   *manifestations / wooing*
Nor would I have him till I do deserve him,
185 Yet never know how that desert should be.
I know I love in vain, strive against hope:
Yet in this captious° and intenible° sieve   *receptive / unretentive*
I still° pour in the waters of my love   *continually*
And lack not to lose still.° Thus, Indian-like,   *And keep losing it*
190 Religious in mine error, I adore
The sun that looks upon his worshipper
But knows of him no more. My dearest madam,
Let not your hate encounter with° my love   *oppose*
For loving where you do; but if yourself,
195 Whose agèd honor cites° a virtuous youth,   *testifies to*
Did ever, in so true a flame of liking,
Wish chastely and love dearly, that your Dian
Was both herself and Love[8]—oh, then give pity
To her whose state is such that cannot choose
200 But lend and give where she is sure to lose;
That seeks not to find that° her search implies,   *what*
But riddle-like[9] lives sweetly where she dies.
COUNTESS   Had you not lately an intent—speak truly—
To go to Paris?
HELEN   Madam, I had.
COUNTESS   Wherefore? Tell true.
205 HELEN   I will tell truth; by grace itself I swear.
You know my father left me some prescriptions
Of rare and proved effects, such as his reading
And manifest° experience had collected   *obvious*
For general sovereignty;° and that he willed me   *effectiveness*
210 In heedfullest reservation° to bestow them,   *With most sparing care*
As notes whose faculties inclusive were

---

6. You have made a fine tangle of thread (mess).
7. Don't beat around the bush.
8. Venus, goddess of erotic love, is usually the antag-   onist of Diana, goddess of chastity; Helen's love reconciles them.
9. Paradoxically; retaining her secret.

More than they were in note.[1] Amongst the rest
There is a remedy, approved,° set down,   *tested*
To cure the desperate languishings whereof
215   The King is rendered lost.°   *held to be dying*
COUNTESS   This was your motive for Paris, was it? Speak.
HELEN   My lord your son made me to think of this;
Else Paris, and the medicine, and the King
Had from the conversation of my thoughts
Haply° been absent then.   *Perhaps*
220   COUNTESS   But think you, Helen,
If you should tender° your supposèd aid   *offer*
He would receive it? He and his physicians
Are of a° mind: he, that they cannot help him;   *one*
They, that they cannot help. How shall they credit
225   A poor unlearnèd virgin when the schools,
Emboweled° of their doctrine, have left off   *Emptied*
The danger to itself?
HELEN   There's something in't
More than my father's skill, which was the greatest
Of his profession, that his good receipt°   *prescription*
230   Shall for my legacy be sanctified
By th' luckiest stars in heaven. And would your honor
But give me leave to try success,° I'd venture   *test the outcome*
The well-lost life of mine on his grace's cure
By such a day, an hour.
COUNTESS   Dost thou believe't?
235   HELEN   Ay, madam, knowingly.[2]
COUNTESS   Why, Helen, thou shalt have my leave and love,
Means and attendants, and my loving greetings
To those of mine in court. I'll stay at home
And pray God's blessing into thy attempt.
240   Begone tomorrow, and be sure of this:
What I can help thee to, thou shalt not miss.°   *Exeunt.*   *lack*

2.1

Enter the KING *with diverse young* LORDS, *taking leave for*
the Florentine war[, including BERTRAM,] *Count Roussillon,*
PAROLES[, *and the two* LORDS DUMAINE]. *Flourish cornetts.*

KING   Farewell, young lords: these warlike principles°   *military precepts*
Do not throw from you. —And you, my lords,[1] farewell.
Share the advice betwixt you; if both gain all,
The gift doth stretch itself as 'tis received
And is enough for both.
5   FIRST LORD DUMAINE   'Tis our hope, sir,
After well-entered soldiers,[2] to return
And find your grace in health.
KING   No, no, it cannot be; and yet my heart
Will not confess he owes° the malady   *it owns*
10   That doth my life besiege. Farewell, young lords.

---

1. *As ... note:* As prescriptions of greater powers   1. Presumably leaving to take the opposite side in
than were recognized.   the war.
2. Fully aware of what I am doing.   2. After we are well initiated as soldiers.
2.1 Location: The King's palace.

	Whether I live or die, be you the sons	
	Of worthy Frenchmen. Let higher° Italy—	*northern*
	Those bated° that inherit but the fall	*dwindled peoples*
	Of the last monarchy³—see that you come	
15	Not to woo honor but to wed it, when	
	The bravest questant° shrinks. Find what you seek,	*seeker*
	That fame may cry you loud.° I say farewell.	*acclaim you loudly*

FIRST LORD DUMAINE   Health at your bidding serve your majesty.

KING   Those girls of Italy, take heed of them!

20 They say our French lack language to deny
   If they demand.° Beware of being captives⁴   *request*
   Before you serve.°   *(militarily)*

BOTH LORDS DUMAINE   Our hearts receive your warnings.

KING   Farewell. [*to some* LORDS *as he is helped aside*] Come
   hither to me.

FIRST LORD DUMAINE [*to* BERTRAM]   O my sweet lord, that you
   will stay behind us!

PAROLES   'Tis not his fault, the spark.°   *spirited person*

25 SECOND LORD DUMAINE   Oh, 'tis brave° wars!   *splendid*

PAROLES   Most admirable; I have seen those wars.

BERTRAM   I am commanded° here, and kept a coil° with   *(to stay) / fussed over*
   "Too young," and "the next year," and "'tis too early."

PAROLES   An° thy mind stand to't, boy, steal away bravely.   *If*

30 BERTRAM   I shall stay here, the forehorse to a smock,⁵
   Creaking my shoes on the plain masonry,⁶
   Till honor be bought up° and no sword worn   *all acquired (by others)*
   But one to dance with. By heaven, I'll steal away!

FIRST LORD DUMAINE   There's honor in the theft.

PAROLES   Commit it, Count.

35 SECOND LORD DUMAINE   I am your accessory,° and so farewell.   *accomplice*

BERTRAM   I grow° to you, and our parting is a tortured body.   *am deeply attached*

FIRST LORD DUMAINE   Farewell, Captain.

SECOND LORD DUMAINE   Sweet Monsieur Paroles!

PAROLES   Noble heroes, my sword and yours are kin, good
   sparks and lustrous. A word, good mettles.° You shall find   *spirits; sword blades*
40 in the regiment of the Spinii one Captain Spurio, with his
   cicatrice,° an emblem of war, here on his sinister° cheek; it   *scar / left*
   was this very sword entrenched it. Say to him I live, and
   observe his reports° for me.   *note his reply*

FIRST LORD DUMAINE   We shall, noble captain.

45 PAROLES   Mars dote on you for his novices.

                  [*Exeunt the* LORDS DUMAINE.]

   [*to* BERTRAM] What will ye do?

BERTRAM   Stay° the King.   *Await*

PAROLES   Use a more spacious ceremony° to the noble lords;   *expansive courtesy*
   you have restrained yourself within the list° of too cold an   *limit*
50 adieu. Be more expressive to them. For they wear themselves in the cap of the time;⁷ there do muster true gait;⁸
   eat, speak, and move under the influence of the most
   received° star; and, though the devil lead the measure,°   *fashionable / dance*

---

3. Perhaps the Holy Roman Empire, the Medici, or
the papacy.
4. Of your mistresses.
5. Lead horse of a team driven by a woman (figuratively, part of a dancing couple).
6. Level stonework (of the palace floors, in contrast
to the rough battlefield).
7. Are ornaments of fashion.
8. Display grace of movement.

such are to be followed. After them, and take a more dilated°   *extended*
55 farewell.

BERTRAM   And I will do so.

PAROLES   Worthy fellows, and like to prove most sinewy
swordmen.   *Exeunt* [BERTRAM *and* PAROLES].
     Enter LAFEU [*to the* KING, *who is brought forward*].

LAFEU [*kneeling*]   Pardon, my lord, for me and for my tidings.
60 KING   I'll fee[9] thee to stand up.

LAFEU [*standing*]   Then here's a man stands that has brought
   his pardon.
   I would you had kneeled, my lord, to ask me mercy,
   And that at my bidding you could so stand up.

KING   I would I had, so I had broke thy pate°   *head*
   And asked thee mercy for't.

65 LAFEU   Good faith, across![1]
   But my good lord, 'tis thus. Will you be cured
   Of your infirmity?

KING   No.

LAFEU   Oh, will you eat
   No grapes, my royal fox?[2] Yes, but you will:
   My noble grapes, an if° my royal fox   *an if = if*
70   Could reach them. I have seen a medicine°   *physician; remedy*
   That's able to breathe life into a stone,
   Quicken° a rock, and make you dance canary°   *Animate / a lively dance*
   With sprightly fire and motion; whose simple° touch   *mere; medicinal herb*
   Is powerful to araise King Pépin,[3] nay,
75   To give great Charlemagne[4] a pen in 's hand
   And write to her a love line.

KING   What "her" is this?

LAFEU   Why, Doctor She. My lord, there's one arrived,
   If you will see her—now by my faith and honor,
   If seriously I may convey my thoughts
80   In this my light deliverance,° I have spoke   *mode of speaking*
   With one that in her sex, her years, profession,°   *claims of skill*
   Wisdom, and constancy, hath amazed me more
   Than I dare blame my weakness.° Will you see her—   *(as an old man)*
   For that is her demand—and know her business?
   That done, laugh well at me.

85 KING   Now, good Lafeu,
   Bring in the admiration,° that we with thee   *marvel*
   May spend our wonder too, or take off thine
   By wondering how thou took'st° it.   *came by*

LAFEU   Nay, I'll fit° you,   *satisfy*
   And not be all day neither.

90 KING   Thus he his special nothing° ever prologues.   *trifles*

LAFEU [*going to the door*]   Nay, come your ways.°   *come along*
     Enter HELEN.

KING   This haste hath wings indeed.

LAFEU   Nay, come your ways.
   This is his majesty; say your mind to him.
   A traitor[5] you do look like, but such traitors

---

9. Pay (not merely "pardon").
1. A weak jest: in tilting, a blow "across" is a bad hit.
2. In Aesop, a fox pretends not to want a bunch of grapes he cannot reach.
3. Eighth-century French king.
4. Pépin's son, founder of the Holy Roman Empire.
5. Because she avoids the King's gaze.

95 His majesty seldom fears. I am Cressid's uncle,[6]
That dare leave two together. Fare you well.

Exeunt [all but KING *and* HELEN].

KING Now, fair one, does your business follow us?

HELEN Ay, my good lord.
Gerard de Narbonne was my father,
In what he did profess, well found.°   *found to be good*

100 KING   I knew him.

HELEN The rather will I spare my praises towards him;
Knowing him is enough. On 's° bed of death   *On his*
Many receipts he gave me, chiefly one,
Which as the dearest issue[7] of his practice
105 And of his old experience th'only darling,
He bade me store up as a triple° eye,   *third*
Safer than mine own two. More dear I have so,
And hearing your high majesty is touched
With that malignant cause wherein the honor
110 Of my dear father's gift stands chief in power,[8]
I come to tender it and my appliance°   *treatment*
With all bound° humbleness.   *dutiful*

KING   We thank you, maiden,
But may not be so credulous of cure
When our most learnèd doctors leave us, and
115 The congregated college[9] have concluded
That laboring art° can never ransom nature   *medical skill*
From her inaidable estate.° I say we must not   *condition*
So stain our judgment or corrupt our hope
To prostitute° our past-cure malady   *submit*
120 To empirics,[1] or to dissever so
Our great self and our credit[2] to esteem
A senseless help,° when help past sense we deem.   *An unbelievable cure*

HELEN My duty then shall pay me for my pains.
I will no more enforce mine office° on you,   *service*
125 Humbly entreating from your royal thoughts
A modest one[3] to bear me back again.

KING I cannot give thee less to be called grateful.
Thou thought'st to help me, and such thanks I give
As one near death to those that wish him live.
130 But what at full I know, thou know'st no part:°   *not at all*
I knowing all my peril, thou no art.

HELEN What I can do can do no hurt to try,
Since you set up your rest° 'gainst remedy.   *stake everything*
He that of greatest works is finisher
135 Oft does them by the weakest minister.
So Holy Writ in babes hath judgment shown
When judges have been babes.[4] Great floods have flown

---

6. Pandarus, the go-between for Troilus and Cressida and archetypal pimp.
7. Best product; favorite child.
8. *malignant . . . power:* disease for which my father's honored gift is most effective.
9. Assembled College of Physicians.
1. Physicians whose methods were based on experience rather than on medical theory. In early modern Europe, "theoretical" practitioners, like the members of the French College of Physicians, often considered

their "empirical" colleagues mere quacks; the "empirics" usually hailed from lower social classes and had less formal education.
2. *to dissever . . . credit:* to open such a gap between my royal station and my gullibility.
3. A favorable thought appropriate to a woman and a subject.
4. *So . . . babes:* "Thou hast hid these things from the wise and men of understanding, and hast opened them unto babes" (Matthew 11:25).

From simple sources, and great seas have dried
When miracles have by the greatest been denied.
140   Oft expectation fails, and most oft there
Where most it promises; and oft it hits°   *succeeds*
Where hope is coldest and despair most fits.
  KING   I must not hear thee. Fare thee well, kind maid;
Thy pains not used must by thyself be paid.
145   Proffers not took reap thanks° for their reward.   *only thanks*
  HELEN   Inspired merit so by breath is barred.[5]
It is not so with Him that all things knows
As 'tis with us that square our guess by shows.[6]
But most it is presumption in us when
150   The help of heaven we count the act of men.
Dear sir, to my endeavors give consent;
Of heaven, not me, make an experiment.
I am not an impostor that proclaim
Myself against the level of mine aim,[7]
155   But know I think, and think I know most sure,
My art is not past° power, nor you past cure.   *without*
  KING   Art thou so confident? Within what space
Hop'st thou my cure?
  HELEN   The greatest grace lending grace,
Ere twice the horses of the sun shall bring
160   Their fiery torcher his diurnal ring;°   *daily round*
Ere twice in murk and occidental damp
Moist Hesperus° hath quenched her sleepy lamp,   *the evening star*
Or four-and-twenty times the pilot's glass°   *hourglass*
Hath told the thievish minutes, how they pass,
165   What is infirm from your sound parts shall fly;
Health shall live free and sickness freely die.
  KING   Upon thy certainty and confidence
What dar'st thou venture?°   *risk*
  HELEN   Tax° of impudence;   *Accusation*
A strumpet's boldness; a divulgèd shame
170   Traduced by odious ballads; my maiden's name
Seared.[8] Otherwise, no worse of worst, extended[9]
With vilest torture let my life be ended.
  KING   Methinks in thee some blessèd spirit doth speak
His powerful sound within an organ weak,
175   And what impossibility would slay
In common sense, sense saves another way.[1]
Thy life is dear, for all that life can rate
Worth name of life in thee hath estimate:°   *is present*
Youth, beauty, wisdom, courage, all
180   That happiness and prime[2] can happy call.
Thou this to hazard needs must intimate[3]
Skill infinite or monstrous desperate.
Sweet practicer,° thy physic I will try   *practitioner; schemer*
That ministers thine own death if I die.

---

5. Divinely inspired virtue is thus denied by human speech.
6. Who base our conjectures on appearances.
7. *proclaim . . . aim*: boast in advance of the accuracy of my aim; declare myself to be different from what I am.

8. Branded (like a criminal).
9. Prolonged; stretched on the rack.
1. *sense . . . way*: makes sense in another, uncommon way.
2. That good fortune and the springtime of life.
3. For you to risk this must suggest.

185 HELEN   If I break time or flinch in property[4]
  Of what I spoke, unpitied let me die,
  And well deserved. Not helping, death's my fee,
  But if I help, what do you promise me?
KING   Make thy demand.
HELEN   But will you make it even?°   *satisfy it*
190 KING   Ay, by my scepter and my hopes of heaven.
HELEN   Then shalt thou give me with thy kingly hand
  What husband in thy power I will command.
  Exempted be from me the arrogance
  To choose from forth the royal blood of France,
195 My low and humble name to propagate
  With any branch or image of thy state;°   *royal place*
  But such a one, thy vassal, whom I know
  Is free for me to ask, thee to bestow.
KING   Here is my hand. The premises observed,°   *conditions fulfilled*
200 Thy will by my performance shall be served.
  So make the choice of thy own time, for I,
  Thy resolvèd patient, on thee still° rely.   *always*
  More should I question thee, and more I must,
  Though more to know could not be more to trust—
205 From whence thou cam'st? how tended on?°—but rest   *attended*
  Unquestioned[5] welcome and undoubted blest.
  [*He calls.*] Give me some help here, ho! —If thou proceed
  As high as word, my deed shall match thy deed.
                              Flourish. Exeunt.

2.2

        Enter COUNTESS *and* CLOWN.
COUNTESS   Come on, sir, I shall now put you to the height of
  your breeding.[1]
CLOWN   I will show myself highly fed and lowly taught.[2] I
  know my business is but to the court.
5 COUNTESS   To the court! Why, what place make you special,
  when you put off° that with such contempt? "But to the   *dismiss*
  court"!
CLOWN   Truly, madam, if God have lent a man any manners,
  he may easily put it off° at court. He that cannot make a leg,   *lose it; take it off*
10 put off 's cap, kiss his hand, and say nothing, has neither
  leg,° hands, lip, nor cap; and indeed such a fellow, to say   *bow*
  precisely, were not for the court. But for me, I have an
  answer will serve all men.
COUNTESS   Marry, that's a bountiful answer that fits all
15 questions.
CLOWN   It is like a barber's chair that fits all buttocks: the pin° *pointed*
  buttock, the quatch°-buttock, the brawn buttock, or any   *fat*
  buttock.
COUNTESS   Will your answer serve fit to all questions?
20 CLOWN   As fit as ten groats is for the hand of an attorney, as
  your French crown[3] for your taffeta punk,° as Tib's rush[4]   *prostitute*

---

4. If I fail to meet the deadline or fall short in the
particulars.
5. Not having been asked; unquestionably.
2.2 Location: Bertram's palace.
1. Make you display your best manners.
2. Spoiled children were called "better fed than

taught."
3. Coin; bald head (from syphilis, the "French
disease").
4. Reed twisted into a ring for use in folk marriage,
with sexual innuendo.

for Tom's forefinger, as a pancake[5] for Shrove Tuesday, a
morris° for May Day, as the nail to his hole, the cuckold to   *morris dance*
his horn, as a scolding quean° to a wrangling knave, as the   *whore*
25   nun's lip to the friar's mouth—nay, as the pudding° to his   *sausage*
skin.
COUNTESS   Have you, I say, an answer of such fitness for all
questions?
CLOWN   From below your duke to beneath your constable, it
30   will fit any question.
COUNTESS   It must be an answer of most monstrous size that
must fit all demands.
CLOWN   But a trifle neither,° in good faith, if the learned   *No, just a trifle*
should speak truth of it. Here it is, and all that belongs to't.
35   Ask me if I am a courtier: it shall do you no harm to learn.
COUNTESS   To be young again if we could! I will be a fool in
question, hoping to be the wiser by your answer. I pray you,
sir, are you a courtier?
CLOWN   O Lord, sir![6] —There's a simple putting off. More,
40   more, a hundred of them.
COUNTESS   Sir, I am a poor friend of yours that loves you.
CLOWN   O Lord, sir! —Thick,° thick, spare not me.   *Quick*
COUNTESS   I think, sir, you can eat none of this homely° meat.   *plain*
CLOWN   O Lord, sir. —Nay, put me to't, I warrant you.
45   COUNTESS   You were lately whipped, sir, as I think.
CLOWN   O Lord, sir. —Spare not me.
COUNTESS   Do you cry "O Lord, sir" at your whipping, and
"Spare not me"? Indeed your "O Lord, sir" is very sequent[7]
to your whipping; you would answer very well[8] to a whipping
50   if you were but bound to't.[9]
CLOWN   I ne'er had worse luck in my life in my "O Lord, sir." I
see things may serve long but not serve ever.
COUNTESS   I play the noble housewife° with the time, to   *good steward (ironic)*
entertain it so merrily with a fool.
55   CLOWN   O Lord, sir! Why, there't serves well again.
COUNTESS   An end, sir. To your business.
         [*She hands him a letter.*]
                                      Give Helen this,
And urge her to a present° answer back.   *immediate*
Commend me to my kinsmen and my son.
This is not much.
60   CLOWN   Not much commendation to them.
COUNTESS   Not much employment for you. You understand me?
CLOWN   Most fruitfully. I am there before my legs.
COUNTESS   Haste you again.°   *Exeunt.*   *back again*

                            2.3
         Enter Count [BERTRAM], LAFEU [*holding a broadside*],°   *paper proclamation*
         and PAROLES.
LAFEU   They say miracles are past, and we have our philosophical persons to make modern and familiar things supernatural

---

5. Traditionally eaten on Shrove Tuesday, the day
before the beginning of Lent.
6. A voguish catchphrase that evades an answer by
appearing to wonder at the question. *putting off:*
evasion.

7. Follows naturally upon (as a plea for mercy).
8. Reply cleverly to; be a fitting recipient of.
9. Required to answer; tied to a whipping post.
2.3 Location: The King's palace.

and causeless.[1] Hence is it that we make trifles of terrors,
ensconcing ourselves into° seeming knowledge when we   *sheltering ourselves with*
5   should submit ourselves to an unknown fear.°   *awe of the unknown*
PAROLES   Why, 'tis the rarest argument° of wonder that hath   *best instance*
shot out in our latter° times.   *recent*
BERTRAM   And so 'tis.
LAFEU   To be relinquished of the artists[2]—
10   PAROLES   So I say, both of Galen and Paracelsus[3]—
LAFEU   Of all the learned and authentic fellows[4]—
PAROLES   Right, so I say.
LAFEU   That gave him out incurable—
PAROLES   Why, there 'tis! So say I too.
15   LAFEU   Not to be helped—
PAROLES   Right, as 'twere a man assured of a—
LAFEU   Uncertain life and sure death.
PAROLES   Just.° You say well. So would I have said.   *Exactly*
LAFEU   I may truly say it is a novelty to the world.
20   PAROLES   It is indeed. If you will have it in showing,° you shall   *demonstrated*
read it in what-do-ye-call there.
LAFEU   [*reading from the broadside*]   "A showing of a heavenly
effect in an earthly actor."
PAROLES   That's it. I would have said the very same.
25   LAFEU   Why, your dolphin[5] is not lustier.° For me, I speak in   *more sportive*
respect°—   *respectfully*
PAROLES   Nay, 'tis strange, 'tis very strange, that is the brief°   *short*
and the tedious° of it, and he's of a most facinorous° spirit   *long / wicked*
that will not acknowledge it to be the—
30   LAFEU   Very hand of heaven.
PAROLES   Ay, so I say.
LAFEU   In a most weak—
PAROLES   And debile minister,° great power, great transcen-   *feeble agent*
dence, which should indeed give us a further use to be made
35   than alone the recovery of the King, as to be—
LAFEU   Generally° thankful.   *Universally*
Enter KING, HELEN, *and* ATTENDANTS.
PAROLES   I would have said it; you say well. Here comes the
King.
LAFEU   Lustig,° as the Dutchman says. I'll like a maid the bet-   *Frolicsome*
40   ter whilst I have a tooth in my head.[6] Why, he's able to lead
her a coranto.°   *running dance*
PAROLES   Mort du vinaigre,[7] is not this Helen?
LAFEU   Fore God, I think so.
KING   Go, call before me all the lords in court.
[*Exit an* ATTENDANT.]
45   Sit, my preserver, by thy patient's side,
And with this healthful hand whose banished sense°   *sense of feeling*
Thou hast repealed,° a second time receive   *restored*
The confirmation of my promised gift,
Which but attends° thy naming.   *awaits*

1. To make supernatural things, without apparent
cause, seem commonplace and easily explained.
2. Abandoned by the scholars.
3. Galen was a second-century Greek physician, the
traditional medical authority; Paracelsus was a
sixteenth-century Swiss physician who tried to reform
Galen's teachings.

4. Accredited members of the College of Physicians.
5. Punning on "dauphin," heir to the French throne.
6. *whilst . . . head:* so long as I have a taste for pleasure ("sweet tooth"); until I've degenerated into complete senility.
7. Death of the vinegar—a pseudo-French oath.

Enter four LORDS.

50   Fair maid, send forth thine eye. This youthful parcel°   *group*
   Of noble bachelors stand at my bestowing,[8]
   O'er whom both sovereign power and father's voice
   I have to use. Thy frank election° make;   *free choice*
   Thou hast power to choose, and they none to forsake.
55 HELEN   To each of you, one fair and virtuous mistress
   Fall[9] when love please; marry, to each but one.
   LAFEU   I'd give bay Curtal and his furniture[1]
   My mouth no more were broken[2] than these boys'
   And writ° as little beard.   *laid claim to*
   KING   Peruse them well:
60   Not one of those but had a noble father.
   She addresses her to a LORD.[3]
   HELEN   Gentlemen,
   Heaven hath through me restored the King to health.
   ALL LORDS   We understand it, and thank heaven for you.
   HELEN   I am a simple maid, and therein wealthiest
65   That I protest I simply am a maid.
   —Please it your majesty, I have done already.
   The blushes in my cheeks thus whisper me,
   "We blush that thou shouldst choose but, be° refused,   *if you are*
   Let the white death sit on thy cheek for ever,
   We'll ne'er come there again."
70 KING   Make choice and see;
   Who shuns thy love shuns all his love in me.
   HELEN   Now Dian from thy altar do I fly,
   And to imperial Love, that god most high,
   Do my sighs stream. [*to* FIRST LORD] Sir, will you hear my suit?
   FIRST LORD   And grant it.
75 HELEN   Thanks, sir; all the rest is mute.°   *I will say no more*
   LAFEU [*aside*]   I had rather be in this choice than throw
      ambsace[4] for my life.
   HELEN [*to* SECOND LORD]   The honor, sir, that flames in your
      fair eyes,[5]
   Before I speak too threat'ningly replies.
80   Love make your fortunes twenty times above
   Her that so wishes,° and her humble love.   *makes this wish*
   SECOND LORD   No better, if you please.
   HELEN   My wish receive,
   Which great love grant; and so I take my leave.
   LAFEU [*aside*]   Do all they deny her?[6] An they were sons of
85   mine, I'd have them whipped, or I would send them to th'
   Turk to make eunuchs of.
   HELEN [*to* THIRD LORD]   Be not afraid that I your hand should take;
   I'll never do you wrong for your own sake.
   Blessing upon your vows,° and in your bed   *marriage vows*
90   Find fairer fortune if you ever wed.

---

8. Are in my power to bestow (because they are his wards).
9. Befall, with the suggestion of a sexual "fall."
1. I'd give my dock-tailed bay horse and his trappings.
2. Contained broken teeth; of a boy's voice, "broken" at puberty; of a horse, "broken" to the bit.
3. TEXTUAL COMMENT In the Folio text this stage direction is possibly misplaced. See Digital Edition

TC 5.
4. Two aces (the lowest throw in dice); a joking understatement.
5. The pride of rank that shows in your look.
6. Either Lafeu, standing apart, misunderstands what is happening, or (less probably) the Lords' polite replies are belied by their evident relief when Helen rejects them.

LAFEU [*aside*]   These boys are boys of ice, they'll none have
    her. Sure they are bastards to the English; the French ne'er
    got° 'em.   *begot*

HELEN [*to* FOURTH LORD]   You are too young, too happy, and
    too good
95   To make yourself a son out of my blood.

FOURTH LORD   Fair one, I think not so.

LAFEU [*aside*]   There's one grape° yet! I am sure thy father   *fruit of a noble stock*
    drunk wine.[7] But if thou be'st not an ass, I am a youth of
    fourteen: I have known° thee already.   *found out*

100   HELEN [*to* BERTRAM]   I dare not say I take you, but I give
    Me and my service, ever whilst I live,
    Into your guiding power. [*to the* KING] This is the man.

KING   Why, then, young Bertram, take her; she's thy wife.

BERTRAM   My wife, my liege? I shall beseech your highness:
105   In such a business give me leave to use
    The help of mine own eyes.

KING   Know'st thou not, Bertram,
    What she has done for me?

BERTRAM   Yes, my good lord,
    But never hope° to know why I should marry her.   *expect*

KING   Thou know'st she has raised me from my sickly bed.

110   BERTRAM   But follows it, my lord, to bring me down
    Must answer for your raising? I know her well:
    She had her breeding° at my father's charge.   *upbringing*
    A poor physician's daughter my wife? Disdain
    Rather corrupt° me ever!   *ruin*

115   KING   'Tis only title° thou disdain'st in her, the which   *rank*
    I can build up. Strange is it that our bloods
    Of color, weight, and heat, poured all together,
    Would quite confound distinction,[8] yet stands off°   *is separated*
    In differences so mighty. If she be
120   All that is virtuous, save what thou dislik'st—
    "A poor physician's daughter"—thou dislik'st
    Of virtue for the name.° But do not so: *(lack of) a title*
    From lowest place when virtuous things proceed
    The place is dignified by th' doer's deed.
125   Where great additions swell 's° and virtue none,   *titles swell us up*
    It is a dropsied[9] honor. Good alone°   *in itself*
    Is good without a name. Vileness is so;
    The property° by what it is should go,   *quality*
    Not by the title. She is young, wise, fair;
130   In these to nature she's immediate heir,
    And these breed honor. That is honor's scorn
    Which challenges° itself as honor's born   *makes claims for*
    And is not like the sire. Honors thrive
    When rather from our acts we them derive
135   Than our foregoers. The mere word's a slave
    Debauched° on every tomb, on every grave   *Debased*
    A lying trophy,° and as oft is dumb   *memorial*
    Where dust and damned° oblivion is the tomb   *stopped-up*

---

7. Was red-blooded (wine was supposed to turn
directly into blood).

8. Confuse the effort to distinguish.

9. Unhealthily swollen.

Of honored bones indeed. What should be said?
140 If thou canst like this creature as a maid,
I can create the rest. Virtue and she
Is her own dower;[1] honor and wealth from me.

BERTRAM I cannot love her, nor will strive° to do't. *attempt*

KING Thou wrong'st thyself if thou shouldst strive to choose.

145 HELEN That you are well restored, my lord, I'm glad.
Let the rest go.

KING My honor's at the stake, which to defeat
I must produce my power. Here, take her hand,
Proud, scornful boy, unworthy this good gift,
150 That dost in vile misprision° shackle up *wrongful disdain*
My love and her desert; that canst not dream
We, poising us in her defective scale,
Shall weigh thee to the beam;[2] that wilt not know
It is in us° to plant thine honor where *in our power*
155 We please to have it grow. Check° thy contempt; *Restrain*
Obey our will, which travails in° thy good; *labors for*
Believe not thy disdain, but presently
Do thine own fortunes that obedient right
Which both thy duty owes and our power claims,
160 Or I will throw thee from my care forever
Into the staggers[3] and the careless lapse° *fall; ruin*
Of youth and ignorance, both my revenge and hate
Loosing upon thee in the name of justice,
Without all terms of° pity. Speak! Thine answer! *any concessions to*
165 BERTRAM Pardon, my gracious lord, for I submit
My fancy° to your eyes. When I consider *perceptions; affection*
What great creation[4] and what dole° of honor *portion*
Flies where you bid it, I find that she which late
Was in my nobler thoughts most base is now
170 The praisèd of the King, who, so ennobled,
Is as 'twere born so.

KING   Take her by the hand
And tell her she is thine, to whom I promise
A counterpoise, if not to thy estate,
A balance more replete.[5]

BERTRAM   I take her hand.

175 KING Good fortune and the favor of the King
Smile upon this contract, whose ceremony
Shall seem expedient on the now-born brief[6]
And be performed tonight; the solemn feast
Shall more attend upon the coming space,
180 Expecting absent friends.[7] As thou lov'st her,
Thy love's to me religious:° else, does err. *properly devoted*

  Exeunt [all but] PAROLES *and* LAFEU[, *who] stay
  behind, commenting of this wedding.*

LAFEU Do you hear, monsieur? A word with you.

---

1. *Virtue . . . dower:* Her own marriage gift is virtue and herself.
2. *We . . . beam:* Adding my weight to her deficient side of the balance shall raise your (lighter) side. (The King uses the royal plural.)
3. Confusion (literally, a horse disease).

4. Creating of greatness.
5. *A counterpoise . . . replete:* A dowry equal to, if not greater than, your own estate.
6. Shall expedite this newly made decree.
7. *the solemn . . . friends:* The wedding reception will be postponed until relatives and friends can arrive.

PAROLES   Your pleasure, sir.

LAFEU   Your lord and master did well to make his recantation.

185   PAROLES   Recantation? My lord? My master?

LAFEU   Ay. Is it not a language I speak?

PAROLES   A most harsh one, and not to be understood without
bloody succeeding.° My master?   consequences

LAFEU   Are you companion to the Count Roussillon?

190   PAROLES   To any count; to all counts; to what is man.°   whatever is manly

LAFEU   To what is count's man;° count's master is of another   servant
style.

PAROLES   You are too old, sir; let it satisfy you,[8] you are too old!

LAFEU   I must tell thee, sirrah, I write man,[9] to which title

195   age cannot bring thee.

PAROLES   What I dare too well do, I dare not do.[1]

LAFEU   I did think thee, for two ordinaries,° to be a pretty   meals
wise fellow; thou didst make tolerable vent° of thy travel—it   talk passably
might pass. Yet the scarves and the bannerets[2] about thee

200   did manifoldly dissuade me from believing thee a vessel of
too great a burden.° I have now found thee;[3] when I lose   tonnage
thee again, I care not. Yet art thou good for nothing but taking up,[4] and that thou'rt scarce worth.

PAROLES   Hadst thou not the privilege of antiquity[5] upon thee—

205   LAFEU   Do not plunge thyself too far in anger, lest thou hasten thy trial; which if, lord have mercy on thee for a hen! So,
my good window of lattice,[6] fare thee well; thy casement I
need not open, for I look through thee. Give me thy hand.

PAROLES   My lord, you give me most egregious indignity.

210   LAFEU   Ay, with all my heart, and thou art worthy of it.

PAROLES   I have not, my lord, deserved it.

LAFEU   Yes, good faith, ev'ry dram° of it, and I will not bate°   one-eighth of
thee a scruple.°   an ounce / remit
                                                                   one-third of a dram
PAROLES   Well, I shall be wiser.

215   LAFEU   E'en as soon as thou canst, for thou hast to pull at a
smack o'th' contrary.[7] If ever thou be'st bound in thy scarf
and beaten, thou shall find what it is to be proud of thy
bondage. I have a desire to hold° my acquaintance with   maintain
thee, or rather my knowledge, that I may say in the default,°   in the event

220   "He is a man I know."

PAROLES   My lord, you do me most insupportable vexation.

LAFEU   I would it were hell-pains for thy sake, and my poor
doing[8] eternal. For doing[9] I am past—as I will by thee, in
what motion age will give me leave.   *Exit.*

225   PAROLES   Well, thou hast a son shall take this disgrace off
me. Scurvy, old, filthy, scurvy lord! Well, I must be patient;
there is no fettering of authority. I'll beat him, by my life, if
I can meet him with any convenience, an° he were double   if
and double a lord. I'll have no more pity of his age than I

8. Don't force me to avenge your insult.
9. I claim myself to be a man.
1. What I have the courage for (that is, fighting), your age prevents me from doing.
2. Streamers (which remind Lafeu of a ship's pennants).
3. Discovered what you are.
4. Rebuking; arresting; drafting as a soldier.

5. Exemption (from combat) because of age.
6. Paroles is easily seen through despite his affectation; his fancy "latticework" of scarves suggests a lattice window.
7. *pull . . . contrary:* drink a quantity of the opposite quality.
8. My poor attempt to vex you.
9. Activity (with sexual suggestion).

230 would have of—I'll beat him, an if I could but meet him
again!
    Enter LAFEU.
LAFEU Sirrah, your lord and master's married; there's news
for you! You have a new mistress.
PAROLES I most unfainedly beseech your lordship to make
235 some reservation of your wrongs.° He is my good lord; whom   *restrain your abuse*
I serve above is my master.
LAFEU Who? God?
PAROLES Ay, sir.
LAFEU The devil it is that's thy master. Why dost thou garter
240 up[1] thy arms o'this fashion? Dost make hose of thy sleeves?
Do other servants so? Thou wert best set thy lower part
where thy nose stands. By mine honor, if I were but two
hours younger, I'd beat thee. Methink'st thou art a general
offense,° and every man should beat thee. I think thou wast   *public nuisance*
245 created for men to breathe° themselves upon thee.   *exercise*
PAROLES This is hard and undeserved measure, my lord.
LAFEU Go to, sir: you were beaten in Italy for picking a kernel
out of a pomegranate.[2] You are a vagabond and no true traveler. You are more saucy with lords and honorable person-
250 ages than the commission° of your birth and virtue gives you   *warrant*
heraldry.° You are not worth another word, else I'd call you   *entitles you*
knave. I leave you.   *Exit.*
    Enter [BERTRAM,] *Count Roussillon.*
PAROLES Good, very good. It is so, then. Good, very good. Let
it be concealed awhile.
255 BERTRAM Undone and forfeited to cares forever!
PAROLES What's the matter, sweet heart?
BERTRAM Although before the solemn priest I have sworn,
I will not bed her.
PAROLES   What? What, sweet heart?
BERTRAM O my Paroles, they have married me!
260 I'll to the Tuscan wars and never bed her.
PAROLES France is a dog-hole, and it no more merits
The tread of a man's foot. To th' wars!
BERTRAM There's letters from my mother: what th'import is,
I know not yet.
PAROLES   Ay, that would be known.
265 To th' wars, my boy, to th' wars!
He wears his honor in a box unseen°   *(with sexual innuendo)*
That hugs his kicky-wicky° here at home,   *darling*
Spending his manly marrow in her arms
Which should sustain the bound and high curvet°   *leap*
270 Of Mars's fiery steed. To other regions!
France is a stable, we that dwell in't jades;[3]
Therefore, to th' war.
BERTRAM It shall be so. I'll send her to my house;
Acquaint my mother with my hate to her
275 And wherefore I am fled; write to the King

---

1. Tie up (commenting again on Paroles' outfit).
2. *for picking . . . pomegranate:* on the slightest
pretext.
3. Worthless horses; sluts. Paroles considers staying
in France effeminating.

That which I durst not speak. His present gift[4]
Shall furnish me to° those Italian fields   *equip me for*
Where noble fellows strike. Wars is no strife
To° the dark house and the detested wife.   *Compared to*
280   PAROLES   Will this capriccio° hold in thee, art sure?   *caprice*
BERTRAM   Go with me to my chamber and advise me.
I'll send her straight away. Tomorrow
I'll to the wars, she to her single sorrow.
PAROLES   Why, these balls bound;[5] there's noise in it. 'Tis hard:
285   A young man married is a man that's marred.
Therefore away and leave her bravely. Go.
The King has done you wrong, but hush 'tis so.°   *Exeunt.*   *but don't say so*

2.4
Enter HELEN[, *with a letter,*] *and* CLOWN.

HELEN   My mother greets me kindly. Is she well?
CLOWN   She is not well,[1] but yet she has her health. She's very
merry, but yet she is not well. But, thanks be given, she's very
well and wants° nothing i'th' world. But yet she is not well.   *lacks*
5   HELEN   If she be very well, what does she ail that she's not
very well?
CLOWN   Truly, she's very well indeed, but for two things.
HELEN   What two things?
CLOWN   One, that she's not in heaven, whither God send her
10   quickly; the other, that she's in earth, from whence God
send her quickly.
Enter PAROLES.
PAROLES   Bless you, my fortunate lady.
HELEN   I hope, sir, I have your good will to have mine own
good fortunes.
15   PAROLES   You had my prayers to lead them° on, and to keep   *(your good fortunes)*
them on have them still. —O my knave, how does my old
lady?
CLOWN   So that you had her wrinkles and I her money, I
would she did[2] as you say.
20   PAROLES   Why, I say nothing.
CLOWN   Marry, you are the wiser man, for many a man's°   *servant's*
tongue shakes out[3] his master's undoing. To say nothing, to
do nothing, to know nothing, and to have nothing, is to be
a great part of your title,[4] which is within a very little of
25   nothing.
PAROLES   Away, thou'rt a knave.
CLOWN   You should have said, sir, "Before[5] a knave, thou'rt a
knave"; that's "before me[6] thou'rt a knave." This had been
truth, sir.
30   PAROLES   Go to, thou art a witty fool. I have found° thee.   *seen through*
CLOWN   Did you find me in yourself, sir, or were you taught to
find me?
PAROLES   In[7] myself.

---

4. Wedding present just bestowed.
5. Are bouncing now (from tennis); that is, that's how it should be done.
2.4 Location: Scene continues.
1. The dead were said to be well, because in heaven.
2. Perhaps playing on "died."
3. Inadvertently tumbles out.

4. Status; playing on "tittle," "tiny amount."
5. Even in comparison with; in the presence of.
6. An expression like "Upon my soul"; the Clown insinuates that Paroles is another knave.
7. By (reinterpreted in lines 34–35 by the Clown). This speech is not in F, but clearly some such reply should go here.

CLOWN   The search, sir, was profitable, and much fool may
35   you find in you, even to the world's pleasure and the increase
of laughter.
PAROLES   A good knave, i'faith, and well fed.°   *"better fed than taught"*
—Madam, my lord will go away tonight;
A very serious business calls on him.
40   The great prerogative and rite of love,
Which as your due time claims, he does acknowledge,
But puts it off to a compelled restraint,
Whose want, and whose delay, is strewed with sweets
Which they distill now in the curbèd time,[8]
45   To make the coming hour o'erflow with joy
And pleasure drown the brim.
HELEN   What's his will else?
PAROLES   That you will take your instant leave o'th' King
And make° this haste as your own good proceeding,   *represent*
Strengthened with what apology you think
May make it probable need.[9]
50   HELEN   What more commands he?
PAROLES   That having this obtained, you presently
Attend° his further pleasure.°   *Await / command*
HELEN   In everything I wait upon his will.
PAROLES   I shall report it so.   *Exit* PAROLES.
55   HELEN   I pray you come, sirrah.   *Exeunt.*

<h2 style="text-align:center">2.5</h2>

Enter LAFEU *and* BERTRAM.
LAFEU   But I hope your lordship thinks not him a soldier.
BERTRAM   Yes, my lord, and of very valiant approof.°   *proven value*
LAFEU   You have it from his own deliverance.°   *report*
BERTRAM   And by other warranted testimony.
5   LAFEU   Then my dial° goes not true. I took this lark for a   *clock*
bunting.[1]
BERTRAM   I do assure you, my lord, he is very great in knowl-
edge and accordingly° valiant.   *correspondingly*
LAFEU   I have, then, sinned against his experience and trans-
10   gressed against his valor, and my state that way is danger-
ous,[2] since I cannot yet find in my heart to repent. Here he
comes. I pray you make us friends: I will pursue the amity.
Enter PAROLES.
PAROLES [*to* BERTRAM]   These things shall be done, sir.
LAFEU   Pray you, sir, who's his tailor?[3]
15   PAROLES   Sir?
LAFEU   Oh, I know him well.[4] Ay, "Sir," he. Sir's a good work-
man, a very good tailor.
BERTRAM [*aside to* PAROLES]   Is she gone to the King?
PAROLES [*aside to* BERTRAM]   She is.
20   BERTRAM [*aside to* PAROLES]   Will she away tonight?
PAROLES [*aside to* BERTRAM]   As you'll have her.

---

8. *whose delay . . . time:* the delay of which multiplies   like a lark but does not sing).
its sweetness, as distillation intensifies perfumes.   2. In that respect risks damnation.
9. May make the need for haste probable.   3. Mocking Paroles' clothes.
2.5 Location: Scene continues.   4. Lafeu pretends "Sir" is the tailor's name.
1. I underestimated him (since the bunting looks

BERTRAM [*aside to* PAROLES] I have writ my letters, casketed
    my treasure,
    Given order for our horses, and tonight,
    When I should take possession of the bride,
25   End ere I do begin.
LAFEU [*aside*] A good traveler is something° at the latter end   *an asset*
    of a dinner,[5] but one that lies three thirds° and uses a   *i.e., in all things*
    known truth to pass a thousand nothings with should be
    once heard and thrice beaten. —God save you, captain.
30 BERTRAM [*to* PAROLES] Is there any unkindness between my
    lord and you, monsieur?
PAROLES I know not how I have deserved to run into my
    lord's displeasure.
LAFEU You have made shift° to run into't, boots and spurs and   *arranged*
35   all. Like him that leaped into the custard[6] and out of it, you'll
    run again rather than suffer question for your residence.[7]
BERTRAM It may be you have mistaken him, my lord.
LAFEU And shall do so ever, though I took him at 's prayers.
    Fare you well, my lord, and believe this of me: there can be
40   no kernel in this light nut. The soul of this man is his
    clothes; trust him not in matter of heavy° consequence. I   *serious*
    have kept of them tame[8] and know their natures. —Fare-
    well, monsieur, I have spoken better of you than you have
    or will[9] to deserve at my hand, but we must do good against
45   evil.   [*Exit.*]
PAROLES An idle lord, I swear.
BERTRAM I think not so.
PAROLES Why, do you not know him?
BERTRAM Yes, I do know him well, and common speech
    Gives him a worthy pass.°
          Enter HELEN.
50   Here comes my clog.[1]   *report*
HELEN I have, sir, as I was commanded from you,
    Spoke with the King and have procured his leave
    For present parting. Only he desires
    Some private speech with you.
BERTRAM   I shall obey his will.
55   You must not marvel, Helen, at my course,
    Which holds not color° with the time nor does   *is not in keeping*
    The ministration and required office
    On my particular.[2] Prepared I was not
    For such a business; therefore am I found
60   So much unsettled. This drives me to entreat you
    That presently you take your way for home
    And rather muse° than ask why I entreat you,   *wonder*
    For my respects° are better than they seem,   *reasons*
    And my appointments° have in them a need   *purposes*
65   Greater than shows itself at the first view
    To you that know them not. [*He gives her a letter.*] This
        to my mother;
    'Twill be two days ere I shall see you. So

---

5. When stories are welcome.
6. At the annual Lord Mayor's feast in London, a
jester leaped into an enormous custard pie.
7. Rather than explain how you got there.
8. These kinds of tame animals.

9. The intelligence or intention.
1. Weighty fetter, "ball and chain."
2. *The ministration . . . particular:* The particular
duty incumbent on me (as a husband).

I leave you to your wisdom.

HELEN   Sir, I can nothing say
But that I am your most obedient servant—

BERTRAM   Come, come, no more of that.

70 HELEN   And ever shall
With true observance° seek to eke out that   *dutiful service*
Wherein toward me my homely stars° have failed   *humble birth*
To equal my great fortune.

BERTRAM   Let that go.
My haste is very great. Farewell. Hie° home.   *Hurry*

HELEN   Pray, sir, your pardon.

75 BERTRAM   Well, what would you say?

HELEN   I am not worthy of the wealth I owe,°   *own*
Nor dare I say 'tis mine—and yet it is—
But like a timorous thief most fain° would steal   *gladly*
What law does vouch mine own.

BERTRAM   What would you have?

80 HELEN   Something and scarce so much; nothing, indeed;
I would not tell you what I would, my lord.
Faith, yes:
Strangers and foes do sunder° and not kiss.[3]   *separate*

BERTRAM   I pray you, stay° not, but in haste to horse.   *delay*

85 HELEN   I shall not break your bidding, good my lord.
Where are my other men? [*to* PAROLES] Monsieur, farewell.

                                      Exit.

BERTRAM   Go thou toward home, where I will never come
Whilst I can shake my sword or hear the drum.
Away, and for our flight.

PAROLES   Bravely! *Coraggio!*°   [*Exeunt.*]   *Courage (Italian)*

3.1

Flourish. Enter the DUKE *of Florence, the two
Frenchmen* [*the* LORDS DUMAINE], *with a troop of*
SOLDIERS.

DUKE   So that from point to point now have you heard
The fundamental reasons of this war,
Whose great decision° hath much blood let forth   *process of resolution*
And more thirsts after.

FIRST LORD DUMAINE   Holy seems the quarrel
5 Upon your grace's part; black and fearful
On the opposer.

DUKE   Therefore we marvel much our cousin France
Would in so just a business shut his bosom
Against our borrowing prayers.°   *entreaties for aid*

SECOND LORD DUMAINE   Good my lord,
10 The reasons of our state I cannot yield,
But° like a common and an outward man,°   *Except / an outsider*
That the great figure° of a council frames   *image*
By self-unable motion,° therefore dare not   *inadequate guess*
Say what I think of it, since I have found
15 Myself in my incertain grounds° to fail   *conjectures*
As often as I guessed.

---

3. PERFORMANCE COMMENT The text does not indicate whether Helen and Bertram eventually kiss;
whether and how they do has been used in different
performances to forecast various possibilities for
their relationship. For a discussion of some of the
options, see Digital Edition PC 2.
3.1 Location: Florence.

DUKE   Be it his pleasure.

FIRST LORD DUMAINE   But I am sure the younger of our nature,
That surfeit on° their ease, will day by day   *have had too much of*
Come here for physic.[1]

DUKE   Welcome shall they be,
20   And all the honors that can fly° from us   *proceed*
Shall on them settle. You know your places well;
When better fall,[2] for your avails they fell.
Tomorrow to the field.   *Flourish. [Exeunt.]*

3.2

Enter COUNTESS *and* CLOWN[, *with a letter*].

COUNTESS   It hath happened all as I would have had it, save
that he comes not along with her.

CLOWN   By my troth, I take my young lord to be a very melancholy man.

5   COUNTESS   By what observance, I pray you?

CLOWN   Why, he will look upon his boot and sing; mend° the   *adjust*
ruff° and sing; ask questions and sing; pick his teeth and   *boot's cuff*
sing. I know a man that had this trick of melancholy sold a
goodly manor for a song.

10   COUNTESS   Let me see what he writes and when he means to
come.
          [*She takes the letter and reads to herself.*]

CLOWN   I have no mind to Isbel since I was at court. Our old
lings[1] and our Isbels o'th' country are nothing like your old
ling and your Isbels o'th' court. The brains of my Cupid's
15   knocked out, and I begin to love as an old man loves money,
with no stomach.°   *appetite*

COUNTESS   What have we here?

CLOWN   E'en that you have there.   *Exit.*

COUNTESS [*reads a letter*]   "I have sent you a daughter-in-law.
20   She hath recovered° the King and undone me. I have wedded   *cured*
her, not bedded her, and sworn to make the "not"° eternal.   *punning on "knot"*
You shall hear I am run away; know it before the report come.
If there be breadth enough in the world, I will hold a long
distance. My duty to you.
25   Your unfortunate son, Bertram."
This is not well, rash and unbridled boy:
To fly the favors of so good a king,
To pluck° his indignation on thy head   *pull down*
By the misprizing° of a maid too virtuous   *undervaluing*
30   For the contempt of empire°—   *an emperor*
          Enter CLOWN.

CLOWN   O madam, yonder is heavy° news within between two   *sad*
soldiers and my young lady.

COUNTESS   What is the matter?

CLOWN   Nay, there is some comfort in the news, some comfort:
35   your son will not be killed so soon as I thought he would.

COUNTESS   Why should he be killed?

CLOWN   So say I, madam—if he run away, as I hear he does.
The danger is in standing to't:[2] that's the loss of men, though

1. Cure (through bloodletting).
2. When better places fall vacant.
3.2 Location: Roussillon, Bertram's palace.

1. Salt cod (slang for "penis").
2. In standing one's ground (in love and war).

it be the getting° of children. Here they come will tell you   *begetting*
40   more. For my part I only hear your son was run away. [*Exit.*]
     Enter HELEN *and two Gentlemen*[, *the* LORDS DUMAINE].
SECOND LORD DUMAINE   Save you, good madam.
HELEN   Madam, my lord is gone, forever gone.
FIRST LORD DUMAINE   Do not say so.
COUNTESS   Think upon patience, pray you. —Gentlemen,
45   I have felt so many quirks of joy and grief
  That the first face° of neither on the start°   *appearance* / *suddenly*
  Can woman me unto't.³ Where is my son, I pray you?
FIRST LORD DUMAINE   Madam, he's gone to serve the Duke of
    Florence.
  We met him thitherward,° for thence we came,   *going there*
50   And after some dispatch° in hand at court   *business*
  Thither we bend again.
HELEN   Look on his letter, madam: here's my passport.°   *vagabond's license*
  [*She reads.*] "When thou canst get the ring upon my finger,
  which never shall come off, and show me a child begotten
55   of thy body that I am father to, then call me husband, but
  in such a 'then' I write a 'never.'"
  This is a dreadful sentence.
COUNTESS   Brought you this letter, gentlemen?
FIRST LORD DUMAINE   Ay, madam,
  And for the contents' sake are sorry for our pains.
60 COUNTESS   I prithee, lady, have a better cheer.
  If thou engrossest° all the griefs are thine,   *monopolize*
  Thou robb'st me of a moiety.° He was my son,   *share*
  But I do wash his name out of my blood,
  And thou art all my° child. Towards Florence is he?   *my only*
FIRST LORD DUMAINE   Ay, madam.
65 COUNTESS   And to be a soldier?
FIRST LORD DUMAINE   Such is his noble purpose, and believe't,
  The Duke will lay upon him all the honor
  That good convenience claims.°   *That is suitable*
COUNTESS   Return you thither?
SECOND LORD DUMAINE   Ay, madam, with the swiftest wing of speed.
70 HELEN [*reads*]   "Till I have no wife, I have nothing in France."
  'Tis bitter.
COUNTESS   Find you that there?
HELEN   Ay, madam.
SECOND LORD DUMAINE   'Tis but the boldness of his hand,
    haply,°
  Which his heart was not consenting to.   *perhaps*
COUNTESS   Nothing in France until he have no wife!
75   There's nothing here that is too good for him
  But only she, and she deserves a lord
  That twenty such rude boys might tend upon
  And call her hourly mistress. Who was with him?
SECOND LORD DUMAINE   A servant only, and a gentleman
80   Which I have sometime known.
COUNTESS   Paroles, was it not?
SECOND LORD DUMAINE   Ay, my good lady, he.

---

3. Can make me weep like a woman.

COUNTESS   A very tainted fellow, and full of wickedness.
My son corrupts a well-derivèd° nature   *nobly born*
With his inducement.
85   SECOND LORD DUMAINE   Indeed, good lady,
The fellow has a deal of that too much
Which holds him much to have.[4]
COUNTESS   You're welcome, gentlemen.
I will entreat you, when you see my son,
To tell him that his sword can never win
90   The honor that he loses. More I'll entreat
You written to bear along.
FIRST LORD DUMAINE   We serve you, madam,
In that and all your worthiest affairs.
COUNTESS   Not so, but° as we change° our courtesies.   *except / exchange*
Will you draw near?   *Exeunt [all but* HELEN].
95   HELEN   "Till I have no wife, I have nothing in France."
Nothing in France until he has no wife!
Thou shalt have none, Roussillon, none in France;
Then hast thou all again. Poor lord, is't I
That chase thee from thy country and expose
100   Those tender limbs of thine to the event°   *outcome*
Of the none-sparing war? And is it I
That drive thee from the sportive court, where thou
Wast shot at with fair eyes, to be the mark
Of smoky muskets? O you leaden messengers°   *(bullets)*
105   That ride upon the violent speed of fire,
Fly with false aim, move the still-piecing air[5]
That sings with piercing; do not touch my lord!
Whoever shoots at him, I set him there.
Whoever charges on his forward° breast,   *brave; proud; advancing*
110   I am the caitiff° that do hold him to't,   *wretch*
And though I kill him not I am the cause
His death was so effected. Better 'twere
I met the ravin° lion when he roared   *ravenous*
With sharp constraint of hunger; better 'twere
115   That all the miseries which nature owes°   *human nature possesses*
Were mine at once. No, come thou home, Roussillon,
Whence honor but of danger wins a scar[6]
As oft it loses all. I will be gone;
My being here it is that holds thee hence.
120   Shall I stay here to do't? No, no, although
The air of paradise did fan the house
And angels officed all.[7] I will be gone,
That pitiful° rumor may report my flight   *pitying*
To consolate° thine ear. Come, night; end, day;   *console*
125   For with the dark, poor thief, I'll steal away.   *Exit.*

---

4. Has all too much persuasive power, which greatly
profits him.
5. Air that is constantly repairing itself.

6. *Whence . . . scar:* From where honor at best can
win a scar.
7. Performed all household tasks.

3.3

Flourish. Enter the DUKE *of Florence,* [BERTRAM, *Count*]
Roussillon, drum and trumpets, SOLDIERS, [*and*] PAROLES.

DUKE The general of our horse° thou art, and we,   *cavalry*
    Great in our hope, lay° our best love and credence°   *wager / trust*
    Upon thy promising fortune.

BERTRAM   Sir, it is
    A charge° too heavy for my strength, but yet   *load*
5   We'll strive to bear it for your worthy sake
    To th'extreme edge of hazard.°   *limit of danger*

DUKE   Then go thou forth,
    And fortune play upon thy prosperous helm
    As thy auspicious mistress.

BERTRAM   This very day,
    Great Mars, I put myself into thy file.°   *line of soldiers*
10 Make me but like my thoughts, and I shall prove
    A lover of thy drum, hater of love.   *Exeunt all.*

3.4

Enter COUNTESS *and* STEWARD[, *with a letter*].

COUNTESS Alas! And would you take the letter of her?
    Might you not know she would do as she has done
    By sending me a letter? Read it again.

STEWARD [*reads the letter*[1]] "I am Saint Jacques' pilgrim,[2]
    thither gone.
5 Ambitious love hath so in me offended
    That barefoot plod I the cold ground upon
    With sainted vow my faults to have amended.
    Write, write, that from the bloody course of war
    My dearest master, your dear son, may hie.°   *hurry*
10 Bless him at home in peace, whilst I from far
    His name with zealous fervor sanctify.°   *(in prayer)*
    His taken° labors bid him me forgive.   *undertaken*
    I, his despiteful Juno,[3] sent him forth
    From courtly friends with camping foes to live,
15 Where death and danger dogs the heels of worth.
    He is too good and fair for death and me,
    Whom[4] I myself embrace to set him free."

COUNTESS Ah, what sharp stings are in her mildest words!
    Rinaldo, you did never lack advice° so much   *discretion*
20 As letting her pass so. Had I spoke with her
    I could have well diverted her intents,
    Which thus she hath prevented.

STEWARD   Pardon me, madam.
    If I had given you this at overnight,°   *last night*
    She might have been o'erta'en, and yet she writes
    Pursuit would be but vain.

25 COUNTESS   What angel shall
    Bless this unworthy husband? He cannot thrive

3.3 Location: Florence.
3.4 Location: Roussillon. Bertram's palace.
1. The letter forms a sonnet.
2. A pilgrim to the shrine of St. James (presumably
in Santiago de Compostela, in Spain).

3. Cruel goddess of marriage (who oppressed Hercules by assigning him twelve supposedly impossible
tasks).
4. Death (but the suggestion "Bertram" may be
deliberate).

Unless her prayers, whom heaven delights to hear
And loves to grant, reprieve him from the wrath
Of greatest justice. Write, write, Rinaldo,
30 To this unworthy husband of his wife.
Let every word weigh heavy of° her worth   *emphasize*
That he does weigh too light. My greatest grief,
Though little he do feel it, set down sharply.
Dispatch the most convenient messenger.
35 When haply° he shall hear that she is gone   *Perhaps when*
He will return, and hope I may that she,
Hearing so much, will speed her foot again,
Led hither by pure love. Which of them both
Is dearest to me, I have no skill in sense
40 To make distinction. Provide° this messenger.   *Make ready*
My heart is heavy and mine age is weak;
Grief would have tears, and sorrow bids me speak. *Exeunt.*

3.5

A tucket° afar off. Enter [an] old WIDOW *of Florence,* *trumpet call*
*her daughter [*DIANA*], and* MARIANA, *with other citizens.*
WIDOW Nay, come, for if they do approach the city we shall
lose° all the sight.   *miss*
DIANA They say the French count has done most honorable
service.
5 WIDOW It is reported that he has taken their° great'st com- *(of the Sienese)*
mander, and that with his own hand he slew the Duke's
brother. We have lost our labor; they are gone a contrary
way. Hark, you may know by their trumpets.
MARIANA Come, let's return° again and suffice ourselves with *go home*
10 the report of it. Well, Diana, take heed of this French earl.
The honor of a maid is her name,° and no legacy is so rich as *reputation*
honesty.°   *chastity*
WIDOW [*to* DIANA] I have told my neighbor how you have been
solicited by a gentleman, his companion.
15 MARIANA I know that knave, hang him! One Paroles: a filthy
officer° he is in those suggestions° for the young earl. Beware *agent / solicitings*
of them, Diana: their promises, enticements, oaths, tokens,
and all these engines° of lust are not the things they go[1] *devices*
under. Many a maid hath been seduced by them, and the
20 misery is example that so terrible shows in the wreck of
maidenhood cannot for all that dissuade succession but that
they are limed with the twigs that threatens them.[2] I hope I
need not to advise you further, but I hope your own grace° *virtue*
will keep you where you are, though there were no further
25 danger° known but the modesty which is so lost. *(pregnancy)*
DIANA You shall not need to fear° me.   *fear for*
Enter HELEN[, *dressed as a pilgrim*].
WIDOW I hope so. Look, here comes a pilgrim. I know she
will lie at my house; thither they send one another. I'll question her.

3.5 Location: Florence.
1. Conceal themselves.
2. *the misery is . . . threatens them:* Unfortunately,
the example of those women ruined by the loss of

their virginity does not prevent others from falling
victim to the same deceptions. (Sticky lime was applied
to twigs to catch birds.)

30   —God save you, pilgrim, whither are you bound?

HELEN   To Saint Jacques le Grand.

    Where do the palmers° lodge, I do beseech you?   *pilgrims*

WIDOW   At the Saint Francis, here beside the port.°   *city gate*

HELEN   Is this the way?

    A march afar.

35 WIDOW   Ay, marry, is't. Hark you, they come this way.

    If you will tarry, holy pilgrim,

    But till the troops come by,

    I will conduct you where you shall be lodged,

    The rather for I think I know your hostess

40   As ample° as myself.   *well*

HELEN   Is it yourself?

WIDOW   If you shall please so, pilgrim.

HELEN   I thank you and will stay upon° your leisure.   *await*

WIDOW   You came, I think, from France?

HELEN   I did so.

45 WIDOW   Here you shall see a countryman of yours

    That has done worthy service.

HELEN   His name, I pray you?

DIANA   The Count Roussillon. Know you such a one?

HELEN   But by the ear that hears most nobly of him;

    His face I know not.

DIANA   Whatsome'er° he is,   *Whatever kind of man*

50   He's bravely taken° here. He stole from France,   *highly regarded*

    As 'tis reported, for the King had married him

    Against his liking. Think you it is so?

HELEN   Ay, surely, mere° the truth. I know his lady.   *simply*

DIANA   There is a gentleman that serves the Count

    Reports but coarsely of her.

55 HELEN   What's his name?

DIANA   Monsieur Paroles.

HELEN   Oh, I believe with him.

    In argument of praise,[3] or to° the worth   *compared to*

    Of the great Count himself, she is too mean°   *lowly*

    To have her name repeated. All her deserving°   *Her only merit*

60   Is a reservèd honesty,° and that   *preserved chastity*

    I have not heard examined.°   *questioned*

DIANA   Alas, poor lady!

    'Tis a hard bondage to become the wife

    Of a detesting lord.

WIDOW   I warrant, good creature, wheresoe'er she is,

65   Her heart weighs sadly. This young maid might do her

    A shrewd turn° if she pleased.   *nasty trick*

HELEN   How do you mean?

    Maybe the amorous Count solicits her

    In the unlawful purpose.

WIDOW   He does indeed,

    And brokes° with all that can in such a suit   *bargains*

70   Corrupt the tender honor of a maid.

    But she is armed for him and keeps her guard

    In honestest defense.

---

3. As a topic of praise.

Drum and colors. Enter [BERTRAM,] *Count Roussillon,*
PAROLES, *and the whole army.*

MARIANA   The gods forbid else.

WIDOW   So, now they come.
That is Antonio, the Duke's eldest son;
That Escalus.

HELEN   Which is the Frenchman?

75 DIANA   He,
That with the plume. 'Tis a most gallant fellow;
I would he loved his wife. If he were honester[4]
He were much goodlier.
Is't not a handsome gentleman?

HELEN   I like him well.

80 DIANA   'Tis pity he is not honest. Yond's that same knave
That leads him to these places. Were I his lady,
I would poison that vile rascal.

HELEN   Which is he?

DIANA   That jackanapes° with scarves. Why is he melancholy?   *monkey*

HELEN   Perchance he's hurt i'th' battle.

85 PAROLES   Lose our drum?[5] Well!

MARIANA   He's shrewdly° vexed at something. [PAROLES *bows*   *badly*
to them.] Look, he has spied us.

WIDOW [*to* PAROLES]   Marry, hang you!

MARIANA [*to* PAROLES]   And your courtesy,° for a ring-carrier.°   *bow / go-between*
                    Exeunt [BERTRAM, PAROLES, *and the army*].

90 WIDOW   The troop is passed. Come, pilgrim, I will bring you
Where you shall host.° Of enjoined penitents[6]   *lodge*
There's four or five to great Saint Jacques bound
Already at my house.

HELEN   I humbly thank you.
Please it° this matron and this gentle maid   *If it please*
95 To eat with us tonight, the charge and thanking
Shall be for me, and to requite you further
I will bestow some precepts of° this virgin   *advice on*
Worthy the note.

MARIANA *and* DIANA   We'll take your offer kindly.°   *Exeunt.*   *gratefully*

3.6

Enter [BERTRAM,] *Count Roussillon, and the* [*two*]
Frenchmen [*the* LORDS DUMAINE], *as at first.*

SECOND LORD DUMAINE   Nay, good my lord, put him to't.° Let   *(to the test)*
him have his way.

FIRST LORD DUMAINE   If your lordship find him not a hilding,°   *worthless wretch*
hold me no more in your respect.

5 SECOND LORD DUMAINE   On my life, my lord, a bubble.

BERTRAM   Do you think I am so far deceived in him?

SECOND LORD DUMAINE   Believe it, my lord, in mine own direct
knowledge, without any malice, but to speak of him as° my   *as if he were*
kinsman, he's a most notable coward, an infinite and endless
10 liar, an hourly promise breaker, the owner of no one good
quality worthy your lordship's entertainment.°   *patronage*

---

4. More honorable (and chaste).   6. Those sworn to a penitential pilgrimage.
5. A military disgrace.   3.6 Location: The Florentine camp.

FIRST LORD DUMAINE   It were fit you knew him, lest reposing°   *trusting*
too far in his virtue—which he hath not—he might at some
great and trusty business in a main danger fail you.

15 BERTRAM   I would I knew in what particular action to try him.

FIRST LORD DUMAINE   None better than to let him fetch off°   *back*
his drum, which you hear him so confidently undertake to do.

SECOND LORD DUMAINE   I, with a troop of Florentines, will
suddenly surprise° him; such I will have whom I am sure he   *ambush*
20 knows not from the enemy. We will bind and hoodwink°   *blindfold*
him so that he shall suppose no other but that he is carried
into the leaguer° of the adversaries when we bring him to   *camp*
our own tents. Be but your lordship present at his examination: if he do not, for the promise of his life, and in the high-
25 est compulsion of base fear, offer to betray you and deliver
all the intelligence° in his power against you, and that with   *information*
the divine forfeit of his soul upon oath, never trust my judgment in anything.

FIRST LORD DUMAINE   Oh, for the love of laughter, let him
30 fetch his drum! He says he has a stratagem for't. When your
lordship sees the bottom° of his success in't, and to what   *entirety*
metal this counterfeit lump of ore will be melted, if you give
him not John Drum's entertainment[1] your inclining° cannot   *partiality*
be removed. Here he comes.

     Enter PAROLES.

35 SECOND LORD DUMAINE [*aside to* BERTRAM]   Oh, for the love of
laughter, hinder not the honor of his design! Let him fetch
off his drum in any hand.°   *case*

BERTRAM   How now, monsieur? This drum sticks sorely in
your disposition.°   *troubles you sorely*

40 FIRST LORD DUMAINE   A pox on't, let it go, 'tis but a drum.

PAROLES   But a drum! Is't "but a drum"? A drum so lost!
There was excellent command, to charge in with our horse°   *cavalry*
upon our own wings° and to rend our own soldiers!   *flank units*

FIRST LORD DUMAINE   That was not to be blamed in the com-
45 mand of the service. It was a disaster° of war that Caesar   *an accident*
himself could not have prevented if he had been there to
command.

BERTRAM   Well, we cannot greatly condemn our success.[2]
Some dishonor we had in the loss of that drum, but it is not
50 to be recovered.

PAROLES   It might have been recovered.

BERTRAM   It might, but it is not now.

PAROLES   It is to be recovered. But that the merit of service is
seldom attributed to the true and exact performer, I would
55 have that drum or another, or *hic iacet*.[3]

BERTRAM   Why, if you have a stomach° to't, monsieur, if you   *an inclination*
think your mystery in stratagem° can bring this instrument   *tactical skill*
of honor again into his native quarter,° be magnanimous°   *back home / valiant*
in the enterprise and go on; I will grace° the attempt for a   *honor*

---

1. *John Drum's entertainment*: ignominious dismissal
(proverbial).
2. The general success of the battle.

3. Here lies (Latin): Paroles imagines himself dyi⸱
in an attempt to recover the drum.

60 worthy exploit. If you speed° well in it, the Duke shall both   *succeed*
speak of it and extend to you what further becomes his
greatness, even to the utmost syllable of your worthiness.

PAROLES   By the hand of a soldier, I will undertake it.

BERTRAM   But you must not now slumber in it.

65 PAROLES   I'll about it this evening, and I will presently pen
down my dilemmas,[4] encourage myself in my certainty, put
myself into my mortal preparation,[5] and by midnight look to
hear further from me.

BERTRAM   May I be bold to acquaint his grace you are gone
70 about it?

PAROLES   I know not what the success will be, my lord, but
the attempt I vow.

BERTRAM   I know thou'rt valiant, and to the possibility° of thy   *utmost capacity*
soldiership will subscribe° for thee. Farewell.   *vouch*

75 PAROLES   I love not many words.   *Exit.*

SECOND LORD DUMAINE   No more than a fish loves water. Is
not this a strange fellow, my lord, that so confidently seems
to undertake this business which he knows is not to be
done, damns himself to do, and dares better be damned
80 than to do't?

FIRST LORD DUMAINE   You do not know him, my lord, as we
do. Certain it is that he will steal himself into a man's favor
and for a week escape a great deal of discoveries,[6] but when
you find him out, you have° him ever after.   *understand*

85 BERTRAM   Why, do you think he will make no deed° at all of   *endeavor*
this that so seriously he does address himself unto?

SECOND LORD DUMAINE   None in the world, but return with
an invention° and clap upon you two or three probable° lies.   *tall tale / plausible*
But we have almost embossed[7] him. You shall see his fall
90 tonight, for indeed he is not for your lordship's respect.

FIRST LORD DUMAINE   We'll make you some sport with the fox
ere we case° him. He was first smoked[8] by the old lord   *skin*
Lafeu. When his disguise and he is parted, tell me what a
sprat° you shall find him, which you shall see this very   *tiny fish*
95 night.

SECOND LORD DUMAINE   I must go look my twigs.° He shall be   *see to my bird trap*
caught.

BERTRAM [*to* FIRST LORD DUMAINE]   Your brother, he shall go
along with me.

100 FIRST LORD DUMAINE   As't please your lordship. I'll leave you.
[*Exit.*]

BERTRAM   Now will I lead you to the house and show you
The lass I spoke of.

SECOND LORD DUMAINE   But you say she's honest.°   *chaste*

BERTRAM   That's all the fault. I spoke with her but once
And found her wondrous cold. But I sent to her
105 By this same coxcomb that we have i'th' wind°   *are stalking*
Tokens and letters, which she did resend,°   *return*

---

4. I will immediately reflect on my difficulties.
5. Spiritual preparation for death; readying of fatal
weapons.
6. *escape . . . discoveries:* largely get away with it.

7. Cornered; run to exhaustion (hunting term).
8. Forced into the open, like a fox smoked from its
hole.

And this is all I have done. She's a fair creature.
Will you go see her?
SECOND LORD DUMAINE   With all my heart, my lord. *Exeunt.*

3.7

Enter HELEN *and* WIDOW.

HELEN   If you misdoubt° me that I am not she,   *doubt*
  I know not how I shall assure you further
  But I shall lose the grounds I work upon.[1]
WIDOW   Though my estate° be fallen, I was well born,   *fortune*
5 Nothing acquainted with these businesses,
  And would not put my reputation now
  In any staining act.
HELEN   Nor would I wish you.
  First give me trust° the Count he is my husband,   *trust me that*
  And what to your sworn counsel° I have spoken   *secrecy*
10 Is so° from word to word, and then you cannot,   *true*
  By° the good aid that I of you shall borrow,   *With respect to*
  Err in bestowing it.
WIDOW   I should believe you,
  For you have showed me that which well approves°   *confirms*
  You're great in fortune.
HELEN   Take this purse of gold,
15 And let me buy your friendly help thus far,
  Which I will overpay and pay again
  When I have found it.° The Count he woos your daughter;   *succeeded*
  Lays down his wanton siege before her beauty;
  Resolves to carry° her. Let her in fine° consent,   *conquer / in the end*
20 As we'll direct her how 'tis best to bear° it.   *manage*
  Now his important blood° will naught deny   *importunate passion*
  That she'll demand. A ring the County° wears   *Count*
  That downward hath succeeded in his house
  From son to son some four or five descents°   *generations*
25 Since the first father wore it. This ring he holds
  In most rich choice,° yet in his idle° fire   *estimation / crazy*
  To buy his will° it would not seem too dear,   *lust*
  Howe'er repented after.
WIDOW   Now I see the bottom of your purpose.
30 HELEN   You see it lawful, then. It is no more
  But that your daughter, ere she seems as won,
  Desires this ring; appoints him an encounter;
  In fine, delivers me to fill the time,°   *keep the appointment*
  Herself most chastely absent. After,
35 To marry her,° I'll add three thousand crowns   *As her dowry*
  To what is passed already.
WIDOW   I have yielded.
  Instruct my daughter how she shall persever[2]
  That time and place with this deceit so lawful
  May prove coherent.° Every night he comes   *fitting*
40 With musics of all sorts and songs composed

3.7 Location: The Widow's house, Florence.
1. *But . . . upon:* Unless I give up what my plot depends upon (and reveal my identity to Bertram).

2. Follow through, persevere (obsolete); pronounced with the accent on the second syllable.

To her unworthiness.[3] It nothing steads° us   *avails*
To chide him from our eaves, for he persists
As if his life lay on't.
HELEN   Why, then, tonight
Let us assay° our plot, which if it speed°   *attempt / succeed*
45   Is wicked meaning° in a lawful deed   *intention (Bertram's)*
And lawful meaning° in a lawful act,   *intention (Helen's)*
Where both not sin, and yet a sinful fact.[4]
But let's about it.

4.1

Enter one of the Frenchmen [the FIRST LORD
DUMAINE], *with five or six other* SOLDIERS *in ambush.*

FIRST LORD DUMAINE   He can come no other way but by this
    hedge corner. When you sally° upon him, speak what terri-   *rush*
    ble° language you will. Though you understand it not your-   *ferocious*
    selves, no matter, for we must not seem to understand him,
5   unless° someone among us, whom we must produce for an   *except*
    interpreter.
FIRST SOLDIER   Good captain, let me be th'interpreter.
FIRST LORD DUMAINE   Art not acquainted with him? Knows
    he not thy voice?
10   FIRST SOLDIER   No, sir, I warrant you.
FIRST LORD DUMAINE   But what linsey-woolsey[1] hast thou to
    speak to us again?
FIRST SOLDIER   E'en such as you speak to me.
FIRST LORD DUMAINE   He must think us some band of strang-
15   ers° i'th' adversary's entertainment.° Now, he hath a smack[2]   *foreigners/ service*
    of all neighboring languages; therefore we must everyone be
    a man of his own fancy, not to know what we speak one to
    another. So° we seem to know is to know straight° our pur-   *Provided / suffices for*
    pose. Choughs'° language, gabble enough, and good enough.   *Crows'*
20   As for you, interpreter, you must seem very politic.° But   *cunning*
    couch,° ho! Here he comes, to beguile° two hours in a sleep   *hide / while away*
    and then to return and swear the lies he forges.
          Enter PAROLES.
PAROLES   Ten o'clock. Within these three hours 'twill be time
    enough to go home. What shall I say I have done? It must
25   be a very plausive° invention that carries it. They begin to   *plausible*
    smoke° me, and disgraces have of late knocked too often at   *suspect*
    my door. I find my tongue is too foolhardy, but my heart hath
    the fear of Mars before it, and of his creatures, not daring
    the reports of my tongue.[3]
30   FIRST LORD DUMAINE   [*aside*]   This is the first truth that e'er
    thine own tongue was guilty of.
PAROLES   What the devil should move me to undertake the
    recovery of this drum, being not ignorant of the impossibility
    and knowing I had no such purpose? I must give myself some
35   hurts and say I got them in exploit. Yet slight ones will not
    carry it. They will say, "Came you off with so little?" And

3. To my humble daughter; to persuade my daughter   wool fibers).
to unworthy deeds.   2. Smattering.
4. Deed (as Bertram intends it).   3. *my heart . . . tongue:* I am frightened by the god of
4.1 Location: Outside the Florentine camp.   war and his followers, not daring to do what I have
1. Hodgepodge (literally, cloth of mixed linen and   boasted.

great ones I dare not give. Wherefore, what's the instance?° *evidence*
Tongue, I must put you into a butter-woman's[4] mouth and buy
myself another of Bajazeth's mute,[5] if you prattle me into
40 these perils.

FIRST LORD DUMAINE [*aside*]   Is it possible he should know
what he is and be that he is?

PAROLES   I would the cutting of my garments would serve the
turn, or the breaking of my Spanish sword.

45 FIRST LORD DUMAINE [*aside*]   We cannot afford° you so. *accommodate*

PAROLES   Or the baring° of my beard, and to say it was in *shaving*
stratagem.

FIRST LORD DUMAINE [*aside*]   'Twould not do.

PAROLES   Or to drown my clothes and say I was stripped.

50 FIRST LORD DUMAINE [*aside*]   Hardly serve.

PAROLES   Though I swore I leapt from the window of the citadel—

FIRST LORD DUMAINE [*aside*]   How deep?

PAROLES   Thirty fathom.° *180 feet*

FIRST LORD DUMAINE [*aside*]   Three great oaths would scarce
55 make that be believed.

PAROLES   I would I had any drum of the enemy's: I would
swear I recovered it.

FIRST LORD DUMAINE [*aside*]   You shall hear one anon.° *immediately*

PAROLES   A drum, now, of the enemy's—
Alarum° within. *Call to arms*

60 FIRST LORD DUMAINE   *Throca movousus, cargo, cargo, cargo.*

ALL   *Cargo, cargo, cargo, villianda par corbo, cargo.*
[*They seize* PAROLES *and blindfold him.*]

PAROLES   Oh, ransom, ransom! Do not hide mine eyes.

FIRST SOLDIER   *Boskos thromuldo boskos.*

PAROLES   I know you are the Moscows'° regiment, *Russian*
65 And I shall lose my life for want of language.
If there be here German or Dane, Low Dutch,
Italian, or French, let him speak to me.
I'll discover° that which shall undo the Florentine. *reveal*

FIRST SOLDIER   *Boskos vauvado.* I understand thee and can
70 speak thy tongue. *Kerelybonto.* Sir, betake thee to thy faith,° *say your prayers*
for seventeen poniards° are at thy bosom. *daggers*

PAROLES   Oh!

FIRST SOLDIER   Oh, pray, pray, pray! —*Manka reuania
dulche.*

75 FIRST LORD DUMAINE   *Oscorbidulchos volivorco.*

FIRST SOLDIER   The general is content to spare thee yet,
And hoodwinked[6] as thou art will lead thee on[7]
To gather from thee. Haply° thou mayst inform *Perhaps*
Something to save thy life.

PAROLES   Oh, let me live,
80 And all the secrets of our camp I'll show—
Their force, their purposes. Nay, I'll speak that
Which you will wonder at.

FIRST SOLDIER   But wilt thou faithfully?[8]

---

4. Proverbially talkative.
5. *of Bajazeth's mute:* from the Turkish sultan's servant (whose tongue was cut off to ensure his discretion). TEXTUAL COMMENT The Folio text reads
"mule," not "mute," almost certainly a misprint. See

Digital Edition TC 6.
6. Blindfolded; punning on "deceived."
7. Will take you elsewhere; will deceive you furthe
8. Truthfully; loyally (ironic).

PAROLES   If I do not, damn me.
FIRST SOLDIER   *Acordo linta.*
  —Come on, thou art granted space.°   *breathing space*
                           Exit [FIRST SOLDIER *with* PAROLES].
                           A short alarum within.
85 FIRST LORD DUMAINE   Go tell the Count Roussillon and my
      brother
    We have caught the woodcock[9] and will keep him muffled°   *blindfolded*
    Till we do hear from them.
SECOND SOLDIER   Captain, I will.
FIRST LORD DUMAINE   'A° will betray us all unto ourselves: *He*
    Inform on° that.   *Report*
SECOND SOLDIER   So I will, sir.
90 FIRST LORD DUMAINE   Till then I'll keep him dark and safely
      locked.
                                            Exeunt.

                              4.2
          Enter BERTRAM *and the maid called* DIANA.
BERTRAM   They told me that your name was Fontibel.
DIANA   No, my good lord, Diana.
BERTRAM   Titled° goddess,   *Called*
    And worth it with addition.[1] But, fair soul,
    In your fine frame hath love no quality?
5   If the quick° fire of youth light not your mind   *vital*
    You are no maiden but a monument.°   *statue*
    When you are dead you should be such a one
    As you are now. For you are cold and stern,
    And now you should be as your mother was
    When your sweet self was got.°   *begotten*
10 DIANA   She then was honest.
BERTRAM   So should you be.
DIANA   No.
    My mother did but duty: such, my lord,
    As you owe to your wife.
BERTRAM   No more o'that.
    I prithee do not strive against my vows.[2]
15 I was compelled to her, but I love thee
    By love's own sweet constraint and will forever
    Do thee all rights of service.
DIANA   Ay, so you serve us
    Till we serve you.° But when you have our roses,   *(sexually)*
    You barely° leave our thorns to prick ourselves,   *only; nakedly*
    And mock us with our bareness.
20 BERTRAM   How have I sworn!
DIANA   'Tis not the many oaths that makes the truth
    But the plain single vow that is vowed true.
    What is not holy, that we swear not by,
    But take the high'st to witness. Then pray you, tell me:

---

9. Proverbially stupid bird.
4.2 Location: The Widow's house, Florence.
1. *worth it with addition:* you more than deserve to
be called a goddess; with wordplay on "addition" as

an honorific title. The goddess Diana was the patroness of chastity, an "addition" that hardly bodes well
for Bertram.
2. Do not quarrel with me about my wedding vows.

25   If I should swear by Jove's great attributes
    I loved you dearly, would you believe my oaths
    When I did love you ill?° This has no holding,[3]   *poorly; irreligiously*
    To swear by him whom I protest to love
    That I will work against him. Therefore your oaths
30   Are words and poor conditions but unsealed,[4]
    At least in my opinion.
    BERTRAM   Change it, change it!
    Be not so holy cruel. Love is holy,
    And my integrity ne'er knew the crafts°   *deceptive plays*
    That you do charge men with. Stand no more off,
35   But give thyself unto my sick desires,
    Who then recovers. Say thou art mine, and ever
    My love, as it begins, shall so persever.
    DIANA   I see that men may rope's in such a snare[5]
    That we'll forsake ourselves. Give me that ring.
40   BERTRAM   I'll lend it thee, my dear, but have no power
    To give it from me.
    DIANA   Will you not, my lord?
    BERTRAM   It is an honor 'longing to our house,°   *family line*
    Bequeathèd down from many ancestors,
    Which were the greatest obloquy° i'th' world   *disgrace*
    In me to lose.
45   DIANA   Mine honor's such a ring;
    My chastity's the jewel of our house,
    Bequeathèd down from many ancestors,
    Which were the greatest obloquy i'th' world
    In me to lose. Thus your own proper wisdom[6]
50   Brings in the champion, Honor, on my part,°   *side*
    Against your vain assault.
    BERTRAM   Here, take my ring.
    My house, mine honor, yea, my life be thine,
    And I'll be bid° by thee.   *commanded*
    DIANA   When midnight comes,
    Knock at my chamber window;
55   I'll order take my mother shall not hear.
    Now will I charge you in the band of truth,
    When you have conquered my yet maiden bed
    Remain there but an hour, nor speak to me.
    My reasons are most strong, and you shall know them
60   When back again this ring shall be delivered.
    And on your finger in the night I'll put
    Another ring, that what° in time proceeds   *whatever*
    May token° to the future our past deeds.   *betoken*
    Adieu till then; then fail not. You have won
65   A wife of° me, though there my hope be done.[7]   *in; through*
    BERTRAM   A heaven on earth I have won by wooing thee.
    DIANA   For which, live long to thank both heaven and me.
                              [*Exit* BERTRAM.]

---

3. Consistency; binding power.
4. *words . . . unsealed:* contracts without the validating seal.
5. I see that men may entrap us with such trifles.
TEXTUAL COMMENT The Folio text is corrupt here and

has been emended in various ways; for the rationale behind the Norton version, see Digital Edition TC 7.
6. Wisdom in your own affairs.
7. My marriage hopes are ruined; my hope of aiding Helen is accomplished.

You may so in the end.
My mother told me just how he would woo,
70 As if she sat in 's heart. She says all men
Have the like oaths. He has sworn to marry me
When his wife's dead; therefore I'll lie with him
When I am buried. Since Frenchmen are so braid,°   *deceitful*
Marry° that will, I live and die a maid.   *Let those marry*
75 Only in this disguise I think't no sin
To cozen° him that would unjustly win.   *Exit.*   *cheat*

4.3

Enter the two French captains [the LORDS DUMAINE],
and some two or three SOLDIERS.

FIRST LORD DUMAINE You have not given him his mother's
letter?

SECOND LORD DUMAINE I have delivered it an hour since.
There is something in't that stings his nature, for on the
5 reading it he changed almost into another man.

FIRST LORD DUMAINE He has much worthy° blame laid upon   *deserved*
him for shaking off so good a wife and so sweet a lady.

SECOND LORD DUMAINE Especially he hath incurred the everlasting displeasure of the King, who had even tuned his
10 bounty to sing happiness to him.[1] I will tell you a thing, but
you shall let it dwell darkly° with you.   *secretly*

FIRST LORD DUMAINE When you have spoken it 'tis dead, and
I am the grave of it.

SECOND LORD DUMAINE He hath perverted a young gentle-
15 woman here in Florence of a most chaste renown,° and this   *reputation*
night he fleshes his will[2] in the spoil of her honor. He hath
given her his monumental° ring and thinks himself made in   *memorial*
the unchaste composition.°   *bargain*

FIRST LORD DUMAINE Now God delay our rebellion!° As we   *stifle our unruliness*
20 are ourselves,° what things are we!   *without divine aid*

SECOND LORD DUMAINE Merely° our own traitors. And as in   *Absolutely*
the common course of all treasons we still° see them reveal   *always*
themselves,° till they attain to their abhorred ends, so he   *(their true nature)*
that in this action contrives° against his own nobility, in his   *plots*
25 proper stream o'erflows himself.[3]

FIRST LORD DUMAINE Is it not meant damnable° in us to be   *meant to be mortal sin*
trumpeters of our unlawful intents? We shall not then have
his company tonight?

SECOND LORD DUMAINE Not till after midnight, for he is
30 dieted° to his hour.   *restricted*

FIRST LORD DUMAINE That approaches apace. I would gladly
have him see his company anatomized,° that he might take   *companion exposed*
a measure of his own judgments, wherein so curiously° he   *carefully*
had set this counterfeit.[4]

35 SECOND LORD DUMAINE We will not meddle with him° till   *(Paroles)*
he° come, for his presence must be the whip of the other.   *(Bertram)*

4.3 Location: The Florentine camp.
1. Who had previously readied his generosity to
make him happy (with musical metaphor).
2. He feeds his lust (hounds were "fleshed," or
rewarded, with a piece of meat from their prey, or

"spoil").
3. *in his . . . himself:* dissipates himself outside his
appropriate channel.
4. False jewel (Paroles).

FIRST LORD DUMAINE   In the meantime, what hear you of these wars?

SECOND LORD DUMAINE   I hear there is an overture of peace.

40   FIRST LORD DUMAINE   Nay, I assure you, a peace concluded.

SECOND LORD DUMAINE   What will Count Roussillon do then? Will he travel higher° or return again into France?   *farther*

FIRST LORD DUMAINE   I perceive by this demand you are not altogether of his counsel.°   *in his confidence*

45   SECOND LORD DUMAINE   Let it be forbid, sir. So should I be a great deal of his act.⁵

FIRST LORD DUMAINE   Sir, his wife some two months since fled from his house. Her pretense° is a pilgrimage to Saint   *purpose* Jacques le Grand, which holy undertaking with most aus-

50   tere sanctimony° she accomplished. And, there residing, the   *piety* tenderness of her nature became as a prey to her grief; in fine,° made a groan of her last breath, and now she sings in   *in conclusion* heaven.

SECOND LORD DUMAINE   How is this justified?°   *verified*

55   FIRST LORD DUMAINE   The stronger part of it by her own let- ters, which makes her story true even to the point of her death; her death itself, which could not be her office to say is come, was faithfully confirmed by the rector of the place.

SECOND LORD DUMAINE   Hath the Count all this intelligence?

60   FIRST LORD DUMAINE   Ay, and the particular confirmations, point from point, to the full arming° of the verity.°   *corroboration / truth*

SECOND LORD DUMAINE   I am heartily sorry that he'll be glad of this.

FIRST LORD DUMAINE   How mightily sometimes we make us
65   comforts of our losses!

SECOND LORD DUMAINE   And how mightily some other times we drown our gain in tears! The great dignity that his valor hath here acquired for him shall at home be encountered°   *opposed* with a shame as ample.

70   FIRST LORD DUMAINE   The web° of our life is of a mingled   *fabric* yarn, good and ill together: our virtues would be proud if our faults whipped them not, and our crimes would despair if they were not cherished by our virtues.

*Enter a [*SERVANT as*] Messenger.*

—How now? Where's your master?

75   SERVANT   He met the Duke in the street, sir, of whom he hath taken a solemn leave. His lordship will° next morning for   *intends to leave* France. The Duke hath offered him letters of commenda- tions to the King.

SECOND LORD DUMAINE   They shall be no more than needful
80   there, if they were more than they can commend.⁶

*Enter [*BERTRAM,*] Count Roussillon.*

FIRST LORD DUMAINE   They cannot be too sweet for the King's tartness. Here's his lordship now. —How now, my lord, is't not after midnight?

BERTRAM   I have tonight dispatched sixteen businesses a
85   month's length apiece. By an abstract of success:° I have   *list of items*

_____

5. An accessory to his deeds.
6. Even if they were more commendatory than they possibly could be.

congéd with° the Duke, done my adieu with his nearest,   *taken leave of*
buried a wife, mourned for her, writ to my lady mother I am
returning, entertained my convoy,° and between these main   *arranged my transport*
parcels of dispatch° effected many nicer° needs. The last *business / more delicate*
90 was the greatest, but that I have not ended yet.

SECOND LORD DUMAINE   If the business be of any difficulty,
and this morning your departure hence, it requires haste of
your lordship.

BERTRAM   I mean the business is not ended as fearing to
95 hear of it hereafter. But shall we have this dialogue
between the Fool and the Soldier? Come, bring forth this
counterfeit model;° he's deceived me like a double-   *image (of soldiership)*
meaning° prophesier.   *ambiguous*

SECOND LORD DUMAINE   Bring him forth. [*Exeunt* SOLDIERS.]
100 He's sat i'th' stocks all night, poor gallant knave.

BERTRAM   No matter. His heels have deserved it in usurping
his spurs[7] so long. How does he carry himself?

SECOND LORD DUMAINE   I have told your lordship already: the
stocks carry him. But to answer you as you would be under-
105 stood, he weeps like a wench that had shed° her milk. He   *spilled*
hath confessed himself to Morgan, whom he supposes to be
a friar, from the time of his remembrance[8] to this very
instant° disaster of his setting i'th' stocks. And what think   *present*
you he hath confessed?

110 BERTRAM   Nothing of me, has 'a?°   *he*

SECOND LORD DUMAINE   His confession is taken, and it shall
be read to his face. If your lordship be in't, as I believe you
are, you must have the patience to hear it.

     Enter PAROLES, [*blindfolded,*] *with his*
     interpreter[*, the* FIRST SOLDIER].

BERTRAM   A plague upon him! Muffled!° He can say nothing   *Blindfolded*
115 of me.

FIRST LORD DUMAINE [*aside*]   Hush, hush! Hoodman[9] comes.
—Portotartarossa.

FIRST SOLDIER   He calls for the tortures. What will you say
without 'em?

120 PAROLES   I will confess what I know without constraint. If ye
pinch me like a pasty° I can say no more.   *piecrust*

FIRST SOLDIER   *Bosko chimurcho.*

FIRST LORD DUMAINE   *Boblibindo chicurmurco.*

FIRST SOLDIER   You are a merciful general. —Our general
125 bids you answer to what I shall ask you out of a note.

PAROLES   And truly, as I hope to live.

FIRST SOLDIER [*reads*]   "First demand of him how many horse°   *horsemen*
the Duke is strong." —What say you to that?

PAROLES   Five or six thousand, but very weak and unser-
130 viceable. The troops are all scattered and the commanders
very poor rogues, upon my reputation and credit and as I
hope to live.

FIRST SOLDIER   Shall I set down your answer so?

---

7. Symbolic of knightly valor.   9. The blindfolded player in blindman's buff.
8. As far back as he can recall.

PAROLES   Do. I'll take the sacrament on't, how and which way
135   you will.[1]
BERTRAM [*aside*]   All's one to him. What a past-saving slave is
this!
FIRST LORD DUMAINE [*aside*]   You're deceived, my lord. This
is Monsieur Paroles, the gallant militarist—that was his
140   own phrase—that had the whole theoric° of war in the   theory
knot of his scarf and the practice in the chape° of his   scabbard tip
dagger.
SECOND LORD DUMAINE [*aside*]   I will never trust a man again
for keeping his sword clean, nor believe he can have every-
145   thing in him by wearing his apparel neatly.
FIRST SOLDIER   Well, that's set down.
PAROLES   Five or six thousand horse, I said. I will say true.
"Or thereabouts" set down, for I'll speak truth.
FIRST LORD DUMAINE [*aside*]   He's very near the truth in this.
150   BERTRAM [*aside*]   But I con him no thanks° for't in the nature° *feel no gratitude / manner*
he delivers it.
PAROLES   Poor rogues, I pray you say.
FIRST SOLDIER   Well, that's set down.
PAROLES   I humbly thank you, sir. A truth's a truth: the rogues
155   are marvelous poor.
FIRST SOLDIER [*reads*]   "Demand of him of what strength they
are a-foot." —What say you to that?
PAROLES   By my troth, sir, if I were to live but this present hour,
I will tell true. Let me see: Spurio a hundred and fifty, Sebas-
160   tian so many,° Corambus so many, Jacques so many; Guiltian,   *the same number*
Cosmo, Lodowick, and Gratii, two hundred fifty each; mine
own company, Chitopher, Vaumond, Bentii, two hundred fifty
each. So that the muster file, rotten and sound,[2] upon my
life amounts not to fifteen thousand poll,° half of the which   *heads*
165   dare not shake the snow from off their cassocks° lest they   *cloaks*
shake themselves to pieces.
BERTRAM [*aside*]   What shall be done to him?
FIRST LORD DUMAINE [*aside*]   Nothing, but let him have
thanks. [*aside to* FIRST SOLDIER] Demand of him my condi-
170   tion and what credit I have with the Duke.
FIRST SOLDIER   Well, that's set down. [*He pretends to read.*]
"You shall demand of him whether one Captain Dumaine be
i'th' camp, a Frenchman: what his reputation is with the
Duke, what his valor, honesty, and expertness in wars, or
175   whether he thinks it were not possible with well-weighing°   *heavy; persuasive*
sums of gold to corrupt him to a revolt." What say you to
this? What do you know of it?
PAROLES   I beseech you, let me answer to the particular of the
interrogatories.° Demand them singly.   *judicial questions*
180   FIRST SOLDIER   Do you know this Captain Dumaine?
PAROLES   I know him. 'A was a botcher's° prentice in Paris,   *clothes mender's*
from whence he was whipped for getting the sheriff's fool[3]
with child, a dumb innocent° that could not say him nay.   *idiot*

1. According to whatever rite you prefer.   3. Mentally retarded girl.
2. The total roll, sick and able-bodied.

BERTRAM [*to* FIRST LORD DUMAINE] Nay, by your leave, hold
185   your hands, though I know his brains are forfeit to the next
    tile that falls.[4]
FIRST SOLDIER Well, is this captain in the Duke of Florence's
    camp?
PAROLES Upon my knowledge he is, and lousy.
190 FIRST LORD DUMAINE [*aside*] Nay, look not so upon me; we
    shall hear of your lordship anon.
FIRST SOLDIER What is his reputation with the Duke?
PAROLES The Duke knows him for no other but a poor officer
    of mine, and writ to me this other day to turn him out o'th'
195 band. I think I have his letter in my pocket.
FIRST SOLDIER Marry, we'll search.
PAROLES In good sadness,° I do not know; either it is there or   *all seriousness*
    it is upon a file with the Duke's other letters in my tent.
FIRST SOLDIER Here 'tis, here's a paper. Shall I read it to you?
200 PAROLES I do not know if it be it or no.
BERTRAM [*aside*] Our interpreter does it well.
FIRST LORD DUMAINE [*aside*] Excellently.
FIRST SOLDIER "Dian, the Count's a fool and full of gold."
PAROLES That is not the Duke's letter, sir. That is an adver-
205 tisement° to a proper maid in Florence, one Diana, to take   *admonition*
    heed of the allurement of one Count Roussillon, a foolish,
    idle boy, but for all that very ruttish.° I pray you, sir, put it up   *lecherous*
    again.
FIRST SOLDIER Nay, I'll read it first, by your favor.
210 PAROLES My meaning in't, I protest, was very honest in the
    behalf of the maid, for I knew the young Count to be a dan-
    gerous and lascivious boy who is a whale to virginity and
    devours up all the fry° it finds.   *tiny fish*
BERTRAM [*aside*] Damnable both-sides rogue!
FIRST SOLDIER [*reads the*] letter
215 "When he swears oaths, bid him drop gold and take it;
    After he scores he never pays the score.°   *bill*
    Half-won is match well made; match and well make it.[5]
    He ne'er pays after-debts;[6] take it before.
    And say a soldier, Dian, told thee this:
220 Men are to mell° with, boys are not to kiss.   *meddle (sexually)*
    For count° of this: the Count's a fool, I know it,   *on account*
    Who pays before° but not when he does owe it.   *in advance*
    Thine as he vowed to thee in thine ear,
                Paroles."
225 BERTRAM [*aside*] He shall be whipped through the army with
    this rhyme in 's[7] forehead.
SECOND LORD DUMAINE [*aside*] This is your devoted friend,
    sir, the manifold linguist and the armipotent° soldier.   *mighty-in-arms*
BERTRAM [*aside*] I could endure anything before but a cat,[8]
230 and now he's a cat to me.
FIRST SOLDIER I perceive, sir, by the general's looks, we shall
    be fain° to hang you.   *obliged*

---

4. I know he's close to sudden death.
5. Negotiating a good bargain is half the battle, so be
sure to bargain well.
6. Debts payable after receipt of goods.
7. On his (whores and their customers, when pun-

ished by public whipping, were often made to wear
signs indicating their transgressions).
8. A common phobia, but "cat" is also a term of contempt, usually referring to a spiteful or sluttish
woman.

PAROLES   My life, sir, in any case! Not that I am afraid to die,
but that my offenses being many, I would repent out the
235   remainder of nature.° Let me live, sir, in a dungeon, i'th'   *my natural life*
stocks, or anywhere, so I may live.
FIRST SOLDIER   We'll see what may be done, so you confess
freely. Therefore once more to this Captain Dumaine. You
have answered to his reputation with the Duke and to his
240   valor. What is his honesty?
PAROLES   He will steal, sir, an egg out of a cloister. For rapes
and ravishments he parallels Nessus.[9] He professes° not   *makes a practice of*
keeping of oaths; in breaking 'em he is stronger than Her-
cules. He will lie, sir, with such volubility that you would
245   think truth were a fool. Drunkenness is his best virtue, for
he will be swine-drunk, and in his sleep he does little harm
save to his bedclothes about him—but they know his condi-
tions° and lay him in straw. I have but little more to say, sir,   *habits*
of his honesty. He has everything that an honest man
250   should not have; what an honest man should have, he has
nothing.
FIRST LORD DUMAINE [aside]   I begin to love him for this.
BERTRAM [aside]   For this description of thine honesty? A pox
upon him! For me, he's more and more a cat.
255   FIRST SOLDIER   What say you to his expertness in war?
PAROLES   Faith, sir, he's led the drum before the English tragedians.[1] To belie him I will not, and more of his soldiership
I know not, except in that country he had the honor to be
the officer at a place there called Mile End,[2] to instruct for
260   the doubling of files.[3] I would do the man what honor I can,
but of this I am not certain.
SECOND LORD DUMAINE [aside]   He hath out-villained villainy
so far that the rarity° redeems him.   *uniqueness*
BERTRAM [aside]   A pox on him! He's a cat still.
265   FIRST SOLDIER   His qualities being at this poor price, I need
not to ask you if gold will corrupt him to revolt.
PAROLES   Sir, for a *quart d'écu*[4] he will sell the fee-simple° of   *absolute ownership*
his salvation, the inheritance of it, and cut th'entail from all
remainders,[5] and a perpetual succession for it perpetually.
270   FIRST SOLDIER   What's his brother, the other Captain Dumaine?
SECOND LORD DUMAINE [aside]   Why does he ask him of me?
FIRST SOLDIER   What's he?
PAROLES   E'en a crow o'th' same nest: not altogether so great
as the first in goodness, but greater a great deal in evil. He
275   excels his brother for a coward, yet his brother is reputed
one of the best that is. In a retreat he outruns any lackey;[6]
marry, in coming on° he has the cramp.   *advancing*
FIRST SOLDIER   If your life be saved, will you undertake to
betray the Florentine?
280   PAROLES   Ay, and the captain of his horse, Count Roussillon.
FIRST SOLDIER   I'll whisper with the general and know his
pleasure.

9. Centaur who attempted to rape Hercules' wife.
1. He's banged the drum to help advertise plays.
2. Where the London citizen militia drilled.
3. Simple drill exercise, in which the men stand in
two rows.
4. Quarter-crown, French coin of small value.
5. Prevent its succession to any future heirs.
6. Footman who runs before his master's coach.

PAROLES [*aside*] I'll no more drumming. A plague of all
drums! Only to seem to deserve well, and to beguile the sup-
285 position° of that lascivious young boy the Count, have I run   *judgment*
into this danger. Yet who would have suspected an ambush
where I was taken?
FIRST SOLDIER There is no remedy, sir, but you must die. The
general says you that have so traitorously discovered° the   *revealed*
290 secrets of your army and made such pestiferous reports of
men very nobly held° can serve the world for no honest use.   *regarded*
Therefore you must die. Come, headsman, off with his head.
PAROLES O Lord, sir, let me live, or let me see my death.
FIRST SOLDIER That shall you, and take your leave of all your
295 friends. [*He removes the blindfold.*] So, look about you.
Know you any here?
BERTRAM Good morrow, noble captain.
SECOND LORD DUMAINE God bless you, Captain Paroles.
FIRST LORD DUMAINE God save you, noble captain.
300 SECOND LORD DUMAINE Captain, what greeting will you° to   *do you desire*
my lord Lafeu? I am for° France.   *off to*
FIRST LORD DUMAINE Good captain, will you give me a copy
of the sonnet you writ to Diana in behalf of the Count Rous-
sillon? An° I were not a very coward, I'd compel it of you, but   *If*
305 fare you well.   *Exeunt* [*all but* FIRST SOLDIER *and* PAROLES].
FIRST SOLDIER You are undone, captain, all but your scarf;
that has a knot on't yet.
PAROLES Who cannot be crushed with a plot?
FIRST SOLDIER If you could find out a country where but
310 women were that had received so much shame, you might
begin an impudent° nation. Fare ye well, sir, I am for France   *a shameless*
too. We shall speak of you there.   *Exit.*
PAROLES Yet am I thankful. If my heart were great
'Twould burst at this. Captain I'll be no more,
315 But I will eat, and drink, and sleep as soft
As captain shall. Simply the thing I am
Shall make me live.° Who knows himself a braggart,   *sustain me*
Let him fear this; for it will come to pass
That every braggart shall be found an ass.
320 Rust sword, cool blushes, and Paroles live
Safest in shame. Being fooled, by fool'ry thrive;
There's place and means for every man alive.
I'll after them.   *Exit.*

4.4

Enter HELEN, WIDOW, *and* DIANA.
HELEN That you may well perceive I have not wronged you,
One of the greatest in the Christian world
Shall be my surety,° fore whose throne 'tis needful,   *guarantee*
Ere I can perfect mine intents, to kneel.
5 Time was I did him a desired office
Dear almost as his life, which gratitude

4.4 Location: The Widow's house, Florence.

Through flinty Tartar's bosom[1] would peep forth
And answer thanks. I duly am informed
His grace is at Marseilles, to which place
We have convenient convoy.° You must know   *suitable transport*
I am supposèd dead. The army breaking,°   *disbanding*
My husband hies him home, where heaven aiding,
And by the leave of my good lord, the King,
We'll be before our welcome.°   *before we're expected*

WIDOW   Gentle madam,
You never had a servant to whose trust
Your business was more welcome.

HELEN   Nor you, mistress,
Ever a friend whose thoughts more truly labor
To recompense your love. Doubt not but heaven
Hath brought me up to be your daughter's dower,
As it hath fated her to be my motive°   *means*
And helper to a husband. But, oh, strange men,
That can such sweet use make of what they hate!
When saucy trusting of the cozened° thoughts   *deceived*
Defiles the pitchy night,[2] so lust doth play
With what it loathes for° that which is away.   *in the place of*
But more of this hereafter. You, Diana,
Under my poor instructions yet must suffer
Something in my behalf.

DIANA   Let death and honesty°   *chastity*
Go with your impositions, I am yours,
Upon° your will to suffer.   *At*

HELEN   Yet,° I pray you,   *A little longer*
But with the word° "the time will bring on summer,"   *("Yet")*
When briars shall have leaves as well as thorns
And be as sweet° as sharp. We must away.   *fragrant*
Our wagon is prepared, and time revives us.
All's well that ends well; still the fine's° the crown.   *end*
Whate'er the course, the end is the renown.°   *Exeunt.*   *what is remembered*

4.5

Enter CLOWN, *old Lady* [COUNTESS], *and* LAFEU.

LAFEU   No, no, no, your son was misled with a snipped taffeta[1] fellow there, whose villainous saffron[2] would have made
all the unbaked and doughy youth of a nation in his color.
Your daughter-in-law had been alive at this hour, and your
son here at home, more advanced by the King than by that
red-tailed humble-bee[3] I speak of.

COUNTESS   I would I had not known him. It was the death of
the most virtuous gentlewoman that ever Nature had praise
for creating. If she had partaken of my flesh and cost me the
dearest groans of a mother I could not have owed her a more
rooted love.

LAFEU   'Twas a good lady, 'twas a good lady! We may pick a
thousand salads ere we light on such another herb.

---

1. Even from a savage's stony heart (Tartars, residents of central Asia, were considered barbaric by
western Europeans).
2. *When . . . night:* When lascivious yielding to
deceit defiles even the black night.

4.5 Location: Bertram's palace.
1. Silk slashed to show a contrasting lining.
2. Yellow dye, used for pastry; the coward's color.
3. Bumblebee (noisy, colorful, and useless).

CLOWN   Indeed, sir, she was the sweet marjoram of the salad,
15   or rather the herb of grace.°   rue
LAFEU   They are not salad-herbs,[4] you knave, they are nose-herbs.°   fragrant plants
CLOWN   I am no great Nebuchadnezzar,[5] sir: I have not much
    skill in grass.
LAFEU   Whether° dost thou profess thyself, a knave or a fool?   Which
20   CLOWN   A fool, sir, at a woman's service, and a knave at a
    man's.
LAFEU   Your distinction?
CLOWN   I would cozen° the man of his wife and do his service.   cheat
LAFEU   So you were a knave at his service indeed.
25   CLOWN   And I would give his wife my bauble,[6] sir, to do her
    service.
LAFEU   I will subscribe° for thee: thou art both knave and fool.   vouch
CLOWN   At your service.
LAFEU   No, no, no.
30   CLOWN   Why, sir, if I cannot serve you, I can serve as great a
    prince as you are.
LAFEU   Who's that, a Frenchman?
CLOWN   Faith, sir, 'a has an English name, but his physiog-
    nomy[7] is more hotter in France than there.
35   LAFEU   What prince is that?
CLOWN   The Black Prince,[8] sir, alias the prince of darkness,
    alias the devil.
LAFEU   Hold thee, there's my purse. I give thee not this to sug-
    gest° thee from thy master thou talk'st of. Serve him still.   lure
40   CLOWN   I am a woodland fellow, sir, that always loved a great
    fire, and the master I speak of ever keeps a good fire. But
    sure he is the prince of the world. Let his nobility remain in
    's court. I am for the house with the narrow gate,[9] which I
    take to be too little for pomp to enter. Some that humble
45   themselves may, but the many will be too chill and tender,[1]
    and they'll be for the flowery way that leads to the broad
    gate and the great fire.
LAFEU   Go thy ways, I begin to be a-weary of thee, and I tell thee
    so before° because I would not fall out with thee. Go thy ways.   in advance
50   Let my horses be well looked to without any tricks.
CLOWN   If I put any tricks upon 'em, sir, they shall be jades'
    tricks,[2] which are their own right by the law of nature.
                                                        Exit.
LAFEU   A shrewd° knave and an unhappy.   bitter
COUNTESS   So 'a is. My lord that's gone made himself much
55   sport out of him. By his authority he remains here, which he
    thinks is a patent° for his sauciness, and indeed he has no   license
    pace° but runs where he will.   restraint

---

4. Misconstruing "grace" as "grass."
5. In Daniel 4:28–34, the King of Babylon who, lacking spiritual "grace," went mad and ate "grass."
6. Fool's rod (suggesting "penis").
7. Physiognomy, face (in Elizabethan pronunciation,
punning on "nomy" and "name").
8. Punning on the nickname of Edward III's eldest
son, who conquered the French, and whom the Clown
equates to the devil, also as "black prince."
9. "Enter in at the strait gate; for it is the wide gate,

and broad way that leadeth to destruction, and many
there be which go in thereat. Because the gate is
strait and the way narrow that leadeth unto life, and
few there be that find it" (Matthew 7:13–14; see also
Luke 13:24). The devil is called the "prince of this
world" in John 12:31 and elsewhere.
1. Fainthearted and self-indulgent.
2. Contemptible tricks; playing on the sense "tricks
played on horses."

LAFEU   I like him well; 'tis not amiss. And I was about to tell
you: since I heard of the good lady's death, and that my lord
60   your son was upon his return home, I moved the King my
master to speak in the behalf of my daughter, which in the
minority of them both his majesty out of a self-gracious
remembrance[3] did first propose. His highness hath promised me to do it, and to stop up the displeasure he hath
65   conceived against your son there is no fitter matter. How
does your ladyship like it?
COUNTESS   With very much content, my lord, and I wish it
happily effected.
LAFEU   His highness comes post° from Marseilles, of as able   *speedily*
70   body as when he numbered thirty. 'A will be here tomorrow,
or I am deceived by him° that in such intelligence° hath sel-   *someone / information*
dom failed.
COUNTESS   It rejoices me that I hope I shall see him ere I die.
I have letters that my son will be here tonight. I shall
75   beseech your lordship to remain with me till they meet
together.
LAFEU   Madam, I was thinking with what manners I might
safely be admitted.°   *invited to be present*
COUNTESS   You need but plead your honorable privilege.[4]
80   LAFEU   Lady, of that I have made a bold charter,[5] but I thank
my God it holds yet.
       Enter CLOWN.
CLOWN   O madam, yonder's my lord your son with a patch of
velvet[6] on 's face. Whether there be a scar under't or no, the
velvet knows, but 'tis a goodly patch of velvet. His left cheek
85   is a check of two pile and a half,[7] but his right cheek is worn
bare.
LAFEU   A scar nobly got, or a noble scar, is a good liv'ry° of   *uniform*
honor. So belike° is that.   *probably*
CLOWN   But it is your carbonadoed[8] face.
90   LAFEU   Let us go see your son, I pray you. I long to talk with
the young noble soldier.
CLOWN   'Faith, there's a dozen of 'em, with delicate fine hats
and most courteous feathers, which bow the head and nod
at every man.   *Exeunt.*

5.1

       Enter HELEN, WIDOW, *and* DIANA, *with two* ATTENDANTS.
HELEN   But this exceeding posting° day and night   *this hasty riding*
Must wear your spirits low. We cannot help it.
But since you have made the days and nights as one
To wear° your gentle limbs in my affairs,   *tire*
5   Be bold° you do so grow in my requital°   *confident / repayment*
As nothing can unroot you.
       Enter a GENTLE[MAN] *austringer.*[1]
                 In happy time!°   *Just at the right time*

3. Recollection prompted by his own graciousness.
4. Privilege due your honor.
5. Made as bold a claim as I dare.
6. Used to cover a battle wound or a facial sore from
syphilis.
7. The thickest velvet was three-piled; the Clown
invents an imaginary next-best.

8. Slashed (like meat for broiling) in battle or by a
surgeon, to treat a syphilitic eruption.
5.1 Location: Marseilles.
1. TEXTUAL COMMENT An austringer is a falconer, or
keeper of hunting hawks. For a discussion of this
unusual stage direction, see Digital Edition TC 8.

This man may help me to his majesty's ear
If he would spend his power. —God save you, sir.
GENTLEMAN   And you.
10 HELEN   Sir, I have seen you in the court of France.
GENTLEMAN   I have been sometimes there.
HELEN   I do presume, sir, that you are not fallen
From the report that goes upon your goodness;
And therefore goaded with most sharp occasions,°   urgent circumstances
15 Which lay nice° manners by, I put° you to   scrupulous / urge
The use of your own virtues, for the which
I shall continue thankful.
GENTLEMAN   What's your will?
HELEN   That it will please you
To give this poor petition to the King,
20 And aid me with that store of power you have
To come into his presence.
GENTLEMAN   The King's not here.
HELEN   Not here, sir?
GENTLEMAN   Not indeed.
He hence removed° last night, and with more haste   departed
Than is his use.°   custom
WIDOW   Lord, how we lose our pains!
25 HELEN   All's well that ends well yet,
Though time seem so adverse and means unfit.
—I do beseech you, whither is he gone?
GENTLEMAN   Marry, as I take it, to Roussillon,
Whither I am going.
HELEN   I do beseech you, sir,
30 Since you are like to see the King before me,
Commend° the paper to his gracious hand,   Present
Which I presume shall render you no blame
But rather make you thank your pains for it.
I will come after you with what good speed
Our means will make us means.°   resources will permit
35 GENTLEMAN   This I'll do for you.
HELEN   And you shall find yourself to be well thanked,
Whate'er falls more.   [Exit GENTLEMAN.]
We must to horse again. [to ATTENDANTS] Go, go, provide.
                                        [Exeunt.]

5.2

Enter CLOWN and PAROLES.
PAROLES   Good Monsieur Lavache, give my lord Lafeu this
letter. I have ere now, sir, been better known to you, when I
have held familiarity with fresher clothes. But I am now, sir,
muddied in Fortune's mood and smell somewhat strong of
5   her strong displeasure.
CLOWN   Truly, Fortune's displeasure is but sluttish if it smell
so strongly as thou speak'st of. I will henceforth eat no fish
of Fortune's butt'ring.° Prithee, allow the wind.[1]   prepared by Fortune
PAROLES   Nay, you need not to stop your nose, sir. I spake but
10   by a metaphor.

5.2 Location: Roussillon.   1. Stand downwind of me.

CLOWN   Indeed, sir, if your metaphor stink I will stop my nose, or against any man's metaphor. Prithee, get thee further.

PAROLES   Pray you, sir, deliver me this paper.

CLOWN   Foh! Prithee, stand away. A paper from Fortune's
15 close-stool,° to give to a nobleman! Look, here he comes   *toilet*
himself.

Enter LAFEU.

Here is a pur² of Fortune's, sir, or of Fortune's cat—but not
a musk cat³—that has fallen into the unclean fishpond of
her displeasure and, as he says, is muddied withal. Pray you,
20 sir, use the carp⁴ as you may, for he looks like a poor,
decayed, ingenious, foolish, rascally knave. I do pity his
distress in my similes of comfort and leave him to your
lordship.

PAROLES   My lord, I am a man whom Fortune hath cruelly
25 scratched.

LAFEU   And what would you have me to do? 'Tis too late to
pare her nails now. Wherein have you played the knave with
Fortune that she should scratch you, who of herself is a good
lady and would not have knaves thrive long under her? There's
30 a *quart d'écu* for you. Let the justices⁵ make you and Fortune
friends; I am for other business.

PAROLES   I beseech your honor to hear me one single word.

LAFEU   You beg a single penny more. Come, you shall ha't.
Save your word.°   *breath*
35 PAROLES   My name, my good lord, is Paroles.

LAFEU   You beg more than one word,⁶ then. Cox my passion,°   *By God's passion*
give me your hand! How does your drum?

PAROLES   Oh, my good lord, you were the first that found me.

LAFEU   Was I, in sooth? And I was the first that lost thee.

40 PAROLES   It lies in you, my lord, to bring me in some grace,⁷
for you did bring me out.°   *out of favor*

LAFEU   Out upon thee, knave, dost thou put upon me at once
both the office of God and the devil? One brings thee in
grace and the other brings thee out. The King's coming; I
45 know by his trumpets. Sirrah, inquire further after me. I had
talk of you last night. Though you are a fool and a knave,
you shall eat. Go to, follow.

PAROLES   I praise God for you.   *[Exeunt.]*

5.3

Flourish. Enter KING, *old Lady* [COUNTESS], LAFEU,
the two French LORDS [DUMAINE], *with* ATTENDANTS.

KING   We lost a jewel of° her, and our esteem°   *in / (own) worth*
Was made much poorer by it, but your son,
As mad in folly, lacked the sense to know
Her estimation home.°   *value to the full*

COUNTESS   'Tis past, my liege,
5 And I beseech your majesty to make° it   *consider*

---

2. Piece of dung; cat's purr; knave (in the card game
post and pair).
3. Civet cat, a source of perfume.
4. Fish often bred in mud ponds; chatterbox.
5. Of the peace, responsible for beggars.

6. Playing on "Paroles," "words."
7. Into some favor (but Lafeu takes "grace" in its
religious sense).
5.3 Location: Scene continues.

Natural rebellion, done i'th' blade° of youth,   *greenness*
When oil and fire, too strong for reason's force,
O'erbears it and burns on.

KING   My honored lady,
I have forgiven and forgotten all,
10   Though my revenges were high[1] bent upon him
And watched° the time to shoot.   *vigilantly awaited*

LAFEU   This I must say,
But first I beg my pardon. The young lord
Did to his majesty, his mother, and his lady
Offense of mighty note, but to himself
15   The greatest wrong of all. He lost a wife
Whose beauty did astonish the survey°   *observation*
Of richest° eyes; whose words all ears took captive; *most experienced*
Whose dear perfection hearts that scorned to serve
Humbly called mistress.

KING   Praising what is lost
20   Makes the remembrance dear. [*to* ATTENDANT] Well, call him
      hither.
We are reconciled, and the first view shall kill
All repetition.[2] Let him not ask our pardon.
The nature of his great offense is dead,
And deeper than oblivion we do bury
25   Th'incensing relics° of it. Let him approach   *infuriating reminders*
A stranger, no offender, and inform him
So 'tis our will he should.

ATTENDANT   I shall, my liege.   [*Exit.*]

KING [*to* LAFEU]   What says he to your daughter? Have you
      spoke?

LAFEU   All that he is hath reference° to your highness.   *is submitted*

30 KING   Then shall we have a match. I have letters sent me
That sets him high in fame.
                Enter Count BERTRAM.

LAFEU   He looks well on't.

KING   I am not a day of season,°   *constant weather*
For thou mayst see a sunshine and a hail
In me at once. But to the brightest beams
35   Distracted° clouds give way. So stand thou forth;   *Agitated; broken*
The time is fair again.

BERTRAM   My high repented blames,°   *much-repented faults*
Dear sovereign, pardon to me.

KING   All is whole.°   *healed*
Not one word more of the consumèd time.
Let's take the instant by the forward top,[3]
40   For we are old, and on our quick'st decrees
Th'inaudible and noiseless foot of time
Steals ere we can effect them. You remember
The daughter of this lord?

BERTRAM   Admiringly, my liege. At first
45   I stuck° my choice upon her, ere my heart   *fixed*
Durst make too bold a herald of my tongue;
Where the impression of mine eye infixing,[4]

---

1. To the utmost (like a taut bow).
2. Rehearsal of past grievances.
3. Let's seize time by the forelock; proverbial for

"taking a present opportunity."
4. Once the impression of Lafeu's daughter was implanted in my heart.

Contempt his scornful perspective[5] did lend me,
Which warped the line of every other favor,°   *face*
50   Scorned a fair color° or expressed it stolen,[6]   *complexion*
Extended or contracted all proportions
To a most hideous object. Thence it came
That she° whom all men praised, and whom myself   *(Helen)*
Since I have lost have loved, was in mine eye
The dust that did offend it.
55   KING   Well excused.
That thou didst love her strikes some scores° away   *debits*
From the great count.° But love that comes too late,   *reckoning*
Like a remorseful° pardon slowly carried,   *compassionate; regretful*
To the great sender turns a sour offense,
60   Crying, "That's good that's gone." Our rash faults
Make trivial price of° serious things we have,   *Underestimate*
Not knowing them until we know their grave.°   *lose them forever*
Oft our displeasures, to ourselves unjust,
Destroy our friends and after weep° their dust.   *mourn over*
65   Our own love waking° cries to see what's done,   *coming to its senses*
While shameful hate sleeps out the afternoon.
Be this sweet Helen's knell, and now forget her.
Send forth your amorous token for fair Maudlin.°   *Lafeu's daughter*
The main consents are had, and here we'll stay
70   To see our widower's second marriage day.
COUNTESS[7]   Which better than the first, O dear heaven, bless
Or, ere they meet, in me, O Nature, cease.[8]
LAFEU   Come on, my son, in whom my house's name
Must be digested,[9] give a favor from you
75   To sparkle in the spirits of my daughter,
That she may quickly come. [BERTRAM *offers a ring.*] By my
     old beard
And ev'ry hair that's on't! Helen that's dead
Was a sweet creature; such a ring as this,
The last° that ere I took her leave at court,   *last time*
I saw upon her finger.[1]
80   BERTRAM   Hers it was not.
KING   Now pray you, let me see it. For mine eye,
While I was speaking, oft was fastened to't.
This ring was mine, and when I gave it Helen
I bade her if her fortunes ever stood
85   Necessitied to° help, that by this token   *In need of*
I would relieve her. Had you that craft to reave° her   *deprive*
Of what should stead° her most?   *aid*
BERTRAM   My gracious sovereign,
Howe'er it pleases you to take it so,
The ring was never hers.
COUNTESS   Son, on my life
90   I have seen her wear it, and she reckoned it
At her life's rate.°   *value*

5. Distorting optical glass.
6. Declared it artificial.
7. In F, the King speaks these lines.
8. Before they come to resemble one another, let me

die.
9. Absorbed (because Maudlin is his only child and will take Bertram's name).
1. See 4.2.61–64.

LAFEU   I am sure I saw her wear it.

BERTRAM   You are deceived, my lord; she never saw it.
In Florence was it from a casement thrown me,
Wrapped in a paper which contained the name
95   Of her that threw it. Noble she was, and thought
I stood engaged,[2] but when I had subscribed
To mine own fortune,° and informed her fully   admitted my situation
I could not answer in that course of honor
As she had made the overture, she ceased
100 In heavy satisfaction° and would never   sad acceptance
Receive the ring again.

KING   Plutus° himself,   god of riches
That knows the tinct and multiplying med'cine,[3]
Hath not in nature's mystery more science°   expertise
Than I have in this ring. 'Twas mine, 'twas Helen's,
105 Whoever gave it you. Then if you know
That you are well acquainted with yourself,[4]
Confess 'twas hers and by what rough enforcement
You got it from her. She called the saints to surety°   guarantee
That she would never put it from her finger,
110 Unless she gave it to yourself in bed,
Where you have never come, or sent it us
Upon° her great disaster.   On the occasion of

BERTRAM   She never saw it.

KING   Thou speak'st it falsely, as I love mine honor,
And mak'st conjectural fears to come into me
115 Which I would fain° shut out. If it should prove   gladly
That thou art so inhuman—'twill not prove so—
And yet I know not. Thou didst hate her deadly
And she is dead, which nothing but to close
Her eyes myself could win me to believe
120 More than to see this ring. —Take him away!
—My forepassed proofs,[5] howe'er the matter fall,°   befalls
Shall tax° my fears of little vanity,°   accuse / foolishness
Having vainly feared too little. —Away with him!
We'll sift this matter further.

BERTRAM   If you shall prove
125 This ring was ever hers, you shall as easy
Prove that I husbanded her bed in Florence,
Where yet she never was.   [Exit, guarded.]
          Enter a GENTLEMAN [austringer].

KING   I am wrapped in dismal thinkings.

GENTLEMAN   Gracious sovereign.
Whether I have been to blame or no, I know not.
130 Here's a petition from a Florentine,
Who hath for four or five removes come short
To tender it herself.[6] I undertook it,
Vanquished thereto by the fair grace and speech
Of the poor suppliant, who by this° I know   now
135 Is here attending. Her business looks° in her   shows itself

---

2. Pledged to her (alternatively, "ungaged," not promised to anyone else).
3. Alchemical elixir for turning other metals into gold.
4. That you know who you are; that you are willing to admit your actions.
5. My evidence already in hand.
6. Who . . . herself: Who has for four or five changes of royal residence failed to arrive in time to deliver it herself.

With an importing° visage, and she told me   *urgent*
In a sweet verbal brief° it did concern   *summary*
Your highness with herself.

KING [*reads the*] *letter*   "Upon his many protestations to marry
140   me when his wife was dead, I blush to say it, he won me. Now
is the Count Roussillon a widower. His vows are forfeited to
me,[7] and my honors paid to him. He stole from Florence,
taking no leave, and I follow him to his country for justice.
Grant it me, O King; in you it best lies. Otherwise a seducer
145   flourishes and a poor maid is undone.
                                                Diana Capilet."

LAFEU   I will buy me a son-in-law in a fair[8] and toll for this.[9]
I'll none of him.

KING   The heavens have thought well on thee, Lafeu,
150   To bring forth this discov'ry. —Seek these suitors.
                                    [*Exit* GENTLEMAN *austringer.*]
—Go speedily, and bring again the Count.
                                    [*Exit an* ATTENDANT.]
I am a-feared the life of Helen, lady,
Was foully snatched.

COUNTESS   Now justice on the doers!
            Enter BERTRAM.

KING   I wonder, sir, since wives are monsters to you,
155   And that° you fly them as you swear them lordship,[1]   *since*
Yet you desire to marry.
            Enter WIDOW [*and*] DIANA.
                        What woman's that?

DIANA   I am, my lord, a wretched Florentine,
Derivèd° from the ancient Capilet.   *Descended*
My suit, as I do understand, you know,
160   And therefore know how far I may be pitied.

WIDOW   I am her mother, sir, whose age and honor
Both suffer under this complaint we bring,
And both° shall cease without your remedy.   *(age and honor)*

KING   Come hither, Count. Do you know these women?
165   BERTRAM   My lord, I neither can nor will deny
But that I know them. Do they charge me further?

DIANA   Why do you look so strange upon your wife?

BERTRAM   She's none of mine, my lord.

DIANA   If you shall marry
You give away this° hand, and that is mine;   *(Bertram's)*
170   You give away heaven's vows, and those are mine;
You give away myself, which is known mine.
For I by vow am so embodied yours
That she which marries you must marry me,
Either both or none.

175   LAFEU   Your reputation comes too short for my daughter. You
are no husband for her.

BERTRAM   My lord, this is a fond° and desp'rate creature   *foolish*
Whom sometime I have laughed with. Let your highness
Lay a more noble thought upon mine honor
180   Than for to think that I would sink it here.

---

7. His promises have fallen due.
8. Notorious for unreliable merchandise.   (Bertram).
9. Pay a tax for the privilege of selling this one   1. As soon as you vow to wed them.

KING   Sir, for my thoughts, you have them ill to friend²
    Till your deeds gain them. Fairer prove your honor
    Than in my thought it lies!
DIANA   Good my lord,
    Ask him upon his oath if he does think
185   He had not my virginity.
KING   What say'st thou to her?
BERTRAM   She's impudent, my lord,
    And was a common gamester° to the camp.   *prostitute*
DIANA   He does me wrong, my lord. If I were so
    He might have bought me at a common price.
190   Do not believe him. Oh, behold this ring,
    Whose high respect° and rich validity°   *worth / value*
    Did lack a parallel. Yet for all that
    He gave it to a commoner o'th' camp
    If I be one.
COUNTESS   He blushes, and 'tis hit.°   *it hit the mark*
195   Of six preceding ancestors that gem,
    Conferred by testament to th' sequent issue,°   *following generation*
    Hath it been owed° and worn. This is his wife;   *owned*
    That ring's a thousand proofs.
KING   Methought you said°   *(perhaps in the letter)*
    You saw one here in court could witness it.
200 DIANA   I did, my lord, but loath am to produce
    So bad an instrument. His name's Paroles.
LAFEU   I saw the man today, if man he be.
KING   —Find him and bring him hither. [*Exit an* ATTENDANT.]
BERTRAM   What of him?
    He's quoted° for a most perfidious slave   *noted*
205   With all the spots o'th' world, taxed and debauched,
    Whose nature sickens but to speak a truth.
    Am I or° that or this for what he'll utter   *either*
    That will speak anything?
KING   She hath that ring of yours.
BERTRAM   I think she has. Certain it is I liked her
210   And boarded° her i'th' wanton way of youth.   *made advances to*
    She knew her distance and did angle for me,
    Madding° my eagerness with her restraint,   *Maddening*
    As all impediments in fancy's° course   *love's*
    Are motives° of more fancy. And in fine,°   *causes / the end*
215   Her infinite cunning with her modern° grace   *commonplace*
    Subdued me to her rate.° She got the ring,   *price*
    And I had that which any inferior might
    At market price have bought.
DIANA   I must be patient:
    You that have turned off a first so noble wife
220   May justly diet° me. I pray you yet—   *starve (of favor)*
    Since you lack virtue, I will lose a husband—
    Send for your ring, I will return it home,
    And give me mine again.
BERTRAM   I have it not.
KING   What ring was yours, I pray you?
225 DIANA   Sir, much like the same upon your finger.

---

2. *you . . . friend:* they are no friends of yours.

KING   Know you this ring? This ring was his of late.

DIANA   And this was it I gave him being abed.

KING   The story then goes false you threw it him
Out of a casement.

DIANA   I have spoke the truth.

Enter PAROLES.

230   BERTRAM   My lord, I do confess the ring was hers.

KING   You boggle shrewdly;³ every feather starts° you.   *startles*
—Is this the man you speak of?

DIANA   Ay, my lord.

KING   Tell me, sirrah—but tell me true, I charge you,
Not fearing the displeasure of your master,

235   Which on your just proceeding I'll keep off—
By° him and by this woman here, what know you?   *About*

PAROLES   So please your majesty, my master hath been
an honorable gentleman. Tricks he hath had in him which
gentlemen have.

240   KING   Come, come, to th' purpose. Did he love this woman?

PAROLES   Faith, sir, he did love her, but how?

KING   How, I pray you?

PAROLES   He did love her, sir, as a gentleman loves a woman.

KING   How is that?

245   PAROLES   He loved her, sir, and loved her not.

KING   As thou art a knave and no knave. —What an equivocal
companion is this!

PAROLES   I am a poor man and at your majesty's command.

LAFEU   He's a good drum,⁴ my lord, but a naughty° orator.   *bad*

250   DIANA   Do you know he promised me marriage?

PAROLES   Faith, I know more than I'll speak.

KING   But wilt thou not speak all thou know'st?

PAROLES   Yes, so please your majesty. I did go between them,
as I said, but more than that, he loved her. For indeed he

255   was mad for her, and talked of Satan, and of limbo, and of
furies, and I know not what. Yet I was in that° credit with   *so much*
them at that time that I knew of their going to bed, and of
other motions,° as promising her marriage, and things which   *proposals*
would derive me ill will to speak of. Therefore I will not

260   speak what I know.

KING   Thou hast spoken all already, unless thou canst say
they are married. But thou art too fine° in thy evidence: *hairsplitting*
therefore stand aside.
[*to* DIANA] This ring, you say, was yours.

DIANA   Ay, my good lord.

265   KING   Where did you buy it? Or who gave it you?

DIANA   It was not given me, nor I did not buy it.

KING   Who lent it you?

DIANA   It was not lent me neither.

KING   Where did you find it then?

DIANA   I found it not.

KING   If it were yours by none of all these ways,
How could you give it him?

---

3. You take fright violently; you attempt to evade the
point wickedly (or incompetently).

4. Capable only of noise; Lafeu probably also refers
to Paroles' earlier adventures.

270 DIANA   I never gave it him.

LAFEU   This woman's an easy glove, my lord: she goes off and
on at pleasure.

KING   This ring was mine. I gave it his first wife.

DIANA   It might be yours or hers for aught I know.

275 KING   Take her away; I do not like her now.
To prison with her! And away with him!
[*to* DIANA] Unless thou tell'st me where thou hadst this ring,
Thou diest within this hour.

DIANA   I'll never tell you.

KING   Take her away!

DIANA   I'll put in bail, my liege.

280 KING   I think thee now some common customer.°   prostitute

DIANA   By Jove, if ever I knew° man, 'twas you.   (carnally)

KING   Wherefore hast thou accused him all this while?

DIANA   Because he's guilty and he is not guilty.
He knows I am no maid and he'll swear to't;

285 I'll swear I am a maid and he knows not.
Great King, I am no strumpet, by my life;
I am either maid or else [*pointing at* LAFEU] this old man's° wife.   (Lafeu's)

KING   She does abuse our ears. To prison with her!

DIANA   Good mother, fetch my bail.   [*Exit* WIDOW.]
                    —Stay, royal sir.

290 The jeweler that owes° the ring is sent for   owns
And he shall surety me.° But for this lord,   be my security
Who hath abused me as he knows himself,
Though yet he never harmed me, here I quit° him.   acquit; repay; leave
He knows himself my bed he hath defiled,

295 And at that time he got his wife with child.
Dead though she be, she feels her young one kick.
So there's my riddle: one that's dead is quick.°   alive; pregnant
And now behold the meaning.
                    Enter HELEN *and* WIDOW.

KING   Is there no exorcist°   conjurer
Beguiles the truer office° of mine eyes?   function
Is't real that I see?

300 HELEN   No, my good lord.
'Tis but the shadow° of a wife you see,   ghost; imitation
The name and not the thing.

BERTRAM   Both, both! Oh, pardon!

HELEN   O my good lord, when I was like° this maid   in the place of
I found you wondrous kind. There is your ring,

305 And look you, here's your letter. This it says:
"When from my finger you can get this ring,
And are by me with child," etc. This is done,
Will you be mine now you are doubly won?

BERTRAM   If she, my liege, can make me know this clearly,

310 I'll love her dearly, ever, ever, dearly.

HELEN   If it appear not plain and prove untrue,
Deadly divorce step between me and you.
O my dear mother, do I see you living?

LAFEU [*to* PAROLES]   Mine eyes smell onions; I shall weep anon.

315 Good Tom Drum, lend me a handkerchief.
So. I thank thee. Wait on me home, I'll make sport with
thee. Let thy curtsies alone, they are scurvy ones.

KING Let us from point to point this story know
       To make the even° truth in pleasure flow.   *plain*
320   [*to* DIANA] If thou beest yet a fresh uncroppèd flower,
       Choose thou thy husband and I'll pay thy dower.
       For I can guess that by thy honest aid
       Thou kept'st a wife herself, thyself a maid.
       Of that and all the progress more and less⁵
325   Resolvedly° more leisure shall express.   *So questions are resolved*
       All yet seems well, and if it end so meet,°   *properly*
       The bitter passed, more welcome is the sweet.
            Flourish.
       The King's a beggar now the play is done.
       All is well ended if this suit be won,
330   That you express content,° which we will pay   *(by applause)*
       With strife° to please you, day exceeding° day.   *trying / after*
       Ours be your patience, then, and yours our parts;⁶
       Your gentle hands lend us, and take our hearts.   *Exeunt.*

---

5. The course of events, great and small.
6. *Ours . . . parts:* We will wait patiently, like an audience, while you take the active part.

APPENDICES

Early Modern Map Culture

In the early modern period, maps were often considered rare and precious objects, and seeing a map could be an important and life-changing event. This was so for Richard Hakluyt, whose book *The Principal Navigations, Voyages, Traffics and Discoveries of the English Nation* (1598–1600) was the first major collection of narratives describing England's overseas trading ventures. Hakluyt tells how, as a boy still at school in London, he visited his uncle's law chambers and saw a book of cosmography lying open there. Perceiving his nephew's interest in the maps, the uncle turned to a modern map and "pointed with his wand to all the knowen Seas, Gulfs, Bayes, Straights, Capes, Rivers, Empires, Kingdomes, Dukedomes, and Territories of ech part, with declaration also of their speciall commodities and particular wants, which by the benefit of traffike, and entercourse of merchants, are plentifully supplied. From the Mappe he brought me to the Bible, and turning to the 107 Psalme, directed mee to the 23 and 24 verses, where I read, that they which go downe to the sea in ships, and occupy [work] by the great waters, they see the works of the Lord, and his woonders in the deepe." This event, Hakluyt records, made so deep an impression on him that he vowed he would devote his life to the study of this kind of knowledge. *The Principal Navigations* was the result, a book that mixes a concern with the profit to be made from trade and from geographical knowledge with praise for the Christian god who made the "great waters" and, in Hakluyt's view, looked with special favor on the English merchants and sailors who voyaged over them.

In the early modern period, access to maps was far less easy than it is today. Before the advent of printing in the late fifteenth century, maps were drawn and decorated by hand. Because they were rare and expensive, these medieval maps were for the most part owned by the wealthy and the powerful. Sometimes adorned with pictures of fabulous sea monsters and exotic creatures, maps often revealed the Christian worldview of those who composed them. Jerusalem appeared squarely in the middle of many maps (called T and O maps), with Asia, Africa, and Europe, representing the rest of the known world, arranged symmetrically around the Holy City. Because they had not yet been discovered by Europeans, North and South America were not depicted.

Mapping practices changed markedly during the late fifteenth and sixteenth centuries both because of the advent of print and also because European nations such as Portugal and Spain began sending ships on long sea voyages to open new trade routes to the East and, eventually, to the Americas. During this period, monarchs competed to have the best cartographers supply them with accurate maps of their realms and especially of lands in Africa, Asia, or the Americas, where they hoped to trade or plant settlements. Such knowledge was precious and jealously guarded. The value of such maps and the secrecy that surrounded them are indicated by a story in Hakluyt's *Principal Navigations*. An English ship had captured a Portuguese vessel in the Azores, and a map was discovered among the ship's valuable cargo, which included spices, silks, carpets, porcelain, and other exotic commercial objects. The map was "inclosed in a case of sweete Cedar wood, and lapped up almost an hundred fold in fine calicut-cloth, as though it had been some incomparable jewell." The value of the map and an explanation for the careful way in which it was packed lay in the particular information it afforded the English about Portuguese trading routes. More than beautiful objects, maps like this one were crucial to the international race to find safe sea routes to the most profitable trading centers in the East.

In the sixteenth century, books of maps began to be printed, making them more affordable for ordinary people, though some of these books, published as big folio volumes, remained too dear for any but wealthy patrons to buy. Yet maps were increasingly a part of daily life, and printing made many of them more accessible. Playgoers in Shakespeare's audiences must have understood in general the value and uses of maps, for they appear as props in a number of his plays. Most famously, at the beginning of *King Lear*, the old king has a map brought onstage showing the extent of his kingdom. He then points on the map to the three separate parts into which he intends to divide his realm to share among his daughters. The map, often unfurled with a flourish on a table or held up for view by members of Lear's retinue, signals the crucial relationship of the land to the monarch. He is his domains, and the map signifies his possession of them. To divide the kingdom, in essence to tear apart the map, would have been judged foolish and destructive by early modern political theorists. Similarly, in *1 Henry IV*, when rebels against the sitting monarch, Henry IV, plot to overthrow him, they bring a map onstage in order to decide what part of the kingdom will be given to each rebel leader. Their proposed dismemberment of the realm signifies the danger they pose. Treasonously, they would rend in pieces the body of the commonwealth.

Maps, of course, had other uses besides signifying royal domains. In some instances, they were used pragmatically to help people find their way from one place to another. A very common kind of map, a portolan chart, depicted in minute detail the coastline of a particular body of water. Used by sailors, these maps frequently were made by people native to the region they described. Many world or regional maps, because they were beautifully decorated and embellished with vivid colors, were used for decorative purposes. John Dee, a learned adviser to Queen Elizabeth and a great book collector, wrote that some people used maps "to beautifie their Halls, Parlers, Chambers, Galeries, Studies, or Libraries." He also spoke of more scholarly uses for these objects. They could, for example, be useful aids in the study of history or geography, enabling people to locate "thinges past, as battels fought, earthquakes, heavenly fyringes, and such occurents in histories mentioned." Today we make similar use of maps, like those included in this volume, when, in reading Shakespeare's plays, we resort to a map to find out where the Battle of Agincourt took place or where Othello sailed when he left Venice for Cyprus.

The print edition of *The Norton Shakespeare* includes five maps; the Digital Edition seven. Four of these maps, found in both editions, are modern ones drawn specifically to show the location of places important to Shakespeare's plays. They depict the British Isles and western France, London, and the Mediterranean world, in addition to a map of England showing the typical routes the Chamberlain's Men followed when they went on tour outside of London. The print and digital editions also both contain a period map of the Christian Holy Lands at the eastern tip of the Mediterranean Sea. This map was included in what was known as the Bishops' Bible, first printed in London in 1568. Put together under the leadership of the Archbishop of Canterbury, Matthew Parker, working with a committee of Anglican bishops, the 1568 edition featured beautiful typography and illustrations. The text continued to undergo revisions, and twenty editions of it were published between 1568 and 1602.

This last map shows places mentioned in the first four Gospels (Matthew, Mark, Luke, and John), which collectively tell of the life and deeds of Jesus. It indicates, for example, the location of Bethlehem, where he was born; Nazareth, where he spent his youth; and Cana of Galilee, where he turned water into wine at a marriage. It suggests that, to the English reader, this particular territory was overwritten by and completely intertwined with Christian history. Yet in the Mediterranean Sea, on the left of the map, several large ships are visible, reminders of another fact about this region: it was a vigorous trading arena where European Christian merchants did business with local merchants—Christian, Jew, and Muslim—and with traders bringing luxury goods by overland routes from the East. A number of Shakespeare's plays are set in this complex eastern Mediterranean region where several religious traditions laid claim to

territory and many commercial powers competed for preeminence. *Pericles*, for example, has a hero who is the ruler of Tyre, a city on the upper right side of the map. In the
course of his wanderings, Pericles visits many cities along the eastern coasts of the
Mediterranean. The conclusion of the play, in which the hero is reunited both with his
long-lost daughter and with the wife he believes dead, has seemed to many critics to
share in a sense of Christian miracle, despite its ostensibly pagan setting. *The Comedy
of Errors* and parts of *Othello* and of *Antony and Cleopatra* are also set in the Eastern
Mediterranean. One of Shakespeare's earliest plays, *The Comedy of Errors*, is an urban
comedy in which the protagonists are merchants deeply involved in commercial transactions. It is also the first play in which Shakespeare mentions the Americas, which he
does in an extended joke in which he compares parts of a serving woman's body to the
countries on a map including Ireland, France, and the Americas. In *Othello*, the eastern Mediterranean island of Cyprus is represented as a tense Christian outpost defend-
ing Venetian interests against the Muslim Turks. In *Antony and Cleopatra*, Egypt
figures as the site of Eastern luxury and also of imperial conquest, an extension of the
Roman Empire. Clearly, this region was to Shakespeare and his audiences one of
the most complex and highly charged areas of the world: a site of religious, commercial, and imperial significance.

Two other maps occur only in the Digital Edition, where their colors and their
details can be appreciated. The first is a map of London that appeared in a 1574 edition
of a famous German atlas, *Civitates Orbis Terrarum* (*Cities of the World*), compiled by
George Braun with engravings by Franz Hogenberg. This remarkable atlas includes
maps and information on cities throughout Europe, Asia, and North Africa; the first
of its six volumes appeared in 1572, the last in 1617. Being included in the volume
indicated a city's status as a recognized metropolitan center. In a charming touch,
Braun added to his city maps pictures of figures in local dress. At the bottom of the
map of London, for example, there are four figures who appear to represent the city's
prosperous citizens. In the center, a man in a long robe holds the hand of a soberly
dressed matron. On either side of them are younger and more ornately dressed figures. The young man sports a long sword and a short cloak, the woman a dress with
elaborate skirts. In the atlas, the map is colored, and the clothes of the two young
people echo one another in shades of green and red.

At the time the map was made, London was a rapidly expanding metropolis. In
1550, it contained about 55,000 people; by 1600, it would contain nearly 200,000. The
map shows the densely populated old walled city north of the Thames River, in the
middle of which was Eastcheap, the commercial district where, in Shakespeare's plays
about the reign of Henry IV, Falstaff holds court in a tavern. The map also shows that
by 1570 London was spreading westward beyond the wall toward Westminster Palace.
This medieval structure, which appears on the extreme left side of the map, was where
English monarchs resided when in London and where, at the end of *2 Henry IV*, the
king dies in the fabled Jerusalem Chamber of the Westminster complex. On the far
right of the map, one can see the Tower of London, where Edward IV's young sons
were imprisoned by Richard III, an event depicted in Shakespeare's *The Tragedy
of King Richard the Third*. The map also indicates the centrality of the Thames to London's commercial life. It shows the river full of boats; some of those on the east side of
London Bridge are large oceangoing vessels with several masts. South of the river,
where many of the most famous London theaters, including Shakespeare's Globe, were
to be constructed in the 1590s, there are relatively few buildings. By 1600, this
would change, as Southwark, as it was known, came to be an increasingly busy
entertainment, residential, and commercial district.

The final map, of Great Britain and Ireland, comes from a 1612 edition of John
Speed's *The Theatre of the Empire of Great Britain*, an innovative atlas containing
individual maps of counties and towns in England and Wales, as well as larger maps
that include Scotland and Ireland. Speed was by trade a tailor who increasingly
devoted his time to the study of history and cartography. Befriended by the antiquarian

scholar William Camden, he eventually won patronage from Sir Fulke Greville, who gave him a pension that allowed him to devote himself full-time to his scholarly endeavors. *The Theatre* was one product of this newfound freedom. The map included here, one of his most ambitious, shows the entire British Isles, nominated by Speed as "The Kingdome of Great Britaine and Ireland," though at this time Ireland was far from under the control of the English crown and Scotland was still an independent kingdom. James I, a Scot by birth, had unsuccessfully tried to forge a formal union between England and Scotland. This problem of the relationship of the parts of the British Isles to one another, and England's assertion of power over the others, is treated in *Henry V*, in which officers from Wales, Ireland, and Scotland are sharply delineated yet all depicted as loyal subjects of the English king.

One striking aspect of Speed's map is the balance it strikes between the two capital cities, London on the left, prominently featuring the Thames and London Bridge, and Edinburgh on the right. This would have pleased James, whose interest in his native country Shakespeare played to in his writing of *Macbeth*, which is based on material from Scottish history. Speed's map acknowledges the claims of the monarch to the territory it depicts. In the upper left corner, the British lion and the Scottish unicorn support a roundel topped with a crown. When James became king of England in 1603, he created this merged symbol of Scottish-English unity. The motto of the Royal Order of the Garter, *"Honi soit qui mal y pense"* (Shamed be he who thinks ill of it), is inscribed around the circumference. In the bottom left corner of the map, another locus of authority is established. Two cherubs, one holding a compass, the other a globe, sit beneath a banner on which is inscribed "Performed by John Speed." If the territory is the monarch's, the craft that depicts it belongs to the tailor turned cartographer.

Today, maps are readily available from shops or on the Internet, but in early modern England they were rare and valuable objects that could generate great excitement in those who owned or beheld them. Along with other precious items, maps were sometimes put on display in libraries and sitting rooms, but they had functions beyond the ornamental. They helped to explain and order the world, indicating who claimed certain domains, showing where the familiar stories of the Bible or of English history occurred, helping merchants find their way to distant markets. As John Dee, the early modern map enthusiast concluded, "Some, for one purpose: and some, for an other, liketh, loveth, getteth, and useth, Mappes, Chartes, and Geographicall Globes."

JEAN E. HOWARD

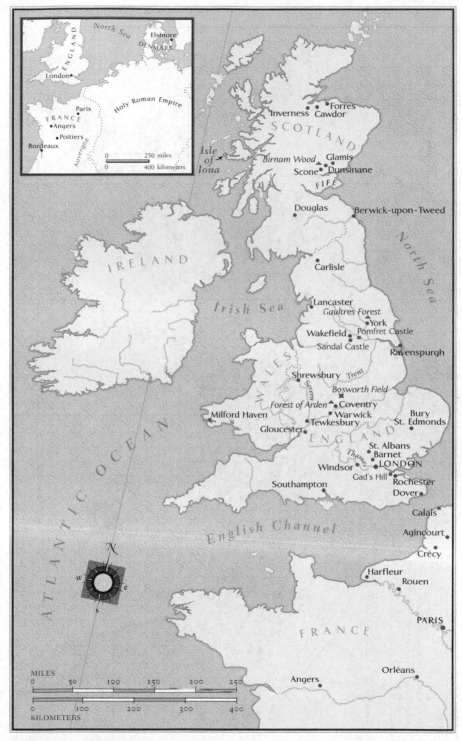

Ireland, Scotland, Wales, England, and Western France: Places Important to Shakespeare's Plays

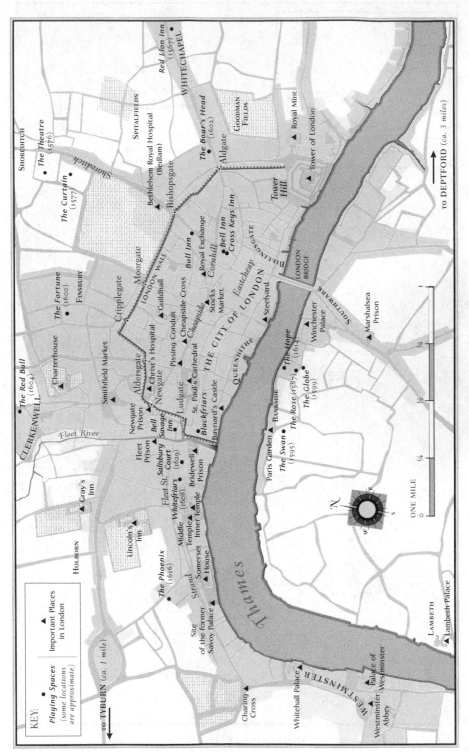

London: Places Important to Shakespeare's Plays and London Playgoing

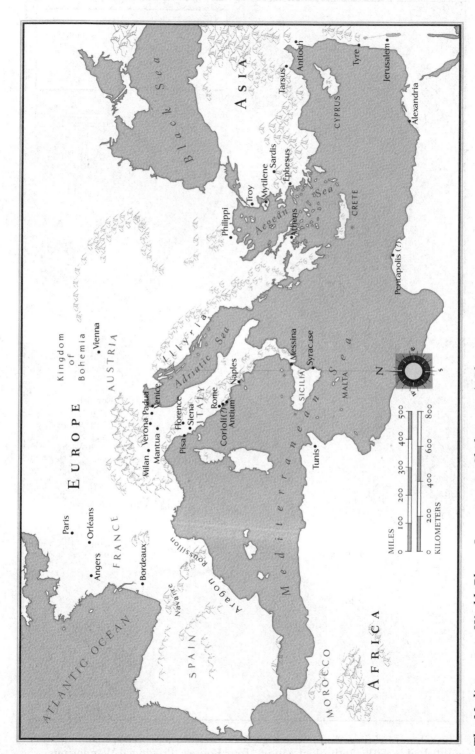

The Mediterranean World: Places Important to Shakespeare's Plays

The Chamberlain's Men and King's Men on Tour (adapted from a map first published by Sally-Beth MacLean in "Tour Routes: 'Provincial Wanderings' or 'Traditional Circuits'?" *Medieval and Renaissance Drama in England* 6 [1992]: 1–14).

Map of the Holy Land, from the Bishops' Bible, printed in London, 1568

Map of the British Isles, from the *Atlas of Italy*, printed by Leyden, 1508.

Documents

The documents in this section provide some early perspectives on Shakespeare's reputation and the works included in this volume. A much more extensive selection of documents can be found in the Digital Edition of *The Norton Shakespeare,* which offers a broad range of contemporary testimony about Shakespeare's character, his art, and the social and institutional conditions under which his art was produced. The first digital section, "Shakespeare and His Works," contains traces of Shakespeare's life and career, evidence of his reputation in the literary community, and a variety of reactions to his plays and poems. The second section, "The Theater Scene," takes a wider view of Shakespeare's professional world with playhouse documents that offer a behind-the-scenes glimpse of companies acquiring scripts and properties, actors rehearsing their parts, and new theaters being constructed, while government documents show dramatic patronage, regulation, and censorship in action.

MISHA TERAMURA

Gesta Grayorum on *The Comedy of Errors*
(December 28, 1594)

[*Gesta Grayorum* is the title of an account of the holiday revels conducted by the law students of Gray's Inn. It was first published in 1688 from a manuscript that apparently had been handed down since the previous century. The subtitle of the book, "The History of the High and Mighty Prince, Henry Prince of Purpoole," alludes to the ceremonial ruler chosen for the occasion, the "Prince of State" referred to in the excerpt below. (The name Purpoole, or Portpool, alludes to the manor house on whose site Gray's Inn was established.) The performance of *The Comedy of Errors* was evidently part of the entertainment for the second night of revels. The text is modernized from the first published edition of the *Gesta Grayorum* (London, 1688).]

The next grand night was intended to be upon Innocents' Day at night, at which time there was a great presence of lords, ladies, and worshipful personages that did expect some notable performance at that time, which, indeed, had been effected if the multitude of beholders had not been so exceeding great that, thereby, there was no convenient room for those that were actors. By reason whereof, very good inventions and conceits could not have opportunity to be applauded, which otherwise would have been great contentation to the beholders. Against which time, our friend, the Inner Temple,[1] determined to send their Ambassador to our Prince of State, as sent from Frederick Templarius, their Emperor, who was then busied in his wars against the Turk. The Ambassador came very gallantly appointed and attended by a great number of brave gentlemen, which arrived at our Court about nine of the clock at night. . . . He was received very kindly of the Prince and placed in a chair besides His Highness, to the end that he might be partaker of the sports intended. . . .

---

1. Another of the Inns of Court, whose students participated in the game of make-believe by sending their own "Templarian" ambassador to the revels.

When the Ambassador was placed, as aforesaid, and that there was something to be performed for the delight of the beholders, there arose such a disordered tumult and crowd upon the stage that there was no opportunity to effect that which was intended. There came so great a number of worshipful personages upon the stage that might not be displaced, and gentlewomen, whose sex did privilege them from violence, that, when the Prince and his officers had in vain, a good while, expected and endeavored a reformation, at length there was no hope of redress for that present. The Lord Ambassador and his train thought that they were not so kindly entertained, as was before expected, and thereupon would not stay any longer at that time, but, in a sort,[2] discontented and displeased. After their departure, the throngs and tumults did somewhat cease, although so much of them continued as was able to disorder and confound any good inventions whatsoever. In regard whereof, as also for that the sports intended were especially for the gracing of the Templarians, it was thought good not to offer anything of account, saving dancing and reveling with gentlewomen; and after such sports, a *Comedy of Errors* (like to Plautus his *Menaechmus*) was played by the players. So that night was begun and continued to the end in nothing but confusion and errors, whereupon it was ever afterwards called "The Night of Errors." . . .

The next night upon this occasion, we preferred judgments thick and threefold, which were read publicly by the Clerk of the Crown, being all against a sorcerer or conjurer that was supposed to be the cause of that confused inconvenience. Therein was contained how he had caused the stage to be built and scaffolds to be reared to the top of the house to increase expectation; also, how he had caused divers ladies and gentlewomen, and others of good condition, to be invited to our sports; also our dearest friend, the state of Templaria, to be disgraced, and disappointed of their kind entertainment, deserved and intended; also, that he caused throngs and tumults, crowds and outrages, to disturb our whole proceedings; and lastly, that he had foisted a company of base and common fellows[3] to make up our disorders with a play of errors and confusions; and that that night had gained to us discredit, and itself a nickname of "Errors"—all which were against the Crown and dignity of our sovereign lord, the Prince of Purpoole. . . .

The next grand night was upon Twelfth Day at night. . . . First, there came six Knights of the Helmet, with three that they led as prisoners and were attired like monsters and miscreants. The Knights gave the Prince to understand that, as they were returning from their adventures out of Russia, wherein they aided the Emperor of Russia against the Tartars, they surprised these three persons, which were conspiring against His Highness and Dignity.[4] . . . Which being done, the trumpets were commanded to sound, and then the King at Arms came in before the Prince and told His Honor that there was arrived an ambassador from the mighty Emperor of Russia and Muscovy that had some matters of weight to make known to His Highness. So the Prince willed that he should be admitted into his presence, who came in attire of Russia, accompanied with two of his own country in like habit.

Francis Meres on Shakespeare (1598)

[Francis Meres (1565–1647) was educated at Cambridge and was active in London literary circles in 1597–98, after which he became a rector and schoolmaster in the country. The descriptions of Shakespeare are taken from a section on poetry in *Palladis Tamia. Wits Treasury*, a work largely consisting of translated classical quotations

---

2. Departed.
3. That is, the actors.
4. This last paragraph has been included because of the theory that this ostensible visit of the Russian ambassador to the court of the Prince of Purpoole provided a model for the masque of Muscovites in *Love's Labor's Lost* 5.2.

and *exempla*. Unlike the main body of the work, the subsections on poetry, painting, and music include comparisons of English artists to figures of antiquity. Meres goes on after the extract below to list Shakespeare among the best English writers of lyric, tragedy, comedy, and love poetry. The text is modernized from the first edition of *Palladis Tamia* (London, 1598).]

As the Greek tongue is made famous and eloquent by Homer, Hesiod, Euripides, Aeschylus, Sophocles, Pindarus, Phocylides, and Aristophanes, and the Latin tongue by Virgil, Ovid, Horace, Silius Italicus, Lucanus, Lucretius, Ausonius, and Claudianus, so the English tongue is mightily enriched and gorgeously invested in rare ornaments and resplendent habiliments[1] by Sir Philip Sidney, Spenser, Daniel, Drayton, Warner, Shakespeare, Marlowe, and Chapman. . . .

As the soul of Euphorbus was thought to live in Pythagoras, so the sweet witty soul of Ovid lives in mellifluous and honey-tongued Shakespeare. Witness his *Venus and Adonis*, his *Lucrece*, his sugared sonnets among his private friends, etc.

As Plautus and Seneca are accounted the best for comedy and tragedy among the Latins, so Shakespeare among the English is the most excellent in both kinds for the stage. For comedy, witness his *Gentlemen of Verona*, his *Errors*, his *Love Labor's Lost*, his *Love Labor's Won*,[2] his *Midsummer's Night Dream*, and his *Merchant of Venice*; for tragedy, his *Richard the 2*, *Richard the 3*, *Henry the 4*, *King John*, *Titus Andronicus*, and his *Romeo and Juliet*.

As Epius Stolo said that the Muses would speak with Plautus' tongue if they would speak Latin, so I say that the Muses would speak with Shakespeare's fine-filed phrase if they would speak English.

John Manningham on *Twelfth Night* (1602)

[John Manningham (ca. 1575–1622) kept a diary during his time as a law student at the Middle Temple, recording the witticisms of his colleagues and a rich variety of anecdotes. The vibrant and boisterous life of the Inns of Court is also illustrated by the *Gesta Grayorum* (see above). The February 1602 entry describes the festivities organized for Candlemas Day at the Middle Temple. As in most early modern English documents, any date before March 25 is assigned to the following year according to our calendar, so that 1601 here becomes 1602 (New Style). The text is modernized from the 1976 edition of Robert Sorlien (Hanover, NH: University Press of New England).]

Febr. 1601

2. At our feast we had a play called[1] *Twelve Night, or What You Will*, much like *The Comedy of Errors*, or *Menaechmi*[2] in Plautus, but most like and near to that in Italian called *Inganni*.[3] A good practice in it to make the steward believe his lady widow[4] was in love with him by counterfeiting a letter as from his lady, in general terms telling him what she liked best in him and prescribing his gesture in smiling, his apparel, &c., and then when he came to practice, making him believe they took him to be mad.

1. Sumptuous clothing.
2. Either the play has not survived, or it is now known by a different name. However, this title is recorded elsewhere, in a bookseller's jottings of 1603, where it again appears following *Love's Labor's Lost*.
1. A deletion in the manuscript suggests that Manningham began to write "*Midsummer Night's Dream*" before correcting himself.
2. Source for *The Comedy of Errors*.
3. The two plays with this exact title (1562

and 1592) seem less likely to be "most like" *Twelfth Night* than another Italian play, *Ingannati* (1537), which has characters named Fabio and Malevolti and makes reference to Twelfth Night (Epiphany).
4. Olivia is not a widow in the version of Shakespeare's play that has come down to us, though she is so described in one of Shakespeare's principal sources for the play.

Front Matter from the First Folio
of Shakespeare's Plays (1623)

After Shakespeare's death in 1616, his friends and colleagues John Heminges and Henry Condell organized this first publication of his collected (thirty-six) plays. Eighteen of the plays had not appeared in print before, and for these the First Folio is the sole surviving source. Only *Pericles, The Two Noble Kinsmen, Sir Thomas More,* and *Edward III* are not included in the volume. Reproduced below in reduced facsimile are the title page (which includes Droeshout's famous portrait of Shakespeare), Heminges and Condell's prefatory address "To the great Variety of Readers," the book's table of contents, and the first page of text from *The Tempest*. Following the facsimile images is a commendatory poem by Shakespeare's great contemporary Ben Jonson (1572–1637), which was also published in the First Folio's front matter.

Mr. WILLIAM
SHAKESPEARES

COMEDIES,
HISTORIES, &
TRAGEDIES.

Published according to the True Originall Copies.

Martin Droeshout sculpsit London.

LONDON
Printed by Iſaac Iaggard, and Ed. Blount. 1623.

To the great Variety of Readers.

Rom the moſt able, to him that can but ſpell: There you are number'd. We had rather you were weighd. Eſpecially, when the fate of all Bookes depends vpon your capacities : and not of your heads alone, but of your purſes. Well! It is now publique, & you wil ſtand for your priuiledges wee know : to read, and cenſure. Do ſo, but buy it firſt. That doth beſt commend a Booke, the Stationer ſaies. Then, how odde ſoeuer your braines be, or your wiſedomes, make your licence the ſame, and ſpare not. Iudge your ſixe-pen'orth, your ſhillings worth, your fiue ſhillings worth at a time, or higher, ſo you riſe to the iuſt rates, and welcome. But, what euer you do, Buy. Cenſure will not driue a Trade, or make the Iacke go. And though you be a Magiſtrate of wit, and ſit on the Stage at *Black-Friers*, or the *Cock-pit*, to arraigne Playes dailie, know, theſe Playes haue had their triall alreadie, and ſtood out all Appeales; and do now come forth quitted rather by a Decree of Court, then any purchas'd Letters of commendation.

It had bene a thing, we confeſſe, worthie to haue bene wiſhed, that the Author himſelfe had liu'd to haue ſet forth, and ouerſeen his owne writings; But ſince it hath bin ordain'd otherwiſe, and he by death departed from that right, we pray you do not envie his Friends, the office of their care, and paine, to haue collected & publiſh'd them; and ſo to haue publiſh'd them, as where (before) you were abuſ'd with diuerſe ſtolne, and ſurreptitious copies, maimed, and deformed by the frauds and ſtealthes of iniurious impoſtors, that expos'd them : euen thoſe, are now offer'd to your view cur'd, and perfect of their limbes; and all the reſt, abſolute in their numbers, as he conceiued thē. Who, as he was a happie imitator of Nature, was a moſt gentle expreſſer of it. His mind and hand went together: And what he thought, he vttered with that eaſineſſe, that wee haue ſcarſe receiued from him a blot in his papers. But it is not our prouince, who onely gather his works, and giue them you, to praiſe him. It is yours that reade him. And there we hope, to your diuers capacities, you will finde enough, both to draw, and hold you : for his wit can no more lie hid, then it could be loſt. Reade him, therefore; and againe, and againe : And if then you doe not like him, ſurely you are in ſome manifeſt danger, not to vnderſtand him. And ſo we leaue you to other of his Friends, whom if you need, can bee your guides : if you neede them not, you can leade your ſelues, and others. And ſuch Readers we wiſh him.

A 3   *Iohn Heminge.*
                                 Henrie Condell.

Line 8. *Stationer:* bookseller.
Line 13. *Iacke:* machine.
Lines 13–14. *And though . . . dailie:* addressed in particular to men of fashion who occupied seats onstage so they could be seen while watching the play.
Lines 15–17. *these Playes . . . commendation:* The legal puns that began with "Magistrate of wit" (fashionable playgoer) in line 13 continue here. The "purchas'd Letters of commendation" refer to escaping the conse- quences of a crime by means of bribery or other undue influence; Shakespeare's plays, by contrast, have been acquitted after a proper and rigorous trial (approved by theater audiences and not insinuated into the public favor by some outside influence).
Line 27. *absolute in their numbers:* correct in their versification. *thē:* them.
Line 28. *a happie:* an apt; a successful.

A CATALOGVE

of the feuerall Comedies, Histories, and Tragedies contained in this Volume.

Troilus and Cressida, despite its absence from the "Catalogue," was in fact printed in the First Folio. Due to negotiations over printing rights, it was included only at the last minute and placed between the histories and tragedies.

THE TEMPEST.

Actus primus, Scena prima.

A tempestuous noise of Thunder and Lightning heard: Enter a Ship-master, and a Botefwaine.

Master.

Ote-swaine.

Botef. Heere Master: What cheere?

Maft. Good: Speake to th'Mariners: fall too't, yarely, or we run our selues a ground, bestirre, bestirre.   *Exit.*

Enter Mariners.

Botef. Heigh my hearts, cheerely, cheerely my harts: yare, yare: Take in the toppe-sale: Tend to th'Masters whistle: Blow till thou burst thy winde, if roome enough.

Enter Alonso, Sebastian, Anthonio, Ferdinando, Gonzalo, and others.

Alon. Good Botefwaine haue care: where's the Master? Play the men.

Botef. I pray now keepe below.

Anth. Where is the Master, Boson?

Botef. Do you not heare him? you marre our labour, Keepe your Cabines: you do assist the storme.

Gonz. Nay, good be patient.

Botef. When the Sea is: hence, what cares these roarers for the name of King? to Cabine; silence: trouble vs not.

Gon. Good, yet remember whom thou hast aboord.

Botef. None that I more loue then my selfe. You are a Counsellor, if you can command these Elements to silence, and worke the peace of the present, wee will not hand a rope more, vse your authoritie: If you cannot, giue thankes you haue liu'd so long, and make your selfe readie in your Cabine for the mischance of the houre, if it so hap. Cheerely good hearts: out of our way I say.   *Exit.*

Gon. I haue great comfort from this fellow:methinks he hath no drowning marke vpon him, his complexion is perfect Gallowes: stand fast good Fate to his hanging, make the rope of his destiny our cable, for our owne doth little aduantage: If he be not borne to bee hang'd, our case is miserable.   *Exit.*

Enter Botefwaine.

Botef. Downe with the top-Mast: yare, lower, lower, bring her to Try with Maine-course. A plague——

A cry within.   Enter Sebaftian, Anthonio & Gonzalo.

vpon this howling: they are lowder then the weather, or our office: yet againe? What do you heere? Shal we giue ore and drowne, haue you a minde to sinke?

Sebaf. A poxe o'your throat, you bawling, blasphemous incharitable Dog.

Botef. Worke you then.

Anth. Hang cur, hang, you whoreson insolent Noysemaker, we are lesse afraid to be drownde, then thou art.

Gonz. I'le warrant him for drowning, though the Ship were no stronger then a Nutt-shell, and as leaky as an vnstanched wench.

Botef. Lay her a hold, a hold, set her two courses off to Sea againe, lay her off.

Enter Mariners wet.

Mari. All lost, to prayers, to prayers, all lost.

Botef. What must our mouths be cold?

Gonz. The King, and Prince, at prayers, let's assist them, for our case is as theirs.

Sebaf. I'am out of patience.

An. We are meerly cheated of our liues by drunkards, This wide-chopt-rascall, would thou mightst lye drowning the washing of ten Tides.

Gonz. Hee'l be hang'd yet, Though euery drop of water sweare against it, And gape at widst to glut him.   *A confused noyse within.*

Mercy on vs.

We split, we split, Farewell my wife, and children, Farewell brother: we split, we split, we split.

Anth. Let's all sinke with' King

Seb. Let's take leaue of him.   *Exit.*

Gonz. Now would I giue a thousand furlongs of Sea, for an Acre of barren ground: Long heath, Browne firrs, any thing; the wills aboue be done, but I would faine dye a dry death.   *Exit.*

Scena Secunda.

Enter Prospero and Miranda.

Mira. If by your Art (my deerest father) you haue Put the wild waters in this Rore, alay them: The skye it seemes would powre down stinking pitch, But that the Sea, mounting to th'welkins cheeke, Dashes the fire out. Oh! I haue suffered With those that I saw suffer: A braue vessell

A   (Who

To the memory of my beloved,
The AUTHOR
Mr. William Shakespeare:
And
what he hath left us.*

To draw no envy, Shakespeare, on thy name,
  Am I thus ample to° thy book and fame,   *copious in praising*
While I confess thy writings to be such
  As neither man nor muse can praise too much:
5 'Tis true, and all men's suffrage.° But these ways   *agreement*
  Were not the paths I meant° unto thy praise,   *(to take)*
For seeliest[1] ignorance on these may light,
  Which, when it sounds, at best, but° echoes right;   *merely*
Or blind affection, which doth ne'er advance
10 The truth, but gropes, and urgeth all by chance;
Or crafty malice might pretend this praise,
  And think° to ruin, where it seemed to raise.   *intend*
These are as° some infamous bawd or whore   *as though*
  Should praise a matron: what could hurt her more?
15 But thou art proof against° them, and indeed   *impervious to*
  Above th' ill fortune of them, or the need.
I therefore will begin. Soul of the age!
  The applause, delight, the wonder of our stage!
My Shakespeare, rise! I will not lodge thee by
20 Chaucer or Spenser, or bid Beaumont lie
A little further to make thee a room;[2]
  Thou art a monument without a tomb
And art alive still while thy book doth live,
  And we have wits to read and praise to give.
25 That I not mix thee so, my brain excuses,
  I mean with great but disproportioned° muses.   *not comparable*
For if I thought my judgment were of years°   *mature*
  I should commit° thee surely with thy peers,   *compare*
And tell how far thou didst our Lyly outshine,
30 Or sporting Kyd, or Marlowe's mighty line.[3]
And though thou hadst small Latin and less Greek,[4]
  From thence to honor thee I would not seek°   *lack*
For names, but call forth thund'ring Aeschylus,
  Euripides, and Sophocles to us,

* By Ben Jonson.
1. Silliest; blindest (falcons' eyelids were "seeled," or stitched shut, while they were being tamed).
2. Geoffrey Chaucer, Edmund Spenser, and Francis Beaumont were all buried near each other in Westminster Abbey (known today as the "Poets' Corner"), while Shakespeare was buried in Stratford-upon-Avon. An earlier elegy for Shakespeare had begun: "Renownèd Spenser, lie a thought more nigh / To learned Chaucer, and, rare Beaumont, lie / A little nearer Spenser to make room / For Shakespeare . . ."
3. John Lyly, Thomas Kyd, and Christopher Marlowe were all celebrated Elizabethan playwrights. *sporting:* gamesome; frolicking (like a young goat, or "kid").
4. The underrating of Shakespeare's Latin was likely influenced by Jonson's pride in his own impressive classical learning.

35 Pacuvius, Accius, him of Cordova dead,[5]
   To life again, to hear thy buskin tread
   And shake a stage; or, when thy socks were on,[6]
   Leave thee alone for the comparison
   Of all that insolent Greece or haughty Rome
40   Sent forth, or since did from their ashes come.
   Triumph, my Britain; thou hast one to show
   To whom all scenes° of Europe homage owe.   *stages*
   He was not of an age, but for all time!
   And all the Muses still were in their prime
45 When like Apollo° he came forth to warm   *god of poetry*
   Our ears, or like a Mercury° to charm!   *god of eloquence*
   Nature herself was proud of his designs,
   And joyed to wear the dressing of his lines,
   Which were so richly spun and woven so fit
50   As, since, she will vouchsafe° no other wit.   *grant*
   The merry Greek, tart Aristophanes,
   Neat Terence, witty Plautus[7] now not please,
   But antiquated and deserted lie,
   As they were not of Nature's family.
55 Yet must I not give Nature all; thy art,
   My gentle Shakespeare, must enjoy a part.
   For though the poet's matter° nature be,   *raw material*
   His art doth give the fashion.° And that he°   *form / that he=he*
   Who casts° to write a living line must sweat   *intends*
60 (Such as thine are) and strike the second heat
   Upon the Muses' anvil, turn the same,
   And himself with it, that he thinks to frame,
   Or for the laurel he may gain a scorn;[8]
   For a good poet's made as well as born,
65 And such wert thou. Look how the father's face
   Lives in his issue;° even so, the race   *offspring*
   Of Shakespeare's mind and manners brightly shines
   In his well-turnèd and true-filèd° lines,   *truly polished*
   In each of which he seems to shake a lance,[9]
70   As brandished at the eyes of ignorance.
   Sweet swan of Avon, what a sight it were
   To see thee in our waters yet appear,
   And make those flights upon the banks of Thames
   That so did take° Eliza and our James![1]   *transport*
75 But stay; I see thee in the hemisphere
   Advanced and made a constellation there.[2]
   Shine forth, thou star of poets, and with rage
   Or influence,[3] chide or cheer the drooping° stage,   *dejected*
   Which, since thy flight from hence, hath mourned like night,
80   And despairs day, but for thy volume's light.

BEN: JONSON.

5. While the Latin tragedians Marcus Pacuvius and Lucius Accius were known to Jonson only by reputation, Seneca the Younger ("him of Cordova") was a major influence on Renaissance revenge tragedies.
6. The boots ("buskins") and shoes ("socks") worn by classical actors were symbolic of tragedy and comedy, respectively.
7. Aristophanes was a Greek writer of satirical comedies; Terence and Plautus were Roman comic dramatists.

8. Or else, instead of the laurel (the symbol of poetic accomplishment), he may gain derision.
9. Punning on Shakespeare's name.
1. Queen Elizabeth and King James.
2. It was a commonplace in classical literature that those who lived glorious lives became constellations after death.
3. Stars and planets were thought to affect human affairs. "Rage" suggests poetic inspiration.

Timeline

Dates for plays by Shakespeare and others are conjectural dates of composition, based on current understanding of the evidence. Works of poetry and prose are listed by date of publication.

TEXT	CONTEXT
	1558 Queen Mary I, a Roman Catholic, dies; her sister, Elizabeth, raised Protestant, is proclaimed queen.
	1559 Church of England is reestablished under the authority of the sovereign with the passage of the Act of Uniformity and the Act of Supremacy.
1562 *The Tragedy of Gorboduc*, by Thomas Norton and Thomas Sackville; the first English play in blank verse.	**1563** The Church of England adopts the Thirty-nine Articles of Religion, detailing its points of doctrine and clarifying its differences both from Roman Catholicism and from more radical forms of Protestantism.
	1564 William Shakespeare is born in Stratford to John and Mary Arden Shakespeare; he is christened a few days later, on April 26.
	1565 John Shakespeare is made an alderman of Stratford.
	1567 Mary Queen of Scots is imprisoned on suspicion of the murder of her husband, Lord Darnley. Their infant son, Charles James, is crowned James VI of Scotland. John Brayne builds the first English professional theater in the garden of a farmhouse called the Red Lion on the outskirts of London.
	1568 John Shakespeare is elected Bailiff of Stratford, the town's highest office. Performances in Stratford by the Queen's Players and the Earl of Worcester's men.
	1572 An act is passed that severely punishes vagrants and wanderers, including actors not affiliated with a patron. Performances in Stratford by the Earl of Leicester's men.

TEXT	CONTEXT
	1574 The Earl of Warwick's and Earl of Worcester's men perform in Stratford.
	1576 James Burbage, father of Richard, later the leading actor in Shakespeare's company, builds The Theatre in Shoreditch, a suburb of London.
1577 First edition of Holinshed's *Chronicles*.	**1577** The Curtain Theater opens in Shoreditch.
	1577–80 Sir Francis Drake circumnavigates the globe.
	1578 Mary Shakespeare pawns her lands, suggesting that the family is in financial distress. Lord Strange's Men and Lord Essex's Men perform at Stratford.
1579 Sir Thomas North's English translation of Plutarch's *Lives*.	**1580** A Jesuit mission is established in England with the aim of reconverting the nation to Roman Catholicism. Francis Drake returns from circumnavigation of globe.
	1582 Shakespeare marries Anne Hathaway.
	1583 The birth of Shakespeare's older daughter, Susanna.
	1584 Sir Walter Ralegh establishes the first English colony in the New World at Roanoke Island in modern North Carolina; the colony fails.
	1585 The birth of Shakespeare's twin son and daughter, Hamnet and Judith. John Shakespeare is fined for not going to church.
	1586 Sir Philip Sidney dies from battle wounds.
1587 Thomas Kyd, *The Spanish Tragedy*; Christopher Marlowe, *Tamburlaine*.	**1587** Mary Queen of Scots is executed for treason against Elizabeth I. Francis Drake, leading a daring raid at Cádiz, destroys many Spanish naval vessels and materiel. John Shakespeare loses his position as an alderman. Philip Henslowe builds the Rose theater at Bank-side, on the Thames.
	1588 The Spanish Armada attempts an invasion of England but is defeated.

TEXT	CONTEXT
1589 Robert Greene, *Friar Bacon and Friar Bungay*. Thomas Kyd(?), *Hamlet* (not extant; perhaps a source for Shakespeare's *Hamlet*). Christopher Marlowe, *The Jew of Malta*. Anonymous, *The True Chronicle History of King Leir, and His Three Daughters*.	**1589** Shakespeare is possibly affiliated with Strange's men, Pembroke's men, or both between this time and 1594.
1590 Edmund Spenser, *The Faerie Queene* (1st edition, Books 1–3). Sir Philip Sidney, *Arcadia*.	**1590** James VI of Scotland marries Anne of Denmark. James believes that witches raised a magical storm in an attempt to sink the ship carrying him home with his bride. Witch trials in Scotland.
1591–92 *Two Gentlemen of Verona*. *2 and 3 Henry VI*. *The Taming of the Shrew* *1 Henry VI*.	**1592** The theatrical entrepreneur and financial manager of the Admiral's Men, Philip Henslowe, begins a diary—an important source for theater historians—recording his business transactions; continued until 1604.
1592–93 *Titus Andronicus*. *Richard III*. *Edward III*. *Venus and Adonis*.	From June 1592 to June 1594, London theaters are frequently shut down because of the plague; acting companies tour the provinces.
1594 *The Rape of Lucrece*. *The Comedy of Errors*.	**1594** Roderigo Lopez, a Christian physician of Portuguese Jewish descent, is executed on slight evidence for having plotted to poison Elizabeth I. The birth of James VI's first son, Henry.
1594–96 *Love's Labor's Lost*. *Richard II*. *Romeo and Juliet*. *A Midsummer Night's Dream*. *King John*.	**1595** Shakespeare lives in St. Helen's Parish, Bishopsgate, London. Shakespeare apparently becomes a sharer in (provides capital for) the newly formed Lord Chamberlain's Men. The Swan Theater is built in Bankside. Hugh O'Neill, Earl of Tyrone, rebels against English rule in Ireland. Walter Ralegh explores Guiana, on the north coast of South America.
1596 Edmund Spenser, *The Faerie Queene* (2nd edition, with Books 4–6).	**1596** John Shakespeare is granted a coat of arms; hence the title of "gentleman." William Shakespeare's son Hamnet dies. James Burbage buys a medieval hall in the former Blackfriars monastery and transforms it into an indoor theater.
1596–97 *1 Henry IV*. *The Merchant of Venice*.	
	1597 The landlord refuses to renew the lease on the land under The Theatre in Shoreditch.

TEXT	CONTEXT
1598 *2 Henry IV.* *Much Ado About Nothing.* George Chapman begins to publish his translation of Homer. Ben Jonson, *Every Man in His Humor,* which lists Shakespeare as one of the actors.	1598 Unable to renew the lease, the Chamberlain's Men move from The Theatre to the nearby Curtain Theater. The Edict of Nantes ends the French civil wars, granting toleration to Protestants. Materials from the demolished Theatre in Shoreditch are transported across the Thames to be used in building the Globe Theater, which opens in the following year.
1599 *The Merry Wives of Windsor.* *Henry V.* *As You Like It.* *Julius Caesar.* *The Passionate Pilgrim*, attributed entirely to Shakespeare. Michael Drayton and several collaborators, who object to Shakespeare's depiction of Oldcastle-Falstaff in the *Henry IV* plays, write *The First Part of the True and Honorable History of the Life of Sir John Oldcastle, the Good Lord Cobham.*	1599 The Queen's favorite, Robert Devereux, Earl of Essex, leads an expedition to Ireland in March, but returning home without royal permission in September, is rebuked by the Queen and imprisoned. Satires and other offensive books are prohibited by ecclesiastical order. Extant copies are gathered and burned. Two notorious satirists, Thomas Nashe and Gabriel Harvey, are forbidden to publish.
1600–1601 *Hamlet.* *Twelfth Night.*	1600 The Earl of Essex is suspended from some of his offices and confined to house arrest. The birth of James VI's second son, Charles. The founding of the East India Company. Edward Alleyn and Philip Henslowe build the Fortune Theater for the Lord Admiral's Men.
1601 "The Phoenix and Turtle" published in Robert Chester's *Love's Martyr.* In the "War of the Theaters," Ben Jonson, John Marston, and Thomas Dekker write a series of satiric plays mocking one another.	1601 The Earl of Essex leads a rebellion against the principal adviser to Elizabeth I and possibly against the Queen herself. The previous afternoon, hoping to enlist support, some of the rebels pay for a performance of *Richard II.* Implicated in the uprising, which is quickly quelled, Shakespeare's patron, the Earl of Southampton, is imprisoned. The Earl of Essex is convicted of treason and beheaded, along with several of his chief supporters. Shakespeare's father dies.
1601–02 *Troilus and Cressida.*	1602 Shakespeare makes substantial real-estate purchases in Stratford. The opening of the Bodleian Library in Oxford.

TEXT	CONTEXT
1601–03 *Othello.*	
1603 John Florio's translation of Montaigne's *Essays.* Ben Jonson, *Sejanus*, which lists Shakespeare as one of the actors.	**1603** Queen Elizabeth dies; she is succeeded by her cousin, James VI of Scotland (now James I of England).
1603–04 *Sir Thomas More* (revised version).	
	Plague closes the London theaters from mid-1603 to April 1604. Hugh O'Neill surrenders in Ireland.
1604 *Measure for Measure.*	**1604** The conclusion of a peace with Spain makes travel across the Atlantic safer, encouraging plans for English colonies in the Americas.
1605 *The History of King Lear.*	**1605** The discovery of the Gunpowder Plot by some radical Catholics to blow up the Houses of Parliament during its opening ceremonies, when the royal family, Lords, and Commons are assembled in one place. The Red Bull Theater built.
1606–07 *Timon of Athens.* *All's Well That Ends Well.* *Macbeth.* *Antony and Cleopatra.* Middleton(?), *The Revenger's Tragedy.*	**1606** The London and Plymouth Companies receive charters to colonize Virginia. Parliament passes "An Act to Restrain Abuses of Players," prohibiting oaths or blasphemy onstage.
1607–08 *Pericles.*	**1607** An English colony is established in Jamestown, Virginia. Shakespeare's daughter Susanna marries John Hall. Shakespeare's brother Edmund (described as a player) dies.
1608 *Coriolanus.*	
1609 *Shakespeare's Sonnets.*	
1610 *Cymbeline.* Ben Jonson, *The Alchemist.*	**1610** Henry is made Prince of Wales. Shakespeare probably returns to Stratford and settles there. The King's Men begin using Blackfriars Theater as a second, indoor venue.

TEXT	CONTEXT
1611 *The Winter's Tale.* *The Tempest.* Francis Beaumont and John Fletcher, *A King and No King.* Publication of the Authorized (King James) Bible.	**1611** Plantation of Ulster in Ireland, a colony of English and Scottish Protestants settled on land confiscated from Irish rebels.
1612–13 *Cardenio*, with John Fletcher (not extant). *Henry VIII*, with John Fletcher. John Webster, *The White Devil.*	**1612** Prince Henry dies.
1613–14 *The Two Noble Kinsmen,* with John Fletcher.	**1613** Princess Elizabeth marries Frederick V, Elector Palatine. The Globe Theater burns down during a performance of *Henry VIII.*
1614 Ben Jonson, *Bartholomew Fair.* John Webster, *The Duchess of Malfi.*	**1614** Philip Henslowe and Jacob Meade build the Hope Theater, used both for play performances and as a bearbaiting arena. The Globe Theater reopens.
1616 Ben Jonson publishes his *Works*, including the first collection of plays by a commercial English dramatist.	**1616** William Harvey describes the circulation of the blood. Shakespeare's daughter Judith marries. Shakespeare dies on April 23.
1623 Members of the King's Men publish the First Folio of Shakespeare's plays.	

Glossary

STAGE TERMS

"above"   The gallery on the upper level of the stage's back wall (see *frons scenae*). In open-air theaters, such as the Globe, this space may have included the lords' rooms. The central section of the gallery was sometimes used by the players for short scenes. Indoor theaters such as Blackfriars featured a curtained alcove for musicians above the stage.

"aloft"   See *"above."*

amphitheater   An open-air theater, such as the Globe.

arras   See *curtain.*

cellarage   See *trap.*

chorus   In the works of Shakespeare and other Elizabethan playwrights, a single individual (not, as in Greek tragedy, a group) who speaks before the play (and sometimes before each act or, in *Pericles*, at other times), describing events not shown on stage as well as commenting on the action witnessed by the audience.

curtain   Curtains, or arras (hanging tapestries), probably covered a part of the stage's back wall (see *frons scenae*), thus concealing the discovery space, and may also have been draped around the edge of the stage to conceal the open area underneath.

discovery space   A central opening or alcove concealed behind a curtain in the center of the stage's back wall (see *frons scenae*). The curtain could be drawn aside to "discover" tableaux such as Portia's caskets, the body of Polonius, or the statue of Hermione. Shakespeare appears to have used this stage device only sparingly.

doubling   The common practice of having one actor play multiple roles, so that a play with a large cast of characters might be performed by a relatively small company.

dumb shows   Mimed scenes performed before a play or as part of the play itself, summarizing or foreshadowing the plot. Dumb shows were popular in early Elizabethan drama; although they already seemed old-fashioned in Shakespeare's time, they were employed by writers up to the 1640s.

epilogue   A brief speech or poem addressed to the audience by an actor after the play. In some cases, as in *2 Henry IV,* the epilogue could be combined with, or could merge into, the jig.

frons scenae   The wall at the back of the stage, behind which lay the players' tiring house. The *frons scenae* of the Globe featured two doors flanking the central discovery space, with a gallery "above."

gallery   Covered seating area surrounding the open yard of the public amphitheater. There were three levels of galleries at the Globe; admission to these seats cost an extra penny (in addition to the basic admission fee of one penny to the yard), and seating in the higher galleries another penny yet.

gatherers Persons employed by the playing company to take money at the entrances to the theater.

groundlings Audience members who paid the minimum price of admission (one penny) to stand in the yard of the open-air theaters; also referred to as "understanders." "Groundling" is an unusual word, possibly coined by Shakespeare; it is unclear whether it was in common usage at the time.

heavens The canopied roof over the stage in the open-air theaters, protecting the players and their costumes from rain. The "heavens" may have been brightly decorated with sun, moon, and stars, and perhaps the signs of the zodiac.

jig A song-and-dance performance by the clown and other members of the company at the conclusion of a play. These performances were frequently bawdy and were officially banned in 1612.

lords' rooms Partitioned sections of the gallery above the stage, or just to the left and right of the stage, where the most prestigious and expensive seats in the public playhouses were located. These rooms did not provide the best view of the action on the stage below. They were designed to make their privileged occupants conspicuous to the rest of the audience.

open-air theaters Unroofed public playhouses in the suburbs of London, such as The Theatre, the Rose, and the Globe.

part The character played by an actor. In Shakespeare's theater, actors were given a roll of paper called a "part" containing all of the speeches and all of the cues belonging to their character. The term "role," synonymous with "part," is derived from such rolls of paper.

patrons Important nobles and members of the royal family under whose protection the theatrical companies of London operated; players not in the service of patrons were punishable as vagabonds. The companies were referred to as their patrons' "Men" or "Servants." Thus the company to which Shakespeare belonged for most of his career was first known as the Lord Chamberlain's Servants, then became the King's Men in 1603, when James I became their patron.

pillars The "heavens" were supported by two tall painted pillars or posts near the front of the stage. These occasionally played a role in stage action, allowing a character to "hide" while remaining in full view of the audience.

pit The area in front of the stage in indoor theaters such as Blackfriars; unlike an open-air playhouse's yard, the pit was designed for a seated audience.

posts See *pillars*.

proscenium The arch that divides the stage, scenery, and backstage area from the auditorium in many theaters built in and after the eighteenth century. It also separates actors and audiences, potentially creating the so-called fourth wall. The stages on which Shakespeare's plays were first performed had no proscenium.

repertory The stock of plays a company had ready for performance at a given time. Companies generally performed a different play each day, often more than a dozen plays in a month and more than thirty in the course of the season.

role See *part*.

sharers   Senior actors holding shares in a joint-stock theatrical company; they paid for costumes, hired hands, and new plays, and they shared profits and losses equally. Shakespeare was not only a longtime "sharer" of the Lord Chamberlain's Men but, from 1599, a "housekeeper," the holder of a one-eighth share in the Globe playhouse.

tiring house   The players' dressing (attiring) room, a structure located at the back of the stage and connected to the stage by two or more doors in the *frons scenae*.

trap   A trapdoor near the front of the stage that allowed access to the cellarage beneath and was frequently associated with hell's mouth. Another trapdoor in the heavens opened for the descent of gods to the stage below.

"within"   The tiring house, from which offstage sound effects such as shouts, drums, and trumpets were produced.

yard   The central space in open-air theaters such as the Globe, into which the stage projected and in which audience members stood. Admission to the yard in the public theaters cost a penny, the cheapest admission available.

TEXTUAL TERMS

aside   See *stage direction*.

autograph   Text written in the author's own hand. With the possible exception of a few pages of the collaborative play *Sir Thomas More*, no dramatic works or poems written in Shakespeare's hand are known to survive.

"bad quartos"   A polemical term for a group of Shakespeare quartos that are different from and often demonstrably inferior to other versions of the plays in question as they are found in later quartos or in the First Folio. Some of these texts are very short; others include notable distortions of language. Explanations for the "bad quartos" (or, more neutrally, "short quartos") include the possibility that they were Shakespeare's early drafts, abbreviated scripts prepared for performance under circumstances such as touring, or "memorial reconstructions."

base text   The early text upon which a modern edition is based, also known as a "control text."

canonical   Of an author, the writings generally accepted as authentic. In the case of Shakespeare's dramatic works, only two plays that are not among the thirty-six plays contained in the First Folio, *Pericles* and *The Two Noble Kinsmen,* have won widespread acceptance into the Shakespearean canon, but recent scholarship suggests that he wrote parts of a number of others, including *Edward III* and *Sir Thomas More*.

casting off   The practice of dividing up a manuscript to anticipate the number of pages needed to contain it in print. Errors in casting off sometimes led compositors to crowd lines, abbreviate spellings, and print verse as prose. If on the contrary a compositor found he had too much space remaining, he might leave spaces around stage directions, add ornaments, or break prose up into short "verse" lines.

catchword   A word printed below the text at the bottom of a page, matching the first word on the following page. The catchword enabled the printer to keep the pages in their proper sequence. Where the catchword fails to match the word at the top of the next page, there is reason to suspect that something has been lost or misplaced.

collaboration   The practice of two or more writers working together to create a play (or other literature). More than half of the plays in Shakespeare's period were collaborative. Shakespeare collaborated with John Fletcher on *Henry VIII*, *The Two Noble Kinsmen*, and the missing *Cardenio*; with George Wilkins on *Pericles*; and with Thomas Middleton on *Timon of Athens*. Shakespeare plays that probably have sections composed by others include *Titus Andronicus*, *1 Henry VI*, and *Macbeth*; in turn, Shakespeare seems to have contributed a section to *Sir Thomas More*.

compositor   A person employed in a print shop to set type. To speed the printing process, most of Shakespeare's plays were set by more than one compositor. Compositors were expected to adjust spelling and provide punctuation and can often be identified by their different habits and preferences (e.g., *been/beene* or *O/Oh* and speech prefixes such as *Que./Queene*). They invariably introduced errors into the texts—for instance, by selecting the wrong letter from the type case or by setting the correct letter upside down.

conflation   A version of a play created by combining readings from more than one substantive text. Since the early eighteenth century, for example, most versions of *King Lear* and of several other plays by Shakespeare have been conflations of quarto and First Folio texts.

deus ex machina   Literally, "god from a machine," the term can refer to any plot device introduced to resolve a seemingly insurmountable problem.

dramatis personae (or The Persons of the Play)   A list of the characters that appear in the play. In the First Folio such lists, called "The Names of the Actors," were printed at the end of some but not all of the plays. In 1709 the editor Nicholas Rowe first provided lists of dramatis personae for all of Shakespeare's dramatic works.

emendation   A correction made in a text by an editor where he or she believes on the basis of evidence and/or inference that it has been corrupted in transmission and needs to be altered for coherence or sense.

exeunt / exit   See *stage direction*.

fair copy   A transcript of the "foul papers" made either by a scribe or by the playwright.

folio   A bookmaking format in which each large sheet of paper is folded once, making two leaves (a leaf is part of a folded sheet of paper with a page on each side). This format produced large volumes, generally handsome and expensive. The First Folio of Shakespeare's plays was printed in 1623.

forme   A body of type secured in a chase, or wooden frame, ready for printing. The forme would be placed into the press and inked and a sheet of paper lowered onto it for imprinting.

foul papers   A term for a playwright's working draft of a play, which is presumed to have contained "false starts," blotted-out passages, ghost characters, and revisions. To judge by apparent errors in the printed texts, several of Shakespeare's plays appear to have been printed from foul papers rather than fair copy; however, no clearcut instance of his foul papers survives, though certain pages in the manuscript of *Sir Thomas More* may represent this stage of the writing process.

ghost characters   Characters named in a stage direction who have no lines during the ensuing action. They may represent a "false start" as the author composed the play, and may not have actually appeared onstage in performance.

licensing By an order of 1581, new plays could not be performed until they had received a license from the Master of the Revels. A separate license, granted by the Court of High Commission, was required for publication, though in practice plays were often printed without license. From 1610, the Master of the Revels had the authority to license plays for publication as well as for performance.

manent / manet See *stage direction*.

massed entry The grouping of all characters who will appear at any point in a scene into a single opening direction. Playwrights such as Ben Jonson preferred this style because of its conformity with classical practice, and it was followed by certain scribes. Modern editors write entry directions to show the point in the scene at which each character enters.

memorial reconstruction The theory that some texts may have been reconstructed from memory by one or more actors, either because a promptbook had been destroyed or because it was not available—for example, while touring. It has been proposed that memorial reconstruction might explain the existence of "bad" or inferior quartos of some of Shakespeare's plays, though this is no longer universally accepted.

octavo A bookmaking format in which each large sheet of paper is folded three times, making eight leaves (sixteen pages front and back). Only one of Shakespeare's plays, *3 Henry VI* (1595), was published in octavo format.

playbook See *promptbook*.

press variants Minor textual variations among pages in books of the same edition, resulting from corrections made in the course of printing or from damaged or slipped type.

promptbook A manuscript of a play (either foul papers or fair copy) annotated and adapted for performance by the theatrical company. The promptbook incorporated stage directions, notes on properties and special effects, and revisions, sometimes including those required by the Master of the Revels. Promptbooks may be identifiable by the replacement of characters' names with actors' names.

quarto A bookmaking format in which each large sheet of paper is folded twice, making four leaves (eight pages front and back). Quarto volumes were smaller and less expensive than books printed in the folio format.

recto Literally, the right-hand page; in a quarto volume, each signature consisted of four leaves each of which had a recto and a verso; the pages were then numbered 1r[ecto], 1v[erso], 2r, 2v, 3r, 3v, 4r, 4v.

scribal copy A transcript of a play produced by a professional scribe (or "scrivener"). Scribes tended to employ their own preferred spellings, abbreviations, and punctuation and could be responsible for introducing a variety of errors.

signature A section of an early book consisting of one group of folded pages (e.g., in a quarto, four leaves or eight pages). Early modern printers indicated each signature by a letter (e.g., A) to assist them in keeping track of the parts of the book to bind together.

single-text editing Editing a work by staying as close as possible to a single early authoritative base text, emending only where necessary for sense and without either conflating by incorporating words or passages from other cognate texts or by reconstructing passages from source materials or other forms of inference.

speech prefix (SP) The indication of the identity of the speaker of the following line or lines. Early editions of Shakespeare's plays often use different prefixes at different points to designate the same person. On occasion, the name of the actor who was to play the role appears in place of the name of the character.

stage direction (SD) The part of the text that is not spoken by any character but that indicates actions to be performed onstage. Stage directions in the earliest editions of Shakespeare's plays are sparse; some necessary directions, most notably exits, are missing, and others may appear earlier or later than the plot requires. Directions for action (e.g., "Pray you, undo this button") may be implied in the dialogue but are not necessarily followed in a given production. By convention, the most basic stage directions were written in Latin. "Exit" indicates the departure of a single actor from the stage, "exeunt" the departure of more than one. "Manet" indicates that a single actor remains onstage, "manent" that more than one remains. Lines accompanied by the stage direction "aside" are spoken so as not to be heard by the others onstage. This stage direction appeared in some early editions of Shakespeare plays, but other means were also used to indicate such speech (such as placing the words within parentheses), and sometimes no indication was provided.

Stationers' Register The account books of the Company of Stationers (the guild of printers, publishers, and booksellers that controlled the London book trade), recording the fees paid by publishers to secure their rights to certain texts, as well as the transfer of these rights between publishers. The Stationers' Register thus provides a valuable if incomplete record of publication in England.

substantive text The text of an edition based upon access to a manuscript, as opposed to a derivative text based only on an earlier edition.

typecase The compartmentalized box in which movable type (metal letters, punctuation, etc.) was stored; capital, or "upper-case," letters were traditionally stored at the top of the typecase, "lower-case" letters at the bottom. Compositors drew individual type from the typecase for placing into a "compositor's stick" that held one line of type; from there the type would be transferred to a chase and secured to create a forme. Mistakes in sorting used type back into the typecase may account for some textual errors.

variorum editions Comprehensive editions of a work or works in which the various views of previous editors and commentators are compiled.

verso See *recto*

Essential Reference Books

Bate, Jonathan, and Russell Jackson, eds. *Shakespeare: An Illustrated Stage History.* New York: Oxford UP, 1996.

Bullough, Geoffrey, ed. *Narrative and Dramatic Sources of Shakespeare.* 8 vols. New York: Columbia UP, 1957–75.

Chambers, E. K. *The Elizabethan Stage.* 4 vols. Oxford: Clarendon, 1923.

———. *William Shakespeare: A Study of Facts and Problems.* 2 vols. Oxford: Clarendon, 1930.

Crystal, David. *Pronouncing Shakespeare: The Globe Experiment.* Cambridge: Cambridge UP, 2005.

Dent, R. W. *Shakespeare's Proverbial Language: An Index.* Berkeley: U of California P, 1981.

Dessen, Alan C., and Leslie Thomson. *A Dictionary of Stage Directions in English Drama, 1580–1642.* New York: Cambridge UP, 1999.

Dobson, E. J. *English Pronunciation, 1500–1700.* 2nd ed. 2 vols. Oxford: Clarendon, 1968.

Dobson, Michael, and Stanley Wells, eds. *The Oxford Companion to Shakespeare.* Oxford: Oxford UP, 2001.

Duffin, Ross W. *Shakespeare's Songbook.* New York: Norton, 2004.

Foakes, R. A. *Illustrations of the English Stage, 1580–1642.* Stanford: Stanford UP, 1985.

Greenblatt, Stephen, and Peter G. Platt, eds. *Shakespeare's Montaigne: The Florio Translation of the Essays, a Selection.* New York: New York Review Books, 2014.

Greg, W. W., ed. *Dramatic Documents from the Elizabethan Playhouses: Stage Plots: Actors' Parts: Prompt Books.* 2 vols. Oxford: Clarendon, 1931.

Gurr, Andrew. *Playgoing in Shakespeare's London.* 3rd ed. New York: Cambridge UP, 2004.

———. *The Shakespearean Stage, 1574–1642.* 4th ed. New York: Cambridge UP, 2009.

Henslowe, Philip. *Henslowe's Diary.* Ed. R. A. Foakes. 2nd ed. New York: Cambridge UP, 2002.

Hosley, Richard, ed. *Shakespeare's Holinshed: An Edition of Holinshed's Chronicles, 1587.* New York: Putnam, 1968.

Murphy, Andrew. *Shakespeare in Print: A History and Chronology of Shakespeare Publishing.* New York: Cambridge UP, 2003.

Oxford Dictionary of National Biography. Oxford: Oxford UP, 2004. www.oxforddnb.com/

Oxford English Dictionary. Oxford: Clarendon, 1989. www.oed.com/

Partridge, A. C. *Orthography in Shakespeare and Elizabethan Drama.* London: E. Arnold, 1964.

Partridge, Eric. *Shakespeare's Bawdy: A Literary and Psychological Essay and a Comprehensive Glossary.* 3rd ed. New York: Routledge, 2001.

Schoenbaum, Samuel. *William Shakespeare: A Documentary Life.* New York: Oxford UP, 1975.

Spevack, Marvin. *A Complete and Systematic Concordance to the Works of Shakespeare.* 9 vols. Hildesheim: George Olms, 1968–80.

Stern, Tiffany. *Documents of Performance in Early Modern England.* Cambridge: Cambridge UP, 2009

Tilley, Morris Palmer. *A Dictionary of the Proverbs in England in the Sixteenth and Seventeenth Centuries*. Ann Arbor: U of Michigan P, 1950.

Wells, Stanley. *A Dictionary of Shakespeare*. 2nd ed. New York: Oxford UP, 2005.

———. *Re-Editing Shakespeare for the Modern Reader*. New York: Oxford UP, 1984.

Wickham, Glynne. *Early English Stages, 1300 to 1660*. 4 vols. New York: Routledge, 2002.

Williams, Gordon. *A Dictionary of Sexual Language and Imagery in Shakespearean and Stuart Literature*. 3 vols. London: Athlone, 1994.

For a much fuller bibliography, including critical and historical works bearing on the study of Shakespeare, see the Digital Edition of *The Norton Shakespeare*.

ILLUSTRATION ACKNOWLEDGMENTS

THE HOUSE OF LANCASTER

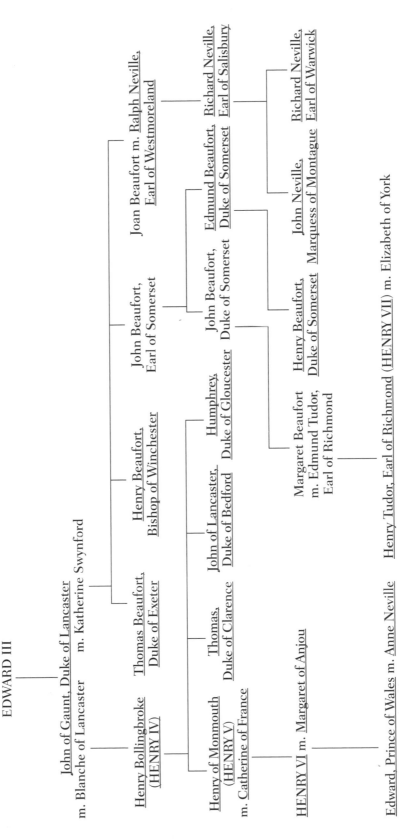

EDWARD III

John of Gaunt, Duke of Lancaster   m. Katherine Swynford
m. Blanche of Lancaster

Henry Bollingbroke
(HENRY IV)

Henry of Monmouth
(HENRY V)
m. Catherine of France

HENRY VI m. Margaret of Anjou

Edward, Prince of Wales m. Anne Neville

Thomas,
Duke of Clarence

John of Lancaster,
Duke of Bedford

Humphrey,
Duke of Gloucester

Henry Beaufort,
Bishop of Winchester

Thomas Beaufort,
Duke of Exeter

John Beaufort,
Earl of Somerset

Joan Beaufort m. Ralph Neville,
Earl of Westmoreland

John Beaufort,
Duke of Somerset

Edmund Beaufort,
Duke of Somerset

Richard Neville,
Earl of Salisbury

Margaret Beaufort
m. Edmund Tudor,
Earl of Richmond

Henry Beaufort,
Duke of Somerset

John Neville,
Marquess of Montague

Richard Neville,
Earl of Warwick

Henry Tudor, Earl of Richmond (HENRY VII) m. Elizabeth of York

The House of York

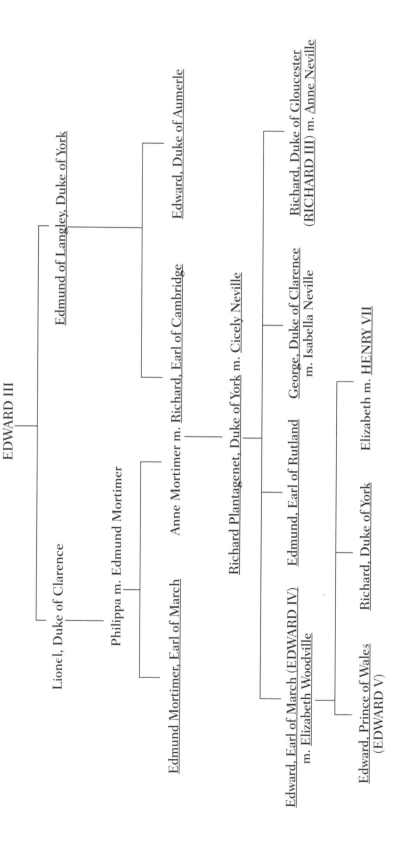

EDWARD III

- Lionel, Duke of Clarence
  - Philippa m. Edmund Mortimer
    - Edmund Mortimer, Earl of March
    - Anne Mortimer m. Richard, Earl of Cambridge
      - Richard Plantagenet, Duke of York m. Cicely Neville
        - Edward, Earl of March (EDWARD IV) m. Elizabeth Woodville
          - Edward, Prince of Wales (EDWARD V)
          - Richard, Duke of York
          - Elizabeth m. HENRY VII
        - Edmund, Earl of Rutland
        - George, Duke of Clarence m. Isabella Neville
        - Richard, Duke of Gloucester (RICHARD III) m. Anne Neville
- Edmund of Langley, Duke of York
  - Edward, Duke of Aumerle
  - Richard, Earl of Cambridge

Tudors (1485–1603) and Stuarts (1603–1714)

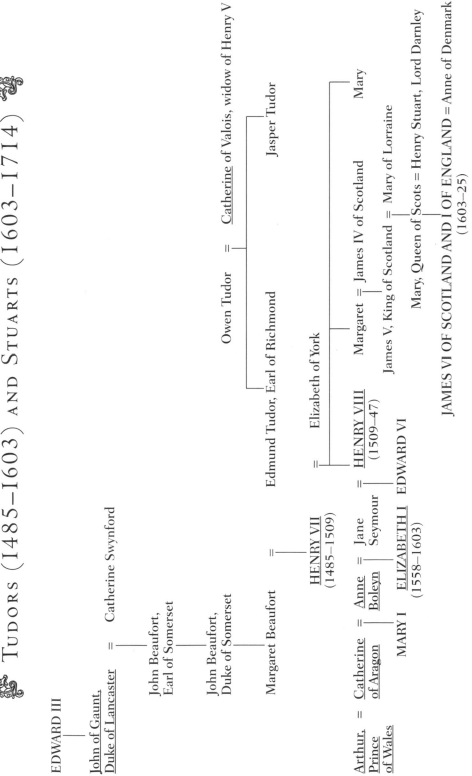

An equal sign (=) stands for marriage. Underlined names indicate characters in the plays. Capitals note reigning Kings and Queens.